Encyclopedia of Psychology and Religion

David A. Leeming, Kathryn Madden, Stanton Marlan (Eds.)

Encyclopedia of Psychology and Religion

Volume 2

L–Z

With 15 Figures and 2 Tables

 Springer

Editors-in-Chief:
David A. Leeming, Ph.D.
Blanton-Peale Institute
3 West 29th Street
New York, NY 10001
USA

Kathryn Madden, Ph.D.
National Institute for the Psychotherapies
250 West 57th Street, Suite 501
New York, NY 10019
USA

Stanton Marlan, Ph.D.
Pittsburgh Center for Psychotherapy and Psychoanalysis
4527 Winthrop Street
Pittsburgh, PA 15213-3722
USA

A C.I.P. Catalog record for this book is available from the Library of Congress
Library of Congress Control Number: 2009934794

ISBN: 978-0-387-71801-9
The electronic version will be available under ISBN 978-0-387-71802-6
The print and electronic bundle will be available under ISBN 978-0-387-71803-3

© Springer Science+Business Media LLC 2010 (USA)

springer.com

Printed on acid-free paper

SPIN: 11528708 2109 — 5 4 3 2 1 0

Preface

Mr. Kenneth Giniger some time ago suggested to Dr. Holly Johnson, then President of Blanton-Peale Institute, New York, NY, that Blanton-Peale compile an encyclopedia of psychology and religion, a comprehensive reference work consisting of articles contributed by scholars of importance in the fields of religion, psychology, psychology and religion, and psychology of religion. Dr. Johnson also saw the need for such an information source and began planning work on the project with the assistance of Blanton-Peale colleagues, Dr. Walter Odajnyk and Dr. David A. Leeming. Long working together with Blanton-Peale on behalf of *Journal of Religion and Health*, Springer Science+Business Media became publisher, with Dr. Leeming, Dr. Kathryn Madden, and Dr. Stanton Marlan named as Editors-in-Chief. Dr. Leeming became Managing Editor of the project. He has taught courses in myth, religion, and literature for many years and has published several books on these subjects, including the *Oxford Companion to World Mythology*, and until recently was Editor-in-Chief of the award-winning *Journal of Religion and Health* and Dean of Blanton-Peale's Graduate Institute. He is currently President of Blanton-Peale Institute. Dr. Madden served as Dean and later President of Blanton-Peale, was Associate Editor and later Executive Editor of the *Journal of Religion and Health*, and has recently published *Dark Light of the Soul* (Lindisfarne Books). She teaches and lectures regularly and is in private practice. She received her M.A., M.Phil., and Ph.D. degrees in Psychology and Religion from Union Theological Seminary in New York City. She has published many articles in her field and is Editor of *Quadrant*. Dr. Marlan is a clinical psychologist in private practice. He is a training and supervising analyst for the Inter-Regional Society of Jungian Analysts and is President of the Pittsburgh Society of Jungian Analysts. He is also Adjunct Clinical Professor of Psychology at Duquesne University and holds diplomates in both Clinical Psychology and Psychoanalysis from the American Board of Professional Psychology. He has been Editor of the *Journal of Jungian Theory and Practice* and is the author of numerous articles and books in the field of Jungian psychology. Parentage of the *Encyclopedia of Psychology and Religion* comes naturally to the Blanton-Peale Institute. Founded in 1937 by Dr. Norman Vincent Peale and psychologist Smiley Blanton, the Institute is a mental health clinic and psychological training institute dedicated to the constructive integration of religion and psychology. The *Encyclopedia of Psychology and Religion* provides a crucial new resource for the collaboration and mutual illumination of these two fields.

Entries are drawn from a wide variety of religious traditions, not only modern world religions, such as Christianity, Judaism, Islam, Buddhism, and Hinduism, but also, for example, African Animism, pre-Christian Celtic and Germanic traditions, Egyptian, Greek, Gnostic, and Native North American and Mesoamerican religious movements. Approaches to the subjects demonstrate a broad range of methodologies. Each entry is intended to create a tension of meaning between traditional religious terms and psychological interpretations. The goal is not to impose *the* correct or definitive meaning, but to explore new and latent deposits of meaning that bear implications for human self-understanding, cross-cultural interpretation, and therapeutic possibilities.

Occasionally, more than one article on a given subject is included to present different points of view. Extensive cross-referencing allows the reader to enhance understanding of particular subjects through direct access to related topics. The *Encyclopedia of Psychology and Religion* will serve as a valuable and accessible reference work in both electronic and print versions for academic libraries and their patrons and will be of particular use to the growing community of researchers, academics, teachers, clergy, therapists, counselors, and other professionals who are involved in the developing reintegration of the fields of religion and psychology.

Acknowledgment

The Editors and Blanton-Peale Institute thank the members of Springer Science+Business Media staff in both Germany and the United States for their support on this project. We are particularly grateful to Carol Bischoff, Thomas Mager, Susanne Friedrichsen, Heike Richini, and Christine Hausmann for their consistent help and support.

David A. Leeming, Kathryn Madden, and Stanton Marlan

Introduction

The world's great religions have always served as the repository of the psychological truths and values of mankind. Religions address the fundamental questions of human existence: the purpose and meaning of life; our relationship with God; the nature of the soul; the existence of evil, suffering, and death; ethical behavior and conscience; our search for happiness, redemption, and salvation. In previous centuries theologians and religious philosophers were not inclined to differentiate between matters of "soul" or "psyche." Figures such as St. Paul, St. Augustine, Martin Luther, Pascal, and Kierkegaard were people of faith who also grappled with the mysteries of human interiority, will, and motivation.

In the course of addressing these issues, every religion has developed a definition of human nature and examined our fundamental motivations, drives, and desires. Religions have been crucibles for the time-tested psychological principles that assure a sense of identity, community, and meaningful life. All religions, for example, have discovered that negative psychological states, such as pride, anger, hatred, lust, envy, ignorance, selfishness, and egotism, lead to personal and social conflict, injustice, and pain. On the other hand, positive mental and emotional attitudes, such as love, altruism, forgiveness, compassion, generosity, humility, equanimity, and wisdom, lead to a sense of personal well-being and social harmony. From a psychological perspective, religions are all-encompassing therapeutic systems that deal with major life events, transitions, and crises and respond in a healing, often life-saving way to the travails of the suffering soul and the impoverished spirit.

With the emergence and then dominance of scientific rationalism, however, the fields of religion and psychology diverged and entered into a relation of mutual suspicion. Beginning with the Enlightenment and its materialistic, secular, and rationalistic *weltanschauung*, the previously generally accepted religious and spiritual delineation of human nature was seriously challenged. In time, a split occurred between studies of human nature based on secular definitions and the age-old religious knowledge of the human soul and spirit. The two fields that should have been allied and in creative dialogue instead became estranged from each other, and often ignored or rejected the knowledge that each could have contributed to the enterprise of understanding human nature. Purely secular notions of human nature emerged: human beings were seen as rational animals; a person was born a *tabula rasa*, neither good nor evil, with parenting and education forming the personality; human beings were a composite of their economic and social relations; human beings were initially motivated by instinctive, irrational, and unrealistic drives and desires; all human behavior, emotions, and motivations and those most sublime cultural creations, religious beliefs and experiences, were the result of complex organic, neurological, and biochemical interactions. The tradition inspired by Sigmund Freud tended to view religion as an illusion, a cultural vestige of immaturity and projection. Consequently, those in the religious camp came to view psychology as a reductionist enterprise that denied the sacred and transcendent aspects of reality.

While some continue to subscribe to such stereotypes, a more sophisticated understanding of religion – particularly as advanced by the field of depth psychology – has done much to overcome them. The secular paradigm that has ruled the domain of psychology for the past centuries was challenged early on by pioneers such as William James, C. G. Jung, Roberto Assagioli, Viktor Frankl, Erik Erikson, and the humanistic psychologists Gordon Allport, Erich Fromm, and Abraham Maslow. During the 1970s, these thinkers were joined by the transpersonal psychologists, who have sought a synthesis between secular psychology and the great spiritual traditions. While they have accepted the stages of personal development described by various exponents of secular psychology, they have added the stages of transpersonal development evidenced in the world's contemplative and meditative traditions. Because of the cultural shift represented by the above and the persistence of religious beliefs in the vast majority of populations worldwide, contemporary psychologists are beginning to recognize that a purely secular approach to the study and treatment of human beings is inadequate. A science dedicated to the exploration of the basic characteristics and strivings of human beings and to the classification of the laws of human behavior needs to be inclusive and not exclusive of the religious dimension.

The need to address religious and spiritual problems is now deemed not only legitimate, but also clinically and ethically imperative. The 1994 edition of the *Diagnostic and Statistical Manual of Mental Disorders* published by the American Psychiatric Association, for example, contains a new classification, "Religious or Spiritual Problems."

This *Encyclopedia of Psychology and Religion* grows out of the developing awareness of the need to reintegrate the sciences of the mind with the science of the spirit. By bringing together the disciplines of psychology and religion, it unites the two areas of study concerned with the behavior and motivations of human beings and provides a crucial new resource for the collaboration and mutual illumination of these two fields. For those in the study of religion, it offers new tools for understanding the images, structures, symbols, and rhythms that constitute the vocabulary of religious experience. For those in the field of psychology it reveals deep patterns of meaning and practice that inform human culture and the personal identity of millions.

This *Encyclopedia of Psychology and Religion* illustrates, even to the skeptical, the vital importance of religion in our world and the serious depths of its symbolic universe. For those already immersed in religious studies, it demonstrates layers of meaning that are enriched – not reduced – by the tools of psychological investigation.

We trust this encyclopedia provides comprehensive timely accessible information from a multi-faceted perspective that reflects the intersection and the growing synthesis of psychology and religion.

David A. Leeming, Kathryn Madden, and Stanton Marlan

Editors-in-Chief

David A. Leeming
Blanton-Peale Institute
3 West 29th Street
New York, NY 10001
USA

Kathryn Madden
National Institute for the Psychotherapies
250 West 57th Street, Suite 501
New York, NY 10019
USA

Stanton Marlan
Pittsburgh Center for Psychotherapy and Psychoanalysis
4527 Winthrop Street
Pittsburgh, PA 15213-3722
USA

Managing Editor

David A. Leeming
Blanton-Peale Institute
3 West 29th Street
New York, NY 10001
USA

Associate Managing Editor

Felice Noelle Rodriguez
Blanton-Peale Institute
3 West 29th Street
New York, NY 10001
USA

List of Contributors with Contributions

Don Allen, Jr.
Christian Life Center
West Chester, OH 45069
USA
Pastoral Counseling

Jennifer Amlen
The Second Wind
New York, NY 10016
USA
Dance and Religion
Twelve Steps

Lucinda Antrim
Blanton-Peale Graduate Institute
New York, NY 10001
USA
Rumi, Celaladin

Jamie D. Aten
Department of Psychology
The University of Southern Mississippi
Hattiesburg, MS 39406-0001
USA
African-American Spirituality
Religious Coping

Galit Atlas-Koch
New York, NY 10003
USA
Postmodernism

Ali Ayten
Department of Psychology of Religion
Marmara University
Istanbul 34662
Turkey
Hafiz
Hajj
Ka'bah

Anthony Badalamenti
Scientific Support
Westwood, NJ 07675
USA
Mysticism and Psychotherapy

Claudia Bader
Institute for Expressive Analysis
New York, NY 10025
USA
Astrology and Alchemy
Astrology and Mandalas
Astrology and the Transitional Object
Duende and Psychoanalysis

Lee W. Bailey
Department of Philosophy and Religion
Ithaca College (Retired)
Ithaca, NY 14850
USA
Amita Buddha
Animism
Anthropomorphism
Dying and Rising Gods
Golden Bough, The
Guan Yin
Mandala
Myth
Myths and Dreams
Projection

David C. Balderston
New York, NY 10128
USA
Love
Shakers

Matthias Beier
Drew Theological School
Madison, NJ 07940
USA
Drewermann, Eugen

Benjamin Beit-Hallahmi
University of Haifa
Haifa 31905
Israel
Bahais
Conversion
Ego
Freud, Sigmund
New Religions

Object Relations Theory
Primal Horde Theory
Super-Ego
Transference
Women and Religion

David M. Bell
Department of Religious Studies
Georgia State University
Atlanta, GA 30322-4089
USA
Religious Identity

David Berman
Philosophy Department
Trinity College
Dublin 2
Ireland
Panaceas and Placebos
Schopenhauer, Nietzsche, and Atheism
Socrates' Daimonion

Rod Blackhirst
Philosophy & Religious Studies
La Trobe University
Bendigo, VIC 3550
Australia
Astrology
Creation
Plato and Religion
Sacred Time

Nicholas Grant Boeving
Rice University
Houston, TX 77251
USA
Hallucinations
Paranormal Experience
Ramana Maharshi
Spiritualism
Swamis
Transcendental Meditation
Transpersonal Psychology
Unconscious
Visions

Meg Bowles
Westchester Institute for Training in
Psychoanalysis and Psychotherapy
New Fairfield, CT 06812
USA

Music Thanatology
Shamanic Healing

Jeffrey H. Boyd
Waterbury Hospital
Waterbury, CT 06708
USA
Biblical Psychology

Dianne Braden
Inter-regional Society of Jungian Analysts
Solon, OH 44139
USA
Compulsion

Roger Brooke
Psychology Clinic
Duquesne University
Pittsburgh, PA 15282
USA
Jung, Carl Gustav, and Phenomenology

Charlene P. E. Burns
Department of Philosophy & Religious Studies
University of Wisconsin-Eau Claire
Eau Claire, WI 54702
USA
Incarnation
Reductionism
Stigmata

Daniel Burston
Psychology Department
Duquesne University
Pittsburgh, PA 15282-1707
USA
Anti-Semitism
Authoritarian Personality
Laing, Ronald David
Luther, Martin
Nazism
Réssentiment and Religion
Stern, Karl

Joe Cambray
Providence, RI 02906
USA
Amplification
Emergentism

Frances Campbell
New York, NY 10001
USA
Synchronicity

Nathan Carlin
Department of Religious Studies
Rice University
Houston, TX 77251-1892
USA
Augustine
Melancholia
Pruyser, Paul
Thanatos

Ann Casement
The British Association of Psychotherapists
London
UK
Archetype
Numinosum
Persona
Self
Transcendent Function

Wing-Shing Chan
Faculty of Medicine
The Chinese University of Hong Kong
Shatin, N.T.
Hong Kong
Hong Kong Special Administrative Region of the
People's Republic of China
Chan Buddhism
Enlightenment
Enlightenment Initiation

F. X. Charet
Aion Center for the Study of Spirituality and Culture
Montreal, QC H2V 3A3
Canada
Consciousness

Stuart Z. Charmé
Department of Philosophy and Religion
Rutgers University
Camden, NJ 08102
USA
Adam and Eve

Kathy Coffman
ACA, MCA
Hattiesburg, MS 39402
USA
African-American Spirituality

Allan Hugh Cole, Jr.
Pastoral Care
Austin Presbyterian Theological Seminary
Austin, TX 78705
USA
Anxiety
Prayer

Michael Conforti
The Assisi Institute
Brattleboro, VT 05302
USA
Objective Psyche

Paul C. Cooper
New York, NY 10016
USA
Koan
Mu Koan or Joshu's Dog
Prajna
Sunyata
Zen

Lionel Corbett
Pacifica Graduate Institute
Carpinteria, CA 93013
USA
Depth Psychology and Spirituality
Soul: A Depth Psychological Approach

Elisa Bernal Corley
Castaic, CA 91348
USA
Evangelical
Orthodoxy

Bonnie Smith Crusalis
Albuquerque Psychiatry and Psychology Associates
Albuquerque, NM 87104
USA
Death Anxiety
Wounded Healer, The

Sam Cyrous
Faro
Portugal
Sabeanism
Zoroastrianism

Don E. Davis
Virginia Commonwealth University
Richmond, VA 23284
USA
Forgiveness

Gerardo James de Jesus
Philadelphia, PA
USA
Shame and Depth Psychology

Laurence de Rosen
75116 Paris
France
Music and Religion
Sound

Miriam Dean-Otting
Religious Studies
Kenyon College
Gambier, OH 43022
USA
Prophets

Ingeborg del Rosario
Emmaus Center
Loyola Heights, Quezon City
Philippines
USA
Doubt
Exodus
Genesis
Job
Psalms
Song of Songs

Valerie DeMarinis
Uppsala University
Uppsala 75120
Sweden
Migration and Religion
Syncretism

Ryan M. Denney
Department of Psychology
University of Southern Mississippi
Hattiesburg, MS 30406-0001
USA
African-American Spirituality
Religious Coping

Stephen A. Diamond
Center for Existential Depth Psychology
Los Angeles, CA 90048
USA
Daimonic
Existential Psychotherapy
Possession, Exorcism, and Psychotherapy
Shadow

Marta Dominguez Diaz
SOAS
University of London
London WC1H 0XG
UK
Traditionalism

Todd DuBose
The Chicago School of Professional Psychology
Chicago, IL 60610
USA
Daseinsanalysis
Existentialism
Fate
Heidegger, Martin
Hermeneutics
Homo Religiosus
Lived Theology
Meaning of Human Existence
Phenomenological Psychology
Psychotherapy
Purpose in Life
Transcendence
Trauma

Anthony J. Elia
JKM Library Lutheran School of Theology at Chicago
McCormick Theological Seminary
Chicago, IL 60615
USA
Rome
Vatican
Virgin Mary

Robert S. Ellwood
Ojai, CA 93023
USA
Eliade, Mircea
Shinto
Theosophy
Watts, Alan Wilson

James G. Emerson
San Francisco, CA 94109
USA
Bonnell, John Sutherland
Forgiveness and the Brain
Hiltner, Seward
Rogers, Carl

Mark William Ennis
Clinton Ave. Reformed Church
Bergenfield, NJ 07621
USA
Cain and Abel
Predestination

Stacey Enslow
Anthropology Department
Purdue University
West Lafayette, IN 47907-2059
USA
Anthropocentric View
Sacred King

Amani Fairak
Heythrop College
University of London
London W8 5HQ
UK
Analogy (Islamic)
Sharia

Sukey Fontelieu
Pacifica Graduate Institute
Carpinteria, CA 93013
USA
Chthonic Deities
Pan

Andrew J. P. Francis
Division of Psychology
School of Health Sciences
RMIT University
Bundoora, VIC 3083
Australia
Locus of Control
Water

Regina A. Fredrickson
Blanton-Peale Institute
New York, NY 10001
USA
Mary

Maurice Friedman
San Diego State University
Solana Beach, CA 92075
USA
Buber, Martin

James Markel Furniss
University of Connecticut
Canton, CT 06019
USA
Oedipus Myth

Tiffani Futch
Department of Psychology
The University of Southern Mississippi
Hattiesburg, MS 39406-0001
USA
African-American Spirituality

Daniel J. Gaztambide
Union Theological Seminary Program
in Psychiatry and Religion
New York, NY 10027
USA
Liberation Psychology
Liberation Theology
Martín-Baró Ignacio
Miracles

Giorgio Giaccardi
London SE4 1TR
UK
Defenses

Paul Giblin
Loyola University
Chicago, IL 60611
USA
Ignatius of Loyola
Jesuits

Ann Gleig
Department of Religious Studies
Rice University

Houston, TX 77005-1892
USA
Narcissism
New Age Movement
Psychology as Religion
Psychospiritual

David M. Goodman
Danielsen Institute at Boston University
Boston, MA 02215
USA
Levinas, Emmanuel

Marta Green
New York, NY 10025-3586
USA
Gnosticism
Kingdom of God
Meister Eckhart

Mark Greene
Department of Counselling and Psychology
Hong Kong Shue Yan University
North Point, Hong Kong
Hong Kong Special Administrative Region of the
People's Republic of China
Happiness as a Goal
Orpheus and Orphism
Spirit Writing
Wong Tai Sin

Christopher S. M. Grimes
Saint Louis Behavioral Medicine Institute
St. Louis, MO 63110
USA
Religion and Mental and Physical Health

Halina Grzymala-Moszczynska
Department of Psychology of Religion
Jagielonian University
Cracow
Poland
Cultural Psychology

Robert Kaizen Gunn
United Church of Rockville Centre
Rockville Centre, NY 11570
USA
American Buddhism
Poverty
Religious Experience

Louis Hagood
Oxbridge Communications Inc. & MediaFinder.com
New York, NY 10010
USA
Dreams

Fredrica R. Halligan
MindBodySpirit Institute
Stamford, CT 06905
USA
Asceticism
Atman
Avatar
Bhagavad Gita
Chaos
Gayatri
Ibn al-'Arabi
Mantra
Merton, Thomas
Om
Omega Point
Ramakrishna Paramahansa
Sai Baba
Sufis and Sufism
Surrender
Taoism
Teilhard de Chardin
Vedanta

Jaco J. Hamman
Western Theological Seminary
Holland, MI 49423
USA
Calvinism
Masochism
Protestantism
Winnicott, Donald Woods

Curtis W. Hart
Weill Cornell Medical College
New York, NY 10065
USA
Boisen, Anton
Dunbar, Helen Flanders
Faith Development Theory
James, William
Worcester, Elwood (Emmanuel Movement)

John Ryan Haule
C.G. Jung Institute Boston
Chestnut Hill, MA 02467
USA

Anima and Animus
Collective Unconscious
Communal and Personal Identity
Feeling
Participation Mystique

Philip Browning Helsel
Pastoral Theology
Princeton Theological Seminary
Princeton, NJ 08540
USA
Child, The
Faith
Father
Gender Roles
Transitional Object
Via Negativa

Louis Hoffman
Colorado School of Professional Psychology
University of the Rockies
Colorado Springs, CO 80903
USA
Fundamentalism
Interfaith Dialog

C. Harry Hui
Department of Psychology
University of Hong Kong
Hong Kong
Hong Kong Special Administrative Region of the
People's Republic of China
Chinese Religions
Extra-Sensory Perception (ESP)

James W. Jones
Department of Religion
Rutgers University
New Brunswick, NJ 08901
USA
Violence and Religion

Kalman J. Kaplan
Departments of Psychiatry and Medical Education
University of Illinois in Chicago
Chicago, IL 60612
USA
Biblical Narratives Versus Greek Myths
Judaism and Psychology

Bobbi Dykema Katsanis
Graduate Theological Union

Berkeley, CA 94709
USA
Antichrist

Ronald Katz
New York, NY 10010
USA
Adoption

Peregrine Murphy Kavros
Department of Psychology
Pace University
New York, NY 10038
USA
Religion
Religiosity
Religious

John Eric Killinger
The Intermundia Foundation for Vocation
and Calling, Inc.
Warrenton, VA 20188-1243
USA
Animectomy Complex
Bion, Wilfred Ruprecht, and "O"
Communitas
Hanging and Hanging God
Hierosgamos
Revelation
Uroboros

Haddon Klingberg, Jr.
Evanston, IL 60201
USA
Frankl, Viktor

Elisabeth Koenig
Ascetical Theology
New York, NY 10003
USA
Discernment

Ali Kose
Ilahiyat Facultesi
Marmara Universitesi
Istanbul 34662
Turkey
Conversion (Islam)
Kabir
Miraj
Qur'an

Richard L. Kradin
Departments of Medicine and Psychiatry
Massachusetts General Hospital
Harvard Medical School
Boston, MA 02114
USA
Judaism and Christianity in Freudian Psychology
Judaism and Christianity in Jungian Psychology

Alexandra Krithades
CG Jung Institute of New York
New York, NY 10003
USA
Dionysos

Steven Kuchuck
Institute for Expressive Analysis
New York, NY 10011
USA
Relational Psychoanalysis

Ryan LaMothe
Pastoral Care and Counseling
St. Meinrad School of Theology
St. Meinrad, IN 47577
USA
Emotional Intelligence

Paul Larson
The Chicago School of Professional Psychology
Chicago, IL 60610
USA
Ananda
Arhat
Bodhi Tree
Bodhisattva
Breathing
Buddhism
Circumambulation
Dalai Lama
Divination
Esoteric Buddhism
Hermits
Hierophany
Homosexuality
Hormic Psychology
Iconography
Immanence
Initiation
Karma

Liminality
Locutions
Mormonism
Occultism
Oracles
Pantheism
Paracelsus
Polytheism
Puer Aeternus
Rites of Passage
Sacred Prostitution
Sangha
Smith, Joseph
Tulku

David A. Leeming
Blanton-Peale Institute
New York, NY 10001
USA
Apollo
Apollonian and Dionysian
Axis Mundi
Baptism
City
Cosmic Egg
Culture Heroes
Deity Concept
Deluge
Deus Otiosus
Divine Child
Eleusinian Mysteries
Gardens, Groves, and Hidden Places
Jihad
Monomyth
Monotheism
Pilgrimage
Primordial Waters
Quest
Resurrection
Sex and Religion
Shakti
Trickster
Vestments

Lorna Lees-Grossmann
Department of Psychosomatic Medicine
Klinikum Rechts der Isar
Munich 81675
Germany
Delusion
Evil

Freud, Sigmund, and Religion
Schreber, Daniel Paul

Meredith Lisagor
New York, NY 10025
USA
Deus Absconditus
Logos
Native American Messianism

Kate M. Loewenthal
Psychology Department
Royal Holloway
University of London
Egham
Surrey TW20 0EX
UK
Charity
Conscience
Depression
Hasidism
Psychology
Psychosis
Psychotherapy and Religion
Zionism

George A. Looks Twice
Oglala Lakota Sioux Tribe
SD
USA
Black Elk

Georgine Leona Looks Twice
Oglala Lakota Sioux Tribe
SD
USA
Black Elk

Sana Loue
Center for Minority Public Health
Case Western Reserve University ·
School of Medicine
Department of Epidemiology and Biostatistics
Cleveland, OH 44106-4945
USA
Curanderismo
Santería

Alex Lunderman, Jr.
Rosebud Sioux Tribe
Ring Thunder Community

Mission, SD
USA
Black Elk

Kathryn Madden
National Institute for the Psychotherapies
New York, NY 10019
USA
Abyss
Dark Mother
Dark Night of the Soul
Descent to the Underworld
Eros
Homo Totus
Mary Magdalene
Tantrism
Transfiguration
Winnicott, Donald Woods, and Religion

Ronald Madden
New York, NY 10025
USA
Dragon Slaying
Temenos

Stanton Marlan
Pittsburgh Center for Psychotherapy and
Psychoanalysis
Pittsburgh, PA 15213-3722
USA
Hillman, James, and Alchemy

Kelly Murphy Mason
The Blanton-Peale Institute
New York, NY 10001
USA
Epiphany
Labyrinth
Story as Scripture, Therapy, Ritual
Wisdom

Mathew Mather
Centre for Psychoanalytic Studies
University of Essex
Wivenhoe Park, Colchester
Essex CO4 3SQ
UK
Alchemical Mercurius and Carl Gustav Jung

Kelley Raab Mayo
Royal Ottawa Mental Health Centre
University of Ottawa

Ottawa, ON K1Z 7K4
Canada
Psychiatry

Pittman McGehee
Saybrook Graduate School and Research Center
San Francisco, CA 94111-1920
USA
Jungian Self

Jill L. McNish
Union Theological Seminary
Swedesboro, NJ 08085
USA
Fall, The
Julian of Norwich
Shame and Guilt

Alice Mills
University of Ballarat
Ballarat, VIC 3353
Australia
Apotheosis and Return
Call, The
Cupid and Psyche
Dismemberment
Etiological Myth
Refusal of the Call

Jessica Mitchell
Blanton-Peale Institute
New York, NY 10001
USA
Dissociation

Ann Moir-Bussy
Department of Counselling and Psychology
Hong Kong Shue Yan University
Hong Kong
Contemplative Prayer
John of the Cross
Tara

David M. Moss III
Atlanta, GA 30305
USA
God
Providence
Psychoanalysis
Theodicy

Claudia Nagel
Mercurius Management Consulting
Königstein 61462
Germany
Analytical Psychology
Ethics and Ethical Behavior

Jo Nash
Mental Health Section
School of Health and Related Research
University of Sheffield
Sheffield S1 4DA
UK
Affect
Ecstasy
Libido
Mindfulness

Annabelle Nelson
The WHEEL Council
Flagstaff, AZ 86002
USA
Sophia

Eddie C. W. Ng
Victoria University
Melbourne, VIC
Australia
Chinese Religions

Kenneth L. Nolen
Salinas Valley Memorial Healthcare System
Salinas, CA 93930
USA
Glossolalia
Personal God
Spiritual Direction

V. Walter Odajnyk
Pacifica Institute
Carpinteria, CA 93013
USA
Angels

Thomas St. James O'Connor
Waterloo Lutheran Seminary
Waterloo, ON N2L 3C5
Canada
Healing
Narrative Therapy
Purgatory

Trish O'Sullivan
New York, NY 10023
USA
Ahimsa
Buddha-Nature
Chakras
Meditation

John Pahucki
Department of Humanities
SUNY Rockland
Suffern, NY 10901
USA
Lacan, Jacques
Plato on the Soul
Quaternity
Rank, Otto
Twice Born

Erica Palmer
Center for Growth
Colorado Springs, CO 80918
USA
Fundamentalism

Ginette Paris
Pacifica Graduate Institute
Santa Barbara, CA 93105
USA
Redemption, the Problem with

Annette Peterson
Riverside, IL 60546
USA
Female God Images
God Image and Therapy
God Image in Dreams
Male God Images

Jeffrey B. Pettis
Department of Theology
Fordham University
New York, NY
USA
Androgyny
Ascension
Bible
Christianity
Confucianism
Eclipses
Elixir
Hinduism

Islam
Jesus
Kabbalah
Magic
Moon and Moon Goddesses
Mummification
Mystery Religions
New Testament
Virgin Birth

Nathalie Pilard
King's College
School of Divinity
University of Aberdeen
Aberdeen AB24 3UB
UK
I Ching
Intuition

Mark Popovsky
Department of Pastoral Care
Weill Medical College of Cornell
New York Presbyterian Hospital - Chaplaincy
New York, NY 10021
USA
Baal Shem Tov
Circumcision
Heschel, Abraham Joshua
Jerusalem Syndrome
Jewish Law
Jewish Mourning Rituals
Jewish Sexual Mores
Maimonides, Moses
Midrash
Shekhinah
Talmud

Robert Prue (Sicangu Lakota)
School of Social Welfare
University of Kansas
Kansas City, MO 64109
USA
Peyote Ceremony
Peyote Religion
Vision Quest

Thomas C. Putnam
Cambridge, MA 02138
USA
Mountain, The
Rinpoche

Robert Quackenbush
New York, NY 10075
USA
Oedipus Complex

Brandon Randolph-Seng
Department of Psychology
Texas Tech University
Lubbock, TX 79409
USA
Altered States of Consciousness
Method
Personal Unconscious
Prejudice

Roberto Refinetti
Psychology
University of South Carolina
Walterboro, SC 29488
USA
Body and Spirituality
Relativism

Jennifer S. Ripley
School of Psychology and Counseling
Regent University
Virginia Beach, VA 23464-9956
USA
Forgiveness

Joenine E. Roberts
Blanton-Peale Institute
Association for Psychoanalytic Self Psychology
New York, NY 10024
USA
Kohut, Heinz

Alan Roland
National Psychological Association for Psychoanalysis
New York, NY 10014
USA
Mysticism and Psychoanalysis

Ann M. Rothschild
Private Practice
New York, NY 10003
USA
Teresa of Avila
Waiting

Tadd Ruetenik
St. Ambrose University
Davenport, IA 52803
USA

Kierkegaard, Søren
Scapegoat

Jeffrey Burton Russell
Department of History
University of California
Santa Barbara, CA 93106-9410
USA
Devil

Krystyna Sanderson
The Blanton-Peale Institute
New York, NY 10001
USA
Compassion
Crucifixion
Grace
Holocaust

Alane Sauder-MacGuire
New York, NY 10016
USA
Jung, Carl Gustav, and Alchemy
Osiris and the Egyptian Religion

Frank Scalambrino
Department of Philosophy
Duquesne University
Pittsburgh, PA 15282
USA
Samsara and Nirvana

Leon Schlamm
School of European Culture & Languages
Religious Studies Section
University of Kent
Canterbury
Kent CT2 7NF
UK
Active Imagination
Individuation
Inflation
Jung, Carl Gustav, and Eastern Religious Traditions
Jung, Carl Gustav, and Gnosticism
Jung, Carl Gustav, and Religion
Wilber, Ken

Magda Schonfeld
Hudson Holistic Health Care
Cold Spring, NY 10516
USA
Yoga

Matthew B. Schwartz
Department of History
Wayne State University
Detroit, MI 48202
USA
Biblical Narratives Versus Greek Myths
Judaism and Psychology

Carol L. Schnabl Schweitzer
Pastoral Care Union-PSCE
Richmond, VA 23227
USA
Kristeva, Julia
Sacraments
Self Psychology
Vocation

Robert A. Segal
School of Divinity, History and Philosophy
King's College
University of Aberdeen
Aberdeen AB24 3UB
UK
Hero

Erel Shalit
Israel Institute of Jungian Psychology
Ra'anana 43104
Israel
Dreams in the Old Testament
Jerusalem
Sacrifice of Isaac

Jane Simon
New York, NY 10023
USA
Mirroring

D. Brian Smothers
The Counseling Center of Milwaukee
Milwaukee, WI 53202
USA
Repression
Self Object

Melissa K. Smothers
School of Education
Department of Educational Psychology
University of Wisconsin-Milwaukee
Milwaukee, WI 53201-0413
USA
Adler, Alfred
Sullivan, Harry Stack

Lynn Somerstein
Institute for Expressive Analysis
New York, NY 10028
USA
Akedah
Erikson, Erik
Ethics of the Fathers
Hillel
Mikveh
Seder
Shema
Western Wall

M. J. Drake Spaeth
The Chicago School of Professional Psychology
Chicago, IL 60610
USA
Celtic Shamanism
Celtic Spirituality
Psyche

Bernard Spilka
Psychology Department
University of Denver
Denver, CO 80208
USA
God Image
Psychology and the Origins of Religion
Ritual

Anais N. Spitzer
Department of Religious Studies
Hollins University
Roanoke, VA 24020
USA
Abraham and Isaac
Campbell, Joseph

Morgan Stebbins
Faculty of the New York C.G. Jung Foundation
New York, NY 10128
USA
Confession
Heaven and Hell
Immortality
Sacrifice
Sin
Taboo

Murray Stein
International School for Analytical Psychology
Goldiwil 3624
Switzerland
Jung, Carl Gustav

Craig Stephenson
La Presbytère
Mondion 86230
France
Complex
Demons
Possession

Emily Stetler
Department of Theology
University of Notre Dame
Notre Dame, IN 46545
USA
Eschatology
Soteriology
Theophany

James H. Stover
Department of Philosophy
Wheeling Jesuit University
Wheeling, WV 26003
USA
Nirvana
Vivekananda

Charles B. Strozier
Brooklyn, NY 11215
USA
Apocalypse

M. Hannah Tai
University of Hong Kong
Hong Kong
Hong Kong Special Administrative Region of the
People's Republic of China
Chinese Religions

Stefanie Teitelbaum
Institute for Expressive Analysis (IEA) and National
Psychological Association for Psychoanalysis
New York, NY 10003
USA
Castration
Clitoridectomy
Drives
Id
Instinct

Matt Thelen
Center for Growth
Colorado Springs, CO 80918
USA
Interfaith Dialog

Chad Thralls
Harrisburg, PA 17102
USA
Centering Prayer

Migmar Tseten
Sakya Center
Harvard University
Cambridge, MA 02139
USA
Rinpoche

Adele Tyler
Life Journeys
Nashville, TN 37212
USA
Extraversion
Introversion
Psychological Types

Daniel Eugene Tyler
Nashville, TN 37212
USA
Urantia Book

Jessica Van Denend
Union Theological Seminary
New York, NY 10023
USA
Criminality

Gilbert Todd Vance
Department of Psychology
Virginia Commonwealth University
Roanoke, VA 24108
USA
Genetics of Religiosity
Hope
Skinner, Burrhus Frederic
Substance Abuse and Religion

Richard W. Voss
Department of Undergraduate Social Work
West Chester University of Pennsylvania
West Chester, PA 19383
USA
Black Elk
Peyote Ceremony
Peyote Religion

Shamans and Shamanism
Vision Quest

Lori B. Wagner-Naughton
Western Connecticut State University
Danbury, CT 06810
USA
Power
Vicarious Traumatization

David Waldron
Department of Social Science and the Humanities
University of Ballarat
Ballarat, VIC 3350
Australia
Celtic Religions
Folk Magic
Great Mother
Holy Grail
Paganism
Wicca
Witchcraft

Sharn Waldron
Bungay
Suffolk NR35 1BJ
UK
Christ
Christ as Symbol of the Self
Religious, Role of
Symbol

Minqin Wang
College of Foreign Languages
Hunan University
Changsha
Hunan Province 410082
People's Republic of China
Amita Buddha
Guan Yin

Hillary S. Webb
Saybrook Graduate School and Research Institute
Portsmouth, NH 03802
USA
Coincidentia Oppositorum
Dualism
Nonduality
Spiritual Emergence

Clodagh Weldon
Dominican University
River Forest, IL 60305
USA

Heresy
Judas Iscariot
Original Sin

Elizabeth Welsh
Fuller Graduate School of Psychology
Pasadena, CA 91182
USA
Femininity
Matriarchy
Mother

Ruth Williams
Association of Jungian Analysts
London E14 0SL
UK
Atonement
Elan Vital
Witch

Benjamin T. Wood
Virginia Commonwealth University
Richmond, VA 23284
USA
Forgiveness

Everett L. Worthington, Jr.
Psychology
Virginia Commonwealth University
Richmond, VA 23284-2018
USA
Forgiveness

David M. Wulff
Department of Psychology
Wheaton College
Norton, MA 02766
USA
Psychology of Religion

Susan Wyatt
Antioch University
Los Angeles, CA 94041
USA
Hestia

Vern Ziebart
Rapid City, SD
USA
Black Elk

L

Labyrinth

Kelly Murphy Mason

The labyrinth is an archetypal form found in disparate cultures across eras spanning from prehistory and to the present day, when it has experienced resurgence in popularity due to interest in its psychospiritual applications. Regardless of how it is styled, a labyrinth is marked by a shape, usually a symmetrical one, containing a unicursal path to or through a center point. This distinguishes it from a maze, which is multicursal and contains dead ends. Following the path of the labyrinth, the traveler is eventually and inevitably brought to the center and then back out again. While travelers may not know where exactly they are on this labyrinthine path, they are never lost, but rather, somewhere along the way they need to travel. As a result, the labyrinth has become common both as a metaphor and as a symbol of the human pilgrimage through life. A great deal of conjecture exists about its history, origins, and purposes, suggesting that the labyrinth has proven fertile ground for the imagination for millennia.

Its universality among prehistoric cultures indicates the so-called classical labyrinth was a primitive form of symbolic communication, perhaps an earliest form of written transmission. It was drawn from a central cross surrounded by four angles and four seed points that were connected until seven circuits were contained in its circle. Cave etchings of this particular labyrinth appear circa 2000 BCE in Spain (Saward, 2002). These symbols appear at approximately the same time in the Indian subcontinent, as well. Later, multitudinous stone arrangements of the similar symbols appeared in Scandinavian soil, often near the coast, leading some to speculate that seafarers would walk them in preparation for their journeys over water.

In mythology, the labyrinth first appears in the Greek lore surrounding the Minotaur of Crete. Unmistakably, the Cretan labyrinth was a built environment, an architectural structure, yet coins from Knossos featured the rounded, two-dimensional form of the classical labyrinth as its signifier. Later, Romans exported labyrinth mosaics throughout the Roman Empire (Kern, 2000), from Great Britain to Eastern Europe to North Africa. Some were purported to be sizable enough for people to travel on horseback; others were too intricate to serve anything other than decorative purposes. Roman labyrinths are distinct for their sharp angularity, both in their pathways and their outlines.

The Hopi tribes of North America had a squared version of the labyrinth that they used in addition to the classical labyrinth (Conty, 2002); it was unique in having two entrances. The Pima tribes, in their depictions of labyrinths, placed a human figure at the very entrance, in what later became known as "The Man in the Maze" pattern. This man was thought to be seeking the mythic place of his origin as a place of eternal return. Labyrinths were associated with a variety of burial rituals in Celtic cultures as well as Egyptian society, where they were believed to protect the sanctity of the tomb.

Despite its strong association with pagan rituals, the labyrinth was adopted rather quickly by the early church. In an Algerian church was found a labyrinth dating from the fourth century BCE (Matthews, 1970); its center circle contained the slogan "Sancta Eclesia," translated "Holy Church." The destination of the spiritual journey was no longer reunion with the earth, but inclusion in corporate Christendom. Interestingly, there was a profusion of varying forms of labyrinths across different churches during the Middle Ages, some square, some circular, a few octagonal.

At Glastonbury Tor, thought to be site of the first church built in England, an oval-shaped labyrinth appears to have been carved into the landscape the tower sat atop, so that entrance to it would be gained by walking the steep incline of winding circuits. Such large-scale, three-dimensional labyrinths also appeared in Peru, where they figured as features in the geoglyphs of totemistic animals used in the rituals of indigenous earth-centered religions.

By and large, Christian labyrinths belonged in the interiors of churches rather than their exteriors, although turf

D. A. Leeming, K. Madden, S. Marlan (eds.), *Encyclopedia of Psychology and Religion*, DOI 10.1007/978-0-387-71802-6,
© Springer Science+Business Media LLC 2010

and hedge labyrinths were fairly frequently found in English gardens and church grounds. Often, the labyrinth was placed near the entry of the church building. These labyrinths were sometimes called "Chemin de Jerusalem," the Way to Jerusalem, because they allowed European churchgoers to enact a pilgrimage to the Holy Land at a time when both its distance and ongoing Crusades made such travel nigh impossible. Members of the clergy would walk the labyrinth as an Easter ritual representing Christ's decent into hell, bodily resurrection, and ascent into heaven. Many monks traveled the labyrinth on their knees.

Perhaps the best known Christian labyrinth is found on the floor of Chartres Cathedral. Completed sometime in the early thirteenth century, its eleven-circuit course led to a six-petalled rosette in the center, outlined in more than a hundred lunations. Much speculation has existed around the esoteric numerology and sacred geometry of the various labyrinths that appeared in churches (Lonegren, 2007). Whether or not the Chartres labyrinth was devised as a specifically Marinal devotion, it was obviously not cruciform, as was the octagonal Maltese labyrinth so suggestive of more martial Roman forms.

General consensus holds that the Chartres labyrinth pays homage to the feminine aspect of the divine dimension with its womb-like appearance evocative of not only actual birth and death but also spiritual rebirth. The continuous pathway can be viewed as representative of the original passage through the birth canal. Some have even suggested that the Chartres labyrinth was actually used as a birthing instrument; either way, its feminine form would be unmistakable to worshippers.

Many churches and cathedrals saw their labyrinths removed or hidden in the centuries that followed, quite possibly as part of a larger repression of the feminine principle or a backlash against vestigial Goddess worship from older traditions. Evidence exists that some pagans may even have used the labyrinth in their mating rituals. The obvious physicality of a walking the labyrinth might have suggested a sensuous and immediate experience of the Divine that organized religion would attempt to control more closely in the West.

It is precisely such kinesthetic engagement that has recently made the labyrinth so appealing to contemporary travelers whose spiritual yearnings have been unfulfilled by religious dogma and formalized worship. In a contained and sanctified way, it offers travelers a chance to practice walking meditation and full-body prayer. In doing so, it combines active and contemplative approaches to self-realization (Artress, 1995).

A labyrinth is clearly an exercise in intentionality. Its traveler is no further along spatially than when the walk was begun and actually backtracks at several different points. The labyrinth thereby challenges some dominant notions of linear progression, time urgency, and outward orientation, suggesting that meaningful personal journeys might involve internal shifts that are as significant as external ones.

As a visual metaphor for journeying within, the labyrinth has also served as a powerful imagistic representation of the psychotherapeutic process, as well as the spiritual quest. The circuits of a labyrinth are vaguely reminiscent of the whorl of a fingerprint, that powerful symbol of personal identity (Attali, 1999). The possibility of truly knowing one's own self emerges as one looks inwards.

The existence of a sacred interiority becomes recognized and transitional/transformational space gets created in depictions of the labyrinth. Today people may trace finger labyrinths as a meditative practice, or else contemplate line drawings of the labyrinth which they can either "walk" with their eyes or consider as a unified symbol of wholeness. Entire classical labyrinths can be easily constructed from just a few simple marks drawn in the earth. The labyrinth can in turn serve as a sacred experience, sacred space, or sacred image.

Such versatility allows the labyrinth to help its travelers bridge some of the mind-body divide, paradoxically by allowing them to ground themselves in the numinous. Circumambulating the labyrinth is a right-brained activity that allows for flashes of intuition. The winding way become clear and in that process, wandering suddenly becomes purposeful. For this reason, ritual use of the labyrinth now often occurs at liminal times (Curry, 2000), whenever people find themselves at a threshold in their lives.

Commentary

The labyrinth has been called the Mandala of the West because of its apparent usefulness as a meditative tool and non-linear activity. It seems to be a culturally consonant symbol that expands consciousness and contains the potential for both psychospiritual integration and healing. The strong revival of interest in labyrinths in Western societies has given rise to numerous organizations promoting their use, organizations that are religious and secular alike, resulting in an international movement to increase their availability in shared spaces. Literature on the topic has proliferated in recent decades.

Even as research into the past and future uses of the labyrinth continues, however, it runs the risk of remaining speculative on the question of its distant origins and almost global ubiquity. What seems clear is that the growing popularity of the labyrinth is a response to a contemporary spiritual yearning to feel more grounded and centered. Through its indirection and reversals, the labyrinth appears to provide people an alternative to the frenetic pace of modern life and a greater sense of continuity with the past, possibly by suspending animation to a degree. Its symbolism has remained alluring and evocative through millennia of human history.

See also: ❷ Biblical Narratives Versus Greek Myths ❷ Biblical Psychology

Bibliography

Artress, L. (1995). *Walking a sacred path: Rediscovering the labyrinth as a spiritual tool*. New York: Riverhead Books.

Attali, J. (1999). *The labyrinth in culture and society: Pathways to wisdom* (J. Rowe, Trans.). Berkley, CA: North Atlantic Books.

Conty, P. (2002). *The genesis and geometry of the labyrinth: Architecture, hidden language, myths, and rituals*. Rochester, VT: Inner Traditions.

Curry, H. (2000). *The way of the labyrinth: A powerful meditation for everyday life*. New York: Penguin Compass.

Kern, H. (2000). *Through the labyrinth: Designs and meanings over 5000 years*. New York: Prestel.

Lonegren, S. (2007). *Labyrinths: Ancient myths and modern uses* (Revised 4th ed.). Somerset, UK: Gothic Image Publications.

Matthews, H. W. (1970). *Mazes and labyrinths: Their history and development* (New ed.). New York: Dover Publications.

Saward, J. (2002). *Magical paths: Labyrinths and mazes in the 21st century*. London: Mitchell Beazly.

Lacan, Jacques

John Pahucki

Jacques Lacan (1901–1981) was a French psychoanalyst associated with the literary and philosophical movements of structuralism and post-structuralism. A notoriously abstruse thinker, Lacan, like many French intellectuals associated with postmodern thought, has often been accused of being deliberately obscure in his writings. This is particularly true of his major work, the *Écrits*, which is noted for its difficulty.

Lacan is known for his claim of a "return to Freud," though in actual practice this amounted to a radical reconfiguration of Freudian psychoanalysis as Lacan attempted to effect a synthesis between Freud's biologically driven psychology and the linguistic theory of structuralists like Ferdinand de Saussure and Roman Jakobson. Freud's biologically founded subject is thus replaced, by Lacan, with a linguistically constituted subject, with the Freudian drives and even the body itself transliterated or overwritten by culturally specific signifying activities. In this view, the linguistic register of one's culture channels and determines the directionality and movements that the biological drives assume. The Freudian unconscious, formerly the a priori wellspring of irrational drives and biological pulsations, is also viewed as a linguistic product, an a posteriori consequence of our entry into the linguistic register. The unconscious possesses rules analogous to the syntactical structures which govern the conscious linguistic subject, hence Lacan's famous claim that the "unconscious is structured like a language."

Lacan is perhaps best known for the three orders of the *imaginary*, the *symbolic*, and the *real*. The imaginary order is inaugurated by what Lacan described as the "mirror phase" which occurs roughly at six months of age. In this phase the child identifies with a "specular" and exteriorized image of itself, in an actual mirror or in the mirror of the "other," which it then introjects in order to stabilize and master its bodily sense. The imaginary order, being based on this fundamental misrecognition of the self in the form of a falsifying image, thus results in a state of alienation.

This alienation is compounded by entry into the symbolic order (or linguistic register) which occurs when the child is forced to accept the "law" of the *Name-of-the-Father* (*le Nom du Pére*). With the adoption of language the subject is inscripted or overwritten by signifiers, thus being made subject to the regulative strictures and organizational principles embedded within the culture's system of signification. The symbolic order is therefore *Other* to the subject, being imposed and not truly adopted. Lacan's ubiquitous use of the term Other most often refers to this otherness of language. The direct consequence of entry into the linguistic register is "symbolic castration," a notion which replaces Freud's oedipal drama and its threat of actual physical castration with the subject's loss of *jouissance*, an untranslated term that refers to a pre-Oedipal enjoyment of the object no longer possible for the linguistic subject. In keeping with this rejection of Freud's biological schema, Lacan replaces the organ of the penis with the symbolic *phallus*, a term which refers to this pre-Oedipal state of dyadic fusion with the maternal object.

The real is much more difficult to describe, as it is the order of experience which completely resists symbolization. It may be the undifferentiated state of being that precedes linguistic acquisition or it may refer to significantly traumatic experiences which resist articulation.

Lacan's theories have generated considerable interest among philosophers, literary and religious studies scholars, and feminists preoccupied with continental thought generally and the postmodern "de-centered" subject specifically. His influence is particularly evident in the psychoanalytic work of Julia Kristeva.

See also: ❯ Kristeva, Julia ❯ Postmodernism

Bibliography

Fink, B. (1994). *The Lacanian subject: Between language and jouissance.* Princeton, NJ: Princeton University Press.

Fink, B. (1996). *A clinical introduction to Lacanian psychoanalysis: Theory and practice.* Boston, MA: Harvard University Press.

Lacan, J. (2007). *Écrits: The complete edition* (B. Fink, Trans.). New York: W.W. Norton.

Laing, Ronald David

Daniel Burston

Life and Career

Ronald David Laing was born on October 7, 1927 on 26 Ardbeg Street in the Govanhill district of Glasgow, and died on August 23, 1989 in St. Tropez, France. Like his father, Ronald Laing was musically gifted, and received a Licentiate in music from the Royal Academy of Music at age 16. At 17, he enrolled in Glasgow University, and at 18, specialized in medicine. Because of the Korean war, military service was mandatory, and so in 1949, Laing did basic training. H After a brief apprenticeship in neurosurgery at Killearn in 1950, Laing spent 1951–1952 as an army psychiatrist. In 1953, now a captain, Laing was placed in charge of the Army hospital in Catterick, in Yorkshire. Soon thereafter, he left the Army for the Royal Gartnavel Hospital and Southern General Hospital (Glasgow), where he worked under Dr. Ferguson Rodger. Rodger brought Laing to the attention of Dr. J. D. Sutherland, the Director of the Tavistock Clinic. With the help of Sutherland, and his successor, John Bowlby, Laing came to London in 1956 to train as a psychoanalyst (Burston, 1996).

During his psychoanalytic training, Laing completed *The Divided Self*, a classic in existential psychotherapy (Laing, 1960). His second book, *Self and Others*, appeared in 1961 (Laing, 1961). From 1962–1965, he worked as the Director of the Open Way Clinic, founded by E. Graham Howe, one of the few places in Britain were Freudian and Jungian therapists worked together comfortably. In 1964, Laing and Aaron Esterson, another Glaswegian psychiatrist, published *Sanity, Madness & The Family* (Laing and Esterson, 1964). Laing also published *Reason & Violence: A Decade of Sartre's Philosophy* with South African psychiatrist Dr. David Cooper that same year (Laing and Cooper, 1964).

Critique of Normality

In February of 1967, Laing published *The Politics of Experience* (Laing, 1967) Though not his best book, it was the most influential, and one feature of the book that gripped many readers was Laing's sweeping critique of "normality," which Laing described as a state of profound self-estrangement or alienation – alienation being a hot topic at the time. By Laing's reckoning, the galloping self-estrangement that plagues Western civilization fosters a progressive attenuation of the average, adjusted person's critical faculties and their openness to transcendental experience; a state more akin to a deficiency disease than to genuine mental health. What is lost to normal people are not merely instinctual urges, or the memory of specific events or losses, as Freud suggested. The awareness of the tragic, the sublime, the absurd, of the prevalence and persistence of evil, of the peace that passes understanding – these innately human sensibilities are severely stunted, if not entirely extinguished in the struggle to adapt to an increasingly one-dimensional world.

In retrospect, it is interesting to note how often Laing disparaged normality with religious tropes and metaphors. In chapter 3, for example, he says (p. 68): "We are all fallen Sons of Prophecy, who have learned to die in the Spirit and be reborn in the Flesh" (Laing, 1967). And again, in chapter six:

> ▶ There is a prophecy in Amos that a time will come when there will be a famine in the land, 'not a famine for bread, nor a thirst for water, but of hearing the words of the Lord.' That time has now come to pass. It is the present age (Laing, 1967: 144).

Without saying so in quite so many words, passages like these implied that the loss of the sacred as a feature of *normal* experience is linked with the problem of individual and collective violence. But according to Laing, the escalating scale and widening scope of violence in our time is *not* the result of innate propensities to violence and indiscipline – a "death instinct," as Freud thought – but of *the violence we do to ourselves* in our efforts to adapt to an increasingly irrational world that is bereft of genuine transcendence. In other words, Laing implied that there is a strong correlation between the numbing routine, the mindless consumerism and the shabby ethical compromises of daily life in postindustrial society and the steady proliferation of evil.

That being so, it is important to note that *The Politics of Experience* was published at the height of the Vietnam war, when Christian, Jewish and Muslim fundamentalism had no appreciable impact on world affairs. For members of Laing's generation, who came of age during the Korean war, religious wars were a distant memory, rather than a growing and undeniable threat to global stability. Much as he lamented the loss of the numinous, Laing was not advocating a return to a repressive, theocratic society, or advocating the revival of religious creeds based on the unreflective embrace or vehement defense of particular forms of belief. Had he lived to witness our present global predicament, Laing would probably have characterized the resurgence of Jewish, Christian and Islamic fundamentalism as a reversion to *pseudo-religious* attitudes and passions, rather than the genuine article.

Metanoia

In any case, in contrast to mere normality, Laing maintained that true sanity can only be achieved through the dissolution of the socially adjusted ego (or persona) in a process which he termed "metanoia." Ego transcendence, said Laing, can be sought gradually and deliberately through meditation and spiritual practices, or it can occur spontaneously. The mad person, said Laing, is often catapulted into this process unawares, and without skillful guidance, will go astray, exiled indefinitely in the daemonic realms that enshroud and obstruct our access to the holy. However, given appropriate care, many psychotics can recover their emotional and intellectual equilibrium without recourse to psychotropic medication or other intrusive or coercive treatments, with the help of a seasoned therapist who is in touch with his or her own psychotic core, and is not intimidated or overwhelmed by the severity of the patient's symptoms.

Like Jung before him, Laing borrowed the word "metanoia" from the New Testament to describe the dissolution of normal egoic consciousness. When translated from the original Greek, this word it usually rendered as "repentance." The problem with this commonplace translation is that it dwells primarily on the subject's sense of sinfulness, and his (or her) earnest desire to shed sinful habits and desires. But in the original Greek, the term "metanoia" connotes an epistemological upheaval, a radical change of perspective, a total and irreversible change in one's view of oneself and the world – in short, an epiphany or enlightenment experience more akin to the ancient idea of "gnosis" than to moral reform or reconstruction.

Laing's Christian Roots

Though few readers were aware of it, R. D. Laing combined a rare appreciation of Asian wisdom and spiritual practices with a heartfelt immersion in Christian spirituality – a trait that he shared with E. Graham Howe and Alan Watts. Nowhere is this more apparent than in an interview with Yoga scholar George Feuerstein, entitled "Sparks of Light," which appeared in 1983. "Sparks of Light" contains many of his most profound reflections on spirituality, but was not delivered in his usual style. Laing himself acknowledged this, admitting that he was finally expressing himself in a Christian idiom that he had become "... less embarrassed about affirming in the course of the last thirty years or so" (Feuerstein, 1983).

Why embarrassed? During the Cold War Era, when Laing rose to prominence, people tended to regard anyone who spoke often and earnestly of their faith outside of their immediate circle as being somewhat odd and ill-educated. However, this statement also conveys the misleading impression that though his reluctance to speak about it had diminished in the last few decades, his faith had been constant throughout. This is simply not so. Indeed, the cumulative impression one gets is that Laing spent most of adult life as a reluctant and sometimes deeply anguished agnostic who longed for the consolations of faith, but could not overcome his doubts and misgivings sufficiently to affirm what he desired to belief – sometimes ambivalently, sometimes wholeheartedly. This is the real source of his "embarrassment."

What kind of Christian was Laing, when he was not overwhelmed by doubt? As a teenager, Laing was exposed to the Evangelical-cum-fundamentalist variety of Calvinism, and to the older "Celtic Christianity" that arrived in Scotland with Brendan the Navigator (c. 484– c. 578) and St. Columba (521–597), both of whom played a significant role in the building of Iona Abbey on the Isle Iona, in the Lower Hebrides. By the age of 14, Laing claimed, he had emphatically Evangelical Christianity in favor of the latter, Celtic variety. This claim is born out by his on again/off again relationship with the Very Reverend George MacLeod (1895–1991), who like Laing, incidentally, was a native of Glasgow who rose to the rank of Captain in the British Army. McLeod was the founder of The Iona Christian Community, an ecumenical community dedicated to the preservation of Celtic Christianity and the erasure of world hunger and poverty, based on the Isle of Iona in the Lower Hebrides. Though few people are aware of it, Laing spent many weeks there over the course of his career. Indeed, in the early 1980s, Laing even pondered the possibility of situating a foundation to be called St. Oran's Trust on this fair island.

Laing's leanings toward Celtic Christianity are also evident in his remark to Feuerstein that we are all one in "the Universal Fire." Indeed, said Laing, our individual souls are nothing but "sparks" emanating from this universal fire. Classicists contend that the idea that the soul is a "spark" of a Divine Fire probably originates in the Orphic religion, but gets taken up by Plato in the fourth century BCE, and subsequently, by the Stoics and neo-Platonists in the Hellenistic-Roman era. While originally a school of pagan philosophy, Neo-Platonism and the emanationist approach to theology later took on Jewish, Christian and Islamic forms, and as we survey the history of Western spirituality, the imagery of the soul as a Divine spark becomes a common idiom for mystics of all three monotheistic traditions.

Another striking feature of his talk with Feuerstein, is that when asked to share the fruits of a lifetime of introspection, Laing responded that he discovered "that hope is justifiable." The term "hope" does not surface often in Laing's work, and though he vigorously repudiated the suggestion, many readers – friends and critics alike – found *The Politics of Experience* to be an angry and eloquent expression of overwhelming despair. If so, of course, Laing had clearly recovered some of his optimism in the interim. Meanwhile, the suggestion that hope is justifiable, and that this represents a hard won discovery on his part, says a great deal about him personally.

That being so, it is also instructive to note that Laing tries here – and not for the first time – to link the idea of love to the project of scientific inquiry, and that Laing often despaired of getting psychiatrists to see that viewing their patients primarily or exclusively through the lenses of the natural scientific attitude is profoundly dehumanizing. The idea that science is (or ought) to be informed by a loving, reverential attitude toward nature was self-evident to someone like Einstein, but is odd and incongruous to most scientists, so Laing justified this linkage by pointing to the destructive potential of scientific research that lacks this basis. He said:

▶ If you investigate and inquire into the world without love, you don't find anything worthwhile. If you look at a tree or a frog or anything at all without the eyes of love, then you obtain only loveless, heartless knowledge. When such knowledge is accumulated and applied to practices of scientific technology, it becomes the most destructive form of knowledge ever discovered. Even the worst black magic cannot vie with the destructive capacity of science. Its very method is to destroy what it looks at in order to discover its elements.

See also: ❯ Ego ❯ Existential Psychotherapy ❯ Jung, Carl Gustav ❯ Psychoanalysis ❯ Self

Bibliography

Burston, D. (1996). *The wing of madness: The life and work of R. D. Laing*. Cambridge, MA: Harvard University Press.

Burston, D. (2000). *The crucible of experience: R. D. Laing and the crisis of psychotherapy*. Cambridge, MA: Harvard University Press.

Feuerstein, G. (1983). Sparks of light: Interview with R. D. Laing. *The Laughing Man, 5*(12), 19–21.

Laing, R. D. (1960). *The divided self*. London: Tavistock Publications.

Laing, R. D. (1961). *Self and others*. London: Tavistock Publications.

Laing, R. D. (1967). *The politics of experience and the bird of paradise*. New York: Pantheon.

Laing, R. D. (1976). *The facts of life*. New York: Pantheon.

Laing, R. D. (1982). *The voice of experience*. New York: Pantheon.

Laing, R. D. (1985). *Wisdom, madness & folly: The making of a psychiatrist*. New York: McGraw Hill.

Laing, R. D., & Cooper, D. (1964). *Reason and violence: A decade of Sartre's philosophy*. New York: Pantheon.

Laing, R. D., & Esterson, A. (1964). *Sanity, madness and the family*. London: Tavistock Publications.

Levinas, Emmanuel

David M. Goodman

Emmanuel Levinas (1906–1995) was a Talmudist, ethicist, and continental philosopher whose thought has left a lasting imprint on contemporary philosophy and theology. His sophisticated ethical system that understands the self to be radically responsible for the Other has challenged conventional theories of selfhood, subjectivity, consciousness, ethics, metaphysics, language, and social relations. Furthermore, his ethical philosophy is beginning to find its way into psychological discourse concerning psychotherapy, human development, and definitions of selfhood.

Levinas was born in Kaunas (a.k.a. Kovno), Lithuania in 1906 to a moderately affluent, Orthodox Jewish family. In his formative years, he was educated in traditional Hebrew school and was also heavily influenced by the work of Russian novelists such as Tolstoy and Dostoyevsky. In 1923, Levinas traveled to Strasbourg, France for formal education in philosophy. Shortly after, he went to Freilburg, Germany where he studied phenomenological theory and methodology under both Edmund Husserl and Martin Heidegger. These experiences impacted Levinas for the remainder of his intellectual career. Levinas translated Husserl's work into French, making him the first to introduce Husserlian phenomenology into the French academy (later read by Sartre and other prominent thinkers). Husserl and Heidegger remained the primary dialogue partners within Levinas' philosophical works. He viewed their thoughts on consciousness, history, ontology, and metaphysics to be representative of the greater Western philosophical tradition he wished to engage and challenge.

Conversant in both Hebrew Scriptures and Western philosophy, Levinas represents a unique perspective on ethics. His project is sometimes described as *translation*, a communicating of ancient Hebrew wisdom through the more dominant and universalizing trends of Greek rationality and the academy. Levinas' project continues to be mined for its far reaching implications upon religious studies, philosophical systems, and psychological paradigms.

The historical context of Levinas' life further enriched the content of his writings and critique. Levinas' loss of his father, mother, and two brothers at the hands of Nazi soldiers, along with his own imprisonment for five years during World War II, left a profound impression on Levinas' thought and interaction with Western philosophy. He claimed that many trends within Western thought had created an allergy to ethics and a form of ethical immunity for persons in the world. He understood many Western systems of morality to be failures and dangerous appendages to the violence making of the ego and human history as a whole. Levinas argued for movement away from the *love of wisdom* that had sustained Western thought since the ancient Greeks (and can be seen in modern science and psychology) to a *wisdom of love at the service of love* recognized within biblical tradition. Levinas called for "ethics as first philosophy" rather than ontology, traditional metaphysics, epistemology, doctrine, or sacraments.

Levinas' concern about violence, along with his desire to provide an account of human experience/phenomenology that recognized the inherent ethical call in the face of the Other, provided the basis of his first magnum opus, Totality and Infinity. In this work, he argues that the ego is not at rest within itself, but rather has a metaphysical desire for something beyond its own sameness (or immanence). Though the ego often defends against otherness by reducing the Other to totalizing depictions (through intentional consciousness), there is a compelling command within the face of the Other that calls for responsibility. Levinas understood the face of the Other to be a trace of the Divine (or infinity/transcendence). The dialogical philosophies of Martin Buber and Franz Rosenzweig were indelible influences upon Levinas' assertions concerning the irreducibility of the Other and the requirement of justice in human relations. As Levinas' work evolved, this responsibility became even more radical and his language for it more intense. By his second magnum opus, Otherwise than Being or Beyond Essence, Levinas had come to emphasize the Other as bearing an alterity as radical as God's alterity. Furthermore, the Other's otherness, in Levinas' thought, wounds the banality and complacency of the ego and denucleates and decenters it. The ego loses its primacy and sovereignty and, instead, is hostage, persecuted, and traumatized by its inexhaustible responsibility for the Other. Ultimately, Levinas worked to uncover the phenomenological experience in face-to-face relation.

For Levinas, one's psyche is ethically constituted and called forth into identity. The Hebrew expression, *hineni*, meaning "here I am," was his most succinct definition of the human psyche and the human self. That is, the self is always an ethical responsiveness, not a self-assertion or noun. To argue these points, Levinas engages in complex analysis about intersubjectivity and time, primordial encounter, interhuman subjectivity, and sensate experience.

Interestingly, Levinas peppers much of his philosophical treatises with rich religious terminology and illustrations (e.g., substitution, expiation, glory, Divine, transcendence, hineni, idol, Abraham's departure from his homeland, etc.). This has created significant contention in the field of Levinas studies concerning the theological characteristics of Levinas' thought. Some argue that his philosophy was fundamentally Jewish while others want to preserve a purist depiction of his thought as philosophical. This issue is complexified by Levinas' confessional writings and Talmudic commentaries. Levinas was not entirely clear about the relation of his religious beliefs to his philosophical works. However, he was clear that he considered himself a translator of Hebrew thought (ethical concern for the Other as represented in ancient tradition) into and through Greek thought (dominant Western tradition). Though, he did not like the title "Jewish thinker" or "Jewish philosopher" to describe his work.

In addition to the works listed above, Levinas wrote many other social and religious commentaries, and philosophical articles and books. By the end of Levinas' career, he had taught in the prestigious philosophy departments at the University of Poitiers, University of Nanterre, and University of Sorbonne. His impact on the landscape of 20th European continental philosophy has been and continues to be quite significant. Such thinkers as Blanchot, Derrida, Merleau-Ponty, Sartre, Lyotard, Marion, Pope Jean-Paul II, and Ricoeur are just a few of the many notworthy figures within Western thought that came under Levinas' influence.

Commentary

Levinas did not write directly about psychology in most of his works. Scattered references can be found – mostly of a critical nature – about the naturalistic, mechanistic, and reductive practices of psychoanalysis and behaviorism. Despite this, Levinas' thought has slowly begun to make its way into psychoanalytic dialogues, with comparisons done between Levinas and Winnicott, Lacan, Freud, and Jung. Existential-Phenomenological schools utilize Levinas' work to further bolster claims about the irreducibility of the human person. Conferences and journals are forming that specifically target the interaction between Levinas' ethical philosophy and psychological systems and practices. Often, this interface takes the form of a fundamental challenging of dominant paradigms within modern psychologies. Reductive theoretical systems and practices have come under serious critique utilizing Levinas' methodology. Furthermore, the nature of consciousness, subjectivity, the ego, and the relation between self and the Other are often the topics addressed in these conversations.

Modern psychologies have frequently functioned as an extension of Western philosophical frameworks and out of a long lineage of Greek thought. As such, the Greek emphasis upon generalization, universalization, rationality, and immanence remains the preponderant base of contemporary psychology. Consciousness and rationality have been emphasized alongside of naturalistic and universalizing depictions of selfhood.

Furthermore, the individual ego is often valorized, with individuation and independence as core goals of human flourishing (in Western psychologies). Language of coping, cohesion, adaptation, and integration are among the many descriptors of a higher functioning self within the world. Seldom are theories and practices developed that understand the self as a "moral event" or emergent from ethical interchange and justice. Some theories recognize the need for social interest (e.g., Alfred Adler) or

interpersonal engagement (e.g., Harry Stack Sullivan), but are far from making ethics a "first philosophy".

Levinas' critique of Western consciousness and the Western ego as self-reflexive and transfixed with itself is a frequent theme throughout his work. His depiction of an ethically constituted self challenges the fundamental primacy of the ego and construes the ego as vulnerable and exposed to the calling of the Other. Psychological appropriators of Levinas' work often accuse psychoanalysis, cognitive-behavioral theories, and a variety of other paradigms as being caught up in this "egology" wherein the monadic individual and his or her rationality, affective functioning, and behavioral repertoires constitute the human person. The Western ego, in Levinas' thought, has become an idolatrous entity within which persons became trapped, pre-occupied, and tormented. Persons cannot find escape from themselves. Levinas uses the story of Odysseus and his return to his homeland as an example of the prodigal and self-returning version of the ego in Western thought. In contrast, he describes the story of Abraham – who is exiled from his homeland and journeys to a land unknown – as an illustration of a self lived beyond the confines of itself.

Instead of freedom being understood as individuation, living congruently with one's biological needs/drives, or self-actualization, Levinas suggested that freedom is born from responsibility for the Other. Ethical interchange and moral attunement are more original than ontological expressions of personhood. Instead of the "I" being sovereign and imperial, it is a response to the imperative found in the needs of the Other. The ego is perpetually called outside of itself and into a selfhood beyond the practices and history of itself (sameness). Levinas utilizes the illustration of God commanding Adam into being at creation, thus showing that the self is first commanded before anything else.

The prophetic quality of Levinas' work and the translation of Jewish ethics into contemporary systems of thought is poignant and a powerful corrective to dominant skews in modern, Western psychologies.

See also: ❯ Anti-Semitism ❯ Bible ❯ Buber, Martin ❯ Communal and Personal Identity ❯ Consciousness ❯ Ego ❯ Ethics and Ethical Behavior ❯ Existentialism ❯ God ❯ Heidegger, Martin ❯ Holocaust ❯ Immanence ❯ Jewish Law ❯ Kristeva, Julia ❯ Lacan, Jacques ❯ Liberation Theology ❯ Love ❯ Narcissism ❯ Nazism ❯ Phenomenological Psychology ❯ Postmodernism ❯ Power ❯ Psyche ❯ Psychoanalysis ❯ Psychology ❯ Psychotherapy ❯ Reductionism ❯ Relational Psychoanalysis ❯ Sacrifice ❯ Self ❯ Talmud ❯ Transcendence ❯ Wisdom

Bibliography

Bloechl, J. (Ed.) (2000). *The face of the other and the trace of God: Essays on the philosophy of Emmanuel Levinas*. New York: Fordham University Press.

Burggraeve, R. (2007). *The wisdom of love in the service of love: Emmanuel Levinas on justice, peace, and human rights*. Milwaukee, WI: Marquette University Press.

Cohen, R. (1994). *Elevations: The height of the good in Rosenzweig and Levinas*. Chicago, IL: The University of Chicago Press.

Critchley, S., & Bernasconi, R. (Eds.) (2002). *The Cambridge companion to Levinas*. Cambridge, England: Cambridge University Press.

Ford, D. (1999). *Self and salvation: Being transformed*. Cambridge, England: Cambridge University Press.

Gantt, E. E., & Williams, R. N. (Eds.) (2002). *Psychology for the other: Levinas, ethics, and the practice of psychology*. Pittsburgh, PA: Duquesne University Press.

Gibbs, R. (1992). *Correlations in Rosenzweig and Levinas*. Princeton, NJ: Princeton University Press.

Kosky, J. L. (2001). *Levinas and the philosophy of religion*. Bloomington, IN: Indiana University Press.

Kunz, G. (1998). *The paradox of power and weakness: Levinas and an alternative paradigm for psychology*. New York: State University of New York Press.

Levinas, E. (1969). *Totality and infinity: An essay on exteriority* (A. Lingis, Trans.). Pittsburgh, PA: Duquesne University Press (Original work published 1961).

Levinas, E. (1989). *The Levinas reader* (S. Hand, Ed. & Trans.). Cambridge, MA: Blackwell Publishers.

Levinas, E. (1990). *Difficult freedom: Essays on Judaism* (S. Hand, Trans.). Baltimore: The Johns Hopkins University Press (Original work published 1976).

Levinas, E. (1994). *Nine talmudic readings*. (A. Aronowicz, Trans.). Bloomington, IN: Indiana University Press (Original work published in 1968, 1977).

Levinas, E. (1998a). *Of God who comes to mind*. (B. Bergo, Trans.). Stanford, CA: Meridian Press (Original work published in 1982).

Levinas, E. (1998b). *Otherwise than being: Or, beyond essence* (A. Lingis, Trans.). Boston, MA: M. Nijhoff (Original work published 1974).

Malka, S. (2006). *Emmanuel Levinas: His life and legacy* (M. Kigel & S. Embree, Trans.). Pittsburgh, PA: Duquesne University Press (Original work published 2002).

Liberation Psychology

Daniel J. Gaztambide

Liberation psychology is a umbrella term for a cross-disciplinary movement in psychology which originated in Central and South America as a response to grievous social injustice, civil war, and political turmoil. It is most often associated with the work of Jesuit priest and social psychologist Ignacio Martín-Baró (1942–1989) in El Salvador. Although he is often credited with popularizing the term in social and community psychology, it was "coined" and employed independently by Nancy Caro Hollander in her assessment of the progressive social justice initiatives of psychoanalysts who integrated the psychological insights of Freud with the social and economic analysis of Marx.

Liberation psychology is a broad movement in psychology comprised of multiple schools with different cultural and ideological origins. It is perhaps most often associated with the work of Jesuit priest and social psychologist Ignacio Martín-Baró (1942–1989) in El Salvador, who called for a psychology which relinquished its aspirations for social, political, and "scientific" prestige in order to make "a preferential option for the poor," those people who are oppressed by unjust social conditions and political regimes. This liberation psychology entailed a fusion of liberation theology, the political analysis of psychology from critical psychology, Paulo Freire's radical pedagogy, and the methodological tools of social psychology. The social ethics and theological assertions of liberation theology in particular were of great import in the development of Martín-Baró's thinking, who maintained a close relationship with renown liberation theologian and philosopher Ignacio Ellacuría.

Three tenets of liberation theology crucial to Martín-Baró's development of liberation psychology were the belief in a God of life and justice who scorned oppression, the importance of orthopraxis over orthodoxy, and the preferential option for the poor. Using these three principles Martín-Baró proposed three essential elements of liberation psychology: a new horizon by which psychology would not concern itself with maintaining a privileged political or social position but with employing itself in the service of the poor and oppressed, a new epistemology that attempts to understand psychological dynamics from the perspective of the dominated poor Salvadorans instead of the perspective of the dominant elite, and a new praxis by which knowledge and research developed from the perspective of the oppressed then becomes used to empower them by developing critical consciousness regarding their psycho-social-political reality (*concientización*), in order that they may liberate themselves and change that reality. Given these elements, Martín-Baró outlined for liberation psychology three urgent tasks. Firstly, there needs to be a recovery of historical memory, by which one discovers those behaviors of the past which instill a sense of collective identity and help a oppressed community survive and struggle toward liberation. Secondly, there needs to be a de-ideologizing of everyday experience through the subversion of dominant narratives by psychologists participating in the life of the poor, recovering their experience and "returning" it to them, so that they may reflect upon it and form a broader consciousness of their reality. Thirdly, psychologists in El Salvador should shun the importation of ethics, cultures, and values alien to the country's people and instead use the people's own values and virtues as represented in the cultural, social, and religious institutions that have aided in their survival during the civil war and struggle toward social justice.

Using this liberation psychology, Martín-Baró developed social psychological research projects that aimed to understand phenomena as varied as the effects of war on mental health (especially that of children), the psychological dynamics of state terrorism and oppression, the ways that psychology can collude with or go against the status quo, the use of religion as an instrument of psychological warfare, and the experiences of the Salvadoran people in the midst of social and political violence. This research was not simply published in academic journals but was likewise used to develop critical consciousness (*concientización*) among the Salvadoran people. Due to the political implications of this perspective for psychology and Salvadoran society, Martín-Baró was murdered in 1989 along with seven others on the campus of the Central American University in San Salvador. His vision, however, lives on as it has influenced many social and clinical psychologists in Latin America, North America, and Europe.

Parallel to the development of Martín-Baró's thinking, in 1981 the North American psychoanalyst Nancy Caro Hollander became interested in the work of Marie "Mimi" Langer (1910–1987) and other psychoanalysts in the Southern Cone countries (Argentina, Chile, Uruguay, Paraguay, and Brazil) who also struggled against unjust political regimes, by relating psychoanalysis and Marxism in both theory and clinical practice much in the same way that liberation theology had related theology and Marxism in liberatory reflection and praxis. Hollander worked with Marie Langer and her colleagues clinically and academically, and as a result of their relationship subsequently began writing a group biography detailing their life and work in the midst of war and oppression. In that biography it was detailed how Marie Langer and many of her colleagues had originally migrated from Europe to South America due to the growing threat of Nazism to Europe and toward their communist and Marxist political views.

Much like their counterparts in North America, in South America Langer and other migrating psychoanalysts initially found it necessary to keep a low profile on their Marxist ideologies for fear of retribution from more conservative colleagues and the local right-wing governments.

As conditions in Latin America continued to deteriorate due to civil wars, revolutions, and economic-political oppression, psychoanalysts began to speak out against injustice and take steps to both make sense of the escalating conflicts psychoanalytically as well as develop treatment relevant to the needs of oppressed and displaced people, hence making a preferential option for the poor people of Latin America. Freud's theories concerning the intrapsychic dynamics of repression, splitting, and projection were related to Marx's theories regarding the repressive and alienating dynamics of economic and structural injustice. The function and role of a overly-harsh and persecutory super-ego likewise became contextualized and related to the imposition of the bourgeoisie morality and right-wing politics of the governing classes. The work of Melanie Klein in particular became very influential in understanding how human destructiveness was affected by interpersonal, economic, and societal dynamics, such as genocidal ideologies molding everyday poor people into soldiers for the all-good regime against the all-bad civilians or insurgents (in many cases seen as one and the same).

In clinical practice, social justice oriented psychoanalysts in Latin America would contextualize developmental (oedipal, pre-oedipal) difficulties and mental illness in the historical economic and political oppression that their patients' experienced in society and through family life, providing interpretations that would encourage them to speak and give voice to their psychosocial trauma. Apart from individual treatment, Langer and others also practiced group psychotherapy as a liberating practice, providing a much more socially relevant service extending mental health services to wider communities in need of support. A variety of pragmatic methodologies were developed in relation to the social ambivalence that surrounded treatment with particular clients (whether it was working with a torturer, a victim of torture, or an insurgent), including encouraging patients to become politically active in order to give voice to their fears and anxieties, a move that was found to be clinically useful in helping the healing process as well as inviting patients to work toward changing their social reality. Due to such consciousness raising and revolutionary clinical work, Hollander used the phrase liberation psychology to describe the labors of social justice oriented psychoanalysts like Marie Langer, a use that was reinforced after she found that Martín-Baró had coined the phrase earlier to describe his social psychological work in El Salvador.

Commentary

A liberation psychology of religion would be concerned with the ways that religion could be a force of prophetic and critical consciousness for social change or a tool of psychosocial domination upholding the interests of those in power. In the specific case of El Salvador, Martín-Baró was concerned with a model of intervention the United States had developed known as "low-intensity conflict," which emphasized sociopolitical psychological warfare which sought to "win the hearts and minds" of the people who supported the insurgency against the U.S.-backed regime. It would pursue this goal through the use of propaganda, harassment, sanctions, and even torture to make people feel insecure about their basic beliefs and shift political orientation in favor of U.S. interests in the region. Religion, as a central institution for many Salvadorans, enters the picture as one possible tool of such psychological manipulation.

In a series of studies starting in 1984, Martín-Baró and his colleagues did empirical research on the relationship between different types of religiosity and sociopolitical attitudes, which compared Catholic Christian Base Communities (groups that use the perspective of liberation theology to reflect upon their spiritual and material conditions in order to organize social justice efforts) to converts to Evangelical Pentecostalism, and charismatic Catholics. These studies took place during a time in which North American evangelical churches intensified missionary efforts into the area, thanks in part to the support of conservative political groups in the U.S. It was found that while the catholic Christian Base Communities displayed a "horizontal" religiosity which emphasized God among the people working toward a more just society, the church as a prophetic voice in society, and the war in El Salvador as a result of structural injustice which must be responded to by a socially active church, evangelical Pentecostals and charismatic Catholics alike displayed a "vertical" religiosity which emphasized God as mysterious and distant, the church as a house of prayer apart from society, with the war a result of man's sinfulness and divine will, which will end only by praying to God and asking for mercy. As a result of these respective theologies, "horizontal" religiosity tended to lead people from the Christian Base Communities to become conscious of their social conditions, to organize and mobilize in the interest of social justice, and to have more progressive views on child rearing, education, work, and politics, while "vertical" religiosity tended to legitimize the policies and behaviors of the government as inevitable and necessary, to become complacent and conforming to the status quo, and to have more conservative views on child rearing, and etc. Type of religiosity, then, was tied to sociopolitical attitudes which either maintained or brought into question the policies and ideologies of oppressive political regimes.

A more psychoanalytic approach to a liberation psychology of religion would attempt to correlate the effects of different types of theologies and religiosity on the psyche, and the way that particular religiosities organizes the psyche are related to the economic and power structures of society. For example, one could take James W. Jones's study of how religion can be both a source of terror and violence or revelation and transformation, and relate that analysis to a social analysis of political power. If what Jones calls fanatical religion fosters deep psychological splits in the self between "good" and "bad," with all the good projected onto an over-idealized God-image, and all the bad projected outside into groups designated as "other," it carries the potential of infantilizing adherents before an awesome and magnanimous parental figure, rendering them submissive and unable of exercising critical thinking in relation to other idealized figures, such as the state, an ethnic group, patriarchy, or a nationalistic identity. The over-idealized social institution may then invoke such sentiments to maintain a particular social order and label those who would upset that social order as enemies who must be silenced or destroyed. Alternatively, Jones also refers to religion's transformative capacity, its ability to create a space from which new insights and truths may emerge in new permutations of consciousness through a relationship – not of submission but of surrender – to a teacher, a text, a empathic community, or a spiritual practice. This transformative function may liberate the true self, and allow space for a critical voice to develop which may be able to de-idealize and critically examine the structures of power and politics within religion, culture, and society. This process may initially be deconstructive as one breaks down the over-idealization of God-images, the ethnic group, or the state, but may also become constructive as new idealizations and permutations of religious experience may emerge from within a de-idealized void. New conceptions of religion may arise with a prophetic vision of a more just society.

Bibliography

Adams, G. (2008). Commemorating Brown: Psychology as a force for liberation. In G. Adams, M. Biernat, N. R. Branscombe, C. S. Crandall, & L. S. Wrightsman (Eds.), *Commemorating Brown: The social psychology of racism and discrimination* (pp. 3–25). Washington, DC: American Psychological Association.

Aldarondo, E. (Ed.) (2007). *Advancing social justice through clinical practice.* Mahwah, NJ: Lawrence Erlbaum Associates.

Alschuler, L. R. (2006). *The psychopolitics of liberation: Political consciousness from a Jungian perspective.* New York: Palgrave Macmillan.

Altman, N. (1995). *The analyst in the inner city: Race, class, and culture through a psychoanalytic lens.* Hillsdale, NJ: The Analytic Press.

Carrette, J. (2007). *Critical psychology and religion.* London: Routledge.

Enriquez, V. (1992). *From colonial to liberation psychology: The Phillipine experience.* Quezon City, Philippines: University of the Philippines Press.

Hollander, N. (1997). *Love in a time of hate: Liberation psychology in Latin America.* New Brunswick: Rutgers University Press.

Jones, J. W. (1997). *Terror and transformation: The ambiguity of religion in psychoanalytic perspective.* New York: Brunner-Routledge.

Martin-Baro, I. (1994). *Writings for a liberation psychology.* Cambridge, MA: Harvard University Press.

Pattison, S. (1994). *Pastoral care and liberation theology.* Cambridge, UK: Cambridge University Press.

Watkins, M. (2002). Seeding liberation: A dialogue between depth psychology and liberation psychology. In D. Slattery & L. Corbett (Eds.), *Depth psychology: Meditations in the field* (pp. 204–224). Einsiedeln, SW: Daimon Verlag.

Watkins, M. (2003). Dialogue, development, and liberation. In I. Josephs (Ed.), *Dialogicality in development* (pp. 87–110). Westport, CT: Greenwood.

Liberation Theology

Daniel J. Gaztambide

Liberation Theology is a Christian theology that originated in the Latin American Catholic Church in the 1960s, but which can today can be found around the world in North America (e.g., Black Liberation Theology), Africa (e.g., African Women's Theology), and Asia (e.g., Minjung Theology). In Latin America it grew out of the efforts of Catholic priests who related theology to Karl Marx's theories of social analysis in order to become more socially conscious of the conditions of political and state oppression, and to relate theological reflection about the nature of economic and social oppression to the needs of the Latin American poor for social justice. Considering God to be a God of justice, and Jesus as not only the savior of mankind but the liberator of the oppressed, liberation theologians lived among the poor as an act of solidarity, making a preferential option for the poor and protesting the unjust conditions that afflicted them through political activism, community work, and academics. Liberation theology has also been of interest to social justice oriented mental health care workers, inspiring not only a variety of liberation psychologies (i.e., the work of Ignacio Martín-Baró, Mary Watkins, and Lawrence Alschuler), but also an integration of liberation theology and pastoral care (e.g., the work of Stephen Pattison).

See also: ⊘ Liberation Psychology

Libido

Jo Nash

Libido is a term used in psychoanalytic psychology to denote the fundamental sexual energy of the human organism, either a sexual "instinct" or "drive" which in simple terms compels us to reproduce the species. In Freud's economic theory of the psyche, libido is proposed as the sexual source of all mental energy, which flows towards objects of our attention, thereby investing them with interest or *cathecting* those objects. In this way, libido establishes a psychic relationship with the object whether in fantasy or reality. The sublimation of libido into creative activity is the source of civilisation for Freud, achieved through the complex processes of displacement of sexual energy away from the gratification of our individual desires, towards servicing the wider purposes of the social groups and institutions to which we belong.

Freud also described how libido cathects zones of the body during the early life of the child in phases called the oral, anal and genital stages of development. These different stages evolve as the child's awareness and interest is invested in progressively more complex activities focused on different parts of the body; beginning with the mouth during feeding, then the anus during potty training, before moving onto the genitals, which continue to absorb more and more attention and interest into adulthood.

For Klein, however, her clinical work with children revealed that the development of these phases was not as staged as Freud proposed, but that at any time from early life onwards, a mixture of these phases of interest could be observed, with some impulses prevailing over other impulses at different times, in order to defend the infant, child and later adult against primitive anxieties of a sadistic nature. Hinshelwood writes,

➤ ...the sequence of dominance was the effect of the sadism, the fear of retaliation, and the anguished wish to restore damage. [...] She also thought of the genital phase as a particular upsurge of libidinal feelings, and that there may therefore be a precocious surge towards the genital phase as a reassurance against the sadistic impulses of the pre-genital phases (Hinshelwood, 1989: 338–339).

In other words, the premature development of genitally focused sexual activity may indicate that deeper impulses of oral and anal aggression are being warded off by the child, out of a fear of retaliation for the harm the expression of these impulses might cause. For Klein, libido pervades all object relationships channelled through various erotogenic zones of the body at various levels of intensity from early life to death. Libido is depicted as something of a rapacious, greedy and visceral force fundamental to the presence of life and its complex quest to sustain itself.

In the analytic psychology of Jung however, the term "libido" is deployed to denote a more generic psychic energy or life force that propels the personality towards individuation through the enlargement of the "self." For Jung libido has a spiritual dimension which did not exist for Freud or Klein. In this way, Jung proposes that libidinal energy is invested in all forms of intentional activity, from individual developmental "tasks" such as symbolism and the acquisition of language, to increasingly complex creative activities, including art, science and religion, that aid increased psychological and spiritual integration. Libido is depicted as a benevolent force which invests both subjectivity and the world around us with the intentional activity of life itself.

See also: ❂ Freud, Sigmund ❂ Jung, Carl Gustav

Bibliography

Freud, S. (1905). *Three essays on the theory of sexuality* (J. Strachey, Trans.), *SE 7* (pp. 125–245). London: Hogarth Press.

Hinshelwood, R. (1989). *The dictionary of Kleinian thought.* London: Free Association Books.

Jung, C. G., & Hinkle, B. M. (1912). *Psychology of the unconscious: A study of the transformations and symbolisms of the libido.* London: Kegan Paul (Revised in 1952 as *Symbols of transformation, CW* 5.).

Liminality

Paul Larson

Origin

Liminality is a term used to describe the psychological process of transitioning across boundaries and borders. The term "limen" comes from the Latin for threshold; it is literally the threshold separating one space from another. It is the place in the wall where people move from one room to another. Often a door is placed across the threshold to close up and restrict access between rooms. The concept was first applied to psychology as the technical name for the perceptual threshold, the degree of stimulus intensity that would just be noticed as audible or visible or detectable in any sensory mode. But its contemporary usage comes from the anthropologist Arnold van Gennep (1873–1957). In his study of religion as a cultural artifact, he saw that many, if not all of the rituals across cultures have the function of moving a person from one status or social circumstance to another. His major work, *Rites of Passage,* or *Les Rites du Passage* in the original French (1909/1960), sets out the thesis that at a psychological and cultural level, religion and its rituals give us the means by which we cope with change, whether it be from childhood into adulthood, from single to married, from lay to clerical, and to mourn the loss of a beloved as they transition from this world to whatever lies beyond. His student Victor Turner (1920–1983) continued and expanded his analytic framework and integrated it into role theory and the relationship of social action to drama.

Psychological Liminality

As a psychological capacity, liminality is the ability to bridge between self and the other. At an interpersonal level this is called empathy. We come to know the other by entering into their phenomenological space to some degree. We begin to see things from their perspective. At the level of social groups, it can be described as the capacity for moving toward an insider's perspective. Pike (1954) coined the terms "emic" and "etic" to refer to the insider's and outsider's perspectives with respect to language, and this now has been broadly adopted in cross-cultural psychology for the knowledge of any social group. So limenality with respect to social groups is gaining the knowledge that approaches what an insider would have; we bridge the gap between our own groups and those of the other. Both the interpersonal and the group levels of limenality requires us to see and appreciate the other and to find bridges that would allow harmonious relationships as opposed to conflict. Liminality, therefore, is a requirement for any effective interpersonal or intercultural communication.

At the intrapsychic level, liminality is the capacity to move within and between the boundaries of one's psychological structure. Lewin (1936/1966) first used the metaphor of space in his topological psychology, defining life spaces and discussing the relative permeability of the boundaries between areas of the person's experiential world. At one extreme, on has the rigid compartmentalization characteristic of dissociation and multiple personalities; at the other is the failure of boundaries found in borderline personality disorders and termed "confluence" in Gestalt therapy.

Joseph Campbell's (1949) *Hero with a thousand faces* was much influenced by van Gennep's basic outline of the three-fold structure of liminal processes; preliminary, liminaire, and post-liminaire. He took the concept and applied it to the transitional phases between the beginning and the end of a journey or transformational process. Liminality is the process of going in between two states and the time spent in that transitional zone when one is neither one nor the other but in the process of becoming. Liminality is the journey of transformation.

Finally, the therapeutic process is itself a literal rite of passage. We can view the relationship of therapist and client as a process of helping the client move from a state of unhappiness to some greater degree of either internal peace or interpersonal harmony and adjustment. The role of patient arises out of the medical role, part of a complementary pair, physician and patient. The various sessions within the relationship, whether in brief therapy or long-term dynamic work are each small steps in the ritual of healing. Liminality describes any process of transformation from one state of being to another in human society; it is a key psychological concept.

See also: ❂ Archetype ❂ Campbell, Joseph ❂ Rites of Passage

Bibliography

Campbell, J. (1949). *The hero with a thousand faces*. Princeton, NJ: Princeton University Press.

Lewin, K. (1966). *Principles of topological psychology* (F. Heider, Trans.). New York: McGraw-Hill (Original work published 1936).

Pike, K. L. (1954). *Language in relation to a unified theory of structure of human behavior* (Parts I, II, and III). Glendale, CA: Summer Institute of Linguistics.

Turner, V. (1995). *The ritual process: Structure and anti-structure*. New York: Aldine de Gruyter (Original work published 1969).

Van Gennep, A. (1960). *The rites of passage*. Chicago, IL: University of Chicago Press (Original work published 1909).

Lived Theology

Todd DuBose

Lived theology is a phrase that describes a process more than an academic discipline. Our lived theology is the enactment of that, which is most significant to us at any given moment, and as lived out in our everyday existence, rather than the systemization of creedal propositions of any given faith tradition. Borrowing from the thought of both the philosopher Martin Heidegger (1889–1976) and the theologian Paul Tillich (1886–1965), and others who have furthered their thought, such as Langdon Gilkey (1919–2004), one's lived theology is one's "enactment of significance" in the world.

Theology, or speech about the divine, is traditionally seen as an academic discipline in which authoritative sources are interpreted and subsequently inform various doctrines and practices respective to one's religious tradition. An understanding of lived theology, though is aligned with existential and empirical-phenomenological traditions, and views the divine is an experiential phenomenon rather than a substantial and delimited thing, and sees speech about this experiential phenomenon is phenomenological in nature. The divine is not considered as an *object* of experience, but a *quality* of experience related to living out significance in the world, a living out of what matters most to one in any given situation. In this way, lived theology is not an exclusive property of elite academicians, but an existential of every human being. Hence, if human being enact significance in every moment of their lives, and if we understanding *lived* theology as those enactments of significance, we can conclude, therefore, that to be a human being *is* to be a theologian. The human being is *homo religiosus*, or more specifically, *homo theologicus* (DuBose, 2000).

To be alive is to enact significance. Theological discernment from this perspective views how one is comporting oneself in one's everydayness as disclosing what Tillich called one's "ultimate concern" (Tillich, 1952). These ultimate concerns, or as I call them, enactments of significance, are not cognitively "thought out" propositions described in abstract, traditional religious discourse, but chosen ways of being-in-the-world. Agency inherent in comportment is lived out long before thought about. Such comportments are "prereflective," as Maurice Merleau-Ponty (1908–1961) argued (Merleau-Ponty, 1964). This perspective privileges a different knowing prior to cognitive reconsideration.

Given these premises, enactments of significance are known only after the fact, or only when reflecting on comportment as it is in operation or having just passed. Life is lived rather than objectified, as the French radical phenomenologist, Michel Henry (1922–2002) proposed (Henry, 2002a). Moreover, when enactments are translated into conceptualizations, such as when an experience of the numinous is translated as "an encounter with the Holy Spirit," the product of the translation is merely a "representation" of the experience and not the experience itself. Lived theology is not reflection on "that which is over there," but a living out of significance rather than a living in relation to a representation of that experience.

Lived theology further presumes that if we are inherently theological, then our very nature as human beings is formed and led by what is of ultimate concern in our lives. Viktor Frankl's (1905–1997) logotherapy is likened to this perspective in the conviction that meaning lures and constructs human development (1946/1997). We live and intend towards meaningful and fulfilling projects and relationships in life. Our enactments of significance, and, hence, any lived theology, is naturally transcendent seeking, but delimited by one's unalterable finitude, facticity, contingency, and "throwness," to use phraseology from Martin Heidegger (Heidegger, 1962). The very delimitation of one's "throwness" enframes the meaningful possibilities of significance enacted in each moment, and are free to change as significance shifts.

Commentary

A word about therapeutic care for, and as, lived theology is in order. Therapeutic practice based on this model begins and ends with attunement toward enactments of significance in particular life-world comportments. It then explores constrictions, that is, how one's enactments of significance are restrained, inhibited, or confined. Finally, it has as the therapeutic goal a free and authentic living into one's cleared and lightened possibilities within one's embraced limitations. All symptoms of the suffering soul are constricted enactments of significance and related to the inextricable interplay of death, transcendence, and radical subjectivity, and are always and already lived out in equiprimordial ways. An obvious alignment with Daseinsanalytic phenomenology and practice is clear (Boss, 1979; Heidegger, 2001).

Often, discussants of this issue quibble about whether one considers oneself religious, spiritual, or theological. I choose to use the word "theology," rather than "spirituality" or "religion," because I believe the latter two concepts are less personal and too amorphous to disclose the specificity of one's very particular enactments of significance in the world. Moreover, one's comportment in existence discloses what one considers significant with much more veracity than what one verbalizes as significant. If you want to know someone's theology, look at their enactments of significance *in the world*. At no time are we absent from living out enacted significance, even (and especially) in despair. Paraphrasing once again Tillich's argument that doubt shows the significance of faith (Tillich, 1957), I say that despair is an enacted significance *of lost significance*, which is perhaps the greatest of all therapeutic challenges.

See also: ❷ Daseinsanalysis ❷ Existential Psychotherapy ❷ Faith ❷ Frankl, Viktor ❷ Heidegger, Martin ❷ Hermeneutics ❷ Homo Religiosus ❷ Kierkegaard, Søren ❷ Meaning of Human Existence ❷ Phenomenological Psychology

Bibliography

Boss, M. (1963). *Daseinsanalysis and psychoanalysis*. New York: Basic Books.

Boss, M. (1977). *I dreamt last night....* New York: Gardner Press.

Boss, M. (1979). *Existential foundations of medicine and psychology* (S. Conway & A. Cleaves, Trans.). New York: Aronson.

DuBose, T. (2000). Lordship, bondage, and the formation of *Homo Religiosus. Journal of Religion and Health, 39*(3), 217–226.

Driver, T. (1985). *Patterns of grace: Human experience as word of God.* Lanham, MD: University of America Press.

Frankl, V. (1946/1997). *Man's search for meaning.* New York: Perseus Books.

Gilkey, L. (1976). *Naming the whirlwind: The renewal of God-language.* Indianapolis, IN: Bobbs-Merrill Educational Publishing.

Heidegger, M. (1962). *Being and time* (J. MacQuarrie, Trans.). New York: Harper and Row.

Heidegger, M. (2001). *Zollikon seminars: Protocols – conversations – letters* (R. Mayr & R. Askay, Trans.). Evanston, IL: Northwestern University Press.

Henry, M. (2000). Speech and religion: The word of God. In *Phenomenology and the "Theological Turn": The French debate* (pp. 217–241). New York: Fordham University Press.

Henry, M. (2002a). *I am the truth: Toward a philosophy of Christianity* (S. Emanuel, Trans.). Stanford, CA: Stanford University Press.

Henry, M. (2002b). Phenomenology of life. *Angelaki, 8*(2), 97–110.

Merleau-Ponty, M. (1964). *The primacy of perception.* Chicago, IL: Northwestern University Press.

Tillich, P. (1952). *The courage to be.* New Haven, CT: Yale University Press.

Tillich, P. (1957). *Dynamics of faith.* New York: Harper and Brothers.

Tillich, P. (1966). *Systematic theology* (Vols. I–III). Chicago, IL: University of Chicago Press.

Locus of Control

Andrew J. P. Francis

The Locus of Control (LOC) of reinforcement construct was originally developed by Rotter (1954, 1966) within the framework of his Social Learning Theory, along a unidimensional internal-external continuum. An important elaboration by Levenson (1981) divided the external contingencies into separate "powerful others" and "chance" dimensions. Broadly, the LOC construct measures the degree to which people believe that reinforcements (rewards and punishments) from the environment are contingent on their own efforts, actions and personal decisions (internal LOC) on the one hand, versus luck, fate, external circumstance and powerful others (external LOC) on the other. A more internal LOC is generally positively associated with a range of indices of psychological and physical health. It is argued that many of these positive health effects reflect the adoption of more positive coping strategies in such individuals. Conversely, externality is typically associated with negative coping styles and poorer physical and mental health outcomes.

In some LOC scales (e.g., the religious revision of Rotter's internal-external scale) the external "powerful others" set of contingencies includes reference to a deity. Thus the individual believes that, to some degree, the circumstances of their life are controlled by a god, goddess or other spiritual force. The belief that an external deity may be controlling some contingencies in a person's life suggests a type of external (powerful other) LOC, and might be expected to be associated with generally poorer health outcomes according to secular LOC theory. Certainly Sigmund Freud and Albert Ellis characterized religious belief in terms of defensive functioning and psychopathology; whereas Carl Jung and Gordon Allport suggested that religion may have important psychological functions and produce positive effects on mental health.

Contemporary scientific literature would suggest that degree of religiosity is positively (albeit mildly) associated with better mental health outcomes; in particular where the type of religiosity is "intrinsic" versus "extrinsic" according to Allport's (1961) taxonomy. It has also been suggested that a person's dispositional "spiritual/religious coping style" will influence how they respond to stressors and challenges and, in a sense, specifies the nature of the control relationship they share with their god. In a self-directing style, a person functions in an active manner, independent of god (essentially a form of internal LOC). When a person adopts a deferring style they will take a more passive role and wait for god to resolve a situation (thus adopting an external LOC). In a collaborative style the person engages with their god in a mutual problem-solving process (mixed internal/external LOC). A surrendering style involves an active decision to release personal control over circumstances beyond personal control to god (external LOC). Depending on the situation, a collaborative style is generally associated with more positive mental health outcomes; although it has been argued that even the surrendering style can provide relief, comfort and security in highly stressful situations. No matter which spiritual/religious coping style is adopted, it is also certainly the case that the use of prayer, ritual and observance can instill an element of control into one's relationship with god.

See also: ❯ Freud, Sigmund ❯ Jung, Carl Gustav

Bibliography

Allport, G. W. (1961). *Pattern and growth in personality.* New York: Holt, Rinehart & Winston.

Carone, D. A., & Barone, D. F. (2001). A social cognitive perspective on religious beliefs: Their functions and impact on coping and psychotherapy. *Clinical Psychology Review, 21*(7), 989–1003.

Contrada, R. J., et al. (2004). Psychosocial factors in outcomes of heart surgery: The impact of religious involvement and depressive symptoms. *Health Psychology, 23*(3), 227–238.

Gall, T. L., et al. (2005). Understanding the nature and role of spirituality in relation to coping and health: A conceptual framework. *Canadian Psychology, 46*(2), 88–104.

Levenson, H. (1981). Differentiating among internality, powerful others, and chance. In H. M. Lefcourt (Ed.), *Research with the locus of control construct:* Vol. 1. *Assessment methods* (pp. 15–63). London: Academic Press.

Rotter, J. B. (1954). *Social learning and clinical psychology.* New York: Prentice-Hall.

Rotter, J. B. (1966). Generalized expectancies for internal versus external control of reinforcement. *Psychological Monographs, 80*(1), 1–28.

Smith, T. B., et al. (2003). Religiousness and depression: Evidence for a main effect and the moderating influence of stressful life events. *Psychological Bulletin, 129*(4), 614–636.

Locutions

Paul Larson

Locutions are inner experiences of hearing a divine voice or receiving revelation. The broader category is theophany or epiphany, which means any revelation or manifestation to humans by God or the divine, or their agents such as angels etc. Visions, or apparitions, are epiphanies which are primarily visual, while locutions are the auditory aspect of contact with or from an external transcendent source. The experience can range from very realistic dialog with an angel (including an apparition) to a subtle and sudden feeling of inspiration coming in linguistic form. It is not uncommon for these visitations to be accompanied by other sorts of miracles, such as healing. St. Theresa of Avila is one of the classic examples of a mystic whose experience included locutions. Bernadette Soubirou (1844–1879) was a young French woman who also received locutions attributed to Our Lady of Lourdes. The Virgin Mary in both Roman Catholic, Eastern Orthodox and Anglican traditions is a frequent source of apparitions and locutions. The Roman Catholic Church has a fairly detailed procedure devised over many years for checking the bona fides of claims for visions or locutions.

See also: ❂ Hierophany ❂ Miracles ❂ Virgin Mary

Bibliography

Freze, M. (1993). *Voices, visions and apparitions.* Huntington, IN: Our Sunday Visitor.

Ghezzi, B. (2002). *Mystics and miracles: True stories of lives touched by God.* Chicago, IL: Loyola Press.

Logos

Meredith Lisagor

Earliest Use of Term

Logos, a noun, derives from the Greek verb legein, originally *to count,* later *to give an account,* finally as lego, *to say.* It enjoys an array of nuanced translations: *utterance, word, speech, thought, meaning, reason, argument, ratio, measure, standard,* or *principle.* Yet whatever distinctions exist among thinkers who employ the term, Logos is consistently used to denote something about creative unifying forces or functions in the composition of reality – cosmologic, religious, philosophical, or psychological.

As a concept, Logos is first encountered in the fragments of Heraclitus of Ephesus (ca. 500 BCE.), where it identifies the underlying ordering principle or plan of the universe, which is itself a hidden unity of opposites in tension. The Logos is not the source of creation, but rather the way in which creation operates, the flux in which "diversity comes out of unity and unity out of diversity" [Frag 10]. Although all creation is elemental of the "One," humanity must "listen" for the Logos in order to comprehend it.

Platonic and Aristotelian use of the term was largely confined to the fact and consequences of human reason. Stoicism, however, took the term beyond the limits of philosophy. Heraclitus' Logos became equated with a dynamic divine reason. Here, humanity did not merely participate in Logos, but was infused with it: Discourse, meaning-making, and life in accord with natural law – or the order given the cosmos by an all-virtuous God/Logos – were products of a "seed" or "ratio" of divinity within each human being.

As Divine in Judeo-Christian Tradition

The divine character of Logos underwent subtle but profound change, when Jewish and Greek thought converged in the works of Philo of Alexandria (30 BCE–50 CE), who enlisted the term to place Torah on equal footing with Greek philosophy. Adapting Jewish Wisdom speculation – and often using "word" and "wisdom" Interchangeably – Logos became both the intelligible world in the mind of God, after which the created world was modeled, and the agency by which it was actually made. By Hellenizing notions found in Jewish texts, canonical (e.g., Proverbs 8:22) and apocryphal (e.g., Wis. 7:22 and 9:1), Philo made the Logos a virtual hypostasis of God, His "Firstborn Son," and "Image."

Philo's syncretism had arisen in an environment that also sustained popular belief in Apollo (especially surnamed Loxias, *fr.* legein) as the "spokesman" of his father Zeus. Thus, it was a short step to dubbing Jesus the Logos and Son of God – which the prologue to the Gospel According to St. John (1:1–18) did near the beginning of the second century. Where St. Paul, had declared Jesus Christ the one "through whom are all things and through whom we exist" (I Corinthians 8:6), the Johannine authors (adapting a Wisdom hymn) trumpeted that the creative Word of God became flesh and entered the world it had created; no less, it "was God."

Early Christian writers would employ Logos broadly and idiosyncratically: Justin Martyr followed a Philonic impulse in his *Apologies* (ca. 55 CE) to liken Christianity to stoic and platonic philosophies; Clement of Alexandria (ca. 150–215) even identified the eternal Christ/Logos as the giver of philosophy to the Greeks; and Christian Gnostics had at least three different notions of Logos – all disdaining the occurrence of actual incarnation. Significantly, Origen (ca. 182–254) saw Logos as a kind of effluence of God's creativity, truth, and wisdom. It could be called God's "Firstborn Son," but in fact it was not only uncreated but co-eternal ("there was no *when* it was not"). Moreover, Jesus was not really an incarnation of the Son, but rather a sinless human being who followed the Logos so closely as to be indistinguishable from it. This set the stage for the great Trinitarian and creedal debates of the next two centuries. In the end, Logos language was replaced by the term "Son."

Logos and Other Traditions

Development of the Logos concept continued into late antiquity: Hermetics declared that the "lightgiving word who comes from [God's] mind is the son of God" (Copenhaver, 1992: 2); Plotinus (205–270 CE), deemed Logos to be a divine entity of creation, unity, and order, but denied it rationality, since reasoning-out should be unnecessary to the mind of God in which all is immediate intelligibility; and the Jewish Wisdom tradition grew to identify the whole of Torah with the plan by which God created the world (Midrash Rabbah).

While one cannot argue a hereditary relationship between Logos and eastern religious thought, Logos is sometimes likened to the ultimate principle of Self in Buddhism, and the Way of Taoism. As the second person of the Christian Trinity, Logos has also been compared to the second facet of the Hindu formula *sac-cid-ananda* or Being-Awareness-Bliss.

Logos and Depth Psychology

Modern depth psychologists have adapted Logos in a range of ways. Freud makes the most limited use, ironically calling Logos the "god" of his argument for rational acceptance of reality against the illusion(s) of religion. Analytical Psychology often equates Logos with the Self, archetype of psychic wholeness and unity of all opposites. The most noteworthy application of the term may be that of Viktor Frankl. Based on his own experience and observation of fellow concentration-camp survivors, his Logotherapy speaks to a meaning-seeking will at the center of human existence. In even the worst objective circumstances, he contends, one has freedom as well a "responsibility" to seek transformative subjective meaning. It is exercise of this will that defines an authentic life.

See also: ⊗ Analytical Psychology ⊗ Archetype ⊗ Buddhism ⊗ Christ ⊗ Christianity ⊗ Freud, Sigmund ⊗ Gnosticism ⊗ Jesus ⊗ Self ⊗ Taoism

Bibliography

Aeschylus. (1992). *Eumenides*, line 19. In D. Grene & R. Lattimore (Eds.), *The complete Greek tragedies* (Vol. 1). Chicago, IL: University of Chicago Press.

Aristophanes. (1952). *The Plutus*, line 8. (B. B. Rogers, Trans.). In R. M. Hutchinson (Ed.), *Great books of the western world* (Vol. 5). Chicago, IL: Encyclopedia Britannica.

Barrett, C. K. (1970). *The prologue of St. John's gospel*. Ethel M. Wood Lecture, University of London. http://www.biblicalstudies.org.uk/articles_ethel_m_wood.php. Accessed December 8, 2006.

Clement of Alexandria. (1885). *Stomata, Book I*. In A. Roberts & J. Donaldson (Eds.), *The ante-nicene fathers* (Vol. 2). Online Edition. Retrieved October 6, 2005 from http://www.newadvent.org/fathers/02105.htm.

Copenhaver, B. P. (1992). *Hermetica*. Cambridge, UK: Cambridge University Press.

Couliano, I. P. (1992). *The tree of Gnosis*. San Francisco, CA: HarperCollins.

Dodd, E. R. (1970). *Pagans & Christians in an age of anxiety*. New York: Norton.

Frankl, V. (1986). *Doctor of the soul* (R. & C. Winston, Trans.). New York: Vintage Books.

Frankl, V. (1992). *Man's search for meaning*. Boston, MA: Beacon Press.

Frend, W. H. C. (1982). *The early church*. Minneapolis, MN: Fortress Press.

Freud, S. (1957). Future of an illusion. In J. Strachey (Ed. & Trans.), *SE* (Vol. 21). London: Hogarth Press.

Geldard, R. (2000). *Remembering Heraclitus*. Great Barrington, MA: Lindisfarne Books.

Gordis, R. (1965). *The book of God and man*. Chicago, IL: University of Chicago Press.

Horowitz, M. C. (1998). *Seeds of virtue and knowledge.* Princeton, NJ: Princeton University Press.

Jaeger, W. (1961). *Early Christianity and Greek paideia.* Cambridge, MA: Harvard University Press.

Jung, C. G. (1989). *Psychology and religion: West and East* (R. F. C. Hull, Trans.), *CW* (Vol. 11). Princeton, NJ: Princeton University Press.

Niebuhr, R. (1955). *The self and the dramas of history.* New York: Scribner's.

Norris, R. A. (1995, Fall). *Lectures.* Union Theological Seminary in the City of New York. New York.

Origen. (1979). *De principiis, Book IV: 4 ff* (G. W. Butterworth, Trans.). Gloucester, MA: Peter Smith.

Perkins, P. (1981). Logos christologies in the nag hammadi codices. *Vigiliae Christianae, 35*(4), 379–396.

Perkins, P. (1987). Jesus: God's wisdom. *Word & World, 7*(3), 273–280.

Philo. (2004). On the creation, IV. 18, V *ff,* VI *ff,* X. 36, Allegorical interpretation III, XXXI. In *The works of Philo* (C. D. Yonge, Trans.). Peabody, MA: Hendrickson Publishers.

Plotinus. (1992). *Enneads, VI. 7* (S. MacKenna, Trans.). Burdett, NJ: Larson Publications.

Reischauer, A. K. (1913). Japanese Buddhism and the doctrine of the logos. *Biblical World, 41*(4), 245–251.

Ricoeur, P. (1970). *Freud & philosophy* (D. Savage, Trans.). New Haven, CT: Yale University Press.

Walker, W., Norris, R. A., Lotz, D. W., & Handy, R. T. (1985). *A history of the Christian church.* New York: Scribner's.

Young, F. (1977). Two roots or a tangled mass. In J. Hicks (Ed.), *The myth of God incarnate.* Philadelphia, PA: Westminster Press.

Zaehner, R. C. (1961). *Mysticism sacred and profane.* New York: Oxford University Press.

Logotherapy

◉ Frankl, Viktor

Love

David C. Balderston

Love is a powerful force that connects and energizes people. It has long been a theme of religions and literatures around the world. More recently, love has been studied by social scientists. This article surveys the major meanings of love, as used in various religions and in modern psychological thought.

Introduction

Love means several different things. Other languages have two, three, or more words with different meanings, where English has only the one, to use in many different situations. The authoritative *Oxford English Dictionary* describes over 30 uses of "love." Like many writers, Scots poet Robert Burns (1759–1796) used literary devices to heighten the effects of his thoughts, e.g., "O, my luv's like a red, red rose" – here, a simile to dramatize love's power of attraction. In contrast, a modern definition strives for neutral objectivity: "Love is the creating and/or sustaining of the connections of mutual support in ever-widening ranges of significance" (Carothers, 1968). Shakespeare noted love's mystery: "I know not why I love this youth, and I have heard you say, Love's reason's without reason" (*Cymbeline,* IV.2.20–22).

Here are some of love's emphases:

1. A *desire for physical closeness* that connects people, to touch and be touched, whether they be sexual partners, parent and child, other family relations, or close friends.
2. *Compassion* of one person toward another, sometimes one who is in need. Altruistic self-sacrifice and empathic understanding of how another feels are components of such love, often recommended by religions.
3. A *mutual affinity* in a friendship that is not primarily sexual but emotional and value-laden, with shared interests and sensibilities, and actions of mutual generosity.
4. A *religious regard* for another, where a human and a spiritual being (a god or a saint) are linked in a relationship of gratitude and devotion by the human, and scrutiny and/or caring by the spiritual figure.

Religion

The world's five largest religions, arranged here from the oldest to the newest, are surveyed for their uses of love. Judaism, which provided the scriptural foundation of monotheism for Christianity and Islam, is also included.

Hinduism, the dominant religion of India and of Indians living elsewhere, is a sprawling, decentralized complex of many parts. Hence the place of love in Hinduism is more diffuse compared to other religions. The following Sanskrit terms suggest the range of loving experiences. *Kama* is sensual pleasure and erotic love. It is also seen as a fundamental life force, a necessary ingredient in other human desires and strivings. *Karuna* refers to compassionate actions to reduce the sufferings of others. *Bhakti* is devotional love, adoration, and service directed at one's chosen deity. *Prema* is an intense and altruistic longing for God, and is considered Hinduism's highest form of love.

Judaism, the religion of Jewish people worldwide, stresses ethical behavior and devotion to a single God, who formed a covenant relationship with "his people" in which He would protect, chasten, and love them, while expecting their grateful adoration and obedience to his laws. This is elaborated in the Hebrew *Bible*, where love is translated from two primary words (and cognates), *ahab* and *khesed*, plus six other less frequent Hebrew words, as desire, mercy, beloved, steadfast love, loyalty, kindness, devotion, and faithfulness.

The great ritual phrase, the *shema* (Deut. 6: 4–5), calls upon the people of Israel to love God with all their heart, soul, and might. Elsewhere, God directs them to love their neighbors and also the stranger in their midst (Lev. 19: 18 and 34). The prophet Hosea used the imagery of an unfaithful wife, lovingly sought out and forgiven by her husband, to stand for God's undying love toward his sometimes unfaithful people.

In *Buddhism*, love has a central place: its founder, Siddartha Gautama (563–483 BCE), is typically referred to as the "compassionate Buddha." The earlier branch of Buddhism, called Hinayana or Theravada, focuses on love as *metta* (in Pali, or *maitri* in Sanskrit), a kindness or benevolence toward all. The later branch, Mahayana, emphasizes *karuna*, compassion, and its ultimate embodiment in a bodhisattva, one who has attained full enlightenment. The bodhisattva most identified with loving compassion is Avalokitesvara (Sanskrit), or Chenrezi in Tibet, often depicted with a multitude of arms and hands, to reach out and help multitudes.

Since Buddhism, a non-theistic religion, teaches that all reality is illusory, one's sense of self-importance is to be devalued, and one is to act as a vehicle of compassion toward others. The various schools of Buddhist meditation, based on deep psychological and philosophical analysis, may focus on neutralizing the mind of its self-centeredness, or filling the mind with compassion toward others.

Confucianism has long been the dominant religion of China and of millions of ethnic Chinese overseas. Confucius (551–479 BCE) taught a version of right living, preserved in the *Analects,* which emphasized the good of society more than the individual. Confucian ethics codified the "five relationships," which stressed "filial piety" (love as respect) between pairs of family members, and others. Confucius taught that the "way of Heaven" (*T'ien*), or a moral life, should be lived by *jen* (translated as benevolence, uprightness, or love) and *li* (proper etiquette and rituals – to preserve social harmony). The Confucian emphasis, on reciprocity (mutual expectations of appropriate role behavior in social relations), was opposed by the radical views of Mo Ti, who followed Confucius about a century later. Mo Ti (or Tzu) promoted *ai*, a universal love that ignored all distinctions of rank or family position, which he said caused trouble. Mo Ti had many followers, but his ideas died out after the counter efforts of Mencius, a follower of Confucius. This conflict is an example of how different values, reciprocity and universality, can pull love in opposite directions.

Christianity, the world's largest religion, relies on the New Testament of the *Bible,* which used two Greek words for "love," *agape* (self-sacrificing love) and *filia* (friendship love), while ignoring a third word, *eros* (erotic love), also in common usage then.

Jesus, the central figure of the New Testament and the Christ of Christianity, was a Jew living in a Jewish society in the land of Palestine, then governed politically by Roman rulers and religiously by Jewish high priests. Love was a major theme of Jesus' message. In the "great commandment," (Matt. 22: 35–40, Mark 12: 28–34, and Luke 10: 25–28), Jesus rebutted Jewish leaders trying to entrap him doctrinally, saying that people should love God with all their heart, soul, and mind (or strength), *and* their neighbors as themselves – just as the scriptures had said earlier but in two separate passages (see Judaism, above). When asked a follow-up question, "Who is my neighbor?" Jesus told the story of a compassionate Samaritan who helped an injured Jew, even though Samaritans were despised by Jews.

Jesus also preached the radical notion of loving one's enemies (Matt. 5: 43–48 and Luke 6: 27–28, 32–36). Twentieth century examples are the effective non-violent protest campaigns of Mahatma Gandhi and Martin Luther King, Jr.

During Jesus' ministry, his ethical message became layered with the additional identification of himself as the Son of God, as he anticipated his death, as a chronic disturber of the Jewish and Roman status quo, to be the necessary means of conveying God's ultimate message of self-sacrificing love: "For God so loved the world that he gave his only Son..." (John 3: 16).

After the death of Jesus (ca. 30–33 CE) and his followers' experience of his resurrection, the apostle Paul emerged as the leading missionary to the Gentiles. His letters to the non-Palestinian churches often develop the dual themes of God's salvational love through the sacrifice of his Son, Jesus (now the Christ), plus the need for Christians to love one another. Paul made explicit the universal quality of this love of Christ that recognized no distinctions of gender, ethnicity, or social status (Gal. 3: 28 and Rom.

10: 12). Paul glorified the ultimate virtue of love in 1st Corinthians, chapter 13. A later apostle also wrote to exalt love, declaring that "God is love" (1 John 4: 7–21).

St. Francis of Assisi (ca. 1182–1226 CE) expanded the scope of love to include animals and all of creation.

A tension has always existed between the commandment to love your neighbor *as yourself*, and the *selfless* love exemplified by Jesus. A balance is needed between loving oneself too much and not enough: both extremes prevent one from loving God and others, although finding that balance can be difficult.

Modern Christian theology and devotional literature continue to confront this tension regarding "self," and the human tendency for self-serving self-deceptions. Psychology has also studied this tendency. Theologian Reinhold Niebuhr wrote, "Goodness, armed with power, is corrupted; and pure love without power is destroyed," (Niebuhr, 1937) a theme developed later by Paul Tillich (1954).

In *Islam*, God (Allah) is always referred to in the *Koran* (*Qur'an*) at the beginning of every chapter (sura) as "the merciful, the compassionate," or as "most gracious, most merciful." These phrases come from one of four frequently used Arabic word groups that convey various Koranic nuances of love, from the roots of *hbb, rdy, rhm,* and *wdd.*

Of the Five Pillars of Islam, the injunction to give alms to the poor is the one most directly connected to loving activity, but the Koran is suffused with themes of benevolence, kindness, and mercy – variants of love.

One movement within Islam is Sufism, which promotes an intimate personal connection between the believer and Allah through a mystical development of love.

Overall, the message about love from various religions might be summarized in interfaith terms something like these, with "God" representing the various names and conceptions of the Ultimate Reality or Ground of Being:

Love is what God is – the energy that binds together Creation and all its creatures.

Love is what God offers *to* humans – a way to be Alive despite imperfections, anxieties, and suffering.

Love is what God expects *from* humans – respect for the Creator and all Creation, with awe at its vastness and complexity.

Love is what God desires *between* humans – to give unselfishly. . .

Psychology

Psychology has studied love from five different perspectives: (1) as an individual emotion, especially in romantic love, (2) as individual behavior, (3) as a relationship between two (or more) people, (4) developmentally over time, and (5) socially as influenced by various social and cultural group norms. Psychotherapists also deal with the absence and failures of love in crumbling marriages, child neglect and abuse, adolescent problems, addictions, depression, and other anxious and lonely states.

1. *Love as a feeling of an individual* is a wonderful, tumultuous experience. In romantic love, a person who has "fallen" in love experiences a heightened sense of well-being: one feels special in the eyes of the beloved, understood as never before, with an improved sense of one's sexual identity as a man or woman. One may be preoccupied by frequent thoughts of the beloved or inspired to act in unusual ways on behalf of the beloved. Sexual desire – or at least the desire to touch, be physically close, and kiss – is a major part of romantic love, along with an idealization of the beloved. This is in contrast to a depersonalized lust for a sexual "object."

The emotion of love contains strong elements of wish, hope, longing, and fantasy. What is often sought is a sense of being made whole, through closeness with another. This goal is also a theme of religious devotion: that divine love will make a flawed human whole: worthy of being loved by another being (human or spiritual), and capable of giving love to others.

Romantic love began in the twelfth century CE songs of European troubadours celebrating the courtly love of knights of chivalry, who labored dramatically to impress and woo their chosen, often married noblewomen. While this love never applied to the rest of the population, it did idealize the quest for a pure love (later portrayed by Dante and Petrarch), and it promoted tenderness and a better view of women (Hunt, 1959).

The emotional intensity of romantic love can have drawbacks: it may be blind to reality, unrequited, or obsessional, and be the excuse for negative behaviors such as manipulative game-playing and revenge-seeking. As a feeling, romantic love is bound to fluctuate, as do all feelings, and thus is unreliable as the sole criterion of true love.

2. *Loving behaviors by an individual* are many: touching and hugging, complimenting, offering help, paying attention to what the beloved is saying and feeling, sacrificing one's time or money for the sake of the beloved, being on time and especially presentable when seeing the beloved, being patient with the other's imperfections, being willing to apologize for one's own – to name a few.

Psychology usually sees outward behavior as an indicator of a person's inner motivation: we often convert our feelings into action. One is held responsible for how one behaves, but not for what one is feeling. Behavior, since it is normally under one's control, can also be used to change one's feelings – the opposite of emotions shaping behavior, as in psychodynamic theory (see an integration of psychodynamic and behavioral approaches at Weinberg, 1981). Thus, a person can learn to behave and feel more lovingly.

3. *Love is a relationship between two people* (or between a human and a divine being) and how the two respond to each other can be studied to see their patterns of interaction. Is there equality between the two, or domination by one? Is one's frequent criticism followed by the other's frequent withdrawal or defensive outburst? Repeated arguments about money, in-laws, friends, or work often conceal an underlying concern: "Do you really love *me*?" In parent-child relations, does the parent feel (and act) more tender or more frustrated? What kind of attachment behavior does the child show toward a parent: secure, avoidant, anxious/ambivalent, or disorganized? (Cassidy and Shaver, 1999)

4. *Love can be understood as a process of development.* Erikson's eight stages of human development (Erikson, 1963) expresses this idea: adolescence is the stage for developing an Identity (finding oneself), during a period of experimentation after the childhood self has been discarded. But if Identity is not adequately developed before entering the next stage, sharing Intimacy with a partner in young adulthood, then the lover will not have enough of a self to share, and the relationship will suffer. On the other hand, while "puppy love" of earlier childhood may be mocked, developmentally it is age-appropriate; it is the extent of love that youngsters are capable of, as they imitate adult behaviors and attitudes.

5. *All of the above aspects of love take place within systems of social expectations.* National, racial, religious, social class, and other cultural norms are always present, exerting limits on the permissible range and appropriate forms of expression of love. The family everywhere is a major human institution, upholding these wider norms and also containing its own local rules, rewards, and understandings of love. When a modernized culture emphasizes individualism, romantic love can happen freely, but where collective stability of the larger family or social system is emphasized, as in traditional cultures, such love is seen as a threat and arranged marriages are more typical.

Culture may also affect parent-child love, when it favors one gender over the other. Birth order customs may require that the oldest and youngest child receive different kinds or amounts of love than other siblings (Toman, 1976). A child's inborn characteristics of temperament (Chess and Thomas, 1984), intelligence, or sexual orientation may affect the ability of parents to love a child who is "different." These psychosocial and situational factors contribute to making love a highly complex phenomenon.

Among psychological *theories* about love are these: *Freud* developed theories about basic drives (especially sex), unconscious wishes and fears, and delayed adult reactions to childhood emotional experiences, all with implications for human love. Freud turned the Golden Rule on its head: you will do to others (in the present) as you have been done unto (in your past). *Maslow* posited an ascending hierarchy of human needs, with love midway (Maslow, 1987). *Harlow* showed, by depriving young monkeys of their mothers, that the normal development of an infant requires what might be called primate love – a stable caregiver that can offer regular, warm physical contact; otherwise, adult mating and parenting abilities will be devastated (Blum, 2002). *Sternberg* sees three dimensions to adult love: intimacy (sharing oneself), commitment (to the relationship), and passion (physical and emotional) (Sternberg and Weis, 2006). In addition, *Rogers* believed that effective psychotherapy requires that a therapist demonstrate "unconditional positive regard," a professional kind of loving (Rogers, 1961).

The opposite of love may be hatred (another kind of powerful interpersonal connection), but sometimes it is the absence of love. A loveless childhood may lead to a loveless adulthood, where a person is unable to care about the feelings of anyone else – in the extreme, an unloving, antisocial personality, previously known as psychopathic or sociopathic. By comparison, the narcissistic personality has mostly given up on ever finding, yet secretly longs for, the love of another person.

Love can be austere: a self-help group uses the concept of "tough love" to help parents cope with the emotional manipulations of wayward offspring. In such situations, religion can remind one of images of steadfast love, while psychology can recommend empathy, to feel in oneself the other's distress and alienation, plus the objective compassion of therapy.

The philosophy of existentialism has contributed Buber's "I – Thou" relationship as a model for responsible loving (Buber, 1923/2000), and Sartre's comment that there was no such thing as love, only loving acts.

In summary, love, while subject to various interpretations by different psychologies (and also religions), is a prominent, complex, and sometimes problematical feature of close personal relationships. Growth in love relationships usually requires persistence in communications of all sorts to nurture the relationship, honesty about one's shortcomings, willingness to make sacrifices for the sake of the relationship, and acceptance of a measure of uncertainty in our still-limited understanding of how, why, and when love fails or succeeds.

In conclusion, while scientific research will continue to study love's intricacies, and psychological understandings will continue to enhance our ways of improving interpersonal relationships, religion (and popular culture) will continue to put forward the belief that love is both necessary and mysterious – a positive force in human relations that we all can be thankful for.

See also: ❖ Buddhism ❖ Christianity ❖ Islam ❖ Judaism and Psychology

Bibliography

Blum, D. (2002). *Love at God park: Harry Harlow and the science of affection.* Cambridge, MA: Perseus.

Buber, M. (2000). *I and Thou.* (R. G. Smith, Trans.). New York: Scribners (originally published 1923).

Carothers, J. E. (1968). *The pusher and puller: A concept of God.* Nashville, TN: Abingdon.

Cassidy, J., & Shaver, P. R. (Eds.) (1999). *Handbook of attachment: Theory, research, and clinical applications.* New York: Guilford.

Chess, S., & Thomas A. (1984). *Origins and development of behavior disorders.* New York: Bruner/Mazel.

Erikson, E. (1963). *Childhood and society* (2nd ed.). New York: W. W. Norton.

Hunt, M. (1959). *The natural history of love.* New York: Knopf.

Maslow, A. (1987) *Motivation and personality* (3rd ed.). New York: Addison-Wesley.

Niebuhr, R. (1937). *Beyond tragedy.* New York: Scribners.

Rogers, C. (1961). *On becoming a person.* Boston: Houghton Mifflin.

Shakespeare, W. (1974). Cymbeline. In G. B. Evans (Ed.), *The Riverside Shakespeare.* Boston, MA: Houghton Mifflin [originally written ca. 1609-10 and first published in the "First Folio" of Heminge, J., & Condell, H. (Eds.) (1623). *Mr. William Shakespeares comedies, histories, & tragedies.* London: Isaac Iaggard & Ed. Blount, printers].

Simpson, J. A., & Weiner E. S. C. (Eds.) (1989). *The Oxford English dictionary* (2nd ed., 20 Vols.). Oxford, England: Oxford University Press.

Sternberg, R., & Weis, K. (Eds.) (2006). *The new psychology of love.* New Haven, CT: Yale University Press.

Tillich, P. (1954). *Love, power, and justice.* London: Oxford University Press.

Toman, W. (1976). *Family constellation* (3rd ed.). New York: Springer.

Weinberg, G. (1981). *The pliant animal: Understanding the greatest human asset.* New York: St. Martin's.

Luther, Martin

Daniel Burston

The Rise of a Reformer

Martin Luther (1483–1546) was born on March 10, 1483, in the small Saxon town of Eisleben. His father, Hans Luther, a peasant turned copper miner, was shrewd, hardworking and prosperous. In 1501, Luther commenced studies in philosophy at the University of Erfurt, where Ockham's nominalistic philosophy (or the *via moderna*) contended with the prevailing Thomistic worldview. In 1505, at his father's urging, he embarked on the study of law. One day, shortly after, he was stranded in a field during an immense thunderstorm, and was so shaken by the experience that he vowed to St. Anne that he would enter a monastery if she spared his life. The storm abated, and to his father's considerable disappointment, he kept his promise, entering an Augustinian monastery in Erfurt. He was ordained in 1507, and the following year, followed his mentor, Dr. Johannes von Staupitz, to Wittenberg to found an Augustinian university, which was outspokenly critical of medieval scholasticism and Aristotelian philosophy. For the following ten years, Luther studied, lectured and prayed dutifully. But his anger toward Roman – and increasingly, Papal – authority grew steadily, influenced in part by *In Praise of Folly* (1511) by Erasmus of Rotterdam, a leading Hebraist and humanist, who criticized the practice of selling "indulgences." On the eve on All Saints Day in October, 1517, Luther published 95 theses of his own criticizing the sale of indulgences. (The story about Luther nailing his theses to the door of the Cathedral is apocryphal. There were no eyewitnesses!) As his fame and notoriety grew, so did his theological daring. In the space of a few years, he went from criticizing a lucrative and hypocritical (but highly specific) practice of the Church to challenging the basic legitimacy of the Pope's authority, eventually labeling him the "anti-Christ."

Luther and Erasmus

While he leaned on him initially, Luther broke with Erasmus and the humanists in 1525. Erasmus resembled Aristotle and St. Thomas in having some faith in our innate sociability, our ability to govern ourselves, and in the efficacy of good works, carried out in the proper spirit, to ennoble and edify the human spirit (Green, 1964). Some humanists and their fellow travelers, the Unitarians, even allowed for the possibility that Jews, Muslims and Hindus, if they conducted their lives in a Christian spirit, could commend themselves to God, and be welcomed into Heaven in the hereafter.

Heresy! thundered Luther. Salvation is always an unmerited gift of God. There is nothing we can do in this world to really merit salvation. Luther argued that works without faith are of no avail, and indeed, are idolatry, and that only those who embrace Jesus Christ as their personal savior will enter the kingdom of heaven. By some accounts, at the end of his life, Luther hated Erasmus even more than he hated the Pope! Another contentious issue was that Erasmus and his circle interpreted scripture allegorically, for the most part, and made ample allowance for the existence of more than one valid interpretation of a text. Though not enamored of Aristotle, whose authority was generally invoked to stifle, rather than to promote free inquiry, at least in those days, Erasmus and the humanists also acknowledged the wisdom of many pagan poets and philosophers, arguing that they are perfectly compatible with a Christian way of life. In short, they were averse to a rigid or doctrinaire attitude toward religious faith. Not so Luther. Though he put a selective emphasis on certain Biblical texts, and deliberately ignored others, Luther maintained that the Bible is the literal and infallible word of God. He also claimed to know precisely what the Bible meant in any given instance, even if the text itself was deeply obscure to other learned commentators who were more deeply versed in Hebrew and Greek – like Erasmus, for example.

Apart from their doctrinal differences, Erasmus was repulsed by the violence of Luther's feelings and exhortations, and the copious blood shed that accompanied the Reformation. Erasmus deplored violence, and spotted Luther's tendencies in that direction early on. Reflecting on their disparate agendas, Erasmus said: "I layed a hen's egg; Luther hatched a bird of quite a different breed" (Green, 1964: 164). Despite these differences, Luther and Erasmus shared was the belief that the Bible should be accessible to all. In fact, Luther stressed that *all* men should read the Bible and pray in their own tongue, rather than in Latin. This doctrinal shift not only undermined the Roman monopoly on the reading and interpretation of scripture, but placed a considerable premium on literacy, creating an urgent demand for public education – an idea unheard of in feudal times. Fortunately for Luther, it also coincided with the invention of the Gutenberg's

printing press, and Gutenberg himself became a staunch ally, printing hundreds of Luther's pamphlets to spread opposition to Rome and its cunning machinations to enslave men's souls. But while it hastened the dissolution of the feudal order (and the creation of public schools,) Luther sought to keep certain features of the feudal hierarchy intact. Luther's religious revolution undermined the ecclesiastical hierarchy in Rome, but enjoined strict obedience to secular authority – even for unfortunate peasants who were thrust to the brink of destitution and beyond (Green, 1964). Indeed, a pamphlet entitled *Against the Thievish and Murderous Hordes of Peasants* (1525) explicitly encouraged German princes to suppress peasant revolts with ruthless violence – which they did, of course.

Marxist and Freudian Readings

Luther's behavior in the peasant wars (1524–1526) invited a Marxist interpretation, and in 1936, Herbert Marcuse published a brief study on Luther in a series called *Studies in Authority*, published by Felix Alcan (Paris), and reprinted in *Studies in Critical Philosophy* (Marcuse, 1973). Marcuse construed Luther's authoritarian tendencies and his growing contempt for the peasantry as an early expression of a nascent bourgeoisie starting to flex its muscles, because it was linked, in his mind, to Roman law, which Luther studied before entering the monastery. (Roman law was used by the burghers of Luther's era to undermine or circumvent the legal constraints on commerce imposed by the Church.) In *Young Man Luther,* the best known biography of Luther by a psychoanalyst (Erikson, 1958), Erik Erikson chided Marxists for being one sided and reductionistic in their emphasis on economic motives, and inattentive to the powerful "psychic reality" behind Luther's teaching. But even he conceded the element of truth in these approaches.

In 1941, Horkheimer and Adorno drew clear links between Luther's anti-Semitic statements and then-current Nazi propaganda in a report on their *"Research Project on Antisemitism"* (Horkheimer and Adorno, 1941). Initially, in more charitable moods, Luther had explained the Jewish refusal to convert to Christianity as rooted in a sensible mistrust for the Papacy, and the pagan elements (including "mariolatry") that Catholicism had introduced into Christian teaching. For a few years, Luther even deluded himself into thinking that once he had purged the Christian faith of these sordid accretions the Jews would convert *en masse*. However, after many abortive efforts to convert local Jewry, in 1543, at age 60, Luther exhorted his contemporaries:

▷ First, to set fire to their synagogues or schools.

▷ Second, I advise that their houses also be razed and destroyed.

▷ Third, I advise that all their prayer books and Talmudic writings, in which such adultery, lies, cursing and blasphemy are taught, be taken from them.

▷ Fourth, I advise that their rabbis be forbidden to teach henceforth on pain of loss of life and limb.

▷ Fifth, I advise that safe-conduct on the highways be abolished completely for Jews.

▷ Sixth, I advise that... all cash and treasure of silver and gold be taken from them.

▷ Seventh... Let whomsoever can, throw brimstone and pitch upon them, so much the better... and if this be not enough, let them be driven like mad dogs from the land (cited in Burston, 2007: 115).

This inflammatory speech was not an isolated incident. Luther's last sermon, was another attack upon Jews, and the Kristllnacht pogrom which swept Germany in 1938 was deliberately timed to coincide with Luther's birthday. Luther's utterances were often read in Protestant Churches during the Nazi era to incite violence and hatred toward Jews (Burston, 2007).

Erik Erikson's biography, *Young Man Luther*, minimized Luther's anti-Semitic outbursts and his destructive attitude toward peasants, dwelling instead on Luther's audacity, originality, resilience, sincerity and wit. While more sympathetic than many treatments of Luther's life, Erikson did strain credulity at times. He credited Luther's confessor, von Staupitz, with rare therapeutic abilities that supposedly saved the sanity of this prodigiously gifted but deeply disturbed young man, and helped him find his "voice," and to trust his own, inner authority, though von Staupitz remained completely loyal to the Church. Odder still, Erikson interpreted a disputed passage in Luther's *Table Talk* to mean that the decisive moment in his religious development - Luther's epiphany - took place while he was evacuating his bowels. Erikson reasoned that for someone who suffers from chronic constipation, having a splendid bowel movement could easily engender a "religious" experience; an idea echoed by Norman O. Brown 2 years later, in *Life Against Death* (Brown, 1960). If Erikson was right, Luther was the first (and perhaps *only*) specimen of *homo religiosis* to have his crucial revelation

during the act of defecation. W. H Auden welcomed Erikson's interpretation. According to Auden (1960),

▷ There must be many people to whom religious, intellectual or artistic insights have come in the same place, for excretion is both the primal creative act – every child is the mother of its own feces – and the primal act of revolt and repudiation of the past – what was once good food has become bad dirt and must be gotten rid of. From then on, Luther's fate became his own (Auden, 1960: 17).

Well, perhaps. But if many people have religious experiences while defecating, very few actually report them. So the question becomes: why did Luther, of all people, have this experience? Or more to the point: did he, really? We may never know, but in retrospect, Luther's epiphany probably did *not* occur in the way or in the place that Erikson imagined it. Luther's account is worded more ambiguously than Erikson allowed, and could be construed as saying that the blessed event occurred in meditation cells *adjacent to* the monastery's privy (Green, 1964; Marius, 1999). But whatever you believe on this point, the fact remains that Luther was an intriguing character. He attacked the selling of indulgences and cult of saintly relics with a clarity and indignation worthy of Voltaire. But he was also deeply superstitious, a believer in witchcraft who claimed to literally "see" demons and evil spirits lurking about the Prussian landscape. As a good medieval cleric must, Luther dutifully reviled "the flesh," echoing centuries of Christian tradition. But he was bitterly opposed to priestly celibacy, spoke frankly of conjugal pleasures, and in later years, ate and drank with deliberate abandon to "mock the devil" – or, as Erikson said, to chase away bouts of anxiety and depression. A man of great vigor and industry, who survived three epidemics of Bubonic plague and lived to the age of 63 Luther was also a legendary neurasthenic, who was prone to bouts of constipation and dizziness, and other diffuse bodily ailments. But for all his faults and frailties, Luther was still what Hegel termed a "world-historical individual," whose writings, utterances and deeds transformed the world irrevocably, for good and for ill. His illustrious contemporaries included Copernicus, Erasmus, Thomas More, Rabelais and Machiavelli – the last of the medievals, or first of the moderns, depending on how you juggle your historical schemata. Looking backwards, it is hard to think of a generation who had more impact on modernity than they. And with the possible exception of Copernicus, Luther was the most influential of them all.

See also: ❷ Christianity ❷ Erikson, Erik

Bibliography

Auden, W. H. (1960, June). Greatness finding itself. *Mid Century, 13*, 9–18.

Brown, N. O. (1960). *Life against death*. New York: Vintage.

Burston, D. (2007). *Erik Erikson and the American psyche*. New York: Jason Aronson.

Erasmus, D. (1511/1876). *In praise of folly* (W. John, Trans.). London: Reeves & Turner.

Erikson, E. (1958). *Young man Luther*. New York: W. W. Norton.

Green, V. H. H. (1964). *Luther and the reformation*. London: New English Library.

Horkheimer, M., & Adorno, T. (1941). Research project on anti-semitism. *Studies in Philosophy and Social Science, 9*, 124–143.

Luther, M. (1569). *Table talk* (W. Hazlitt, Trans.). Philadelphia, PA: The Lutheran Publication Society.

Marcuse, H. (1973). *Studies in critical philosophy*. Boston, MA: Beacon Press.

Marius, R. (1999). *Martin Luther: The Christian between God and death*. Cambridge, MA: Harvard University Press.

M

Magic

Jeffrey B. Pettis

Magic involves the practice of what is perceived to be the direct manipulation of material and spirit realms by human initiative. This action is meant to bring about definitive, tangible results. The Greco-Roman Egypt source entitled the Greek Magical Papyri (second century BCE–fifth century CE) provides an array of kinds and forms of magic used during this time. The spells, for instance, bring favor, produce a trance, drive out daemons, question a corpse, induce insomnia, catch a thief, cause evil sleep, break enchantment, and induce childbearing. They occur as charms, oracles, dreams, saucer divination, magical handbooks, magical rings, astrological calendars, horoscopes, lamp inquiry, and magico-medical formulae. Many of the spells require complex procedures. To control one's shadow, the subject must make an offering of wheaten meal, ripe mulberries, and un-softened sesame. After making the offering, she must go into the desert on the sixth hour of the day and lay prostrate toward the rising sun, hands out-stretched, saying a formula which begins: "Cause now my shadow to serve me …" (Betz, 1986 PGM III: 612–632). The shadow will come before the face of the subject on the seventh hour, and is to be addressed with the command: "Follow me everywhere." A charm for sending a dream requires picking three reeds before sunrise, and incanting a formula after sunset while facing, respectively, east, south, west, and north (Betz, 1986 PGM IV: 3172–3208). The range and extent of forms and purposes of magic relate the human desire to address the complexity of day-to-day life situations. They are meant as wish-fulfillment response to human limitation and anxiety. Coursing through the material there occurs the influence of ancient Egyptian temple religion, worship of the sun, and notions of the regenerative potencies in nature seen in the ritual practices of mummification. At the same time, these magical formulae are representative of a cultural syncretism which includes Babylonian, Greek, Jewish, and Christian religions, and as such evidence the extent to which magic was used within the ancient world. By 13 BCE however, the influence of magic becomes stemmed by Augustus' burning of 2,000 magical scrolls (Seutonius, *Augustus* 2.31). The early church reaction against magic as pagan practice contributes further to the suppression of magical handbooks and magicians. St. Augustine (d. 430 CE) makes it a point to say how the raising of Samuel from the dead by the witch of Endor (1 Sam. 28.8–25) occurred through the work of daemons (*Ad Simplicianum* II, III). The Medieval text *De Magis*, which is part of a larger treatise entitled *Etymologies* by St. Isidore of Seville (d. 638 CE), denounces magic as having originated with *angelorum malorum* ("evil angels"). He says that "hidden knowledge" resulting in the taking of oracles and the raising of the dead (*dicuntur oracula et necromantia*) was first employed by Zoroaster, King of Persia, and even more by the Assyrians beginning with King Ninus (9.1–3). Subsequent church figures including Archbishop Hincmar of Rheims (d. 881), and Bishop Burchard of Worms (d. 1025) rely on Isidore to denigrate magic even further in their own writings. However, by the tenth and eleventh centuries astrological handbooks reappear within the domain of the Church. Demons are perceived to exist under the rule of the Church and the raising of the symbol of the cross. Earth magic, which includes the supernatural marking of shrines, wells and springs, *sculptilia*, and *simulacra* also emerges. The European Enlightenment and its focus upon reason and religious dissociation results in the eventual demise of magic however, while contemporary intrigue seems to be occurring through attention given to books and films such as Harry Potter.

See also: ❯ Astrology ❯ Demons ❯ Zoroastrianism

Bibliography

Betz, H. D. (1986). *The Greek magical papyri in translation.* Chicago, IL: University of Chicago Press.

Flint, V. I. J. (1991). *The rise of magic in early medieval Europe.* Princeton, NJ: Princeton University Press.

D. A. Leeming, K. Madden, S. Marlan (eds.), *Encyclopedia of Psychology and Religion*, DOI 10.1007/978-0-387-71802-6,
© Springer Science+Business Media LLC 2010

Lindsay, W. M. (Ed.) (1911). *Etymologiarum* VIII, ix. *Isidori Hispalenis Episcopi Etymologiarum sive Originum Libri.* Oxford: Oxford University Press.

Mutzenbecher, A. (Ed.). (1970). *De diversis quaestionibus ad Simpliciаnum.* CCL 44. Turnbout: Brepols.

Rolfe, J. C. (Trans.) (1998). *Seutonius.* Loeb classical library, Cambridge, MA: Harvard University Press.

Maimonides, Moses

Mark Popovsky

General

Born in Cordova, Spain, Moses Maimonides (1135–1204) achieved fame as a rabbinic authority, legal codifier, philosopher, physician and astronomer. Religious persecution sent him into exile throughout Spain and northern Africa before he eventually settled in Cairo serving as the physician to the vizier al-Fadil in 1185.

Philosophical Views

Strongly influenced by Aristotelian philosophy popular in the surrounding Muslim culture, Maimonides is regarded as the supreme rationalist of Jewish tradition. He asserted the doctrine of the incorporeality of God and devoted much of his major philosophical work, *A Guide for the Perplexed*, to reinterpreting biblical passages which suggest an anthropomorphic deity. Maimonides wrote the *Guide* in an effort to resolve the apparent contradictions between Aristotelian philosophy and traditional Judaism which were challenging the faith of well-educated Jews at the time. He argued that biblical texts have a spiritual meaning beyond their literal one – a meaning which points to the ultimate authority of reason. He attempted to prove the existence of God using exclusively Aristotelian terms without relying on the bible. Maimonides maintained that Jewish laws – even those of a seemingly ritual nature – are products of divine wisdom and, thus, wholly rational. In the *Guide* and in his work, *The Book of Commandments*, Maimonides dedicates himself to explicating the rational principles underpinning particular Jewish laws.

As in Aristotelian thought, Maimonides believed that moral behavior, while important, was simply a means to attaining intellectual virtue, the highest ideal. He argued that the mind's ability to reason represents the divine image reflected in human beings and thus individuals have a moral imperative to develop their intellectual faculties. Maimonides asserted that morality consists of following the mean which is attained as the well-cultivated mind controls a person's desires. In an exception to this appeal for moderation, Maimonides encouraged his readers to avoid even slight traces of anger or pride and his later writings display an increasingly ascetic inclination.

In the *Guide*, Maimonides shows special interest in the interpretation of dreams and prophetic visions which he views as wholly natural events. Maimonides diverges from earlier Jewish tradition which generally regarded dreams as manifestations of divine communication. In a process similar to what Freud calls the "dream work," Maimonides interprets dream material by retracing how the dream was created in the mind of the individual, focusing on the latent context instead of the dream content itself. He argues that dreams mark the nexus point between the rational and imaginative faculties, two aspects of the mind that the Hebrew prophets and some later rabbinic figures were successfully able to synthesize.

In the *Guide*, Maimonides put forward the argument that ascribing any individual attribute to God denies God's unity and omnipotence. Consequently, one may only speak of what God is not (i.e., God is not nonexistent.) but one commits heresy when attempting to define what God is. Similarly, Maimonides held the neoplatonic doctrine that evil does not exist independently but simply reflects an absence of good. While arguing that the world as a whole is good, Maimonides attributed the suffering that individuals experience to divine justice and man's misuse of free will. He rejected the claims of previous Jewish philosophers that God intentionally causes suffering to a righteous person in order to reward that person in the afterlife. Maimonides' own view of the afterlife drew heavily from the Hellenistic model of the immortality of the soul, downplaying rabbinic notions of physical resurrection.

Legal Writing

Maimonides did not write exclusively for the philosophical elite. He is most famous among Jews today for his legal code, the *Mishneh Torah*. This 14 volume work endeavors to distill the whole of rabbinic literature, rich with arguments, tangents, loose associations and dialog, into a systematic and comprehensive catalog of conclusive legal rulings in clear Hebrew accessible to the lay reader.

The topics covered include family law, torts, criminal law and ritual practice. The code also contains within it a complete system of metaphysics, refutations of Christianity and Islam, and a discussion of eschatology. This project was controversial from its inception, drawing criticism that Maimonides was interpreting previous legal debates idiosyncratically and denying his reader access to dissenting arguments. Nevertheless, the code gained immediate popularity throughout the Jewish world, strongly influencing the language, structure, and content of Jewish legal writings into the modern era.

See also: ◉ Dreams ◉ Freud, Sigmund ◉ Judaism and Psychology

Bibliography

Nuland, S. B. (2005). *Maimonides (Jewish encounters)*. New York: Schocken Books.

Twersky, I. (1972). *Maimonides reader*. Springfield, NJ: Behrman House Publishing.

Male God Images

Annette Peterson

God images are psychological constructs of thoughts and feelings, coalesced into a complex relational gestalt. God images were once critiqued by psychologists of religion as projections, personifications to be rejected. Now they are recognized by contemporary psychologists of religion for their ability to provide psychological strength and resilience. They provide structure and improve functioning on the individual and the social level, by helping us internalize a moral code and a shared world view.

Male God images hold sway over the mainstream religious imagination, affecting conscious and unconscious cultural mores and theological traditions. Male God images are particularly effective in structuring and strengthening the individual and his/her society. Replicating the Western traditional father's role of provider, role model and disciplinarian on the cosmic stage, male God images provide a sense of belonging, safety, and a clear moral compass. However, these benefits are not without risk: these God images may also cause us to suffer perpetual childhood, gender imbalance and guilt/shame complexes.

In the triad of Western monotheisms, Judaism, Christianity, and Islam, gendered and sexualized language is used to express the divine nature. Although Islam eschews divine images, the male referent is used. In the Judaism and Christianity, as in the Bible, masculine language for God is overwhelmingly predominant. God is consistently depicted in a paternal role, as external to but actively involved in his creation. God is a divine king, lord over all the universe, husband to his chosen nation of Israel, and father to us all. The father–child relationship functions particularly effectively as a metaphor for the relationship between God and humans. The term father conveys authority as well as kinship.

The dominant God image of recent history is of a male, divine king, who rules over all, meting out justice, demanding obedience, caring for those on his good side, and smiting those who fail to please. This historical trend dates back several thousand years, to early urban civilizations. Although earlier tribal societies favored more animistic (nature/animal Gods) or feminine (Earth Mother) God images, when humans coalesced into larger societies, the male God image was strengthened as a way of stabilizing the social structure and enforcing a shared code of ethics (Edinger, 1996). Cultures who serve a "divine king" will achieve a greater civilization than if these roles are disparate or conflicting.

Although male God images may strengthen us culturally, they can weaken us individually. Sigmund Freud critiqued the male god image of mainstream monotheism as a projection of our earthly fathers onto the heavens. Freud declared, "God is in every case modeled after the father, and that our personal relation to God is dependent upon our relation to our physical father, fluctuating and changing with him, and that God at bottom is nothing but an exalted father" (1918/1950: 244).

Freud dismissed God as a glorified father figure and rejected religion as a psychological crutch based in illusory wish-fulfillment (1928/1975). He believed that we would remain psychologically crippled until we rejected our parentified God images. Freud compared our projection of the divine father to the story of Oedipus, with God as a psychological creation to assuage our guilt for having usurped our earthly fathers, and as a means to maintain a sense of perpetual childhood, buffered and cradled by God. With God the Father as the ultimate authority figure, it is easy to shrug off free will and personal responsibility and bow to God's greater will.

Since Freud, psychoanalytic object relational theory has elaborated and amended the Freudian critique with studies demonstrating the validity of the parental projection theory. However, these studies have correlated God images with early images of both father and mother, and often the preferred or opposite-sex parent (e.g., Beit-Hallahmi and Argyle, 1975; Rizzuto, 1979; Vergote and Tamayo, 1981). Further, these studies have corrected Freud by showing the positive effects of the God relationship, demonstrating that it provides psychological strength and resilience.

Carl Jung offered a different perspective on the God-as-father hypothesis. Rather than a larger than life father figure, Jung believed that the God image is an archetype, or symbolic representation, of the self. He wrote, "[O]ne can never distinguish empirically between a symbol of the self and a God-image, the two ideas, however much we try to differentiate them, always appear blended together" (Jung, 1958: 156).

If the God image is also a self image, its examination reveals much about the psyche and its complexes. The God image may reflect our personal world view on a cosmic level, or it may be an idealized image that compensates for our inherent deficiencies.

The male God image appears to be a conglomerate of parental and self images, a synthesis of our relational experiences and expectations that is coalesced into a singular divine Person. The God image provides an anchor in our relation to the divine, yet it is also flexible, changing alongside our own faith development. In theories of faith and spiritual development, the personification of the divine occurs in the middle developmental stages, and later gives way to a more universal, inclusive God image (Fowler, 1981; Genia, 1995; Meissner, 1984). With developmental maturity, the God image has greater tolerance for diversity and ambiguity. It is possible that a parallel developmental trajectory also exists in our collective cultural God image development, and gendered, personified God images may gradually give way to more transcendent and inclusive God images (Edinger, 1996; Peterson, 2005).

Commentary

God images can deepen our connection to ultimate reality, but they can also limit or distort our ability to encounter it. A God image based on one's father unavoidably has both positive and negative psychic consequences. Even within a single God image, qualities of God-as-parent have equal and opposite ramifications. For example, a God who provides safety can also be perceived as restrictive; a God who provides for our needs usually requires much in return; a God who gives loving approval can also be a source of rejection.

Similarly, a God image based on our self image can limit our openness to experiencing the divine.

The masculine emphasis in prevalent God images is symptomatic of psychological misalignment. Jung argued that a healthy God image needed to reflect the balance of male and female, which he called anima and animus. A gender imbalance results in psychological one-sidedness, limiting freedom of experience and expression. This problematic imbalance occurs on individual and cultural levels, and has resulted in fierce polemic debate.

Feminist theologians have argued bitterly against male-only language for God. They believe that God's maleness deifies the masculine, which appears as divine sanction for patriarchy and the devaluation of women. Male God images, therefore, perpetuate injustices against women in societies across the world.

Mary Daly quipped, "If God is male, than the male is God" (1973: 19). The dominance of male God images has been used to elevate men in society, under the belief that male authority is God given and sanctioned.

In verbalizing our experience of God, both male and female traits are needed. However evident this may be from a psychological perspective, it remains a source of theological debate in religious circles. Biblical precedent (e.g., 1 Corinthians 11:7) is used to argue for solely masculine names/titles for the divine, even to assert that women do not bear the image of God to the extent that men do. Theologians debate over whether the masculine language is culturally-dependent or Self-revelatory. In view of the furor involving gendered language for the divine, it is helpful to step back and acknowledge the radical difference between human sexuality and divine reality. God by nature encompasses and exceeds all our efforts to express "him."

See also: ❯ Female God Images ❯ God ❯ God Image ❯ God Image and Therapy

Bibliography

Beit-Hallahmi, B., & Argyle, M. (1975). God as father projection: The theory and the evidence. *British Journal of Medical Psychology, 48*, 71–75.

Daly, M. (1973). *Beyond God the father: Toward a philosophy of women's liberation*. Boston, MA: Beacon.

Edinger, E. F. (1996). *The new God-image: A study of Jung's key letters concerning the evolution of the western God-image* (D. D. Cordic & C. Yates, Eds.). Wilmette, IL: Chiron.

Fowler, J. W. (1981). *Stages of faith: The psychology of human development and the quest for meaning*. San Francisco, CA: HarperCollins.

Freud, S. (1918/1950). *Totem and taboo: Some points of agreement between the mental lives of savages and neurotics* (A. A. Brill, Trans.). SE 13. New York: Norton.

Freud, S. (1928/1975). *The future of an illusion* (J. Strachey, Trans.). New York: Norton.

Genia, V. (1995). *Counseling and psychotherapy of religious clients: A developmental approach.* Westport, CT: Praeger.

Jung, C. G. (1958). A psychological approach to the dogma of the trinity. In H. Read, M. Fordham & G. Alter (Eds.), R. F. C. Hull (Trans.), *Psychology and religion: West and East, CW* 11 (Vol. 11, pp. 107–200). New York: Pantheon, Bollingen Series XX.

Meissner, W. W. (1984). *Psychoanalysis and religious experience.* New Haven, CT: Yale University Press.

Peterson, A. O. (dissertation) (2005). *The dynamic God image: Psychoanalytic object relational, developmental and Jungian theories of God image and their implications for psychotherapy.* UMI: California Institute of Integral Studies.

Rizzuto, A.-M. (1979). *The birth of the living God: A psychoanalytic study.* Chicago, IL: University of Chicago Press.

Vergote, A., & Tamayo, A. (1981). The parental figures and the representation of God: A psychological and cross-cultural study. In *Religion and society* (Vol. 21). The Hague, the Netherlands: Mouton.

Mandala. Figure 1 Double sand spiral by Jim Denevan at Ocean Beach, San Francisco, March 6, 2005. Photo by Lee Bailey.

Mandala

Lee W. Bailey

The Sanskrit word *mandala* means "circle" – circular images drawn, built, painted, danced or lived, expressing many qualities of nature and culture. Many mandalas are unnoticed images of peace, power, oneness, and transcendence. Circular fountains in cities, for example, simultaneously send out a circle of energy and bring to the "center" the community around it. Mandalas are a sacred visual art about the silent center within, the endless circumference without, an art with psychological, biological, and spiritual significance. Some are evident in nature, others products of art and religion. Cultures embroider the form with many unique variations. The focus is often on the center of the circle, which is commonly a geometric symbol of the eternal source. Mandalas with symmetry imply a tension or balance and harmony of spiritual forces. The mandala is an orienting map of the soul, the world, and the cosmos, a microcosm and macrocosm.

Natural Mandalas

We live amid nature's own wondrous mandalas – flowers, age-rings of a tree-trunk, or the cycling of the earth and celestial lights. Sit quietly and watch a shadow move along and feel yourself sitting on the vast earth's globe rotating around its axis, through its seasons. Enjoy a campfire circle in the darkness, friends linking souls and fire thrusting and sparking upward. Feel the cycles of your breathing. Think of the plant cycles, such as trees, that absorb the carbon dioxide we breathe out, and produce oxygen for us to breathe in. Sit by a stream and recall the cycle of water, rising in mist to the sky, drifting in the wind as clouds, then falling in lifegiving rain, flowing over waterfalls to the ocean. Wonder at the complex variety of circular seashells – delicate sand dollars or spiraling conches. Study snowflakes, their tiny, delicate crystalline, symmetrical structure, each completely unique in design. Look at a satellite photo of a vast hurricane swirling in a powerful circle.

As you grow up and grow older, think of the birthdays, births, and deaths of your life as part of earth's life cycles. These simple yet cosmic wonders are doorways to a higher consciousness and infinite power beyond mundane consciousness. Intuitively we can see in them reminders of our place in the grander scheme of nature. This opens up their sacredness, the geometry of life and the endless beyond within it. The cosmic cycles of reincarnation are a basic assumption of Asian religions, so historical time and life experiences are belived to be cyclical, not linear.

The ancients personified the sky's magnificent powers with the circles of starry astrological symbols, such as

Taurus the Bull, as divinities in daily cycles, and closer stars as gods and goddesses, such as Venus and Jupiter, in planetary processions. The beauty they emanate has long seemed to be a channel to the divine.

Animals also live with cycles. A circular bird nest is the safe haven home for the oval eggs of a new year's generation of the winged nation. The old image of the serpent, that sheds its skin as it grows, in a circle eating its tail, or wrapped around an egg, evokes the cycle of life eating life and birthing it again. The complex eyeball is a circle that draws the visual and soulful world into our brains and connects us with the world. Watch the seasonal cyclical migration of birds such as graceful geese, honking in their formations as they fly thousands of miles north and south each year. Remember the hidden fish and whales that also migrate long distances with the seasons to reproduce underwater, replenishing the earth.

The plant nation also springs forth with many circles, from the sunflower's whirled center to the unfolding delicate beauty of a royal English rose or royal Chinese peony. Flowers, the perfumed sex organs of the plant world, symbolize at weddings the beauty of erotic love and family fertility, and at funerals the beauty of human and eternal life. The Christmas tree is a mandala, a miniature cosmos on an *axis mundi* with lights like tiny suns, globes like planets, and soul symbols such as children's toys all around. The lotus is an image of the divine in Asia. Hindu gods and Buddhas sit on lotus thrones.

The mineral world has its mandalas, also, from common rounded stones washed smooth by running water to precious diamonds, shaped in a circle to reflect the divine treasure of light. Gold wedding rings symbolize the loving union of marriage. The stone seen as the center or belly-button of the world, *omphalos* in Delphi, or the central Ka'bah stone in Mecca for Islam, are world-orienting mandalas. Stone circles, notably England's Stonehenge, over 5,000 years old, apparently a cosmic calendar, mark for the ages the cycles of nature, such as the solstices. Egyptian, Mayan, and many other pyramids are model holy mountains, often four-sided, orienting to earthly directions and pointing above to the eternal divine powers. The Egyptian pyramids are positioned to imitate the belt of the Osiris [or Orion, in Greek] constellation of stars, toward which the spirit of the deceased Pharaoh was to ascend.

Mandala Psychology

Carl Jung, after undergoing a confusing period of encounters with unconscious material, began in 1916 to draw mandala images spontaneously, at first not knowing what they meant. As he came to understand it, he saw the mandala as a picture of the complete soul, conscious and unconscious, with the center as the pointer to an authority far larger than the ego, which he later called the "Self," or psychological experience of the divine within.

Jung collected numerous mandalas drawn by his patients (Jung, 9,1: para. 627–712). They pictured images sometimes seen in dreams: squares, circles, spirals, flowers, crystalline reflections, geometric multiplications, eyeballs, animals, light rays, serpents, fish, or a glowing egg. Jung saw circular UFOs as mandala symbols in machine form, bringing cosmic energies down to earth. He found that mandalas reduced confusion and panic and introduced order, balance and wholeness. Mandalas, he saw, urged one to become more truly what one is, overcoming fear, chaos, and balancing opposites, guided by the healing energy of the central image. In his translation of *The Golden Flower*, Richard Wilhelm introduced Jung to Chinese mandalas. Jung envisioned a shadow negative force in each archetypal image, so in our time a shadow of the mandala would be the swastika, which Hitler took from a Hindu tradition and transformed its meaning into one of hatred and death.

Here is an example of the dynamic energy that a mandala can have. A college girl, scornful of religion, sullen and sad, had a dream of an energetic three-inch sphere, that she found in a field, that suddenly came alive, pulsating with lightning bolts, driven by dangerous electricity. The threatening ball swooped around her as the sky became menacing. She ran and ran, until the ball faced her as she gave up and repeatedly cried out "I do believe in God!" The sky calmed, the now lifeless ball dropped to the ground and flowers grew all around. She woke up in a sweat, and soon became a Religion major (Federico, 2008). This sphere emerged from her unconscious soul with a fright that transformed her consciousness into a search for spiritual peace.

Indigenous Peoples

Of all the indigenous peoples' mandalas, we can note a few. Many dance in a circle around a fire, and some prefer to live in circular tipis. The Mexican God's Eye of cross-shaped sticks is woven with brightly colored threads, making a diamond shape. The great Aztec Sunstone has at its center the symbol of the present age *Ollin,* surrounding with calendar and cosmic images, two cosmic fire serpents, and pictures of a coming cataclysm. The Australian Aborigine Tjuringa stone, shows the map of the journeys of the Ancestors of the Dreamtime. They build large mandala circles made of natural colors and feathers in the desert, covering two or three acres.

Celtic Mandalas are full of endless knots – ropes and vines twined in and out of each other in manifold knots, like a maze or pilgrimage through life, not to be untied, but to be followed in its endlessness. Some have women entwined as in a dance, or men whose beards are entwined with their limbs, as if swimming in a wild lake of seaweed. Others have the tidy order of linear lines and crosses or triangles. Beastly creatures chase each other in a circle, paws entwined. One anthropomorphic mandala celebrated in carved circles on United Kingdom churches, in dances, and in processions, is the Green Man, whose beard is entwined with wings, leaves and branches. Leaves may grow out of his mouth (Holitzka, 1996).

In Native American mandalas, the four directions often appear, pointing to the horizon, the powers and colors of the cardinal directions, and the cosmic forces they embody. Feathers and wings carry the powers of the winged beings of the sky. In the Lakota Sioux shaman Black Elk's great vision, he saw a cloud teepee in the center of a camp with grandfathers in it who gave him powers, and four ceremonial horses dancing at each of four directions (Neihardt). Some Native Americans make circular dream catchers or outdoors stone circles in places of power. Navahos make sand mandalas for healing ceremonies, seeking to balance spiritual forces to overcome sickness. Some call mandalas "medicine wheels." The dazzling sun may send its rays in a mandala circle mixed with images of serpents, humans, lizards, and shimmering zig-zag lines.

Rock drawings, or petroglyphs, may be mandalas marking a vision, a spirit, an ancestor spirit, or a deity, such as a rain god. Animals are prominent, such as the wolf, bear, eagle, or buffalo. The peace pipe, bows and arrows, and jagged "thunder arrows" of lightning, or a thunder bird illuminate some mandalas. The Great Mother and her growing plants, or male figures may stand arms upraised, or dancing. A ritual such as the Plains peoples' sun dance has the cottonwood tree in the center, warriors dancing around it in a circle, tipi lodges around them, mountains, and clouds, all pointing upward to the Great Spirit.

Flowers may grace a mandala, or the spiral of a tornado with jagged lightning powers swirling toward the center. Horses may stand in lines facing the central sun, with a surrounding image of a Great Spirit. A basket or plate often has woven images of human figures, spirals, suns, abstract geometric designs, or sacred foods. A Pueblo kachina dancer with elaborate mask and imagery such as wings may dominate a mandala. These images convey the powers of the universe that appear in nature, for in many forms the ancestor spirits and the Great Spirit lives in all the world (Holitzka, 2000).

Judaism

The Jewish Star of David is a mandala, with two inverted triangles intersecting. Jerusalem and its ancient temple mount is the geographic center of historical Israel, so this holy land is the central focus of the faith. Jewish traditional dances frequently move in a circle. The family dining table is also a central focus of Judaism. Torah scrolls are cylindrical mandalas of sacred texts. The menorah candelabrum is a half-circle of nine candles, an ancient symbol of Judaism. The tree inspired Jewish Kabbalist mystics to organize their metaphysical vision of the universe as a tree, a circle on an axis. The top is the Ein Sof, the infinite creative spirit, and the various revealed aspects of God (Sepiroth) take their place as branches, until the bottom is reached as the Shekinah, the presence of God for humans.

Christianity

The labyrinth is an archaic symbol adopted by Christians, a maze, perhaps meant to trap evil spirits. At the Cretan palace of Knossos, there are reports of a labyrinth as a dancing ground, and the myth of the Minotaur at the center. Pliny reports others in Italy And Lemnia, and, like Pliny, Herodotus records a huge labyrinthine building in Egypt (Pliny, Bk. 36:xix, Herodotus, Bk. 2, p. 149, Ramsay, 664–65). Some ancient versions seem to induce confusion and being lost or trapped. Some were later altered to focus on finding the center and then a way out. They were made with stones and bushes, and one notable one remains in the floor just inside the entrance of Chartres Cathedral in France. The one in Reims Cathedal is more square (*Paroisse*) with four larger corners, and the Virgin Mary at the center. The one at Amiens Cathedral is square. The winding passages portray the sufferings on this earth, and the center depicts the divine peace. The journey is a descent into oneself to find inner divinity. A 21st-century revival of labyrinth meditative walking began at Grace Cathedral in San Francisco.

The cross is also a mandala, focusing on the center of meaning in the faith, the incarnation and sacrifice of Christ, which stripped his humanity bare, returned his spirit to the center of being, and left the Holy Spirit on Earth. The Latin cross has one long side. The Celtic cross has long side with a small circle around the center of the cross inscribed with designs. Eastern Orthodox crosses may have the four sides of equal length, or an angled short piece on the longer side. The circular stained glass rose window is a large mandala in churches with pictures and colors illuminated by sunlight, developed by Gothic cathedral designers. Cathedral ground plans are cross-mandalas with high ceilings or domes.

Islam

Muslims worldwide face Mecca when they bow in prayer, forming a vast human mandala. At the Haaj pilgrimage journey to Mecca, itself a mandala journey, there is the central ritual circumambulation of Ka'aba stone in the Great Mosque. The new moon and nearby star are a Muslim symbol, appearing on the flag of Turkey. The huge dome in many mosques symbolizes the arch of heaven, and the typical four minaret towers at the mosque periphery form a symmetrical square. Muslim art forbids human images, so many designs, as on Turkish tiles, include s symmetrical plants and calligraphy. Classic carpet designs often have mandala designs. The mystical Whirling Dervishes dance in a circular spinning form.

Taoism

Chinese Taoism emphasizes the ancient Yin-Yang circle, in which black and white halves flow into each other and each contains a circle of the opposite within itself, showing the inadequacies of rigid dualisms, flowing paradoxically in tension and harmony in the Way of deepest eternal mysteries. The *Tao te Ching* says: "The Tao is an empty vessel; it is used, but never filled. . .hidden deep but ever present" (Tao te Ching, poem 4).

Tibetan Buddhism

Today's most complex mandalas are the colorful Tibetan Buddhist sand mandalas. They are elaborate, detailed circular designs made with colored sand by monks, with well-developed metaphysical interpretations. A mandala in Tibetan Buddhism is a map of the spiritual cosmos, an *axis mundi,* a cosmic center whose purpose is, like smoke going up the smoke hole of a circular tent, to commune with the transcendent realms. This results in a sacred spiritual transformation for those who make it. Tibetans believe that the mandala was invented by the Buddha, who is said to have designed the first Kalachakra ("time-wheel") mandala after reaching enlightenment. A *yantra* is a purely geometric mandala, with no deity pictured, typically with several overlapping triangles.

Another type of Tibetan mandala is the "world wheel," held by the god of death Yama, portraying the various forms of suffering in the world, from the central rooster (lust) snake (envy), and pig (unconsciousness) to death holding all the earth's suffering, surrounded by garden-like, peaceful trees, ducks, clouds, and birds.

A master monk supervises the highly liturgical mandala construction for a novice initiate. A deity is commonly pictured at the geometric center and is the central theme of a mandala. The making of a mandala is a ritual of restoring the ideal principles of things to earth. The adepts involved both bring the cosmic energies down into the mandala and reawaken the immaculate principles within themselves. Giuseppe Tucci describes the ritual of making and contemplating a mandala as an "epiphany":

▶   . . .[one] comes to be identified with the center of the *mandala,* the point from which all goes forth and to which all returns and from where the archetypal essence stream forth in luminous rays which pervade the whole world. . . (1973: 105).

The mandala is intended to balance, like spokes around the center of a wheel, the confused mixture of earthly passions and consciousness, good and evil. In some mandalas a god and goddess may embrace in Tantric fashion, making love to release the divine light within. Other mandalas reflect the kundalini tradition of locating various archetypal cosmic powers on the line of the spine, rising from the most coarse to the most refined, each chakra spot symbolized by a mandala. The most important dynamic of the making and contemplation of a mandala is to visualize a divine principle or divinity, bring it down from the transcendent realm, realize that it is already in one's own heart, and awaken it.

Kalachakra Mandala

The Tantric Kalachakra mandala has roots in Indian tradition. The "wheel of time" is now the favorite of the 14th Dalai Lama. Making it is to promote spiritual peace in individuals and on earth. It portrays a square divine palace within a circle of colorful symbols, full of deities. Journeying toward the center, the god Kalachakra is visualized embracing his female partner Vishvamata in his arms. He is the sun, she is the moon. Together they unite compassion with absolute wisdom. In the center is the Tibetan blue vajra, symbol of the diamond scepter or thunderbolt. This the participants must melt into in order to be purified and be reborn beyond this world into the pure essence of the emptiness of the absolute (Crossman). When the mandala ceremony is complete, the sand is swept into a container that is retuned to the earth or waters, an expression of the impermanence of all things, even sacred mandalas.

Industrialism

The industrial era also has its mandalas, such as the early, oversimplified model of the atom as a miniature solar system with a nucleus surrounded by cycling electrons, symbolizing the foundation of material/electronic existence. The culminating space age mandala is the earth seen from outer space. This has morphed from a proud image of technological space conquest to a more awesome vision of the delicacy of our home in the vastness of space, needing ecological harmony more than the spirit of conquest of nature.

See also: ❯ Circumambulation ❯ Great Mother ❯ Hajj ❯ Jung, Carl Gustav

Bibliography

Anderson, W. (1990). *Green man: The archetype of our oneness with the Earth*. London: HarperCollins.
Argüelles, J., & Argüeles, M. (1972). *Mandala*. Berkeley, CA: Shambhala.
Cornell, J. (1994). *Mandala: Luminous symbols for healing*. Wheaton, IL: Quest Books.
Crossman, S., & Jean-Pierre, B. (Eds.) (2004). *Tibetan mandala: Art and practice*. Old Saybrook, CT: Konecky & Konecky.
Doob, P. R. (1990). *The idea of the labyrinth: From classical antiquity through the middle ages*. Ithaca, NY: Cornell University Press.
Federico, C. (2007). The ominous sphere: A transforming dream. In M. P. Fisher & L. W. Bailey (Ed.), *An anthology of living religions* (pp. 25–26). Upper Saddle River, NJ: Prentice-Hall.
Herodotus. *The histories*. "The Labyrinth" (A. Selincourt, Trans.) (Book. II, p. 149). Baltimore, MD: Penguin Books.
Holitzka, K. (1996). *Mandalas of the celts*. New York: Sterling Publishing.
Holitzka, K. (2000). *Native American mandalas*. New York: Sterling Publishing.
Jung, C. G. (1979). *The collected works of C. G. Jung* (R. F. C. Hull, Trans.). Princeton, NJ: Princeton University Press.
Lao-Tzu. (1972). *Tao Te Ching* (Gia-Fu Feng & J. English, Trans.). New York: Random House.
Neihardt, J. G. (1961). *Black Elk speaks* (Ch. 3, *The Great Vision*). Lincoln, NE: University of Nebraska.
Paroisse notre dame saint Jacques de reims. "Le Labyrinthe." http://www.cathedrale-reims.com/notre dame-saint-jacques-reims/groupe [Italics here indicate the French.]
Pliny (The Elder). *Natural history. Loeb classical library* (D. E. Eichholz, Trans.) (Book XXXVI: xix, Vol. 10, pp. 67–73). Cambridge, MA: Harvard University Press.
Ramsay, W. (1875). "Labyrinthus" A dictionary of Greek and Roman antiquities (pp. 664–665). London: John Murray. http://penelope.uchicago.edu/Thayer/E/Roman/Texts/secondary/SM/CRA*/Labyrinths.html.
Tenzin-Dolma, L. (2006). *Natural mandalas*. London: Duncan Baird.
Tucci, G. (1973). *The theory and practice of the mandala* (A. H. Broderick, Trans.). New York: Samuel Swiser.
Wilhelm, R., & Jung, C. G. (1962). *The secret of the golden flower: A Chinese book of life*. New York: Harcourt Brace Jovanovich.

Mantra

Fredrica R. Halligan

Many adherents of eastern religions, especially Buddhism and Hinduism, use brief verbal phrases or verses as objects for meditation. Such *mantras* are numerous, but best known are the *Avalokiteshara mantra* of the Tibetan Buddhists: "*Om mani padme hum*," and the *Gayatri Mantra* which is widespread among the Hindus:

▶ *Om Bhur Bhuva Svaha*
Tat Savitur Varenyam
Bhargo Devasya
Deheemani
Dhi Yo Yonah Prachodayat.

Any personally-meaningful sacred word or phrase can be used as a *mantra* or as a focus for centering prayer. Well known among Christians is the "Jesus Prayer" described in *The Way of A Pilgrim*, a famous Hesychast text: "Lord Jesus Christ, have mercy on me, a sinner." In Judaism the simple word "*Shalom*" can be used repetitively as a *mantra*, or the *Shema Israel* can be said, affirming the unity and love of God. The comparable verse in Islam is called *Dhikr*.

Recent psychosomatic research (e.g., following Benson, 1976) has shown *mantra* meditation to be very beneficial in eliciting the "Relaxation Response," thus attenuating anxiety and improving physical (especially cardiac) health and pain reduction.

See also: ❯ Buddhism ❯ Gayatri ❯ Hinduism

Bibliography

Anonymous. (1996). *The way of a pilgrim* (O. Sarin, Trans.) Boston, MA: Shambhala.

Benson, H. (1976). *The relaxation response.* New York: Avon.

Borysenko, J. (1987). *Minding the body, mending the mind.* Reading, MA: Addison-Wesley.

Kabat-Zinn, J. (n.d.) *Audio tapes of mindfulness meditation.* Stress reduction tapes. Worcester, MA: University of Massachusetts Medical Center.

Martín-Baró, Ignacio

Daniel J. Gaztambide

Ignacio Martín-Baró (1942–1989) was a Jesuit priest, philosopher, and social psychologist who is most recognized for using the theological-ethical-political insights of liberation theology to develop a social justice oriented liberation psychology. Drawing on insights from liberation theology, Paulo Freire's pedagogy of the oppressed, critical/political psychology, and social psychology, Martín-Baró conducted research projects with a "preferential option for the poor" and oppressed people of El Salvador, with the intention of raising awareness and empowering them in the midst of social, political, and war-related trauma. Due to his political positions and socially progressive psychological research, he was murdered by the Salvadoran army along with five other Jesuits and two employees at the Central American University in El Salvador.

Ignacio "Nacho" Martín-Baró was born on November 7, 1942, in the municipality of Valladolid, Spain. He became a novice of the Society of Jesus in 1959, and was transferred first to Villagarcía and then to Santa Tecla in El Salvador for his second year. From 1961 to 1965 he was sent to study at the Catholic University of Quito (Ecuador), and later to the Javeriana University in Bogotá, earning a bachelors degree in philosophy and a licentiate in philosophy and literature. He returned to El Salvador in 1966 to teach at the *Externado* San José, and in 1967 also began teaching philosophy and theology at the *Universidad Centroamericana "José Simeón Cañas"* (UCA; or Central American University) in San Salvador, the capital. This was short lived, as Martín-Baró left that very year for Frankfurt and then Leuven to study theology. He returned once again to El Salvador in 1970 to finish his last year of theology, due to encouragement from his close friend, the liberation theologian Ignacio Ellacuría. Due to a prior interest he developed in Bogotá, whereby he consumed a variety of writings from psychology, Martín-Baró began studies in the field at UCA. He earned a licentiate in psychology in 1975, during which time he was also teaching the subject in the National Nursing Academy of Santa Ana. Desiring to expand his knowledge of psychology, he earned a Masters degree in social sciences and a Doctorate in social and organizational psychology from Chicago University from 1977 through 1979. Although he was in the United States during this time, both his master's and doctoral thesis showed a deep concern with the growing social and political turmoil of El Salvador, as he wrote about group conflict and the living conditions of the lower classes in the Central American country. Although deeply involved in his studies, he was attentive to the latest news from El Salvador.

After completing his studies in the United States he returned to El Salvador to become a lecturer and head of the psychology department at the UCA. From 1981 through 1989 he acquired numerous administrative and academic positions within the university as well as became member of the editorial board of numerous social science journals, such as *Estudios Centroamericanos* (Central-American Studies), and the *Journal of Salvadoran Psychology.* Apart from these endeavors as a scholar, Martín-Baró in his capacity as a priest first served in the district of Zacamil, which lacked a clergyperson in the early 80's, and afterwards performed sacramental duties in the parish of Jayaque, a poor rural municipality some 30 km from San Salvador. It was in this role that he appeared closest to the Salvadoran people, involving himself through pastoral and community care, and helping construct necessary structures to improve their living conditions (such as a new bridge, or providing wood and materials to fix their homes, etc).

As a result of his studies in liberation theology and social psychology, of Paulo Freire's pedagogy of the oppressed, political/critical psychology, as well as his experiences as a Jesuit in El Salvador before and during the Salvadoran Civil War (1980–1992), Martín-Baró developed a system of psychological thought he termed "liberation psychology." In developing liberation psychology, he critiqued the general state of Latin American psychology for its "slavery" and "scientist mimicry"- the uncritical importation of North American psychologies for the purposes of gaining prestige and power, as ideologies alien to the experiences of the Latin American people, with its attending positivism, individualism, hedonism, and ahistoricism. He argued that such imported constructs tended to problematize the experiences of the common and poor people of El Salvador while ignoring structural injustice, and thus serving the interests of the ruling classes. In the stead of imported psychology, he proposed a liberation psychology based on three guiding principles of liberation theology: a Christian God of life who scorns injustice, the primacy of orthopraxis over orthodoxy, and the preferential option for the poor. Based on these ethical and philosophical commitments, Martín-Baró argued that psychology should ally itself with the oppressed people of El Salvador and develop research projects that would help articulate and give voice to their experiences, fostering the development of a critical consciousness (*concientización*) of their personal, social, and political conditions. This liberatory aim would be accomplished by psychology working not for but with the Salvadoran people and their cultural and religious values, recovering their historical memory as people and as communities surviving in limit situations, and by subverting the dominant narratives of the powerful and allowing people to experience their reality in more critical and liberatory ways, giving them the tools necessary for psychological and collective liberation. One particularly important application of this theoretical lens was in the development of the University Institute for Public Opinion in 1986, which Martín-Baró (as the only doctorate level psychologist in the country at the time) used to study popular opinions about the war, the U.S. government's involvement, and the Salvadoran government itself. He in turn reflected these opinions back to the common people in order to inspire discourse, reflection, and critical consciousness.

Because of this liberation psychology, its political ramifications, and the research projects undertaken through this lens, Martín-Baró's life became threatened by the dominant conservative political forces of El Salvador. In order to protect his colleagues and allies at the UCA and himself, he made numerous trips outside the country, especially to the United States, to have intellectual exchanges with colleagues in social psychology, and increase the visibility of the work being done in El Salvador. Such academic rapport led to his group and some North American colleagues extending his public opinion research more broadly to Central America, through the establishment of the Central American Program of Public Opinion in 1988.

Tragically, on the evening of November 16, 1989, Ignacio Martín-Baró was killed along with five other priests and two employees on the UCA campus by U.S.-trained Salvadoran troops. It is reported that he spoke out against injustice to the very end. His last words, spoken over the gunfire directed at his close friend Ignacio Ellacuría, were "Esto es una injusticia!" meaning "This is an injustice!"

Commentary

George Atwood and Robert Stolorow in their classic text *Faces in a Cloud* argued that all psychological theories are the product (at least in part) of the intricate and idiosyncratic cultural, historical, and subjective experiences of the theorist. Their intersubjective systems approach would contextualize all psychological theories, then, within the respective lives of their theorists. Such an approach to the study of psychological theory would be undertaken not as an attempt to invalidate the theory, but to comprehend the theorist's intent and vision.

Atwood and Stolorow studied various meta-psychologies which claimed different universal forces motivated human behavior (Freud's drives, Jung's archetypes, Reich's bioorganic energy, and Rank's notion of the will), but in the end revealed the deep texture of the meta-psychologist's subjectivity. This subjectivity with its particular personal-social-historical location, it appeared, was in many ways forgotten (was unconscious) in the construction of theory.

In Martín-Baró's construction of liberation psychology one does not find de-contextualized meta-constructs which claim universal validity and influence on human behavior (something he himself criticized of much North American psychology), but rather a set of assertions and theories developed out of his experiences as a Jesuit priest working with the Salvadoran people in the years before and during the Salvadoran Civil War. In his writings and work he himself contextualized his theories as the product of political, historical, and personal circumstances, developing research that unapologetically made a preferential option for the poor and displaced people of El Salvador. He made repeated conscious efforts to construct a psychology that validated the experiences of the Salvadoran people, allowing them to give voice to socially and psychologically repressed emotions and opinions. Liberatory psychological theories were to be crafted not as abstract universal principles developed in order to safeguard a subjectivity that craves recognition and social status, but by immersing one's subjectivity as a researcher-in-solidarity in the subjectivity of the oppressed. In Martín-Baró's case the oppressed were not abstract political entities but the particular people suffering under oppressive regimes in El Salvador and Latin America.

Encounters with the Salvadoran people in a religious and rural context, and with liberation theology and with liberation theologians such as Ignacio Ellacuría were of crucial import to Martin-Baró's development both as a Jesuit priest and as a social psychologist. Although he was born and raised in Spain, liberation theology's God of the oppressed with its preferential option for the poor can be seen as having fomented in him an identification with the people of El Salvador. Alternatively, it could be argued that his empathy and experiences with the Salvadoran people in a condition of socio-political oppression made him more attracted to the discourse of liberation theology. From the perspective of relational psychoanalytic research on God-images, the former case could be understood as the image of a God of justice and the oppressed affecting the transference-counter-transference relationship between Martin-Baró and his parishioners in El Salvador, while the latter suggestion could be understood as that same transference relationship affecting his image of God. Intersubjectively speaking, both dynamics could have been present, his experiences among the poor affecting his theology and his theology affecting his experiences among the poor. Martin-Baró's patterns of relating himself with his environment, his experiences and his theology, can be seen as deeply affecting his liberation psychology in an especially self-conscious way.

See also: ❯ Christianity ❯ Communal and Personal Identity ❯ Cultural Psychology ❯ Ignatius of Loyola ❯ Jesuits ❯ Liberation Psychology ❯ Liberation Theology ❯ Poverty ❯ Psychology

Bibliography

Atwood, G., & Stolorow, R. (1993). *Faces in a cloud: Intersubjectivity in personality.* New York: Jason Aronson.

Hasset, J., & Lacey, H. (1991). *Toward a society that serves its people: The intellectual contribution of El Salvador's murdered jesuits.* Washington, DC: Georgetown University Press.

Hollander, N. (1997). *Love in a time of hate: Liberation psychology in Latin America.* New Brunswick, NJ: Rutgers University Press.

Jones, J. W. (1991). *Contemporary psychoanalysis & religion: Transference and transcendence.* New Haven, CT: Yale University Press.

Martin-Baró, I. (1994). *Writings for a liberation psychology.* Cambridge, MA: Harvard University Press.

The Ignacio Martin-Baró fund for mental health and human rights. Retrieved August 30, 2008 from: http://www.martinbarofund.org/.

UCA Department of Psychology. Retrieved August 30, 2008 from: http://di.uca.edu.sv/deptos/psicolog/nacho.htm.

Universidad Centro-Americana "José Simeón Cañas"; Martyrs of the UCA. Retrieved August 30, 2008 from: http://www.uca.edu.sv/martires/new/baro/fbaro.htm.

Mary

Regina A. Fredrickson

Mary, maiden of Nazareth, Mother of God, pre-eminent follower of Jesus, has seized the personal and communal religious imagination of believers. Down the ages and across cultures, Mary has been heralded in painting, poetry, prayer and pageantry. Most often the intuitive psychology of personal and communal sentiments predates the theological articulation or liturgical celebration of Mary as virgin, mother, companion.

Whether masterpiece or indigenous work, Mary's person is inextricably bound to her assent to her role in the Incarnation-Redemption and by appropriation to her foremost place within the Church, and within the pilgriming people of God. She is the attentive, inclined young woman whispering a thunderous *Fiat mihi* (Luke 1.38). She is the rounded, redolent Madonna gazing, swaddling, and nurturing her Son (Luke 2.7). She is the restrained, resplendent Hodigitria icon beckoning and presenting her regaled Emmanuel Child (Matthew 1.11). She is the wise woman crone surrounded by prophets and populace, penitents and patrons pictured in catacomb Orans etchings, sketched Coptic depictions or embellished Renaissance family commissioned works.

The people of the early waves of evangelization were steeped in the mythology and archetypes of the goddess trilogy of maiden, mother, and crone. Agricultural peoples felt the power of the fecund, nourishing and sometimes punishing Great Mother, while others were comfortable with images of the mother-son, queen consort-ruler representations. Vestal rituals and festivals abounded. Paul preached amid Diana's temples. From a psychological developmental lens the maiden becomes mother then evolving to the wise and companioning crone. Within faithful and orthodox tradition and theology, Mary was never deemed a goddess yet there were epochs of popular excess, political contrivances, misguided homage, and stark purgings.

Mary: Maternal Theotokos

British pediatrician and psychoanalyst, D. W. Winnicott, wrote of the intensity and perduring influence of the mother's early "primary maternal occupation" [with her child]. His works convey the ongoing function of the mother's presence, her ordinary ministrations and her facilition of the integration of her child's psyche, soma and mental development (Winnicott, 1992: Ch. XXIV).

Both psychological constructs are applicable to the centrality of Mary's motherhood as theologically defined in the patristic church. Her singular relationship to her Son, who was both the *Logos* and *Verbum* of God, and her evolving presence within the soma of the church were hailed at the Council of Ephesus in AD 431. Mariology followed Christology and Mary was decidedly declared Mother of God, Theotokos, God-bearer. This proclamation affirmed that Christ was one divine Person, with both a divine and human nature. The emphasis of the Council was to refute the several variations of heresy concerning the Person and nature(s) of Jesus. Mary was deemed mother of the fully human incarnate, second creation, nature of the one Person. The response of the people further enunciated Mary as Mother of God.

The psychological literature is replete with references to the essentiality of the mother. The love relationship between the mother and son was seminal in Freudian thinking. For child analyst, Margaret Mahler, the mother's capacity of attentive empathy made her "a beacon of orientation [for the child] in the world of reality"(Bacal, & Newman, 1990). The pastor and psychoanalyst Harry Guntrip, writing of the mother-infant dyad, asserted that "the deepest thing in human nature is 'togetherness.' After passing through separation at birth to 'aloneness'. . . there still persists that oneness of the child with the mother . . . . It remains as the secret foundation of the stillness, security and peace of the Brughes Madonna . . ." (1992: 269).

Scarce are the Scriptural accounts of Mary's lived and shared experiences. Yet what is recorded of her is analogous to the motherhood constellation posited by Daniel Stern, infant researcher and psychoanalyst. For the new mother there is the life growth concern for the physical and psychological well-being of her child. There is the oscillating questioning of her capacity for "primary relatedness" and her efforts to secure the ties of attachment, security, cohesion, and affection. The synoptic Gospel accounts of the Incarnation, the infancy and early hidden life of Jesus suggest that Mary's relational self was analogous to that of other mothers. She exhibited the normal tensions between her hopes and expectations and her fears and premonitions keeping all these things in her heart.

Stern continues in his delineation of this motherhood constellation affirming that the mother herself demands a "supportive matrix" and that she undergoes an "identity reorganization" as she evolves over time. The pericopes of Jesus' ministry and the subsequent Pentecost event reveal Mary's evolving communal self and the consequent demands for her psychological reorganization from virgin, mother, pre-eminent companion to the followers of Jesus.

The mother-child dyad is a continuous flowing of mutual-reciprocal influencing and while the externals of the early and deep maternal musings and preoccupations may dissipate, they are subject to reactivation over the mother's lifespan. Within the child these early and intense emotional and neurological working models of the mother's presence, containment, and soothing can be elicited again as the "evoked companion" (Stern, 1995: 171–185). Through the centuries, such had been the reactivation of Mary's natural protection and the pilgrim peoples' eliciting of her evoked presence.

Mary: Strong Maiden

Were we to visualize the maternity of Mary as a triphytic with its two covering panels, the first panel would depict Mary as a daughter of Abraham and virgin of Nazareth. This historical Mary and her choice of virginity is indeed a paradox, personally, religiously, and culturally. Mary lived in a multicultural milieu, a multi-governed political regime, a marginalized position of poverty, gender and religion. From another perspective she was deeply knowledgeable and rooted in the Messianic prophecies and their reference to the Virgin (Genesis 3.15 and Isaiah 7.14). Living near trade routes, hearing many languages, coping with competing cultural values, Mary could not be naïve or complacent about her volitional virginity. This virginity grounded her personal sense of self as a singular "at-one-ness" yet positioned her communal self with respect to her people and her God. Upon her visit to Elizabeth, her kinswoman (Luke 1. 46–58), Mary proclaims her integral fullness and magnifies and rejoices in her God. She aligns herself intergenerationally and affectively to our father Abraham and his descendants. She resonates with a fundamental option for the poor and oppressed. She acknowledges that her grace-filled person will be called blessed through the generations.

Reflecting on the poet William Wordsworth's words, she was indeed ". . . our tainted nature's solitary boast" (Wordsworth, 1977). Her call to this virginity went beyond physical intactness and integrity to that of psychological attentiveness and attunement. It was a transformative source of personal cohesion and spiritual unity culminating in both virginal sufficiency and maternal abundance. Her stance of introspection and interiority moved outward in Mary's embrace of the virgin-mother paradox and encircled ever-widening communities.

Mary: Companion in Our Pilgrimage

The second panel covering the maternity triphytic would elaborate Mary's position within the ever-widening communities of the followers of Jesus. The wise woman, crone, holds the traditions and companions the pilgrim people. Psychologically and developmentally she is a grounded, seasoned and tested woman abounding in lived and shared experiences, relieved of individual family responsibilities and available for those generative and integrative functions in the larger community. From the Pentecost event emerge two Marian considerations. She was among the disciples who "were constantly devoting themselves to prayer, together with certain women, including Mary, the mother of Jesus" (Acts 1. 14). She is both locus and encounter for the new community of Jesus' followers, and again she receives the fullness of the Holy Spirit. She is commissioned to minister among the diverse peoples "from every nation … [who] at the sound [of the rush of violent wind] gathered and were bewildered, because each one heard them [the disciples] speaking in the native language of each" (Acts 2. 5). The Pentecost paradigm is the nodal psychological and life cycle event that thrusts Mary into her relational and communal vocation of companion to the journeying people of God.

Jaroslav Pelikan, eminent historian and scholar in the humanities, in his exhaustive and artistic volume on Mary's place in culture, proposes that the Maryam of the Qur'an, and the Miriam of Zion may function "as a bridge builder to other traditions, other cultures and other religions" (1996: 67). In the Christmas greeting (2007), "A Common Word," addressed to the Christian communities, leading Muslim teachers opened their letter quoting from the Chapter of Mary. The metaphor of Mary, as the bridge builder and its psychological implications are not lost in considering her most documented apparitions. While assent is not incumbent, these apparitions show a predilection for the poor and unlearned, the young and the indigenous peoples as seen at Lourdes, Fatima and Tepeyac (Guadalupe).

The merciful and powerful queen, advocate, and refuge theme runs deep in the religious psyche. Personal and communal blessings, victories, rescues and restorations have been attributed to Mary's presence and patronage. While miracles and apparitions do not require belief among Roman Catholics, the Church has declared two dogmas for ecclesial assent concerning Mary, namely, the Immaculate Conception (1854) and the Assumption into heaven (1950). The first defines Mary as free from any or all sin from the first moment of her conception and throughout her life. This singly graced position distinguished her and was prescient and orienting for her role in the Incarnation. The second definition, that of the Assumption, follows the long tradition in both the Eastern and Western churches of Mary's dormition, of her incorruptible body and soul being taken up into the glory of her Son and the fittingness of her hailed position

relative to her Son's glory. Neither declarations supported Carl G. Jung's attempts to feminize the Triune Godhead as depicted in the quaternity image of the feminine and the goddess within the Trinity. Both declarations bring to prominence the integrative wholeness of body and spirit but they have limited accessibility and intensity for the religious imagination of other communities.

Righting this tendency to imbalance in Marian devotion and theology, the Second Vatican Council (1966) in the decree *Lumen Gentium*, the Dogmatic Constitution on the Church, situates the statements on Mary within the schema dealing with the total community of the Church, with her living as a "pilgrim of faith" (no. 58), and being "one with all human beings" (no. 53). In Chapter VIII of the document, the council fathers renew the concept of Mary as model of the Church, citing her obedience, faith, hope, burning charity and perfect union with Christ (nos. 61 and 63). Such virtues together with her solidarity with the poor, strength in faith and response to grace, and her call to ongoing justice ministry speak to a wider ecumenical fellowship and are vital to dialog with the present culture. Such virtues appeal to the broader human community, address the ruptures of the human condition and culture, and resonate with acts of global concern, conscience, and care.

Our psychological and religious sensibilities about Mary's companioning function strain between the beautiful enthroned woman ushering Dante in the final steps to *Paradiso* to the graphic and palpable image of Mary the single, unwed mother whose son will be executed, an image offered in Pax Christi reflections. Theologian Elizabeth Johnson gives us a creative and thoughtful biblical paradigm in which Mary is partner and companion, comrade and co-disciple (2003: 313). The historical virgin of Nazareth, the theological maternal Theotokos and the psychologically evoked companion crone, ever enfold in our personal and communal imagination.

See also: ❯ Christianity ❯ Pilgrimage ❯ Virgin Mary

Bibliography

Bacal, H. H., & Newman, K. M. (1990). Theories of object relations: Bridges to self-psychology. In *Margaret Mahler* (Ch. 5). New York: Columbia University Press.

Guntrip, H. (1992). *Schizoid phenomena: Object relations and the self*. Madison, CT: International Universities.

Johnson, E. A. (2003). *Truly our sister: A theology of Mary in the communion of saints*. New York: Continuum.

Metzger, B. M., & Murphy, R. E. (Eds.) (1991). *The new Oxford annotated Bible: New revised standard version*. New York: Oxford University Press.

A Muslim message of thanks and of Christmas and New Year greetings. (December 2007). www.acommonword.com.

Pelikan, J. (1996). *Mary through the centuries: Her place in the history of culture.* New Haven, CT: Yale University Press.

Stern, D. N. (1995). *The motherhood constellation: A unified view of parent-infant psychotherapy.* New York: Basic Books.

The Teachings of the Second Vatican Council. (1966). *Chapter VIII: "The Blessed Virgin Mary, Mother of God, in the mystery of Christ and the Church."* Westminster, MD: The Newman Press.

Winnicott, D. W. (Ed.) (1992). *Through paediatrics to psycho-analysis: Collected papers* (Ch. XXIV). New York: Brunner/Mazel, Inc.

Mary Magdalene

Kathryn Madden

The figure of Mary Magdalene depicted in the New Testament of the Christian tradition was the first witness to the Resurrection of Jesus Christ. Specific New Testament references to Mary Magdalene include the Gospel of Luke 8:2–3 in which Mary Magdalene is described as one who ministered to Jesus. This passage also describes an exorcism of demons, which according to current biblical scholarship, may not refer definitely to the Magdalene.

Over the centuries of Christian history and reflection, many scholars have accepted the identification of Mary Magdalene with Mary of Bethany and with a woman sinner who anointed Jesus' feet. Yet, Eastern Orthodox Christians and the Catholic Encyclopedia of 1910 distinguish these women as three different persons. Although, Mary Magdalene has often been claimed to have been a prostitute, there is no specific biblical reference in the New Testament. This misappropriation most likely arises from the town she originated from. Migdal, originally called Magdala, was a fishing town known for women who consorted freely with men.

In the Gospel of Matthew 27:55–56; Mark 15:41; and Luke 23:55, the Magdalene and Mary, the mother of James, came to the Jesus' tomb at dawn on the first day of the week to anoint his body with oils and spices. The tomb was empty. The Magdelene ran to tell Simon Peter and another disciple (John 20:1–2). Then she returned to the tomb and, alone, she waited there.

The brief historical evidence we find about the Magdalene paired with poetic imagination and combined with certain concepts of psychodynamic and analytical psychology usher us toward meaning at the most definable character of essences. Interweaving psychology with scripture, we see in the narrative of the Magdalene a transformed disposition of mind, body and soul animated by spirit in relationship to Jesus Christ. Further, the Magdalene's relationship with Jesus allows us to discern deeper knowledge and insight about the value of symbol and metaphor.

Etymologically, the Hebrew form of the name *Mary*, or *mirjam*, derives from the Egyptian *mr'* (to be loved) and from *rà a*: to see, the seer (Ricci, 1994: 129). Her receptivity to "waiting" at the tomb is analogous to the depth psychological notion of "seeing" and "seeking." Her witness to the Risen Christ represents a transformation of consciousness, profound change inclusive of the notion of re-collected memory at the level of the archetypal and numinous.

The root of the word memory in its most reduced form is *mr.* Closely associated to this root is the Egyptian *mr'.* Imaginatively splitting the m and the r, and locating the earliest graphic sign for the letter *M* in the image of water, *m-a* also becomes the imitative root for the sound a child makes when it desires the source of its nourishment. The reduplicated form of *mr* is "*murmur*" which can be associated with the sound that water makes (Ricci, 1994: 129). The two roots combined become a metaphor for the source of nurture, a moist, soothing, maternal, watery reality (Dunne, 1988: 116–120).

The letter R originally meant "*head*" and is close to the Proto-Indo-European roots *ar-, or-,* and *er-.* Ar- which means "*to fit together*," gives us the Latin *ordiri,* the root of "primordial." Primordial refers to the original order of things, at-one-ness, har mony. Primordial also refers to that which fuels inspiration, what developmental psychologist D. W. Winnicott tells us is the goal of developmental maturity: creativity and *art.*

The basic meaning of *er*-means "*to set in motion*." Also from *er-* comes the Latin *oriri* which means "*to be born*," or "*origin*." If we put the *m* and the *r* together again, we arrive at an image of maternal head-waters giving birth to us, setting us in motion. Psychologically speaking, the transformed Magdalene is analogous to how a mature ego provides a center from which we can generatively unfold, an interior previously unknown or unconscious. This core opens to us in numinous experience, receives us and renews us.

At a deep unconscious level, our "forgotten" or repressed memory strives for *this* source, or perhaps something beyond this foundation. Archetypal spirit – original unity or wholeness – is represented in the first figure a child knows: its mother, or primary caregiver. Developmental child psychologist, D. W. Winnicott reminds us that ideally our biological mother mirrors the archetypal feminine and imparts to the infant the deep inheritance of the Self. Yet, due to early developmental trauma sometimes what we long for can only be experienced as an absence.

Even if we cannot "re-member" the source of our being because of developmental injury, there is yet a bridging possibility that will restore to us what was lost or dissociated. St. Augustine of Hippo claims that what we yearn for is the soul we have been dissociated from at birth. We remain in this state until God belongs to the soul in totality: "O truth, everywhere" (Chadwick, 1991, *Book Ten* 26:37).

Re-establishing the psychological traces of murmurings in the treasure house of the imagination – what Augustine identified as *memoria*, the infinite halls of the unconscious – we make our way inward into these spacious caverns, seeking to make conscious what is at "the bottom of the trough." In the process of depth psychoanalysis and various religious practices, we regress and feel as if we are once again "inside of the mother's body," or held by spirit, that feeling of oneness we still had as infants. We can locate a new vantage point from which the ego forms a relationship with the archetypal Self of the psyche. Mary Magdalene re-connected to this archetypal Self, which crosses the divide between soul and spirit. She ventured into the depths of memory, mourning, and "*mr.*" Whereas the etymological root of *ma*-resonates with the notion of the archaic maternal, *mr*, in contrast, leads us to the *ground* level, to the Magdalene and the empty tomb. Here we find psyche and soul rising to greet the source of spirit.

We can only speculate upon the specifics of the Magdalene's life. In scriptural accounts, there is evidence that something had caused a breakage in her inner world triggering fragmentation for which she sought healing. Whether or not she had been possessed by demons, she had become dispossessed of an authentic self. She needed help to mourn and to remember, to re-collect that part of herself that had fallen away. Jesus offered this relationship. Jesus took root in her psychic soils and led her into the well of her own rich archetypal femininity. In learning to yield to the antinomies within her psyche, fertile soil was prepared for spirit.

Mary Magdalene willingly waited at the tomb. As in the Old-Irish extension of the root *memor*, or *miraim*, which translates as "I remain," Mary remained, even though the disciples and other women departed. Remaining provides the necessary period of preparation and formation for the depth of interior feelings in relation to spirit to evolve.

At the intersection of mourning and re-membering, a phenomenon emerges where there is a necessary breakthrough to something else, a new sphere of experience (Haughton, 1981: 18–47). Winnicott speaks of this breakthrough phenomenon as "*indwelling*," meaning that psyche comes to dwell in the body-soma, which leads to an "integrated unit self." Receptivity does not preclude suffering. Suffering and brokenness at times of psychological crisis, emptiness, or loss translates as living through the death of the ego in its old form, the space of dead-nothing. The Magdalene entered "the gap," the dark interval.

The Empty Tomb

In John's account of the Easter story, (1991, John 20: 1–18), Mary Magdalene arises the day after the Sabbath and comes to the tomb "while it was still dark" to anoint Christ's body before his burial. After the disciples depart, Mary stands vigil. Jesus' crucifixion has caused such a profound reaction that the event of his death is experienced as a *void*.

In Winnicott's terms, one who feels "dead, empty, nothing" has not arrived at the stage of security that he calls the "I am" state of being. Unclaimed and repudiated parts of the self still accompany the individual preventing wholeness because these parts are yet unintegrated bits of being. The ego suffers tremendous anxiety and threat upon nearing integration of these bits, fearing what feels like certain death. To prevent what the ego perceives as its own potential annihilation, it sometimes defends itself by *breaking down or falling into* the gap of madness.

Beneath the defenses of the person is a "something else" which potentially integrates the dissociated aspects of the infantile or child self which, have become split off. These defenses prevent us from experiencing certain intrapsychic dynamics that lead to mature development and the depressive position. The depressive position pertains to overcoming the earlier developmental stage called the paranoid-schizoid position, which is equivalent to a less mature psychological constitution. The depressive position also relates to the capacity to mourn.

In "The Manic Defense" (1935: 134–35), Winnicott speaks of the manic defenses as the way human beings typically defend against the depressive position. These defenses are related to omnipotent fantasies, "flight to external reality, suspension of inner objects, and denial of sensations." As means of control, these forms of resistance offer us reassurance through external reality. Rather than experience emptiness, we fill ourselves up; instead of being still, we move; we seek to know and to understand instead of entering the unknown. Above all, we deny death as the ultimate fact of life.

They defenses are resilient because they prevent the innocent pre-egoic self from the beginning of life from being overcome by intense affect that an infant cannot yet tolerate such as severe dissociation. These defenses are still active beneath the surface of the adult psyche. The goal of healing is to get to the experience of emptiness and nothingness and to discover the true self which is creatively alive and real in contrast to the false self of defenses and repression. Only by entering into the original anxiety and experiencing the primal agony can we re-collect the missing bits of being and become alive again. Healing entails building belief in good internal objects; lessening the manic defenses, which, in turn, shrinks depressive and persecutory anxieties. We are enabled to link imagination (in contrast to fantasy) to our physical experiences whereby we can create freely from an unlimited imagination, which is preliminary to the evolution of symbolic consciousness. We move beyond shame to healthy guilt.

The Stone Had Been Removed

At the empty tomb, the Magdalene faces dread, emptiness, and non-existence. Fearing that Jesus' body might have been stolen, she turns to external sources. The two disciples she turns to metaphorically represent the false-self reality. The disciple who outruns Peter represents the manic defenses. He runs ahead, but he does not *go in;* he does not enter interiorly. Simon Peter follows the other disciple and goes into the tomb. Yet, both return to their homes. The Magdalene waits.

Woman Why Are You Weeping?

Mary's tears at the empty tomb express grief, loss, and suffering over Jesus' absence. Tears are also a way of seeking, desiring, and restoring. Bending over to look inside, she confronts the darkness. As we enter the empty tomb of our own subjective interior, the ego fears the depths of the unconscious and the death of the false self. Without projections, we feel an acute emptiness.

When She Has Said this, She Turned Around

This phrase represents a first "turning." The first turning still belongs to the transitional arena in which our imagination is churning with new images and feelings. When

we continually long for something, it builds its image into us by depositing "a seed" in our psyche. The seed germinates and grows when it finds itself in a nurturing and moist soil (maternal love, Eros, desire, agape love). When the inspired image is secured internally, eventually something new is born of the two, a living third thing which exists midway between our idealized images and the essence of the thing-in-itself (von Baader, 1850–1860: 8: 96).

In contrast, if an infant is surrounded by an environment in which it does not *see itself being seen* by the mother-mirror, but instead perceives an expressionless canvas, then the looking-glass mother becomes an external thing to be looked at but not to be looked into. A seed does not sprout and take root.

Woman Why Are You Weeping? Whom Are You Looking for?

At this point in the scriptural narrative, Mary Magdalene sees Jesus but she does not recognize him. Jesus asks, "woman why are you weeping, *whom are you looking for?*" In the therapeutic arena, we are often mourning the self we have never known. We struggle to gather up the disparate pieces of self that are dissociated and scattered.

When Jesus asks Mary "*whom* are looking for," however, this phrase underscores the distinction that for the Magdalene to *re-member* and to re-collect the unity of her self is distinct from *mourning*. To remember has do with spirit beyond the psyche, yet bridged by the psyche.

The Magdalene first *mourns the dead Christ and seeks "the living among the dead" in order to anoint him.* Only when the Magdalene *waits* by the empty tomb of death and descent and faces its depths is she able "to anoint" the dead Christ. Encountering this space of emptiness, where our own images do not reign, allows something more profound to occur within our psyche. "Anointing" the dead Christ has to do with receiving new life, new possibility in this imageless space. The images emerge from the union of psyche and soul, not solely from our egos, and are now in-fleshed.

Tell Me Where You Have Laid Him and I Will Take Him Away

When she first sees Jesus, the Magdalene thinks he is the gardener. Winnicott (1958: 133) speaks of how some persons do not recognize that the people who inhabit them psychologically are a part of themselves.

Mary!

When Mary sees Jesus, he *calls her by name*. As Mary is named by Jesus, he endows Mary with an identity specifically her own. As a distinct and separate being, she is able *to respond* and to name Jesus in return. Analogous to a child that separates from the mother at the appropriate stage of its development, Mary can now witness Jesus from her own subjective nature as a separate person. Similarly, a therapist, as a significant other "names" a patient through reliable person-to-person presence, receiving the spontaneous gesture, and allowing for the omnipotent infant self to come forward to achieve the developmental culmination of the early stages of life. A container is provided for spirit to enter and to engage with psyche reminiscent of the image of the well-known attribute of the Magdalene – the alabastron – a symbol in ancient and modern times of the eternal feminine.

She Turned and Said to Him, "Rabbouni"

The scriptural narrative does not indicate that Mary has ever turned away from Jesus in the first place. The *pivotal point* is that when the angels first ask Mary why she is weeping, she cannot recognize Jesus as the risen Christ but only through her own projections, as a gardener. Then, in contrast to a bodily act, when we turn the second time, we come to know that we are separate but related to the *divine* source who meets us in the dark night of the imageless space. There is no one other than God who is capable of being such a reliable and eternal mother-mirror. If we are fully given to this source, we are transformed into the same image. In psychological terms, this moment of self reflection would be an instant when perception gives way to apperception, when "object" turns into a "subject."

The text of a prayer by St. Anselm of Canterbury (1033–1109) grasped this complex transformation when he said of Mary Magdalene that "Christ was *hiding* himself from you when you were *seeing him* and *revealed himself to you when you were not seeing him*; until he whom you were seeking, *asked you whom you were seeking and why you were weeping*" he could not be anointed. Only when the risen Christ is present to her *actually*, flesh resurrected in spirit, and *anoints her* does she recognize him.

We can look into the psyche and think we "see him," but he is hidden from us, for whatever reasons of human defense structures. When Christ does reveal himself, we may *not* "see him" because we are caught in our own projections. The second turning, then, is a profound transfigurative moment for Mary as well as the Risen Christ. We see all essences in their restored, eternal form. It is the eternal essence of the Risen Christ who Mary greets as "Rabbouni."

Master!

The Magdalene returns to the starting point, – *memor*, – something folding back upon itself. Making conscious the depths of *memoria*, gives us witness to the true source that the Magdalene perceives when she exclaims, "Master."

Do not Hold on to Me

Jesus is both human and divine, never merely an *image* of God, nor merely a psychic internalization. Yet, his image received and internalized in Mary is a portal to the mysteries of the trinity and a presence that will never leave her. "*From now on you do know him and have seen him*" (John 14: 7). This phrase translated in the *New English Bible* as "do not cling to me," urges the Magdalene not to cling to old projections, nor to dismiss the efficacy of what she has witnessed thus far.

I Am Ascending to My Father and Your Father, to My God and Your God

Jesus includes Mary Magdalene in his final transformation, indicating the potential for others to become whole selves. The phrase "my father and your father, my God and your God," infers a specific kind of dependency that is beyond psychological categories and belongs more to the arena of faith.

What the Magdalene experiences is definitively more than the restoration of the lost object in the psyche, more than the integration of psychic contents. In the first turning, she mourns the loss of the idealized object in relationship to the historical person of Jesus. She encounters *a new psychical reality*. In the second turning, she encounters *the spiritual reality* of the Risen Christ in which spirit has bridged psyche and psyche, spirit, making it possible for her to participate in *actual* presence, resurrected presence.

As this love comes back into the world, we find a mother restored. His death becomes our death, his resurrection, our resurrection. Our participation leads us into the maternal headwaters to the mother before the mother, the object behind the object, who becomes a subjective interior reality, as well as a lived, embodied reality. Mary Magdalene re-turns to her community. True to the derivatives of her name, she becomes "rà a," a seeker and seer of internals and eternals, a woman of multiple realities, one who participates in two worlds, an inner and an outer world which leads her to exclaim:

"I Have Seen the Lord"

The glory of Christ is not visible in itself. Glory is a reality that can be expressed only as recognized by an other, at a juncture where the opposites of otherness are met and suffered. The impact of this notion is that Christ dies and rises in a way that is visible to others, which others can attain.

Mary Magdalene not only witnesses Christ's second birth, *she rises with him.* As Jesus sheds his burial cloths, the Magdalene sheds the skins of her former self. Jesus gives her everything that is *already* hers. She dies unto him whose body disappears, but rises. In his return, she is born with a physical meaning of her own. Spirit conjoins with flesh, and flesh returns to life and incarnates. Her resurrection is different from his and her response has its own characteristics. Mary, too, has risen.

The redemption of matter might be configured in the psychological arena as two persons in relationship who comprise opposite but complimentary terms. A third constituent arises from the psychic vessel that the two persons create together. The opposites undergo a process of transformation and restoration. As the life-giving essence is restored, a fourth element arises which is spirit-in-matter. This becomes the basis for our wholeness and grounds us in space, time, history (Von Baader, 1851–1860 2:243).

In re-turning, our relationship to material reality changes. We participate in our own freedom and also in a redemptive historical process. As nature is redeemed, so is the creative feminine element, the god-bearer. Mary Magdalene offers an exquisite feminine ground to illustrate the embodiment of a psychological principle: that beyond our internal projections and introjections, beyond history, but in history – *when we mourn, when we remember* – we anoint: *but first we must wait to be anointed.*

See also: ❖ Archetype ❖ Depth Psychology and Spirituality ❖ Jesus ❖ Self ❖ Winnicott, Donald Woods

Bibliography

Dunne, C. (1988). The roots of memory. *Spring*, 116–120.
Haskins, S. (1993). *Mary Magdalen.* New York: Harcourt, Brace & Company.
Haughton, R. (1981). *The passionate God.* New York: Paulist Press.
Metzger, B. M., & Murphy, R. E. (Eds.) (1991). *The new Oxford annotated Bible.* New York: Oxford University Press.
Ricci, C. (1994). *Mary Magdalene.* Minneapolis, MN: Fortress Press.
St. Augustine. (1991). *Confessions* (H. Chadwick, Trans.). England: Oxford University Press.
Von Baader, F. (1851–1860). *Sämtliche Werke* (F. Hoffman, Ed.) (16 vols.). Leipzig, Germany: Bethman.
Winnicott, D. W. (1958). *Collected papers: Through paediatrics to psychoanalysis.* London: Tavistock Publications.
Winnicott, D. W. (1989). *Psychoanalytic explorations.* Cambridge, MA: Harvard University Press.

Masochism

Jaco J. Hamman

German psychiatrist Richard von Krafft-Ebing coined the word masochism in 1869 after his reflection on the life of novelist Leopold von Sacher-Masoch (Nacht, 1995). A paraphilia, masochism's primary context is sexual relationships, describing the experience of an individual receiving erotic satisfaction from real or imagined personal suffering, in being humiliated, and in the relinquishment of power. Masochism is often identified with sadism in sado-masochistic relationships (Loewenstein, 1957).

As self-inflicted suffering, however, masochism can have a moral character as satisfaction is gained by becoming a victim. In religious masochism, the body is hurt for the sake of the soul (Ghent, 1999; Glucklich, 2001). In many western as well as eastern religions, experiencing personal pain becomes sacred as the producer of altered states of consciousness, a pathway to detachment, or an agent of purification.

Psychological understandings of masochism are diverse, ranging from the suppression of inner guilt caused by outward aggressive drives (Freudian) (Freud, 1957); activity of the shadow and the archetypal need to worship (Jung); the persecution of internal objects (Object relations theory) (Berliner, 1995); frustration with a primary, non-nurturing self-object (Self psychology) (Menaker and Barbre, 1995); a disembodied self

(Gestalt theory); or, a significant cognitive distortion (cognitive therapy).

Increasingly and especially in the context of religious experience, the portrayal of masochism in pathological terms is questioned.

See also: ❯ Affect ❯ Altered States of Consciousness ❯ Dissociation ❯ Freud, Sigmund, and Religion ❯ God Image ❯ Homo Religiosus ❯ Job ❯ Jung, Carl Gustav, and Religion ❯ Object Relations Theory ❯ Psychology of Religion ❯ Religion and Mental and Physical Health ❯ Repression ❯ Self Object ❯ Self Psychology ❯ Shadow ❯ Shame and Guilt ❯ Soul: A Depth Psychological Approach

Bibliography

Berliner, B. (1995). The role of object relations in moral masochism. In M. A. F. Hanly (Ed.), *Essential papers on masochism*. New York: New York University Press.

Cowan, L. (1982). *Masochism: A Jungian view* (1st ed.). Dallas, TX: Spring Publications.

Freud, S. (1957). A child is being beaten: A contribution to the study of the origin of sexual perversions (1919). In J. Strachey (Ed.), *The standard edition of the complete psychological works of Sigmund Freud* (Vol. 17, pp. 179–204). London: The Hogarth Press.

Ghent, E. (1999). Masochism, submission, surrender: Masochism as a perversion of surrender. In S. A. Mitchell & L. Aron (Eds.), *Relational psychoanalysis: The emergence of a tradition* (pp. 211–242). London: Analytic Press.

Glucklich, A. (2001). *Sacred pain: Hurting the body for the sake of the soul*. Oxford, England: Oxford University Press.

Loewenstein, R. (1957). A contribution to the psychoanalytic theory of masochism. *Journal of American Psychoanalytical Association, 5*, 197–234.

Menaker, E., & Barbre, C. (1995). *The freedom to inquire: Self psychological perspectives on women's issues, masochism, and the therapeutic relationship*. Northvale, NJ: J. Aronson.

Nacht, S. (1995). Le Masochisme, Introduction. In M. A. F. Hanly (Ed.), *Essential papers on masochism*. New York: New York University Press.

Matriarchy

Elizabeth Welsh

The term is defined in three ways. One refers to gynecocracy, or a family, group, or nation governed by a dominant woman, and more specifically, a mother who is the head and ruler of her family and descendants. A second meaning refers to matrilineal organization, or a social system in which descent and inheritance is passed on through the female lineage. A third meaning, matrifocality, refers to the centrality (though not domination) of women, especially mothers.

Gynocentric organization can be found in many non-human populations which are centered around alpha females. Examples include ants, bees, pygmy chimpanzees, elephants, killer whales, spotted hyenas, desert mole rats, and termites. Another notion linked to the hypotheses of matriarchy is parthenogenesis, or asexual reproduction in females which continues to exist in most lower plants as well as in some invertebrates and vertebrates. Parthenogenetic reproduction has been connected to the origin myths circulating among primitive cultures which recognized the role of female primacy in the creation of human societies. The idea of the female primeval creative force could be found in many of the earliest human writings and art forms such as those of Ancient Egypt.

The notion of matriarchy in humans emerged within the field of anthropology in the context of nineteenth century theory of cultural evolution. The latter posited that the human species "advanced" from primitive matriarchal social organization to patriarchal systems at the same time as it progressed from a polytheism that included the worship of multiple great goddess figures to a monotheism centered on a single male divinity. Anthropologists have also hypothesized that patriarchal impositions developed as people realized the link between paternity and pregnancy, however, clear evidence for this theory has been lacking. Nonetheless, in some fields such as comparative religion and archeology the hypothesis of pre-ancient matriarchal systems has continued to be explored and used as basis for various ethnographic theories which have attempted to resurrect the female elements from a misogynistic and sexist cultural history and reestablish gender balance. In spite of the disparity of views regarding the actual gender relations in pre-ancient societies, scholars generally agree that Neolithic societies were more egalitarian than those of later periods.

Currently, most anthropologists concur that there is no evidence for the existence of matriarchal societies in the primary sense of the term, but that matrilineal/matrifocal groups have existed in various places for many centuries. The following are current examples of social structures which have maintained an ancient tradition of passing on of inheritance, name, or group membership through the female line and of giving women central roles in family and community affairs (though religious and political affairs are still reserved for the male domain): various communities in South India (e.g., in Kerala, Tulu Nadu, Mangalore, Udupi, Tamil Nadu) and Northeastern India (in Meghalaya), the Malikun on Minicoy Island, the Minang communities in West Sumatra, Indonesia, the Masuo people of Southwestern China, the Tuareg communities of Western Sahara, the people of the Huron, Cherokee, and Iroquois Confederacy, the Navajo, Hopi, and Gitksan groups in North America. Furthermore, in Orthodox Judaism, while the laws of inheritance follow the father, the laws of descent are matrilineal.

Theories of matriarchy have received most attention in the field of archeology. The notion of an archaic matriarchy that was subsequently overturned by patriarchal rule was primarily introduced by Johann Jakob Bachofen in his 1861 publication, *Mother Right: An Investigation of the Religious and Juridical Character of Matriarchy in the Ancient World*. A systematic study of myth traditions led Bachofen to propose that the prehistoric civilizations were marked by three stages: in the first hetaeric stage, males had unrestricted access to all females; in the second stage, females overturned this unfavorable arrangement and established monogamous relationships and mother right, or matriarchal groups, along with an extremist variant, the Amazons; in the third stage, matriarchy was permanently ousted by patriarchy with its male-dominated institutions which marked the beginning of women's disenfranchisement.

Although the exact characteristics of these hypothesized archaic matriarchal systems cannot be established with certainty, some general features have been proposed: (1) the female family name is retained; (2) children follow the female line; (3) movable and immovable property remains in the hands of the woman and is inherited by daughters, while sons only receive a dowry; (4) the difference between legitimate and illegitimate birth disappears; (5) the woman becomes the wooer. The least disputed features are those that pertain to matrilineality. Examples include records concerning the prehistoric Lycian people whose families appeared to be organized according to the matrilineal principle, as evidenced in the Herodotus accounts of the Lycians who did not name their children after their fathers like the Hellenes but after their mothers, and the testimony of Nicolaus of Damascus who asserted that only the daughters possessed the right of inheritance, a tradition traced to the Lycian common law.

Other characteristics are not as clear. There are inconsistencies in the delineations of matriarchal features regarding sexual relations. For instance, some scholars like Bachofen, argue that it was through matriarchal rule that monogamous relationships were instated not through patriarchy. Others say that matriarchy was characterized by promiscuity, that women were having sex indiscriminately and that through patriarchy men established monogamous marriage relationships so as to ensure that their progeny was indeed theirs. In support of this latter thesis, scholars have turned to the patriarchal rhetoric of various Greek myths which contain traces of possible preexisting or contemporary forms of matriarchy. For example, female rule was equated with animal bestiality and promiscuity which patriarchal rule "corrected" by establishing the institution of marriage (one woman for each man) so that men knew who their children were. Greek myths also reveal that underneath various marital conflicts was the male effort to suppress the woman's attempts to overthrow the established male-dominant order and the set up of a bestial, promiscuous, and female dominated arrangement (matriarchy implied). A prominent example is that of Agamemnon and Clytemnestra. Clytemnestra's reprehensible repudiation of marriage and revenge on her husband for sacrificing their daughter, Iphigenia, were explicitly portrayed as disastrous to cosmic order for the implied reason that her acts were negating the male order and overturning patriarchal institutions and values.

Bachofen's theory has inspired numerous studies as well as controversies regarding the characteristics of such Neolithic matriarchal communities as well as the historical process that led to their development. Many scholars have subsequently argued that the ancient struggle between matriarchal and patriarchal rule is implicit in the rhetoric of numerous Greek myths. However, most of the arguments for the existence of matriarchal societies are based on speculation.

Commentary

The question of the existence of matriarchy poses difficulties for feminists because it is asked within a historical framework that is phallocentric, or based on the accounts and interpretations of ancient texts and artifacts have been written by males. Recent trends in feminist thought (also named "third wave feminism") have abandoned matriarchal theories and critiqued the notions of any one gender, race, or social group holding power over another. In fact, the very term "matri-archy," or rule by a female/mother implies a notion of power that is more congruent with the misogynist hierarchies of patriarchy than with any form of female social influence that may have characterized the pre-ancient world. Thus, the language itself used in the discussions of matriarchy is questionable because it emerged within a discourse tainted by oppressive systems of power that were based on exclusion, domination, and violence.

In psychoanalysis also, the question of whether matriarchy ever existed is problematic since from the psychic perspective historical reality is never objective, but it is always an amalgam of actual or imagined events and unconscious fantasies which shape our collective unconscious. The latter is expressed in the myths as well as the interpretive narratives we call "history." The archaeological examination of ancient myths, art, and artifacts clearly assume the existence of a "matriarchal consciousness" (which may or may not have had a material component) which early civilizations vehemently attempted to exclude and destroy by means of adopting its opposite: the patriarchal male-centered consciousness. From the psychoanalytic perspective, the very rancor of the misogyny in some early cultures, the extreme forms of patriarchy adopted in certain groups, as well as the eventual universality of the patriarchal system point to a violent repression of the generative powers of female sexuality in the ancient world.

Freud recognized the dynamics of the repression of incest love for one's mother which characterizes identity development, but his phallocentric interpretations have offered a limited understanding of the patterns of patriarchal oppression of females. A more recent psychoanalytic scholar, Julia Kristeva, explains that the roots of the cultural abjection and fervent efforts to dominate women stem from aspects of the individual's early psychic processes of separation from the mother. In early infancy, the newborn exists in a state of undifferentiated physical and psychic fusion with the mother. This maternal space in which the baby is immersed is characterized by fluid physical and psychic boundaries as well as undifferentiated emotions and sexual drives. It precedes language it is capable of generating the energy which helps fuel the subject's meaning-making, or signifying process, which, at this point consists of echolalia, glossolalia, rhythms, and intonations of an infant who does not yet know how to use language to refer to objects. In this early psychic space the infant experiences a wealth of drives (feelings, instincts etc.) that could be extremely disorienting and destructive were it not for the infant's tactile relation with its mother's body which provides orientation for the infant's drives. At the same time as the maternal realm provides emotional exhilaration and jouissance for the infant, it can also become suffocating and stifling as the infant becomes increasingly aware of its separateness from the mother as well as its continued dependence on her. The infant must gradually reject and expel the mother's realm from which it must emerge and separate in order to develop as an autonomous subject. The violence of the expulsion attempts reflect the infant's arduous struggle to resist the powerful pull of fusion with the mother's body and return to the uterine realm of plentitude. Thus the maternal space represents at once abundance and sufficiency as well as the threat of suffocation and death of the emerging subject. From this perspective, the ancient lure as well as inconceivability of matriarchy and the extreme imposition of patriarchy would seem to have its roots in the psychic rejection of the ever-seductive maternal realm and the idealization of the paternal image in the hope of permanently erasing the threat of undifferentiated/psychotic fusion with the mother. In modern Western consciousness this dynamic seems to have become even more entrenched and solidified during modernity when philosophical rationalism and scientific reasoning led to the conceptualizations of human identity as a rational and carefully-bounded entity that could be studied scientifically.

See also: ❷ Femininity ❷ Freud, Sigmund ❷ Great Mother ❷ Mother

Bibliography

Bachofen, J. J. (1967). *Myth, religion, and mother right.* Princeton, NJ: Princeton University Press, Bollingen Series LXXXIV.

Diner, H. (1973). *Mothers and Amazons: The first feminine history of culture.* Garden City, NY: Anchor Press/Doubleday.

Moi, T. (Ed.) (1986). *The Kristeva reader.* New York: Columbia University Press.

Ruether, R. R. (2005). *Goddesses and the divine feminine.* Berkeley, CA: University of California Press.

Tyrrell, W. B. (1984). *Amazons: A study in Athenian mythmaking.* Baltimore, MD: The Johns Hopkins University Press.

Meaning of Human Existence

Todd DuBose

The question of the meaning of human existence holds the longest running place on the best seller list of vital questions among human beings, and the plethora of answers to this question have been complementary, redundant, and contradictory, and expressed in philosophical arguments, theological apologetics, literary narratives, and a myriad of expressive arts. The meaning of human existence, though, is found by exploring situations in which, as Joseph Campbell (1904–1987) was apt to say, one is experiencing oneself as alive in meaningful and fulfilling ways. The experience of being alive in meaningful and fulfilling ways, however, is still described in nearly as many diverse ways as there are those asking the question, which is as it should be.

Descriptions of meaningful and fulfilling kinds of existence are plentiful in the history of philosophy and religion. These descriptions include notions of Platonic attainment of the ideal good to Aristotelian practices of the virtuous life, from Epicurean achievement of pleasurable absence from pain and suffering, to Stoic self-control, indifference, and freedom from obsession and compulsion, or the Cynic's self-sufficiency and release from external attractions and controls. For the pragmatist, the meaningful life is one lived with utility and practicality, while the Utilitarian finds meaning in life by submitting to the higher spiritual goal of all actions being done with the intention of achieving the greatest good for the greatest number of people. The existentialist seeks freedom and the transcendent experience of creating one's meaning in life, while the humanist seeks the actualization of one's potential, even to the transhumanist's desire for overcoming all limitation, even death. Logical positivistic meaning is found in objective, empirical verification. The Abrahamic religions find meaning in pleasing and loving the divine, while the Eastern religious traditions include Confucian emphasis on social education and proper relationships, Taoist alignment with the flow of nature, Shinto movement toward collaboration with nature spirits in the path toward immanent immortality, Buddhist awakening from suffering, Hindu liberation from cycles of repetition through alignment of one's soul with the supreme soul, Bahai's spiritual unity of all humankind, to Zoroastrian rewards in blissful life for right actions and avoidance of the hellish life for destructive living.

The history of discovering meaning in existence is not without the challenge of absurdity, meaninglessness, and despair. More formally expressed in the nineteenth century and early twentieth century, and resurrected more explicitly in postmodernity, nihilism in various forms attempts to deconstruct any conception of transcendent meaning, and most importantly, any meaning deemed static, secure, or eternal. Whether it is a Nietzschean devaluation of all values (Nietzsche, 1967), or Heidegger's destruction of metaphysics (Heidegger, 1962), or the reduction of value to merely exchange value, or the relativism of linguistic meaning, one is left often with the lived experience of meaninglessness and despair. Yet, the very diversity of meaningful experiences articulated and expressed in history need not nullify the experience of meaning-making as central to human well-being. On the contrary, the diversity of searches and experiences for meaning validates its significance. Sounding somewhat circular, the meaningfulness of the search and expression of meaning in human existence gains its reliability and validity from its inescapable and unavoidable presence across all qualifications of diversity in history, culture, and life span.

Meaning making in psychology finds its most formal handling in depth psychologies of various sorts, including psychoanalysis, Jungian analytic psychology, and a range of existential-phenomenological perspectives. Kegan (1982) has described the process of developmental psychology as a series of meaning-making stages. The most familiar of the approaches to meaning-making is Viktor Frankl's (1905–1997) perspective on meaning in human existence called, logotherapy, as formulated by Frankl under the extreme duress of enduring and surviving a concentration camp (1946/1959). Other explorations of meaning making in psychology would include personal construct theory (Kelly, 1963), and positive psychology (Seligman, 2004) – the latter finding significance in discerning what is satisfying to others.

Commentary

The aforementioned compressed history offers vital themes or questions for further reflection. Is meaning created or found? Is meaning cognitively constructed or existentially lived out? Is meaning found in the absence of suffering, or does meaning arise from the edifying encounters with suffering, conflict, and pain? Is meaning a product of one's neurophysiology? Is it evoked by intimate relationships or the desire for them? Is it found in cultural discourse, symbols, or artifacts? Commentary on a few vital points of consideration may provide answers to these questions.

The experience and hope for freedom is central to most any description of a meaningful and fulfilling life, even though different types of freedom are meaningful to different persons: freedom from suffering and political oppression, from oppressive values, from a cycle of rebirth, from one's bodily existence, from disintegration, alienation, and dualism, from violence, from hegemony of ideas and practices, from illusion, or from limits of any sort. But our desires for freedom from situations is accompanied by desires of freedom toward other possibilities: toward a freedom to act, to connect, to decide, to eternal life, to purity, to intimacy, to justice, to synchronicity with nature, to a peaceful existence, to overcome evil, to authenticity, to productivity, to actualize one's potential, to truth, to satisfaction, to union with the divine.

Our desire for freedom in its kaleidoscopic manifestations reinforces the conviction that transcendence is at the heart of meaning-making. The experience of transcendence is the *sine qua non* phenomenon that weds psychology and religion, and is the existential life force operative in the formation of *homo religiosus*. Transcendence as freedom, if experienced in the here and now mode of existence, is an immanent experience of actualizing possibilities within one's ways of being-in-the-world. Even for those who seek freedom beyond-the-world, this otherworldliness is existentially experienced at any given moment in this world's modes of existence, and finds pathways and expressions of transcendence in our everydayness.

The cultural expressions of meaning and transcendence in and through cultural artifacts suggest meaning is embedded in the world's webs of significance. In this way, meaning is discovered in an already and always pre-established context in which we find ourselves. Webs of meaning differ given particular multicultural contexts, including economic contexts. For instance, in a capitalist economic system, profit bestows meaning, as does promotion, and other such experiences of ascendancy, in what could be considered a "commodified" experience of existence. In other contexts, the giving of gifts without expectations of remuneration or return or payback shapes and is shaped by what is considered a "gifting" kind of meaningful and fulfilling existence. Conflicts about what is meaningful among individuals are inevitable within and among cultures.

Relational patterns also construct space in which meaning occurs, such as in egalitarian and inclusive communal encounters that offer transcendence from hierarchical oppression and ostracization. For others, though, freedom from sharing, belonging, and difference has led to more exclusive and hierarchical patterns of relating, that, although oppressive for most individuals, is nonetheless meaningful to those in power. Transcendence in this latter situation may be skewed in that freedom is a freedom to control others. But inviting other possibilities of communal liberation freed from commodification and paternalization as prime bestowers of significance ultimately requires starting from an understanding of the significance of control and destruction for those who exact these patterns of being. Inevitably, conflicts of competing contingencies occur between competing enactments of significance, though resolution of conflict is facilitated more readily when mutual, empathic understanding is risked

regarding how the other comes to find his or her respective life patterns meaningful is granted a hearing.

Another point to consider and clarify is that meaning-making is more than cognitive formulations of propositions created by the neo-cortex. Hence, meaning making in existential psychology is often confused with schema formation in the cognitive sciences. Clarifying this distinction is vital. Neuropsychological insights offer us brain mapping of those undergoing experiences of significance, which makes us aware of how embodied meaning-making is, but this process extends beyond the activity of the frontal lobe to other emotional and narrative centers of brain functioning. Helpful as this information may be, if would be a mistake to conclude that the brain "causes" meaning. Critiques of unilinear causality and biological determinism takes us beyond the scope of this entry, but suffice it to note that even within neurophysiology we know that dendritic branching rewires itself in relation to significant experiences in our lives, particularly traumatic ones. Significant experiences are experiences in which we have attributed or found meaning in one way or another, that can "cause" dendritic rewiring as much as be "caused" by it. It would be more appropriate to speak of our bodying forth in meaningful, transcendent possibilities as co-constructed and pre-reflective. Maurice Merleau-Ponty (1908–1961), the French existential-phenomenologist, brought our attention to how meanings are pre-reflective and lived out long before being conceptualized, which corroborates the neuropsychological findings mentioned above (Merleau-Ponty, 1964).

The plurality of transcendent possibilities in meaningful and fulfilling modes of existence still leaves us with the specter of nihilism. If everything is meaningful then can anything be meaningful? The counter question is just as fair and perhaps more accurate in its presumptions about existence: If everything is meaningful, how could anything be truly meaningless? It is a mistake to assume meaning-making can be avoided or escaped in existence. Even the apparent absence of meaning is always juxtaposed against an already and always posited presence of meaning. Despair would not be painful were it not for alternative enactments of significance in other desired lifeworld comportments that are absent, lost, or inaccessible for the one in despair. Even in "the pit," despair discloses its own embedded hope for transcendence. In fact, we enact significance every moment of our lives.

See also: ◉ Dark Night of the Soul ◉ Daseinsanalysis ◉ Doubt ◉ Faith ◉ Frankl, Viktor ◉ Hermeneutics ◉ Homo Religiosus ◉ Kierkegaard, Søren ◉ Lived Theology ◉ Phenomenological Psychology ◉ Trauma

Bibliography

Campbell, J., & Moyers, B. (1991). *The power of myth*. New York: Anchor.

Driver, T. (1985). *Patterns of grace: Human experience as word of God*. Lanham, MD: University of America Press.

DuBose, T. (2000). Lordship, bondage, and the formation of *Homo Religiosus*. *Journal of Religion and Health, 39*(3), 217–226.

Eliade, M. (1959). *The sacred and the profane: The nature of religion* (W. Trask, Trans.). New York: Harper & Row.

Frankl, V. (1946/1959). *Man's search for meaning*. New York: Washington Square Press.

Gilkey, L. (1976). *Naming the whirlwind: The renewal of God-language*. Indianapolis, IN: Bobbs-Merrill Educational Publishing.

Heidegger, M. (1962). *Being and time* (J. Macquarrie & E. Robinson, Trans.). Oxford: Basil Blackwell.

Heidegger, M. (1987/2001). *Zollikon seminars: Protocols – conversations – letters*. Evanston, IL: Northwestern University Press.

Kegan, R. (1982). *The evolving self: Problem and process in human development*. Cambridge, MA: Harvard University Press.

Kelly, G. (1963). *Theory of personality: The psychology of personal constructs*. New York: W.W. Norton.

Merleau-Ponty, M. (1964). *The primacy of perception* (W. Cobb, Trans.). Chicago, IL: Northwestern University Press.

Nietzsche, F. (1967). *The genealogy of morals and Ecce Homo* (W. Kaufman, Trans.). New York: Vintage.

Otto, R. (1917/1958). *The ideal of the hold: An inquiry into the non-rational factor in the idea of the divine and its relation to the rational* (J. Harvey, Trans.). New York: Oxford University Press.

Schleiermacher, F. (1893). *On religion: Speeches to its cultured despisers* (J. Oman, Trans.). London: Kegan Paul, Trench, and Tribner.

Seligman, M. (2004). *Authentic happiness: Using the new positive psychology to realize your potential for lasting fulfillment*. New York: Free Press.

Tillich, P. (1952). *The courage to be*. New Haven, CT: Yale University Press.

Tillich, P. (1957). *Dynamics of faith*. New York: Harper and Brothers.

Van der Leeuw, G. (1986). *Religion in essence and manifestation* (J. E. Turner, Trans.). Princeton, NJ: Princeton University Press.

Mecca

◉ Hajj ◉ Pilgrimage

Meditation

Trish O'Sullivan

Meditation is a practice wherein active thinking is suspended and mind activity is focused and stilled. There are three meditation subtypes – concentration, contemplation and mindfulness. Concentration involves focusing the mind on one object; contemplation involves the summoning of an image or thought and then holding or examining it in the mind; and mindfulness is paying complete attention to the here and now including thoughts and feelings without engaging with them. In actuality, these practices are often intermingled. Some religious groups, however, emphasize one or the other e.g., concentration in Zen meditation, mindfulness in Vipasanna or insight meditation, contemplation in Christian and Tantric meditation.

Meditation Techniques

Meditation is generally concerned with calming and controlling the mind. There are various techniques for achieving this:

1. mantra is focusing the mind on a thought, word(s), or sounds;
2. breath – focusing the mind on the breath as it enters and leaves the body –(anapanasati)
3. image – a spiritual image is focused on in the mind's eye.
4. guided – a theme or structured map is followed
5. mindfulness – observing thoughts and feelings that arise (vipassana)

Meditation Postures

The most common meditation posture is sitting crosslegged on a cushion with the hands forming a mudra in the lap or on the knees. However, there are various forms of sitting postures, including sitting in a chair. Sitting without moving allows the mind to concentrate fully. Other forms of meditation postures are standing, bowing or walking. Meditation can be continued throughout daily activities through the practice of mantra repetition or mindfulness – present awareness.

Spiritual or Religious Meditation

There are differences between the emphasis, approach and techniques used by various religious traditions. Sometimes the meditation practices are utilized by mystics only or otherwise hidden while some religions consider meditation to be a central practice for all adherents. Goals of meditation practices also vary and they include contact with the divine, spiritual insight, self-refinement, self-knowledge, purification of consciousness and/or enlightenment. The practice itself is done within each unique religious framework and has that religion's particular emphasis as well as flavor or imprint.

Buddhism

The Buddha attained nirvana or enlightenment by meditating. He then devised the Noble Eightfold Path out of suffering of which correct meditation (concentration or dhyana in Sanskrit) is the eighth practice on this path and mindfulness the seventh. Buddhists strive to purify the heart and mind of greed, hatred, ignorance, fear, envy, jealousy and other attributes of mind that produce suffering as well as to achieve enlightenment by realizing their own true or Buddha Nature.

Although the goals are similar, the practice methods within the major Buddhist traditions differ in emphasis and sometimes overlap. There are three main groupings within the Buddhist meditation tradition:

Zen – emphasis on concentration through the practice of Zazen or sitting meditation. The word *Zen* is a Japanese term which comes from the Chinese ch'an which is a transliteration of the Sanskrit term dhyana or meditative absorption.

Vipassana or Insight (Theraveda) – the practice of mindfulness and analysis of phenomena to facilitate inquiry into the true nature of things.

Tantric or Tibetan –in addition to concentration and vipassana, the distinctive practices of this branch often include visualization and contemplation of mandalas, deities, etc.

All three of these traditions include Metta or loving kindness practices although in different forms i.e., chanting in Zen, and visualization in Vipassana and Tibetan.

Christianity

Meditation has not been a central spiritual activity for ordinary people within Christianity where the emphasis is more on prayer, although some of the prayers chanted over and over again silently with the aid of rosary beads are like mantras which concentrate the mind. Religious and mystics have and do practice both concentrative and contemplative forms of meditation. The presence of God is the object of Christian contemplation. There is also the objective of

becoming more holy or Christlike. In the Eastern Orthodox tradition there is a practice known as repetition of the "Jesus Prayer." "Lord Jesus Christ, Son of God, have mercy on me." This is similar to a mantra used in the concentrative practices. St. John of the Cross taught silent, imageless meditations not unlike Zen meditation. Similar to Sufism, the basis of Christian meditation is to open one's heart to both human and divine love. In current times, there has been cross-fertilization from East to West and many Christian meditation practices now incorporate Eastern techniques while maintaining the unique Christian perspective.

Hinduism

Most Eastern meditation practices have their roots in ancient India. A classical meditation technique of ancient India is Pranava or the repetition of the sacred sound of AUM. Yoga and Vedanta are the two prominant philosophies of the Indian tradition. With both, the goal of meditation is to lose the subject/object distinction and realize the truth of Ultimate Reality. Meditation is the only way to achieve this goal of Samadhi or blissful superconsciousness. Patanjali (second–third century CE) is clear in his Yoga Sutras [1.2] that the purpose of Yoga is stilling the mind or "restricting the whirls of consciousness" – "*Yogas citta vritti nirodha*". With Vedanta, meditation is seen as purifying the mind through intense mental worship and the goal is union of the individual consciousness with the all-pervading consciousness. This worship entails symbols and images, repetition of a sacred word (japa), meditation on the qualities of the divine, and meditation on oneness with the divine. In Tantric Yoga, yantras (geometric designs representing universal forms) are internalized through intense concentration and visualization.

Islam

Sufism, considered the mystical form of Islam, incorporates meditation practice. In Sufism, meditation and contemplation are considered essential for purification of the heart. Remembrance of God is the primary focus. There are many forms of meditation/contemplation including breath control, visualization, chanting the names of God, recollecting verses of the Koran, use of a *zikr* or phrase concentrating on God chanted either silently or out loud, etc. There is also a mindfulness practice wherein one contemplates the self: analyzing weaknesses and negative qualities with the intention of purging them. Freeing oneself from the illusion of separation from nature and the universe by the suspension of rational thinking in meditation is also a focus.

Judaism

Jewish meditations come from the tradition of Jewish understanding, and include Jewish symbols, words, images and visualization practices. Regardless of the approach, the focus and aim of Jewish meditation is the union of the self with the divine. While some form of Jewish meditation is believed to have existed in ancient times, over time meditative techniques became largely confined to esoteric Kabbalah practices. Beginning in the eighteenth century, the Hasidic movement attempted to bring meditation into the lives of ordinary Jews. They taught prayer as mantra and contemplative forms of meditation aimed at refining character traits and awareness of the divine. This practice consisted mainly of focusing on the letters of the divine name in various combinations; the Tree of Life symbol, a candle flame or chants. Jewish meditation is today making a comeback based on recorded practices from historical Jewish texts including Kabbalah and meditation practices created by Jewish meditation teachers or borrowed from eastern traditions.

Taoism

Taoists believe that mind and body are intimately connected to one another. Therefore, in Taoism, meditation is both for improving and maintaining the health of the body and attaining enlightenment. The focus is on stilling the mind and attaining present awareness by keeping the mind and breath together. This helps to simplify life and increase awareness of the Way. There are many "inner alchemical" practices as well as physical practices such as Tai Chi, for balancing the Yin and Yang energies and the five elements.

Secular Meditation

Within secular society, meditation is sometimes used for self-improvement purposes. This type of meditation is without spiritual goals and is utilized more to obtain good feelings, to improve concentration and performance in some activity, to help solve emotional or mental problems, or to relieve physical and mental stress.

Meditation is said to have physiologic benefits. It helps slow down the impulse to rush into the next moment and since much stress is caused by anticipation, it reduces stress and promotes a relaxed state. This rested state is believed to have health benefits. Many studies have reported that brain rhythms, heart-beat, blood-pressure, skin resistance, etc. are changed by meditation with resultant health benefits. There are ongoing studies on the beneficial effects of meditation and mindfulness to the mind and body.

Meditation and Psychotherapy

The goals of psychotherapy and spiritual meditation differ in that many types of psychotherapy aim to strengthen the ego and the self with the goal of improving the client's personal and social functionality while meditation aims to free the individual from own identification with the ego and the self for the purpose of increasing awareness of the self as part of a whole and attaining spiritual realization. They are similar in that with both disciplines the focus is on exploring consciousness both within the self and between the self and the other. With both, the habits of mind are observed with the intention of letting go of illusion, unhappiness, suffering and self-alienation. In both meditation and psychotherapy the process involves freeing the self from illusion and reducing alienation from the self.

Knowledgeable therapists often teach their clients meditation techniques for use outside of the office since the meditation process is an individual internal experience. One of the benefits of meditation for both therapists and clients is the improvement of concentration and mindfulness or the ability to be fully present in the here and now of the psychotherapy session. Mindfulness of both the self and each other is an important aid to the therapeutic process for both the client and therapist.

Self-refinement and personality transformation through meditation are goals in many religious traditions but Buddhism and Yoga both especially emphasize psychology. In both Buddhist and Yoga psychology freeing oneself from the grip of attachments is central to personal growth and development. Both traditions hold that past thoughts form impressions or samskaras (skrt) which form habitual patterns of thinking and behavior. Through concentrating the mind in meditation, the unconscious can be penetrated and the samskaras loosened, observed and eventually dissipated. The Sufi's through a similar process, tap into unconscious forces and become aware of and transcend the egoistic nafses.

The use of meditation techniques within the therapy or advocacy of meditation for clients should be carefully considered. Many teachers do not advocate meditation for those who are emotionally or psychologically unstable as both the detachment process and the surfacing of intense emotions can be overwhelming for unstable patients. There is a also a phenomena known as "meditation sickness" wherein headaches, chest pain or stomach aches may occur when the beginner practices excessively. This is believed to result from chi or kundalini energy rising too fast.

On the other hand, meditation is said to help patients with objectivity which can increase emotional stability. This skill in observing emotions rather than acting upon them helps to counter impulsive behavior. Self-detachment rests and rejuvenates the mind. Mindfulness practices are sometimes used in psychotherapy to increase the patient's awareness of their inner state. Dialectical Behavior Therapy, for example, teaches unstable clients mindfulness skills in order to increase their capacity for staying in the moment and balancing the mind. The taking apart of self-concepts in mindfulness meditation allows clients to increase self-knowledge and correct mis-identifications with negative aspects of their personalities. One can train oneself to identify and then relinquish painful mental habits. Meditation is also believed to increase compassion towards others, thus, improving relationships.

Currently in the West, there is an increasing interest in the integration of meditation, specifically Buddhist meditation practices, and psychotherapy.

See also: ⊗ Buddhism ⊗ Christianity ⊗ Hinduism ⊗ Islam ⊗ Judaism and Psychology ⊗ Mantra ⊗ Om ⊗ Psychotherapy

Bibliography

Adiswarananda, S. (2003). *Meditation and its practices: A definitive guide to techniques and traditions of meditation in yoga and vedanta*. Woodstock, VT: SkyLight Paths Publication.

Besserman, P. (1997). *The Shambhala guide to Kabbalah and Jewish mysticism*. Boston, MA: Shambhala.

Bhaskarananda, S. (2001). *Meditation, mind and patanjali's yoga: A practical guide to spiritual growth for everyone*. Seattle, WA: Viveka Press.

Cleary, T. (Compiled and translated) (2000). *Taoist meditation: Methods for cultivating a healthy mind and body*. Boston, MA: Shambhala.

Cooper, R. D. A. (2000). *The handbook of Jewish meditation practices: A guide for enriching the Sabbath and other days of your life*. Woodstock, VT: Jewish Lights.

Davich, V. (1998). *The best guide to meditation*. Los Angeles, CA: Renaissance Books.

Fadiman, J., & Frager, R. (Eds.) (1997). *Essential Sufism*. San Francisco, CA: HarperCollins.

Farrer-Halls, G. (2000). *Illustrated encyclopedia of Buddhist wisdom*, Wheaton, IL: Quest Books.

Feuerstein, G. (2001). *The yoga tradition: Its history, literature, philosophy and practice*. Prescott, AZ: Holm Press.

Gefen, N. F. (1999). *Discovering Jewish meditation: Instruction and guidance for learning an ancient spiritual practice*. Woodstock, VT: Jewish Lights Publishing.

Goldstein, J. (1984). *Seeking the heart of wisdom: The path of insight meditation*. Boston, MA: Shambhala.

Goleman, D. (1988). *The meditative mind: Varieties of meditative experience*. Los Angeles, CA: J. P. Tarcher (Distributed by St. Martin's Press, New York.)

Hsing Yun, Master. (1999). *Only a great rain: A guide to Chinese Buddhist meditation*. Boston, MA: Wisdom Publications.

Joeng, B. (2006). *The mirror of Zen: The classic guide to Buddhist practice by Zen Master So Sahn*. Boston, MA: Shambala.

Johnston, W. (1997). *Silent music: The science of meditation*. New York: Fordham University Press.

Keema, A. (1999). *Visible here and now: The Buddha's teaching on the rewards of spiritual practice*. Boston, MA: Shambhala Publications.

Main, J. (1984). *Moment of Christ: The path of meditation*. New York: Crossroad.

Mishra, R. (1973). *Yoga sutras: The textbook of yoga psychology*. New York: Anchor Books.

Nelson, J. E. (1994). *Healing the split: Integrating spirit into our understanding of the mentally ill*. Albany, NY: State University of New York.

Odier, D. (2003). *Meditation techniques of the Buddhist and Taoist masters. inner traditions*. Rochester, VT: Inner Traditions.

Rama, S., Ballentine, R., Ajaya, S. (Weinstock, A) (1976). *Yoga and psychotherapy: The evolution of consciousness*. Glenview, IL: Himalayan International Institute.

Seung, Sahn, Zen Master. (1999). *The Compass of Zen*. Boston, MA: Shambhala.

Shafii, M. (1985). *Freedom from the self: Sufism, meditation and psychotherapy*. New York: Human Sciences Press.

Smith, J. (Ed) (1998). *Breath sweeps mind: A first guide to meditation practice*. New York: Berkeley Publishing.

Meister Eckhart

Marta Green

Life

Johannes Eckhart (also called Eckhart von Hocheim, also spelled Eckehart) was born around 1260 in Thuringia in what is now Germany. He entered the Dominican priory around 1275. He studied in the University of Paris, receiving his master's degree in 1302 and the title of Meister meaning Master. In his lifetime he became famous as an administrator, scholar, preacher and spiritual director. In 1323, the Archbishop of Cologne inaugurated proceeding against him for heresy. After publicly declaring that he had no intent to preach heresy, Eckhart appealed to Pope John XXII but died some time before he was to appear before the Pope in April of 1328. In 1329, the Pope issues a bull condemning 28 of Eckhart's propositions (Smith, 1987: 6–8).

Thought

Meister Eckhart was most concerned with the *union* of the soul to God. Of the birth of the Word in the soul he writes, "What does it avail me if this birth take place unceasingly and yet does not take place within myself?"(Eckhart, 1980: 293–312).

Eckhart is concerned with knowing God, but for him knowledge is in the form of union with God. You know about something by joining with it, the way Adam knew Eve. Knowing God can not be achieved in the outer world, but only by turning inward and experiencing God in the *"Foundation of the Soul."* Eckhart conceived The Foundation of the Soul as a place of pure emptiness and receptivity, unformed, unconditioned. Being that humans are made in the image of God, God also has a *Foundation*, a place Eckhart calls "the desert," "the abyss," where God also purely empty. It is at the Foundation of the Godhead that the Foundation of the Soul finds union with God.

To achieve this place of union individuals must practice *detachment*. We must detach not only from material possessions, relationships, and our sense of who we are as individuals but even our means of experiencing reality: memory, reason, images, sensations, perception. We are to become empty, sounding boards for God (Smith, 1987: 64). Eckhart writes: "Avoid the restlessness of external deeds! Flee and hide yourself before the storm of inner thoughts, for they create a lack of peace! If God therefore is to speak the Word within the soul, the soul must be in peace and at rest" (Fox, 1980: 298).

When one has completely emptied oneself, then one can receive God (The Word) completely without reservation or thought and *"Breakthrough* into the Godhead." Breaking through means that God completely lives in the person so that the life of God becomes the person's life. "The eye with which I see God is the same with which God sees me. My eye and God's eye, and one sight, and one knowledge, and one love" (Fox, 1980: 83–86, Sermon IV). When we are united with God, we can see the world not as creatures, but as God does (Kelley, 1977; Smith, 1987: 65).

There is one more step. Eckhart understands that God does not reside only in God's Foundation but that God flows out into the world. God animates the world by breathing out into it and then withdraws His breath into the silence and emptiness of His solitude. In doing so God enacts a never-ending eternal process of life and death (Smith 1987: 70). As we are united with God, we also flow out into the world and return back to union with God.

Relationship to Psychotherapy

Although Eckhart's concern is union with God, not the healing of souls, aspects of his thought can inform the practice of psychotherapy, especially if psychotherapy does not limit itself to symptom relief, but is concerned with the development of the inner world of the patient.

One place where the thought of Eckhart and modern psychotherapy meet is in the commitment to radical interiority. Eckhart's insistence on and detachment from all is not dissimilar to the sort of discipline required of those in psychoanalysis. The analysand is asked to examine the inner meaning of outward events; sometimes to such an extent that the events of one's "real life" became nothing more than a screen for one's projected inner contents. This is certainly a process of detachment from the "reality" of every day life All internal contents are examined for their unconscious symbolic value in a detached manner and interpretations are offered. Eckhart would eschew interpretations and insist on a complete house cleaning, sweeping away all labels and preconceived concepts. Eckhart doesn't even want to label God as "good" for fear that the word would be too confining (Fox 1980: 177–180, Sermon XII).

Meister Eckhart taught a radical presence to God by cultivating a mind completely clean of pre-existing categories. In this his thought is very similar to that of the Easter mystics. The concept of radical emptiness may be of help in the work of psychotherapy. To the extent that therapists are able to become aware of the contents and categories of their minds and detach from them, maintaining an evenly hovering attention, to that extent they are able to be wholly present to their patients. As Eckhart warned about images, so counselors must detach themselves from all images of who they are, of what therapy is and allow each session to come alive in the spontaneity of the moment.

Eckhart's concept of image is also helpful in considering the self-image of the patient or counselor. Patients are people who have become attached to a few very rigid ideas of who they are and what is possible for them: "I am not good enough." "I am no one unless I am loved." They block out much of life returning to their core images (Shainberg, 1983: 11f). Clearly, such individuals can be helped by learning to let go of their grip on such limited

M

life scripts. Much can be gained by honoring Eckhart's in-depth understanding of detachment from images especially in detaching from self-images in the service of freeing up inner space for the client. The images must be dissolved not to be replaced with other supposedly superior images, but to permanently free up the inner world of the client, enabling them to live spontaneous, less scripted lives.

While the therapist may detach in approaching the patient and in helping the patient let go of inner clutter, for Eckhart, detachment creates a space for God which he defines as The Word entering human life. To experience the, Word Eckhart counsels not-knowing or as his seventeenth sermon is titled: "Letting the Intellect Go and Experiencing Pure Ignorance" (Fox, 1980: 238). Is this not also a useful model for a therapist? Can we likewise practice entering each session without "desire, memory or understanding" as Bion has counseled to await the birth of the one word that needs to be said in that session? The one word that will define and heal and connect the moment. Is that not the point of the session to sit and wait for the one right word to emerge spontaneously, in the session, out of the communion of the unconscious?

See also: ◉ Christianity ◉ Psychotherapy and Religion

Bibliography

Eckhart, J. (1980). Three births, ours, God's, and ourselves as God's children. In M. Fox (Ed.), *Breakthrough: Meister Eckhart's creation spirituality in new translation* (pp. 325–330). Garden City, NY: Doubleday & Company.

Fox, M. (1980). *Breakthrough: Meister Eckhart's creation spirituality in new translation.* Garden City, NY: Doubleday & Company.

Kelley, C. F. (1977). *Meister Eckhart on divine knowledge,* New Haven, CT: Yale University Press.

Shainberg, D. (1983). *Healing in psychotherapy: The process of holistic change.* New York: Gordon & Breach Science.

Smith, C., OSB. (1987). *The way of paradox: Spiritual life as taught by Meister Eckhart.* New York: Paulist Press.

Melancholia

Nathan Carlin

Notes on the Term

The term "melancholia" comes from Greek and literally means "black bile." The condition of melancholia in ancient times, according to the medical theory of the four humors, was thought to be caused by an excess of black bile in the human body. Since ancient times, we have a great deal of writing on melancholia, including works by such thinkers as the Hippocratics, Rufus of Ephesus, Galen, and Avicenna, to name only a few of the most prominent names (cf. Jackson, 1986). While Robert Burton's (1979) *The Anatomy of Melancholy,* published in 1621, is generally regarded as the most extensive and detailed treatment of the term, Sigmund Freud's (1963) "Mourning and Melancholia," published in 1917, is perhaps the work most well-known on the issue of melancholia, likely because of Freud's enormous influence on culture in general and because of his impact on the practice of psychiatry in America in the twentieth century in particular. In this essay, Freud gave a psychological or mental, as opposed to a biological, explanation for melancholia in that he argued that mourning and melancholia are two kinds of reactions to losing an object, where mourning represents the normal grieving process and melancholia a pathological response. In melancholia, one is prevented from mourning, Freud argues, because the object is "still in the neighbourhood" but is still nevertheless lost.

The term "melancholy" today is often associated with sadness (a feeling or mood) and depression (a clinical disorder or symptom). In clinical circles, the term melancholia has fallen out of favor, much like the term manic-depression. In *The Diagnostic and Statistical Manual of Mental Disorders-IV-TR,* for example, there is no melancholia diagnosis, but there is a sub-section titled "Melancholic Features Specifier" that is used to help clarify diagnoses of mood disorders, such as Bipolar I and II Disorders. However, melancholia as a term is making a comeback. William Styron (1990) writes in his memoir that

▸ "Depression," most people know, used to be termed "melancholia," a word which appears in English as early as the year 1303 and crops up more than once in Chaucer, who in his usage seemed to be aware of its pathological nuances. "Melancholia" would appear to be a far more apt and evocative word for the blacker forms of the disorder, but it was usurped by a noun with a bland tonality and lacking any magisterial presence, used indifferently to describe an economic decline or a rut in the ground, a true wimp of a word for such a major illness (p. 36–37).

Donald Capps and I (2007; cf. Capps, 2005) have endorsed Styron's view in our own writings in the fields of pastoral psychology and psychology of religion. In psychiatric literature, Michael Taylor and Max Fink

(2006) have also endorsed Styron's view, as they quoted this very passage for one of their chapter epigrams, and they argue that melancholia has a more precise meaning than depression in terms of clinical diagnosis (p. 15). In any case, time will tell what the status of melancholia will be in *The Diagnostic and Statistical Manual of Mental Disorders-V*.

Melancholia and Religion

Historically, melancholia has also had religious significance. Jackson (1986) notes that "Whether the gods, a god, or the God, the supernatural being (or beings) visited the distressing state on the sufferer as punishment for his sin or because of his lack of repentance for his sin" (p. 325). Jackson also notes variations on these themes, that sometimes, for example, it was and is still sometimes believed that God can use mental illness as a means for growth, or that the Devil, too, may be allowed to test God's faithful from time to time, as in the *Book of Job*. Such explanations for melancholia will likely sound offensive to the contemporary reader because these explanations appear to be blaming the victim, rationalizing, trivializing, or romanticizing suffering.

In any case, mental and emotional disorders in general continue to have religious significance today. While psychological insights into religion have not fared well among theologians (cf. Scharfenberg, 1988), Paul Tillich is certainly an exception, and his theological thinking does not blame the victim, rationalize, trivialize, or romanticize suffering. Tillich's project was to correlate the teachings of the church with modern day experience, and so he redefined many traditional theological concepts, like sin. He argued for understanding sin as estrangement from God, others, and self. And he also argued that everything in existence is also in estrangement. Existence, in other words, is estrangement. The upshot here is that, for Tillich, it would be correct to say that mental illness is a manifestation of estrangement or sin, but it would not be correct to say that it is the result of a particular sin. Tillich wrote regularly for the journal *Pastoral Psychology* in its early years, and he (2000) also wrote at length about the religious significance of anxiety and despair. In terms of the religious significance of melancholia today, particularly for men, Donald Capps, whose work I will discuss briefly below, has written prolifically (see, for example, Capps, 1997, 2001, 2002, 2004, 2005, 2007a, and 2007b).

Jackson (1986) also notes Burton's introduction of the term "religious melancholy" in his *The Anatomy of Melancholy*. Burton defined religious melancholy as a kind of desperation and "sickness of the soul without any hope or expectation of amendment" (quoted in Jackson, 1986: 331; cf. Rubin, 1994). Significantly, then, Capps (2001) has argued for the image of the pastor as an agent of hope (on depression, cf. pp. 101ff.). Depression and melancholia are obviously significant to pastoral care professionals, though mental illness in general receives very little attention in seminary education (Capps, 2005: 1), even while there are excellent books available (Ciarrocchi, 1993; Collins and Culbertson, 2003).

Donald Capps on Male and Female Melancholia

Capps defines male melancholia as a form of religiousness that emerges in men's early childhood through their relationship to their mothers. This male melancholic religion "may or may not manifest itself in religious observances, commitment to spiritual disciplines, or religious participation in social causes or in acts of personal sacrifice" (Capps, 2002: xvi). In fact, it is more often the case that men are *not* religious in these conventional ways but are often religious in experiential (in contrast to institutional) ways (cf. Capps, 2007a: 256). As strange as it might sound, men are often religious in ways that, on the surface, do not resemble religion. But by understanding the origins of male melancholia, one can then see how men are religious in unconventional ways.

When boys emotionally separate from their mothers (normally between ages 3 and 5), they acquire an ambivalent attitude toward their mothers because, even though, or precisely because, she is still around, things are not the same. "Why has mother abandoned me?" the boy asks himself. He also wonders, "Can this loss be reversed? And, if so, what can I do to reverse it?" "[T]he very ambiguity of this situation," Capps writes, "and the anxieties that such ambiguity promotes are of key importance to the emotional separation that occurs between a small boy and his mother, and this separation is reflected in the form and style of men's religious proclivities" (2004: 108). Since all boys separate from their mothers, all men suffer from melancholia, and all men, therefore, are religious in this sense.

Capps suggests that male religiousness takes three forms, which are all directly related to the boy's separation from his mother. The first of men's religious proclivities is the religion of honor. By being a "good boy," men attempt to "win" their mothers back, perhaps by doing well in school, by earning a lot of money, or by achieving remarkable social standing. The second main proclivity is the religion of hope, and here men attempt to find a replacement for their mothers by finding someone like her or something to replace her. Here men might take interest in literal quests, such as traveling, or the quests can be of a more symbolic nature. The third religious proclivity, which Capps (2002) added in his *Men and Their Religion: Honor, Hope, and Humor*, is the religion of humor, "which stands overagainst the first two ways of being religious in the sense that it humors them" (2004: 108). This way of being religious asks, "Can one really win mother back, and can one really find a replacement?" It may also ask, "And why would one *want* to win mother back?" The religions of honor and hope may have their successes, but they have their defeats and disappointments as well, and one way that a man might cope with the latter is to develop a humorous attitude toward the first two ways of being religious. Here men make light of the commitments and efforts that they engender, and by doing so, they save themselves from bitterness and despair. The religion of humor accepts the reality of the loss, yet refuses to be defeated by this loss. If male melancholia has no cure, Capps suggests that humor is a pretty good antibiotic. Put in theological terms, if the religion of honor correlates with what Christian theology calls "works," and the religion of hope fits with a mystical searching, often marked by tentativeness and doubt, the religion of humor, for Capps, paves the way for the religious notion of grace. The other forms of religion involve doing, whether by working or searching, but the religion of humor is simply being, mocking and relativizing doing. Honor and hope are retained, but in a chastened, relativized form.

But what about women? Where do they fit into Capps's theory? In *Men and Their Religion*, a sequel to *Men, Religion, and Melancholia*, Capps (2002) notes psychoanalyst Julia Kristeva's view on the etiology of female melancholia. In *Black Sun*, Capps notes, Kristeva argues that female melancholia "is traceable to the two to three-year-old girl's need to begin adopting the dominant ('symbolic') language of her culture, which is male-oriented, and thus to leave the security of her mother's language world (which is 'semiotic')" (p. 5). Capps notes that Kristeva cites studies that link signs of depression with language acquisition. If this theory is correct, Capps suggests, then "it would follow that boys adapt more naturally to the symbolic language of patriarchal culture and are therefore less subject to lasting melancholia as a consequence of language acquisition" (2002: 5). Capps believes this argument has considerable merit. And it may also explain why more women than men suffer from depression.

In his work on the psychology of men, Capps has been greatly influenced by his mentor James Dittes. On the differences between boys and girls, men and women, Dittes (1996) writes:

> ▸ Girls have the advantage that their primary caregiver (and life-giver) can be their primary role model. They know they are to grow up female, and to learn how to do that – how to behave and feel and think of themselves as female – they have both model and encouragement at hand in the person they are already closest to and dependent on (p. 24).

"For a boy," Dittes writes, "it is not that easy. He knows he is to grow up male, and he also recognizes early on that to achieve this he must not honor and strengthen but disrupt the bonds between himself and his primary caregiver, his life-giver" (1996: 24). And so "being male costs a connectedness with life" (1996: 25). If Kristeva is correct, being female also costs a connectedness with life, but this cost is different than the one men pay, and it is one in fact that they would share with their mothers, perhaps even strengthening their bond. For more discussion on melancholia and gender, see Schiesari (1992), and for more of a discussion on mourning and melancholia in light of Kristeva's work, see Diane Jonte-Pace (2008).

See also: ◉ Depression ◉ Freud, Sigmund ◉ Psychology of Religion

Bibliography

American Psychiatric Association (2000). *Diagnostic and statistical manual of mental disorders (DSM-IV-TR)* (4th ed., text revision). Washington, DC: American Psychiatric Press.

Burton, R. (1979). *The anatomy of melancholy*. New York: Frederick Ungar.

Capps, D. (1997). *Men, religion, and melancholia: James, Otto, Jung, and Erikson*. New Haven, CT: Yale University Press.

Capps, D. (2001). Male melancholia: Guilt, separation, and repressed rage. In D. Jonte-Pace & W. B. Parsons (Eds.), *Religion and psychology: Mapping the terrain* (pp. 147–159) London: Routledge.

Capps, D. (2002). *Men and their religion: Honor, hope, and humor*. Harrisburg, PA: Trinity Press International.

Capps, D. (2004). Leonardo's Mona Lisa: Iconic center of male melancholic religion. *Pastoral Psychology, 53*, 107–137.

Capps, D. (2005). *Fragile connections: Memoirs of mental illness for pastoral care professionals*. St. Louis, MO: Chalice Press.

Capps, D. (2007a). The making of a reliably religious boy. *Pastoral Psychology, 55*, 253–270.

Capps, D. (2007b). Augustine's *Confessions*: Self-reproach and the melancholy self. *Pastoral Psychology, 55*(5), 571–592.

Capps, D., & Carlin, N. (2007). Mental illness publications in major pastoral care journals from 1950 to 2003. *Pastoral Psychology, 55*, 593–600.

Ciarrocchi, J. (1993). *A minister's handbook of mental disorders*. Mahwah, NJ: Paulist Press.

Collins, G., & Culbertson, T. (2003). *Mental illness and psychiatric treatment: A guide for pastoral counselors.* New York: The Haworth Press.

Dittes, J. (1996). *Driven by hope: Men and meaning.* Louisville, KY: Westminster John Knox Press.

Freud, S. (1963). Mourning and melancholia. In P. Rieff (Ed.), *General psychological theory: Papers on metapsychology* (pp. 164–179). New York: Collier Books.

Jackson, S. (1986). *Melancholia and depression: From Hippocratic times to modern times.* New Haven, CT: Yale University Press.

Jonte-Pace, D. (2008). Melancholia and religion in French feminist theory. In W. B. Parsons, D. Jonte-Pace, & S. Henking (Eds.), *Mourning religion* (pp. 81–94). Charlottesville, VA: University of Virginia Press.

Kristeva, J. (1989). *Black sun: Depression and melancholia.* New York: Columbia University Press.

Mitchell, S. (1992). *The book of Job.* New York: Harper Perennial.

Rubin, J. (1994). *Religious melancholy and protestant experience in America.* New York: Oxford University Press.

Scharfenberg, J. (1988). *Sigmund Freud and his critique of religion* (O. Dean, Trans.). Philadelphia, PA: Fortress Press.

Schiesari, J. (1992). *The gendering of melancholia: Feminism, psychoanalysis, and the symbolics of loss in renaissance literature.* Ithaca, NY: Cornell University Press.

Styron, W. (1990). *Darkness visible: A memoir of madness.* New York: Random House.

Taylor, M., & Fink, M. (2006). *Melancholia: The diagnosis, pathophysiology, and treatment of depressive illness.* New York: Cambridge University Press.

Tillich, P. (2000). *The courage to be.* New Haven, CT: Yale University Press.

Merton, Thomas

Fredrica R. Halligan

For Catholics and other Christians, Thomas Merton (1915–1968) has been a role model both for the contemplative life and for openness to the interfaith dialogue, in particular the sharing and learning from Eastern religions. A best-selling author, Merton first became famous for his autobiography *Seven Story Mountain*, in which he documented his conversion to the Roman Catholic faith. Death touched him early: he lost his mother at age six and his father at fifteen. Both his parents had been artists and Protestants. Tom traveled extensively in Europe and was deeply moved by religious art. After he was orphaned, he was raised by his grandfather and attended private school in England, followed by a flamboyant and disastrous year at Cambridge. He returned to the U.S. and attended Columbia where, under the mentoring of Mark Van Doren, he began serious writing. While at Columbia he also turned to Catholicism, and in 1938 he was baptized a Catholic. Three years later he joined the contemplative Cistercian (Trappist) Abby in Gesthemani, Kentucky. He chose the strictest order to do penance for his sins.

Contemplation and Activism

In his twenty-seven years of religious life, Merton struggled with the contrast of strict monastic rule and the role he played in "the world" as he became increasingly popular, writing poetry, fiction, journals and spiritual prose. Among his fellow monks and priests, Merton (who was known there as Fr. Louis) was both fun-loving and deeply serious in this spiritual quest. He became novice master and was much beloved for his wisdom and his wit.

Thomas Merton was highly intelligent, a voracious reader, and deeply interested in all forms of contemplative experience. He corresponded with some of the great spiritual leaders of the East, including Buddhists, Hindus and Moslems. He was spiritually nourished by this correspondence and by his own exploration of the inner life. In 1960 he was granted special permission to spend his days (part-time) as a hermit where, in addition to praying, he joyfully continued to study, write and communicate via letters in a vast and burgeoning interfaith dialogue. The Dalai Lama, for example, treasured Thomas Merton for his intelligence, creativity, wisdom, humor, openness, commitment and religious zeal.

In the 1960s when the Church was changing due to Vatican II and the U.S. was changing due to the civil rights movement and the Viet Nam war protests, Merton became an activist by the "power of his pen." *Conjectures of a Guilty Bystander* is an example of this social activism. He wrote passionately about the Christian's responsibility for humanity, including responsibility to speak up against injustice, prejudice and war. Thomas Merton, the man, knew both pleasure and pain in his life; he shied away from neither. As a monk and writer his genius lay in his capacity to express both intense pleasure and intense suffering, all with a sense for the whole.

Turning Eastward

Merton found in Eastern contemplation the same emphasis he valued from Western monasticism: silence, solitude, simplicity, emptiness, treasuring the sacred in the ordinary, surrender, meditation and prayer. In 1968 he was invited to give two talks at interfaith events in Bangkok and India. In preparing for that journey, he read extensively in Tibetan Buddhism and Zen, Islam and Sufism, and Vedanta. He wrote a journal during his travels in the East which was published as *The Asian Journal of Thomas Merton.* In it he reflected on every aspect of his thought and varied experiences. He wrote, for example, about the abiding value of the interreligious dialogue:

> ...we can see the special value of dialogue and exchange among those in the various religions who seek to penetrate the ultimate ground of their beliefs by transformation of religious consciousness. We can see the point of sharing in those disciplines which claim to prepare the way for "mystical" self-transcendence.... Without asserting that there is complete unity of all religions at the "top," the transcendent or mystical level...it is certainly true to say that even where there are irreconcilable differences in doctrine and in formulated belief, there may still be great similarities and analogues in the realm of religious experience....[H]oly men like St. Francis and Ramakrishna (to mention only two) have attained to a level of spiritual fulfillment which is at once universally recognizable and relevant to anyone interested in the religious dimension of existence. Cultural and doctrinal differences must remain, but hey do not invalidate a very real quality of existential likeness (Merton, 1975: 311f).

Merton was on the cutting edge of East-West dialogue and he opened the door for believing Christians to follow his footsteps in the dialogic encounter with Eastern thought. In October 1968, just after completing one of his planned talks, he went to his room to shower and rest. He accidentally touched a fan in the bathroom that had faulty wiring and was immediately electrocuted. His death was a blow to all who knew him.

But his death itself gave a final exclamation to his closing offering at the first spiritual summit conference in Calcutta. He so eloquently expressed this prayer which remains as his final wisdom for all spiritual aspirants:

> Oh God, we are one with You. You have made us one with You. You have taught us that if we are open to one another, You dwell in us. Help us to preserve this openness and to fight for it with all our hearts. Help us to realize that there can be no understanding where there is mutual rejection. Oh God, in accepting one another wholeheartedly, fully, completely, we accept You, and we thank You, and we adore You, and we love You with our whole being. Our spirit is rooted in Your Spirit. Fill us then with love, and let us be bound together with love as we go our diverse ways, until in this one spirit which makes You present in the world, and which makes You witness to the ultimate reality that is love. Love has overcome. Love is victorious. Amen (Merton, 1975: 318f).

See also: ◉ Meditation ◉ Prayer

Bibliography

Merton, T. (1965). *Conjectures of a guilty bystander.* Garden City, NJ: Image/Doubleday.

Merton, T. (1975). *The Asian Journal of Thomas Merton.* In M. Burton, P. Hart, & J. Loughlin (Eds.), New York: New Directions.

Method

Brandon Randolph-Seng

Religion's method is based on faith, while psychology is a science. Therefore, both religion and psychology have a different yet complimentary way of dealing with and understanding existential questions such as the meaning and purpose of life (Greenberg, 2004). For psychology, the scientific method, the research process, and critical thinking are all going to be important. The scientific method is a cyclical process with the scientific cycle of theory building consisting of two complimentary forms of reasoning: induction and deduction. Therefore, factual findings can either contribute to theory development (induction) or theory can serve as a basis for hypotheses that may or may not be verified by factual findings (deduction). Programmatic research is a systematic step-by-step approach to theory development (Randolph-Seng, 2006). In order to make a contribution to the understanding of human thought and behavior, contemporary psychologists must have a program of research in place (Klahr and Simon, 2001). For religion or the religious believer, science-like critical thinking processes are important, but ultimate understanding of self and others must come through a trust and belief in those things that cannot be tested through traditional scientific methods. Evidence for the meaning and purpose of life comes through the fruits (outcomes) of those beliefs (see Matt. 7 King James Version). Religion's method is also a cyclical process with faith and action serving as two complimentary forms of belief. Therefore, the outcome of action based on faith grows into knowledge for the believer. In order for the religious believer to come to a sense of religious knowledge, faith in those things that are not seen or scientifically testable must come first (see Heb. 11 King James Version).

See also: ◉ Faith

Bibliography

Greenberg, J., Koole, S. L., & Pyszczynski, T. (Eds.) (2004). *Handbook of experimental existential psychology*. New York: Guilford.

Klahr, D., & Simon, H. A. (2001). What have psychologists (and others) discovered about the process of scientific discovery? *Current Directions in Psychological Science, 10*, 75–79.

Randolph-Seng, B. (2006). Doing programmatic research: Two case studies from social psychology. *The New School Psychology Bulletin, 4*, 73–90.

Midrash

Mark Popovsky

Midrash refers to a genre of classical Jewish biblical interpretation which flourished from the third century through the thirteenth century. The term derives from the Hebrew verb "to pound" – suggesting that midrash *pounds out* meaning from the biblical text. The literary form refrains from determining one interpretation as normative, allowing for multiple and mutually exclusive interpretations of the biblical text to coexist.

Rarely does midrash attempt to comment on an entire biblical passage; rather it almost always focuses on a particular word, phrase, or individual verse. Following an extremely close reading of the biblical text, the interpreter will point out a textual oddity such as an unusual word choice, a variant spelling, or unexpected syntax. Holding the premises that the bible's author is divine and that the text was composed with ultimate economy, an individual midrash endeavors to show how the apparent error was actually intended by God to teach an additional lesson. The remainder of the midrash will expound that point, often making liberal use of wordplays, puns, and convergences of sounds. Similar to psychoanalysis, the midrashic process seeks to find latent meaning implied in the manifest material of the biblical text. Few Jews composed works of philosophy or systematic theology prior to the medieval period; midrash serves as the primary window into how the rabbis of the ancient world viewed God, morality, and the world around them.

Midrash can loosely be divided into two categories: narrative (*aggadic*) and legal (*halakhic*). Biblical style is typically laconic. The text provides only flashes of dialog and almost never directly reveals a character's thoughts or emotions. Narrative midrash attempts to fill these gaps in the text, playfully imagining missing dialog, background stories, and motivations for behavior. One common method is to shift the reader's point of view, retelling the story from the perspective of a peripheral or altogether invented character. This undermines the reader's confidence in objective inquiry and directs his or her attention towards the relational field. Like many psychological interventions, the midrashic process provides individuals with license to explore, question and refashion narratives that may initially appear immutable.

Legal midrash purports to deduce practical rules for worship, daily life, and moral behavior from a biblical text which appeared sometimes too vague and sometimes simply outdated to its rabbinic interpreters. For example, the Bible commands that Israelites refrain from work on the Sabbath, but it provides no definition of work. The Sabbath laws observed today by religious Jews develop directly from midrashic efforts to elucidate specific practices relying on subtle clues within the generally silent biblical text.

Midrashic interpretation is traditionally viewed as divine in origin; consequently, rules derived through legal midrash are considered by rabbinic authorities as if they were stated explicitly in the Bible. Midrash served as a tool to connect sometimes radical innovations in religious practice to the biblical text itself, thus maintaining a direct link between devotee and scripture despite significant transformations in normative behavior over time. As Jewish tradition evolved through its encounters with other cultures and new technologies, midrash became the primary means by which rabbis validated these developments as consistent with divine will.

See also: ◉ Jewish Law ◉ Judaism and Psychology ◉ Psychoanalysis

Bibliography

Hammer, R. (1995). *The classic Midrash: Tannaitic commentaries on the Bible (Classics of Western Spirituality)*. Mahwah, NJ: Paulist Press.

Katz, M., & Schwartz, G. (2002). *Searching for meaning in Midrash: Lessons for everyday living*. Philadelphia, PA: Jewish Publication Society of America.

Migration and Religion

Valerie DeMarinis

Introduction

The relationship between and psychological consequences of migration and religion are topics of historically long standing. The age of globalization and patterns of forced migration have brought new attention to this topic. The text is organized into the following sections: cultural function and worldview; voluntary and forced migration; host culture analysis and operant refugee paradigm; and, mental health, religion, and trauma.

Cultural Function and Worldview

To understand the psychological implications of the interaction between migration and religion, the function of religion in cultural context needs to be studied. The pioneering work of Arthur Kleinman in cultural psychiatry (1980) introduced a now internationally used model of the dimensions of culture for analysis of how healthcare systems, types of interaction in healthcare contexts, and patients' cultural understandings of illness and health are constructed. In this model the symbolic dimension, which includes religious elements and rituals, is pivotal for understanding the deepest levels of how concepts of illness and of health are understood in a given cultural context. As illness and health are culturally-influenced constructions, the religious or spiritual way in which these are approached inform the psychosocial and psychoexistential functioning of individuals and groups within the culture. Cultural psychologists Marsella and Yamada (2000) note that culture is a living entity that provides both internal and external artifacts. Included in the external category are societal institutions including religious and healthcare organizations. Included in the internal category are beliefs, rituals, and symbols, including those of a religious or existential nature. A change in one category necessitates attention to the need for change in the other as the internal and external categories are interdependent. The religious or spiritual systems operant in a mono-cultural or stable multi-cultural situation provide a means for creating a functioning worldview in which psychosocial and psycho-cultural understandings and behaviors are contained. Approaching the concept

of worldview as a psychological construct Koltko-Rivera (2004) defines it as a set of assumptions about physical and social reality that may have powerful effects on cognition and behavior. An individual's worldview needs to be studied in relation to personality traits, motivation, affect, cognition, behavior, and culture.

Religious and spiritual beliefs, rituals, and symbols can and very often do function as resources in such mono- or stable multi-.cultural contexts. In cultural contexts where political stability, safety, and religious toleration exist, migration of different minority groups representing different religious traditions can have a positive outcome for both minority and majority groups. Perhaps the most salutogenic and health-enabling acculturation process, in such cases, would mean that the migrant minority group members find ways to incorporate aspects of the majority culture's external and internal artifacts while maintaining and developing central resources for their psychosocial health and spiritual resilience originating from their original culture (DeMarinis, 2003). Thus a syncretism of cultural resources would emerge over time, experience, and exposure. Majority culture members would also be a part of the acculturation process, learning from and respecting the resources of the minority groups.

Voluntary and Forced Migration

International migration implies a shift from one cultural context to another. Depending on the differences between the old and new cultural contexts, the role of religion or spirituality can have very different consequences for psychosocial adjustment and development. Migration takes place in both voluntary and forced situations. The term "refugee" denotes an individual who is forced to flee in search of safety, in contrast to someone who chooses of their own volition to relocate. Bascom (2001) provides a helpful overview of the geographical and geopolitical dimensions of refugee (forced) migration patterns.

Migration of any kind can cause a dramatic change in the way in which and means by which a person or a group's religious or spiritual expression may function. The more dramatic and traumatic the situation of migration, the more one may expect situations of dysfunction. As Silove (2005) points out, it is important to pay attention to how changes in existential meaning are being handled, especially in situations of forced migration. Values and belief systems, the inner artifacts of culture, can become dysfunctional leading in extreme cases to alienation and loss. Thus addressing these areas in response to trauma may assist with the move from trauma to survival. It therefore becomes necessary through both social and psychological interventions to include room for religious and spiritual expression in cultural reconstruction and adaptation processes. Elements of humanistic and existential material need to be included in counseling and psychotherapy.

Host Culture Analysis and Operant Refugee Paradigm

Another important psychosocial aspect regarding migration and religion is the fit between the host culture and the cultures of the migrating groups, with special attention to refugees. This aspect of research has been understudied but is now receiving much-needed attention. One of the central results of a research study on Polish children's attitudes to refugees (DeMarinis, Grzymala-Moszczynska, and Jablonski, 2001) points to the need for an analysis of functioning religious culture when investigating attitudes of the host culture population. Analysis of this dimension is important when conducting research or designing intervention programs in countries that have a defined religious tradition such as Poland but also as in countries that represent a more secular orientation such as Sweden. Concepts and policies such as religious freedom and tolerance may appear as simple and straightforward on the surface but may be impeded by underlying and underexplored worldview conceptions that often contain suspicious attitudes to certain religious traditions or religious expressions.

Host culture analysis in relation to refugee groups needs to be understood in relation to the operative refugee paradigm. Clearly, a paradigm shift has occurred in international responses to refugees. After September 11, 2001, the *security paradigm* has taken form, where refugees are not infrequently viewed with deep suspicion, and in the extreme as being terrorists (Frelick, 2007). A sign of this paradigm shift is reflected in the decline of asylum applications in the Western industrialized countries. Refugees are often viewed as moral blackmailers, exploiting the goodwill of the host nations (Ingleby, 2005), or as a result of terrorist threats, a major devaluing of refugees among receiving countries has taken place (Frelick, 2007).

In a comparison of European and North American attitudes to immigration (Livi-bacci, 1994), noted that the factors explaining the different immigration policies in North America and Europe are not economic or demographic, but stem rather from history, social structure, the functioning of the labor market and social mobility. European countries tend to perceive themselves as totally formed and not requiring further cultural contribution. Homogeneity in culture, language, and religion is valued. Finally, in Europe, restrictive policies are in perfect harmony with public opinion.

A study of refugee problems in Europe (Veiter, 1988) points out the large influx of refugees coming from places with other cultural and religious attributes. Accordingly, the Islamic immigrants often declare themselves as political refugees and hope to be acknowledged as such by the receiving state. The fear of the governments and populations of the receiving countries is that it will not be possible to assimilate refugees who do not belong to the Christian culture of Europe (Veiter, 1988).

Mental Health, Religion, and Trauma

Research on mental health and religion has become timelier because of a resurgence of interest in religious belief and practice in many parts of the world, and because of the increased movement of the world's population (Boehnlein, 2006). Mental health providers in developed countries increasingly are treating immigrants and refugees whose backgrounds are much different from their own, so it is important for them to understand cultural belief systems, including religious thought and practice that relate to mental health and illness (Ingleby, 2005; Bhugra, 2004).

During and after traumatic events, individuals frequently report great cognitive dissonance between what they observe and experience in reality and what they previously believed were stable, secure, and predictable relationships, not only with other individuals but also with the supernatural or the metaphysical (Boehnlein, 1987). Incorporating religious and spiritual perspectives in the clinical assessment of patients takes into account the effects of philosophical viewpoints, cultural values, and social attitudes on disease (Fabrega, 1977). Religious teachings recognize the transcendental meaning of suffering and the fact that suffering, such as agony, despair, pain and conflict, belongs to the totality of life (Rhi, 2001; Kirmayer, 2008).

In PTSD recovery, spiritual awakening can play a role in relieving survivor guilt (Khouzam and Kissmeyer, 1997). Traumatic memory and unresolved issues may be helped in psychotherapy through an understanding of and addressing of the rituals of importance to the patient. Working with re-ritualization in the new cultural context, through connection to the patient's religious or meaning making system, may help to create a new perspective and a means of containing painful memory as well as providing a new memory resource (DeMarinis, 1996).

Exposure to inexplicable evil, cruelty, and extreme violation can shake and sometimes shatter the foundations of the survivor's existential worldview. The survivor and the community face crises of trust, faith, and meaning (Silove, 2005).

A very useful conceptual framework for understanding the existential meaning-system in mental health initiatives among refugees in post-conflict societies is the *survival and adaptational model* by Silove (2005). On the level of existential meaning-system, the challenges are to the undermining of cultural and belief systems values. The adaptive responses are existential doubts and the adoption of new/ hybrid identities, while the extreme responses are alienation and loss of faith. The social interventions can be made on religious, political, and cultural reconstruction levels. The psychological interventions may include elements of humanistic and existential therapy (Silove, 2005).

Several recent studies in different contexts point to the importance of religious coping strategies and resources in the management of traumatic stress after forced migration: Gozdziak (2002), Hagan and Ebaugh (2003), Myers (2000), and Shoeb et al. (2007). These and other studies are providing a base for understanding the potential of certain kinds of religious engagement and involvement for identifying resources for coping and moving beyond surviving. However, there is the need for caution in examining these results as so many factors are involved at many different levels. Keeping such cautions in mind, three initial observations can be made. First, that religion and spirituality can be beneficial to people in dealing with the aftermath of trauma. Second, that traumatic experience can lead to a deepening of religion or spirituality. Third, that positive religious coping, religious openness, readiness to face existential questions, religious participation, and intrinsic religiousness are factors that may be associated with posttraumatic growth.

See also: ❂ Cultural Psychology ❂ Syncretism

Bibliography

Bascom, J. (2001). Refugees: Geographical aspects. In *International encyclopedia of the social and behavioral sciences* (pp. 12895–12901). Oxford: Elsevier Science Ltd.

Bhugra, D. (2004). Migration and mental health. *Acta Psychiatriska Scandinavia, 109,* 243–259.

Boehnlein, J. K. (1987). Clinical relevance of grief and mourning among Cambodian refugees. *Social Science and Medicine, 25,* 765–772.

Boehnlein, J. K. (2006). Religion and spirituality in psychiatric care: Looking back, looking ahead. *Transcultural Psychiatry, 43,* 634.

DeMarinis, V. (1996). A psychotherapeutic exploration of religious rituals as mediators of memory and meaning. A clinical case presentation of the therapeutic efficacy of incorporating religious ritual into therapy. In M. B. Aune & V. DeMarinis (Eds.), *Religious and social ritual: Interdisciplinary explorations* (pp. 235–266). Albany, NY: State University of New York Press.

DeMarinis, V. (2003). *Pastoral care, existential health, and existential epidemiology: A Swedish postmodern case study.* Stockholm: Verbum Press.

DeMarinis, V., Grzymala-Moszczynska, H., & Jablonski, S. (2001). Polish children and refugees: The role of religious culture in the host community acculturation process. *International Review of Religious Research, 23*(1), 177–199.

Fabrega, H., Jr. (1977). *Origins of sickness and healing.* Berkeley, CA, University of California Press.

Frelick, B. (2007). Paradigm shifts in the international responses to refugees. In J. D. White & A. J. Marsella (Eds.), *Fear of persecution: Global human rights, international law, and human well-being.* (pp. 33–58). New York: Lexington Books.

Gozdziak, E. (2002). Spiritual emergency room: The role of spirituality and religion in the resettlement of Kosoval Albanians. *Journal of Refugee Studies, 15,* 136–153.

Hagan, J., & Ebaugh, H. (2003). Calling upon the sacred: Migrants' use of religion in the migration process. *International Migration Review, 37,* 1145–1162.

Ingleby, D. (Ed.) (2005). *Forced migration and mental health: Rethinking the care of refugees and displaced persons.* New York: Springer.

Khouzam, H. R., & Kissmeyer, P. (1997). Antidepressant treatment, post-traumatic stress disorder, survivor guilt, and spiritual awakening. *Journal of Traumatic Stress, 10,* 691–696.

Kirmayer, L. (2008). Culture and the metaphoric mediation of pain. *Transcultural Psychiatry, 45,* 318–338.

Kleinman, A. (1980). *Patients and healers in the context of culture.* Berkeley, CA: University of California Press.

Koltko-Rivera, M. (2004). The psychology of worldviews. *Review of General Psychology, 8,* 3–58.

Livi-Bacci, M. (1994). "Us" and "them": European and North American attitudes to immigration. *Politique Étrangère, 59*(3), 661–70.

Marsella, A., & Yamada, A. (2000). Culture and mental health: An introduction and overview of foundations, concepts and issues. In I. Cúellar & F. A. Paniagua (Eds.), *Handbook of multicultural health: Assessment and treatment of diverse populations* (pp. 3–26). San Diego, CA: Academic Press.

Myers, S., (2000). The impact of religious involvement on migration. *Social Forces, 79*(2), 755–783.

Rhi, B. Y. (2001). Culture, spirituality, and mental health. *Psychiatric Clinics of North America, 24,* 569–579.

Shoeb, M., Weinstein, H. M., & Halpern, J. (2007). Living in religious time and space: Iraqi refuges in Dearborn, Michigan. *Journal of Refugee Studies, 20,* 441–460.

Silove, D. (2005). From trauma to survival and adaptation: Towards a framework for guiding mental health initiatives in post-conflict societies. In D. Ingleby (Ed.), *Forced migration and mental health: Rethinking the care of refugees and displaced persons* (pp. 29–51). New York: Springer.

Veiter, T. (1988). Juridical structures: refugees and migration. *Migration World Magazine, 14,* 3–28 (Staten Island, NY: Center for Migration Studies of New York.).

Mikveh

Lynn Somerstein

The mikveh, a word denoting "the collection or gathering of water" is a ritual bath used for purification purposes by women, after their menstrual cycle is completed, or after childbirth, making a woman ready to resume intimate relations with her husband, and by men, to achieve ritual purity. Women also immerse themselves before the day of their wedding. Immersion in the mikveh is part of the conversion experience, too, symbolizing the change from the old identity to the new Jewish identity. Immersion in the mikveh marks an intermediate step towards a new state. The entire body, including the hair on one's head, must be totally immersed in the waters of the mikveh.

The mikveh is a deep pool filled with a mixture of pure spring water or rain water, called living water, and tap water. Tap water alone can not be used because it is pumped. Mikveh water must flow into the pool by natural means, such as gravity, although tap water can be mixed with what is called "living water." The emphasis on the use of "living water" symbolizes water from the earth, like amniotic fluid from mother earth.

The narrow deep pool of water symbolizes the amniotic fluid; the pool itself is like the womb, a return to the mother. A person totally immersed in the mikveh is like a fetus inside the mother's body.

New cooking implements are also immersed in the mikveh to ready them for kosher use.

See also: ❯ Judaism and Psychology ❯ Primordial Waters ❯ Ritual

Bibliography

Skolnik, F. (Ed.) (2006). *Encyclopedia Judaica*. New York: MacMillan.

Mindfulness

Jo Nash

Historical and Religious Origins of the Term "Mindfulness"

The Buddhist practice of mindfulness is described in detail in the Satipatthana Sutra (*Satipatthana Sutra* is also known as "The Foundations of Mindfulness" translated in Rahula (1959) *What the Buddha Taught)*, and also comprises the seventh aspect of the Noble Eightfold Path to end all suffering as explained by Siddartha Gautama

Buddha. Each aspect of the Eightfold Path is an interdependent principle of Dharma practice, and Right Mindfulness involves cultivating insight into how our minds work, using both the conceptual mind and the direct perceptions of our bodily senses to refine our awareness of how different aspects of the mind and body inform each other, through observation and acceptance of their fluctuating nature. This enables Dharma practitioners to notice the arising and dissolution of changing states of awareness and cultivate an acceptance of the impermanence of bodies, emotions, thoughts and environmental phenomena. This increases equanimity which is a mind free of attachment or aversion to what occurs. Ultimately it prepares the practitioner for the realisation of the peace of Nirvana. Rahula writes, "Right Mindfulness is to be diligently aware, mindful and attentive with regard to (1) the activities of the body, (2) the sensations or feelings, (3) the activities of the mind and (4) ideas, thoughts, conceptions and things" (1959: 48).

Contemporary Psychological Definitions

Mindfulness has now been adopted as a contemporary practice beyond the Buddhist community, used to tackle stress and modify distortions in thinking. It involves paying full attention to the present moment through the direct perceptions of our bodily senses, emotions and thoughts, without judgment. It is understood as the antithesis of time referenced action, where our feelings, thoughts and behavior are rooted in an evaluative assessment of the efficacy of past actions and the anticipation of future consequences, which may be more or less consciously available to us. When practising mindfulness we observe the present moment in all its fullness to access an awareness unencumbered by the distortions of memory or desire. Mindfulness is thereby the opposite of "mindlessness," or a mind susceptible to unconscious feelings and reactive thoughts, leading to automatic, habitual or impulsive actions.

Mindfulness Based Health Interventions

Contemporary health practitioners of various kinds understand the latter to be the root of much stress and psychological distress. Mindfulness techniques are being taught by a range of health education professionals to help cultivate the self management of health problems which may be compounded by the tendency of the mind to react impulsively rather than observe and reflect; from acute stress to chronic pain, substance abuse, and severe, recurring mood disorders.

In more complex cases of recurring major depression, mindfulness techniques have been used as an adjunct to other forms of psychological intervention, primarily in conjunction with cognitive therapy to produce the hybrid "Mindfulness Based Cognitive Therapy" or MBCT. Recent research has demonstrated that MBCT is especially effective at preventing relapse in patients suffering with a history of three or more episodes of major depression, the most recent of which has not been precipitated by significant life events (Ma and Teasdale, 2004). MBCT helps these patients "... learn to be aware of negative thinking patterns reactivated during dysphoria and disengage from those ruminative depressive cycles" (Ma and Teasdale, 2004: 31). It facilitates this by enabling the patient to experience changes in affect and thinking with acceptance, rather than the controlling, clinging mind of aversion or attachment. This cultivates a de-centered approach to fluctuations in emotions and thoughts through an awareness of their impermanence, or ultimately changing nature. It can thereby avert the downward spiral of rumination on previous experiences of feeling "stuck" with negative emotions such as sadness or anger, which has in the past precipitated a depressive mood, and developed into a major depression. In short, the adoption of MBCT techniques enables the patient to choose to observe their ever changing emotions and thoughts rather than become them.

Mindfulness Based Stress Reduction is a more generic form of health care intervention aimed at facilitating the self-management of chronic pain and stress, pioneered by John Kabat Zinn (1990). He describes the practice he teaches his clients at the stress clinic as follows,

> ...the essence of mindfulness is paying attention on purpose. [. . .] being awake, owning your moments. As long as you are awake you can be mindful.[. . .] bringing your attention into the present moment [. . .] it [. . .] does not mean 'thinking about.' It means directly perceiving what you are attending to. [. . .] direct seeing, direct hearing, direct feeling (1990: 438).

Through the increased awareness of the here and now, we tune into our thoughts, feelings, sensations and those of other people too, so that "we can respond more appropriately to change and to potentially stressful situations, because we are aware of the whole and our relationship to it" (1990: 438). We can make more informed choices about how to act, because we have more information about what is going on inside us and around us, through the cultivation of focused attention on what is there, rather than what we want to be there, or fear may be there. In this way MBSR side steps the stress created by the limitations of our time referenced mind, which is prone to get stuck in the past or worry about the future, neither of which exist right now.

In summary, mindfulness is an ancient Buddhist contemplative practice that can lead the Dharma practitioner to the fulfillment and peace of Nirvana, as well as having a range of tangible health benefits for the non-Dharma practitioner. In both it requires the sustained cultivation of non-judgemental attention to the present moment, in all its fullness.

See also: ⊙ Buddha-Nature ⊙ Buddhism ⊙ Meditation ⊙ Nirvana

Bibliography

Kabat-Zinn, J. (1990). *Full catastrophe living: How to cope with stress, pain and illness using mindfulness meditation*. London: Piatkus.

Ma, S. H., & Teasdale, J. (2004). Mindfulness based cognitive therapy for depression: Replication and exploration of differential relapse prevention effects. *Journal of Consulting and Clinical Psychology, 72*(1), 31–40.

Rahula, W. (1959). *What the Buddha taught*. New York: Grove Atlantic.

Miracles

Daniel J. Gaztambide

In philosophy and theology, miracles are wondrous events generally conceived as violations of the immutable laws of nature by divine or supernatural forces such as god/s or other spiritual beings. Depending on one's philosophical or theological position, they are argued to either be impossible events without any verifiable evidence due to the contradiction inherent in the notion of violating immutable natural laws, or possible events enacted by a deity who has the capacity to momentarily suspend, abrogate, or transform the laws of nature. A psychological approach influenced by this debate over immutable natural laws and the supernatural would be tempted to problematize either party as neurotic and lacking good reality testing, depending again on the philosophical orientation of the psychologist- one who does not believe in miracles might see those who do as irrational and mentally ill and vice-versa. A different psychological approach would be interested not in the particular truth claims of philosophical inquiry but on the way miracles and miraculous experiences express the deep structure of a person's subjectivity and their relations to personal, communal, and religious experience.

See also: ◉ Myth

Miraj

Ali Kose

Miraj is an Arabic word meaning "ladder, to elevate, or to ascend". In Islamic literature it is used for the night journey of Prophet Muhammad when he was miraculously taken to the presence of Allah (God) in Heaven. According to the Islamic faith it is one of the major miracles of the Prophet. It happened on the night of the 26th of *Rajab*, the seventh month of the Islamic calendar, in the year 621 AD, which is one year before the Prophet's migration to Medina. How the miraculous journey occurred is a matter of differing opinions among Muslim theologians. Some maintain that, it occurred only spiritually while others assert that it happened both bodily and spiritually.

Stages of Miraj

Miraj happened in two stages. In the first, the Prophet was taken from *Masjid al-Haram*, the mosque which surrounds the *Ka'bah*, in Mecca to *Masjid al-Aqsa*, the mosque just south of the Dome of the Rock, in Jerusalem. This stage, which is mentioned in the Qur'an, is named *al-isra*, the night journey (Qur'an 17: 1). In the second stage, the Prophet miraculously ascends from *Masjid al-Aqsa* to God in Heaven. This stage, called miraj, is not mentioned in the Qur'an, but it is narrated in detail in various sayings of the Prophet (al-Bukhari, *al-Salat*, 1; al-Muslim, *al-Iman*, 259).

According to the sayings of the Prophet, the Archangel Gabriel took the Prophet to Heaven riding on a mount called *Burak*. He was elevated through seven levels of Heaven where he met seven former prophets; Adam, Jesus, Joseph, Enoch, Aaron, Moses, and Abraham, one at each level respectively. His ascension was accompanied by the Archangel Gabriel until the lotus tree called *sidra al-munteha* in the Seventh Heaven. Then he continued his journey riding on another mount called *Rafraf* and not accompanied by the Archangel Gabriel until he arrived to God's presence. There, he was given the good news that his people, except those who attribute partners to God, would eventually be allowed into Paradise. It was here where God enjoined five daily prayers. On his descending from Heaven, he rode *Rafraf* until the lotus tree where he took *Burak* again until Jerusalem before returning to Mecca.

While in God's presence, the Prophet was also given the following 12 commandments: (1) Do not worship any God, but Allah, (2) Treat parents well, (3) Lend help to kin, the stranded one, and the poor, (4) Do not be mean and do not waste, (5) Do not kill your child due to the fear of poverty, (6) Do not approach adultery, (7) Do not kill, (8) Do not usurp orphan's belongings, (9) Keep your promise, (10) Do not deal in fraud, (11) Do not follow an idea which you know nothing about, (12) Do not be arrogant.

Reactions of Muslims and Idol-Worshippers

The following day, the Prophet told the Meccans about his journey to Heaven. The idol-worshippers tested him asking questions about a caravan traveling from Jerusalem. His answers were satisfactory, but the idol-worshippers did not believe in him even though they cross-checked all with the members of the arriving caravan. Some idol worshippers went to Abu Bakr, who was one of the first Muslims, saying that Muhammad had gone crazy claiming that he had ascended to Heaven. Abu Bakr surprised them saying that he would believe anything Muhammad had said. After this event Abu Bakr was given the title of "The Trustworthy." In general, Muslims believe that Miraj is a test of their faith.

Miraj has a symbolic meaning for Muslims. They are supposed to experience the journey of the Prophet in their five-daily prayers feeling themselves in the presence of God as the Prophet did at Miraj. In order of importance of sacred occasions, it is after the Night of Power (*Lailatu'l Qadir*), when the Qur'an is believed to have been revealed.

See also: ◉ Islam ◉ Jerusalem ◉ Qur'an

Bibliography

Ahmad ibn Hanbal. (1895). *al-Musnad* (Vol. I, pp. 309). Cairo, Egypt.
al-Dihlavi. (1992). *Hujjatullah al-Baligha* (Vol. I, pp. 115). Beirut.

Mirroring

Jane Simon

The intrigue with the *mirror* leads down a corridor of a long, variegated history to involve the profound subject of identity. Who are we to self? Who are we to the world? What is reality? What is distortion? How much can we alter our perceptions?

The earliest hominid gazed at his image in the still water following a rainstorm. The question of identity and the soul concerned the ancient Egyptians, Chinese, and Aztecs. Present-day astronomers turn their big mirrors out toward space and ask "Who are we; what is our place in the universe?"

Uses of the Word "Mirror"

The noun mirror is an object which reflects back to the onlooker a more or less distorted image, most commonly reversing right and left or presenting the onlooker with a "mirror image." The verb "to mirror" is to offer a verbal feedback, an aspect of the subject "*mirrored*" by an onlooker.

Superstitions and the Mirror

Many people from Europe to Madagascar, and sects of Mohammedans and Jews, cover mirrors in the house after a death because they believe the soul of a living person in the form of his reflection, may be carried off by the ghost of the deceased which hovers around the house until the burial (Goldberg, 1986: 3).

Seven years bad luck to one who breaks a mirror is related to the belief that the image is the soul. Since the mirror supposedly captures the soul, if it breaks, the soul breaks too. British anthropologist, Sir James Frazer, found that the Greeks believed water spirits could drag a person's reflection under water, leaving him soulless to perish. This superstition explains the myth of Narcissus who perished from the frustration of inordinate love for his mirror image (Goldberg, 1985: 6). Universal mystery of the mirror involves divination, the art which seeks to foretell the future and discover hidden knowledge (1985: 7).

Philosophy and History

Plato argued that it was often impossible to see the idea, just as the true nature of the sun...cannot be viewed directly...can only be seen imperfectly reflected in a mirror. And by extension, the material world known through our senses, was regarded as a reflection of the "other world," of ideals which we cannot see, feel, or hear unless possessed of universal wisdom. Socrates and Plato asserted that our illusory reality is only the reflection of a greater, abstract Goodness that lies in a hypothetical upper world beyond the *mirror-like* dome of the sky. Even though he considered this world a mirror-illusion. This Platonic concept prevailed for over fifteen hundred years in Europe, in religion, art and morality (Goldberg, 1985: 114, 115).

Socrates urged his followers to study themselves in mirrors in order to make sure their faces did not reflect dishonorable thoughts or deeds, apparently assuming that they could "monitor their inner reality by their outer appearance" (Pendergrast, 2003: 12).

Seneca, who lived during the time of the Roman Empire (AD 40), thought mirrors were invented so man might gain knowledge of himself and thereby wisdom. With the mirror's help, the handsome man may avoid infamy; the young man be reminded that youth is a time of learning, and "the old man, set aside actions dishonorable to his gray hair, to think some thoughts about death. This is why nature has given us the opportunity of seeing ourselves" (Goldberg, 1985: 112–113).

The *Book* of *Wisdom* of the second century BC echoes an aspect of the Platonic mirror. In AD 54, Paul, at the church in Corinth, addressed his Epistle, "For now we see in a mirror dimly, but then face to face. Now I know in art: then I shall understand fully, even as I have fully understood" (Goldberg, 1985: 115). In the authorized translation: "For now we see through a glass, darkly" (I Corinthians 13:12).

From these beginnings the mirror analogy took on significance in Christian thought. From "spotless mirror" in the *Book of Wisdom* was drawn the attribute of the purity of the Virgin Mary.

The metaphor of the mirror lent itself to the Christian belief that all existence is understood as a relation between paragon and image, between a reality and its innumerable reflections. Contempt for the world of matter and belief in the liberation of the soul through asceticism and mystic revelation made this congenial to many believers. (Goldberg, 1985: 116).

Through the writings of Augustine and others, basic theological mirror analogies were formulated: the mirror of the soul and the mirror of the mind. The mirror of the soul was the image of the ideal, or archetypal idea. This led to mirrors knows as compendiums of knowledge and idealized virtues. The mirror of the mind was ambivalent; it reflected the shadow world of the senses and led to mirrors that warned of the transience and illusiveness of this world. But concerned itself with religious truth. The Holy Scripture was called a mirror from which could be drawn models of holy living either as biography or as religious rule (Goldberg, 1985: 118–119).

In Kabbalistic doctrine the goal is to meditate on the Hebrew letters in order to pass beyond the control of the natural mind, first by means of script and language and then by means of imagination to reach the stage where you can't speak. Through the power of sheer imagination one's inmost being is something outside of self which takes on "the form of a polished mirror" (Scholem, 1995: 154–155).

Shakespeare's Hamlet, Yahweh of the Hebrew Bible, and Jesus of the Greek New Testament, each provide mirrors in which we see ourselves reflected in their faith and in their skepticism, with the ultimate hope for transcendence. Jesus Christ may be seen as "a concave mirror" in which we see the distortions we have become (or a "theological labyrinth") while Yahweh, the Hebrew God is a "mad moralist" (Bloom, 2005: 9).

Like Hamlet, Jesus is a mirror in which we see ourselves. "Endless questing for the historical Jesus has failed, in that fewer than a handful of searchers come up with more than reflections of their own faith or their own skepticism." . . . Jesus is to the Greek New Testament what Yahweh is to the Hebrew Bible, or Hamlet to Shakespeare's play: the vital protagonist, the principle of apotheosis, the hope for transcendence" (Bloom, 2005: 12–13).

History has altered our perceptions and with it perceptions of soul, self, mirror, and mirroring. At first images reflected in water, did not appear to belong to us, but rather to the deities.

During the nineteenth Century, the concept of the double, an alternate version of self, was perceived to turn against self. The Russian symbolist Andrei Bely produced a body of literature in which the reflected image plays a role often portending a tragic end. Gogol in *The Nose* and Dostoyevskii in *The Double* through the use of the mirror, describe the worlds of their characters.

In 1924, Otto Rank a renowned Austrian psychoanalyst, published a psychological treatise *The Double* which theorized that the double or soul and man's need to immortalize himself led to the development of civilization and its spiritual values. Rank shared the preoccupation of the Russian symbolist writers in his observation that the double represented the problems of man's relationship to himself. Both novelists and psychologists were affected by the impact of nineteenth-century science which seemed to destroy the soul. The mirror became a symbol of man's rejection of materialistic reason in his search to repossess his lost soul (Goldberg, 1985: 242).

When our conception of the universe changed to a more objective view of reality, we were freed of earlier misapprehensions about self, and in turn, our conception of the mirror was altered. Looking outward, the modern mirror contributes to the broadening of scientific and technological horizons. Looking inward, the mirror remains a powerful tool of introspection, a metaphor to help distinguish outward appearance and inner truth.

Poetry

Poet Margaret Atwood writes a powerful poem in which she equates the absence of a mirror to living without the self.

"To live in prison is to live without mirrors. To live without mirrors is to live without the self. She is living selflessly, she finds a hole in the stone wall and on the other side of the wall, a voice. The voice comes through darkness and has no face. This voice becomes her mirror" (Artwood, 1978).

I interpret Atwood's words as an expression of our a human desperation for "mirroring."

Another contemporary poet, *former* laureate, Billy Collins writes about the mirror as an informer in a poem entitled "In the Moment":

➤ As I closed the book on the face
of Thomas Traher and returned to the house
where I lit a flame under a pot
full of floating brown eggs,
and while they cooked in their bubbles,
I stared into a small oval mirror near the sink
To see if that crazy glass
Had anything special to tell me today.

Theoretically the glass "mirrors" back something we know or informs of what is there, but it may surprise us with *something* we haven't seen before.

In the 20th century psychologists became intrigued with the significance of mirroring as a vital process to self *development*. Today 'mirroring neurons' have been anatomically defined and observed in action on a functional magnetic radiological imaging of the living brain.

The study of how mirroring and the activities of mirroring cells affects us has been extended from the major role *they* play during the years of child development to their everyday role in influencing our actions in subtle ways often outside our awareness.

M

Mirroring and Development

Does the mirror corrupt or enhance a sense of self for a young child? Psychologist Fritz Wittels* found as a boy that the mirror helped identify his ego to himself (Goldberg, 1985: 249; *year of Wittels' writing is not provided).

Child psychiatrist, Robert Coles recognized the role of the mirror in developing a positive self image. He studied American children of well-to-do parents. These children were exposed to many mirrors in their homes, which were used for inspection of their appearance to "insure neatness and cleanliness, and "as a means of nurturing self-esteem." These children became leaders in society. By contrast, in his study of underprivileged children, Coles found this emphasis lacking (Goldberg, 1985: 250).

Psychology

In the 1970's, psychoanalyst Heinz Kohut described the concept of mirror transference in two seminal books, *The Analysis of the Self* and *Restoration of the Self.*

In Kohut's words, "The genetic matrix of the primary defect-stunted development of the grandiose-exhibitionistic aspects of the self-was insufficient mirroring from the side of the mother..." (Kohut, 1977: 7–8).

Margaret Mahler studied the interaction and interrelationship between mother and infant and categorized a variety of mothering styles based on the mother's ability to recognize and mirror the affect, cognition, and behavior of her young child.

The goal for the mother to respond with sufficient accuracy determines the development of a healthy sense of self for the infant. If her mirroring doesn't relate, or approximate the inner feeling state of the infant/child, he develops an inadequate or distorted sense of self.

Mahler cites the example of Charles who could not be alone or in the company of another person for extended periods of time; he had lost his "symbiotic mother" "at a time in his development when this loss was equivalent to losing part of the self." He tried to learn how to have emotions...to maintain a sense of identity by mirroring others (Mahler, 1968: 30–31).

A decade later, child psychiatrist Daniel Stern based much of his study on significant developmental processes of mirroring, attunement, and empathy between infant and caretaker. To a great degree, these processes determine our identity, a sense of who we are and how we interact with others.

Stern elaborates on the development of several forms of the self which are essential for functioning. The self as *agent* grants us ability to perform in the inanimate and social worlds. If this sense is lacking, paralysis may result. The sense of physical cohesion prevents fragmentation with depersonalization, out of body experiences, de-realization. Memory aids a sense of continuity and prevents temporal dissociation which is seen in fugue states and amnesias. An affective sense prevents anhedonia and enables a person to connect to the culture, to socialize and avoid cosmic loneliness.

Kohut, Mahler and Stern all focus on the preverbal self and damage to the sense of self and psychopathology which result from failure of good enough mirroring whether the problem exists in the emotional/affective, cognitive, or behavioral realm.

Used in the clinical theories of Mahler et al. (1975); Kohut (1977), Lacan (1977) reflecting back an infant's inner feeling state, remains a key to the infant's development in learning about his or her own affectivity and sense of self. "Mirroring" then implies that the mother is helping to create something within the infant that was only dimly or partially there until her reflection acted to solidify its existence. Based on these studies, mirroring lies at the basis of healthy development and constitutes the foundation of the authentic self.

Mirror Neurons

In the 1990's, mirror neurons were discovered by an Italian team who happened to be snacking on ice cream cones in front of macaque monkeys. These monkeys imitated the scientists by beginning to eat too.

Mirror neurons are housed in several areas of the brain. One of these, the insula is responsible for social emotions like guilt, shame, pride, embarrassment, disgust and lust.

We humans are "hard-wired" for imitation. Mirror neurons begin working at birth. Watching his mother stick out her tongue, an infant a few days old will imitate her behavior by protruding his own.

Through the operation of mirror neurons we learn many behaviors. Our survival depends on understanding actions, intentions and emotions of others which in turn depends on the existence of mirror neurons.

The function of mirror neurons extends beyond *actions* to involve *intentions* and *emotions* which contribute to make us social animals.

According to researcher Rizzolatti, mirror neurons have been found to mediate a broad range of human experiences that were previously thought too subjective to be characterized experimentally. Emotions such as empathy, theory of mind (the ability to perceive another person's intent), and even the reaction to a loved one's pain have been characterized at the neuro-anatomical level and appear to involve mirror neurons (Blakeslee, 2006).

Whether a person performs the action, observes the action done by someone else, or hears a sentence describing the action, activates the same mirror regions in the brain which has led researchers to "speculate that syntactic understanding involves mirror regions that are normally associated with action recognition."

Neuroscientist Marco Iacoboni who studies mirroring cells in human brains links empathy with strength of mirror neuron response suggests that the mirror system opens the gate to understand other cultures (Blakeslee, 2006: 4; Hotz, 2007).

A kind of mirroring or mimicry, "a synchronized and usually unconscious give and take of words and gestures" has been found to foster the subtle art of persuasion. Researchers find that when a persons' posture and movements are mirrored with a one-to two-second delay, namely, to create an imperfect mirror, they are more receptive to the suggestion to try a new soft drink. Subtle mimicry, perceived as flattery, has the opposite effect of social mimicry which is likely to be perceived as mockery (Carey, 2008).

Biology, Anatomy and Pathology

Humans possess multiple mirror systems located in diverse areas of the brain responsible for language, emotions, and perceptions. Researchers seem to agree there are multiple mirror systems and neurons have connections to thousands of other cells which create intricate constellations of relationships.

Faulty mirroring most likely lies at the root of psychopathology of many diagnoses, perhaps excluding only those which fall primarily in the biochemical realm.

Normal function helps determine what goes wrong in pathological conditions such as autism, a disorder manifested in failure to respond to social cues.

This mirror of neurons may be broken with greater disruption of mirror networks implicated in worse symptoms of autism, that is, more severe impairment of language, behavioral and social skills.

Unresolved as to etiology and now attributed to the realm of the biological is the malady known as Body Dysmorphic Disorder which manifests as faulty, inaccurate thoughts and perceptions about appearance. Variations on distorted body image include anorexics who look into a mirror and see too much body fat and male bodybuilders who suffer from "bigorexia" a condition in which their mirror image looks too weak.

Many schizophrenics react oddly to mirrors, sometimes staring at them for hours. Curiously, there are no blind schizophrenics, and in the single known case where a long-term schizophrenic went blind, she went into remission within a few days (Pendergrast, 2003: 360).

Astronomy

The use of mirrors extends beyond psychology and religion to astronomy. Astronomers attempt to build the biggest telescope with huge mirrors to learn about the universe and the dark energy that seems to be splitting the universe apart. Patrick McCarthy of the Carnegie Observatories told the group, "The most important tool we take to the observatory is an open mind."

The open mind is a kind of two way mirror: we present (an aspect of) self to the world and the world reflects back. Our chore, with an openness or questioning of self, to what resides within (our thoughts, dreams, fantasies) with what the environment mirrors back to us about the aspects of self we present to the world, is an ongoing dynamic process. Perceptions, like waves of the ocean, can reinforce or interfere/ or negate our self concept.

Although the formation of the self depends on the mirroring process, and since the sense of self varies from culture to culture, characteristics of mirroring also vary. For example, the sense of self in India is intricately woven into the fabric of the family. By contrast the American culture to a large degree focuses on the individual. The process of mirroring is a learning tool. We learn by imitating others, parental figures, mentors both consciously or unconsciously.

And as one would expect, mirroring is culturally conditioned. An involuntary sense of empathy responds differently depending on whether we're looking at someone who shares our culture (Hotz, 2007).

Cultural and Future Implications

Mirroring affects us to the core of our being, yet the major significance is only beginning to be recognized. To a large extent, murderers and lovers are made, not born (unfortunately, not always mutually exclusive). From the above observations, an understanding and acting upon mirroring may be important in the process of establishing world peace. The history and role of the mirror and mirroring over the centuries reflects the human evolution from placing our Fate in the Deities, to claiming our role of self identity down to the unique sub-molecular composition of each of us and embodies the potential of humans to evolve. Dire world conditions result from the human capacity both to destroy and to re-build, create, and problem-solve. Based on research in writing this article, I am hopeful that we have the biological capacity (some of which lies in our in mirroring neurons) to achieve increasing harmony in the future.

See also: ❯ Kabbalah ❯ Rank, Otto ❯ Virgin Mary

Bibliography

Atwood, M. (1978). *"Marrying the hangman, two-headed poems".* Canada: Oxford University Press.

Blakeslee, S. (2006, January 10). Cells that read minds. *The New York Times*, p. F1.

Bloom, H. (2005). *Jesus and Yahweh: The names divine.* New York: Riverhead Books.

Carey, B. (2008, February 12). You remind me of me. *The New York Times*, p. F1, 6.

Collins, B. (2005). *The trouble with poetry and other poems* (p. 16). New York: Random House.

Dostoevsky, F. (2006). *The double. West valley city.* West Valley City, UT: Waking Lion Press.

Gogol, N. (1985). *The complete tales of Nikolai Gogol* (Vol. I). Chicago, IL: University of Chicago Press.

Goldberg, B. (1985). *The mirror and man.* Charlottesville, VA: University Press of Virginia.

The Holy Bible. King James Version. (2000). United States: Oxford University Press.

Hotz, R. L. (2007, August 17). How your brain allows you to walk in another's shoes. *WSJ*, p. 31.

Kohut, H. (1971). *The analysis of the self.* New York: International Universities Press.

Kohut, H. (1977). *The restoration of the self.* New York: International Universities Press.

Lacan, J. (1977). *The four fundamental concepts of psycho-analysis.* London: Tavistock.

Mahler, M. (1968). *On human symbiosis and the vicissitudes of individuation.* New York: International Universities Press.

Mahler, M., Pine, F., & Bergman, A. (1975). *The psychological birth of the human infant.* New York: Basic Books.

McCarthy, P. (2005, August 30). Mirror, mirror: Astronomers race to build the biggest telescope ever. *The New York Times*, p. F1, 4.

Medina, J. J. (2007, September). Mirroring in the human brain. *Psychiatric Times*, p. 14.

Overbye, D. (2005, August 30). Mirror, mirror: Astronomers race to build the biggest telescope ever. *The New York Times*, p. F1, 4.

Pendergrast, M. (2003). *Mirror, mirror a history of the human love affair with reflection.* New York: Basic Books.

Robert, C. (1977). *Privileged ones*, Boston, MA: Little, Brown.

Scholem, G. G. (1995). *Major trends in Jewish mysticism, Abhlafia and the doctrine of prophetic kabbalism* (pp. 154–155). New York: Schocken Books.

Stern, D. N. (1985). *The interpersonal world of the infant.* New York: Basic Books.

Monomyth

David A. Leeming

Mythologist Joseph Campbell has demonstrated that when we consider heroes and their myths comparatively we discover a universal hero myth that speaks to us all and addresses our common need to move forward psychologically as individuals and as a species. "The Hero," writes Campbell, "is the man or woman who has been able to battle past his personal and local historical limitations to the generally valid, normally human forms" (1949/1972: 19–20). The hero does not stand for the status quo; he or she breaks new ground. The striving hero is our cultural and collective psyche out on the edges of knowledge and existence.

Taking a word coined by James Joyce, Campbell calls the archetypal hero the "monomyth." The hero of the monomyth, our representative of Self, the totality of our individual and collective unconscious and conscious psyches, passes in his "adventures" through a series of transformative thresholds, which are representative of the psychic and, to an extent, the physical life. The middle of the hero's life, mirroring the passage of our conscious search in the conscious life and the progress of the inner psychic journey into the unconscious, a journey undertaken consciously in the process of psychotherapy, is made up of three essential elements: the *Departure* from home (the status quo), the *Adventure* in the unknown world, and the *Return* with some new understanding. These three elements are framed by an appropriately heroic beginning and ending.

The beginning is often a miraculous conception and birth. The Tewa hero, Waterpot Boy, is conceived when a piece of clay enters his mother. The Aztec man-god Quetzalcoatl is conceived when a god breathes on his mother. A Ceramese heroine, Hainuwele, is born of the combination of coconut sap and a drop of blood. Often the hero, the divine child, is born of a virgin. Almost always he or she comes at a time of great need – the darkest night of the cultural year, a time of general suffering, a period representing the darkness and, more often than not, the suffering that exists in our unconscious or subconscious individual and collective selves.

The hero birth is the hope for a new beginning, a ubiquitous hope. He or she is our second chance. The hidden place – the stable, the grove of trees, the cave – where the hero is born and the painful times in which he emerges remind us that even the gods require the elements associated with the mother – earth, flesh, pain – to enter the world as one of us. The birth also stands for the loneliness and the pain of the beginnings of the psychic journey towards wholeness, or self discovery.

Not surprisingly, the new born hero is almost immediately threatened by the first of the "guardians at the gate" of the status quo, the preconceptions and habits that say "no" to the journey. These guardians are the kings, jealous fathers, or demons who cannot tolerate the presence of a force for new understanding. Thus Herod sends soldiers to kill any child who might be what the magi have called a new king in the Jesus birth myth. And when other magi announce the birth of Zoroaster to King Duransarum, he attempts to stab the child himself. Sigurd and Moses are hidden away for their own protection.

As a child, the hero must somehow prove himself/herself. Signs of the divine essence must shine through. Krishna, the avatar of the god Vishnu, kills a demoness while still in the cradle. The boy Arthur removes the sword from the rock. Theseus retrieves his father's shoes and sword. The Irish hero Cuchulainn, still a mere boy, kills the giant watchdog of Culann. Jesus amazes the Elders in the Temple. As the young wife of the Pandava brothers in the Indian epic the *Mahabharata*, Draupadi reveals her inner divinity when, through Krishna's power, the evil Kauravas fail to strip her of her miraculous sari. So it is that as we begin the journey outlined by depth psychology we must confront the obvious barriers to the journey – our own monsters of the status quo.

Once adulthood is achieved, the hero frequently undergoes a preparatory period of isolation before receiving a call to action, which the hero sometimes initially refuses. Moses, the shepherd alone in the fields, is called from the burning bush, and his reluctance must be overcome by Yahweh himself. The Ojibwa Hiawatha prototype Wunzh is called during his lonely vision quest, but before he can begin his adult journey he must wrestle with the corn god, with divinity itself. Jesus must be tempted in the wilderness, and the Buddha must be tempted by the fiend Mara.

All of these events are preparation for the beginning of the hero journey, and our psychic journey. Like Odysseus, who is reluctant to accept the call of the Greeks to leave wife, child, and possessions to fight in Troy, or like Tolkien's Bilbo and Frodo, who would rather not leave the comforts of Hobbit ways, the hero, must leave home precisely because he must break new ground in the overall human journey. The old ways must be constantly reviewed and new understandings developed. The knights of the Round Table must give up the comforts of Camelot for adventure, and Gilgamesh must leave home to seek eternal life.

The adventure of the hero is marked by several universal themes. The first of these is the search. Sometimes the questing hero looks for something lost as we do if we journey into our unconscious world. Odysseus' son Telemachos, Theseus, and Waterpot Boy all search for the Father. Gilgamesh, Jason, the Knights of the Round Table, Moses, seek objects or places – often lost ones – of potential importance to their cultures – the plant of immortality, the Golden Fleece, the Holy Grail, the Land Where the Sun Rises, the Promised Land. More overtly "religious" or philosophical heroes such as the Buddha or Jesus look to less tangible goals: Enlightenment or Nirvana, the Kingdom of God.

The quest always involves difficult trials. There are frightening and dangerous guardians at each threshold the hero must cross – giants, dragons, sorcerers, evil kings. And there are tests. Herakles must perform the 12 labors, the Grail heroes must prove themselves through various deeds and, like heroes of many cultures, are tested by a femme fatale. This enchantress, a particularly popular nemesis of the patriarchal hero – Adam's Eve, Aeneas's Dido, Samson's Delilah – is the archetypal image of the dangerous alternative to the true goal.

Many heroes must die and descend to the place of death itself, sometimes as scapegoats for the mistakes of others. Jesus and Osiris die, as does the Ceramese Hainuwele. In death, the hero is planted in mother earth and during that period, which we recognize as the ultimate "dark night of the soul," a period of dark gestation, he confronts the most terrifying terrors and demons of the underworld and our own depths.

But the hero returns, usually in the spring. He or she is resurrected, as in the cases of Hainuwele and Jesus. Many returning heroes become material or spiritual food for their people: Osiris emerges from the earth as the god of grain; Hainuwele's buried limbs become vegetables; numerous Native American corn heroes and heroines become the staple food for their people; for the Christian the resurrected Jesus is the "bread of life." These are all images of the boon or great gift that the hero or harrowers of the unconscious bring upon returning from the depths of the quest.

As an epilog to the Departure, the Adventure, and the Return, the hero can make a second return, this time to achieve union with the cosmic source of his or her being. Jesus and the Virgin Mary ascend to God, and a legend has it that Abraham did too. The Buddha, King Arthur, and Moses all undergo a kind of apotheosis, a union with the ultimate mystery. Like myths of creation and deities, those of heroes all seem to lead inevitably to that very strangest and most mystical expression of the human imagination, the concept of union which, depending upon era and tradition, has been called by many names, of which nirvana, enlightenment, the God within, individuation, self-identity, wholeness and Self are a few.

See also: ❯ Campbell, Joseph ❯ Dark Night of the Soul ❯ Hero ❯ Myth ❯ Quest ❯ Self

Bibliography

Campbell, J. (1949/1972). *The hero with a thousand faces*. Princeton, NJ: Princeton University Press.

Jung, C. G. (1969). *Archetypes of the collective unconscious*. CW, 9,1.

Leeming, D. A. (1998). *Mythology: The voyage of the hero*. New York: Oxford University Press.

Leeming, D. A. (2005). *The Oxford companion to world mythology* (p. 179ff). New York: Oxford University Press.

Lord Raglan, F. (1937/1966). *The hero: A study in tradition, myth, and drama*. New York: Vintage.

Rank, O. (1936/1966). *The myth of the birth of the hero*. New York: Knopf.

Monotheism

David A. Leeming

Monotheism is necessarily understood in opposition to polytheism. Do we believe in one god or several gods (or one god more powerful than other gods)? The struggle between monotheism and polytheism can be seen as a metaphorical representation of an essential struggle in the human psyche.

We almost always associate monotheism with Judaism, Christianity, and Islam. The assumption in these religious traditions is that there is one deity, conceived of as a personality with mind, a deity who acts through history and ultimately rules and controls the universe. Because of the dominance of the three "monotheistic religions" there has been a general assumption in the western world that monotheism is an important part of a general path towards enlightenment. Polytheism is a belief system postulating many gods representing the many facets of creation and is often dismissed by the western mind as a "primitive" phenomenon.

Freud, in his *Moses and Monotheism*, suggested that monotheism originated not in Judaism but in Egypt, in the religion fostered by the pharaoh Amenhotep IV (renamed Akhenaton after the Aton, the sun god he worshipped as the one god or at least the most important god). And it can certainly be argued that Ahura Mazda in Zoroastrianism and the concept of *Brahman* in branches of Hinduism can be understood in terms of the monotheistic paradigm. In short, some humans have long searched for a sense of a unified cosmic power, even as other humans – in ancient cultures such as those of the Mesopotamia, Egypt, and Greece, and animist cultures such as those of Africa and Native America – have been content to see nature and the cosmos reflected in a variety of divine beings.

Psychologically speaking, the belief in monotheism is the result of an archetypal or cultural search for a father – a source of being. This is certainly so of patriarchal cultures, which is to say, most of the world's cultures.

Mircea Eliade sees the monotheistic god as a sky god, as opposed to an earth god or goddess. In terms of psychic imagery and conception, the sky god is generally visualized as a male who creates ex nihilo – from nothing – that is, not from pre-existing material, but from his mind. And to one degree or another, we are said by the monotheists to have been created in God's image, that is with something of God's creative mind, making it possible for us to continue the creative process. In short, monotheism is a metaphor for who we are, for what Carl Jung and others have articulated in the concept of Self or potential wholeness. Monotheism and the concept of Self imply a rational progress toward self-knowledge. But, as world history demonstrates, it can also support tendencies towards exclusivism, intolerance and lack of imagination – in short, lack of creativity. A father god who, through perceived sacred scripture and religious law, prescribes our actions might be seen as limiting our potential for psychological and emotional growth. It is for this reason that religious and psychological scholars such as David Miller and James Hillman have argued for a "new polytheism" that emphasizes more feminine and earth based qualities such as feelings and emotions and intuition rather than obedience and unbridled rationalism. In this sense polytheism stands as a metaphor for a life of many possibilities and perceptions, for tolerance, for freedom from what is seen as a limiting monotheism.

See also: ❯ Christianity ❯ Eliade, Mircea ❯ Freud, Sigmund ❯ God ❯ Islam ❯ Judaism and Psychology ❯ Polytheism ❯ Self

Bibliography

Eliade, M. (1963). *Patterns in comparative religion*. Cleveland, OH: Meridian.

Freud, S. (1939/1961). *Moses and monotheism*. New York: Random House.

Hillman, J. (1971). *Psychology: Monotheistic and polytheistic* (pp. 193–208). New York: Spring Publications.

Jung, C. G. (1976). *Symbols of transformation*. Princeton, NJ: Bollingen.

Miller, D. (1974). *New polytheism: Rebirth of the Gods and Goddesses*. New York: Harper & Row.

Moon and Moon Goddesses

Jeffrey B. Pettis

The Greek astronomer Claudius Ptolemaeus (100 CE–178 CE) writes in his *Tetrabiblos* ("Four Books") how the moon (*selēnē*) gives its effluence (*aporroia*) abundantly upon the earth: "the rivers increase and diminish their streams with her light, the seas turn their own tides with her rising and setting, and plants and animals in whole or in part wax and wane with her" (Ptolemy, 1940 I.2). For Ptolemaeus, the power (*dunameōs*) of the moon consists of humidifying (*tō hugrainein*) and having also the sun's heat, its action (*diatithēsin*) for the most part being one of softening and putrefying bodies (1940 I.4). According to Ptolemaeus, the moon is by nature associated with Venus and the person of the mother (*Aphroditēs tō metrikō*), the sun with Saturn and the person of the father (1940 III.4). In Christian Patristics the moon appears as a symbol of the Church which puts to flight all wintry clouds (Methodius of Philippi, *Symposion*, VIII: 12). In this way she is likened to her spouse who is Christ the Sun who at dawn releases all "evil odors and vapors that infect (*inficientes*) the mind" (von Franz, 2000 *Aurora Consurgens* 4.7–12). She is sister and bride, mother and spouse of the sun, often seen by alchemists as the lover in the Song of Songs. As the vessel and universal receptacle of the sun, she receives and disseminates the powers of heaven. The moon is often a symbol for certain aspects of the unconscious in a man. In females the moon refers to aspects of consciousness and the sun to the unconscious. Jung says this comes from the contrasexual archetype in the unconscious – animus in a woman, anima in a man (Jung, 1963: 135). The ancient notion that the moon promotes all plant-life led alchemists to regard the moon itself as a plant, having parallels with the "Tree of Eternity" in Hindusim (Easwaran, 1987 *Katha Upanishad* II.3.1), for example, and the divine feminine *Malkhut*, the tenth *sefirot* associated with earth and moon on the Cabalistic tree. Compare mystical reading of the tree of Zacchaeus in Luke 19.1–10 by the Christian Flemish mystic John of Ruysbroeck (1214–1381 CE) in his *The Adornment of the Spiritual Marriage*. The moon occurs in a variety of ways as a goddess symbol. In ancient Greek myth the moon goddess Hekate is the daughter of Gaia and Uranus, Earth and Sky. She is the deity loved most of all by Zeus (Hesiod, 2006: 411f.), and she has special powers given by Zeus to use as she wills. Originally worshipped as a mother goddess in Asia Minor, Hekate eventually is presented as the goddess of sorcery in Ptolemaic Alexandrian culture. Other Greek moon goddesses include Selen, Phoebe, Artemis, Luna, and Rhea. In Zoroastrianism the moon goddess Mah possesses, according to Avestan hymns, wealth, knowledge, and discernment. She is the "queen of the night." In Hinduism the moon goddess Anumati ("divine favor") represents spirituality, intellect, children, and prosperity. A variety of masculine moon deities occur in history, including Sin (Arabiac myth), Jarih (Canaanite myth), and Thoth (Egyptian myth). Compare the Hindu god Chandra, which although male, has masculine-feminine, androgynous qualities.

See also: ❯ Female God Images ❯ Great Mother ❯ Hinduism ❯ Jung, Carl Gustav

Bibliography

Easwaran, E. (Trans.) (1987). *The Upanishads*. Tomales, CA: Nilgiri Press.

Hesiod. (2006). *Theogony, works and days and testimonia* (G. W. Most, Trans.). Loeb Classical Library, Cambridge, MA: Harvard University Press.

Isidore of Seville. (1911). *Isidori Hispalensis Episcopi Etymologiarum sive Originum Libri XX* (W. M. Lindsay, Ed.). Oxford: Oxford University Press.

John of Ruysbroeck. (1995). *The adornment of the spiritual marriage; The sparkling stone; The book of the supreme truth* (C. A. Wynschenk, Trans.). Felinfach [Lampeter, Wales]: Llanerch Publishers.

Jung, C. G. (1963). *Mysterium Coniunctionis: An inquiry into the separation and synthesis of psychic opposites in alchemy* (R. F. C. Hull, Trans.). Princeton, NJ: Princeton University Press.

Methodius of Philippi. (1885/1994). *Symposion. The Ante-Nicene fathers: Writings of the fathers down to A.D. 325* (Vol. VI) (A. Roberts & J. Donaldson, Ed.). Peabody, MA: Hendrickson.

Ptolemy. (1940). *Tetrabiblos* (F. E. Robbins, Trans.). Loeb Classical Library, Cambridge, MA: Harvard University Press.

Von Franz, M.-L. (Ed.). (2000). *Aurora Consurgens: A document attributed to Thomas Aquinas on the problem of the opposites in alchemy* (R. F. C. Hull & A. S. B. Glover, Trans.). Toronto, Canada: Inner City Books.

Mormonism

Paul Larson

Mormonism is a colloquial term for several Christian denominations which constitute restorationist theology. The two leading groups are the Church of Jesus Christ of Latter Day Saints (LDS) and the Reorganized Church of Jesus Christ of Latter Day Saints (RLDS), now known as the Community of Christ. There are several smaller offshoots, including a fundamentalist LDS church, recently in the news from a controversy involving polygamy and marriage of underage girls. All of the Mormon groups claim descent from the teachings of Joseph Smith Jr. (1805–1844), who was the first Prophet, Seer and Revelator of this dispensation.

Restoration theology holds that there have been several "dispensations" of the true religious doctrine and priestly authority to perform sacraments, and within a century or so after the dispensation originated by Jesus Christ, there was a "great apostasy" where doctrine was corrupted and the authority of the priesthood was withdrawn by God because of the falling away from the correct path. The next dispensation began with the first vision of Joseph Smith in 1820 and continued through subsequent angelic visits, including the ones leading to finding a set of golden plates containing writing which he claimed to translate and publish as the *Book of Mormon*. Besides that book, two other books, the *Doctrine and Covenants* and the *Pearl of Great Price* are also viewed as canonical scripture, along with the *Bible* (the Protestant version without the Apocrypha). Smith and others founded the LDS church in 1830. Mormons generally claim to have the exclusive truth and authority to conduct the sacraments that result in spiritual growth and ultimately lead to salvation.

Mormon theology rejects many of the doctrines of orthodox Christianity. It does not accept the various creeds propounded by the Ecumenical Church Councils and rejects the validity of Apostolic Succession claimed by both the Roman Catholic, the various Orthodox churches, or the liturgical Protestant churches (Anglican, Lutheran) which uphold the importance of bishops and priestly authority. The basic statement of beliefs is contained in the Articles of Faith, which is now found in the *Pearl of Great Price.*

LDS theology has a particularly American flavor, in that it offers the opportunity of continual evolution and growth. This is best expressed in a couplet articulated by Lorenzo Snow (nineteenth century/1994), who became the fifth President of the LDS Church, "As man is, God once was, and as God is, man may become" (p. 1). This holds out the possibility of apotheosis as the ultimate goal of spiritual development. When this doctrine is coupled with the doctrine of marriage for time and eternity, rather than till death do us part, then the family can become an eternal unit. The idea that spiritual evolution can lead to become a divinity in one's own right and create worlds is radically different from mainstream Christian belief.

These teachings, though available in public sources are part of the esoteric part of LDS practice involving temples. These are buildings for special rites that are open only to devote members of the church who received clearance from their religious leaders. The ceremonies conducted in the temples are secret, though documents purporting to be accurate redactions are available on the Internet. The temple endowments and marriage ceremony are held out as the most important parts of religious development, while the ordinary weekly activities of church members are designed to prepare people for those rites and support their continued involvement in church teachings and practices. The endowments and sealing of marriages are done not only for living members of the church, but by proxy for dead ancestors and others, along with proxy baptisms. There has been recent complaints from Jewish groups and others about proxy baptisms.

The public LDS church is organized into local units, known as "wards," led by a bishop and regional units or "stakes" (these are equivalents to parishes and dioceses in other denominations). In areas where there are fewer members, these are known as missions. There is no professional clergy. Priestly authority is only held by males and is lay, in the sense that all priestly duties are in addition to civil jobs. There are two orders of priesthood, the Aaronic and Melchizadek. Boys age 12 are ordained into the Aaronic priesthood first as deacons, then passing into the quorum of teachers, then priests. Most males are ordained into the Melchizadek priesthood when they are called to go on a 2-year mission for the church at age 19, though sometimes those who do not go on missions are ordained into that level of priesthood in adulthood. The ranks of the Melchizadek priesthood start with the quorum of Elders, then the quorum of Seventies, and the highest order is the quorum of High Priests. Each ward is led by a Bishop and two counselors, the stakes by a President and two counselors. The church as a whole is led by the First Presidency, the Quorum of 12 Apostles, their assistants and other "General Authorities." The President of the church is deemed the current Prophet, Seer and Revelator and is believed to guide the church's activities by divine revelation. The church promulgates changes in policy and conducts major teachings at two semi-annual conferences, usually in April and October.

Members are kept very active in multiple meetings at their local level. Each Sunday, men have weekly meetings of their priesthood quorums, families attend Sunday School and Sacrament meeting. During the week there are meetings of the women's auxilliary, the Relief Society, and youth meetings, Primary for pre-adolescent children, and the Mutual Improvement Associations (MIA) for adolescents and early adults. Various other activities are available, embodying the idea that the church should provide opportunities covering all of life's domains.

Jackson's (2008) book is clearly written by an outsider and from an evangelical Christian point of view, but is relatively accurate and non-judgmental in tone. Mauss's (1994) account is more of an insider's one, though his voice is clearly scholarly and reflective on the religion of his cultural background. The McMurrin books (1959, 1965) are from the standpoint of a professional philosopher within the Mormon tradition and are excellent sources for understanding the ideological context of the Mormon religion.

See also: ◈ Christianity ◈ Smith, Joseph

Bibliography

Jackson, A. (2008). *Mormonism explained: What Latter-Day Saints teach and practice*. Wheaton, IL: Crossway Press.

Mauss, A. L. (1994). *The angel and the beehive: The Mormon struggle with assimilation*. Urbana, IL: University of Illinois Press.

McMurrin, S. M. (1959). *The philosophical foundations of Mormon theology*. Salt Lake City, UT: University of Utah Press.

McMurrin, S. M. (1965). *The theological foundation of the Mormon religion*. Salt Lake City, UT: University of Utah Press.

Snow, L. (1996). *The teachings of Lorenzo Snow* (C. J. Williams, Ed.). Salt Lake City, UT: Bookcraft. (Original works published late 19th century).

Mother

Elizabeth Welsh

The mother is the biological and/or social female parent. From a psychological perspective, the mother is the female caregiver who may or may not be biologically related to the infant but who assumes the parental role. The mother-infant dyad represents the primary form of human attachment based on physical dependence as well as affection, both of which are vital for survival. The word "mother" is also used in reference to the source or origin of things. In ancient religions, the earth was referred to in feminine terms as "Mother Earth" and represented the divine figure that was the source of all life. In addition, ancient myths included various female divinities that possessed maternal qualities or fulfilled mother roles for other gods or for humans. With the rise of monotheistic religions, however, the divine maternal images were eradicated, but in Western Christianity, the icon of Mary, the Mother of Jesus gradually rose to cult status.

The primary cultural scripts for mothers and motherhood have been shaped heavily by religious discourses or myths, and today, these scripts continue to be reflected in the cultural norms for maternal roles. Although through secularization religion has lost its centrality in society, on the linguistic level, the impact of the religious heritage continues to be felt.

In Western history, until recently, the Judeo-Christian worldview provided the dominant categories for the meaning and role of mothers. However, through the developments in the fields of anthropology and archeology in the nineteenth and twentieth centuries, there has been a renewed interest in studying the ancient cultural myths and religions which in turn have given impetus to a variety of theoretical developments in religious, feminist, and psychoanalytic studies. The foundation of Freudian theory, the Oedipus complex, is based on an ancient Greek myth.

Religious Myths and Legendary Mothers

Ancient myths highlight several legendary mother figures that represent powerful creative forces of fertility as well as social influence. Given the precariousness of life in the ancient world, it may be easy to see why the act of procreation and the bringing forth of life through birthing had such a miraculous and divine significance. In Egypt, Isis, also named "the kingmaker," was the goddess who generated her son, the living king, from the dead body of her brother/husband Orisis. The image of her son's throne as her own lap on which he sat as an infant and suckled was representative of her function as the pharaoh's source of power and influence. Isis was a wifely figure whose nature was centered on maternal devotion but she was also the powerful patron of nature and magic. In Greece, Gaia was the primeval goddess representing the earth, the

Mother Goddess, who birthed Uranus, the sky, through parthenogenesis, and later lay with her son to give birth to a series of other gods including Oceanus, the World-Ocean, as well as the Titan gods. Also in Greece, Demeter was the goddess of fertility as well as a symbol of the mother who fights to protect the bond with her daughter (Persephone who was raped and abducted by Hades) and revolts against the male usurping power of Hades and Zeus. In the Hindu traditions, Parvati was the supreme Divine Mother who was beautiful and gentle but also fearsome. In the ancient Buddhist myths, Queen Maya was said to have become pregnant during a vision in which the divine Buddha reincarnated as a white elephant touched her and she later given birth to Prince Siddhartha, the Buddha-to-be. Scholars have pointed out the similarities between Maya and the Virgin Mary who also becomes pregnant without having intercourse. The mythical models of motherhood in the ancient religions were quite diverse and influential.

In the Abrahamic traditions the pagan goddess cults were eradicated though scholars have pointed out that, while the male monotheistic cult took over, the language used to talk about the divine figure retained some inexplicit but clearly maternal elements such as the images of God nursing, gathering, or holding his people. The female biblical figures that do stand out are several women who were important in the development of the Israelite and Islamic nations. Eve, the first woman created by God and mother of all living, has been a disputed figure in theological debates on prescriptions for women's societal roles because of her depictions in later Jewish, Christian, and Muslim sources as a temptress and an archetype of sin. Feminist theologians have attempted to reconceptualize her as a prototype of motherhood pointing out that her name meant "mother of all living" and that, although her role is not described in much detail, she did play a significant role in naming her sons. In the Bible, the most prominent mothers are the matriarchs Sarah, Rebecca, Rachel, and Leah the wives of the patriarchs Abraham, Isaac, and Jacob respectively as well as the mothers of the budding Israelite nation. Other biblical female figures such as Deborah are metaphorical representations whose "mothering" provides a model for large-scale leadership in the community which greatly differs from the male style of leadership.

Perhaps the most influential mother figure within the Western religious tradition has been Mary, the young virgin who became the mother of Jesus, and who remained present at significant points in her son's life according to the biblical text. From the fifth century onward, Mary became the subject of much veneration in the Catholic tradition which has devoted an entire branch to Mariology, or the study of Mary's role and significance within the Christian faith. Catholic theology maintains the doctrine of the Immaculate Conception of Mary, or the idea that Mary was born without original sin and remained sinless throughout her life. Mary is believed to have conceived Jesus through an act of the Holy Spirit and not through sexual intercourse; this is the doctrine of the "virgin birth." Catholics also maintain that Mary remained a virgin for the rest of her life and was taken up into heaven upon her death. Orthodox theologies reject the Immaculate Conception but affirm the "virgin birth" and celebrate Mary's "Dormition" (or "falling asleep") and her being taken up into heaven. The Protestant views affirm that Mary was "blessed among women" and a virgin when she conceived Jesus, but do not believe in the veneration of Mary or in her role as mediator between humans and God, pointing out that Mary's role diminished after the birth of Christ. Nonetheless, within traditional Christian discourse, Mary became the antithesis of Eve. The latter was the temptress who was responsible for bringing sin into the world, while the former was a symbol of meekness, holiness, and the way to salvation.

Many scholars have argued that the conceptualization of Eve and Mary within the Western religious tradition has had a strong impact on societal views of women and especially mothers. Feminist critics have pointed out that neither of the two have provided redemptive models for women since they have both been set up to represent two extreme opposites: the one who was deemed responsible for bringing sin into the world versus the asexual, self-abnegating saint. The former represents a condemned view of womanhood, while the other a romantic idealization of motherhood. Most revolutionary feminist thinkers have abandoned the traditional religious motifs of Western Christianity and turned instead to religious themes found in various ancient goddess cults or to their emergence within New Age religions. Revisionist feminist theologians, however, in addition to redeeming these prominent biblical female figures, also attempt to resurrect the feminine and motherly aspects of God which have been traditionally been eclipsed by patriarchal categories within the biblical language of God. According to this view, the language of God is inadequate inasmuch as it does not include equivalent images of God as male and female. For example, it is peculiar that in traditional theology, the speech about God as the origin and caregiver of all things omits, as if by default, the maternal aspect of these images, and attributes them to a paternal relationship, as the opening of the Nicene Creed indicates: "God, the Father, the Almighty, maker of heaven and earth, of all that is seen and unseen. . .". Since religious myths and traditions have a profound impact on cultural conceptions of motherhood and thus on women's identities as mothers revisionist feminist theologians want to offer renewed and redemptive perspectives for women and mothers.

The Psychological Perspective

Much of psychoanalytic theory has dealt with the child's relationship with the mother. Freud posited that at the heart of psychosexual development was the Oedipus complex, or the child's desire for an incestual relationship with his/her mother. The dynamics of psychic development emerge out of this basic but prohibited desire which the child learns to defend against through various patterns of repression, displacement, sublimation, and other neuroses. Both boys and girls are primordially in love with the maternal parent but Freud believed that for girls this changes when they realize that the mother lacks a penis, at which time they begin to develop sexual desires for their fathers.

In Melanie Klein's work, the focus shifted to the pre-Oedipal relationship between the infant and the mother, through which the child develops and internalizes a basic psychic structure of object relations. For example, the infant's sometimes satisfying and sometimes frustrating experiences with the mother's body become internalized as split-off "part-objects" ("good breast" vs. "bad breast"). Through adequate mothering, the infant can gradually begin to integrate these separate experiences into whole internal representations and learns that the mother who is generally loving and responsive is the same one who is sometimes frustrating and disappointing.

British psychoanalyst Donald Winnicott also focused on the primacy of the maternal role in psychic development, coining terms such as "holding environment," "good-enough mother," "primary maternal preoccupation," "subjective omnipotence" and others to describe how the mother's behavior and state of mind function to help the newborn transition from a terrifying world of disconnected experiences to a progressive internalization of objective reality and development of a cohesive "true self." Winnicott's concept of the "good enough mother," who is neither stiflingly perfect nor abusive and neglectful but who provides an optimal level of frustration, has also served as a model for an effective psychotherapist.

Some psychodynamic frameworks, such as attachment theory, relational psychoanalysis, and intersubjectivity, have begun to recognize that not only mothers but fathers, grandparents, or other caregivers, insofar as they are intensively involved in providing care, can become primary relational or attachment figures. However, psychoanalytic approaches that have continued to draw from Freudian theories maintain their emphases on the mother's primordial role in the identity formation of infants.

See also: ❂ Femininity ❂ Freud, Sigmund ❂ Great Mother ❂ Mary ❂ Matriarchy ❂ Virgin Mary

Bibliography

Bronner, L. L. (2004). *Stories of biblical mothers: Maternal power in the Hebrew Bible.* Lanham, MD: University Press of America.

Johnson, E. A. (2002). *She who is: The mystery of God in feminist theological discourse.* New York: The Crossroad Publishing Company.

Lawson, R. B., Graham, J. E., & Baker, K. M. (2007). *A history of psychology: Globalization, ideas, and applications.* Upper Saddle River, NJ: Pearson-Prentice Hall.

Prochaska, O. J., & Norcross, J. C. (2004). *Systems of psychotherapy: A transtheoretical analysis.* Pacific Grove, CA: Thomson-Brooks/Cole.

Ruether, R. R. (2005). *Goddesses and the divine feminine.* Berkeley, CA: University of California Press.

Mountain, The

Thomas C. Putnam

Mountain symbolism occurs throughout history: the peoples of one of the earliest known civilizations, the Sumerians built mountain-like ziggurats in the desert, which they believed to be the dwelling places of the gods; in contemporary times we climb, conquer and marvel at the beauty of natural mountains. Mountains symbolize constancy, eternity, firmness, and stillness. They have been used to represent the state of full consciousness: in Nepal the sacred mountain Everest ("Mother Goddess of the world") is thought of as the "navel of the water." The image of the mountain as a *center* is one of the most important and widespread throughout history. Many ancient cultures considered the mountain the "Center of the World." It often serves as a cosmic axis linking heaven and earth and providing *order* to the universe. Mountains evoke a special sense of awe and power and no single image or meaning can capture or express every facet of its symbolic significance.

Being close to the heavens, the mountain is often the place of revelation, as it was in the epiphany of Moses and the transfiguration of Christ. Jesus retired to the mountains when confronted with a problem that needed reflection. Buddha gave his first significant teaching on the summit of Vulture Peak in India.

Native Americans made frequent pilgrimages to mountains, which they saw as abodes of the Great Spirit. The Elders sent tribal members, who were found guilty of wrongdoing, the mountains to do penance, and to benefit from the healing influence of these surroundings. Many believe that the archetypal container is inherent in the image of the mountain because it is ordered and organized by the laws of nature; it reflects the internal experience of a "parental" container. It is important to note, however, that this image does not imply "paradise" but a *self-regulating* system that provides *continuity of being*. Traversing mountains requires human effort and they mark a place in mythological stories where heroes, after the arduous effort of climbing, gain steadfastness and self-knowledge. Mountain climbing gives the ego something to conquer and to move against, potentially imparting a sense of being capable and self-sufficient.

Mountain imagery also represents the unconscious, the earth, our mother and "mother nature." We live with these constructs in a "participation-mystique." It is here that the archetypes live and also where the *instincts* reside. C.A. Meier states, "The wilderness mountain is really the original biotope of the Soul" (Meier, 1985: 13).

Consequently, mountains can be seen as both a desire and an unconscious attempt to reconnect with the archetypal core of the personality, which also offers recovery of the lost capacity for experience and meaning. In sum, the mountain image gives us a sense of relatedness and ontological security by connecting us to the universe.

See also: ❂ Great Mother

Bibliography

Evans-Wentz, W. Y. (1981). *Chauchoma and sacred mountains*. Stanford, CA: Stanford University Press.

Herzog, M. (1953). *Annapurna*. New York: Dutton.

Meier, C. A. (1985). *A testament to wilderness*. Culver City, CA: The Lapis Press.

Searles, H. F. (1960). *The non-human environment*. New York: Inter-University Press.

Stewart, L. H. (1986). Affect and archetype: A contribution to a Comprehensive theory of the structure of the psyche. In N. Swartz-Salant (Ed.), *Chiron: A review of Jungian analysis*. Brooklyn, NY: Chiron Publications.

Mu Koan or Joshu's Dog

Paul C. Cooper

Introduction

▸ *A monk once asked Joshu, 'Has a dog the Buddha Nature or not?' Joshu said, 'Mu!'* (Shibayama, 1974: 19).

The "Mu Koan" or "Joshu's Dog" introduces the thirteenth century koan collection, *Mumonkan* (Gateless Gate or Gateless Barrier), which was compiled by the Chinese monk Mumon (1183–1260). This terse koan expresses the irresolvable paradox between dualism and non-dualism, which is a common theme throughout the various koan collections. As a basis of practice it serves to cut through all dualities, the most significant of which is that between being and non-being.

Mumon attributes no significance to the order of the koans in *Mumonkan*; however, scholars underline the importance of the koan by its placement as first in the collection. The American Zen master Phillip Kapleau observes that "Even to this day no koan is assigned to novices more often" (1966: 63).

Transcending Dualism and Non-Dualism

For the Zennist, being and non-being are inclusive and intertwined. This seemingly irrational paradox flies in the face of the western positivism that influenced Freud and early psychoanalytic thought. From this perspective, "gate" or "barrier" refers to the discriminating mind which interferes with spiritual freedom. Viewed dualistically as elements, "Buddha nature or not" and "Mu" reflect polarized extremes of affirmation and negation. However, when understood as a whole, the koan serves as an expression of inclusive non-dualism. That is, as a whole, the text of the koan initiates an investigation that induces intuited self-realization. This tactic places total responsibility for spiritual development on the student.

Practice supported by Joshu's Mu dovetails with the psychoanalytic process of developing autonomy, mature relatedness and accepting personal responsibility for one's actions. For example, through the psychoanalytic process, the patient will become aware of the irrational hold of infantile wishes, the tendency to blame others for one's failures and to establish developmentally more adaptive and constructive forms of human relatedness.

In response to the student's question, Joshu simply says "Mu." Joshu would sometimes say "U" (yes) or remain silent. Joshu's response (Mu, U, or silence) exemplifies the Zen challenge of all reifications and deconstructs all assertions and negations. In this regard Joshu's response is both informative and performative and engenders what Michael Sells (1994) views as a "meaning event," which he describes as the moment when expression and meaning are fused. Similarly, the meaning event is the moment that occurs during psychotherapy when the therapist's comments and the patient's responses are no longer exclusively hypothetical, speculative, informative and based solely on discovered "evidence," and words, but are spontaneously emerging expressions of in the moment emotional truth; deeply felt, lived, experiences that can be transformative for both individuals.

D. T. Suzuki emphasizes this unity and he notes that "Enlightenment was to be found in life itself, in its fuller and freer expressions, and not in its cessation" (1948: 85). The notion of "fuller and freer expression" that Suzuki articulates finds a parallel in Wilfred Bion's work. He notes that as a result of the therapeutic encounter; the patient will display a fuller and wider range of emotional experience and he writes that "'Progress' will be measured by the increased number and variety of moods, ideas and attitudes seen in any given session" (1967: 18).

Alternative Intuitive Model

As an alternative intuitive model the Mu koan can contribute to enriching our understanding, use and further development of psychoanalytic theory and technique. For example, viewed holistically, the Mu koan can serve as a prototype for integrating and synthesizing seemingly contradictory theoretical models and for organizing and articulating the resulting technical implicatigns. Fgr instance, contemporary intersubjectivity theorists have offered cogent and convincing critiques of the tendency in the literature on self psychology and object relations toward reification and personification of the metapsychological concepts of "self" and "object" (Stolorow and Atwood, 1992). As a result, the intersubjectivists completely dismiss basic concepts that are central to object relations theory such as projective identification. From the Zen perspective, as noted above, all reifications are ultimately false and in this respect the intersubjectivists rightfully question the misuse of these important concepts. However, a total dismissal of these concepts reflects an underlying nihilism, which is also subject to reification. Relatively speaking, as Zennists point out, reification is an active process that functions to defend against existential anxiety. This deeply rooted emotional response to our ultimate insubstantiality can't be worked out simply through new theoretical constructs. The illusion of solidity and separateness holds very real consequences that require intuitive and experiential responses. We can think of Joshu's Mu and the monks' "Buddha nature" as symbolic of this human tendency toward reification and we can also think of intersubjectivity theory and object relations theory as highly rarified and well-thought out theoretical manifestations of these basic human tendencies. However, when considered holistically as differing aspects of one reality, they point to varying aspects of human experience.

See also: ❯ Buddism ❯ Koan ❯ Self ❯ Zen

Bibliography

Aitken, R. (1991). *The gateless barrier: The Wu-Men Kuan (Mummonkan).* New York: North Point.

Bion, W. (1967/1988). Notes on memory and desire. In E. B. Spillius (Ed.), *Melanie Klein today developments in theory and practice: Volume 2: Mainly practice* (pp. 17–21). London: Routledge.

Heine, S. (1994). *Dogen and the Koan tradition: A tale of two Shobogenzo texts,* Albany, NY: State University of New York Press.

Kapleau, P. (1966). *The three pillars of Zen.* New York: Harper & Row.

Sells, M. (1994). *Mystical languages of unsaying.* Chicago, IL: University of Chicago Press.

Shibayama, Z. (1974/2000). *The gateless barrier: Zen Comments on the Mumonkan.* Boston, MA: Shambala.

Stolorow, R., & Atwood, G. (1992). *Contexts of being: The intersubjective foundations of psychological life.* Hillsdale, NJ: The Analytic Press.

Suzuki, D. T. (1948). *Essays in Zen Buddhism.* London: Ryder.

Yamada, K. (1979). *Gateless gate.* Los Angeles, CA: Center Press.

Mummification

Jeffrey B. Pettis

Mummification is part of ancient Egyptian religious belief concerning the afterlife. It entails preserving the body of one who has died for his/her journey into the next world. Initially provided for Egyptian Pharaohs, mummification is founded on religious fertility rites and notions of vegetative processes of regeneration. It is understood in relation to the natural ebb and flow of the Nile River agrarian life cycles. Extant ancient Egyptian instructions held in the Cairo Museum tell of the special care given to the procedures of dissection and embalmment which constitute mummification (Arabic *mūmiyā*) and the process of desiccation. Every part of the body receives a ritual anointing with special oils and plant derivatives. The spine is soaked with oil. The head is twice anointed. The fingernails are gilded, the fingers are wrapped with linen bandages, each of which is attributed to a single god. The entire body is contained in linen wrappings, excluding the inner organs. These are removed (with exception of the heart) due to the rapidity of decay, and held in funerary vases called canopic jars. The jars are a sign of physical immortality and set (with other possessions of the deceased) alongside the mummy in the tomb. In later times, the organs were wrapped in linen cloth and set back into the body. The mummification ritual evidences what is perceived to be the deification of the corpse, and connects with the myth of the god Osiris who dies and is brought back to life by the queen goddess Isis. Resurrected, Osiris becomes the god of "the things in heaven and in the lower world" (Plutarch, 1936 *Isis and Osiris* 61E). The soul (Ba) of the deceased journeys in order to enter into eternal life – the field of reeds. It must pass through seven gates to obtain lasting union with the sun-god Ra. The names of demons, shades, gods, and monsters encountered on the journey, along with magical formulae to disarm them, are provided to the deceased in such funerary "handbooks" as the *Coffin Texts* (ca. 2000 BCE), the *Pyramid Texts* (ca. 2600 BCE–ca. 2300 BCE), and *Book of the Dead* (sixteenth century BCE). The funerary text is placed between the wrapped hands of the mummy for the journey of the soul which occurs in the "light of day," so that the journeyer has consciousness while passing through the land of the dark (unconscious) world. Egyptians placed wheat grains and flower bulbs inside the wrappings of mummies, watering the seeds and watching for growth as a sign of resurrection. The mummification practice is perceived this way to involve an inseparable connection between matter and spirit. Resurrection occurs through and from the old body, which itself contains the mystery of the new life. In one Coffin text the deceased declares: "I live, I die. . . . I live in wheat, I grow in wheat which the gods sow, hidden in Geb [the earth]." In Egyptian myth Osiris himself is referred to as wheat and barley. The first century CE alchemical text entitled "Isis to Horus" says how "nature delights (*pereptai*) in nature, and nature overcomes (*nika*) nature" (7). *Mumia* is thought to have contained medicinal value in European pharmacy, and the German-Swiss physician and alchemist Paracelsus (d. 1541) refers to it as having elixir potency (Jung, 1963: 391). The preparation of the body with cloth wrappings and plant derivatives referenced in the New Testament gospels (e.g., Mark 15.42–47) may be representative of ancient Egyptian mummification practices (cf. John 12.24). Origen of Alexandria speaks of the old body as *seminarium*, seed-plot from which springs new life (Jerome's *Epistle to Pammachius* IV, 38).

See also: ❯ Jung, Carl Gustav ❯ Osiris and the Egyptian Religion ❯ Ritual ❯ Soul: A Depth Psychological Approach

Bibliography

Berthelot, M., & Ruelle, Ch.-Em. (1967). *Collection des Anciens Alchimistes Grecs.* Asnabruck, Germany: Zeller.

Jung, C. G. (1963). *Mysterium Coniunctionis: An inquiry into the separation and synthesis of psychic opposites in alchemy* (R. E. C. Hull, Trans.). Princeton, NJ: Princeton University Press.

Plutarch. (1936). *Moralia, volume V* (F. C. Babbitt, Trans). Loeb Classical Library, Cambridge, MA: Harvard University Press.

Schaff, P. (Ed.). (2007). *Nicene and Post-Nicene fathers: Second series, volume VI Jerome.* New York: Cosimo Classics.

Music and Religion

Laurence de Rosen

Since the dawn of time, music has been man's medium of communication with its divinity/divinities. Views of the origin of both religion and music swing between two poles: the belief in a reality that is essential and independent of an observer and a view that neither music nor religion exist on its own, challenging their independent existence. Both views address the question, did music and religion exist prior to our having discovered them or did they exist all along, whether we knew them or not? In modern psychology Jung answered this by positing that the world comes into its being when man discovers it.

In monotheism, Music and religion are means of accessing the invisible, unseen, and untouchable, what is beyond what man can comprehend. They both refer to the Almighty God, the Divine, the One which is called in religion and psychology the Numinous, holy, and tremendous. Their common ground is archetypal and relates to the experience of loss through rituals of death and rebirth. The relationship between religion and music can be coined as the "spirit" of the "sound." Both provide a means of transcending human existence. In polytheism, syncretic religions, and animism, there is no need to reach out the invisible in a way the spirit is present and embodied. Immanence represents the other side of the dichotomy transcedence (monotheism) – immanence (polytheism).

The archetypal ground of music and religion:

* Reflects an ordering principle that brings in music, harmony out of chaos, and dissonance and rituals and pilgrimages in religion. This principle moves from fragmentation toward a human need for wholeness. There is an expression of this universal human need in Chinese literature, the *I Ching or Book of Change* (see Chapter 16: Religion and Music).
* Refers to memory: music and religion are intimately entwined with memory. Western mythology encapsulates this through the figures of the muses, daughters of Mnemosyne, goddess of memory. The oral tradition is still very much alive in the non-Western and Native American worlds, depends on memory, and stimulates it through repetition that is rhythmic and that is built into the body. In the Western world, this tradition is represented primarily by Homer. The oral tradition experiences time, essential in music as well as in religion, as circular, while the written tradition perceives it as linear.
* Embraces a dichotomy, identified at a collective level with the dualities of the Western/Eastern, and the Apollonian/Dionysian, as well as in the individual level as an inner struggle such as experienced by Mozart, in which Salzburg came to symbolize sacred music, and Vienna secular. Tension and release, dissonance and consonance, silence and chant, are the kinds of opposites that express the energy carried by music and religion that eventually may find transformation through these channels.
* Holds the experience of mystery, whose Greek root means "to close, to have a mouth and the eyes closed," probably coming from the onomatopoeia *mu*, symbol of inarticulate sound. There is an intimate relationship between music and faith across all civilizations.
* Appeals to irrational, emotional, and instinctive processes. Because of their archetypal nature, no scientific approach can capture them in their entirety. Indeed, a large part of our understanding of both comes from a place before words. The body, with its taboos and shadows, is the main channel through which music and religion express themselves, by means of voice and dance. In ancient Greece, the secret of the Eleusian Mysteries could be more readily revealed by dancing than by speaking.

In ancient times, the oral tradition was predominant in both music (poetry) and religion (chant and dance). The figure of the shaman seems to be the oldest to embody the convergence of music and religion. The English word shaman (cf. Eliade, Frazer, Levi Straus) comes from the Tungusic language of Siberia – saman – broadly meaning "mastery over fire," "magical flight," and "communion with spirit." With his ritual of dance, chant, and musical instrument (drums and rattle) the shaman was and still is a healer. Among the 17,000-year-old cave painting at Les Trois Frères in France, we see a shaman playing a resonating musical bow.

With the development of consciousness, music and religion which were combined in the figure of the shaman, began to differentiate, mythos and Eros giving way to logos. According to tradition, Orpheus, grandson of Mnemosyne, came out of the shamanic mists, stepping into the fifth century, a period of great changes in the Greek world. Built on the older form of the shaman, the figure of Orpheus stands as the medial term between the Apollonian and the Dionysian modes of thought, holding the tension, pre-figuring the dualities of Christianity.

With the emergence of patriarchy, as music and religion became separated and differentiated, oppositions arose: spirit/matter (e.g., Hildegard von Bingen), male/female (e.g., castrato), lyric/melody (e.g., Querelle de Bouffons, in France), and so on. Figures, which had combined the agencies of music, religion, and healing, in the past began to specialize. For example, in the Celtic tradition, the roles of the shaman were split into the druid, who accessed the spiritual and healing realm, and the bard, artist, poet, musician. Under Christianity, a polarization between external/internal, physical/spiritual, emotion/thought, and text/context increased in music as well as in religion, separating one from the other.

In all cultures, a tension between text and music exists in the most primitive as well as most sophisticated forms. On the one hand, chant, a codification or an amplification of words from a litany, represented by the monosyllabic song of the Greek tragedies to the psalmodies of the Buddhist monks. On the other, the enjoyment of singing, independent of text: melisma, "bel canto," and ornamentation can be found in a Gregorian Alleluia, in Islamic and Spanish chant, and in the Messiah of Handel.

Judaism

For over 3,000 years Jewish people have come together to worship by way of songs. "Man is like a ram's horn. The only sound he makes is that which is blown through him," said a Chassidic master. The horn of ram is the oldest Jewish musical instrument, the shofar, with an extremely profound symbolic, religious, and spiritual significance.

Judaism developed an ancient and annotated system (called *trope*) for chanting the Bible, with particular scales and melodies for each book and musical modes (called *musah ha-tefillah*) for every category of prayer and for different holidays, passed on to observant Jews through oral tradition. The rich garden of mystical tradition known as the Kabbalah states, "Come, I will show you a new way to the Lord, not with words but with song." (Chassidic masters)

Christianity

The Christian tradition, while recognizing the great psychological value of Music, has seldom used it for esoteric or initiatory purpose. Like other religions, it experiences the opposition between words and music. Early in Christian history, Saint Augustine declared that "To sing is to pray twice" and sung prayers have always been central. Christian forms of chant wear many faces from Gregorian chant to the African drums and rhythms of the monks in Senegal, from stately Lutheran hymns to gospel music. Among theses practices, Gregorian chant is unique in providing an unbroken link not only to the prayers of early Christians, but also to the Jewish tradition of chanting texts more than 3,000 years ago. The Bible is full of musical references, particularly in the Psalms, in the Songs of the Songs, and in the Lamentation of Jeremiah. The oldest instrument in the Bible is an organ originally made of pipes. In the New Testament, Paul instructs the Ephesians "to sing and psalmodize to the Lord with your heart and for everything giving thanks in the name of our Lord." The Christian monastic tradition represents the combined heritage of religious life and music (Gregorian chants), including the practice of medicine (culture of medicinal herbs). Bach, recognized as one of the greatest composers in Western history, was also a devout Christian and understood the profound meaning of the texts he set to music. The text of the Cantata BWV 20 is amazingly closed to the number 16 of the *I Ching*: "O Eternity, you word of thunder..."

Islam

The Prophet Muhammad is said to have recited the Qur'an, whose root means *to[recite]*. Therefore Imams are not selected for their musical abilities. Although Islamic tradition in general frowns upon instrumental music and music in general as a sensual distraction from a devout life, there exists a rich tradition of chanting Qur'an and intoning prayers. The Sama is a practice of mystical listening. While orthodox Muslims have an uncanny relationship to music, most Sufis, a mystical branch of Islam, embrace it (e.g., dervishes).

African

While chants have been orally passed down from generation to generation since the dawn of history, individuals are also free to improvize and express their own unique style and personality. Drumming uplifts the Spirit of African chant on a tide of rhythm more sophisticated than almost anywhere else in the world. And where there are drums playing, bodies start to move. Chanting is always done in groups, rarely, if ever, alone.

Hinduism

All forms of yoga make use of chant. The word *yoga* means "yoke" or union with God and the purpose of these practices and Sanskrit chanting is to become One with God, the *Atman,* our own inner Self. Of all the religious traditions there is none in which chant and dance play a more central role than Hindu/Vedic culture.

Buddhism

The word *Buddha* comes from Sanskrit word meaning literally "to wake up." This is the true message of Buddhism. In Buddhism the chant is a tool for awakening consciousness. Originating in India, Buddhism shares with Hinduism use of Sanskrit and the practice of chanting mantram. Many Buddhist monks practice visualizations and sacred hand gestures, called *mudras,* while chanting. Tibetan monks produce unique deep-throated vocal tones with such powerful harmonics that each voice is able to sound three separate notes at the same time. The overtones that emanate from their voices are extraordinary phenomenon of sound, generating a high level of scientific interest and research. There are many faces and many voices of Buddhist chant. It invokes the clarity, emptiness, and compassion of the Buddha's teaching. Buddhist chant is slow, meditative, and dispassionate, a far cry from the ecstatic devotional chant practices of Hinduism or the sensual rhythms of Africans.

In psychoanalysis, the relation between music and religion remains relatively untrodden territory. The analytical approach, influenced by its fathers, swings between suppression and repression. Freud was very sensitive to music and could not bear the amount of affect triggered by anything musical, from a singing voice to a performed piece of music. Yiddish and Czech, languages of religious songs and feelings dominated his early childhood in Freiberg. Music drew him irresistibly closer to his mother and grandmother, symbol of incestual love, object of repression. While son of a protestant minister, Jung was not a musician, as he explicitly said and wrote. Jung emphasized the visual image.

See also: ◉ Crucifixion ◉ Dalai Lama ◉ Eleusinian Mysteries ◉ Jung, Carl Gustav ◉ Lacan, Jacques ◉ Mantra ◉ Psalms ◉ Rank, Otto ◉ Rumi, Celaladin

Bibliography

Adler, G., & Jaffe, A. (Ed.) (1953). *Jung C. G. letters* (Vol. 2). Princeton, NJ: Princeton University Press.

Becker, J. (2004). *Deep listeners: Music, emotion, and trancing*. Bloomington, IN: Indiana University Press.

The Bhagavad Gita. (2001). New York: Harpercollins.

The Bible. King James Version. (2002). Grand Rapids, MI: Zondervan.

During, J. (1988). *Musique et Extase, l'Audition dans la Tradition Soufie*. Paris: Albin Michel.

Eliade, M. (1964). *Shamanism: Archaic techniques of ecstasy*. Princeton, NJ: Princeton University Press.

Eschyle. (2001). *The mysteries: Dionysus, Orpheus, Artemisia, Demeter*. Paris: Robert Laffont.

Euripides. (2001). *The Bacchanales*. Paris: Robert Laffont.

Frager, R. (1997). *Essential Sufism*. San Francisco, CA: Harper San Francisco.

Freud, S. (1983). *Totem et Taboo*. Paris: Payot.

Freud, S. (1986). *L'Homme Moise et la Religion Monotheiste*. Paris: Gallimard.

Halifax, J. (1979). *Shamanic voices*. New York: Dutton.

Huron, D. (2006). *Sweet anticipation: Music and the psychology of expectation*. Cambridge, MA: The MIT Press.

I Ching or Book of change. (1950). Princeton, NJ: Princeton University Press.

Jung, C. G. (1952a). *Symbols of transformation*. Princeton, NJ: Princeton University Press.

Jung, C. G. (1958). *Psychology and religion: West and East, CW 11*.

Jung, C. G., & Kerenyi, C. (1949). *Essays on a science of mythology*. Princeton, NJ: Princeton University Press.

Jung, C. G. (1988). *Nietzsche's Zarathustra seminars 1934–1939*. Princeton, NJ: Princeton University Press.

Kerenyi, C. (1940). *Pythagoras and Orpheus*. Amsterdam.

Kerenyi, C. (1944). *The Gods of the Greeks* (Penguin ed.).

Kerenyi, C. (1962). *The religion of the Greeks and Romans*. London.

Lacan, J. Le Seminaire, Livre XI (1973) et Livre XX (1975).

Libsker, E., & Pasternak, V. *Chabad melodies*. Owings Mills, MD: Tara Publication.

Mozart, W. A. (1972). *Letters of W. A. Mozart*. New York: Dover Publication.

Nietzsche, F. (1993). *The birth of tragedy: Out of the spirit of music*. London: Penguin Books.

Otto, W. F. (1933). *Dionysos. Myth and cult*. Bloomington, IN: Indiana University Press.

Otto, W. F. (1955). *The Homeric Gods: The spiritual significance of Greek religion*. New York: Harper & Row.

Otto, W. F. (1955). *The meaning of the Eleusinian mysteries*, Eranos Yearbooks (Vol. 2). New York: Pantheon Books.

Poizat, M. (1991). *La Voix du Diable* (Edition Metaille). Paris.

The Quran. (2003). New York: Olive Branch Press.

Radha, Swami S. (1994). *Mantras: Words of power*. Spokane, WA: Timeless Book.

Rouget, G. (1985). *Music and trance: A theory of the relation between music and possession*. Chicago, IL: University of Chicago Press.

Reik, T. (1974). *Le Ritual. Psychanalyse des rites religieux*. Paris: Denoel.

Rudhyar, D. (1982). *The magic of tone and the art of music*. Boston, MA: Shambhala.

Shankar, R. (1968). *My music, my life*. New Delhi, India: Vikas Publishing House.

Shiloah, A. (1995). *La Musique dans le Monde de l'Islam*. Paris: Fayard.

Surya, D. (1997). *Awakening the Buddha within*. New York: Broadway Books.

Wallin, N., Merker, B., & Brown, S. (Ed.). (2000). *The origin of music*. Cambridge, MA: MIT Press.

Zuckerlandl, V. (1956). *Sound and symbol: Music and the external world*. New York: Pantheon Books.

Zuckerlandl, V. (1973). *Man the musician*. Princeton, NJ: Princeton University Press.

Music Thanatology

Meg Bowles

Definition

Thanatology, from the Greek word "*thanatos*," meaning death, refers to the study of the death and dying process from various interdisciplinary perspectives including physiology, psychology, and spirituality. Music thanatology is a contemplative practice within the field of thanatology, where prescriptive music, usually via the medium of harp and voice, is delivered live in clinical settings as a form of palliative medicine for patients who are dying.

While there is little doubt that many forms of live and pre-recorded music delivered *to* an audience can be experienced as profoundly healing, prescriptive music differs in that it is intentionally delivered solely *for* the dying patient. The practitioner of music thanatology uses her instrument in a way that attunes to the dying person's unique and individual needs from moment to moment, as opposed to a performing musician who delivers a preset program which is informed and shaped in advance by the energies of desire.

Origins

Although the field of music thanatology in its contemporary form originates from the visionary opus of harpist, musicologist, and clinician Therese Schroeder-Sheker (Founder and Director of the Chalice of Repose Project™ and Dean of the Chalice of Repose School of Music Thanatology, which has offered a highly specialized and rigorous graduate program in the field for decades), its ancestral roots stretch back to the monastic medicine practiced in the eleventh century Benedictine monastery of Cluny in Burgundy, France. At Cluny, rituals of prayer and what became known as "infirmary music" were used in bedside vigils to attend to the physical, emotional, and spiritual suffering of the dying. The relief of pain in both body and soul was considered essential for the experience of a peaceful and blessed death. The seeds of this holistic philosophy continue to bear fruit today, in the many different branches of modern palliative care. While the field of music thanatology does not seek to replicate the Benedictine approach to serving the dying, it deeply embraces the cultivation of a vital inner life through a contemplative spiritual practice, as an essential companion to doing clinical work.

Comparison with Music Therapy

Music thanatology shares much in common with music therapy in that both disciplines work intimately and powerfully with the healing potential of sound. However, music therapy differs in one important respect in that usually the therapeutic process assumes the presence of, and then harnesses, an innate capacity in the patient to be an active participant in the session. The music therapist, in collaboration with the patient, chooses the specific musical interventions which tend to elicit the physiological and emotional responses that are desired. Even during altered states involving deep relaxation or cathartic release, the patient usually has access to an observing ego and can process the experience with the therapist afterwards so that the material can be integrated into consciousness. A music thanatologist, on the other hand, is usually invited to work with a patient in the active phase dying. The patient may be agitated and in pain, or comatose, or pulled in and out of various altered states of consciousness, or otherwise unable to communicate. As the patient moves more deeply into the territory of a liminal world between life and death, she is in a sacred state of extraordinary vulnerability which needs to be supported as the natural "unbinding" processes in the body and the psyche take hold. Where there is resistance and struggle, carefully chosen prescriptive music will help the patient's connections with this world to be softened and loosened gently so that the energies moving her towards death and beyond may do so unimpeded.

In order to support a patient's physical and spiritual transition, or "transitus," (from the Latin *transire*, to cross over) into the territory of death and beyond, a practitioner of music thanatology allows herself to be guided both internally and externally by experiences of attunement and entrainment which mysteriously arise in the vibrational field between the practitioner and patient. The word "entrain" means "to pull or draw along after itself." Entrainment is a universal phenomenon appearing in nature, where two oscillating bodies begin to vibrate together, in harmony, due to their mutual influence upon each other. Engaging in a process of nonverbal attunement similar to what occurs between mother and infant, the practitioner gradually synchronizes the music to the patient's physiology. For example, as the practitioner adjusts the meter and phrasing to mirror the breathing patterns she observes, the patient, whose body is literally absorbing and responding to the music, will often begin to "vibrate" at a frequency of greater relaxation and peace. The breathing slows and eases. This musical flexibility which also includes an adept use of the power of silence and rest, tends to draw one into the more fluid, non-ordinary soul-space of *kairos* time, as opposed to the linear, precisely metered *chronos* time which can bind one to ordinary reality.

Conclusion

The practitioner of music thanatology (whether male or female) functions as a spiritual midwife and a comforting maternal presence. Perhaps she (along with the harp, which has a mythology of its own) also carries a bit of an angelic or shamanic projection as well. There is little doubt that the beauty in the music itself, expressed through the exquisitely refined craft of a skilled, trained instrumentalist, and mediated by the humble, compassionate presence of a fellow human being who is called to serve, has the potential to create and hold a space for an experience of the transcendent. Although the delivery of prescriptive music is not designed to cure, it does heal by supporting the patient to release her engagement with life in this linear time-space dimension so that ultimately her consciousness and spirit as we know it can become gathered back into the Greater Mystery.

See also: ❷ Healing ❷ Music and Religion ❷ Thanatos

Bibliography

Kossak, M. (2008). *Attunement and Free Jazz. Voices: A world Forum for Music Therapy*. Retrieved May 20, 109, from http://www.voices.no/mainisuses/mi40008000271.php.

Schroeder-Sheker, T. (1994). Music for the dying: Using prescriptive music in the death bed vigil. *Noetic Sciences Review*, 31, 32–33.

Schroeder-Sheker, T. (1996). *What is prescriptive music?* www.chaliceo frepose.org/

Schroeder-Sheker, T. (2001). *Transitus: A blessed death in a modern world*. St. Dunstan's Press.

Mystery Religions

Jeffrey B. Pettis

Mystery religions flourished in the Hellenistic world. They centered around deities including Mithras (Persia), Atargatis (Syria), Dionysos, Demeter and Core (Greece), Meter, (Anatolia) and Isis (Egypt). Most of the deities associated with these cults have their beginning as agricultural fertility gods and the notion of the great divine Mother who begets and receives life force. The word "mystery" comes from the Greek *muein*, "to initiate." Membership in the Mysteries occurred on an individual and voluntary basis. Ritual practices, worship, and "inner" teachings were privy only to cult members – this contributing to the prestige of the cult. Subsequently, little is known about worship and the Mysteries. Apuleius (Lucius Apuleius Platonicus ca. 123/125 CE–ca. 180 CE), in his *Metamorphoses* provides a glimpse into the nature of the Isis cult in second century CE. He explains how he was directed in a night dream by Isis "the mother of the universe" to become an initiate (1989, XI.5), and how he undergoes purification rituals, observes ten days of celibacy and fasting from meat and wine, and receives secret instructions (1989, XI.23). At the culmination of the rite he emerges from the inner sanctuary reborn in "the likeness of the sun" (1989, XI.24). He writes how he came to the boundary of death and... traveled through all the elements... and in the middle of the night came face to face with the gods below and the gods above" (XI.23). Plato also refers to ecstatic experience and the Mysteries in the *Phaedrus*, where he says one who is taken up with True Beauty (*kallos tou alēthous*) cannot help but be euphoric – something the common world sees as madness

(*parakinōn*) not knowing it to be inspiration (*enthousiazōn*)(249D). Plato says that the soul forms wings (*pterōtai*), and that it "throbs and palpitates... it is feverish and uncomfortable and itches when they [wings] begin to grow" (251C). The Roman Emperor Marcus Aurelius (161–180 CE), a stoic philosopher, writes how the Mysteries place one between dream visions and miraculous healings, suggesting some kind of psyche-soma, liminal experience. In this state of disorientation the initiate may undergo an altered state of consciousness. Dramatic rituals involving strong contrast between light and dark, and movement through interior and exterior spaces become part of a rebirth experience. Initiates of the Anatolian Mysteries of Kybele and Attis enter into the sacred wedding chamber to experience the Great Mother. Fanatical members of this cult flagellate themselves to the point of bleeding, sprinkling their blood across the sanctuary altar. Members of the Mithras cult worship in subterranean caves before a graphic depiction of Mithras slaying the bull. The Mother Goddess Cult of Meter includes self-castrating priests (*galloi*), and from the second century CE on drenched initiates in the blood of a slaughtered bull. The notion of ascending also occurs as a quality of the Mysteries. Apuleius speaks of traveling through "all the elements" (*omnia elementa*) (1989, XI.23), and Plato speaks of the chariot of the soul rising into the region above the heavens (*huperouranion topon*) which have a colorless, formless, and intangible essence (1914, *Phaedrus* 247C). The Mithras Liturgy found in the ancient source called the Great Magical Papyri of Paris tells of the ascent through seven levels which include the lower powers of the air, Aion and his powers, Helios, and Mithras (751–834). The Mysteries can be understood then as cults which make conscious the symbols and movements of the unconscious and processes these in the formation of rituals as part of religious experience. Not being self-sufficient, the Mysteries diminish with the demise of the ancient world upon which they depend. Following the imperial decrees of 391/92 CE against all pagan cults they suddenly and permanently disappear.

See also: ❂ Eleusinian Mysteries ❂ Great Mother ❂ Osiris and the Egyptian Religion ❂ Ritual

Bibliography

Apuleius. (1989). *Metamorphoses* (J. A. Hanson, Trans.). Loeb Classical Library, Cambridge, MA: Harvard University Press.

Aurelius, M. (1930). *Meditations* (C. G. Haines, Trans.). Loeb Classical Library, Cambridge, MA: Harvard University Press.

Betz, H. D. (1986). *The Greek Magical Papyri in translation.* Chicago, IL: University of Chicago Press.

Plato. (1914). *Phaedrus* (H. N. Fowler, Trans.). Loeb Classical Library, Cambridge, MA: Harvard University Press.

Mysticism and Psychoanalysis

Alan Roland

Introduction

In the last 30 years, two broad attempts have been made to challenge the classical Freudian psychoanalytic narrative on mysticism in which spiritual experiences and practices have been viewed as regressive and/or psychopathological, personified by Jeffrey Masson (1976, 1980), noted Sanskritist turned psychoanalyst. The first attempt centered on South Asian studies, particularly but not exclusively on major Hindu spiritual figures, similar to Masson. Methodologically, it uses applied psychoanalysis involving textual analyses and ethnographic interviews. Those who have contributed most directly to this new psychoanalytic perspective are the Indian psychoanalyst, Sudhir Kakar, psychoanalytically-oriented professors of religion, Jeffrey Kripal and William Parsons, and the anthropologist, Gananath Obeyesekere. The second movement involves psychoanalysts (Nina Coltart, Paul Cooper, Michael Eigen, Alan Roland, and Jeffrey Rubin among others), who are involved in one or another spiritual practice, overwhelmingly but not exclusively Buddhist, and who work psychoanalytically with some patients seriously involved in their own spiritual disciplines. This movement is thus more clinically and experientially oriented than the applied psychoanalysis of the first group.

In the first group, almost all are in agreement that there needs to be a seismic shift from what they view as a highly pejorative and reductionistic Freudian psychoanalytic rendering of religious experiences and practices. Kakar (1978, 1991) is the first Freudian psychoanalyst to openly challenge the psychoanalytic establishment to accord the mystic a similar respect to that given the artist in the West. They all agree that religious experiences are valid in and of themselves but all assert that these experiences can at least be partially if not fully explained by psychoanalytic considerations. It is to this inherent tension between the spiritual experience being considered sui

generis and their psychoanalytic explanations of it that shall be addressed in this section of the chapter. With the exception of Obeyesekere, and to some extent Kripal, they rely on more current Freudian psychoanalytic theorists than classical Freudian theory. Thus Wilfred Bion, Heinz Kohut, Jacques Lacan, Anna Maria Rizzuto, and D. W. Winnicott are cited for a new psychoanalytic rendering of mysticism.

Sudhir Kakar

This chapter shall address what is problematic in this new Freudian psychoanalytic discourse on mysticism before advancing the other perspective. It shall critique Sudhir Kakar as he has greatly influenced the others through writing extensively on the subject of psychoanalysis and mysticism, beginning with his analysis of Swami Vivekananda in *The Inner World* (1978), then on Gandhi in *Intimate Relations* (1989), and finally on Ramakrishna in *The Analyst and the Mystic* (1991). Kakar is to be applauded for his courage in the Freudian psychoanalytic world for advocating for a radical reconsideration of the mystic. His description of the lives of Vivekananda, Gandhi, and Ramakrishna are very well done in his gifted style of writing. But what happens when he actually applies his psychoanalytic understanding to these three spiritual figures? His analyses are as fully reductionistic as those of Jeffrey Masson. This chapter shall cite just one of what could be many examples.

After disavowing the pathographic approach (1978: 164), Kakar cites the following:

▶ With the advent of adolescence... he (Vivekananda) found he could not always cope with the claims of archaic grandiosity and the anxiety and guilt associated with its breakthrough. Increasingly, he experienced periods of hypomanic excitement; once... when he was fifteen... Narendra 'spied a large bee-hive in the cleft of a giant cliff and suddenly his mind was filled with awe and reverence for the Divine Providence. He lost outer consciousness and lay thus in the cart for a long time' (1978: 178–179).

Thus, Kakar equates Vivekananda's spiritual experience with archaic grandiosity and hypomanic excitement.

This stems in good part from the second problem in his work, his theoretical understanding of mysticism from a psychoanalytic standpoint. In *The Inner World*, Kakar states "real knowledge is only attainable through direct primary-process thinking and perception..." (1978: 107).

▶ In the Hindu ideal, reality is not primarily mediated through the conscious and preconscious perceptions, unconscious defenses, and logical rational thought processes that make up the ego; it emanates from the deeper and phylogenetically older structural layer of personality – the id, the mental representation of the organism's instinctual drives. Reality, according to Hindu belief, can be apprehended or known only through those archaic, unconscious, preverbal processes of sensing and feeling (Kakar, 1978: 20).

To what extent primary-process thinking and the id constitute spiritual knowing is highly questionable to say the least. The primary process, perhaps Freud's most original discovery, constitutes certain mechanisms (condensation, displacement, symbol formation, dramatization, and such), symbolic processes essential in dreams, symptoms, and in certain ways in artistic creativity. In Freud's view, they give disguised expression to the instinctual wishes; in later contributions (Deri 1984; Noy 1969; Roland 1972), they also give excellent metaphorical expression to various facets of the self. In *The Inner World* it is Kakar's inaccurate use of Freudian psychoanalytic concepts such as the primary process and the id as a Procrustean Bed to encompass psychological processes involved in spiritual realization that results in his reverting to traditional psychoanalytic reductionism in his analyses of mystics.

His theoretical understanding of mysticism shifts from the use of the primary process and the id in *The Inner World* to current psychoanalytic relational theories in *The Analyst and the Mystic*. Kakar in this latter work fully accepts the reductionistic psychoanalytic premise that spiritual experiences and motivation are essentially a regression to the preverbal, symbiotic experiences of the mother-child relationship.

▷ The vicissitudes of separation have been, of course, at the heart of psychoanalytic theorizing on mysticism. The yearning to be reunited with a perfect, omnipotent being, the longing for the blissful soothing and nursing associated with the mother of earliest infancy... has been consensually deemed the core of mystical motivation (Kakar, 1991: 29).

Only Kakar puts a more positive spin on this regression than do the classical Freudian analysts, in as much as he sees the mystic as able to effect a deeper regression than that which occurs in psychoanalysis to repair what Kakar deems is the essential depressive core of life; and in Winnicottian terms, the mystic is involved in a creative experiencing through this regression to infancy. Again, it is highly questionable whether spiritual aspirations, practices, and experiences essentially involve regression.

Psychoanalytic Therapy with Indian and American Mystics

From those psychoanalysts and psychoanalytic therapists who have worked with patients deeply involved in spiritual disciplines, and who are themselves practicing meditation, a newer narrative has emerged on psychoanalysis and mysticism. Or perhaps more accurately, on psychoanalysis and mystics. In general, the spiritual self of the mystic and psychopathology/normality are seen on two separate continua. Thus, a mystic, even an advanced one, can range from being mentally healthy to having various kinds of psychopathology. Conversely, mentally healthy and mature persons can range from not being in the least interested in a spiritual quest to being very involved. The same is true of persons who are emotionally disturbed.

Correspondingly, the spiritual self of the mystic cannot be reduced to any psychoanalytic theory with the possible exception of Wilfred Bion's concept of "O." Both Kakar (1991) and Parsons (1999) cite Lacan's theory of the Real but according to a recognized Lacanian authority, Paola Mieli, they misunderstand the meaning of the Real (Personal communication).

Similarly, attempts to link spiritual experiences with various developmental stages are seen by this group as being highly reductionistic: whether it is Freud's primary narcissism of infantile merger with the mother, or a Winnicottian creative experiencing of a transitional space between mother and child, or Rizzuto's god-images from different developmental stages, or Kurtz's (1992) concept of later childhood merger with the extended family. These views simply do not take sufficiently into account the existential nature of spiritual experiences. Nor can these experiences be categorized by regression of one sort or another, or to one or another stage of development, or to one or another kind of inner representation of either the mother or father. If anything, clinical experience indicates that spiritual practices and experiences are a strong counterpoint to regression and childhood merger experiences with the mother.

If psychopathology does not enter into spiritual experiences, where does psychoanalysis fruitfully enter the picture with mystics? First and foremost, it is in their relationships with others, often love relationships affected by earlier difficult family relationships, but also friends and work relationships, any or all of which can sometimes be truly problematic, and also to their everyday sense of self. Psychoanalytic therapy with those patients who are mystics is often of considerable help in their functioning much better in their relationships while simultaneously freeing them to be more involved on a spiritual path.

How then does unconscious motivation and psychopathology enter into a mystic's spiritual practices? Two women in psychoanalysis with highly distressful love relationships were first drawn to Vipassana meditation, which helped them attain an inner calm. On the other hand, an advanced mystic like Shakuntala (Roland, 1988) began having spontaneous, intense spiritual experiences by age fourteen while on a family pilgrimage to a shrine of a goddess. Other persons with a spiritual inclination may be drawn to spiritual disciplines out of defensive needs to resolve some kind of psychopathology (Coltart, 1996), while still others may become openly psychotic if they have a psychotic core. One patient was attracted to an ashram and guru known for both its spiritual powers and its sexual licentiousness. While progressing there on her spiritual path, she unconsciously repeated the childhood sexual abuse she had once experienced. The decision to embark on a spiritual quest may sometimes result from some of the hard knocks of life, but not always. Even then, the person must be strongly inwardly inclined in this direction for it is still a rare pursuit.

A psychoanalytic discourse on mystics can fruitfully comment on that which has only been minimally discussed, the guru or teacher-disciple relationship. Besides the important teachings that are conveyed by a suitable teacher, there can also be multiple transferences from both the disciple and the teacher, depending on the individual personality. Rubin (1996) has commented on this at length.

To what extent can spiritual practices alleviate emotional problems? While most agree they can be helpful, it is generally considered that they cannot resolve deep-seated psychopathology. Coltart (1996) noted that some people who seek out spiritual practices to resolve their emotional problems would do much better being in psychotherapy. On the other hand, these psychoanalysts have noted that patients involved in spiritual disciplines can usually tolerate a greater degree of anxiety in facing inner conflicts and/or deficits in the psychoanalytic process.

See also: ❸ Bion, Wilfred Ruprecht, and "O" ❸ Lacan, Jacques ❸ Mysticism and Psychotherapy ❸ Psychoanalysis

Bibliography

Coltart, N. (Ed.) (1992). The practice of psychoanalysis and Buddhism. In *Slouching toward Bethlehem* (pp. 164–175). New York: Guilford Press.

Coltart, N. (Ed.) (1996). Buddhism and psychoanalysis revisited. In *The baby and the bathwater* (pp. 125–140). New York: International Universities Press.

Cooper, P. (1998). The disavowal of the spirit: Integration and wholeness in Buddhism and psychoanalysis. In A. Molino (Ed.), *The couch and the tree: Dialogues in psychoanalysis and Buddhism* (pp. 231–246). New York: North Point Press.

Cooper, P. (1999). Buddhist meditation and countertransference: A case study. *American Journal of Psychoanalysis, 59*, 71–86.

Deri, S. (1984). *Symbolization and creativity*. New York: International Universities Press.

Eigen, M. (1998). *The pyschoanalytic mystic*. Binghamton, NY: ESF Publications.

Kakar, S. (1978). *The inner world: A psychoanalytic study of childhood and society in India*. New Delhi: Oxford University Press.

Kakar, S. (1989). *Intimate relations: Exploring Indian sexuality*. Chicago, IL: University of Chicago Press.

Kakar, S. (1991). *The analyst and the mystic: Psychoanalytic reflections on religion and mysticism*. New Delhi: Viking by Penguin Books India.

Kurtz, S. (1992). *All the mothers are one: Hindu India and the cultural reshaping of psychoanalysis*. New York: Columbia University Press.

Masson, J. M. (1976). The psychology of the ascetic. *Journal of Asian Studies, 35*, 611–625.

Masson, J. M. (1980). *The oceanic feeling: The origins of religious sentiment in ancient India*. Dordrecht, Holland: D. Reidel.

Noy, P. (1969). A revision of the psychoanalytic theory of the primary process. *International Journal Psycho-Analysis, 50*, 155–178.

Parsons, W. B. (1999). *The enigma of the oceanic feeling: Revisioning the psychoanalytic theory of mysticism*. New York: Oxford University Press.

Rizzuto, A. (1979). *The birth of the Living God: A psychoanalytic study*. Chicago, IL: Chicago University Press.

Roland, A. (1972). Imagery and symbolic expression in dreams and art. *International Journal of Psycho-Analysis, 53*, 531–539.

Roland, A. (1988). *In search of self in India and Japan: Toward a cross-cultural psychology*. Princeton, NJ: Princeton University Press.

Roland, A. (1996). *Cultural pluralism and psychoanalysis: The Asian and North American experience*. New York: Routledge.

Roland, A. (1999). The spiritual self and psychopathology: Theoretical reflections and clinical observations. *Psychoanalysis and Psychotherapy, 16*, 211–234.

Roland, A. (2005). Psychoanalysts and the spiritual quest: Framing a new paradigm. In A. Roland, B. Ulanov, & C. Barbre (Eds.), *Creative dissent: Psychoanalysis in evolution*. New York: Praeger.

Rubin, J. (1996). *Psychotherapy and Buddhism: Toward an integration*. New York: Plenum Press.

Mysticism and Psychotherapy

Anthony Badalamenti

The goal of psychotherapy is either to relieve distressing symptoms such as anxiety, depression, phobias and so on, or to enable a person to better manage his or her life. These two goals usually overlap and this fact is a key to understanding the general principle by which psychotherapy works. Whatever the issue that brings a person to therapy, the therapist sees the desired improvements as the natural expression of a needed form of personal growth. The work to create this growth uses a person's perceptual and cognitive powers to bring about a change that takes place mostly in the emotional system.

A major difference between emotional and cognitive processing is the degree of automatism versus choice in each. Most people can call upon their ability to understand something by an act of will, that is, by the wish to have the given understanding. This is rarely true of the emotional system, which tends to be evoked involuntarily by perceptions arising either from within a person or from the person's environment. It is the lack of conscious control over emotional responses that troubles people with emotional problems because the wish to be free of a symptom has little or no effect on it. One of the main characteristics of an emotionally healthy person is that his or her emotional responses tend to be adaptive, and therefore welcome, with respect to what provokes them. This is why spontaneity is often taken as a sign of emotional health, where it is assumed that the spontaneous response is appropriate. In this framework the general goal of psychotherapy is to create a fitting spontaneous response to certain parts of the subject's life. This involves taking measures to realize the potential within the subject to become what is needed to be free of the distressing symptom or presenting complaint. It is this relationship of potential to actual that begins a natural relationship between mysticism and psychotherapy.

The general goal of mysticism is to achieve ever-increasing levels of awareness of the cosmos. This involves training exercises in attitudes and orientations toward the self and the world that promote the emergence of another level of awareness. This other level is best understood as experiential rather than cognitive or emotional or even intuitive, although it is important to note that the experiential level of understanding includes all of these three. Achieving this experiential level of understanding enters a domain where words, emotions and even intuition can no longer be used to communicate what is apprehended. Here the way cosmic reality is apprehended is neither by words nor by emotions but by a direct experience of the continuity of the psyche with the cosmos.

This mode of knowing and being presupposes a kind of human potential and here the connecting link to psychotherapy again surfaces. Within psychotherapy the desired growth, or realization of potential, is located in the emotional system and to a lesser degree in the cognitive system. Within mysticism, the desired growth refers to the entire person. In this sense the goal of mysticism is a generalization of the goal of psychotherapy. The idea that mysticism subsumes psychotherapy is not new and has long been a familiar to mystics of all traditions. Before the nineteenth century mystics did not frame this idea in terms of psychology, as now understood, but in more home-spun terms such as growing up, carrying one's cross, coming into one's own and so on. When psychotherapy emerged, adepts in mysticism were quick to see that their tradition was a generalization of the psychological one.

Psychotherapy has a variety of tools, all accessing the emotional and cognitive powers, to use to stimulate needed growth. Mysticism also has tools to achieve its ends but here the two part ways in a paradoxical manner that also brings them back together. Since the object of mysticism is accessed outside feeling and rational knowing, the training for this goal involves weaning a person away from his or her familiar reliance on feeling, thinking and choosing. A redirection of attention takes place, usually involving long and diligent training before first fruits appear. One of the major tools in all mystical traditions is the koan.

A koan is a riddle presented as if solvable by using cognitive or emotional intelligence. For example, "what is the sound of one hand clapping?" or "what did you look like before your parents were born?" The koan is meant to be vexing because its purpose is to bring the subject to see that rational processing cannot be of service in certain parts of life. This is a first step, usually under the direction of a spiritual director, toward disengaging attention from its ordinary use. The long-term goal of the exercises is to get attention off of any one thing, a state usually termed "letting go and letting be." The major reason for this goal is that the more a person holds on to any one state, the more the person interferes with the inflow and creation of more of the psyche. This is another connection with psychotherapy.

One of the major obstacles to successful psychotherapy is the subject's unwillingness to release former ways of living and adapting. As a rule new and better ways cannot be evolved except by also clearing behaviors that stand in the way. Thus, the idea of letting go and letting be enters psychotherapy at the level of emotional, and to some degree, cognitive processing. Within psychotherapy one lets go of behaviors that either do not work well enough or that do harm in favor of growing new behaviors that make for a better adaptation. The goals of mysticism include a sound adaptation but this is more of a starting point for what mysticism aims at and here the idea that mysticism subsumes psychotherapy enters in a natural way.

The goal of mysticism is to directly experience the cosmos, an event whose higher levels are outside the domain of words, thoughts, feelings and images. The onset of mystical experience takes place with the emergence of new perceptual powers in the psyche. The first experiences along these lines involve the intuition of being in which a person begins to experience the "isness" of things. It is very important for the subject to train in moving attention away from emotional, cognitive and other familiar modes of knowing and adapting for this to take place. The intuition of being is usually the very first of a sequence of experiences that build to mystical experience. The mystical experience proper is more an event of growth than of a new kind of perception, but it is the case that the growth precedes and enables the perception. This kind of perception is an experience outside of and different from all the subject's prior modes of knowing and apprehending, a thing suggested by the need for some prerequisite growth of the psyche to first take place. This is parallel to many therapeutic events.

Within psychotherapy a person first realizes a needed potential to live and adapt in a new way before the person becomes able to see what it means. This actualization process is what extinguishes the distressing symptoms and the more willing the subject is to release the prior way of adapting, the quicker this takes place. In the mystical experience, the more the subject has learned to release prior attachments of *all* kinds, the more quickly the growth needed for the next level of mystical experience takes place. Here again the idea that mystical experience is a generalization of the therapeutic experience presents itself.

The goal of psychotherapy is to increase the "isness" of the subject in the affective or emotional domain, and to some degree in the cognitive domain also. This has traditionally been regarded as the event of turning potential into actual, where the "'isness" of the potential is already in place and the therapeutic process results in the "isness" of its actual form. The outcome, in practical terms, is that the subject feels and functions better as a result of the leap from potential to actual in target areas. In mystical terms, the subject's ontology has increased and the subject is literally more than he or she was before the realization of potential took place. Put differently, the subject's powers to adapt increase.

The ontological increases in mystical experience include the issue of here and now adaptation because the entire psyche increases as a result. That is, the mystical experience is enabled by the growth of new psychic capacity whose object is to engage the cosmos itself. However, the psyche is itself an expression of the cosmos and therefore any increase in the psyche affects the person's relationship to all parts of life, simply because all events take place in the cosmos. What this means in practical terms is that the subject's emotional life is not only enriched for adaptation in the usual sense, but more, the emotional system begins to respond to the

new life in the psyche that has the capacity to directly experience the cosmos in ways that are outside the reach of the emotional, rational and intuitive domains. The emotions of awe and trust take on new meanings as the mystical experience develops, just as these same emotions take on fresh meaning as a person grows new here-and-now adaptive powers within psychotherapy.

In sum, the goals of mysticism may be regarded as a generalization of those of psychotherapy, or those of psychotherapy may be regarded as a specialization of those of mysticism. One major difference between the two is that mysticism results in the emergence of another way of becoming and knowing not achievable by the emotional and cognitive systems alone. One major parallel between the two is that both require the releasing of former ways of living and being, this release being a completely general one in mysticism and a more particular one in psychotherapy. Both mysticism and psychotherapy address the realization of potential, and both regard potential as unlimited, but what potential refers to is man's relation to all things in the first and man's relation to matters of love and work in the second. This too fits the idea that mysticism is a generalization of psychotherapy.

See also: ❯ Biblical Psychology ❯ Collective Unconscious ❯ Depth Psychology and Spirituality ❯ Jung, Carl Gustav, and Eastern Religious Traditions ❯ Mindfulness

Bibliography

Benoit, H. (1990). *Zen and the psychology of transformation*. Rochester, VT: Inner Traditions International.

Freud, S. (1966). *The complete introductory lectures on psychoanalysis*. New York: W.W. Norton.

Jaeger, W. (1995). *Search for the meaning of life*. Chicago, IL: Triumph Books.

Johnston, W. (Ed.) *The cloud of unknowing*. Brooklyn, NY: Image Books.

Jung, C. G. (1966). *Psychology and religion*. New Haven, CT: Yale University Press.

Myth

Lee W. Bailey

The study of myth is an ancient topic that has expanded greatly in the last 200 years. The foci of studies are commonly: *literary* – clarifying texts, translating, categorizing [Greek myths, Irish myths], or *religious* – labeling other culture's religions as false [pagan, heathen, primitive]

while typically preserving the truth value of one's own religion, or *psychological* – exploring the psychological themes expressed in myths [Freudian, Jungian], or *sociological/anthropological/political* – bringing out the ideological symbols of social structures such as class, nation, patriotism, and similar themes in myths [Marxist, capitalist], or *philosophical* – efforts to determine the truth or reality of mythic accounts, historical or imaginative [Plato, deconstructionists]. Some theories of myth focus on stories accepted as myth, others point to mythic themes in unexpected places. Some combine various methods. The emergence of depth psychology gave a new prominence and new important methodology for interpreting myth and religions.

Many theories of interpreting myths see "*mythos* as inferior to *logos.*" But the theory that myth is simply an archaic literary genre or social ideology replaced by modern rational thought has been radically questioned by the development of depth psychology. Its opening to the unconscious soul and intuitive blend with reasoning now lets us see "*mythos* dancing poetically with *logos.*" In the psychology of religion, the approach to myth depends less on rational, conscious, historical, factual *logos* to establish truth, but rather moves in the realm of poetic, metaphoric symbolic language – *mythos,* a different kind of truth that still interacts significantly with *logos,* open to unconscious dynamics. Myth is not a literary museum of a consciousness outdated by rational science, but a living symbolic language of a continuing consciousness important to understand. Oedipus, the cowboy, the king, the prophet, and the astronaut, whether or not they have a historical background, have far broader horizons than any factual basis, guiding the soul through collective unconscious paths of tragic, comic, transforming, saving, and heroic journeys. The mythic narratives of historical figures may be far more significant that the bare factual bones of the biographies.

Myths still need to be distinguished from factual knowledge, as in propaganda or ideology. Myths cannot provide a reliable basis for deductions about historical facts, such as facts about Santa Claus. Yet, myth is indispensable, for it symbolizes the soul's desires, positive and negative. Myths are living, powerful stories, although sometimes unacknowledged and unconscious, articulating essential meanings (Bailey). Awareness of them can prevent disaster and soothe the soul. The modern turning point came with Freud.

Sigmund Freud

Sigmund Freud (1856–1939), the Viennese physician turned psychotherapist, made the major leap out of *logos* rationalism and materialism in psychology by showing the reality and symbolic meaningfulness of the unconscious mind for medical treatment by taking seriously its languages, such as dreams, errors and symptoms. He saw the unconscious mind as largely composed of repressed desires. Freud used some myths in his exploration of the unconscious, notably Oedipus, Narcissus, Moses, Eros and Thanatos. He elevated the Oedipus complex to be the foundation of most all neurosis, myth, art, religion, and therapy. This gave a new, powerful methodology for interpreting myths as expressions of the unconscious mind.

Freud's elevation of the Oedipus myth was part of the end of the Victorian era, but finally was too narrow. He universalized his love for his mother and jealousy of his father into the Oedipus complex, which he found to be basic to his patients' neuroses. This was part of Freud's strong emphasis on the centrality of sexuality as the main dynamic of the psyche. He was widely reviled for this during the closing years of the Victorian era in Europe, which stifled sexuality [in public, anyway], but his work actually contributed to the spreading collapse of strict Victorian sexual customs, along with the development of contraceptives and women's education by the 1920s. Openness to sexuality can lead to openness to the unconscious and its mythic expressions.

Freud's residual nineteenth-century materialism prevented him from allowing non-pathological truths to be seen as true in the mythic expressions of the unconscious mind. Rather, he let conscious reason be the final arbiter of truth, which conflicted with his readings of mythic material. In his 1927 *Future of an Illusion,* he argued that religion is a universal neurosis founded on ignorance and weakness. It is an illusion of wish-fulfillment, he envisioned, a consolation for fate, and an effort to exorcize the terrors of nature with faith. God is an infantile neurosis, a dreaded yet trusted mythic figure carried over from infancy that maintains the believers' helplessness. A secular ethics is workable and science has no illusions, since conscious knowledge can purge itself of unconscious errors, Freud fervently believed. Uncovering the powerful unconscious mind, Freud kept it in the realm of the pathological, so neither myth nor religion could be allowed to carry much truth-value. "Religion would thus be the universal obsessional neurosis of humanity; like the obsessional neurosis of children, it arose out of the Oedipus complex, out of the relation to the father" (1927/1961: 70–71).

The follower of Freud who made the most out of certain types of myths was Bruno Bettelheim (1903–1990), who wrote *The Uses of Enchantment: The Meaning and Importance of Fairy Tales* in 1975. He defined myths as stories that are pessimistic and superhuman (such as Oedipus), fables as moralistic and cautionary (such as the Ant and the Grasshopper), and fairy tales as optimistic, taking place in the ordinary world, for children and guides to growing up (such as the Three Little Pigs). His Freudian analysis was tinged with the existential principle that fairy tales help children find hopeful meanings and moral education as they grow up. At their best fairy tales take children's predicaments seriously and provide confidence that they can be overcome. They relieve unconscious pressures and strengthen the child's growing ego. Such problems include narcissistic disappointments, Oedipal dilemmas, sibling rivalries, gaining independence from parents, increasing a sense of self-worth and a sense of moral obligations. Fairy tales help release repressed dark feelings, and help overcome fears that they present, such as abandonment. They simplify but do not suppress evil. Bethlehem believes that fairy tales should not be prettified, for that makes them too shallow to solve the real problems that monsters and fearful plots present.

Fairy tales offer valuable heroes for children to identify with in combating fears and strengthening their blossoming egos. Fairy tales should not be mis-interpreted as neurotic symptoms, Bettelheim stresses, but be seen as positive guides to growth because they help the child feel understood and offer hope for overcoming anxieties. Nor should they be taken as guides to behavior in the external world; they are symbolic expressions of deep unconscious childhood processes. Religious themes in fairy tales are common, such as references to Islam in *The Thousand and One Nights*, (Tales, 1975) and the references to God and the Virgin Mary in original Grimm's tales, which are often edited out in modern versions. Unlike moralistic biblical tales, fairy tales allow more expression of dark feelings – monsters, beasts, big bad wolves – and more psychological solutions than divine interference.

Carl Jung

Carl Jung (1875–1961) was the Swiss psychologist who provided the strongest theory of myth for understanding religion positively. His major theoretical foundation is the archetype: innumerable unconscious, collective, psychological patterns or instincts, positive and negative. An archetype is an invisible [inaccessible in itself] pattern that appears in numerous images. They appear worldwide in myths and dreams, shaped by local cultures.

Unlike Freud, Jung does not see the unconscious as primarily repressed desires, but as far more complex archetypal patterns. Myth functions to reveal the unconscious to consciousness and to guide the conscious ego's relation to it by showing its typical patterns. Myth is neither indispensable nor sufficient for the psyche. The unconscious must co-operate with the conscious ego's guidance also. Unlike many Eastern religions, the ego is not meant to dissolve into the unconscious. While uncovering valuable mythic guides, psychotherapy can provide more functions, such as seeing the symbolism of dreams, symptoms, or myths, and integrating these meanings into life.

Jung focuses on the archetypal images of the ego/hero (such as Odysseus), the shadow (such as the Devil), the anima/animus contrasexual lover images in each person (such as Tristan and Iseult), the child (such as Cinderella), the trickster (such as Hermes), the wise old man or woman (such as Merlin), the dual mother (wicked stepmother), and the Self (such as God). The Self is the central guiding, healing archetype for Jung, perhaps the center of the mandala image, that regulates and balances the dynamics of the numerous archetypal patterns that emerge in the psyche. The challenge of psychotherapeutic healing is to identify one's influencing archetypes, become aware of their dynamics and influences on feeling and behavior, help the ego and Self control shadows, and strengthen the positive aspects.

An important part of Jung's archetypal theory is that each archetype has a shadow. Even the Self, paradigm of divinity, has a shadow in doubts, demon figures, and limits to divine power in the world. Jung pioneered the elaboration of the introvert/extravert pattern in his theory of psychological types, and this pattern was widely adopted. The extreme introvert is shy, quiet, socially inept, inward, intuitive, and isolated. The extreme extravert is socially adept, outspoken, concerned with what others think of him/her, often a performer anxious for approval, or a conformist. One-sided people may see the other side as a shadow figure to be fought in outward life. However, the ideal is to balance the two in one's life, so the advantages of each side of the continuum are available to consciousness.

Jung and Freud became close collaborators between 1907 and 1913. Freud hoped that the younger Jung would become his successor, but Jung developed key disagreements with Freud. His theory of archetypes saw myths as more important collective symbols of many archetypes, as opposed to Freud's central Oedipus theory. He also rejected Freud's emphasis on sexuality as the major psychological dynamic, and came to regard religion far more positively as psychological events than Freud, who dismissed it as illusory. Nor did Jung accept Freud's causal-reductive method by which he reduced unconscious images to his theoretical framework, mainly the Oedipal drama. Rather, Jung saw a purposeful dynamic in each archetypal pattern [especially the Self], a teleology of sorts that could point the ego in healing directions, even a transcendent quest for the divine.

The divine Jung sees not just in narrow biblical terms, but also as a global phenomenon that appears in endless symbols in dreams, literature, art, and myth. He stresses that he speaks as a psychologist describing a psychological phenomenon, not a metaphysical one, which he said he leaves to the theologians. This wide variety of images of the divine is an important theme for Jung's impact on culture, because it throws open the door to seeing the divine symbolized in many ways – from non-anthropomorphic stones, waterfalls and cosmic phenomena to anthropomorphic prophets and gurus. This supports the field of comparative and phenomenological studies of religions worldwide, as well as the growing feminist quest to positively re-evaluate the goddesses.

Jung's view of the collective archetypal unconscious explains the arising of mythic themes around the world without recourse to the theory of diffusion from an original source. Although some myths can be traced along a trail of diffusion [such as Cinderella coming from China to Europe], other themes such as virgin births in the Americas can be explained as archetypal images emerging completely independent of parallel themes on other continents [such as the Aztec virgin birth story].

Jung's view of religion is rooted in his Swiss Protestant emphasis not on formal and textual doctrines, but on personal experiences of the divine. He was frustrated with the lack of this authentic religious experience and came to see psychotherapy as a way out of superficial, even infantile dogmatism, into a genuine experience and deep understanding of divinity in its many expressions. The psyche, Jung stresses, has a natural religious function, an ability to experience the sacred or numinous. Myth can be seen as symbolic expressions of archetypal powers, real as such, and thus authentic, so changing religion need rely less on historical facts than on informed archetypal experiences. The hero, the savior, the father, mother, guru, etc. are active collectively and "within" – not merely historical figures of the past or of metaphysical constructs. This does not make Jungian "analytical" or "archetypal" therapy a religion, but it is more open to the reality of spiritual experiences. Against Freud, Jung argued that it is not the presence of religious images in the psyche, but their absence and lack of conscious respect for them that lead to neurosis.

As Jung's thought developed, he came to see divinity as a union of opposites, a totality of good and evil, masculine and feminine, and spirit and body, that he had discovered in his clinical and comparative cultural research, pictured in images of the Self. In his important lectures on "Psychology and Religion" in 1937 (1953–1979, CW 11), Jung clarified that we cannot know metaphysical entities such as God in themselves. We can only know the psychic images of them that we experience. "Withdrawing projections" from enemies, lovers, or priests also helps uncover deeper truths about one's experience of divinity. The goal of therapy is not perfection or salvation, but completeness, finding the most refined way of integrating unions of opposites, often symbolized by mandalas. This is all essential in a time when industrial society has challenged and weakened the traditional authority of conventional religions.

After 1938, Jung also studied Eastern religions and traveled to India. One theme that emerged from this period was Jung's view that Christ is an inadequate image of divinity because he is one-sidedly good, masculine and spiritual. A more adequate image would include evil, the feminine, and the body (1953–1979, CW 9,ii). For him evil is real, and not just Augustine's *privatio boni,* or lack of goodness. Jung saw this also in his *Answer to Job* (1953–1979, CW 11:553–758). Christ's incarnation did not solve the problem of one-sidedness, and Jung explores figures such as Sophia, then proposes that Mary complete God's image by becoming the fourth member of the incomplete Trinity, to add femininity and body to God's masculinity and spirituality (1953–1979, CW 11:122–127).

Jung's challenge, particularly in view of his near-death experience in 1944 (Jung, 1961 MDR: 289ff), is this: "The decisive question for a [person] is: is he [/she] related to something infinite or not?" (1961, MDR: 300). Mere mortals may err by falling into one of two camps: by reifying parochial beliefs [such as patriarchy or our version of God] into metaphysical universals or "archetypes," or, at another extreme, rationalistic scientism's omni-competent claim to be the only valid method of knowledge.

In the late twentieth century, the major overlapping schools of Jungian psychotherapy emerged: the Classical, the Archetypal, and the Developmental (Samuels).

Jung's fertile thought on religion and myth has continued and is being expanded by numerous successors such as Aniela Jaffé (Jung's biography), Marie-Louise von Franz (folktales), Edward Edinger (the ego-Self axis), Victor White (Jung and religion), Sylvia Brinton Perera (the scapegoat, gods and goddesses), Edward Whitmont (symbolic quest), (Jean Bolen (Greek goddesses), John Dourley, Ann Ulanov (Jung and Christianity), James Hillman (many radical revisions), David L. Miller (polytheism), Thomas Moore (soul and re-enchantment), Clarissa Pinkola Estés, (*Women who Run With the Wolves*), and Joseph Campbell (*Hero with a Thousand Faces*). Jung's archetypal theory has made its way into numerous approaches to myth and religion, whether acknowledged or not.

See also: ⊗ Depth Psychology and Spirituality ⊗ Freud, Sigmund ⊗ Hero ⊗ Jung, Carl Gustav ⊗ Monomyth ⊗ Myths and Dreams

Bibliography

Bailey, L. W. (2005). *The enchantments of technology*. Champaign-Urbana, IL: University of Illinois Press.

Bettelheim, B. (1975). *The uses of enchantment: The meaning and importance of fairy tales*. New York: Knopf.

Bolen, J. S. (1984). *Goddesses in everywoman: A new psychology of women*. San Francisco, CA: Harper & Row.

Brown, J. A. C. (1961). *Freud and the Post-Freudians*. Middlesex, England: Penguin.

Campbell, J. (1949). *The hero with a thousand faces*. New York: Pantheon Books.

Casement, A., & Tracey D. (Eds.) (2006). *The idea of the numinous: Contemporary Jungian and psychoanalytical perspectives*. London: Routledge.

Dawood, N. J. (Trans.) (1973). *Tales from the thousand and one nights*. Baltimore, MD: Penguin.

Doty, W. G. (1986). *Mythography: The study of myths and rituals*. Tuscaloosa, AL: University of Alabama Press.

Dourley, J. (1984). *The illness that we are: A Jungian critique of Christianity*. Toronto: Inner City Books.

Edinger, E. (1972). *Ego and archetype; individuation and the religious function of the psyche*. New York: Putnam.

Estés, C. P. (1992). *Women who run with the wolves*. New York: Random House.

Freud, S. (1927/1961). *The Future of an illusion*. Garden City, NY: Doubleday.

Freud, S. (1973). *Abstracts of the standard edition of the complete psychological works of Sigmund Freud* (C. L. Rothgeb, Ed.). New York: International Universities Press.

Freud, S. (1974). *The standard edition of the complete psychological works of Sigmund Freud* (J. Strachey, Trans.) (24 Vols.). London: Hogarth.

Hillman, J. (1975). *re-visioning psychology*. New York: Harper & Row.

Hopke, R. H. (1999). *A guided tour of the collected works of C. G. Jung*. Boston: Shambhala.

Jung, C. G. (1953–1979). *The collected works of C. G. Jung* (W. McGuire, Ed., R. F. C. Hull, Trans.) (20 Vols.). Princeton, NJ: Princeton University Press.

Jung, C. G. (1961). *Memories, dreams, reflections*. (A. Jaffé, Ed.) New York: Random House.

Miller, D. L. (1974). *The new polytheism*. New York: Harper & Row.

Moore, T. (1996). *The re-enchantment of everyday life*. New York: HarperCollins.

Perera, S. B. (1981). *Descent to the Goddess: A way of initiation for women*. Toronto: Inner City Books.

Perera, S. B. (1986). *The scapegoat complex: Toward a mythology of shadow and guilt*. Toronto: Inner City Books.

Perera, S. B. (2004). *The Irish bull God: Image of multiform and integral masculinity*. Toronto: Inner City Books.

Samuels, A. (1975). *Jung and the Post-Jungians*. London: Routledge & Kegan Paul.

Ulanov, A. B. (1999). *Religion and the spiritual in Carl Jung*. New York: Paulist Press.

Von Franz, M.-L. (1970). *An introduction to the interpretation of fairy tales*. Dallas, TX: Spring Publications.

White, V. (1982). *God and the unconscious*. Dallas, TX: Spring Publications.

Whitmont, E. (1978). *The symbolic quest: Basic concepts of analytical psychology*. Princeton, NJ: Princeton University Press.

Myths and Dreams

Lee W. Bailey

The Common Well

Dreams and myths have striking parallels. They are different, of course, in that dreams are personal and raw products of the unconscious. Myths, on the other hand, may have dream backgrounds, but are the product of sometimes elaborate artistic narrative shaping by consciousness. They develop variants and historical associations with collectives, such as religious texts, rituals, literature, or national legends with political purposes, such as the national hero or goddess. But dreams and myths are both rooted in unconscious depths, the well of the soul, and thus have parallels. Carl Jung made the strongest connection between them. Jungian analyst Marie von Franz saw fairy tales as in-between – less influenced by cultural elaboration than myths, thus closer to their unconscious source: "Fairy tales are the purest and simplest expression of collective and unconscious psychic processes" (von Franz 1970: 40). Many later Jungians, such as Andrew Samuels and Jean Shinola Bolen, have emphasized that mythic images are not jut a list of images to be checked off from a mental distance, but are pervasive themes in everyday life. James Hillman emphasizes that soul is also in the world, anthropomorphized and personified, and mythic images can help us descend into these depths. It is blindness to identify completely with images in dreams, fairy tales or myths, but, conversely, over-intellectualizing not to feel them at all. Keeping the dreaminess in myths helps prevent over-systematizing and rationalizing them.

The modern connection between myth and dream was articulated by Sigmund Freud, who saw myths as dreamlike events. He saw them as distorted wish-fulfillments of whole nations rooted in the unconscious. Otto Rank and Karl Abraham said the same. These Freudians saw an infantile element in myths. Abraham said: "The myth is therefore a fragment preserved from the infantile psychic life of the race, and dreams are the myths of the individual" (Abraham, 1913: 36, 72). It is useful to contrast the personal and the mythic amplifications of a dream, but not by labeling them "subjective" and "objective." These labels place the process in the scientific metaphysic that overall strives to deny the meaningfulness of dreams.

Carl Jung also saw the myth-dream connection rooted in the unconscious: "myths are dreamlike structures" (Jung, *CW* V: para. 28). But Jung rejected the Freudian emphasis on wish-fulfillment and the infantile nature of myths. He saw myths as the most mature product of early humanity, and a continuing important expression of civilization's collective unconscious (Jung, *CW* V: 28–29). Jungian analysts methodically use myths to amplify clients' dreams, bringing out unsuspected unconscious meanings. Myths echo individual dreams, both emerging from the collective unconscious. Joseph Campbell put it in a nutshell: "Dream is the personalized myth, myth the depersonalized dream" (1949: 19).

A Prom Night Dream

An example of this correlation, that Jung would call a "big" dream, is a college student's dream reported to me that echoes the mythic text of an ancient goddess.

▸ In 1980 this girl wrote that she dreamed that when she was getting ready for her high school prom dance, she grew curious about her home's basement. She crept down the stairs and came to a door at first hard to open, but she pushed again and it flew open into a dark room. She fell inside and caught her shawl on a nail. Curious, she left behind the shawl and entered another dark room, She saw another door that was also stuck at first, but soon opened easily. She tripped and lost a shoe, which she left behind. She saw a third door, which was already open. She walked through it and removed her second shoe. Everything was dark and dirty. She found a fourth door, at first locked, but when she pushed again, it also opened. Suddenly a gold necklace she was wearing fell down from her neck and she left it, planning to pick it up on her way back. She looked around and found a fifth door, dirty and slimy. She decided to wipe off the doorknob with her dress, then she took off the now dirty dress. She then spied a sixth door in the dark room that was slightly ajar. She passed through it, but caught her panties on a nail, and they ripped and fell off. She was naked, and slowly lifted her head; she was horrified.

▸ She saw heaps of dead and decaying animals, covered with mud and dust. An old decrepit man was sitting atop of a pile. But it could have been a male/female figure. The door slammed shut, and she was trapped, frightened, and naked in this dark, smelly, hellish place. She was stuck there for what seemed forever, though it was actually a few months. She ate the dust and mud just as the old woman/man did.

▸ Back home upstairs, everyone became sick. Her father wondered what had happened to her, and recalled her interest in the basement, so he went down the same stairs and followed her trail of dropped clothing through the six doors. As he entered the last door, he too was horrified, for his daughter had become just as decrepit as the old woman/man, in this hellish place. Her father fought with the androgynous beast as he tried to reach her, and he finally won. He put his arms around her and took her back through the six doors. She collected her clothes and dressed. They slowly mounted the stairs, and as they reached the top, she suddenly became radiant and everything became well.

The Ishtar Myth

Struck by the parallels, I showed this dreamer the text of "Descent of Ishtar to the Nether World" in James Pritchard's classic *The Ancient Near East* (Pritchard, 1958, I: 80–85). She said that she had never heard this story. Indeed it was an obscure scholarly text at the time. She agreed with my suggestion that her dream, which on the surface had nothing to do with her personal experiences, was obviously connected with the ancient religious myth. She gave me permission to publish it. Over twenty years later, I found her online and asked her if she recalled the dream. She did not, but told me that she had become a successful business woman, married, and a mother, but was not interested in exploring much further personal information.

I described the correlation to a noted Jungian analyst, Sylvia Brinton Perera, author of *Descent to the Goddess: A Way of Initiation for Women*, which analyzes in detail the Inanna-Ishtar myth. She replied that the dream-myth parallel frequently appears for Jungian analysts. In analysis, she added, of course much more personal information would also be explored. Also in therapy the ego-consciousness may well need to stand back and make discriminations and judgments about both dreams and myths. Both may have shadowy beasts or seductive lovers, for example, projected onto real-world figures that need to be re-interpreted or disconnected.

Pritchard's text has subsequently been amplified in later scholarship by others, notably Samuel Kramer and

Diane Wolkstein. This literature reveals fascinating connections with the dream. The Akkadian goddess Ishtar is closely related to the Sumerian Inanna, both early cultures that emerged into Babylonia, now Iraq. Pritchard's text, translated from ancient clay tablets, can be summarized:

▶ Ishtar, queen of life, set her mind to go down to the dark underworld abode of Irkalla, the realm of her sister Ereshkigal, queen of the dead. Hers is the dreadful dark realm from which no one returns, "Where dust is their fare and clay their food ... (And where) over door and bolt is spread dust" (lines 8–11). When Ishtar reached the front gate of the Land of no Return, she imperiously demanded that the gatekeeper open the gate, threatening to smash the gate and raise the dead. The humble gatekeeper ran off to his queen announcing Ishtar's arrival. Ereshkigal angrily, cruelly replied, "What drove her heart to me? ... Should I bemoan the maidens who were wrenched from the laps of their lovers? Or should I bemoan the tender little one who was sent off before his time? Go, gatekeeper, open the gate for her, Treat her in accordance with the ancient rules" (lines 31–38).

▶ The gatekeeper welcomed her to enter, but at each of seven gates, he stripped away one of her royal garments: her great crown, her earrings, her necklaces, her breast ornaments, her birthstone belt, her wrist and ankle ornaments, and finally her dress. At each gate she ritually asked: "Why, O gatekeeper, didst thou take the great crown on my head?" To which the gatekeeper replied: "Enter, my lady, thus are the rules of the Mistress of the Nether World" (lines 42–66).

▶ The goddesses of life finally stood before the goddess of death and angrily flew at her. But Ereshkigal responded by giving orders to release the forces of death against her: "Go, Namtar, lock [her] up [in] my [palace]! Release against her, [against] Ishtar, the sixty mis[eries]" (lines 64–69). When this happened, the energies of reproduction in the world above ceased: "The bull springs not upon the cow, [the ass impregnates not the jenny], In the street [the man impregnates not] the maiden" (lines 71–81). Then the advisor to the great god Ea goes to him and bemoans the lack of the life-force on earth, repeating ritually the above impregnation chorus. Ea responded by sending a eunuch to journey to the underworld, who somehow manipulated Ereshkigal into sprinkling the water of life on Ishtar. The queen then returns above, passing through the same seven gates, and at each one her discarded royal clothes and ornaments are ritually returned to her by the gatekeeper for her to wear.

▶ The text ends with obscure hints. Ereshkigal apparently says: "If she does not give thee the ransom price, bring her back" (line 51), and ..."On the day when Tammuz (lover of Ishtar) comes up to me, When with him the lapis flute (and) the carnelian ring up to me, When with him the wailing men and the wailing women come up to me, May the read rise and smell the incense" (lines 61–66) (Pritchard, 1958: 80–85).

While the Sumerian and Babylonian versions are very similar, there are important differences between them. In one version, Inanna is hanged on a hook on the wall, like a piece of meat (Wolkstein and Kramer, 60). But these differences have little effect the thematic similarities with the contemporary dream, which sounds more like the Babylonian Ishtar's myth.

The more recent work of Kramer and Wolkstein, collecting and assembling tablet fragments, has added new versions and details to the myth. Inanna's text comes from the older Sumerian culture, dating as far back as about 4000 BCE. The Sumerians apparently invented cuneiform writing and built the first ziggurats. The majority of the fragments of Inanna's ancient Sumerian tale were first unearthed in the ruins of the city of Nippur, Sumer's spiritual and cultural center, by a University of Pennsylvania archaeological dig in 1889 and 1890. The Babylonians began invading Mesopotamia with their Semitic language about 2000 BCE, and absorbed much of the earlier Sumerian and Akkadian language and mythology. So the later Babylonian Ishtar's story is not surprisingly similar to the earlier Sumerian Inanna's. For example, On Inanna's way back to the earthly realm, the Annuna, the judges of the underworld, seized her. They said: "No one ascends from the underworld so unmarked. If Inanna wishes to return from the underworld, she must provide someone in her place." They sent merciless demons above that passed by those on earth who humbled themselves, but they took Dumuzi, Inanna's husband, who had too proudly usurped the throne. He escaped the demons for a while by turning into a serpent or a gazelle, but ended up in the underworld of the dead (Wolkstein and Kramer, 1983: 52–73).

The layers of symbolism are many, as Perera shows, but the themes, some in remarkable detail, paralleled in, the modern girl's dream, are evident: A woman descends to a dark, unconscious underworld, where "over door and bolt is spread dust." She passes through six or seven doors, and at each door an item of clothing or jewelry is removed, until she stands, naked as she was born, before a scene of death and a powerful ruling figure. She is held captive among the dead, "Where dust is their fare and clay their food." While she is captive in the land of the dead, life is interrupted above. She is finally rescued by a person from above who wrestles with the master of the dead and succeeds in leading her out of that hell. As they return through each doorway, she regains her clothing. The myth has far more collective and religious themes – the queens of life and death, love and grief, the royal clothing and ornaments, the rescuer sent by a god, the obscure ending hinting at the need for a ransom for her return, and a general resurrection.

The dream is more personal and modern, centered on a teen-aged girl, on the eve of her ritual prom dance, signifying passage into adulthood, encountering the dark mysteries of the collective unconscious, nakedness and fertility, where passionate love helps overcome horrifying death, and comforting family – her rescue by her personal father. Freud would stress the Oedipal father-daughter erotic overtones, and Jung the archetypal collective life-death struggle, androgyny, and initiation. The myth is more collective, ritualized, and religious, with feminine images of life and death and their struggle. The seven gates image may be rooted in the seven stars visible to the unaided eye, seen as gates of a cosmic journey through the ancient cosmological image of seven heavenly spheres below the disc-like earth. The theme of a ransom echoes later in the theology of Jesus as an atoning sacrifice demanded by a god, and the resurrection expresses the general return from the dead in Western traditions of dying and rising gods. These parallel images arise in both this contemporary personal dream and the 4,000-year old ritualized, religious myth, indicating the ancient dream-myth connection and the modern mind's astonishing well of archaic images, bursting up with sparkling, age-old, deep, mysteriously meaningful images, as fearful as death, as beautiful as love.

See also: ❂ Depth Psychology and Spirituality ❂ Dying and Rising Gods ❂ Freud, Sigmund ❂ Jung, Carl Gustav ❂ Myth

Bibliography

Abraham, K. (1913). *Dreams and myths.* New York: Journal of Nervous and Mental Diseases Publishing Co.

Bolen, J. S. (1984). *Goddesses in everywoman.* San Francisco, CA: Harper & Row.

Campbell, J. (1949). *The hero with a thousand faces.* New York: World/Meridian.

Freud, S. (1974). *The standard edition of the compleate psychological works of Sigmund Freud* (J. Strachey, Trans.) (24 Vols.). London: The Hogarth Press.

Hillman, J. (1979). *The dream and the underworld.* New York: Harper & Row.

Jung, C. G. (1953–1979). *The collected works of C. G. Jung* (W. McGuire, Ed., R. F. C. Hull, Trans.). (20 Vols.). Princeton, NJ: Princeton University Press.

Perera, S. B. (1981). *Descent to the Goddess: A way of initiation for women.* Toronto: Inner City.

Pritchard, J. B. (Ed.). (1958). *The ancient near East* (Vol. 1). Princeton, NJ: Princeton University Press.

Rank, O. (1914). *The myth of the birth of the hero.* New York.

Samuels, A. (1985). *Jung and the Post-Jungians.* London: Routledge & KeganPaul.

Von Franz, M.-L. (1970). *An introduction to the interpretation of fairy tales.* Dalls, TX: Spring Publications.

Wolkstein, D., & Kramer, S. N. (1983). *Inanna: Queen of Heaven and Earth, her stories and hymns from sumer.* New York: Harper & Row.

M

N

Narcissism

Ann Gleig

Narcissism played a key role in the development of psychoanalysis and has been pivotal to contemporary revisionings of psychoanalytic theory and technique. Freud discussed narcissism in a number of texts including *Leonardo da Vinci and a memory of his childhood* (1910/1975), *On Narcissism: An Introduction* (1914/1975b), *Three Essays on Sexuality* (1915/1975a) and *The Ego and the Id* (1923/1960) yet his writings are inconsistent and have been subject to different interpretations. There are disputes on the exact relationship between primary narcissism and autoeroticism; on whether the state of primary narcissism is free of object relations or contains primitive object relations; and on whether primary narcissism is experienced as a prenatal state, by the infant at the breast, or both.

In his first systematic discussion of narcissism, Freud (1905/1975a) distinguishes between primary narcissism and secondary or pathological narcissism. Defining primary narcissism as "the libidinal complement to the egoism of the instinct of self-preservation," (1915: 73–74) Freud states it is a normal developmental state during which the infant takes its own ego as a libidinal object, thereby experiencing the self as perfect and omnipotent. During this stage the infant does not differentiate between self and object but with the emerging experience of, and attachment to, the primary caretaker, usually the mother, libido is transformed and redirected from the pleasurable and self-sufficient narcissistic stage to the need-satisfying object. Freud called this outward directed libido "object libido," and claimed that there was an inverse relationship between object libido and inwardly invested "ego libido."

The departure from primary narcissism leaves the individual with a desire to recover narcissistic perfection. One way this is recovered is through the cathexis of an ideal ego – an idealized projected image of the self formed from the internalized demands and restrictions of authoritative figures (a concept which later develops into the superego)– which replaces the actual ego as the object of primary narcissism. Other attempts at recovery include a narcissistic object choice in which the object resembles the subject's idealized self-image as opposed to the anaclitic object choice in which the object resembles the primary caretaker.

Like object libido, narcissistic libido can suffer from fixation and become pathological. Freud observed that in a variety of traumatic situations – including organic diseases such as schizophrenia-object libido is withdrawn from objects and reinvested in the ego. This renewal of libidinal investment in the ego is "secondary or pathological narcissism," a regressive state experienced as a grandiosity and omnipotence of the self.

The concept of secondary narcissism has been utilized to interpret a range of religious phenomena including animism, magic, psychologized spirituality, and mysticism. In *Totem and Taboo,* (1913/1950), Freud discusses narcissism in relation to omnipotence, claiming that primitives who believed that external events occurred because of the magical power of their own thought processes were suffering from pathological narcissism. More influentially, in *Civilization and its Discontents,* (1930/1975), Freud explained the "oceanic feeling" of unity experienced in mysticism as the preservation of and return to the stage of primary narcissism in which boundaries between self and other are undifferentiated. This established the classic reductive psychoanalytic view of mysticism as narcissistic, regressive and pathological as illustrated by early studies such as Morel's *Essai Sur l' Introversion Mystique* (1918) and Theodore Schroeder's *Prenatal Psychisms and Mystical Pantheism* (1922) and the more recent work of Jeffrey Masson (1974, 1980).

The use of narcissism to explain certain types of religion is also found in the work of the Norwegian brothers Harald and Kristian Schjelderup (1932). On the basis of both contemporary and historical evidence, they identify three main types of religious experience: father religion, mother religion and self-religion each of which corresponds to a different stage of childhood development. Self-religion, such as Zen Buddhism and yoga, is marked by a quest for and fantasies of self-deification which is a

D. A. Leeming, K. Madden, S. Marlan (eds.), *Encyclopedia of Psychology and Religion*, DOI 10.1007/978-0-387-71802-6,

result of narcissistic withdrawal of libido from external objects and a regression to infantile self-grandiosity.

The Schjelderup's analysis anticipates psychoanalytic readings of contemporary forms of self-spirituality, such as the New Age and the human potential movement, which have also been interpreted as narcissistic. M. D. Faber (1996) argues that New Age thinking is a regression to primary narcissism in which the adult is returned to an infantile state of omnipotence, magical wish fulfillment and merger with the mother. While Christopher Lasch's influential *The Culture of Narcissism* (1979) explains the rise of the new psychospiritual therapies and their quest for self-realization as being both a product and perpetuation of a narcissistic personality structure that because of recent socio-cultural changes has become the predominant psychopathology of contemporary life. To counter this narcissism, Lasch suggests a return to and renewal of Christian commitment and ethics. However this assumes Christianity is immune from narcissism, an assumption undermined by Paul Pruyser's (1978) targeting of the narcissistic strands within evangelical Christianity. He claims the evangelic practices of witnessing and testifying are often beset by "reflective narcissism" the need to have one's own self-love mirrored back in the affirmation and admiration of others. However, unlike self-spirituality, Pruyser argues that Christianity contains abundant resources to counter such narcissistic trends. For example, the story of Paradise in the book of Genesis rejects the desire to become omnipotent and omniscient like God – which Pruyser interprets as a mythic expression of primary narcissism-as the root of original sin.

Interpretations of religious phenomena, therefore, that utilize Freud's understanding of narcissism are unremittingly negative; focusing on its regressive, defensive and grandiose nature. However, Heinz Kohut's (1971, 1977) highly influential psychoanalytic revisioning of narcissism has opened up a much more positive dialog between narcissism and religion. Kohut believed that the pejorative classical Freudian evaluation of narcissism which cast it in an inverse relationship to object love reflected an intrusion of western altruistic cultural values into psychoanalysis. While accepting Freud's stage of primary narcissism, Kohut claimed that narcissism followed its own developmental line in which the two primary archaic configurations of narcissism-the grandiose self and the idealized parent imago-had the potential to transform respectively into a cohesive sense of self with healthy self-esteem and a set of mature goals, values and ideals. Crucial to this transformation was the ability of the primary caretakers to act as selfobjects. Kohut coined the term selfobject to describe how an infant's earliest experience of the other is

not as a separate object but as part of oneself. Parents are the earliest selfobjects and they perform crucial psychological functions which the child's own psychic structure will later transmute into internal structures. However, if caretakers fail to respond empathetically to the child's experience, or if the child is subject to premature or traumatic separation, the integration of archaic narcissism is disturbed and the repressed strands emerge unresolved in later life; in a clinical condition designated as the narcissistic personality disorder. This is characterized by states of emptiness and despair, feelings of unreality, excessive self-consciousness, oscillation between experiences of inferiority and grandiosity, an intense desire to merge with an idealized other, uncontrollable rage and an absence of empathy.

Unlike Freud, however, Kohut believed that narcissistic disturbances could be rectified through the establishment of empathetic communication in the analytic relationship which enabled the working through of traumatic failures of early selfobjects and a more conscious negotiation of legitimate narcissistic needs. Kohut claimed that a mature ego had the capacity to tame and employ narcissistic cathexes for its highest developmental aims, namely; creativity, empathy, contemplation of ones own impermanence, a sense of humor and wisdom.

Moreover, Kohut saw mysticism as engaging the developmental line of narcissism and affecting a transformation of the narcissistic elements of one's personality into the higher religio-ethical goal of what he termed, "cosmic narcissism." This is the transformation of narcissism into a type of mature, state-like mysticism in which the subject participates in a supraindividual and timeless existence. Although rooted in the mother-child symbiosis, this differs from the transient oceanic feeling of unitive mysticism which Kohut reads as the preservation of the early mother-child unity. Neither transient nor unitive, cosmic narcissism is an ethical and existential developmental achievement of an autonomous ego. Kohut hoped that the transformation of narcissism into cosmic narcissism would signal the emergence of a new unchurched tradition of mystical rationality which would replace traditional religions and rejuvenate the west (Parsons, 1999).

Following Kohut, Peter Homans (1979) has claimed that unchurched psychologized religiosity, such as that of Carl Jung, displays an authentic engagement with narcissism. Homans argues that due to secularization traditional religion lost its ability to organize personal and social life and this has resulted in the emergence of a diffuse and heightened form of self-consciousness in which legitimate narcissistic needs are now satisfied primarily in the context of personal and psychological experience. Hence, while psychologized spirituality, with its themes of unity, wholeness, self-actualization and individuation, is indeed reflective of the contemporary emergence of narcissistic disorders it is also an authentic attempt to maturely heal and transform them.

The German theologian Hans-Gunter Heimbrock (1977) has applied Kohut's revisioning of narcissism to Christianity, claiming that the biblical image of God has advanced along the very lines laid down by Kohut's analysis of transformed narcissism. Heimbrock reads the omnipotent and moralistic God of the Hebrew Bible as an example of archaic narcissism and self-grandiosity. However, through Jesus' crucifixion and suffering, the New Testament God renounces self-grandiosity and frees the individual from the need to shore up the weak self through an omnipotent self-ideal. The suffering of God enables a person to empathize with the suffering of others and to accept one's own finitude both of which represent a mature and creative transformation of narcissism.

Other writers have drawn on Kohut's concept of the selfobject to interpret and legitimate religious phenomena. Robert Fuller (1989) claims that New Age healers act as mature selfobject for clients and analyst Sudhir Kakar (1991) has argued that the Indian guru is the primary cultural selfobject experience for adults in Hindu tradition and society. Such work demonstrates that narcissism in both classical and contemporary psychoanalytic theoretical formations continues to play an important role in the psychological interpretation of and dialog with religion.

See also: ❂ Freud, Sigmund ❂ Jung, Carl Gustav ❂ Psychoanalysis

Bibliography

Faber, M. D. (1996). *New age thinking*. Ottawa, ON: The University of Ottawa Press.
Fonagy, P., Person, E., & Sandler, J. (1991). *Freud's on Narcissism: An introduction*. Yale University Press.
Freud, S. (1910/1975). Leonardo da Vinci and a memory of his childhood. In *The standard edition of the complete psychological works of Sigmund Freud* (Vol. 11) (J. Strachey, Trans.). London: Hogarth Press.
Freud, S. (1913/1950). *Totem and taboo, SE*. New York: W.W. Norton & Company.
Freud, S. (1915/1975a). Three essays on sexuality. In *The standard edition of the complete psychological works of Sigmund Freud* (Vol. 14) (J. Strachey, Trans.). London: Hogarth Press.
Freud, S. (1914/1975b). On Narcissism, An introduction. In *The standard edition of the complete psychological works of Sigmund Freud* (Vol. 14) (J. Strachey, Trans.). London: Hogarth Press.
Freud, S. (1923/1960). The Ego and the Id. In *The standard edition of the complete psychological works of Sigmund Freud* (J. Strachey, Trans.). New York: W.W. Norton.
Freud, S. (1930/1975). Civilization and its discontents. In *The standard edition of the complete psychological works of Sigmund Freud* (Vol. 21) (J. Strachey, Trans.). London: Hogarth Press.
Fuller, R. C. (1989). *Alternative medicine and American religious life*. New York: Oxford University Press.
Heimbrock, H.-G. (1977). *Phantasie und Christlicher Glaube: Zum Dialog Zwischen Theologie und Psychoanalyse*. Kaiser: Grunewald.
Homans, P. (1979). *Jung in context*. Chicago, IL: University of Chicago Press.
Kakar, S. (1991). *The mystic and the analyst*. Chicago, IL: University of Chicago Press.
Kohut, H. (1966). Forms and transformations of Narcissism. *Journal of the American Psychoanalytic Association, 14*, 243–272.
Kohut, H. (1971). *Analysis of the self*. New York: International University Press.
Kohut, H. (1977). *The restoration of the self*. New York: International University Press.
Lasch, C. (1979). *The culture of Narcissism*. New York: W.W. Norton.
Masson, J. (1974). Sex and yoga: Psychoanalysis and the Indian religious experience. *Journal of Indian Philosophy, 2*, 307–320.
Masson, J. (1980). *The oceanic feeling: The origin of the religious sentiment in ancient India*. Dordrecht, the Netherlands: D. Reidel.
Morel, F. I. (1918). *Essai Sur l'Introversion Mystique*. Geneva: Kundig.
Parsons, W. B. (1999). *The enigma of the oceanic feeling*. New York: Oxford University Press.
Pruyser, P. (1978). Narcissism in contemporary religion. *Journal of Pastoral Care, 32*, 219–231.
Schjelderup, H., & Schjelderup, K. (1932). *Über drei Haupttypen der Religiösen Erlebnisformen und ihre psychologische Grundlage*. Berlin: De Gruyter.
Schroeder, T. (1922). Prenatal psychisms and mystical pantheism. *International Journal of Psychoanalysis, 3*, 445–466.
Wulff, D. M. (1997). *Psychology of religion: Classic & contemporary* (2nd ed.). Hoboken, NY: Wiley.

Narrative Therapy

Thomas St. James O'Connor

Introduction and Assumptions

Narrative therapy is more of an approach than a defined theory (O'Connor, Meakes, Pickering, and Schuman, 1997). This approach works from the premise that each person's life is a series of stories on many levels similar to a novel with many chapters. Stories are used to make meaning of a situation and to make sense of one's life. Some of these stories and chapters are given to the person by family, context, culture, religion, gender, etc. One of the key aspects of narrative is to re-author one's own story so that one is not living a story that does not fit with one's identity. In narrative therapy, a person and/or family seek therapy when there is a problem that cannot be fixed. In fact, there is a story around a problem that oppresses the family. This story about the problem also fits into the larger stories about oneself.

In terms of its philosophical underpinnings, narrative therapy is a post modern approach (White and Epston, 1990; White, 2007). Stories are socially constructed and are not objective truth. They are interpretations of experience and narrative is a hermeneutical project. This hermeneutical understanding challenges the notion of objective truth and diagnosis based on norms. In this post modern view, the categories of the DSM IV are viewed as social constructions and not as objective truth.

The most prominent writer in narrative therapy is Michael White, an Australian therapist who with David Epston wrote *Narrative Means to Therapeutic Ends* in 1990. Other names associated with narrative are K. Thomm (1989), J. Freedman and G. Combs (1996) and H. Andersen and H. Goolishian (1988). In the field of theology and spirituality, Charles Gerkin (1982) and Thomas St. James O'Connor (1998, 1999; Bloos & O'Connor, 2002) have also made contributions using a narrative perspective in theology and spirituality. Since the early 1990s Michael White's work has grown in popularity in the field of family therapy.

Michael White and Key Ideas

In examining the work of Michael White a number of points stand out. White uses the philosophy of Michel Foucault and the anthropology of Jerome Bruner and Gregory Bateson in developing his view of narrative therapy (White and Epston, 1990; White, 2007). Drawing on Foucault, White believes that knowledge is power and within society there are dominant narratives that privilege certain groups and oppress others. The notion of the dominant narrative is a key idea. In therapy, there is a problem that has developed an oppressive narrative and dominates the thinking of the individual and family. In the midst of this narrative there is an alternative narrative that has moments when the family and/or individual have overcome the problem. These are called unique outcomes. However, the power of the dominant narrative of the problem is so strong that it often robs the person of memory of the alternative narrative. The work of narrative therapy is to facilitate the client in uncovering these unique outcomes and developing them into an alternative narrative.

Another key idea is separating the problem from the person. White believes that the person is not the problem; the problem is the problem. Narrative therapy externalizes the problem and takes it out of the person and moves it into the external world. This is done through the use of language. Narrative therapy uses active verbs and not being verbs. Instead of saying the client is depressed, the narrative therapist might say that 'depression pushes against John or oppresses John at times or jumps all over Mary or kidnaps Mary.' This externalization of the problem, i.e., putting the problem on the outside separates the person from the problem and moves it from the intrapsychic to the interpersonal. This separation of the problem from the person using active verbs is known as an externalizing conversation. The narrative therapist also seeks to map the influence of the problem on the individual and family. When did depression start pushing against John?

Another key idea is widening the audience for change. White (2007) also describes this as developing witnesses. Narrative therapy seeks to include other people in helping the person re-story the problem. These witnesses often include a team observing the session with the client behind a one-way mirror. This group is called the reflecting team. Reflecting teams offer reflections to the clients on the problem as well as commenting on family members and friends or anyone significantly involved in the story of the problem. This audience is meant to be supportive and to work with the client in reducing the problem. The audience for change or witnesses emphasizes team work which is very important to help make the change. Narrative therapy seeks to develop a team of people (audience or witness) who work together against the problem and not against the client. The client is a main person on the team.

Another aspect of narrative therapy that stands out is the facilitation of personal agency. Some of the research clearly indicates that narrative therapy is very helpful in reducing the presenting problem. Personal agency is facilitated by the therapist working with the client(s) in developing an understanding of the problem and its effects on the persons involved, drawing on key metaphors of the problem that can be developed into an externalizing conversation and searching for unique outcomes to the problem that are developed into an alternative narrative. Crucial to facilitating personal agency is the involvement of the client. The therapist does not work out of an expert position with special knowledge but rather views the client as the expert on the experience of the problem with a belief that the client already has resources to help with the problem. Here, the therapist works from a position of not knowing and curiosity and follows the maps of the client.

Narrative therapy as constructed by White and Epston (1990) also uses letters and certificates. These are sent or given to clients. The letters most often underline the client's strengths and pose some wonderings about possible directions and are sent by the therapist after a session or sessions. Similar to solution focused therapy, narrative therapy emphasizes the strengths of the client especially in dealing with challenging problems. It uses scaling questions that put the problem or its effects on a scale of 1–10. The scale is meant to gauge the progress of clients in dealing with their problems. Certificates are used to celebrate the growth of clients. For example, a child who has progressed in terms of management of angry outbursts could be given a certificate celebrating that he/she is now a "temper buster."

Research on Narrative

The research on narrative therapy is at the beginning. Published research involves qualitative and case studies. O'Connor, et al. (1997) found that in a qualitative study of 8 clients that narrative therapy significantly reduced the presenting problem. Smith, et al. (1992) and Sells, et al. (1994) using qualitative research found reflecting teams used in narrative therapy for the most part to be effective. Coulehan, Freilander and Heatherington (1998) used grounded theory in interviewing 8 clients of Carlos Sluzki who is a narrative therapist about how they changed their views of the problem construction. Results were mixed. Four clients thought that they could see the problem in a more helpful way and four did not. O'Connor, et al. (2004) examined therapists' experiences of using narrative therapy utilizing an ethnographic research design. This research indicated that therapists found narrative therapy helpful in reducing the presenting problem and also reported some limitations of narrative therapy. There have been a few qualitative studies of children and narrative therapy (Focht and Beardslee, 1996; Larner, 1996; Weston, Boxer and Heatherington, 1998). All of these qualitative studies found narrative therapy helpful to children. In the area of teaching, Morrison, et al. (1997) found in a qualitative study that students reported positive learning in narrative therapy.

Case studies on narrative include Kogan and Gale (1997) who did a study of a videotape of Michael White with a client. They examined how White managed talk in the session and used the metaphor of "de-centring." Kahle and Robbins describe a case study of a family where success over the problem is externalized. Michael White has provided numerous case studies outlining the effectiveness of narrative therapy with a wide range of clients.

Little has been written on spirituality and narrative therapy. However, narrative therapy has many commonalities with Judeo-Christian spiritualities. O'Connor (1999) notes the similarities and differences between Dante's *Purgatio* and narrative therapy. O'Connor argues that Dante's notion of the cure of souls that takes place through climbing mount Purgatory has many similarities in narrative therapy. In particular, the externalizing conversation, the separation of the problem from the person and the development of personal agency based on strengths is similar to sin as object and the work of grace. Bloos and O'Connor (2002) also examine the use of the labyrinth as a spiritual experience that has similarities to the experience of narrative therapy.

Charles Gerkin (1982) describes a narrative hermeneutical theory of practical theology. Gerkin's understanding of narrative has many similarities to White's notions as well as difference. For Gerkin, theology is described in many narratives. Working from a Christian standpoint, Gerkin believes that the Christian narrative of creation, sin, redemption is what gives Christians a sense of identity and is the lens through which one interprets and makes meaning of experience. Gerkin believes in this meta-narrative and argues that identity is rooted in the meta-narratives. Certainly, there are many narratives in one's life. Like White, Gerkin believes that there are a multitude of chapters in our stories. Gerkin's narrative hermeneutical theory of practical theology can be divided into four elements (O'Connor, 1998): (1) rooted in the Christian heritage; (2) uses a multi-disciplinary approach; (3) based in practical theology and the practices of ministry; (4) and uses the hermeneutical and narrative theory of Paul Ricoeur and Hans-Georg Gadamer.

See also: ❯ Psychotherapy and Religion

Bibliography

Andersen, H., & Goolishian, H. (1988). Human systems as linguistic systems: Preliminary and evolving ideas about implications for clinical practice. *Family Process, 27*, 371–393.

Bloos, I., & O'Connor, T. (2002). The ancient and medieval labyrinth and narrative therapy: How do they fit? *Pastoral Psychology, 50*(4), 219–230.

Coulehan, R., Freilander, M., & Heatherington, L. (1998). Transforming narratives: A change event in constructivist family therapy. *Family Process, 37*, 17–33.

Focht, L., & Beardslee, W. R. (1996). Speech after long silence: The use of narrative therapy in a preventative intervention for children of parents with affective disorder. *Family Process, 35*, 407–422.

Freedman, J., & Combs, G. (1996). *Narrative therapy: The social construction of preferred identities.* New York: W.W. Norton.

Gerkin, C. (1982). *The living human document: Revisioning pastoral counseling in a narrative hermeneutical mode.* Nashville, TN: Abingdon.

Kahle, P. A., & Robbins, J. M. (1998). Reauthoring therapeutic success: Externalizing the success and unpacking marginalized narratives of competence. *Journal of Systemic Therapies, 17*, 58–69.

Kogan, S. M., & Gale, J. E. (1997). Decentering therapy: Textual analysis of a narrative therapy session. *Family Process, 36*, 101–126.

Larner, G. (1996). Narrative child family therapy. *Family Process, 35*, 423–440.

Morrison, N. C., Hunt, T., Natoli, D., & DiTiberio, T. (1997). Narrative of change: Teaching from a social constructionism perspective. *Journal of Systemic Therapies, 16*, 83–92.

O'Connor, T. (1998). *Clinical pastoral supervision and the theology of Charles Gerkin.* Waterloo, ON: WLU Press.

O'Connor, T. (1999). Climbing Mt. Purgatory: Dante's cure of souls and narrative family therapy. *Pastoral Psychology, 47*(6), 445–457.

O'Connor, T., Davis, A., Meakes, E., Pickering, R., & Schuman, M. (2004). Narrative therapy using a reflecting team: An ethnographic study of therapists experiences. *Contemporary Family Therapy, 19*(4), 23–40.

O'Connor, T., Meakes, E., Pickering, R., & Schuman, M. (1997). On the right track: Clients' experience of narrative therapy. *Contemporary Family Therapy, 19*(4), 479–496.

Sells, S. P., Smith, T., Coe, M. J., Yoshioka, M., & Robbins, M. (1994). An ethnography of couple and therapists experiences of reflecting teams. *Journal of Marriage and Family Therapy, 20*, 247–266.

Smith, T., Winston, M., & Yoshioka, M. (1992). A qualitative understanding of reflecting teams II: Therapists perspectives. *Contemporary Family Therapy, 14*, 419–432.

Thomm, K. (1989). Externalizing the problem and internalizing personal agency. *Journal of Marital and Family Therapy, 8*, 54–59.

Weston, H. E., Boxer, P., & Heatherington, L. (1998). Children's attributions about family arguments: Implications for family therapy. *Family Process, 37*, 35–49.

White, M. (2007). *Maps of narrative practice.* New York: W.W. Norton.

White, M., & Epston, D. (1990). *Narrative means to therapeutic ends.* New York: W.W. Norton.

Native American Messianism

Meredith Lisagor

The envisioning of a radical change in world order through the leadership of a divinely-informed prophet or actual messiah is a response to similar spiritual and psychosocial stressors wherever it is found – across cultures, and from primal to post-industrialized societies. The empirical needs that occasion a collective readiness to receive divine intervention usually relate to the intensity of exploitation a society perceives itself to have suffered from a hegemonic alien culture. And the anticipation of a messianic figure is most usually phenomenal of a general movement to revitalize the oppressed society, which may seek to restore its integrity and sense of autonomy by: comprehensively rejecting the alien culture, while reviving or recalibrating traditional institutions, practices and values; or incorporating elements of the oppressive alien culture into a new foundational vision.

The literature, ethnographic and anthropological, points to revitalization impulses in the way of apocalyptic expectations at work in many quarters of the Americas well before encounters with white culture. And of prophet-led movements among indigenous Americans, it has been suggested that nascent messianic impulses in the visionary programs of communities already in crisis may have been ripe for taking a decisive shape and energy from first contact with Christian Europeans, while owing nothing to Christian theology.

Because of the rapid growth and domination of Christian European culture in the Americas after the late fifteenth century, there has, indeed, been debate about the likelihood of messianism in some Northern Native American enclaves being unique and organic. However, cases of messianic movements in Central and South America that clearly pre-date native first contact with Christianity (e.g., Tupinamba migrations of Brazil searching for the "Land of Immortality and Perpetual Rest") support arguments in favor of Northern American instances independent of European influences. Of religious and psychological importance is that even where elements of Christianity are identified in an otherwise nativistic movement, selective recourse to the person of a messiah by primal Americans (to someone who straddles the gap between time and eternity, who corrects severe psychosocial imbalance in the subjective field of history) supports the universality of a human capacity to envision engagement with transcendent reality and its association to a concept of absolute justice.

Messiahs and messianic solutions to oppression can be seen as a natural outgrowth of the prophetic and shamanic domains of tribal structure. Even where the prophet who launched a given movement is not ascribed personal divinity, there seems to be a template for the process by which he arrived at his charismatic influence and the strategy that promised to liberate his people: He received a vision of high detail about why misfortune had befallen his people and what they must do to restore social equilibrium. Often the prophet or shaman was beset by a near-death illness (likely, a somatization of the collective plight) before this presentment, and emerged physically and spiritually revitalized himself. He began to evangelize, and followers experienced an ecstatic charge from him similar to his own from the supernatural sponsor of his vision. The message of salvation was similar from visionary to visionary, frequently demanding the end of inter- and intra-tribal strife, exogamy, any sort of dishonesty, and the drinking of alcohol, (which had quickly become a scourge to indigenous Americans). It alternately encouraged co-existence with enemies, ensured their surrender, or guarantied apocalyptic destruction of them; sometimes it promised a welcome return of the dead.

More usual in South America was the prophet's announcement that he was a divine hero or god (often the creator or law-giver, as with the Latin American prophets called *pagé*), who had returned to bestow eternal life on the faithful. Generally, South American movements sought an earthly paradise and the patently supernatural benefit of eternal youth, like the Tupis' ongoing pursuits of the alternatively-called "Land without Evil." And while a more religio-political movement, like that of the early nineteenth century Incan Tupac Amuru, looked forward to a cosmic cataclysm from which a new world order could spring, native millenarianism of Paraguay and Brazil outside the context of messianism could be merely terrifying: In contemporary literature about the Brazilian Nãndeva-Guanari, where this kind of mythology conflated with Christian teachings about the Day of Judgment, a fear of returning dead bent on vengeance has been associated with collective depression and suicidality into the twentieth century.

In both Americas, movements that sought to reinstate, reinforce or perpetuate native culture tended to arise during earlier stages of European impingement and were marked by revolutionary aggression. Those that could tolerate syncretism of European tradition and indigenous beliefs developed later, and/or where social cohesion had become profoundly eroded.

The former type of movement is exemplified by the holy wars of the Pueblo Indians at Taos Mexico in 1680 under the leadership of the messianic Popé, which exterminated hundreds of Spanish settlers, and of the Delaware Indians under a nameless prophet from Michigan, whose 1762 movement aimed to do away with every European influence on tribal culture in the Great Lakes area – and doomed its success by restricting its weapons to bows and arrows against colonial fire power.

An exemplar of syncretistic movements is that of Handsome Lake, a Seneca, whose visions occurred after the American Revolution, a time of deep internal discord, economic collapse, and moral indifference for the Iroquois confederacy as a whole. Although he made no claim to divinity, his visions began after an illness from which he was thought to have died and returned. They instructed him in a new religion of the "Good Message" that borrowed from Quakerism to renovate native

religion, retaining what had well-served social and spiritual stability, eliminating contaminants like alcohol, abortion, and witchcraft. It emphasized marriage, adoption of orphans, and care for the aged. It also crafted a social model for the disenfranchised trader-hunter-warrior who would otherwise have been emasculated by cultivation of the land, which was now a necessity.

Still, syncretism could signal intractable defiance to white culture, as with the "Dreamers" cult of Northwestern America, ca. 1870. Its founder Catholic-educated Smohalla was believed to have died and been resurrected. In his trances or "dreams," the Great Spirit censured his people for apostasy from native ways. Smohalla instituted religion with Roman Catholic trappings, but doctrine that held whites to be inferior creations and Indians alone to have rights to the land – cultivation of which, as ordered by the whites, was violation of Mother Earth from whose bosom the Indian dead would one day rise. The "Dreamers" cult would be the basis of two armed insurrections near the end of the century.

By far the best-known Native American messianic movements are the Ghost Dances of 1870 and 1890. They arose in a family of movements that employed lengthy, repetitive, communal dance to effect the prophetic vision – which varied with different tribes' adoption, but held close to the original script everywhere on the restoration of lands and game to the Indians and, most importantly, on the return to life of their dead. During a period of rapid depopulation, Wodziwob the Paviotso prophet of the 1870 Ghost Dance foresaw the return of the ancestors via train with concomitant destruction of the whites – in which, however, the tools of their culture would be left behind for Indian use. Though variations anticipated rapprochement with whites, when neither had occurred, and social and political traumata continued, the movement died out.

In 1890, the prophet Wovoka claimed to be the messiah awaited by the Mormons (some of whom had joined the original Ghost cult). This time the movement spread widely with magical details, such as belief in an immunity to the white man's bullets, that would have disastrous consequences for 350 Sioux prisoners at Wounded Knee, South Dakota. It was not long before the movement died again. The Kiowa of the Southwest would revive the Ghost Dance in 1894 and sustain its practice until 1916; but resurrection failing to occur, the focus of the dance became the trance state achieved by participants and the opportunity thence to communicate immediately with ancestors.

Ascending gradually (even before the advent of the Ghost Dance) as a psycho-spiritual tool in the Native American struggle to resist assimilation was the ritual ingestion of the vision-producing *peyote*. While the Peyote Cult may not always be classed with messianism, as a medium of personal emancipation in the collective setting of what has become the Native American Church, the drug by all reports is salvational. As dancing was used in the cults of the latter nineteenth century and early twentieth for crossing the barrier to the divine realm, so peyote has been used to this day. Parallels to both practices are found universally, as in the dances of the South-African Bushmen or the use of *soma* by the ancient Hindus.

The Native American response to the encroachment of Europeans, whose policies in the encounter amounted to ethnic and political castration, can easily be said to model Freud's theory for the etiology of religion. With or without messianic leadership, the renewal movements of the fifteenth to twentieth centuries were driven in classical psychoanalytic terms by anxiety over murder of the primal father as described by Freud in *Totem and Taboo* (and developed further in *Moses and Monotheism*). Under the coercive advances of white settlers, memory traces of a primal conflict had been aroused, and the tribal psyche returned to the repressed trauma of the original sons' dispatch of a father who stood between them and the object of their Oedipal desire, i.e., the mother – indeed, barely disguised here as Mother Earth. Where a charismatic leader arose we would observe the tribe's correlative longing for the return of that father whom it had vanquished. And where a redeemer figure was said to have had a near-death experience or could claim to have died and returned, we would note both an atonement for the ancient murder and full emulation of the father through which the new leader would unconsciously be received as his replacement.

The significance of this kind of person to society, however, should not be dismissed as a mere artifact of psychosocial regression. As the Oedipal drama leads to development of the individual's super-ego, its recapitulation at the social level under the influence of a great leader is the origin of a culture's super-ego (*Civilization and Its Discontents*). So we may liken the movement of Handsome Lake (or even Smohalla) to the ethical monotheism developed by the Jews under Moses.

Nevertheless, confining messianism to the Oedipal context is relegating it to social order-keeping – making the revival of movements that clearly failed to eliminate exogenous stressors amount to little more than corporate repetition compulsion. To typify these movements as compulsions to repeat is to miss the ways in which they succeeded in counterbalancing the psychosocial problems of forced acculturation. For instance, through the filter of Self Psychology, we recognize in almost all instances attempts to revitalize an *idealized values system*. And movements carried by a charismatic leader demonstrate

the collective compensatory activation of an *idealized parent imago*, which, along with an agenda to foster family cohesiveness, is the basis of a society prepared to adjust to any environmental changes.

Implicit in the foregoing is the fact that what compels a people to accept an individual as messiah or charismatic leader rests on the extent to which the person addresses the deepest unconscious needs and wishes of the believers, Oedipal or otherwise. Additionally, it can be said that the degree of a leader's charisma relates to the level of the group's sense of desperation. One pre-condition for desperation would be the deep cleft indigenous people came to feel between themselves and nature. Erich Fromm who sees the messianic age as a human achievement (not the product of divine intervention) locates the existential problem it is meant to end in the individual's sense of estrangement from him- or herself and nature. It is essentially a problem of *splitting* – here, meaning the dichotomy between one's animal and transcendent natures – and is resolved when one (with one's society) can command reason, love, truth, and justice well enough to attain harmony. The actualization of Fromm's messianic age can be said to have been consistently pushed farther from the grasp of indigenous peoples, each time reason, love, truth, and justice were transgressed from the outside.

What we may conjecture to be the intra-psychic result of such transgressions is social regression to a pre-Oedipal stage. Borrowing from Object-Relations, where relationships are severely disrupted, there is risk of regression to the *schizoid position*, a psychic space of womblike safety but indifference to relationships – between internal and external objects, or self and nature. To defend against what the conscious mind would experience as intolerable loss, the individual or social group could instead withdraw to the *paranoid* or *depressive position*. Messianism animated by paranoia, with fantasies of persecution projected onto neutral as well as persecutory external realities, would resemble some of the millenarian Tupi quests for paradise, or the early dance movements that promoted emancipation through violence; while regressions to the depressive position (and its remorse) would be characteristic of movements that associated liberation with renovation of social morality, or later dance movements distinguished by some tolerance of acculturation. The choice would depend on a kind of tribal personality style.

Later Ghost Dances invite further Object-Relational review. In the language of D.W. Winnicott, the dance was manifest *potential space*, or that hypothetical realm between internal and external realities in which the psyche both creates and finds play, art, or religion. The shift from a hopeless expectation for the return of the dead to trance-encounters with them connotes the ghost-dancers' creative enlistment of their deceased as revivals of *transitional objects* to reconnect the community with a sense of, at least, its cultural environment's reliability.

From the Analytical Psychology perspective, a messianic movement as a symptom of cultural crisis would be teleological, pointing to, in fact representing, its own solution. A leader who experienced a rebirth or became divine, would be symbolic of the *Self*, archetype of wholeness, which for the individual or the collective is "an image of the goal of life, spontaneously produced by the unconscious, irrespective of the wishes and fears of the conscious mind" (Jung, 1989: 459). Rituals like the Ghost Dance and peyote use would be media through which members of the community participated in the kind of encounter with objective (i.e., transcendent) reality to which their messiah laid claim through near-death experiences and visions. And whatever the cause of disturbance in the tribal psyche, any socio-spiritual programs stipulating endogamy, marital fidelity, and eradication of practices (such as alcohol consumption) that effected schizoid retreats or the ego's collapse into the unconscious, would be expressions of the integrative drives that gave rise to the messianic movement. Messianic moral prescriptions, then, would betoken progressive rather than regressive tendencies. By this interpretation, retreats to pre-Oedipal positions or abandonment of a movement suggests either psychic unreadiness for a major emergence of deep psychic contents or merely a phase of the regressive struggle that normally accompanies such emergence.

See also: ❂ Analytical Psychology ❂ Archetype ❂ Depression ❂ Freud, Sigmund ❂ Jung, Carl Gustav ❂ Object Relations Theory ❂ Oedipus Complex ❂ Self ❂ Self Psychology ❂ Super-Ego ❂ Transitional Object ❂ Winnicott, Donald Woods

Bibliography

Brown, D. (1991). *Bury my heart at Wounded Knee: An Indian history of the American west.* New York: Henry Holt.

Farb, P. (1978). *Man's rise to civilization: The cultural ascent of the Indians of North America.* New York: Dutton.

Freud, S. (1957). Totem and taboo. In J. Strachey (Ed. & Trans.), *SE* (Vol. 13). London: Hogarth Press.

Freud, S. (1961). Civilization and its discontents. In J. Strachey (Ed. & Trans.), *SE* (Vol. 21). London: Hogarth Press.

Freud, S. (1964). Moses and monotheism. In J. Strachey (Ed. & Trans.), *SE* (Vol. 23). London: Hogarth Press.

Fromm, E. (1964). *The dogma of Christ.* New York: Holt, Rinehart & Winston.

Guntrip, H. (1992). *Schizoid phenomena, object-relations and the self.* Madison, CT: International Universities Press.

Hultkrantz, A. (1979). *The religions of the American Indians.* In M. Setterwall (Trans.). Berkeley, CA: University of California Press.

Jung, C. G. (1989). Answer to Job. In R. F. C. Hull (Trans.), *Psychology and religion: West and East, CW* (Vol. 11). Princeton, NJ: Princeton University Press.

Jung, C. G. (1990). *The archetypes and the collective unconscious* (R. F. C. Hull, Trans.), *CW* (Vol. 9, Part 1). London: Routledge.

Kohut, H. (1987). *The Kohut seminars on self psychology and psychotherapy with adolescents and young adults* (M. Elson, Ed.). New York: W. W. Norton.

Kracht, B. R. (1992). The Kiowa ghost dance, 1894–1916: An unheralded revitalization movement. *Ethnohistory, 39*(4), 452–477.

La Barre, W. (1971). Materials for a history of studies of crisis cults: A bibliographic essay. *Current Anthropology, 12*(1), 3–44.

Lanternari, V. (1965). *The religions of the oppressed: A study of modern messianic cults* (L. Sergio, Trans.). New York: Alfred A. Knopf.

Linton, R. (1943). Nativistic movements. *American Anthropologist, New Series, 45*(2), 230–240.

Ribeiro, R. (1992). Messianic movements in Brazil. *Luso-Brazilian Review, 29*(1), 71–81.

Riley, C. L., & Hobgood, J. (1959). A recent nativistic movement among the Southern Tepehuan Indians. *Southwestern Journal of Anthropology, 15*(4), 355–360.

Smith, H. (2000). *Cleansing the doors of perception: The religious significance of entheogenic plants and chemicals.* New York: Penguin Putnam.

Thornton, R. (1986). *We shall live again: The 1870 and 1890 ghost dance movements as demographic revitalization.* New York: Cambridge University Press.

Tooker, E. (1968). On the new religion of Handsome Lake. *Anthropological Quarterly, 41*(4), 187–200.

Wallace, A. F. C. (1956). Revitalization movements. *American Anthropologist, New Series, 58*(2), 264–281.

Wallace, A. F. C., & Steen, S. C. (1970). *The death and rebirth of the Seneca: The history and culture of the great Iroquois nation, their destruction and demoralization, and their cultural revival at the hands of the Indian visionary, Handsome Lake.* New York: Alfred A. Knopf.

Wallis, W. D. (1915). Individual initiative and social compulsion. *American Anthropologist, New Series, 17*(4), 647–665.

Werblowsky, R. J. (1965). A new heaven and a new earth: Considering primitive messianisms. *History of Religions, 5*(1), 164–172.

Winnicott, D. W. (1994). *The maturational processes and the facilitating environment.* Madison, CT: International Universities Press.

Nazism

Daniel Burston

The Menace of Modernity

After the Reformation, the development that shaped European civilization the most was the Age of Enlightenment, which began around 1720, and culminated shortly after the American Revolution in 1776. The Enlightenment rejected supernaturalism, the divinity of Jesus and the authority of the Church. Nevertheless, they said, there is a natural or built in *telos* to historical development, called "Progress" – a slow but inexorable process that, through the dissemination of science and literacy, would eventually envelope the whole planet. Among the moral and material benefits "Progress" would presumably confer is a much greater degree of human equality.

Though it is hard to credit nowadays, many religious people were utterly opposed to the Enlightenment's promotion of reason and human equality. Medieval Christians believed that all believers are equally important in the eyes of God, and that on the Day of Judgment, God will judge each personal impartially, ignoring their worldly status and accomplishments. In the meantime, they said, as far as *this* world goes, it is sinful to question the feudal hierarchy. Individuals can "progress" in their moral or spiritual growth, in their relationship with God. But that is an individual, not a societal affair. Medieval minds dismissed the idea of collective human emancipation, fostered by the growth of literacy and the dissemination of reason, because since the Fall, humankind is enmeshed in a world of suffering and woe, and attempts to improve our earthly condition through "works," or our own worldly efforts – including science and technology – are sinful, and distract us from our true spiritual vocation.

Nevertheless, in the eighteenth century, Deists and free thinkers began to make human equality a political norm or ideal, which meant translating the old belief in equality before God on Judgment Day into a political reality in *this* world. The growing demand for equality took several forms. The first was equality before the law, creating one system of justice, one law for the rich and the poor, commoners and the aristocracy, and increasingly, for Catholics and Protestants as well. In time, this emphasis on equality was extended to *all* religious creeds, including Jews. A second form the call for equality took was in terms of equality of access or opportunity, which required that the state provide free public education so that members of all social classes would have the chance to improve and to prosper. By the middle of the nineteenth century, Western European (and British and American) Jews benefited enormously from access to public education, and this is a feature of modernity that anti-Semites rejected. From the 1860s onwards, anti-Semites all across Europe, Britain and the United States argued that Jews *still* belong at the bottom of the social ladder, as in medieval days, and that their current prosperity was a symptom of a widespread social disorder. Indeed, if they will not return to their "natural" place in the social order, Jews should be intimidated, harassed and if need be, slaughtered *en masse*.

Nazism, Mysticism and the Occult

Given this background, the Nazi Party was not some weird aberration that sprang up overnight. The Treaty of Versailles made conditions for the spread of anti-Semitism in German speaking countries more favorable, but in the end, Nazism was a continuation of the older anti-Semitism, albeit with a fierce anti-Christian component that was well hidden from the rank and file. It also had an occult dimension. Much as they feared and detested them, the Nazis emulated the Masons in several respects, and borrowed some racist ideas from the Theosophical Society of Madame Helena Blavatsky, a Russian medium, who introduced the Swastika, an ancient Asian symbol, into Western occultist circles. They also had contact with Gregory Ivanovich Gurdjieff, another Russian mystic, and studied Anthroposophy, Sufism, Kundalini yoga, Zen Buddhism and so on. Most of these eclectic explorations in mysticism, meditation and the occult were carried on in the SS, under Himmler's oversight.

Having said that, many occult and spiritual practices the Nazi elite embraced were associated with movements and teachers who were not particularly racist, and whose overall objectives focused on individual development, rather than world domination or genocide. So to insure that these occult techniques were practiced in the proper spirit, the Nazis borrowed even more heavily from ultranationalist German or Austrian occultists and neo-pagans. One was the Austrian writer Guido von List (1848–1919). List founded an "Armanist" Brotherhood of Wotan worshippers who were obsessed with racial purity. In 1911, List codified a set of racial and marriage laws that bear an uncanny resemblance to the Nuremberg racial laws, that he claimed would be enacted in 1932. (He wasn't far off!)

Another important influence was Lanz von Liebenfels, a former Cistercian monk who founded the *Ordo Novi Templi*, or The New Templar Order, in 1907. Lanz was the editor of *Ostara*, a journal read by future Nazi stalwarts like Alfred Rosenberg, Heinrich Himmler, Julius Streicher and Rudolph Hess long before Hitler became leader of the Nazi Party. As Morris Berman points out: "Castration, sterilization and extermination of 'inferior' races are all present in Ostara. Subsidies for 'blond marriages' made available by Hitler in Norway and Holland during the war are advocated, as well as a ban on interracial ones" (Berman, 1989: 265).

Another important influence on the Nazis was Rudolf von Sebottendorf. Seboddendorf studied Islamic mysticism in Turkey and Egypt, and by his own admission, was strongly influenced by List and Lanz. In 1917, as Germany slouched towards defeat, Seboddendorf founded the

Thule Society – a violently anti-Semitic, ultra-nationalist group whose newspaper, *The Munich Observer*, attracted the aristocratic Dietrich Eckart and the lesser known Anton Drexler, a railroad mechanic who founded the ultra-Right wing German Workers Party. Drexler persuaded Sebottendorf and Eckart that it was time to turn the Thule Society into a mass movement. And when Adolf Hitler wrested control of The German Workers Party from Drexler, and renamed it the National Socialist Workers Party, *The Munich Observer* became the official organ of the Nazi organization.

And what about Hitler himself? What did he study? As far as we know, Hitler never belonged to any secret society, but was personally coached by his mentor Dietrich Eckart. Just what Eckart taught Hitler is not known, though it is the subject of some lively scholarly conjecture. In any case, the real inspiration for Hitler's occult leanings may have been more chemical than personal in nature. While serving as a soldier, Hitler was hit by British mustard gas on October 15th, 1918, and became blind. As he was recovering in hospital in Pasewalk, north of Berlin, his vision was gradually restored, until November, when he learned that Germany had been declared a Republic, which caused him to relapse completely. Whilst lying on his cot in despair, Hitler experienced as a call "from the other world" naming him the savior of the German people. After that, he started back on the road to recovery, and as they say, found "his voice." Thus a failed artist and a brain injured veteran was transformed into a charismatic political speaker, who transfixed the entire German people, putting them into a collective trance. The Nazi elite were as transfixed as the general population by Hitler's hate filled rants. The main difference between the elite and the rank and file was that the elite were never taken in by Hitler's public professions of support for Christianity. They knew that Hitler aimed to replace Christianity with an improvised pastiche of Wotanist and occultist beliefs and rituals in the fullness of time.

Hitler: The Aryan Messiah

Critics and supporters of the Enlightenment have noted that the modern myth of progress is a kind of secularized Messianism, in which the era of universal brotherhood, peace and prosperity is brought on, not by a divine messenger or intercessor, but by the growth of reason, science and technology. Viewed through the lenses of a secular, scientific mindset, the Nazi elite's involvement with the occult represents no more than a foolish reversion to magic and superstition – a puzzling anomaly,

given that they were enthusiastic promoters of science and technology. But the tendency to oppose magic and superstition to scientific method is a product of a modern mindset, and the Nazis were at war with modernity. Indeed, their hatred of Jews and of modernity were inseparably linked. They blamed Jews for the twin evils of modernity – capitalism and communism – and depicted them as incorrigibly materialistic, opposed to every noble, spiritual tendency in the "Aryan" psyche, which is inherently hierarchical in outlook.

So when all was said and done, Nazism embraced modern science and technology, but rejected modernity's characteristic emphasis on human equality, and the modern separation of the sacred and the secular in the political arena. In its place, they created a neo-feudal system based on hereditary rank and privilege, and sought to fuse the sacred and the secular in their political ideology. But instead of reviving the Church, they sought to destroy it, and to replace Christianity with a cult of the Fuehrer. As Morris Berman points out, the cult of the Fuehrer was much more than a political movement. It was a state religion. Berman writes:

> ➤ At the Nazi rally in Nuremberg in September of 1937, a huge photo of Hitler was displayed with the inscription beneath it: 'IN THE BEGINNINING WAS THE WORD...' William Teeling, who visited Germany in the late thirties, was told by the Mayor of Hamburg: We need no priests or parsons. We communicate directly with God through Adolph Hitler. Dorothy Thompson, writing in the December 1934 issue of Harper's Magazine (Good Bye To Germany) told the following story: 'At Garmisch I met an American from Chicago. He had been at the Oberammergau to see the Passion Play. 'These people are all crazy," he said. 'This is not a revolution, it is a revival. They think Hitler is God. Believe it or not, A German woman sitting next to me at the Passion Play and when they hoisted Jesus on the Cross, she said: 'There he is. That is our Fuehrer, our Hitler.'" And when they paid out the thirty pieces of silver to Judas, she said: "That is Roehm, who betrayed the Leader'" (pp. 277–278).

Berman gives more examples, but there is no need to belabor the issue. Nazi propaganda *deliberately* displaced Jesus with Hitler at every opportunity, because the German populace wanted a *savior*. Hitler and his followers discerned this (largely unconscious) desire, and used techniques culled from black magic and modern advertising techniques to create a demonic new race-based religion of state.

Why then, beginning in 1935, did Hitler suppress all secret societies – even the Thule Society, and other racist ones that were precursors to his movement? Hitler aimed to create a complete police state – one which would harness people's yearning for a savior and for a sense of belonging to something bigger, something powerful and spiritual. In Hitler's utopia, no one would belong to any organization that harbored secrets from the state, or nourished competing loyalties or differences of opinion with Hitler – on any subject pertaining to spirituality. For a brief period of time, Hitler was a kind of Emperor and demonic Pope rolled into one – the final authority on all matters temporal and spiritual. His authority was beyond question, and brooked no challenges. The brief but astonishing career of Adolf Hitler, and the lingering appeal of Nazism to this day are potent reminders of the limits of progress. As we enter our present "postmodern" historical era, science and technology develop apace, but genuine equality, brotherhood and peace are as elusive as ever.

See also: ⊙ Anti-Semitism ⊙ Theosophy

Bibliography

Berman, M. (1989). *Coming to our senses: Body and spirit in the hidden history of the West*. New York: Simon & Schuster.

Lacquer, W. (2006). *The changing face of anti-semitism: From ancient times to the present day*. New York: Oxford University Press.

New Age Movement

Ann Gleig

The New Age burst into public consciousness in a buzz of media attention around crystals, reincarnation, and channeling in the 1980s, but it has its immediate roots in the 1960s and 1970s counterculture. Tracing this history, Wouter Hanegraaff (1998) and Steven Sutcliff, (2003) have delineated two understandings of the New Age: the New Age in the Strict Sense and the New Age in the General Sense. The Strict Sense New Age refers to an apocalyptic/millennial movement that emerged in the 1940s and 1950s when a number of Anglo-American groups announced they were receiving messages from intelligent beings from other planets who were coming to bring a New Age to the Earth. These groups believed there would be an apocalyptic catastrophe followed by a new era of spiritual evolution, peace, and prosperity with only those attuned to "new age" consciousness surviving. Predominantly populated by white, middle-aged, and elderly adherents and characterized by a culture of austerity and morality that emphasized community and service, these groups reflected a strong British influence.

In response to the absence of an actual apocalypse, the Strict Sense New Age underwent a radical shift, internalizing the apocalyptic narrative and relocating the New Age to the inner psychospiritual landscape. Hence, from the 1970s onwards, the New Age was revisioned as the replacement of an old, rationalistic, negative mind-set with a radically new state of human consciousness – famously characterized as the "Age of Aquarius." Now promoting a constructive and participatory attitude, these Utopian communities and discourses were assimilated into the wider counterculture identified by sociologist Colin Campbell (1972) as the "cultic milieu." This refers to a plethora of diverse new religious movements ranging from those stable entities with definite organizational structures, doctrines and rules of conduct, to much more fluid, inclusive and undemanding groups. Attracting individuals who are dissatisfied with mainstream options, cultic groups are often in flux and members may participate in more than one group. According to Hanegraaff, it was when the cultural milieu became conscious of itself in the late 1970s as constituting a more or less unified movement that the New Age Movement in the general and popular sense was born.

The General Sense New Age has a dominant American influence, from New Thought to the more recent human potential movement, and has significantly assimilated Asian religions. Adherents tend to be middle class, mostly Caucasian, and value emotional expressiveness, body awareness, and the belief that world transformation is dependent upon individual transformation. Classic texts include David Spangler's *Revelation: The Birth of a New Age* (1976), Marilyn Ferguson's *The Aquarian Conspiracy: Personal and Social Transformation in the 1980's* (1979), Shirley MacLaine's, *Out on a Limb* (1986), and James Redfield's, *The Celestine Prophecy* (1995).

Having no founder, no set canon, binding creed or definite organization structure, the General New Age is broader and more diverse than what is normally understood as a religious tradition, yet one can still identify a number of shared themes/beliefs, practices and general characteristics. Hanegraaff names one of the defining marks of the New Age as "the psychologization of religion and the sacralization of psychology," in which personal growth and religious salvation merge to such an extent that it is difficult to distinguish between the psychological and spiritual. He delineates two major lineages for this occurrence: American metaphysical movements and Carl Gustav Jung. The American lineage is divided into two separate but related streams. The first, the metaphysical movements, includes Mesmerism, Mind-Cure, the New Thought movement, and positive thinking/self-help popular psychology. The second, functionalist psychology, embraces William James, Carl Rogers, and humanistic psychology.

The second major source is Jung who Hanegraaff sees as the link between traditional esotericism, Naturphilosophie, Romanticism, and the New Age. Jung both psychologized esotericism by presenting an esoteric worldview in psychological term and providing a scientific alternative to occultism and sacralized psychology by filling it with the contents (e.g., archetypes, the transcendent function, and individuation) of esoteric speculation rather than empirical realities. The result was a theory which allowed people to talk simultaneously about God and the psyche, thus anticipating and producing the major themes of the New Age.

Fundamental to these themes is a "metaphysics of mind," a philosophical idealism in which the distinction between mind and matter and subjective and objective reality is undermined. With mind or consciousness as the ultimate reality, the psychological takes on an unprecedented importance; the psyche is celebrated as the locus of the sacred and reality is seen as created by the mind. This leads to a sacralization of the Self, not the conventional individual ego, but rather an inner divinity, a Higher Self which is the source of all value and meaning. Unlike Asian monistic mysticism which aims at the dissolution of individual consciousness in the universal, impersonal consciousness of the Self, the New Age champions the infinite evolution of a unique individual soul/Self. A core mythology of the New Age is the journey of the Self through many incarnations towards increasing levels of spiritual knowledge with the world being embraced as a school for spiritual growth and life situations framed as being pre-chosen by the Self according to the lessons it needs to learn.

The basic ontology in the New Age is a Neoplatonic model of a hierarchical cosmos with a myriad number of spiritual beings existing on ascending planes of existence, each corresponding to progressively higher levels of spiritual development and culminating in an impersonal monistic Absolute. Pantheism; the concept that the Absolute is identical with the natural universe and Panentheism; the belief that the Absolute contains but is not reducible to the natural world are also popular models. Most importantly, the New Age rejects dualistic and materialist ontologies in favor of holistic and interdependent models.

In terms of practices, Hanegraaff has helpfully grouped an incredibly broad range of activities, from aromatherapy to astral projection to channeling to various forms of "energy work," into four major streams: channeling, healing and personal growth, New Age science, and New Age Neopaganism. Particularly significant to psychology is healing and personal growth. Hanegraaff has divided the wide array of alternative therapies falling under the broad rubric of healing and personal growth into two main currents: the holistic health movement and the human potential movement. Mention should also be made of "prosperity consciousness," those American healing systems that claim the full attainment of health and spiritual wellbeing includes material prosperity and utilize positive thinking and affirmation techniques to this end. Many of these systems and texts fall under the rubric of "popular psychology," with a classic example being Norman Vince Peale's bestseller, *The Power of Positive Thinking* (1952/1990).

Fundamental to the holistic health movement is the belief that that each human being is a unique, holistic, interdependent, relationship of body, mind, and spirit and that healing is achieved through an alignment with the underlying power of the universe. It stresses the central role the mind plays in healing, believing that psychological conditions can both cause and cure physical illness. Hence, the individual is challenged to discover and take responsibility for the deeper meaning of his/her illness and use it as an instrument for inner growth. Varieties of holistic healing include acupuncture, biofeedback, kinesiology, homeopathy, iridology, reflexology, massage and bodywork.

Utilizing a range of therapies such as Holotropic breathing, encounter groups, gestalt therapy, Neo-Reichian bodywork, Bioenergetics, and shamanic consciousness, the basic goal of the human potential movement is to help people connect with and integrate suppressed and alienated parts of the self in order to develop their full human potential. It is strongly associated with Abraham Maslow's humanistic psychology with its self-actualization needs and promotion of B-values such as wholeness, aliveness and uniqueness. With the increasingly assimilation of Asian mysticism, the movement has shifted more and more into the spiritual sphere, reflected in the establishment, in 1969, by Abraham Maslow and Anthony Sutich, of the "fourth force" of psychology, transpersonal psychology, in order to scientifically investigate altered states of consciousness, such as unitive consciousness, peak experiences, mystical experiences, self-transcendence and cosmic awareness. Seeing western psychology as only addressing the lower levels of the psyche and being inadequate for dealing with the higher or transpersonal levels which have traditionally been the province of spiritual traditions, particularly Asian ones, transpersonal psychology aims for a more integrated approach to the human being through a synthesis of western psychology and Asian spirituality.

It should be noted, however, that although transpersonal psychology is commonly associated with the New Age and while they share many overlapping themes, transpersonalists have distanced themselves from the New Age. This is because transpersonal psychology is primarily an academic discipline (recognized by the British Psychological Society but not yet the American Psychological Association) rather than a spiritual movement, and many transpersonal psychologists have critiqued what they perceive as a superficiality and lack of rigor within the New Age movement.

Some general characteristics, mirroring the themes outlined above, have also been identified across the New Age. First, the General Sense New Age tends to be highly *individualistic* where each person is seen as the highest authority for themselves and as the final arbiter of truth and *experiential* with personal experience valued above tradition or dogma. Second, New Age practice tends, at least on the surface, to embrace a *democratic* position that rejects, or is highly suspicious of, various forms of authority; with most New Age practice claiming to be available for all individuals. Third, the New Age tends towards the *relativistic*, where contrasting claims about ultimate reality are seen as "different," rather than "better or worse" or "true and false." This relativism legitimates the incredible diversity and *syncretic/eclectic* nature of the New Age, whereby elements from different traditions may be simultaneously embraced and/or combined into new and innovative forms of spiritual activity. Finally, this eclecticism exists hand in hand with *perennialism*, where all spiritual traditions are seen as being paths to and manifestation of a common sacred Absolute.

The New Age has come under increasing scholarly attention with a growing number of sociological, anthropological and historical academic studies produced. In a groundbreaking sociological study Paul Heelas (1996) describes the New Age as Self-Spirituality: a spiritualized form of humanism that sacralizes the modern values of freedom, authenticity, equality, and the uniqueness and goodness of the individual. From a history of religions perspective, Hanegraaff's (1998) seminal study of the New Age identifies it as "secularized estericism"; the transformation of traditional esotericism as it adapted to a modern, scientific and disenchanted world. He identifies four mirrors of secular thought through which traditional esotericism was refracted: scientific materialism and positivism; the comparative study of religion; evolution; and modern psychology. In a later analysis, he draws attention to the impact of the capitalist market economy on spirituality during the 1980s and 1990s which has created a "spiritual supermarket," where religious consumers pick and choose those spiritual products which suit their own needs.

There have also been a number of attempts at psychological profiles of New Agers. These are helpfully summarized by Daren Kemp (2004) in his meticulously researched overview of different etic and emic approaches to the New Age. The most prominent psychological claim is that New Age thinking is regressive and narcissistic. Christopher Lasch (1987) states that the New Age attempts to restore the symbiotic state of primary narcissism by denying the reality of the differentiated material world. Similarly, M. D. Faber (1996) argues that New Age thinking is a regression to primary narcissism in which the adult is returned to an infantile state of omnipotence, magical wish fulfillment and merger with the pre-Oedipal mother. Leading transpersonal theorist, Ken Wilber has described the type of argument employed by Lasch and Faber as examples of the "pre/trans fallacy," in which pre-personal (narcissistic) and transpersonal (genuinely transcendent) experience is conflated. However, Wilber (1991) himself estimates that four-fifths of the New Age is prepersonal and only one fifth is transpersonal.

In conclusion, due to its associations with commercialism and predominantly negative media attention, the term "New Age" itself has fallen out of favor. This is reflected in both the academic and commercial worlds: "alternative spirituality" is becoming the preferred term in scholarship, and it is more common in bookstores to see sections marked as "Spirituality," or "Mind-Body-Sprit" than "New Age." At the same time, practices and themes associated with the New Age are gaining in their mainstream acceptance and integration into existing social and religious structures (for example, the growing attention to "holistic" practices in mainstream medicine or the increasing use of Asian meditation in various forms of Christian practice). From this perspective, there is little evidence that the practices and concerns of the General Sense New Age are diminishing; indeed, if anything, the movements and practices that fall under the rubric of the New Age are growing and seem sure to shape future religious landscapes.

See also: ❂ James, William ❂ Jung, Carl Gustav ❂ Self

Bibliography

Albanese, C. (2007). *A republic of mind and spirit: A cultural history of American metaphysical religion.* New Haven, CT: Yale University Press.

Campbell, C. (1972). The cult, the cultic mileu, and secularization. In *A sociological yearbook of religion in Britain 5* (pp. 119–136). London: SCM Press.

Christopher, P. (2006). *The re-enchantment of the West: Alternative spiritualities, sacralization, popular culture and the occulture* (Vol. 1). London: T & T Clark/Continuum.

Faber, M. D. (1996). *New age thinking.* Ottawa, ON: The University of Ottawa Press.

Ferguson, M. (1982). *The aquarius conspiracy: Personal and social transformation in the 1980's.* London: Paladin/Grafton Books.

Fuller, R. C. (1989). *Alternative medicine and American religious life.* New York: Oxford University Press.

Fuller, R. C. (2001). *Spiritual, but not religious: Understanding unchurched America.* New York: Oxford University Press.

Hammer, O. (2004). *Claiming knowledge: Strategies of Epistemology from Theosophy to the new age.* Leiden: Brill.

Hanegraaff, W. (1998). *New age religion and Western culture.* Albany, NY: State University of New York.

Hanegraaff, W. (2005). The New Age. In L. Jones (Ed.), *The encyclopedia of religion* (2nd ed., 15 Volume Set) New York, MI: MacMillan Reference Books.

Heelas, P. (1996). *The New Age Movement and the sacralization of the Self.* Oxford, England: Blackwell Publishers.

Kemp, D. (2004). *New age: A guide.* Edinburgh, England: Edinburgh University Press.

Lasch, C. (1979). *The culture of Narcissism.* New York: W.W. Norton.

Lasch, C. (1987). Soul of a New Age. *Omni,* 10.1, 78–85.

MacLaine, S. (1983). *Out on a limb.* Toronto: Bantam Books.

Pearle, N. V. (1952/1990). *The power of positive thinking.* New York: Prentice-Holt.

Redfield, J. (1997). *The celestine prophecy.* New York: Warner Books.

Spangler, D. (1977). *Revelation: The birth of a new age.* Forres: Findhorn Foundation.

Sutcliffe, S. J. (2003). *Children of the new age: A history of spiritual practices.* London: Routledge.

Wilber, K. (1991). *Grace and grit: Spirituality and healing in the life and death of Treya Killam Wilber.* Boston: Shambhala.

New Religions

Benjamin Beit-Hallahmi

The Phenomenon

Right now, there may be more than 10,000 living religions in the world, each promoting a separate belief system and having its own organizational structure. What makes a religious group unique are its own distinct beliefs, practices, authority structure, and leadership. Quite often the group's history starts with a new claim to authority on the part of a new leader.

As used here, the term new religions, or new religious movements (NRMs) refers to groups founded after the year 1750. In recent years, such movements have been examined under the rubrics of religious experimentation, marginal religions, or oppositionist religions.

Quite interestingly, most of the religions that have ever been in existence were founded after 1750. The modern age, while being marked by secularization, is also marked by the appearance (and disappearance) of thousands of new religious movements. This may actually be directly related to secularization and the decline in the authority and political power of major historical religions. Democracy and the idea of freedom in religion and political expression create a free market for religious entrepreneurs. While declaring oneself to be in possession of a new religious truth was, in most parts of the world, quite risky or fatal 300 years ago, it carries little risk in the modern world.

In looking at any new religion, we should focus on the most important thing in forming its unique identity, and that is its beliefs. A belief system makes a movement distinct, and these beliefs change little over time, as opposed to other aspects of a group's history, which are likely to change, such as organizational structure. Many aspects of a group's history may be in dispute. Such facts as membership numbers are changing and often impossible to determine. Members of new religious movements, which are historically and developmentally young, show high levels of involvement and commitment, unlike many in the "old," historical, religions, and this attracts much attention. Some groups have received much media attention around scandals and crimes. This is because many of these groups deliberately and explicitly challenge existing traditions.

Looking at a particular religious group, our diagnostic and predictive efforts are severely hampered by the complexity of interactions between beliefs, individual members, leadership, and the surrounding environment. A new group's claim to originality and uniqueness in its beliefs may lead to what the world around it perceives as deviance, leading to friction and arousing resistance. What we have learned over the years is that predicting the future fate or development of a religious movement is impossible. Groups that today seem marginal may rise to prominence, while groups which are at the moment well-known decline into obscurity. The history of new religious movements is replete with such cases. Developments in religion today are not just international but global, and belief systems cross borders easily. A little known group in South America or Africa may gain followers in Europe or the United States.

Research on NRMs

Some NRMs have attracted the attention of researchers in psychology. Such was the case of the group described by Festinger, Riecken, and Schachter, in *When Prophecy Fails*

(1956). The group was founded by a woman named Marian Keech in the study, claimed to have received messages from a space being named Sananda, a source that was both extraterrestrial (i.e., outer space) and divine (Jesus in Christian tradition) about the coming end of the world. On a specified date, which she announced to the world, all of humanity would perish, save the group membership, who would be taken away in a spaceship. This date was announced (December 1953), and group members expected the end of the world, and their own salvation by a spaceship sent by Sananda. After the prophecy failed, some of the group members maintained their faith. The group did not survive this crisis, but its disintegration was not immediate. Actually, the disconfirmation caused some committed members to proclaim their faith even more vigorously by proselytizing.

Mrs. Martin claimed that the world was saved by their full faith. She also made additional predictions about various disasters, which also failed to materialize. These events took place in Chicago in late 1953, but the leader continued her activities into the 1980s.

There are cases where prophecy failures have not led to a visible crisis or collapse, possibly because the prophecies are only subject to disconfirmation in terms of timing. Thus, a prediction about the coming end of the world in 1984 may be re-interpreted as true in principle, and only temporarily delayed by other events. A belief system may be flexible enough to accommodate such failures. Some groups have survived disconfirmation through some effort, but in other cases a direct disconfirmation of claims leads to crisis and sometimes decline or disintegration.

New religions in Western societies, often subject to external opposition, are mostly unstable groups with unstable members, which need extraordinary luck and leadership to survive and prosper. NRMs suffer from high rates of defection, and many religious movements have been started through schisms in existing groups.

We should pay attention to the special situation of NRMs as belief minorities in modern society, which dictates certain behaviors to the groups and their members. This means that NRMs are sometimes not completely truthful about their doctrines or practices, out of concern for possible majority reactions. At other times, deception in fund raising, practiced by some groups, may be justified in religious terms. New religious movements (NRMs) are groups in which membership in most cases, is achieved, rather than ascribed, through voluntary conversion and recruitment.

Numerous examples of millennial movements which followed on the heels of social dislocations, catastrophes, plagues, famines, and massacres, are known.

In pre-industrial societies, NRMs in recent times have been known as "crisis cults", including so-called Cargo Cults and Ghost Dances. Cargo cults and ghost dances represent desperate efforts to cope with terrible realities. The Sabbatian movement in the seventeenth century is another example. It was a messianic upheaval unprecedented in Jewish history, which engulfed the whole Jewish world at the time. A crisis may sometimes lead to a complete surrender, and religious movements may express resignation and hopelessness. Some religious movements are attempts to respond to crisis by revitalizing collective faiths. An example of a successful revitalization movement is the case of the Seneca tribe in North America, suffering every possible disaster since 1650, and a total disintegration at the end of the eighteenth century, which was reborn in the nineteenth century thanks to a religious vision.

When religious renewal movements appear in modern societies, and attract individuals who are sometimes quite well off, their growth has been interpreted as a response to what has been called ethical and psychic deprivations. In modern society, joining an NRM has been interpreted as a response to crisis situations and individual alienation, relieved in the religious group setting with its promise of salvation.

Among historical cases of crisis religions in modern society, we should mention those in the United States in the nineteenth century, with a wealth of private and collective salvation movements, the rise of Spiritualism, and the founding of so many new religions (e.g., Christian Science, Mormonism, Seventh Day Adventists, Theosophy), and the United States in the 1960s, another Great Awakening of salvation movements.

When dealing with NRMs, we have to explain not only recruitment and growth, but also disaffection and failure, which are quite common. New religious movements in modern societies receive much attention, which is out of all proportion to their success in recruiting members or their overall growth. Many religious groups fail to grow because of their opposition to society around them, which leads to their encapsulation. They are able to survive, but not grow. Another problem NRMs face is that the number of seekers, motivated or open to identity change in any society, is limited, for social and psychological reasons. There are cases where joining an NRM will lead to improved individual functioning and the group environment is clearly therapeutic. There are also opposite cases of deterioration and pathology in individuals and groups where there is clear evidence of destructive and self-destructive behavior.

NRMs are often highly vulnerable, always struggling, and seeking legitimacy, while internally preoccupied with issues of authority, leadership, and identity. New religions face both internal and external tensions as they struggle to achieve survival and stability in an environment that is often or always indifferent and non-supportive, and sometimes hostile. This struggle, often marked by desperation as outside pressures mount, colors the psychological development of both the group in its members in most new religions. What defines the dynamics of many NRMs is the actual presence of the founder or founders and the founding generation of members. Most groups are relatively small and so relationships and activities are more intense and personal. Because many members in NRMs are coverts and the group relatively young, we can observe high levels of ego involvement, which do not characterize most members of historically established religions. While in "old" religions personal involvement takes the form of an identity label and often little else, in NRMs belonging is central and salient in terms of identity and action, and members typically devote much of their energy, time, and money to the group.

Charisma in NRMs

In terms of their organizational character, NRMs are based on charisma rather than any routinization or evolved hierarchy. In many new religions, leadership is personal and charismatic. Charisma is something that we may find hard to predict, but easy to recognize. It is needed to attract new recruits to a small group and keep them, and maintain the leader's authority. In most cases, founders of NRMs have sufficient charisma to attract relatively the numbers of followers necessary to keep the group alive. An effective leader, in this case and in others, creates a mutually empowering relationship with his followers, at least for a while.

The charismatic and direct nature of leadership, in the absence of articulated structures involving multiple levels of hierarchy, will lead to internal tensions. The idea that leaders are chosen through the power of revelation or religious creativity legitimizes schisms. Being a successful leader facing both internal tensions and a hostile environment is a challenge rarely met. It requires creativity in the midst of competition and resistance, but some leaders, and some groups, have shown remarkable resilience.

One the more interesting cases of leadership in a new religious movement in the face of adversity and opposition involves the tragic early history of the Church Of Jesus Christ Of Latter-Day Saints (LDS), informally known as Mormons, and sometimes as LDS, "Latter-day Saints" or "Saints." This Christian-polytheistic millenarian group was founded by Joseph Smith, Jr. (1805–1844) in 1830 in northern New York State. At age 14 Joseph Smith declared he had spoken with God. Later he had other visions, during some of which, he claimed, an ancient book, written on four tablets, was given to him. This text has become known as *The Book of Mormon* and has given its name to the Church.

Smith announced to the world that he was "seer, translator, prophet, apostle of Jesus Christ, and elder of the church." According to some reports, Smith was crowned as a king in 1844. In 1835 12 apostles were appointed and sent to gain converts in the United States. In 1835 Joseph Smith also prophesied the Second Coming. In 1837 the first Mormon missionaries arrived in Britain, and met some success, as well as some prejudice.

In its early years, the movement encountered much violence because of its unconventional beliefs and its advocacy of polygamy, which was first renounced in 1890 and then rescinded in 1904. Opposition forced the group to move first to Ohio, then to Missouri, and then to Illinois, where the city of Nauvoo was founded in 1840. In 1844 Joseph Smith and his brother were killed by a mob there. Again the members embarked on a long voyage away from the Eastern United States, led by Brigham Young (1801–1877) and settled in Salt Lake City. In 1850 Brigham Young became the first governor of the territory of Utah, which became a state in 1895.

Over the past few decades, much attention has been given to tragic cases of violence in NRMs, including the murders and terrorist attacks by Aum Shinrikyo in Japan, and mass killings in the Peoples Temple, the Branch Davidians, the Solar Temple, and Heaven's Gate. The victims often included dependents of group members, and not just members. Deviant and destructive groups such as Aum Shinrykio and the Order of the Solar Temple must be viewed against a background of severe personal and social pathology, related to histories of vulnerability and deprivation among members. When it comes to evaluating the leaders in these cases, using the psychological (hypothetical) systems of individual personality and individual psychopathology in which we analyze our observations, one prominent issue is that of the limitations psychopathology puts on performance. Pathology must limit the ability to carry out complicated acts of destruction, or self-destruction, must be limited. Still, we see cases of religious leaders where presumed insanity still leaves much room for successful leadership and organizational talent, as well as fairly sophisticated acts of violence, which involve planning and preparation.

Summary

The impact of NRMs is much narrower than often perceived. They are small and marginal, and touch the lives of fewer than 1% of all religious believers. Most are so unstable as to be ephemeral. A look at the history of twentieth century NRMs is quite sobering in this respect. Movements that once seemed on the verge of becoming global powers are now remembered only by historians. Moral Rearmament (the "Oxford Group Movement"), the best known NRM of the 1930s in Britain and the United States, is today totally forgotten. The Jesus Movement of the early 1970s in the United States, with its hundreds of communes in major US cities, has similarly disappeared. It seems that high utopian excitement cannot be maintained for long, and that adolescence is more of a factor than is often realized. When enthusiastic members get older, commitment wanes in favor of more conventional pursuits. Nevertheless, like the phenomenon of conversion, NRMs deserve, and get, attention, just because of their rarity and intensity.

See also: ❯ Conversion ❯ Prophets

Bibliography

Beit-Hallahmi, B. (1992). *Despair and deliverance*. Albany, NY: SUNY Press.

Beit-Hallahmi, B., & Argyle, M. (1997). *The psychology of religious behaviour, belief and experience*. London: Routledge.

Festinger, L., Riecken, H. W., & Schachter, S. (1956). *When prophecy fails*. Minneapolis, MN: University of Minnesota Press.

Lincoln, C. E. (1961). *The Black Muslims in America*. Boston, MA: Beacon Press.

New Testament

Jeffrey B. Pettis

The New Testament consists of 27 writings representative of various cultural and socio-political backgrounds. As canonical texts they represent only a portion of early Christian scriptures and were frequently used in preaching, teaching and worship. The Pauline letters constitute the earliest material, written in the middle of the first century CE. These include 1 Thessalonians, Philippians, 1 Corinthians, 2 Corinthians, Galatians, Philemon, and Romans. Scholars are more divided on the authorship of Colossians, Ephesians and 2 Thessalonians, which are attributed to Paul, although probably written near the end of the first century. The remaining writings attributed to Paul and known traditionally as the Pastoral Epistles were probably written early in the second century. These include 1 and 2 Timothy, and Titus. The Pauline corpus as a whole evidences the processing of some significant and deeply felt religious experience by Paul. This processing (something Jung might refer to as the reforming of an *a priori* archetype, *Aion* pars. 73) includes the translating and re-presenting of what is understood to be the meaning of that experience by Paul, as well as the way(s) that experience both forms and is shaped by later Christian communities. Paul offers little detail with regard to his conversion (see Gal. 1.13–17; Rom. 1.1) suggesting the ineffable nature of the encounter. Several decades later the author of Luke-Acts presents a dramatic account of the event, giving nuances and psyche-soma movements to detail the encounter (Acts 9.1–22). These include Paul's being acted upon by what is perceived to be a divine presence, heightened auditory and ocular sensory awareness and disorientation, and a definitive shift of consciousness as one being "set apart (*aphōrizmenos*) for the gospel of God" (1 Cor. 1.1). The experience orients Paul toward a new understanding with regard to the meaning and significance of the life, death and post-mortal accounts of Jesus, whom Paul understands to be *Iēsous Christos*, the "Anointed One" (1 Cor. 3.11). Religious experience occurs as a foundation for other writings within the NT canon. The author of Mark (ca. 70 CE) presents Jesus baptized in the Jordan River as the heavens split, a voice is heard, and a dove descends (Mark 1.4–13). Immediately Jesus is driven into a wilderness encounter with Satan amidst wild animals and angels (1.12–13). The author of Matthew (ca. 90 CE) roots the birth of the "Messiah" in a series of dreams (Matt. 1.18–2.23) which occur within a cosmic orientation and the coming of Magi from the East to worship the child. The author of Luke mixes angelic visitations and the pregnancies of Elizabeth and Mary in an elaborate birth narrative (Luke 1.5–2.20), while the school of John speaks of the "Word become flesh" (*logos sarx egeneto*, John 1.14), and tells of what appears to be a numinous encounter involving touch, hearing and sight (1 John 1.1–4). This notion of incarnation – inter-relating and inter-mixing earth and heaven – occurs as real, re-orienting, and efficacious event for the writers of the gospel narratives who tell in declarative story form (*euaggelion*) the Jesus event. For all these writers the relationship between the human and the divine must be negotiated. This includes the *Book of Revelation*, which as *apokalupsis* ("revealing") literature having to do with divine intervening and judgment ("a new heaven and a new earth"), gives especial focus to divinity definitively encountering the material realm. For none of the writings, apart from Paul, are scholars certain about historical authorship; rather, observations about religious, cultural, and socio-political biases and interests of authorship can be made. The Hellenistic orientation of the Gospel of Luke points toward a Gentile author writing for a Gentile audience. The heightened, visual, and urgent language in the *Book of Revelation* points toward an author connected with a community threatened by and/or suffering some kind of religious persecution. Later writings in the NT tend to emphasize the practice (*praxis*) of Christian faith. First Timothy 2.8–15, for example, has as its focus codes of Christian behavior (see also Eph. 5.22–33; Col. 3.18ff.; 1 Pet. 3.1–7), and the pseudonymous second century Letter of James is actually an extended parenesis on moral behavior and how it is a Christian community should live. Other examples include the ritual instituting of Christian baptism (1 Pet. 1.3, 23; 2.2; 3.2), the development of church government (1 John and 2 John), and the Luke-Acts narrative presentation of the emerging church establishing itself in the Greco-Roman world.

See also: ❯ Bible ❯ Christianity

Nietzsche, Friedrich

❯ Schopenhauer, Nietzsche, and Atheism

Night Journey

❯ Miraj

Nirvana

James H. Stover

Nirvana (Sanskrit) or *nibbana* (Pali) literally means "extinction" or "blow out." Negatively articulated, it is detachment from the cycle of death and rebirth (*samsara*) and the cessation of suffering (*dukkha*). Positively articulated, it may be rendered as a transcendent, blissful mode of existence. To this extent, it is associated with both liberation and enlightenment and is the goal of Buddhism.

Siddhartha Gautama is said to have experienced two kinds of nirvana. The first nirvana was experienced at the moment of his awakening (*bodhi*) when he was meditating under the Bodhi Tree and actually became a Buddha. Subsequently, no longer bound by ignorance or the desires of this world, he carried on his earthly ministry for the next 45 years in this enlightened state of nirvana. His teaching (*dharma*) was that one could experience awakening or nirvana by practicing the Eightfold Path, a synergism of moral conduct, mental discipline, and wisdom. The second nirvana was that which Siddhartha Gautama (now the Buddha) experienced at death. This *parinirvana* is the doing away with the personality and all links to the phenomenal world. It is the ultimate state or final nirvana. Having an ineffable character, it cannot be adequately conveyed with words.

Since Buddhism includes a variety of systems, it is not surprising that nirvana takes on various inflections. In Theravada Buddhism, which focuses on individual liberation, it is the *arhat* (literally, "worthy one") that experiences nirvana for himself. Non-monks do not experience nirvana, but are inspired by the idea that they may some day, perhaps after many reincarnations, become an arhat. Theravada also reflects the idea of two nirvanas (see above). The first is nirvana with residue. It is experienced in this life, and results from the overcoming (or extinguishing) of desire, hatred, and delusion. Here, although enlightened, one is still experiencing the limitations of the personality: form, sensation, perception, mental formations, and consciousness. The second is nirvana without residue, which is a complete break from the world of death and rebirth, i.e., samsara.

In Mahayana Buddhism we see the development of the *bodhisattva* ideal rather than the more narrow and so-called selfish perspective of the arhat. The bodhisattva, motivated by compassion, forgoes nirvana until others experience it first. Everyone is a candidate for nirvana, not just certain monks, since everyone possesses buddha-nature. In various groups of Mahayana Buddhism the nirvana/samsara dichotomy is deemphasized. These concepts are perceived more as a matter of spiritual perspective than a polarization of opposites. Hence, nirvana and samsara are both identified with emptiness (*sunyata*). They are best described as interdependent rather than self-existent. Thus, the strict boundary separating nirvana and samsara is removed. This is seen in Zen where nirvana is not only revealed in meditation, but through such common activities as eating, drinking, and washing dishes. On the contrary, one Mahayana tradition denies the possibility of experiencing nirvana in this corrupt world altogether. Here, individuals, assisted by Buddhas or Bodhisattvas are reborn in a Pure Land, which provides the ideal setting for attaining nirvana.

Although nirvana is generally thought of as a Buddhist concept, its later Hindu understanding is associated with the realization that the soul (*atman*) is one with Brahman – ultimate or absolute reality. Typically Hinduism uses the term *moksa* rather than nirvana. In Jainism, nirvana may be attained by the most accomplished yogis at death. This is an eternal state in which suffering is absent. It is preceded by the continual reduction of life's activity and many reincarnations.

Commentary

Jung often stressed the differences between the psychologies of East and West and warned against problems resulting from Western people participating in Eastern practices. Nevertheless, he immersed himself in the study of Asian perspectives and found its rich symbolism provided many helpful parallels, such as nirvana. From a Jungian perspective nirvana symbolizes the mature unification process of individuation. It is the reconciliation of opposites through transcendence, which is indicative of self-realization. Here the symbols of the unconscious are appropriated by consciousness and the ego. Although the ego previously held the central place of the psyche, it now gives way to the Self – that archetype of wholeness which reconciles consciousness with unconsciousness. Just as nirvana in Buddhism is not annihilation, but reconciliation, so too is the process of individuation and the discovery of the Self.

Freud, less immersed in Asian psychology than his former student, indirectly engages this concept by borrowing Barbara Low's term "nirvana principle." For Freud, the nirvana principle is ultimately affiliated with the death instinct, which he juxtaposes with the libidinal life instincts. As an unconscious propensity away from the activity of life, the nirvana principle shows itself in such activities as rest, sleep, and even suicide. This retreat from the exasperating striving for life is a natural response and ultimate goal for a return to inactivity, ultimately transforming life back to its previous inorganic state. With the nirvana principle, Eros confronts Thanatos, destruction engages construction. Both Eros and Thanatos are helpful

aspects of life as they provide a necessary balance for activity. Trouble often ensues if they become imbalanced.

See also: ❷ Amita Buddha ❷ Arhat ❷ Atman ❷ Bodhisattva ❷ Bodhi Tree ❷ Buddha-Nature ❷ Buddhism ❷ Eros ❷ Freud, Sigmund, and Religion ❷ Individuation ❷ Jung, Carl Gustav, and Eastern Religious Traditions ❷ Samsara and Nirvana ❷ Self ❷ Sunyata ❷ Thanatos ❷ Transcendence ❷ Zen

Bibliography

Anonymous. (1881). Buddhist Suttas. In T. W. Rhys Davids (Trans.), F. Max Müller (Ed.), *Sacred books of the East* (Vol. 11). Oxford, England: The Clarendon Press. From http://www.sacred-texts.com/bud/sbe11/index.htm [CW].

Anonymous. (1881). The Dhammapada and the Sutta-Nipâta. In F. Max Müller & V. Fausböll, (Trans.), F. Max Müller, (Ed.), *Sacred books of the East* (Vol. 10). Oxford, England: The Clarendon Press. Retrieved June 16, 2008 from http://www.sacred-texts.com/bud/sbe10/index.htm [CW].

Anonymous. (1896). Buddhism in translations. In H. C. Warren (Trans. & Ed.), *Harvard oriental series* (Vol. 3). Cambridge, MA: Harvard University Press. From http://www.sacred-texts.com/bud/bits/index.htm [CW].

Anonymous. (1991). Nirvana. In I. Fischer-Schreiber, F. -K. Ehrhard, & M. S. Diener (Eds.), *The Shambhala Dictionary of Buddhism and Zen*. Boston, MA: Shambhala.

Freud, S. (1961). *Beyond the pleasure principle*. New York: W.W. Norton & Company.

Jung, C. G. (1958). *Psychology and religion: West and East*. In R. F. C. Hull, (Trans.), H. Read & G. Adler (Eds.), *The collected works of C. G. Jung* (Vol. 11). New York: Bollingen Foundation.

Kasulis, T. P. (1987). Nirvāna. In M. Eliade (Ed.), *The encyclopedia of religion* (Vol. 10). New York: Macmillan.

Nonduality

Hillary S. Webb

While "duality" as an ontological construct refers to a philosophical system in which existence is believed to consist of two equally real and essential substances (such as mind and matter) and/or categories (such as "being" and "nonbeing," "good" and "bad," "subject" and "object"), philosophies of "nonduality" emphasize the fundamental nature of reality as being a single, undifferentiated essence or consciousness. Although the term "nonduality" comes from the Sanskrit word *advaita*, meaning, "not two," forms of nondual philosophies have found articulation in a number of spiritual traditions around the world, including Christian and Jewish mysticism, Sufism, Taoism, Madyamika Buddhism, and various branches of Hinduism. Certain Western theologians and philosophers (among them Plotinus, Meister Eckhart, and G. W. F. Hegel, to name a few) have also embraced forms of nondualism as being representative of ultimate reality.

It is, of course, important to point out that while a belief system may be identified as "nondual," the various systems are not necessarily identical to one another. Despite sharing a similar ontological basis, nondual philosophies can be quite different in their particular perspectives and practices. For example, the extent to which each tradition rejects the reality or importance of the material world varies. Some nondual systems deny the ultimate reality of the phenomenal world to such an extent that all "knowledge" attained through the physical and mental senses is seen as being more or less empty of absolute value (e.g., Advaita Vedanta Hinduism). Others, while ultimately nondual, place greater value on the material realm, considering it to be the means by which one can come to understand the ultimately singular nature of reality (e.g., many of the Mahayana, Theravada, and Vajrayana Schools of Buddhism).

For the purposes of this article, the term "nonduality" will be used as a way of describing spiritual systems based on the underlying presumption that the phenomenal world of forms is an illusion – albeit perhaps a *necessary* illusion – and that through making shifts in consciousness one can escape the delusion of separation and distinction created by the dualizing mind (perhaps most importantly and most challengingly, that of having a separate "I" self) and achieve what Evelyn Underhill (1911/2002) described as, "that perfect unity of consciousness, that utter concentration on an experience of love, which excludes all conceptual and analytic acts" (p. 371).

From Wholeness to Separation

In his book *Nonduality: A Study in Comparative Philosophy*, author David Loy (1988) provides an interesting deconstruction of what has been suggested are the three stages that the mind passes through in its transition from an initial non-dual, undifferentiated state of consciousness, to that of a dualistic, ego-identified awareness (that is, one in which the "I-self" becomes dis-identified from all other aspects of existence).

To begin, one's attention is drawn toward a stimulus. In this, nondual state of awareness, there is a split-second of "being with" the object or sensation in its "bare existence," during which time it is unnamed and undistinguished. The object of attention just is what it is, without judgment or distinction. This non-dualistic way of knowing is "unassociated with name," "undifferentiated," and "non-relational." It is "immediate apprehension" and "direct sense experience" (Loy, 1988). This initial, often unconscious, state of awareness is followed by a second, in which what was initially perceived as a "pure concept" is now identified and made determinate by giving it a linguistic label. The original, undifferentiated stimulus becomes identified as, say, "cat." The third and final stage in this process is what Loy describes as "an occasion for entrancement." While in the first stage, I experience the initial, nondual sensation of a stimulus, and in the second I identify the stimulus and give it the linguistic label of "cat," in this third stage, an emotional and/or intellectual response based on memory of past experiences attaches itself to the object of attention. For example, I see "my cat" and I imagine him sitting in my lap, purring, and I desire to pick him up. Or, I remember finding a dead chipmunk in my closet the night before and I am angry and shoo him away.

Falsely believing the conceptualizations created by language, memory, and emotion to be reflective of ultimate reality itself, pure consciousness moves deeper and deeper into a self-created illusion, until the world we experience becomes no more than a projection, a habitual fiction of our minds. With the world split up into a multiplicity of forms, linguistic labels, and emotional conceptualizations, life becomes a never-ending struggle between that which is considered to be "good" and therefore desirable and that which is "bad" and to be avoided. The aim of many of the nondual traditions is, therefore, to help the individual return to the initial, *spontaneous* stage of pure awareness that occurs just before the conceptualization process begins. By returning to a nondual state of awareness – one in which no distinctions exist between things (including the self) – the individual will cease to desire one thing over the other, and, in doing so, will cease to suffer.

Nondual Psychologies

What have emerged out of the nondual philosophies' goal of complete liberation from suffering through achieving a state of "pure perception" (Loy, 1988) are psychological approaches to dealing with the human condition. This is especially evident when compared with the more mechanistic and behaviorally oriented perspectives of traditional Western psychologies, which originally emerged out of a scientific worldview based on the assumption that all human functioning is the result of material causes. Given this ontological presumption that all things can be reduced to the material, some early pioneers in Western psychology (e.g., behavioralists John B. Watson, B. F. Skinner) denied consciousness as a thing in and of itself, believing all psychological states to be products of behavior. Others (e.g., Sigmund Freud) acknowleged the existence of consciousness but attributed mental states to be ultimately rooted in physical and/or external influences such as social environment, biochemical or evolutionary processes, personal history, and so on. In cases such as these, with biological and/or social elements seen as constituting the "first cause" of human suffering, the human psyche becomes entrapped in a kind of psychological determinism based on the assumption that the individual is unable to escape his or her history and/or biology unless some secondary factors are introduced. In contrast, however, within the context of several of the nondual traditions (e.g., Advaita Vedanta Hinduism, Madhyamika Buddhism), cause and effect are considered ultimately illusory. Rather than being a product of his or her environment, biology, or past history, nondual psychologies maintain that suffering originates within the consciousness of the individual, and that the answer to suffering lies in making shifts in one's consciousness to return to a pure, undifferentiated state. Once the individual's thinking changes, the outer world in which he or she exists will shift to an equal degree (Loy, 1988).

And, yet, even this notion of "change" may be considered illusory within the nondual context. While some psycho-therapeutic systems seek to first identify deficiencies or distortions in the psyche and then alter the mental behavior seen as responsible for these dysfunctions, nondual thinkers assert that attempts to "fix" ourselves only trap us deeper into our suffering, for to "fix" something implies a distinction between a desired state and an undesired state. But because from the nondual point of view all things are considered to be ultimately singular and undifferentiated, no one need "become" anything (Ajaya, 1983; Prendergast, Fenner, and Krystal, 2003).

As is said in the *Katha Upanishad*, "What is within us is also without. What is without is also within. He who sees difference between what is within and what is without remains trapped in the drama of struggling unceasingly to find that which is already within" (as cited in Ajaya, 1983: 66).

"Trying to transcend our human shortcomings and imperfections, our 'sins and defilements,' does not liberate them," notes John Welwood (2003) in his essay *Double Vision: Duality and Nonduality in Human Experience*. Rather, he claims, "Only entering into them and suffering them consciously allows us to exhaust their momentum, move through them, and be done with them" (p. 159).

With this in mind, within the nondual framework, "problems" or "dysfunctions" are not considered negative events that must be resolved or avoided, but rather are seen as tools to lead one towards greater awareness of the true nature of the self. Instead of trying to alter one's mental state, these systems suggest that one just "be with" phenomenal experience without judgment or attachment to outcome (Prendergast, Fenner, and Krystal, 2003).

What may perhaps be the most distinctive, and most challenging feature of nondual psychologies is what Underhill (1911/2002) calls the "last and drastic purgation" (p. 396), that is, the individual's attempt to "disidentify" with the illusion of having a separate ego or I-self. The goal of both nondual psychologies and the more materially/behaviorally based Western psychologies is to help the individual to "know" him or herself, and yet each does so from a very different frame of reference. While certain branches of Western psychology (e.g., various psychoanalytic schools) focuses on helping the individual become *more* identified with the ego (thereby establishing a stronger and more distinctive sense of self) as part of the development of the personality, many nondual traditions (e.g., Advaita Vedanta Hinduism, Madhyamika Buddhism, as well as many of the theist mystical traditions) assert that this reinforcement of the ego's separateness from the rest of existence reinforces duality and leads to further isolation, anxiety, and, ultimately, suffering. In order for suffering to cease, absolutely and completely, only a total dissolution of ego-hood and return to a state of undifferentiated awareness will suffice. Nondual practices therefore seek to dissolve the individual's sense of having a separate "I-hood" so that the individual can come to identify with his or her more true nature as pure consciousness (Ajaya, 1983).

Says the Hindu sage, Shankara (1978), "[The ego] robs you of peace and joy... By identifying yourself with it, you have fallen into the snare of the world – the miseries of birth, decay, and death" (p. 83).

For obvious reasons, the separation between the individual ego self and the unified, non-dual self is the hardest division of all to reconcile, for it requires that the individual surrender all that he or she identifies with as "I." Through the various meditative and/or ascetic practices, a more comprehensive center of consciousness develops within the psyche of the individual. Subject-object, I-thou distinctions begin to dissolve, until the practitioner experiences a state of consciousness in which all conceptual distinctions disappear. This is the Buddhist awakening experience of *nirvana* or *satori*, or Hinduism's liberation from the cycle of death and rebirth through *moksha*. It has been equated with the *illumination* experience described by Christian mystics, as well as the experience of *ein sof* of Jewish mysticism and *fanaa* of Sufism, to name a few. Descriptions of this ineffable state of "no-self" vary from tradition to tradition, but is most consistently described as a state of being in which all multiplicity and distinction dissolve and the finite and differentiated I-self enters into divine union with the infinite Oneness of all existence. It is said that one who has achieved this state of consciousness still exists in and interacts with the phenomenal world, but now does not attach him/herself to the superimpositions created by the multiplicity of forms (Loy, 1988).

Says John Prendergast, "When we awaken from the sense of personal identity, we also awaken from all our role identities, even as these roles continue. We are like the actor who snaps out of his trance while onstage and suddenly realizes that he had lost himself in his role. . . . Freed of the role identity, we are more authentic, transparent, available, and creative in the moment" (Prendergast, 2003: 6–7).

While many of the beliefs and practices of nondual psychologies may seem irrational or even insane by non-nondual standards, nondual psychologies have, over the years, had a profound influence on the more human-centered Western psychotherapeutic practices, particularly within the field of transpersonal psychology. More recently, an emerging discipline of psychotherapeutic practice called "nondual therapy" has begun to emerge, on that seeks to integrate the philosophies and practices of nondual psychologies within the consciousness of a Western clientele (Prendergast, Fenner, and Krystal, 2003).

Acknowledgement

The author would like to thank Francis X. Charet and Donald Rothberg for their assistance with this very nuanced subject.

See also: ❷ Buddhism ❷ Freud, Sigmund ❷ Hinduism

Bibliography

Ajaya, S. (1983). *Psychotherapy East and West*. Honesdale, PA: Himalayan Publishers.

Loy, D. (1988). *Nonduality: A study in comparative philosophy*. Amherst, NY: Humanity Books.

Prabhavananda, S., & Isherwood, C. (1978). *Shankara's crest-jewel of discrimination*. Hollywood, CA: Vedanta Press.

Prendergast, J. J. (2003). Introduction. In J. J. Prendergast, P. Fenner, & S. Krystal (Eds.), *The sacred mirror: Nondual wisdom and psycho-therapy* (pp. 1–22). St. Paul, MN: Paragon House.

Prendergast, J. J., Fenner, P., & Krystal, S. (2003). *The sacred mirror: Nondual wisdom and psychotherapy*. St. Paul, MN: Paragon House.

Underhill, E. (2002). *Mysticism: A study in the nature and development of spiritual consciousness*. Mineola, NY: Dover Publications. (Original work published 1911)

Welwood, J. (2003). Double vision: Duality and nonduality in human experience. In J. J. Prendergast, P. Fenner, & S. Krystal (Eds.), *The sacred mirror: Nondual wisdom and psychotherapy* (pp. 138–163). St. Paul, MN: Paragon House.

Numinosum

Ann Casement

Numinosum is the term Jung appropriated from Rudolf Otto's *The Idea of the Holy: An Inquiry into the non-rational factor in the idea of the divine and its relation to the rational*, produced during the First World War. It is a philosophical work showing the influence of Schleiermacher, Marett, Husserl, and Neo-Kantianism but the central experience depicted in it, referred to as the *numinous*, particularly attracted Jung's attention. Otto adopted the term from a word coined from the Latin *numen* defined in the Oxford Dictionary as a presiding deity or spirit. The Latin dictionary further defines *numen* as "nod" or "will" both of which are important in Jung's usage of the term numinous. For instance, he often refers to a numinous experience as a "hint" that there are greater powers in the psyche than ego is conscious of. He was also influenced by Schopenhauer's use of the term "will" which derived from the numinous depths of the psyche. "Hence it is that we can often give no account of the origin of our deepest thoughts. They are the birth of our mysterious inner life" (Schopenhauer, 1883: 328).

Otto was a theologian who traveled widely in the West (Europe and the United States), the Middle-East (Palestine and Egypt), and the East (India, China and Japan). As the sub-title of the book shows, Otto pointed to the need to keep the rational and non-rational in some kind of relationship when dealing with religious matters. Furthermore, he depicted the *numinous* as both attractive and repellent in giving rise to feelings of supreme fascination and tremendous mystery, of nameless dread and fear, and of submergence and personal nothingness before the awe-inspiring directly experienced object, the numinous raw material for the feeling of religious humility. Otto quotes from the philosopher, William James, as follows: "The perfect stillness of the night was thrilled by a more solemn silence. The darkness held a presence that was all the more felt because it was not seen. I could not any more have doubted that *He* was there than that I was. Indeed, I felt myself to be, if possible, the less real of the two" (Otto, 1923: 22).

Otto's influence on Jung is to be found in frequent references to the numinous in the latter's work from the mid 1930s on though Jung adapted this to fit with his empirical psychological approach to religious issues. For instance, he states it would be a regrettable mistake to assume from archetypal God-images that they prove the existence of God. Instead, they are "...the most we can assert about God psychologically." But "...since experience of this archetype has the quality of numinosity, often in very high degree, it comes into the category of religious experiences" (Jung, 1958a: 59). Both writers draw on the *Book of Job* from the *Old Testament* but here again Jung's focus is on the "psychic nature and effects" of "the extraordinary numinosity" of the God-images (Jung, 1958b: 363).

The Numinous Mystery of "I"-ness

The central place of the numinous in Otto's theological reflections and Jung's psychology has inspired a recent book, *The Idea of the Numinous*, from which the following extracts are taken.

The psychoanalyst, James Grotstein's *Foreword* shows the close connection between Jung and Bion's later work in their approach to numinosity. This is in sharp contrast to Freud as Grotstein makes clear in the following statement: "The concept of the numinous offers a dimension to our unconscious lives that is utterly missing in Freud" (Grotstein, 2006: xiv). As David Tacey says: "Jung does not challenge us with sexuality, but with something equally primary and perhaps more terrifying; the reality of the *numinous*" (Tacey, 2006: 219). Similarly, Grotstein points to the psychoanalytic realization of the primacy of affects rather than the primacy of the instinctual drives arising from the postmodern trend towards subjectivity and intersubjectivity where they "begin to approximate the numinous because they are, originally, infinite in nature – and numinosity does seem to constitute an expression of affect, all be it, an affect of a very particular and ineffably distinctive nature" (Grotstein, 2006: xii). Furthermore "Jung's allusions to the numinous are many, and most often concern the emotional, affective experience of the unconscious..."(Huskinson, 2006: 202).

References from other contributors to the book underline Grotstein's statement as follows: "Jung...personally engaged the 'God within' in a wholly psychological manner, and while he related to the *imago Dei* with the same passion and feeling for its mystery and awesome emotional power as did Otto, he related to it psychologically" (Stein, 2006: 43). "For Jung, God seemed to be both divine and, in a terrible way, anything but divine...'on the one hand a bloody struggle, on the other supreme ecstasy'" (Bishop, 2006: 120). "...archetypal representations referring to Apollo and Dionysus...show how they seem to be pointing at underlying psychic structures which are involved in the experience of that emotionally charged and consciousness-transforming *mysterium tremendum* which Otto named 'numinous'" (Giaccardi, 2006: 138). "What Jung calls 'the numinous' and Derrida the 'sublime'...engages the passions of ...the struggle between the logos god and eros goddess...wrestling for the soul of modernity" (Rowland, 2006: 116). "The numinous affects what is uncontrolled in people and so can let loose dangerous psychic reactions in the public" (Main, 2006: 159).

Numinosity and the Alchemy of Individuating

Jung's writings often demonstrate his psychological approach to analysis centered on the numinous as follows: "...the main interest of my work is not concerned with the treatment of neuroses but rather with the approach to the numinous" (Jung, 1973: Vol. 1, 377). The following writers acknowledge this as in Murray Stein statement: "The individuation process...typically includes experiences of a numinous nature" (Stein 2006: 34). John Dourley says: "Jung's equation of therapy with the experience of the numinous and with religious conversion has little or nothing to do with religion as commonly understood" (Dourley, 2006: 172). "The psychological reality of Christ is the numinous experience of the self becoming incarnate in consciousness" (Dourley, 2006: 181). And Lucy Huskinson writes: "The numinous object cannot be forced or summoned into consciousness; it is not subject to the ego's control. Rather, the numinous object is discovered in its autonomous manifestation where it calls the ego into response" (Huskinson, 2006: 200). As Edward Edinger says about Job in his inspiring "little" book *Encounter with the Self*: "If he were to decide that his misfortunes were all his own fault he would preclude the possibility of a manifestation of the *numinosum*. The ego-vessel would be broken, would lose its integrity, and could have no divine manifestation poured into it. By holding fast to its own experience as an authentic center (*sic*) of being, the Job-ego brings about the visible manifestation of the 'other,' the transpersonal center" (Edinger, 1986: 43).

Jung says, archetypes possess a certain numinosity so that "(i)t is a psychological rule that when an archetype...becomes identified with the conscious mind of the individual...(it) produces an inflation of the subject" (Jung, 1958c: 315). "I think that Genesis is right in so far as every step towards greater consciousness is a kind of Promethean guilt: through knowledge, the gods are as it were robbed of their fire, that is, something that was the property of the unconscious powers is torn out of its natural context and subordinated to the whims of the conscious mind" (Jung, 1953: 156). The knowledge meant here is that of greater consciousness which leads to an enlargement or inflation of the ego. This is an inevitable part of the individuating process but not without its dangers as the ego that remains identified with "unconscious powers" may become grandiose. It is this grandiosity that can be punctured and bring the person crashing down to earth.

The Concept of Dread

At the time of the Enlightenment, the contents of the Bible, in particular the myth of the fall of Adam and Eve, came under fresh scrutiny depicting as it does the numinous conflict between good and evil. "Our angst-ridden age was heralded by Kierkegaard's *The Concept of Dread*, which postulates that dread is a *prelude* to sin not its *sequel* and may precede a shift from a state of ignorance to attainment of new awareness" (Casement, 1998: 70) (Original italics.) Adam is forbidden to eat of the tree of the knowledge of good and evil but he cannot understand this for the distinction between the two would only follow as a result of his eating the fruit. "Thus Adam is in a state of ignorance when the voice of prohibition awakens in him a new set of possibilities, including the possibility of disobedience" (Casement, 1998: 70). Thus dread is a prelude to sin which precedes the attainment of new awareness, therefore, it follows logically on that dread is prospective.

This prospective component of numinous dread is akin to Jung's thinking on the prospective or purposive nature of unconscious psychic contents. Huskinson contrasts Otto's non-purposive interpretation of Job's numinous encounter with God with the purposive orientation of the "Jungian psyche" stating the latter is grounded in the *holy* as "that which instils meaning and content in the *tremendum* ...(as the wrath of God)...Without such mediation, we are unable to make sense of, and thus utilize, the creative energies unleashed in the numinous experience" (Huskinson, 2006: 208).

Bishop, in his turn, points to Goethe's "...the Numinous, in the sense of the Monstrous" which links to "analogous experiences in the case of C. G. Jung" and back to the Goethe quotation in Otto's work: "When our own eyes have glimpsed a monstrous act" (Bishop, 2006: 118). It is this monstrous core of the numinous that "shows" (from the Latin *monstrare* to show) ego consciousness the way towards what Jung terms individuation and the fateful transformations that are encountered by any individual journeying along that path. It is in this way that the Jungian psyche relates to the numinous.

See also: ⊚ Apollo ⊚ Bion, Wilfred Ruprecht, and "O" ⊚ Dionysos ⊚ Job ⊚ Jung, Carl Gustav ⊚ Kierkegaard, Søren

Bibliography

Bishop, P. (2006). *The idea of the numinous in Goethe and Jung*. In A. Casement & D. Tacey (Eds.), *The idea of the numinous: Contemporary Jungian and psychoanalytic perspectives*. Hove, England: Routledge.

Casement, A. (1998). The qualitative leap of faith: Reflections on Kierkegaard and Jung. In A. Casement (Ed.), *Post-Jungians today: Key papers in contemporary analytical psychology*. Hove, London: Routledge.

Dourley, J. (2006). Rerooting in the mother: the numinosity of the night. In A. Casement (Ed.), *The idea of the numinous: Contemporary Jungian and psychoanalytic perspectives*. Hove, England: Routledge.

Edinger, E. F. (1986). *Encounter with the self: A Jungian commentary on William Blake's illustrations of the Book of Job*. Toronto: Inner City Books.

Giaccardi, G. (2006). Accessing the numinous: Apolline and Dionysian pathways. In A. Casement & D. Tacey (Eds.), *The idea of the numinous: Contemporary Jungian and psychoanalytic perspectives*. Hove, England: Routledge.

Grotstein, J. (2006). Foreword. In A. Casement (Ed.), *The idea of the numinous: Contemporary Jungian and psychoanalytic perspectives* (pp. xi–xv). London: Routledge.

Huskinson, L. (2006). Holy, Holy, Holy: The misappropriation of the numinous in Jung. In A. Casement & D. Tacey (Eds.), *The idea of the numinous: Contemporary Jungian and psychoanalytic perspectives*. Hove, England: Routledge.

Jung, C. G. (1953). The persona as a segment of the collective psyche. In *Two essays on analytical psychology*. Princeton, NJ: Princeton University Press.

Jung, C. G. (1958a). Psychology and religion. In *Psychology and religion: West and East* (Vol. 11). London: Routledge & Kegan Paul Ltd.

Jung, C. G. (1958b). Answer to job. In *Psychology and religion: West and East* (Vol. 11). London: Routledge & Kegan Paul Ltd.

Jung, C. G. (1958c). Foreword to Werblowsky's "Lucifer and Prometheus" In *Psychology and religion: West and East* (Vol. 11). London: Routledge & Kegan Paul.

Jung, C. G. (1973). *C. G. Jung Letters* (selected and ed. G. Adler with A. Jaffé) (2 Vols.). Princeton, NJ: Princeton University Press.

Main, R. (2006). Numinosity and terror: Jung's psychological revision of Otto as an aid to engaging religious fundamentalism. In *The idea of the numinous: Contemporary Jungian and psychoanalytic perspectives*. Hove, London: Routledge.

Otto, R. (1923). *The Idea of the holy: An inquiry into the non-rational factor in the idea of the divine and its relation to the rational*. London: Oxford University Press.

Rowland, S. (2006). Jung and Derrida: The numinous, deconstruction and myth. In A. Casement & D. Tacey (Eds.), *The idea of the numinous: Contemporary Jungian and psychoanalytic perspectives*. Hove, England: Routledge.

Schopenhauer, A. (1883). *The World as will and idea* (R. B. Haldane & J. Kemp, Trans.) (Vol. 3). London: Routledge & Kegan Paul.

Stein, M. (2006). On the importance of numinous experience in the alchemy of individuation. In A. Casement (Ed.), *The idea of the numinous: Contemporary Jungian and psychoanalytic perspectives*. Hove, England: Routledge.

Tacey, D. (2006). The role of the numinous in the reception of Jung. In A. Casement (Ed.), *The idea of the numinous: Contemporary Jungian and psychoanalytic perspectives* Hove, England: Routledge.

O

Object Relations Theory

Benjamin Beit-Hallahmi

The concept of "Object relations" in psychoanalytic writings means relations with significant others and their internal representations, starting with infancy and the mother ("object" in psychoanalytic writings always refers to another person). Primitive, early, object relations are the starting point for personality development. Whereas, for Freud, the drive-based quest for sensuous gratification conditions the structure of the personality, object relations theorists argued that the individual seeks relationships before seeking gratification. The pattern taken by the individual's relationship with others, internalized during early childhood, structures the adult personality as well as adult spirituality.

What is known as psychoanalytic object-relations theory represents the psychoanalytic study of the nature and origins of interpersonal relations, and, more significantly, of the nature and origins of internal, unconscious, structures deriving from interpersonal contacts and experiences. Present interpersonal relationships are regarded as the reactivation of past internalized relations with others. Psychoanalytic object-relations theory focuses upon the internalization of interpersonal relations, their contribution to normal and pathological personality development, and the mutual influences of internal fantasies and the reality of interpersonal relations.

Individual personality is formed through object relations patterns which are set up in early childhood, become stable in later childhood and adolescence, and then are fixed during adult life. The functioning of the adult personality depends on the maturity of one's object relations. Object relations theorists propose that the ego, which is the center of the personality, seeks objects, and this is the basic drive animating the human personality. The role played by the mother's constant presence during the first stages of life makes it the factor around which personality is organized. The mode by which one manages one's dependence on and differentiation from the mother is the structuring force of the individual mind. Psychoses and neuroses are accounted for by the complications of parental care rather than by eruptions of repressed desire.

Motivations experienced by the individual's body alone are thus deemphasized, and, correspondingly, the formative significance of relating to others is played up. Sexuality is demoted to a secondary role. It may complicate the relationship with the object, but it does not by itself constitute that relationship. Body sensations carry messages, but are not equivalent to the contents of these messages. Communication is channeled through the surface of the body, the sensitivity of which intensifies with the child's age. At all stages, bodily sensation is a means rather than an end of communication.

While classical psychoanalytic theory viewed the personality as an information processing system, in touch (or out of touch) with reality, in object relations theory the emphasis is on internalized and projected ideas, leading to a total distortion of reality. Compared to classical approaches, object relations theory is even more pessimistic. It views personality as less reality-oriented, and its structure as determined earlier in life. While in Freud's version the "critical period" in personality development is the Oedipal stage, years 3–6 of life, here it is during the first year that object relations patterns are determined.

The common core of classical psychoanalytic theory and object relations theory can be summarized in the two concepts of a search (for an object or for instinctual gratification), and an experienced distance from the object. Both approaches agree that it all starts with the young child and its understanding of sex, birth, and family relations, with the inevitable results in the form of confused and confusing ideas that stay with us for life. Object relations theory claims that the process all starts very early, which means that the cognitive confusion is greater and deeper.

Donald W. Winnicott asserted that at the original point from which all humans start there is already a relationship. The baby is an aggregate of sensations and

D. A. Leeming, K. Madden, S. Marlan (eds.), *Encyclopedia of Psychology and Religion*, DOI 10.1007/978-0-387-71802-6,
© Springer Science+Business Media LLC 2010

body parts without an organizing principle, which may only be provided by the parent "who is holding the child" physically, and whose presence functions as an external perimeter that contains the various stimuli and so orders them into a meaningful whole. Thus, relationship precedes individuality. There is no such thing as a baby, because there is always, attached to it, someone caring for the baby. The lack of individual separateness in the initial stages of life goes beyond the fact of physical dependence. It involves the absence of inner cohesion.

At this point the child creates what Winnicott calls the transitional object. This object appears when the reassuring internal representation of the mother is projected onto a tangible item, such as a blanket or a soft toy, which the child invests with special meaning and identity. The transitional object helps the child bridge the frustration of parental unavailability. That object is simultaneously internal and external: it carries a subjective meaning, but, being tangible, it is also objectively perceived. In later life the soft toy or blanket is substituted by games, artistic creativity and intellectual discussion. Such activities provide individuals with spaces where they can externalize their internal images. Winnicott's concept of transitional states and transitional objects has been applied to religious ritual and belief, assuming that religion tries to elaborate an experiential space between the self and reality.

Regarding religious beliefs, most object relations theorists follow Sigmund Freud in viewing any religious belief system as based on projections. While Freud emphasized the projection of the father, the so-called Oedipal object, object relations theory suggests that what is projected is the maternal image, formed earlier in the child's development. The objective existence of the caring figure, without whom the infant would not survive is the source of fantasies about caring spirits, who promise eternal love and boundless happiness. As the developing child internalizes hope and trust he comes to live within an inner psychic universe of unseen, but providential presences. When he is subsequently introduced to supernaturalist beliefs through cultural experience (God, angels), he takes to it naturally.

Cultural fantasies expressed in so-called mystical experiences reflect an attempt to recreate the mother-child symbiotic encounter. The early experience of creating a substitute for the mother, known as the transitional object is the model for cultural rituals and beliefs. This experience is one case of transitional states, where a real stimulus near the person starts a fantasy process in which object relations are projected on it. This "substance of illusion," as Winnicott described it, is the starting point for the creation of art and religion. The behavior in an individual of turning to "spiritual search" is most likely to be caused by a loss of a significant other or a significant relationship. This search makes possible an imaginary contact with the lost object. Loss or absence in the child's relations with parental figures may lead to the appearance of religious experiences.

See also: ❂ Freud, Sigmund ❂ Psychoanalysis ❂ Winnicott, Donald Woods

Bibliography

Beit-Hallahmi, B. (1996). *Psychoanalytic studies of religion: Critical assessment and annotated bibliography.* Westport, CT: Greenwood Press.

Fairbairn, W. (1953). *Psychoanalytic studies of the personality.* London: Tavistock Publications.

Greenberg, J. R., &. Mitchell, S. A. (1983). *Object relations in psychoanalytic theory.* Cambridge, MA: Harvard University Press.

Winnicott, D. W. (1965). *The maturational process and the facilitating environment.* London: Hogarth Press.

Objective Psyche

Michael Conforti

In 1633, Galileo Galilei was forced to his knees by the Catholic Church, and with his hands on the Bible, demanded to retract his comments that the earth was not the center of the universe. Drawing on his years of scientific inquiry, he found that it was the *earth* which rotated around the sun and not the other way around. His was a heliocentric view of the universe, not a geocentric approach. Perhaps using science to refute religious dogma was not the best approach in the 1600s, but Galileo's search for truth knew no limits. Those near him during the inquisition heard him whisper under his breath the words, *eppure si muove* (and yet it moves), as he completed his testimony to the Papal See.

Eppure si muove speaks to the issue of relative and fixed space and movement. The Church needed to see the earth as center of the universe to justify its position of moral and spiritual supremacy. However, his utterance that "the earth moves" urges us to re-consider the relationship between relative and objective meaning. This theme remains crucial to our understanding not only of the world, but also the human psyche and in many ways has influenced the practice of psychotherapy and psychoanalysis.

Jung's discovery of the Objective Psyche closely parallels Galileo's findings, in that the ego, like the earth, was not to be viewed as the center of the personality. For Jung, the objective psyche allows us to determine the distinction between a relative and subjectively derived meaning from what is objective and invariant. While in relation to the ego, the matrix for this objective psyche exists independently of the conscious mind, and its contents are not acquired through personal experience. Like a compass pointing due north or a bird's innate capacity for building intricate nests and traveling thousands of miles during its migratory journeys, there is an internal wisdom and directionality within the psyche- a psychic "due north."

Like his mentor Freud, Jung sought to understand the workings of a personal unconscious. Our personal history clearly shapes our experience of the world. Freud's theory of the unconscious evolved into a topological model, comprised of a number of invariants, such as the *id, ego* and *superego*. While these can be viewed as inherent, universal components within the psyche, existing much like our biological inheritance, Freud tended to stress the personal aspects of each. On the contrary, Jung's discoveries identified the existence of non-personally derived, archetypal substrata inherent within the psyche, which continued to shape and effect the personality even without the conscious awareness of the individual.

Analogous to the workings of the biological unfolding of human life, we see that individual form is directly influenced by our genetic, personally acquired inheritance – blue eyes, brown hair, etc. However, prior to the emergence of these individual features, they exist *in potential* until a series of pre-figured, morphogenetically determined processes unfold.

Developmental biologists have discovered that fetuses develop in highly characteristic ways, according to a seemingly pre-determined schedule. At about eight weeks the heart beat can be heard. At different stages other features appear, as if by magic, in virtually the same sequence as all other babies since the beginning of humanity.

This unfolding of specificity in human form occurs against the backdrop of a set of universal, objective processes encoded within the body. The human psyche also follows a deeply etched riverbed traversed by humanity since the beginning of time. What are these silent codes that guide the development of our physical, psychological and spiritual life? The plethora of books available on infant and child development informs us about these "predictable," highly patterned processes.

While the emotions and perceptions of the ego and personal unconscious are influenced by experience and subjective reactions, the matrix from which the objective psyche gathers its impressions and information exists independent of individual experience.

With the eye of a scientist and the heart of a mystic, Jung sought to understand these other influences shape human experience. Familiar with the Freudian ethos, he realized that drive theory did explain the commonality of experience found throughout our collective history. Freud looked to drives, especially sexuality, as the primary mover of human experience. Jung understood the limitations of these ideas. Through many years studying different cultures and religions, he posited the existence of a set of universals within the human psyche. This point was especially evident in one of Jung's last recorded interviews, *Face to Face* (BBC Interview with John Freeman, October 22, 1959). Jung was asked if he believed in God. He smiled and said that he did not *believe* in a God, but *knew* there was a God. Belief, he explained, relied on faith, while knowing is arrived at through direct experience. He explained that every culture throughout history has some form of a God as a central component of their world. The constancy and universality of this *image* of a God suggests that a God or "God concept" exists as a living entity and an objective fact within the psyche.

The extensive body of Jung's writing details those universal portals which every individual must traverse, and a methodology for distilling an objective, ontological truth from the Scylla and Charybdis of bias and personal opinion. Like Galileo and the biologists who came after him, Jung demonstrated the effects of these objective aspects of life on individual development. He suggests that the Objective Psyche functions much like a magnet, constantly oriented towards true north. Consciousness, on the other hand, functions all too often as a faulty compass creating due north wherever one chooses to point it. Truth, meaning, and spirit, become relative terms, shaped by the individual's needs. One can take an objective fact, for instance entrance into mid-life, and create one's own meaning of it. For instance one can say, "I don't feel any different" and "I can do almost all of the things I did in my forties." Or, "I feel so much older and more worn our," and on an on. Clearly each of us will experience mid-life in our own way. The point here is that no matter how we subject this stage of life to the Procrustean Bed of personal opinion, there remains an objective fact- namely that one is at the mid-point of life.

Religious traditions have provided a rich body of literature regarding the universal features of these stages of life, and an awareness of the deep psychological and spiritual needs related to each stage. Mid-life requires us to attend to a particular set of issues that were not part of our concerns during the first half of life.

The existence of an "objective," ontologically based psychology is now supported by discoveries in the sciences, which address the concept of self-organizing systems. The self-regulatory functioning of the body is one illustration of such tendencies. For example, our blood sugar levels are governed by the presence of what are called *periodic attractors*. Like a pendulum moving 30 degrees to the right or to the left, biological rhythms are governed by an innate ordering principle, which serves to maintain our metabolic reactions within a certain, pre-determined range.

Jung's (1969) work on the symbolism in the Mass provides a compelling illustration of the objective psyche. In his essay, " *Transformation Symbolism in the Mass*," he looks beyond individual experience to the ontological, symbolic meaning of the Mass. Writing of its psychological significance, Jung states:

▶ ...human consciousness (represented by the priest and congregation) is confronted with an autonomous event which is taking place on a "divine" and "timeless" plane transcending consciousness, is in now way dependent on human action, but which impels man to act by seizing upon him as an instrument and making him the exponent of a "divine" happening. In the ritual action, man places himself at the disposal of an autonomous and "eternal" agency operating outside the categories of human consciousness. . . . . It is something outside, something autonomous which seizes and moves him (1969: 249–250, 379).

Jung takes a similar approach to symbolic imagery found in dreams, fantasies and hallucinations. Traditional psychotherapeutic approaches seek to understand symbols through clients' associations. Jung looked to the inherent, innate and universal meaning of these symbols. This approach is illustrated in the following analysis of a dream.

Dream

▶ I am visiting Florida during a March vacation. I go to the beach on a lovely sunny day, and suddenly see baby turtles emerging from a mound in the sand. Hundreds of them are emerging from the sand, and moving towards the sea. It is such a beautiful sight, that I am moved to tears.

While it is essential to ask for the client's associations and feelings about the dream, for this example, I will present the approach used in working with the Objective Psyche in clinical material.

Since this dream presents the motif of turtles hatching, we need to enter the "field" (Conforti, 2004) of turtles born on Florida beaches in March. While it is possible for the patient and analyst to have impressionistic or circumstantial information about this topic, it is important to seek out objective and accurate details about the birth of turtles and the conditions required to insure successful completion of the gestation period. In this dream the turtles hatch in March. However, turtles actually *lay their eggs* in March, and they lay burrowed in the sand as a protection against the hot Florida sun. We also learn that predation results in only 1 out of 10,000 hatchlings ever surviving to maturity. Now with these objective facts, we are prepared to work with this dream.

The material provided by our specialist, enables us to see that something within the patient's psyche, and perhaps also within the analysis, is occurring out of sequence. What has just begun its gestation is now hatching, during a time when prospects for reaching maturation are minimal, at best. The requisite incubation period was, for some reason, interrupted, thus jeopardizing what was seeking expression within the patient.

Let's now explore the image of the turtle. One of the most salient features of turtles is their shell. Their protection is external, whereas with humans and most other mammals the protective skeletal structure is internal. In many earlier life forms, protective defenses remained external. So the turtle's ecto-skeletal make up may symbolize an early and somewhat primitive system of defense, which is also very vulnerable. In the dream, what is attempting to born is a somewhat primitive and necessary system of defense, but one that will in all probability, not survive.

Recent studies have found that our conscious mind generally perceives only 7.4% of the information available in our field of data. Translated, this means that the ego is aware of only a small portion of its experiences. Jung's discovery of the objective psyche encourages us to look beyond the confines of what we generally perceive, thus allowing for a wisdom far greater than that derived from our conscious minds.

Religious traditions and the world's great spiritual teachers have always spoken about a world far wiser than the one we habitually inhabit. Spirituality is an accessing of the transcendent. In virtually every religious tradition, one has to undergo a series of rituals meant to lessen the hold of conscious reality, to allow for the unknown to enter. Meister Eckart echoes this point: "All the different religions traditions can be traced back to the experience of communion with the Ultimate. . .(with) the one and the same mystical core-experiences of the sense of ultimate belonging" (Fitz-Gibbon: 2008: 196).

Our wisdom traditions seek to move beyond the veil of conscious reality a greater knowledge for our understanding about life. This point is beautifully made in *Saul Lieberman: Talmudic Scholar and Classicist* (2002).

Discussing Rabbi Lieberman's approach to reading a sacred text we find him suggesting that:

> (...) We are always on safer ground when the reading is sure, and all that remains for us to do is to explain it. Of course a scholar's understanding of a given text depends on what he brings to it: the more he knows the less likely he is to engage in conjectures not justified by the facts; the less likely he is to doctor a text that should be left alone, the less likely he is to offer a labored, intricate explanation, when he should be saying; "I don't know." On the other hand, the more he knows, the more likely he is to select the correct meaning and when necessary, amend one that has been corrupted in transmission (2002: 4/5).

In summation, Jung's discovery of the Objective Psyche follows in the rich traditions of scientists, theologians, mystics and investigators of the human mind, whose search for knowledge about the psyche brought them into dialog with the eternal wisdom traditions, which have shaped personal and spiritual development throughout human history.

See also: ❂ Freud, Sigmund ❂ God Image ❂ Jung, Carl Gustav ❂ Meister Eckart ❂ Personal Unconscious

Bibliography

Conforti, M. (2004). *Field, form and fate: Patterns in mind, nature and psyche*. New Orleans, LA: Spring Journal Books.

Fitz-Gibbon, A. (2008). Spiritual practice as a foundation for peacemaking. In D. Poe & E. Souffrant (Eds.), *Parceling the globe: Philosophical exploration in globalization, global behavior, and peace*. The Netherlands - New York: Editions Rodopi B.V.

Hawking, S. (Ed.) (2002). *On the shoulders of giants: Dialogues concerning two new sciences*. Philadelphia PA: Running Press Book Publishers.

Jung, C. G. (1969). *Psychology and religion: West and East*. Princeton, NJ: Princeton University Press.

Jung, C. G. (1984). Transformation symbolism in the mass. In *Psychology and Western Religion*. Princeton, NJ: Princeton University Press.

Lubutski, M. (Ed.). (2002). *Saul Lieberman (1898–1983) Talmudic scholar and classicist*. New York: The Edwin Mellon Press.

Occultism

Paul Larson

The term "occult" means hidden and has been used for over two centuries to describe a variety of esoteric philosophies grounded in the Western philosophical tradition. Esoteric doctrines are passed among a smaller group of people than the outer more public, or exoteric forms of spirituality and philosophy. The word "occult" and its derivatives are often used in a pejorative way by religious conservatives who view the wide range of views subsumed under this label as evil and involving devil worship. Rejection of esoteric forms occurs in many religious traditions, but has an especially violent history in the Christian tradition.

Occult philosophy, or the western esoteric tradition (WET) is thoroughly syncretic, blending ideas, practices, and symbols of the divine from several streams. Western culture incorporates elements from both classical Greece and Rome, with ideas and practices taken from Judaism. Christianity represents a fusion of Judaic roots and Greco-Roman philosophy. Into this mix is poured ample elements of eastern thought and practice. Religious syncretism characterizes the Western esoteric tradition.

From the Greek inheritance comes the font of much Western magic with Pythagoras (ca. 582–507 BCE). He first used the five-pointed star which has now been adopted by Wiccans and other pagans as a religious symbol. Among the oldest of sources, we have less of his thought preserved. He was insightful and skilled in mathematics, his theorem on right angled triangles is the contribution for which he is best known, but he also saw the relationship between length of string and pitch, another aspect of mathematics. He founded the first Western mystery school in Croton, Italy.

The mystery religions of classical Greece, the Eluesian mysteries, those of Dionysos and the Orphic mysteries were a major counter-current to the exoteric worship of the Olympian deities. Other mystery religions in Egypt (Isis) and the Levant (Cybelle and Attis) came to be very influential in Roman times as well as Mithraism which incorporated much of the earlier Persian dualistic religious stream from Zoroastrianism. By the time of the late Hellenistic world and the advent of Rome as the dominant political force in the Mediterranean, all these stream flowed together and mixed. From this the broader streams of Hermetic philosophy and Gnosticism emerged as traditions that would be passed on to the West after the rise of Christianity and the fall of Rome.

Plato's thought tended to dominate the world of Hermetic philosophy through a series of great teachers who were prominent Neo-Platonists. The first important figure was Plotinus (205–270 CE) whose cosmology of emanations was carried on by his students. Porphyry (233–309 CE) and Iamblichus (245–325) were among the followers of Plotinus whose work became the basis of later medieval esoteric philosophy. Iamblichus brought in expertise in ritual to a tradition that had been mostly contemplative, the philosophical Neo-Platonists. Their influence on occult philosophy is significant. The divine is unitary and ineffable, all other forms of spirit are emanations of the One. The creator God, or demiurge is different from the One. From that creator god other spiritual beings emanate, and ultimately the material world and all its creatures are formed. In Iamblichus this evolutionary path was expressed by way of a mathematical analogy, unity, dyad, triad and hebdomad (group of seven). It was also expressed philosophically as *nous* (unity, mind), *psyche* (duality, subject/object). The goal of life is re-unification with the divine, Porphyry believed this could be accomplished through contemplation, but Iamblichus held that ritual (theurgy) is needed. He contrasted theurgy with thaumaturgy, the working of ordinary magic for such mundane things as love, health and wealth. These were and remain the staples of common esoteric practices. But theurgy, or the divine work, has always been held out to be the loftiest ambition.

There is a strong dualistic trend in Neo-Platonism; the realm of spirit, of Platonic forms has a fundamental reality and goodness that the material world lacks. Indeed, the body-mind dualism that permeates much Western thought shows the influence of Plato and his later followers. This dualistic trend found favor with early Christian mystics in the rejection of the temptations of the flesh in favor of ascetic practices. Christians, both orthodox and heretical, as in the gnostics, were influenced by the heightened dichotomy of self-mortification for achieving spiritual growth.

Another stream from classical antiquity feeding into modern occult philosophy is the Hermetic Corpus, or group of writings attributed to Hermes Trismegistus, or thrice-great Hermes; especially important is the dictum from the *Emerald Tablet*, "as above, so below." This references the basic tenet of magic that action on either the spiritual or material plane can influence the other; this belief underlies the theory of efficacy of both prayer, ritual invocation or evocation, and divination. Gnosticism is a more specific stream within this broad area of occult philosophy, and includes Christian as well as non-Christian versions.

The hermetic tradition became influential in the Renaissance. Marsilio Ficino (1433–1499) translated Plato into Latin and wrote on astrology, Giovani Pico della Mirandola (1463–1499) translated the Hermetic Corpus and works of the classical Neo-Platonists into Latin. Finally, Giordano Bruno (1548–1600) went too far and was burned at the stake for his promotion of hermetic ideas.

Alchemy was a practical as well as an esoteric discipline and one of its leading exponents, Paracelsus (1493–1541) influenced Franz Anton Mesmer (1734–1815) in the development of what is now known as hypnosis. The Elizabethan magicians John Dee (1527–1608) and Edward Kelley (1555–1597) are important figures as well. But the leading theoretician was Cornelius Agrippa (1486–1535) whose *Three books on occult philosophy* (1531–1533) remains a much reprinted classic. Giabatista Vico (1668–1744) is a key figure in the recovery of the status of imagination. His principle of "verum factum" holds that truth is established when an idea is able to bring forth some sort of concrete manifestation or invention. Ideas help create new realities.

In the seventeenth century, the Rosicrucian manifestos stimulated a lot of interest in occult philosophy, though the origins of those documents has never been completely determined. The alleged secret college of adepts sent teachings to benefit humans. Whatever one makes of their foundational mythos, the Rosicrucian documents circulated widely and would later find echoes in any sort of claim of communications from higher spiritual forces or entities, including the Theosophic movement and many modern authors who channel dictated material, (e.g., the Seth material etc.)

The modern occult movement begins in earnest in the late eighteenth and early nineteenth century with such figures as Allesandro di Cagliostro (1743–1795) and Francis Barrett (ca. 1770–1780) who wrote *The Magus* in 1801. Albert Louis Constant who wrote under the name Papus was another early figure in nineteenth century occultism and his work on the Tarot remains a classic.

But by far the most important developments occurred in the latter part of the nineteenth century when a variety of movements including Theosophy and the Golden Dawn were started. It was in this late Victorian era that modern occultism got a big boost in popularity. In mid to late 1800s the spiritualist movement reached its zenith and the use of mediums to contact spirits of the dead was relatively common, which encouraged many charlatans to practice as well as more sincere believers. Theosophy was a spiritual movement started by Elena Petrovna Blavatsky (1831–1891). She is the first of the modern mediums who writings claim to be received or channeled from Eastern "ascended masters." Her co-founder Col Henry Olcott (1832–1907) helped spur on a revival of Buddhism and was among the first Westerners to adopt Buddhism. He even designed the Buddhist flag. The Hermetic Order of the Golden Dawn was a group of ceremonial magicians centered around the figure of

MacGregor Mathers (1854–1918). In Bavaria, Adam Weisthaupf (1748–1830) formed an occult group known as the Illuminati. All sorts of conspiracy theorists now use this group as a starting point for their worries. The New Thought movement of Phineas Quimby (1802–1866) sparked a whole host of esoteric schools, including Christian Science.

Of all the psychologists and psychiatrists, Carl Gustav Jung (1875–1961) has been the most favorable in his assessment of the value of occult philosophy, or the western esoteric tradition (WET). He made the detailed links between personal unconscious processes and the wealth of cultural symbolism that has been handed down across time and culture. Myth is a primary medium for conveying symbolic meanings in the collective or cultural unconscious. He wrote about how alchemy is an apt metaphor for the transformations of personality than can occur in analysis or psychotherapy.

Witchcraft was revived, reconstructed or brought out into the open in the early twentieth century, depending on how you view the likelihood of a continuous tradition as Gerald Gardner (1884–1964) claimed. His lineage survives as do numerous off shoots as well as some others who have announced their teachings. By the 1960s and 1970s a widespread interest in the occult led to a flowering of all sorts of new amalgams of ancient lore. Some sought to reconstruct the ancient pre-Christian pagan religions of Europe, others sought to come up with their own blends of traditions and new age thought.

See also: ❂ Gnosticism ❂ Jung, Carl Gustav ❂ Ritual ❂ Wicca ❂ Witchcraft ❂ Zoroastrianism

Bibliography

Adler, M. (1986). *Drawing down the moon: Witches, druids, Goddess-worshipers and other pagans in America today* (Revised. ed.). Boston, MA: Beacon Press.

Godwin, J. (1981). *Mystery religions in the ancient world*. San Francisco, CA: Harper & Row Publishers.

Higginbotham, J., & Higgenbothm, R. (2006). *Pagan spirituality: A guide to personal transformation*. Woodbury, MN: Llewellyn Publications.

Jones, P., & Pennick, N. (1995). *A history of pagan Europe*. New York: Routledge.

Mishlove, J. (1975). *The roots of consciousness: Psychic liberation through history, science and experience*. New York & Berkeley, CA: Random House/Bookworks.

Starhawk. (1979). *The spiral dance: A rebirth of the ancient religion of the Goddess* (p. 196). San Francisco, CA: Harper & Row Publishers.

York, M. (2003). *Pagan theology: Paganism as a world religion*. New York: New York University Press.

Oedipus Complex

Robert Quackenbush

Oedipus Complex, in psychoanalytic theory, is based on the premise of incestuous fantasy in which a child desires the parent of the opposite sex. Sigmund Freud (1921/1955), the father of psychoanalysis, held that children pass through a stage from about ages three to six in which they develop a lively curiosity about sex. The son desires his mother and wants the father dead. The daughter wants sex with the father and hates the mother. ("Electra Complex" may be used to label the girl's feelings.) Freud believed that many adult neuroses originate with the Oedipus Complex. He derived his theory from the Oedipus myth revealed in the oracles of ancient Greece.

The tragic story of Oedipus Rex (Oedipus the King) has been told many times through the ages in literature and plays. According to the fifth-century BC play by Socrates, an oracle tells King Laius and Queen Joscasta of Thebers that a son will be born to them who will kill the king and marry the queen. When the son is born, the king and queen order a trusted slave to take the infant to the mountains to die. The slave takes pity on the infant and gives him to a childless royal couple in Corinth who name him Oedipus. When Oedipus grows into young manhood he goes on a journey to Delphi and meets an oracle who tells him that he will kill his father and marry his mother. Knowing this, he is afraid to return to Corinth and goes on to Thebes. At the crossroads between Corinth, Delphi and Thebes, he gets into a quarrel with an old man in a chariot who pushes him aside to go past him on the road. The old man attacks Oedipus with his long scepter. Oedipus grabs the scepter and kills the old man. Still at the crossroads, Oedipus is confronted by Sphinx who demands that he solve a riddle of what walks on four legs in the morning, what walks on two legs in the afternoon, and what walks on three legs in the afternoon. Oedipus guesses the right answer, which is a man (baby – adult – old person), and Sphinz leaps to her death over a cliff. His trails over, Oedipus goes on to Thebes and receives a hero's welcome for saving the city from Sphinx. He is crowned the new king to replace the old king who has just died. At the same time he marries the widowed Queen Jocasta. They have a happy life together and produce four children. Years later, a plague strikes Thebes. Oedipus learns that the Gods are angry and brought forth the plague because the murder of King Laius has not been avenged. He goes on a quest to find the murderer and discovers that the old man he killed at the crossroads was King Laius, his father, and that he has married his mother, Queen Jocasta. The terrible news reaches the castle and the queen hangs herself in the bedroom she has shared with her son and Oedipus's father. Oedipus is so horrified by what he has done that he pokes out his eyes with a pin from her body. Blinded, he goes into exile and mysteriously dies in Athens. Thus ends the myth of Oedipus, who brought about the very prophecy he had been trying to escape from all his life.

Freud (1927/1955) extended the Oedipus Complex into his theories about religion. He called religion "the universal obsessional neurosis of humanity; like the obsessional neurosis of children, it arose out of the Oedipus Complex, out of the relation to the father." Ernest Jones (1953) wrote that Freud "grew up devoid of any belief in a God or Immortality, and does not appear ever to have felt the need of it." Thus, Freud looked at all religions with a jaundiced eye. Based on his theory (1923/1955) of the ego, the id, and the super-ego, he called God the super ego. To him the super ego is ever observing of the contact between the ego and the id and intervenes when necessary to impose rules and regulations that were learned by every person from their early caretakers during their formative years. The id is our basic needs for survival and comfort and wants what it wants when it wants it. The word "no" is not in id's vocabulary. The ego helps the id to get what it wants in an appropriate manner. Freud's theory places the super ego in the role of a father who supervises the interaction between the id and ego.

The theory of the presence of oedipal phenomenon in religious ideation has not been accepted as a universal construct and has been argued since its inception. Some of Freud's followers, including Otto Rank, Alfred Adler, and C. G. Jung, broke away from Freud and went on to form their own schools based on their own philosophies. Rank (1929) elevated the maternal role at the expense of the paternal by arguing that the experience of birth is the primary psychological event. Adler (1948) explored nonsexual reasons for neurosis, in particular the role of inferiority feelings. Contrary to Freud's emphasis on the sex drive, Adler believed strivings for social success and power as fundamental in human motivation. Jung (1906) did not support Freud's ideas of infant sexuality and went on to develop his own theories about the psyche, which he called the Self. He said, "as for Freud's therapy, it is at best one of several possible methods and perhaps does not always offer in practice what one expects from it in theory." Freud (1914/1955) responded by saying, "All the changes that Jung has proposed to make in psycho-analysis flow from his intention to eliminate what is objectionable to the family-complexes, so as not to find it again in religion and ethics." He explains that to Jung "the Oedipal Complex has a merely 'symbolic' meaning: the mother in it means the unattainable, which must be renounced in the interests of civilization; the father who is killed in the Oedipus myth is the 'inner' father, from whom one must set oneself free in order to become independent."

The debate between psychology and religion over Freud's Oedipus Complex theory has been ongoing for over a hundred years. On the religious side of the debate some analysts and theologians have called for an abandonment of the oedipal theory. Brothers and Lewinberg (1999) argue that "so-called oedipal passions" result when children, forced to dissociate aspects of themselves as gendered, find these aspects of their self-experience embodied in caretakers. They go on to say, "In light of recent advances in theory and research that starkly reveal the shortcomings of oedipal theory, we ask the reader to consider laying Oedipus to rest once and for all." They also question the Oeidpus myth by calling attention to Kohut (1981) and his last paper in which he argued that analysts have "reversed their usual stance as regards King Oedipus by taking the manifest content – father, murder, incest – as the essence." Kohut believed the story's "most significant genetic dynamic feature" is that "oedipus was a rejected child" and that a replacement is needed for the Oedipus myth.

In keeping with the thoughts of Brothers and Lewinberg (1999), Judith Van Herik (1983) suggests that Freud's psychology and his theories about religion "are about patriarchal culture, and therefore about mental expression and reproduction of gender asymmetry." She states that Freud's oedipal theory acts as a constraint that has the same psychical structure as religious attachment to the father. Freud's psychology, says Van Herik, "is primarily about the socialized son and secondarily about the socialized daughter in a situation where father-son dynamics are primary." More directly, Gary Ahlskog (2001) says that he is not sure there is even one piece of Freudian theory so sacrosanct that it deserves allegiance and discipleship, which "proper" therapists are supposed to endorse. He goes on to say, "Nominating the Oedipus Complex won't do because of the need to specify 'which Oedipus Complex'? – an indefinite and endless task, since variations of sexual, aggressive, social, and intergenerational conflict are as innumerable as there are individuals on the planet." On a positive side, Esther Menaker (1995) says that the individual self is structured by the internalization of emotional experience with significant others – preferable with those who we have admired and to whom we have been attached and that the "other" lives on – is immortalized – within ourselves. Theologian Paul Tillich (1956) confirms this by stating simply that it is "the activity of God *within man* that grounds and makes possible the experience of God *beyond* man."

Today many caregivers in the mental health field do not believe as Freud did and include spirituality with psychotherapy. Hyman Spotnitz, M.D. (1985), for one. He is a pioneer of group therapy and founder of Modern Psychoanalysis that addresses the treatment of traumas incurred from infancy to the Oedipal stage that Freud did not believe were treatable. He believes that Freud was wrong in calling God the super-ego. To Spotnitz (1990) religion and going to church is ego supportive and a strong ego is what enables a person to tolerate all their impulses, all of their thoughts, all of their feelings, and what everybody else is doing to them.

The debate over Freud's Oedipus Complex is never-ending. Through it all, as Spotnitz, Tillich, and others have maintained, every school of thought works in psychology and religion when it is ego enhancing and helps people to find their way in life and to realize their full potentials and to form meaningful, lasting relationships. This is confirmed in a forward Erik H. Erikson (1963) wrote for his book *Childhood and Society*. He says that Freud was once asked what he thought a normal person should be able to do well. Freud is reported to have said: "Lieben und arbeiten" ("To love and to work").

See also: ◉ Freud, Sigmund ◉ Psychoanalysis

Bibliography

Adler, G. (1948). *Studies in analytical psychology.* London: Routledge & Kegan Paul.

Ahlskog, G. (2001). Reclaiming Freud's seven articles of faith. *The Journal of Pastoral Care.* 55(2), 2131–2138.

Brothers, D., & Lewinberg, E. (1999). Contemplating the death of Oedipus. *Gender & Psychoanalysis an Interdisiplinary Journal,* 4(1), 497–498.

Erikson, E. (1963). *Childhood and society, Forward.* New York: W. W. Norton.

Freud, S. (1913/1955). *Totem and taboo, SE* 13 (p. 136, 157). London: Hogarth Press.

Freud, S. (1914). *A history of the psycho-analytic movement, SE* 14 (p. 62). London: Hogarth Press.

Freud, S. (1921/1955). *Group psychology and the analysis of the ego, SE* 18 (pp. 105–106). London: Hogarth Press.

Freud, S. (1923/1955). *The ego and the Id, SE* 19 (pp. 31–32, 173, 177–179, 244–247, 251–253). London: Hogarth Press.

Freud, S. (1927/1955). *The future of an illusion, SE* 21 (p. 43). London: Hogarth Press.

Jones, E. (1953). *The life and work of Sigmund Freud* (Vol. 1, p. 19). New York: Basic Books.

Jung, C. G. (1906). *The collected works of C. G. Jung* (Vol. 3, p. 4). New York: Pantheon Books.

Kohut, H. (1981). Introspection, empathy, and the semicircle of mental health. In P. H. Ornstein (Ed.), *The search for the self: Selected writings of Heinz Kohut* (Vol. 4, pp. 537–568). New York: International Universities Press.

Menaker, E. (1995). *The freedom to inquire: Self psychological perspectives on women's issues, masochism, and the therapeutic relationship.* Northvale, NJ: Jason Aronson, 1995.

Rank, O. (1929). *The trauma of birth.* New York: Harcourt & Brace.

Spotnitz, H. (1985). *Modern psychoanalysis of the Schizophrenic patient.* New York: Human Sciences Press.

Spotnitz, H. (1990). Schizophrenia, alcoholism, and addiction (interview conducted by Dr. Jeff Landau). *Let's Talk: The Relationship Newsletter,* 3(2).

Tillich, P. (1956). *The dynamics of faith.* New York: Harper & Row.

Van Herik, J. (1983). *Freud on femininity and faith* (p. 48, 51). Berkeley, CA: University of California Press.

Oedipus Myth

James Markel Furniss

The Myth

Oedipus is a mythic Greek character thought to originate in Mycenaean folklore. His story is cited by Homer and was central in the lost Theban cycle of post-Homeric epics, before becoming a subject in tragedies written for the Festival of Dionysius in fifth-century BC. Athens, most notably in the three Theban plays by Sophocles. Sophocles' plays provide the best-known modern version of the myth, though the story differs to varying degrees in works by Aeschylus and Euripides as well as in the epics and in the original folklore.

The first of Sophocles' Theban plays in story chronology (though second in order of composition) is *Oedipus Tyrannus*. The play begins as Oedipus, King of Thebes, is asked by his subjects to rescue the city from a devastating plague. Brother-in-law Creon brings news from Apollo's oracle at Delphi that the murderer of previous Theban king (and former husband of Oedipus's wife Jocasta), Laius, must be destroyed before the plague can end. In the course of the ensuing investigation we learn the back-story of Sophocles' drama.

Laius and Jocasta, King and Queen of Thebes, have been warned by an oracle that Laius would die at the hands of his own child. (One reason offered for this terrible fate, found in other mythic sources, is Laius' former kidnaping and rape of the boy Chrysippus.) When a male child is born to the couple, they send him off to be abandoned on Mt. Cithaeron. The servant charged with the task, however, takes pity on baby Oedipus and gives him to a shepherd, who then delivers the infant to childless Corinthian King Polybus and Queen Merope. They raise Oedipus as their own. When, as an adult, Oedipus hears a prophecy that he will kill his father and marry his mother, he leaves Corinth to escape the dire prediction but on the road argues with and kills another traveler, who (unbeknownst to Oedipus) is his real father, Laius. Oedipus proceeds to Thebes, where he answers the riddle of the Sphinx, thereby freeing the city of this monster's murderous siege and winning the hand of Queen Jocasta.

Sophocles has Oedipus conduct a determined murder investigation, which reveals the facts of his past one by one. By the play's end Jocasta has committed suicide and Oedipus has both blinded himself and insisted to new king Creon that he be exiled from Thebes.

In *Oedipus at Colonus*, last in composition and second in story order, we meet Oedipus some twenty years after his exile from Thebes; he is a blind old man being guided by daughter Antigone. When they reach the village of Colonus, Oedipus discovers that he is in a grove sacred to the Eumenides. Here, he claims, Apollo's oracle has foretold his life's journey will end and the hosts of his burial ground will be blessed.

Oedipus's other daughter, Ismene, arrives with news about his sons, Eteocles and Polyneices, and Creon, all of whom have heard oracles about the significance of Oedipus's burial site and who want control of that site for various reasons. King Theseus of Athens then arrives, hears Oedipus's story, and gives his sanction to Oedipus for burial in the holy grove, for which Athens will be blessed in future conflict with Thebes.

Later in the play Oedipus bitterly denies the entreaties of Creon (who attempts to compel Oedipus to come with him and must be thwarted by Theseus) and Polyneices, who – like his uncle/great-uncle – wants to avoid the consequences of Oedipus's burial in a foreign land. Oedipus proclaims his innocence of responsibility for his terrible fate and denounces both Creon and his sons for maintaining his banishment before they knew of his new favor with Apollo. Oedipus condemns both sons to die in the assault on Thebes Polyneices is about to launch. Zeus's thunder signals Oedipus that his time has come to die. Theseus alone is allowed to see the place of Oedipus's death, for its blessing on Athens depends upon its secrecy.

Oedipus is present in *Antigone* (composed first though last in story chronology) as the spirit of the curse which has been fulfilled in the deaths of his sons in their battle for control of Thebes before the tragedy begins. The play tells the story of Antigone's refusal to accept Creon's decree that Polyneices be denied burial because he had led the attack on Thebes. Their conflict of wills results in the deaths of Antigone, Haemon (Antigone's fiancé and Creon's son), and Eurydice (Haemon's mother and Creon's wife), as well as Creon's ruin by the play's conclusion.

Oedipus and Freud

The Oedipus myth, particularly *Oedipus Tyrannus*, has had an enduring fascination for western audiences and readers, as evidenced by many retellings of the story and perennial production of Sophocles' original. Sigmund Freud was both exemplar and student of that fascination when he proposed that the Oedipus story – specifically, patricide and mating with one's mother – depicts a universal stage of human development. This proposal occurred as Freud formulated his theories of psychoanalysis in the late nineteenth and early twentieth centuries.

Freud's Oedipal theories begin in *The Interpretation of Dreams* (1899), although there is preliminary mention of them in earlier letters. Freud claims that there exists an Oedipal relationship between all children and their parents in early childhood.

➤ According to my already extensive experience, parents play a leading part in the infantile psychology of all persons who subsequently become psychoneurotics. Falling in love with one parent and hating the other forms part of the permanent stock of the psychic impulses which arise in early childhood, and are of such importance as the material of the subsequent neurosis. But I do not believe that psychoneurotics are to be sharply distinguished in this respect from other persons who remain normal. . . .[they] do no more than reveal to us, by magnification, something that occurs less markedly and intensively in the minds of the majority of children. Antiquity has furnished us with legendary matter which corroborates this belief, and the profound and universal validity of the old legends is explicable only by an equally universal validity of the above-mentioned hypothesis of infantile psychology.

I am referring to the legend of King Oedipus and the *Oedipus Rex* of Sophocles.

Freud supports his idea that the story depicts a universal psychic reality by emphasizing the uniquely enduring power of the Oedipus myth to move audiences:

▶ If the *Oedipus Rex* is capable of moving a modern reader or playgoer no less powerfully than it moved the contemporary Greeks, the only possible explanation is that the effect of the Greek tragedy does not depend upon the conflict between fate and human will, but upon the peculiar nature of the material by which this conflict is revealed. There must be a voice within us which is prepared to acknowledge the compelling power of fate in the Oedipus, while we are able to condemn the situations occurring in... other tragedies of fate as arbitrary inventions (Brill, 1995: 274–276).

Over time Freud's Oedipus theories became a crux of his construct for human psychosexual development and crucial in his understanding of neurosis. He also attributed the development of such superego constructs as religion to repression of the Oedipal drives. In the third stage of development ("phallic," age 3–6), children experience the Oedipal "complex," which involves erotic attraction toward the opposite-sex parent and jealousy toward the same-sex parent. In normal development a "dissolution" of the Oedipus complex takes place when fear of castration by the father (or, for girls, envy of the father's penis together with a belief that castration has already been brought about by their mothers) causes children to repress their incestuous desires. This results in the beginning formation of superego, Freud's conception of an unconscious psychic component which enforces the father's/culture's prohibitions. Freud also suggested that the individual psychic process of the Oedipus conflict and its dissolution originally played out collectively in history. He first addresses this theory in the final section of *Totem and Taboo* (1913), "The Return of Totemism in Childhood." In this passage Freud imagines a "primal horde," Darwin's speculative idea of an early human society, in which a group of brothers have banded together and killed their father, who had banished them from the social group to deny their lust for their mother, his mate.

▶ We need only assume that the group of brothers banded together were dominated by the same contradictory feelings towards the father which we can demonstrate as the content of ambivalence of the father complex in all our children and in neurotics. They hated the father who stood so powerfully in the way of their sexual demands and their desire for power, but they also loved and admired him. After they had satisfied their hate by his removal and had carried out their wish for identification with him, the suppressed tender impulses had to assert themselves. This took place in the form of remorse, a sense of guilt was formed which coincided here with the remorse generally felt. The dead now became stronger than the living had been, even as we observe it today in the destinies of men. What the fathers' presence had formerly prevented they themselves now prohibited in the psychic situation of "subsequent obedience" which we know so well from psychoanalysis. They undid their deed by declaring that the killing of the father substitute, the totem, was not allowed, and renounced the fruits of their deed by denying themselves the liberated women. Thus they created two fundamental taboos of totemism out of *the sense of guilt of the son*, and for this very reason these had to correspond with the two repressed wishes of the Oedipus complex. Whoever disobeyed became guilty of the two only crimes which troubled primitive society (Brill, 1995: 884–885).

Freud ends this imagined scenario with his "conclusion that the beginnings of religion, ethics, society and art meet in the Oedipus complex" (Brill, 1995: 895).

Oedipus After Freud

Freud's linkage of myth with psychic processes has had a profound impact on subsequent psychology as well as on western culture generally. Over the last century a great number of thinkers in diverse disciplines have responded to Freud's Oedipal theories either to confirm, deny, or retool to fit their own purposes. Oedipus has also become, post-Freud, an even more pervasive presence in literature, the fine arts, and popular culture.

One important effect of Freud's Oedipal theories has been their impact on the interface between psychology and religion. The idea that a myth could depict a universal psychic reality raised the possibility that individual psyches are retellings of a greater, mythic reality, where – by searching, interrogating, recognizing – human beings can find their place in a coherent whole. James Hillman remarks, "What holds us to Freud... is not the science in the theory but the myth in the science," and also, "Freud brought in myths and myth brings in God" (1995: 102, 124).

For some in psychology – behaviorists, for example – myth and gods are not objective enough means or content for the conduct of scientific inquiry. Others, however, who share some of Freud's basic ideas (such as the importance of the unconscious), have continued and expanded what the Oedipal theory began in what is broadly referred to as Depth Psychology. The central early figure in this endeavor was Carl Jung, a one-time disciple/colleague of Freud, who split with his mentor over a fundamental difference in their concepts of human nature.

Jung expanded upon Freud's recognition of the universality of Oedipus in his idea of a "collective unconscious," where primal forms (archetypes) of all human experience exist in a subliminal reservoir, from which individual psyches draw guidance and energy as they seek to realize the potential of their own natures. While Freud implies that the Oedipus myth is a later, cultural construct representing the historical experience of certain instinctive sexual drives, Jung's collective unconscious suggests a more complex origin for myth. In a manner similar to dreams for an individual, myth emerges into consciousness out of the collective unconscious, from whose mysterious depths it derives symbolic content implying a natural teleology not limited to physical evolution of the species. Jung claimed, for instance, that myth and dream contain evidence for the existence of Self, an archetype of the collective unconscious which is the universal potential for human beings: a perfect merger of individual and the whole of creation, a concept analogous to God.

Jung's extension of the Oedipal theories to the collective unconscious and to his study of world myth and symbology can be cited as having a seminal influence on the development of later twentieth-century psychological fields that emphasize human spirituality over instinct, such as Transpersonal Psychology and Archetypal Psychology. Broadly speaking, these may be thought of as religious psychologies in that they premise a link between individuals and enduring, perhaps timeless, forms. In such approaches to psychology, the entire body of human myth – including all the stories of Oedipus – is a context in which the stories of individual lives declare their meaning.

Also, Freud's Oedipal explanation for the origins of religion instigated reactions and accelerated the development of the Psychology of Religion, a field to which such figures as Erik Erikson and Erich Fromm have made significant contributions. Among contributors to this field are psychoanalytical theoreticians who revise founder Freud's Oedipal theories and – instead of regarding religion as a neurosis to be outgrown – propose a newly harmonious relationship between psychoanalytic theory and religious thought.

See also: ❂ Collective Unconscious ❂ Depth Psychology and Spirituality ❂ Dreams ❂ Freud, Sigmund ❂ Jung, Carl Gustav ❂ Oedipus Complex ❂ Psychoanalysis ❂ Self

Bibliography

Brill, A. A. (Ed.) (1995). *The basic writings of Sigmund Freud*. New York: Modern Library.

Hillman, J. (1995). Oedipus revisited. In *Oedipus variations*. Dallas, TX: Spring Publications.

Roche, P. (Trans.) (1958). *The Oedipus plays of Sophocles*. New York: New American Library.

Om

Fredrica R. Halligan

In the Eastern religions, which grew out of the Vedic tradition, sound vibrations are thought to have great power in both the spiritual and physical domains. *Om* is believed to be the first sound of the universe, the creative power from which all else emerged. Pronounced A-U-M (Ah-oo-mm), all sounds are believed to be contained in this *Prandava* or primal sound. A favorite mantra (chant) in Hinduism and Buddhism, *Om* is believed to be the Name – the very Presence – of the Absolute. Many individual or communal rituals begin or end with the chanting of *Om*.

In psychotherapy, if meditation is recommended, the practice of mantra meditation may be very calming and/or uplifting for the client. *Om* is an appropriate mantra for many clients. An alternative sacred word for meditation in the Judeo-Christian tradition is "Shalom" which ends with the same sound vibrations.

See also: ❂ Buddhism ❂ Hinduism ❂ Mantra ❂ Meditation ❂ Psychotherapy

Bibliography

Dattatreya, A. (1994). *Avadhuta Gita: The song of the ever-free* (S. Chetanananda, Trans.). Calcutta, India: Advaita Ashrama.

Shraddhananda, S. (1996). *Seeing God everywhere: A practical guide to spiritual living*. Hollywood, CA: Vedanta Press.

Yatiswarananda, S. (1995). *Meditation and spiritual life*. Bangalore, India: Ramakrishna Math.

Omega Point

Fredrica R. Halligan

The forthcoming unity of all humanity was defined as the "Omega Point" by Jesuit paleontologist and mystic, Fr. Pierre Teilhard de Chardin. (q.v.) In most mystical traditions, the idea of union with God is preceded by the experiential recognition of loving unity with all humanity. Sai Baba (q.v.), for example, recently has stated that:

> All the resources of nature like air are available to all irrespective of nationality or creed or race. This is the unity in diversity that has to be realized. . . . All should seek to live as brothers and sisters. No one should criticize any nation, faith or culture. When you cultivate this broad outlook, your culture will be respected by others. It is this spirit of unity that the world needs today (Sai Baba, 1995: 214).

In medieval times, the Sufi mystic Ibn al-'Arabi (q.v.) wrote of similar, cross-cultural breadth of love:

> My heart has become capable of every form:
> It is a pasture for gazelles and a convent for Christian monks,
> And a temple for idols and the Pilgrim's Ka'ba
> And the tables of the Tora and the book of the Qur'an.
> I follow the religion of Love; Whatever way Love's camels take,
> That is my religion and my faith (cited in Halligan, 2003: 1).

With the rapid advance of globalization, our society is currently undergoing many challenges related to the interface of various cultures, both those within our midst and those external to our borders. Psychotherapy frequently deals with relationship issues that are tinged by cultural differences. When the therapist maintains a broad, accepting perspective she or he can more readily facilitate resolution to the interpersonal and group struggles that are inevitable as we try to unite into one world.

See also: ❂ Ibn al-'Arabi ❂ Psychotherapy ❂ Teilhard de Chardin

Bibliography

Halligan, F. R. (2003). *Listening deeply to God: Exploring spirituality in an interreligious age.* Mystic, CT: Twenty-third Publications.
Sai Baba. (1995). *Sathya Sai speaks* (Vol. XXVIII). Prashanti Nilayam, India: Sri Sathya Sai Books & Publications Trust.

Oracles

Paul Larson

The term "oracle" can refer to a specific person who practices divination or to the mechanism used to read the portents (e.g., cards, trance possession, reflecting bowl of water, etc.). The oracle is the medium either as person who channels the guidance from the spiritual realm, or who interprets the display pattern of some physical oracle device.

Two important personal oracles have received some broad public attention. The oracle of Apollo at Delphi is perhaps the most famous oracle, but that position has been vacant since the Christian Church persuaded the Roman emperor Theodosius I to close pagan temples in 393 CE The oracle, known as the Pythia, had provided guidance to both persons and city states since the eighth century BCE., so it represents a very long standing social and spiritual tradition. One of the most famous sayings from classical Greek antiquity was reputed to have been inscribed on the lintel to the temple of Apollo at Mt. Parnassus, where the oracle resided. "Gnothi seauton," or "know thyself" echoes across the ages as surely sage advice.

The service (Gk. chresmos) provided was "gnosis," or knowledge (Burkert, 1985). There was an implicit assumption that a special type of knowledge was needed to resolve a troubling circumstance in the individual. This shows the therapeutic effect of knowledge, an idea which continued throughout the gnostic traditions of the mystery religions and early Christian heresy. It is also the basis upon which reason was used in philosophy, there is something corrective about knowing the truth, whether it is in abstract matters or mundane affairs needing decision. Healing is a special type of gnosis, it involves two aspects, diagnosis and treatment. The diagnostic phase is easily seen as open to oracular spirituality. The means of healing can be prescribed in dreams as will be described below.

There are many theories about how the oracle entered into an altered state of consciousness. Some of speculated that the temple lay upon a fissure where intoxicating fumes emerged. The priestess would sit over the fumes. Others speculate that the intoxicant was some psychoactive plant, cannabis or opium being common and known for their psychotropic properties. But evidence remains mixed and more speculative than consistent. Without reference to intoxicants, there is clear evidence of human ability to enter into trance and perform oracular functions, so the specific details are less important.

O

The Pythia illustrates one type of oracle, a localized connection between earth and spirit. This oracle remained at Delphi and was indeed part of the sacredness of Delphi. At the very heart of the temple of Apollo at Delphi, where the Pythia made her pronouncements was the Omphalos, a large stone believed to be the navel of the world. This anchored the place at a spiritual level dating back to animistic times, well before the classical polytheisms. Because of this, those that seek advice must come from afar, this creates a link to the act of pilgrimage as a motive force in human spiritual psychology. The record of the pronouncement mostly concerns the issues of important people, Alexander the Great consulted the Pythia, or affairs of state. He also later consulted the older oracle of Amun at the Siwa oasis in Egypt. Little remains of the pronouncements for more mundane querants.

Healing also was a possible focus as in the case of the temples of Asklepios where the oracular function came to the querant themselves in dreams and the divination in the exegesis given by the priest upon awakening in the morning (Kerenyi, 1959). Epidauros was the main site for the cult of Asklepios, though the practical advantages of a dispersed expertise in healing led his cult to spread more widely in the Greco-Roman world of the Mediterranean. The island of Kos had a sanctuary and in the heart of Rome on an island in the Tiber River the temple of Asklepios, Latinized as Asklepios, was established. Asklepian dream incubation illustrates an interesting variation on the oracular process. In most instances the divine speaks through the seer, but in this case it comes to the seeker by night. Part of the ritual was entering into sleep with a group of fellow seekers.

An oracle who is still practicing, is the Nechung oracle. He is the state oracle of Tibet and serves the court of the Dalai Lama as leader of the Tibetan people in exile (http://www.tibet.com/Buddhism/nechung_hh.html). The movies *Kundun* and *Seven years in Tibet* portray this figure. Like many oracular experiences, the film portrays a fairly active trance state with convulsive movements and guttural vocalizations. Like many senior Tibetan religious officials he is considered a tulku that is a continued stream of incarnated lamas, or teachers. Since oracular traditions in this region date back to the aboriginal Bon religion, we can wee in this instance a layered texture to the spiritual experience. The Vajrayana Buddhism overlays an earlier animistic spirituality. The modern form of spirituality was influenced by a degree of formalism, yet more archaic forms such as spirit possession are retained and shaped by the newer world view of Tantric or esoteric Buddhism.

In modern revival/recreation of Norse religion, the oracular "seidh" ceremony is used to offer advice on personal decisions. The deities that possess the oracle in Seidh, of course, are Norse or Germanic in mythic frame, Odin, for example. The same basic formula of spirit possession serves to channel spiritual advice and guidance. The time of spirit possession is a limenal one; the oracle is physically present in the mundane world, but is mentally and spiritually engaged in the realm of the spirit and literally sees and hears things from beyond the veil. Indeed, the physical use of a veil to cover the head is a fairly common physical prop for the performance. In the seidh, one person allows him or herself to become possessed for the duration of the ceremony and enters into a trance state for the pronouncements.

There is a formal process of querants coming forth and asking specific questions. As with all divination, this is a dialectical process, that is, one governed by the formal social and communicational properties of question and response. The advice of the oracle is couched to be responsive to the needs of the querant, yet bringing in an outside perspective on the decision or trajectory about which the querant seeks guidance. The advice is also vague enough to leave a number of things unclear. This adds a degree of openness to unfolding possibilities that makes the divination of an oracle a flexible guide rather than a deterministic or fatalistic prediction.

See also: ⊙ Apollo ⊙ Buddhism ⊙ Divination ⊙ Esoteric Buddhism ⊙ Ritual ⊙ Tulku

Bibliography

Burkert, W. (1985). *Greek religion* (J. Raffan, Trans.). Cambridge, MA: Harvard University Press.

Kerenyi, C. (1959). *Asklepios: Archetypal image of the physician's existence.* New York: Pantheon Books.

Original Sin

Clodagh Weldon

Original sin is the Christian doctrine which says that because of the sin of Adam and Eve, original innocence is lost and all subsequent human beings are born into a state of sinfulness. The doctrine states that human beings do not commit this sin but rather contract it from the Fall of Adam and Eve (CCC: 404). In other words, original sin is an inherited condition.

The doctrine of original sin was most famously formulated by North African theologian St. Augustine of Hippo (354–430) following his conversion to Christianity (Augustine, *Confessions* 8:12). His theology was deeply influenced by Plato's separation of the body and soul, a dualistic vision in which the pure and immutable soul is trapped in the prison house of a corruptible body. Upon his conversion to Christianity, Augustine renounced all pleasures of the flesh and, embracing the spiritual world, chose the celibate life. But he soon realized that the mind could not suppress the desires of the body, and concluded from this that there must be some defect in human nature. That defect, he argued, came from original sin.

Although the words "original sin" do not appear in the Bible, the doctrine of original sin is implicit in the writings of the apostle Paul. In his letter to the Romans, Paul says that it is by one man that sin entered the world (Romans 5:12) and that by one man's disobedience all were made sinners (Romans 5:19). Central to Augustine's argument is the premise that all of humanity was summed up in Adam. Thus when Adam disobeyed God by eating of the fruit of the tree of the knowledge of good and evil, it was not just Adam who sinned but all of human nature that sinned. Augustine argued that original sin was transmitted through concupiscence, an idea affirmed by the Council of Trent (1545–1563). As a result of original sin, humanity is condemned. Hope for redemption comes with the death of the second Adam, Jesus, who atones for the sins of humanity. Participation in his death by baptism washes away the stain of original sin (Romans 6:3–11).

Not all agreed with Augustine in his day. Most notable was a British monk by the name of Pelagius. He argued that human beings sin not because they are predisposed to do so due to the disobedience of Adam and Eve, but because they utilize free will and choose to imitate bad example. He was condemned by the Church at the Council of Orange (529 AD), and it was Augustine's view that prevailed. Some believers today, most notably the Disciples of Christ and Mormons, side with Pelagius in rejecting the doctrine of original sin as unbiblical. They argue that human beings are only responsible for the sins that they commit, and not the sins of the fathers (see for example Deut. 24:16; Ezek. 18:20; Jer. 31:29–30).

Commentary

From Freud's perspective, original sin has a parallel in the guilt of oedipal transference, an idea he articulates in his *Totem and Taboo*. Here Freud argues that the killing of the primal father creates man's sense of guilt. In "*Our Attitude to Death*" (14: 292–293), Freud argues that the Christian doctrine of original sin further allows us to deduce the nature of this primal guilt. If humanity, he argues, is redeemed from original sin by the sacrifice of Jesus, then by implication there must have been a murder. Freud therefore concludes that original sin is the primal crime of the killing of the primal father.

Jung was deeply critical of the traditional Christian doctrine of original sin, his principle critique being that it implied that man rather than God is responsible for evil. However, he thought that if psychologically interpreted, it is "...of profound therapeutic significance" (Jung 16 § 186), particularly if understood as an expression of the archetype of the shadow.

See also: ❯ Adam and Eve ❯ Augustine ❯ Christianity ❯ Freud, Sigmund ❯ Genesis ❯ God ❯ Jung, Carl Gustav ❯ Plato on the Soul ❯ Soul: A Depth Psychological Approach

Bibliography

The Catholic Church. (1994). *Catechism of the Catholic Church*. London: Geoffrey Chapman.

Freud, S. (1976). Our attitude to death. In *The complete psychological works of Sigmund Freud*, SE 14 (pp. 292–293). New York: W.W. Norton.

Freud, S. (1976). *The complete psychological works of Sigmund Freud*, SE 13 (pp. 1–161). New York: W.W. Norton.

Freud, S. (1976). *The complete psychological works of Sigmund Freud*, SE 23 (pp. 7–137). New York: W.W. Norton.

Jung, C. G. (1966). *Collected works of C. G. Jung* (2nd ed., Vol. 16, p. 186). Princeton, NJ: Princeton University Press.

New American Bible.

Warner, R. (1963). *The confessions of St. Augustine*. New York: Penguin Books.

Orpheus and Orphism

Mark Greene

The image of Orpheus as a semi-divine mythological being and perhaps an actual person has inspired countless works of art for well over two and half millennia. Within the domains of myth and art, he is primarily associated with his renowned abilities as poet and musician. Many versions of his story describe the captivating power his music exerted over anyone or thing near him while he played his cithara. Equally compelling is the story of the death of his newlywed bride, Eurydice, and his journey to the underworld to attempt her retrieval. He also plays a crucial role aboard the Argos accompanying Jason and fellow Argonauts on the quest for the Golden Fleece. Perhaps most intriguing, from the perspective of religious studies, is his purported role as the founder of a non-Hellenic renunciation cult called Orphism that condemned animal sacrifice and produced a large body of works describing a cosmogony and eschatology that stand in sharp contrast to those described in Homer and Hesiod.

The Orphic doctrine views all of humanity as semi-divine in origin due to our having sprung from the ashes of the Titans after they had tricked, killed and then eaten the infant Dionysos, the divine ruler of the universe. In retribution, Zeus immolated the Titans but only after the infant god had been ingested. Those calling themselves followers of Orpheus based their belief system upon this divine somatic origin myth. Accordingly, the Orphic believer was asked to renounce the mundane and concentrate on cleansing himself of his Titanic ancestry through purification rituals and certain life-style choices. Such precepts included vegetarianism and the prohibition from using any sort of animal product, including wool, as it was believed the animal's soul could actually be human and that shearing it could cause the soul harm. The initiate was told of the possibility that several incarnations would be necessary as preparation for his eventual apotheosis. These followers of the priest-initiate Orpheus are also believed to have propagated the literature that scholars nowadays refer to as the *Orphica*. These unearthed texts describe the worshippers' insistence on bodily purification so that the soul could be deemed worthy of returning to its original divine state in the afterlife.

The figure of Orpheus with his lyre first appears in the early to mid-sixth century BCE. on the metopes of the Sikyonian *monopteros* at Delphi, although his name is spelled Orphas (ΟΡΦΑΣ). In Greek literature towards the middle of the same century, he is referred to as "famous Orpheus" by the poet Ibykos. Also beginning at this time his image is often depicted on vase paintings. No mention of Orpheus is made anywhere in Homer or Hesiod, those two poets whose works provide us with the earliest recorded Greek myths. This is probably due to the rapid southward movement and re-popularization of the cult of Dionysos which occurs less than two centuries after the written appearance of Hesiod's *Theogony* and Homer's

epics. It is from Dionysos' legendary birthplace of Thrace – a territory considered wild by the Greeks and on the fringes of the geographical domain encompassed by the principal Hellenic cults of worship – that Orpheus is also said to have come.

Whether a historical figure named Orpheus actually lived and delivered the mysteries, or *teletae*, which are said to reside at the ritual heart of such Orphic beliefs is an open question.

Commentary

Thematically, Orpheus occupies an intermediary position between the Dionysian (earth, moon, body) and Apollonic (sky, sun, spirit) forms of worship. Indeed, most versions of the myths recounting his story acknowledge these contrasting influences upon him in their attribution of paternity to Apollo and his death by dismemberment at the hands of the Maenads (female worshippers of Dionysos). Originally a worshipper of Dionysos, Orpheus travels a narrative arc from the chthonic, earthy domain of Dionysos to the rarefied heights of Apollonian worship.

Images of Christ as Orpheus appear frequently during early Christianity, examples of which can been seen in the catacombs of Peter and Marcellus in Rome and in the catacomb of Domitilla. In most cases, Orpheus is seen holding his lyre surrounded by animals that sit calmly at his feet. Arguably, there are many thematic parallels between Orpheus' life and those of the life of Christ. Although Orpheus communicated his message in song and word and Christ just with words, the results were captivating for all those within earshot and highlighted by accounts of miracles surrounding their actions. Both were said to have ventured to the underworld and both died violent deaths on behalf of the salvation of their respective believers.

Viewing the story of Orpheus psychoanalytically reveals a fixation based on the unsuccessful resolution of psychodynamic conflicts experienced during the Oedipal stage of psychosexual development. The death of Eurydice on their wedding day may indicate a son who is still sexually fascinated with the mother and for whom the wife's image carries no potency. The hero's descent into Hades where he converses with the King and Queen of the underworld represents the ego's attempt to negotiate with the subconscious aspects of the parental images that comprise his superego. The warning to not turn back and look at Eurydice as he leads her to the upper world is reminiscent of the incest taboo. That Orpheus does indeed turn to look back at Eurydice suggests an attempt to resolve his Oedipal anxiety by actually violating the taboo. His losing his wife a second time causes him to suffer a great depression.

The Orphic doctrine's primary tenet of repeated reincarnation with an eventual return to godliness stated as a goal appears an attempt to reduce the individual's anxiety over dying. The image of returning to a divine state functions as compensation for life's mundane qualities and the individual's limitations, especially mortality. Curiously, Orpheus establishes a cult of renunciation. In Freudian terms this is reminiscent of the child's attempts to manipulate the parent by controlling the amount and types of food ingested. This behavior indicates further regression to the anal and oral stages.

From the point of view of Jungian psychology, Orpheus is a hero who conquers his desire to return to the mother and thus provides a template for the successful canalization of libido that is necessary for the individual's individuation. In the case of Orpheus, the obstacle to the flow of libido is represented by Eurydice's death on their wedding day. Her death by snakebite indicates that the complexes awakened in Orpheus are from those domains occupied by images of both the father and the mother. These constellate on the son's wedding day and propel the narrative forward until resolution is achieved at the threshold between the lower and upper worlds when Orpheus looks back at Eurydice. That this look back prevents Eurydice from joining Orpheus in life can be seen to represent his failure to integrate the anima's position into consciousness. Still, as a variation on the night sea journey motif, Orpheus' journey to the underworld does result in the tempering of his soul. In accordance with the motif of the hero's journey, Orpheus is ultimately reborn as the head of a mystery cult. In this sense he successfully canalizes the blocked libido by sublimating it to a higher cultural purpose.

The figure of Orpheus the poet/musician distinguishes himself from other Greek heroes in that he feels compelled to transcend the boundary between the upper and lower worlds for love. In some versions of the myth, he undertakes this journey for the love of his wife. In others, he descends to the underworld to secure special consideration by Persephone for his followers upon their entry into Hades. In both of these examples, Orpheus transcends the physical boundary defined by death in an attempt to intercede for the benefit of others. Perhaps for this reason, and coupled with his reputation as a poet and a musician, his image is often co-opted as an emblem of romantic creativity and inspiration, two qualities revered and required by all artists.

In modern interpretations of the myth, a rich panoply of images emerge depicting other, hybrid modes of masculinity – characterized by corporeal depth and spiritual inspiration – that manifest themselves as amalgams of solar (traditionally masculine) and lunar (traditionally feminine) aspects of psyche. Indeed, the image of Orpheus brandishing a musical instrument instead of a sword to overcome the obstacles he encounters is emblematic of a form of masculinity that successfully integrates these two poles. In this view, Orpheus' look back to Eurydice is an act that follows conscious deliberation, an act that paradoxically results from and causes an integration of unconscious elements into consciousness. Here Orpheus is now privy to the secrets of the underworld and understands that Eurydice's death is part of her own process within a larger framework. His look back allows her to return to her path, although the cost to him is great. Sacrificing his personal wishes propels Orpheus fully onto his path of individuation, or self-actualization, in that he finds his true calling as the founder of a mystery cult with the image of Eurydice and her assumed eventual apotheosis functioning as an inspiration.

See also: ⊚ Apollo ⊚ Apollonian and Dionysian ⊚ Apotheosis and Return ⊚ Biblical Narratives Versus Greek Myths ⊚ Christianity ⊚ Dionysos

Bibliography

Burkert, W. (1985). *Greek religion* (J. Raffan, Trans.). Cambridge, MA: Harvard University Press.

Burkert, W. (1977). Orphism and bacchic mysteries: New evidence and old problems of interpretation. In W. Wuellner (Ed.), *Protocol of the 28th Colloquy of the Center for Hermeneutical Studies* (pp. 1–4). Berkeley, CA: Center for Hermeneutical Studies.

Gantz, T. (1993). *Orpheus Early Greek myth* (Vol. 2). Baltimore, MD: Johns Hopkins University Press.

Greene, M. (1999). *Re-imagining as a method for the elucidation of myth: The case of orpheus and eurydice*. Doctoral dissertation, Pacifica Graduate Institute, Carpinteria, CA.

Guthrie, W. K. C. (1993). *Orpheus and Greek religion*. Princeton NJ: Princeton University Press.

Irwin, L. (1991). The orphic mystery: Harmony and mediation. In *Alexandria* (pp. 37–55). Grand Rapids, MI: Phanes Press.

Orthodoxy

Elisa Bernal Corley

"Orthodoxy" means "right belief." The term comes from the combined Greek words *orthos*, meaning "right, true, straight," and *doxa*, meaning "praise." In early Christian history, it was used in contrast with heresy, which literally means "choice." The classical view of orthodoxy refers to the right belief that Jesus taught his disciples and handed down by them to the leaders of the Christian church. Its most basic form is found in the creedal statements adopted by the four ecumenical councils of the early Church and held by the majority of the believers in early Christian period.

In the history of Christianity, belief in Orthodoxy is tied with the idea of primacy or originality. Early Christian theologians emphasized the view that orthodoxy is *primary* and heresies are deviations and corruptions of the original and pure orthodoxy. Eusebius, Bishop of Caesarea (263–339 CE) established this view of orthodoxy during the time of Emperor Constantine (c. 275–337). The former is considered the most influential proponent of the standard that orthodoxy is primary and innovation is heresy. Other prominent Church Fathers like Irenaeus (c. 130–200) and Tertullian (c. 155–222) expressed the same opinions regarding the opposition between orthodoxy and heresy.

Orthodox Sunnis of Islam and Neo-Confucian scholars also tie orthodoxy with the idea of primacy and early origins. Orthodox Sunnis represent their faith as pure and primary because it has remained unchanged from the beginning. For Sunni Islam, ideal faith meant adherence to the time-honored practice of the tribe and clan. In fact, the word *Sunna*, means, "beaten path or standard practice of the Prophet." Thus, orthodox faith is one that is free from any historical developments or innovations. Any innovation or change to the primal path established by the Prophet is heretical. This tradition of Sunni Orthodoxy emerged during the latter half of the ninth century.

The Neo-Confucian scholars of the Sung dynasty (960–1279) also affirm the primacy of Confucianism in the world. Chu-Hsi (1130–1200), who synthesized Buddhist teachings with Confucianism, designated the "transmission of the Way" as the core concept of *Tao* Learning. He gave it the name *Tao-T'ung*. The *Tao-T'ung* is understood to have been transmitted from the ancient sage kings to Confucius and his original heirs. The works of the Sung thinkers who inherited this philosophical tradition were deemed orthodox in contrast with the writings of their rivals. The principal Neo-Confucian scholar of the modern times, Mou Tsung-san (1909–1995) formulated a new version of the *Tao-T'ung*, but continued to highlight the importance of traditional Chinese philosophical lineage in establishing orthodoxy.

Thus, for early Christians, Orthodox Sunnis, and Neo-Confucians, any claim to primacy of teaching must be authenticated by the manner of transmission, which assumes the direct contact between the master-teacher and his disciples. The idea of chain of transmission or chain of traditions validates the truth of orthodoxy. Modern ideologies and scientific history also reveals the pursuit of the same standard of transmission.

In addition to the notions of primacy and fidelity, a third feature, unity, was essential to the establishment of Christian and Sunni Islam orthodoxy. In early Christianity, unity of faith and practice was contrasted with the multiplicity that characterized heretical groups and their teachings. Similarly, in Sunni Islam, the concept of *ijma'* or consensus, became a central pillar of orthodoxy. In their writings, Sunni scholars are known to diminish the sectarian controversies plaguing the early history of Islam, in order to promote a more harmonious picture of Islamic faith and tradition.

Commentary

Since beliefs are often translated into some form of social behavior, concern for tradition, fidelity, and unity within religious orthodoxy remains relevant to identity-formation and social adaptation. Studies have shown a positive correlation between religion and life-satisfaction, revealing that a person's quest for the meaning of life is strongly associated with psychological well-being. Current research also demonstrates that religion plays a role in the development of a person's meaning-system, which in turn allows the believer to weave a coherent life-story. In other words, religious tradition helps individuals construct their own sense of order as well as find meaning out of life's failures and achievements.

Devotion to religious orthodoxy, coupled with personal faith and church involvement is important to the formation of a person's identity. As part of the religious community, people can learn about who or what they are. Such religious identification influences how they interpret the world. Studies reveal that those who consider themselves as having more orthodox religious beliefs have no problem attributing life events to divine intervention. They are willing to give up total control, believing that with denouncement of the self comes greater mastery of life. In addition, as people root their own personal experiences within a fixed and broader narrative, community teachings and practices become part of the person's orienting system for relating to the world. Thus, they are able to face personal limitations and move beyond themselves to find solutions for life's problems and crises. Worldly cares and troubles do not threaten their unity, fidelity, and commitment to faith. In a sense, religious truth becomes a most powerful coping and defense mechanism for the preservation of one's self.

Nevertheless, external forces can challenge the potency of religious orthodoxy as a coping mechanism. Although many studies found that orthodox beliefs help individual attain psychological well-being, there are also those that find religious orthodoxy, in the Fundamentalist form, to be more authoritarian and dogmatic, and more racially prejudiced.

When a believer is intent to preserving religious orthodoxy, like the attempt of early Christians to rid the Church of heretics and infidels, an inflexible and rigid personality may develop. Such inflexible and rigid personalities seem to be more common among the Christian Fundamentalist groups, for example. Research has implicated the latter with prejudice and more discriminatory attitudes towards blacks, women, and homosexuals. Personal rigidity leaves a Fundamentalist susceptible to prejudice when responding to peoples and perspectives perceived as threats to religious traditions.

When people are unwilling to question what is believed to be true teachings about God and humanity, and to discard an inherited set of life's practices, they become vulnerable to the rapidly changing and diverse world. They can acquire "closed minds" and develop a defensive constricted personality generally linked with a religiously orthodox upbringing. In the attempt to protect what is considered the greatest significance to the individual, ideological self-identifications may flourish among the religious orthodox and conservatives.

See also: ❂ Christianity ❂ Confucianism ❂ Faith ❂ Fundamentalism ❂ Heresy ❂ Islam ❂ Meaning of Human Existence ❂ Prejudice ❂ Prophets ❂ Purpose in Life ❂ Religion

Bibliography

Argyle, M. (2000). *Psychology and religion.* London and New York: Routledge Press.

Chan, W.-T. (1987). *Chu-Hsi. Life and thought.* Hong Kong: Chinese University Press.

Ehrman, B. D. (2003). *Lost Christianities. The battles for scripture and the faiths we never knew.* New York: Oxford University Press.

Henderson, J. B. (1998). *The construction of Orthodoxy and Heresy.* Albany, NY: State University of New York Press.

Pargament, K. I. (1997). *The psychology of religion and coping.* New York: Guilford Press.

Schumaker, J. F. (1992). *Religion and mental health.* New York: Oxford University Press.

Tu, W.-M. (1996). *Confucian tradition in East Asian modernity. Moral education and economic culture in Japan and the four mini-dragons.* Cambridge, MA: Harvard University Press.

Osiris and the Egyptian Religion

Alane Sauder-MacGuire

Although the Osiris story represents only one stream of a complex and multifaceted ancient Egyptian religion, the story is perhaps the Egyptian myth that most permeates later religions, alchemy and the psychology of Carl Jung.

The cosmology in which Osiris originated was located at Heliopolis. There the followers of the creator god, Ra, first achieved the unification of upper and lower Egypt and set up a capital which remained the major theological and academic center through many dynasties.

The creation of the world in this cosmology began with the masturbation of Ra or Atum. From his seed Shu, the airs, and, his sister, Tefnut, the moisture, were created. They were the first couple. They, in turn, gave birth to Geb, the earth, and his sister, Nut, the sky. Geb and Nut bore Osiris, Isis, Set, and Nephthys. Osiris married his sister, Isis, and his younger brother, Set their sister, Nephthys.

Osiris and Isis were the parents of Horus. In one version of the myth, Isis and Osiris fell in love in the womb of Nut and produced Horus in utero.

Osiris was a talented musician who came to rule an Egyptian land afflicted by cannibalism and other ills. He converted the Egyptian people into civilized ways not by force, but by persuasion and by his music.

After he had brought civilization to Egypt, he left the lands of Egypt under the rule of his sister-wife, Isis to continue the spread civilization throughout the world. His brother, Set, coveting both Isis and the kingship, devised a plan to murder Osiris. He lured him into a box that he then cast into the sea.

Isis and Nephthys searched for Osiris and saved him, but the frustrated and vicious Set the again captured Osiris and this time cut him into pieces that he scattered throughout Egypt. A grieving and sorrowful Isis collected the scattered limbs of his body and bathed them with her tears.

However, she could not find the phallus so she fashioned one out of wood. Although she could not revive Osiris to the state of living, she was able to vivify him sufficiently as to impregnate herself.

In this version of the myth, Horus was born of Isis's efforts and he avenged his father and fought the forces of chaos represented by a battle with his evil uncle, Set. In the Egyptian mythology the soul resided in the eye and Osiris was said to be located in Horus's eye. The struggle between Set and Horus was prolonged and both suffered grave wounds. Eventually a council of the gods declared Horus the victor. Thus, order was restored.

After Isis impregnated herself, Osiris descended into the underworld and became its god. Through this mythic understanding of Osiris's death and resurrection as the god of the underworld, the Egyptians explained the path of the sun and its renewal from its setting in the evening to its rising in the morning.

It was believed the evening sun penetrated a cave in the west, and over a period of twelve hours passed through the underworld from which it emerges the next morning, regenerated. At midcourse the sun met Osiris and drew the energy from him for its renewal.

Also in his role as ruler of the underworld, Osiris was thought of as the judge who allows or disallows the dead the passage into the rebirth of an idealized afterlife.

Philosophically, the Egyptian religion professed the belief that the gods had laid down universal laws of order and justice (maat) at the moment of creation. The conflict between the forces of evil or chaos as represented by Set and Osiris represented the disruption of this order, the redemption by Horus, the restoration of it. This also provided a way of understanding the chaos that at times affected the Egyptian political system.

The Egyptian political system itself was based on an identification between the rulers and the Osiris/Horus myth. The Egyptians believed their pharaoh to be both human and divine. Horus was the chief god of the upper world and became the symbol of kingship with which the living pharaohs identified with. Osiris who resided in the underworld was identified with the living pharaoh's deceased father.

The pharaoh was assimilated into Osiris in the afterlife. The process was dynamic with the living king understood as Horus in life and then Osiris after death. Most Pharaoh's coffins were fashioned in the shape and pose of Osiris with his distinctive flail and crook held in arms crossed at his chest as a symbolic representation of this transition. It was from this relationship between the upper world and the underworld that the pharaoh derived his power and wisdom in the Egyptian imagination.

In classical antiquity Osiris's fame spread outside of Egypt through the writings of Plutarch and Apuleius among others. In fact, the myth of Osiris became the basis of a religion of salvation widely practiced in the ancient world.

Commentary

The mystique of the Egyptian kingship exemplified for Jung, the force of the archetype in creating a symbolic image that can channel human experience. An archetype can be defined, as a predisposition to experience and the symbolic image it creates is the best possible description of that experience. In the case of the Egyptian kingship this would be the experience of the mysterious incarnation of the divine within.

In this mystique of kingship, Horus incarnated in the form of the pharaoh and then at his mortal death the Pharaoh was reincarnated into the eternal realm of all pharaohs past held in the image of Osiris.

Thus creating a mythic picture and explanation of the soul's experience of eternity.

Because of this move from eternal being into mortality and then to immortality, Osiris acts as an archetypal image for the human experience of having an eternal soul within a mortal body. His story creates a philosophical metaphor for this human experience that defeats rational understanding. In other words, it creates, in a mythic form accessible to the individual psyche, a way of reconciling the experience of being alive with the knowledge of physical death.

Important, too, for the myth's psychological power is the fact that good eventually outweighs evil – meaningfulness prevails over meaninglessness. The archetypal battle of good and evil so much a part of the Christian era was arguably missing from the Hellenistic world, the Christian era's closer ancestor.

Osiris was originally the good divine king of the upper world who kept the cosmos in order. He was also fertility god associated with the force that generated the growth and life of crops. His brother, Seth, represented the forces of chaos and was associated with the desert, which for the ancient Egyptian was associated with all manner of evil.

To understand the importance of Osiris/Set/Horus myth as an archetypal image to the ancient Egyptians, it is helpful to take into consideration just how perilous the climate and conditions they lived under were.

For the Egyptian the sun was a destructive as well as creative force. To produce crops, the rains had to come and the Nile had to flood. This allowed the land which every summer the relentless sun turned into desert to flood and be saturated, restoring its fertility. This usually happened, but frequently enough it did not and the result was disorder and famine.

Thus, the Egyptians had much less faith in the cycle of nature than the Europeans did. The sun, without adequate rainfall to produce the floods, turned the fertile land into a dead zone indistinguishable from the surrounding desert. The myth of Osiris, his destruction by Seth, and the redemption of Set's evil by Horus as described above invested a meaning to the cycles experienced by the ancient Egyptian. The drama of the two brothers, Osiris and Seth provided a mythic understanding of the perilous fertility cycle which was at times disrupted by disorder as it held the hope of a reordering in the eventual dominance of Horus.

Jung believes that the Christian era itself owes its significance, in part, to this archetypal form of kingship and the antique god-man mystery that has its roots in the story of the Osiris–Horus myth.

There is in the relationship between Horus and Osiris a symbolic equivalency to Christ and God the father. In Genesis, the Judeo-Christian god created an order, which became disrupted by Satan, an equivalent of Seth, and was then to be restored by the birth of Christ. The Christian story like the Egyptian myth represents the idea of the good god restoring the original order of creation after it is disrupted by an evil divinity.

From another perspective, Osiris, himself, represents, as did Christ, the god who incarnates and then dies a brutal death to be reborn back into immortality.

Unlike the other Egyptian gods, Osiris shows vulnerability. Though not as immanent as Jesus because Osiris was always god, he shows pathos. He alone of the Egyptian gods does not transcend the vicissitudes of human existence – specifically death. He, in fact, seems completely defenseless against his evil brother, Set, and without the intervention of Isis would have been completely destroyed.

At the same time, Osiris represented fertility and life. Therefore, even as he was dead Osiris was the source of life. The ancient Egyptians believed he was the source of growth and reproduction for all animals and plants. He was both dead and the source of life.

As such, Osiris can be understood as a vivid and complex achievement of the Egyptian imagination. He answered the psychological paradox and dilemma of grappling with death even as an eternal life force is experienced.

In sum, the ancient Egyptian imagination created in the archetypal image of Osiris a symbol that explained not only the experience of their particular existence, but also the universal experience of humanity in reconciling the immortal experience of soul with the knowledge of physical death. It also provided a mythic carrier for the archetypal battle between good and evil.

See also: ❯ Astrology and Alchemy ❯ Dying and Rising Gods ❯ Jung, Carl Gustav

Bibliography

Clark, R. T. (1978). *Rundle, myth and symbol in ancient Egypt*. London: Thames & Hudson.

Frankfort, H. (1948). *Ancient Egyptian religion*. New York: Harper Torchbooks.

Ions, V. (1982). *Egyptian mythology*. New York: Peter Bedrick Books.

Jung, C. G. (1953). *The collected works of C.G. Jung*. Princeton, NJ: Princeton University Press.

Otherworld

❯ Heaven and Hell

P

Paganism

David Waldron

The Origins of the Term Paganism

The term Pagan etymologically derives from the Latin adjective *Paganus* which, typically is taken to mean of the rural countryside. It is also a term which has been used pejoratively from its inception as uncivilized, uncouth and rustic. However, this interpretation has come under criticism by historians Robin Lane Fox and Pierre Chauvin due to the term being utilized widely in Early Christian Rome when the bulk of the urban population remained Pagan in today's terms. Like Chauvin, Ronald Hutton proposes that a more accurate meaning of the term in antiquity is that of followers of the customs and religions of locality (i.e., *Pagus*) rather than one of the many cosmopolitan, universalist and transcendent faiths of the early Christian period (Hutton, 1993).

Paganism and the Countryside

The perceived high prevalence of localized pre-Christian customs, idolatry and ritual surviving in the countryside led to the association of the *Paganus* with the uncivilized and rural. This distinction between rural and urban religious practices also links closely with the intensely urban and cosmopolitan demography of early Christianity. In the early Christian era the term Pagan came to represent those who still practiced the predominantly rural and localized expressions of pre-Christian belief in contrast to the predominantly urban and educated Christianity of the middle ages. In this sense western thought has typically presented a universal divide between Christianity and, by association, the other Abrahamic faiths of Islam and Judaism, and that of the incredibly diverse and wide ranging other faiths of antiquity, indigenous cultures and contemporary pagan revivals. The adoption of this dualist distinction by cotemporary pagan revivalists has led to numerous conflicts between western pagan revivalists, eager to integrate traditional pre-Christian religious practices with pagan revivals, and members of indigenous cultures and non-Christian religions (Mulcock, 1998, 2001).

Paganism and the Abrahamic Faiths in Antiquity

With regards to interpretations of the Paganism of antiquity, the central distinction that can be made with the Abrahamic faiths is that of locality and cultural pluralism. This distinction is pointed out by Martin Bernal in his discussion of the rise of the transcendent monotheistic and dualist cosmopolitan religions of the second and third centuries C.E., particularly in Egypt, the supposed heartland of the Temple based urban paganism of antiquity. He argues that by the third century the breakdown of traditional local structures of social and religious practice combined with rising urban cosmopolitanism placed enormous pressures on the localized basis of the traditional pagan religious institutions. These pressures were linked to long term class and social tensions that gave Christianity and other universalist faiths, such as Manichaenism, an appeal when linked with Hellenic philosophy, with which the traditional localized temple religions could not compete. This in turn led to class prejudice and hostility to the old pagan religious practices that were inevitably strongest in the rural sector where traditional structures of community, folklore and religion held sway and the localized ethnic identity of the religions of the *Pagus* held more significance than in the cosmopolitan urban sectors (Bernal, 1991).

This construction of a duality between Christianity (or more broadly Abrahamic faiths) and Paganism and its pejorative use against non-Christian peoples, customs and faiths came to dominate perceptions of religious diversity in Western thought. A vast array of divergent religious practices, customs and folklore were linked together by association as the antithesis of Christian values, culture and ideals. Even

D. A. Leeming, K. Madden, S. Marlan (eds.), *Encyclopedia of Psychology and Religion*, DOI 10.1007/978-0-387-71802-6,
© Springer Science+Business Media LLC 2010

where Pagan writers were rehabilitated by the intelligentsia, as with the Greek and Roman philosophers and poets such as Virgil, Aristotle and Plato, the re-appropriation of pagan writers was carefully constructed within a dualist world view of Christian and Pagan. In this sense the term Pagan was reconstructed as the shadow side of Christian civilization with the term applied indiscriminately to disparate religious traditions. The notion of the Pagan also came to serve as a crucible of symbolic and psychological projections of varying constructions of Christianity. These ranged from demonized images of traditional societies and non-Christian civilizations such as the Norse, to extensively idealized representations of Pagan Greece and Rome.

Paganism as a Pejorative and Reactionary Term

In this sense, as well as becoming a pejorative construction of anti-Christianity, ironically enough utilized by Protestants in their criticism of Catholicism as "Pagan", Paganism also came to represent a symbolic construction for people's frustration and dissatisfaction with what they perceived as the ills of Christian society. If Christianity, and by association Western civilization, was intolerant, destructive, patriarchal and rapacious, Paganism could then be perceived in antithesis as matriarchal, tolerant and living in harmony with natural world and society. This particular construction of Paganism came to predominance during the massive social upheavals of the nineteenth century and the rise of the Romantic movement in literature and philosophy. Even as early as the seventeenth century there were prominent cultural trends that described the Noble Savage as evidence of the innate goodness of man in his perceived natural state. In the seventeenth and eighteenth century writers such as Gabriel de Foigny, Jonathon Swift, Denis Diderot and Jean-Jaques Rousseau commonly utilized primitivist and utopian notions of "natural man" based on the descriptions of "pagan societies" living close to the earth and following nature. These "neo-Pagan" movements served to connect an idealized past to the present through ritual, symbolism and aesthetics, constructing an alternative vision for society and an alternative struggle for cultural and social renewal. This construct attempted to ground itself in notions of historical and cultural authenticity and autonomy as set over and against the repressive and destructive aspects of western modernity, caricatured as universalist reason or an irrational, violent and patriarchal Christianity.

Neo-Paganism and the Contemporary Pagan Revival

The term neo-Pagan appeared in the late nineteenth century and was used to refer to Romantic discourses that supported the ideal of a Pagan revival as an antidote to the ills of industrialization and the perceived restrictive nature of conservative Christian morality. During this period a plethora of new movements arose seeking to reclaim the past as a means of transcending the social ills, conflicts and destructive aspects of the tumultuous present. These ranged from extensive searches for a historical authentic pagan religious practice to searches for Pagan survivals in the present. There was also widespread embracing of the religious practices of indigenes peoples perceived to offer an antidote to the ills of Christianity and industrialism. Perhaps the most famous of these new movements was Gerald Gardner's Wiccan movement founded in the 1950s which came to be the foundation of the later pagan revival in the 1960s and 1970s. Central to these movements was the sense of looking back to an idealized past as a means of shaping the future and transcending the ills of the techno-centric or Christo-centric present. Whilst a full discussion of the myriad movements and versions of neo-Paganism is beyond the scope of this entry there are four main approaches to the past, to symbolism and to symbolic constructions of identity in neo-Pagan movements (Waldron, 2000).

Reconstructionist: Those groups who rely on traditional historiography and empirical veracity in defining their historical legitimacy and socio-cultural identity. Also included in this grouping are the various national and ethnic groups such as Odinist, Celtic or Creole based practitioners who utilize the recreation of magical ritual as a means of defining a national cultural identity in the confines of traditional historiography.

Traditionalist: These groups derived from ritual magic intensive witchcraft such as Gardnerian and Alexandrian Wicca. These groups tend to be more concerned with the precision of ritual activity and magical practice than the veracity of their historical claims. Some people have used the term "Traditionalist" to describe those claiming to have a hereditary or pre-industrial background to their witchcraft beliefs.

New Age/Eclectic: These groups are heavily reliant on the work of Carl Jung and his theory of the collective unconscious. New Age/Eclectic neo-pagans are particularly concerned with the psychological impact and universality of symbols. They posit the psychic truth of symbolic representations manifested in history and other cultures as the ultimate source of authenticity in ritual opposed to the empirical veracity of truth claims.

Eco-feminist: Those groups that are particularly concerned with the plight of women and utilize the symbol of the witch as an ultimate expression of the persecution of women within patriarchal culture and society. These movements typically focus on the capacity of ritual and historical reclamation to empower women to deal with the social and environmental ills created by patriarchal forms of social control.

While these four models of neo-Pagan approaches to symbolism and historicity have different structures for legitimating historical interpretation and ideological/cultural perspectives, there are several elements which link them together. The first is a belief that the application of the enlightenment and industrialization represent a distancing of humanity from its more authentic and natural existence uncorrupted by the influence of western civilization. Secondly, the neo-pagan movement is generally unanimous in the belief that western Christianity is guilty of suppressing much of what is free, creative and autonomous in human nature – in support of a static oppressive patriarchal system of morality and social control. Thirdly, the witch crazes of the early modern period are taken as representative of a conscious attempt to oppress and destroy the vestiges of pre-Christian nature religions. And finally, the reclaiming and recreating of the pre-Christian agrarian past is perceived as the best way for contemporary society to evolve in such a way as to transcend the ills caused by the oppressive aspects of Christianity, the enlightenment and western modernity.

Whilst most of the neo-Pagan movement's attempted initially to ground themselves in claims to empirical historical authenticity, recent historical findings led to the collapse of many of the arguments upon which the movements were based. Most notable of these was the almost complete collapse of Margaret Murray's thesis of the witch persecutions of Early Modern Europe being an attempt by the Catholic church to stamp out surviving pagan practices (Ankarloo and Henningsen, 1990) and (Ginzberg, 1992). In the aftermath of this collapse, many neo-Pagans have abandoned empirical history as the basis of religious legitimacy and shifted onus for perceived veracity of ritual and symbolism in the psychological impact of the symbolism and ritual as archetypal forms. Often this approach quite consciously embraces the analytical psychology of Carl Jung (Waldron and Waldron, 2004). Perhaps the most recognizable exponent of this is Wiccan author Vivian Crowley, author of *The Old Religion in the New Age* (1998). This approach tends to

focus on the psychological power of ritual and symbolism to evoke psychological truths whilst utilizing post modern critiques of positivism to critique empirical constructions of the past by professional historians. Similarly, Michael York in "Defining Paganism" argues that definition rooted in the cultural forms and rituals of a particular movement is impossible. Instead he argues that what links neo-Pagan movements together is their shared attitude towards culture, nature and spirituality, defined as "an affirmation of interactive and polymorphic sacred relationships, by individuals or communities, with the tangible, sentient and/or non empirical" (York, 2000).

Paganism Old and New

This particular approach illustrates just how far the original distinction between the religions of the *pagus* or locality and the Christian or monotheistic has shifted in terms of defining what Paganism means. It also illustrates just how far many schools of Pagan thought have shifted from ritual, philosophical and symbolic legitimacy rooted in historicity and ethnicity. That being said, it is worth noting that this approach is largely rejected by reconstructionist neo-Pagans who immerse themselves in the material culture of the various Paganisms of antiquity. These movements are typically closely attached to empirical forms of historical legitimation as both an expression of religious belief and ethnic identity, albeit often a reclaimed version.

The primary ideological basis of neo-Pagan is the belief that it is necessary to gaze inwards and to appropriate images from the past to find forms of identity and symbols of meaning perceived as natural, culturally authentic and in opposition to the forces of the enlightenment and industrialism. Conversely, this also involves a belief in the veracity of symbols, images and feelings over empirical experience and logic and thus emphasises the feminine aspects of the psyche over the masculine. Like much of western romantic literature, neo-paganism is fundamentally dominated by a reification of beliefs and images. Quintessentially modern ideological and symbolic socio-cultural formations are reinforced by interpretations of a past that is dogmatically protected as a particular symbolic construction that is defined as authentic. Similarly, neo-paganism and romanticism both share a focus on the new and the modern. Whilst neo-paganism and romanticism gaze into representations of the past for symbols of authenticity and meaning, they are far more than simply a reaction of traditionalism against industrialization and the objectification of society. What they represent is a search for cultural authenticity and creative autonomy and a redefinition of the modern as a search for that which is creative, authentic and autonomous.

See also: ❯ Christianity ❯ Islam ❯ Jung, Carl Gustav ❯ Polytheism ❯ Wicca

Bibliography

Adler, M. (1986). Drawing down the moon: Witches, druids, Goddess worshipers and other pagans in America today. New York: Penguin Group.

Ankarloo, B., & Henningsen, G. (1990). Early modern European witchcraft: Centres and peripheries. Oxford: Clarendon Press.

Bernal, M. (1987). Black athena. London: Vintage Books.

Crowley, V. (1989). The old religion in the new age. New York: Harper Collins.

Ginzberg, C. (1992). The night battles: Witchcraft and agrarian cults in the sixteenth and seventeenth centuries. Baltimore, MD: Johns Hopkins University Press.

Hutton, R. (1991). Pagan religions of the British Isles: Their nature and legacy. Oxford: Oxford University Press.

Mulcock, J. (1998). (Re) Discovering out indigenous selves: The nostalgic appeal of Native Americans and other generic indigenes. Australian Religious Studies, 14(1), 45–64.

Mulcock, J. (2001). Creativity and politics in the cultural supermarket: Synthesizing indigenous identities for the r/evolution of spirit. Continuum: Journal of Media and Cultural Studies, 15(2), 169–185.

Waldron, D. (2001, February). Post modernism and witchcraft histories. The Pomegranate: The International Journal of Pagan Studies, 1(15), 16–22.

Waldron, D., & Waldron, S. (2004). Jung and the neo-Pagan movement. Quadrant: The Journal of the C.G. Jung Foundation for Analytical Psychology, XXXIV(1), 29–46.

York, M. (2000, February). Defining paganism. The Pomegranate: The International Journal of Pagan Studies, 1(15), 4–9.

Pan

Sukey Fontelieu

The goat god Pan was a god of flocks and shepherds in ancient Greece. His cult began in Arcadia and was elevated from its rustic status after the Battle of Marathon when the Athenians, out of gratitude for Pan's help in their victory, dedicated a cave, Long Cliffs, to Pan beneath the city of Athens (Herodotus, 1992). His cult took root and rapidly spread through the Mediterranean basin.

Pan was above all a chthonic nature god. His body was half divine and half goat. He lived outside of the civilized world, sometimes near its borders in huts or hidden, shady glens, but also dwelled in the wilderness in dark caves and on mountain peaks. He was a solitary and rustic god. From his earliest origins he was expected to induce fertility. Pan is an archetypal image of nature's cornucopia of sexual heat, which ensures life will endure. In character, locales, and functions Pan is seen in service to nature.

Fear and Panic

Pan is associated with panic and all its legion of psychological burdens. Panic is with him from the moment of his birth when his mother took one look at him and, as told in the Homeric hymn "sprang up and fled" (1976: 63). Pan suffered the loss of his mother because his body was monstrous (even Hephaestus with his broken body could still count on his mother's love), which led to a recurring motif for Pan of unrequited love for the feminine. Paradoxically, Pan was the beloved of the gods. In the Homeric hymn Pan's father, Hermes, wrapped him in the pelt of a hare and carried him up to Mt. Olympus where he charmed the Olympians with his laughter and was named Pan, which the hymn tells us meant "all."

But the themes of panic and a lack of self-control dogged Pan throughout his myths. His unbridled sexuality created panic in the objects of his desire. Yet panic is also a tool that Pan skillfully wields in his role in battle, where he found victory without the aid of his keen eyed marksmanship, but rather by instilling fear and confusion in the hearts of the enemies of his friends. Pan did not instigate wars or fight for his own gain, but his role as an arouser of fear naturally led him to the battlefield. As well as his intervention at the battle of Marathon, he was also present during Zeus' rise to power and assisted him in his battle with the Typhoeus (or Typon) (Kerenyi, 1998), was a general in Dionysus' army in his invasion of India (Polyaenus, 1994), and Pausanius reported Pan's aid in a battle with the Gauls. He caused panic to enter the hearts of the Gauls so they could no longer understand their mother tongue and killed each other instead of the Greeks (1935/1961 [VIII: xxiii]).

Pan and the Nymphs

Pan was said to have caused panolepsy, a seizure that brought laughter and ecstatic rapture. They nymphs were also, and more commonly, associated with inducing altered states in humans. Both *panolepsy* and *nympholepsy* were believed to be gifts that inspire. But these healing trances were also feared because they were thought to sometimes cause a person to be carried off by Pan or a nymph. Untimely deaths were attributed to them (Borgeaud, 1979/1988). A recurrent theme, linking danger and ecstasy with Pan, echoes through his stories. Pan's intensity, often dangerous, is a touchstone for the life force. It is associated in different myths with creativity, fertility, and survival.

Pan played his pipes at the center of the nymph's dances, yet even then was not allowed to touch them. The nymphs, besides representing the freedom of feminine sexual expression, were nurses and mothers to Greek gods and heroes. They were a soothing balm, a natural force that emitted from thousands of springs, rivers, trees, and knolls. These healers were also associated with the power to engender metamorphosis and served as a balance or an antidote to the over reaching excesses of Pan. His self absorbed sexual intensity is feared by them, and yet he is the one they run to in the evenings when he returns from his day's hunt, joyfully dancing to the strains of his pipe. The nymphs are near to Pan, but untouchable, even though they are all divinities of fertility.

Pan's myths recount his overwhelming sexual desire and consequent pursuit of many nymphs. The extant primary sources, from Pindar, c. 522–433 BCE (1997a, 1997b) and Apollodorus, second century BCE (1997) to Nonnus in the early fifth century (1940/1962), do not report any stories where Pan actually rapes the nymph he is chasing after. The pattern in the myths follows this recurring storyline: he chases a nymph and out of fear she asks for help and is metamorphosed. She is still alive but in a different form, transformed by the interaction. Her new form has less of its own power of volition. For Pan, his chases turned up empty. Yet, rapist is a common epithet today for Pan (Hillman, 1988) and is perhaps the way he is most often considered.

Geneology

In genealogy the Greeks were less inclined to insist on historical veracity then is the prevailing sentiment today, since their tendency to imagine numerous sets of parents for their gods and goddesses occurs frequently. Pan is a case in point and is a god with more sets of mothers and fathers than most (Nonnus, 1940/1962). A popular version of Pan's birth in ancient texts named Penelope, the reserved wife of long-suffering Odysseus, as his mother.

She is best known for the subtle wiles with which she handled her suitors while she waited and waited for her husband's return from Troy. Her history with Hermes and Pan is less known, though well recorded by the ancients. The historian Herodotus, b. c. 484 BCE, is the oldest source. His histories (1921/1960) makes reference to "Pan, the son of Penelope (for according to the Greeks Penelope and Hermes were the parents of Pan)" (p. 453 [II. 145]).

Squilling Ritual

Pan Agreus (the hunter) was invoked when the Arcadians needed to find game to supplement their sparse agricultural returns. If the kill was small and so meat on the table was sparse, or the hunters returned empty handed, then the young men of the village would perform a ritual called *squilling* (Edmonds, 1912/1977). This involved a ceremonially circumambulation of a statue of the god while whipping him around the genitals and shoulders with large onions still attached to their stalks. The onions, squills, were believed to be a healing agent, and were used to ward off evil spirits, to promote growth, and, like nettles, were an irritant to the skin (Dioscorides, 1934/1959).

The Death of Pan

Plutarch, a Greek scholar and priest of Delphi, in 83 or 84 CE, recorded the legend of the death of Pan (1936/2003). He told of a group traveling by ship who heard a voice call out that the "Great Pan is dead!" and that the ship's helmsman was to sail north and call out these same words when they reached Palodes. He did so and his call was met with a "a great cry of lamentation, not of one person, but of many" (1936/2003: 403 [419D]). This story is an anomaly in Greek theology, since the gods were believed to be immortal (Borgeaud, 1983).

On the one hand, the story of the death of Pan had no verifiable impact on the cults of Pan, which are known to have continued to thrive (Pausanias, 1935/1961). On the other, the legend's historical context places it in close proximity to Jesus' crucifixion. Both happened during Tiberius Caesar's short reign. The juxtaposition of these two events led to speculation and conjectures about Pan by early Christian writers such as Eusebius in the third century and in medieval times by Rabelais, to a fascination with Pan among the Romantics (Russell, 1993), and even today we can witness Pan's reemergence in modern stories such as the film *Pan's Labyrinth* (Navarro, Cuoron, Terresblanco and Augustin, 2006).

Pan and Christ are associated with each other by some of these thinkers. Both were thought of as shepherds, both offered their bodies as sacrifice, and both were thought of as containers of "all" to their worshippers. Pan has also been associated with the Christian devil, both in countenance and in spirit.

The death of Pan would not be worth noting as anything more than one of the historical record's many oddities except that, over the centuries, it has obstinately continued to linger; it has been used to argue positions diametrically opposed to one another. The fascination with his death indicates that the story has an archetypal nature because it refuses to die.

See also: ❖ Chthonic Deities ❖ Circumambulation

Bibliography

Apollodorus. (1997). *The library of Greek mythology* (R. Hard, Trans.). Oxford: Oxford University Press.

Borgeaud, P. (1983). The death of great Pan: The problem of interpretation. *History of Religions, 22*(3), 254–283.

Borgeaud, P. (1988). *The cult of Pan* (K. Atlass & J. Redfield, Trans.). Chicago, IL: University of Chicago Press. (Original work published 1979).

Dioscorides. (1959). *The Greek herbal of Dioscorides: Materia medica* (R. T. Gunther, Ed., J. Goodyer, Trans.). New York: Hafner Publishing. (Original work published 1934).

Edmonds, J. M. (Trans.) (1977). *The Greek bucolic poets.* Cambridge, MA: Harvard University Press. (Original work published 1912).

Herodotus. (1960). *Herodotus* (A. D. Godley, Trans.) (Vol. III). Cambridge, MA: Harvard University Press.

Herodotus. (1992). *The history* (H. Cary, Trans.). Buffalo, NY: Prometheus Books.

Hillman, J. (1988). *Pan and the nightmare.* Dallas, TX: Spring Publications.

Homer. (1976). *The Homeric hymns* (A. Athanassakis, Trans.). Baltimore, MD: John Hopkins University Press.

Kerenyi, C. (1998). *The Gods of the Greeks.* London: Thames and Hudson.

Navarro, B., Cuarón, A., Torresblanco, F., & Augustin, A. (Producers), & Del Torro, G. (Director) (2006). *Pan's Labyrinth.* [Film]. Mexico: Picturehouse Films.

Nonnos. (1962). *Dionysiaca* (W. H. Rouse, Trans.). London: William Heinemann. (Original work published 1940).

Pausanias. (1961). *Pausanias: Description of Greece.* (W. H. S. Jones, Trans.) (Vol. IV). Cambridge, MA: Harvard University Press. (Original work published 1935).

Pindar. (1997a). *Nemian odes, Isthmian odes. Fragments* (W. H. Race, Ed. & Trans.) (Vol. I). Cambridge, MA: Harvard University Press.

Pindar. (1997b). *Olympian odes, Pythian odes* (W. H. Race, Ed. Trans.) (Vol. II). Cambridge, MA: Harvard University Press.

Plutarch. (2003). *On the obsolescence of the oracles. Moralia* (F. C. Babbitt, Trans.) (Vol. 5, pp. 350–501). Cambridge, MA: Harvard University Press. (Original work published 1936).

Polyaenus. (1994). *Stratagems of War* (P. Krentz & E. L. Wheeler, Eds., Trans.) (Vol. 1). Chicago: Ares Publisher.

Russell, D. (1993). Introduction. *Plutarch: Selected essays and dialogues* (D. Russell, Trans.) (pp. ix–xxii). Oxford: Oxford University Press.

Panaceas and Placebos

David Berman

Of the two terms in the title of this article, panacea is probably the clearer and least equivocal. By panacea is meant a medicine, treatment or therapy that can cure or alleviate all illnesses. From that definition it is clear that any alleged panacea must work, according to present-day scientific thinking, at least partly as a placebo. A placebo (Latin for "I will please") can be defined as a medical treatment that works (satisfies the patient) not through its apparent agency, but by the belief in its efficacy. And since no medical scientist of repute would seriously hold that there is any one medical treatment that can relieve every known illness, it follows that if a treatment appears to be working universally, or even widely, it must be doing so at least partly as a placebo, by virtue of the belief in it.

Yet panaceas have been proposed in the past. Here I look at two panaceas, arguably the two most serious and instructive of the past 300 years. The first was proposed by George Berkeley, now best-known as the philosopher, the father of idealism, who denied the existence of matter. But in his lifetime, Berkeley was better known for his advocacy of tar-water as a universal medicine, which he published in *Siris* (1744). The other panacea was developed by Mary Baker Eddy, the founder of Christian Science, who published her treatment for all illnesses in *Science and Health* (1903).

Berkeley's Tar-Water

Tar-water is made by mixing wood tar with cold water and allowing the tar to settle, after which the clear infused water can be descanted and drunk. In *Siris*, sect. 71,

Berkeley (1744) says that "there will not perhaps be found any medicine more general in its use, or more salutary in its effects," than tar-water, and catalogues the many illnesses it has cured. But he stops short of saying directly that it is a panacea. However, in his later *Letter to Prior* (1744), sect. 11, he is prepared to "speak out": "I freely own that I suspect tar-water is a panacea." And in the pamphlet's next section, he says: "Having frankly owned the charge, I must explain … that by a panacea is not meant a medicine which cures all individuals (this consists not with mortality) but a medicine that cures or relieves all different species of distempers."

Berkeley had two justifications for this claim: one theoretical, the other empirical. The theoretical reason is complex, involving chemistry, botany, physics, philosophy, theology and Scripture. But, as I have suggested elsewhere, the main idea is that tar-water is the closest natural, ingestible thing to fire; and as fire, Berkeley believes, is the natural substance closest in nature to God, it follows that tar-water is drinkable spirit or God, and that is why it is so efficacious as a medicine. Berkeley's empirical justification was the experiments on tar-water which he carried out on himself, his family, his neighbors, as well as the cures that were gathered by his friend Prior from those who had benefitted from his medicine.

Eddy's Christian Science

If anything, Eddy's panacea was and is even more ambitious than Berkeley's. For not only did she believe that Christian Science could cure all physical ills, but she also believed that it was effective even against death itself. And one main way that Christian Science works is by bringing its subjects to the truth that matter is an illusion. This follows largely from the principle that God is a perfect, infinite spiritual being, the creator of this world; so everything in this world is perfect. Therefore since matter and illness are imperfect, it follows that they do not exist. Hence, for the Christian Scientist, whole-heartedly embracing these truths about matter and God is the way to health and immortality. But there is also a third key element in Eddy's cure, which is what gives it its name. This is the role played by Jesus Christ, who showed how apparent illness and death in the world can be overcome by the belief or faith of the sufferers. In short, Jesus found a way to eliminate the illusion of illness and death. Christ was a scientist. What he discovered was essentially Christian Science, which was lost until it was re-discovered by Mrs Eddy.

Placebos and Panaceas

We now need to look at the two panaceas from the perspective of medical science in order to see how far they must be considered placebos.

The judgement of medical science on tar-water, briefly, is that it can be useful externally against certain skin diseases and internally against chronic coughs and chest-diseases; but as one medical writer put it, its "therapeutic properties are, however, too limited to account for more than a small proportion of the diseases given by Berkeley and Prior" (Bell, 1933).

So, the inference is that the great majority of cures must have been brought about by placebo action. But if medical science judges that tar-water was partly a placebo, its verdict on Christian Science must be that it is a pure placebo, since it does not use any physical agency.

That tar-water worked largely as an impure placebo would not have been welcome to Berkeley, even though he believed that ultimately the only real cause is mental or spiritual, in fact God. But his argument in *Siris* is that tar-water works not by any actual physical agency it possesses, but only because its observable, sensory properties are followed unerringly by observable physical cures, whose explanation lies in the laws of nature established by God. So, despite Berkeley's positive attitude to mental agency, he shows no sign of appreciating placebo action either in *Siris* or any other work. Probably the main reason for this is his sensitivity to the criticism that his idealist philosophy seems to break down the hallowed distinction between reality and appearance. Hence Berkeley is reluctant to recognize the power of the human mind in affecting the physical world. Berkeley is prepared to acknowledge that we have agency, but only over our thoughts or mental images, not the sense data which for Berkeley constitute the physical world.

Another way that Berkeley's concern for keeping the objective, physical realm safe from human agency comes out in his attitude to miracles. As an Anglican clergyman, Berkeley does not deny that there have been miracles, and he believes that God did in the past sanction those of Moses but especially those of Jesus Christ and his disciples. But for Berkeley, miracles ended in the first century AD, one reason being that their continuing occurrence would undermine our confidence in the objective or natural realm, upon which we depend.

Christian Scientists have an entirely different attitude to what are called miracles, placebos and faith healing. But here, especially, we need to recognize the equivocal nature of these terms and put aside their negative connotations. If a putative placebo does actually work by the action of mind or spirit, then I think a Christian Scientist could agree that placebo action is an acceptable description, although for her a more accurate description would be cures resulting from Divine Truth and Science.

Of course, for medical science this is all perfect nonsense. Illness and disease as material conditions can only be cured by material agents. Miracles and faith healing are superstitions. Here the issue becomes complicated, because we are getting into a deeper debate, where materialistic or natural science itself has to be- at least for the purpose of this debate- called into question. If that is not done, then this ceases to be a debate and becomes a begging of the question; which, no doubt, most scientists would say is entirely appropriate.

Material Versus Mental Agency

Yet where the naturalistic attitude of science becomes doubtful is just in the area of placebos, which seem to work not by material but by mental causation, by belief. This suggests that the human mind can bring about cures that appear miraculous. And although this is denied by medical science, it does seem that the mind can, working through belief, cause certain observable physical changes in the body. This was dramatically demonstrated to the first important champion of placebos, H. K. Beecher- best known as the author of the influential 1955 article, "The Powerful Placebo"– when he was working as a medic during World War II. On one occasion, there was no morphine to give a soldier who required a major operation. In a moment of inspiration or craziness, a nurse injected the soldier with a harmless water solution, which amazingly produced virtually the same effect on him as morphine. This converted Beecher to the power of placebos.

This crux comes out in a related way in probably the second most important medical article on placebos, that by Levine, et al., published in 1978. Levine's team administered a placebo and found, as expected, that it produced a decrease in pain in their subjects, as well as increasing their endorphins, the body's natural morphine. Going further, however, Levine and his colleagues then injected the subjects with nolaxine, which works against morphine. The result was that the subjects's pain returned. The conclusion, which was hailed as an important step towards discovering the mechanisms of placebos, was that the endorphins were the physical agents producing the placebo effect. So the endorphins, it was hoped, would be the beginning of the trail leading to the chemical agents that work directly on illnesses responsive to placebos.

What appears to have passed unnoticed, however, is that, prima facie, the endorphins came into being directly from mind action- from belief. But if so, then why, in principle, couldn't the agency that works DIRECTLY on the illness also be belief or some other form of mind agency?

For Berkeley, all power or agency in the physical world is mental, namely God's; but God produces the train of sensory data in accordance with His laws of nature; hence physical cures must be brought about in this indirect, law-abiding way. To be sure, God could allow a change or violation in these laws, thereby permitting a human agent to effect a cure more directly, as with Jesus's miracles, but He doesn't now, as that dispensation ended with Jesus's disciples.

Most natural scientists, especially nowadays, would take a far harder line on this, holding that there is no such spiritual agency and hence no way that that the natural laws and processes can be contravened even for such good ends as cures. Thus in his helpful book *Placebos* (2003), Dylan Evans, speaking for natural science, tells us that "We know now that the processes of thinking and wishing that Descartes ascribed to the ethereal, invisible mind are, in fact, complex patterns of electro-chemical activity that swirl around in the lump of fatty tissue we call the brain" (p. xi). So for Evans, materialism has been proved to be true and dualism and idealism false. Hence there MUST have been something material operating in the belief of Beecher's soldier which caused his body to behave as though it had been given morphine. This material something, which we know introspectively as belief, must have been the actual cause of the numbing of his pain and the endorphines which Levine's team discovered in the placebo effect. But so far no scientist has found this material stuff, either in the brain or anywhere else, which we, in our quaint folk-psychological way, identify as belief. Hence what Evans and other materialists take to be proven science is in fact an article of faith.

Indeed, I think we can go further and say that materialism and medical science can themselves be described as placebo sciences in the same way as they would describe Christian Science as a placebo science- given, that is, one important condition being fulfilled. The condition is that idealism should prove true. If that were the case, then matter and hence material medicines would be placebos, as things that do not exist, but which are vitally practical to believe in, as enabling us to live in and make sense of the apparent or sensory world. And, in the final analysis, that is what Berkeley held.

See also: ❯ Body and Spirituality ❯ Christ ❯ Healing ❯ Jesus ❯ Psychotherapy and Religion

Bibliography

Barrett, W. (1925). *The religion of health*. London: Dent.

Bell, J. (1933). Bishop Berkeley on tar-water. *Irish Journal of Medical Science. 99*, 629–633.

Berkeley, G. (1744). Siris: A chain of philosophical reflections. In *Works* (vol. 5). Dublin: Rhomes.

Berkeley, G. (1744). Letter to Thomas Prior. In *Works* (vol. 5). Dublin: Faulkner.

Berkeley, G. (1953). *Works* (Vol. 5) (T. E. Jessop, Ed.). Edinburgh: Nelson.

Berman, D. (1994). *Berkeley: Idealism and the man*. Oxford: Oxford University Press.

Eddy, M. B. (1903) *Science and health*. Boston, MA: The First Church of Christ, Scientist.

Evans, D. (2003). *Placebos: The belief effect*. London: HarperCollins.

Pantheism

Paul Larson

Pantheism is the religious doctrine that the divine is infused within all existent beings. The phrase "the divine" is used as a short-hand label for both theistic (personal) and non-theistic (impersonal) definitions of the sacred ground of being. Virtually all pantheistic thought involves a belief in the immanence of the divine, though the doctrines are distinguishable. In many forms of immanence, particularly within theistic traditions, the deity is not limited to being infused into the material world, it can be beyond it as well. In the case of pantheism, however, there is an identity between the phenomenal world and the divine. God is the natural world personified.

A distinction needs to be made between true pantheism, which equates the divine with the totality of the natural world and panentheism with accepts that idea but adds that the divine is both immanent in the world yet still somehow transcendent in some manner. This view allows some "otherness" to god beyond his or her presence within the natural world. In panentheism god suffuses the world but is not exhausted by the immanence in the world. There is a sense in which the fullness of god goes beyond the material world of nature.

Pantheism is also contrasted with the view of strict creationism, which holds that the divine is the source of, but cannot be identified with the natural world. God, being eternal and infinite, cannot be limited by being part of his own creation. He stands over it as ruler and Lord. In western monotheisms (Judaism, Christianity, Islam) creationism is a foundational doctrine rooted in Biblical and Q'uranic texts. But God is not the same as his creation.

True pantheism, as distinguished from panentheism, is found in only a few positions, as it requires exclusion of the concept of transcendence and confines understanding of the divine to the totality of existent and experienced objects in the world. The identification of the natural world with the divine is appealing to secular thinkers who still have a sense of awe at the majesty of the created world, including life and consciousness.

It is not surprising then, that early in the Enlightenment when secular thought was emerging, a pantheistic school emerged. Deism, the is a spiritual philosophy which fairly clearly identified the divine with nature. The God of the Deists creates and sets in motion the world and its deterministic causal mechanisms and laws, but does not actively intervene in human history. A Deist who coined the term pantheism was John Toland (1670–1722). His views on both politics and religion were quite radical for his day. But he sought to keep a religious sentiment based in nature and aided by reason as opposed to based in obedience to and faith in established authorities. He founded the Ancient Druid Order, so his views would today be closer to the sort of Gaian nature spirituality of neo-Pagans.

Among those philosophers who are clearly pantheists and who Toland refers back to would be Spinoza and Leibniz. Baruch de Spinoza (1632–1677) was born to Portuguese Jews, though he spent most of his life in the Netherlands. His religious ideas were far enough outside the Judaism of his own day that he was excommunicated from the synagogue in Amsterdam. He rejected Descartes dualism and held instead a type of naturalistic monism, where all the world in its diversity was nonetheless dependent on one substance behind the variety of manifest beings and objects.

Such a comprehensive and abstract concept is, of course, difficult to hold on to so the experience of pantheism is generally fleeting and imperfect. Humans have found the metaphor and primary cognitive structure of personhood to be more compelling and so theistic spirituality and religious formations have predominated throughout history. The pantheistic vision is a heady one and not shared by most exoteric religious forms and expressions, which are decidedly personalistic.

The philosophic concepts involved in defining pantheism as well as its alternatives requires a discussion of primary theological distinctions, whether there is a divine realm of being or not, and if so, what is its nature. The empirical study of the variety of comparative world religions suggests that the primary boundary is between the sacred and divine, on the one hand, and the secular or mundane, on the other. If we look at the variety of world views held by most people this primary distinction can be sustained a major dividing point. But within those who espouse one or another of the spiritual world view, the next division of ideas is between those who espouse the existence of personal or impersonal basic natures of the divine.

The impersonal nature of the divine is found in such concepts as "chi," "ki," "prana," "pneuma" and other labels. Those terms comes from Chinese, Japanese, Indian, and Greek cultural spheres, respectively. These embody a force which was also described by Newton and the other formative thinkers in the modern scientific world view. Indeed, the very nature of the modern scientific world view is the metaphysical existence of impersonal forces which determine the manifestation we experience as the phenomenal world. So the spiritual philosophies which incorporate an impersonal force as a significant concept are part of a pantheistic tradition. In Christianity, by counter example, the role of the impersonal force in traditional eastern and pagan western philosophies has been replaced by the person of the Holy Ghost as the third person in the orthodox definition of the Christian trinity of Godhood.

Theistic religions see the divine as manifested in the form of persons. These are the one God in monotheistic traditions and the family of gods in the polytheistic traditions. From a psychological perspective, theism is quite understandable. We understand our selves as persons, which means we experience our ability to create and govern, rule and determine. These are the qualities we project onto the divine and transcendent realm and whatever quality it has. As human beings we can only relate to the greatest concept of existence beyond our self and other than our self as if they were like us, as sentient, active agentic persons. But that very ability to experience the divine as other as person requires an accommodation with the experience of the divine as immanent.

In theism, pantheism is generally thought of as the suffusion of the divine spirit within creation, including human beings. The classical example comes from Hinduism where the seed or "atman" of Brahman, the divine ground of being, is implanted in each individual human soul. This provides the motive force for the individual to seek reunion with the divine through the course of spiritual evolution across many lifetimes via reincarnation (Daniélou, 1964). The mystic vision of the unity of all things can be seen as the experiential side of the idea of pantheism.

A related idea is panpsychism, which holds that every thing in the universe has some form of consciousness or mind. The early psychologist, Gustav Fechner (1801–1887) held this belief. Edwards (1967) quotes him directly in a rapturous meditation on a water-lily during which he accepted the possibility of a mental or psychological life in some manner for lower orders of animate beings. Panpsychism is the chief assumption of animism as a world view (Pepper, 1942). All things are alive and have or are spirits in their essential nature, including things science and common sense deems inanimate.

See also: ❂ Animism ❂ Atman ❂ Christianity ❂ Hinduism ❂ Immanence ❂ Islam ❂ Judaism and Psychology ❂ Paganism

Bibliography

Daniélou, A. (1964). *Hindu polytheism*. New York: Pantheon Books.
Edwards, P. (1967). Panpsychism. In P. Edwards (Ed.), *The encyclopedia of philosophy* (8 Vols.). New York: Collier MacMillan Publishers.
MacIntyre, A. (1967). Panetheism. In P. Edwards (Ed.), *The encyclopedia of philosophy* (8 Vols.). New York: Collier MacMillan Publishers.
Pepper, S. C. (1942). *World hypotheses: A study in evidence*. Berkeley, CA: University of California Press.

Paracelsus

Paul Larson

Paracelsus is the professional name of Theophrastus Phillipus Aureolus Bombastus von Hohenheim (1493–1531), a German alchemist, physician and occultist. The professional name was a reference back in time to the Roman physician Celsus (ca. 25 BCE–50 CE). He adopted much of the previous theories of magic passed on from classical antiquity in the writings of the Hermetic corpus and Neo-Platonic thought. He wrote at a time when alchemists were beginning extensive studies with metals and he sought to propagate a theory metallic magic to supplement or supplant the older magic which concentrated on empirical herbal lore and angelic or spiritual manifestations. In addition to his own work on the newly discovered property of magnetism, he served as an influence for Franz Anton Mesmer's (1734–1815) dissertation for the doctor of medicine degree. Mesmer's theory of animal magnetism served as the initial basis of the psychological technique now known as hypnosis.

See also: ◉ Astrology and Alchemy

Paranormal Experience

Nicholas Grant Boeving

Although the word itself did not come into common usage until at least 1920 (from the Latin *para*: counter, against) the cluster of phenomena generally agreed upon as being "paranormal" have appeared in every culture, age and era of which we have written record. As is the case in every historical excavation, one must take note of the fact that the taxonomies used are indeed our own, and in the particular case of this category, entirely new. What we, in the modern age consider outside or next to the limen of experience, other cultures included with the mysteries of the circulation of the blood and the wind, harsh demarcations being the province of the modern age. Generally speaking however, the paranormal is an umbrella term used to describe unusual experiences or events that resist scientific explanation. The term is frequently found in conjunction with parapsychology, the scientific field dedicated to the gathering and analysis of paranormal data, under which the following are generally categorized: telepathy, extrasensory perception, psychokinesis, ghosts, hauntings, spirit possession, xenoglossia, angel hair, cryptozoology, paracryptozoology, materialization, UFOlogy, automatic writing, channeling, telepathy, spirit photography, spirit possession, medical intuition, psychic surgery, lycanthropy, and some, such as ball lightening, which have recently been empirically confirmed.

The investigation into the paranormal has taken many forms, from the stringently scientific, to the Fortean practice of gathering anomalous anecdotal evidence. The difficulty lies in winnowing away what is (not) to be included in the study as well as what lens should be used. As a recent Gallup poll (2005) indicates, among ten listed paranormal phenomena, 73% of people believed in at least one, while only 1% believed in all. Obviously, there is little consensus – even within the religious and psychological communities – as to what warrants actual investigation. And certainly efforts at debunking paranormal claims have exposed many charlatans, leading many in the scientific community to summarily dismiss the entire project.

Collective perceptions of the origin, manifestation, and even veracity of these wide-ranging phenomena are intimately dependent on the socio-cultural ecologies within which they occur and arguably determine the very possibility of the event in question. The literatures of ethonopsychology are replete with examples of paranormal "afflictions" that manifest in one culture, but not in any others (e.g., Windigo). Still others, such as the "night mare" appear to arise cross-culturally, though not by diffusion, lending the interpretation that these "events" may be rooted in physiological, rather than in esoteric, processes – or of course, in the night mare herself.

Several theoretical orientations are possible when apprehending the paranormal.

The Orthodox Approach

These are the "traditional" explanations as they surface from culture to culture. An example, in the Christian tradition, is the interpretation of possession as not being caused by unresolved psychosexual suppression, but by the actual presence of a discrete demonic entity in the body of an individual. Different religious systems offer different explanations of paranormal events. Whereas Sai Baba's ability to materialize objects is understood in Hinduism to be a result of a perfected understanding of the intrinsic unreality of whatever it is he is materializing – and as evidence of *siddhis*, or yogic powers – other religious systems might see this as evidence of Satanic intervention or, less spectacularly, simple chicanery.

The Bicameral Mind

A novel theory that seeks to understand the origin and persistence of clairvoyant phenomena by right-hemispheric dominance in the brains of those genetically predisposed to this type of experience. More finely nuanced depictions of neurological correlations to paranormal phenomena will undoubtedly be revealed as the fledgling field of neurotheology experimentally matures.

The Pluralist/Inclusivist Approach

This approach aligns itself with the constructivist tendency to view language as the arbiter of what is real. In this model of culturally dependent ontologies, certain phenomena exist because there are certain *words* that circumscribe their manifestations.

The Psychoanalytic Approach

The hermeneutic of suspicion. A powerful tool for the exploration of the underlying neurotic conflicts and wish-fulfillment fantasies seen by this school as the actual bases for all events erroneously perceived to be paranormal. This approach is related to other psychological theories that ground belief in the paranormal as evidence of psychopathologies such as Schizotypal Personality Disorder or Schizophrenia.

Progressive Paradigms

When viewed from within the cause-and-effect-bound Newtonian cosmology, these phenomena simply don't seem to "fit;" they are *para*, in every sense of the prefix. With the advent of Quantum Theory, however, the mystery becomes, not why these events happen, but why they don't happen more often. A science of possibilities, quantum mechanics allows for what once was once seen as *para*, to fit snugly within the realm of the expected.

Commentary

If taken seriously, the claims of paranormal research impact every domain of human knowledge and experience, challenging us to expand our notions of the body, the mind, and indeed the universe itself, beyond our linear geometries; from the relationship of man and machine (see Pears), to occult influences on evolution (see Noetic Institute), investigation into the paranormal is becoming increasingly integral to evolving understandings of consciousness itself, as well as understandings of the chimerical helices of matter and mind.

Psychology and Religion

With the advent of The Fourth Force in psychology (the previous three being Behaviorism, Psychodynamism, and Humanistic psychology) the inclusion of the transpersonal has been taken seriously for the first time in the discipline's history. Whereas psychoanalytic theory offers richly nuanced and psychologically mature analyses of the paranormal, it is reductive none-the-less, while the other two simply do not deign to discuss it. Transpersonal psychology allows for the existence of the "paranormal" as standing outside the limen of egoic experience – in other words, outside the "visible" bands of the spectrum of consciousness. Whether they be unconscious projections of the lower spectra (as may be the case with possession) or transrational transmissions of higher states of being, or simply transmissions from higher beings themselves, transpersonal cartographies of consciousness are theoretical maps of the intersection of psychology and religion that describe, in Wilber's famous phrase, the marriage of sense and soul.

For psychology, the resuscitation and integration of the paranormal from out of the pseudoscientific hinterlands, demands radical reformulation of the psyche. One might even argue that the "repression" of this dimension of experience has returned as any number of "disorders of the spirit" – addiction, narcissism, etc (see Hillman).

For religion, an honest understanding and inclusion of the aforementioned demands both self-reflection and eventually change – self-reflection in the sense that there must be more to the human condition then dreamt of in their philosophies, and change, in the sense of expanding theological purviews to include the possibility of multiple truths.

And as for where they intersect, both religion and psychology are potentially transformative in their respective understandings of the paranormal, psychology lending academic rigor and a scientific orientation to its study, while religion a sensitivity to the subtleties of spirit.

Perhaps the most pragmatic approach is to use a theoretical "toolbox." Are Yeti sightings to be lumped with those of UFO's – or do they mean different things and require different lenses? A psychoanalytic approach might make sense for a poltergeist or channeling (reference) but not for remote viewing or spirit photography. And of course, the question becomes then, is a psychoanalytic reading as reductive as it sounds? Or does a truly comprehensive estimation have room for this perspective as well as something else? Whatever hermeneutic one employs to read it will certainly color the *way* it is read; which is why, if anything, a perpsectival plurality should be conscientiously employed when doing so.

See also: ❯ Christianity ❯ Hinduism ❯ Psychoanalysis ❯ Psychology as Religion

Bibliography

Alleau, R. *History of occult sciences* (Series: The new illustrated history of science and invention.) London: Leisure Arts Limited Publishers. No date appears, but probably 1960s.

Cohen, D. (1971). *A natural history of unnatural things.* New York: McCall Pub. Co.

Cohen, D. (1979). *Ceremonial magic.* Cincinnati, OH: Four Winds Press.

Condon, E. U. (1969). *Scientific study of unidentified flying objects.* Report commissioned by the U. S. Air Force. Introduction by Walter Sullivan. New York: Bantam Books.

Fort, C. (1919). *The book of the damned*. Boni and Liveright.

Fort, C. (1923). *New lands*. New York: Boni and Liveright.

Fort, C. (1931). *Lo!*. New York: Claude Kendall.

Fort, C. (1932). *Wild Talents*. Charles Fort.

Kreskin. (1974). *The Amazing World of Kreskin*. (c. 1973 by Kreskin). New York: Avon.

Krupp, E. C. (Ed.) (1978). *In Search of Ancient Astronomies*. New York: McGraw-Hill.

Kusche, L. D. (1975). *The Bermuda triangle mystery-solved*. New York: Harper & Row.

Larue, G. A. (1975). *Ancient myth and modern men*. Englewood Cliffs, NJ: Prentice-Hall.

Lewinsohn, R. (1961). *Science, prophecy and prediction*. New York: Bell.

Ley, W. (1969). *Another look at Atlantis, and fifteen other essays*. New York: Bell.

MacDougall, C. D. (1983). *Superstition and the press*. Buffalo, NY: Prometheus.

MacDougall, C. D. (1958). *Hoaxes*. (c. 1940 by C. D. MacDougall). Mitchell, WJ: Dover. Hoaxes in art, history, science, literature, politics and journalism. {A6253.M3}

Mackay, C. (1892). *Memoirs of extraordinary popular delusions and the madness of crowds*. London: George Routledge & Sons, Ltd.

McCain & Segal. (1994). *The game of science* (5th Ed.). Pacific Grove, CA: Brooks-Cole.

McIntosh, C. (1969). *The astrologers and their creed, an historical outline*. London: Praeger.

Neher, A. (1980). *The psychology of transcendence*. Englewood Cliffs, NJ: Prentice-Hall.

Randi, J. (1975). *The Magic of Uri Geller, as Revealed by The Amazing Randi*. New York: Ballantine.

Randi, J. (1986). *The Faith Healers*. Seattle, WA: Prometheus.

Shirley, R. (1972). *Occultists & mystics of all ages*. Buffalo, NY: University Books.

Stiebing, W. H., Jr. (1984). *Ancient astronauts, cosmic collisions, and other popular theories about man's past*. Buffalo, NY: Prometheus.

Tompkins, P. (1973). *The secret life of plants*. Kent, U.K.: Avon.

West, J. A. & Toonder, J. G. (1970). *The Case for Astrology*. London: MacDonald.

Zölner, J. C. F. (1888). Transcendental Physics, *An Account of Experimental Investigations from the Scientific Treatises of Johann Carl Friederich Zölner*. Boston, MA: Colby & Rich.

Participation Mystique

John Ryan Haule

Mode of Thinking

"Mystical participation" is an idea introduced by Lucien Lévy-Bruhl in 1910 to identify what it is about the mentality of so-called primitives that makes them understand things differently from Westerners. Lévy-Bruhl began his lifework as a professional philosopher in search of "unimpeachable truths" that would be universally human in their validity. To escape his own cultural limitations, he began studying the reports of missionaries and colonialists working among pre-literate peoples in Africa, Australia, the Americas, and Oceania – all baffled by what they took to be absurd beliefs on the part of the natives. Finding the same sorts of "absurdities" in all parts of the world, Lévy-Bruhl proposed that, while Europeans find meaning in events by looking for causal, empirical theories to explain what made them happen, "primitives" find meaning by seeing empirical events as "participating" in a larger, invisible reality – something on the order of myth, made up of what he called "collective representations" – very similar to Jung's idea of archetypal images. By 1927 he had identified the powerful emotions that accompany mystical participation as the crucial factor in "primitive mentality." He argued that *participation mystique* is in some ways superior to our European way of thinking, insofar as it gives natives' experience a greater depth and meaningfulness than our materialistic empiricism allows us.

Shared Identity

C. G. Jung borrowed the term for his psychology and expanded its meaning, although he was aware of what a controversial figure Lévy-Bruhl had become – unjustly burdened with a racist reputation for having described "primitive mentality" as "inferior" to the European sort. In Jung's hands, participation mystique came to mean, not only "mythic thinking," but also the partial loss of individuality that people commonly suffer in crowds, tribes and families, usually without knowing it. Jung found participation mystique to be characteristic of all human psychology, modern Westerners included.

Most frequently, when used in a Jungian context, participation mystique refers to a regrettable state of unconsciousness: as when parents cannot appreciate the individuality of their children but see them primarily as advertisements for their own honor or shame, or when an analyst becomes so unconsciously identified with an analysand as to lose the capacity for objective critique. In truth, however, every interpersonal relationship has elements of participation mystique in it; and when one recognizes this element and makes use of it, a higher level of consciousness can be attained. A state of participation mystique between mother and infant is an essential part of the bonding between them, and it is the platform of trust and immediate understanding which makes their emotional/gestural communications possible and effective. The infant is socialized and begins to learn language within a cocoon of participation mystique.

Similarly, the rapport or transference relationship between analyst and analysand inevitably involves mystical participation. Whether one thinks in terms of empathy (literally, "feeling into" another person's state of mind) or of an "interpersonal field" of mutuality, there is always a background condition in which the distinction between "me" and "you" is greatly diminished. By directing attention to the background state of participation mystique, an analyst is able to gain access to the analysand's condition and by articulating it raise consciousness. Toward the end of his life, Jung often spoke of this participation mystique based transference relationship in terms of a two-million-year-old man, the personification of the collective unconscious, who brings to the analytic meeting the wisdom of the human race. The mutual field becomes an age-old source of insights relevant to both parties.

Society and Myth

Every society that shares a mythic narrative which gives meaning and shape to its communal life inhabits a world of participation mystique in both senses of the term: (1) the members share a mutual identity to a greater or lesser degree and (2) they make sense of their communal life and the events they experience by reference to "collective representations" derived from their myth. Meditative states of consciousness are more easily and dependably achieved in ashrams and monasteries where all participate in the same rituals and practices, because the communal activities build a participation mystique with a character that supports those states. Shamans exploit the background state of participation mystique when they make visionary journeys on behalf of a patient, to diagnose an illness or to seek out and retrieve a lost soul. Yogis and Sufi masters confer meditative powers upon their disciples by *shaktipat* (Sanskrit, "transmission of psycho-spiritual energy"), which is a form of participation mystique.

See also: ◉ Collective Unconscious ◉ Communal and Personal Identity ◉ Jung, Carl Gustav ◉ Meditation ◉ Mysticism and Psychoanalysis ◉ Mysticism and Psychotherapy ◉ Myth ◉ Shamans and Shamanism ◉ Sufis and Sufism

Bibliography

Jung, C. G. (1966). *Two essays on analytical psychology* (2nd ed.). Princeton, NJ: University Press.

Jung, C. G. (1977). *C. G. Jung speaking: Interviews and encounters* (W. McGuire & R. F. C. Hull, Eds.). Princeton, NJ: University Press.

Lévy-Bruhl, L. (1922/1966). *Primitive mentality*. Boston, MA: Beacon.

Lévy-Bruhl, L. (1927/1966). *The "Soul" of the primitive*. Chicago, IL: Henry Regnery.

Lévy-Bruhl, L. (1945/1975). *The notebooks on primitive mentality*. New York: Harper Torchbooks.

Pastoral Counseling

Don Allen, Jr.

Over the centuries pastoral counseling has been one of the main responsibilities of pastors throughout the church. Jesus provided pastoral counseling to his disciples and to the crowds that followed Him. He talked regularly with those who were physically sick and emotionally hurting. The Apostle Paul also gave pastoral counseling to his young students and preachers such as Timothy and Titus. He also gave pastoral counseling through his letter to Philemon to address the issue of Onesimus returning home. He even gave pastoral counsel to Peter as he attempted to correct the issues facing the church in book of Acts.

Throughout all church history, pastoral counselors have been the foundational and focal point of helping people deal with all sorts of issues and problems. Pastors are frequently the first person church members will seek help from when dealing with grief and death issues, crisis situations, marriage struggles, family issues, health problems, job-related problems, etc.

The goals of pastoral counseling are really quite simple:

(1) To develop a relationship based on trust that supports the person seeking help.
(2) To provide wise Biblical counseling and spiritual resources for church members and others seeking help.
(3) To provide a safe environment offering confidentiality to people dealing with problems and issues.

Pastoral is defined as "Relating to the care of souls, or to the pastor of a church; as, pastoral duties; a pastoral letter" (http://dictionary.reference.com/browse/pastoral).

Counseling is defined as "professional guidance of the individual by utilizing psychological methods especially in collecting case history data, using various techniques of the personal interview, and testing interests and aptitudes" (http://www.merriam-webster.com/dictionary/counselor).

According to American Association of Pastoral Counselors, "Pastoral Counseling is a unique form of psychotherapy which uses spiritual resources as well as psychological understanding for healing and growth" (http://www.aapc.org/about.cfm#intro).

When you combine the two words you have a pastor (shepherd) caring for the souls (members) of his/her congregation by providing a listening ear, guidance, prayer, hope and wisdom in how deal with crisis, family issues, spiritual dilemmas, etc.

It is recommended that we give the same consideration to people with emotional/mental health issues that we do when we help individuals deal with physical problems (such as a physical illness). Just as pastors refer people to seek appropriate medical care, we need to refer people to seek appropriate help to deal with issues of mental illness. As pastors, it is important to understand that unless we have had specific training in the field of mental health it is dangerous (and, in some cases, criminal) to deal with mental health issues as well. Over the years there have been a number of cases where churches and pastors have be sued and lost because of the information and advice they provided to someone dealing with a mental health problem.

Another essential area of pastoral counseling is hospital and nursing home ministry. Pastors are generally the first ones called to come and minister to a patient just before a surgery. Pastors are summoned to comfort the sick and dying. He/she will address fears and spiritual conditions and provide comfort from a spiritual perspective. Pastoral counselors often deal with the aftermath of a patient's hospital admittance or the grief of a family mourning the death of a loved one.

Pastoral counselors are also often called upon to minister in the prisons. He/she is asked to provide wisdom, comfort, hope and Biblical outlook for the inmate and the suffering family on the outside. The word chaplain refers to that person who feels a special call to minister in jails, hospitals, military bases and workplaces. The chaplain's role is to provide support, encouragement, spiritual perspective and Biblical guidance in their place of ministry.

A relativity new and developing part of Pastoral Counseling is the professional Pastoral Counselor. This individual often has a Practice of Pastoral Counseling, which is not only their ministry, but also their employment. A professional Pastoral Counselor is often employed by the local church or social agencies that specialize in helping Christians or other religious groups address their issues in an office setting. The professional Pastoral Counselor studies counseling from a Christian or Biblical view and challenges clients to seek out answers and spiritual truth. Many states require that Pastoral Counselors be certified or licensed just as other professional counselors. A few states even offer credentials for those serving in the developing field of Pastoral Counselors.

Education Requirements

There is a wide range of education and training available for pastoral counselors, including seminars, workshops, distant learning programs and college level programs covering undergraduate, graduate, and doctoral programs. Many major Christian universities and seminaries offer degree programs in Pastoral Counseling or Christian Psychology. It is very important to review the college or seminary's accreditations and to understand the state laws regarding licensure of pastoral counseling within the local church and at private agencies.

Types of Counseling Performed

The content and practice of pastoral counseling is as diverse as psychology. There are generally three distinct groups: The first group is typically referred to as "Bible Only." This group uses the Scripture as their only tool for counseling. A foundational verse for this is "All Scripture is God-breathed and is useful for teaching, rebuking, correcting and training in righteousness" (II Timothy 3:16). The Bible is their main authority and they feel that one can find all the answers to life's questions within the context of Scripture. The second group believes it is appropriate to take from both the Bible and the scientific discipline of psychology to help people address the problems they are dealing with. This group has no conflict using cognitive therapy to help individuals address substance abuse problems or Gestalt therapy to address an individual's personal decisions in seeking direction for their lives. The third point of view is that a counselor should only use only proven psychological methods to treat mental/emotional problems. This group and views pastoral counseling as only an extension (not an integral treatment partner) of the mental health community.

Several therapies are commonly used by pastors when they provide pastoral counseling. Some of those therapies include:

* Rational Emotive Behavioral Therapies
* Solution Focus or Brief Therapies
* Cognitive Behavioral Therapy
* Person Centered Counseling
* Gestalt therapy
* Behavior Therapy and
* Reality Therapy

There are also several professional organizations for pastoral counselors:

* American Association of Pastoral Counselors (AAPC)
* Association for Clinical Pastoral Education (ACPE)
* Association of Professional Chaplains
* American Association of Christian Counselor
* National Association of Nouthetic Counselor (NANC)
* Association of Biblical Counselors (ABC) and
* National Association of Catholic Chaplains.

Professional Journals of interest in the field of Pastoral Counseling include:

* The Journal of Pastoral Care Publications, Inc. (JPCP)
* The Journal of Pastoral Counseling
* The Journal of Pastoral Theology
* The Journal of Biblical Counseling and
* Christian Counseling Today

See also: ❱ Jesus ❱ Psychotherapy and Religion

Bibliography

American Association Pastoral Counselors. Retrieved September 15, 2008 from http://www.aapc.org/about.cfm

The Holy Bible, New International Version. (1984). International Bible Society. Grand Rapids, MI: Zondervan.

Merriam-Webster Online Dictionary. Retrieved 15 September 2008 http://www.merriam-webster.com/dictionary/counselor.

Dictionary.com Unabridged (v 1.1). Retrieved September 15, 2008, from Dictionary.com website: http://dictionary.reference.com/browse/pastoral.

Porter, N. (Ed.) (1998). *Webster's Revised Unabridged Dictionary,* Version published 1913, by the C. & G. Merriam Co., Springfield, MA. 1996, 1998 by MICRA, Inc. of Plainfield, NJ. Last edit February 3, 1998.

Patriarchy

❱ Father

Persona

Ann Casement

Persona is the term Jung used to denote the outer face that is presented to the world which he appropriated from the word for the mask worn by actors in antiquity to indicate the roles they played. Jung conceived of it as an archetype meaning that it is universal and it is the archetypal core of persona that facilitates the relating that has evolved as an integral part of humans as social beings. Different cultures and different historical times give rise to different outer personas as do different life stages and events in an individual's development. However, the archetypal core gives the persona its powerful religious dimension that raises it from the banal, workaday outer vestment of an individual via its connection to the depths of the psyche.

In his writings on persona, Jung often emphasizes its superficial aspects as, for instance, in his paper *The persona as a segment of the collective psyche,* where he makes the point that the contents of the persona are similar to the impersonal unconscious in being collective. "It is only because the *persona* represents a more or less arbitrary and fortuitous segment of the collective psyche that we can make the mistake of regarding it *in toto* as something individual" (Jung, 1953: 157) (Original italics). He goes on to say: "It is. . .only a mask of the collective psyche, a mask that *feigns individuality,* making others and oneself believe that one is individual, whereas one is simply acting a role through which the collective psyche speaks" (Jung, 1953: 157) (Original italics).

He goes on to say the essential components of the persona may be summarized as a compromise between individual and society, a semblance, and a two-dimensional reality. However, in the course of analysis, the persona often begins to break down with the result that the conscious mind can become suffused with material from the collective unconscious. The resultant release of involuntary phantasy material seems to be the specific activity of the collective psyche. As the influence of the latter increases, the conscious personality loses its power of leadership and is "pushed about like a figure on a chess-board by an invisible player" (Jung, 1953a: 161). Jung illustrates this process with case material from a patient whose persona was identified with that of the supremely wise, grown-up, all understanding mother-daughter-beloved behind which her authentic self lay hidden. Her transference onto Jung consisted of the intellectual father who would collude with her intellect as her actual father had done. In the course of analysis she had dreams that brought up material from the collective unconscious which in turn led to her realizing her own real potential instead of her previous role-playing.

From these brief comments, it can be seen that persona has a paradoxical nature in lying between consciousness and the contents of the unconscious so it is important to stress that the persona is not itself pathological but may become so if an individual is too identified with their social role of mother, lawyer, teacher and so on. This kind of persona identification which is concerned with conscious and collective adaptation leads to rigidity and an ego which is capable only of external orientation so that unconscious material will tend to erupt into consciousness rather than emerging in a more manageable form.

Persona Versus Vocation

As has been said above, the persona is the psychic mechanism that consciously adapts an individual to the demands of the external world, but, being an archetype, a part of it lies in the unconscious. There may come a time in any individual's life when conscious adaptation proves insufficient and the unconscious part of the persona becomes active often through neurotic symptoms which can lead the person into therapy. Jung's view of anyone seeking that kind of help was that they were ultimately seeking a spiritual solution to problems. Paradoxically, the path to the inner spiritual quest for anyone lies in the unconscious part of the persona: "But since the soul, like the persona is a function of relationship, it must consist in a certain sense of two parts – one part belonging to the individual, and the other . . .in the unconscious" (Jung, 1971: 167–168).

On the whole, Jung's view of persona was somewhat negative equating it with unconscious adaptation to mass demands. He poses the question of what induces anyone to emancipate themselves from the "herd and its well-worn paths" (Jung, 1954: 175) the latter induced by identification with a collective persona. The answer lies in "*vocation*" (p. 175) which "puts its trust in it as in God. . .vocation acts like a law of God from which there is no escape"(p. 175). This vocation or inner voice is a different one to the voice of the persona (from the Latin *personare*: to make resound)

which can boom loudly in order to compensate for feelings of inferiority: ". . .whenever people are called upon to perform a role which is too big for the human size, they. . .inflate themselves – a little frog becomes like a bull. . ." (Jarrett, 1988: 1213).

The religious life is the one that follows its own destiny by separating from identification with the herd persona. As Jung says: "We can point to Christ, who sacrificed. . .to the god within him, and lived his individual life to the bitter end without regard for conventions. . ." (Jung, 1958: 340). And as Jung goes on to say about the god archetype: ". . .since experience of this archetype has the quality of numinosity, often in very high degree, it comes into the category of religious experience" (Jung, 1958: 59). What the conscious part of the persona may regard as evil is a perception based on it not conforming with what an individual considers to be good so that paradoxically it is through confrontation with and conscious integration of the evil, and, therefore, rejected parts of the personality that a truly religious and meaningful attitude to living evolves. As Jung states: ". . .all religious conversions that cannot be traced back directly to suggestion and contagious example rest upon independent interior processes culminating in a change of personality" (Jung, 1953b: 175).

Jekyll and Hyde

A fictional example of where an individual cannot perform the task of confronting the evil that lies in the psyche is attested to by Murray Stein in his writings about the persona in his book *Jung's Map of the Soul*, wherein he highlights Jung's special interest in this phenomenon which has to do with playing roles in society. "He was interested in how people come to play particular roles. . .and represent social and cultural stereotypes rather than assuming and living their own uniqueness. . . It is a kind of mimicry" (Stein, 1998: 111). He goes on to say that character is often situational and cites the Jekyll and Hyde story as an extreme form of that. In looking more closely at that particular story, one could say that Jekyll was identified with the persona of the caring doctor whose sole aim was to be in the service of humankind. He was in denial of his more animal instinctual side, which, through being repressed, grew in force until eventually it got the upper hand and gained control of his whole personality. The latter exemplifies what Jung calls *shadow* which stands in relation to the persona as polarities of the ego and, in this way, they represent a classic pair of opposites. Where there is a weak ego, shadow and persona can split into extreme polarities leaving no possibility of a dialog between the two as in the fictional case of Jekyll and Hyde. It may be of interest to note that Robert Louis Stevenson said that much of his writing was developed by "little people" in his dreams, and specifically cited the story of *Dr. Jekyll and Mr. Hyde* in this context. This writer has speculated on his use of the name "Jekyll" for the human side of the character he was depicting as it bears an obvious resemblance to the word jackal. It may be that, in choosing this ambiguous name, Stevenson is drawing attention to the animal nature from which the persona evolves.

Soul as Persona

Jung's interest in the persona arose out of his study of multiple personalities and dissociation in an individual which, in turn, was sparked by his experience with the French school, in particular the work of Pierre Janet. "'One has only to observe a man rather closely, under varying conditions, to see that a change from one milieu to another brings about a striking alteration of personality...'Angel abroad, devil at home" (Jung, 1971: 464). Different environments demand different attitudes which depend on the ego's identification with the attitude of the moment. This personality-splitting is by no means only abnormal but led Jung to state that "such a man has no real character at all: he is not *individual* but *collective*, the plaything of circumstance and general expectation" (Jung, 1971: 465) (Original italics).

Jung links *soul* to *persona* by differentiating the former from *psyche* in the following way: "By psyche I understand the totality of all psychic processes, conscious as well as unconscious. By soul, on the other hand, I understand a clearly demarcated functional complex that can best be described as a 'personality'" (Jung, 1971: 463). Jung gives an instance of a man whose persona was identified with the soul leading to "a lack of relatedness, at times even a blind inconsiderateness" (Jung, 1971: 467). This kind of rigid persona can result in a person "who blindly and pitilessly destroys the happiness of those nearest to him, and yet would interrupt important business journeys just to enjoy the beauty of a forest scene" (Jung, 1971a: 467). In other words, persona identification with soul can lead to a deep aesthetic sensibility but also to a lack of heart and a capacity for relatedness.

On the other hand, a lack of connection between soul and persona can have grave consequences as Jung demonstrates with Spitteler's prose epic *Prometheus and Epimetheus*. In this work, Prometheus is depicted as having sacrificed his ego to the soul, the function of inner relation to the inner world, in the process losing the counterweight to the persona, which would connect him with external reality. An angel appears to Prometheus saying: "It shall come to pass, if you do not prevail and free yourself from your forward soul, that you shall lose the great reward of many years, and the joy of your heart, and all the fruits of your richly endowed mind" (Spitteler, 1931: 23). As Jung points out, the soul, like the persona, is a function of relationship and hence consists of two parts – one belonging to the individual and the other to the object viz. the unconscious.

In conclusion, it should be clear from the above that the development of a well-functioning persona is an essential task for any individual but in the process two major pitfalls must be avoided. The first is an over-valuing of the outer persona which leads to dissociation from its unconscious side and hence from connection to the symbolic life; the second is an under-valuing of the persona which can result in dissociation from the external world of reality. Jung cites Schopenhauer's claim that the persona is how one *appears* to oneself and the world but not what one *is*. In view of this, it is wise to bear in mind the well-known saying that one should never judge a book by its cover. As Jung states: "...the temptation to be what one seems to be is great, because the persona is usually rewarded in cash" (Jung, 1959: 123).

See also: ❂ Jung, Carl Gustav ❂ Psyche

Bibliography

Jarrett J. L. (Ed.) (1988). *Nietzsche's Zarathustra: Notes of the seminar given in 1934–1939 by C. G. Jung*. Princeton, NJ: Princeton University Press.

Jung, C. G. (1953a). The persona as a segment of the collective psyche. In *Two essays on analytical psychology*. Princeton, NJ: Princeton University Press.

Jung, C. G. (1953b). The relations between the ego and the unconscious. In *Two essays on analytical psychology*. Princeton, NJ: Princeton University Press.

Jung, C. G. (1954). The development of personality. In *The development of personality* (Vol. 17). London: Routledge & Kegan Paul.

Jung, C. G. (1958). Psychotherapists or the clergy: Psychology and religion: West. In *Psychology and religion: West and East* (Vol. 11). London: Routledge & Kegan Paul.

Jung, C. G. (1959). Concerning rebirth. In *The archetypes and the collective unconscious*. London: Routledge & Kegan Paul.

Jung, C. G. (1971a). Definitions. In *Psychological types* (Vol. 5). London: Routledge & Kegan Paul.

Jung, C. G. (1971b). The type problem in poetry. In *Psychological types*. London: Routledge & Kegan Paul.

Spitteler, C. (1931). *Prometheus and Epimetheus: A prose epic*. London: James Fullarton Muirhead.

Stein, M. (1998). *Jung's map of the soul*. Peru, IL: Open Court Publishing Company.

Personal God

Kenneth L. Nolen

A personal God is a supreme being with self-consciousness and will, capable of feeling, has the attributes and desires of a person, and enters into relationships with individuals and people groups. Although not all Christians believe in a personal God, the belief is integral to and most prevalent in Christianity. Atheists do not believe in God or gods. Agnostics believe that there is a God or gods but that they are unknowable, and Deists believe in an impersonal supreme God that exists and created the universe, but does not intervene it its normal operations. Other god or gods may have human characteristics and feelings that encompass the entire range of human attributes, emotions, and abilities, but lack the holiness and relational attributes of the unique God of Judaism and Christianity.

A major survey by the Pew Forum on Religion and Public Life finds that 6-in-10 adults in the United States believe in a personal God. However, to say that God is a person is to affirm the divine ability and willingness to relate to others and does not imply that God is human, evolved from humanity, or is located at a specific point in the universe. Although the Christian concept of a triune God, Father, Son, and Holy Spirit, could imply a belief in three gods, Christian creeds are quick to clarify that there are not three gods, but only one God existing in three persons. In this sense the word, "God" must apply to a person or a whole composed of interrelated persons. A personal God has all of the maximum attributes of a human person and in addition is omniscience, omnipotence, omnipresence, eternal, and morally perfect. The belief in a personal God presupposes that God is active in the affairs of humanity while enacting an eternal plan for humankind and all of creation. God, who has attributes of male and female, is usually referred to in the masculine. He is actively sustaining and preserving his creation for his own purpose. Since God is divine and may have attributes unknown and unknowable by humanity, God must be self-revealing.

Christians believe that God is self-revealing in nature, in special relationships with individuals and groups of people, but especially in Christian scriptures or Bible. Although the Christian Bible does not try to prove the existence of God, it does give insights into God's nature and attributes. From this self-revelation, God is described as a spirit, who wants to be known by humanity, who has a name or names, who is wise, faithful, truthful, patient, good, loving, gracious and merciful, holy, righteous and just. Many of these same moral attributes are found in the characteristics of humankind, but God's attributes are exceedingly greater in intensity and holiness. The God of Judaism and Christianity emulates the positive absolutes that humanity strives for but fails to achieve.

Commentary

The presuppositions that an investigator brings to the discussion will have a bearing upon his or her belief or disbelief in a personal God. Psychology and religion have had an ongoing tenuous relationship. At times, their relationship could be described as warfare between science and religion with psychology attempting to replace religion or at the very least enter into the discussion of the origins and functions of religious beliefs and practices. For some, a personal God is an anthropomorphic human creation and a mere reflection of humanity and has no place in the world of science. While others who understand the positive effects of faith and belief, blend psychology with religion until a belief in a personal God is no longer necessary. At other times, psychology and religion agree as they consider spirituality a central part of the human journey seeking ways in which psychology could deepen the understanding of the foundation and positive effects of religion on the human condition including the belief in a personal God.

See also: ❯ Anthropomorphism ❯ Biblical Psychology ❯ Christianity ❯ Freud, Sigmund, and Religion ❯ God ❯ God Image

Bibliography

Broad, C. D. (1925). The validity of belief in a personal God. *Hibbert Journal, 24,* 32–48.

Burgess, S., & Van der Maas, E. M. (Eds.) (2002). *International dictionary of Pentecostal and charismatic movements.* Grand Rapids, MI: Zondervan.

Erickson, M. J. (1985). *Christian theology.* Grand Rapids, MI: Baker book House.

Horton, S. M. (Ed.) (1994). *Systematic theology: A Pentecostal perspective.* Springfield, MO: Logion Press.

Kilpatrick, W. K. (1985). *The Emperor's new clothes: The naked truth about the new psychology.* Wheaton, IL: Good News Publishers.

Koenig, H. G., (Ed.). (1998). *Handbook of religion and mental health.* San Diego, CA: Academic Press.

McGrath, A. (2006). *Christian theology: An introduction.* Oxford: Blackwell Publishing.

P

Menzies, W. W. & Horton, S. M. (Eds.) (1993). *Bible doctrines: A Pentecostal perspective*. Springfield, MO: Logion Press.

Pew Forum on Religious & Public Life. (n.d.). *US Religious Landscape Survey*. Retrieved September 24, 2008, from The Pew Forum on Religion and Public Life Website: http://religions.pewforum.org/reports.

Personal Unconscious

Brandon Randolph-Seng

The unconscious has a long history in psychology. Although Freud in credited for his contributions on the understanding of the unconscious, contemporary psychology has failed to find evidence for much of Freud's assertions concerning what the unconscious part of human beings contains. The unconscious is now considered to be indicative of automatic thought processes. Automatic thought is generally characterized as nonconscious processing. Automatic thought processes involve reflexive responses to certain triggering conditions. These processes require only that a stimulus event or object be detected by an individual's sensory system. Once that triggering event is detected, the process runs to completion without awareness (for a review see Wegner and Bargh, 1998). Such nonconscious influences on thoughts can, in turn, automatically influence behavior. One frequently-cited demonstration of this effect involved the priming of some participants with the concept of the elderly. Results showed that these elderly-primed participants subsequently walked slower than did control participants (Bargh, Chen, and Burrows, 1996).

What are the nonconscious components of thought for religion and the religious believer? Is it possible that mental representations that shade the way an individual interprets a variety of situations, such as religious beliefs, could have automatic influences? Research in this area suggests the answer to this question is yes, particularly for religious individuals. For example, using a method designed to measure implicit (i.e., automatically activated) evaluations, Hill (1994) found that religious and nonreligious people made similar implicit evaluations towards religiously neutral objects. In contrast, implicit evaluations of religious objects were stronger among religious people than among nonreligious people. Going one step further, recent research has shown that subliminal (i.e., outside of conscious awareness) presentations of the concept of God actually reduce causal attributions to the self for believers of God (see Dijksterhuis, Aarts, and Smith, 2005). Can religious representations in turn automatically influence behavior outside of awareness? Research once again says yes. Subliminal presentation of religious words (e.g., amen, faith, saved) have been shown to increase prosocial behavior (helping, honesty) and do so without participants' conscious awareness of such influence (Pichon, Boccato, and Saroglou, 2007; Randolph-Seng and Nielsen, 2007). Furthermore, these behavioral effects are not moderated by self-reported religiosity (Randolph-Seng and Nielsen, 2007; Shariff and Norenzayan, 2007).

See also: ❷ Freud, Sigmund ❷ Unconscious

Bibliography

Bargh, J. A., Chen, M., & Burrows, L. (1996). Automaticity of social behavior: Direct effects of trait construct and stereotype activation on action. *Journal of Personality and Social Psychology, 71*, 230–244.

Dijksterhuis, A., Aarts, H., & Smith, P. K. (2005). The power of the subliminal: On subliminal persuasion and other potential applications. In R. Hassin, J. Uleman, & J. A. Bargh (Eds.), *The new unconscious* (pp. 77–106). New York: Oxford.

Hill, P. C. (1994). Toward an attitude process model of religious experience. *Journal for the Scientific Study of Religion, 33*, 303–314.

Pichon, I., Boccato, G., & Saroglou, V. (2007). Nonconscious influences of religion on prosociality: A priming study. *European Journal of Social Psychology, 37*, 1032–1045.

Randolph-Seng, B., & Nielsen, M. E. (2007). Honesty: One effect of primed religious representations. *The International Journal for the Psychology of Religion, 17*, 303–315.

Shariff, A. F., & Norenzayan, A. (2007). God is watching you: Priming God concepts increases prosocial behavior in an anonymous economic game. *Psychological Science, 18*, 803–809.

Wegner, D. M., & Bargh, J. A. (1998). Control and automaticity in social life. In D. T. Gilbert, S. T. Fiske, & G. Lindzey (Eds.), *Handbook of social psychology* (4th ed., pp. 446–496). Boston, MA: McGraw-Hill.

Petitionary Prayer

❷ Contemplative Prayer ❷ Prayer

Peyote Ceremony

Richard W. Voss · Robert Prue (Sicangu Lakota)

The Peyote ceremony has been described in a number of ethnographic works (Steinmetz, 1990; Anderson, 1996; Schaefer and Furst, 1996; Hultkranz, 1997). While the interpretations these works offer are suspect for their enthnocentrism, the ritual descriptions are largely consistent with observations of the ceremonies. The second author has attended peyote ceremonies, on both personal and professional levels, as both an invited guest and as part of his research, and will describe the process of the peyote ceremony. The conduct of the peyote meeting is fairly simple when compared to the complex rituals many of the shamanistic societies of the plains have or had (Wissler, 1916).

The ceremony is typically held in either a plains style tipi or a Navajo hogan, although some chapters have buildings set aside for their services. In any case, there is always a dirt floor and participants sit or kneel on blankets for the duration of the 8–10 h service. Exceptions are made for elderly, who may sit in a chair, or for prepubescent children, some who will lie down being their adult guardians, being allowed to sleep. The ceremony itself begins with the lighting of the fire at sunrise on the morning of the service. A Fire-keeper tends the fire throughout the day praying. Participants arrive in the hours preceding the service proper, which usually begins at about 4 h before midnight. There are opening prayer songs, prayers and words of instruction by the Roadman. Each person present is usually acknowledged and made welcome, with special attention being given to the elderly, youth, those who have traveled far and individuals new to the religion.

A Roadman is a man qualified to conduct the ritual who serves in the role of facilitator more than medicine man, priest or minister, although some Roadmen are also highly skilled shamans and orators. The service continues with the sponsoring party saying a "few" words about the nature of the service, why and in some cases for whom the service was called. Peyote Way services are not routine, for the most part, but are called a specific purpose of healing, thanksgiving or celebration. While the opening of the ceremony is happening corn husks and tobacco are passed to all participants, who roll prayer smokes. Some participants carry ground peyote into the ritual that they add to the prayer smokes. These prayer smokes are than smoked in unison with all participants addressing the Chief Peyote to intervene on behalf of their prayers. The Chief Peyote is a whole dried peyote plant placed prominently on the altar (viewed as the symbolic road of life), and is not thought of as a deity itself, but as an intercessor to God.

Many peyotists profess to be Christian and view the Chief Peyote to be a manifestation of Christ. Once the initial prayers and songs have been said, the peyote is passed around. Referred to as medicine in both English and most Indigenous languages, the peyote is consumed either green or fresh, in powdered form, in slurry of ground peyote or as a tea. Medicine is passed around after several rounds of singing, however, individuals can usually ask for more throughout the ceremony. Once the medicine has been passed a staff, fan and rattle are passed sequentially to each participant who then prays silently or sings four songs, accompanied by a drummer.

The Peyote Way services use a water drum, usually made of a cast iron kettle and partially filled with water, which produces a unique droning sound. The drummers are usually highly skilled and fast paced beat contributes to the transcendent state. The drumming, rattling and singing continues for about 4 h until midnight when there is ritual water brought in by the sponsoring woman or the wife of the Roadman. Participants usually leave the tipi to stretch, or relieve themselves. The service resumes following the short break and continues in a similar manner to the first round. The water woman brings in more water at sunrise, again offering words of gratitude and thanksgiving, usually addressing each participant personally. She then smokes over the water and which is then passed around for participants to take a drink. The water is followed by a ceremonial meal consisting of dried pulverized deer meat, corn meal, a fruit pudding and a sweet desert. Then the service is ended, but the ceremonial space is not disbanded until after the participants have taken a lunch meal.

The atmosphere of the service is usually quite reverent and sedate. This is in striking contrast to the atmosphere when the service is completed which is quite animated, with humor being the order of the day, with old and new acquaintances poking good-natured fun at themselves and each other. People appear quite emotionally open during this period. Individuals that I have known for years and thought to be quiet and reserved, openly shared personal challenges or intimate concerns about themselves or others. The ceremony seems to help participants become more vulnerable and emotionally connected with one another. Caution is advised in assuming that this animation and openness is caused by the intoxicating effects of peyote alone. The same behavior can be observed following other intense indigenous rituals, (e.g., Sundance, Vision Quest or Sweat Lodge Ceremonies).

Ceremonial Use of Peyote and the Professional Healthcare System

Beginning Discussion

There is evidence that the medical community in the United States is ambivalent about how to comprehend and view the ceremonial use of peyote (Salladay, 2005; Yuill, 2006). How should a professional healthcare provider react or respond when he or she learns that one's patient is active in the peyote religion and periodically attends a peyote ceremony? While there are emerging studies that show that the ceremonial use of peyote does not correlate to increased risk of psychological or cognitive deficits (Halpern, Sherwood, Hudson, Yurgelun-Todd, and Pope, 2005), there is also evidence that the illicit use of peyote (outside a ceremonial context) is associated with low levels of social support, low levels of self-esteem, and low identification with American Indian culture (Fickenscher, Novins, and Manson, 2006), more research needs to be done looking at the interactions between peyote and prescribed medications.

Peyote has been classified under federal law as a Schedule I controlled substance, however exemptions have been enacted, through the American Indian Religious Freedom Amendments Act of 1991 (AIRFAA) to protect members' exercise of traditional peyote ceremonies of the Native American Church. While there are exemptions for members of the Native American Church of Native American descent, the interpretation of this federal legislation has been subject to various interpretations by the states (Parker, 2001). Parker notes, "While current exemption structure seems to provide ample protection to Native Americans practicing peyote religion, continuing challenges to the constitutionality of the exemptions by non-Native Americans indicates that Congress could strengthen and clarify the exemption to avoid future problems and court challenges" (2001: 13).

See also: ❂ Christ ❂ Native American Messianism ❂ Ritual ❂ Shamans and Shamanism

Bibliography

Anderson, E. G. (1996). *Peyote: The divine cactus*. Tucson, AZ: University of Arizona Press.

Fickenscher, A., Novins, D. K., & Manson, S. M. (2006). Illicit peyote use among American Indian adolescents in substance abuse treatment: A preliminary investigation. *Substance Use & Misuse, 41*(8), 1139–1154.

Halpern, J. H. (2004). Hallucinogens and dissociative agents naturally growing in the United States. *Pharmacology & Therapeutics, 102*(2), 131–138.

Halpern, J. H., Sherwood, A. R., Hudson, J. L., Yurgelun-Todd, D., & Pope. H. G. (2005). Psychological and cognitive effects of long-term peyote use among Native Americans. *Biological Psychiatry, 58*(8), 624–631.

Hultkranz. (1997). *The attraction of Peyote: An inquiry into the basic conditions for the diffusion of the Peyote religion in North America. Stockholm studies in comparative religion*, No. 33. New York: Coronet Books Inc.

Parker, C. (2001). A constitutional examination of the federal exemptions for native American religious peyote use. *BYU Journal of Public Law, 16*(1), 89, 24 p. Retrieved February 4, 2007 from [EBSCOhost %20E-mail%20Result-5E].

Salladay, S. A. (2005). Sacramental Peyote: Standing on ceremony. *Nursing, 35*(10), 66.

Schaefer, S. B., & Furst, P. T. (1996). *People of the Peyote: Huichol Indian history, religion, & survival*. Albuquerque, NM: University of New Mexico Press.

Steinmetz, P. B. (1990). *Pipe, Bible, and Peyote among the Oglala Lakota: A study in religious identity*. Knoxville, TN: University of Tennessee Press.

Wissler, C. (1916). General discussion of shamanistic and dancing societies. *Anthropological Papers on the American Museum of Natural History, 11*(12), 853–876.

Yuill (February, 2006). Retrieved on June 17, 2009 from http://www.nursing2004.com/pt/re/nursing/abstract.00152193-200602000-00005.htm;jsessionid=K5pCjqKVJHBWLfzpyLdJ5rp1q2H6kM8whQxVwh4Kq35BktL9pWYG!713060492!181195629!8091!-1.

Peyote Religion

Richard W. Voss · Robert Prue (Sicangu Lakota)

Peyote Way: Background and Cultural Context

The term "Peyote Religion" describes a wide range of spiritual practices primarily from tribes of the American Southwest that has expanded into a kind of pan-Indian movement under the auspices of the Native American Church (NAC). Peyote religion, formally recognized as the Native American Church (NAC) incorporates the ritual use of peyote, the small spineless peyote cactus *Lophophora Williamsii*, into its spiritual and healing ceremonies. The peyote ceremony is led by a recognized practitioner who is referred to as a Roadman who is sponsored by an individual or family requesting a ceremony, usually for some specific need or healing or to recognize some event, such as a birthday or an important life transition.

Derived from the Aztec word *Péyotl*, the Peyote Way religions have expanded their spheres of influence from an area around the Rio Grande Valley, along the current US-Mexico boarder, to Indigenous groups throughout Central and North America (Anderson, 1996).

The ritual use of peyote has roots in antiquity. A ritually prepared peyote cactus was discovered at an archeological site that spans the US-Mexico border dated to 5,700 years before the present. Other archeological evidence, paintings and ritual paraphernalia, indicates that the Indigenous people of that region have been using both peyote and psychoactive mescal beans ritually for over 10,500 years (Bruhn, et al., 2002).

The Peyote Way is a complex bio-psycho-social-spiritual phenomenon that encompasses much more than the pharmacology plant. The contemporary peyote practice found in the United States, Canada and by Mestizo peoples in Mexico differs significantly from the older rites that continue to be practiced by the Huichol, Cora and the Tarahumar in Mexico (Steinberg, et al., 2004). The forebearers of the modern Native American Church were the Lipan Apache, who brought the practice from the Mexican side of the Rio Grande to their Mescalero Apache relatives around 1870. From the Mescalero it spread to the Comanche and Kiowa in Oklahoma and Texas. It quickly spread to most of the Eastern Tribes forcibly relocated to the Oklahoma Territory. The quick spread from the Mescalero to most of the Oklahoma Tribes has been attributed to the loss of traditional religions due to oppression (Anderson, 1996).

The psychedelic properties of peyote are just a part of the whole spiritual package "this is not to say that peyote does not facilitate visions but rather that it is only one influence in a total religious setting" (Steinmetz, 1990: 99). It is important to note that describing peyote as a "psychedelic" while accurate, is fraught with problems, particularly when the Peyote religion is studied outside its indigenous context. Here, one needs to differentiate the ritual use of peyote by indigenous practitioners, called Roadmen, and Native American Church participants from use or abuse of peyote by curiosity seekers and experimenters who are simply seeking a "high" devoid of a ceremonial and cultural context. Peyote has been described as both a psychedelic as well as an entheogen. An entheogen is a chemical or botanical substance that produces the experience of God within an individual and has been argued to be a necessary part of the study of religion (Roberts and Hruby, 2002). Elsewhere, an entheogen has been defined as a psychoactive sacramental plant or chemical substance taken to occasion primary religious experience. Within such an understanding the complementary use of Peyote Ceremony within the context of mental health treatment has been viewed as a form of cultural psychiatry (Calabrese, 1997). Other entheogens include psilocybin mushrooms and DMT-containing *ayahuasca*, which, similar to the use of peyote, have been used continuously for centuries by indigenous people of the Americas (Tupper, 2002).

Civil Rights Versus Indigenous Rites: New Pathways for Treatment

Mental health practitioners from across disciplines may view Peyote Religion and the Native American Church with some degree of suspicion, if not, with downright skepticism. Mack (1986) discussed the medical dangers of peyote intoxication in the peer-reviewed *North Carolina Journal of Medicine*. Mack refers to the users of peyote as "the more primitive natives of our hemisphere" (p. 138), and gives repeated attention to details of nausea, vomiting and bodily reactions that happen, at doses that he failed to mention were 150–400 times higher than the ceremonial amount reported nearly a century prior (Anderson, 1996). So, there is need for reasoned and open discourse on this important resource and potential partner for the mainstream mental health practitioner.

Psychiatric researchers, Blum, Futterman and Pascarosa (1977), looked at the mildly psychedelic effects of the peyote, coupled with Native American Church ritual and exposure to positive images projected by the skillful use of folklore by the road man. They found these components facilitated an effective therapeutic catharsis. Albaugh and Anderson (1974) hypothesized that the effects of peyote created a peak psychedelic experience that were similar to those found when using LSD as an adjunct to psychotherapy with alcoholics. In their study of a group of lifelong drug and alcohol abstaining Navajo, Halpern, Sherwood et al. (2005) found no evidence of psychological or cognitive deficits associated with regularly using peyote in a religious setting. However, the placement of peyote, LSD and other psychedelics on the Schedule 1 classification of drugs has eliminated public funding of psychedelic research (Strassman, 2001), and has limited scientific inquiry on the effects of such. The current bio-medical opinion on efficacy of entheogens is inconclusive (Halpern, 2001) and yet there is limited evidence that further study is warranted. Wright has suggested that the behavioral sciences should once again open its mind to the incorporation of mind expanding substances in the psychiatric or psychotherapeutic treatment milieu (2002). As science takes a more benign look at the effects of traditional healing practices and brain chemistry, new pathways for treatment and renewed discussions about traditional indigenous healing methods may be opened up for study (see Hwu and Chen, 2000).

See also: ❯ Peyote Ceremony ❯ Ritual

Bibliography

Albaugh, B. J., & Anderson, P. O. (1974). Peyote in the treatment of alcoholism among American Indians. *American Journal of Psychiatry, 131*(11), 1247–1250.

Alcoholics Anonymous. (1984). *"Pass it on": The story of Bill Wilson and how the A.A. message reached the world.* New York: Alcoholics Anonymous World Services.

Anderson, E. F. (1996). *Peyote: The divine cactus.* Tucson, AZ: University of Arizona Press.

Blum, K., Futterman, S. L., & Pascarosa, P. (1977). Peyote, a potential ethnopharmacologic agent for alcoholism and other drug dependencies: Possible biochemical rationale. *Clinical Toxicology, 11*(4), 459–472.

Bruhn, J. G., DeSmet, P. A., El Seedi, H. R., & Beek, O. (2002). Mescaline use for 5700 years. *The Lancet, 359*(9320), 1866.

Calabrese, J. D. (1997). Spiritual healing and human development in the Native American Church: Toward a cultural psychiatry of peyote. *Psychoanalytic Review, 84*(2), 237–255.

Grof, S. (1987). Spirituality, addiction, and western science. *ReVision, 10*(2), 5–18.

Halpern, J. H. (2001). Research at Harvard Medical School. *Newsletter of the Multidisciplinary Association for Psychedelic Studies, 11*(2), 2.

Halpern, J. H., Sherwood, A. R., et al. (2005). Psychological and cognitive effects of long-term peyote use among Native Americans. *Biological Psychiatry, 58*(8), 624–631.

Hwu, H. -G., & Chen, C. -H. (2000). Association of 5HT2A receptor gene polymorphism and alcohol abuse with behavior problems. *American Journal of Medical Genetics, 96*(6), 797–800.

Mack, R. B. (1986). Marching to a different cactus: Peyote (mescaline) intoxication. *North Carolina Medical Journal, 47*(3), 137–138.

Roberts, T. J., & Hruby, P. J. (2002). Toward an Entheogen Research Agenda. *Journal of Humanistic Psychology, 42*(1), 71–89.

Schaefer, S. B., & Furst, P. T. (1996). *People of the peyote: Huichol Indian history, religion & survival.* Albuquerque, NM: University of New Mexico Press.

Sherwood, J. N., Stolaroff, M. J., & Harman, W. W. (1962). The psychedelic experience: A new concept in psychotherapy. *Journal of Neuropsychiatry, 4*(2), 96–103.

Steinberg, M. K., Hobbs, J. J., & Mathewson, K. (2004). *Dangerous harvest: Drug plants and the transformation of indigenous landscapes.* New York: Oxford University Press.

Steinmetz, P. B. (1990). *Pipe, Bible, and peyote among the Oglala Lakota a study in religious identity.* Knoxville, TN: University of Tennessee Press.

Strassman, R. (2001). *DMT: The spirit molecule: A doctor's revolutionary research into the biology of near-death and mystical experiences.* Rochester, VT: Park Street Press.

Tupper, K. W. (2002). Entheogens and existential intelligence: The use of plant teachers as cognitive tools. *Canadian Journal of Education, 27*(4), 499–516.

Wissler, C. (1916). General discussion of shamanistic and dancing societies. *Anthropological Papers of the American Museum of Natural History, 11*(12), 853–876.

Wright, S. (2002). Open your mind. *Nursing Standard, 16*(48), 20–21.

Phenomenological Psychology

Todd DuBose

Phenomenological psychology is a type of human science psychology that emphasizes close attention to, and rigorous, detailed description and understanding of, personal lived experiences within respective lifeworlds. One's lived experience within one's lifeworld is how one experiences and makes sense of everyday events *as it is to the one experiencing* those events or happenings. Entry into meaningful experiences is accessed by descriptive approaches, rather than explanative ones, and through intuitive, empathic resonance with the intersubjective meaningfulness of an individual's enactments of significance in the world.

The formal discipline of phenomenological psychology was founded by Wilhelm Dilthey (1833–1911; 1989). Dilthey distinguished between the natural sciences (*Naturalwissenschaften*) and the human sciences (*Geisteswissenschaften*), believing the latter to be the more appropriate approach to understanding human existence. He used hermeneutical theory, or the art and science of interpretation, as the earlier hermeneuticist and theologian Freidrich Schleiermacher (1768–1834; 1893) understood it, and broadened its scope. For Schleiermacher, interpretative skills were tools used for textual analysis, particularly sacred texts, and interpretation was partly accomplished though empathic resonance with an author's intentions for textual meaning. Dilthey expanded the interpretive process beyond textual analysis to include an analysis of human experience as disclosed in actions, experiences, products, and cultural artifacts. For Dilthey, though, meaning cannot be experienced directly and must be "decoded" through interpretive inquiry. On the other hand, Dilthey argued that what allows for empathic and communal sharing at all is that, mediated as it is, we all share a common human existence (Burston and Frie, 2006). Moreover, Dilthey rejected any sense of unconscious representation, thus founding a central tenet of phenomenological psychology, namely, that what shows itself in existence is inextricably intertwined with the *ways* in which we experience those things (Burston and Frie, 2006).

Edmund Husserl (1859–1938; 1962), furthered Dilthey's project, and, through the influence of his teacher Franz Brentano (1838–1917), developed what became known as transcendental phenomenology. Husserl and his teachers were influenced by Immanuel Kant's (1724–1804) work on the possibilities and limitations of knowledge. Husserl insisted that the phenomenologist remain focused on "the things themselves," bracketing biases and assumptions that would prevent a clear perception of things as they presented themselves to our consciousness. For Husserl, borrowing from his teacher Brentano, experience, or consciousness, is intentional, which is to say that experiences, objects, persons, things, and events are taken up by each of us in meaningful ways. We are always "about" some directive. Objects, for instance, are objects for us, have a certain calling to us, and are placed within a particular project and direction or goal of significance for us. Husserl fused the traditional distinction between noesis, or the thinking process itself, and noema, or the meaning attributed to objects experienced in consciousness. This move steps beyond a Kantian loyalty to the conditions of knowledge over the objects of knowledge and, instead, refigures knowledge as a co-construction between how we experience things and how the things themselves shape and delimit how we experience them.

Transcendental phenomenology developed into phenomenological research methodology. The challenge for transcendental phenomenological psychology became how one could move from particular experiences to general claims. Although we may have different lived experiences of any given event, human experience is structured in such a way that if we can understanding the general structure of how things come to be experienced as they are, potentially anyone undergoing the same experience could find resonance with any other person having encountered it. The experience of being anxious, or angry, or desirous, albeit from differing life stories, nonetheless has the potential of sharing a common human "way" of undergoing these experiences. Arriving at this common structure of experience for any given event, though,

necessitates an act of "bracketing" pre-understandings, biases, prejudices or other assumptions about how an experience should be, in order to clear a space for things to show themselves as they are to us.

Martin Heidegger (1889–1976), Husserl's student, concurred that experienced was structured, but understood this fact in very different ways. Heidegger became known as the founder of hermeneutical or existential phenomenology, and saw all experience as conditioned by common, existential givens: temporality, spatiality, mortality, co-existence, mood/attunement, historicity, and bodyhood (Heidegger, 1962). Heidegger thought that the idea of an objective, isolated, egoistic ego that is separate from the world in which he experiences things as a dualistic illusion, and instead, considered the person-world co-construction an inseparable process.

Heidegger described this process as being-in-the-world, with "being" described as a comportment of existence rather than an isolated and self-contained ego, and thus, preferred to use the intentionally untranslated German word, *Dasein*, or "being-there," for "being," in order to accentuate a process rather than a "thing." Existential-phenomenological psychology became a practice of interpreting the presencing of *Dasein* in eventful situations. Interpreting *Dasein* required an acknowledgment of one's own biases and pre-understandings, rather than rid oneself of them, as any understanding presupposes an already pre-understanding. Our pre-understandings are ways in which we enter a phenomenon we want to understand better, and use what we do know about it as points of entry. One leads with the bit of awareness and experience one knows of a phenomenon and dialogues with the undulation of concealment and disclosure.

Commentary

Contemporary expressions of phenomenological psychology include methodological applications to a wide range of psychological subjects, such as assessment, diagnostic, and research practices (Fischer, 1994; 2006), Jungian studies (Brooke, 1991), stress (Kuglemann, 1992), and in critically analyzing technological impact on lived experience (Idhe, 1995; Romanyshyn, 1989). There are a plethora of countries around the world in which formal phenomenological organizations are operating, and in which research is thriving. One only need explore the umbrella organization known as the *Organization of Phenomenological Organizations*, or peruse the *Journal of Phenomenological Psychology* to find how many possibilities are available for interested human scientists.

Phenomenological psychology as a collective field of research today centers around the debate of whether the focus should be on description or interpretation. Most theorists agree that the dichotomy is false. Any description is an interpretation, and an interpretation, at least in phenomenological circles, is descriptive rather than explanative, and is an invitation to further disclosure rather than a reductive pronouncement of "what is the case." Reliability and validity are understood in very different ways than in natural science research. What is true is not what can be objectively isolated, operationalized, and controlled in order to pin down unilinear causal relationships as is the case in logical positivistic styles of scientism. Truth as valid and reliable, for a phenomenologist, rests in how well one is able to describe the depth and breath of a phenomenon as it shows itself in the world. The structure of an experience is discerned through imaginative variation in which every manner of a phenomenon's presentation is considered from all advantage points until no matter how one looks at it, certain meaningful aspects of the experience are always present. One's validation as a phenomenological researcher comes when a human experience is so well disclosed by way of rigorous description that any human being undergoing that experience can find it familiar. Nevertheless, there is always a mystery to phenomenological disclosure in that the undulation of concealment and disclosure is never finished.

The spiritual themes within phenomenological psychology are numerous. To start with, the phenomenological psychology of religious experience has a long and brilliant history, and includes Friedrich Schleiermacher (1768–1834), William James (1842–1910), Gerardus van der Leeuw (1890–1950), Rudolf Otto (1869–1937), Mircea Eliade (1907–1986), Paul Tillich (1886–1965), Langdon Gilkey (1919–2004), and David Tracy (1939–) just to name a few scholars. The process itself can be compared to a type of spiritual discipline. Within the emphasis on bracketing to allow things to show themselves lies the heart of a spirituality of freedom, respect and mystical – though not mystifying – openness. Meaning making and the primacy of validating lived experience privileges depth relating in intersubjective ways. Phenomenological psychology warns against the hubris of a "god's eye view," in which we presume to step out of our horizons or perspectives to "know" about phenomena more objectively. On the contrary, objective knowing misses the richness of truth revealed to us subjectively. Knowing about swimming theoretically is very different from jumping in a pool and doing it. Subjective experiencing does not mean isolationist experiencing. We co-construct experiences, and thus build communion in our co-dwellings as we ready ourselves to receive revelations of Being itself.

Finally, the French phenomenologist Michel Henry (2003) has taken phenomenology in its most radical direction to date, thus challenging many foundational assumptions of phenomenological psychology, while ironically returning to Husserl's thought to do so. For Henry, life is "invisible" in that it is lived rather than abstracted, conceptualized, or objectified. Interestingly enough, Dilthey was found of a similar way of thinking, noting often the Latin phrase, "*individuum est ineffabile*" to describe the unfathomable nature of human existence (Burston and Frie, 2006). Henry's work not only radicalizes phenomenology, but also radicalizes Christian thought as his work is in essence a radical phenomenology of Christianity (Henry, 2003). If Life is invisible, then I would argue that it is likewise immeasurable and incomparable. We may hear the sound of it, and may very well succeed in describing it to some extent, but we cannot know from where it comes or to where it will go from here.

See also: ❂ Daseinsanalysis ❂ Heidegger, Martin ❂ Hermeneutics ❂ Homo Religiosus ❂ Lived Theology ❂ Meaning of Human Existence ❂ Psychology

Bibliography

Brooke, R. (1991). *Jung and phenomenology*. London: Routledge.

Burston, D., & Frie, R. (2006). *Psychotherapy as a human science*. Pittsburgh, PA: Duquesne University Press.

Creswell, J. W. (2006). *Qualitative inquiry and research design: Choosing among five approaches* (2nd ed.). Thousand Oaks, CA: Sage Publications.

DeRobertis, E. (1996). *Phenomenological psychology: A text for beginners*. New York: University Press of America.

Dilthey, W. (1989). *Selected works* (Vol. 1). Princeton: Princeton University Press.

Eliade, M. (1959). *The sacred and the profane: The nature of religion* (W. Trask, Trans.). New York: Harper & Row.

Fischer, C. (1994). *Individualizing psychological assessment*. Hillsdale, NJ: Lawrence Erlbaum Associates.

Fischer, C. (2006). *Qualitative research methods for psychologists: Introduction through empirical studies*. San Diego, CA: Elsevier Academic Press.

Fuller, A. (1990). *Insight into value: An exploration of the premises of a phenomenological psychology*. Albany, NY: State University of New York Press.

Gilkey, L. (1976). *Naming the whirlwind: The renewal of God-language*. Indianapolis, IN: Bobbs-Merrill Educational Publishing.

Giorgi, A., Knowles, R., & Smith, D. (1980). *Duquesne studies in phenomenological psychology*. Pittsburgh, PA: Duquesne University Press.

Heidegger, M. (1962). *Being and time* (J. Macquarrie & E. Robinson, Trans.). Oxford: Basil Blackwell.

Heidegger, M. (1987/2001). *Zollikon seminars: Protocols—conversations—letters.* Evanston, IL: Northwestern University Press.

Henry, M. (2003). *I am the truth: Towards a philosophy of Christianity* (S. Emanuel, Trans.). Stanford, CA: Stanford University Press.

Husserl, E. (1962). *Ideas: General introduction to pure phenomenology* (W. Gibson, Trans.). New York: Collier.

Idhe, D. (1995). *Postphenomenology: Essays in the modern context.* Evanston, IL: Northwester University Press.

James, W. (1902/1982). *The varieties of religious experience.* New York: Penguin.

Kuglemann, R. (1992). *Stress: The nature and history of engineered grief.* Westport, CT: Praeger Publishers.

Merleau-Ponty, M., & Merleau-Ponty, M. (1964). *The primacy of perception* (W. Cobb, Trans.). Chicago, IL: Northwestern University Press.

Moustakas, C. (1994). *Phenomenological research methods.* Thousand Oaks, CA: Sage Publications.

Otto, R. (1958). *The ideal of the holy: An inquiry into the non-rational factor in the idea of the divine and its relation to the rational* (J. Harvey, Trans.). New York: Oxford University Press.

Romanyshyn, R. (1989). *Technology as symptom and dream.* London: Routledge.

Schleiermacher, F. (1893). *On religion: Speeches to its cultured despisers* (J. Oman, Trans.). London: Kegan Paul.

Spinelli, E. (2005). *The interpreted world: An introduction to phenomenological psychology.* London: Sage Publications.

Van der Leeuw, G. (1986). *Religion in essence and manifestation* (J.E. Turner, Trans.). Princeton, NJ: Princeton University Press.

Pilgrimage

David A. Leeming

Pilgrimages in various cultures are remarkably similar in essential form. The pilgrimage, whether to Lourdes, Jerusalem, Banaras, Ise, or Mecca, involves three essential steps, suggesting a rite of passage and a process of curative renewal. The first step involves a significant separation of the pilgrim from home and ordinary life and the journey to a sacred center. The separation can be signified by particular clothes, by rituals of departure or any consciously unusual behavior. It is usually characterized by a deep sense of religious community, a concept suggested by the etymology of the word religion, suggesting a binding back or gathering together under the influence of the numinous. The second and most important step is the interaction with the sacred, the given culture's spiritual energy source. Typically this aspect involves certain ritual acts, most notably circumambulation, a gathering up of energy in the creation of a living mandala of completeness, a ritual cleansing, or ablution in preparation for a new beginning and the recitation of certain sacred formulae, or mantras. The third step is the return home. The return is always marked by a sense of renewal. The pilgrim has been re-created by the encounter with the numinous center of the collective being.

It is important to differentiate the pilgrimage from its close relative, the quest. Both the questor and the pilgrim go on journeys that can be difficult, even treacherous, and both have some goal in mind, but the questor is in search of the goal while the pilgrim knows exactly where it is and how to get there. The questor never knows what might happen on the journey, whereas the pilgrim's "progress" is essentially a ritual process. One might say that the labyrinth is the pilgrim's signifying model while the maze is the questor's.

Important examples of pilgrimage exist in most religious systems. The Hindu might visit Banaras (Kashi) and bathe ritually in community with thousands of fellow pilgrims in the sacred living waters of the Ganges. There he will recite certain mantras and circumambulate important shrines. If particularly devout, the pilgrim might make a point of literally circumambulating sacred India herself, creating a gigantic mandala of completeness by visiting the seven sacred cities. The Buddhist can visit the footprint of the Buddha on Adam's Mount in Sri Lanka. For the Christian or Jew the footprint is said to be Adam's, for the Hindu it is Siva's. Again, circumambulation and mantras are important, and sometimes ablutions. In keeping with ancient traditions of prescribed visits to the Temple in Jerusalem, the Jew in our time will visit the Wailing Wall of the old Temple. The Christian will circumambulate the sacred places in Jerusalem associated with the passion of Jesus or visit curing shrines such as Lourdes, or, like Chaucer's famous pilgrims, travel to the shrines of martyrs. People of animistic traditions tend to see the whole world as a sacred place, so that anywhere one is can be a pilgrimage site, and buildings, such as Navajo hogans and Pueblo kivas are themselves metaphors for constant pilgrimage to the center.

Perhaps the most elaborate pilgrimage is the Hajj, one of the five essential "Pillars" of Islam. For this pilgrimage, taken by the community of Muslims, there are special requirements for the home-leaving and the journey, very specific rules of behavior while at Mecca, and clear rituals that involve ablutions various sub-pilgrimages to outlying areas, and a sacred mantra of humility and obedience recited during a circumambulation of the Kab'ah, the structure in the great mosque of Mecca

P

that is the center of the Muslim world. As in the case of all great pilgrimages, the Hajj-pilgrim, or Hajji, returns home re-newed and re-created by his experience. It should be noted that back home, the Muslim makes the pilgrimage symbolically and spiritually every time he faces Mecca and prays.

Liturgies are, in fact, often symbolic pilgrimages. The Eucharist of the Catholic tradition, for example, is an elaborate symbolic communal pilgrimage to the sacred center, reinforced even by the architecture of the various types of church building. Holy Water at the door (in ancient times the baptismal font was there as well), the ablutions of the priest, processions, the circumambulating of the altar, or sacred center, during its censing, and the complex system of mantras all suggest the pilgrimage.

Having once more noted the aspect of community or communitas in pilgrimage, it must be noted that this element is associated more with external as opposed to internal pilgrimage. External pilgrimage has been called "exteriorized mysticism." To the extent that such a characterization is valid, interior pilgrimage might be equated with mysticism itself. Thus, the pilgrim who travels to Mecca or Banaras is acting out the interior journey taken by the Yogi or the contemplative nun to the sacred center. The process for the mystic, which involves communitas only in the sense that nuns or monks, for instance, are a community of contemplative prayer, nevertheless resembles that of the external pilgrim in its basic plot. The interior pilgrim establishes a separation from ordinary life by accepting some prescribed discipline, involving such matters as clothing, breathing, posture, or particular objects of meditation.

The Pilgrim then proceeds to the sacred center found within. John of the Cross enters upon the Dark Night of the Soul, the purifying process by which God prepares the mystic for Union. The Hindu ascetic – the yogi – never moving from one place, can visit the seven sacred cities. The Mevlevi (Mawlawiya) Sufis, or Whirling Dervishes are perhaps unique in that each dancer, turns on his own axis, entering a trance-like ecstatic state even as he circles the sacred center in an intricate expression of perfect community with his fellow interior pilgrims. Upon his return, the interior pilgrim, whether the Yogi, the Mevlevi or the Christian mystic, like the external pilgrim, is a person who has been renewed by the numinous power of the center.

The idea of the pilgrimage as spiritual therapy, then, is universal, and humans of all sorts – mystical and otherwise – have traditionally turned to pilgrimage as a source of curing. People go to Lourdes and other holy places to be cured of physical disease, of course, but the 'more typical pilgrim is the one who is experiencing a malaise of the soul or the psyche. A person who is in this sense "lost" takes a journey to his/her culture's spiritual center, participates in the prescribed activities, and returns home in a centered state. A similar goal is achieved through participation in religious ritual. It is not surprising that Jung and other modern psychotherapists have suggested religious activity for persons whose backgrounds provide an opening to the numinous through such activity.

An attempt to interpret the pilgrimage psychologically can begin with the assumption that human beings are naturally attracted to the phenomenon by reason of their consciousness of what Aristotle called "plot." A defining characteristic of our species is our universal and perhaps even obsessive concern with questions of beginnings, middles, and ends. We see life as a journey, and to the extent that we are goal-oriented, we see it sometimes as a quest, but often as a pilgrimage. For the human species, pilgrimage may be said to be an archetypal pattern, a representation of an essential collective psychological tendency. We understand that if we are in any sense broken – collectively or individually – we would do well to take the difficult journey to the center and work towards a state of renewal or re-creation. As in the case of all pilgrimages, to reach this center we are greatly helped by an experience of the numinous, whether induced through sectarian religious activities, meditation, love, music, or various kinds of mantra. When we speak of the individual journey, our pilgrimage analogy is that of the interior pilgrimage, which, in psychological terms, becomes a journey to the Self. The Self is the totality of personality from which we can receive the ablutive power that renews and leads towards Individuation, that is, Self-realization. In short, the psychological pilgrimage, if accomplished, takes the individual to a curing circumambulation of or assimilation of the sacred center of one's very Being.

See also: ❱ Christianity ❱ Circumambulation ❱ Communitas ❱ Hajj ❱ Islam ❱ Ka'bah ❱ Mandala ❱ Ritual ❱ Self

Bibliography

Kamal, A. (2000). *The sacred journey: The pilgrimage to Mecca.* Bloomington, IN: i-Universe.

Turner, V. (1975). Pilgrimage as a social process. In *Dramas, fields, and metaphors* (pp. 167–230). Ithaca, NY: Cornell University Press.

Plato and Religion

Rod Blackhirst

Plato (428/427BC – 348/347BC) was a Greek philosopher, a citizen of Athens and follower of Socrates. He founded the Academy, a school for statecraft, circa 387BC, his most famous student being Aristotle. His work – in the form of dialogues – has had an immeasurable influence upon Western civilization. The modern philosopher, Whitehead, once famously quipped that "the whole of Western philosophy is nothing but a series of footnotes on Plato." The same might be said of other fields of learning where Plato's thought has been seminal. He has made a profound contribution to both the arts and sciences, including psychology. Many aspects of his thinking foreshadows modern theories. In psychology, for example, his teachings regarding *eros* as a foundation for human motivation clearly foreshadow the theories of Freud or, as some prefer, Freud's theories are a decadent version of Plato's earlier theory. In religious thought, Plato has long been acknowledged as prefiguring aspects of the Christian faith, even to the extent that some Churches have canonized him as a pre-Christian saint. More generally, he has influenced important streams of mystical thought and spiritual psychology in Judaism, Christianity and the Sufi schools of Islam.

It should be noted that while we commonly attribute theories and ideas to Plato himself, these are usually taken from the words of Socrates as presented in Plato's philosophical dramas and that, in a famous passage in a letter to a friend called Dion, Plato states that his own ideas are nowhere to be found in his dialogues. This is the so-called "Socratic problem" – to what extent does Plato's Socrates speak Plato's mind? All the same, the teachings and arguments of Plato's Socrates are, for convenience, referred to as "Platonic" and it is common to refer to the "Platonic tradition" of thought that has its roots in Plato's dialogues. This tradition extends across the last 2000+ years of occidental culture and has penetrated most fields of learning. Nearly all of the dialogues might be construed as contributing to Platonic psychology but the main contributions are found in the dialogues called *Republic, Phaedo, Phaedrus, Symposium* and to some extent *Timaeus*.

Plato (i.e., Plato's Socrates) argues that there is a mental, supra-physical realm of "Forms" or "Ideas" or "archetypes" that is beyond the restraints and limitations of time and space and that the spateo-temporal realm is related to this archetypal realm as a copy is related to a model. Plato's psychology, like his political philosophy and everything else, needs to be understood in the context of the metaphysical framework of this pervasive "Theory of Forms." For Plato, for example, human beings – as creatures of time and space – yearn for eternity and for the pure reality of the Forms. This is the basis of all human motivation. It is why the hero does brave deeds – he seeks the immortality of fame. And it is at the root of the sexual drive – lovers seek a surrogate immortality through procreation. By extension, the religious impulse is an expression of the same urge but on a higher plane.

An important corollary of the Theory of Forms is the Theory of Recollection. This states that human beings possess a faculty (*nous*) that comprehends the traces of the Forms in their physical copies. When we see beauty in a rose, for example, it is because the rose *reminds* us of the Form of Beauty, i.e., Beauty Itself. The Forms are structural and innate. Plato is at pains to insist that our senses are unreliable and that the mind, not the senses, is the agent of cognition. When we see a circle our eyes merely register an unintelligible set of data; it is our mind (or the faculty of *nous*) that matches this data to its innate knowledge of the Form of Circle, thus making the sensory impression intelligible. That is, Plato proposes that we are born with a stock of (supra-physical) mental templates and that these are the basis of all cognition.

Exploring this theory throughout his dialogues, Plato next proposes that there must be a hierarchy of such Forms and that at the pinnacle of this hierarchy there must be a Form of the Forms, namely what he styles "The Form of the Good." The theory seems to be an adaptation of aspects of ancient Greek religious thought where natural phenomena were understood as expressions of various simple allegorical deities such as Love, Night, Chaos etc. For example, Plato's Forms of Sameness and Difference (two of the most basic Forms) seem to be extrapolations from the deities Love and Strife, a principle of union or similarity and a principle of dissolution or differentiation. In a similar way, Plato's creator-god, the "Demiurge," appears to be a philosophical rendering of the Olympian craftsman god, Hephaestus. Whereas Greek religious thought personified such principles, Plato's Forms are non-personal archetypes. His "Form of the Good" is very like the Judeo-Christian/Islamic notion of God but, importantly, has no personhood. In modern terms we would say it is an "abstraction" but for Plato this is exactly wrong since the world is "abstracted" from the Forms not the other way around.

There are several descriptions of the human psyche given in the dialogues, most notably in the form of allegories. In the *Phaedrus* (246a–254e) Plato compares the human soul (*psyche*) to a chariot with a charioteer driving two horses, one white and one black. The white horse is well-trained while the black horse is ill-bred and unruly. The charioteer represents the intellect or reason (*nous*) that must reconcile conflicting impulses as it steers the vehicle (body) through life's journey. In the *Republic* (514a–520a) Plato offers a parable of the human condition in which prisoners have been held in a cave since childhood and compelled to watch a puppet-play of shadows on the cave wall. Not knowing any better, they mistake this for reality. It is only with great effort that they might escape from their bonds and eventually discover the source of these shadows and, beyond the cave, the light of day. This is an epistemological parable but also a model of human psychology with the shadows on the wall representing the conscious realm, that small portion of the mind we regularly assume to be reality with the rest of the cave representing other hidden levels of consciousness.

This line of thinking is often criticized for being counter-intuitive, dualistic and life-hating. The world is a mere copy of the "true" world which is beyond death. The body of flesh, with the vicissitudes of pleasure and pain, is a prison in which the mind is trapped. In the *Phaedo* Socrates seems to regard life as a disease and as a punishment with death as a cure and a release. Platonic psychology, therefore, is deemed anti-naturalistic. To a great extent the entire modern scientific enterprise can be seen as a process of shedding the influence of Plato in that it situates man in a natural context and attempts to understand human beings as a product of natural rather than supernatural forces. For Plato, the natural world is derivative and therefore fundamentally unreal – he presents the study of natural science (*phusis*) as an inherently unworthy enterprise that offers a "likely tale" at best.

There are readers of Plato, however, who argue that on closer examination this dualism is only a first step in the Platonic enterprise and that, ultimately, Plato is fully aware of the shortcomings of the Theory of Forms. In the dialogue called Parmenides, in particular, Plato seems to demolish the theory and looks beyond the duality of copy and model. Others point out that Plato is not a pessimistic philosopher with a bleak view of the human condition. One of the most notable correlatives of the Theory of Forms and its culmination in the Form of the Good is the Socratic dictum that ignorance is the root of evil. According to this theory, no one does evil willingly; rather, the evil-doer has made a miscalculation and mistakenly supposes that his evil deeds will bring himself or others some good. This is a profoundly optimistic view of the human state since it proposes that people can be taught to be good, that education is the key to human advancement and that evil-doers can be shown their miscalculations and that they will then correct their ways since they, like everyone else, are in pursuit of the transcendent Good (whether they are aware of it or not). For Plato, the highest human achievement is the "Vision of the Good", the pneumatic apprehension of the Good Itself, equivalent to the mystical vision of God in religious systems.

Regarding popular religion the indications throughout the dialogues are conflicting. Socrates is presented as being dutifully obedient to the established religious cults and yet elsewhere is so opposed to anthropomorphism that he would ban Homer and other poets from his ideal society. In an infamous provision of the dialogue called Laws, atheism is made a crime punishable by execution. In Plato's account of the trial of Socrates, Socrates is accused of introducing false gods and, by implication, impiety regarding the established religious order.

The influence and reputation of Plato has declined especially since World War II and the publication of such works as *The open society & its enemies* by Karl Popper (1945) which paint him, with some exaggeration, as the father of both right and left-wing totalitarian ideologies. The main exception to this waning influence has been a revival and reinterpretation (some would say perversion) of Plato's political philosophy through the teachings of Leo Strauss, regarded as one of the intellectual founders of contemporary neoconservatism in the United States. Strauss' studies concentrate on the so-called 'Noble Lie' passage in the *Republic* where Plato justifies rulers creating myths to pacify the ruled. For Strauss, an atheist, this is the role of religion. Most people, he argues, are not psychologically or emotionally equipped to be atheists and to face the bitter meaningless of existence; it is better if the rulers of society maintain religion as a "Noble Lie" to help preserve psychological stability in individuals and cohesion in society as a whole. This is surely a far cry from Plato's intention but it illustrates the ways in which, for good or for bad, Plato's works continue to stimulate contemporary ideas.

See also: ❂ Christianity ❂ Freud, Sigmund ❂ Plato on the Soul ❂ Psyche ❂ Sufis and Sufism

Bibliography

Allen, R. E. (2006). *Studies in Plato's metaphysics II*. Las Vegas, NV: Parmenides Publishing.

Gregory, V. (Ed.) (1971). *The philosophy of Socrates*. New York: Anchor.

Hamilton, E., & Cairns, H. (1961). *The collected dialogues of Plato*. Princeton, NJ: Princeton University Press.

Jackson, R. (2001). *Plato: A beginner's guide*. London: Hodder & Stroughton.

Mohr, R. D. (2006). *God and forms in Plato – and other essays in Plato's metaphysics*. Las Vegas, NV: Parmenides Publishing.

Nails, D. (2006). *The life of Plato of Athens*. In H. H. Benson (Ed.), *A companion to Plato*. Hoboken, NJ: Blackwell Publishing.

Strauss, L. (1964). *The city and man*, Chicago, IL: Rand McNally.

Taylor, A. E. (2001). *Plato: The man and his work*. Chelmsford, MA: Courier Dover Publications.

Plato on the Soul

John Pahucki

The ancient Greek philosopher Plato (424–348 BC) wrote copiously on the question of the human soul. The soul is given substantial treatment in many of his dialogs – the *Phaedo, Republic, Symposium, Phaedrus,* and *Timaeus* primarily, though the *Meno, Ion,* and *Philebus*, as well as other dialogs, are at least tangentially concerned with topics related to his view of the soul as well. Of these treatments, two particular items of interest to the student and historian of psychology are his "tripartite" theory of the soul and his epistemological theory of *anamnesis*, or learning by recollection.

Plato's tripartite theory is given most explicit expression in Book IV of the *Republic*. According to Plato's view, there are three elements which constitute the life of the soul. Of these the one that is unique to human beings, and thus privileged by Plato, is *reason*. Plato's accent on reason would be the impetus behind Aristotle's – and historically, the Western tradition's – characterization of man as *animal rationale*. The other aspects of the soul are the *spirited* element, which seems to correspond to the emotions, and the *appetites* of the body which we share in common with the beasts. Reason and the appetites are often in conflict, with the spirited element capable of lending its weight to either side in this internecine struggle of the soul. The individuals lauded by Plato are those in whom reason successfully reigns, though these would seem to always constitute a minority.

Plato's theory is a historical curiosity, as it seems to anticipate Freud's psychodynamic model of the mind and its intrapsychic conflicts among the id, ego, and superego. Indeed, Freud may have been aware of Plato's theory as he employed a metaphor similar to the one from Plato's *Phaedrus* where the philosopher compares the appetites to an obstinate horse who must be firmly guided by the charioteer of reason (a second horse, corresponding to the spirited element, does not resist the commands of its master).

Plato's epistemological theory of *anamnesis*, or learning by recollection, is based on what has come to be described as the *learning paradox*, first formulated by Plato in his dialog the *Meno*. There Socrates asks the question how learning is possible. If we are seeking after something we do not know, we will be unable to recognize it if and when we do encounter it. If we do recognize it, we must have had some previous knowledge of it in order for this recognition to occur in the first place. Either way, learning seems to be a paradoxical enterprise. This leads Plato to present his own theory of learning as recollection based on his belief in the reincarnation of the soul. In dialogs like the *Symposium* and *Phaedrus*, Plato will argue that learning/knowledge is possible based on our pre-earthly existence in the realm of divine forms. These forms are the templates of all sensible objects, undergirding the sensible realm and giving the world its rational structure. When the soul incarnates in matter, it temporarily "forgets" its previous experience of the forms. Learning occurs when certain earthly experiences "trigger" these memories. Anamnesis is thus a form of "cryptomnesia" as described by Jung. It should be stated that Plato's belief in the transmigration of the soul had strong precedent in the Pythagorean cult as well as other mystery cults extant at the time.

The linguistic and cognitive theorist Noam Chomsky has identified his own "innateness" theory of linguistic acquisition as based on a kind of Platonic learning paradox. According to Chomsky's theory, linguistic ability may be structurally fixed or "hardwired" into the mind; we may be able to postulate a "universal" a priori grammar based on what has been described as "the poverty of the stimulus." Put simply, we evidence a degree of intricacy and depth in our knowledge and utilization of language far in excess of what we could have formally learned.

See also: ❯ Freud, Sigmund ❯ Plato and Religion

Bibliography

Lavine, T. Z. (1984). *From Socrates to Sartre: The philosophic quest*. New York: Bantam.

Plato. (1961). *Plato: The collected dialogues* (E. Hamilton & H. Cairns, Eds.). Princeton, NJ: Bollingen Books.

Polytheism

Paul Larson

Polytheism is the worship of many forms of the divine. Etymologically it means many gods, but to say that is to delve into the nature of personhood. Pepper (1942) in his summary of epistemologies set out six world hypotheses, four of which he felt were minimally acceptable in rational discourse, and two unacceptable because of their reliance on faith. Each of the six world hypotheses (similar to the modern concept world view) is grounded in a root metaphor. The two unacceptable world views were animism and mysticism. The former was based on the root metaphor of the person. He was less clear on the distinction between animism and mysticism but seems to refer to the distinction between the natural religions and revealed religions. His identification of the concept of the person as being at the heart of a spiritual world view was correct. Indeed, to understand theism whether mono- or poly- requires understanding the nature of the person.

Pepper's psychologism was saying that because we experience the divine in us and we are people, we project out onto the world our own experience of personhood. We attribute all the experiences we have to the power(s) which are divine. Since we have consciousness, our gods must have consciousness, since we have choice and agency, our gods must have nothing less than that since they are transcendent to us and greater than us, much like a whole is greater than the sum of its part. Whatever is divine must be no less than what we are, and must be anywhere from somewhat to immensely greater than us.

There are several types of spiritual world views, so polytheism must be set into its context. Though it may not have been the first spiritual view to arise historically, the belief in some impersonal divine ground of being that is the source of life, and all that is, is possible. The clearest example of this type of belief comes from Chinese traditional religion and philosophy. Chi (Jap. Ki) is the impersonal force that animates all living being and is imbued within even inanimate matter as well. This life force is also found in the Indian concept of "prana," common to both Hindu and Buddhist philosophy. It is also found in Stoic philosophy as "pneuma." Both literally mean the breath of life.

To some with a completely secular scientific world view, the very laws of nature may be likened to an impersonal divine ground of being in an existential sense. This is basically the position of either pantheism or its close variant panentheism. Spinoza and Leibniz are two early modern philosophers who represent this stream of belief. This is also the position of the Deists; that group of Enlightenment thinkers who first articulated a basically secular philosophy while preserving that sense of reverence and awe to the existence of life itself.

What, of course, makes the respect for the impersonal forces behind life and existence divine is the religious experience. Both James (1902/1958) and Otto (1917/1958) support the notion that the beginning of the life of the spirit is religious experience; not belief, not acts, but the experience of awe in the face of the great *mysterium tremendum*. Belief in the near universality of religious or spiritual experience makes us all mystics at the core; some may tenderly stick their toes in these deep waters while others jump in with both feet in ecstatic joy.

The next question is whether we ascribe personhood to the divine force and whether belief in an inanimate divine force or power is incompatible with personhood. On the basis of the principle that the lesser is included in the greater, the burden of proof rests with those who would exclude an impersonal force as not present with the divine person(s) to say why.

Assuming that the divine can take on the qualities of a person, the next question is one or many. This is related to the philosophical debate as to whether the "physis." or stuff of the universe is one or many, perhaps no more resolvable now than to the Pre-Socratics who took up the question in the first millennium BCE. It is also related to the related debate between Parmenides and Heraclitus as to whether stasis or change in more fundamental. Belief in stasis tends to favor ontological monism, which would include monotheism. Belief in change tends to favor polytheism by providing the means by which the divine may be ever-present, though the actors may shift among the many masks of God (Campbell, 1955, 1962, 1964, 1968).

The historical records supports a vigorous and ancient period where polytheism was the dominant spiritual world view. Part of the rhetorical appeal of monotheism is the rejection of the confusion multiplicity of divine coupled with a moral rejection of the all to close modeling of human foibles and flaws into the biographies of the gods. But across the widest reach of the planet and throughout all human times polytheism has continued despite competition from monotheism with its aggressive proselytizing.

One instructive development was the synthesis of Hindu polytheism to harmonize with an underlying spiritual monism. Behind Brahma, Shiva, Vishnu and all the other Hindu gods was Brahman. Although it was based in earlier statements in the Upanishads, it took

Adi Shankaracharya to provide a coherent integration of polytheistic outer forms with a single unifying singleness beyond all concept or duality, the ground of being. So even in the midst of polytheism one can see a sort of monotheism as consistent. It should be noted that Brahman, like prana, chi/ki and pneuma is impersonal in nature, beyond all human concepts. In Buddhism the Vajrayana as well as Mahayana schools accept an impersonal unity beyond the obvious multiplicity of the world. The Vajrayana Buddhism of Tibet in particular has a whole catalog of personal forms of the deity and an equal number of demi-gods, dharma protectors, dakhinis and so on. Yet with Nagarjuna's Madhyamakha philosophy the unity of non-duality and emptiness provides a fertile ground upon which phenomenal existence can play out our many incarnations in the samsaric wheel of life. In the Western Esoteric Tradition (WET), or occultism as it is often known, the first model of this same sort of co-existence of impersonal monism as an originating point for a phenomenal polytheism is the Neo-Platonic hierarchy of emanations found in Gnosticism in its many forms.

The next question is whether there are any true polytheisms, given that the most sophisticated forms of philosophy and theology among historically and culturally poltheistic religions? The answer is yes, at least in the sense that in polytheistic systems there is at least a modeling of the male/female dimorphism of human persons. If we allow that the divine can be said to be a person, then why would we use just one gender? Many contemporary positions within the Western monotheisms that are response to the feminist critique of patriarchy allow that what may have been historically gender biased language can be best understood as inclusive of both genders or beyond both genders, whether we continue to use the male oriented language or modify our liturgies and prayers. The whole leverage about Brown's *DaVinci Code* sought to raise the magnitude of awareness about the divine feminine. Polytheism provides the minimal coverage of both genders, and in nearly all historical settings had several families of deities modeling the diversity of the human family, complete with extensive genealogies.

One curious case is Mormonism, the major type of restorationist theology in Christianity, and associated with the Church of Jesus Christ of Latter Day Saints (LDS). They are explicitly and clearly monotheistic in the aim of their worship, but their theology implies a Heavenly Mother as well a Heavenly Father. Implicit is an unknown possibility for an endless series of gods of both genders stretching back in ageless time and moving forward as individual humans deceased, now existent,

or yet to come achieve salvation at the highest level, in the celestial kingdom. Mormonism expresses a radical doctrine of spiritual evolution arising out of its American historical roots and a philosophy of progress (McMurrin 1959, 1965).

Contemporary Paganism or earth-centered religions are all clearly poltheistic in their worship and spiritual focus. The primacy of the Divine Earth Mother and her Consort (the Horned God, under various names) in Wicca and similar movements affirms a multiplicity of divine personifications. There are many reconstructionist groups come with many names; those in the Norse or Germanic traditions prefer being called heathens. The varieties of traditions in occultism (cf.) as it is often called, likewise are polytheistic.

In summary then, the veneration, worship and mythological narratives of multiple gods and goddesses is alive and flourishing through contemporary animistic aboriginal or native religions, through highly evolved religious traditions such as Hinduism and many forms of Buddhism where multiple deities are yet subsumed into a non-personal divine ground of being beyond human labels or names. It has also been reconstructed as part of a revival of earth based religious movements founded in Western Europe and America from the nineteenth century onward. Even an explicit monotheism such as Mormonism contains some elements of polytheistic theology. So polytheism is alive and well. It was never completely supplanted by monotheism, though the two forms of theism are shaking hands in some instances.

See also: ⊗ Animism ⊗ Buddhism ⊗ Gnosticism ⊗ James, William ⊗ Mormonism ⊗ Occultism ⊗ Paganism ⊗ Pantheism ⊗ Wicca

Bibliography

Campbell, J. (1955). *The masks of God: Primitive religions*. New York: Viking.

Campbell, J. (1962). *The masks of God: Oriental mythology*. New York: Viking.

Campbell, J. (1964). *The masks of God: Occidental mythology*. New York: Viking.

Campbell, J. (1968). *The masks of God: Creative mythology*. New York: Viking.

James, W. (1958). *The varieties of religious experience*. New York: Mentor Book. (Original work published 1902).

McMurrin, S. M. (1959). *The philosophical foundations of Mormon theology*. Salt Lake City, UT: University of Utah Press.

McMurrin, S. M. (1965). *The theological foundation of the Mormon religion*. Salt Lake City, UT: University of Utah Press.

Otto, R. (1958). *The idea of the holy*. New York: Oxford University Press. (Original work published 1917).

Possession

Craig Stephenson

In common usage, "to possess" means "to hold as property," "to own," "to occupy." The English word derives from the French *posséder* and originally from the Latin *possidere*, from *potis* meaning "able" and *sedere*, "to sit." The metaphoric image which resides behind the concept of possession is perhaps, then, of a being successfully claiming space, perhaps "sitting" in a position of power. Hence, the suffering and distress associated with "possession" we attribute to foreign entities or partial aspects of the personality occupying the seat of selfhood by virtue of a tyrannical overthrow. For example, in the Christian tradition, according to the Synoptic Gospels of Mark, Matthew and Luke, Jesus cures people suffering from various mental and physical ailments caused by occupying demons (daimonia) which he drives out of them (see Demons); in the Gospel of John, while Satan as "adversary" confronts and tempts Jesus, he enters Judas (John 13:27). Inherent in the Christian understanding of evil, then, is the notion of an "obstruction" (*skandalon*, Matthew 16:23) that "holds," "claims" or "occupies" the embodied self (Kelly, 2006).

The subsequent language of possession in the history of European religion has been far more fluid than one might imagine, and the set texts identifying orthodox criteria for establishing legitimate cases of possession were very much of a specific time and place. For example, in Christianized Europe's early Middle Ages, the possessing devil's field of action is defined as the imagination, not the body or corporeal reality. As portrayed in the writings of Tertullian, Augustine, and John Cassion between the third and fifth centuries, the devil is most importantly a deceiver who employs *fantasmata* in order to take possession of the soul, and it is particularly in dreams that we fall prey to the devil. True dreams come from God; the devil fills dreams with false and tempting images. However, in 1233 the pontifical constitution *Vox in Rama* described the ritual homage to Satan as a feudal *osculum* in reverse (that is to say, by kissing the devil's buttocks), and what the Church once considered nocturnal dream voyages were now redefined as sectarian meetings marked by physical (not imaginary) acts of incest, sodomy, infanticide and cannibalism. By 1484, according to the Papal Bull *Summis desiderantes affectibus* promulgated by Innocent VIII, witches and sorcerers abjured their faith by inviting the devil to enter their bodies. Since the body became increasingly the subject of diabolical attack in the higher Middle Ages, terms such as "possession" and "obsession," which had been used almost synonymously to describe the intermittancy of manic attacks, come to be more highly differentiated. Etymologically, *obsidere* denotes "to sit at or opposite to," "to sit down before," "to beseige" as when an enemy force sits down before a fortress. Hence, an obsessive spirit is perceived as assailing, haunting, harrassing a person from outside, while a possessing spirit is considered to have taken up residence inside the human body. Such distinctions are not so very far away from current Western psychopathological diagnostic criteria which differentiate, for example, between paranoid feelings of being persecuted from without and delusional notions of being preoccupied by thoughts which are not one's own but which one believes have been inserted into one's mind. While psychiatry coopted the word "obsession" and stripped it of its religious connotation, the word "possession" has remained outside psychiatric discourse (until its recent tentative entry into the appendix of the DSM IV as a dissociative disorder currently under review).

The most important source for contemporary literature on possession is anthropological. As a social anthropologist, I. M. Lewis (1971) argues in an objectivist manner that possession and shamanism are two components of ecstatic religion which can best be interpreted from within a structural functionalist framework of delineating power and social status. From within this perspective, possession functions as an obliquely aggressive strategy with which disempowered or marginalized individuals, especially women, seek to redress their political subordination within oppressive, predominantly patriarchal cultures. Lewis defines the suffering caused by possession as linked to status deprivation and portrays possession cults as socially-motivated manoeuvres which heal, at least in part, by enhancing the social status of sufferers, recasting them in fantasy or belief as humans "seized by divinity."

Paul Stoller (1989) emphasizes the particularity of Songhay possession in Tillaberi, Niger, as a fusion of human and spirit. Possession as "fusion" signifies a white-heat meshing of elements foreign to each other, an active seizing, a loss of identity for each of the elements, a loss of soul, an interpenetration. Stoller describes how the Songhay sorcerers perform rituals of separation or cleansing to alleviate suffering caused by fused states, for example, leading their mediums to a crossroad where they fling millet seeds (which correspond in number to the possessing spirits) onto an anthill and flee from their state of fusion and oneness to the enclosed compound, to a separated state of twoness. Stoller investigates possession through its theatricality, the possession troupe functioning like a repertory company, the *zima* as stage director and dramaturge, the mediums as actors. The ceremonies are theatrical events in which possession troupes offer healing through compensatory existential reenactments of an ancestral world, replete with historical, sociological and cultural themes, in which mediums learn to fuse with and later separate from a collective *imaginaire*.

Janice Boddy (1989) delineates in terms of cultural symbolism and morality several levels at which *zar* possession in the northern Sudanese village of Hofriyat performs a therapeutic function. For instance, when *zar* spirits usurp and block a woman's fertility, the husband must enter into an exchange relationship with her spirits and thereby implicitly renegotiates his relationship with his wife, both human beings being equally powerless before a transcendent third, the *zar*. Boddy argues that Lewis's social functionalist analysis of *zar* possession is inadequate because it glosses over the issue of belief. *Zar* practitioners, though not with conscious intent, take the potentially destructive ambiguities in a marriage and open them up to a symbolic performance and subsequently to interpretations which might lead the marriage in a positive direction. The performance does not necessarily resolve the conflict or its ambiguities, despite the adoption of a spirit idiom. Part of its therapeutic potential resides in the fact that the ceremony articulates a possible world and a possible way of orienting oneself within it. If the husband chooses to receive this other language elucidated by the adepts, the marriage relationship may be enriched by new meanings and by new ways of communicating.

According to Boddy, the *zar* possession cult is a resource used only by specific individuals within the culture. A spirit must make sense to those whom it encounters; the sense it makes is a product of human and spirit collaboration. Consequently, possession by a *zar* requires control on the part of the possessed. The hosts must have the ability to enter trance, at the same time remaining alert to their surroundings. Even when the spirits descend, the hosts are expected to be sensitive to cues from other spirits and the audience of human observers. Seriously disturbed people would focus on their own intentions and neglect those of the spirits, and would be classed as misdiagnosed, seen as engaging in idiosyncratic fantasy which the *zar* patently are not; or accused of playing with the spirits and provoking their wrath. Individuals who can successfully enact such dramas become increasingly familiar with the "roles" they may – as spirits – be required to play. Paradoxically, then, the possessed are able to bracket their own substantial concerns and suffering in deference to those of the *zar*.

Central to the experience of possession is the diagnostic act, that is to say, testing the spirits, to see whether they are of God (1 John 4:1). Boddy emphasizes that the Hofriyati differentiate between *zar* spirits (whom the culture believes can be integrated through ceremonial marriage) and others (such as black *jinn* which must be exorcized if possible), and that the diagnostic act of giving the spirit its right and proper name, of differentiating between *zar* spirits and black *jinn*, already contributes a positive effect to a suffering individual. Subsequent marriage with correctly identified spirits in a rite of passage suggests that the status of the sufferers changes paradoxically for good, that thereafter the spirits will not simply possess them; rather, they will allow themselves to be invoked, and the interplay will be potentially productive.

In analytical psychology, Jung describes a similar apotropaic effect of diagnosis, a partial alleviation of suffering when a repressed complex is identified and thereby acknowledged by ego consciousness (see Complex): "The true symbol, the true expression of the psychological fact, has that peculiar effect on the unconscious factor, that is somehow brought about by giving it the right name" (Jung, 1984: 581). And describing the psychological life-process of differentiating and, as much as possible, integrating otherwise dangerous and difficult unconscious complexes/spirits into consciousness (a process he called "individuation"), Jung argues that the goal is best symbolized by the alchemical image of a "marriage of opposites." By the time he writes *Aion* in 1951, Jung has revised that notion, taking it from a universalist symbol of marriage as representing ordered wholeness, to cross-cultural images of an intricate and neverending interplay of opposites, of an Otherness inherent in experiences of selfhood.

Writing about cannibalism, Claude Lévi-Strauss argues:

> It would be tempting to distinguish two contrasting types [of societies]: those which practice cannibalism – that is, which regard the absorption of certain individuals possessing dangerous powers as the only means of neutralizing those powers and even of turning them to advantage – and those which, like our own society, adopt what might be called the practice of anthropemy (from the Greek *émein*, to vomit); faced with the same problem, the latter type of society has chosen the opposite solution, which consists in ejecting dangerous individuals from the social body and keeping them temporarily or permanently in isolation, away from all contact with their fellows, in establishments specially intended for this purpose (Lévi-Strauss, 1955: 388).

Michel de Certeau (1970) applies Lévi-Strauss's structuralist distinction between ingurgitating and vomiting to the most famous case of possession in the Western history of religion, the possession of the Ursuline nuns at Loudun, France in 1631. Certeau suggests that there exist two opposing responses to the suffering caused by spirit possession: to vomit out and exorcize the spirit, or to absorb, literally incorporate and integrate the spirit as Other, in an attempt to neutralize and even turn to one's advantage its dangerous power. Most of the iconography of the Christianized West confirms the extent to which its societies have one-sidedly identified with anthropemy, although there exists with the canonical literature the possibility of divine as well as demonic possession. In this regard, Lacan (1966) as the great reader and interpreter of Freud, rescues psychoanalysis from the positivist medical interpretation that rendered Freud exclusively "anthropemic" in his approach to the unconscious; that is to say, Lacan corrects the inclination to read Freud as characterizing all psychological symptoms as foreign elements which ought to be expelled.

The goal of contemporary psychotherapy is for the patient to be "self-possessed": at its most banal, this suggests the ability to habitually exercise control of one's self, as when, for example, one is said to possess oneself in patience; at its most profound, it evokes the image of selfhood as "able to sit" squarely in its own seat. In this context, it may be important to note that the English verb "exorcize" comes from Greek *exorkizein* meaning "an oath," and is translated into Latin as *adjuro* or *conjuro*. Etymologically, then, the verb *exorkizo*, "to exorcise," originates in attaching the prefix *ex* meaning "out" to the root *[h]orkos* "the daemon of oaths." The Greek divinity Horkos is the daemon-son of Eris, goddess of Discord or Strife, who punishes those who do not honor oaths they have sworn. But his name also denotes "fence" or "bulwark," suggesting that taking an oath functions as a protective enclosure. The etymological image behind exorcising is of casting "out" a "daemon" but also of "invoking and putting on oath." That is to say, hidden behind the onesided anthropemy of the Christianized West may reside also the image of an exorcist solemnly (by naming God) invoking a devil ironically in an attempt to thereby establish a truth.

See also: ❂ Complex ❂ Devil ❂ Dreams

Bibliography

Boddy, J. (1989). *Wombs and alien spirits: Women, men and the Zar Cult in Northern Sudan*. Madison, WI: University of Wisconsin Press.

De Certeau, M. (1970). *La Possession de Loudun*. Paris: Julliard. [M. B. Smith, (Trans.). (2000). *The Possession at Loudun*. Chicago, IL: University of Chicago Press.].

The Jerusalem Bible, Reader's Edition. (1968). Garden City, New York: Doubleday and Company.

Jung, C. G. (1951). *Aion: Researchers into the phenomenology of the self*. Princeton, NJ: Princeton University Press.

Jung, C. G. (1984). *Dream analysis: Notes of the seminar given in 1928–1930*. Princeton, NJ: Princeton University Press.

Kelly, H. A. (2006). *Satan: A biography*. Cambridge, England: Cambridge University Press.

Lacan, J. (1966/1989). *Écrits*. Paris: Éditions du Seuil. A. Sheridan (Trans.) (1977). *Écrits: A Selection*, London: Tavistock Books/Routledge].

Lévi-Strauss, C. (1955). *Tristes Tropiques*. Paris: Plon. [J. and D. Weightman, (Trans.). (1973). London: Jonathan Cape].

Lewis, I. M. (1971/1989). *Ecstatic religion: A study of shamanism and spirit possession*. London: Routledge.

Stoller, P. (1989). *Fusion of the Worlds: An ethnography of possession among the Songhay of Niger*. Chicago, IL: University of Chicago Press.

Possession, Exorcism, and Psychotherapy

Stephen A. Diamond

What is Exorcism?

Exorcism – the ritualistic expulsion of malevolent spirits inhabiting body, brain or place – has been practiced in some form throughout human history, and is probably the primeval prototype for psychotherapy. Exorcism is a traditional treatment for possession by evil spirits or demons, and was a method employed for millennia by prehistoric shamans, witch doctors, priests and medicine men prior to and during ancient Greek and Egyptian cultures. Hippocrates, the father of western medicine, was purportedly trained as an exorcist.

Exorcism is deeply rooted in demonism and demonology, presuming that the "victim's" symptoms are caused by evil entities that have invaded and taken possession of body and soul. Jesus of Nazareth reputedly practiced exorcism in healing "demoniacs," as described in the New Testament: "They brought unto him all that were diseased, and them that were possessed with devils. . . And he healed many that were sick of divers diseases, and cast out many devils" (Mark 1:32, 34). The Roman Catholic, Anglican, Lutheran, and Protestant (especially Methodist, Charismatic, Evangelical and Pentecostal) Church still practice exorcism in extraordinary cases deemed – usually after at least some scientific scrutiny and in keeping with current Vatican policy – to be bona fide demonic possession. References to exorcism and possession can also be found in Judaism, Hinduism, and Islam, as well as Scientology.

Exorcism entails forcing the evil spirits out of the victim by religious ritual, prayer, supplication, admonition, threats, bargaining, enticement, confrontation, and other means. Typically, the victim's symptoms of possession worsen as an exorcism is initiated and the ceremonial symbols of the higher power (incantations, holy relics, crucifix, holy water, Bible, etc.) are introduced. Rage is notably and predictably the predominant response to exorcism, traditionally known as the "rage of the demon" resisting expulsion, and the possessed person is frequently physically restrained so as to prevent hurting themselves or others while in this enraged state. *Exorcistic catharsis* consists of the unbridled expression of the anger, or rather, the demon's rage expressing itself autonomously through the victim. However, unlike in psychodynamic psychotherapy, there is no conscious ownership of the anger required during this primitive process: the rage belongs instead to the demon, to whom it is attributed, not to the victim. Once the victim is cathartically purged (abreaction) of the demonic (see demonic), he or she returns to a normal, albeit still relatively unconscious, naïve, and tenuous state of psychological equilibrium – the demon or devil having evidently been driven out.

Demonic Possession

The idea of demonic possession is a theological or spiritual explanation for human evil, suffering and aberrant behavior. Possession has been a well-documented phenomenon occurring across cultures in virtually every era. But the term *possession* is seldom mentioned in the mainstream psychiatric and psychological literature. Instead, psychiatry and psychology speak of *obsession*, which has similar intrusive, involuntary, ego-dystonic qualities. Mild cases of demonic possession were referred to by the Catholic Church as obsession as far back as the fifteenth-century, and psychotherapists still use that diagnostic term today. Or we refer to "multiple personality disorder" (dissociative identity disorder) in which one or more so-called subpersonalities temporarily take total possession of the person against his or her will. Or we diagnose *bipolar disorder* in those possessed by mania, irritability or melancholy; and intermittent explosive disorder to describe someone possessed or overtaken by uncontrollable rage. Indeed, the subjective experience of possession – being influenced by some foreign, alien force beyond the ego's ken or control – can be considered more or less a phenomenological aspect of most psychiatric disorders. Today, this "possession syndrome" (Diamond, 1996) is seen by psychiatrists and psychologists as a mental disorder more often than not caused by some underlying neurological or biochemical aberration. Biochemistry, in the form of the tiny neurotransmitter, has become our demon du jour to which all manner of psychopathological evils are attributed. But despite its obscurity in the psychiatric and psychotherapeutic texts, it must be admitted that the enigmatic experience known for millennia as "demonic possession" persists today in differing forms and varying degrees. The only difference is the way in which we now attempt to explain and treat it.

Exorcism Versus Psychotherapy

At least since Freud's day, it has become commonplace to refer metaphorically or poetically to struggling with one's vexing psychological problems as wrestling with "demons." Carl Jung (1921, 1971) theorized that, from a psychological perspective, "demons are nothing other than intruders from the unconscious, spontaneous irruptions of unconscious complexes. . . " (cited in Diamond, 1996: 64–65). Psychotherapy, a structured process of psychological treatment originating in the pioneering work of Freud and Jung, has been practiced now for little more than a century, and has deep roots in and remarkable similarities to exorcism. According to psychiatric historian Henri Ellenberger (1970), "Exorcism is the exact counterpart of possession and a well-structured type of psychotherapy." He explains that the exorcist typically addresses the possessed and the demons in the name of a higher power, as for example, when the priest invokes the power of Jesus Christ in the Christian ritual of exorcism. Complete conviction in both the demonic and spiritual power, and confidence in his or her own skills are essential for the exorcist's success. Psychological and spiritual support for the victim is provided, while at the same time, the possessing evil spirits are verbally attacked, challenged, and provoked to speak directly to the exorcist. In some cases, contentious negotiations are engaged in between the demonic powers and exorcist, in an effort to have them release their disturbing grip on the victim. This demanding, dangerous, arduous process can last for days, months or years, and is not always successful.

Much the same can be said about the psychotherapist. Despite the ostensibly secular, scientific persona of most practitioners, scratching the surface of rationality and objectivity reveals a latent exorcist. Psychotherapists also speak in the name of a "higher power," be it science, psychology or some metaphysical belief system. They too firmly believe in the reality of the pathological problem manifested in the patient's symptoms and suffering. And they dispense encouragement to troubled patients while joining with them in a sacred "therapeutic alliance" – the common healing denominator in all types of psychotherapy – against the wicked and destructive forces bedeviling them. Psychotherapy can, of necessity, consist of a prolonged, bitter, soul-wrenching, sometimes tedious battle royale with the patient's diabolically obdurate behaviors and emotional "demons," a war frequently waged over the course of years rather than months, and not always with a victorious result. And, as in exorcism, there is recognition by psychodynamic psychotherapists of the very real dangers and risks of "psychic infection" or counter-transference, which can cause the therapist to suffer similarly disturbing, subjective symptoms during the treatment process. Hence the ever-present importance for both the exorcist and psychotherapist to perform his or her sacred duties within a formally ritualized structure; to make full use of collegial support, cooperation, and consultation; and to maintain inviolable professional boundaries. To paraphrase Freud: No one wrestles with demons – not even the demons of others – and comes away unscathed. Psychological infestation (counter-transference) is an occupational hazard shared by both the exorcist and psychotherapist that can undermine or sabotage the process, and must therefore be consciously recognized and constructively resolved.

Italian psychiatrist Gaetano Benedetti (1960) compared exorcism to his own therapeutic work with schizophrenics. Benedetti points out the many parallels between the process of exorcism and psychotherapy, noting how both the exorcist and psychotherapist must tend first to themselves spiritually or psychologically prior to entering the chaotic inner world of the victim or patient. The standard worsening of symptoms as the process proceeds is psychologically understood as a form of *resistance* to the treatment or remedy. The psychotic or demonically possessed person attempts to overpower the therapist, who must maintain control of the process, set consistent limits and boundaries, and not retreat from or submit to the patient's anger, rage and aggression. Both the exorcist and psychotherapist align themselves with the healthy part of the personality against the evil or pathological aspects, repudiating all destructive, defensive expressions of the latter. Toward the end of such intensive treatment for schizophrenia, during the final "rebuilding" phase of what psychologist Jack Rosberg calls Direct Confrontation Therapy,

> the patient doesn't understand all of what has happened and is happening to him, and he [or she] is very angry with the therapist.... The patient must be kept from regressing and must be increasingly motivated to get out into the world... Thus, slowly, gradually and painfully, healthy defenses are substituted for unhealthy [ones], and strengthened (cited in Diamond, 1996: 213).

Born-again Christian psychiatrist M. Scott Peck (1983) noted that, unlike exorcism, traditional psychotherapy "is conducted in an atmosphere of total freedom. The patient is free to quit therapy at any time.... Except for the threat of refusing to see the patient anymore, ... the therapist has no weapons with which to push for change beyond the persuasive power of his or her own wits, understanding, and love" (cited in Diamond, 1996: 214). In stark contrast, exorcism makes full use of power to overcome the patient or victim's illness. Almost always conducted by a team or group as opposed to the one-to-one relationship of psychotherapy, exorcism controls the situation completely. Whereas the duration of a psychotherapy session is typically predetermined,

> The length of an exorcism session is not preset but is at the discretion of the team leader. In ordinary psychotherapy the session is no more than an hour, and the patient knows this. If they want to, patients can evade almost any issue for an hour. But exorcism sessions may last three, five, even ten or twelve hours.... Exorcism is psychotherapy by massive assault (Peck, cited in Diamond, 1996: 214–215).

As in exorcism, the constructive use by the therapist of power is essential in psychotherapy, particularly in the treatment of the most debilitating mental disorders.

In Christian exorcism, writes Peck, "the exorcism team, through prayer and ritual, invokes the power of God in the healing process. Indeed, as far as the Christian exorcist is concerned, it is not he or she who successfully completes the process, it is God who does the healing" (1983: 186). This attitude can also frequently be found in secular or even atheistic psychotherapy, with the healing power being attributed not to God, but to the palliative nature of the treatment process itself. Peck draws a distinction between human evil and supernatural, metaphysical or demonic evil, the latter being the cause, he contends, of *genuine possession*. Peck further distinguishes demonic possession from mental illness, stating that though in such cases "there has to be a significant emotional problem for the possession to occur in the first place, ... the proper question to pose diagnostically would be: 'Is the patient just mentally ill or is he or she mentally ill and possessed?'" (1983: 121).

For Dr. Peck and others of his spiritual persuasion, the demonic – unlike the *daimonic* – is purely negative, a power so vile it can only be exorcized, expelled, and excluded from consciousness. It has no redeeming qualities and is unworthy of redemption. On the contrary, the daimonic incorporates the potentially healthy, vital, creative, compensatory forces whose conscious integration is required for any real, lasting therapeutic transformation. Psychiatrist C.G. Jung (see the *shadow*) and existential analyst Rollo May (1969) provide psychologically sophisticated, secular theories of human evil and *daimonic* (as opposed to demonic) possession which, unlike Peck's, do not demand literal belief in the Devil or demons.

Out of vogue for centuries since the Enlightenment, exorcism is experiencing a twenty-first century rebirth in Europe, the United States and elsewhere. Growing numbers of postmodern pilgrims are turning desperately to exorcism to alleviate their psychological or spiritual suffering, due, in part, to a dissatisfaction with contemporary psychiatric and psychological treatment. William Peter Blattey's popular film The Exorcist (1973), derived from his book about an actual reported case, as well as the *Exorcism of Emily Rose* (2005) presented a highly dramatized picture of possession and exorcism, restimulating public fascination with this bizarre phenomenon. Based on the current resurgence in exorcism – being met by an acceleration in the formal training of priests as exorcists by the Vatican – it appears that, for many, the archetypal myths of "demonic possession" and "exorcism" offer a more meaningful and compelling explanation for such powerful experiences than do the conventional scientific theories of biological psychiatry and cognitive-behavioral psychology. If secular psychotherapy as a true healing of the soul or spirit (*psyche*) is to survive and thrive into the future, it will need to more meaningfully address the archetypal phenomenon of possession and the psychology of human evil.

Acknowledgement

Derived and reprinted by permission from *Anger, Madness, and the Daimonic: The Psychological Genesis of Violence, Evil, and Creativity* by Stephen A. Diamond, the State University of New York Press ©1996, State University of New York. All rights reserved.

See also: ❯ Daimonic ❯ Demons ❯ Depth Psychology and Spirituality ❯ Devil ❯ Evil ❯ Existential Psychotherapy ❯ Freud, Sigmund ❯ Jesus ❯ Psychoanalysis ❯ Psychotherapy ❯ Psychotherapy and Religion ❯ Shadow

Bibliography

Benedetti, G. (1960). Blumhardts Seelsorge in der Sicht heutiger psychotherapeutischer Kenntnis. *Reformatio, 9,* 474–487; 531–539.

Diamond, S. (1996). *Anger, madness, and the daimonic: The psychological genesis of violence, evil, and creativity* (Foreword by Rollo May. A volume in the SUNY series in the Philosophy of Psychology). Albany, NY: State University of New York Press.

Ellenberger, H. F. (1970). *The discovery of the unconscious: The history and evolution of dynamic psychiatry.* New York: Basic Books.

The Holy Bible. Containing the Old and New Testaments. Revised Standard Edition (1952). New York: Thomas Nelson & Sons.

Peck, M. S. (1983). *People of the lie: The hope for healing human evil.* New York: Simon & Schuster.

Postmodernism

Galit Atlas-Koch

Postmodernism refers to a body of ideas that represent a new era succeeding modernism and in response to it. Postmodern thought characteristically undermines modernist assumptions concerning the universal, rational, non-historic foundations of human society. It is based on perception of multiplicity, complexity, or chaos of experience, rather than unity or organization, while repudiating meta-narratives. Postmodernism inclined towards relativistic, irrational, and nihilistic conceptions of human reality. Postmodern theorists reject the concepts of foundational knowledge, essences and universals, cause-and-effect relationships and the notion of scientific progress. They prefer theoretical pluralism over the claims of any single explanation and assert that all knowledge is partial.

There is no absolute agreement as to precisely when the postmodern era first appeared on the time axis. In economic-political terms, the main reference point is the Second World War, during which acts of slaughter and warfare on an unprecedented scale were committed in the name of different ideologies, including the Holocaust and the atomic bombs over Hiroshima and Nagasaki. This war left the Western world pessimistic about progress, rationality, and science. The renouncement of Newtonic science's mechanistic thought and the change over to electronic and photonic thought (the relativity revolution, the quantum revolution, and the digital revolution) are considered significant points in postmodernism.

Another reference point is the end of the cold war between the Soviet Union and the United States and the latter's becoming the only superpower, as well as the demise of the imperialistic era and the establishment of new countries around the world; the formation of a new political world, divided into hundreds of autonomous political and cultural units, seeking pluralism and acknowledgment. Emanuel Kant conceders to be one of the first postmodernists, as well as Friedrich Nietzsche who was the first to criticize modernist thought.

For those who lived during the nineteenth century, "god died," as articulated by Nietzsche, and science provided a hedge to nihilism. In modern times, scientific truth resided in the space previously taken by religious truth. While in the modernistic era many believed that science could provide humans with the tools through which to gain access to the enigmas and structure of the universe, one of the main tenets of postmodernism is that there is no one objective truth. Accordingly, it is now plausible to assume that postmodern western religious pluralism led to a search for spiritual alternatives such as Westernized versions of Hinduism and Buddhism.

Postmodernism asserts that every view of the world is a view from a specific perspective, and that there is no external viewpoint from which one can see everything objectively. Michel Foucault wrote that there is no truth to uncover, but rather control mechanisms that produce truth. This conception emphasizes the relation between words and truth, as discourse is produced through language; usually the language of hegemonic groups, thereby increasing their power.

The postmodern claim concerning science is that science, like literature and art, is a text that each reader interprets on his or her own through deconstruction (the disassembly of the text and its restructuring) in any way one wishes. Science, they believe, depends on contemporary needs and social interests. Therefore, science does not provide correct objective knowledge, but rather depends on society, and each period has the science that befits it and that maintains power in the hands of the dominate elites.

Postmodern psychology emphasizes process over structure in conceptualizing the mind, and nonlinearity over linearity in conceptualizing development. While modern psychological concepts, as expressed by Freud and developmental psychologists such as Piaget, articulated set developmental stages of the human psyche, postmodernism rejects the assumptions regarding an invariant, stable core; one self. This newer way of thinking concerns itself with the meaning of different kinds of discourse and interactions with the world, and with the conception of multiple selves.

Freud viewed the intellect and the brain as objects of scientific research in the modernistic sense. To him, the analytic method provides a "correct" understanding of the mind. By contrast, Relational psychoanalytic theory is considered to be a postmodern, post-scientific theory, and as written by Mitchell, Aron, Benjamin and others, it stresses our inability to stand outside nature so as to objectively describe what happens within it. All types of knowledge are therefore pluralistic, not singular; contextual, not absolute; constructed, not uncovered; changing and dynamic. Michael Eigen and Lew Aron are both important postmodern psychoanalysts who also consider religious themes in their writing. Among other prominent postmodern thinkers whose ideas are reflected in the psychology literature are Martin Heidegger, Michel Foucault, Friedrich Jameson, Jacques Derrida, and gender researcher Judith Butler.

See also: ❯ Buddhism ❯ Freud, Sigmund ❯ God ❯ Heidegger, Martin ❯ Hinduism ❯ Holocaust ❯ Relational Psychoanalysis ❯ Self

Bibliography

Aron, L. (1996). *A meeting of minds: Mutuality in psychoanalysis.* New York: Analytic Press.

Benjamin, J. (1988). *The bonds of love.* New York: Pantheon.

Butler, J. (1990). *Gender trouble: Feminism and the subversion of identity.* London: Routledge.

Derrida, J. (1978). *Writing and difference* (A. Bass, Trans.). Chicago, IL: University of Chicago Press.

Foucault, M. (1997). *The Archaeology of knowledge.* London: Routledge.

Foucault, M. (2001). *Dits et écrits* (Vol. 1: 1954–1975, Vol. 2: 1976–1988). Paris: Gallimard, coll. Quarto.

Jameson, F. (1991). *Postmodernism: Or, The cultural logic of late capitalism.* London: Verso.

Mitchell, S. (1993). *Hope and dread in psychoanalysis.* New York: Basic Books.

Nietzsche, F. (1973). *Beyond good and evil.* New York: Penguin Books (Original edition 1886).

Postmortal Existence

❯ Heaven and Hell

Poverty

Robert Kaizen Gunn

After a brief consideration of how poverty is viewed in five world religions, some psychological aspects of poverty will be considered.

Attitudes and Actions Concerning Poverty Among the Five Major World Religions

Poverty is a major concern for every world religion. Every religion makes room for a conscious consideration of what one is to do with and for the poor. Each religion gives instruction regarding the proper attitude and action to take regarding the poor. These attitudes and actions affect one's own life, for faithfulness in each religion requires attitudes and actions of compassion and the sharing, to whatever degree, of what one has with those who have significantly less. Poverty thus directly affects oneself. Indeed, for most religions one's attitude and actions toward the poor is an essential element in the determination of one's own spiritual development and destiny.

Poverty in Judaism

- The concern for the poor is closely linked to the maintenance of justice:

  ▶ you shall not side with the majority so as to pervert justice; nor shall you be partial to the poor in a lawsuit.... You shall not pervert the justice due to your poor in their lawsuits (Exodus 23: 2b-3, 6).

  (All quotations from the Hebrew and Christian Bibles are taken from *The New Oxford Annotated Bible*, 1994)

  ▶ from the profit of their trading they will get no enjoyment. For they have crushed and abandoned the poor, they have seized a house that they did not build (Job 20:19).

  ▶ Thus says the Lord of hosts: render true judgments, show kindness and mercy to one another; do not oppress the widow, the orphan, the alien or the poor... (Zechariah 7:10).

- Leaving fields and crops for the poor is a religious duty:

  ▶ In the seventh year you shall let (the land) rest and lie fallow, so that the poor of your people may eat (Exodus 23: 11).

  ▶ When you reap the harvest of your land, you shall not reap to the very edges of your field, or gather the gleanings of your harvest. You shall not strip your vineyard bare, or gather the fallen grapes of your vineyard; you shall leave them for the poor and the alien: I am the Lord your God (Leviticus 19: 9–10).

- God is compassionate toward the poor and judges those who oppress them:

  ▶ May he defend the cause of the poor of the people, give deliverance to the needy, and crush the oppressor....for he delivers the needy when they call, the poor and those who have no helper. He has pity on the weak and the needy and saves the lives of the needy (Ps 72:4,12, 19, 21).

  ▶ Incline your ear, O Lord, and answer me, for I am poor and needy (Psalm 86:1).

  ▶ This was the guilt of your sister Sodom: she and her daughters had pride, excess of food, and prosperous ease, but did not aid the poor and needy (Ezekiel 16:49).

  ▶ Hear this word, you cows of Bashan who are on Mount Samaria, who oppress the poor, who crush the needy... (Amos 4:1).

Poverty in Christianity

- The poor receive God's favor:

  ▶ Blessed are the poor in spirit, for theirs is the kingdom of Heaven (11:5). Go and tell John what you hear and see: the blind receive their sight, the lame walk, the lepers are cleansed, the deaf hear, the dead are raised and the poor have good news brought to them (Matthew 5:3).

  ▶ Blessed are you who are poor, for yours is the kingdom of God (Luke 6:20).

- Disciples are sometimes urged to become poor themselves:

  ▶ He ordered them to take nothing for their journey except a staff; no bread, no bag, no money in their belts; but to wear sandals and not to put on two tunics (Mark 6:8–9).

P

▶ You lack one thing: go, sell what you own, and give the money to the poor and you will have treasure in heaven; then come, follow me (Mark 10:21, cp Luke 18:22, and John 12:1–8 where words are spoken by Judas).

● Poverty for disciples is recommended because it is following Jesus' example:

▶ For you know the generous act of our Lord Jesus Christ, that though he was rich, yet for your sakes he became poor, so that by his poverty you might become rich (I Corinthians 8:9).

● The surrender of private ownership to communal property is a natural expression of the new life found in Christ:

▶ Now the whole group of those who believed were of one heart and soul, and no one claimed private ownership of any possessions, but everything they owned was held in common.....There was not a needy person among them, for as many as owned lands or houses sold them and brought the proceeds of what was sold. They laid it at the apostles' feet, and it was distributed to each as any had need (Acts 4:32).

● And yet there is a place for extravagance and abundance:

▶ Now while Jesus was at Bethany in the house of Simon the leper, a woman came to him with an alabaster jar of very costly ointment, and she poured it on his head as he sat at the table. But when the disciples saw it, they were angry and said, 'Why was the ointment wasted in this way? For this ointment could have been sold for more than three hundred denari, and the money given to the poor,' and they scolded her. But Jesus said, 'Let her alone; why do you trouble her? She has performed a good service for me. For you always have the poor with you and you can show kindness to them whenever you wish; but you will not always have me' (Matthew 26: 9–11).

● A distinction is made between those who are materially poor and those who appear to have everything, but have nothing:

▶ For you say, 'I am rich, I have prospered, and I need nothing.' You do not realize that you are wretched, pitiable, poor, blind and naked (Revelation 3:17).

In a contemporary expression of Christian concern about poverty, people at Union Theological Seminary in New York City started The Poverty Initiative to raise awareness and take action on behalf of the poor. Their perspective is reflected in an essay entitled "*Who are the poor?*" written by Willie Baptist and Liz Theoharis, August 2008:

▶ If you can't get the basic necessities of life, you're poor. The poor and dispossessed today differ from the poor and dispossessed of the past. They are compelled to fight under qualitatively new conditions and to creatively wield new weapons of struggle. In other words, the socio-economic position of the low waged, laid off, and locked out is not that of the industrial poor, the slave poor, or of the colonial poor of yesterday. The new poor embody all the major issues and problems that affect the majority of other strata of the country's population. Presently, we are experiencing the wholesale economic destruction of the so-called "middle class" in this country. This is huge in terms of political power relations and of strategy and tactics. This "middle class" is beginning to question the economic status quo. The point here is that the economic and social position of the poor is not one to be pitied and guilt-tripped about, but that it indicates the direction this country is heading if nothing is done to change it. Poverty is devastating me today. It can hit you tomorrow. The crisis of healthcare is currently the cause of half of all the bankruptcies in this country (see www.povertyinitiative.org and www.universityofthepoor.org).

Poverty in Islam

According to Osman Guner, in an essay on "Poverty in Traditional Islamic Thought: Is It Virtue or Captivity?", the Islamic words for poverty occur in the Qu'ran twelve times. Two of those times refer to spiritual poverty, meaning human finitude and humans' absolute need for Allah; the other ten refer to material poverty and how Muslims should help them. Additionally, in the Sufi tradition of Islam, the giving up of property and goods is an essential aspect of emphasizing one's utter dependence on Allah.

For most Muslims, however, there is nothing wrong with acquiring material goods, and material well being is seen as an imperative. Nevertheless, greed and oppression are considered unlawful and poverty is considered a social anomaly that should be changed. The poor are looked upon with favor both in this world and the next: "While the food of the poor will be delicious, the food of the rich will not be....Allah certainly gives the deliciousness of the food of the rich to that of the poor....The superiority of the poor over the rich will continue in the Hereafter too....the poor of your community enter the Paradise five hundred years before the rich."

According to one author, Islam has the key to solving the world's problems of poverty and hunger through its tradition of **Zakat**. *Zakat* is an obligatory gift to be distributed among the poor and needy. Muslims are expected to give 2.5% of money that they have had in their possession for over a year. The author concludes:

Now consider this simple fact: Forbes Magazine reported that in 2004 there were 587 billionaires worldwide, with a combined net worth of $1.9 trillion dollars. If in 2004, these 587 richest people in the world paid zakat, we would have had $47.5 billion dollars distributed among the poor (http://www.al-islami.com/islam/islam_solves_poverty.php).

Poverty in Hinduism

Hinduism has sometimes been accused of creating and exacerbating poverty because of its caste system. In Hindu tradition, humankind is divided into four castes, called *varnas*: the highest is the Brahmin, which is for priests, teachers and wise men. The second is that of *Kshatriya*, which is for warriors, rulers and leaders. The third varnas is *Vaishya*, which includes merchants, farmers and those who work in commerce. The lowest *varna* is *Sudra* for those who do manual labor and service. One is born into one of the levels at birth based on one's karma, that is to say, the effect of how one has lived in previous lifetimes. Each *varna* has its own set of rules and expectations, its particular *dharma*, which, if one follows it well, will enable one to be born at a higher level *varna* in one's next lifetime.

Thus understood, although people in the lowest level often live in serious poverty, in Hindu thought it is not a source of disapprobation since everyone is, in every *varna*, in each person's current lifetime, working out their own karma and anticipating raising the level of their *varna* in the next lifetime. Westerners may see a parallel between the Hindu notion of karma and the tradition in both Judaism and Christianity that assumes one's status of both physical and economic well-being to be determined, when negative, by one's own sin or the sins of forebears.

Far from seeing poverty as a virtue, however, Hindu thought emphasizes the value of acquiring wealth and a better standard of living, often through prayers to Lakshmi, the goddess of wealth.

As Hindus have experienced globalization, however— both in terms of Hindus going to other cultures and others coming to them through business and media— there is a significant shift taking place in the understanding of caste and its place in Hindu spiritual development.

Poverty in Buddhism

Buddhism's attitude toward poverty stems from its understanding of all existence according to the first two of the Four Noble Truths propounded by Shakyamuni Buddha in the fifth century, B.C.E. Taken together, the first two Noble Truths comprise a profound critique of the role of poverty in the conditions of all people around the world.

The First Noble Truth is that all of life is *dukkha*, usually translated as suffering, sometimes as anxiety, frustration of dissatisfaction. Poverty– meaning not having enough material goods for health, safety and the kind of well-being needed to realize oneself– is bad, therefore, because it usually entails suffering, and the loss of conditions needed to flourish. It was Shakyamuni's experience that ascetic practices did not, in themselves, lead to enlightenment, and therefore even voluntary poverty— the deliberate surrender of worldly goods– for the Buddhist requires the meeting of ordinary conditions for health, safety and well-being, which is called the "middle way" in between ascetic denial and personal riches.

The Second Noble Truth is that the cause of suffering is *tanha*, perhaps best translated as "craving" or "desire." In the Buddhist analysis, poverty is one of the primary conditions that give rise to craving, because one's ordinary needs for food, clothing, shelter and care have not been met. Thus, poverty is bad because it gives rise to the kind of craving that increases suffering, leading people to extreme behaviors that add suffering to oneself and others.

Any social, economic and political conditions, therefore, that create poverty are bad because they thereby increase the suffering in the world. Thus, Buddhists are urged to engage in "right livelihood," ways of making a living that do not create further suffering in the world, as part of the Fourth Noble Truth concerning the following of the Buddha Way. It follows from this concern that a society that is built on creating desire in order to induce people to acquire goods and be consumers of more goods than are needed will be a society that increases the suffering in the world. When the wealth of the few requires the inordinate consumption of the many because of artificially induced desires, poverty becomes a necessary corollary to wealth.

It is one of the primary insights of Buddhism that dualistic views– perspectives or attitudes in which reality is divided into two opposing positions—will necessarily increase the suffering in the world, because one side has been reified, elevated into a fixed position, at the expense of the other. Buddhist analysis pays keen attention, therefore, whenever dualism appears, and finds there another cause of suffering. Seen this way, poverty is but one side of human life, of which the other extreme is riches, and the Buddhist point of view is that such dualisms are entirely inter-related and interdependent, such that you cannot have one without the other. Poverty so seen is a direct outcome of the accumulation of wealth by one group at the expense of another.

▶ For Buddhism, such a proliferation of wants is the basic cause of unnecessary ill-being. This implies that poverty can never be overcome by proliferating more and more desires which are to be satisfied by consuming more and more goods and services....In short, there is a fundamental and inescapable poverty "built into" a consumer society (Loy, 1999).

In this sense, even the affluent suffer in a consumer-oriented society, because their desires are never satiated. The poor in material goods suffer additionally because they do not have their basic needs for safety, health and well-being met. Morever, the many efforts by governments and institutions such as the World Bank to eliminate poverty may be seen as serving the needs of development for the purpose of creating and sustaining consumers, thus increasing the wealth of the rich, while making others poor.

▶ Global poverty is thus conceptually necessary if the world is to be completely commodified and monetarized...The poverty of others is...necessary because it is the benchmark by which we measure our own achievements....In all these ways, then, we need the poor....among the causes of poverty today are the delusions of the wealthy...(therefore) we should not allow ourselves to be preoccupied only with the poverty side of the problem; to correct the bias, we should become as concerned about the wealth side: the personal, social, and environmental costs of our obsession with wealth-creation and collective growth. (Loy, 1999).

Some Psychological Aspects of Poverty

The Buddhist concern for dualism finds its psychological corollary in the Jungian concepts of persona and shadow. Carl G. Jung, founder of analytical psychology, noted that personality may be divided between the *persona* and the *shadow*. The *persona* is the "mask" or "face" that one presents to the world, and includes all aspects of the person which the person consciously wants to be seen. It generally includes everything about one that may be expected to receive approval, and consists, therefore, in all aspects that one considers good and acceptable.

The *shadow*, on the other hand, contains all those attributes about oneself of which one disapproves or those of which one believes others will disapprove; it includes all things about which one might feel shame, and which one therefore hides or denies. When it comes to the poor, the psychological situation was articulated by Malthus:

▶ Even in the relief of common beggars we shall find that we are more frequently influenced by the desire of getting rid of the importunities of a disgusting object than by the pleasure of relieving it. We wish that it had not fallen in our way, rather than rejoice in the opportunity given us of assisting a fellow-creature. We feel a painful emotion at the sight of so much apparent misery; but the pittance we give does not relieve it. We know that it is totally inadequate to produce any essential effect. We know, besides, that we shall be addressed in the same manner at the corner of the next street; and we know that we are liable to the grossest impositions. We hurry therefore sometimes by them, and shut our ears to their importunate demands. (Malthus, 1992: 283, quoted in Johnson 2007)

Poverty thus constitutes society's shadow, for the poor elicit an uncanny loathing on the part of those who are not poor. The loathing is uncanny precisely in the way Malthus describes, in which the giving of a "pittance" does not relieve the "painful emotion at the sight of so much apparent misery." It is uncanny further because, as Malthus says, the sheer scope and intractability of poverty baffles the mind, invoking an unshakeable ambivalence.

The direct experience of the people who are poor—if one is not–is unsettling. To put oneself in their shoes is to imagine who and what we are underneath our clothing, our roles, our relationships, our money, credit rating or house or car—it is to become aware of how thin and arbitrary the line is between the haves and the have-nots. In manifesting this core vulnerability and fragility, the poor live close to the border of life and death, which is the province of all spirituality. (It is to be that intimate with the divine that some people choose poverty voluntarily.)

The psychological point reinforces the Buddhist point regarding the dualism of poverty and wealth: the persona by definition requires the shadow. Indeed, the persona requires the shadow, for the persona itself is based on what it consciously declares it is not, namely, it is not the shadow. Without the shadow, the persona would not exist; without the persona, the shadow would not exist. They are interdependent. The rich require the poor psychologically, just as the poor require the rich.

Insofar as an individual accepts this division of reality into personality/shadow, rich/poor, and identifies with only one aspect, one will be locked in, psychologically, into only one half of one's actual possibilities, and in denial about the other half. For the wealthy, they will be locked into maintaining their persona aspects: qualities of competence, superiority of ability and virtue, worthiness and the right to all that is considered good in life, including creativity, power, dignity and pursuit of happiness. To maintain the split, to make sure the shadow is suppressed, whole systems of thought will be devised to justify their position and to manifest *les droits du seigneur*—the rights of the lord. This psychological position will seek manifestation in every aspect of the social structure, from the economy to the politics, to the arts and religions. All of society will become organized around the split between the persona and shadow, the rich and the poor, in such a way as to insure the split and thus insure each side remains what it is and remains separate from the other.

The poor, for their part, insofar as they accept this division of reality, will become entirely identified as the poor, with all the psychological expectations demanded by their status as separate from the rich. They will not expect themselves to have a voice in the society, nor a place; they will not expect to be treated with full human dignity; they will not expect to contribute to the arts, nor have any place in religion except that of helpless victim, and thus they will adopt a form of a religion that reinforces their helpless status.

Consciousness and liberation for all people require the integration of split-off aspects of the personality. Programs to help the poor or end poverty will necessarily serve the divided psyche unless it speaks to the psychopathology of the division itself. Such a perspective cannot be imposed from only one aspect of the population, but must come from the ground up, from the people as a whole.

It is almost impossible to understand the psychological power built into the dynamics between the persona/shadow dynamics of rich and poor. It is cross-cultural, at least among developed nations. It is built into the nature of what it is to be human, because to be poor is to express and manifest the core powerlessness and vulnerability of the human condition, and to recognize how tentative and fragile human life is.

A psychological consideration of the persona/shadow dynamics of the rich and poor requires a spiritual vision, a vision of the whole, in which wealth and poverty are each integrated in relation to the other in mutual interdependence, and only from such a vision can the division between rich and poor even be imagined.

Bibliography

Loy, D. (1999). "Buddhism and Poverty" in *Kyoto Journal*.
Johnson, K. S., 2007. *The Fear of Beggars: Stewardship and Poverty in Christian Ethics*, Grand Rapids, Michigan: Wililam B. Eerdmans Publishing Company.
The New Oxford Annotated Bible. (1994). New York: Oxford University Press.
Rahula, W. 1994. *What the Buddha taught: Revised and expanded edition with texts from the Suttas and the Dhammapada*. New York: Grove/Atlantic, Inc.
www.povertyinitiative.org
www.universityofthepoor.org
www.al-islami.com/islam/islam_solves_poverty.php

Power

Lori B. Wagner-Naughton

Defined as the ability to influence other's thoughts, feelings, or behaviors in order to achieve one's own agenda. Power can be communicated through indirect methods (i.e., nonverbal behaviors) or direct verbal exchange. Intimate relationships, such as spouse, parent, or sibling may engender a different influence compared to religious or political leaders. French and Raven (1959) assert that there are five social bases of power that influence relationships. These include: reward, coercive, expert, legitimate, and referent. Raven (1999) further explains how reward power can be defined through rewards or approval from other's whereas coercive exchanges encompass punishment or disapproval. Expert power gives strength to the "influencer" through their knowledge or skill set. Legitimate power signifies a hierarchical structure or position within the relationship. Lastly, referent power describes the influential nature of identifying with or caring about another individual.

See also: ⊙ Communal and Personal Identity

Bibliography

French, J., & Raven, E. (1959). The bases of social power. In D. D. Cartwright (Ed.), *Studies on social power*. Ann Arbor, MI: University of Michigan, Institute for Social Research.
Raven, B. H. (1999). Kurt Lewin address: Influence, power, religion, and the mechanisms of social control. *Journal of Social Issues, 55*, 161–186.

Prajna

Paul C. Cooper

Prajna is the Sanskrit term for wisdom, intuitive knowing or "quick – knowing" (Evans-Wentz, 1954: 208). For the Zen practitioner it is the direct seeing into reality "beyond words and letters." Prajna stands in contradistinction to knowledge based cognition or discursive, linear thinking, which from a Buddhist perspective would be considered dualistic and therefore limited. Prajna is the intuitive wisdom that reveals the truth of reality as embodied in the doctrine of emptiness and dependent-arising and that frees one from suffering. The important Buddhist scripture, *Prajna-paramita Sutra* (*Perfection of Wisdom Sutra*) describes prajna as unsurpassed and unequalled.

A direct parallel to psychoanalytic thinking can be found in the writings of the British psychoanalyst Wilfred R. Bion who makes a distinction between "K," knowledge that is known discursively and through the senses and "O," which is his symbol for ultimate Truth, and that can be intuited but not known. He writes: "O does not fall into the domain of knowledge or learning save incidentally; it can 'become,' but it cannot be 'known'" (1970: 26).

See also: ❯ Bion, Wilfred Ruprecht, and "O" ❯ Zen

Bibliography

Bion, W. R. (1970). *Attention and interpretation*. London: Karnac Books.
Evans-Wentz, W. Y. (1954). *The Tibetan book of the great liberation*. Oxford, England: Oxford University Press.

Prayer

Allan Hugh Cole, Jr.

Prayer is a central act of religion that involves seeking and responding to the presence, interest, will, purposes, and aid of the Divine. It entails orientation toward the transcendent realm, whereby expression is given to one's own, and others', struggles, regrets, needs, and desires. This expression occurs in individuals and groups, in verbal and non-verbal forms, through conscious and unconscious states, and according to ritualized and non-ritualized methods. Motivations and effects of prayer may be understood in religious and psychological terms.

Religious Understandings

William James called prayer "the very soul and essence of religion" (James, 1902/1987). Viewing prayer religiously can involve appeal to objective and subjective factors (Pratt, 1920; Wulff, 1997). Objective factors generally pertain to two matters. The first is the belief that prayer is offered to, received by, and acted upon by an ontologically real and supernatural divine being. Many religious traditions, particularly monotheistic ones (e.g., Judaism, Christianity, and Islam), refer to this being as God. When human beings pray to God, they do so to one that exists and functions outside of their own subjectivity. They seek an encounter with or relationship to an objective, transcendent, but living and acting entity. A second matter involving objective factors of prayer concerns its effects. Appeal is made to tangible external criteria to discern prayer's benefits, such as improvement in physical or emotional state, or provision for one or more needs. In many Jewish and Christian religious traditions, prayer is viewed as a human response to God's acting on our behalf, such that God always acts first and, even in prayer, human beings act subsequent to God's initial action. Even so, many of these same traditions subscribe to belief in divine passibility (i.e. God's capacity to feel and empathize). God's nature is such that human prayer can affect God's will and purposes, and enlist God's concern and help.

Subjective factors of prayer relate to how it involves and changes the one who prays. Søren Kierkegaard, a nineteenth century philosopher, claimed that one should pray out of devotion to God, but especially to bring one's own will, efforts, and needs in line with those of God (Kierkegaard, 1990). Kierkegaard held that prayer does not change God, for God is unchangeable. Rather, prayer changes us. Herein lay its purpose and value.

Twentieth century theologian Paul Tillich echoed this perspective. He claimed that in prayer we surrender to God, "the ground of being," and are taken into God's creative acts (Tillich, 1951; McKelway, 1965). In prayer, we become part of God's "directive creativity" in the world. Kierkegaard and Tillich stressed the role of human subjectivity in religion. Kierkegaard anticipated psychological perspectives on matters of religion, faith, and practices such as prayer, while Tillich appropriated these perspectives for theology and the philosophy of religion. Support for the veracity of both objective and subjective claims concerning prayer is found in sacred texts of many religions.

Psychological Understandings

Psychological perspectives on motivations and effects of prayer consider how it relates to religious practices and experiences, but especially as these involve what transpires within the praying subject with respect to cognitive, emotional, relational, and behavioral states.

Some psychological perspectives, particular those tied to Freudian thought, view prayer negatively. Like all religious beliefs and practices, it is said to involve an infantile form of seeking wish fulfillment (Freud, 1961). In this view, one pursues in prayer the presence and provision of an all powerful deity that compensates for human limitations and unmet needs or desires. As we look to parents to meet our needs in childhood, we look to God as we age. Such pursuit is viewed negatively because of its basis in irrational thinking and delusion, and its appeal to superstition or magical powers.

Other psychological perspectives hold a more positive view of prayer and stress its potential benefits for human wellbeing. Some like William James and other psychologists of religion who were his contemporaries have suggested that prayer is "the religious experience *par excellence*" (see Capps, 1982). Others have found that prayer is a common source for religious experience, second only to music (Greeley, 1975, Argyle 2000/2004). Prayer promotes a particular type of consciousness, including inward communion marked by earnestness, openness, and expectancy; and something is "transacted" in prayer that involves "spiritual energy" and which can promote therapeutic gain (James, 1901). Moreover, prayer may lead to enhanced self-awareness, which can include a deeper consideration of held values, ideals, goals, and responsibilities (Jung, 1961/ 1989). Prayer can also promote "active cognitive coping" (Argyle, 2000/2004) and cognitive restructuring, particularly as understood by principles of cognitive therapy (Beck and Emery, 1985; Cole, 2008a, 2008b). In this view, how one feels and acts is directly related to how one thinks. As one becomes more aware of one's thoughts, patterns of thinking, and how these inform one's feelings and behaviors, one may then alter how one feels and behaves by altering what and how one thinks. Prayer has the capacity to foster thinking, and thus feeling and behaving, in more faithful, peaceful, healthy, and whole ways. Seeking a type of cognitive restructuring through prayer parallels what occurs in various methods employed in a therapeutic setting.

Types of Prayer

In the early twentieth century, the German historian of religion Friedrich Heiler (1892–1967) proposed a typology of prayer consisting of nine distinct forms (Heiler, 1932). These include: primitive, ritual, hymns, Hellenistic, philosophical, prayer of the religious expert or genius, prayer of great poets and artists, prayer in public worship, and prescribed and meritorious prayer. Heiler's typology still has value, but a simpler and perhaps more relevant approach considers four primary types of prayer: meditative, ritualistic, petitionary, and colloquial (Poloma and Pendleton, 1991, Argyle, 2000/2004).

In meditative prayer, one attends to acts of contemplation and seeks the presence of God and communion with God. Meditative prayer usually results in altered states of consciousness. Although practiced less frequently than other types, its effects can be significant (Argyle, 2000/ 2004). In ritualistic prayer, spontaneity gives way to more formulaic, if not prescriptive, forms. Ritualistic prayer also tends to be practiced among groups whose leadership consists of an identified priestly class that regularizes expectations and practices of prayer life (Heiler, 1932). This form of prayer is often practiced in particular places held to be sacred, which informs a degree of emotional investment and perceived power in praying that otherwise may be lacking (Argyle, 2000/2004). Petitionary prayer is the most spontaneous form. In using it one makes explicit requests of God for intervention or help, but this generally lacks critical reflection (Heiler, 1932). Whether offered by individuals alone or collectively by a group, it usually involves more intense emotional states, and it often issues from a need for God's aid amidst a perceived threat (Heiler, 1932). Colloquial prayer shares many qualities with petitionary prayer, and especially relates to efforts for "religious coping" (Argyle, 2000/ 2004). As the most common form of prayer, it involves talking with God as a friend or close associate, and using a familiar tone with ordinary language (Poloma and Pendleton, 1991). A major study has shown that among conservative Protestant Christians, experience with prayer is predictive of overall existential wellbeing, whereas for mainline Protestants prayer is less predictive of wellbeing than regular church attendance (Poloma and Pendleton, 1991; Argyle, 2000/2004).

See also: ❯ Christianity ❯ Freud, Sigmund ❯ Islam ❯ James, William ❯ Judaism and Psychology ❯ Kierkegaard, Søren

Bibliography

Argyle, M. (2000/2004). *Psychology and religion: An introduction*, New York: Routledge.

Beck, A. T., & Emery, G. (1985). *Anxiety disorders and phobias: A cognitive perspective*. New York: Basic Books.

Capps, D. (1982). The psychology of petitionary prayer. *Pastoral Psychology, 39*(2), 130–141.

Cole, A. H., Jr. (2008a). *Good mourning: Getting through your grief*. Louisville, KY: Westminster John Knox Press.

Cole, A. H., Jr. (2008b). *Be not anxious: Pastoral care of disquieted souls*. Grand Rapids: William. B. Eerdmans.

Freud, S. (1961/1989). *The future of an illusion* (Rev. ed.) A. Strachey (Trans.) J. Strachey (Ed.) (Introduction by Peter Gay). New York: W. W. Norton.

Greeley, A. M. (1975). *The sociology of the paranormal*. London: Sage.

Heiler, F. (1932). *Prayer: A study in the history and psychology of religion*. London: Oxford University Press.

James, W. (1902/1987). *The varieties of religious experience*. New York: Library Classics of the United States.

Jung, C. G. (1961/1989). *Memories, dreams, reflections*. R. Winston & C. Winston (Trans.) A. Jaffé (Ed.). New York: Vintage Books.

Kierkegaard, S. (1990). *Eighteen upbuilding discourses* (H. V. Hong & E. H. Hong, Trans.). Princeton, NJ: Princeton University Press.

McKelway, A. J. (1965). *The systematic theology of Paul Tillich: A review and analysis* (Introduction by Karl Barth). Richmond, VA: John Knox Press.

Poloma, M. M., & Pendleton, B. F. (1991). *Exploring neglected dimensions of religion in quality of life research*. New York: Lewiston.

Pratt, J. B. (1920). *The religious consciousness: A psychological study*. New York: Macmillan.

Tillich, P. (1951). *Systematic theology*, Vol. 1. Chicago, IL: University of Chicago Press.

Thomte, R. (1948). *Kierkegaard's philosophy of religion*. Princeton, NJ: Princeton University Press.

Wulff, D. M. (1997). *Psychology of religion: Classic and contemporary* (2nd ed.). New York: John Wiley and Sons.

Predestination

Mark William Ennis

Predestination (election) is an ancient Christian concept that is, perhaps the most widely misunderstood of all Christian doctrines. In the Christian Canon it is mentioned first in the Pauline literature, Ephesians chapter 1 in which Paul defines the Christian community as being "pre-ordained" by God for adoption since before the beginning of creation.

In many respects this assurance to the congregation in Ephesus establishes the "legitimacy" of gentile Christians amid an atmosphere of largely Jewish Christians. As Jews became a chosen people because of the unilateral covenant that God made with Abraham and his descendents, so God now makes a unilateral covenant with gentiles. Gentile Christians are thus "pre-destined" and are the equals of God's chosen people; the Jews.

The church in Ephesus to whom this was written, suffered under great persecution in the Roman Empire. Paul's assurance of God's choice of them serves to give courage to this persecuted community. Viktor Frankl observed during World War II that harsh conditions can be endured with the knowledge of a deeper meaning to life. Love, he reasoned, could enable people to live through conditions that might seem to be unlivable.

In early Christian times the Church Fathers wrestled with the concept of predestination (election) feeling the tension between this doctrine and "free will." Others confused this doctrine with "fatalism" in which one's life is scripted by God and each second of life is predetermined. Scripture however says nothing of a life script. It speaks of God's irresistible love that will ultimately bring those elect to salvation. It describes the ultimate destination but does not in any way suggest a scripted life.

During the Protestant Reformation, John Calvin in order to combat what he perceived to be the salvation by works taught by the Roman Catholic Church, expanded this doctrine to include a "double decree" of predestination (election). This double decree put forth the thesis that as some people are predestined for heaven, others are predestined for damnation. Calvin, although putting forth this idea, did warn that speculating on the roster of such a list would not be productive.

In later years Arminian thought challenged Calvinists. James Arminius, who studied under Beza, a student of Calvin's, put this thought forth. Arminius argued that God's grace was indeed resistible and humans ultimately participate in their own salvation through their decisions. Thus began in the Netherlands, the controversy between Arminianism and Calvinism led to the Synod of Dort (1618). This synod affirmed predestination (election), repudiated Arminianism and cemented the rift between believers in each of these schools of thought.

In the twentieth century, Swiss theologian Karl Barth again tackled the doctrine of preordination (election). He upheld the double decree of election but argued that in the atoning work of Jesus, God leaves the list of those damned under the double-decree, vacant, thereby opening up the role of the elect to all people.

The doctrine of predestination (election) represents the full unconditional love of God for an individual. Much like a child yearns for parental acceptance so those adhering to this doctrine know the true joy of acceptance by their creator. They are chosen, as were the ancient Jews through the Abrahamic covenant. In a world where often we see the break down of traditional social groups and institutions, this doctrine emphasizes belonging and can be seen as an antidote for an anomic person. During personality development the knowledge of this connection by election gives a person a grounding of belonging.

See also: ❯ Augustine ❯ Frankl, Viktor

Bibliography

Barth, K. (1976). Church dogmatics. In *The doctrine of God* (Vol. II). Edinburgh, England: T & T Clark.

Brouwer, A. R. (1977). *Reformed church roots*. New York: Thirty-Five Formative Events Reformed Church Press.

Buttrick, G. A. (Ed.). (1980). *The interpreters dictionary of the bible*. Nashville, TN: Abingdon.

Frankl, V. E. (1977). *Mans search for meaning*. Boston, MA: Beacon Press.

Hageman, H. G. (1963). *Predestination*. Minneapolis, MN: Fortress Press Library of Congress 63–12533.

McNeill, J. T. (Ed.). (1977). *Calvin: Institutes of the Christian religion* (Vol. 1). Philadelphia, PA: Westminster Press.

McNeill, J. T. (Ed.). (1977). *Calvin: Institutes of the Christian religion* (Vol. 2). Philadelphia, PA: Westminster Press.

Plantinga, C., Jr. (1981). *A place to stand: A study of ecumenical creeds and reformed confessions*. Grand Rapids, MI: Board of Publication of the Christian Reformed Church.

Simpson, E. K., & Bruce, F. F. (1982). The new international commentary on the New Testament. In *The epistles to the ephesians and colossians*. Grand Rapids, MI: Wm. B. Eerdmans Publishing.

persecution of Muslims to Muslim persecution of Jews. Therefore, a powerful justification for prejudice is the religious belief that God has ordained a specific social order. However, a powerful justification against prejudice for a religious believer is the belief that God has ordained that "all are created equal." Many historical examples could also be cited as evidence to this association (Meyers, 2008). What then is the connection between prejudice and religion? The answer to this seeming contradiction can be resolved upon closer examination of the psychological components of an individual's religious belief and action (Donahue and Nielsen, 2005). Individuals with an intrinsic religious orientation understand all of life by their religion. Religion is an essential part of their orienting system towards themselves, others, and the world at large. Individuals with an extrinsic religious orientation on the other hand see religion as a means to other types of ends like social activity or power (Allport and Ross, 1967). Compared to more extrinsically motivated religious individuals, these intrinsically religious believers tend to be less prejudice. Therefore, depth of religious commitment may be the key to either making or unmaking prejudice in religious domains (Meyers, 2008).

See also: ❯ Christianity ❯ God ❯ Islam ❯ Judaism   and Psychology

Bibliography

Allport, G. W., & Ross, J. M. (1967). Personal religious orientation and prejudice. *Journal of Personality and Social Psychology, 5*, 423–443.

Donahue, M. J., & Nielsen, M. E. (2005). Religion, attitudes, and social behaviour. In R. F. Paloutzian, & C. L. Park (Eds.), *Handbook of the psychology of religion and spirituality* (pp. 274–291). New York: Guilford.

Meyers, D. G. (2008). *Social psychology* (9th ed.). New York: McGraw-Hill.

Prejudice

Brandon Randolph-Seng

Psychologically, prejudice can be defined as a predetermined judgment of a group of people including its individual members. This preconceived judgment is usually considered to be negative. Within religion, many historical examples of prejudice can be found from Christian

Primal Horde Theory

Benjamin Beit-Hallahmi

In *Totem and Taboo* (1913/1955) Freud analyzed the phenomenon of totemic religion, characterized by the centrality of the totemic animal, symbolizing the clan, in worship, and the incest taboo applied to all members of the same clan. This could still be observed directly among pre-literate cultures in our time. Freud asserted a connection between totem, taboo, and paternal authority.

He suggested that this connection stemmed from human pre-history, when humans lived in large groups, the primal horde, dominated by one older male, who could monopolize all females (this was first proposed by Charles Darwin). This tyrannical father was murdered and then eaten by the resentful young males, his sons, who then possessed all females, including mothers and sisters. The murdered father was then symbolized in the totem animal, which holds the authority within the horde. Through the sacrifice of the totem animal, the sons could try to allay their burning sense of guilt and to bring about a reconciliation with their father.

The primal crime, and the resulting guilt, where the starting point for civilization, morality, the incest taboo, and religion. The guilt-stricken brothers agreed to a social contract: Stop the war of all against all and to prohibit copulations within the clan, thus controlling, if not conquering, the disruptive and destructive impulses of sex and aggression.

The primal crime left a legacy found everywhere in culture. From the pre-historical to the more abstract and symbolic, the functions of commemoration, appeasement, and renunciation of instinct remained integral to the cultural compromise of the Oedipus complex expressed through religion. Religious myths and rituals obsessively re-enacted the primal crime, and the totemic meal, in which the primal crime was celebrated and atoned for, became the Christian Eucharist, and the Jewish Passover.

While Freud's assertions regarding the events of human pre-history have been rejected by most scholars, his psychological observations regarding the dynamics of totemism and ritual have been treated with respect.

Some of the best known anthropologists of the twentieth century, while critical of the Freud's thesis about the primal crime in the primal horde, embraced his phylogenetic insights. These included A. L. Kroeber, Ernest Becker, Meyer Fortes, and Derek Freeman. Margaret Mead speculated that Freud was, after all, right about the "primal crime," except that this deed was committed much earlier in the evolutionary history of humanity. It was a pre-human horde, when sexual maturity was reached at age seven or eight, and life was much shorter. And the deed was committed repeatedly, as each generation got rid of the earlier one over hundreds of thousands of years, until these pre-humans became real humans.

See also: ❯ Freud, Sigmund ❯ Oedipus Complex

Bibliography

Beit-Hallahmi, B. (1996). *Psychoanalytic studies of religion: Critical assessment and annotated bibliography.* Westport, CT: Greenwood Press.

Freud, S. (1913/1955). Totem and taboo. In J. Strachey (Ed.), *The standard edition of the complete psychological works of Sigmund Freud* (Vol. 13, pp. 1–164). London: Hogarth Press, 1953–1974.

Primordial Waters

David A. Leeming

All cultures naturally recognize water as a necessary source of life and survival, making it a useful symbol of creative fertility – spiritual and psychological fertility as well as physical fertility. At the same time, large masses of water are uncontrollable and, therefore, aptly representative of chaos – the chaos that precedes creation. Together, these two symbolic functions lead us, like the cosmic egg symbol, to the idea of potential, as yet unformed reality. The primordial waters figure strongly in creation myths from all corners of the world. The waters speak to the larger metaphor of creation as birth. We are all born of the maternal waters and so, in creation mythology, worlds are typically born of the waters.

In the earth diver type of creation myth a diver, usually a humble animal, is sent by the creator to the depths of the waters to find soil with which to begin the creation of Earth. In several Native American myths a toad or a muskrat, for instance, succeeds after much difficulty, in penetrating the waters, like the lonely sperm which penetrates the egg, and brings back the fertilizing germ of creation, a tiny bit of earth, a fetus to be nurtured. In India the Garo people say it was Beetle who succeeded in the dive. The Gond people say that the creator, sitting on a lotus leaf on the waters, sent the crow to find the seed of life. The Birhor creator also sits on the lotus, by means of which he himself has emerged from the waters, and he sends the lowly leech to find the germ of creation. In a Hungarian myth the sun takes the form of a duck and makes the successful dive for the "seed." Out of this small beginning in several Native American myths – particularly of the Iroquoian speaking peoples – a woman who falls from the sky, the heavens, now an Earth Mother, directs the process of creation and civilization resulting from the bit of earth. The maternal birth-giving waters are, after all, feminine.

In a Polynesian myth of Samoa, the creator broke out of a cosmic egg and allowed parts of the shell to "fertilize" the Primordial waters causing the formation of the Samoan Islands. Some Samoans say that the creator himself dove to the depths to find the stone that would form the basis of creation. A myth of the Papago of Arizona tells how in the beginning darkness rubbed with the primordial waters and so impregnated "her" with the first human. A Mongolian myth relates how the creator simply stirred the waters – perhaps a veiled image of intercourse – and filled them with creation.

The primordial water can stand as a symbol of the possibility of rebirth, a psychological and spiritual new beginning. Baptism contains the elements of this symbolism. The initiate dies to the old life in a kind of symbolic drowning but is reborn from the maternal and cleansing water as a new "whole" being. The water is also an archetypal representative of the unconscious, in the depths of which the earth diver, – the individual – can, sometimes at great risk, discover the seeds of individuation. The waters are the amniotic fluid in which preconscious Self is formed and from which conscious Self will emerge.

See also: ❂ Baptism ❂ Chaos ❂ Cosmic Egg ❂ Creation ❂ Myth ❂ Self ❂ Unconscious

Bibliography

Eliade, M. (1958). *Patterns in comparative religion* (Chap. V) (R. Sheed, Trans). Cleveland, OH: Meridian, 1967.

Leeming, D. A. (2005). *The Oxford companion to world mythology*. New York: Oxford.

Leeming, D. A. & Leeming, M. (1994). *Encyclopedia of creation myths*. Santa Barbara, CA: ABC-CLIO. (Revised as *A dictionary of creation myths*, New York: Oxford, 1994).

Von Franz, M. L. (1972). *Patterns of creativity mirrored in creation myths*. Zurich, Switzerland: Spring Publications. (Revised as *Creation myths*, Boston, MA: Shambala, 1995).

Projection

Lee W. Bailey

Projection is the term used to describe a common psychological dynamic, well known in psychotherapy and critical studies of religion. It means the attribution of qualities of person A to person or thing B that can be traced back to the unconscious contents of person A, such as love, hate, or divinity. It is a useful theory that describes both normal and pathological ways of involvement in the world, such as falling in love at first sight. It has been used to attack religion as "nothing but" illusory projections of an infantile father complex, but recent thinkers have challenged this Pre-theoretical "projections" are described in ancient literature.

Ancient Greeks

Pre-theoretical "projections" are described in ancient literature. Xenophanes proclaimed: "But if cattle and horses or lions had hands, or were able to draw with their hands and do the works that men can do, horses would draw the forms of the gods like horses, and cattle like cattle, and they would make their bodies such as they each had themselves" (Kirk & Raven, 169). Xenophanes' critique is not atheist, but is an effort to clear away attributions ["projection" is a modern term] that distort his view of a refined monotheism: "One god, greatest among gods and men, in not way similar to mortals either in body or in thought" (Kirk & Raven, 169).

Plato reports on a Sophist argument that the differences between different tribal gods reflect merely tribal qualities: "This party asserts that gods have no real and natural, but only an artificial being, in virtue of local conventions, as they call them, and thus there are different gods for different places, conforming to the conventions made by each group" (1961, *Laws* X, 889E).

Plato also describes what psychologists commonly call "projection" in a lover's passion, rooted in an unconscious complex: "So he loves, yet to knows not what he loves; he does not understand, he cannot tell what has come upon him" (1961, *Phaedrus* 255D). Lovers attribute qualities to their beloved ones, Plato says, because they are unconsciously adoring a god:

▷ All this, mark you, they attribute to the beloved, and the draughts which they draw from Zeus they pour out, like bacchants, into the soul of the beloved, thus creating in him the closest possible likeness to the god they worship (1961, *Phaedrus* 253A).

Similarly, Freud says centuries later, parents project royalty onto "His Majesty the Baby," because "they are under compulsion to ascribe every perfection to the child" (1974 *SE* XIV: 91). Like Plato's lover, Freud's theoretical parents project god-like perfections onto their beloved children.

Plato's lover is projecting forth a flowing stream that originates in Zeus, for example, and floods his beloved with a passion. But "he cannot account for it, not realizing that his lover is as it were a mirror in which he beholds himself" (1961 *Phaedrus* 255D). Like Freud, Plato recognizes that the lover is unconsciously looking in a mirror, but unlike Freud, Plato believes that what we call "projections" originate in gods, not in subjectivity.

Ludwig Feuerbach

Plato's theory was theological, but in the nineteenth century, Ludwig Feuerbach reversed Plato's theology, arguing that "The personality of God is nothing other than the projected personality of man" (1957: 226). Unlike Xenophanes and Plato, Feuerbach did not want to clear the way of projections so we could see a purified divinity or Being. On the contrary, he was immersed in the materialist subject-object metaphysic that sought to reduce religious metaphysics to the metaphysics of subjective contents. He stresses not just the illusions of such projections. The positive contents of religion Feuerbach wants to return to human self-awareness:

▸ God is the manifested inward nature, the expressed self of a man – religion the solemn unveiling of a man's hidden treasures, the revelation of his ultimate thoughts, the open confession of his love-secrets (12–13).

Although Feuerbach's theory of projection was adopted widely by atheists, ironically he did not use the term "projection," that was available in German as *projicieren*. His English translator George Eliot provided this word. Feuerbach used the terms *Entäusserung* ("externalization" or "alienation") and *Vergegenständlichung* ("objectification" or "alienation"), so his theory is better termed one of "theological alienation." Marx borrowed this.

Camera Obscura

Where did the image of "projection" originate that was attached to these early psychological and religious insights? Two old related machines were the experiential collective source: the *camera obscura* and the "magic lantern." The *camera obscura* is a dark room with a small hole allowing the external scene to be projected onto an internal screen. In the tenth century, Alhazen experimented with solar eclipses projected into a dark room. Roger Bacon also experimented with the dark room, using mirrors (Bacon, 1614). Leonardo DaVinci also experimented

with a small *camera obscura* and made the first surviving comparison to the human eye:

▸ When the images of illuminated bodies pass through a small round hole into a very dark room, if you receive them on a piece of white paper placed vertically in the room at some distance from the aperture, you will see on the paper all those bodies in their natural shapes and colors, but they will appear upside down and smaller ... the same happens inside the pupil (DaVinci, 1490).

Descartes explored the *camera obscura* with an ox-eye in the aperture to invert and focus the image. He considered the results unreliable, but John Locke believed the images to be reliable pictures of the outer world, which supported his psychology of representation. The *camera obscura* was a widespread instrument by the Renaissance, and fed both the collective images of mental projection and of mental subjectivity.

The Magic Lantern

While the *camera obscura* received external images into a dark room, the "magic lantern" projected images, painted on mirrors or glass, into a dark room, often with dramatic intent. The Dutch physicist Christian Huygens first combined the elements of candlelight, lens and picture on glass around 1659. The Jesuit Athanasius Kircher published the first illustration in his *Ars Magna* (see *Fig. 1*). The magic lantern spread around Europe with traveling magicians and carnivals using images such as angels and

Projection. Figure 1 The first known illustration of the magic lantern, by Kirchner (1671: 768–769).

demons that produced shocking effects on audiences. Diderot's *Encyclopedie* explained the technique in 1753, but many were still in the dark.

A Belgian magician named Etienne Robertson's traveling *Phantasmagorie* show used the magic lantern dramatically. He tossed chemicals into a brazier in front of an audience, producing smoke, and images were projected from concealed magic lanterns onto the smoke. Demons, skulls, skeletons, and dead heroes appeared in the smoke (the "smoke screen"). Spectators sank to their knees, drew their swords, or covered their eyes in terror. Such shows multiplied, and their tricks were exposed in popular magazines (Barnouw, 1981). By the nineteenth century the magic lantern was spreading the idea that angels and demons alike were "nothing but" projections from a magic lantern into a dark room. Thus, Feuerbach was able to translate this collective image into a philosophical theory by 1841.

Sigmund Freud

By 1895, when the movie projector was finally working in Edison's lab, Freud's first formulation of the theory of psychological projection also appeared. He proposed that paranoia uses projection as a defense: "The purpose of such delusions, "Freud writes, "is to fend off the idea that is compatible with the ego, by projecting its substance into the external world" (1974 *SE* I: 209). Freud added to the popular image of projection by a magic lantern, and to Feuerbach's philosophy of projection from subjectivity, not only psychological depth, but the notion of projection as a mental "mechanism," modeling on nineteenth century technological inventions (such as magic lanterns). He used the theory commonly, from clinical analyses to cultural criticisms of religion:

> ▶ I believe that a large part of the mythological view of the world, which extends a long way into the most modern religions, is nothing but psychology projected into the external world (1974, *SE* VI: 258–259).

Here Freud illustrates the positivist effort to reduce religion to subjective contents using the theory of projection. Projection became a major argument for atheism in the twentieth century by reducing gods to subjective illusions. It also offered a useful perspective for cleansing religions of inappropriate projected accretions, such as nationalism and racism.

The theory of projection was applied in the clinical development of analysis of psychological transference and counter-transference between patients and therapists.

The "withdrawal" of projections was the description often used in the therapeutic work of "owning" or recognizing one's own unconscious feelings initially experienced in other people or in the world in many developing schools of psychotherapy.

Carl Jung

When Jung developed his theory of the collective unconscious and archetypes, he welcomed Freud's theory of projection, but modified it. Like Freud, he saw projection in culture saying: "All human relationships swarm with these projections" (*CW* XIII, paragraph 507). Projections generated "blinding illusions which falsify ourselves and our relations to our fellow men, making both unreal" (*CW* VII, 373). Jung agrees with Freud that in transference projections are often rooted in unreal infantile and erotic fantasies. However, he rejected Freud's theory that projection is primarily a defense mechanism, infantile and personal in content. Jung also rejected the view that projections are caused by individual repression, as he realized the collective, impersonal contents in projections. Patients not only fell in love with him, but also fantasized that he was a devil or a savior (*CW* VII, 99). Not only illusions, but also strengths may appear in projections, Jung found.

Jung did keep projection largely in the subject-object metaphysic (*CW* XVIII, 367). However, he occasionally questioned this dualism, saying: "The word 'projection' is not really appropriate, for nothing has been cast out of the psyche" (*CW* IX, i, 53). He came to reject the positivist view of projections as "nothing but" subjectivity. Throughout his work, Jung says that gods in themselves are beyond the grasp of human consciousness, but have real psychological, symbolic meanings that are important, not illusory.

After his 1944 near-death experience, Jung's mystical explorations into alchemy led him to see projections not as simply part of the subject-object metaphysic of empirical sciences. He saw projections as part of an ontologically deeper participation in the depths of existence. This was expressed in the paradoxical and obscure symbolic alchemical language that he translated. Here *proiectio* is part of the casting forth of the philosopher's stone (which is not a stone but a wisdom) into the banal world, which transforms it into a precious mystical treasure, including awakening to the *unus mudus* (one world), below its multiplicity. Jung agrees with projection theory's separation of inner from outer, but he is also compelled to describe the one world containing the collective unconscious, below the subject-object divide. This paradox of the one and the many and their relations is a deep mystery explored by philosophers since Plato. Jung enriched its psychological dimension.

The Jungian analyst Marie-Louise von Franz explored projection thoroughly in 1980. She shows the value of projection theory and touches on the difficulty of its subjectivism: "outward-material and inner-spiritual are only characteristic labels" (Von Franz, 1980). This theme makes projection less of a serious critique of religion. The archetypal psychologist Wolfgang Giegerich criticizes the theory of projection as the servant of physics, withdrawing soul and Being from its mechanistic framework.

Object-relations psychology expands projection theory with Melanie Klein's theory of introjection (the opposite of projection), the process of taking external images and reality into the inner world of the self.

The Netherlands

In the Netherlands after World War II, the study of projection theory was greatly expanded (but not translated from the Dutch) by several thoughtful scholars, notably Simon Vestdijk, Fokke Sierksma, and Han Fortmann (Bailey, 1988). Vestdijk and Fortmann, for example, both stressed that projection is not a psychological fact, but an explanatory hypothesis. In his 1947 *De Toekomst der Religie* (The Future of Religion) Vestdijk criticized absolute metaphysical religion as a projection, but argued for a mystical, introspective religion that withdraws projections in Buddhist fashion. The book evoked a storm of protest in Holland.

Fokke Sierksma's 1956 *De Religieuze Projectie* (Religious Projection) placed projection in a framework of a psychology of perception, taking it out of the theory of being a pathological defense. Han Fortmann, a phenomenologist of religion, influenced by Jung and Heidegger, dismantled the subjectivist philosophy underneath the theory of projection in his 1968 *Als Ziende de Onzienlijke* (As Seeing the Invisible). For him projection is not subjective interiority projected into an objective world, but participation in qualities in the lived world (*Lebenswelt*). Participation in the world, as in ritual, is not just primitive, delusory or infantile, but a normal way of being-in-the-world, as in Feuerbach's and Buber's I and Thou relations, Freud's "oceanic feeling," Jung's collective unconscious, Heidegger's ontology, Vestdijk's mysticism, and Sierksma's perceived world. There are no subjects, no objects, no projections, for these concepts are reified theories of the mechanical metaphysic. Thus a door to religion

in a new key is opened. The theory of "projection" is a useful tool in psychotherapy and religion to separate personal feelings from outer situations, but its philosophical foundations have been deepened enough to challenge its use in dismissing religions.

See also: ◉ Buber, Martin ◉ Collective Unconscious ◉ Freud, Sigmund ◉ Jung, Carl Gustav ◉ Object Relations Theory ◉ Plato and Religion ◉ Plato on the Soul

Bibliography

Alhazen. (1970). *Optics and the shape of the eclipse.* A.I. Sabra, "Ibn al-Haytham," in the *Dictionary of Scientific Biography,* VI, pp. 195–196.

Bacon, R. (1614). *Perspectiva.* Frankfurt: Richteri.

Bailey, L. W. (1983). Myths of projection. Doctoral dissertation, Syracuse University, Syracuse, New York.

Bailey, L. W. (1986). Skull's lantern: Psychological projection and the magic lantern. *Spring: A Journal of Archetypal Psychology and Jungian Thought,* 72–87.

Bailey, L. W. (1988). Religious projection: A new European tour. *Religious Studies Review, 14*(3) 207–211.

Bailey, L. W. (1989). Skull's Darkroom: The *Camera Obscura* and Objectivity. *Journal of Philosophy and Technology, 6,* 63–79.

Barnouw, E. (1981). *The magican and the cinema.* New York: Oxford University Press.

DaVinci, L. (c. 1490). Manuscript D; see Gernsheims, *Photography,* p. 19.

Descartes, R. (1913). "*La Dioptrique*," Discourse 5, *Oeuvres de Descartes* Paris: Vrin, VI: 81–228.

Feuerbach, L. (1841/1957). *The essence of Christianity* (G. Eliot, Trans.). New York: Harper & Row.

Fortmann, H. (1964–1968). *Als ziende de onzienlijke: een cultuur psychologische studie over de religieuze projectie* (4 vols. Rpt. in 2 vols). Hilversum Netherlands: Gooi en Sticht, 1974. [Faber, J. (1991). As seeing the invisible. Ann Arbor, MI: UMI, Books on Demand].

Freud, S. (1974). *The standard edition of the complete psychological works* (J. Strachey, Ed.) (24 vols.). London: Hogarth.

Gernsheim, H., & Gernsheim, A. (1969). The history of the Camera Obscura. In *The History of Photography.* New York: McGraw-Hill.

Giegerich, W. Der Spring nach dem Worf: Über das Einholen der Projektion und den Ursprung der Psychologie. *Gorgo, 1,* 49–71.

Huygens, C. *Oeuvres Completes.* Le Havre: Nijhoff, 188–1967, IV:102–111, 125, 197, 269. [Wagenaar, W. A. (1979). The True Inventor of the Magic Lantern. *Janus, 66,* 193–207].

Jung, C. G. (1953–1978). *The collected works of C. G. Jung* (R. F. C. Hull, Trans., W. McGuire, Ed.) (20 vols.). Princeton, NJ: Princeton University Press.

Kircher, A. (1646/1671). *Ars magna lucis et umbrae.* Book I, Magic, Part III (pp. 768–769). Rome and Amsterdam.

Kirk, G. S., & Raven, J. E. (Eds.). (1957). *The presocratic philosophers.* Cambridge, England: Cambridge University Press.

Locke, J. (1976). *Essay on human understanding* (J. Yolton, Ed.). New York: Dutton.

Plato. (1961). *The collected dialogues* (E. Hamilton & H. Cairns, Ed.). Princeton, NJ: Princeton University Press.

Sierksma, F. (1956). *Der religieuze projectie.* Delft: Gaade. [Faber, J. (1990). *Religious projection.* Ann Arbor, MI: UMI, Books on Demand].

Vestdijk, S. (1947). *De toekomst der religie.* Arnhem: Slaterus. [Faber, J. (1989). *The future of religion.* Ann Arbor, MI: UMI, Books on Demand].

Von Franz, M.-L. (1980). *Projection and re-collection in Jungian psychology* (W. Kennedy, Trans.). LaSalle, IL: Open Court.

Prophets

Miriam Dean-Otting

Eleventh-Ninth Century BCE

The most highly developed manifestation of prophetic activity in the Ancient Near East is to be found in the Hebrew Scriptures. In examining the words and actions of these ancient prophets one can discern many psychological factors that describe and explain prophetic behavior. These include possession, ecstatic behavior, altered consciousness, obsession or compulsion, having an unmediated relationship with the Divine, visionary experience and irrationality. For the earliest prophets we can begin with Abraham and Moses and conclude with Deborah, Samuel, Nathan, Elijah and Elisha. There is a single reference to Abraham as a prophet, "for he is a prophet and he will pray for you, and you shall live" (Genesis 20:7). According to Genesis 15 Abraham has an ecstatic experience, especially if the Greek translation (*exstasis*) of the Hebrew *tardemah* (deep sleep), is taken into consideration. The case of Moses warrants particular attention, both as a paradigm for other prophets, and as an anomaly: "Never since has there arisen a prophet in Israel like Moses – whom the Lord knew face to face" (Deuteronomy 34:10).

Each of the other prophets listed above is an example that contributes to a composite portrait of the eleventh–ninth century BCE prophets. For instance, Deborah, seated under a palm tree in the hills of Ephraim, functioned as a judge and advisor (Judges 4 and 5). Samuel was dedicated to the Lord and served in the Temple at Shiloh, where he was called to be a prophet (I Samuel 1–3). Saul is seized by a prophetic frenzy, caught up with the guild prophets (e.g., I Samuel 10:9). He also practices necromancy when he causes the medium of Endor to call up Samuel from the dead (I Samuel 28). David's court prophet, Nathan, condemned the actions of his king and employer. Questioning the authority of the ruler and advocating for the powerless, Nathan thus embodies two of the characteristics of the later Hebrew prophets (II Samuel 11–12). Elijah, "troubler of Israel" (I Kings 18:17), and Elisha, his heir, work magic, perform miracles and speak unwelcome truths to the kings of Israel. In addition, their ecstatic behavior is a model for the visionary experience of the prophets described next.

Eighth-Sixth Century BCE

Fifteen books in the Hebrew Scriptures are named after individuals, with Isaiah assigned to three distinct historical periods. In chronological order these book are Amos, Hosea, I Isaiah, Micah, Zephaniah, Nahum, Habakkuk, Jeremiah, Ezekiel, II Isaiah, Haggai, Zechariah, Malachi, III Isaiah, Obadiah, Joel, and the folktale of Jonah. There is a breadth of prophetic voice and a range of personalities and professions found in the prophetic canon. For instance, Amos claims to be simply a shepherd and a farmer: "I am no prophet, nor a prophet's son; but I am a herdsman, and a dresser of sycamore trees, and the Lord took me from following the flock, and the Lord said to me, 'Go, prophesy to my people Israel'" (Amos 7:14–15). Isaiah, on the other hand, is a priest in the Temple in Jerusalem, truly part of the institutional religion (Isaiah 6). Jeremiah laments and suffers abuse. Both Jeremiah and Ezekiel go into exile. Jonah sulks.

Characteristics of the Prophet

A prophet is not a fortuneteller, nor is the prophet particularly interested in the distant future, except in so far as it is influenced by actions taken in the present. In fact, the portrait of a prophet is rather complex. First of all a prophet must experience some kind of *calling*. In the biblical tradition this comes from God. This *calling awakens the prophet to injustice*, elicits both a feeling of *impending doom* and a *deep compassion for the oppressed*. *Drama and passion* energize the message of the prophet. The task is onerous and, thus, prophets frequently express *reluctance to accept the role*. Even so, a prophet is *compelled to speak* out and may seem, to others less sympathetic, to be a fanatic or zealot. In psychology we might deem this obsession. The prophet's words carry a clout that does not spare those responsible for the suffering of others. Yet it is important that the prophet's *perspective is rooted in a broad view of humanity*; she or he *must work for the good of all people*. Furthermore, a prophet must be *selfless* and *self-confident*, but also *provocative*. The prophet's *charisma* draws followers but, nevertheless, the prophet frequently experiences *loneliness*, and *may even be cast out*, for the message is one that few want to hear. Above all the prophet's message *challenges the status quo* and *questions the authority of those in power*. Prophetic arguments are *articulate* and *persuasive*, often *fueled by ecstatic behavior*, supported by *visions*, and voiced in *powerful poetic meter*. Finally, a prophet most often *rejects the designation* and, *never receives remuneration* for prophesying. Above all, prophets emphasize *justice, righteousness, humility* and *kindness*. A summary of these central concepts is voiced in Micah: "He has told you, O mortal, what is good; and what does the Lord require of you, but to do justice, love kindness and walk humbly with your God" (6:8).

Psychology of the Prophet

The prophet's relationship with the Divine, the prophetic call, ecstatic behavior, visions and poetry are all facets of what we might treat in any study of the psychology of the prophet. Passages from the texts of the classical Hebrew prophets illustrate these characteristics.

The prophet's relationship with God is profound, and often disturbing. "The lion has roared, who will not fear? The Lord has spoken, who can but prophesy? (Amos 3:8). A shocking example, even if it is only a metaphor, is the expectation that Hosea's life will mirror God's relationship with Israel: "Go, take for yourself a wife of whoredom, for the land commits great whoredom by forsaking the Lord" (Hosea 1:2). The central phrase *neum Adonai* ("Thus says the Lord"), repeated throughout the prophets, and many other metaphors leave no doubt that, according to the biblical perspective, the prophet is a vessel for God's words. This implies that prophet must lose sight of all personal needs and be subsumed in divine expectations.

Most prophets experience a call, but the circumstances vary considerably. For instance, Isaiah encounters a numinous vision of God in the Temple in Jerusalem, his lips are seared and purified by a burning coal born by a fantastic creature, and he is forewarned that the people will turn a tin ear to his prophecy (Isaiah 6). Jonah responds to his call by fleeing in the other direction (Jonah 1), a radical and physical denial of the call. Jeremiah is summoned as a youth, and learns that he had been appointed a prophet even before he was born. He depicts his call as a physical gesture, "Then the Lord put out his hand and touched my mouth; and the Lord said to me, 'Now I have put my words in your mouth'" (Jeremiah 1:9).

Often ecstatic behavior precedes the voicing of the prophetic message and this is where we can point to a kind of possession, what might be called, in psychological terms, an "altered consciousness." "As for me, I am filled with power, with the spirit of the Lord, and with justice and might" (Micah 3:8). Jeremiah echoes a metaphor common in the prophets, the swallowing of God's words: "Your words were found, and I ate them, and your words became a joy and the delight of my heart; for I am called by your name, O Lord, God of hosts" (Jeremiah 1:16). Significantly, he denies that he has used wine to evoke this state: "I did not sit in the company of merrymakers, nor did I rejoice; under the weight of your hand I sat alone for you filled me with indignation" (1:17). Several psychological states of mind, that might be called "unbalanced," irrationality, enthusiasm, possession, in sum, a variety of states of altered consciousness, activate prophetic speech. The words of the prophets are met with utmost seriousness, whether out of fear or reverence. Ecstatic behavior, then, enhances rather than diminishes the power of the message.

Out of ecstasy come visions, and prophetic texts are rife with revelations of both wrath and restoration. Perhaps the most well known is Ezekiel's colorful vision of the fiery chariot (Ezekiel 1), but plenty of visions are more mundane by comparison. Everyday objects might become catalysts for vital lessons, such as when Jeremiah visits the potter's house and watches as the potter reshapes a spoiled vessel. This sight is understood symbolically as an indication of God's intention to break down and rebuild the people Israel (Jeremiah 18:1–12). For Joel armies of locusts, surely observed in times of natural disaster, become signs of invading armies (Joel 1). Visions reveal much about the environment of ancient Israel, and demonstrate the practice of the prophets to be out and about, in the marketplace, at sacred centers, at the city gates and walking the streets, anywhere where people are gathered, so that an audience is always at hand.

Many of the passages cited in these samples are rendered in the meter of Hebrew poetry, an aspect of biblical prophecy that lends the prophetic words dignity and elegance. It is poetry that allows the prophet to ascribe to God both the power of a warrior and the empathy of a laboring woman: "The Lord goes forth like a soldier, like a warrior he stirs up his fury; he cries out, he shouts aloud, he shows himself mighty against his foes. For a long time I have held my peace, I have kept still and restrained myself; now I will cry out like a woman in labor, I will gasp and pant" (Isaiah 42:13–14). Hebrew poetic lamentation meter enhances the grief already inherent in Amos' words: "Fallen no more to rise is maiden Israel; forsaken on her land, with no one to raise her up" (Amos 5:2).

Questions have been raised about whether prophetic possession should be described as a kind of neurosis or madness. Clearly prophetic behaviors are not average or muted in any way. For instance, some assert that Hosea's willingness to marry a prostitute, as a concrete symbol of Israel's rejection of God, was indicative of his madness. Isaiah's walking naked for three years to call attention to the captivity of the Assyrian king could indicate some exhibitionism. But this is mere speculation at a distance of well over 2000 years and is, perhaps, not so instructive. At most it seems that we can only point to some marginal behaviors in addition to the characteristics of possession, ecstatic behavior, altered consciousness, obsession or compulsion, having an unmediated relationship with the Divine, visionary experience and irrationality outlined above.

See also: ❯ Bible ❯ Biblical Psychology

Bibliography

Meeks, W. A. (Ed.). (1993). *The Harper-Collins Study Bible*. New York: Harper Collins Publisher.

Protestantism

Jaco J. Hamman

Protestantism is a general term describing a third main form of Christianity alongside Roman Catholicism and Orthodox Christianity. It originated in the sixteenth century when in 1529 German princes presented a *Protestatio* or letter of protest against the Catholic Church's prohibition on innovation in the field of religion. This act by the "Protestants" – later also called "Evangelicals" – initiated a movement called the Christian Reformation asking "Who is the true and holy church?"

Despite holding worldviews ranging from open and liberal to nationalist conservative and even fundamentalist, Protestantism is most often characterized by: proclaiming that all glory belongs to God (*soli Deo Gloria*); salvation is by grace alone (*sola gratia*); the centrality of the spoken and written Word (*sola Scriptura*); freedom and independence; truth and the church are ever evolving; baptism and communion as the only sacraments; and, placing a person's relationship with God above allegiance to the church. These traits can be summarized as: only grace, faith, and Scripture should govern life inside and outside the church. The church, therefore, is not the carrier of grace and salvation. In light of this belief, baptized believers are called, through the priesthood of all believers, to be instruments of grace and salvation empowered by God's Spirit.

A strength of Protestantism is its critical nature, but the same orientation has created lack of unity in dogma and institutional structure. After nearly 500 years of experiencing schisms and internal conflict over doctrinal issues such as infant or adult baptism and the nature of Holy Communion, Protestantism incorporates many different traditions. There traditions have a unique character as they developed around spiritual leaders in a specific social context. Groups include: Anglican (Episcopal), Congregationalist, Lutheran, Methodist (including the Salvation Army), Reformed (Calvinist/Presbyterian), Waldensian, Zwinglian, and also Baptist, Anabaptist (Mennonite, Brethren), and charismatic Pentecostal Protestants. Most of these groups experience secularization, loss of church membership, and internal struggles. The cultural and doctrinal diversity within Protestantism is best expressed in numerous confessions of faith. Traditionally an Anglo-Saxon faith, forms of Protestantism are growing rapidly in the developing world (African Independent Churches; South America) and in Asia (especially South Korea) due to Protestantism's missionary fervor.

Protestantism's general orientation to critical distinction rather than synthesis impacts its relationship with psychology. Yet Protestantism's search for truth brings interdisciplinary exploration. Protestants engage in *critical evaluation or correlation* of psychological theories and use whatever is deemed compatible with their worldview. Others engage in *theory building*, reworking psychological theories, especially cognitive theories, according to Protestant presuppositions. Some seek a *dialectical* approach, holding the tension between two diverse disciplines. Others yet argue that postmodern rationality, refusing objective truth, allows different disciplines to speak into each other's world without losing unique identities. Protestants also use psychology as a lens through which to read Scripture.

One goal that Protestants and psychology share is seeking ways to facilitate the good life. Typical topics of contention Protestantism has with psychology, however, are: wholeness found through a personal relationship with Jesus; Scripture as a special revelation; the problem of suffering; the reality of evil and sin; what it means to be a human being; and how truth is defined. Protestantism can inform psychology on the human spirit's search for meaning around ultimate concerns. Psychology, in turn, can educate Evangelicals on the depths of an embodied existence. In dialog, mutual illumination is possible around concerns such as models of personhood, disease and health, individuality and community, and how transformation occurs.

See also: ⊗ Baptism ⊗ Biblical Psychology ⊗ Calvinism ⊗ Christianity ⊗ Evangelical ⊗ Fundamentalism ⊗ Grace ⊗ Luther, Martin ⊗ Meaning of Human Existence ⊗ Original Sin ⊗ Religion

Bibliography

Browning, D. S. (1987). *Religious thought and the modern psychologies: A critical conversation in the theology of culture*. Philadelphia, PA: Fortress Press.

Carroll, A. J. (2007). *Protestant modernity: Weber, secularization, and Protestantism*. Scranton, PA: University of Scranton Press.

Eppehimer, T. (2007). *Protestantism*. New York: Marshall Cavendish Benchmark.

Griffith, R. M. (2004). *Born again bodies: Flesh and spirit in American Christianity*. Berkeley, CA: University of California Press.

Guntrip, H. (1957). *Psychotherapy and religion*. New York: Harper.

Harrison, P. (1998). *The Bible, protestantism, and the rise of natural science*. Cambridge, MA: Cambridge University Press.

Holifield, E. B. (1987). *A history of pastoral care in America: From Salvation to self-realization*. Nashville, TN: Abingdon Press.

Hunsinger, D. V. D. (1995). *Theology and pastoral counseling: A new interdisciplinary approach*. Grand Rapids, MI: Eerdmans.

Jones, J. W. (1991). *Contemporary psychoanalysis and religion: Transference and transcendence*. New Haven, CT: Yale University Press.

Jonte-Pace, D., & Parsons, W., B. (2001). *Religion and psychology: Mapping the terrain*. New York: Routledge.

Malony, H. N. (1995). *The psychology of religion for ministry*. New York: Paulist Press.

McGrath, A. E. (2007). *Christianity's dangerous idea: The Protestant revolution – a history from the sixteenth century to the twenty-first* (1st ed.). New York: HarperOne.

McMinn, M. R., & Campbell, C. D. (2007). *Integrative psychotherapy: Toward a comprehensive Christian approach*. Downers Grove, IL: InterVarsity Press.

Oates, W. E. (1962). *Protestant pastoral counseling*. Philadelphia, PA: Westminster Press.

Oates, W. E. (1973). *The psychology of religion*. Waco, TX: Word Books.

Pearce, J. C. (2007). *The death of religion and the rebirth of spirit: A return to the intelligence of the heart*. Rochester, MN: Park Street Press.

Pruyser, P. W. (1968). *A dynamic psychology of religion*. New York: Harper & Row.

Pruyser, P. W. (1991). *Religion in psychodynamic perspective: The contributions of Paul W. Pruyser*. New York: Oxford University Press.

Shults, F. L., & Sandage, S. J. (2006). *Transforming spirituality: Integrating theology and psychology*. Grand Rapids, MI: Baker Academic.

Watts, F. (2002). *Theology and psychology*. Aldershot: Ashgate.

Providence

David M. Moss III

This is a critical theological term of profound psychological significance. Providence refers to God's creative and sustaining care of the universe. In the Judaeo-Christian tradition it identifies events or circumstances of divine interposition. It also signifies revelation through insight.

In 400 BC Greek philosophers used the word *prónoia* to describe a power which rationally guides the world and human destiny by a fixed set of natural laws. This became a dogma of Stoicism. It also bears points of contact with the biblical idea of the Creator being directly involved with creation. The Old Testament records a gradual development of the *belief* in providence. Nevertheless, the Hebrew scriptures reveal a dynamic theme: God guides history in such a way that independent and free human actions are not annulled. Unlike the impersonal Stoic concept, this conception requires the Creator's intimate involvement with humanity. The New Testament develops this view but not as a theoretical explanation. It is an eschatological perspective, inherently implied far more than explicitly mentioned. The incarnation was providence personified.

Early patristic literature was strongly influenced by Greek philosophy, particularly cosmology. Clement of Alexandria (c. 150–215) best expressed the synonymous relationship of God and providence. Conversely, he contended that the denial of providence was to be equated with atheism. The Church Fathers also explored the biblical idea of freedom with responsibility under God's provision. During the Middle Ages, the Scholastic theologians set forth philosophical speculations about the nature and meaning of providence. Inspired by Augustine of Hippo (354–430), Thomas Aquinas (1224–1274) produced a penetrating examination of this belief. Subsequently, the Council of Trent (1545–1563) designated providence as a *doctrine* of the Church. However, the Reformation was already underway. This represented a break with Catholic intellectualism. Reason was not dismissed but experience was elevated to a primary importance. The Reformers also presented new views about providence. Their writings no longer centered on an explanation of the universe, but in realizations of *faith* and practical living. John Calvin's (1509–1564) teaching on predestination was exceptionally controversial. In his theological system providence was restricted and free will was restrained. Popular expressions of the Protestant belief in providence were published chiefly in devotional literature and hymns. In the eighteenth century scholars of the Enlightenment viewed providence from a more rationalistic position. As a result, this dimension of reality became the fulcrum of Natural Theology. G. W. Leibniz (1646–1716) described providence as the rational and meaningful order of human history and the cosmos.

Systematic explanations of providence eventually raise problems of theodicy, questions about the goodness and fairness of God given the evil and suffering in creation. Pastoral theology emphasizes the ascendancy of the former over the latter. Consequently, providence is the basic source of hope for human development. In the twentieth century this belief was reemphasized by the growth of pastoral counseling as a specialized ministry. From such a therapeutic perspective, providence can be defined as an *awareness* that out of every unfortunate experience, as long as one chooses to look with insight, beneficial results will be revealed.

See also: ❷ Augustine ❷ Incarnation

Bibliography

Gilkey, L. (1976). *Reaping the worldwind: A Christian interpretation of history*. New York: Seabury.
Hodgson, P. (1989). *God in history: Shapes of freedom*. Nashville, TN: Abingdon.
Scheffczy, L. (1970). *Creation and providence*. New York: Herder & Herder.
Tillich, P. (1951). *Systematic theology* (Vol. 1). Chicago, IL: University of Chicago Press.

Pruyser, Paul

Nathan Carlin

Paul W. Pruyser (1916–1987) was a clinical psychologist who, especially by means of his prolific writing, contributed greatly to the psychology of religion while working at the Menninger Clinic in Topeka, Kansas (now located in Houston, Texas). His monographs include *A Dynamic Psychology of Religion* (1968), *Between Belief and Unbelief* (1974), *The Psychological Examination* (1979), and *The Play of the Imagination* (1983). He edited *Diagnosis and the Difference it Makes* (1976b) and *Changing Views of the Human Condition* (1987). And, with Karl Menninger and Martin Mayman, he wrote *The Vital Balance* (1963). In addition to these books, he also wrote some 30 book chapters and 80 journal articles. Pruyser also contributed to the field of psychology of religion by serving as President of the Society for the Scientific Study of Religion and by serving on the editorial boards for *The Journal for the Scientific Study of Religion* and *Pastoral Psychology*.

Pruyser and the Menninger Clinic

Pruyser moved to Topeka, Kansas in 1954 to work in the Topeka State Hospital. He joined the staff of the Menninger Clinic in 1956 and worked there until his death. He developed a close relationship with Karl Menninger, founder of the Menninger Clinic. Karl was psychoanalyzed by Franz Alexander and received the first psychoanalytic certificate from the training institute in Chicago (Wallerstein, 2007). At Menninger, Pruyser rose through the ranks – but never to the very top, because he was "a psychologist among psychiatrists" – and eventually participated in "the palace revolt" that removed Karl from power in his own institution, a revolt that Karl believed had affinities to Freud's (1913/2001) *Totem and Taboo*. Nevertheless, Pruyser still viewed Karl as a father figure, perhaps because Pruyser's own father had died at a young age. Pruyser wrote Karl these words in 1971: I hope you would "appraise the last ten years as a period in which I have not only kept your great heritage, but nurtured, fostered and expanded it" (Friedman, 1990: 324). In any case, after the overthrow, Pruyser developed a facial tic and aged "precipitately," perhaps an indication of Pruyser's guilt and a testimony to Karl's interpretation of the overthrow (1990: 324). In the political struggles that followed, Pruyser was able "to retain a significant position," but he was eventually pressured into resigning from his position as Education Department director, then to assume the post of resident teacher-scholar (1990: 338).

Pruyser's Contributions to Psychology of Religion

Pruyser's contributions to the psychology of religion are sadly overlooked today. Sometimes Ana-Maria Rizzuto is thought to be the first person to have brought the ideas of D. W. Winnicott, a major proponent of a British appropriation of psychoanalysis known as object relations theory, to the psychoanalytic study of religion, as she does in her classic *The Birth of a Living God*, published in 1979.

However, Pruyser (1974) had already done so in his *Between Belief and Unbelief* (cf. Hamman, 2000: 137–138). A few major points that Pruyser makes in this book – insights that are still valuable today – include: (1) "it is implied in Freud's approach to religion that many forms of unbelief can be at the same developmental level as belief itself" (1974: 61); (2) "unbelief can be just as primitive, neurotic and drive-determined as belief" (1974: 61); and (3) "[i]f belief is personal, so is unbelief" (1974: 65). While Pruyser, following Freud, did see religion as an illusion, he did not, as opposed to Freud, view illusion or religion pejoratively. Using Winnicott's notion of illusion – which departed greatly from Freud's usage (cf. Jones, 1991: 38ff.) – Pruyser viewed illusion as something deeply positive, transformative, and creative.

But this is not to say that Pruyser uncritically or simplistically accepted religion. While he served as an elder in the Presbyterian Church, he stopped going to church services in his later years, apparently because he was unsatisfied with such services. He also held the view that "much of the force of current religion comes from the persistence of irrationality in both culture and our individual lives" (Spilka and Malony, 1991: 14). Jansje Pruyser, his wife, once described her late husband as a "rebel" in an interview with H. Newton Malony and Bernard Spilka, two other leading scholars in the psychology of religion. They added, "Indeed he was a rebel, but not one who was strident, noisy, or bellicose. . . . He had the rare knack of propounding controversial and iconoclastic ideas in a manner that might elicit disagreement but never hostility" (Spilka and Malony, 1991: 3). And so Pruyser was a man who struggled deeply with matters of faith and reason, matters of subjectivity and objectivity, matters of the inner and the outer worlds. And the way in which he could stand by his own idiosyncratic faith was by means of a middle way, a way inspired by Winnicott's psychology, a way, finally, that enabled him to make his own faith real to him.

Pruyser and Practical Theology

In addition to writing for the field of psychology of religion, Pruyser also wrote for pastors, including works such as *The Minister as Diagnostician* (1976a) and an important essay in *The Journal of Pastoral Care* (now called *The Journal of Pastoral Care and Counseling*) titled "Religion in the Psychiatric Hospital" (1984). Both of these works call pastors to bring the tools that are unique to their trade – especially theology – when dealing with people's problems.

Pruyser's work has influenced many thinkers in the field of psychology of religion. H. Newton Malony and Bernard Spilka (1991), themselves significant contributors in the psychology of religion, edited a volume of Pruyser's work and dedicated it to his wife. Pruyser also greatly influenced Princeton Seminary's Donald Capps, the most prolific writer in the fields of psychology of religion and pastoral care today. Princeton Seminary had tried to recruit Pruyser to teach in their practical theology department, but he declined the offer and instead recommended to the President that they hire Capps. And so Pruyser's influence still lives on in the work of Capps (2001) and his protégés, notably in the eloquent writing and preaching of Robert Dykstra (2001, 2005).

See also: ❂ Freud, Sigmund ❂ Winnicott, Donald Woods

Bibliography

Capps, D. (2001). *Agents of hope: A pastoral psychology*. Eugene, OR: Wipf and Stock Publishers.

Dykstra, R. (2001). *Discovering a sermon: Personal pastoral preaching*. St. Louis, MI: Chalice Press.

Dykstra, R. (2005). *Images of pastoral care: Classic readings*. St. Louis, MI: Chalice Press.

Freud, S. (1913/2001). Totem and taboo. In J. Strachey (Ed. & Trans.), *The standard edition of the complete psychological works of Sigmund Freud* (Vol. 13, pp. 1–162). London: Vintage.

Friedman, L. (1990). *Menninger: The family and the clinic*. New York: Alfred A. Knopf.

Hamman, J. (2000). *The restoration of Job: A study based on D. W. Winnicott's theory of object usage and its significance for pastoral theology*. Unpublished doctoral dissertation, Princeton Theological Seminary, Princeton, NJ.

Jones, J. (1991). *Contemporary psychoanalysis and religion: Transference and transcendence*. New Haven, CT: Yale University Press.

Menninger, K., Mayman, M., & Pruyser, P. (1963). *The vital balance*. New York: Viking Press.

Pruyser, P. (1968). *A dynamic psychology of religion*. New York: Harper & Row.

Pruyser, P. (1974). *Between belief and unbelief*. New York: Harper & Row.

Pruyser, P. (1976a). *The minister as diagnostician: Personal problems in pastoral perspective*. Philadelphia, PA: Westminster Press.

Pruyser, P. (1976b). *Diagnosis and the difference it makes*. New York: Aronson.

Pruyser, P. (1979). *The psychological examination: A guide for clinicians*. New York: International Universities Press.

Pruyser, P. (1983). *The play of the imagination: Towards a psychoanalysis of culture*. New York: International Universities Press.

Pruyser, P. (1987). *Changing views of the human condition*. Macon, GA: Mercer University Press.

Pruyser, P. W. (1984). Religion in the psychiatric hospital: A reassessment. *Journal of Pastoral Care*, 38(1), 5–16.

Rizzuto, A. (1979). *The birth of a living God: A psychoanalytic study*. Chicago, IL: University of Chicago Press.

Spilka, B., & Malony, H. N. (1991). *Religion in psychodynamic perspective: The contributions of Paul W. Pruyser.* New York: Oxford University Press.

Wallerstein, R. (2007). Karl Menninger, M.D.: A personal perspective. *American Imago, 64*(2), 213–228.

Psalms

Ingeborg del Rosario

The Book of Psalms, also known by its traditional Hebrew title *tehillim* (praises), belongs to the Wisdom literature of the Hebrew Scriptures and the Old Testament of the Christian canon. Comprising 150 individual psalms (from the Greek word *psalmoi* or songs sung to a harp), the Book of Psalms is both the longest and most varied in tone, content and message of its individual religious lyrical poems. While authorship of the psalms is attributed to King David, biblical scholars note that the period of their composition spanned half a millennium (c. 1000 BCE–c. 500 BCE) and its compilation most likely took place after the end of the Babylonian captivity (c. 537 BCE), with reference to the Book of Psalms as an entity around the first century AD, in the New Testament books of the Gospel of Luke (20:42) and the Acts of the Apostles (1:20). The psalms have been classified under different genres, such as praise, thanksgiving, supplication psalms, individual and communal lament psalms, songs of trust and confidence, pilgrimage, historical, wisdom or instructional psalms, royal and messianic psalms, and temple or liturgical songs; however, these distinctions do not take into account the psalms' fluidity of message and intent. Walter Brueggemann, an Old Testament scholar, has proposed taking the Book of Psalms in its entirety and organizing them under three themes: orientation, disorientation and reorientation. This thematic organization of the psalms supports the wholistic understanding that human life and ordinary experience, along with one's faith life and relationship with the Divine are not about the occurrence of single events but are taken within the process and flow of an unfolding and ever evolving complex life journey.

What is commonly recognized is that the Book of Psalms reflects themes universal to human life and experience as well as particular to the divine-human relationship: creation, destruction and transformation; death and life; suffering and relief; good and evil; sin and contrition; repentance and forgiveness; justice and judgment; war and triumph; injustice and loss; betrayal and vengeance; wisdom and worship; darkness and light. Many believers of both the Jewish and Christian traditions cyclically recite or sing the entire Book of Psalms, thus acknowledging how its prayers embrace and encompass the totality of human reality, how they mirror the diversity of life's facets and textures.

There are psalms and verses favored and held in memory to bring comfort and courage, strength and hope, such as Psalm 8 ("When I consider your heavens, the work of your fingers, the moon and the stars, which you have set in place; what are human beings that you are mindful of them, mortals that you care for them?"); Psalm 23 ("The Lord is my shepherd, I shall not be in want"); Psalm 51 ("Have mercy on me, God, according to your unfailing love; according to your great compassion, blot out my transgressions. Wash away all my iniquity and cleanse me from my sin"); Psalm 63 ("O God, you are my God, earnestly I seek you, my soul thirsts for you; my body longs for you, in a dry and weary land where there is no water"); Psalm 121 ("I lift up my eyes to the hills – where does my help come from? My help comes from the Lord, the maker of heaven and earth"); Psalm 127 ("Unless the Lord builds the house, its builders labor in vain"); and Psalm 139 ("O Lord, you have searched me and you know me").

The lament psalms, which make up more than a third of the book's composition, are given less focus and attention in individual prayer and liturgical worship. While the Book of Psalms mirrors all of humanness and life, the lament psalms (3, 5–7, 9, 10, 12, 13, 17, 22, 25–28, 31, 35, 38, 39, 41–44, 51, 52, 54–57, 59–61, 63, 64, 69–71, 74, 79, 80, 82, 83, 85, 86, 88, 90, 94,102, 106, 108, 109, 120, 123, 126, 130, 137, 140–143) are particularly about life assailed by suffering and pain, brokenness and dislocation, anguish and affliction. All have some experience of betrayal, rejection and abandonment, illness and death of a loved one, emotional and relational conflicts, crisis and powerlessness, oppression or abuse, even trauma. In them, the encounter with emotions of fear and terror, anxiety and bewilderment, loneliness and despair, grief and sadness, anger and resentment, rage and hatred is palpable.

In the human search for words with which to speak of experiences of disruption and express vital emotions, the lament psalms provide speech and language that reverberate through centuries and are relevant across cultures. The psalms provide vivid imagery, provocative metaphor, piercing, pointed words, offering a way of expression that resonates with the ache and agony accompanying the tearing and breaking of every human heart.

The lament psalms provide voice to speak of the pain, from the pain. In and through the psalms, one may give vent to the most intense hurt, the deepest rage, the most profound grief with words that are neither meek nor polite but are bold and direct, harsh and biting, cutting and honest, at times brutally frank.

Lament psalms also contain imprecatory verses, those that invoke curses of violence and vengeance. The Christian Psalter excludes these verses, setting them off in bracketed form. Ordinarily, they are not recited or sung in communal prayer nor are they used in liturgical readings and rites. Some examples of these verses are: Psalm 3: "Deliver me, O my God! Strike all my enemies on the jaw; break the teeth of the wicked"; Psalm 11: "On the wicked he will rain fiery coals and burning sulfur; a scorching wind will be their lot"; Psalm 69: "May their eyes be darkened so they cannot see, and their backs be bent forever. Pour out your wrath on them; let your fierce anger overtake them. May their place be deserted, let there be no one to dwell in their tent... May they be blotted out of the book of life and not be listed with the righteous"; Psalm 137: "O Daughter of Babylon, doomed to destruction, happy is he who repays you for what you have done to us – he who seizes your infants and dashes them against the rocks"; and, perhaps the most detailed and elaborate of the imprecatory psalms, Psalm 109: "May his days be few... may his children be fatherless and his wife a widow. May his children be wandering beggars; may they be driven from their ruined homes. May a creditor seize all he has; may strangers plunder the fruits of his labor. May no one extend kindness to him or take pity on his fatherless children. May his descendants be cut off, their names blotted out from the next generation. May the iniquity of his fathers be remembered before the Lord; may the sin of his mother never be blotted out... He wore cursing as his garment; it entered into his body like water, into his bones like oil. May it be like a cloak wrapped about him, like a belt tied forever around him."

Many individuals in psychotherapy struggle with allowing themselves the space, freedom and spontaneity to enter into and express emotions that accompany their wrenching stories. They might speak of their sufferings from the outside, looking in, rather than speak from the heart of their suffering. They might talk about their feelings rather than talk from the depth of these feelings. Some patients profess not to have the words and the language with which to identify and distinguish their feelings of grief, anger, fear, rejection and humiliation. Others are unable to give voice to emotion for fear these feelings might intensify and overpower, leaving them out of control. One resists giving in to her grief for fear she might never stop weeping once she begins. Another resists giving voice to his anger for fear he might become violent and unmanageable. Because of the fear of feeling, patients will split-off from these emotions and disavow their presence. Ironically, when emotions are banished from the space of conscious awareness and dissociated, when they are unsymbolized, unrecognized and unarticulated, they gather greater energy, power and force in the shadows of unconsciousness than they would have in being given space and voice to be put into words, heard, held and contained in speech and language. Just as the imprecatory verses are excluded from the Christian liturgy and Psalter, so too are the urges for violence and vengeance left unspoken. When fragmented from consciousness, this powerful energy of hatred, rage and aggression becomes manifest in relational enactments. Cut-off from this vital force, one is unable to fully connect with the totality of all that is human, unable to take in shadow experiences and emotions whose release into the light of consciousness and verbal expression permit a full experiencing of all that is authentic and real.

Patients may be helped to discover emotional speech and language, to identify and distinguish, to give voice and words to the mélange of sensations and feelings that can seem chaotic. A therapeutic relationship that provides emotional safety and consistency allows patients to become more secure in the capacity to acknowledge, engage and befriend the expansive range of their inner life without fear of being overwhelmed. As with the God of the psalms who receives profound angst and the most vicious urges in the lament, no part of life need ever be beyond speech or conversation in the therapeutic space. For the psychoanalyst who has undergone intensive personal analysis, an internal space opens to hold and contain more of the patient's deepest experiences and emotions, to enable a total presence to courageous efforts to encounter and put into words whatever feelings might emerge, be they anger and rage, envy and jealousy, hatred and wrath, shame and guilt, or kindness and tenderness. For the patient to engage and be present to the immediacy of the experience of the inner world, the analyst must be in this immediacy, with a fullness of presence. For patients to feel greater ease and comfort with their aggression, the analyst must be capable of receiving, holding and containing the power and energy of this verbalized force without censure, judgment or condemnation. As in the psalms, with even the imprecatory verses, everything that can be said may be said in the safety of the analytic space. Before the analyst who holds her own experiences and emotions, the patient need not be nice, well mannered, meek or polite. The patient need only be as the self presents and is present to self, with a growing range of experiences and their accompanying emotions being given voice.

The Book of Psalms acknowledges that pain and suffering are an intrinsic part of life. That the lament psalms significantly comprise the Book of Psalms emphasizes that one must deal with chaos, disruption and disorientation, the agony and anguish of life's difficulties not by denying, ignoring or minimizing their presence in life nor by splitting them off, shunning this darker and seemingly less tolerable aspect of oneself by relegating their emotional impact to unconsciousness. The Book of Psalms offers voice and language with which to speak and entrust the depth and breadth of fear, frustration, rage, grief, despair, bitterness, meanness, spite and desire for vengeance. It provides a way to give expression to these experiences and emotions with powerful yet finite, containable words, rather than by impulsive, destructive activity. The therapeutic process shares this way of the Book of Psalms in the acknowledgment of the need for language that is forthright, for containment and verbalization in words that are honest, in the moving through intense emotions which enables a delving into the meaning and depths of one's humanity and the dark corners of one's humanness. These processes awaken the possibility and potential for metabolizing and transforming the energy and power of such emotions and experiences. In the sacred space held by the Book of Psalms echoed in the therapeutic space come a gentle reorientation of life-meaning, a more profound connection with self and with all who partake and share in the universality of lived humanness and reality, and a more profound awakening to the freedom, receptivity and compassion of God who hears, welcomes and holds all, spoken, unspoken and unspeakable, in the Divine lyrical embrace.

See also: ❂ Affect ❂ Bible ❂ Defenses ❂ Dissociation ❂ Feeling ❂ Psychotherapy ❂ Trauma ❂ Unconscious

Bibliography

Alter, R. (2007). *The book of psalms: A translation with commentary*. New York: W. W. Norton & Company.

Brueggemann, W. (1984). *The message of the psalms: A theological commentary*. Minneapolis: Augsburg Press.

Del Rosario, I. (1997). At evening, morning and noon I will cry and lament: Praying our distress. *Conversatio, 28*(10), 3–22.

The Holy Bible: New International Version (2005). Grand Rapids, MI: The Zondervan Corporation.

Psyche

M. J. Drake Spaeth

Psyche, the ancient Greek word meaning "soul" or "spirit," is also the name of the Greek goddess of the Soul, one of whose symbols is the butterfly. The term was employed by Sigmund Freud to describe the unity of unconscious and conscious, the tripartite structure of the mind divided into Id (i.e., the repository of unconscious drives and wishes that determine our conscious behaviors); Super-Ego (i.e., the repository of superconscious extreme moralistic elements that compensate for the opposite extremes of the id); and the Ego (i.e., the conscious referee between the dichotomous ongoing conflict between id and superego). It was also adopted by Freud's student Carl Jung to encompass the mind and its evolving, developing relationship with the world over the course of life, manifest in the individuation of the Self from the more limited ego (Jung, 1978).

The concept of psyche links psychology and spirituality in several ways. In the Greek myth of the goddess Psyche, a human woman becomes elevated to the status of a goddess through her tumultuous relationship with Eros, the god of Love. She at first loses Eros through the machinations of his mother Aphrodite and later is restored to him through the intervention of Zeus, king of the Gods. Symbolically, this myth illustrates how the human spirit/soul is elevated and ultimately transformed through the vicissitudes love, and how sexuality and spirituality spring from the same libidinal source – a connection recognized by Freud in his theory of psychosexual development. In Jungian terms, the myth calls to mind the unity of anima (the feminine aspect of the psyche) and animus (the masculine aspect of the psyche), the Hierosgamos (i.e., the sacred marriage of opposites) in the quest of the ego to become the Self. Moreover, the butterfly aspect of Psyche evokes the image of the caterpillar building and ultimate discarding the cocoon, which it sheds upon its transformation into a butterfly. This image brings to mind Platonic dualism – in which the soul or spirit sheds the outer physical flesh in death, flying free – an idea that is still found in many religious traditions throughout the world. Ulanov and Ulanov (1991) point out that Jung regarded Psyche as the "mother of consciousness" – that which joins with the father that is spirit (p. 12), effectively linking Christian ideology with the older Greek images described above.

See also: ❂ Anima and Animus ❂ Cupid and Psyche ❂ Drives ❂ Ego ❂ Eros ❂ Freud, Sigmund ❂ Hierosgamos ❂ Id ❂ Jung, Carl Gustav ❂ Jungian Self ❂ Self ❂ Super-Ego

Bibliography

Jung, C. G. (1978). *Aion: Researches into the phenomenology of the self.* Princeton, NJ: Princeton University Press.
Ulanov, A., & Ulanov. B. (1991). *The healing imagination: The meeting of psyche and spirit.* Canada: Daimon Verlag.

Psychiatry

Kelley Raab Mayo

Introduction

Psychiatry and religion have had a complicated, at times collaborative and at times competitive, relationship over their respective histories. Since the earliest days of Western medicine, scientifically-trained physicians have recognized that religion and spirituality can affect the mind for both good and ill. Historically regarded as the first spiritual healer, the shaman is a prototype of the modern physician and psychotherapist. Prior to the fall of the Roman Empire and the growth of the Catholic Church, priests and physicians were often the same individuals in different civilizations around the world.

For all cultures, it has been a long journey to look for natural rather than supernatural explanations for mental illness. Ancient Jews seemed to have viewed madness in both natural and supernatural terms. Most Christian thinkers saw no inherent contradiction between a medical view of madness and a Christian view. Islam has a long tradition of compassion for those who were labeled mad. On the other hand, religions of Asia and Africa tended to fuse ideas of madness and demonic possession. Enlightened views on the mentally ill were found in early Christian hospitals, by Buddhist missionaries, Confucian scholars, medieval Jewish physicians, and in the Islamic hospitals of the Middle Ages. However, many societies later reverted to unscientific and at times inhumane practices. These were epitomized in the medieval Christian Inquisition, where mentally ill individuals, accused of being possessed by the devil, were put to death as witches.

Background: Science Versus Religion

Fundamental controversies between science and religion laid the groundwork for the modern origin of the antagonism between psychiatry and religion. Concerning psychiatry, a number of prejudices have stood in the way of a closer relationship with religion: the view that religions attract the mentally unstable, that religions may have their origins in madness, that religious experience is phenomenologically similar to psychopathology, that paranormal experiences are a product of definable patterns of brain functioning, that religions are harmful – inducing guilt – or that religious belief is ineffective. Research has proven these prejudices false.

Deeper reasons for the separation between psychiatry and religion have to do with the identification of psychiatry with the "medical" model. As a science, psychiatry is assumed to be based on observation and experiment and in principle open to objective testing. Religion, on the other hand, is said to be "revealed." Psychiatry employs an essentially deterministic model, whereas religion assumes freedom of action. Yet the separation between science and religion is perhaps a peculiarly Western phenomenon.

During the early years of the twentieth century, psychiatry in the US and Europe underwent a number of changes, most notable an increasing focus on social progress and general societal welfare. In addition to an evolving body of literature on psychoanalysis, other forces that shaped the field included new religious movements such as New Thought, Christian Science, theosophy, and spiritualism, as well as the growing social marginalization of fundamentalism. Moreover, in terms of diagnosis psychiatry began moving away from classifications based on course and prognosis of disease. Specifically, "religious insanity" or "religious mania" – diagnoses based on the content of a delusion – became irrelevant to classification and treatment.

Influence of Freud

Although the notion of religious insanity faded with the coming of twentieth century psychiatry, it lived on in some form in the ideas of Sigmund Freud. Challenging the notion that truth can be found in religion, Freud viewed religious faith as based in the illusion of an idealized Father God who provides needed comfort and security; Freud in turn understood religion as a "universal obsessional neurosis." A goal of psychoanalysis was to trust in the scientific method as a source of truth concerning the nature of one's being and the world.

Since Freud, modern psychiatry and psychology make claims to have supplanted a number of religious concepts central to understanding human nature. Among these are notions of a soul, of sin, and of morality. Soul and sin have been replaced by notions of human consciousness and psychological and social pathologies. Deficiencies in morality are understood as products of inadequate socialization processes, thus obviating the need for confession and redemption. Religious teachings traditionally promoted the view that unhappiness, despair and other physical and mental suffering are meaningful events. While Western religious traditions recognize illness to have a purpose within a grander design and emphasize the spiritual meaning of suffering, conservative psychiatry maintains a materialistic and mechanistic orientation. Thus, the two disciplines have functioned as competing belief systems for providing life meaning and purpose.

From Freud's work through the 1976 report on mysticism by the Group for the Advancement of Psychiatry (GAP), there has been a tendency to associate spiritual experiences with psychopathology. The report of GAP on "The Psychic Function of Religion in Mental Illness and Health" (1968) acknowledged that religious themes often surfaced during psychoanalysis and that religion could be used in both psychically healthy and unhealthy ways. Yet the residue of nineteenth century interest in religious insanity could still be found in the glossary of the Third Edition of the DSM (Diagnostic Statistical Manual) and in the 1989 edition of the Oxford Textbook of Psychiatry.

DSMIV: Religious or Spiritual Problem

In order to redress lack of sensitivity to religious and spiritual dimensions of problems that may be the focus of psychiatric treatment, a new Z code category for DSM IV was proposed, "psychoreligious or psychospiritual problem." The impetus for the proposal to add a new diagnostic category emerged from transpersonal clinicians and the work of the Spiritual Emergence Network. Their focus was on spiritual emergencies – forms of distress associated with spiritual practices and experiences. The proposal had the following goals: (1) to increase accuracy of diagnostic assessments when religious and spiritual issues were involved, (2) to reduce occurrence of medical harm from misdiagnosis of religious and spiritual problems, (3) to improve treatment of such problems by stimulating clinical research, and (4) to encourage clinical training centers to address the religious and spiritual dimensions of experience.

The DSM IV category was accepted under Religious or Spiritual Problem as follows: "This category can be used when the focus of clinical attention is a religious or spiritual problem. Examples include distressing experiences that involve loss or questioning of faith, problems associated with conversion to a new faith, or questioning of other spiritual values that may not necessarily be related to an organized church or religious institution" (APA, 2000: 741). Frequently reported religious problems in the literature are a loss or questioning of faith, change in denominational membership or conversion to a new religion, intensification of adherence to the beliefs and practices of one's own faith, and joining, participating in, or leaving a new religious movement or cult. Spiritual problems cited in the literature involve conflicts concerning an individual's relationship to the transcendent and questioning of spiritual values. Moreover, questioning of spiritual values can be triggered by an experience of loss or a sense of spiritual connection. Spiritual problems also may arise from spiritual practices, e.g., someone who begins a meditation practice and starts to experience perceptual changes. As well, mystical experiences and near-death experiences can lead to spiritual problems and were a focus for concern by the Spiritual Emergence Network. It was argued that inappropriately diagnosing disruptive religious and spiritual experiences as mental disorders can negatively influence their outcome. For example, some clinical literature on mysticism has described mystical experience as symptomatic of ego regression, borderline psychosis, a psychotic episode, or temporal lobe dysfunction. As well, "dark night of the soul" experiences have been equated to clinical depression. Moreover, the interaction of contemporary psychiatry and religion can take place at several levels: patients may have religious beliefs that need to be taken into consideration when planning treatment, and patient's values may affect acceptance of treatment.

While introduction of the V-code represents a significant first step toward explicit delineation of religious and spiritual clinical foci, it is but a modest accommodation. One limitation is the tendency to compartmentalize clinical focus on religious or spiritual issues, versus viewing them as interwoven among all other areas of functioning. With the secularization of medicine, mental health practitioners increasingly have assumed three functions traditionally recognized as being in the realm of religion: explanation of the unknown, ritual and social function, and the definition of values.

Training and Research

On average, psychiatrists hold far fewer religious beliefs than either their parents or their patients, and little if any attempt is made to explore the relevance of faith to illness or health. Moreover, despite the importance of religion and spirituality to most patients' lives psychiatrists are not given adequate training to deal with issues arising from disturbances in these realms. C. Jung's work on the importance of recognizing the "shadow" in healing of minds and souls has contributed a great deal to cementing productive relationships between patient and therapist, priest and counselor.

Disorders of the mind raise questions about the meaning of life, the presence of evil, and the possibility that forces beyond the senses are influencing one's life. Contemporary psychiatry and religion can be viewed as parallel and complementary frames of reference for understanding and describing human experience and behavior. Thus, while they place different degrees of emphasis on body, mind, and spirit, integration is possible to achieve comprehensive patient care.

It is only recently that religion and mental health issues have been addressed through research. In large part, results from studies have indicated a salutary relationship between religious involvement and health status. The consistency of findings, despite diversity of samples, designs, methodologies, religious measures, health outcomes and population characteristics, serves to strengthen the positive association between religion and health. For several decades, empirical research findings and literature reviews have reported strong positive associations between measures of religious involvement and mental health outcomes. A beneficial impact of religious involvement has been observed for outcomes such as suicide, drug use, alcohol abuse, delinquent behavior, marital satisfaction, psychological distress, certain functional psychiatric diagnoses, and depression. A next logical step for research on religion and mental health is to explore possible explanations for this mostly positive religious effect. A variety of possible factors have already been identified, such as social cohesiveness, the impact of internal locus of control beliefs, religious commitment, and faith. Among older adults, for example, it has been shown that: (1) religious faith provides hope for change and healing, (2) religious involvement influences well-being by providing social support, and (3) prayer and religious worship affect mental health through the effects of positive emotions.

Future: Religion and Culture

In the twenty-first century, religious and spiritual dimensions of culture remain important factors structuring human experience, beliefs, values, behavior, and illness patterns. Sensitivity to the cultural dimensions of religious and spiritual experiences is deemed essential for effective psychiatric treatment. The majority of the world's population relies on complementary and alternative systems of medicine for healing. It follows that in order for a psychiatrist to effectively work with an indigenous healer, he or she must have some understanding of the patient's cultural construction of illness, including the meaning of religious content. Religious cultures are powerful factors in modifying individual attitudes toward life and death, happiness and suffering. The subspecialty of transcultural psychiatry has gained momentum and clinical relevance from an interest in similarities and differences between cultures and the effect of culture on treatment plan. In this view, religion is a "container of culture": rituals, beliefs, and taboos of religion are profoundly important to the nature and structure of society as vehicles whereby values, attitudes, and beliefs are transmitted from generation to generation.

Finally, religion and spiritual issues have been identified as a research agenda for the development of DSM V. Examination of religion in history-taking and cultural formation processes and spirituality as a factor in self-identity, self-care, insight, self-reliance, and resiliency, are being promoted. Research on the similarities and differences of religious and spiritual issues across ethnic and cultural groups is being encouraged, as is research on the transgenerational process of acquisition or transmission of religious and spiritual norms and their impact on diagnosis.

See also: ◉ Freud, Sigmund ◉ Jung, Carl Gustav

Bibliography

American Psychiatric Association. (2000). *Diagnostic and statistical manual of mental disorders* (4th ed., Text Rev.). Washington, DC: Author.

Bhugra, D. (Ed.). (1996). *Psychiatry and religion: Context, consensus and controversies.* London: Routledge.

Boehnlein, J. (Ed.). (2000). *Psychiatry and religion: The convergence of mind and spirit,* Washington, DC: American Psychiatric Press.

Group for the Advancement of Psychiatry. (1968). *The psychic function of religion in mental illness and health.* New York: Author.

Jung, C. (1933). *Modern man in search of a soul.* London: Routledge.

Jung, C. (1964). *Man and his symbols.* London: Aldus Books.

Koenig, H. (Ed.). (1998). *Handbook of religion and mental health.* San Diego, CA: Academic Press.

Kupfer, D., First, M., & Reiger, D. (Eds.). (2002). *A research agenda for DSM-V.* Washington, DC: American Psychiatric Association.

Lukoff, D., Lu, F., & Turner, R. (1992). Toward a more culturally sensitive DSM-IV: Psychoreligious and psychospiritual problems. *The Journal of Nervous and Mental Disease, 180*(11), 673–682.

Lukoff, D., & Turner, R. (1998). From spiritual emergency to spiritual problem: The transpersonal roots of the new DSM-IV category. *Journal of Humanistic Psychology, 38*(2), 21–50.

Mansager, E. (2002). Religious and spiritual problem V-code: An Adlerian assessment. *The Journal of Individual Psychology, 58*(4), 374–387.

Peck, M. S. (1993). *Further along the road less traveled: The unending journey toward spiritual growth.* New York: Simon & Schuster.

Rhi, B. -Y. (2001). Culture, spirituality, and mental health: The forgotten aspects of religion and health. *Cultural Psychiatry: International Perspectives, 24*(3), 569–579.

Scott, S., Garver, S., Richards, J., & Hathaway, W. (2003). Religious issues in diagnosis: The V-code and beyond. *Mental Health, Religion and Culture, 6*(2), 161–173.

Psychoanalysis

David M. Moss III

Psychoanalysis is a school of psychology originated by the Austrian psychiatrist Sigmund Freud (1856–1939). Born out of struggle, it is a scientific approach to the investigation of conscious and unconscious processes, as well as a clinical discipline of artistic application and therapeutic scrutiny. Psychoanalysis is the *sine quo non* of modern psychology.

Philosophically, psychoanalysis is based on psychic determinism, a theory of human behavior rooted in a premise that certain causes predictably engender particular psychological effects. Prior to Freud, psychiatric studies theorized that organic conditions were the elementary basis of human behavior. Freud asserted that deep personality conflicts shaped the psyche, as did interpersonal and cultural influences. These dynamic forces became the psychic determinants of attitudes, opinions and behavioral patterns – including religious practices and faith convictions. Psychoanalysis, by pointing to their roots, offers a mode of shifting or managing and, to some extent, changing the consequences of these influences. This hope is Freud's major gift to depth-psychology.

Personality Constructs

Freud's belief in unconscious motivation was the foundation from which he developed an elaborate theory of personality that virtually reshaped Western thought. He believed that the fundamental source of psychic energy underlying human behavior stems from an instinctive drive called libido which is sexual in nature. By "sexual" he meant any type of physically pleasurable activity, particularly those of the mouth, anus and genitals. The libido also enables an individual's survival, motivating one to eat and drink. Along with propagation, this survival drive is the essence of what Freud termed Eros, the life instinct. The opposite of Eros is Thanatos, the death instinct aimed at a return of the human organism to an inorganic state.

While Thanatos has been debated and denied by countless critics, Freud's personality divisions have been well-accepted as psychodynamic constructs. Basically he contends that the interaction of the id, ego and superego forms the personality. The id is an unconscious dimension of the mind that serves as a storehouse for the libido. Freud claimed that this "dark, inaccessible...cauldron full of seething excitations" composes all instinctive organic cravings. The id is a substratum characterized by unrestrained pleasure-seeking impulses constantly demanding expression *via* thought and behavior.

Ideally, these unconscious libidinal drives are controlled by the conscious ego. This is the rational aspect of the personality which governs the activities of the id and directs a person's behavior so that the demands of reality are met. The ego is basically concerned with the maintenance of social approval, self-esteem and the alteration of libidinal drives so that they are in compliance with normative society.

Morality is not necessarily the product of the ego though. Ethics, folkways and mores reside in the third part of Freud's personality schema, the superego. A product of parental authority and institutional standards – especially religion – the superego uncompromisingly guards ideas of right and wrong. In turn, the superego's wishes continually conflict with those of the id and both battle for expression through the ego. When their tension is relatively acute the latter employs compromise mechanisms such as sublimation or compensation. Generally, such a compromise is aimed at satisfying both the id and superego. However, if the ego fails to accomplish this goal, neurotic symptoms may result, symbolically venting the frustrated libidinal impulses.

Developmental Stages

Psychoanalytic theory claims that the first exposures to crises shape the child's personality and therefore the ways in which he or she handles stress throughout life. Like his personality structure, Freud believed that early growth can be dynamically differentiated into three parts, each of which is a stage of development during the first five years of life. He defined these stages mostly in terms of the individual's awareness and the basic reaction of particular erogenous zones. For example, the oral stage is the first or infantile stage in a person's psychosexual maturation. The anal is the second stage and the phallic is the last pregenital phase. The next period of development is latency, a time during which pregenital impulses are repressed. These impulses are then reawakened during adolescence when the genital phase is reached.

Although family influence is important during all of these stages, Freud laid particular weight upon the pregenital periods. During the oral period one may form certain dominant character traits as a result of feeding, weaning and the mother's attention. For instance, an overprotective mother may cause a child to be abnormally dependent. Another sign of oral fixation is the argumentative person, one who displaced an early need to bite with sarcasm or quibbling.

Usually a child is toilet trained at the anal phase. Like weaning (and delivery before) this, too, is a crucial experience that may determine future attitudes and behavioral characteristics. A strict mother may produce an anally-retentive child who will continue to be obstinate and stingy. She may also encourage an explosive type of personality who will be cruel, destructive and disorderly. Conversely, a mother who coaxes and rewards may help her child to become creative and productive.

The most important point about the phallic stage is that it is the period during which the child experiences an unconscious sexual attachment to his mother and a feeling of jealousy toward his father. Freud called this the Oedipus complex and said that it results in a feeling of guilt and emotional conflict on the part of the child. Yet, like the oral and anal phases, the danger of such conflict is relative to the individual. In other words, fixation is not inevitable even though most males supposedly have this experience.

Again, latency is a period generally characterized by repression. However, if painful conflicts are repressed without being adequately resolved, they will continue to unconsciously influence the individual's thought, feelings and behavior. This will cause emotional tension or anxiety and possibly an inability to adjust. Such anxiety manifests itself in varying degrees. Freud used two standard categories to portray the magnitude of a person's maladjustment: neuroses and psychoses. To him, the former is chiefly a product of id versus ego, while the latter is a breakdown of ego, defense mechanisms and the projection of unconscious wishes onto the external world.

Religion

The projection of wishes is a key factor in Freud's use of dreams as "the royal road to the unconscious." While dream work is a central ingredient of psychoanalytic interpretation, it is also a medium of religion. Yet Freud contended that religion was an illusion, a belief system largely based on wishes. He appreciated the particularity of religion in providing a sense of emotional protection from external threat, as well as a cultural reservoir of ethical standards. Nevertheless, he believed modern mankind was capable of maturing beyond the irrational, superstitious and magical thinking of religious ideation.

Freud was an atheist who referred to himself as a "godless Jew." He saw God as a magnified father figure or parental ideal at the hub of a social neurosis one must grow beyond to be truly educated and able to cope with reality. He believed that primitive religions in patriarchal societies with strong totemic beliefs were profoundly influenced by the Oedipus complex. Young men of a tribal horde murdered their father to possess his wives. Totemic worship was to atone for such death and reinforce ethical restrictions founded on shame and guilt.

Struggle

Freud's beliefs about religion have been criticized since their first publications. They are intellectually valuable but they do not represent the driving force of psychoanalysis the way his personality constructs do. These models – especially infantile sexuality – have also been challenged since their initial presentations more than a century ago. Such controversies have led to the development of other schools of depth-psychology. These range from Analytic Psychology and Individual Psychology to Ego Psychology and Self Psychology. Clinically, all of these orientations use Freud's basic tools – free association, transference and interpretation.

Schools of Psychoanalysis vary in their expectations about treatment length and frequency of sessions. Customarily, an analyze will spend at least three hours a week on the couch for months if not years. This is because the process of analysis is not symptomatic in focus. Psychoanalysis is insight oriented psychotherapy devoted to a reeducation of the self. An effective analysis can enable one to harness neurotic energy in the interest of interpersonal responsiveness and intrapsychic balance.

Shortly before his death Freud made a brief recorded public message in which he noted his "good fortune" in the discovery of psychoanalysis. Yet he concluded, "People did not believe in my facts and thought my theories unsavory. Resistance was strong and unrelenting: In the end, I succeeded in acquiring pupils and bringing up an international psychoanalytic association. But the struggle is not yet over."

See also: ❯ Analytical Psychology ❯ Depth Psychology and Spirituality ❯ Freud, Sigmund ❯ Jung, Carl Gustav ❯ Psyche

Bibliography

Freud, S. (1957). *The standard edition of the complete psychological works of Sigmund Freud* (vols. 3–6, 11–15, 19–23). London: Hogarth Press.

Gay, P. (1987). *A godless Jew: Freud, atheism, and the making of psycho-analysis.* New Haven, CT: Yale University Press.

Jones, J. W. (1991). *Contemporary psychoanalysis and religion: Transference and transcendence.* New Haven, CT: Yale University Press.

Makari, G. (2008). *Revolution in mind: The creation of psychoanalysis.* New York: HarperCollins.

Meissner, W. W. (1986). *Psychoanalysis and religious experience.* New Haven, CT: Yale University Press.

Psychological Types

Adele Tyler

A theory of personality developed by Swiss psychiatrist Carl Jung in the early years of the twentieth century. Jung theorized that people's behaviors are directed by inborn tendencies to think and act in different but equally valid ways. His theory posits two basic orientations to the world, called *attitudes*, and four main mental processes, called *functions*. He considered these psychological preferences innate tendencies, like a preference for right or left-handedness, and speculated they were biologically based.

Jung's stated purpose in developing a theory of psychological types was not to sort people into box-like categories but rather to expand the language of the then-new science of psychology to facilitate more methodical, empirical research on human behavior. He developed his ideas on psychological types in part from observations of his patients, both individuals and couples. In his book *Psychological Types*, first published in 1921, Jung acknowledged the historical roots of personality types in oriental astrology, Hippocrates' theories on the four elements (earth, air, fire, and water) and Greek physician Galen's system of four temperaments (sanguine, phlegmatic, choleric, and melancholic), among others.

Extraversion and Introversion

Jung's first and central idea on psychological types was that people prefer one of two fundamentally different attitudes toward the world. A tendency to focus on the outer world of objects and people he deemed *extraversion* and an orientation toward and preference for the inner world of ideas and emotions he called *introversion. Extraversion* and *introversion* describe two opposite ways of using and renewing one's psychic energy. Extraverts direct energy to and receive energy back from the external world and introverts direct energy to and receive energy from the inner world of reflection.

The preference for extraversion or introversion is easily understood by most people in their recognition of extraverted people who are outgoing, talkative, uninhibited, and involved in multiple groups and activities, and introverted persons who are more reserved, quiet, and harder to know. These differences can be observed in infancy in an extraverted child's quicker and easier adaptation to and participation in the outer world and an introverted child's tendency toward shyness and reluctance to engage with objects and people. The innate nature of the preference for one or the other attitude helps explain differences in personalities of children raised in the same family. Jung stated that it was incorrect to assume extraverts were active people and introverts were passive people, saying instead that extraversion correlates with acting in an immediate, unreflective way, whereas introversion correlates with acting after reflecting or acting with forethought. He emphasized that neither way was better or more valid except as called for in a particular situation.

The Four Functions

In addition to a preference for an attitude of extraversion or introversion, Jung theorized four different mental processes that explain how people use their minds. Two of these, which explain how people gather information, are called the perceiving functions, *sensing* and *intuition*. The two ways people make judgments and decisions are called the judging functions, *thinking* and *feeling*.

When using one of the perceiving functions, *sensing* or *intuition*, people become aware of what is happening, without interpreting or evaluating the experience. Sensing, which is perceiving through the five senses, is concerned with concrete realities and is therefore focused in the present, the "what is." Intuition, which is perceiving information through a "sixth sense" or the unconscious, looks for hidden possibilities and is therefore more concerned with the future, the "what ifs." A person whose dominant function is sensing focuses on facts, and one whose dominant function is intuition prefers using imagination.

Evaluating the information that has been gathered via the perceiving functions is done by one of the two judging functions, *thinking* or *feeling*. Thinking relies on logic to make decisions and judgments, weighing the pros and cons to decide whether something is "right or wrong." The feeling function makes judgments based on one's personal values, deciding with compassion and empathy whether something is "good or bad." The thinking function is more concerned with truth and justice, and the feeling function more concerned with kindness and harmony. Thinking makes judgments from the outside, using an objective viewpoint, and feeling makes judgments from the subjective viewpoint of "standing in another person's shoes."

Jung observed that an innate preference for one of these four functions emerges in early childhood and develops as the dominant mental process. Later, a second or auxiliary function emerges. The other two functions remain less developed but available to the individual through the unconscious. As with the attitudes of extraversion and introversion, Jung emphasized that all four functions are equally valid and useful.

Type Dynamics

All four of these functions are used in either the extraverted or introverted attitude, which led to eight possible combinations of preferred attitude and function, which Jung called the eight function types. It is important to understand that Jung's is a dynamic system of personality. Rather than static boxes, these eight type combinations interact in the conscious and unconscious mind of each individual in unique ways. Each set of preferences are like poles on a continuum, with most people's strength of preference somewhere along the continuum. Some more developed and some less developed, the functions and attitudes work as templates for potential behaviors that result in infinite varieties of individual expression, much the way that the template that governs the crystallization of frozen water into six-sided figures produces an infinite variety of snowflakes.

Throughout life a person will have an interaction and flow of energy between the poles of extraversion and introversion, sensing and intuition, and thinking and feeling.

Because one's preferences are viewed as innate, they do not change during a lifetime, but with normal development people learn to use all the functions in both attitudes to some degree. Jung postulated that a "falsification of type" sometimes occurs where cultural influences cause a person to develop a lesser preference, much as left-handed children once were forced to use their right hands, and that this condition is a primary cause of neurosis.

Application of Psychological Type Theory

Jung's type theory has been popularized through the Myers-Briggs Type Indicator, a questionnaire based on Jung's typology developed by the mother-daughter team of Katherine Briggs and Isabel Briggs Myers. The Myers-Briggs Type Indicator, referred to as the MBTI, includes the additional category of Judging/Perceiving to indicate a person's preference for the perceiving functions or the judging functions. The MBTI gives scores for one's preference for E or I (extraversion or introversion), S or N (sensing or intuition), T or F (thinking or feeling), and J or P (judging or perceiving). These four categories yield 16 combinations of preferences, called the 16 types, thus doubling Jung's original 8 types to 16. The types are referred to by a four- letter designation that shows these preferences. For example, a person whose scores showed a preference for Extraversion over Introversion, Sensing over Intuition, Thinking over Feeling, and Judging over Perceiving would have the designation ESTJ.

The MBTI, a practical application of type theory, is the most widely used personality test in the world and has made Jung's ideas useful for ordinary people in understanding themselves and developing their potentials. This tool is commonly used in career counseling, marriage and family counseling, education, and in organizations. Recent works in psychological type have examined the role of type in religion and spirituality, studying the ways in which each of the 16 types approaches worship and engages in spiritual practices and works. A less-recognized test of psychological types called the Singer-Loomis Inventory of Personality (the SLIP) was developed by two Jungian analysts and uses as categories the eight function types originally described by Jung.

In recent years a worldwide community of type practitioners, called typologists, has developed. Hundreds of books have been written and studies conducted applying typology to numerous fields of human activity. The prevalence of the MBTI and typology indicate that Jung's theories on personality type continue to have value in helping increase self-awareness and self-acceptance in individuals and by promoting better understanding and communication in human relationships of all kinds.

See also: ❯ Depth Psychology and Spirituality ❯ Extraversion ❯ Introversion ❯ Jung, Carl Gustav ❯ Unconscious

Bibliography

Jeffries, W. C. (1991). *True to type*. Charlottesville, VA: Hampton Roads Publishing Company.

Jung, C. G. (1971). *Psychological types, a revision by R.F.C. Hull* (H. G. Baynes, Trans.). Princeton, NJ: Princeton University Press, Bollingen Series XX.

Myers, I. B. (1998). *Introduction to type*. Mountain View, CA: CPP, Inc.

Myers, I. B., & Myers, P. B. (1980). *Gifts differing*. Palo Alto, CA: Davis-Black Publishing.

Spoto, A. (1995). *Jung's typology in perspective*. Wilmette, IL: Chiron Publications.

Von Franz, M.-L., & Hillman, J. (1971). *Lectures on Jung's typology*. Dallas, TX: Spring Publications.

Psychology

Kate M. Loewenthal

What is psychology? There is little dispute about the broad definition of psychology as the study and understanding of human behavior, cognitive processes, experience and emotion. However the history of psychology has been colorful, peppered with disputes about how such understanding and study should be done. The different views on the "how" of psychology have impacted on the psychological study of religion.

This essay will highlight some important features of the history of psychology, and suggest how these features may have impacted on the psychological understanding of religion.

Psychology and the Early Study of Religion

In its early days, in the nineteenth and very early twentieth centuries, psychologists had no problems with asking people to introspect or report on their "inner" experiences. Two often-cited examples are (1) the Wurzburg school (Wundt, 1902), who asked for detailed introspective reports on what went through people's minds when they saw or picture, for example, or solved a problem, (2) psychoanalysis (e.g., Freud, 1964) in which people were asked to free-associate, to talk about the first things that came to mind. In this climate, the work of William James, described in *The Varieties of Religious Experience* (1902) was perfectly at home. James described pioneering uses of the psychological questionnaire method in which people were asked to describe their religious development.

But as the twentieth century grew older, scientific psychology was dominated by positivism, in which it was held that the objects of scientific investigation should be publicly observable and measurable. This entailed a shift from a focus on experience, to a focus onbehavior, epitomized in Watson's *Psychology from the Standpoint of a Behaviorist* (1919). The psychological study of religion was seen to be incompatible with behavior – since the object of religious activity and feeling cannot be observed and measured, this was thought to make the study of religious activity and feeling unworthy of scientific attention. The psychological study of religious fell into a decline, and this decline was assisted by the influential and rather derogatory views of Freud on religion (e.g., Freud, 1927). Religion was seldom indexed in psychology textbooks, and where it was indexed, the explanations of religious behavior and feeling were almost always pejorative (Loewenthal, 2000).

Within psychology, there remained considerable interest in personality, and in the psychometric assessment of personality and social attitudes, using psychological tests and measures. This was reflected in the psychological study of religion, particularly the seminal work of Gordon Allport on religious orientation and prejudice (1966), followed by pioneering works on the psychology of religion involving extensive use of psychological and social attitude measures (e.g., Argyle and Beit-Hallahmi, 1975; Francis, Pearson, Carter, and Kay, 1981).

Recent Shifts in Psychology and the Study of Religion

Towards the end of the twentieth century and the early twenty-first century, there were important shifts in psychological methodologies and perspectives, reflecting a general post-modern tolerance of different perspectives.

This resulted in a growth of the range of methods used to study religious behavior and experience. Religion was indexed more frequently in psychology textbooks, and explained and studied in non-pejorative ways. The most important shifts were (1) the development of qualitative research methodologies (Elliott, Fischer, & Rennie, 1999). This went alongside the acceptance of experiential and phenomenological perspectives, and enabled the development of valuable work on the experiential aspects of the psychology of religion, and the emergence of interest in spirituality (Hay and Morisy, 1978; Tacey, 2004; Paloutzian and Park, 2005), (2) the development of experimental methodologies, in particular their applications to areas of psychology other than the cognitive domains to which experimental methodology had traditionally been applied. Experimental work on social cognition and attachment theory, for example, is being usefully extended to the understanding of religion in relation to social cognition, and religious feelings (e.g., Islam and Hewstone, 1993; Birgegard and Granqvist, 2004), (3) the development of cognitive science has included the study of cognitive universals in religion (e.g., Andresen, 2001) (4) the development of neuroimaging techniques in the study of psychological processes has included the use of neuroimaging in the study of religious thinking and experience (e.g., Azari, Missimer, and Seitz, 2005).

Conclusions

In brief, then, the twentieth century saw the development of psychology into a positivist discipline. Then from the mid-twentieth century onwards, psychology developed into a discipline involving a broad range of approaches and methodologies, all impacting on the way the psychological processes involved in religion have been studied.

See also: ❯ Freud, Sigmund ❯ James, William ❯ Psychoanalysis

Bibliography

Allport, G. W. (1966). The religious context of prejudice. *Journal for the Scientific Study of Religion, 5*, 448–451.

Andresen, J. (Ed.). (2001). *Religion in mind: Cognitive perspectives on religious ritual, belief and experience.* Cambridge, England: Cambridge University Press.

Argyle, M. (2000). *Psychology and religion.* London: Routledge.

Argyle, M., & Beit-Hallahmi, B. (1975). *The social psychology of religion.* London: Routledge & Kegan Paul.

Azari, N. P., Missimer, J., & Seitz, R. J. (2005). Religious experience and emotion: Evidence for distinctive cognitive neural patterns. *International Journal for the Psychology of Religion, 15*, 263–282.

Birgegard, A., & Granqvist, P. (2004). The correspondence between attachment to parents and God: Three experiments using subliminal separation cues. *Personality and Social Psychology Bulletin, 30*, 1122–1135.

Elliott, R., Fischer, C. T., & Rennie, D. L. (1999). Evolving guidelines for publication of qualitative research studies in psychology and related fields. *British Journal of Clinical Psychology, 38*, 215–229.

Francis, L., Pearson, O. R., Carter, M., & Kay, W. K. (1981). Are introverts more religious? *British Journal of Social Psychology, 20*, 101–104.

Freud, S. (1927). *The future of an illusion.* London: Hogarth Press.

Freud, S. (1964). *New introductory lectures on psychoanalysis.* London: Hogarth Press.

Hay, D., & Morisy, A. (1978). Reports of ecstatic, paranormal, or religious experience in Great Britain and the United States: A comparison of trends. *Journal for the Scientific Study of Religion, 17*, 255–268.

Islam, M. R., & Hewstone, M. (1993). Intergroup attributions and affective consequences in majority and minority groups. *Journal of Personality and Social Psychology, 64*, 936–950.

James, W. (1902). *The varieties of religious experience.* New York: Collier.

Loewenthal, K. M. (2000). *A short introduction to the psychology of religion.* Oxford, England: Oneworld.

Paloutzian, R. F., & Park, C. (2005). *Handbook of the psychology of religion and spirituality.* New York: Guilford.

Tacey, D. T. (2004). *The spirituality revolution: The emergence of contemporary spirituality.* Hove, England: Brunner-Routledge.

Watson, J. B. (1919). *Psychology from the standpoint of a behaviorist.* Philadelphia, PA: Lippincott.

Wundt, W. (1902). *Outlines of psychology* (W. H. Judd, Trans.). Leipzig, Germany: Engelman.

Psychology and the Origins of Religion

Bernard Spilka

The Danger in Analyzing Religion

To pose questions regarding the origin of religion from a social scientific stance is to enter dangerous territory. For millennia, deviation from the views espoused by religious authorities has always been negatively viewed and where possible, suppressed. This inclination is still present, but skepticism and challenge to monolithic religion now has a considerable likelihood of eventuating in diverse positions.

A Safe Understanding

Anthropologists introduced such variation in the nineteenth century. Their orientation was not to analyze the Judeo-Christian tradition, but to follow a safe path by examining the faiths of peoples they termed primitive. This approach did not threaten the Western religious establishment and was intellectually and emotionally accepted. Another major factor was that the religious perspectives of native groups in obscure locations were largely discussed in terms of the mythology of those studied. F. Max Muller (1879) wrote on the religions of India and Edward B. Tylor (1896) referred to the "religion of the lower races," "uncultured races," and "savages and barbarians" (1896: 342). Readers of Muller, Tylor, and their ilk considered themselves "civilized" as opposed to the "primitives" whose faiths were treated as naïve mythological tales.

Psychology and Religion

Muller (1879), however, initiated a cognitive approach to the issue of religious origins by claiming that sensory experience with the finite world plus reason leads a person to contemplation of the infinite. He further asserted that from this "sprang the first impulse to religion" (1879: 360). Concurrently, the notion of a religious instinct was rejected. He correctly argued that it did nothing more than substitute one unknown for another. His reservations did little to deter many who endorsed the idea of a religious instinct. The death knell to this approach was sounded in 1924 by L. L. Bernard who found 83 religious instincts in the literature.

The next development emanated from Behaviorism when the search for religious origins stressed natural processes such as evolution and neural processes. Given the substrate of human biology, emphasis shifted to learning and the influence of environmental forces. Objectivity and measurement now dominated Psychology and since theories of religious origins could not be empirically verified, they were relegated to the realm of opinion and simply ignored.

Classical learning theory gave way to cognition and the revival of Muller's stance via John Dewey (1929) who crossed both philosophy and psychology. Dewey saw the difficulty as experiential. Attempts to understand life's uncertainty implied a basic cognitive weakness which aroused insecurity and a "quest for certainty." According to him "Religion was, in its origin, an expression of this endeavor" (1929: 292).

Religion, Evolution and Genetics

Increasing conceptual sophistication replaced the absolutist hereditary-environment distinction. One now calculated the degree to which environment and genetics separately contributed to the phenomenon in question. A new perspective in which psychological processes and behavior were examined in twin studies plus the idea of heritability entered the picture. Reviews of this rapidly developing literature suggest that up to 50% of the variance in religion measures may be referable to genetics. Keep in mind that heritability estimates are derived from group data and do not hold for any specific person.

The first major effort along these lines was E. O. Wilson's 1978 formulation of Sociobiology. His basic principle is that evolution has endowed the human mind with some basic guiding rules. Though these are concerned with collective social behavior, including religion, he cautiously invoked the joint influence of both genetics and environment. Wilson (1978) claimed that religion "can be seen to confer biological advantage" (p. 188). He attempted to support this position via an understanding of the role and function of myth for both society and the individual. His argument enlisted natural selection in the process.

This approach contributed to the growing school of evolutionary psychology. Its advocates embrace both genetic and environmental influences, but there is a tendency for the latter to be minimized in favor of a search for biological bases of behavior.

Interestingly, the Psychology used to theorize possible religious origins has been largely employed by anthropologists who exclusively look to cognition. Usually, without elaboration, they refer to biology and evolution for their final answer.

Pascal Boyer (2001) has been in the forefront of this movement. He initially claimed that religious ideas must be influenced by the way the brain are organized to make inferences. Theoretically, the seeking of causes and the making of attributions are given a biological foundation. This position is buttressed by noting the involvement of emotion in religious expression. Biology is joined with environment by acknowledging the important individual and social functions that religion plays in life. Above all, genetics and evolution loom in the background primarily for handling cognition. In addition Boyer appreciates religion's function in maintaining the group. Group selection, however, is largely rejected by the biological community. Hypotheses are then posited regarding the association of cognition and social behavior with natural selection. Religion thus develops because there is need for these concepts, socially, culturally and biologically.

Among a number of others who look to cognition for religion's origin is Stewart Guthrie (1993) who extensively and impressively details the tendency of people to anthropomorphize virtually anything that may provide meaningful explanations. The result is that religion is reduced to anthropomorphism and ritual and all other religious forms fall into line.

Anthropologist James McClenon (1994, 2002) has taken an approach that explicitly combines cognition with emotion while assuming an evolutionary foundation though the latter remains vague and undefined. His emphasis is on the experiences of early humans with what he terms "wondrous events." Though "wondrous healing" is stressed as a basis for religion, religion is primarily treated as belief. Leading also to this conclusion are trance states, hypnotizability, out-of-body experiences and the like. Helplessness in the face of the unknown especially death results in the development of Shamanism and ritualization which offer the delusion of meaning and control. The theoretical views of Freud and Malinowski among others are used by McClenon to buttress his arguments.

Cognition, Heritability and Faith

Cognitive theory offers a powerful entrée into questions about the psychological origin of religion. One can, however, argue that it may not enough. Religion does much more than help make life and the world sensible. From a motivational perspective, it aids people to maintain and/or enhance personal control over themselves and their environment. Lack of control is also one correlate of lack of meaning. Religion not only has the potential to satisfy needs for meaning and control, but furthermore brings people together, supporting them both individually and collectively. Natural selection may be invoked for all three of these functions as it can easily be shown that survival and reproductive success follow from meaning, control, and sociality. Furthermore biological and evolutionary bases for these factors are available and researchers are continually discovering their neuropsychological and hormonal correlates. In all likelihood, these elements account for the observation that there is a moderate component of heritability in religious belief and adherence. For example, data suggest that up to 50% of the variability in measures of control motivation is heritable. This overall framework is introduced

and discussed elsewhere (Spilka, Hood, Hunsberger, and Gorsuch, 2003). Inherited hormonal factors in sociality have also been identified. An indirect test of these views is possible. One can hypothesize that partialling out these factors from the religion – genetics relationship in twin studies should make this association disappear. This does not deny the necessity of conducting additional research to define other neurobiological possibilities for understanding the place of heritability in personal faith. The content of the three domains just cited still has to be defined though excellent insights have been offered by Boyer, Guthrie and Kirkpatrick (2004).

Religion as an Evolutionary By-Product

Kirkpatrick (2004) rejects the role of natural selection and religion as basically a biological adaptation. He sees it as a set of evolved by-products that involve cognitive, motivational and social factors. Further development should not gainsay the role of environment in the learning and expression of religious beliefs, experience and behavior. In coming to understand the nature of religion cross-culturally, naturalistic approaches ought not be viewed as threatening and blasphemous. There is room for comprehending the character of faith and spirituality from as broad a perspective as possible.

See also: ❯ Psychology

Bibliography

Bernard, L. L. (1924). *Instinct*. New York: Henry Holt.

Boyer, P. (2001). *Religion explained*. New York: Basic Books.

Dewey, J. (1929). *The quest for certainty*. New York: Minton, Balch.

Guthrie, S. E. (1993). *Faces in the clouds: A new theory of religion*. New York: Oxford University Press.

Kirkpatrick, L. A. (2004). The evolutionary social psychology of religious beliefs. *Behavioral and Brain Sciences, 27*, 741.

McClenon, J. (1994). *Wondrous events: Foundations of religious belief*. Philadelphia, PA: University of Pennsylvania Press.

McClenon, J. (2002). *Wondrous healing: Shamanism, human evolution and the origin of religion*. DeKalb, IL: Northern Illinois University Press.

Muller, F. M. (1879). *Lectures on the origin and growth of religion as illustrated by the religions of India*. New York Charles Scribner's sons.

Spilka, B., Hood, R. W., Hunsberger, B. & Gorsuch, R. L. (2003). *The psychology of religion: An empirical approach* (3rd ed.), New York: Guilford.

Tylor, E. (1896). *Anthropology*. New York: D. Appleton.

Wilson, E. O. (1978). *On human nature*. Cambridge, MA: Harvard University Press.

Psychology as Religion

Ann Gleig

In a useful survey of the terrain between religion and psychology, William Parsons and Diane Jonte-Pace (2001) note that the multiple and diverse approaches now utilized within this area have replaced its identity as a single field, traditionally know as the psychology "of" religion, with the more inclusive "religion and psychological studies," within which reside the subsets of "psychology of religion," and "psychology in dialogue with religion." What distinguishes the dialogical approach is that it moves beyond using psychology as a method of analysis to interpret religious phenomena to employ psychology as a tool to extend, through conversation, the aims of religion.

An additional subset appearing within, although arguably threatening to undermine, the dialogical enterprise is an approach that seeks less to relate psychology to religion than to offer psychology *as* a religion. Despite eliciting controversy for blurring the boundaries between the two fields, psychology as religion cannot be dismissed as there is little doubt that the functioning of psychology in ways comparable to religion is widespread within contemporary western culture. This is attested to by the popularity of best-selling texts offering a mix of therapeutic and spiritual advice such as Scott M. Peck's *The Road Less Traveled* (1978) and Thomas Moore's *Care of the Soul* (1994). Presenting itself as a modern unchurched way to experience one's religiosity, psychology as religion has flourished within a wider therapeutic climate as an alternative method to guide an individual's quest for meaning and the sacred.

Before proceeding to the socio-historic development of psychology as religion and notable cultural commentaries and critiques, further clarification of terms is useful. As William G. Barnard (2001) notes, the type of psychology utilized here is a humanistically oriented psychotherapy that is harnessed in service of psychospiritual wholeness and replaces religion as a way to develop existential meaning and enable a direct experience of the sacred. Similarly, religion is interchangeable with spirituality referring to a personal transformative experience of the essential core of religion, often rendered as a divine force, energy, or consciousness, that is distinct from traditional religious institutions, creeds and praxis. When

these two particular strands of psychology and religion overlap to such a degree that they fulfill the same purposes we have psychology as religion.

This merging occurs at a variety of intersections as a multitude of cultural strands converge, intertwine and trail off. Such interlacing complicates a tracing of the history of psychology as religion but one can certainly identify significant junctures and key figures. William Parsons (2008) has teased out one dominant strand, which he labels as the "*psychologia perennis*," an unchurched, psychological form of spirituality whose origins can be seen as early as the sixteenth and seventeenth centuries with the appearance of mysticism as a subjective "experience" divorced from church and tradition. The emergence of a universal, sacred inner dimension of human beings allowed for the psychologization of mysticism and links the figures of William James, Carl Jung, Romain Rolland, Richard Maurice Bucke and humanistic and transpersonal psychologists such as Abraham Maslow, Roberto Assagioli and Ken Wilber. While recognizing differences in metapsychology and therapeutic techniques among these thinkers, Parsons offers a list of shared characteristics that unite them as perennial psychologists: the championing of the individual as an unchurched site of religiosity, the search for the origin of mysticism in the unconscious, a valorization of personal unchurched mystical experiences, an advocacy of perennialism, the discernment of innate, intuitive, mystical capacities, the development of psycho-mystical therapeutic regimens and a social vision grounded in the rise of *homo mysticus*.

As Parson notes, such characteristics are similar to those identified as definitive of the New Age. Indeed, Wouter Hanegraaff (1998) has described one of the major trends of the New Age as "healing and personal growth," in which psychological development and religious salvation merge to such an unprecedented extent that it is difficult to distinguish between the two. Setting it within the wider context of the secularization of traditional esotericism as it adapted to the emerging scientific worldview, he argues that one of the defining marks of the New Age is "the psychologization of religion and the sacralization of psychology," and delineates two major lineages for this occurrence: American metaphysical movements and Carl Gustav Jung. Regarding the first, drawing heavily on a series of works by Robert Fuller (1982, 1986, 1989) which traces the emergence of a distinctively American religious psychology, Hanegraaff divides the American lineage into two separate but related streams. The first, the metaphysical movements, includes Mesmerism, Phineas Parkhurst Quimby's Mind-Cure, the New Thought movement, and positive thinking/self-help popular psychology. The second, functionalist psychology, has its roots in the thought of Ralph Waldo Emerson, embraces William James, Carl Rogers, and humanistic psychology, and is best represented by James's classic *The Varieties of Religious Experience*.

Common to the American lineage are the following themes: an understanding of the unconscious as a site of harmony, reparation and revitalization; the casting of the unconscious as the locus of or a doorway to the sacred; a concept of a spectrum of consciousness in which different layers of consciousness correspond to different psychic capacities, mystical experiences and metaphysical realms; and the development of a pragmatic attitude and scientific techniques to access the resources of the sacralized unconscious.

The second major source for the psychologization of religion is Jung who Hanegraaff sees as the link between traditional European esotericism, Naturphilosophie, Romanticism, and the New Age. According to Hanegraaff, Jung united science and religion by presenting an esoteric worldview in psychological term and providing a scientific alternative to occultism. Not only did Jung psychologize esotericism, he also sacralized psychology by filling it with the contents (e.g. archetypes, the transcendent function, and individuation) of esoteric speculation rather than empirical realities. The result was a theory which allowed people to talk simultaneously about God (the Self) and the psyche, thereby collapsing the categories of religion and psychology and anticipating the rise of New Age self-spirituality.

There have been a number of cultural commentaries on the recent spread of psychology as religion. Attending to the wider contemporary therapeutic culture within which it has flourished, Philip Rieff (1966) posits a radical break between religion and psychology with a discussion of the replacement of early religious "positive communities" by therapeutically-orientated "negative communities." Traditional societies were "positive communities" governed by a cultural symbolic which encouraged restraint of behavior and an ethic which favored the group over the individual. The repression of socially destructive instincts was achieved through the acceptance of an authoritative "language of faith" and the idealization of a cultural super-ego. The institutions of the "Church" and the "Party" enabled positive communities to prevent anomie and reintegrate neurosis through religious forms of healing in which the unconscious was encountered in a non-direct manner.

In contrast, negative communities encourage a direct engagement with the unconscious and foster a therapeutic mode of self-awareness. They are suspicion of cultural

forms like religion and politics which are understood as symbolic representations of unconscious content. The shift from repression to direct engagement with the unconscious leads to the collapse of the cultural super-ego and the replacement of the "Church" and the "Party" with the "Hospital" and "Theatre" as the new cultural spaces for the working out of previously repressed psychic contents. The individual is privileged over the group and a new character type emerges, namely, "psychological man."

Critiques of psychological man and the psychologization of religion have come from Paul Vitz, (1977) Christopher Lasch (1979) and Richard King and Jeremy Carrette (2005) on the grounds of narcissism, individualism and apoliticism. The charge of narcissism is most notably filed in Lasch's *The Culture of Narcissism*. Echoing Vitz, he laments that the quest for self-realization promoted by the new psychospiritual therapies has encouraged an indulgent self-preoccupation and created a crisis in personal and social relationships. Moreover, in addition to being narcissistic in the self-absorbed colloquial sense, Lasch utilizes Heinz Kohut to argue that psychologized spirituality reflects and exacerbates an actual clinical disorder; a narcissistic personality structure that because of recent socio-cultural changes had become the predominant psychopathology of contemporary life. Lasch argues that the deification of the self within psychologized religiosity appeals to and feeds narcissistic grandiosity. Accusing the psychospiritual therapies of contributing to an amoral society, he calls for the creation of new communities of competence which foster civil commitment and draw out the moral energies of the Protestant work ethic.

A more recent critique by Jeremy Carrette and Richard King (2005) has targeted the twentieth century assimilation of the religious into the psychological arguing that psychology has diluted the social and ethical aspects of religion to form a privatized religion amenable to the demands of neoliberal ideology. Highlighting the roles of James, humanistic, transpersonal and popular psychology, Carrette and King argue that the individualism of psychologized spirituality allows for the infiltration of capitalist logic into religious discourse and the wise-scale commodification of spiritual "products."

However, there have also been a number of more optimistic appraisals of psychology as religion. Peter Homans (1979, 1989) has undermined the opposition between a traditional moral religious community and a contemporary amoral psychologized culture and challenged the charge of narcissism. According to Homans, critiques such as Rieff's and Lasch's fail to appreciate how much of a generative force religion was in the formation of the current psychological climate. He argues that due to secularization, the western religious traditions were deidealized and this resulted in a period of mourning; a regressive process involving a direct encounter with the unconscious no-longer externally expressed in the form of religious symbols and ideation. While religious disillusionment may lead to despair or cynicism, there is also the possibility of a more creative response; an opportunity for individuation and the reintegration of unconscious contents into new meaningful symbols and values. Moreover, these new systems of meaning–such as the analytic psychology of a forefather of psychology as religion, Jung–not only reject but also assimilate religion so that to various degrees it lives on within them.

Homans also critiques Lasch of misreading Kohut, pointing out correctly that for Kohut narcissism was not in itself a pathological condition but rather a normal developmental stage which not only had the potential to transform into a healthy valuing of the self and empathy for the other, but also to reach the higher religio-ethical goal of "cosmic narcissism." The issue, therefore, is not narcissism per se but whether narcissistic needs are repressed and acted out, or positively transformed. For Homans, and Kohut, therapeutic culture, with its themes of idealization, self-esteem, and grandiosity, displays a genuine engagement with narcissism and a desire for a more complete and satisfying subjectivity.

Additional defenses have come from sociologists of religion such as Robert Wuthnow (1998), Wade Clarke Roof (1999) and Robert Fuller (2001) who have convincingly attempted to rescue unchurched religion from unfounded generalizations, unfair stereotypes and pessimistic evaluations. Arguing that contemporary forms of psychologized spirituality generally display a legitimate quest for self-transformation, these works challenge the elevation of traditional religion over unchurched spirituality, the caricatures of its proponents as superficial and self-absorbed and its proposed inability to foster a social and relational ethic.

Such scholarship shows that many charges against psychology as religion are exaggerated and unsubstantiated. However, while it is necessary to temper unequivocal condemnations, many proponents of psychology as religion have recognized that certain accusations of individualism and narcissism are legitimate and have embarked on self-critiques to correct the elements that threat to undermine its status as an authentic form of religiosity. Jorge Ferrer's (2002) postmodern deconstruction and participatory revisioning of transpersonal psychology is a sophisticated example of this. Combining proponents growing self-reflexivity and relational turns, with the increasing academic scholarship on unchurched psychologized spirituality and the proliferation of Mind-Body-Spirit sections in bookstores with their best-selling psychology/spirituality titles, demonstrates that psychology as religion has established itself as a popular and increasingly sophisticated way to frame one's religiosity in the contemporary cultural climate.

See also: ❯ James, William ❯ Jung, Carl Gustav ❯ Mysticism and Psychoanalysis ❯ Psyche ❯ Psychology ❯ Psychology of Religion ❯ Self

Bibliography

Barnard, W. G. (2001). Diving into the depths: reflections on psychology as a religion. In W. B. Parsons & D. Jonte-Pace (Eds.), *Religion and psychology: Mapping the terrain* (pp. 297–318). London: Routledge.

Carrette, J., & King. R. (2005). *Selling spirituality.* London: Routledge.

Ferrer, J. (2002). *Revisioning transpersonal theory.* Albany, NY: State University of New York Press.

Fuller, R. C. (1982). *Mesmerism and the American cure of souls.* Philadelphia, PA: University of Pennsylvania Press.

Fuller, R. C. (1986). *Americans and the unconscious.* New York: Oxford University Press.

Fuller, R. C. (1989). *Alternative medicine and American religious life.* New York: Oxford University Press.

Fuller, R. C. (2001). *Spiritual, but not religious: Understanding unchurched America.* New York: Oxford University Press.

Hanegraaff, W. (1998). *New age religion and western culture: Esotericism in the mirror of secular thought.* Albany, NY: State University of New York Press.

Homans, P. (1979). *Jung in context.* Chicago, IL: University of Chicago Press.

Homans, P. (1989). *The ability to mourn: Disillusionment and the social origins of psychoanalysis.* Chicago, IL: University of Chicago Press.

Lasch, C. (1979). *The culture of Narcissism.* New York: W. W. Norton.

Moore, T. (1994). *Care of the soul: A guide for cultivating depth and sacredness in everyday life.* New York: Harper Paperbacks.

Parsons, W. B. (2008). Psychologia perennis and the academic study of mysticism. In W. B. Parsons, D. Jonte-Pace & S. Henking (Eds.), *Mourning religion* (pp. 1–29). Charlottesville, VA: University of Virginia Press.

Parsons, W. B., & Jonte-Pace, D. (2001). Introduction: Mapping religion and psychology. In W. B. Parsons & D. Jonte-Pace (Eds.), *Religion and psychology: Mapping the terrain* (pp. 97–123). London: Routledge.

Peck, S. M. (2003). *The road less travelled 25th anniversary edition: A new psychology of love, traditional values and spiritual growth.* New York: Touchstone.

Rieff, P. (1966). *The triumph of the therapeutic.* Chicago, IL: The University of Chicago Press.

Roof, W. C. (1999). *The spiritual marketplace.* Princeton, NJ: Princeton University Press.

Vitz, P. (1977). *Psychology as religion: The cult of self-worship.* Grand Rapids, MI: William B. Eerdmans Publishing Company.

Wuthnow, R. (1998). *After heaven: Spirituality in America since the 1950's.* Berkekely, CA: University of California Press.

Psychology of Religion

David M. Wulff

Introduction

Classically defined, the psychology of religion consists of the systematic application of psychology's methods and interpretive frameworks to the broad domain of religion. As strictly a nonsectarian scholarly discipline, it should be carefully distinguished from "religious psychology," which is the psychology that in varying degrees is explicit in the texts and teachings of a religious tradition; from "psychology *and* religion," a phrase intended to suggest a mutually respectful dialogue between psychological theories and various perspectives in religious studies; "psychology *as* religion," which designates clinically oriented forms of psychology grounded in "spiritual" conceptions of human existence; and "integration of psychology and religion," which constitutes variously conceived (and usually religiously conservative) efforts to critique, recast, and apply psychology within a particular theological framework. The boundaries of the psychology of religion have from the beginning been difficult to draw, especially given the field's long history of providing foundations for religious education and pastoral care.

Beginnings in America

Of the many specialized areas of psychology, the psychology of religion was among the first to emerge out of the new empirical science of psychology that established itself late in the nineteenth century in both Europe and the United States. The extraordinary success of the physical sciences in understanding the natural world suggested to various nineteenth-century scholars that scientific methods might be applicable in the human realm as well. Thus arose scientific psychology as well as the *Religionswissenschaften*, the sciences of religion, or what today is called the history of religions.

The American founders of the psychology of religion, including Stanley Hall, William James, Edwin Starbuck, James Leuba, James Pratt, George Coe, Edward Ames, and George Stratton, understood "religion" to encompass both individual piety and the historic religious traditions. Using methods that were both qualitative and quantitative, these scholars were well informed by the burgeoning literatures on religion authored by anthropologists, sociologists, linguists, and historians of religion. Among the field's early proponents, Pratt stands out for his systematic efforts – including extensive travel in India, Burma, Ceylon, Vietnam, China, Japan, and Korea – to acquaint himself with the major Eastern traditions in both their corporate and individual embodiments. And more than anyone else, he strove to grasp and sympathetically convey the worldviews and experiences of his informants. But it was William James, Pratt's thesis advisor and author of the field's signature classic, *The Varieties of Religious Experience* (1902), who brought the field most prominently into view.

A further impetus for the new psychology – and for the psychology of religion in particular – came in no small measure from the spirit of Progressivism. Near the end of the nineteenth century, the increasingly evident deleterious effects on society of the industrial revolution prompted in the United States an assortment of reform efforts that together became known as Progressivism. Among them was the Social Gospel movement, which centered on the conviction of many liberal Protestants that the traditional teachings of Jesus are aimed chiefly at righting the wrongs in this world, not preparing believers for the next. Hall, Coe, and Ames were themselves involved in this movement, including the social services offered by the various missions and settlement houses. But others, too, shared their conviction that the psychology of religion could help to reconceive or reform religion in such a way that it would more directly address the personal, social, and spiritual needs of the modern world. Thus the early psychologists of religion were by and large active proponents of religion, but in liberal versions compatible with the rationalistic worldview shaped by modern science, including the theory of evolution.

Two Methodological Principles

Fundamental principles for the new psychology of religion were laid out in 1902 by the Swiss psychologist Theodore Flournoy, who was a close friend of William James and, like Coe, a student of theology before he found it problematical. According to Flournoy's *Principle of the Exclusion of the Transcendent*, psychologists of religion should neither affirm nor reject the independent existence of the object of religious experience and reflection. Restated in contemporary terms, their posture should be one of methodological agnosticism. But the *experience of* the transcendent object is most certainly not to be excluded from their province; indeed, such experience should be observed with the closest attention to its nuances and variations.

The second of Flournoy's guidelines, the *Principle of Biological Interpretation*, lays out a broadly inclusive framework for the psychological study of religion. Such study, as the principle's name indicates, should search for the *physiological* conditions of its object of study, conditions that today are naturally far better understood than in Flournoy's time. But Flournoy had more in mind than biology. The psychology of religion should also incorporate a *developmental* perspective, giving attention to both hereditary and environmental factors that play a role in the human species as a whole and in individual lives. It should be *comparative* in the sense of being sensitive to and taking into account individual differences. And it should be *dynamic* by recognizing that the religious life is a complex living reality representing the interplay of a great diversity of factors. Flournoy assigns to the field, in sum, a broadly inclusive agenda, according to which its proponents should welcome guidance and insights from many different areas of psychology. It might also hope to reciprocate by sharing insights of its own.

Two Methodological Traditions

In laying out these principles, Flournoy did not address the difficult question of what specific research methods to use. In his own investigations, he drew on case studies and personal documents, much as did James. He was thus a qualitative researcher in the tradition of the *Geisteswissenschaften*, the human sciences, one of the two main traditions constituting both psychology and the psychology of religion. Hall and his Clark School of Religious Psychology inaugurated the alternate tradition, which cast itself in the empirical model represented by the *Naturwissenschaften*, the natural sciences, most notably by the use of systematic measurement and the quest for causal interpretations. Even though the natural-scientific approach won the day both in psychology and in the psychology of religion, the human-scientific perspective continued to attract proponents, especially among clinical practitioners as well as scholars specializing in the history of religions.

In the United States today, the empirical psychology of religion finds its organizational home mainly in Division 36, Psychology of Religion, of the American Psychological Association (APA) and in the Society for the Scientific Study of Religion, even though in both organizations it is

distinctly a minority undertaking. Advocates of the human-scientific approach can be found chiefly in the Person, Culture, and Religion Group of the American Academy of Religion. In Europe, the International Society for the Psychology of Religion is inclusive of both traditions.

Three General Goals

Implicit in Flournoy's methodological principles are three goals that are more explicit in James's *Varieties* and that have characterized the psychology of religion to this day. The first one – the one for which James is most famous – is the descriptive task: identifying and describing the field's object of study. When the aim is a *psychology of religious persons*, as it was for James and Flournoy, the object is religious experience or – more broadly – religious attitudes, sentiments, and other such terms intended to encompass religion as it becomes embodied over time in individual lives. When, on the other hand, the aim is a *psychology of religious content or tradition*, as it was for Sigmund Freud and C. G. Jung, the object becomes particular religious content that is shared by adherents of a specific tradition or that is found in a variety of traditions: images, symbols, stories, doctrines, scriptures, rituals, and so forth. Such shared religious content typically serves as the focus of individual religious experience and hence contributes to the shaping of it.

With the object of study well delineated, the psychologist of religion may then pursue either of two further goals: (1) accounting for the object's causal origins – what James called existential judgments – and (2) evaluating the fruits, or correlates, of the religious life, James's so-called spiritual judgments. The first of these goals, uncovering religion's causal origins, naturally requires some reconstruction of the past, whether it be an individual's past or a tradition's. This demand is particularly problematic for empirical researchers, who are by and large limited to measures obtained in the present. But retrospective measures – say, of parental religiosity when the respondent was a child or of family religious practices – along with contemporary assessment of a great variety of other psychological variables (e.g., attachment style) does allow for some meaningful inferences regarding causal associations in individual lives. Interpretive psychologists, on the other hand, may freely draw on a variety of resources for reconstructing the past, of both individuals and traditions.

As a self-acknowledged defender of the religious outlook if not its popular forms, James was most interested in revealing the fruits of the religious life. That goal today dominates the work of empirical researchers. Having constructed a variety of measures for assessing individual differences in religiosity, such investigators have for more than half a century sought to identify its correlates in a diversity of realms. Initially, in an effort to understand the impulses underlying the appalling inhumanity of World War II, the focus was mainly on negative social attitudes, including authoritarianism, ethnocentrism, dogmatism, and prejudice. Religious persons, it was found, tended to score higher than nonreligious persons on measures of these attitudes. Subtler measures of religiousness were subsequently developed, mainly of "intrinsic" and "extrinsic" religious orientations, to demonstrate that it is not religiousness per se that is associated with such negative social attitudes, but superficial or inauthentic forms of it. In time, attention shifted from social attitudes to mental and physical health, once again anticipating that intrinsic, or sincere, religiosity would be associated with more positive outcomes. Today, especially with the encouragement of munificent Templeton Foundation grants, there is increasing interest in demonstrating religion's positive association with certain classic virtues, including forgiveness, gratitude, and humility.

Challenges to the Psychology of Religion

From its beginnings, the psychology of religion has faced a number of critics. Psychologists, who tend in general to be less religious than many other academic and professional groups, have long been suspicious of any interest in religion on the part of their colleagues. Scholars of religion, on the other side, are often critical of what seem to them to be reductionistic if not also hostile views of religion among its psychological interpreters. Thus the psychology of religion has been an academic stepchild from its beginnings. Graduate programs and academic positions in the field have always been scarce, and where they appear they are usually subordinated to theological or pastoral training. Undergraduate courses on the psychology of religion are most often taught in departments of religion at church-related schools; otherwise they are likely offered only because some faculty member has a personal interest in the subject matter. Nonsectarian programs in the psychology of religion have been more common in England and Europe, where chairs in the field were founded beginning early in the twentieth century. Yet even there the field has never been widely pursued, and recent changes in economic conditions, in conjunction with the traditional priorities of theological faculties, have brought

reductions in both chairs and programs, most notably in the Scandinavian countries.

Such external difficulties are complicated by challenges that are intrinsic to the field. Most apparent is the debate between empirical and interpretive approaches, between quantitative and qualitative methodologies, which, beyond determining the research methods used, have broad implications for how religion is constructed and what questions are posed. Less obvious and more difficult is the conundrum of addressing a phenomenon that interprets itself in relationship to a transcendent dimension that by definition lies beyond the conceptual tools and understanding of psychology. Flournoy's exclusion principle suggests the possibility of bracketing such interpretations, but in reality all researchers come to the field with personal religious views that inevitably shape the questions they address. If one takes a religious outlook to be fundamentally mistaken, as it was by Freud, one will naturally ask how it may have arisen, either in human history or in an individual life. If one has oneself a sense of the transcendent, on the other hand, one will naturally be inclined to ask why it eludes other persons. Given the obvious diversity of religious constructions of reality, the latter question would likely be posed from within a particular theological or religious framework, inevitably threatening to transform the psychology of religion into a sectarian enterprise.

One solution would be to pursue a purely descriptive psychology of religion. But that, the German philosopher Max Scheler once argued, would require a separate psychology of religion for every tradition. Another seeming solution would be the strategy of setting aside any questions about the nature or origins of religion and merely examining its fruits instead. Although widely embraced, this strategy has long been recognized as likewise shaped by religious agendas, which affect the religiosity scales one adopts or devises, the variables one investigates, and the conclusions one draws. Of the respondents to a 1998 survey of the members of Division 36 of APA, the majority of whom are clinical practitioners, nearly all reported themselves to be moderately or highly religious or spiritual. Thus it is not surprising that most research is aimed, subtly or not, at demonstrating the value of religion, and that there is a parallel burgeoning of works on the integration of spirituality into psychotherapy, some published by the APA.

Most of the religiously liberal founders of the psychology of religion sought to reinterpret or even transform religion to make it serviceable in the modern world. Today, the psychology of religion serves as a rubric under which more religiously conservative psychologists act as caretakers and promoters of traditional religious convictions. The ideal, most fully realized by James Pratt, of a truly disinterested discipline that investigates a broad range of phenomena drawn from a diversity of religious traditions thus seems today evermore elusive.

See also: ❧ Analytical Psychology ❧ Authoritarian Personality ❧ Depth Psychology and Spirituality ❧ Erikson, Erik ❧ Faith Development Theory ❧ Freud, Sigmund, and Religion ❧ Genetics of Religiosity ❧ God Image ❧ James, William ❧ Judaism and Christianity in Freudian Psychology ❧ Judaism and Christianity in Jungian Psychology ❧ Jung, Carl Gustav ❧ Jung, Carl Gustav, and Religion ❧ Meditation ❧ Mysticism and Psychoanalysis ❧ Object Relations Theory ❧ Pruyser, Paul ❧ Psychology and the Origins of Religion ❧ Psychology as Religion ❧ Religion and Mental and Physical Health ❧ Religious Coping ❧ Religious Experience ❧ Self Psychology ❧ Sex and Religion ❧ Winnicott, Donald Woods

Bibliography

Batson, C. D., Schoenrade, P., & Ventis, W. L. (1993). *Religion and the individual: A social-psychological perspective*. New York: Oxford University Press.

Belzen, J. A., & Wikström, O. (Eds.). (1997). *Taking a step back: Assessments of the psychology of religion*. Uppsala: Acta Universitatis Upsaliensis.

Flournoy, T. (1902). Les principes de la psychologie religieuse. *Archives de Psychologie, 2*, 327–366.

Hill, P. C., & Hood, R. W., Jr. (Eds.). (1999). *Measures of religiosity*. Birmingham, AL: Religious Education Press.

Hood, R. W., Jr., Hill, P. C., & Spilka, B. (2009). *The psychology of religion: An empirical approach* (4th ed.). New York: Guilford.

Hyde, K. E. (1990). *Religion in childhood and adolescence: A comprehensive review of the research*. Birmingham, AL: Religious Education Press.

James, W. (1902/1985). *The varieties of religious experience: A study in human nature*. Cambridge, MA: Harvard University Press.

Jonte-Pace, D., & Parsons, W. B. (Eds.). (2001). *Religion and psychology: Mapping the terrain*. London: Routledge.

Paloutzian, R. F., & Park, C. L. (Eds.). (2005). *Handbook of the psychology of religion and spirituality*. New York: Guilford.

Pargament, K. I. (1997). *The psychology of religion and coping: Theory, research, practice*, New York: Guilford.

Pratt, J. B. (1920). *The religious consciousness: A psychological study*. New York: Macmillan.

Roelofsma, P. H. M. P., Corveleyn, J. M. T., & Van Saane, J. W. (Eds.). (2003). *One hundred years of psychology of religion: Issues and trends in a century long quest*. Amsterdam: VU University Press.

Wulff, D. M. (1997). *Psychology of religion: Classic and contemporary* (2nd ed.). New York: John Wiley & Sons.

Wulff, D. M. (1998). Rethinking the rise and fall of the psychology of religion. In A. L. Molendijk & P. Pels (Eds.), *Religion in the making: The emergence of the sciences of religion* (pp. 181–202). Leiden: Brill.

Wulff, D. M. (2001–2002). The psychology of religion and the problem of apologetics. *Temenos: Studies in Comparative Religion, 37–38*, 241–261.

Psychosis

Kate M. Loewenthal

What is psychosis? How is it related to religion and religious factors?

Psychoses are psychiatric illnesses, normally distinguished from neuroses, the other main group of psychiatric disorders. In psychosis the degree of impairment and lack of insight are said to be more severe than in neurosis. Psychotic illnesses have been categorized into two broad groups, the schizophrenic disorders and the bipolar disorders. There are significant concerns about the use of these diagnostic categories, but they are likely to remain in use for the foreseeable future. In schizophrenia, the individual normally shows a marked deterioration in self-care, work functioning, and/or social relations, but no major changes in mood. There is no evidence of an organic cause (drugs, or a medical condition). Symptoms normally include two or more of: delusions, hallucinations, incoherent speech, catatonic behavior (rigid, frozen posture), flat or very inappropriate mood. The DSM-IV classification lists a large number of related disorders in the schizophrenia group, such as the paranoid or catatonic types, but here we will consider schizophrenia as an overall diagnostic category. The other general form of psychosis is considered to be bipolar (manic-depressive, cyclothymic) mood disorder, swinging from high to low moods, sometimes with intervening periods of "normal" mood. The most striking feature of bipolar disorders is mania, euphoric joy out of proportion to circumstances, plus at least some of the following irritability and anger especially if plans are frustrated, hyperactivity, going without sleep, poor judgment, following ones own grandiose ideas and plans and feeling others are too slow, self-esteem approaching grandiosity, flamboyance, delusions or hallucinations (Comer, 1999: 352–357). About one person in a hundred may be affected by a psychotic disorder at some time in their lives. It may pass, or respond to medication or other treatment, or the person may continue significantly disturbed.

How do psychoses relate to religion? There are several important questions for discussion.

Do Religious Factors Correlate with or Cause Psychosis?

The short answer is that there are no clear associations between schizophrenia – or possibly predisposing personality traits – and religious factors. There is some tentative evidence that psychotic episodes may be precipitated in those already prone to disturbance, by some religious practices such as meditation, but this evidence is currently very thin.

The associations between religious factors and psychotic illness have been difficult to disentangle. This is partly because some religious behaviors and beliefs – especially if they stem from a tradition alien to clinicians – may be seen as symptoms of illness, and a misdiagnosis may be made. For example a devout woman who had been sexually abused began to pray and bible-study frequently and eat moderately in an attempt to purify herself. This was interpreted as symptomatic of schizophrenia (Loewenthal, 2007: 37). Beliefs that the evil eye, spells or spirits are causing somatic symptoms may be seen as delusory, even though in contemporary transcultural psychiatry, good clinical outcomes have been reported when clinicians treat these beliefs respectfully. A further set of factors complicating the picture is that stress may well induce mood disturbances and other psychiatric symptoms, and in an attempt to cope, individuals may resort to prayer and other religious practices (Bhugra, 2002; Siddle, Haddock, Tarrier, and Faragher, 2002). Indeed there is considerable evidence that prayer and other religious practices may relieve distress (Pargament, 1997; Maltby, Lewis, and Day, 1999; Loewenthal, 2007: 59–67). Thus there may be the appearance of an association between mental illness and religiosity, but religiosity is an effect, not a cause. Furthermore, if and when stress is reduced and symptoms alleviate, religious coping is reduced – again, giving the appearance of an association between better mental health and lower religiosity. Only longitudinal studies, in which individuals are followed-up over time, can tell us more about whether religion plays a causal role in psychosis and other mental illnesses. At the moment, this does not seem likely, for schizophrenia.

There are a number of personality traits which have been suggested to relate to the tendency to schizophrenia and psychotic illness. The most heavily-researched of these is the so-called Psychoticism (P) measure in the Eysenck Personality inventory. This is negatively associated with religiosity (Eysenck, 1998). A more complex set of traits fall under the head of schizotypy, which involves personality traits which might indicate prodromal schizophrenia, including discomfort in close relationships, and odd forms of thinking and perceiving. The different aspects of schizotypy relate in complex ways to religiosity (Joseph and Diduca, 2001), with no substantial evidence to support the idea that religious factors are related to schizophrenia or possible predisposing personality factors.

It has been suggested that meditation and possibly other religious practices and experiences may precede episodes of manic disorder in individuals who are susceptible (Wilson, 1998; Yorston, 2001; Kalian and Witztum, 2002). However this suggestion is based on clinical case histories, and there is insufficient quantitative evidence in further support of this suggestion.

Can We Distinguish Between Pathological and Benign Visions and Voices?

This has been a longstanding problem for well-intentioned and culturally-sensitive psychiatrists, given that visions and voices are supposed to be symptoms of schizophrenia. Littlewood and Lipsedge (1997), and Greenberg and Witztum (2001) offer fascinating and often tragic examples of diagnostic and therapeutic difficulties. It has now been well-documented that visions and voices are commonly-experienced by healthy individuals, and cannot be regarded in themselves, as symptoms of psychosis (see Loewenthal, 2007: 17–21). Some religious groups encourage or praise the experiencing of visions, or the hearing of voices, and these can be valued aspects of spirituality. Recent work examining the comparing the experiences of members of religious groups, and of others without psychiatric illness, with experiences of psychotic individuals indicates that the visions and voices experienced by the psychotically ill are significantly more unpleasant and uncontrollable than those experienced by others (Peters, Day, McKenna, and Orbach, 1999; Davies, Griffiths, and Vice, 2001). This work does give clues as to how psychotic visions and voices might be identified. Importantly, we can conclude that the experiencing of visions and voices should no longer in itself be treated as symptomatic of psychosis.

What Is the Significance of Belief in Demons, Evil Spirits and the Like, in Relation to Psychotic Illness?

Belief in evil spirits, demons, and other malignant spiritual forces is surprisingly widespread, including highly-developed, urbanized countries. A striking example involves sleep paralysis, which is as often reported in highly developed countries in which belief in evil spirits is not well-supported, as in less developed countries. The individual feels wakeful but unable to move, and is conscious of a shadowy presence (Hufford, 2005). The experience is usually unpleasant, interpreted as involving evil forces, and seldom mentioned for fear of being thought insane. In fact this condition is not a psychiatric problem at all, in spite of the fears and beliefs of those who have experienced it. This example highlights the existence of a widespread and popular idea that the experience of malign spiritual forces is closely related to insanity. Lipsedge (1996), and Kroll, Bachrach, and Carey, (2002) have shown that in medieval times demons and other malign spiritual forces were only occasionally seen as possible causes of psychiatric illness. Contemporary studies have examined beliefs that malign spiritual forces can be causes of insanity. Such beliefs have been reported in many countries, for example Egypt (Coker, 2004), Israel (Heilman and Witztum, 2000), South Africa (Ensink and Robertson, 1999) and Switzerland (Pfeifer, 1994), and there has been some success reported in deploying healing methods which are believed by patients to dispel evil spiritual forces. It has been suggested that the experience of demons and the like may be regarded as an "idiom of distress" (Heilman and Witztum, 2000). Contemporary clinical practitioners with experience in different cultural settings would advocate incorporating beliefs about spiritual forces as causes of disturbance into treatment plans, wherever possible.

What Is the Current Status of the Concept of Religious Mania?

Religious monomania is a now-discarded diagnostic category. At one time it was popular, and used to denote intense religious excitement and enthusiasm, to the extent that the individual had gone beyond the bounds of the acceptable and containable. For example Jonathan Martin, a fundamentalist preacher, who thought the clergy of his time (early nineteenth century) were too lax. He had some dreams which seemed to him significant, for example in one he saw a black cloud over York Minster. These dreams inspired him to set fire to York Minster (Lipsedge, 2003). At the time this act was a capital offence, but the diagnosis of monomania helped to get the death sentence commuted to imprisonment. With religious and other monomanias, there were difficulties in distinguishing between acceptable and pathological levels of behavior – one group's terrorist is another group's martyr, for example.

Conclusions

There is little to support the idea that religious factors play a role in causing psychotic illnesses. It is likely that religious coping may be helpful in relieving the distress associated with psychotic illness, and the appearance of "religious symptoms" may indicate attempts to cope with distress, rather than as symptoms as such. However, as with other psychiatric illnesses, the religious context may shape the occurrence of stress, often a factor in psychiatric breakdown. The religious context may also shape expressions of distress.

See also: ❂ Demons ❂ Psychiatry ❂ Religious Coping ❂ Visions

Bibliography

Bhugra, D. (Ed.). (1996). *Psychiatry and religion: Context, consensus, and controversies*. London: Routledge.

Bhugra, D. (2002). Self-concept: Psychosis and attraction of new religious movements. *Mental Health, Religion and Culture, 5*, 239–252.

Coker, E. M. (2004). The construction of religious and cultural meaning in Egyptian psychiatric patient charts. *Mental Health, Religion and Culture, 7*, 323–348.

Comer, R. J. (1999). *Abnormal psychology* (2nd ed.). New York: Worth/Freeman.

Davies, M. F., Griffiths, M., & Vice, S. (2001). Affective reactions to auditory hallucinations in psychotic, evangelical and control groups. *British Journal of Clinical Psychology, 40*, 361–370.

Ensink, K., & Robertson, B. (1999). Patient and family experiences of psychiatric services and African indigenous healers. *Transcultural Psychiatry, 36*, 23–44.

Eysenck, M. W. (1998). Personality and the psychology of religion. *Mental Health, Religion and Culture, 1*, 11–19.

Greenberg, D., & Witztum, E. (2001). *Sanity and sanctity: Mental health work among the ultra-orthodox in Jerusalem*. New Haven, CT: Yale University Press.

Heilman, S. C., & Witztum, E. (2000). All in faith: Religion as the idiom and means of coping with distress. *Mental Health, Religion and Culture, 3*, 115–124.

Hufford, D. J. (2005). Sleep paralysis as spiritual experience. *Transcultural Psychiatry, 42*, 11–45.

Joseph, S., & Diduca, D. (2001). Schizotypy and religiosity in 13–18 year old school pupils. *Mental Health, Religion and Culture, 4*, 63–70.

Kalian, M., & Witztum, E. (2002). Jerusalem syndrome as reflected in the pilgrimage and biographies of four extraordinary women from the 14th century to the end of the second millennium. *Mental Health, Religion and Culture, 5*, 1–16.

Koenig, H. (Ed.). (1998). *Religion and mental health*. San Diego, CA: Academic Press.

Kroll, J., Bachrach, B., & Carey, K. (2002). A reappraisal of medieval mysticism and hysteria. *Mental Health, Religion and Culture, 5*, 83–98.

Lipsedge, M. (1996). Religion and madness in history. In D. Bhugra (Ed.), *Psychiatry and religion: Context, consensus, controversies*. London: Routledge.

Lipsedge, M. (2003). Jonathan Martin: Prophet and incendiary. *Mental Health, Religion and Culture, 6*, 59–78.

Littlewood, R., & Lipsedge, M. (1997). *Aliens and alienists: Ethnic minorities and psychiatry* (3rd ed.). London: Oxford University Press.

Loewenthal, K. M. (2007). *Religion, culture and mental health.* Cambridge, England: Cambridge University Press.

Maltby, J., Lewis, C. A., & Day, L. (1999). Religious orientation and psychological well-being: The role of the frequency of personal prayer. *British Journal of Health Psychology, 4*, 363–378.

Pargament, K. (1997). *The psychology of religion and coping.* New York: Guilford Press.

Peters, E., Day, S., McKenna, J., & Orbach, G. (1999). Delusional ideas in religious and psychiatric populations. *British Journal of Clinical Psychology, 38*, 83–96.

Pfeifer, S. (1994). Belief in demons and exorcism in psychiatric patients in Switzerland. *British Journal of Medical Psychology, 67*, 247–258.

Siddle, R., Haddock, G., Tarrier, N., & Faragher, E. B. (2002). Religious delusions in patients admitted to hospital with schizophrenia. *Social Psychiatry and Psychiatric Epidemiology, 37*, 130–138.

Wilson, W. P. (1998). Religion and psychoses. In H. Koenig (Ed.), *Religion and mental health* (pp. 161–172). San Diego, CA: Academic Press.

Yorston, G. (2001). Mania precipitated by meditation: a case report and literature review. *Mental Health, Religion and Culture, 4*, 209–214.

Psychospiritual

Ann Gleig

The term psychospiritual has entered psychological and religious discourse as a loose designation for the integration of the psychological and the spiritual. As a broad term it can denote a variety of positions between psychology and spirituality: a supplementation, integration, identification or conflation of the two fields. It is commonly used to describe a wide range of therapeutic systems which embrace a spiritual dimension of the human being as fundamental to psychic health and full human development and which utilize both psychological and spiritual methods (such as meditation, yoga, dream-work, breathwork) in a holistic, integrated approach to healing and inner growth. Included here are Jungian psychology, Roberto Assagioli's Psychosynthesis, the post-Jungian archetypal psychology of James Hillman, transpersonal psychology, such as the work of Abraham Maslow, Stanislav Grof, Ken Wilber, Michael Washburn and Charles Tart, the spiritual psychology of Robert Sardello and a plethora of contemporary spiritual therapies which are being developed within an East-West framework.

William Parsons (2008) offers some useful historical contextualization for the western lineage of the psychospiritual through his discussion of the "*psychologia perennis,*" an unchurched, psychological form of spirituality whose origins can be seen as early as the sixteenth and seventeenth centuries with the appearance of mysticism as a subjective experience divorced from church and tradition. The emergence of a generic "Absolute" framed as an inner universal, sacred dimension of man allowed for the psychologization of mysticism and links the figures of Romain Rolland, William James, Carl Jung, and Richard Maurice Bucke with humanistic and transpersonal psychology. While recognizing significant differences in metapsychology and therapeutic techniques among these thinkers, Parsons identifies a number of common characteristics: a championing of the individual as an unchurched site of religiosity, the search for the origin of mysticism in the unconscious, a valorization of personal unchurched mystical experiences, an advocacy of perennialism, the discernment of innate, intuitive, mystical capacities, the development of a technology of altered states, the institutionalization of psycho-spiritual therapeutic regimens and a vision of social transformation grounded in the psychospiritual transformation of the individual.

Psychospiritual therapies explicitly protest against the reductive and materialist assumptions of mainstream behavioral and cognitive psychology and seek to return the soul or psyche to psychology. While traditionally associated with the humanistic-existential strands within depth psychology, as Parsons (2007) points out there has also been a recent wave of interest in spirituality within the psychoanalytic field. Much of contemporary psychoanalytic literature suggests that spirituality has seeped into many aspects of the practice of analysts and of the therapeutic expectations of analysands. For example, the analyst Michael Eigen, who is particularly influenced by Jewish mysticism and Zen, describes psychoanalytic therapy as "a psychospiritual journey," and argues that meditative practices and psychoanalysis are not separate but rather integral parts of the growth process (Molino, 1998). Similarly, analyst Paul Cooper claims that spiritual practices have influenced many dimensions of psychoanalytic therapy, such as theory, technique, training, and supervision, and draws attention to the important empirical fact that many of his analysands understand psychoanalytic therapy as part of their spiritual growth. Furthermore, Cooper argues that there is undeniable cultural drift in this direction (Molino, 1998).

In a similar vein, concerns with the psychospiritual have entered into mainstream psychotherapy. This is reflected in both the professional psychotherapeutic accrediting of spiritual therapies and the establishment of a number of associations that seek to integrate the two fields of spirituality and psychotherapy, for example, the Institute for Psychotherapy, Science and Spirituality, formerly the Center for Spirituality and Psychotherapy, established in 1997 to study how psychotherapy can foster the emergence of the spiritual dimension in life and how spiritual practice may enhance the psychotherapeutic encounter.

The term psychospiritual has also been applied to mystical traditions, particularly Asian, which include psychological development as an indispensable component of spiritual growth or see psychological and spiritual development as inseparable. Some of these traditions are seen as inherently containing a psychospiritual approach. A notable example, here, is Sufism which aims for a psychospiritual transformation of the human being from a state of ego-centeredness to a state of purity and submission to the will of God (Frager, 1999). Other spiritual traditions have incorporated western psychology into traditional mysticism to create new psychospiritual integrations. An influential example of this is integral psychology, a synthesis of the Indian mystic Sri Aurobindo's teachings with the findings of depth psychology as developed by his disciple, Haridas Chaudhuri (Cortright, 2007). Another contemporary psychospiritual tradition which incorporates the insights of psychoanalytic theory to aid spiritual realization is A. H. Almaas's Diamond Approach (2004).

Finally, the psychospiritual is a term often used interchangeably with the cultural phenomena referred to as psychology *as* religion and to signify the psychologization of religion and the sacralization of psychology that is a defining mark of the New Age. Hence, commentaries on, critiques of, and predications for, these two related, if not identical, strands are indispensable in illuminating different aspects of the psychospiritual.

See also: ❂ Depth Psychology and Spirituality ❂ Psyche ❂ Psychology as Religion ❂ Psychology of Religion ❂ Transpersonal Psychology ❂ Zen

Bibliography

Almaas, A. H. (2004). *The inner journey home.* Boston, MA: Shambhala.
Assagioli, R. (1965). *Psychosynthesis.* New York: Viking Press.
Cortright, B. (2007). *Integral psychology: Yoga, growth and opening the heart.* Albany, NY: State University of New York Press.
Frager, R. (1999). *Heart, self and soul: The Sufi psychology of growth, balance and harmony.* Wheaton, IL: Quest Books.
Hardy, J. (1987). *A Psychology with a soul: Psychosynthesis in evolutionary context.* London: Routledge & Kegan Paul.
Maloney, A. (2007). *Alchemy of the soul: Integral healing: The work of psychology and spirituality.* Nevada City, CA: Blue Dolphin Publishing.
Mijares, S. (Ed.) (2005). *The psychospiritual clinician's handbook: Alternative methods for understanding and treating mental disorders.* Binghamton, NY: Haworth Press.
Molino, A. (Ed.). (1998). *The couch and the tree.* New York: North Point Press.
Parsons, W. B. (2007). Psychoanalytic spirituality. In J. Winer & J. Anderson (Eds.). *Spirituality and religion: Psychoanalytic perspectives.* Catskill, NY: Mental Health Resources.
Parsons, W. B. (2008). Psychologia Perennis and the academic study of mysticism. In W. B. Parsons, D. Jonte-Pace, S. Henking (Eds.), *Mourning religion.* Charlottesville, VA: University of Virginia Press.
Sardello, R. (2001). *Love and the world: A guide to conscious soul practice.* Herndon, VA: Lindisfarne Books.
Wilber, K. (2000). *Integral psychology: Consciousness, spirit, psychology, therapy.* Boston, MA: Shambhala.

Psychotherapy

Todd DuBose

On Caring Rather than Curing

Psychotherapy is an art and a science of caring for those in distress with the goal of helping others toward more fulfilling and meaningful experiences in their everyday existence. The ways in which this project is done is extremely diverse, and in fact, there are hundreds of practices in our contemporary situation that would claim the name "therapy." Although various kinds of histories have been written, I would like to offer a read of this history that highlights its inherent religiosity.

Discerning the beginnings of psychotherapy depends on how one defines this process, and whether or not one understands psychotherapy as a science, an art, or both. I argue that its foundation rests in both the history of the *cura animarum,* or the care of souls, and in the history of consolation literature and practices across a variety of religious traditions, "*Cura*" originally meant "care" rather than "cure" (McNiell, 1977; Jalland, 2000). The psychotherapist was an *iatros tes psuche,* or physician of the soul. Much as changed since these originations. Thomas Szasz (1988) notes that psychotherapy as a talk therapy originated in ancient rhetorical traditions, but, over time, psychotherapy has become a medical treatment. Szasz has argued, and I think correctly, that psychotherapy is not a medical treatment, evoking Aristotle's warning against the confluence of science and rhetoric.

Although aligned with Szasz's general project as a clarification and differentiation of psychotherapy from medical modeled practices, I nonetheless agree with Ernesto Spinelli's (2007) proposal that psychotherapy, or therapeia, should be understood in light of its true etiological foundation as less an art of persuasion and more a process of "walking with" another who suffers and is in distress. If cura is care and therapy is more a "walking with" rather than a "doing to," then contemporary practices of psychotherapy as problem solving and repairing brokenness are practices far from their origins. The conceptualizations of Spinelli, Szasz, and other like minded theorists and clinicians are much closer to the tradition of pastoral counseling as a companioning with another through existential transitions in life.

Another important distinction to be made about psychotherapy as seen from the field of psychology and religion concerns what is meant by the "psyche." Early Greek formation of this concept did not start with the psyche as a self-encapsulated thing or ego. Psyche was more closely aligned with nous, or mind (Louth, 1981). Mind, however, did not mean "brain," which is another confluence of irreconcilable differences based on a categorical mistake of fusing mind and brain (Brothers, 2001). Nous was "soul" and specifically the experiencer of meaning, significance and purpose, or telos (Louth, 1981). Hence, Viktor Frankl (1905–1997) developed his existential approach to psychotherapy and called it Logotherapy, basing logos on a noosological discernment of how meaning motivates our existential comportment in our lives (1946/1959). Bruno Bettleheim (1903–1990) has further pointed out that Sigmund Freud's (1856–1939) position on the psyche has been grossly misunderstood, often due to Freud's mechanistic conceptualizations of the psyche (Bettelheim, 1983). Freud's understanding of psyche, as Bettleheim argues, is the German word, Seele, or soul. This conceptualization is aligned with Martin Heidegger (1889–1976) and the psychiatrists with whom he dialogued regarding the implications of his philosophy for psychotherapy, Ludwig Binswanger (1881–1966) and Medard Boss (1903–1990). Whereas Binswanger (1967) understood the goal of therapy to be soul oriented goals, such as the ability to love and trust again, Boss and Heidegger described psychotherapy as a process of Seelsorgen, or soul care (Boss, 1963; Heidegger, 1987/2001). Heidegger (1962) still wanted to destruct any conception of the psyche or soul as a substantial entity, and so shift the focus from psyche as thing to human existence as Dasein. Dasein, or literally, "being there," is the unfolding of being amid the clearing and unburdening of human existence. Psychotherapy, or Daseinsanalysis, allows for the particular kinds of disclosure of one's existence and relationship to existential givens that give rise to symptomatic constrictions of one's freedom in the world.

Therapy as "Begin With"

This genealogical interlude shows how current practices of psychotherapy have been consistent with its origins the origins in some cases, and in other practices have diverged from its foundations. Therapy can be a fixing of broken psyches, a walking with persons, a "being with" and description of ways of being-in-the-world, an interpretation of relational patterning, or the regulation of unbalanced chemical processes, among other possibilities. Heidegger and Medard Boss considered this process more one of analysis than therapy, in which one loosens constrictions of Dasein's ways of being-in-the-world (Boss, 1979; Heidegger, 1962, 1987/2001). Regarding the psychology and religion field, at first glance "loosening throughout" seems at odds with the definition of religion as a "binding back." Nevertheless, with transcendent liberation as the goal of both processes, we can see how psychotherapy is itself a spiritual discipline.

An understanding of the spirituality of psychotherapy, then, depends on how one understands psyche and therapy or analysis. Although distinctions have been made between counseling, therapy, and spiritual direction, I believe these distinctions presuppose functional and content differences that are secondary to what is shared by all of these practices: therapeutic presence. The current consensus among meta-analysts of successful psychotherapeutic practice is that the therapeutic relationship is the key factor in therapeutic change and positive outcome. Training programs, therefore, should focus most of its emphasis on teaching trainees how to establishment and foster therapeutic relationships. With this focus, intangibles arise that are nonetheless significant factors in therapeutic outcome: empathic presence, depth of compassion, degrees of self and other acceptance, risks of transparency and disclosure, the quality of discernment, the felt sense of being understood, and so forth. These qualities of therapeutic presence are well grounded in all traditions of religious care of however the soul is conceived.

The therapeutic intangibles mentioned above require discipline to achieve that necessitates risk, sacrifice, and patience – again, familiar words to all spiritual traditions. Participation in these intangibles transforms all participants in the therapeutic process, including the therapist. Both participants are on a journey toward liberation and transformation, which is the lived experience of transcendence.

Commentary

One point for discussion in this commentary is how one adjudicates between the current insistence on providing evidence-based practices with this history of psychotherapy as spiritually informed by invisible, incommensurate, immeasurable phenomena that make up what is considered the sine qua non aspects of therapeutic change: therapeutic presence. Mere assessment from an outside position belies the history of concerned involvement and thousands of years of care and consolation. People do come to treatment in order to experience transcendence-as-transformation in their lives. Yet, being prescriptive about how one should live one's life can be intrusive at least and downright controlling at best, thus disempowering another's journey. An alternative is available, and one that is understood in light of its inherent religiosity: therapy as the clearing of space and lightening of burdens so being can unfold towards its ownmost potential in light of its embrace limitations. This is neither analysis alone, nor psycho-therapy, but a type of therapy nonetheless. One doesn't direct the future, but open possibilities towards it. Doing psychotherapy this way necessitates a less than controlling experimental approach to discerning therapeutic quality.

At the forefront of the edification debates is a competition around which style of psychotherapy should be considered the most successful. Again, success depends on what counts as data and outcome, and, in fact, meta-analyses consistently suggest that all styles are more or less equally successful – depending, again, on the quality of the therapeutic relationship, which in turn depends on the quality of the therapeutic presence. Questions about therapeutic presence should be directed to the ancient spiritual traditions, particularly the ascetic and mystical dimensions of those traditions. What isn't discusses as much as it should be is the fact that no one really knows how change occurs, in spite of our obsessive attempts to predict and control change factors. In other words, we should include more discussion about one change factor in the therapeutic process that is as old as the traditions that can inform it: mystery.

Finally, the development and choice of therapeutic modality should also be a consideration in the process of soul care. With the shift of psyche to more than an isolated ego, and/or a growing awareness of systems, relational processes, and like kind phenomena, therapeutic modalities have expanded to include group, family, couple, and play therapy. At the same time, psychotherapy still remains within a medically-modeled format as long as those who come for help are seen as compromised and those who help them are seen as experts. Psychotherapy in the future could break this hegemony by focusing more on communities becoming more therapeutic and therapeutic milieus expanding toward more invitation to true *koinonia*, or the experience of freely being oneself as affirmed and affirming otherness.

See also: ❯ Hermeneutics ❯ Homo Religiosus ❯ Lived Theology ❯ Meaning of Human Existence ❯ Phenomenological Psychology

Bibliography

Bettelheim, B. (1983). *Freud and man's soul: An important re-interpretation of Freudian theory*. New York: Vintage Press.

Binswanger, L. (1967). *Being-in-the-world: Selected papers of Ludwig Binswanger* (J. Needleman, Trans.). New York: Harper & Row.

Binswanger, L., & Foucault, M. (1993). Dream and existence. K. Hoeller (Ed.). Atlantic Highlands, NJ: Humanities Press International.

Boss, M. (1963). *Daseinsanalysis and psychoanalysis*. New York: Basic Books.

Boss, M. (1977). *I dreamt last night. . . .* New York: Gardner Press.

Boss, M. (1979). *Existential foundations of medicine and psychology* (S. Conway & A. Cleaves, Trans.). New York: Aronson.

Breggin, P. (2006). *The heart of being helpful: Empathy and the creation of a healing presence*. New York: Springer.

Brothers, L. (2001). *Mistaken identity: The mind-brain problem reconsidered*. Albany, NY: State University of New York Press.

Burston, D., & Frie, R. (2006). *Psychotherapy as a human science*. Pittsburgh, PA: Duquesne University Press.

Clebsch, W., & Jaekle, C. (1964). *Pastoral care in historical perspective: An essay with exhibits*. New York: Prentice-Hall.

Clinebell, H. (1966). *Basic types of pastoral counseling*. Nashville, TN: Abington Press.

Frankl, V. (1946/1959). *Man's search for meaning*. New York: Washington Square Press.

Heidegger, M. (1962). *Being and time* (J. Macquarrie & E. Robinson, Trans.). Oxford, England: Basil Blackwell.

Heidegger, M. (1987/2001). *Zollikon Seminars: Protocols – Conversations – Letters*. Evanston, IL: Northwestern University Press.

Jalland, P. (2000). *Death in the victorian family*. Oxford: Oxford University Press.

Louth, A. (1981). *The origins of the Christian mystical tradition: From Plato to Denys*. Oxford, England: Clarendon Press.

McNiell, J. (1977). *History of the cure of souls*. New York: Harper.

Spinelli, E. (2006). *Demystifying therapy*. London: PCCS Books.

Spinelli, E. (2007). *Practicing existential psychotherapy: The relational world*. London: Sage.

Szasz, T. (1988). *The myth of psychotherapy: Mental healing as religion, rhetoric, and repression.* Syracuse, NY: Syracuse University Press.

Wise, C. (1983). *Pastoral psychotherapy: Theory and practice.* New York: Jason Aronson.

Psychotherapy and Religion

Kate M. Loewenthal

This essay briefly outlines some of the varieties of psychotherapy practiced today, and looks at the development of the relationship between psychotherapy and religion under two broad headings: independence, and integration.

The Varieties of Psychotherapy

Freud (e.g., 1933) is usually credited with the discovery of the "talking cure" for psychiatric illness: psychoanalysis. Although in the late nineteenth and early twentieth centuries, psychiatric illness was dealt with by medical practitioners, the chief disturbances are those of behavior, thinking and feeling, often with no clear organic cause. The era of humane treatments had dawned, and pioneers such as Tuke, Pinel and Dix had established humane institutions for the care of the insane, in England, France and the USA respectively. But effective medical treatments were lacking. Psychoanalysis, the talking cure developed by Freud, was not always totally effective in producing improvements, but it was sufficiently effective to survive, expand and develop enormously during the twentieth century. Its development still continues and its clinical efficacy has been placed on a firm footing (e.g., Sandell, Blomberg, Lazar, Carlsson, Broberg, & Schubert, 2000). The theories, aims and methods of psychoanalysis can only be summarized briefly here. Psychoanalysis aims to enable to client to develop a conscious awareness of the feelings and ideas that underlie his or her habitual style of living and relating to others. These feelings and ideas have ruled his/her life in a powerful way. The origins of these feelings and ideas are unconscious. Awareness allows the possibility of assuming a level of control. One view of psychoanalysis, therefore, is that it helps make the unconscious, conscious. One route by which this is often achieved is via the "transference relationship," in which the client displays powerful feelings towards the analyst – anger, dependency, idealization – feelings which are not realistically related to the current context. The analysis of transference – the examination of these feelings and their earlier occurrences and origins – is an important route towards therapeutic improvement.

From its earliest days, psychoanalysis has engendered new theories and methods. Some are regarded as recognizably psychoanalytic – for example the neo- and post-Freudians (e.g., Horney, 1963), and Klein (1955) and her followers. Others, for example Rogers (1961), have developed schools of counseling in which a primary vehicle of improvement has been the therapist's support and regard for the client. Cognitive Behavior Therapy (CBT) (e.g., Beck, 2005) has begun to exert a very important influence in clinical practice, since it has been able to demonstrate effective outcomes in relatively few sessions. CBT functions by enabling the client to examine and evaluate his/her habitual thoughts, behaviors and feelings in a manner which is focused on the client's immediate problems and agreed-upon areas of improvement, and is therefore less wide-ranging than psychoanalytic therapy. There are many other varieties of psychological therapies, but this brief account has hinted at the range and approach of some of the dominant influences in this very active field.

Independence

A starting-point is to note Freud's apparent distaste for religion, for instance his view of religion as a universal obsessional neurosis (e.g., Freud, 1907). Spilka (1986), Loewenthal (1995) and others have described as the enormous range of ways in psychotherapists have seen and described the role of religion: religion may be a socializing and suppressing force, a source of guilt, a haven, a source of abuse, a therapy, and a hazard. Many of the views of religion expressed in the early days of psychoanalysis and psychotherapy were detrimental: religion was seen as damaging to mental health. One response to these views is to attempt to leave religion out of the picture in any attempt to work with mental health issues.

During the twentieth century, the mental health and religious leadership professions were often seen as parallel and largely independent, each offering solutions to human misery that were alternative rather than complementary. There was some antagonism. Some psychotherapeutic writers perceived only damaging effects of religion. Some religious leaders saw psychotherapy as a spiritually damaging venture (Loewenthal, 1995).

One reasonable justification for the independence of the psychotherapy and religious professions was advanced by Neeleman and Persaud (1995). While decrying the fact that mental health professionals overlook the often important religious concerns of their patients, they observe that mental health and religion are two largely independent areas of professional expertise. The mental health professional may feel – wisely – that s/he does not have the expertise to tackle religious issues. These, it might be felt, should be left to the chaplaincy. Similarly the religious leader may feel that s/he does not have the expertise to tackle mental health problems.

These concerns gave rise to the development of pastoral counseling among the ministry, and to transcultural psychiatry and spiritual counseling among mental health professionals. Both developments aim to give professionals awareness of and training in issues in mental health and religion, including sufficient knowledge of when to cross-refer. Many mental health practitioners and religious leaders/chaplains work now harmoniously with each other, and earlier mistrust and antagonism have generally been laid to rest.

Integration

The history of peace between psychotherapy and religion is almost as old as the history of war. Carl Gustav Jung was the prominent early exponent of harmony, with his view of spirituality as intrinsic to human nature, suggesting that spiritual growth and psychological growth involved the same processes – an inner journey involving the healing of fragmented aspects of the self, and the development of individuation (e.g., Jung, 1958). The Jungian influence was almost certainly the strongest in the early development of pastoral psychology.

Other prominent exponents of harmony include Rizzutto (1974) and Spero (1992). Both these authors use objects-relations theory (a development of Kleinian thinking), which deals with how from infancy onwards, the individual internalizes, splits, and harmonizes "objects" from his/her social world. G-d is an internal "object" and the relationship with G-d may be examined, developed and healed in the course of psychotherapy.

There has been a strong growth of interest in psychotherapy and religion, as seen for instance in the psychoanalytic explorations in Stein's (1999) *Beyond Belief: Psychotherapy and Religion*. David Black (2000: 25) explores recent thinking involving a neuro-scientific model. In Black's view some of the values of psychotherapy and religion are remarkably similar, for example love, mourning and reparation. Nevertheless their goals are different – psychoanalytic therapy proceeds by the analysis of transference to allow the ego to achieve optimal functioning in the individual's social world. The goal of religion is to achieve "a true view of the universe and our relations to it." Black believes that mature religions aim to give access to positions which differ from what can be established and worked through in psychoanalysis. "A religious vision opens up the possibility of other sorts of development which go beyond the world of human object relations" (p. 22). Thus, interestingly, Black appears to suggest that in object-relations terms, the potential for spiritual and personal development may differ in the religious life, from what can be achieved in psychoanalysis.

In a different vein, Viktor Frankl (1986) has explored the importance of the will to meaning, and the role of purpose in life in psychological health. His introduction of these concepts into the practice of psychotherapy has enabled a positive approach in working with troubled individuals.

Attending to the client's spiritual problems has become a strong focus of attention in the twenty-first century (Pargament and Tarakeshwar, 2005; Pargament, 2007). One noteworthy point is that the term *spirituality* has become increasingly popular as an alternative and substitute for the term *religion* – the implications of this shift are reviewed by Pargament, also Loewenthal (2007) and others. In *Spiritually Integrated Psychotherapy,* Pargament defines spirituality as *the search for the sacred*. He argues that spiritual concerns are often salient for many clients and therapists need to be equipped to deal with them. Therapists need to be able to recognize spirituality which can lead to growth, and spirituality which can lead to a decline, also spirituality which is part of the problem, and spirituality which is part of the solution.

Another development has been the question of examining different cultural-religious traditions. In what ways do different traditions differ in the extent and manner of their integration into psychotherapeutic practice? Such issues are explored in Richards and Bergin (2000), in their *Handbook of Psychotherapy and Religious Diversity,* and Dowd and Nielsen (2006), in their *Exploration of the Psychologies in Religion.*

Conclusions

The early development of psychotherapy featured some mistrust as the proponents of psychotherapy and religion viewed each others' ideas. Nevertheless from the early stages there were noteworthy attempts to integrate the practice of psychotherapy with the religious and spiritual concerns of clients, and such attempts are now flourishing. On the whole, it is the psychoanalytic and counseling schools of psychotherapy, rather than the cognitive-behavioral school, that have been responsible for these developments.

See also: ⊚ Depth Psychology and Spirituality ⊚ Freud, Sigmund ⊚ Jung, Carl Gustav ⊚ Psychoanalysis ⊚ Psychology as Religion ⊚ Psychology of Religion ⊚ Psychotherapy

Bibliography

Beck, A. T. (2005). The current state of cognitive therapy: A 40-year retrospective. *Archives of General Psychiatry, 62*, 953–959.

Black, D. M. (2000). The functioning of religions from a modern psychoanalytic perspective. *Mental Health, Religion and Culture, 3*, 13–26.

Dowd, T., & Nielsen, S. (Eds.). (2006). *Exploration of the psychologies in religion.* New York: Springer.

Frankl, V. E. (1986). *The doctor and the soul.* New York: Basic Books.

Freud, S. (1907). Obsessive acts and religious practices. In *Collected Papers* 1907/1924 (pp. 25–35). London: Hogarth Press.

Freud, S. (1933). *New introductory lectures on psychoanalysis.* Harmondsworth: Penguin.

Horney, K. (1963). *The collected works.* New York: W. W. Norton.

Jung, C. G. (1958). *Psychology and religion: East and west.* London: Routledge & Kegan Paul.

Klein, M. (1955). *On envy and gratitude and other works.* New York: Delacourte Press.

Loewenthal, K. M. (1995). *Mental health and religion.* London: Chapman & Hall.

Loewenthal, K. M. (2007). *Religion culture and mental health.* Cambridge, England: Cambridge University Press.

Neeleman, J., & Persaud, R. (1995). Why do psychiatrists neglect religion? *British Journal of Medical Psychology, 68*, 169–178.

Pargament, K. I. (2007). *Spiritually integrated psychotherapy.* New York: Guilford Press.

Pargament, K. I., & Tarakeshwar N. (Eds.). (2005). Spiritually integrated psychotherapy [Special Issue]. *Mental Health, Religion and Culture, 8*(3), 155–238.

Richards, P. S., & Bergin, A. E. (Eds.). (2000). *Handbook of psychotherapy and religious diversity.* Washington DC: American Psychological Association.

Rizzutto, A. M. (1974). Object relations and the formation of the image of God. *British Journal of Medical Psychology, 47*, 83–89.

Rogers, C. R. (1961). *On becoming a person.* Boston, MA: Houghton Mifflin.

Sandell, R., Blomberg, J., Lazar, A., Carlsson, J., Broberg, J., & Schubert, J. (2000). Varieties of long-term outcome among patients in psychoanalysis and long-term psychotherapy: A review of findings in the stockholm outcome of psychoanalysis and psychotherapy project. *International Journal of Psycho-Analysis, 81*, 921–942.

Spero, M. H. (1992). *Religious objects as psychological structures: A critical integration of object relations theory, psychotherapy and judaism.* Chicago, IL: University of Chicago Press.

Spilka, B. (1986). *Spiritual issues: Do they belong in psychological practice?* Philadephia, PA: Haworth Press.

Stein, S. (Ed.). (1999). *Beyond belief: Psychotherapy and religion.* London: Karnac.

Puer Aeternus

Paul Larson

"*Puer Aeternus*" is a Latin phrase for "eternal child." It is an archetypal complex; that is, a psychological and mythical amalgam of symbols and images of eternal youth. It is embodied in the literary work, *Peter Pan* by the British author James Barry (1860–1937), which has been adapted numerous times in plays, movies and television. It is often used as a pejorative phrase to denote a young man who will not make the emotional commitments of adulthood and prefers to continually "play the field."

Pushing the archetypal image backward in time from Victorian literature, Pan was the proverbial "naughty boy" in Greek mythology. Like the lost boys in Barry's work, Pan lived out in the wild woods and was notorious for unrestrained sexuality. Other creatures fill this role, centaurs, half man half horse, were notorious for not only their unrestrained sexual appetites, but for their aggression as well. Satyrs, half man, half goat were Pan's species, and he was their chief. Barry's Peter Pan was pre-pubescent and sexually neuter, boyish with charm but without the threat of rising sexuality. But Pan as the archetype of an animalistic approach to sexual relations informs the use of the Peter Pan complex today.

In the gay male imago, *Puer Aeternus* can be seen as the continuation of the mythic image of same-sex attraction begun with the "erastes/eromenos" relationship as well as the Zeus and Ganymede story. The archetype continued through the real historical characters of the Roman emperor Hadrian (76–138 CE) and his adolescent companion, Antinous, a youth from Bithynia in modern day Turkey. After his tragic death by drowning in the Nile river while the two visited that province of Rome, Hadrian had him deified. The godling ephebe, Antinuous, became a late Roman polytheistic cult with particular support from men who sought erotic connection and love with other men. The Antinoan temples lasted until Theodosius closed all pagan temples between 388 and 381 CE.

In Jungian archetypal psychology the *Puer Aeternus*, or eternal child, represents a regressive romanticization of childhood and can be unhealthy, preventing normal adult development, or it can be transformed into an appreciation of one's remaining child-like qualities as one ages. Woman can have "puella eternis" issues as easily as men struggle with the puer. All people struggle with the eternal child as a reaction to aging. The dialectic polarity in the psyche is that of puer and senex. The emulation of youth is a strong tug in the mind fed by our consumer culture. We struggle to hold on to the seemingly unbounded energy, enthusiasm, and vitality as the "eternal child" continues to influence our choices and feelings. The process of self-exploration allows us to confront this archetypal force and through dialectic to transform the energies into an age-appropriate blend of *Puer Aeternus* and the elder, sage and wise one. We start as the former and, should we live so long, embody the other.

See also: ❯ Archetype ❯ Homosexuality ❯ Jung, Carl Gustav

Bibliography

Hillman, J. (1979). *Puer papers.* New York: Spring Publications.
Von Franz, M. L. (2000). *The problem of the puer eternus* (3rd ed.). New York: Inner City Books.

Purgatory

Thomas St. James O'Connor

There are diverse beliefs about the existence of Purgatory. There is little evidence for purgatory in the Scriptures. The notion of Purgatory began in the Patristic period. Purgatory is a time, place and/or moment in the afterlife between God's judgment at death and the final beatific vision. Eastern mystical theology sees purgatory as a time of purification. Humans need to be purged of their sins before seeing God face-to-face. Purgatory is the final step in human growth and divination. In Western theology, purgatory contains the notion of reparation (satisfaction) for one's sins through penance. Sinners take responsibility for the sins and accept the consequences (justice). In the medieval time, Popes and Church councils addressed this doctrine. The Council of Florence (1439) in the *Decree to the Greeks* sought to balance the Western and Eastern notions. The reformers (Luther and Melanchton, Calvin and Zwingli) threw out the notion of purgatory. They believed that God's grace in Christ was more than sufficient and that human purification and satisfaction were part of a salvation-by-works mentality. The reformers were particularly incensed by the selling of indulgences which Tetzel argued helped release souls from Purgatory. The Roman Catholic church in the Council of Trent (1563) re-affirmed the teaching on purgatory while eliminating the excesses like the sale of indulgences. In the twentieth century, Vatican II and Paul VI re-affirmed the doctrine of purgatory.

Praying for the dead (those in purgatory) has been part of Roman Catholic piety since the beginning. Some other denominations share this spiritual practice. The fourteenth century poet Dante devoted one book (*Purgatio*) of *The Divine Comedy* (translated Sayers, 1955) to the journey up Mount Purgatory. His artistic depiction has had an enduring effect. Based on the theology of Thomas Aquinas, Dante portrays purgatory as both purification and reparation for sin. Purgation is God's work and not the result of a human effort. Humans however must cooperate with grace. Unlike Hell, penitents in purgatory gladly take responsibility for their sins, accept the just consequences, are purified and make reparation that is healing.

Some contemporary thinkers believe that purgatory or aspects of purgatory can be helpful today. In family therapy, O'Connor (1999) relates Dante's notion of purgatory to narrative therapy developed by White and Epston (1991). Taking responsibility for self, accepting the consequences for one's actions, and developing personal agency are similar to both narrative therapy and purgatory. Narrative therapy externalizes the problem much in the same way that Dante externalizes the seven deadly sins. Both approaches lead to transformation. Theologian Richard McBrien (1981) believes that purgatory is the shedding of the selfishness of the ego so that humans become more like God who serves others. Similarly, Boszormenyi-Nagy and Krasner (1984) argue that family therapy should be modeled on Martin Buber's (1970) I-Thou that purifies self-centeredness in developing a deep respect and care for others. Hargrave (1994) in his research on forgiveness maintains that reparation of wrong doing is an important aspect of forgiveness and healing. Purgatory in this postmodern era has experienced resurgence while still being disputed.

See also: ❯ Buber, Martin ❯ Forgiveness ❯ Healing

Bibliography

Boszormenyi-Nagy, I., & Krasner, B. (1984). *Between the give and take: A clinical guide to contextual family therapy*. New York: Brunner/Mazel.

Buber, M. (1970). *I and thou* (W. Kaufmann, Trans.). New York: Charles Scribner & Sons.

Hargrave, T. (1994). *Families and forgiveness*. New York: Brunner/Mazel.

McBrien, R. (1981). Purgatory. *Catholicism* (Study Edition, pp. 1143–1147). Minneapolis, MN:Winston Press.

O'Connor, T. (1999). Climbing Mount Purgatory: Dante's cure of souls and narrative therapy. *Pastoral Psychology, 47*(6), 445–457.

Sayers, D. (1955). Introduction. In *The comedy of Dante Alighieri: Cantica II Purgatio* (D. Sayers, Trans.) (pp. 9–71). London: Penguin.

White, M., & Epston, D. (1991). *Narrative means to therapeutic ends*. New York: Winston.

Purpose in Life

Todd DuBose

Purpose in life is the prime motivator for meaningful and fulfilling relationships and projects in existence, without which we can find ourselves in abject despair. Hence, discernment about the nature and edification of the purposeful life is vital to every area of therapeutic care and spiritual well-being. In fact, one could say that the partnership between psychology and religion is found in the understanding and perpetuation of the purposeful life. The purposeful life has been described by such diverse writers as the existential logotherapist, Viktor Frankl (1905–1997), to the current, American, popular culture writers (Tolle, 2008; Warren, 2007).

Originally, "purpose" meant, "aim," "intention," "to put forth," or "by design." Inherent to purpose is some type of directionality that is transfused with significance. A thorough understanding of purpose in life, therefore, entails an investigation of two primary aspects of its character, namely, intentionality and teleology.

Intentionality is our "aboutness" or "oughtness" in any given circumstance and comportment in the world. Beginning with Franz Brentano (1838–1917) in the late nineteenth century and furthered by the founder of transcendental phenomenology, Edmund Husserl (1859–1938), intentionality was defined as a focus on or toward something that is a part of any experience. Experience is always an experience of something, or an experience that is pointed, about which we are attuned or concerned. We are always heading somewhere, in some direction, searching, not only with our consciousness, but also with our entire comportment. Brentano's and Husserl's positions were altered yet again by Martin Heidegger (1889–1976) who saw intentionality as an every moment experience of "care" or "Sorge" (Heidegger, 1962). We find ourselves invested in how we are in the world, to what ends, and with what constitutes our own most possibilities.

Unlike Husserl, Heidegger did not believe we could shed or escape finitude and pre-understanding to achieve a pure phenomenological clarity. Rather, Heidegger believed that our very intentions are called forth by the already and always world of meaning in which we are "thrown" or find ourselves by happenstance. Jean Paul Sartre (1905–1980) furthered Heidegger's work by equating consciousness with intentionality, including an emphasis on deconstructing any assumptions of an unconscious. For Sartre, the unconscious is merely disowned consciousness and an example of bad faith (Sartre, 1956). In short, we are living out a purpose while searching for a purpose, as it the direction in which we are proceeding either has a design to it, or, with each step, gives clues to the construction of a purposeful life. As the debate continues, what is indisputable is that there is teleology to how we experience and for what purposes.

Teleology can mean either "end" or "purpose," but an end or purpose that either is a part of or completes a particular design or another. The existence of something in a purpose-as-plan leaves us with the question of whether the circumstance creates space for something to exist, or if our purposeful comportment would exist no matter what provisions were provided for it. Do we develop certain strengths or illnesses because it fits our culture's needs, or would we have such strengths and/or illnesses regardless of the cultural prescriptions? Contemporary perspectives on this matter, also called a nurture or nature debate, consider our designs as a product of both natural and nurturing processes. The same issue contains another dilemma: are our designs, even if a combination of nature and nurture, a part of hard determined fate or providence, or are we free to create our designs as we choose? Finally, is our purpose serving a means for the ends of a larger purpose, or is our purpose an end in itself that uses the larger context as a means to our own ends? Do we become sensual creatures because we have senses, or do we evolve senses because we need to become sensual creatures? At the same time, much like air shifting towards the most vacuous space, does our direction in life take the shape is does because of opportunity for it to do so? The answers to these and other similar questions are predicated on whether or not one sees teleology as extrinsic, intrinsic, or a combination thereof. Nevertheless, all purpose in life is an intertwining of calling and commitment, of oughtness and response, and most importantly, of an inviting niche matched with a matching fit.

The importance of purpose in life within the field of psychology and religion is probably best known in the work of the logotherapist, Viktor Frankl (1905–1997). Frankl's development of logotherapy evolved from his lived experiences within a concentration camp during World War II. Frankl's now famous book, *Man's Search for Meaning* (1946/1959), showed what human beings could endure anything as long as the purpose and meaning to stay alive is strong enough to overcome one's psychic, physical, and spiritual pain. For Frankl, his purpose to live was two-fold: he had someone who loved him and whom he loved, and he had projects to complete before his death. Frankl's convictions integrate both teleology and intentionality in the will to meaning. Spirituality, contrary to an otherworldly phenomenon, is viewed from this perspective as the meaningful and fulfilling experience of discovering, following, being sustained by, and living out our purposeful existence.

Contemporary articulations of purpose in life continue with strong following. Rick Warren's (2007), *The Purpose Driven Life*, is a very popular text, at least among conservative to moderate Christians, and focuses on the discernment and synchronization of one's life calling and direction with God's providential plan for each person. Eckhart Tolle (2008) advises us that attachment to ego-based consciousness creates our conflicts and suffering, mirroring Buddhist noble truths, and invites us to a new consciousness that moves purpose beyond our egoism toward a deeper connection with that, which is more than us all, which is experienced in the fullness of the present moment. So whether in a popular or more formally academic way, discerning and following our purpose in life spotlights what matters in assessing and committing to live.

Commentary

Several questions remain for consideration in discerning the purposeful life. First of all, one significant concern is clarifying who gets to define what is purposeful. Social construction has shown how powerful the voices of others are in shaping our life direction. Our purposes in life may actually be handed to us by the group, herd, crowd, or status quo. Yet, even though agency is shaped by our environmental and ideological contexts, agency still remains. One still assents or not, interprets or is interpreted, decides or is handed decisions. Merely to fit with the needs of the group's purpose has led to fascist and totalitarian horrors as much as the dictatorship-like apathy regarding how one's intentions impact others. Caution should be exercised in both directions, but all said and done; we are still left with the accountability of our own personal decisions and commitments toward a direction in life. What is purposeful defends on what is valued, be it survivability, safety, or otherwise. But inspiration and motivation seem to entail more than mere self-preservation. Thriving, as the old adage goes, is more than merely existing.

Another issue for consideration is whether purpose is found, discovered, or, as I argue, in line with the tradition of existential phenomenology, that purpose is already and always lived out in the world long before it becomes an object for reflection. Even in the very Sartrean act of creating meaning and purpose out of nothing overrides the obvious meaningful place from which the creation of meaning out of nothing can occur. Our enactments of significance fold in teleology and intentionality, while simultaneously incorporating finitude and freedom. One intends and complies with design based on what is meaningful to us, which at times doesn't show itself until times of great intimacy or crisis. As Will Barrett (1913–1992) noted, we often quibble about free will and determinism until our lives are at stake and our choices become quite pronounced (1979). Our lived purposes are so much a part of our moment to moment existence that Maurice Merleau-Ponty (1908–1961) demonstrated that intentionality (and the reception of the intended response) is even in our reflexology (Merleau-Ponty, 1963).

It should also be kept in mind that intentionality occurs within a context and clearing in which the intention is summoned and recognized. Jan van den Berg (1914–), the Dutch phenomenologist, argued that the metabletic moment, or the moment in which change occurs, is a convergence of many vectors that come together (van den Berg, 1983). A space is created for purpose to become itself, much like the unfolding of Heidegger's *Dasein*.

Finally, we must address the relationship of the purposeful like to nihilism. Albert Camus (1913–1960) knew this relationship well, and perhaps put it most succinctly when we argued that the only question worth asking is whether life is worth living in spite of its absurd constitution (Camus, 1955). His answer was a courageous "yes." It behooves us to be honest about how random and seemingly impersonal tragedy can be in its savagery, often leaving powerful undertows of post-traumatic reactions and/or invitations to suicidal despair. But even suicidal despair is purposeful. One seeks to transcend one state of existence for another, which is driven by the pain of what is and what could be, albeit from a narrowed place of attunement. Each moment, though, we inescapably enact significance, whether or not we are attuned to it, or whether or not we find it pleasing. Each moment is nonetheless a leap of enacted significance and lived out long before analyzed (Kierkegaard, 1843/1941; Henry, 2002). Hence, if we are always and already enacting significance, there can be no purpose-less existence. Knowing this about the purposeful life frees us to embrace the "call of the wild," where the "freedom to be" may actually be the heart of purpose in a life fully lived.

See also: ❯ Daseinsanalysis ❯ Doubt ❯ Faith ❯ Frankl, Viktor ❯ Hermeneutics ❯ Homo Religiosus ❯ Kierkegaard, Søren ❯ Lived Theology ❯ Meaning of Human Existence ❯ Phenomenological Psychology ❯ Psychology as Religion ❯ Trauma

Bibliography

Barrett, W. (1979). *The illusion of technique*. New York: Anchor.

Campbell, J., & Moyers, B. (1991). *The power of myth*. New York: Anchor.

Camus, A. (1955). *The myth of sisyphus and other essays* (J. O'Brien, Trans.) (pp. 51–65). New York: Random House.

Driver, T. (1985). *Patterns of grace: Human experience as word of God*. Lanham, MD: University of America Press.

DuBose, T. (2000). Lordship, bondage, and the formation of *Homo Religiosus*. *Journal of Religion and Health, 39*(3), 217–226.

Frankl, V. (1946/1959). *Man's search for meaning*. New York: Washington Square Press.

Gilkey, L. (1976). *Naming the whirlwind: The renewal of God-language*. Indianapolis, IN: Bobbs-Merrill Educational Publishing.

Heidegger, M. (1962). *Being and time* (J. Macquarrie & E. Robinson, Trans.). Oxford: Basil Blackwell.

Heidegger, M. (1987/2001). *Zollikon seminars: Protocols – Conversations – Letters*. Evanston, IL: Northwestern University Press.

Henry, M. (2002). *I am the truth: Towards a philosophy of Christianity* (S. Emanuel, Trans.). Stanford, CA: Stanford University Press.

Kierkegaard, S. (1843/1941). *Fear and trembling* (W. Lowrie, Trans.). Princeton, NJ: Princeton University Press.

Merleau-Ponty, M. (1963). *The structure of behavior* (A. Fisher, Trans.). Pittsburgh, PA: Duquesne University Press.

Nietzsche, F. (1967). *The genealogy of morals and Ecce Homo* (W. Kaufman, Trans.). New York: Vintage.

Sartre, J. P. (1956). *Being and nothingness: An essay on phenomenological ontology* (H. Barnes, Trans.). New York: Philosophical Library.

Tillich, P. (1952). *The courage to be*. New Haven, CT: Yale University Press.

Tillich, P. (1957). *Dynamics of faith*. New York: Harper & Brothers.

Tolle, E. (2008). *A new earth: Awakening to your life's purpose*. New York: Penguin.

Van den Berg, J. (1983). *The changing nature of man: Introduction to a historical psychology*. New York: W. W. Norton.

Warren, R. (2007). *The purpose driven life: What on earth am I here for?* Grand Rapids, MI: Zondervan Publishing Company.

Q

Quaternity

John Pahucki

A concept in Jungian analytical psychology which refers broadly to images of totality and wholeness – such as the mandala – that appear in dreams or other spontaneous expressions of the unconscious. Jung believed that the quaternity should serve as the primary image of the God-archetype, replacing the Christian trinity which he viewed as psychically obsolescent. The Christian trinity was an inadequate symbol to denote psychic wholeness, Jung contended, as it failed to encompass the shadow and feminine aspects of the psyche. Jung was not clear on which of these two should be accorded priority, arguing for the inclusion of Mephistopheles in the quaternity, as the shadow cast by Christ, while also expressing great enthusiasm for the Catholic Church's adoption of the doctrine of the *Assumption* of Mary. This, he maintained, established a quaternity relation as Mary, representative of the eternal feminine, functioned as counterpart to the bridegroom of Christ.

See also: ◉ Jung, Carl Gustav ◉ Mandala ◉ Shadow ◉ Transcendent Function

Bibliography

Jung, C. G. (1958). A psychological approach to the dogma of the trinity. In *Psychology and religion: West and East*, CW 11. Princeton, NJ: Princeton University Press.

Quest

David A. Leeming

In the cultural dreams that are our myths, heroes serve as our personae, representatives of our collective psyches – first as cultures and then as a species. Gilgamesh reflects a Mesopotamian physical and psychological experience and Odysseus could not be anything else but Archaic Greek. But when we compare the heroes of these various cultures, Joseph Campbell's heroic monomyth pattern emerges and we discover a hero who belongs to all of humanity. "The Hero," writes Campbell, "is the man or woman who has been able to battle past his personal and local historical limitations to the generally valid, normally human forms" (1949/1973 Hero: 19–20).

The central event in the universal hero myth, the heroic monomyth, is the quest, in which a hero – the representative of a culture – seeks some significant goal or boon for his people. Often the voyage involves archetypal stages such as the search for truth or riches or a lost loved one, a struggle with monsters, and the descent to the underworld. Jason goes in search of the Golden Fleece, Parcifal the Holy Grail, and the Buddha Enlightenment.

Interpreted psychologically, the questing hero is our cultural and collective psyche out in search of identity – that is, Self, the point of self knowledge at which the conscious and unconscious come together as a unity.

As we see in the overall heroic monomyth, the archetypal pattern that emerges from a comparison of hero myths, the quest involves several almost ritualistic stages. There is the initial unwillingness to begin the journey – the refusal of the call – reflecting the natural unwillingness of most of us to give up the status quo for a difficult exploration of our inner worlds. But the hero must leave home precisely because he must break new ground in the overall human journey, as we must on the psychological journey towards fulfillment or self identity. The old ways must be constantly renewed and new understandings developed. The knights of the Round Table must give up the comforts of Camelot to achieve renewal through adventure, and Gilgamesh must leave home to seek eternal life.

The questing hero looks for something lost – a father, a sacred icon of the tribe, something that will save the people, the plant of immortality, the Holy Grail. "Religious" or philosophical heroes such as the Buddha or

D. A. Leeming, K. Madden, S. Marlan (eds.), *Encyclopedia of Psychology and Religion*, DOI 10.1007/978-0-387-71802-6,
© Springer Science+Business Media LLC 2010

Jesus look to less tangible goals: Enlightenment, Nirvana, the Kingdom of God.

The quest always involves frightening and dangerous thresholds to be crossed – giants, dragons, evil kings, seemingly impossible labors such as those of Herakles. These all reflect the monsters within our own psyches and the thresholds we must cross on the way to wholeness. When the hero confronts the ultimate threshold and dies, and when he returns to the world after his descent into death, he is an image of our descent into the very depths of the unconscious world in preparation for a new "birth" of the psyche.

See also: ❯ Hero ❯ Monomyth ❯ Pilgrimage ❯ Self

Bibliography

Campbell, J. (1949/1973). *The hero with a thousand faces.* Princeton, NJ: Bollingen.

Leeming, D. (1998). *Mythology: The voyage of the hero* (3rd ed.). Oxford, England: Oxford University Press.

Qur'an

Ali Kose

The Qur'an is the sacred book of Muslims who believe its complete text came through revelation. Each word of it was revealed in Arabic by Allah (God) to Prophet Muhammad through the Archangel Gabriel over a span of 23 years in the seventh century. The revelation of the Qur'an began when the Prophet was 40 years old. It consists of around 600 pages, 114 chapters, and over 6,000 verses. The length of chapters varies with the longest chapter having 286 verses while the shortest one has only three. The word "Qur'an" means recitation, and the first verse of the Qur'an to be revealed to Prophet Muhammad was a command to "read in the name of your Lord, the Creator. . . ." (Ibn Hanbal, 1895: 232).

Given that the Prophet was an unlettered man, his early followers eagerly memorized and recorded each new revelation as it was revealed. By the time the Prophet passed away, the Qur'an had been completed and many had memorized its entirety. Within two years after the death of the Prophet, the first caliph, Abu Bakr, compiled the Qur'an into a manuscript which became the basis for the authorized editions that were distributed to each Muslim province during the rule of Uthman, the third caliph. A few of those early manuscripts have been preserved and can still be viewed in museums today. Thus, there is only one authorized-version in Arabic.

Muslims believe in the original form of all the revealed books which are mentioned in the Qur'an: the Torah of Moses, Psalms of David, and the Gospels of Jesus. The Qur'an also mentions Scrolls of Abraham. Moses' contemporaries were excellent in magic, so his major miracle was to defeat the best magicians of Egypt in his day. Jesus' contemporaries were recognized as skillful physicians; therefore, his miracle was to cure incurable diseases. The Arabs, the contemporaries of Prophet Muhammad, were known for their eloquence and magnificent poetry. Accordingly, Prophet Muhammad's major miracle to prove that he is a messenger of God is believed to be the Qur'an.

Final Scripture

The Qur'an is revered by Muslims as being God's final Scripture. Its verses are and have been recited and memorized by Muslims of every nationality. It is the verses of the Qur'an that Muslims read during their five daily prayers. The faithful ones are inspired, consoled, and often moved to tears by its poetic imagery.

For the past fourteen centuries, Muslims from all over the world have written the Qur'anic verses in various calligraphic forms, which were mainly produced and perfected by the Ottoman Turks. In fact, it was in Istanbul that the finest calligraphic scripts were produced. A famous saying, therefore, goes: "The Qur'an was revealed in Mecca, read in Egypt, and written in Istanbul."

The Qur'an contains many verses which describe natural phenomenon in various fields such as astronomy, geology, and embryology. It is also a law book to provide some basic principles for both individual and social life. Its main message is to call people to turn to the Source of all being and the Giver of life and to serve Him with a pure heart, free of idolatry or superstition. It rejects the concept of salvation or special privilege based on ethnicity, race, or color. Spiritual salvation is to be achieved by an attempt to make amends for one's sins and a sincere intention not to repeat one's mistakes in the future. There is no official priesthood in Islam, and the "imam" is no more than a knowledgeable prayer-leader; one's sins need only be confessed directly to the Creator. The Qur'an presents itself as guidance for mankind as a whole. It is not for any particular people, place, or period in time.

The Qur'an as Source of Culture

Islamic culture is founded on the Qur'an. It is recited on special occasions like wedding ceremonies, and at certain times, such as going to sleep or setting forth on a journey. In this sense, it serves the purpose of a prayer book. Muslims also utilize the Qur'an as a psychotherapeutic book. For example, they read some certain verses and gently blow them upon the sick as well as for the soul of the deceased. Additionally, verses like the eleven in the last two chapters are read to protect against evil temptations or when one fears of possession by a devil. People hang up amulets which has chapters from the Qur'an around their neck, on the main door of houses, and on the rear mirror of automobiles to protect themselves and their belongings from accidents, evil eyes, burglars, etc. The Qur'an is also popularly used as an oath book; people swear by the Qur'an to take an oath.

See also: ❯ God ❯ Hafiz ❯ Hajj ❯ Islam ❯ Pilgrimage ❯ Sharia

Bibliography

The Holy Qur'an. (1934). Translation and Commentary by Abdullah Yusuf Ali (1st ed.). Birmingham, England: Islamic Propagation Centre International.

Ibn Hanbal, A. (1895). *al-Musnad* (Vol. IV, p. 232). Cairo, Egypt.

R

Ramakrishna Paramahansa

Fredrica R. Halligan

One of the most recognized and beloved of the great saints of India, Ramakrishna (1836–1886) is best known for his devotion to the Divine Mother, the Goddess Kali. He was also founder of the Vedanta Society that now has branches in many major cities throughout the world. The doctrine of Vedanta is based on Hindu tradition, but Ramakrishna was also versed in comparative religious traditions as well. It is a characteristic of Hindu tradition to honor and respect all religions.

Ramakrishna's life was marked by many unusual spiritual phenomena. His birth was predicted to both his parents individually as being especially devoted to both Vishnu and Shiva, two of the Hindu Trinity. Early in life Ramakrishna was a nature mystic, occasionally falling into rapturous unconsciousness at the sight of great beauty or, on one occasion, when playing the role of Shiva in a play. He was the youngest son of a poor family that was of the *Brahmin* (priestly) caste. When his oldest brother went to Calcutta to teach Sanskrit and serve as a priest in the temple consecrated to the Goddess Kali, he invited his youngest brother, then 17, to assist him in his priestly duties. When this brother died just 1 year later, Ramakrishna took over as priest in the temple. It was at that point that he underwent a profound change, dedicating himself entirely to the service of the Divine Mother. He became so engrossed in religious life that he sometimes lost track of time. Nonetheless, this was a period of dark yearning for the young Ramakrishna. His ardent spiritual thirst was for *darshan* – a vision and teaching of the Divine Mother. At one point he almost committed suicide, and it was then that the Divine Mother first appeared to him. As he taught later, when yearning is as strong as that of a drowning man gasping for breath, then we will be given the gift of knowing God. (cited in Kakar 1991: 16f).

After this first powerful mystical experience, his appetite was whetted for more. Whenever he received visions of the Goddess, he would beam with joy, and enter into *samadhi*, which is a deep and intense meditative state wherein the ego enters into unspecified, formless, featureless consciousness, and then he would frequently become unconscious. When there was any diminution in the sense of her presence, he would loudly wail and become breathless. His family worried about him; they took him to an *Ayurvedic* doctor for treatment and even tried an exorcist. He gradually passed through this initial intense spiritual phase. Subsequently his family arranged a marriage for him with the 6-year old Sarada Devi. He complied with their wishes but never had any intention of consummating the marriage. In later life he envisioned his wife as the Divine Mother herself and worshiped her.

Teachings

For Ramakrishna taught that *Bhakti yoga*, or the life of devotion, is the quickest, surest path toward union with the Divine. From this perspective, all desire can lead one to God. The passions of life are all redirected toward God rather than toward the objects of the world. Devotional mysticism, rather than eliminating the sense of individuality of the aspirant, seeks to use that sense of ego-identity by recapturing the feelings of childlike innocence and fresh vision. It was in feeling as a child, aware of his total humanity and complete dependence on the Divine, that Ramakrishna prayed:

> ▶ To my Mother I prayed only for pure devotion. I said, 'Mother, here is your virtue, here is your vice. Take them both and grant me only pure devotion to you. Here is your knowledge and here is your ignorance. Take them both and grant me only pure love for you. Here is your purity, and here is your impurity. Take them both, Mother, and grant me only pure devotion for you' (Kakar, 1991: 16).

As a priest in the Kali Temple, Ramakrishna became known as a mystical genius and he was greatly sought after for teachings. He frequently taught that one can

D. A. Leeming, K. Madden, S. Marlan (eds.), *Encyclopedia of Psychology and Religion*, DOI 10.1007/978-0-387-71802-6,
© Springer Science+Business Media LLC 2010

certainly worship God with form – any form – or one can worship God without form. What matters, he said is simply the longing and the intensity of devotion. Not awe, but devotion. He was known to have many occult powers or *siddhis*, but he always made light of them. Ramakrishna conveyed his experiences through devotional songs, myths, analogues, metaphors and parables. He generally transmitted his teachings orally, but also gave special mystical energy transmissions to his close disciples.

Vedanta Society

His key disciples were originally 16 in number. After Ramakrishna's death, which occurred at age 50 due to throat cancer, Swami Vivekananda took over leadership of the spiritual community. Starting in 1893 at the Chicago World Parliament of Religions, the Vedanta Society grew into a world wide movement. Today the spiritual traditions of India are easily accessible through this group; and in particular, when feminists are searching for female god-images, the teachings of Ramakrishna make these ideas more plausible and available to spiritual aspirants.

See also: ❯ Great Mother ❯ Hinduism

Bibliography

Kakar, S. (1991). *The analyst and the mystic.* Chicago, IL: University of Chicago Press.

Ramakrishna, S. (1980). *The gospel of Ramakrishna* (S. Nikhilananda, Ed. & Trans.) (Abridged). New York: Ramakrishna-Vivekananda Center.

Ramakrishna, S. (1994). *Teachings of Sri Ramakrishna.* Calcutta, India: Advaita Ashram.

Satprakashananda, S. (1976). *Sri Ramakrishna's life and message in the present age.* St. Louis, MO: Vedanta Society.

Ramana Maharshi

Nicholas Grant Boeving

Sri Ramana Maharshi (December 30, 1879 – April 14, 1950) was born into a Tamil Brahmin family, though freed himself of any caste restrictions at the age of 16 upon achieving liberation. His initial experience of *moksha* was famously precipitated by an acute psycho-spiritual crisis which manifested in an all-consuming fear of death. His ermergence as an *Atiasrami* was complete with the realization that Spirit is deathless, that it transcends the body and endures after physical expiration. Although he highly reccommended Bhakti as a path to the Absolute, he favored the non-dual system of Advaita Vedanta far more, his primary method of instruction (aside from the knowing radiance of his silence) to encourage seekers to ask of themselves the following all-important query: Who am I? For he understood that this question, if honestly explored with both passion intensity would lead those seeking answers through the tempestuous fog of samsaric confusion to the shining realization of *Tat Tvam Asi* – Thou Art That – the apex of the Vedantic path.

His uniquely Maharshian blend of Advaita Vedanta has influenced untold numbers both East and West. His teachings prefigured and informed in a multitude of ways the kinds of existential inquiry that would later be integrated into the humanistic and transpersonal theories that would dethrone the despots of psychodynamism and behaviorism. But these are modern distinctions; for, in Vedantic understanding the domains of what we perceive to be those of "psychology" and "religion" overlap to the point of indistinctiveness.

Many modern interpreters of Asian religious traditions to the West have embraced the figure of Ramana Maharshi as the exemplar of perfected understanding incarnate in the flesh – most famously Ken Wilber, who in his mapping of the Kosmos, privileges Maharshi beyond all other sages. Subsequent authors critical of Wilberian spiritual politics see Maharshi's complete disregard for his own health and survival not as evidence of spiritual profundity but of severe psychopathology. In the final analysis, perhaps the answer lies not so much in either extreme but in the meeting of the two.

See also: ❯ Death Anxiety ❯ Hinduism

Bibliography

Natarajan, A. R. (1999). *Timeless in time: Sri Ramana Maharshi: A biography.* Ramana Maharshi Centre for Learning.

Osborne, A. (1970). *Ramana Maharshi and the path of self- knowledge.* Weiser Press.

Ramana Maharshi. (1972). *The spiritual teaching of Ramana Maharshi* (Shambhala Dragon Editions).

Rank, Otto

John Pahucki

One of Freud's closest colleagues for 20 years, Rank (1884–1939) was an early and influential member of the Viennese Psychoanalytic Society, serving as its secretary and the editor of two journals, the *Zeitschrift* and *Imago*. He was also a member of Freud's innermost circle, the "Ring" committee. Rank was one of the first lay analysts, a point of contention in the early days of psychoanalysis, receiving his Ph.D. in philosophy from the University of Vienna.

Rank's eventual break with Freud accompanied the publication of his book *The Trauma of Birth*, where he traced the genesis of anxiety neurosis to the birth experience. Rank's claims in this text threatened to subvert Freudian orthodoxy, with suspicious Freudians like Ernest Jones suspecting that Rank was seeking to replace the Oedipal drama with the experience of birth trauma as the central interpretive principle of psychoanalysis. Rank did, at places, call for a reevaluation of the importance of the maternal in psychoanalytic theory, recognizing the overestimation of the role accorded to the paternal in Freud's system. In this sense, Rank's work anticipated the criticisms and constructions of later feminist psychoanalysts like Luce Irigaray and Julia Kristeva.

Rank's subsequent work retained this sense of the importance of birth as a paradigmatic experience in psychic development, arguing that this painful severance from the maternal was to some extent recapitulated in all later relationships as well as the countless "deaths" and "rebirths" the subject undergoes in the process of self-development, described in *Truth and Reality* as the "never completed birth of individuality."

Rank became increasingly critical of the deterministic elements of Freud's thought, arguing that Freud reduced the role of the ego to a mere "showplace" in the war between the biologically driven id and the socially imposed superego. Dissatisfied with Freud's rejection of ego psychology, Rank turned to his early philosophical influences, Arthur Schopenhauer and Friedrich Nietzsche, in developing his own psychotherapeutic system of "will therapy."

The goal for the subject, in the Rankian view, is to marshal his creative powers for the development and pursuit of his own projected ego-ideal. Following Schopenhauer, Rank claimed that self-consciousness had developed evolutionarily as an instrument of the will, eventually becoming capable of autonomous determination. Based on this view, Rank developed a triadic psychological typology. The majority of people, he believed, simply languish in unconsciousness, not nearly self-aware enough to labor under the burden and alienation that self-consciousness imposes. The last two types are the neurotic and the artist. Both the artist and neurotic are akin to Schopenhauer's genius, individuals who are gifted with a kind of surfeit of will that grants them prospects for liberation and self-determination that few can enjoy. The neurotic, however, refuses to embrace his creative powers as this involves conscious acceptance of the conditions of life, namely the isolation and mortality imposed on him by the act of birth. The neurotic is thus, in Rank's term, a failed artist (*artiste manqué*) who turns his tremendous energies in upon himself in constituting his own suffering. The artist, by contrast, embraces life's transience and directs himself toward the formation and establishment of his own considered ego ideal, which often proves at variance with the ideal foisted upon him by parents and society. In this sense, Rank's conception of the artist type has clear resonance with Nietzsche's notion of the "overman" (*Übermensch*) and the "transvaluation of values."

See also: ❯ Freud, Sigmund ❯ Kristeva, Julia ❯ Psychoanalysis ❯ Schopenhauer, Nietzsche, and Atheism

Bibliography

Karpf, F. B. (1953). *The psychology and psychotherapy of Otto Rank*. New York: Philosophical Library.

Lieberman, E. J. (1985). *Acts of will: The life and work of Otto Rank*. New York: The Free Press.

Rank, O. (1964). *Truth and reality*. New York: W. W. Norton.

Rank, O. (1989). *Art and artist*. New York: W. W. Norton.

Rank, O. (1993). *The trauma of birth*. New York: Dover.

Rebirth

❯ Resurrection

Redemption, the Problem with

Ginette Paris

Humanity Redeemed!

The myth of redemption is so pervasive that it permeates global politics, education, ecology, feminism… Depth psychology is not exempt. Ostensibly a depth psychological analysis starts with a pursuit of consciousness, but covertly the process often conceal a quest for redemption, masquerading as individuation, actualization, psychological health, wholeness, centeredness, mindfulness, or whatever new jargon accommodates the Christian myth of redemption. The confusion between those two concepts leads to a belief that analyzing the unconscious will lead to a clean, pure, healthy psyche; that one will evolve into a luminous, loving, dignified, pacified soul. Such a utopian dream would be nice were it not for the fact that it produces an odious, sanctimonious persona. To break the trance, one needs to differentiate redemption from individuation, salvation from wisdom. The time allotted for our life is finite, but the quest for perfection is not and when the pursuit of perfection is ego-driven, it causes psychological exhaustion. The quest for redemption turns the person into a depressed pilgrim, out of spiritual wind from the long ascension towards an impossible apotheosis of individuation. Despite every guru's teaching and Jung's warnings that individuation can never be complete, sparks from the ego are often taken for an "illumination." Because the spiritual need is real, so is the danger of inflation.

For depth psychology to emerge as a force of renewal of the sense of the sacred, it needs to escape from inflation about the quasi-divine principle of the Jungian "Self." Escape from ego fixations includes theoretical fixations upon the masters that have trained us. Deification of the masters and their theories, is, in itself, a sign that the myth of redemption is active. The masters, gurus, leaders who ask to be "adored" by their disciples are usually in the business of selling redemption ("Think like me and you'll be saved!"). When adoring disciples notice that their idols have feet of clay their critique becomes vicious, fueled by a sense of betrayal and disillusionment. However, such decanonization would not have been necessary had they not deified their master in the first place.

Neither Voltaire, nor Nietzsche, nor Freud, nor Jung, nor any of the modern philosophers of atheism were completely free of the redemption myth. The Christian God may have been declared dead, but the mourning is not finished; it is too big a loss to be completed in just a few generations. Jung's nostalgia for the Christian God resurfaces at times in his theory about the Self (capital S); I have met many who *believe* in Jungian theory as one believes in a Savior, because they miss the certainties of faith. Until our mourning of God is done, the fantasy of redemption will grow out of all sorts of grounds.

Zarathustra's rallying cry of "God is dead provided me with an enduring motivation to practice psychotherapy: I felt then – and still do today – that a world without the Christian God need not be a desperate world. Psychotherapy is a daily battle against despair. Nevertheless, the deconstruction of conventional religions does not alleviate the need for a sense of the sacred; but where is it? The desire for redemption resurfaces in every cause that is dear to one's heart: eco-feminist redemption (when women rule, all will be fine on this planet); political redemption (this party will change everything); financial redemption (as soon as I have enough, I'll follow my bliss); romantic redemption (one day my prince/princess will come); psychological redemption (one day, I'll be individuated, one of the Illuminati). Each of these fantasies stems from the monotheistic mythology. Even the ideal of Buddhist detachment can conceal a typical Christian fantasy where the guru replaces God, and an all-encompassing philosophical system serves as faith.

To make sense of my small life, I need the amplification of my ordinary life-journey into something I can call an Odyssey; I want the magnification of my battles at the office into an Iliad; I know my house is not a castle, but in a way it is. This aggrandizement of our story, which is not at all an aggrandizement of the ego, is a valid protection against feelings of absurdity. In times of great difficulty, the narrative logic breaks down and the transformation of facts into a narrative fails. One tries to tell the events this way and that way, from this or that perspective, but the collection of facts remains absurd. The trajectory of one's life appears seemingly random – what was THAT all about? The breakdown in the narrative capacity is usually interpreted as a form of despair, similar to the despair of losing one's faith. Yet, it can also signal a very different kind of breakdown: that of the redemptive myth. Only then can the loss of the redemptive hope appear as a necessary loss.

Life is Absurdly, Awesomely Ugly and Beautiful

Christians come from a culture that has millennia of religious indoctrination in which meaning was defined by hope of salvation in the afterlife. Nietzsche and many others bulldozed the field, but the efforts of many more generations may be necessary to change not only our religious attitudes, but our psychological makeup as well. We have only begun to expose the racist, sexist, oppressive, violent, hypocritical, parasitic, exploitative cowardice present in the cement of actual institutionalized religions. The need to explore the destructiveness of our pervasive redemption myth is as necessary as a good look at the shadow. We could begin with examining how it is very possible and feasible to live outside the redemptive myth, without falling into despair. For example, if one looks at the usual promises of human love – "I'll love you forever" or "I'll never abandon you" – one see the *absurdity* of it. These promises may be sincere, but are *absurd* if one considers that mortality is an absolute limitation to the infinite depth of the experience of love. Nevertheless, this limitation, with all the sweet lies around love, is not reason enough to waste the spiritual value of love. We bring children into this world, and we love them madly, even if we know they will suffer and die. We love them with an intensity that is almost painful, even though we know, despite all our efforts, that they, like ourselves, will suffer and die. It doesn't make much sense, but not loving makes even less sense. The sense of the absurd, which is a consequence of the loss of a religious faith in a literal god may come to be experienced as something as natural as the limitations of human love, a reality that simply is, like other realities that cannot be logically explicated.

The core idea of early twentieth-century existentialists, with respect to the experience of the absurd was to suggest the necessary dissolution of all the meanings that have been taken for granted. Their sense of the "absurd" is often interpreted as meaning "nonsensical" but it does not; I am suggesting it means "mysterious." The notion that existential angst is the unavoidable consequence of the loss of faith in a redemptive god may very well be simply a consequence of a very long domination by the monotheistic God. Religious sentiment, like the sentiment of love, has a history. Building cathedrals was a task carried on by many generations; deconstructing the redemptive obsession may take at least that long. Postmodernism, with its unrelenting attack on ideologies and single meanings, has acted as a sort of collective therapy. It took us to a place in our consciousness where the loss of the redemptive myth is simply equal to the major absurdity of most of life's trajectories.

It is a fact that an acute sense of the death of God can stir up feelings as painful as when experiencing the death of a child, or the loss of a loved one in a car accident. It seems so absurd, so meaningless, the anguish is so acute. The danger is then to invest all of one's psychic energy in *explaining* the absurd, to redeem the tragic event (Why? why? why?) The suffering soul become obsessed with a search for meaning; and because the tragic cannot be redeemed, that search itself becomes tragic. This is where I find that a depth psychological approach can be of immense help, because it moves away from explanations and remains in the territory of the tragic. It leads into the deepest layers of the imagination, where psychic regeneration can occur. It does not offer redemption but a map of the journey through psychic devastation.

Augustine asked himself the age-old question that historians have in common with depth psychologists: can one find meaning in history? (And the corollary: can I find meaning in my story?) Augustine's answer constituted dogma for a very long time. Yes, history has meaning, says Augustine. It is the meaning given by faith. If one loses faith, one also loses meaning. Problem solved! By remaining unconscious of our Christianity, we tend to apply that same logic and replace one bible with another, falling right back into Augustinian dogma. One of the current tasks of depth psychology, as I understand it, involves dumping the last residue of that Augustinian style of consciousness, based in faith. Not that there is a need to bring up Augustine's case again. He has been tried and found guilty over and over. Nevertheless, Augustinian debris is blocking new construction. Depth psychology is experimenting with a next style of consciousness, one that allows a person to endure the absurd, to cope with the insufferable, to lose one's innocence and, instead of turning to Augustinian redemption, to learn to swim in the Styx, imagine life differently, making room for its tragic element. Depth psychology suggests, for example, that you are absolutely free to jump off a bridge, if suicide is what your soul ultimately wants, but before you literalize death into physical death of the body, try a metaphorical death. Try an imaginal trip to the Underworld. Try a form of loving through pain, living with loss, aging in character. Try imagining another self, inventing another myth, writing another chapter in your story. Travel first, see the inner world, and then decide if it is literal or metaphorical death you want.

The desire to find meaning is a human one, and is given expression in the creation of a narrative, but there is too often a contamination with the belief in a redemptive principle which want to turn bad into good. "My baby is dead, but she is now an angel in God's paradise" is a frequent defense against despair, a direct consequence of not having completed the mourning for one particular long-lived God. The almost irresistible reflex of turning everything into morality of good and evil belongs to faith, belongs to a God that defines right and wrong. The adventure of a depth-psychological analysis is a move away from this kind of religious conditioning. The need for redemptive ideals is replaced by another style of consciousness: the capacity to value the awe-inspiring mysteries of the psyche and of the beauty of the sensate world. As one opens up to the possibility of living a full and generous life, the thirst for redemption diminishes and the need to be of service to Others, to culture, and to nature increases.

Human glory, health, and fortune do not suffice to fill the vast inner space. We need to imagine a wider world, one of archetypal dimension. All humans, once they take care of survival needs, feel that there is a beyond-the-ego-realm. Many still choose to call "it" God, or Goddess, or Love, or First Principle, or "any other term of your choice," as they say in Alcoholics Anonymous, with impressive success. Transcendence means a sense of value above, beyond and apart from the material world. Depth psychology has helped many understand and feel that life lived in the service of Justice, Truth, Love, Compassion has enough transcendental value without any imposition of pre-fixed meanings and pre-defined values. This is why the search of a junction between psychology and the various religious traditions feels like a precious alternative to institutionalized religions; it recognizes the human need for something bigger than ego, but refuses to let religious orthodoxies manipulate that need.

Acknowledgment

This article is an adaptation of part of a chapter from the book, *The Wisdom of the Psyche: Depth Psychology after Neuroscience*, Routledge 2007, by Ginette Paris.

See also: ◉ Christ as Symbol of the Self ◉ Christianity ◉ Depth Psychology and Spirituality ◉ Freud, Sigmund ◉ Jung, Carl Gustav ◉ Self

Bibliography

Paris, G. (2007). *The wisdom of the psyche: Depth psychology after neuroscience*. London: Routledge.

Reductionism

Charlene P. E. Burns

Introduction

Reductionism is the process of breaking complex entities, concepts, or phenomena down into their smallest constituent parts or processes in order to more fully understand them. While essential to scientific study, reductionism generates difficulties when dealing with higher level phenomena like those related to human religious experience. The problem is especially difficult for the psychology of religion because of the tendency among many researchers to assume that description is explanation.

Historical Trends

Reductionist tendencies in the psychology of religion have historically led researchers and analysts to commit the fallacy of "nothing buttery" (Paloutzian, 1996). The discovery that certain areas of the brain are active during meditation, for example, has led some to claim that experiences of the one who meditates are *nothing but* byproducts of neurochemistry. From the standpoint of religion, this is obviously problematic. From the standpoint of psychology it is also, if less obviously, problematic since reductionism of this sort ends in loss of important information about the object of study (Zinnbauer and Pargament, 2005). Prior to the advent of neurological and cognitive sciences, the most reductionist approaches were perhaps the Freudian and behaviorist schools of thought. In Freud's framework, the "personal God is, psychologically, nothing other than an exalted father" (Freud, 1910/1957: 123) and religion is illusion, "fulfillments of the oldest, strongest, and most urgent wishes" (1927/1961: 30). For the strictly behaviorist school of thought, religion is reduced to publicly observable behaviors, which are nothing more than operantly conditioned actions. For B. F. Skinner, the father of behaviorism, a god is nothing more than the "archetypal pattern of an explanatory fiction" (1971: 201).

The problematic nature of reductionism was recognized by some from the start. William James wrote against what he called medical materialism and advocated a descriptive approach to the study of religion. Although it is debatable how well he succeeded in avoiding explanation, James' seminal *The Varieties of Religious Experience* (1902) remains the standard for approaching religion from a phenomenological point of view. Theodore Flournoy (1903) identified two fundamental principles for a psychological approach to religion, the first of which is the "exclusion of the transcendent." By this he meant that psychologists should always strive to avoid making claims about the actual existence/nonexistence of God or other aspects of transcendent experience. One can learn a great deal about human psychology by studying the ways people conceive of God without making claims that these ways of conceiving prove anything about the reality of God. Carl Jung also repeatedly attempted to make this distinction clear: "the image [of God] and the statement [about God] are psychic processes which are different from their transcendental object; they do not posit it, they merely point to it" (1976: 556).

Current Thought

Over the course of the twentieth century, the majority of psychologists who studied religious experience tended toward the reductionist explanatory approach. This may in part be accounted for by the apparent "genuine antagonism toward religion among typical psychologists" and may itself account for the fact that this is an under developed field of study (Wulff, 1997: 16–18). But it seems the psychology of religion is in the midst of a paradigm shift. It is now seen as an area rich in research possibilities that overlaps with research on neuroscience, philosophy, anthropology, evolutionary biology, and cognitive science. Emmons and Paloutzian (2003) have shown that religion and spirituality are complex, multifaceted phenomena that cannot be understood from the vantage point of a single discipline. The only viable approach today is one like their "*multilevel interdisciplinary paradigm*" which "recognizes the value of data at multiple levels of analysis while making nonreductive assumptions concerning the value of spiritual and religious phenomena" (2003: 395). Approaching religion in this way is to presuppose different and interrelated "planes of information" wherein the most fundamental are "necessary but not sufficient" for explanation of higher order phenomena (Zinnbauer and Pargament, 2005: 31).

See also: ❯ Freud, Sigmund ❯ James, William ❯ Jung, Carl Gustav ❯ Psychology of Religion

Bibliography

Emmons, R. A., & Paloutzian, R. F. (2003). The psychology of religion. *Annual Review of Psychology, 54*(1), 377–402.

Flournoy, T. (1903). Les principes de la psychologie religieuse. *Archives de Psychologie, 3*, 33–57.

Freud, S. (1910/1957). *Leonardo da Vinci and a memory of his childhood, SE* 11 (pp. 57–137). London: Hogarth Press.

Freud, S. (1927/1961). *The future of an illusion, SE* 21 (pp. 1–56).

James, W. (1902). *The varieties of religious experience: A study in human nature*. Cambridge, MA: Harvard University Press.

Jung, C. G. (1976). Answer to Job. In J. Campbell (Ed.), *The portable Jung* (pp. 519–650). New York: Penguin Press.

Paloutzian, R. F. (1996). *Invitation to the psychology of religion*. Needham Heights, MA: Allyn & Bacon.

Skinner, B. F. (1971). *Beyond freedom and dignity*. New York: Alfred A. Knopf.

Wulff, D. (1997). *Psychology of religion: Classic and contemporary*. New York: Wiley.

Zinnbauer, B., & Pargament, K. (2005). Religiousness and spirituality. In R. F. Paloutzian & C. L. Park (Eds.), *Handbook of the psychology of religion and spirituality* (pp. 21–42). New York: Guilford Press.

Refusal of the Call

Alice Mills

In Joseph Campbell's monomyth model of the hero quest, the hero may not immediately agree to undertake the quest on receiving the call to adventure. Refusals of the call are quite common in fairy tales, myths and other sacred tales. The hero does eventually consent to undertake the quest, but there are plenty of examples of people never undertaking the quest to which they have been summoned. In *The Hero With a Thousand Faces*, Campbell cites an example of a reluctant hero and heroine from the Arabian Nights story cycle and examples of those who altogether refuse from Ovid's *Metamorphoses* and *The Bible*. Refusal in these cases has a calamitous outcome: the nymph is transformed into a tree; God refuses to help those who have refused his call.

For the Christian, human life can be considered a quest to which all are called by the fact of their birth into this world. St. Augustine conceptualizes each Christian as a warrior engaged in spiritual warfare against the devil (though in Augustinian theology, salvation is only possible through the grace of God, not by individual effort alone). Those who refuse the call to champion the Christian cause are damned, just as much as those who actively fight on the side of the devil. According to Jesus, God hates those who are lukewarm even more than those who are either hot or cold. Those who refuse the call must face the consequences; opting out of the spiritual war is not ultimately possible.

Freudian theory does not consistently recommend one response to the call to adventure, understood as an internal process within the psyche. In his earlier writings, Freud considers that the healthy psyche accommodates the desires of the id rather than repressing them. In his later works, however, such as *Civilisation and Its Discontents*, he argues that the id's appetites must be repressed in order for civilization to continue. In terms of this later Freudian theorisation, Campbell's monomyth call would be understood as the id's call to act out its sexual or aggressive impulses with a danger of complete loss of self-control; this call must be refused in order for the social order to be preserved. In Jungian terms, however, the call should in general be accepted, and refusing the call to adventure has deeply undesirable consequences. In the context of the healthy psyche with appropriate inner boundaries, a Jungian would understand the call to come in the first instance from the shadow, signaling its readiness to become gradually more integrated in the process of individuation. The hero's quest is then an internal effort to explore, acknowledge and accept the psyche's unconscious contents. Refusing this call means robbing consciousness of its potential richness and depth. Living thus becomes more like a mere struggle to exist; purpose and happiness are drained away. The repressed will return with increasingly peremptory calls for attention. If the call is refused, the person runs the risk of becoming possessed by unconscious contents in psychosis or of suffering severe psychosomatic illness as the body protests. Ultimately, refusing the call is psychological suicide.

See also: ❂ Augustine ❂ Campbell, Joseph ❂ Hero ❂ Jung, Carl Gustav ❂ Monomyth ❂ Quest ❂ Unconscious

Bibliography

Campbell, J. (1949). *The hero with a thousand faces*. Princeton, NJ: Princeton University Press.

Freud, S. (1961). Civilization and its discontents. In J. Strachey (Trans.), *The standard edition of the complete psychological works*. London: Hogarth Press.

The New Oxford Annotated Bible with the Apocrypha. (1973). New York: Oxford University Press.

Ovid. (1955). *The Metamorphoses* (M. Innes, Trans.). Harmondsworth, England: Penguin Books.

Relational Psychoanalysis

Steven Kuchuck

Introduction to Relational Theory

In addition to other principles that will be discussed below, relational psychoanalysis assumes that psychic structure develops in response to interactions and relations with primary caretakers and is therefore accessible in psychotherapy or psychoanalysis through an examination of the transference-countertransference relationship. Stephen Mitchell was the primary founder and passionate voice at the center of this new way of thinking. With his large body of written work, founding of the journal Psychoanalytic Dialogues and central role in the formation of relational programs in New York and then internationally, Mitchell had a crucial influence on the first generation of relational analysts.

The term relational first appeared in the psychoanalytic literature in 1983, when Mitchell and Jay Greenberg proposed a synthesis of Fairbairn's Object Relations and Sullivan's interpersonal theories. Object relations theory (especially as developed and influenced by Klein, Fairbairn, Guntrip and Winnicott) offered an alternative to Freudian theory based not on drives pressing for discharge, but rather on connections with others as the main motivation in development and later life, and the resulting internalization of objects and self-other relationships. Different theorists emphasize different aspects of this process and while seen as a useful model of development, it nonetheless offers a somewhat disparate set of concepts that are sometimes difficult to apply to clinical practice. Similarly, Sullivan and his followers also emphasized the centrality of relationships to the development of psychic structure. Interpersonal theorists, in an effort to distance from classical, intrapsychic theory, deemphasized internal process in favor of here and now relating as the most accessible and therefore most important unit of study for the psychoanalyst. Originally employing a firm, authoritative style characteristic of its main founder's personality, contemporary interpersonal theory is often indistinguishable from relational psychoanalysis, though there are still sometimes subtle differences in emphasis and technique.

Key Concepts in Relational Thinking

The heart of relational psychoanalysis involves a focus on and mutual understanding with patients that therapist-patient interactions will always reflect the ways in which patients interact with others and as children were interacted with by their primary objects. Often though not always made explicit, there is an additional assumption that the analyst's particular history and internal world will also come to bear on the therapeutic relationship and may in fact influence or even pull for particular transference responses. In this way, relational psychoanalysis is a two-person psychology that while engaged in for the growth and benefit of the patient, must nonetheless take in to account the mind of the analyst as well. Selective self-disclosure, once thought to be taboo, is now seen as an important tool that when used with discretion can both enable the analyst to acknowledge his or her contribution to the current relational dynamics, and also enables the patient to recognize otherwise dissociated material through its impact on the analyst and others.

Departing from the Classical

This shift from a one to two person psychology, and an emphasis on the primacy of relating rather than drives, are two of the major differences between relational psycho-analysis and the classical Freudian theory that preceded it. While still asymmetrical-the analyst sets the parameters and tone of the treatment- relational analysis is co-constructed rather than dictated by an "all knowing" analyst, and is therefore a more mutual endeavor. In this way of thinking, the therapeutic relationship itself serves as the main vehicle for therapeutic action and change. Concepts of intersubjectivity, wherein the interaction between and mutual influence of analyst and patient subjectivities are understood as central to understanding and working through the patient's psychic conflicts and, related to this, the analytic third: the ideas and affects that belong not to analyst or patient alone but rather in the middle, co-constructed space between the two, multiple, shifting self states: there is no singular personality constellation, and enactment as co-determined, inevitable, and crucial to deepening the therapeutic relationship, are just some of the more important hallmarks of relational thinking. Relational psychoanalysis maintains a hermeneutic and also a dialectical approach; an attempt is made to maintain tension between seemingly opposite or opposing principles rather than either-or thinking or complimentarity, which can result in a limiting dichotomy of doer-done to thinking.

Postmodernism

Relational psychoanalysis exemplifies the postmodern tradition in which it evolved. It transcends the notion that one theory or hierarchical, fixed, rigid set of rules and ways of thinking can explain the vast complexity of human behavior. Standing less in opposition to than inclusive of, it's an offshoot of and/or includes aspects of classical theory, self psychology (especially the current thread of intersubjectivity theory as developed by Stollorow and associates), object relations, interpersonal and attachment theories. There has also been an active dialogue with and feed from gender and queer theory, feminism, culture, race, class and political activism. An attempt is made to understand and include many groups that were and felt themselves to be powerless, pathologized and excluded from more traditional psychoanalytic thought (referred to in the relational literature as "the other")-women, lesbians, gays, bisexuals and transgendered, people of color and others previously underrepresented in society and mainstream psychoanalytic teaching and practice.

Believing

Religion was seen by Freud and many of his followers to be the result of regressive fantasy and infantile neurosis. One goal of psychoanalysis then was to free the patient from the illusion of religion. In light of this, we might add people who believe in god or maintain other religious and spiritual attachments to the above mentioned list of those disenfranchised from classical psychoanalysis. As mentioned, postmodernism and contemporary schools of psychoanalytic thought such as relational psychoanalysis are critical of dichotomies. While the ability to reality test is of course still a necessary consideration, automatic, rigid distinctions between fantasy and reality, illusion and "truth" and science versus religion are no longer tolerated. Patient and analyst subjectivity and personal beliefs are given equal weight to or privileged over objective "facts" such as whether or not god exists. In large part as a result of relational psychoanalysis, religion is coming out of the closet. Prominent relational writers such as Lew Aron, Charles Spezzano, Michael Eigen and others write about religion and the influence of their and patients' religious beliefs and practices on the transference-countertransference field. Relational psychoanalysts have committed themselves to welcoming and examining all aspects of the patient's and clinician's subjectivity. In this respect religion-either the presence or absence of spiritual belief and practice, associated thoughts, feelings and fantasies, can come to be an important part of the relational psychoanalytic dialogue.

See also: ❯ Affect ❯ Dissociation ❯ Femininity ❯ Freud, Sigmund ❯ Freud, Sigmund, and Religion ❯ Gender Roles ❯ God ❯ Hermeneutics ❯ Homosexuality ❯ Judaism and Christianity in Freudian Psychology ❯ Object Relations Theory ❯ Postmodernism ❯ Power ❯ Psychoanalysis ❯ Psychotherapy ❯ Religion ❯ Religious ❯ Self ❯ Self Psychology ❯ Sullivan, Harry Stack ❯ Transference ❯ Winnicott, Donald Woods

Bibliography

Aron, L. (1996). *A meeting of minds, mutuality in psychoanalysis*. New Jersey: Analytic Press.

Aron, L. (2004). God's influence on my psychoanalytic vision and values. *Psychoanalytic Psychology, 21*, 442–451.

Aron, L. (2005). The tree of knowledge: Good and evil conflicting interpretations. *Psychoanalytic Dialogues, 15*, 681–707.

Eigen, M. (1981). The area of faith in Winnicott, Lacan and Bion. *International Journal of Psychoanalysis, 62*, 413–433.

Eigen, M. (1998). *The psychoanalytic mystic*. New York: Free Association Books.

Greenberg, J., & Mitchell, S. (1983). *Object relations in psychoanalytic theory*. Cambridge, MA: Harvard University Press.

Mitchell, S. A. (1993). *Hope and dread in psychoanalysis*. New York: Basic Books.

Sorenson, R. (2004). *Minding spirituality*. New Jersey: Analytic Press.

Spezzano, C. (1994). Illusion, faith, and knowledge: Commentary on Sorenson's "ongoing change in psychoanalytic theory". *Psychoanalytic Dialogues, 4*, 661–665.

Relativism

Roberto Refinetti

Relativism refers to the contention that moral values and/or factual beliefs are not good or correct in themselves but are good or correct only in reference to other values or beliefs. The term relativism is often used with a negative connotation, and many relativists prefer the term *relativity* to express the idea that moral values and factual beliefs are *relative to* the context in which they are adopted. The relativist posture is often contrasted with the absolutist posture – that is, the contention that at least some moral values and factual beliefs are *absolute* (i.e., good or correct in themselves).

History

Records of relativistic thought are available since the beginning of written history. Among the pre-Socratic thinkers in Ancient Greece, Heraclitus and Protagoras are often cited for their relativistic pronouncements. Heraclitus' famous metaphor asserting that a person cannot bathe twice in the same river (because the water is constantly moving and the river does not remain the same) implied that everything is in constant change and, consequently, that what is true today may not be true tomorrow. Likewise, Protagoras' relativistic thought is encapsulated in the sentence "Man is the measure of all things," meaning that truth or virtue are not absolute concepts but are rather dependent on who experiences them.

In the middle ages, René Descartes sought certainty and absolute truths but learned in his travels that "those who have views very different from our own are not therefore barbarians or savages, but several use as much reason as we do, or more" (Descartes, 1637). Later on, the 1800s brought to light much relativist activity, including Freud's relativization of the conscious mind, Marx's relativization of the free market economy, and Darwin's relativization of man's place in the animal kingdom.

In the twentieth century, Thomas Kuhn did much for the cause of relativity. Kuhn never saw himself as a relativist, but his analysis of how progress is attained in science led him to question the absolute nature of scientific knowledge. In his classic book, *The Structure of Scientific Revolutions*, he asserted that scientific knowledge is always part of a transitory paradigm that, by necessity, must eventually be discarded in order for scientific progress to take place (Kuhn, 1962). Quite more explicitly, Willard Quine used the expression *ontological relativity* to describe the fact that the objects of a science cannot exist in themselves and must instead be interpreted or reinterpreted by one theory or another (Quine, 1969).

Logical Coherence

Relativity might at first seem intrinsically contradictory, as an absolute proof of relativity would directly contradict the relativist cause. Relativists, however, readily recognize that to say that "everything is relative" is the same as to say that "everything is absolute." That is, when one says that statement x is relative to context y, one says not only that it is possible that statement x will not be true in context z but also that it is actually absolute in context y. This so-called "arbitrary absolute" is just as absolute as it is arbitrary (relative). Thus, the obvious fact that there is a world around us is not denied, but the absolute character of this world is put in question.

The notion of an arbitrary absolute is clearly illustrated by a musical staff with and without a clef. Notes on the staff are musically nonexistent if there is no clef (see *Fig. 1a*). If a treble clef is placed on the staff, such as to provide a frame of reference, then the indeterminate note assumes the absolute ontological identity of an E above middle C (*Fig. 1b*). This absolute E is arbitrary, however, as it becomes a G when a bass clef replaces the treble clef (*Fig. 1c*).

It should be noted that, because absolute relativity is indeed nonsensical, relativists do not fret about exhausting the relativization of the universe. Rather than demonstrating that nothing is absolute, relativists enjoy pointing out instances of relativity. Expunging alleged absolutes – or "questioning authority" – is the true impetus. This relativistic impetus is pervasive among intellectuals in contemporary Western culture and is reflected in the emphasis on "critical thinking" in education.

Antagonism to Science

Relativists are often maligned by scientists. This is not surprising, as science is commonly thought of as an absolutist institution. Many – possibly most – scientists share a positivist view of science, according to which a real world exists independently of science and has structural and functional properties of its own that can be objectively known and understood by scientists. Against this, relativists such as Michel Foucault argued that the language of science is part of the language of a culture and, therefore, it establishes beforehand what can and cannot be discovered by scientific research (Foucault, 1969). Similarly, David Bloor claimed that pieces of scientific knowledge are nothing more than symbols standing for social struggles among scientists (Bloor, 1976), and Helen Longino stressed that the logical and cognitive structures of scientific inquiry cannot even develop without a dynamic interaction between scientific practice and social values (Longino, 1990). This relativization of science was not well received by a number of scientists and philosophers, as is clear in an edited volume entitled *A House Built on Sand: Exposing Postmodernist Myths about Science* (Koertge, 1998). The criticism expressed in this volume was partially justified because quite a few "postmodernists" (relativists) were simply ignorant of science and scientific methods. It is also true, however, that many of the self-appointed defenders of science were ignorant of philosophical relativity and made unjustifiable absolutist claims.

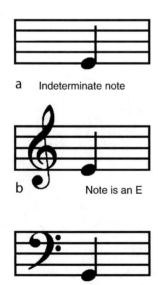

a   Indeterminate note

b   Note is an E

c   Note is a G

Relativism. Figure 1. Musical staffs showing the same quarter note as either an indeterminate note, an E, or a G, depending on the chosen clef (or absence thereof).

Antagonism to Religion

Relativists are equally apt at enraging religious leaders. After all, *faith* (belief in authority) is central to most religions. By doubting religious dogma, relativists act as heretics. That religious leaders despise relativity is exemplified by Pope John Paul II's thoughts as expressed in his encyclical letter *Faith and Reason*. There, he posited that faith and reason are essential human attributes, and that reason without faith leads to nihilism and relativism. He explicitly condemned relativism and asserted that the rejection of relativism is prescribed by the Bible (John Paul II, 1998).

See also: ❷ Doubt ❷ Freud, Sigmund ❷ Postmodernism ❷ Psychology as Religion ❷ Psychology of Religion

Bibliography

Bloor, D. (1976). *Knowledge and social imagery.* London: Routledge.

Descartes, R. (1637/1947). *Discours de la Methode.* Paris: J. Vrin.

Foucault, M. (1969). *L'Archéologie du Savoir.* Paris: Gallimard.

John Paul II (1998). *Fides et Ratio.* Vatican: Libreria Editrice Vaticana.

Koertge, N. (Ed.). (1998). *A house built on sand: Exposing postmodernist myths about science.* New York: Oxford University Press.

Kuhn, T. S. (1962). *The structure of scientific revolutions.* Chicago, IL: University of Chicago Press.

Longino, H. E. (1990). *Science as social knowledge.* Princeton, NJ: Princeton University Press.

Quine, W. V. (1969). *Ontological relativity and other essays.* New York: Columbia University Press.

Religion

Peregrine Murphy Kavros

Introduction

The word religion is derived from the Latin, *religare*, to bind, restrain or tie back, and was first recorded in English in the eleventh century. Religion is defined as a system of faith and worship or faithfulness or devotion to a principle.

Agreement about the definition of religion has been lacking. The West generally views religion as a system of practices and belief towards a sacred or supreme being. Worship in the East has emphasized transcendence or liberation, as opposed to systematic belief. Many definitions of religion have been suggested, but one approach that avoids cultural bias and secular ideologies of human origin has suggested that religion include: doctrine (a creed of belief), myth (an historical sacred narrative), ethics (moral code of sacred origins), ritual (use of sacred objects/ceremony including the historical sacrifice), experience (devotional, mystical, experiential), and social institutions (educational, social gatherings, social service, pastoral care), all of which are inter-related.

Researchers are trying to understand the relationship between religion and health, psychological functioning and decision making. Methods of studying religion are becoming increasingly formal and rigorous. Researchers use multidimensional assessments to evaluate religious affiliation, belief systems and practices. A few of the more commonly used instruments are described below, but for a more thorough review, please refer to the work of Koenig et al. (2001).

Assessments Used in Religion

Affiliation

Roof and McKinney (1987) have developed the most common form of measuring religious affiliation. Duke University has expanded the primarily Western denominational scale to include Muslims, Greek Orthodox, Agnostics, and Atheists.

Belief

Glock and Stark's (1966) Orthodoxy Index identifies beliefs about God, Jesus, miracles, and the devil. Beliefs of orthodoxy, fanaticism, importance, and ambivalence have been measured by Putney and Middleton's (1961) dimensions of religious ideology scale.

Religious Practice

King and Hunt (1967) have assessed participation in church attendance, organizational activities, and related church work. Considering that church attendance may be influenced by relationships, (Fetzer, 1999) evaluates the emotional support provided by a congregation. Murphy et al. (2000) demonstrates the impact of religious and spiritual practices on decision making in long term illness.

Practices of Piety

Stark and Glock (1968) evaluates private prayer; and, Lenski (1963) assesses the extent to which one consults God when making everyday decisions.

Background and Theorists

Early relationships between psychological attitudes and religious belief can be found in the pre-patriarchal rites of the southeastern pre-Indo-European peoples during the Paleolithic era. The religious belief system featured a monotheistic female deity as center and possibly reflected the mother-kinship societal structure. This belief system may have developed to counter fears arising in response to the natural elements, which were beyond their control (ca. 6500–3500 BCE). Within the Greco-Roman culture, the monotheistic God was preferred by Plato to the polytheistic gods that were vulnerable to vice, ignorance and imperfection. An early source of Christian doctrine was the *Didache* (ca. 140). Here, peace is promoted with singularity of thought and avoidance of debate. St. Augustine in *Confessions* describes the emotionally charged psychological turmoil as difficulty with singleness of belief: "My desire was not to be more certain of you but to be more stable in you" (St. Augustine: 133).

William James (1958) explains that there are two aspects to religion: institutional, and personal. Institutional religion includes worship, theology, ceremony, and ecclesiastical organization. Personal religion reflects the inner dispositions, which prompts personal prayer outside of ritual. James believes that religion is the "...feelings, acts and experiences of the individual...in their solitude, as they stand in relation to whatever they may consider the divine." Freud (1856) offered the first of many psychoanalytic interpretations of religion. He observed the rituals of indigenous people and concluded that religion developed from the guilt experienced by the son when he tries to replace the father. Later, in the *Future of an Illusion,* Freud stated that human beings are essentially unhappy, and try to escape their unhappiness by engaging in religious ritual. He believed that religion enabled individuals to externalize religion's precepts while disguising possibly incompatible internal intentions. Jung felt that religion provided something that the external world did not. However, over time he believed that individuals saw that religious truths were sometimes empty and not integrated. Neurosis was the state of being at war with oneself, which he saw could be cured by the Christian virtue of forgiveness. Healing occurred as the representation of religion and the self evolved in the psyche.

More recently, object relations theorists (Rizzuto, 1974, 1979) integrate the representation of the mother (or caretaker) as a central figure in religion. Drawing from the writing of Winnicott (1953, 1975) where he suggests that religion was synonymous with an object that the infant used to help with transitions; this illusory experience provided a bridge from the inner world to the outward reality. The child's representation of God, therefore, evolves from the child's relationship with his/her caretakers. This representation of God is shaped by all of the emotional factors that are dominant in the child at the time of formation, and evolves with the changing representation of the parents and the inner view of the child's sense of self. Theorists (Rizzuto, 1974, 1979) believe that it

is possible that one can hold a representation of God while not believing, but when one believes in the representation of God, one expresses loyalty to the inner representation of the self, and to the ones who nurtured the self into existence.

See also: ❯ Conscience ❯ Faith Development Theory ❯ Forgiveness ❯ Freud, Sigmund ❯ Freud, Sigmund, and Religion ❯ God Image ❯ Great Mother ❯ Healing ❯ Hermeneutics ❯ James, William ❯ Jung, Carl Gustav, and Religion ❯ Myth ❯ New Testament ❯ Object Relations Theory ❯ Psychology as Religion ❯ Psychology of Religion ❯ Ritual ❯ Winnicott, Donald Woods ❯ Wisdom

Bibliography

EPESE. (1984). *NIA Established population for epidemiologic studies of the elderly.* Durham, NC: Center for the study of aging and human development, Duke University Medical Center.

Fetzer Institute (1999). *Multidimensional measurement of religiousness/ spirituality for use in health research.* Kalamazoo, MI: John E. Fetzer Institute.

Freud, S. (1927). *The future of an illusion.* Garden City: Anchor Books, Doubleday.

Freud, S. (1938). Totem and taboo. In A. A. Brill (Ed.), *The basic writings of Sigmund Freud.* New York: Modern Library.

Fowler, J. W. (1996). Pluralism and oneness in religious experience: William James, faith-development and clinical practice. In E. P. Shafranski (Ed.), *Religion and the clinical practice of psychology.* Washington, DC: American Psychological Association.

Glock, C. Y., & Stark, R. (1966). *Christian belief and anti-semitism.* San Francisco, CA: Harper & Row.

James, W. (1958). *The varieties of religious experience: A study of human nature being the Gifford lectures on natural religion delivered at Edinburgh in 1901–1902.* New York: New American Library.

Jung, C. G. (1933). *Modern man in search of a soul* (Harvest Book Series). New York: Harcourt, Brace & World.

Jurgens, W. A. (Ed.). (1970). *The faith of the early fathers.* Collegeville, MN: Liturgical Press.

King, M., & Hunt, R. (1967). Dimensions of religiosity in measuring the religious variable. *Journal for the Scientific Study of Religion, 6,* 173–190.

Koenig, H. G., McCullough, M. E., & Larson, D. B. (2001). *Handbook of religion and health.* New York: Oxford University Press.

Lenski, G. (1963). *The religious factor.* Garden City, NY: Doubleday.

Murphy, P. L., Albert, S. M., Weber, C. M., Del Bene, M. L., & Rowland, L. P. (2000). Impact of spirituality and religiousness on outcomes in patients with amyotrophic lateral sclerosis. *Neurology, 55,* 1581–1584.

Myscofski, C. A. (1995). New religions. In J. Z. Smith (Ed.), *The Harper Collins dictionary of religion.* San Francisco, CA: American Academy of Religion.

Putney, S., & Middleton, R. (1961). Dimensions and correlates of religious ideologies. *Social Forces, 39,* 285–290.

Rizzuto, A.-M. (1974). Object relations and the formation of the image of God. *British Journal of Medical Psychology, 47,* 83–99.

Rizzuto, A.-M. (1979). *The birth of the living God: A psychoanalytic study*. Chicago, IL: University of Chicago Press.

Roof, W. C., & McKinney, W. M. (1987). *American mainline religion*. New Brunswick, NJ: Rutgers University Press.

Simpson, J. A., & Wiener, E. S. C. (Eds.). (2008). *The Oxford English dictionary online*. Oxford, England: Oxford University Press.

Smart, N. (1983). Religion. In A. Richardson, & J. Bowden (Eds.), *The Westminster dictionary of Christian theology*. Philadelphia, PA: The Westminster Press.

St. Augustine. (1991). *Confessions*. Oxford, England: Oxford University Press.

Stark, R., & Glock, C. Y. (1968). *American piety: The nature of religious commitment*. Berkeley, CA: University of California Press.

Taliaferro, C. (2007). Philosophy of religion. In E. N. Zalta (Ed.), *Stanford Encyclopedia of philosophy* (Winter 2007 ed.). Stanford, CA: The Metaphysics Research Lab, Center for the Study of Language and Information.

Winnicott, D. W. (1953). Transitional objects and transitional phenomena. *International Journal of Psycho-Analysis, 34*, 89–97.

Winnicott, D. W. (1975). *Through pediatrics to psychoanalysis*. New York: Basic Books.

Wulff, D. M. (1991). *Psychology of religion: Classic and contemporary views*. New York: Wiley.

Religion and Mental and Physical Health

Christopher S. M. Grimes

Since earliest antiquity humans have theorized and speculated about the relationship of religion and mental and physical health. Early writings, including those contained in Jewish scriptures, demonstrate a belief that mental or physical illness was understood as sometimes resulting from uncleanliness, sinfulness, or as a result of a separation between the individual and God. A period of emotional turmoil in the life of King Saul in 1 Samuel, for example, is attributed to the Spirit of God departing from Saul and an evil spirit tormenting him. These writings are evidence of a belief within earliest cultures of a relationship between religion, spiritual healing, and mental and physical health.

Religious Practices and Healing

In many religions the concept of health refers to a sense of spiritual, mental, and physical wholeness, and in many ancient cultures the healing arts were closely related to religious practices. As early as the fifth century BC followers of Asclepius, the Greek god of medicine and healing, sought services and advice of priests of the cult of Asclepius to find cures to their ailments through, among other things, the interpretation of divinely inspired dreams. There are accounts in the Christian New Testament of Jesus providing healing of physical infirmities such as paralysis, blindness, and leprosy, as well as casting out demons from individuals feared by others because of their aberrant mannerisms and behavior. The cult of Asclepius and the accounts of the miracles of Jesus illustrate how religious leaders, because of their close relationship with the gods, God, or a higher spiritual power, have historically been viewed as healers and sought out by the lame who believed that a religious or spiritual act could restore physical health. Various religious practices ranging from prayer, scripture reading, anointment with oil or perfume, laying on of hands, interpretation of visions, casting out demons, and even sacrifice have been included in healing ceremonies across the ages.

As a result of advances in biology, physiology, and psychology across the millennia, and specifically during the Renaissance and the Enlightenment, a more complete understanding of the causes of physical and mental illness has developed. Presently, within contemporary cultures, treatment of physical and mental illness are predominately based on scientific knowledge or assumptions from previous scientific research. Within Western cultures, medicine and psychology's emphasis on applying scientifically based treatments for physical and mental illnesses, while deemphasizing spiritual matters, resulted in segmented treatment of the individual's concern: Physicians are sought for physical concerns, psychiatrists or psychologists treat mental concerns, and religious leaders tend to the spiritual needs of the individual. However, since the later part of the twentieth century there has been a trend within Western medicine and behavioral healthcare toward increased awareness of the relationship between religion/spirituality and mental and physical health. The segmented treatment of the person has been less pervasive in Eastern cultures where a mind-body-spirit approach to healthcare has remained popular and the distinction between religion, medicine, and psychotherapy are less pronounced. For example, the Chinese medical practice of acupuncture which emphasizes restoring balance and correct flow to the body's Qi, an immaterial substance of vital energy; and the Buddhism emphasis on mindfulness, a concept now gaining popularity in current Western psychotherapy. Indigenous and tribal cultures, even in the West, have tended to maintain a holistic view of the person. Present day Native Americans while heavily influenced by Western culture, may include traditional spiritual ceremonies and interventions alongside interventions informed by modern scientific research. Religious groups who subscribe to only spiritual interventions for physical or mental illness exist as a small minority.

Religion and Wellbeing

Contemporary research has consistently found a relationship between religion and mental and physical health. Generally, researchers have found individuals who practice mainstream religions have fewer physical illnesses and tend to live longer than their nonreligious counterparts (Koenig, 1999; McCullough et al., 2000). George, Ellison, and Larson (2002) propose there are multiple factors that account for these findings. Relevant to physical health, most religions explicitly prescribed good health habits while recommending moderation or abstinence of behaviors that are known to be detrimental. Relative to mental health, individuals who belong to a religious group benefit from social support and gain psychosocial resources as a result of their membership. Religion, especially organized religion, offers adherents coping resources. In times of stress, upheaval, and suffering, individuals often turn to their religious beliefs and/or a religious community to provide comfort, hope, and a sense of belonging and being loved. Generally, religiosity is associated with positive coping in times of distress (Larson and Larson, 2003). Regular attendance and participation in religious services offer members the opportunity to connect with a group of concerned individuals who support one another when there is a need. Religious communities not only care for the spiritual need of their members, but also provide help for those who are ill or in distress. Religion also provides a systematized faith and value system that helps the believer organize and makes sense out of his/her existence and relationships with fellow humans and the natural world.

However, not all forms of religion are equally beneficial to the individuals' overall well-being. Larson and Larson (2003) have noted some individual's religious beliefs lead to a sense of guilt, condemnation, and/or abandonment that can result in poorer coping and increased distress. While there has been relatively consistent support for a positive relationship between well-being and internalized intrinsically motivated religion based on a secure relationship with God, the opposite is true for religion that is imposed, unexamined, and reflective of a tenuous relationship with God; this type of religious belief

has consistently been negatively related to well-being (Pargament, 2002).

Current research on the relationship between religiosity and mental and physical health suggests a complicated multidimensional relationship. Through a review of the literature on religion/spirituality, health, and well-being, Erwin-Cox, Hoffman, Grimes, and Fehl (2007) revealed four models implicit in the current literature to explain this relationship. One model found in the literature suggests that religiosity has a positive impact on physical health as mediated by mental well-being. A second model suggests that religiosity has a positive impact on mental well-being as mediated by physical health. A third model suggests religiosity as that impacts both physical health and mental well-being while at the same time physical health and mental well-being influence each other. Erwin-Cox et al., however, settle on a forth model that suggests: Religion has effects on both physical health and mental well-being; physical health and mental well-being effect each other; and physical health and mental well-being impact religiosity. Erwin-Cox et al.'s model emphasizes the bi-directional and interactional nature of the relationship between religion, physical health, and mental well-being revealed in the current literature.

In conclusion, that there is a relationship between religion and physical and mental health is not in doubt. The relationship between religion and physical and mental health is generally positive, although this is not always the case. Future research will hopefully clarify the multidimensional relationship between religion and mental and physical health allowing for the best possible holistic and integrated care of the individual.

See also: ⊗ American, Buddhism ⊗ Amita Buddha ⊗ Biblical Narratives Versus Greek Myths ⊗ Biblical Psychology ⊗ Buddhism ⊗ Chinese Religions ⊗ Christ ⊗ Christianity ⊗ Demons ⊗ God ⊗ Healing ⊗ Jesus ⊗ Mindfulness ⊗ Miracles ⊗ New Testament ⊗ Psychology ⊗ Psychology and the Origins of Religion ⊗ Psychotherapy ⊗ Psychotherapy and Religion ⊗ Religiosity ⊗ Religious Coping

Bibliography

Erwin-Cox, B., Hoffman, L., Grimes, C. S. M., & Fehl, S. (2007). Spirituality, health, and mental health: A holistic model. In K. Rockefeller (Ed.), *Psychology, spirituality and healthcare*. Westport, CT: Praiger Books.

George, L. K., Ellison, C. G., & Larson, D. B. (2002). Explaining the relationships between religious involvement and health. *Psychological Inquiry, 13*, 190–200.

Koenig, H. G. (Ed.). (1998). *Religion & mental health.* San Diego, CA: Academic Press.

Koenig, H. G. (1999). *The healing power of faith.* New York: Simon & Schuster.

Koenig, H. G., McCullough, M. E., & Larson, D. B. (2001). *Handbook of religion and health.* New York: Oxford University Press.

Larson, D., & Larson, S. (2003). Spirituality's potential relevance to physical and emotional health: A brief review of quantitative research. *Journal of Psychology and Theology, 31,* 37–51.

McCullough, M. E., Hoyt, W. T., Larson, D. B., Koenig, H. G., & Thoresen, C. (2000). Religious involvement and mortality: A meta-analytic review. *Health Psychology, 19,* 211–222.

Pargament, K. (2002). The bitter and the sweet: An evaluation of the costs and benefits of religiousness. *Psychological Inquiry, 13,* 168–181.

Religiosity

Peregrine Murphy Kavros

Introduction

The word religiosity derives from the Latin, religisitas, and was first recorded in English in the fifteenth century. The original sense of religious feeling or sentiment has come to be used to mean excessive or pathological expression of religious feeling.

Religious, religiousness and religiosity are used interchangeably within medical literature. This flexibility in nomenclature is confusing; it is not clear whether the religious behaviors described are excessive, pathological, or customary. Expressions of religiosity vary depending upon the religion and culture. Religiosity includes affected or excessive religious feelings or sentiments and may include behaviors that are dogmatic and pathological; religiosity may manifest as extreme scrupulosity, guilt, worry, or ritual, glossalalia, delusions, distorted beliefs, and desires of persecution or martyrdom. Hebrew and Christian Scripture distinguish between the expressions of religious sentiment. Ecclesiastes (1.16–17) states that it is the "…mind to know wisdom and to know madness and folly…." James (1:26–17) writes "If any think they are religious, and do not bridle their tongues but deceive their hearts, their religion is worthless. [God desires] Religion that is pure and undefiled." Sr. T. More attempted to clarify the heuristic: aberrant religious behavior as "a feverish state of what may better be called religiosity, than religion" (Southey, 1829).

Scientific research on the relationship between religiosity and psychological functioning has contributed to a greater understanding of the field, but one must exercise caution in generalizing assumptions about religiosity across religious groups and cultures. Research findings have demonstrated positive, negative, or nonexistent relationships. Results may be obtained through correlation (how the variables vary together); and it may be difficult to determine whether religiosity affects psychological adjustment or whether psychological adjustment manifests religiosity.

Background and Theorists

Physicians in the nineteenth century were intrigued with manifestations of religiosity. One of the more significant neurologists of the time, and a professor of Freud's, Jean Martin Charcot, demonstrated that professed demonic possession was a form of hysteria. Pierre Janet, another student of Charcot's, described a patient whose religious behaviors reflected a number of mystic stances, including the stigmata. Janet identified early forms of obsessive compulsive disorder in his patient.

Aspects of obsessive compulsive disorder are still associated with religiosity (religious scrupulosity). This crippling association has been observed in the religiosity shown by ultra-Orthodox Jews. Determining when customary religious ritual transcends to pathological religiosity has sometimes, but not always, been determined by how much distress the individual is experiencing and his/her resistance to change.

Some religious experiences such as forms of mysticism have been deemed meaningful. Delacroix studied the mystics for signs of psychopathology/religiosity. After observing fervent signs of religious behavior, Delacroix concluded that mystics were not pathological but that their unconscious life was rich and creative. He believed that the mystics were evolving to new and creative forms of existence, transforming their personalities to achieve selfless unification with God. Although mystics, through prayer, attempted to unite with God, Delacroix felt that this process was not a form of disassociation (the sense of being split off from normal awareness). While extreme and lengthy presentations of dissociation can be manifestations of religiosity, some researchers believe moments of disassociation may occur without one's awareness during religious rituals and may not include aspects of psychopathology or religiosity. One researcher discovered that many people experience being in communion with a holy other (numinous). These experiences are similar to what Otto (1950) described in *The Idea of the Holy – as one transcends* oneself to be in the presence of the sacred.

The religious groups that use extreme ritual, dogma, indoctrination, and alienation from the larger community promote fear and a form of religiosity that is deleterious to physical and mental health. As when the approximately 900 members of the People's Temple, which was led by the Rev. Jim Jones, committed mass suicide in Jonestown, Guyana, on November 18, 1978. The way in which one perceives God can influence how one perceives the external world. When one perceives God as merciful, kind, and forgiving one is more likely to experience positive effects in relation to mental and physical health than when one believes that God is distant, punishing, or vindictive.

Our understanding of religious beliefs has developed from research involving attachment theory. Attachment theory holds that individuals form cognitive representations of the self and others in relationship. These cognitive representations evolve out of the child's interactions with his/her caregivers, which then influence his/her behavior and expectations in relationships. Researchers here observed children's behavior as they were separated and then reunited with their caretaker. Children were classified as: *insecure/avoidant*, when they minimized contact with their caretaker, which was understood to be a defense against rejection; *insecure/ambivalent*, when children desired maximum contact, and expressed considerable distress at separation, which was understood to be reflective of inconsistent caretaking; and, *secure*, when children did or did not show distress at separation, and when they sought closeness, especially at times when they needed comforting. Rizzuto (1979) investigated the effects of attachment on how people perceived God, and their experiences with religious belief. They found that individuals who described their experience with God as *anxious* were more likely to express signs of psychopathology such as, neurotic behavior and a propensity towards negativity. Religious behavior and belief were similar, in that when *insecurely* attached people were in adult relationships that were described as *insecure*, they compensated by increasing their involvement in religious activities. Individuals, who described themselves as *securely* attached, tended to demonstrate stable religious behaviors. *Securely* attached people adopted religious beliefs that were similar to those of their caretaker's, and changed their religious beliefs or activities slowly over time. Alternatively, people who described *insecure* childhood experiences displayed signs of religiosity, which were more often than not highly emotional experiences. These individuals also tended to experience sudden changes in their religious beliefs and were more prone to acts of conversion.

See also: ❂ Altered States of Consciousness ❂ Conscience ❂ Delusion ❂ Discernment ❂ Faith Development Theory ❂ Glossolalia ❂ James, William ❂ Numinosum ❂ Religion ❂ Religion and Mental and Physical Health ❂ Religious Experience ❂ Religious Identity ❂ Unconscious

Bibliography

Ainsworth, M. D., Blehar, M. C., Waters, E., & Wall, S. (1978). *Patterns of attachment: A psychological study of the strange situation.* Hillsdale, NJ: Lawrence Erlbaum.

Allport, G. W., & Ross, J. M. (1967). Personal religious orientation and prejudice. *Journal of Personality and Social Psychology, 5,* 432–443.

Anderson, B. W., Anderson, G. W., Beardslee, W. A., Breck, J., Brueggemann, W., Callaway, M. C., et al. Ecclesiastes, James. In B. M. Metzger & R. E. Murphy (Eds.), *The New Oxford Annotated Bible with the Apocryphal/Deuterocanonical books. New Revised Standard Version.* New York: Oxford University Press.

Bowlby, J. (1969). Attachment. In *Attachment and loss* (Vol. 1). New York: Basic Books.

Granqvist, P., & Hagekull, B. (1999). Religiousness and perceived childhood attachment: Profiling socialized correspondence and emotional compensation. *Journal for the Scientific Study of Religion, 38*(2), 254–273.

Greenberg, D., & Shefler, G. (2002). Obsessive compulsive disorder in ultra-Orthodox Jewish patients: A comparison of religious and non-religious symptoms. *Psychology and Psychotherapy: Theory, Research and Practice, 75*(2), 123–130.

Hackney, C. H., & Sanders, G. S. (2003). Religiosity and mental health: A meta-analysis of recent studies. *Journal for the Scientific Study of Religion, 42,* 43–55.

Hood, R. W. (2005). Mystical, spiritual, and religious experiences. In R. F. Paloutzian & C. L. Park (Eds.), *Handbook of the psychology of religion and spirituality.* New York: The Guildford Press.

Koenig, H. G., McCullough, M. E., & Larson, D. B. (2001). *Handbook of Religion and Health.* New York: Oxford University Press.

Miller, L., & Kelley, B. S. (2005). Relationships of religiosity and spirituality with mental health and psychopathology. In R. F. Paloutzian & C. L. Park (Eds.), *Handbook of the psychology of religion and spirituality.* New York: Guildford Press.

Otto, R. (1950). *The idea of the Holy: An inquiry into the non-rational factor in the idea of the divine and its relation to the rational* (2nd ed., J. W. Harvey, Trans.). London, New York: Oxford University Press.

Pargament, K. I. (1997). *The psychology of religion and coping: Theory, research, and practice.* New York: Guildford Press.

Pargament, K. I., Ano, G. G., & Wachholtz, A. G. (2005). The religious dimension of coping: Advances in theory, research, and practice. In R. F. Paloutzian & C. L. Park (Eds.), *Handbook of the psychology of religion and spirituality.* New York: Guildford Press.

Price, C. A., & Snow, M. S. (1998). Ceremonial dissociation in American protestant worship. *Journal of Psychology and Christianity, 17,* 257–265.

Rizzuto, A.-M. (1979). *The birth of the Living God: A psychoanalytic study.* Chicago and London: University of Chicago Press.

Rowatt, W. C., & Kirkpatrick, L. A. (2002). Two dimensions of attachment to God and their relation to affect, religiosity, and personality constructs. *Journal for the Scientific Study of Religion, 41*(4), 637–651.

Simpson, J. A., & Wiener, E. S. C. (Eds.). (2008). *The Oxford English dictionary online,* Oxford, London: Oxford University Press.

Southey, R. (1829). *Sir Thomas More, or colloquies on the progress and prospects of society*. In J. A. Simpson & E. S. C. Weiner, (Eds.) (2008). The Oxford English dictionary online. Oxford, England: Oxford University Press.

Wulff, D. M. (1991). *Psychology of religion: Classic and contemporary views*. New York: Wiley.

Religious

Peregrine Murphy Kavros

Introduction

The word, religious, derives from the Latin, *religiōs-us*, the suffix, *us*, – *means full of*, and is first recorded in the twelfth century in Old French. Religious is most commonly defined as demonstrating the full practical, or spiritual, (human spirit, soul, or higher moral qualities) effects of religion. The word also refers to a person belonging to or bound by holy orders.

How one demonstrates the full practical or spiritual effects of religion varies. Variables influencing religious behaviors are multidimensional, measurable, and are associated with aspects of interiority. When surveys are conducted on the general population, a single dimension of belief often underlies many religious behaviors. However, when people who claim to be religious are queried, some aspects of religion weigh in more heavily over others. In order to understand how religious behaviors influence outcomes in community life, well being and longevity, many researchers have called for more rigorous investigations. Two of the assessments measuring some of the factors influencing religious behaviors are described, as well as a brief review of the background influencing the dialog between psychology and religion. An expanded review of the instruments measuring dimensions of religious behavior are found in Koenig et al. (2001).

Assessment of Religious Behaviors

Religiousness

Variables influencing religious behaviors can be identified with the Fetzer-NIA Scale, which was developed by a consortium convened by the Fetzer Institute (Idler, Ellison, et al., 2000). The scale assesses belief, religiousness, history, private piety, morals, financial support, social support, experiences, and coping. Among other investigations, the scale has been used to measure the impact of religious behaviors on health outcomes (Murphy, et al., 2000).

Orientation

The Allport & Ross (1967) Religious Orientation scale determines whether individuals are *Intrinsically* motivated and live as though personal and religious beliefs are aligned; *Extrinsically* motivated who use religion to provide security, status, and self-justification; *Indiscriminately Pro-religious* individuals who produce responses falling in both scales, and individuals who are neither *Intrinsic* nor *Extrinsic* and are considered *Indiscriminately Antireligious/Nonreligious*. Intrinsic religious orientation has been significantly associated with many factors, one of which is *Absorption*, openness to experience and the ability to alter one's emotional and belief systems across a variety of situations; a protective mechanism against the effects of morbidity and mortality.

Background

Some researchers, despite the questionnaires wide use, have questioned whether religious orientations such as, Intrinsic and Extrinsic are distinctive. Drawing from Allport's model, Bateson and Ventis (1982) correlated categories of *Internal* and *External* with Intrinsic and Extrinsic. Findings from this study revealed three independent categories: religion as means, Extrinsic; religion as an end, Intrinsic; and, *Quest*, which describes individuals who are still questioning their religious process. More recently, an investigator tackled the questions surrounding the scales, reformatted both models and equalized the questions. Again, Intrinsic, Extrinsic and Quest emerged as three distinct categories. Individuals, who were not religious, had low scores in all three categories. Most importantly, religious orientation was found to vary among the persons, who were sampled, and their particular situation or context.

See also: ❂ Quest ❂ Religion ❂ Religiosity ❂ Ritual

Bibliography

Allport, G. W., & Ross, J. M. (1967). Personal religious orientation and prejudice. *Journal of Personality and Social Psychology, 5,* 432–443.

Batson, C. D., & Ventis, W. L. (1982). *The Religious experience: A social-psychological perspective.* New York: Oxford University Press.

Francis, L. J. (2007). Introducing the new indices of religious orientation (NIRO): Conceptualization and measurement. *Mental Health, Religion & Culture, 10,* 585–602.

Hunt, R., & King, M. (1971). The intrinsic-extrinsic concept: A review and evaluation. *Journal for the Scientific Study of Religion, 10,* 339–356.

Idler, E. L., Ellison, C. G., George, L. K., Krause, N., Levin, J. S., Ory, M., Pargament, K. I., Powell, L. H., Williams, D. R., & Underwood-Gordon, L. (2000). Brief measure of religiousness and spirituality: Conceptual development. Research on Aging.

King, M., & Hunt, R. (1967). Dimensions of religiosity in measuring the religious variable. *Journal for the Scientific Study of Religion, 6,* 173–190.

King, M. B., & Hunt, R. A. (1972). Measuring the religious variable: Reflections. *Journal for the Scientific Study of Religion, 11,* 240–251.

Kirkpatrick, L. A., & Hood, J. R. W. (1990). Intrinsic-Extrinsic religious orientation: The boon or bane of contemporary psychology of religion? *Journal for the Scientific Study of Religion, 29,* 442–462.

Koenig H. G., McCullough, M. E., & Larson, D. B. (2001). *Handbook of religion and health.* New York: Oxford University Press.

Levin, J. S., Wickramasekera, I. E., & Hirshberg, C. (1998). Is religiousness a correlate of absorption? Implications for psychophysiology, coping, and morbidity. *Alternative Therapy Health Medicine, 4,* 72–76.

Murphy, P. L., Albert, S. M., Weber, C. M., Del Bene, M. L., & Rowland, L. P. (2000). Impact of spirituality and religiousness on outcomes in patients with ALS. *Neurology, 55,* 1581–1584.

Simpson, J. A. & Wiener, E. S. C. (Eds.). (2008). *The Oxford English dictionary online,* Oxford: Oxford University Press.

Watts, F., & Williams, M. (1987). *The psychology of religious knowing.* Cambridge, England: Cambridge University Press.

Religious Coping

Ryan M. Denney · Jamie D. Aten

Tix and Frazier (1998) defined religious coping as the "use of cognitive or behavioral techniques, in the face of stressful life events, that arise out of one's religion or spirituality" (p. 411). Religious coping strategies often stem directly from an individual's religious beliefs system, and helps them to construct meaning and form interpretations (both positive and negative) of stressful situations and events (Gall and Cornblat, 2002). Moreover, religious coping has been found to be a distinct form of coping separate from secular forms of coping (e.g., cognitive restructuring) (Tarakeshwar and Pargament, 2001). It has been hypothesized that the incorporation of religion into the process of coping provides a source of meaning that may not be as salient or readily accessed during times of distress with secular forms of coping (Krause, 1998).

Religion and Coping with Trauma

When faced with stressful life events, many people turn to their faith for comfort, support, and a sense of meaning and control (Pargament and Ano, 2006). Most commonly, researchers have found that people use prayer, worship, and social support from a faith community to cope with suffering (Pargament, 2005; Tatsumura, Maskarinec, Shumay, and Kakai, 2003). A study of 586 members of mainline Christian churches in America revealed that 78% of church members utilized religion in their coping with difficult life circumstances (Pargament et al., 1990). A study of 1,000 battered wives revealed that one-third sought help from clergy (Bowker, 1988). Of 1,299 African Americans responding to an interview concerning prayer, 80% reported using prayer to cope (Ellison and Taylor, 1996). Similarly, Kesselring, Dodd, Lindsey, and Strauss (1986) reported that 37% of Swiss respondents and 92% of Egyptian respondents believe that God will help them through their cancer-related illness. Koenig, George, and Siegler (1988) also reported that 45% of older, Protestant adults believed religion to be an important part of coping. In short, many people turn to religious leaders and practices to cope with traumatic or stressful circumstances.

There are other factors and personal predictors that serve to influence the probability religious coping strategies will be utilized (Pargament, 1997). Overall, gender, religious affiliation, level of education, and ethnicity tend to be the most important determining factors in the use religion to cope with major life stress or trauma (Pargament, 2002). For example, minority status has also been correlated with predictors of religious coping (Bearon and Koenig, 1990; Bjorck and Cohen, 1993; Ellison and Taylor, 1996). Furthermore, the fewer resources available to a person, the more likely religious coping strategies will be utilized. Research has also found that the more serious and potentially threatening the stressor, the more likely people are to rely upon religious coping strategies (Pargament, 1997).

Primary Approaches to Religious Coping

Five primary approaches to religious coping have been identified (Pargament et al., 1988; Pargament, 2002). The self-directed approach refers to people relying on their own internal resources to cope, believing they are God-given. The deferring approach occurs when people passively transfer responsibility for problem solution to God. In the collaborative approach, people view themselves as partner with God to solve problems. Pargament et al. (1988) and Pargament (2002) also describes several correlates of these approaches, with the self-directed approach to coping being linked to higher self-esteem and an increased sense of control. The deferring approach has been connected to lower self-esteem, external locus of control, poorer problem-solving skills, and increased intolerance for human diversity. Collaborative religious coping, which involves reciprocation of responsibility between the person and God, has been associated with higher self-esteem, and internal locus of control, and has been described by several researchers as the most psychologically healthy method of religious coping.

Positive and Negative Coping Strategies

Religious coping strategies have also been divided into positive and negative categories (Pargament, 1997). Positive religious coping occurs when people believe that God is guiding and supporting them through their times of trouble. Researchers have shown that those who experience spiritual support often report more positive outcomes (Pargament, 2005; Tatsumura, Maskarinec, Shumay, and Kakai, 2003). Churches and synagogues are used more than any other social support system as a source of social support in times of distress. People sometimes describe their faith communities as "second families" as they rely on the financial, emotional, and spiritual support of members and clergy. This is an especially salient point in light of the cogent empirical evidence that social support is positively related to healthy coping. Additionally, positive religious reframing has been linked to better outcomes, as persons who attribute death, illness, or other major losses to the will of God or to a benevolent God are more likely to experience positive coping, as are persons who frame their experience as an opportunity to grow spiritually (Pargament and Ano, 2006). For instance, cancer patients who attributed more control of their illness to God have reported higher self-esteem and better adjustment (Jenkins and Pargament, 1988). Tarakeshwar et al. (2006) also found that positive religious coping was related to better overall quality of life in persons with advanced cancer.

Negative religious coping mechanisms, which occur when religion and spirituality play a role in coping that is not health-promoting (e.g., feeling abandoned by God) have also been identified. Pargament (2005) found that people who frequently use negative religious coping strategies also tend to report an increase in negative physical and psychological experiences such as depressed mood and a lower quality of life.

Major medical illness, for example, may lead to more distress and even physical symptoms because the illness itself represents a threat to one's foundation of faith (Pargament and Ano, 2006). McConnell, Pargament, Ellison, and Flannelly (2006) found that negative religious coping was significantly linked to various forms of psychopathology, including general anxiety, phobic anxiety, depression, paranoid ideation, obsessive-compulsiveness, and somatization. Also, the relationship between negative religious coping and various forms of anxiety was more pronounced for persons who had recently experienced a serious illness such as cancer (McConnell, Pargament, Ellison, and Flannelly, 2006). Faith communities while often a source of support can also be a source of psychosocial anxiety (Pargament, 1997). Sometimes distressed persons report feeling abandoned by church members and leaders, or they feel they have been a disappointment to their faith community. This can have a negative impact on coping, which can lead to feelings of hopelessness, despair, and resentment. Just as there is positive religious reframing, there can be also be negative reframing. Seeing one's trauma as a deserved punishment from God is one of the most common negative religious reframes reported in the literature, the effect of which is often to stifle adaptive coping (Pargament, 1997). Overall, religious coping is a multifaceted construct that has been found to affect how people understand, interpret, experience, and respond to stressful events.

See also: ◉ Healing ◉ Psychotherapy and Religion

Bibliography

Bearon, L. B., & Koenig, H. G. (1990). Religious cognitions and use of prayer in health and illness. *Gerontologist, 30*, 249–253.

Bjorck, J. P., & Cohen, L. H. (1993). Coping with threats, losses, and challenges. *Journal of Social and Clinical Psychology, 12*, 36–72.

Bowker, L. H. (1988). Religious victims and their religious leaders: Services delivered to one thousand battered women by clergy. In A. L. Horton & J. A. Williamson (Eds.), *Abuse and religion: When praying isn't enough* (pp. 229–234). Lexington, KY: Lexington Books.

Ellison, C. G., & Taylor, R. J. (1996). Turning to prayer: Social and situational antecedents of religious coping among African Americans. *Review of Religious Research, 38*, 111–131.

Ferraro, K. F., & Koch, J. R. (1994). Religion and health among black and white adults: Examining social support and consolation. *Journal for the Scientific Study of Religion, 33*, 362–375.

Gall, T. L., & Cornblat, M. W. (2002). Breast cancer survivors give voice: A qualitative analysis of spiritual factors in long-term adjustment. *Psycho-Oncology, 11*, 524–535.

Jenkins, R. A., & Pargament, K. I. (1988). Cognitive appraisals in cancer patients. *Social Science and Medicine, 26*, 625–633.

Kesselring, A., Dodd, M. J., Lindsey, A. M., & Strauss, A. L. (1986). Attitudes of patients living in Switzerland about cancer and its treatment. *Cancer Nursing, 9*, 77–85.

Koenig, H. G., George, L. K., & Siegler, I. C. (1988). The use of religion and other emotion-regulating coping strategies among older adults. *Gerontologist, 28*, 303–310.

Krause, N. (1998). Neighborhood deterioration, religious coping, and changes in health during late life. *Gerontologist, 38*, 653–664.

McConnell, K. M., Pargament, K. I., Ellison, C. G., Flannelly, K. J. (2006). Examining the links between spiritual struggles and symptoms of psychopathology in a national sample. *Journal of Clinical Psychology, 62*, 1469–1484.

Pargament, K. I. (1997). *The psychology of religion and coping: Theory, research, practice.* New York: Guilford Press.

Pargament, K. I. (2002). The bitter and the sweet: An evaluation of the costs and benefits of religiousness. *Psychological Inquiry, 13*, 168–181.

Pargament, K. I. (2005). The sacred search for significance: Religion as a unique process. *Journal of Social Issues, 61*, 665–687.

Pargament, K. I., & Ano, G. G. (2006). Spiritual resources and struggles in coping with medical illness. *Southern Medical Journal, 99*, 1161–1162.

Pargament, K. I., Ensing, D. S., Falgout, K., Olsen, H., Reilly, B., Van Haitsma, K., et al. (1990). God help me: Religious coping efforts as predictors of the outcomes to significant negative life events. *American Journal of Community Psychology, 15*, 269–286.

Pargament, K. I., Kennell, J., Hathaway, W., Grevengoed, N., Newman, J., & Jones, W. (1988). Religion and the problem-solving process: Three style of coping. *Journal for the Scientific Study of Religion, 27*, 90–104.

Tatsumura, Y., Maskarinec, G., Shumay, D. M., & Kakai, H. (2003). Religious and spiritual resources, CAM, and conventional treatment in the lives of cancer patients. *Alternative Therapies, 9*(3), 64–71.

Tarakeshwar, N., & Pargament, K. I. (2001). Religious coping in families of children with autism. *Focus on Autism and other developmental disabilities, 16*, 247–260.

Tarakeshwar, N., Vanderwerker, L. C., Paulk, E., Pearce, M. J., Kasl, S. V., & Prigerson, H. G. (2006). Religious coping is associated with the quality of life of patients with advanced cancer. *Journal of Palliative Medicine, 9*, 646–657.

Tix, A. P., & Frazier, P. A. (1998). The use of religious coping during stressful life events: Main effects, moderation, and mediation. *Journal of Consulting and Clinical Psychology, 66*, 411–422.

Religious Experience

Robert Kaizen Gunn

Insofar as one defines religious experience as an experience of the transcendent or the supernatural (or some equivalent term), religious experience has been around in some form since humans developed symbols and language. We may look at the full range of religious experience in either of at least four ways: (1) how the experiences of the transcendent are viewed from within the religion itself; or (2) how the experiences may be evaluated and understood from a discipline outside any particular religion; (3) the unique approach to religious experience in a religion based on mind; and (4) the use of various drugs to induce transcendental states of mind.

Religious Experience as Viewed from Within the Particular Religion

Each religion usually begins with a profound experience of the transcendent on the part of the founder. Abraham, Isaac and Jacob, as well as Moses, all had profound experiences of God that were the basis for Judaism. Jesus had direct experiences of God and his followers had direct experiences of him for the founding of Christianity. Many Christians emphasize the importance of having a personal experience of Christ, called "being born again." Islam was founded on the experience of Allah by Mohammed. Buddhism began with the enlightenment experience of Shakyamuni Buddha, and continued, particularly in Zen, to emphasize the importance of one's own direct experience of enlightenment, which would be verified by one's teacher. The value of direct personal experience in religion is in its transformational possibilities: those who have them often claim to have a clearer purpose for living, a shift away from egocentrism in the direction of altruism and identification with the existential plight of all living things; and a sense of time that transcends human chronology. Within each religion there are often criteria by which particular religious experiences are evaluated as to their authenticity.

Within each of the world religions, where the direct experience of the transcendent is not emphasized, emphasis usually falls on correct doctrine, belief or ritual and practice for approval of one's status within the religion. Thus, Judaism has its requirement of circumcision, the Mosaic Laws, the Torah and Talmud; Christianity has its gospels and New Testament canon, its belief in Christ as formulated by one of the ancient creeds (Nicene, Apostles', etc.) and allegiance to the Church; Islam has its daily prayers and weekly gatherings, and reliance on the Koran; Buddhism has its precepts for monks and laity and the teachings of the Buddha as written in the Dhammapada, and the many sutras that followed.

Religious Experience Viewed from Disciplines Outside Religion

As an object or field of study capable of being investigated and understood by someone outside any particular religion, however, the very concept of religious experience is a relatively new idea in the history of civilizations. It requires the conceptual possibility of a secular consciousness, i.e., a consciousness that reflects on itself and on all human phenomena without presuming a priori any particular religious truth. It requires someone to look at religious experience from outside the religion.

In this sense, religious experience is impossible to consider without at least the theoretical possibility of atheism or at least secularization, which is to say, it is impossible without the capacity to stand back from all religions and observe religious activity as an outsider. Such a stance aims to observe, evaluate, categorize and understand religious experience on phenomenological grounds alone, without any reference to the truth claims of any particular religion.

As such, religious experience as a field of study never appeared in the world before the nineteenth century CE, that era in which God was declared dead by Nietzsche, religion was declared an opiate of the masses by Marx, God was seen as a projection of the immature human psyche by Freud, and the entire origin of species was theorized by Darwin without any assumptions of theistic causation.

One might say that the roots of an entirely secular, non-theistic weltanschauung were laid by the Protestant Reformation's break from the Roman Catholic Church (1517–1648), for without the concept of a legitimate consciousness separate from ecclesiastical control, all observations and truth claims were captive to the Church, as attested by the church's condemnation of Galileo (1564–1642) and Spinoza (1632–1677), among others. Although the grounds for separating from the Roman Catholic Church were intra-religious, based on the interpretation of the Biblical text itself, the revolutionary and ground-breaking departure was the concept of the individual conscience and the personal direct access to God as superseding ecclesiastical authority. The conception of the possible validity of an individual's conscience being greater than the consensus ecclesiae was the first step toward the development of a secular consciousness, a consciousness not constricted by and defined by the church's authority. In this sense, the Protestant Reformation was a necessary precursor to the Age of Enlightenment, which provided the humanistic philosophical and political framework from which the natural and social sciences of the nineteenth century sprang. Only after Freud, Marx, Nietzsche and Darwin could the idea of a study of religious experience per se be considered.

William James may easily be called the father of secular studies of religious experience. His book, The Varieties of Religious Experience (James, 2004), published in 1902, remains the classic work in the field. In it he outlined the four characteristics of religious experience as being (1) transient, (2) ineffable, (3) noetic, and (4) passive. The experience is transient in that it occurs in a limited frame of time, after which the person returns to ordinary life. The experience is ineffable in that it is hard for the person to put it into words. It is noetic insofar as the person usually feels that she/he has learned something of deep and lasting value, on the basis of which her/his life is altered significantly for the better. The experience is passive in the sense that it was not created by conscious control, but "just happened." Even if one engaged in deliberate activities to increase the possibility of the experience, the actual experience was not under the person's will power or control.

It was in this book that James distinguished between the "once born" and the "twice born": the once born are people who go through life without having any powerful religious experience that significantly changes them; the twice born are those who do have such a powerful religious experience that they see it as the basis for an entirely new (and improved, from their point of view) way of living.

It was also in this book that James distinguished between the religion of "healthy-minded" people and that of those of a very disagreeable temperament. In James' view, healthy minded people choose a form of religion that is basically positive in its outlook on people and the world, whereas less healthy-minded people choose a religion fraught with the dynamics of judgment, anger and wrath. This distinction was invaluable for future studies on the particular characteristics of healthy/unhealthy people and, by extension, healthy/unhealthy religion.

The value of James' book far exceeded the numerous brilliant insights he offered: it laid the groundwork for the entire field of psychology of religion, and psychology and religion. Moreover, it suggested how religion might be a proper field of study for other sciences. Thus, since James, the many dimensions of religious experience continue to be mapped by the fields of philosophy of religion, phenomenology of religion, sociology of religion, comparative studies in religion, history of religions, neurotheology, transpersonal psychology, and genetics.

Meanwhile, as society has become increasingly secularized and mainstream religion has suffered loss of favor, many people identify themselves as being "spiritual" without being "religious," indicating an interest in experiences of the transcendent but a decidedly negative valuation of both institutionalized religion and monotheism. Such people tend to gravitate toward Eastern, non-theistic religions, or to personally constructed amalgams of religious and spiritual truths and practice. The result is the expansion of the meaning of "religious experience" to include "spiritual experience," in order to include those who intentionally don't want to be identified with institutional or theistic religion.

Religious Experience as Viewed from Within a Religion Based on Mind

More than 2,000 years before Freud, a religion arose in India that was based on the intentional exploration of the nature of mind itself. Standing midway between religions that evaluate religious experience on the basis of his or her own internal standards and scientific disciplines that evaluate religious experience from an outside observer standpoint, Buddhism is entirely based on realizing the nature of mind and what is its ground or source through intensive meditation. Fully aware of the mind's tendency to distort, project, deny, and to engage in whatever activities may confirm a sense of a permanent self, Buddhism trains adherents in awareness of the mind's dynamics in order to break through the delusion of a fixed, separate and immutable self to ultimate reality, the emptiness of all things. Such a breakthrough is what is called enlightenment in Buddhism. From that experience one realizes in a total (whole body and mind), non-conceptual way the basic tenets of Buddhism: the interdependence of all things, the impermanence of all things, wisdom and compassion.

Religious Experience Initiated by the Use of Drugs

The last category of religious experience to be considered is unique in that it is based on the ingestion of some form of chemical, whether found in nature, such as peyote, or manufactured, such as LSD, psilocybin, cocaine, or nitrous oxide, among others. Taking one of these drugs induces an experience with many of the characteristics identified by William James as marks of traditional mysticism: a transient and ineffable feeling of ecstasy, of loss of boundaries, an oceanic feeling of oneness with all; the noetic conviction that one has experienced some profound existential truth about the nature of ultimate reality. On the other hand, since it is prompted by the ingestion of drugs, such experiences do not have the fourth trait of passivity James listed. The significance of the passivity in traditional religious experience is in understanding it as an experience of grace, beyond one's control. This element may be missing for those who use a drug to trigger the experience. For some people, nevertheless, drug-induced experiences of transcendence do become transformative in their day-to-day life. Such a life change is usually made possible by the person's continual reflection on the experience and construction of a method for integrating the experience into their common life. On the other hand, as those religions that have made use of drugs in their rituals (most notably, Native American tribes), certain precautions (such as the presence of a trust other person or community, or the context of a ritual) need to be taken so that the drug functions in a constructive way.

See also: ⊙ Buddhism ⊙ James, William

Bibliography

Abernethy, B., & Bole, W. (Eds.). (2007). *The life of meaning: Reflections on faith, doubt and repairing the world* (see especially Chapter 4, "I'm spiritual, not religious"). New York: Seven Stories Press.

Byrom, T. (1993). *The Dhammapada*. Boston, MA: Shambhala.

Campbell, J. (2008). *The hero with a thousand faces*. Novato, CA: New World Library.

Eliade, M. (1968). *The sacred and the profane: The nature of religion*. New York: Houghton Mifflin Harcourt.

Geertz, C. (1977). *The interpretation of cultures*. New York: Basic Books.

James, G. A. (1995). *Interpreting religion: The phenomenological approaches of Pierre Daniel Chatepie de la Saussaye, W. Brede Krestensen and Gerardus van der Leeuw*. Washington, DC: Catholic University of America Press.

James, W. (2004). *The varieties of religious experience*. New York: Barnes & Noble.

Otto, R. (1958). *The idea of the holy*. New York: Oxford University Press.

Rahula, W. (1994). *What the Buddha taught: Revised and expanded edition with texts from the Suttas and the Dhammapada*. New York: Grove/Atlantic, Inc.

Smith, H. (1991). *The world's religions: Our great wisdom traditions*. San Francisco, CA: HarperCollins.

Smith, H. (2003). *Cleansing the doors of perception: The religious significance of entheogenic planats and chemicals*. Boulder, CO: Sentient Pubs.

Wach, J. (1962). *Sociology of religion*. Chicago, IL: University of Chicago Press.

Wach, J., & Kitagawa, J. (1961). *Comparative study of religions*. New York: Columbia University Press.

Religious Identity

David M. Bell

Introduction

Most scholars in religious studies and the humanities understand religious identity to be a simple matter of self-identification with a religious tradition. The term is popular in these fields, but such an approach offers little in the way of conceptual clarity or insight into the formation or functioning of religious identity. When approached from a psychological perspective, religious identity reveals significant insight into the cognitive role of religion; new research may influence the basic questions asked about the psychology of religious beliefs and practices.

The Psychology of Identity

Erik Erikson (1902–1994), a theorist who essentially began the psychological study of identity, originally spoke of identity as a central ego achievement to be reached in adolescence (1950). One's *ego identity* ("ego" comes from the Latin nominative pronoun "I") is formed from simpler identifications made in childhood and then integrated into a coherent sense of self in adolescence. Through evolution, Erikson theorized that the adolescent is biologically wired to necessarily seek social resources for this identity process during this time of life. This illustrates the interdisciplinary quality of Erikson's *psychosocial model* as being both psychological and sociological. The psychological person is designed to pull identity content from the relative and always changing cultural resources. Observing that identity is often formed and integrated in adolescence only to be later unraveled, Erikson later expanded this stage of human development to also be a constant psychosocial element in adult life as aging individuals encounter other identity crises throughout adulthood.

The current psychological study of identity can be divided into two primary areas. One area of research looks at the cognitive mechanisms and neural structures that are utilized to construct autobiographical memory. There are three primary findings in this relatively new area. First, the field of autobiographical memory emphasizes that identity is more than a mere sociological identification. One's identity is a neurological component of the brain that is formed through memory encoding, selective retrieval, implicit memory schemas, and many factors of psychosocial selective biases. New research in functional magnetic resonance imaging (fMRI) has shown specific modular patterns of long-term memory encoding in which particular regions of the brain are utilized in different types of memory which are complexified by variants in the content of the remembered experiences. Secondly, this research has shown that memories of experiences are re-constructed and that individuals typically overestimate the correctness of their memories. Humans naturally recreate their event memories to fit patterns of belief expectations. As part of this constructive process, implicit memories (subconscious) are formed from a collection of various experiences that then function as a filter through which to interpret later experiences. Finally, researchers in autobiographical memory have demonstrated a psychosocial quality in the cognitive formation of identity. Through developmental studies of autobiographical memory, Fivush and Haden (2003) have shown that children form a coherent sense of identity primarily through learned patterns of adult and peer interaction.

Another area of identity research uses psychometric measures of identity to determine levels of *identity status* formation. Marcia (1966) took Erikson's concept of identity development and sought to break it down into four identity statuses that could be measured. He distinguishes two factors that are relatively independent of each other in identity formation. The crisis axis measures whether a person had ever had an identity crisis, and whether they are currently in an identity crisis. The commitment axis determines whether or not someone has made a commitment to a certain identity. Identity diffusion (no crisis, no commitment), identity foreclosure (no crisis, commitment), identity moratorium (present crisis, no commitment), and identity integration (past crisis, commitment) make up the four identity statuses. The content of the qualitative interview and the psychometric measure of identity neatly divides the questions into primary areas of vocation, gender, politics and religion. Marcia's popular paradigm has been used in hundreds of published articles. The preponderance of research in identity and the psychology of religion has used variations of Marcia's measure with other established psychological measures of religiosity to reveal interesting connections in which religion is often shown to be a positive resource in overall identity achievement (see review by Spilka, Hood, Hunsberger and Gorsuch, 2003: 143–146). Such studies have shown a connection between identity achievement and increased intrinsic religiosity, belief-threatening consultation, and the level of religious commitment. Identity moratorium is positively associated with higher levels of quest, belief threatening consultation, lower levels of religious commitment, and religious doubting. Identity foreclosure is correlated with extrinsic religiosity, religious commitment, and belief-confirming consultation. Overall identity diffusion is generally related to lower levels of overall religiosity.

There are two caveats to this work. First, these findings are limited due to biased sampling with subjects who are: primarily in the United States; primarily adolescents; primarily Christians; and primarily more religious than the norm of American society. More importantly, another limitation lies in the basic theoretical conception of the studies. Using a basic identity status measure (which includes religious content) and a basic measure of religiosity, the researchers end up confounding their results by partly measuring the same factor – religiosity. To show a relationship between religiosity and identity development, one would either have to remove the religious content from the identity measure, or design an entirely new measure of religious identity. This also reveals a problem for identity research in which the primary measure of identity is biased towards more religious people.

Religious Identity Formation and Functioning

In the last decade, researchers in identity studies have begun to focus on specific cognitive domains of identity, which may be neurologically unique from other domains, and may be formed independently of other domains. This finding of *domain specificity* has shown that identity statuses may be entirely different in one identity domain than in another domain. Several recent studies have looked at unique patterns of identity formation in the specific areas of ethnicity, gender, vocation, and politics. But few have considered the unique formation and function of the domain of religious identity. Until recently, there has been no conceptual work in a psychology of religious identity, and no tool with which to measure or establish uniqueness of religious identity. A recently proposed psychometric measure of religious identity seeks to look at identity formation through the lens of religiosity separated from overall global identity (see direction of this research in Bell, 2008). In one study of 650 subjects, four

statuses of religious identity were defined and measured in ways that revealed clear patterns of cultural resources (i.e., particular religious backgrounds) predicting but not determining overall identity formation. The conceptual bases of the four statuses were also reconsidered to avoid simple assumptions by Marcia about identity achievement in the specific content of religion. A fourth status of "religious identity integration" is being proposed that better reflects a more fluid commitment instead of a rigid commitment to a particular form of religion.

Likewise, this conceptual work considers the functioning of religious identity as potentially the most unique domain of identity in which: the focus of religious identity is often away from the self/ego (transcendence to other), much more capable of imagination, and more prone to implicit belief patterns of narrative construction. In the same study of 650 participants, it was demonstrated that people use religious identity in both implicit and explicit ways. In conjunction with the cognitive research in implicit memories, individuals use religious identity in ways in which they may be largely unaware. The importance of one's religious identity often increases in importance due to levels of social approval bias. For example, the explicit functioning of religious identity is often presented as much more important than when measured implicitly. For the researcher, getting at such a disclosure of religious identity is difficult not only due to social approval bias, but also due to "deity approval bias." People may want to say that religion is more important to their identity than it really is not only because of social approval concerns, but also because the deities of their belief system may not approve if it is not important enough.

One goal of this research in religious identity is to discover why it is that for many individuals religious identity lingers in the mind much longer than religious beliefs or the desire to do religious practices. For those who change or lose their religious practices, and even their religious beliefs, individuals may find that their religious identity is still present and continues to keep them somewhat oriented around religion. This illustrates how religious identity, for many individuals, may be a core psychological mechanism that takes on more permanence than beliefs and practices. Such a proposal may significantly influence how researchers in psychology and religion approach and ask the most basic questions about the role of religion in the mind. Another consideration includes the reframing of the notion of religious orientation. Allport and Ross's (1967) measures of extrinsic and intrinsic orientation were efforts to distinguish different motivations in individuals' religiosity as explicitly reported by the participants. By looking at levels of social approval bias, a psychological understanding of implicit and explicit religious identity takes the question of motivation to a different level in which self-reported motivation is only one consideration.

The work should also extend beyond the measures of such factors. With adequate funding, fMRI studies could investigate whether there are unique modular areas of religious identity. To date, studies have shown how general autobiographical memories are retrieved and constructed, but this research has not considered how the content of the identity may affect the retrieval process.

In short, the psychological study of religious identity is fundamentally a psychosocial investigation in which religious content is often a rich identity resource for individuals in most societies. Certainly one does not need to be religious to be able to form an overall, integrated, and healthy global identity. Religion is part of the many cultural resources that are highly relative and prone to changing over time. Yet, the ways in which the individual needs to form a notion of self through adulthood is uniquely affected by the amount of religious resources by which that individual is surrounded. Further, religious identity content, as a cognitive domain, operates differently than other domains, including gender identity, racial identity, and political identity. Finally, it is proposed that the psychological study of religious identity is relatively unexplored and yet foundational to much of the research in the field of psychology of religion. As a new theoretical paradigm, it offers several explanatory insights into the role of religon in the mind.

See also: ❯ Communal and Personal Identity ❯ Erikson, Erik ❯ Religiosity ❯ Self ❯ Self Psychology

Bibliography

Allport, G. W., & Ross, J. M. (1967). Personal religious orientation and prejudice. *Journal of Personality and Social Psychology, 5*, 432–443.

Bell, D. M. (2008). Development of the religious self: A theoretical foundation for measuring religious identity. In A. Day (Ed.), *Religion and the individual: Belief, practice, and identity* (pp. 127–142). Burlington, VT: Ashgate.

Erikson, E. H. (1950). *Childhood and society*. New York: W. W. Norton.

Fivush, R., & Haden, C. A. (2003). *Autobiographical memory and the construction of a narrative self: Developmental and cultural perspectives*. Mahwah, NJ: Lawrence Erlbaum Associates.

Marcia, J. E. (1966). Development and validation of ego identity status. *Journal of Personality and Social Psychology, 3*, 551–558.

Schacter, D. L., & Scarry, E. (Eds.). (2000). *Memory, brain, and belief*. Cambridge, MA: Harvard University Press.

Spilka, B., Hood, R., Hunsberger, B., & Gorsuch, R. (2003). *The psychology of religion: An empirical approach* (3rd ed.). New York: Guilford.

Religious, Role of

Sharn Waldron

Carl Jung defines his understanding of religion in terms that make it apparent that he regards religion as a certain attitude of mind taken towards particular factors of experience that are seen as powerful, dangerous, grand, beautiful or meaningful (Jung, 1938: par. 8). These factors of experience are factors of psychic experience and especially those psychic experiences that arise from the collective unconscious. From in Jung's perspective religious ideas originate with the archetypes and careful consideration of the archetypal symbols and image constitutes the essence of religion.

The Transcendent Quality of Religious Experience

Religion has a transcendent quality because these unconscious processes transcend the realm of the conscious ego, the observing subject, and the ideas and motifs of religion appear to the ego to come from beyond ad revelations. But psychologically speaking this beyond is also within although not restricted to the individuality of the experiencing person. Jung considers that the realm of the unconscious from whence these revelations derive may possess an insight superior to that of the conscious mind. Religious experience is grounded in what is both absolute subjectivity and universal truth, it partakes of the accumulated wisdom of the ages and is not lightly influenced by either the caprices of consciousness or with transcentary cultural trends (Jung, 1952: par. 355).

The images enshrined in such Christian doctrine as the God-man, the Trinity, the Virgin Birth or the Cross, are not peculiarly or exclusively Christian. Not only can they be found in many pagan religions but they may also appear or re-appear spontaneously with all sorts of variations as psychic phenomenon. In Christianity they have been refined and are highly developed but their remote origins are neither faith nor tradition but primitive dreams, visions or trances. They are certainly not conscious interventions but Jung considers that they came into being at that stage of human development in which humans did not so much think as we do today but rather were aware of thoughts coming into them. These dogmas may last for untold centuries: the suffering God-man may be at least five thousand years old and the trinity is probably even older. Jung claimed that the doctrines of a particular religion are expressions of unconscious psychic activity with their roots in humanity's primitive past. The particular religion merely shapes and refines these ancient symbolizations.

In consequence to this common reference of symbols of all religions to the fundamental archetypes, there can be no exclusive claim made by the disciples of any particular religion on behalf of its own God. These claims must rather be regarded as an index of the intensity of the conviction aroused in believers by their experience of the overwhelming numinosity that they call God. The experience is certainly valid, but the interpretation of it may not be. Anything or anyone, any figure or any symbol which, can produce this overwhelming effect is entitled to the name "God" from the point of the believer, but he can also say that, 'every idea of the ultimate, of the first or last, of the highest or lowest. The name makes no difference (Jung, 1952: par. 739 note 1).

As a psychologist then Carl Jung agrees neither with those who see God as absolute that is existing in Himself, nor yet with those who adopt the relative view of God which recognizes at least in an elementary way that there is some personal involvement in the process which produces conception of God (personal here relating to the personal psyche). Within its self-imposed empirical limits, analytical psychology recognizes God as a function of the unconscious and particularly of the collective unconscious. The image of god is, then the symbolic expression of a certain psychological state, or function, which has all the character of absolute superiority to the conscious will of the subject; hence it can enforce or bring about a standard of accomplishment that would be unattainable to conscious effort.

The Impact of the Development of Consciousness on Religious Experience

In the process of the development of consciousness by humanity, Jung argues that two unfortunate but probable unavoidable errors arose in relation to the concept of God. The first of these was materialism that declared in effect that since God could not be found in the galaxies he had never existed. The second error was to psychologise God as an illusion based on the will to power or repressed sexuality. But Jung believes that humanity cannot thus easily dispose of God or of the instinctually or archetypally based religious impulse. From time immemorial human beings have recognized the existence of gods or a God in one form or another and have been unable to do

without them. Consciously or unconsciously the idea of an all-powerful divine Being is everywhere present. He who says with Nietzsche, that "God is dead" does not thereby rid himself of God but rather faces the fatal inflation of becoming his own god – and such gods are but tin gods with thick skulls and cold hearts' (Jung, 1917: par. 113).

The alternative, which Carl Jung propounds to these two errors, is based upon the conviction that the God-images in the psyche have not only numinosity and power, but also an essential autonomy. They exist, and they are not dependent for their existence on any other need, motive, desire, or attribute of human beings. For the empiricist, the unanswerable question concerning the metaphysical reality of God in Himself is irrelevant beside the fact that the "idea of God is an absolutely necessary psychological function of an irrational nature." The idea is archetypal and thus there is that within the human psyche which will behave as a god and which caution, if nothing also, dictates should be consciously acknowledged as God (Jung, 1917: par. 113). Human beings do not create gods for themselves but there is a sense in which they choose the master they wish to serve. In choosing their god humanity necessarily denies their services to other masters and attempts to secure themselves against them. Such choices do define one's God but they do not make intelligible that unknown psychic quantity which implies the choice. For true wholeness and genuine health, or salvation, it is important that the human individual chooses wisely. In other words, humanity can become a Self only by choosing the right God. The live issue for modern humanity is between the archetypal image with its authenticity and its immediacy, on the one hand, and the intellectual constructs of the so-called enlightened mind on the other. In the final analysis these constructs represent the abortive attempt on the part of the enlightened to deny the reality of both the God-image and the realm from which the image derived (Jung, 1933: par. 429).

God as Dangerous

Christianity and Judaism and others of the world religions, recognize God as being not only redemptive but also dangerous. In Judaism for example, the holiness of God is seen as something unapproachable: no man can see God and live'. (Compare the elaborate precautions taken to protect the unwary from the Holy Mountain, from the ark...etc.) God must be mediated to humanity, and this mediatory function finds its highest expression in the figure of Christ. This concept of the danger of the nearness of God, according to Carl Jung is a well established psychological fact (Jung). The concentration of psychic energy in the unconscious can have catastrophic effects upon consciousness and the saving factor is the symbol, "which is able to reconcile the conscious with the unconscious and embrace them both" (Jung, 1921: par. 178). God images are practically indistinguishable from the symbols of the self, this means that these symbols and images serve the very real purpose of putting the human individual in touch with his/ her own depths in such a way that the contact does not destroy him/her but immeasurable enriches his/her life and increases the boundaries of his/her awareness.

Jung is convinced not only that religious dogma and doctrines always express and formulate essential psychological attitudes but also that they are a more satisfactory medium of expression that scientific theories for irrational facts like the psyche. A theory is necessarily highly abstract and exclusively rational whereas the imagery of dogma can encompass psychic totality and can express the living processes of the psyche in suitable dramatic forms, like the drama of creation, sacrifice and redemption.

Thus Jung argues strongly for the positive value of myth and claims that to divest the Gospels of myth would be to sacrifice that very quality in them which conveys wholeness and health. Myth become suspect only when one attempts to take the mythological contents literally and concretely, in which case they come into conflict with the objective knowledge of the external world. Treated symbolically, they have tremendous force and power.

Myth is not to be confused with fiction but should be recognized as the dramatic expression of psychic experience that have been constantly repeated in individual lives and in whole cultures. Since they relate back to the archetypes, their content cannot be exhausted in rational explanation and to dismiss them as primitive is to overlook the fact that humanity still has its primitive nature.

Much unnecessary confusion arises from the failure to distinguish between what Jung calls religion as immediate experience (or, more usually, just religion) and religion as creed. Once again Jung himself is partly responsible for the confusion since he is not always consistent in making it unambiguously clear whether his praise or polemic against religion is directed towards the experience or the creedal variety. Jung writes that

▶ the creeds have accordingly seen themselves obliged to undertake a progressive codification of their views, doctrines, and customs, and in doing so have externalized themselves to such an extent that the authentic religious element in them – the living relationship to an and direct confrontation with their extramundane point of reference has been trust into the background (1957: par. 508).

Religion as immediate experience is grounded in the experience of the numinous, the extra-mundane, which is manifested through the unconscious. Essentially it is personal and individual experience of the collective depths and as such it is superior to even the best traditions, at least with respect to the intensity of the conviction that it imparts. His reflection on his experience may or may not accord with the orthodox conceptions or formulations of particular religious confessions but official pronouncements of Church, Synagogue, Mosque or Temple are comparatively meaningless unless the individuals to whom they are addressed can them selves authenticate them by personal experience.

This experience may well be mediated through the historic religions with their wealth of symbols and images expressive of wholeness and salvation but only if those symbols and images are consciously recognized and valued for what they are,. The whole meaning and purpose of religious experience can be expressed in language more congenial to the great religions of the world by saying that the purpose lies 'in the relationship of the individual to God (Christianity, Judaism, Islam) or to the path of salvation and liberation (Buddhism) (Jung, 1957: par. 507). Psychologically, the meaning and purpose lies in the relationship of the person to his own Self, or to the path of wholeness and health.

See also: ◈ Archetypes ◈ Christianity ◈ Collective Unconscious ◈ Ego ◈ God ◈ Islam ◈ Judaism and Psychology ◈ Jung, Carl Gustav ◈ Self

Bibliography

Jung, C. G. (1970). *Civilisation in transition.* London: Routledge.
Jung, C. G. (1974). *Psychological types.* Princeton, NJ: Princeton University Press.
Jung, C. G. (1977). *Two essays.* Princeton, NJ: Princeton University Press.
Jung, C. G. (1981). *Civilisation in transition.* London: Routledge.
Jung, C. G. (1991). *Psychology and religion: West and East.* London: Routledge.
Waldron, S., & Waldron, D. (2004). Jung and neo-paganism. *Quadrant* XXXXIV, (Summer).

Repentance

◈ Confession ◈ Forgiveness

Repression

D. Brian Smothers

Definition

Repression: (1) The defensive process by which an idea or memory is expelled from the conscious mind. (2) A defense mechanism used to protect the self from unwanted affects associated with instinctual impulses.

Discussion

According to Freud's original childhood seduction theory, an individual repressed unwanted or painful memories associated with childhood sexual experiences which were subsequently reawakened in adult sexuality. As Freud's theory moved away from the actuality of childhood abuse and towards instinctual sexuality, repression played a prominent role as a generic psychological defensive phenomenon in which an individual excluded painful affects and perceptions from consciousness. Repression was one of Freud's earliest discoveries in working with hysterical patients. Freud felt that such patients experienced impulses that were stricken from consciousness and converted into somatic complaints and hysterical symptoms, such as blindness and paralysis. Thus, while the memory my have been expelled from conscious awareness, the event, affect or impulse remained present through a compromise formation within the symptomatic sphere.

Originally, Freud argued that the repression of drives and affect as experienced by hysterical patients resulted in anxiety. As the affects and drives were pressing for release and subsequently repressed, the individual experienced anxious tension. Freud latter amended this theory to suggest that repression was a result rather than a cause of anxiety. Accordingly, a preexisting fear, impulse or anxious tension caused the need to forget. Freud suggested that repression occurred in two separate phases, primary repression, and secondary repression or repression proper. In primary repression a child learns that some aspects of reality are pleasant, while others are unpleasant. The child, on an unconscious level, keeps unpleasant experiences and affects out of conscious awareness. According to Freud, primary repression is thought to be the cause of infantile amnesia. In accordance with the development of the superego and the maturing of the psychic apparatus, the child is able to actively defend the conscious from unwanted perceptions. Thus, in secondary repression the child formally and consciously excludes from consciousness, desires, affects, or perceptions that may cause tension or anxiety.

At its core, repression is motivated forgetting or ignoring. Freud's early drive model suggested that impulses and affects press for release and have to be held in check by a dynamic defensive force. It is important to note that not all forgetting is an example of repression. Repression is primarily defensive, in that it protects the conscious from an overwhelming affect or perception. Classical analytic theory regards repression as a higher-level neurotic defense.

Regarding matters of religion, Freud persuasively argued that repression and obsessional neurosis were at the core of religious traditions and practices. Freud suggested that as instinctual impulses, primarily sexual ones, are repressed, the lurking remnants of the impulses are felt as temptation. Religious practices and traditions are used as a means of defending against the lurking temptation. Additionally, Freud suggested that the anxiety that is defended against in the process of repression is similar to one's fearful experience of an omnipotent God's retribution. Thus, the pious believer will repress the sinful impulse in fear of divine punishment and seek penance or repentance for any temptation. The martial ceremony is an example of this defense in religious life. The church formally prohibits sexual relations outside of marriage though after the ceremony sexual enjoyment is sanctioned. Prior to marriage, any gratification of the sexual impulse is due to temptation and in need of forgiveness or penance.

See also: ❯ Anxiety ❯ Defenses ❯ Freud, Sigmund ❯ Psychoanalysis

Bibliography

Freud, S. (1953–1973). Obsessive actions and religious practices. In *The standard edition of the complete psychological works of Sigmund Freud* (Vol. 9) (J. Strachey, Ed. & Trans.). London: Hogarth Press. (Original work published 1907).

Freud, S. (1953–1973). Repression. In *The standard edition of the complete psychological works of Sigmund Freud* (Vol. 14) (J. Strachey, Ed. & Trans.). London: Hogarth Press. (Original work published 1915).

Freud, S. (1953–1973). The psychopathology of everyday life. In *The standard edition of the complete psychological works of Sigmund Freud* (Vol. 6) (J. Strachey, Ed., & Trans.). London: Hogarth Press. (Original work published 1901).

Réssentiment and Religion

Daniel Burston

Nietzsche, Freud and Christianity

The concept of réssentiment and its role in religious life emerged in the late nineteenth and early twentieth century, and was harnessed in the service of a critique of modernity which often had elitist and anti-democratic overtones. For example, Friedrich Nietzsche (1844–1900) was a classicist who was deeply versed in Greek religion and art, but highly selective in his preferences. Nietzsche admired Homer, who extolled the warrior virtues, but detested Plato's other-worldliness, asceticism and denigration of the body and its passions. According to Nietzsche, the Homeric warrior was uniquely capable of the resounding self-affirmation that also says "Yes!" to life, while Plato presages a "priestly" mentality that is (1) life negating, and which (2) inverts or falsifies the natural scale of values, and is rooted in self-deception.

In *The Genealogy of Morals* (1888), Nietzsche argued that Judaism and Christianity also share a pathos that inverts the noble values of the older pagan aristocracy, one rooted in a subaltern mentality or "slave morality" that results from a frustrated will to power. It is rooted in envy and rancor, traits common among the weak and dispossessed. Those afflicted with réssentiment habitually envy and devalue the attitudes and attributes of their aristocratic masters, who are more prosperous, powerful and favored by fortune. Unlike aristocrats and warriors, who are men of action, slaves and their "priestly" leaders wage a war of words. They rationalize their cowardice and impotent hatred by attacking the good, old-fashioned warrior virtues – courage, individualism and the unfettered expression of instinctual drives – rather than the warriors themselves. They make virtues out of necessities and their own apparent defects, i.e., their meekness, poverty, selflessness, reliance on others, and so on. Lacking the strength or resolve to throw off their oppressors' individually, slaves slowly band together (with the help of ascetic priests) to subdue and subvert the individualism and ferocity of the ruling caste through an increasingly peace-loving, collectivistic and otherworldly ethos.

Nevertheless, said Nietzsche, the newer Christian virtues of meekness, poverty, selflessness, charity and so on, do not alter human nature. They merely distort it, because

the Platonic/Christian tendency to mortify the flesh is unnatural, and a source of suffering to all who embrace it. So underneath the pious surface of Christendom, all the aggression that formerly found a "healthy" expression in individual acts of courage and self-affirmation become distorted and displaced into different forms of institutionalized sadism and revenge fantasies that pass for genuine justice.

Nietzsche's critique of Christendom vividly presages Freud's reflections on the ubiquity of repressed aggression in *Civilization and Its Discontents* (Freud, 1930). But Freud said that Christianity promoted group cohesion through sublimation and aim inhibited love, but being unable to totally transform human nature, deflected the repressed aggression of believers onto external groups, and above all, onto the Jews. In Freud's scenario, then, the containment of collective aggression is a necessary step toward progress, though Jews are but the victims or casualties of progress. By contrast, Nietzsche argued that the triumph of Christianity paved the way for modern socialist and communist movements, which promote leveling, mediocrity and "degeneracy." In Nietzsche's view, Jews are not merely the target of Christian aggression; they are also its secret source. In his own words:

> Jesus of Nazareth, the gospel of love made flesh, the "redeemer," who brought blessings and victory to the poor, the sick the sinners – what was he but temptation in its most sinister form, bringing men by a roundabout way to precisely those Jewish values and renovations of the ideal? Has not Israel, precisely by the detour of this "redeemer," this seeming antagonist and destroyer of Israel, reached the final goal of its sublime vindictiveness? Was it not a necessary feature of the a truly brilliant politics of vengeance, a far sighted, subterranean, slowly and carefully planned vengeance, that Israel had to deny its true instrument publicly and nail him to the cross like a mortal enemy, so that "the whole world" (meaning the enemies of Israel) might naively swallow the bait (Nietzsche, 1956; 168–169).

There are problems with Nietzsche's critique of Christianity, one being that despite the Platonizing Judaism of Philo of Alexandria (and Jewish mystics who followed in his footsteps), normative Judaism emphatically does *not* devalue the body and its appetites, nor treat self-affirmation as inherently sinful. Furthermore, Nietzsche's monstrous (and transparently paranoid) conjecture that the Jews plotted the overthrow of Rome by denying and crucifying one of their own out of "a politics of vengeance" is sheer nonsense, and completely unsupported by any historical evidence. But though nonsense, it is extremely *interesting* nonsense, because most of Nietzsche's Christian readers were anti-Semitic to varying degrees. Many, like Adolph Harnack, the famous Church historian, claimed that the essence of Christianity has nothing to do with Judaism, and chastised Christians who acknowledged any sense of kinship with the Jews (Harnack, 1900). By blaming Christianity on the Jews, and emphasizing the Jewish roots of Christianity, Nietzsche sought to baffle and disconcert pious Christian anti-Semites, including his erstwhile friend Richard Wagner, and others who, like Houston Stewart Chamberlain, fantasized about an "Aryan" Jesus.

Scheler's Critique of Nietzsche

While most Christian scholars simply tuned him out, Max Scheler (1874–1926), a Catholic spokesman, finally grappled with Nietzsche's critique of Christianity in a book called *Réssentiment* published in 1915. Like Nietzsche, Scheler acknowledged the presence of malice, vindictiveness, and a thirst for revenge in religious ideation, and regarded these passions as abiding character traits that warp our judgment, engendering a tendency to disparage or devalue others which is generally rationalized as righteous indignation,. But unlike Nietzsche, Scheler insisted that réssentiment is not a specifically Jewish or Christian trait, but a universal social phenomenon, involving (1) the process of comparing oneself unfavorably to other individuals in one's own reference group, or (2) the process of comparing one's actual power and status with the status one feels one *should* possess, for whatever reason.

With respect to the former, Scheler noted that the process of comparing oneself to others *within one's own reference group* is ubiquitous and by no means necessarily harmful. After all, unless we know how others differ we cannot appreciate or understand them as individuals, or to improve oneself. More importantly, those whose self-esteem is intact can compare themselves to others endowed with greater gifts or material wealth without feeling that their dignity or personal worth is diminished or impugned by the competence, intelligence, vitality or good fortune of the other(s). A person who possesses a calm sense of self-worth weathers such comparisons without repressing his or her feelings, or allowing them to warp their judgment. Rather than responding to the presence of a prodigy, or someone favored by fortune, through a tendency to deprecate, the healthy person sees superior gifts in another person as cause for celebration or, indeed, for love and esteem. Following Nietzsche and Georg Simmel, Scheler called this the "noble" mentality, and fancifully attributed it to aristocrats in bygone days. By contrast, said Scheler, the envious,

vindictive person has a "slavish" cast of mind that was presumably more characteristic of the lower orders. He suffers from (unconscious) feelings of impotence, inferiority and worthlessness, and uses the hostile devaluation of others and copious self-deception to compensate for hidden injuries.

With respect to the latter, Scheler points out that in medieval society, people seldom cherished fantasies of upward mobility. Power and status were hereditary and deemed natural and necessary in the scheme of salvation. Industrial democracies, by contrast, replace the traditional yearning for salvation in the afterlife with the promise of equality, breeding extravagant needs and expectations, and upending traditional class and caste divisions, fostering envy and rancor among those who remained relatively disadvantaged in the struggle to "get ahead," and those whose hereditary status was dwindling, or plummeting downwards in the face of new market pressures.

By Scheler's reckoning then, réssentiment did exist in ancient times, but was not the real basis of the Christian faith which, by Scheler's reckoning, is neither democratic nor pacifist in character, but explicitly hierarchical, leaving ample room for the warrior virtues Nietzsche praised so highly. So the prevalence of réssentiment among all social classes today is not the fault of Christianity per se, but of capitalism, which Scheler, echoing Werner Sombart, likened to "the Jewish spirit." So Scheler had it both ways – declaring réssentiment to be a universal phenomenon, while describing it as being particularly intense in Judaism and capitalism, which he took to be related kindred phenomena. Quite apart from the high-brow, low intensity anti-Semitism on display here, Scheler's spirited defense of Christianity stood in the starkest possible contrast to the ideas of contemporaries better known contemporaries like Leo Tolstoy and Romain Rolland. Unlike these egalitarian pacifists, he was an ardent German nationalist during World War I, and was admired by many Nazis after his death, despite the fact that his mother was Jewish. But whereas Nietzsche, a more prominent fascist icon, flirted with neo-paganism, Scheler's discourse was romantic and neo-feudal, prompting him to dissociate "true" Christianity from socialism or collectivism, on the one hand, and from Judaism on the other.

Réssentiment and "Penis Envy"

Thus far, we have noted anti-democratic and anti-Semitic strains in the literature on réssentiment. But there are notable instances when Jewish theorists used the idea of réssentiment – albeit seldom labeling it as such.

For example, Freud deemed women to be notably inferior to the average male, and psychologically akin to children or "savages" cannot reason properly. By Freud's account, women and girls harbor feelings of envy and inferiority vis a vis their husbands, sons and brothers because their male kin possess a penis; a fact that gives rise to an even more intense enmity to the requirements of civilization among women than in the average man.

The idea that women are anatomically predestined to be the "losers" in the unfolding drama of civilization strikes us as odious or hilarious nowadays. Nevertheless, Freud and his followers maintained that the normal (albeit usually unconscious) experience of a woman is of herself as a castrated (i.e., defective) male, and that the feelings of envy, inferiority and resentment that they harbor unconsciously prompt them to distort reality, and will plague them perpetually, regardless of any efforts to alter their inferior social status. The idea that one half of humanity is doomed to have their self-esteem and judgment diminished by (anatomically preordained) réssentiment regardless of their faith or their moment in history is also quite elitist, and manifestly sexist, but constitutes a considerable shift in emphasis from Nietzsche and Scheler.

Finally, in a series of best selling books on Arab civilization and the Muslim world today, historian Bernard Lewis invokes a version of the theory of réssentiment to explain the widespread fear and antipathy to the West, with its emphasis on democracy, gender equality, freedom of inquiry and expression, and so on. This is another dramatic reversal of emphasis, one laced with considerable irony. Nietzsche and Scheler saw modernity as the problem, and implicated the Jews in the genesis of this problem to an unusual degree. Lewis, who is Jewish, sees modernity as a good thing, but uses réssentiment to explain the roots of Islamic extremism. And while his thesis has some merit, no doubt, it has been used to justify some disastrous foreign policy initiatives, i.e., the second Gulf War.

Reviewing these diverse contributions in chronological order reminds us that the literature on réssentiment and religion contains many worthwhile insights, but is also fraught with bias. The passions that give rise to réssentiment – feelings of powerlessness, envy, the thirst for revenge, the tendency to disparage or devalue others unreasonably – are ever present possibilities of human experience, and only harden into character traits that routinely impair our judgment in adverse social and historical circumstances. Members of both sexes and all faiths are susceptible to it, and any effort to depict one faith (or one gender) as uniquely susceptible to (or representative of) this character deformity should be greeted with considerable skepticism.

See also: ◉ Christianity ◉ Freud, Sigmund ◉ Judaism and Psychology ◉ Schopenhauer, Nietzsche, and Atheism

Bibliography

Burston, D. (2003). Nietzsche, Scheler and social psychology. *Journal of The Society for Existential Analysis, 14*(1), 2–13.

Freud, S. (1930). *Civilization and its discontents* (J. Strachey, Trans.) (1974 ed., Vol. 21). London: Hogarth Press.

Harnack, A. (1900). *Das Wesen des Christenthums*. Leipzig, Germany: J. C. Hindrichs.

Nietzsche, F. (1956). *The birth of tragedy and the genealogy of morals* (F. Golfing, Trans.). New York: Doubelday.

Scheler, M. (2000). *Ressentiment*. Milwaukee, WI: Marquette University Press.

Resurrection

David A. Leeming

The word "resurrection" refers to the return of a dead person to life and is most commonly used in connection with the Christian story of Jesus. The four writers of the biography of Jesus in the Christian section of the Bible (*New Testament*) report the mysterious disappearance of Jesus' body from his tomb after his death by crucifixion and his subsequent appearance to various followers as a living person. This story is central to the Christian belief system.

The story of Jesus' resurrection was by no means the first in the history of world religion and mythology. In some versions of a Greek myth, the god Dionysos rises from the dead, as do the Middle Eastern deities Attis and Tammuz and most especially, the Egyptian Osiris. Sir James Frazer in his *Golden Bough* had much to say about these resurrected man-gods. Many resurrection stories, such as that of the Canaanite Baal, were associated with agriculture, particularly with periods of draught followed by periods of fertility. In Egypt, the resurrection myth of Osiris was associated with the devastating but land renewal process involved in the annual flooding of the Nile.

For non Christians and some non fundamentalist Christians, the story of Jesus' resurrection might be said to become more significant when it is treated psychologically. The same can be said of the earlier resurrection stories. When one applies the approach taken by Jung in his "Christ, a Symbol of Self," the resurrection heroes are freed from the restrictions of the merely local or the merely sectarian, and we are able to see that perhaps the real importance of the resurrection myth, whether or not it is based in some sort of historical fact, lies in resurrection and not in the individuals who are resurrected. As Zen masters say, "The first step of Zen is to kill the Buddha."

For Jung, the archetypal or symbolic Christ as opposed to the historical Jesus is present in the unconscious of each of us as what might be called the "God within" or the "Self" waiting to be realized in our individual egos – our conscious lives. The process of the rising of the Self from our unconscious into our conscious psyches is the process of what Jung called "individuation." The psychological or archetypal meaning of the resurrection, then, is the awakening of the Self and its emergence through the psychological growth process into our psychic lives.

See also: ❯ Christ ❯ Christ as Symbol of the Self ❯ Christianity ❯ Individuation ❯ Osiris and the Egyptian Religion ❯ Self

Bibliography

Frazer, Sir J. (1922). *The golden bough* (Chap. 29–45). New York: Macmillan.
Jung, C. G. (1951/1976). Christ, a symbol of the self. In *Aion, CW* 9ii. Princeton, NJ: Princeton University Press, Bollingen.

Revelation

John Eric Killinger

Introduction

Revelation is derived from the Greek, *apokalypsis* (ἀποκάλψις), *uncovering of the head, disclosure of hidden springs, revelation/uncovering of divine mysteries, manifestation of persons. Apocalypsis* itself is a derivative of *apokalymma* (ἀποκαλύμμα), a revelation, a combination of ἀπό, *away from* + κάλυμμα, *head covering, hood,*

veil, dura mater (lit., "hard [or coarse] mother"), *grave. Kalymma* is related to Calypso (καλύψω), *she that conceals. Apokalyptō* is a *bon mot* (Derrida, 1982: 64) for the Hebrew *galah* (גלה), meaning *to uncover, remove, reveal, emigrate, disclose, discover, display.* Cognates of *galah* include *ger* (גד), *sojourner,* which in the Aramaic sense indicates one who has been accepted from the outside into the YHWH faith; *golah* (גולה), the feminine form of exile (both as a collective and in its abstract sense, to go into exile); and *gilaion* (גליון), a table or tablet – the Talmud uses *gilyōn* (גליון), the empty margin of a page or scroll (Killinger, 2006: 359, 2007: 545). Subsidiary Hebrew words that express the divine act of revelation include *yada'* (ידע), "indicate, announce"; *nagad* (נגד), "publish, declare"; and *dabar* (דבר), "speech, word," and in Greek, *phaneroō* (φανερόω), "I reveal, make known."

Sources of Apocalyptic

Persian religious sources, such as the Zoroastrian *Zand-i Vohuman Yasht,* antedate both the Greek and Jewish forms of apocalyptic genre. Such traditions were carried over into the early Christian church. Apart from *revelatio,* Latin terms for revelation include *visio,* "vision, inspection"; *horama,* "vision in a dream"; and *autopsia,* "direct observation, supernatural vision." In Islam, *Wahy,* "instruction," or "what ought to be read," comes from God, usually through the archangel Gabriel, given to the prophets, but in its definitive form to Muhammad. Content of revelation in the Qur'ān is wisdom and guidance for the living and warnings and the announcement of final judgment. Because it is divine, it is revelation and may not be altered. In Hinduism, the Vedas have the status of sacred revelation: *sruti* ("heard," i.e., revealed directly by the gods to the seers) as distinguished from *smrti* ("remembered," i.e., composed by humans).

In the Judeo-Christian traditions there are two forms of apocalyptic: historical and the otherworldly journey. The latter form is influenced by Greek sources, such as Book 11 of Homer's *Odyssey* (Homer, 1956) and the myth of Er in Book X of Plato's *Republic* (Plato, 1961). Historical apocalypticism with its insistence on a coming utopian age merges well with millenarianism, connecting it with more structured forms of normative communitas. As event or happening, revelation can be said to be spontaneous or existential communitas, especially when it is the communal nature of the community or nations at stake. Numerous apocalypses occur throughout the gnostic texts of the Nag Hammadi writings, the Old Testament pseudepigrapha, the Dead Sea scrolls, and a small but significant number of New Testament apocryphal documents.

Apocalyptic writers were the heirs of the sages, concerned with purity within. As heirs of the prophets they were concerned with both cleanliness and social justice. As heirs of the priestly tradition, they made use of doxology and concern with defilement/purification of the land, as well as concern for restoration of worship and an understanding of *who* could participate in such worship, thus demonstrating the alignment of their views with the sacerdotal praxes of the priestly and cultic. A paraprophetic phenomenon, apocalypses differ from biblical prophecy in their notions of radical transformations of human relation and in the manner of judgment. Akin to wisdom literature, apocalyptic writings possess a supernatural wisdom dependent on revelation rather than empirical wisdom as in, for example, the Book of Proverbs.

Features of Revelation

Judgment upon the nations, a recurring feature, does not come because of failure of nerve and/or pessimism; rather, what is pointed to is the dynamic of an "interim ethics of active waiting and faithfulness to God in all things" (Gammie, 1989: 181). This is, of course, a radical move, for as with the suspension aspect of the Hanging God or Hanged Man of the Tarot (q.v.), it is the sacrifice of all that to which we cling and hold dear, from our defenses and preconceptions to our interpretations. This not only happens communally among all the nations but also to each individual. For the faithful – those who undergo the ruptures caused by suffering whether in liminal suspension or at the hands of the cruel and ruthless (the unjust) – there is a share in the divine majesty.

A prominent feature in revelation is the holy mountain. Bearing the characteristics and potencies of the cosmos, it is the conclave of the gods like those who gather on Olympus, the battleground of opposing natural forces, and the conjunction of heaven and earth. Because of this last attribute, it is the place from which effective decrees are issued. The holy mountain is a place set apart, a margin sanctified by God, aligning it with the feature set of *galah* and its cognates. In other words, sojourners, exiles, and exilic communities go to the mountain to receive the revelation of God on tables or tablets (of stone).

The idea of the Kingdom of God has as its focus the sovereignty of the godhead, as well as its majesty and mystery – its establishment in the heavens is matched by an equivalent establishment on earth (cf. Mt. 16:19 Aland, et al., 1998: 44)—as above, so below, as the alchemists say. The apocalyptic is a true dialectic of power. Even the Lord's Prayer depicts this: "Thy kingdom come, thy will be done on earth as it is in heaven." Natural revelation, expressed in the formula *Deus absconditus/deus revelatus* is not unlike Bion's epistemological move from knowledge (curiosity) to ultimate reality, K → O.

Christian theologians in the main reject the broad usage of *revelation* (any inspiration or new knowledge), preferring instead the narrower definition of revelation as the manifestation of something hidden that cannot be discovered through ordinary and usual means of acquiring knowledge. The neo-orthodox Christian theologian Karl Barth, for example, argued that the only true revelation is through the Word of God incarnate, Jesus Christ. Whereas this might be quite valid in a purely Christian religious milieu, in post-modern religious plurality in which dialogue between the major monotheistic religions is paramount, the Word of God must be accepted along side the words of God, as in the *Wahy* of the Qur'ān, which are also manifestations of the divine transcendence. In Kabbalah, the letters themselves are important sources of revelation; that is, "intentional speech is an ascending human creation complementing the descending divine speech" (Idel, 2002: 182). Jewish tradition realizes that such revelations or apocalypses of the divine add spice – as presentations of a certain point of view they possess a marked exegetical character in that they enlarge scriptural scenes. The theme of apocalypse is primarily the glory or arm of YHWH, and it can be disclosed in one's gaze or ear. Nowhere does it have the sense of fearsome catastrophe with which apocalypse has come to be associated. It is, as André Chouraqui notes, essentially "a contemplation...or an inspiration at the sight, the uncovering or disclosure of YHWH" (Chouraqui, cited in Derrida, 1982: 64).

The narrowness of definition by modern theologians has been called into question in the post-modern era. Thomas J. J. Altizer's apocalyptic is an inversion of "what had heretofore been named and valued as God but is now manifested in emptiness or abyss" (Wyschogrod, 1987: 377), leaving creation and apocalypse in a state of nondifference. In literary theory, Tzvetan Todorov (1973) locates the fantastic narrative (which apocalypses can be) on the frontiers of two genres, the uncanny – *unheimlich* – (supernatural explained) and the marvelous (supernatural accepted).

Taylor (1987) has advanced the Derridean notion of erasure by arguing that words re-veil rather than reveal. The idea of erasure is that when something is written down, when marks are made on paper – inscribed – something (whether or not we know what that something is) is written out, erased; an exscription has to occur, relating again to *galah, ger, gilyon, and gilaion*. This is in opposition to traditional theological thinking that revelation occurs linguistically. Taylor argues therefore that there is no revelation of divine truth but only the endless re-veiling or covering of truth. Truth and meaning: if the search is for ultimate truth such as Bion's O (q.v.), then we might find ourselves crossing the threshold into the creation of a fallacy. *Is the fallacy meaningful or meaning-making?* is the line of questioning one might well take. It is the narrative that provides the raw material. Truth may then be irrelevant, for a good lie can be the enantriodromic end of truth (and vice versa) as in a uroboros (q.v.) or topology of the torus as in early delineations of the Lacanian Real. A hermeneutic approach, interpreting with symbols that still possess cultural validity may be warranted for bringing out the hidden aspects of the narratives developing both in the consulting room and in the world outside its doors.

Drawing significantly on the work of Blanchot (1955/1982, 1969/1993, and 1971/1997a) Taylor (1987) reminds us of the fact that revelation is also tear, interstice, rent, fissure, cleft in not only the language but also the narrative structure as well. Blanchot reports that image is what veils by revealing. If, as Jung argues, image is psyche, then psyche veils by revealing, re-veils through fissure, cleft, interstice, and abyss. Blanchot (1971/1997a) observes how image is capable of negating nothingness as in the Hegelian *Aufhebung* paradigm, and as in the Nietzschean Dionysian dithyrambic view of the abyss, image is also "the gaze of nothingness upon us" (p. 40). This is perhaps why current work on void states (Ashton, 2007) is becoming important in an era when the unreality of dissolution into nothingness seems more real than ever in human history, whether linearly or spatially.

With regard to the apocalypse, the theme is that we must change. Despite concerning himself with the apocalypse as a choice between annihilation via atomic bomb or totalitarianism, Blanchot (1971/1997c) suggests that the apocalypse can be demystified by understanding. All or nothing is therefore far from being our only truth; however, the caveat to removing the projection of mystique is that "it exposes us to a loss of fear…that misleads but also warns" (p. 108). It is an apocalypse without an apocalypse!

Connected with the themes of erasure mentioned above, involvement of the "hard mother" aspect indicates that the word "apocalypse" can mean *away from the hard* (coarse) *mother*. As the tough fibrous outermost membrane enveloping the brain and spinal cord, the *dura mater* is composed of a series of adjacent laminations. Of interest here is not so much the structure but two metaphoric resonances. The first of these is in tandem with the *pia mater* and involves the concepts William James (1907/1987) identified as "tough-minded" and "tender-minded." Whereas tough-minded folk tend toward facts, empiricism, fatalism, and materialism, tender-minded folk tend toward principles, rationalism, free will, and idealism. Such a dichotomy might even relate to Sheldon's (1936) epimethean/promethean understanding of the animectomy complex (q.v.).

The other metaphoric resonance of the *dura mater* is with Grotstein's (1979/2000) laminations of awareness in consciousness. It is tantamount to living a palimpsest self. In other words, it is a kind of development in which what occurs is the smudging of one life script – or a portion or portions thereof – in order to write over and/or re-write the narrative by and through which one lives. But it is not a complete erasure, for the past essence remains, feint (faint) as it is. It's counterpart is the *pia mater* (tender mother), a soft inner membrane enveloping the brain. The brain is thus aligned with Bion's container contained ($♀♂$), or it suffers the ontic psychological dualism of good breast/bad breast.

The revelatory manifestation of the divine life comes from the supramental realm. If any of the following three aspects is neglected, we slip back into mental life, knowledge about rather than becoming being or growing into aesthetic consciousness. For example, neglecting the abysmal aspect (the inexhaustible, ineffable depth characteristic) leads to the transformation of revelation into information via rationalistic deism. Neglecting the logical character of divine life transforms revelation into heteronomous subjection via irrationalistic theism. Finally, neglecting the spiritual character makes a history of revelation impossible. Maurice Blanchot reminds us that the nameless navigator, who first crossed the zero parallel, "was under the impression that he found himself at an exceptional moment and at a unique point, a sacred zone, the passage over which symbolized a crucial initiation" (Blanchot, 1971/1997b: 79).

See also: ❯ Apocalypse ❯ Bible ❯ Christianity ❯ Gnosticism ❯ Hinduism ❯ Islam ❯ Kabbalah

Bibliography

Aland, B., et al. (Eds.). (1998). Κατά Μαθθαῖον [According to Matthew]. In *Greek-English New Testament* (8th Rev. ed., pp. 1–87). Stuttgart, Germany: Deutsche Bibelgesellschaft.

Ashton, P. W. (2007). *From the brink: Experiences of the void from a depth psychology perspective*. London: Karnac.

Blanchot, M. (1982). *The space of literature* (A. Smock, Trans.). Lincoln, NB: University of Nebraska Press. (Original work published 1955).

Blanchot, M. (1993). *The infinite conversation* (S. Hanson, Trans.). Minneapolis, MN: University of Minnesota Press. (Original work published 1969).

Blanchot, M. (1997a). The museum, art, and time. In E. Rottenberg (Trans.). *Friendship* (pp. 101–108). Stanford, CA: Stanford University Press. (Original work published 1971).

Blanchot, M. (1997b). Man at point zero. In E. Rottenberg (Trans.). *Friendship* (pp. 73–82). Stanford, CA: Stanford University Press. (Original work published 1971).

Blanchot, M. (1997c). The apocalypse is disappointing. In E. Rottenberg (Trans.). *Friendship* (pp. 101–108). Stanford, CA: Stanford University Press. (Original work published 1971).

Derrida, J. (1982). Of an apocalyptic tone recently adopted in philosophy (J. P. Leavey, Jr., Trans.). *Semeia, 23,* 63–97.

Gammie, J. G. (1989). *Holiness in Israel.* Minneapolis, MN: Fortress Press.

Grotstein, J. S. (2000). The ineffable nature of the dreamer. In *Who is the dreamer who dreams the dream?: A study of psychic presences* (pp. 1–36). Hillsdale, NJ: Analytic Press. (Original work published 1979).

Homer. (1956). *The Odyssey.* In A. Nicoll (Ed.). & G. Chapman (Trans.), *The Odyssey and the lesser homerica: Vol. 2. Chapman's Homer* (pp. 3–498). New York: Pantheon Books. (Original work published 1614).

Idel, M. (2002). *Absorbing perfections: Kabbalah and interpretation.* New Haven, CT: Yale University Press.

James, W. (1987). Pragmatism. In B. Kuklick (Ed.), *Writings, 1902–1910: The varieties of religious experience, pragmatism, a pluralistic universe, the meaning of truth, some problems of philosophy, essays* (pp. 479–624). New York: Library of America. (Original work published 1907).

Killinger, J. E. (2006). Between the frying pan and fire: The intermundia of clergy transitioning out of parish ministry. *Dissertation Abstracts International 67*(12-B). (UMI No. 3247249).

Killinger, J. E. (2007). Apologia pro intermundia sua. *Journal of Religion and Health, 46*(4), 541–557.

Plato. (1961). *Republic* (P. Shorey, Trans.). In E. Hamilton & H. Cairns (Eds.), *Plato: The collected dialogues* (pp. 575–844). Princeton, NJ: Princeton University Press.

Sheldon, W. H. (1936). *Psychology and the promethean will: A constructive study of the acute common problem of education, medicine, and religion.* New York: Harper & Brothers.

Taylor, M. C. (1987). *Altarity.* Chicago, IL: University of Chicago Press.

Todorov, T. (1973). *The fantastic: A structural approach to a literary genre* (R. Howard, Trans.). Ithaca, NY: Cornell University Press. (Original work published 1970).

Wyschogrod, E. (1987). Value. In M. C. Taylor (Ed.), *Critical terms for religious studies* (pp. 365–382). Chicago, IL: University of Chicago Press.

Rinpoche

Migmar Tseten · Thomas C. Putnam

The Tibetan word "rinpoche," derived from Sanskrit term "ratna," which means "precious," "valuable" and "rare." In general, it is applied for anything that is considered valuable, such as gold and jewel etc. and is also applied to respected teachers and reincarnated lamas as a veneration.

In Jungian theory the title may be understood as a projection of the Self onto a person. Thus the one who has been given the title, "Rinpoche" would symbolically carry the projection of a deeply individuated person who has reached his fullest potential of wholeness. In western psychology this person would carry the projection of the Self for his/her students much like a western psychotherapist does for his/her patients.

See also: ⊙ Buddhism ⊙ Jung, Carl Gustav ⊙ Jungian Self ⊙ Self ⊙ Tulku

Rites of Passage

Paul Larson

The phrase "rite of passage" was coined by the anthropologist Arnold van Gennep (1873–1957) in his 1909 book of that title (Fr. "Les rites du passage"). The phrase has become widely known and used to describe those rituals which mark significant life transitions of individuals in a community. Victor Turner (1920–1983) continued the focus on study of the psychology of rituals and elaborated on the ways in which these rites of passage function to move people from one social status to another (Turner, 1969/1995, 1974).

Many of the life passages which are marked by special rituals are age related, though not all. There is often a ritual at or close to the birth in which the child is named and given a place in the family and community. Another period of transition comes at puberty when boys become men and girls become women. In many pre-industrial societies the arrival of puberty shortly follows with marriage, when the individual chooses or is given a mate. This is another major transition, though in most modern industrialized societies, there is a significant time lag between physical sexual maturation and the assumption of the responsibilities of marriage. Especially in modern societies, there are special occasions to mark the completion of educational preparation and entry into the world of adult occupations and work. The commencement ceremonies at graduation use the pomp of academic regalia to celebrate the accomplishments of the new graduates. Likewise, retirement from the work force sometimes is celebrated with at least a social occasion if not a formal ritual. Finally, at death the body is interred or buried and a memorial service is held to honor the memory of the deceased and ease the loss to those who survive the individual.

In each case, the ritual serves to mark the change in how an individual is to be regarded by the community. Turner elaborated on van Gennep's concept of limenality, that transitional state where one is neither the former status nor the new status, but is in the process of passage. In general, limenality refers to this transitional space and time "in between." There is often a period of time over which the ritual takes place or a period of preparation for it. This allows both the individual or individuals undergoing the transition as well as the rest of the community to psychologically work through the hopes, fears and expectations for the new role which the participants will assume with each other. During the "in between" phase the participants are linked by what Turner calls "communitas," the equality shared by all who are undergoing the transition.

Roles, of course, are not only born by an individual, but are relational. When a person marries, for example, they are treated differently not only by their spouse and family, but other members of the community. Likewise, when an individual is ordained to a sacred role in a community, everyone now relates to them differently. Making these transitions more manageable is the great psychological function of rites of passage. The markers are not only celebratory for the individual but important for the social group as a whole. Our entrances, or shifts in role and our exits are all marked by rituals that serve our needs as well as those who participate with us in our community lives. Thus the rites of passage serve one of the most important functions in a community of the spirit, they guide us through the transitions that inevitably mark our human life trajectory and serve as a means of transmittal of cultural values and meanings.

See also: ◉ Communal and Personal Identity ◉ Cultural Psychology ◉ Ritual

Bibliography

Turner, V. (1974). *Dramas, fields, and metaphors.* Ithaca, NY: Cornell University Press.

Turner, V. (1995). *The ritual process: Structure and anti-structure.* New York: Aldine de Gruyter. (Original work published 1969).

Van Gennep, A. (1960). *The rites of passage.* Chicago, IL: University of Chicago Press. (Original work published 1909).

Ritual

Bernard Spilka

Ritual, in general, refers to patterned behavior, possibly repetitive, that is usually fraught with symbolism. Ritual thus has significance beyond the actions that define it. Simply put, it is a force for connection, communication, cooperation, coordination, cohesion, control, and influence. All of these roles can first be demonstrated in animal ritualization which appears to serve language or signaling functions. Given this potential, evolutionary speculations have been introduced into our understanding of ritual (Huxley, 1966). The essence of ritual is therefore functional and adaptive as these same purposes hold for human beings.

Religious Ritual

Even though religion per se has not been satisfactorily defined in cross-cultural perspective, disagreements appear to be relatively minor. Religious ritual may, however, be distinguished from non-religious forms by its emphasis on ultimate human dependence upon superhuman agents who are not directly observable. Some scholars stress what people simply define as sacred or holy but this tends to be poorly circumscribed. To the best of our knowledge all societies possess religion and religious ritual is likewise found in all known religious traditions.

The terms, rite and ceremony, are often used interchangeably with ritual; however, some scholars distinguish them as formal actions while religious ritual is regarded as informal. Since this distinction is difficult to maintain, all three words are used here to cover both formal and informal behavior.

Patterns of Religious Ritual

Religious rituals do not occur randomly. They are traditionally associated with important cultural and individual events. First, they are annually patterned. For example, annual midnight masses have been viewed as celebrating the opening and closing of the year. Rites often accompany the planting and harvesting of crops plus specific holidays that honor major socio-cultural happenings like military victories, the establishment of nations, or the lives and accomplishments of great historical figures.

Second, ceremonies religiously validate rites of passage such as birth and death, one's coming of age, marriage, graduations from schools and noteworthy anniversaries that occur in long marriages. A third set of religious rituals is commonly associated with such public events as inaugurations of presidents and other high government and public officials. In like manner, legislative bodies open their daily proceedings with a prayer. On a different level rituals mark similar activities like the installation of presiding officers in universities and fraternal bodies. Fourth, one finds group rituals that either call upon the Divine to help persons in dire straits or thank superhuman agents when recovery from serious illness occurs or one's actions result in personal success. Note further spiritual references connote gratitude that is offered when a lottery is won or individual efforts result in athletic triumphs, high examination scores or noteworthy advancements in one's life. Fifth, there are familial religious ceremonies such as saying grace at meals, prayers before facing the rigors of daily life, or upon retiring at night. In addition people frequently develop practices utilizing household shrines, reading from sacred scriptures, intoning prayers before taking trips etc. Depending on one's religious heritage, group associations, or place in a social structure, there is the likelihood of other rituals.

Psychological Approaches to Religious Ritual

Contemporary psychological approaches to ritual usually stress cognition (Boyer, 2001; Guthrie, 1993; Lawson and McCauley, 1990; McCauley and Lawson, 2002). Motivation is much more implied than explicit, a tendency common to both psychologists and anthropologists who also emphasize cognition. The essential component appears to be a search for meaning. From a subjective perspective, the feeling that one is enlightened by ritual participation is common and may enrich the individual spiritually.

Even though Freud interpreted ritual behavior as obsessional neurosis, thereby affiliating it with pathology, modern Analytic views suggest it may be an avenue to religious experience (Pruyser, 1968). Resort to religious ritual is particularly evident under stress that poses cognitive dilemmas. Clarification is sought in ceremonies in which the person attempts to make sense of h/his predicament. People need to understand the causes of events, in other words, attributions are sought that will resolve cognitive difficulties. The intricate matrix of

relationships between ritual and myth may speak to this fundamental human desire to make sense out of life and the world.

The leads offered by these scholars need to explicitly include motivation in order to understand religious ritual more fully. Post Freudians and Jungians recognize ritual behavior as controlling and directing emotion. It may thus act as both means of self-control and a spur to control outside influences (Pruyser, 1968; Jonte-Pace, 1997). Even though these are constructive and adaptive functions, the classical idea of ritual and mental disturbance lurks in the background of many such writings.

Religious Ritual as Connection

The notion of connectivity leads to both humanistic and holistic perspectives, and in doing so tie ritual to spirituality as opposed to treating it as simple religious activity. Utilizing prayer as representative of religious ritual, connection to the supernatural is intended (Foster, 1992; Ladd and Spilka, 2002). This includes worship as public prayer. *Upward Prayer* is an obvious ritual effort to establish this kind of contact. Whether public or private, people introduce their own devices to increase, from their perspective, the efficacy of formal liturgical worship. These regularly encompass changes in body posture such as bowing and kneeling, among other motions. Some settings accept dancing. In the privacy of one's personal life, innovation is frequently present in the prayers addressed to the Divine. Since there are many reasons people desire to connect to superhuman agents, prayer is multidimensional. Foster (1992) theorizes 21 different forms. Empirically, research has distinguished over 10 types via Factor Analytic methodology.

The most common form of prayer has been termed petitionary, a term that is very broad since people may seek innumerable things, to wit, material gain or items, divine protection, God's intervention to help others as in intercessory prayer, personal guidance, self-improvement, religious experience. Prayers of confession, praise, forgiveness or thanksgiving are frequently offered. Contemplation or meditation may be sought. These are some of the more evident contents possible. Verbal ritual is clearly patterned and may be supplemented with "speaking-in-tongues," various body movements, eye-closing, hand clasping etc. When describing personal practices, people readily acknowledge that their prayers are made in a regular, orderly sequence based on individually constructed ritual formats.

According to Foster, connectivity via prayer can also be conceptualized as inward or outward. Though the upward focus remains, *Inward Prayer* stresses the self. Confession and atonement are usually its chief elements. In contrast, *Outward Prayer* emphasizes the external world and others. We witness this in intercessory prayer.

Prayer, as probably the dominant kind of religious ritual, can be viewed from a number of stances, both theoretically and empirically. As connection, it is not a simple phenomenon.

The Social Role of Religious Ritual

Ritual in general and specifically religious ritual as connectivity performs a fundamental communicative role. Recognizing this, Lawson and McCauley (1990) analyze religious ritual in terms of linguistic theory. More than simply the intended communicative substance of the act itself is conveyed to the object of the ritual. Further, the performing person becomes bound to the religious group within which the act is meaningful plus the larger culture in which the actor's faith has meaning. When people jointly participate in religious ritual, they perceive themselves as unified with their like behaving peers. They are not only connected to the supernatural but to each other through common symbolic actions. Particularly within the religious sphere there is the belief that communal rituals are more apt to influence a deity than isolated individual responses. We see this in joint public expressions of intercessory prayer or calls for collective godly blessings.

Increased social coordination and cohesion are part of this process. Implicitly, an interpersonal consensus is intimated since these acts were learned from and usually concern others. Religious institutions openly avow ceremonial messages of mutual support and harmony in public settings. The hoped for result is a reduction of conflict and enhancement of help and cooperation. Again, the enrichment of religious ritual behavior that connotes spirituality is implicit in these activities.

The significance of ritual within the individual personality implies a broad range of possibilities. At one end of this continuum there is an obsessive compulsive approach that is narrow and protective-restrictive. In the extreme, pathology as in scrupulosity may be present. At the other terminus the search for meaning in ritualistic actions can reflect a broadened view as connections to oneself, others, and the sacred come to the fore.

See also: ❯ Freud, Sigmund ❯ Jung, Carl Gustav ❯ Myth ❯ Religion

Bibliography

Boyer, P. (2001). *Religion explained.* New York: Basic Books.

Foster, R. J. (1992). *Prayer: Finding the heart's true home.* New York: HarperSanFrancisco.

Guthrie, S. E. (1993). *Faces in the clouds: A new theory of religion.* New York: Oxford University Press.

Huxley, J. (1966). A discussion on ritualization of behavior in animals and man: Introduction. *Philosophical transactions of The Royal Society of London, Series B., Biological Sciences, 251,* 249–524.

Jonte-Pace, D. (1997). Julia Kristeva and the Psychoanalytic study of religion: Rethinking Freud's cultural texts. In J. L. Jacobs & D. Capps (Eds.), *Religion, society and psychoanalysis* (pp. 240–268). Boulder, CO: Westview Press.

Ladd, K. L., & Spilka, B. (2002). Inward, outward, and upward: Cognitive aspects of prayer. *Journal for the Scientific Study of Religion, 41,* 37–47.

Lawson, E. T., & McCauley, R. N. (1990). *Rethinking religion: Connecting cognition and culture.* Cambridge, England: Cambridge University Press.

McCauley, R. N., & Lawson, E. T. (2002). *Bringing ritual to mind.* Cambridge, England: Cambridge University Press.

Pruyser, P. (1968). *A dynamic psychology of religion.* New York: Harper & Row.

Ritual Curing

❯ Healing

Rogers, Carl

James G. Emerson

Introduction

In most evaluations of psychologists and psychotherapists of the twentieth century, Carl Rogers (January 8, 1902–February 4, 1987) stands amongst the top five or six whether one speaks of his personal ability as a therapist, a theorist, or a student of personality.

Person Centered Therapy

The approach of Carl Rogers, often called "non-directive," was not nearly as absent direction as both critics and supporters claim. The phrase "client-centered" as opposed to "theory centered" or "teacher centered" is a far better statement of his approach and contribution than other terms.

He himself came to focus on the phrase, "person centered."

Seward Hiltner and Carl Rogers

Most in the field of religion became aware of Rogers through the work of Seward Hiltner. An approach to pastoral care that centered on the perspective of the parishioner rather than the perspective of the pastor or the denomination had several values. The first value lies in awareness that the pastor and the parishioner both stand in need of a context of love and care. That holds true whether or not one speaks of the love and care of another human being or of God. The fact that Rogers came to be identified as a humanist simply defines the perspective from which the client or parishioner was viewed. The starting point was still the person and not the professional.

The Role of Empathy

The approach of Carl Rogers had special emphasis on empathy or the capacity for empathy. Empathy is a moment in which the brain of one person fully catches what is happening in the brain of another and therefore allows both people to bring that "happening" into full consciousness. The reaction of more than one student of Rogers after an interchange often resulted in the comment, "My word, he really heard me" (At least, that was my reaction when I met Dr. Rogers again some ten years after I completed my graduate work with him).

The Process and the Dynamic

From a humanist standpoint, Roger's view lifted up the capacity of the individual to find healing of mind and self within himself or herself. The process required a context that allowed that healing to work. The task of the therapist, and by extension the pastor, was/is to bring that context into the individual encounter or the group. Contrary to the view that the pastor should have all the answers and give advice, this approach holds that the capacity and strength is within the individual. The role

of the counselor or pastor, then, is so to hear what is being said and to lift up what is heard so that the counselee or parishioner can "hear" those strengths within himself or herself.

In his book *Psychotherapy and Personality Change* edited with Rosalind F. Dymond, Rogers drew a picture of two sets of overlapping circles. In one set, he listed many types of experiences in which the experiences were distinct and not in the parts of the circles that overlapped. Those outside of the overlapping section indicated experiences that were in the subconscious and not part of conscious awareness. As, through counseling or pastoral care, experiences became more and more available to ones conscious awareness, one became healthy-healed.

From Rogers to Pastoral Care

Although Rogers saw this as a strength of the individual person, it is a simple step for one who believes in God to say that we have not just evidence of the individual at work but of God or of the Holy Spirit at work within an individual. Hence, in the confessional, what happens is that the parishioner brings to the fore events of which he or she feels ashamed. In Penance, then, it is the task of the priest to find those conscious acts that can bring cleansing to the sin or failure of which one is aware. From a Rogerian standpoint, what happens happens because of a dynamic within the individual and not because of priestly authority.

Significance for Pastoral Care

The parishioner-centered pastor finds great resource in the work of Carl Rogers for developing a process of pastoral care and counseling.

A Weakness in Roger's View

One of the weaknesses of Carl Roger's approach lay in the area of the reality of sin. Partly in response to that, Carl Menninger wrote a book entitled, *Whatever Became of Sin*. The approach of Sigmund Freud, which was basic to Dr. Menninger, resulted in Menninger as a Christian developing a strong sense of the negative forces in human nature even as Carl Rogers looked at the positive. (If one may speak editorially, both are needed.)

Other Applications of Rogers

As Carl Rogers went on in life, he more and more developed applications of his insights to businesses, to educational situations, to practices of management, and to international situations. In line with what is said above, from the religious side, what Rogers would have identified as personality forces within the individual or the group the person of faith may identify as a spiritual dimension – as the work of God.

A major contribution of Carl Rogers lay in establishing means of researching what actually happened in therapy and measuring evidence of movement or change in the therapeutic process. The use of taped interviews, of Q-sorts, and of narrative case studies all became part of the scientific testing that Rogers brought to the measurement of the therapeutic experience.

The Scope of His Work

Of his many books, two key publications give the essence of Dr. Rogers' theory and his research.

See also: ● Freud, Sigmund ● Psychotherapy ● Psychotherapy and Religion

Bibliography

Menninger, K. (1973). *Whatever became of sin?* New York: Hawthorne Books.
Rogers, C. (1951). *Client-centered therapy* (p. 560). New York: Houghton Mifflin.
Rogers, C. R., & Dymond, R. F. (Eds.). (1954). *Psychotherapy and personality change.* Chicago, IL: The University of Chicago Press.

Rome

Anthony J. Elia

Rome (Ital. *Roma*) in the state of Lazio, Italy is the capital of the Italian Republic and spiritual center of the Roman Catholic world. The Vatican, which is its own self-governed city-state, is located centrally in Rome, just a few blocks from the Tiber River. Though in most cases Rome indicates the geographical location of the city and its environs, it also refers to a set of ideas ranging from the state functions of the Republic and Empire in antiquity to the centrality of power of the Roman Catholic Church and the seat of the papacy. Rome is often referred to as "The Eternal City" (*la città eterna*), "The City of the Seven Hills" (*la città dei sette colli*), and "Capital of the World" (*caput mundi*).

The centrality of Rome has been recognized for millennia, and written about in literature, theology, and histories (including St. Augustine, Edward Gibbon, and Henry James). Psychologically, its spatial and spiritual centrality may be compared with Jerusalem, which often attracts individuals with the so-called "Jerusalem syndrome," but to a much lesser extent. A comparable condition might best be described as a "Rome neurosis," which Freud described as his anxiety about traveling to Rome while in Italy. As Ginsburg writes "Freud developed what he called his 'Rome neurosis.' He, an avid traveler in Italy, could not get to Rome, though the city haunted his dreams. To do so, he had to dig up the Rome in himself, by analyzing his dreams" (Ginsburg, 1999: 17). Freud eventually got over this neurosis, enjoying Rome tremendously, with even a consideration of retiring to the Italian capital (Jones, 1955: 96).

Rome and the Church

The relationship between Rome and the Catholic Church is inextricable. Since late antiquity and the reign of Constantine, the Church has played a dominant role in forming an identity of the city. Ernest Jones, Freud's biographer, wrote about Freud's idea of the "two Romes," one which embodies classical antiquity, the other which was the Christian Rome, the Rome which superseded the earlier Rome of the Republic and Empire. Freud had great interest and admiration for the first Rome, but conflict with the second. This second or New Rome "could only be an enemy to him, the source of all the persecutions Freud's people had endured throughout the ages" (Jones, 1955: 18).

Rome in Freud's Analyses

Freud encountered the subject of Rome several times in his work, both in his analyses of individuals and his topical interpretations. One of the first accounts of Rome in Freud's works is from a patient "Frau Emmy von N.," whom Freud saw beginning in May, 1889. On the morning session of 15 May, the patient asked Freud if he had heard about a "Countess Sch.," who had been killed in an accident in Rome. The next mention of Rome was from a patient named "Fräulein Rosalia H." in the autumn of 1892, who recounted singing at a rehearsal in Rome, at which point she was in a "state of great emotional excitement," and fell ill upon the stage (Freud, 1953: II, 169n).

R

In his "Infantile Materials as a Source of Dreams," Freud dealt to some extent with the issue of Rome as a topological ideal and the psychological implications of visiting it. When speaking of memories that may have begun in childhood, Freud notes "what I have in mind is a series of dreams which are based upon a longing to visit Rome. For a long time to come, no doubt, I shall have to continue to satisfy that longing in my dreams: for at the season of the year when it is possible for me to travel, residence in Rome must be avoided for reasons of health" (Freud, 1953: IV, 193–194). Freud then recounts the details of a dream about being in a train near the Tiber. Freud did not visit Rome until 1901, at the age of forty-five. And in the footnotes of these discussions on dreams, Freud has successive notes (one added in 1909, another in 1925), which underscore the importance of the city. He writes "I discovered long since that it only needs a little courage to fulfill wishes which till then have been regarded as unattainable; and thereafter became a constant pilgrim to Rome" (Freud, 1953: IV, 194n).

In one of his dreams, Freud described being on a street-corner in Rome and "surprised to find so many posters in German stuck up there," which he then describes as a vision of Prague and a conflation of his early memories of Moravia, where he was born and where German was likely to be more tolerated (Freud, 1953: IV, 195).

Freud, Hannibal, and Rome

Freud's most notable work on Rome is that which de-scribes (1) parallels between Hannibal and Freud himself and (2) the tensions embodied between Jewry and the Catholic Church. Freud wrote in his "Infantile Material" that "I had actually been following Hannibal's foot-steps. Like him, I had been fated not to see Rome; and he too had moved into the Campagna when everyone had expected him in Rome. But Hannibal, whom I had come to resemble in these respects, had been the favourite [sic] hero of my later school days" (Freud, 1953: IV, 196). More importantly, Freud makes the connection between himself and Hannibal as something akin to a more press-ing historical tension, that between the Church and the Jews. He writes "to my youthful mind Hannibal and Rome symbolized the conflict between the tenacity of Jewry and the organization of the Catholic church. ...Thus the wish to go to Rome had become in my dream-life a cloak and symbol for a number of other passionate wishes" (Freud, 1953: IV, 196–7).

Rome appears in additional writings about childhood without significant comment (Freud, 1953: V) and a

handful of times in Freud's commentary "Delusions and Dreams in Jensen's Gradiva" (Freud, 1959: IX). In his piece "Der Moses des Michelangelo," Freud is very inter-ested in the artist's sculpture, and as the editors of his collected works note, "Freud's interest in Michelangelo's statue was of old standing. He went to see it on the fourth day of his very first visit to Rome, . . .as well as on many later occasions" (Freud, 1955: XIII, 210).

Rome is of some importance to Freud in his work "Civilization and Its Discontents," of which "the main theme of the book – the irremediable antagonism between the demands of instinct and the restriction of civilization – may be traced back to some of Freud's very earliest psy-chological writings" (Freud, 1961: XXI, 60). In this work, Freud expresses a comparison between the *past of a city* and the *past of the mind*, which questions the mental imagining of the idea of a city like Rome, as well as the artifacts that create the historical narratives around the location of Rome (Freud, 1961: XXI).

Lacan and Rome

Lacan's vision of Rome is much different than Freud's ideas about Rome. Lacan was not interested in the same historical artifacts or constructions that Freud was. As one scholar has put it, "Lacan's Rome resembled rather the ceilings of the Galleria Farnese, the arch-angels of Andrea Pozzo, or the facades of Francesco Bor-romini. (. . .) Occasionally, antiquity would revive in the form of philosophical references or famous battles, but never ruins. The unconscious discovered by Freud was to be started up anew as a Counter-Reformation, sumptu-ously draped in the folds of Clérambault. Rome would be his palace, the French language his garden" (Roudinesco, 1990: 253). For Lacan, the illustriousness of the Baroque Rome was attractive, as were the trappings of the Chris-tian Rome, which seemed to be anathema to Freud's own vision of what Dr. Jones called his "second Rome" (noted above). Roudinesco writes that "Lacan's Rome began with Ignatius of Loyola and ended in rococo madness. As founder of a new orthodoxy, the master spawned a flam-boyant theory.... Rome emigrated to Versailles and the Holy See to the rue de Lille. Lacan's Rome was that of the Roman Catholic empire, a city in which the Pope was no longer a preacher but a commander in chief. The Rome dreamt of over maps in childhood; the Rome of adolescence and the Collège Stanìslas: everything in the realm of religion, nothing accorded to faith" (Roudinesco, 1990: 253). As for Freud, "Medieval and baroque Rome evoked his hatred of Catholicism once more..."

(Ginsberg, 1999: 18). Lacan presented his *Rome Discourse* in 1953, which is seen as a "first step toward the elaboration of a theory of therapy, of its conduct, temporality, and punctuation" (Ginsberg, 1999: 18). The presentation of this discourse in Rome was symbolic of Lacan's own feelings about the city and what it meant in his overarching thought and work (Amati, 1996).

See also: ❷ Freud, Sigmund ❷ Lacan, Jacques ❷ Vatican

Bibliography

Amati, U. (1996). *Freud e Lacan a Roma: Dal Nome del Padre al Padre del Nome*. Roma: Borla.

Freud, S. (1953). *The standard edition of the complete psychological works of Sigmund Freud* (Vol. IV) (J. Strachey, Trans.). London: Hogarth Press.

Freud, S. (1955). *The standard edition of the complete psychological works of Sigmund Freud* (Vol. II) (J. Strachey, Trans.). London: Hogarth Press.

Freud, S. (1955). *The standard edition of the complete psychological works of Sigmund Freud* (Vol. V) (J. Strachey, Trans.). London: Hogarth Press.

Freud, S. (1955). *The standard edition of the complete psychological works of Sigmund Freud* (Vol. IX) (J. Strachey, Trans.). London: Hogarth Press.

Freud, S. (1955). *The standard edition of the complete psychological works of Sigmund Freud* (Vol. XIII) (J. Strachey, Trans.). London: Hogarth Press.

Freud, S. (1955). *The standard edition of the complete psychological works of Sigmund Freud* (Vol. XXI) (J. Strachey, Trans.). London: Hogarth Press.

Ginsburg, N., & Ginsburg, R. (1999). *Psychoanalysis and culture at the millennium*. New Haven, CT: Yale University Press.

Jones, E. (1955). *The life and work of Sigmund Freud: Years of maturity, 1901–1919* (Vol. 2). New York: Basic Books.

Rizzuto, A. M. (1979). *The birth of the living God: A psychoanalytic study*. Chicago, IL: University of Chicago Press.

Roudinesco, E. (1990). *Jacques Lacan & Company: A history of psychoanalysis in France, 1925–1985*. Chicago, IL: University of Chicago Press.

Rumi, Celaladin

Lucinda Antrim

Introduction

Celaladin (Jalal-ud-Din) Rumi, considered by many to be Islam's greatest mystic, was born in or near Balkh (in present-day Afghanistan) on what is generally accepted to be September 30, 1207 and died in Konya, in what is now southern Turkey, on December 17, 1273. A prolific poet and spiritual writer, his work has influenced not only Islamic literature and thought but the wider Western world. For the first years of his adult life Rumi was a respected Islamic jurisprudent, teacher and writer, as his father was before him. With the arrival in Konya of the wandering mystic Shams-i-Tabriz, when Rumi was 37 years old, Rumi entered a period of creative and mystic fervor that resulted in an outpouring of poetry and teaching. His physical expressions of mystical experience inspired the founding of the Mevlevi order of whirling dervishes.

Life

We are dependent for the specifics of Rumi's life on several early hagiographers, including his son, Sultan Valad. Mevlana (or Our Master) Jalal-ud-Din Rumi was born in either Vakhsh, outside Balkh, or in Balkh itself, a major cultural center where Muslims, Jews, Hindus, and Christians interacted. It was a period of political unrest. Quarrels between dynasties in the region and the impending Mongol threat may have contributed to the decision of Rumi's father, Baha al-Din, a Sunni Muslim, to leave Balkh. It is also possible that Baha al-Din left in search of greater scope for his work, which he may have felt was underappreciated in Balkh. When Rumi was 12, they departed on a journey of about 10 years and 1,500 miles, during which Rumi's mother (one of Baha al-Din's four wives) and a brother died, Rumi was married (to a young woman traveling with the family), and the couple had their two sons. When they arrived in the ancient city of Konya, perhaps at the invitation of the sultan, Konya was still a center of wealth and influence, growing in population with the influx of those fleeing the Mongols. Baha al-Din died in Konya in 1231, when Rumi was 24.

Rumi was well-educated, perhaps spending time in Damascus; he studied under leading Sufi mystics and learned large parts of the *Koran* the holy book of Islam, a record of God's words revealed through the Angel Gabriel to the prophet Muhammad from 610 to 632 C.E. and *diverse Hadith*, commentaries on the Koran and on the saying of Muhammad, by heart. Upon his return to Konya, Rumi assumed a position in the madrase, or religious school, teaching sharia law and Sufi practices and lecturing widely.

After the death of his first wife, Rumi remarried, a woman some believe to have been a Christian and with whom he had a son and a daughter.

In 1244, Shams-i Tabriz arrived in Konya. He was the first of Rumi's three spiritual companions. A relatively uneducated wandering dervish, he was a man of complex personality, experienced by some as dismissive and demanding. He may have been a member of an Islamic order that purposely incited rejection as a path to spiritual growth. For Rumi, the meeting was transformative. Legends grew up around it: one holds that Shams, entering Rumi's home while he was lecturing, looked at a pile of books and asked, "What is this?" Rumi replied, "You don't know." The books burst into flame. Rumi asked, "What is this?" Shams replied, "You don't know."

Many of Rumi's followers reacted to Rumi's intense interest in Shams with jealousy. A combination of this, Shams's own wandering spirit, and Shams's desire to further Rumi's spiritual growth through a period of separation may have caused Shams to leave Konya after several months. Disconsolate, Rumi sent his son Sultan Walad to bring Shams back. After a period of peace when Shams returned in 1247, the jealousy of Rumi's madrase community members returned, and after less than a year together Shams disappeared. Some scholars believe he was murdered, perhaps by Rumi's older son Ala al-Din.

In 1250, after a period of deep mourning and of search for Shams, Rumi connected with his second spiritual companion, also a relatively uneducated man, Salah al-Din, a Sufi and a goldsmith in Konya. Upon Salah al-Din's death in 1258, Rumi chose Husam al-Din as his third and last beloved spiritual companion. Husam, a long-time friend and fellow Sufi, became Rumi's amanuensis and inspiration in the writing of the *Masnavi*.

Rumi died in 1273, welcoming death and telling those left behind not to grieve.

Works

Rumi wrote in Persian, with a few poems of lesser quality in Arabic. He cited a book of poems by a classical tenth century Arab poet as his favorite work but influences on his poetry are diverse, from animal stories of Indian origin to classical Sufi works to Persian love stories. He wrote in classical form, but with living, variously informed content.

In the *Divan-I Kebir*, Rumi documents his love, union, and longing for Shams-i Tabriz, as representative of mystical union and separation from God, in what are considered to be some of the world's great love poems. Rumi signs many of the poems (ghazals, a traditional Persian love poem of 5–12 rhymed lines) as Shams, indicating that he and Shams have become indistinguishable. Many poems speak of spring, intoxication, and of Shams as the Sun, with a musicality that is often lost in translation. All are an attempt to describe inexpressible experience, suffused with a meaning beyond words. Rumi's work is endlessly associative without being dissociated; it is ultimately organized by its object: Allah. Also in the *Divan* is Rumi's Rubaiyat, a series of rhymed quatrains.

The *Masnavi*, a lengthy book of couplets dictated to his last spiritual companion, Husam al-Din, is a famously difficult book: his teachings took as its subjects everything from ribald tales about cheating Sufi wives to parables from the Judeo-Christian Bible to animal fables, through which he hinted at spiritual implications often without specifying them. He charmingly and at times frighteningly personified abstract concepts, and anthropomorphized everything from parts of the body to Sleep.

Rumi was a Neo-Platonist; Aristotelian logic held little interest for him, and he was sometimes castigated by more traditional Muslims for taking too many liberties with the interpretation of the Koran. His whirling, which began with the arrival of Shams, was viewed with suspicion by other teachers and by some of his own disciples. Within the Sufi tradition, he was relatively uninterested in the delineation of Gnostic stages by which one approaches union with God: for Rumi, man was perfected in love and suffering.

His discourses were collected under the title *Fihi ma fihi*. Several collections of his poems and a short selection of his sermons are available. His correspondence has also been preserved.

Influence

Despite the fact that his poetic language is rooted in the conventions of Persian and Sufi literature, informed by a medieval world view very different from our own, and so infused with the Koran that his *Masnavi* was called by some later Muslims "the Koran in Persian," Rumi's poetry quickens the hearts and touches the souls of many today. From providing the text of a Philip Glass/Robert Wilson song cycle to Rumi calendars, cards, and websites, Rumi is threading through the modern Western consciousness. Some trace the common phrase "It is what it is" to the compendium of Rumi's teachings, *Fihi ma fihi*, "In it is what is in it," or "It is what it is." Rumi influenced German and English writers in the 19th Century and was the UNESCO (The United Nations Educational, Scientific, and Cultural Organization) International Man of the Year in 2007 (commemorating the 800th anniversary of his birth).

He is widely influential in the Muslim world: in Iran, he is a household name, his mausoleum in Turkey is a place of pilgrimage, and his influence on later Muslim philosophers and poets is pervasive.

Commentary

Commentary on the intersection of psychology and religion in Rumi is conditioned by the distance from which we view this medieval mystic, who was deeply rooted in the Koran and in the society of his day.

Developmentally, Rumi remained a gifted but unremarkable Sufi scholar until age 37. His flowering as a poet and mystic began at approximately the same age as the prophet Mohammed experienced his spiritual awakening. For Jung, this is the phase of mid-life individuation. For Erikson, it is near the beginning of the middle adulthood stage, generativity versus stagnation.

Rumi's sense of identification with Shams and his identification of Shams with the Sun could be seen to indicate a fusion transference, in Kohutian terms.

Some modern commentators (e.g., Leslie Wines) have linked Rumi's mystical flowering to trauma during the long journey from Balkh to Konya, and perhaps even earlier, to trauma at age 5 as Mongols invaded his home town. The mirroring connection with Shams allowed Rumi to expand a part of self that had been desiccated and begin to process the trauma.

Creatively, Shams could be seen as the precipitant, introduced into Rumi's erudition and talent and yielding an outflow of poetry and teaching.

It is diagnostically interesting to speculate about Rumi's internal motivations: his whirling and its attendant drumming may have harnessed mild compulsive or anxious features. At times he reported that he was impelled to the poetry. Sleeplessness and fasting were a regular part of Sufi discipline and may also be related to psychic states.

Rumi's poetry explores at length and in great depth the wide range of human emotions. His lack of sentimentality allows the participation of others in his experience; he provides for readers the mirror that he found for himself in Shams and his later two spiritual companions. Numerous truths that we now recognize as psychological are found in his writing, for example, "'Flee not from the suffering We (God) inflict, for wherever you find suffering, there also you find a way to the remedy.' No one has ever fled from suffering without finding something worse in return" (*Rumi; Divan*, 1995: 123).

Rumi's relationships with Shams, and to a lesser extent with Salah al-Din and Husam al-Din, were deeply engaging at the expense of other relationships, and aroused fierce, even murderous jealousy in his community. For Bion, the pairing of Rumi with his spiritual companions, especially his first, Shams, may have been experienced by Rumi's madrase community as preventing the work stage. The pairing, very fecund, was not able to contain the heightened anxiety of the group. Some was released in Rumi's poetry, some in Shams's possible murder.

In James Fowler's Stages of Faith, Rumi is in stage 6, a Universalizer. Fowler found those at this stage to be "contagious"; Rumi's influence is still felt after eight centuries.

Psychoanalysts share with Rumi the inability to express in words the experience of the encounter, and theorists from Winnicott to Bollas to Eigen have worked to describe aspects of that experience.

See also: ❯ Islam ❯ Julian of Norwich ❯ Meister Eckhart ❯ Mysticism and Psychoanalysis ❯ Mysticism and Psychotherapy ❯ Sufis and Sufism

Bibliography

Chittick, W. C. (1983). *The Sufi path of love: The spiritual teachings of Rumi*. Albany, NY: State University of New York Press.

Harvey, A. (1999). *Teachings of Rumi*. Boston, MA: Shambhala.

Muhammad. (633). *The Koran*. Any of a number of translations

Rumi, C. (1947/2004). *Discourses of Rumi. (Fihi ma Fihi)* (A. J. Arberry, Trans.). London: RoutledgeCurzon.

Rumi, C. (1995). *Divan-i Kebir (Divan-I Shams), Meters 1- 20* (N. O. Ergin, Trans.). Walla Walla, WA: Current and the Turkish Republic Ministry of Culture.

Rumi, C. (2007). *The Masnavi, books 1 and 2* (J. Mojaddedi, Trans.). Oxford, England: Oxford University Press.

Rumi, C. (2008). *The Quatrains of Rumi* (F. A. G. Rawan & I. W. Gamard, Trans.). San Rafael, CA: Sophia Perennis.

Schimmel, A. (2001). *Rumi's World: The life and work of the great Sufi poet*. Boston, MA: Shambhala.

Wines, L. (2000). *Rumi: A spiritual biography*. New York: Crossroad Publishing.

Yarshater, E. (Ed.). (1991). *The mystical poems of Rumi* (Vols. 1 and 2) (A. J. Arberry, Trans.). Chicago, MA: University of Chicago Press.

S

Sabeanism

Sam Cyrous

An ancient religion which should not be mistaken with the Sabaeanims of Sabá (or Sheba), nor with the Sabianism (with "i" in English rather than with "e") originated from the group of followers of John the Baptist who did not accept Jesus as the Christ.

Term Confusion and History

The confusion of the three is a constant through the literature and it is primarily, due to a translation mistake of the Koran by Marmeduke Pickthall – the term mentioned in the Koran refers to the religious group and it is written with the Arabic letter *sad* and Sabá is written with *sin* and is referred to the people of Sabá, Yemen. Other cause of confusion results from the fact that the Ansar tribe of Sabá adopted the Koranic Sabeanism as a religion. A third cause can be pointed in the fact that the followers of John the Baptist, being persecuted and expelled from Palestine, have settled down in the city of Harran, where Sabeanism was the dominant religion and also, after the conquest of Alexander, the center of religious and intellectual activity. Finally, a historical cause is in the fact that the first commentarists of the Koran, the historians and the jurists of Islam, not seeing a Sabean, concluded that all the peoples of the world that were not Christian, Jews or Muslims, living from India to Spain, were Sabeans.

Only on tenth century, it was known that there were two different groups: the ones living at the area of the Euphrates – the Mandaeans, followers of John the Baptist – and the descendents of the city of Harran – the Harranians (Mehrabkhání, 1995).

In this period, the Mandaeans lived among the Sabeans in Harran, probably, copying some of their cosmology, and later in Babylon, where assimilated local beliefs; posterior to the arrival of Muslims in Iraq (636 AD), they moved to the swampy lands of meridian Iraq (Cárdenas, n.d.).

Sabeanism and Other Religions

According to Mehrabkhání (1995) there are no more living believers of this religion and the only sources referring to it are the Muslim historians of the ninth, tenth and eleventh centuries, the explanations presented in Bahá'í texts, their mention in Judaism – in *Yeshayahu/Isaiah*, 45:14 and *Iyov/Job*, 1:15 – and the existence advocated in the original Islam through quotes that distinguish the followers of the book – by one hand, the Muslims and by the other the Jews, the Christians and the Sabeans (2:62; 5:69; 22:17).

As mentioned, their geographical origin was attributed to the city of Harran (Mesopotamia), destroyed by the Mongol invasions of the twelfth century. In the Bible (Génesis, 12:4) one can read that Abram "departed out of Haran," indicating that he could be from there. In letters, the Guardian of the Bahá'í Faith, Shoghi Effendi, by his turn, mentions that "The followers of this religion lived in Ur of the Chaldees, where Abraham appeared" (1941 cit. in Research Department, 1996) and "Abraham is considered as having been a follower of that Faith" (1939 cit. in Departamento de Pesquisa, 2006). And the Koran describes some beliefs of the land of Abraham as similar to those of the Sabeans.

The founder of Islam Himself is seen as being of Sabean origin, according to some descriptions of His time. About Muhammad, Ibn Jurayi (767) wrote "He is a Sabian," 'Abd al-Rahman 'ibn Zayd (798) mentioned "The polytheists used to say of the prophet and his companions 'these are the Sabians' comparing them to them, because the Sabians who live Jaziartal-Mawsil would say 'La ilaha ila Allah'" (a sentence common in Islamic theology), Rabi'ah 'ibn 'Ubbad (contemporaneous of Muhammad) wrote "I saw the prophet when I was a pagan. (. . .) I noticed a man behind him saying 'he is a sabi.' When I

D. A. Leeming, K. Madden, S. Marlan (eds.), *Encyclopedia of Psychology and Religion*, DOI 10.1007/978-0-387-71802-6,
© Springer Science+Business Media LLC 2010

asked somebody who he was he told me he was 'Abu Lahab, his uncle" (Gündüz, 1994: 18–19).

Religious Life

Sabeans believed in the need of demiurges that had all the virtues and perfections of one God unique, incognoscible, incomprehensible; prophets capable of answering any questions and unite humankind in conciliation and peace. From unknown date of foundations and having a founder or a "Prophet (...) Whose name is unrecorded" (Effendi, 1938 cit. in Departamento de Pesquisa da Casa Universal de Justica, a, 2006), the learned attributed its origin to Seth – son of Adam – or Idris – Enoch –, having in account that their pilgrimage was to Giza, Egypt, where the tombs of Idris and Seth would be, or even to Hermes Trimegistus. This absence of a known founder made them "replace their unknown prophet with these spirits" (Mehrabkháni, 1995), in a total of seven, that govern the earthly world and manage the worldly and the spiritual problems. Those spirits assumed a celestial body as their own physical one – Saturn, Jupiter, Mars, the Sun, Venus, Mercury and the Moon – having erected temples for each one of them, in Harran (possibly, in a total amount of 12).

Each of these temples, without images, possessed a different architecture. The ceremonies in these temples were under the absolute control of the sacerdotal individuals, existing a clear dependence towards them. A detailed analysis of the religious phenomenon would show an increase of need of clergy dominion as one would go back in time, and a consequent apparent loss of responsibility of the believers' personal acts. Nevertheless, in the case of Sabeanism there was a belief that the individual's spirit is conscious of the punishments and rewards he/she was receiving during life, indicating an individual responsibility, despite the need of constant sacerdotal presence and confirmation on the lives and thoughts of the believers: humans were perfect creations, but in potential, and through the intervention of the spirits and through the clergy, it would have its development. Thus, conscience would become the meaning organ, as defined by Frankl (2002), guiding each human being and permitting the maintaining of his/her own identity, making him/her aware of his/her objective in life. In this way, a Sabean was someone that, guided, reflected on his attitudes, because "freedom of adopting an attitude (...) is never completed if it is not converted and transformed in freedom to assume responsibility" (Frankl, 2001: 75). Responsibility is now an essential force in Sabean

psychology, marking as a "distinctive note of man in his humanity" (Guberman & Soto, 2005: 122).

Family Life

The concept of family, by its turn, was one of equality, under the law, between men and women, in a monogamist couple, making more likely to have a more congruent child education, in what couple and family therapist could call balanced, or at least, inclination to a more balanced and healthy family system. Divorce was not forbidden, but it was unadvised and only made possible, once more, through the intervention of a superior and exterior entity: in this case a judge that, after the analysis of the adultery charges (only acceptable cause of divorce).

Collective Life and Individual Life

It was a religion that defended individual role, submissive to an external orientation: from the judge, the clergy, or the spirits. Thábit ibn-i-Qarrah (a devoted Sabean) has written that "some chosen among the people" are those who "have reached all this and have shown the way to heal the badness of the souls and have filled the world with the institutions and centers to fulfill and extend wisdom and piety." These are the few who leaded the matters of the community. A first and superficial analysis could attribute the locus of control of the believers to external variables, but if such was true, the cities where they lived, as was the case of Harran, wouldn't have been the centers of cultural enterprises, where difference was accepted. In reality, respecting the guide of those who were hierarchically superior could be compared to the respect a student has towards the teacher, or the relationship of a patient with his therapist: at the end, responsibility is of he/she who has, initially, lesser information and knowledge and that wants to learn and develop new capabilities. Thus the ninth and tenth centuries recorded great sages of Sabean origin, like philosophers, astronomers, physicians and botanicals.

The existence of a class superior in knowledge and wisdom could also prevent a common individual from imposing his opinions to others: as consequence equality, tolerance to difference and equal opportunities would be as if instituted. The very own diversity of the temples could be seen as an acceptance of difference and diversity. As a consequence, social and moral principles could only result of a social consensus.

Individual Life

At an individual level, like other religions, there were prayers – in a total of three or five obligatory ones, depending on the referral source. They took care of their bodies and clothing, as it would be needed for devotional moments. Such act shows a belief in some kind of relationship between the body and the spirit. They fasted three times an year – in a total of 30–46 days –, believed that circumcision was against divine creation and had as forbidden to eat some sorts of meats, garlic, onion, lentils or broadbeans.

Scholars assume they believed in life after death, due to their erect and without prostration prayers for the dead during funerals, the archeological findings pointing to their burial with fingernails and, in a specific record, the figure of a Phoenix on the tomb with the sentence "let there be the joy of a happy ending!"

They were, besides all these, owners of firmness and constancy before hardships, as reported, once more, by Thábit ibn-i-Qarrah: "when everyone was under the influence of the Cross, our parents, with the help of God, showed firmness (...). Blessed those who show constancy and accept all kinds of calamities for the cause of hanputeh, and manifest certitude and confidence." It was, perhaps under this vision that they reached vast corridors of the African world, despite their Asian origins. There are authors that believe that Sabeanism was the precursor of African religions, as the case of the Ngoni people of the Bantu ethnicity of Swaziland, as described by Cárdenas (n.d.), or even *Santeria* taken to the Americas, centuries later.

See also: ❂ Abraham and Isaac ❂ Adam and Eve ❂ Bahais ❂ Baptism ❂ Christianity ❂ Circumcision ❂ Conscience ❂ Frankl, Viktor ❂ God ❂ Islam ❂ Judaism and Psychology ❂ Locus of Control ❂ Prayer ❂ Purpose in Life ❂ Religion ❂ Santería ❂ Soul: A Depth Psychological Approach

Bibliography

Cárdenas, B. V. (n.d.). *Apuntes sobre los Sabeanos*. http://bahai-library.com/file.php5?file = villar-cardenas_apuntes_sobre_sabeanos&language: Bahá'í Library Online.

Departamento de Pesquisa da Casa Universal de Justiça. (2006). *Sabeísmo, Buda, Krishna, Zoroastro e Assuntos Correlatos*. Mogi Mirim: Editora Bahá'í do Brasil.

Frankl, V. E. (2001). *Psicoterapia y existencialismo – Escritos selectos sobre la logoterapia*. Barcelona, Spain: Editorial Herder.

Frankl, V. E. (2002). *La voluntad del sentido – Conferencias escogidas sobre logoterapia*. Barcelona, Spain: Editorial Herder.

Guberman, M., & Soto, E. P. (2005). *Diccionario de logoterapia*. Buenos Aires, Argentina: Grupo Editorial Lumen Hvmanitas.

Gündüz', Ş. (1994). The knowledge of life, the origins and early history of the Mandaeans and their relations to the Sabians of the Qur'an and to the Harranians. *Journal of Semitic Studies*.

King James Bible.

Mehrabkháni, R. (1995). Los sabeos y el Sabeísmo. *Apuntes Bahá'ís*, II Época. Rivista N°4, 53–72.

The Qur'an. (n.d.) (Yusuf Ali, Trans.).

Research Department of The Universal House of Justice (1996). MEMORANDUM to David Garcia.

Sacraments

Carol L. Schnabl Schweitzer

Sacred Ritual – Public Act

From a religious perspective, a sacrament is a ritual that has been elevated to a special status because it is believed to have been instituted by a divine figure. For Christians, for example, these sacred rituals or sacraments are believed to have been instituted by Christ. Scholars that study ritual are able to agree (mostly) on at least two points: (1) "ritual consciousness is pre-critical"; and (2) "ritual is meaningful and that meaning consists of the words or ideas to which ritual acts refer" (Grimes, 1993: 7). Moreover, ritual is a collective, or corporate and public act, as opposed to an individual or personal and private act; ritual is also traditional as opposed to created or invented. On these points, even Freud would be likely to concur since he declared that an obsessional neurosis was a "half comic and half tragic *private* religion" (Freud, 1907: 119). This is not to say that new rituals are not created or invented and later adopted as sacred, but it is a process that takes place over generations. The generational process points to the need for some kind of ritual authority – especially with regard to sacred rites or sacraments. Authority is ascribed to sacred texts, tradition (the generational process), ecclesiastical hierarchies, and the like. Grimes identifies several other sources of ritual authority: performance according to rules established by sacred or liturgical texts; functions that cohere with the social context and/or work to achieve explicit goals; and, moral criteria which ritual subscribes to and ensures that ritual is just (Grimes, 1993: 50). Thus, as psychologist of religion Paul Pruyser was led to conclude: "in religion, it is folly to ignore the impact of action on belief. Religious belief is embedded in religious practices; creed is grafted onto cult" (Pruyser, 1974: 205). Though doctrine about such religious practices is in some ways inseparable from the culture and the practice it describes, there is an unavoidable "chicken-egg" question about which is prior. What then does psychoanalytic theory teach us about ritual and the sacraments in particular?

Obsession – Private Act

Freud had a less than charitable view of religious ritual and declared that all religion was best understood as a universal obsessional neurosis (Freud, 1907/1959: 126). What Freud labeled as "neurotic ceremonials" are "small adjustments to particular everyday actions... which have always to be carried out in the same, or in a methodically varied, manner" (Freud, 1907/1959: 117–118). If these actions are not carried out methodically and repetitively (daily), the individual experiences intolerable anxiety. Thus, one conclusion pertaining to the function of ritual is that ritual serves as a defense mechanism, which assists in reducing an individual's anxieties about everyday life. Freud attends particularly to the small additions to what would otherwise be "mere formalities" or exaggerations of formal procedures; these additions or exaggerations may have a "rhythmic character" which consists of pauses and repetitions. One could argue that these "neurotic ceremonials" have an almost musical quality about them. Yet even Freud distinguishes between "neurotic ceremonials" and religious rituals as we shall see.

Neurotic Obsession or Sacred Rite?

The similarities that Freud identified between neurotic obsessions and sacred rites include: the conscientiousness with which the practices are observed as well as the attention paid to details; the "qualms of conscience" or guilt that is stimulated by neglecting the rituals; and, the observation or performance of such rituals in isolation from other activities in conjunction with a prohibition against the interruption or disruption of the act. The dissimilarities are equally apparent and include: the "stereotyped" character of religious ritual (Freud cites prayer as an example); the corporate or communal nature of sacred ritual; and, the details or dimensions of religious rituals that are imbued with significance and symbolic meaning consciously by the believer (Freud, 1907/1959: 119). Here we can note the "pre-critical consciousness" and meaning located in words and ideas that Grimes describes. In contrast, an obsessional neurosis is acted out in private

and the meaning (there is always a symbolic meaning) is not known, at least consciously, to the individual who engages in such practices. Finally, Freud contends that if "deeper insight" into the actual mechanism of the obsession is to be attained then one needs to examine what is at the bottom or root of the obsession which is "always *the repression of an instinctual impulse* (a component of sexual instinct)" (Freud, 1907/1959: 124). Here then we see that an obsessional neurotic practice addresses the guilt which is related to the repression of an impulse and by analogy one can see a similarity with the function of sacraments which, at least in part, are rituals performed to cleanse the believer from sin. Thus as Freud concludes, the origins of religion are located in the renunciation or suppression of "certain instinctual impulses" (Freud, 1907/1959: 125). Acts of penance or contrition, which are deemed sacraments in some Christian denominations, are ritual acts engaged in to compensate for the believer's sinful behaviors and these acts have a pathological counterpart in obsessional neuroses. As Pruyser notes, however, this treatment of religious ritual doesn't do justice to religious practice which leads him to render a more favorable reading of sacraments and religious rituals building upon the work of Winnicott and Erikson (Pruyser, 1974: 205–213). What then does this more favorable understanding of sacred ritual look like?

Sacraments as Sacred Ritual

Pruyser takes Winnicott's idea of a transitional object and its transitional sphere (the attention paid to and "goings on" surrounding the transitional object) as his starting place. The transitional object is a ritual or sacred object which, Pruyser argues, is the transcendent. The object is held as sacred; for example, an infant's mother and the rest of the family realize almost intuitively that a blanket or teddy bear is precious and it acquires a "ceremonial focus" within the family. It isn't washed with the rest of the laundry, is often carried everywhere, and is treated with awe or reverence. This transitional sphere wherein the object becomes sacred is also the source of illusion in the positive sense of the word. It is the space between "the mental image produced by the mind itself and the objective perceptual image produced by the real world impinging upon the sensory system. Illusion is neither hallucination nor delusion, nor is it straightforward sense perception. Illusion also includes mystery" (Pruyser, 1974: 11). Thus the transitional object has an almost numinous – even if illusory – quality about it while the transitional sphere is the location for mediation between inner and outer reality and in this way serves as the place from which religion emanates. The first occurrence of ritual takes place when an infant and mother exchange smiles while the infant is nursing (Erikson, 1977: 87). How then does this lead to the development of sacred ritual and the celebration of sacraments? If we consider the Christian sacraments of Baptism and the Eucharist as examples, we can see that they are in some sense religious dramas enacted in a worship context that deal primarily with notions of grace and judgment (or damnation) which invite communal participation. To be sure, the celebration of the sacraments are fraught with symbols, the multi-valent meanings of which perhaps only the clergy or ecclesiastical authorities are able to explain fully, but their absence from the drama of human life would signal nothing short of a person with a negative identity (Erikson) or an individual who has never learned to play (Winnicott).

See also: ❯ Anxiety ❯ Christianity ❯ Compulsion ❯ Defenses ❯ Erikson, Erik ❯ Freud, Sigmund ❯ Instinct ❯ Pruyser, Paul ❯ Psychology of Religion ❯ Psychoanalysis ❯ Ritual ❯ Shame and Guilt ❯ Super-Ego ❯ Symbol ❯ Transitional Object ❯ Winnicott, Donald Woods

Bibliography

Erikson, E. (1977). *Toys and reasons: Stages in the ritualization of experience.* New York: W. W. Norton.

Freud, S. (1907/1959). Obsessive actions and religious practices In J. Strachey, (Trans.). *The standard edition of the complete psychological works of Sigmund Freud* (Vol. 9). London: Hogarth Press (1959).

Grimes, R. L. (1993). *Reading, writing, and ritualizing: Ritual in fictive, liturgical, and public places.* Washington DC: Pastoral Press.

Pruyser, P. W. (1974). *Between belief and unbelief.* New York: Harper & Row.

Pruyser, P. W. (1983). *The play of the imagination: Toward a psychoanalysis of culture.* New York: International Universities Press.

Winnicott, D. W. (1971). *Playing and reality.* London: Tavistock/Routledge.

Sacred King

Stacey Enslow

The Sacred King is a unification of the concepts of the innate self-ruler; the human being as a potentiality expressed in competence, command, resourcefulness and self-control. This is united with the mystical, religious, or psychic self, as the leader of the unearthly aspects of the human. The Sacred king joins the office of the secular King and the holy Priest into a single whole person, one who acts with authority and knowledge in the inner and outer realms of human experience. Sacred King seeks to achieve homeostasis but at an idealized level. He (the Sacred King is a "masculine" aspect – it is understood that archetypes are manifested in both genders and sexes) is the bridge between extremes of human social and personal/religious experience. In Eastern metaphysics the Human is conceived of as a bridge between "heaven" and "earth," whereas in Western metaphysics, humanity is seen as possessing, or linking, the extremes of the "upper" or celestial worlds, and the "lower" or demoniac worlds; Heaven:Hell, Human world:Faery/Other world, Arcadia:Hades.

Mythic correspondences include, as earthly beings; Gilgamesh, Rama, and The Fisher King. Some deities representing Sacred Kingship are Marduk, Prajipati, and Osiris.

As Gilgamesh, the earliest recorded Sacred King in history, the Sacred King represents the culmination of the journey of the soul, from realization of potential, to the limits of the physical self, to the unification of desires and will to achieve the end of the soul's journey. Gilgamesh is the Sacred Warrior, and the Wanderer, who has achieved success in the quest for selfhood and self-mastery. Gligamesh also shows the power of the Sacred King as living and ruling in two worlds: the land of the living and the land of the divine, be they ancestors or gods. Working with the High priestess/Goddess of the Land, the Sacred King is the judge and upholder of sacred law, and by his decree secular and sacred law are joined. The Goddess and the Land are forces with which the Sacred King must remain in balance with, to stay healthy and potent.

Rama is the law-giver: he who arbitrates the sacred law and also keeps the land fertile through fairness and justice. Rama is the Sacred King as universal or social conscience, and the self as a social force; both a binder and administrator. As Rama, the Sacred king represents the idea of latent sovereignty within the self, or self-rulership, as well as the ability to empower, and rule, others. This aspect of the Sacred king is the fulfillment of the social contract between the individual and humanity: as a self-realized human being, the Sacred King performs his duties of office and is in turn sustained within the interconnected energy exchange between himself, the land and society on one hand, and between himself, the goddess of the land and the collective spirit of the people on the other. Thus the Sacred King fulfills the "Divine Mandate" of Eastern metaphysics as a bridge between heaven and earth. By mastering the Shadow within himself, he is also the bridge between the "lower" or demonic, and "upper" or angelic realms as well.

The Fisher king is the wounded self, seeking reconciliation and healing: the Sacred King as victim, and as self-immobilized. Just as the empowered Sacred King represents the self-realized self-ruler, the Fisher King represents the powers of the King: healing, union, justice, rulership, and wisdom, all rendered impotent by the innate power of the King turned against the self. In this aspect of the archetype, the illness of the self is a public role, affecting the health of the entire network he is connected to: the Land, and its divinity, and the people, and their collective spirit.

For the Fisher King, all relationships that the Sacred King needs to fulfill are out of balance, rendering the King unable to perform his functions, and unable to be healed until the inbalances both within and without the self are healed. The Fisher King's illness is reflected in the land, and so the land ceases to nourish the King, or his people. Also, the Land no longer nourishes the social network of the people, and so they cannot heal the King: The Fisher King is sick in body, social function and psyche.

The Sacred King has a strong messianic component: like the Fisher King, Rama and Osiris are embodiments of the Returning King which involves a period away from society and family (through illness, a personal quest or exile, death), and then a return to liberate and rule again.

Sexual potency is an important aspect of the Sacred King; all Sacred Kings excel in combat, and usually possess superlative weapons; when the King's power is lessened, there is a corresponding lessening, or even breakage, of the potent weapon, and vice-versa. The libido is a driving force for the Sacred King; the erotic interplay between Gilgamesh and Innnana, the love affair of Rama/Radhi, the castration and rejuvination of Osiris by Isis illustrate the necessity of the male/female dynamism not only as a catalyst, but also as a means of attainment.

When the role of the Sacred King is fulfilled, he is the idealized ruler of the inner self. For the individual, the Sacred King is a realization of Maslow's self-actualized person. In all his aspects, the Sacred King reflects an integration of the private self and the social self; the King is ruler and hero, healer and warrior. In all instances, the Sacred King is a responsible participant (and even initiator) of social action, for benefit or for ill.

See also: ❯ Angels ❯ Archetype ❯ Christ ❯ Conscience ❯ Demons ❯ Descent to the Underworld ❯ Eros ❯ Heaven and Hell ❯ Libido ❯ Liminality ❯ Love ❯ Monomyth ❯ Mother ❯ Osiris and the Egyptian Religion ❯ Self ❯ Shadow

Bibliography

Jacobsen, T. (1976). *The treasures of darkness*. New Haven, CT: Yale University Press.

Jung, C. G. (Ed.). (1959). *By Violet Staub De Laszlo: The basic writings of C. G. Jung*. New York: Modern Library.

Maslow, A. H. (1968). *Toward a psychology of being* (2nd ed.). New York: Van Nostrand Reinhold Company.

Sacred Prostitution

Paul Larson

Religion has had at best an ambivalent attitude toward human sexuality. All religions recognize the value of sexual union between a man and a woman in a mutually committed relationship and ritually recognized through some sort of rite of marriage. Beyond that type of sexuality, most other forms have received more or less harsh condemnations and proscriptions. Thus, sacred prostitution, or providing sexual acts to strangers as a religious act or in exchange for a donation to a religious organization has had very limited acceptance and much more condemnation.

Where we have record of sacred prostitution it has occurred in association with the older pagan fertility goddesses of the ancient Near East. Since most of the commentators, especially those found in the Bible, have condemned the practice, the accuracy of their description of the practice should be taken with some skepticism. In the Hebrew Bible (*Tanach*), the term for a servant of a temple who would provide a sexual act to a supplicant of the goddess is "K'desh" (male) or "K'deshah" (female), with the plural being "K'deshim" and "K'deshot," though the literal root meaning is closer to "holy one" without any sexual connotation. That additional element is a gloss by the author with a point of view. "Hierodule" is the term in English for this role as translated from ancient works in Hebrew, Greek or Latin. The Greek historian Herodotus (1, 199) noted that in Mesopotamia it was required that a women offer herself sexually at the temple of Mylitta once in her lifetime.

Budin (2008) has taken the position, based on philological analysis of the evidence, that sacred prostitution did not exist. As noted above some of the terminology does not imply sexual action, but has come to be associated with a sexual meaning only through a tradition she claims is fatally flawed. The strong moralistic tone found in the Jewish and Christian writers who are the source of much of the evidence lends weight to her criticism. She also rightfully points out that prostitution was well known in most of those civilizations without any religious overtones and references to sacred prostitutes don't usually use the terms for regular sex workers. Thus one is left with much doubt as to whether or what extent the practice existed. It is probable that there were some associations of ritual sexual activity with religious institutions. There is evidence for the existence of "hieros gamos" (Gk.), a ritual sex act between a king or high priest and a high priestess in ancient Mesopotamia. But Budin's argument is that the practice was not widespread or institutionalized. Greenberg (1988) focuses more on the male hierodule, particularly the "galli" (Lat.), the temple servants of the Phrygian deity Cybele. These men castrated themselves as part of their initiation into their priestly role and donned female garb. There is some evidence that they subsequently were available for sexual liaisons with males, though our most detailed account (Apulius, second century CE/1962) is a satirical work of fiction. Herodotus' note cited earlier is both the earliest reference and the least burdened by judgment as to the practice he describes, so it is harder to dismiss. Nevertheless, the evidence is scanty and imprecise, and the final word should be that controversy surrounding the practice makes firm conclusions difficult.

See also: ❯ Rites of Passage ❯ Ritual ❯ Sex and Religion

Bibliography

Apulius. (1962). *The golden ass* (W. Adlington, Trans.). New York: Collier Books. (Original work published 2nd century CE).

Budin, S. L. (2008). *The myth of sacred prostitution in antiquity.* New York: Cambridge University Press.

Greenberg, D. E. (1988). *The construction of homosexuality.* Chicago, IL: University of Chicago Press.

Sacred Time

Rod Blackhirst

In profane understandings time appears to be a constant linear sequence of moments, but all religious and spiritual traditions conceive of a "sacred time" that is outside of or other than this sequence. Commonly, this sacred time is said to be an "eternal now" that is located "between" (or above or beyond) the moments that make up linear time. Time is an agent of death, corruption and the finite; spiritual traditions seek a realm that is ever-living, incorruptible and infinite and therefore not subject to the flux of time.

The psychological perception of time is inconstant. Time will often seem to either "fly" or "drag" and it seems to pass slower to children and pass faster as we age. Similarly, there are cultural differences in the perception of time. The nomad, for instance, has more of a spatial than a temporal consciousness. For the nomad the starry sky is a map, while for the sedentary city-dweller it is a clock. The decline of nomadic life and the arrival of sedentary life (recorded in such myths as the Biblical story of Cain and Abel) is therefore the passage from the sacred to the profane experience of time.

One of the most primordial accounts of sacred time comes from the Australian Aborigines who describe a period called the "Dreaming" or the "Dreamtime." While this is usually conceived of as a time long before memory, it is also understood to be ever-present and can be accessed at any time by way of religious rites. This same convention is a feature of most religious systems; the liturgical or theurgical elements of the system allow a symbolic relocation from profane to sacred time, which is at the same time a return to the formative and creative period or the point of a sacred theophany (intervention of God into time).

The most conspicuous instance of this in the semitic religions is the Jewish sabbath which is celebrated every 7 days (Saturday) and is a return to the Divine repose after the 6 days of creation. The reiteration of sacred events is the guiding principle of sacred calendars and calendrical systems. The annual reiteration of events is not merely commemorative; it a symbolic return to sacred time. Often, inter-calary days and festivals are regarded as especially sacred because they represent "time outside of (normal) time."

In Judeo-Christian mythology, the period that Adam and Eve spend in the Garden of Eden is the paradigmatic instance of sacred time. Sacred time is Edenic and before the Fall. But, as historical religions, Judaism and Christianity both propose paradixical instances of sacred periods that are within the fold of history. In Judaism, the period during which the Israelites wandered in the wilderness in a sacred time that is "out of history" even though it is understood to have been an historical event. In Christianity, the Last Supper was an historical event at a definite time and place, but it also dwells in sacred time since it can be accessed by the Real Presence of Christ in the Eucharist. Similarly, the crucifixion was an historical event but in Christian theology it is also an eternal event; the sacrifice of Christ is now and on-going. In shamanism and in shamanic practices that persist in later religions – such as fasting, chanting, trances, dancing, auto-hypnosis or the sacramental use of drugs – there is an attempt to have direct and immediate experience of "time beyond time" and to induce a psychological state of timelessness that is not merely symbolic. In folk tales, popular stories or so-called fairy tales sacred time is signaled by the convention "once upon a time" which refers to a mythical time that is no time in particular.

Sacred time is pristine and archetypal; it is the time when the shape and patterns of life and the world were first established. It is therefore mythological and non-historical, history then being defined as a decline, a deviation from or the passing away of sacred time. Plato, giving a very traditional account of it, says in his *Timaeus* that "time is a moving image of eternity" and that the Forms or archetypes of the world reside in eternity, their temporal (and corruptible) manifestations being "images" or copies of the a-temporal originals. In his dialog called *The Statesman* Plato also gives an account of the idea of "eternal return," namely the notion that historical time is circular (rather than linear) and that all events in time are repeated endlessly. This idea is surprisingly widespread, as Mircea Eliade has documented, and follows from the idea that, ultimately, the movement of time is an illusion and that only motionless eternity (sacred time) is real. The myth often takes the form of an era in which the world moves in one direction (with the sun rising in the east and setting in the west) followed by a catastrophic reversal of direction at end of this era (after which the sun rises in the west and sets in the east). Time, so to speak, winds up and then winds down, although in fact both movements cancel each other out and there is really no movement at the level of the principle. The religious mystic or the spiritual seeker aspires to this principle (which is spatially represented as the center or axis of a wheel) and therefore to freedom from the cycles and vicissitudes of time and decay. In the eastern religions this idea is expressed in terms of cycles of birth and rebirth and the timeless realm is attained through liberation from these cycles. In modern thought the idea of "eternal return" was taken up by the German philosopher Nietzsche who presented it as a nihilistic denial of the liberal ideal of progress.

See also: ❯ Christianity ❯ Judaism and Psychology ❯ Myth ❯ Plato and Religion ❯ Ritual ❯ Schopenhauer, Nietzsche, and Atheism ❯ Shamans and Shamanism

Bibliography

Alexander, S. (1920). *Space, time, and deity* (Vol. 2). London: Macmillan.

Brumbaugh, R. S. (1984). *Unreality and time.* Albany, NY: State University of New York Press.

Cowan, J. (1992). *The elements of the aborigine tradition.* Shaftesbury, England: Element.

Eliade, M. (1959). *The sacred and the profane: The nature of religion* (W. Trask, Trans.). London: Harcourt Brace Jovanovich.

Eliade, M. (1971). *The myth of the eternal return: Cosmos and history.* Princeton, NJ: Princeton University Press.

Sacrifice

Morgan Stebbins

The concept of sacrifice was once so important in the study of religions that whole developmental taxonomies were created to define them from this standpoint (Frazer; Hubert and Mauss, 1981). We can still see it as one of the least understood but central ideas in religion, in dynamic psychology, and in common parlance.

Sacrifice, like many words that have crossed from ritual to general usage can be defined in two general ways. On one hand it is giving up something for something else, and on the other it is giving up something precious (anything from grain to animals to goods to humans) to a deity, in usually in supplication. For the former, one might wonder how it is different from the concept of simple exchange – and indeed it seems to be hardly differentiated especially when applying models of social value systems which depend on both cohesion and coercion. For example, a mother is said to sacrifice for her children or a soldier for his or her country, and yet it is hard to see how it was not a matter of job description in the first place. That is, it seems to be more a choice in terms of both having children as well as parenting style, except that socially the value of parenting is higher than that of self-care. The same goes for military sacrifice (the so-called ultimate sacrifice) and other things that benefit a given social group. Both of these examples show that the dynamic involved is that of giving up something personal for something collective or inter-personal (and something that often needs to remain unexamined to retain its influence).

For all of these examples, critical theory in the style of Slavoj Zizek indicates that a form of ideology is active. That is, a master signifier embedded in the language of a particular social group designates collective goals as more valuable than the pursuit of personal consciousness or desire. In this sense, the master signifier acts to justify a regrettable life – if one has sacrificed something major for something else of less tangible import, one could hardly be expected to have excelled as a person. Of course this dynamic can be reversed so that, for example with sports figures, one might be either negatively or positively assessed in terms of sacrifice made for some great achievement. In either case we can see the caustic lens of social reprobation at work. To the extent that ideological cultures can express a sentimentality toward sacrifice we have to remember Jung's words that "sentimentality is the sister of brutality" (Jung, 385).

Before moving to the specifically religious concept of sacrifice, let us notice that the word itself is derived from the Latin words *sacre*, or sacred, and *facere*, the verb meaning to make. So sacrifice is that act which makes something (or someone) sacred. The terrain of the sacred includes a range of experience from sublime experience of union to terrible and destructive acts of the divine. To make sacred then is to approach the meaning of taboo – it is nearing the holy fire, the spark of life, and the dark reaches of the psychoid realm of the psyche. The term "psychoid" refers to a theoretical level of unconscious which can never be plumbed and yet out of which content emerges. One could think of it as the irreducible biological substrate of mind (see Jung, *On the Nature of the Psyche*).

In the realm of religious traditions, sacrifice of some kind in nearly ubiquitous.

It also served a social or economic function in those cultures where the edible portions of the animal were distributed among those attending the sacrifice for consumption. This aspect of sacrifice has recently become the basis of an economic explanatory model (see especially R. Firth, E. E. Evans-Pritchard). Animal sacrifice has turned up in almost all cultures, from the Hebrews to the Greeks and Romans (particularly the purifying ceremony Lustratio and from the Aztecs to the Yoruba. The ancient Egyptians, however, forbade the practice as being primitive, although the entombment of both humans and animals in a sacrificial form with the Pharaoh as companions after death was common.

The Hebrew word for sacrifice is korban, from the root *karov*, meaning to come close to God. This is a more spatial aspect of the quality of making sacred. The opening chapters of the book of Leviticus explain in great detail the various methods of sacrifice, as well as providing a veritable taxonomy of sacrificial victims. Sacrifices were classified as bloody (animals) or un-bloody (grain and wine). Bloody sacrifices were again differentiated into holocausts (whole burnt offerings,), guilt offerings (divided into a burnt part and a part kept by the priest) and peace offerings (also partial burning).

A specific set of sacrificial offerings were the scapegoat, particularly instructive psychologically because these were a pair of goats with different functions. As is well known, the scapegoat was adorned with ribbons representing the sins of the village and driven out into the wilderness. The other goat was an unblemished holocaust or wholly burnt offering to God. Psychologically translated this shows an inability to sustain a proximity to the divine while suffering consciousness of sins. Moreover, in the person manifesting the victim mentality there is a split which both cannot bear responsibility for mistakes and in which there is an unconscious identification with the divine – represented by the wholly burnt and therefore nutritionally unavailable goat. In other words, for this type of split subject the only path to an experience of value is through suffering.

The practice of human sacrifice is a particularly instructive, if brutal, reminder of the power of the gods however imagined. This translates into a personal possession by a transpersonal structure which results in the destruction of anything human. Examples come from all over the world: In the Greek world there are many stories of human sacrifice from youths sent to appease the Minotaur to Iphigenia being sacrificed by her father Agamemnon for the sake of favorable war-wind. There are many conflicting ancient sources and in fact only Aeschylus' *Agamemnon* and Pindar's *11th Pythian Ode* describe her actual sacrifice and her father's blood-guilt, prompted by his eagerness for war.

In Mesoamerica human sacrifice was even more widespread from Aztec sacrifice of many (usually enemy) humans in order to assure the rising of the sun, to common Mayan and Incan sacrifice for astrological and architectural reasons. It has been found in Norse culture, Indonesian tribal society, and in some African cultures, and persisted until recently in India in the form of immolation of the widow of a Brahmin on his death pyre The immolation of the widow is called *sati*. Legislation to outlaw it was passed only as recently as 1987.

Frazer and other early theorists of religion established a dubious but very influential hierarchy or development of sacrifice from the human to the animal to the symbolic to, not surprisingly, the Christian (Frazer, *The Golden Bough*). Of course the latter (the Eucharist) is really a form of human sacrifice, but with the twist that it is also a sacrifice of God, and is self-inflicted. In this model we come very close to a psychological view in that the most valuable thing one can give up for something higher or greater is an aspect of oneself. The factor which keeps this process from becoming merely an exchange is that of uncertainty. Although some anthropologists have seen sacrifice as a fairly transparent manipulation of the divine, the Catholic and Orthodox churches have gone to great lengths to explain that it is not in fact a manipulation of the God-head but rather an offering which is then responded to out of Grace, albeit suspiciously consistently. The instructive Biblical passage is the moment in the garden of Gesthemene in which Jesus admits that he doesn't want to go through with the crucifixion but then assents, saying "Not my will, but thine, be done" (Gospel of Luke, 41:22–24). This is also found in Paul, Galations 2:20, "I have been crucified with Christ, it is no longer I who live, but Christ who lives in me."

We can see that psychologically the dynamic is one of giving up the lesser for a chance at some uncertain greater. This is only viable within depth psychological approaches for which there is a mode of functioning or a psychic structure which is seen as bigger, greater, wiser, or more comprehensive. However within these systems we can see another sort of sacrificial taxonomy. An image of human sacrifice would indicate a blame of the other, of animal sacrifice indicates a relinquishing of instinct, of agricultural offerings shows a dynamic of cultural sacrifice, and a self/symbolic sacrifice shows that a process of giving up something highly valuable and personal for the transpersonal is indicated.

In this process the first victim is instinctive certainty, replaced by doubt and concomitant differentiation. This becomes the development of an evaluating consciousness, one that weighs options and consequences. If successful, personal guidelines emerge in the shape of instinct molded by will. This phrase is instructive as it is Jung's very definition of psyche; it is "instinct modified by will" (Jung, Aion: 56), which if still successful, push the natural impulses into a corner. There is a danger as well as hardship in this, but further sacrifice including spiritual ambition in favor of something still unknown but symbolically indicated reveals the logic of the soul apparent in the present in any given moment.

To turn the image another way, we can see the sacrificial knife (of differentiation) as the instrument of a kind of regeneration. It is one that kills the failing king, or dominant part of consciousness. As such the knife acts like the Lacanian concept of any speech act: it carries content but also carries the implicit world-view in which the content can be viable, thus undercutting the very subject of the utterance. In Lacan's case, what must be given up is the attachment to a specular (that is, apparent in vision only) wholeness in favor of a more authentic experience of fragmentation in the face of ideological social pressure (Lacan, *The Four Fundamental Principles*).

Lacan's analysis indicates the coercive aspect of sacrifice that may be supported by a social agenda. In this we see that the dynamics of sentimentality include brutality, so that a statement of sacrifice of some overt type "I sacrifice for you" (or the call for a patriotic sacrifice under the banner of "us" when what is meant is "you") is revealed as a desperate gambit to maintain control at any price and is the reverse of a personal spiritual process.

Sacrifice is a key aspect of both religion and psychology. In religious terms it was archaically practiced through the sacrifice of an animal in order to change the supplicant's relationship with the divine. It has changed to become a sacrifice of personal intention in favor of divine spirit – although this is ambiguous it brings the concept very close to the psychological meaning in which growth is seen as giving up the smaller for the larger. For Freud this meant giving up the sexual urge, or sublimating it, into cultural pursuits. For Jung there is a definitive religious instinct in which sacrifice is made of the small personality in favor of the large. Although simple to describe, in practice it involves a typically difficult struggle to let go of something that previously defined the subject in favor of something not yet fully known but more comprehensive.

See also: ❯ Christ ❯ Judaism and Psychology ❯ Jung, Carl Gustav ❯ Lacan, Jacques ❯ Osiris and the Egyptian Religion

Bibliography

Bataille, G. (1992). *Theory of religion*. New York: Zone Books.

Carter, J. (2003). *Understanding religious sacrifice*. New York: Continuum.

Davies, N. (1981). *Human sacrifice: In History and today*. New York: Dorset Press.

Eliade, M. (1978). *A history of religious ideas* Vol. I, From the stone age to the Eleusinian Mysteries (W. Trask, Trans.). Chicago, IL: University of Chicago Press.

Frazer, J. (1854–1941). *The golden bough*.

Freud, S. (1913). *Totem and taboo*. New York: W. W. Norton.

Freud, S. (1939). *Moses and monotheism*. New York: Random House.

Heinsohn, G. The rise of blood sacrifice and priest kingship in Mesopotamia: A cosmic decree? (also published in: 1992. *Religion, 22*).

Hubert & Mauss. (1981). *Sacrifice: Its nature and function*. University of Chicago Press (Reprint, original 1898).

Jung, C. G. (1956). *Symbols of transformation*. London: Routledge & Kegan Paul.

Jung, C. G. (1969). *On the nature of the Psyche*. Princeton, NJ: Princeton University Press.

Jung, C. G. (1979). *Aion*. Princeton, NJ: Princeton University Press.

Lacan, J. *The four fundamental principles*.

Sacrifice of Isaac

Erel Shalit

The sacrifice of Isaac, in Hebrew the *akedah*, i.e., the *binding* of Isaac, is one of the Bible's most dramatic stories. In its extreme brevity, the narrative is an archetypal skeleton, not fleshed out by personal details or human feelings. It thus lends itself to innumerable theological explanations, philosophical readings and psychological interpretations.

God tells Abraham to go to the land of Moriah (possibly meaning the land of the Amorites, the land of worship, or the teaching-place of God) and offer his beloved son Isaac for a burnt offering. Abraham does not question his God, with whom he has sealed a covenant. He has been promised that he will "multiply exceedingly," and become a father of many nations. He binds his son Isaac and lays him upon the wood on the altar he has built, but when raising his knife, the angel calls upon him not to slay his son. He has passed God's test of devotion, and a ram is offered in place of Isaac. Abraham then calls the place Adonai-yireh, because "the Lord has been seen" (Genesis 22: 1–14).

For philosophers and religious commentators, the test of Abraham has provided a stage, similar to the trial of Job, for contemplating good and evil. Kierkegaard emphasized Abraham's anguish and suffering in preserving his faith. For him, "only one who draws the knife gets Isaac" (Kierkegaard, 2006: 27). The willingness to fulfill the command (or rather, as phrased in Hebrew, the request) to sacrifice Isaac becomes, then, for Kierkegaard, a rekindling of faith in the good God, while for Kant it represents an act of evil to be rebelled against.

In Jewish thought, the perception of the story has commonly emphasized Abraham's devotion to God, to the extent of sacrificing the embodiment of his future. It has been considered a paradigm of the readiness to give up life in order to sanctify the divine name, but also as punishment for Abraham having sent Ishmael into the wilderness.

Some biblical scholars have read the account as a prohibition against child sacrifice, such as mentioned for instance in Jeremiah (7: 31; see also Exodus 22: 28–29; 2 Kings 3: 27, 16: 3, 21: 6), with the angel intervening to prevent Abraham's act of filicide. The narrative has also served as a model for anti-Semitic blood libels accusing Jews of ritual murder of non-Jewish children.

Already some early legends told the story that Abraham in fact did slay and then burned Isaac. The lad "was reduced to ashes," only to be revived by God's "life-giving dew" (Spiegel, 1993: 37). Thus, Isaac served as a "symbol for the archetypal experience of death and rebirth" (Dreifuss, 1971: 72).

The symbolic death of Isaac has been understood as transformative, confirming him in his role as chosen to carry out God's promise to Abraham, to be the one in whom the seed shall be called (cf. Abramovitch, 1994: 123; Genesis 21: 12). This seed, says St. Augustine, while called in Isaac, is gathered together in Christ by the call of grace. The sacrifice of Isaac becomes the precursor of Christ; like Jesus carried His cross, Isaac himself carried the wood to the place of sacrifice, and like the ram was offered in place of Isaac, so Jesus would die on the cross for humankind.

The name of the sacrificial child is not mentioned in the Quran. Consequently, Muslim scholars have disagreed whether it concerns Ishmael or Isaac. Since it is said that Abraham offered up his only son, scholars have argued this could only mean Ishmael, the elder of the two. The importance ascribed to the sacrifice is reflected in Eid-ul-Adha, the Feast and Festival of Sacrifice, celebrated immediately after the Hajj, the annual pilgrimage to Mecca.

Psychological Aspects

The akedah offers a kaleidoscope of psychological facets and interpretations. Abraham, Urvater of the monotheistic religions, stands in the center, between the Father-God, who now requires of him the sacrifice of his repeatedly promised seed, and the late-born son, predestined to fulfill the covenant and conceive the earthly offspring. The offering of a child to appease the gods is a common theme in myth and legend in many traditions.

Psychological interpretations naturally tend to look at the father-son relation. One aspect of this is submission – both Abraham's and Isaac's – to the command of the father. It entails the recognition of God's supremacy, interpreted on the psychological level as reflecting weakness in relation to authority. Yet, the archetypal scheme seems more important than personal character, since Abraham already had shown himself quite capable of challenging God, as when he argues and negotiates with God to spare the sinners with the righteous in Sodom (Genesis 18: 23–33).

Father's Reluctance Against His Son

In a sense, the akedah is a reversal of and predecessor to the Oedipus complex. A complex would not have been born in Oedipus's name if it were not for his father Laius, who frightened by the oracle's prophesy of his son's patricide and mother-incest exposed Oedipus to certain death. Only the shepherd's compassion saved Oedipus the child from certain death by unprotected and defenceless exposure to archetypal forces. Likewise, Acrisius, fearing the prophesy that his grandson would kill him, locked his daughter Danae and grandson Perseus in a chest and threw them into the river to an unsure fate, though they were saved by the good fisherman. (Later, Perseus saved Andromeda, who was offered by her father, the king, to appease the sea monster Cetus.) The Laius complex, the father's fear of the son, who eventually will destroy and replace him, precedes the son's slaying of the father.

Castration anxiety, in which the child fears the father's anger because of its choice of the mother as love object, is an innate aspect of the Oedipus complex. Theodor Reik refers to *Das Incestmotiv* by Otto Rank, in which he "conceived of Isaac's sacrifice, prevented only at the last moment, as a threat to castrate Abraham's son" (Reik, 1961: 66). The threatened castration and near-sacrifice of the son can be taken to mean that the genitality and vitality of the ego may feel threatened by new instinctual and archetypal elements that arise from the unconscious. Consequently, the ego responds like a vulnerable father who undermines his son's rise to masculinity.

The libido and potency of the son may threaten many a father, and the youthful spirit of the revolting son may pose a challenge to his authority. Jung relates *father-and-son* not only to an interpersonal dynamic, but also to the intrapsychic polarity of *discipline and instinct* (Jung, 1956, CW 5, par. 396). In the individual psyche, the father may represent adherence to the collective consciousness of established norms, rules and principles, whereas the son represents an upcoming, purposeful complex, which by its mere newness may pose a threat, even in the case when, as with Isaac, he collaborates in the sacrifice. In the edifying process of acculturation, aspects of the child's nature are slain.

Rite of Initiation

The sacrifice of Isaac (whose name means *he laughed*, Genesis 21: 6) has been looked upon as a puberty rite of initiation. The characteristics of the divine and innocent child, who has thrived in the delightful embrace of the Great Mother, are shed in juvenile rites-de-passage. In the process of becoming an adult, the child is now exposed to the requirements and principles of the spiritual father. Isaac's age at the time of the sacrifice is unclear; while

phenomenologically he appears to be a child, legends have given his age as twenty-five or thirty-seven. That is, Isaac moves from childhood to maturity, from innocence to consciousness. In some legends Satan tries to prevent Abraham from carrying out the sacrifice, thereby introducing conscious doubt into the otherwise passive submission. Satan is thus found in his role as adversary, instigating toward consciousness.

Rites of initiation require the sharpening of the maturing ego's strengths by exposure to what is experienced as a very real threat to body and soul. The ego is exposed to hardships and extreme conditions, such as sleeplessness and infliction of physical pain. The ego is required to hold out against its own destruction, in order to be rendered adequate to carry the Self or a transcendent principle into living, embodied reality. The danger may entail, as in the case of Isaac, being burned by fire, nature's very essential transformative energy, whether representing Logos and consciousness, Eros and relationship, or Thanatos and destruction (Shalit, 2004a, 5f.) The evolving ego must be able both to endure and revolt against the father's authority, in order to carry, continue and regenerate the collective spirit, whether social, religious or otherwise.

Sacrifice and Transformation

The readiness to sacrifice one's offspring for a higher cause has been prevalent during all times, as the death of the young in innumerable wars testifies. In devotion of a principle, whether transcendent, ideological or intrapsychic, the individual's embodied identity may be sacrificed. Many wars for one's devoted country, religion or ideology, attest to the sacrifice of one's offspring, even if reluctant and painful.

In the sacrifice of Isaac, Abraham succumbs to the command of God to sacrifice the human flesh and ego for divinity and a greater Self. As a prefiguration of Christ, God's test of Abraham "is to determine whether Abraham was willing to share Yahweh's later ordeal of sacrificing his son, Christ. Abraham is asked to participate in the tragic drama of divine transformation" (Edinger, 1984: 98).

Processes of psychological transformation and individuation entail the temporary defeat, or sacrifice, of the ego. Jung writes, "Quite apart from the compassion [Abraham] felt for his child, would not a father in such a position feel himself as the victim, and feel that he was plunging the knife into his own breast?" He continues, "The self is the sacrificer, and I am the sacrificed gift, the human sacrifice," whereby the self can be integrated or humanized, and pass "from unconsciousness into consciousness" (Jung, 1969, *CW* 11, par. 397ff.). With the sacrifice of Isaac, God nearly destroys his own creation (Schärf-Kluger, 1967: 154). Destruction is psychologically crucial in processes of transformation and creativity, and the process of individuation requires sacrifice and near-destruction, or representative, symbolic sacrifice, as in the akedah. However, the individual ego may, likewise, collaborate with an ideology, a mass or a leader claiming God-like proportions, sacrificing mature and critical consciousness.

Psychization

Jung coined the term *psychization* for the process whereby an instinct or a sensory experience is transferred into the psyche and consciousness. The instinctual *reflex* becomes the *reflection* of the psyche, just like soul and psyche constellate by the capacity to reflect. This is the process whereby the actual deed can be psychically represented, and experience becomes consciously *experienced* experience (Shalit, 2004b). The infant comes to *psychically* experience for instance touch and pain to which it is exposed. The concrete deed or physical sensation, such as pain, become represented and imagined in the psyche. This lies at the core of symbol-formation and acculturation, and of the representative dimension of art and literature.

Psychization expands the human sphere, says Neumann, by the withdrawal of "Gods, demons, heaven and hell," in their capacity as psychic forces, "from the objective world," and their incorporation in the human sphere (Neumann, 1970: 338f.).

The binding of Isaac signifies a cultural transition, whereby the sacrifice of the first-born was replaced by animal sacrifice. Whereas there is little or no archeological evidence of the practice of filicide, the binding of Isaac provides a striking archetypal image of the transition from literalness to symbolic representation, from actual deed to image-formation, i.e., of soul-making, in the absence of which the ego is literalized and "trapped in 'reality'" (Hillman, 1992: 51). By substituting the sacrificial animal for the actual son, the akedah represents the separation of meaning from act. The near-sacrifice thus represents the very essence of psychic processes – intrapsychically, interpersonally as well as culturally.

See also: ❂ Abraham and Isaac ❂ Akedah ❂ Augustine ❂ Bible ❂ Christ ❂ Evil ❂ Freud, Sigmund ❂ Hillman, James, and Alchemy ❂ Judaism and Psychology ❂ Kierkegaard, Søren ❂ Oedipus Complex ❂ Rank, Otto ❂ Ritual ❂ Sacrifice ❂ Scapegoat

Bibliography

Abramovitch, H. H. (1994). *The first father*. Lanham, MD: University Press of America.
Dreifuss, G. (1971). Isaac, the sacrificial lamb, *Journal of Analytical Psychology, 16*, 1.
Edinger, E. (1984). *The creation of consciousness: Jung's myth for modern man*. Toronto, Ontario, Canada: Inner City Books.
Hillman, J. (1992). *Re-visioning psychology*. New York: HarperPerennial.
Jung, C. G. (1956). *Symbols of transformation, CW* 5. London: Routledge & Kegan Paul.
Jung, C. G. (1969). *Transformation symbolism in the mass. Psychology and Religion, CW* 11. London: Routledge & Kegan Paul.
Kierkegaard, S. (2006). *Fear and trembling*. New York: Penguin.
Neumann, E. (1970). *The origins and history of consciousness*. Princeton, NJ: Princeton University Press.
Reik, T. (1961). *The temptation*. New York: George Braziller.
Shalit, E. (2004a). *The hero and his shadow: Psychopolitical aspects of myth and reality in Israel* (New revised edition). Lanham, MD: University Press of America.
Shalit, E. (2004b). Will fishes fly in Aquarius -or will they drown in the bucket? *San Francisco Jung Institute Library Journal, 23*(4), 7–33.
Shärf-Kluger, R. (1967). *Satan in the old testament*. Evanston, IL: Northwestern University Press.
Spiegel, S. (1993). *The last trial: On the legends and lore of the command to Abraham to offer Isaac as a sacrifice*. Woodstock, VT: Jewish Lights Publishing.

Sai Baba

Fredrica R. Halligan

Personal History

Sri Sathya Sai Baba is a holy man who was born in the tiny hamlet of Puttaparthi in south central India on November 23, 1926. At age thirteen he declared his spiritual purpose and commenced a ministry that today provides spiritual nourishment for millions of devotees worldwide. Sai Baba is a teacher, healer, and miracle worker. He values all religions and is trans-traditional in outlook. His influence has expanded so that today his organization provides free education and medical care and clean water to countless poor Indians. Similar projects are organized in other countries because Sai Baba's call is to universal love and service. He teaches: "The best way to love God is to love all and serve all."

To his devotees Sai Baba is an *Avatar,* and he is believed to be the second of three Divine Incarnations that all carry the name Sai Baba. The first holy man who was known as Sai Baba lived in the nineteenth and early twentieth century in a mosque in the town of Shirdi, India. Although his parents were Hindu, he was raised by a Moslem holy man, after his parents went off to the forest to become ascetics (*sanyases*). That first Sai Baba was a teacher and healer who used ashes from a fire in the mosque for healing purposes. Shirdi Sai Baba, as he is called today, fostered inter-religious understanding. For example, he taught Hindus about Allah and Moslems about Rama and Krishna. At the time of his death, both Hindus and Moslems claimed him. Shortly before he died in 1918, he confided to a close devotee that he would return in 8 years.

In 1926, a child was born who carried the name of Sathya Raju. There are many stories about miraculous events that attended his conception and birth and, as a young boy, Sathya was known to be very spiritual and loving. His playmates called him *Guru* (meaning "teacher") and he was known for his generosity both to his friends and to wandering beggars. Whenever he witnessed suffering, he provided help in some way.

Sathya's parents were sometimes distressed by his unusual behavior, especially when he quit school at the age of 13 and announced that his devotees were waiting for him. "Who are you?" his perplexed father asked. Sathya replied, "I am Sai Baba," and picking up a handful of jasmine flowers, he threw them on the ground. The flowers are said to have formed themselves into letter shapes that spelled out the name: Sai Baba.

Thenceforth he has been known as Sathya Sai Baba. His miracles are numerous. Among the most frequent and well-documented miracles are materializations. Sai Baba waves his hand and various material objects appear, apparently out of thin air. He sometimes makes jewelry – rings or lockets – or icons for devotees. These religious objects include Hindu images such as Krishna, or Christian icons such as the crucifix. Frequently he materializes *vibhuti,* which is a sacred ash used for healing. In providing this healing ash, he echoes and goes beyond the sacred ash that Shirdi Sai Baba used for similar purposes.

Sai Baba now lives in a large *ashram* in the town of Puttaparthi, where he has also built a hospital and a university, both of which serve the people free of charge. His *ashram* is called *Prashanti Nilayam,* (the Abode of Highest Peace.) At the time of major feast days, hundreds of thousands of devotees flock into the town, to view the holy man (*darshan*) and to receive the spiritual energy of his blessings. Sai Baba has told devotees that he is preparing to "leave this body" at age 92, and he has predicted that the third Sai Baba re-incarnation will occur 8 years later, at which time he will carry the name of Prema Sai Baba (*Prema* means love, and *Sathya* means Truth).

Teachings

In addition to his charitable work, materializations and occasional miraculous healings, Sathya Sai Baba teaches his devotees through public discourses that he gives frequently at his *ashram.* These teachings have been gathered into books, which now comprise over 30 volumes in the *Sathya Sai Speaks* series. There is also a website where his message is articulated. For example, this writing from 1968 describes Sathya Sai Baba's self definition of purpose:

➤ I have come to light the lamp of Love in your hearts, to see that it shines day by day with added luster. I have not come on behalf of any exclusive religion. I have not come on a mission of publicity for a sect or creed, nor have I come to collect followers for a doctrine. I have no plan to attract disciples or devotees into my fold or any fold. I have come to tell you of this unitary faith, this spiritual principle, this path of Love, this virtue of Love, this duty of Love, this obligation of Love (Sathya Sai Baba, 7/4/68, cited on www.sathyasai.org).

Despite his stated lack of specific plans to attract followers, there are over 30 million devotees worldwide who follow the teachings of Sai Baba and believe him to be an *Avatar,* that is, an Incarnation of God on earth. When asked directly whether he is God, Sai Baba will frequently respond, "Yes, and so are you!" A central component of his teaching is that the Divine is omnipresent; Divinity resides in every person and our primary duty in life is to discover that indwelling divine life (*Atman*). In 1997, he spoke to a large group of devotees:

➤ *Embodiments of Love!* Only that person can be said to lead a full human existence whose heart is filled with compassion, whose speech is adorned by Truth and whose body is dedicated to the service of others. Fullness in life is marked by harmony of thought, word and deed.... In every human being Divinity is present in subtle form. But man is deluded.... The innumerable waves on the vast ocean contain the same water as the ocean regardless of their forms. Likewise, although human beings have myriads of names and forms, each is a wave on the ocean of

Sath-Chith-Aananda (Being-Awareness-Bliss). Every human being is invested with immortality. He is the embodiment of love. Unfortunately he fails to share this love with others in society. The root cause of this condition is the fact that man is consumed by selfishness and self-interest. . . . Only when this self-interest is eradicated man will be able to manifest his inner divinity (Sai Baba, 1997: 191f).

Like Jesus, Sai Baba frequently teaches in parables, and these stories are often spoken in modern idiom. Airplanes, for example, become the subject to teach about the presence of an unseen God (the pilot); and electrical energy is used to teach about the inner, unseen current that activates a multiple of appliances, even as God motivates and activates humans. Sometimes Sai Baba teaches from the wisdom on the *Vedas,* the *Bhagavad Gita,* or other ancient Indian scriptures; at other times he speaks quite directly to the needs and problems of twentieth and twenty first century global society. In 1993, for example, he spoke about a problem that is increasingly newsworthy in the twenty first century:

▶ My advice to office-goers and students is that it is good for them to commute by cycle at least 5 or 6 km a day. This cycling exercise is very useful, not only for maintaining health, but also for reducing the expenditure on automobiles . . . . Moreover it serves to reduce atmospheric pollution caused by harmful fumes from automobiles. The carbon dioxide smoke from motor vehicles and factories is already polluting the air in cities and is affecting the ozone layer above the earth. The primary task is to purify the environment, which is affected by pollution of air, water, and food. All the five elements [earth, water, air, fire, and ether] are affected by pollution. People should, therefore, try to reduce the use of automobiles and control the emission of harmful industrial effluents . . . . Trees play a vital role in helping mankind to receive oxygen from the atmosphere while they absorb the carbon dioxide exhaled by human beings. Hence the ancients favored the growing of trees to control atmospheric pollution. But nowadays trees are cut down indiscriminately and pollution is on the increase (Sai Baba, 1993: 35f).

Like Gandhi, Sai Baba emphasizes the importance of the fivefold values: Truth, Love, Peace, Non-violence, and Righteous living (*Sathya, Prema, Shanti, Ahimsa,* and *Dharma.*) Sai Baba treasures the *Bhagavad Gita* and he frequently teaches his devotees the meaning of the metaphors of that archetypal story of the war between good and evil. For example, on the battlefield in the *Gita* Krishna says:

▶ The point, old friend – and this is very important – is to do your duty, but do it without any attachment to it or desire for its fruits. Keep your mind always on the Divine (*Atma,* the Self). Make it as automatic as your breath or heartbeat. This is the way to reach the supreme goal, which is to merge into God (*Gita* 3:19. Hawley, 2001: 32).

Sai Baba teaches that the battlefield is our inner life. Our spiritual aim should be to surrender to the Divine, to be a willing instrument of God's Will, and to leave the results of that action in God's hands. This relatively simple statement is the essence of life's goal; it is a spiritual work worthy of conscious effort (*sadhana*). Sai Baba provides many teachings that support this goal. To keep focused on the Divine, he teaches that the easiest method in this era is, with every breath, to repeat the name of God (*namasmarana,* remembering God through any name that has personal meaning).

Sai Baba's teachings also emphasize the importance of purity of heart, which entails letting go of desires and attachments. The union of opposites involves transcending the natural tendency to have likes and dislikes, attachments, and aversions. Rather, he teaches, one should strive to care equally for friend and foe; to behave calmly whether one receives praise or criticism; to be indifferent to honor and ignominy. Equanimity is fostered when one is able to accept suffering as a blessing in disguise, and to accept adulation with humility.

Psychotherapy with Devotees

In working psychologically with devotees of Sai Baba, or with others who adhere to similar Eastern traditions, it is important to understand and accept their worldview. While anger, jealousy, fear, pride, lust etc. are natural psychological states, the spiritual aim in this Eastern tradition is to transcend those states. World – as we know it – is illusory (*maya*). The only permanent Reality is the Divine, and that permeates everyone and everything. Every situation is a scene in the Divine play (*leela*). Psychologically, this attitude enables devotees to take life a little more lightly and to cope with its vicissitudes a little more gracefully.

Self-Realization

In summary, to the devotee of Sri Sathya Sai Baba, the aim of life is to surrender to God, to be the Instrument of Divine Will, to fight the various battles of life, but to leave the outcome in God's hands. In order to accomplish that aim, the primary purpose of life is to discover the Godlife (*Atman*) within oneself and to honor that same Godlife in others – all others. Self-realization means to know that identity and unity experientially. Sai Baba promises that such Self-realization results in a state of bliss. In essence, he teaches, we are being, awareness and bliss (*sath-chith-ananda*), i.e., when we are fully aware of the Divine within each of us and acting from that awareness, we shall receive bliss as a natural occurrence. Thus when we aspire for world unity and work toward that end, we work in consort with the Divine Will. We merge with the Divine One.

See also: ⊛ Atman ⊛ Avatar ⊛ Bhagavad Gita ⊛ Healing ⊛ Hinduism ⊛ Incarnation ⊛ Psychotherapy and Religion

Bibliography

Hawley, J. (2001). *The Bhagavad Gita: A walkthrough for Westerners.* Novato, CA: New World Library.

Sai Baba. (1993). *Sathya Sai Speaks* (Vol. 26), Prashanti Nilayam, India: Sri Sathya Sai Books & Publications Trust.

Sai Baba. (1997). *Sathya Sai Speaks* (Vol. 30), Prashanti Nilayam, India: Sri Sathya Sai Books & Publications Trust.

Samsara and Nirvana

Frank Scalambrino

The first part of this article discusses the philosophical and religious aspects of nirvana and samsara, and the second part approaches a pyschological articulation. The second part is, of course, not considered exhaustive. In approaching nirvana and samsara, here, we will discuss the related notions of suffering, liberation, and enlightment. Whereas the second part of this article indicates historically related psychological readings of nirvana and samsara, the first part approaches nirvana and samsara hermeneutically, as it were, moving through a number of possible understandings in order to situate our perspective of nirvana and samsara.

We approach nirvana and samsara, here, by discussing suffering, liberation, and enlightenment. Approaching nirvana and samsara hermeneutically, as it were, we will move through a number of possible understandings in order to situate our perspective of nirvana and samsara.

Etymologically speaking, "Nirvana," of Sanskrit origin, is considered a Vedantic notion perhaps best characterized as the culmination of a path of knowledge or wisdom – the end(s) of knowledge or wisdom – like a river leading into an ocean. It is literally rendered as cessation or extinguishing and often coupled with the image of an extinguishing flame. If we were to think of the friction of the phenomenal flow of existence as igniting a flame, then we might think of nirvana as the extinguishing of that flame which in multiple ways distorts a vision of the phenomenal flow of existence.

"Samsara," also of Sanskrit origin refers to a flowing, a wandering, an eternal cycle of (the wheel of) birth and rebirth. In this way, we might think of Samsara as the phenomenal flow of existence which, of its own accord, "ignited," breeds an illusory view of itself. The notion of samsara is operative in both Vedic and Vedantic discourses. However, samsara is often considered a Vedantic notion discussed in relation to *moksha*, also of Sanskrit origin, suggesting liberation or release from that which is referred to as samsara.

Ethically speaking, nirvana and samsara may be explicated by examining their relation to suffering. Within traditional Buddhism we find the "Four Noble Truths" which relate to suffering. First, the truth of suffering (*dukkha*), which is the awareness of suffering, is also thought to be the awareness of samsara. Second, the truth of the origin of suffering refers to an awareness of desire and attachment in relation to suffering. Third, the truth of the cessation of suffering, which is an awareness of the cessation of suffering, is also thought to be an awareness of nirvana. Fourth, the truth of the path to the cessation of suffering refers to the habits and practices involved in maintaining an awareness of the cessation of suffering.

Ontologically speaking, samsara may be thought of as a physical or phenomenal existence or world. In time, then, samsara can be thought similar to a literal reading of Socrates' story about birth and rebirth in Plato's *Phaedo.* Namely, the physical world in which life resides can be thought of as a place into which a person is born and back into which a person is reborn after death. Given this reading, depending upon how you live your life you may or may not be "(re)born" into this place. If you are not "(re)born" into this place, then you reside in a different place. This different place, in so far as it is not the physical or phenomenal world, is of course only a "place" nominally. Such a reading, perhaps over-simplistically, gets paraphrased in the dichotomy life and afterlife. Approaching Samsara by way of a thinking paraphrased by life and afterlife, samsara appears sequentially related to nirvana. It is in this way that nirvana sometimes gets associated with "Heaven" understood as an afterlife event, as if one is transported to a different "place."

To sum, at this point in our possible ontological understanding of samsara and nirvana, consider the following analogy. Let us assume at this point that an understanding of samsara as a physical or phenomenal existence is like looking at a stream. Regardless of whether the stream is muddy, when we first look at a stream we might find our attention focused solely on one aspect of the stream. Perhaps we even understand that part of the stream on which we are focused to be the stream itself (see also "the five aggregates" for a different approach to samsara as an assemblage).

Departing from the above understanding of samsara, we can temporally resituate the dichotomy of samsara and nirvana. In other words, we need not think of nirvana as literally an event at the end of life or a place after life. Rather, we may think of samsara and nirvana as contemporaneous. This is perhaps what the Buddhist monk Dogen (1200–1253) invoked stating, "Most people think time is passing and do not realize that there is an aspect that is not passing" (Dogen, 1975: 70). In so far as it is in and by the world of phenomena that we are able to tell time, to think samsara and nirvana as contemporaneous is to privilege a thinking conditioned by the phenomenal world, a thinking conditioned by samsara. Returning to our analogy, this may be like focusing our attention on both the ground of the stream and the surface, and understanding these aspects to be the stream itself.

Now, ready for a different situation, recognizing what we might refer to as the non-presence and the non-being of nirvana, we can view our current understanding of samsara and nirvana as a moment in the phenomenal flowing, a moment in that which is sometimes referred to as "phenomenal flowing" and sometimes referred to as "life." This non-presence and non-being of nirvana is standardly discussed with terms such as "emptiness" and "nothing." As with nirvana, these terms are difficult to grasp clearly and distinctly. Yet, by following the movement toward that to which these terms are supposed to refer, we may have a clearer vision of what is being discussed as the non-presence and non-being of nirvana.

Like the Heraclitean maxim in regard to not being able to step in the same river twice, returning to our analogy, an insight regarding the identity of the stream is itself a moment in the flowing. It is as if in our seeking to identify the ontology of the stream, we discovered our seeking to be an aspect of the stream or (privileging time) a moment in the flowing. Analogously, we see the ground and the surface of the stream being aware what we see is both the stream and not the stream. Here, up against a threshold of ineffability, we might say there is an experience of the stream but the stream is "more than" (or "less than") this experience of it. Being as it is, we cannot experience or see another aspect or moment of the stream. However, synthesizing the experience of the stream with an awareness of the experience's limits allows for a different awareness. Similar to remembering (above) the "place" of nirvana that is not a place, looking at the stream, seeing that which we are seeing, we "see" what we are not seeing.

Though it is a misnomer to speak as if we can shift our perspective to view, as it would be, from this no place or by this not seeing, perhaps we may at least speak of a new awareness. This awareness, as it relates to the phenomenal world from the perspective of no place, "sees" that which was our point of departure, namely recognition of and belief in the phenomenal world, differently. Such a situation, blossoming out of and intimately involved in non-attachment to the "phenomenal world," may be thought of as an understanding of nirvana and samsara which privileges nirvana. Likewise, given this way of speaking, the understanding with which we began our ontological speaking above may be thought of as an understanding of nirvana and samsara which privileged samsara. An understanding of nirvana and samsara which does not privilege samsara is often described with words such as liberation, freedom, or enlightenment.

Heuristically we may speak of a perspectivism or a contextualism in our attempt to gain an awareness of samsara and nirvana. In other words, depending upon the moment or aspect of exposure, signs may tend toward different interpretations. A striking example, the apparent contradiction within the Mahayana Buddhist *Diamond Sutra*, compare "Save all sentient beings" with the subsequent statement, "There are no sentient beings to be saved" (Soeng, 2000: 80). This Mahayana Buddhist attempt to speak ontologically about nirvana and samsara reveals the importance of the approach and the ineffability in play. The desire to speak ontologically about nirvana and samsara and approaches to such a speaking are each aspects of what we would speak were we able. Hence, beyond a possibly true propositional account, the above attempt to speak ontologically about nirvana and samsara calls for a relationality which allows for an awareness. Though perhaps an ineffable awareness, using the language of perspectivism or constructivism may aid in communicating notions of samsara and nirvana.

Historically speaking, understandings of nirvana help differentiate a number of practices known as Eastern Religions. The textual history from which discussions of samsara and nirvana come to us appears to have originated in India. Tracing the trajectory of an awareness of what we are referring to as samsara and nirvana geographically from India across Asia to Japan and America, from the terrain of Hinduism to Buddhism through the "three vehicles" of Mahayana, Hinayana (a.k.a. Theravada), and Vajrayana (a.k.a. Tantric Buddhism), and textually from the *Bhagavad Gita* (ca. 3000 BC) to the *Upanishads*, we trace a movement of Vedic origin into a Vedantic dimension. Whereas a Vedic dimension is said to include knowledge and wisdom, the Vedantic dimension refers to the end(s) of knowledge and wisdom. Further, in this way we see some affinity between the figures of Buddha and Jesus as they may be seen to relate to the sacred texts of Hinduism and Judaism respectively.

A distinction is often made between those adhering to an understanding of gradual and those adhering to an understanding of instant enlightenment. (Discussion of instant enlightenment derives in part from the *Platform Sutra*.) The difference at work in this distinction characterizes the path to nirvana as a timely and gradual process, which may be thought to encompass a number of life times, on the one hand. On the other hand, as can be seen in the discussion of time above, the prospect of instant enlightenment is often supported by notions associating time with samsara and pointing to the timelessness of nirvana. Whether privileging gradual or instant enlightenment, situating the ineffability of nirvana serves as a point of departure in accounting for the possibility of liberation and enlightenment. Further, in so far as accounts which distinguish between gradual and instant enlightenment hold such liberation as a goal, the privileged relating to the ineffable determines practices and paths taken up toward this goal.

It is in classifying practices in regard to the concerns which helped formulate them that the Zen practices of *Koan* and *Zazen* resonate with other Buddhist practices and notions, even if the proper practice of Zen is ultimately to not be attached to these notions. For example, a concern for liberation, reminiscent of the "Four Noble Truths," seems operative in discussions regarding samsara and nirvana. *The Tibetan Book of the Dead: The Great Liberation through hearing in the Bardo* in its full title suggests a way of speaking from one Bardo to another, as it were, so as to help liberate the inhabitants of a "lower" Bardo. Controversy, then, regarding the inclusion of Zen as a Buddhism does not set Zen, or the above excerpt from the *Diamond Sutra*, apart from these concerns or discussions regarding liberation, samsara, and nirvana. Rather, the controversy involves classifying "traditional" Buddhism with the notion of gradual enlightenment and Zen with the notion of instant enlightenment.

Psychologically speaking, theorists disagree concerning the psychological value of worldviews privileging samsara and nirvana. Striking examples of standard psychological interpretations consider the impact of an individual's awareness of samsara and nirvana in relation to life functioning and notions of self. Looking at Freud, Jung, and Lacan serves to frame a discussion of psychological interpretations and aspects of samsara and nirvana. With these psychological interpretations we commonly find charges of "nihilism" levied by theorists, these charges seemingly serve as a critique for both proponents and opponents alike. Texts such as Sangharakshita's *Survey of Buddhism*, David-Neel's *Buddhism*, and Droit's *The Cult of Nothingness* all point to a correlation between notions of nirvana and death or nirvana and nothingness. After positing a duality, proponents of one side of the binary opposition may levy charges of nihilism against proponents of the other side for an attachment to or belief in "nothing."

Sigmund Freud (1856–1939) employed the term "nirvana principle" in discussing what he referred to as "the Death Instinct." The following quotes support a Freudian psychoanalytic reading of any striving for nirvana as the manifestation of the body's desire to cease its own processes of maintaining the status of "living." Since, in Darwinian fashion, life for Freud emerges from the non-living and struggles to survive, in *Beyond the Pleasure Principle* Freud speculated an "inertia" tending, then, toward non-living. Further, Freud suggested, "everything living dies for *internal* reasons" (Freud's emphasis). (Freud, 1955: 38) Freud unfolds this interiority from which death derives in *Instincts and Vicissitudes (Triebe und Triebschicksale)*, "an 'instinct' appears to us as a concept on the frontier between the mental and the somatic, as the psychical representative of the stimuli originating from within the organism and reaching the mind" (Freud, 1957: 121–122).

What is more,

> by the source of an instinct is meant the somatic process which occurs in an organ or part of the body and whose stimulus is represented in mental life by an instinct. We do not know whether this process is invariably of a chemical nature or whether it may also correspond to the release of other, e.g. mechanical, forces. . . . Although instincts are wholly determined by their origin in a somatic source, in mental life we know them only by their aims (Freud, 1957: 123).

The next two quotes appear later in Freud's writings than the previous two. Further, in the following two quotes Freud speaks directly to suffering and the "nirvana principle."

▶ the derivation of the super-ego ... from the Oedipus Complex ... brings it [the super-ego] into relation with the phylogenetic acquisitions of the id and makes it a reincarnation (*Reinkarnation*) of former ego-structures which have left their precipitates behind in the id. ... In the end we come to see that we are dealing with what may be called a 'moral' factor, a sense of guilt, which ... refuses to give up the punishment of suffering. ... What is now holding sway in the super-ego is, as it were, a pure culture of the death instinct, and it often enough succeeds in driving the ego into death ... the more a man controls his aggressiveness, the more intense becomes his ideal's inclination to aggressiveness against his ego (Freud, 1961: 48–55).

Finally, in his *Economic Problem of Masochism* Freud suggested, "the nirvana principle expresses the tendency of the death instinct" (Freud, 1961: 160). The aim of the "death instincts" is to "conduct the restlessness of life into the stability of the inorganic state, and it would have the function of giving warnings against the demands of the life instincts" (Freud, 1961: 160).

Freud's use of the word "reincarnation" stands as a pivotal point in the interpretation of the Freudian psychoanalytic consideration of samsara and nirvana. On the one hand, we may interpret Freudian psychoanalysis as concerned with the cessation of suffering, and the death instinct with its seemingly divertible, and therefore unnecessary, velocity toward death as excessive and unadvisable. On the other hand, from a less egocentric, and perhaps more instinct-centric view, Freud's highlighting of the repetition of ego structures across organisms, from out of one body and into another body as it were, as a "re(-)incarnation" in conjunction with the association between ego structures and suffering seems open to an interpretation of the cessation of the repetition as the liberation of the ego structure from the wheel of birth and rebirth, liberation from samsara. Such a reading of Freud seems to be one less perpetuated.

With the subversion of the subject as a point of departure, Jacques Lacan (1901–1981) may be read as situated in this space which resonates with samsara and nirvana. Explicitly stating his aversion to a reductive reading rendering Freudian psychoanalysis "biological," Lacan suggests "the notion of the death instinct involves a basic irony ... Hence the congruence of the contrasting terms of the death instinct with the phenomena of repetition, ... would not cause difficulty were it simply a question of a biological notion" (Lacan, 2006: 260–261). Further, for Lacan, "It is not, in fact, a perversion of instinct, but rather a desperate affirmation of life that is the purest form we can find of the death instinct"(Lacan, 2006: 263). The link between the death instinct and the subject which allows for Lacan's non-biological appropriation of Freud's notion is language.

Interrogating Freud's death instinct in *The Ethics of Psychoanalysis*, Lacan asks, "How can man ... have access to knowledge of the death instinct?" Lacan states, "The answer is ... It is in the signifier and insofar as the subject articulates a signifying chain that he comes up against the fact that he may disappear from the chain of what he is" (Lacan, 1992: 295). Ultimately, with Lacan's terminology we can describe samsara and nirvana in different ways. On the one hand, if we consider nirvana as somehow a function of the symbolic order, then we might think of samsara as a function of the imaginary order. On the other hand, if we think of samsara as an identification with the imaginary other or a symbolic Other, we might think of nirvana along lines of a Lacanian real.

In *The Four Fundamental Concepts of Psychoanalysis*, Lacan states, "What I, Lacan, following the traces of the Freudian excavation, am telling you is that the subject as such is uncertain because he is always divided by the effects of language" (Lacan, 1981: 188.) As put by Raul Moncayo in "The Finger Pointing at the Moon: Zen Practice and the Practice of Lacanian Psychoanalysis," from *Psychoanalysis and Buddhism* "Both [the Buddhist and the Lacanian formula] could be said to converge on the Zen formula that 'true self is no-self' or the Lacanian-informed formula that 'true subject is no ego'" (Moncayo, 2003: 349).

Associating his practices with those of the instant awaking of Zen, Lacan specifically speaks of Zen. In the "Overture" of his *Seminar One: Freud's Papers on Technique*, he states, "The master breaks the silence with anything – a sarcastic remark, with a kick-start. That is how a Buddhist master conducts his search for meaning, according to the technique of zen." Again in *The Function and Field of Speech and Language in Psychoanalysis*, regarding (scansion) "short sessions," sessions strategically stopped short by the analyst, Lacan notes, "And I am not the only one to have remarked that it bears a certain resemblance to the technique known as Zen, which is applied to bring about the subject's revelation" (Lacan, 1991: 1). Lastly, in *The Direction of the Treatment and the Principles of Its Power*, "desire is borne by death" stands at the end of a series of words which also acknowledge the "everydayness of human suffering" (Lacan, 2006: 536).

Reporting what may be taken up as a point of departure for Analytic Psychology from Freudian Psychoanalysis, Carl Gustav Jung (1875–1961) in *Freud and Jung: Contrasts* declared, "I prefer to look at man in the light of what in him is healthy and sound, and to free the sick man from just that kind of psychology which colors every page Freud has written." (Jung, 1970: 335). For Jung, then, instincts are intimately connected with his notions of the archetypes, the collective unconscious, and psychological types. Though Jung's discussion of samsara and nirvana shares with Freud's a discussion of instincts, Jung's derivation of an understanding of samsara and nirvana differs from both Freud and Lacan.

According to Jung, "the question of instinct cannot be dealt with psychologically without considering the archetypes, because at bottom they determine one another" (Jung, 1978: 134). In a parallel construction, Jung, then unfolds his understanding of instincts and archetypes. On the one hand, "Instincts are typical modes of action, and wherever we meet with uniform and regularly recurring modes of action and reaction we are dealing with instinct, no matter whether it is associated with a conscious motive or not." (Jung, 1978: 135). On the other hand, "Archetypes are typical modes of apprehension, and wherever we meet with uniform and regularly recurring modes of apprehension we are dealing with an archetype, no matter whether its mythological character is recognized or not" (Jung, 1978: 137–138). Jung's conception, then, holds open the possibility of unconscious apprehension and a way of discussing the apprehension by way of archetypes. "Just as conscious apprehension gives our actions form and direction, so unconscious apprehension through the archetype determines the form and direction of instinct" (Jung, 1969: 137). Further, regarding the archetype in its relation to instinct Jung notes, "the yucca moth must carry within it an image, as it were, of the situation that 'triggers off' its instinct" (Jung, 1978: 137).

Speaking directly to Freud's equation of death and ego dissolution noted above, Jung writes:

> ▷ To us, consciousness is inconceivable without an ego . . . If there is no ego, there is nobody to be conscious of anything. . . . The Eastern mind, however, has no difficulty in conceiving of a consciousness without an ego. Consciousness is deemed capable of transcending its ego condition; indeed, in its 'higher forms, the ego disappears altogether. Such an ego-less mental condition can only be unconscious to us, for the simple reason that there would be nobody to witness it (Jung, 1969: 484).

In this way both Lacan and Jung provide readings which do not reduce instincts to the merely biological. However, Jung goes so far as to explicitly comment here despite the apparent darkness or obscurity of the subject. According to Jung,

> ▷ the higher forms of yoga . . . seek a mental condition in which the ego is practically dissolved . . . whereas what we [in the West] call the 'dark background of consciousness' is [in the East] understood to be a 'higher' consciousness. Thus our concept of the 'collective unconscious' would be the European equivalent of *buddhi*, the enlightened mind (Jung, 1969: 485).

Using his Introversion/Extraversion distinction Jung equates the practice of attaining this "higher consciousness" with introversion. Jung notes "Introversion is felt here [in the West] as something abnormal, morbid, or otherwise objectionable. Freud identifies it with autoerotic, 'narcissistic' attitude of mind. . . . In the East, however, our cherished extraversion is depreciated as illusory desirousness, as existence in the samsara" (Jung, 1969: 481).

To conclude, in the spirit of what we might read akin to the Koan, "Meet the Buddha, kill the Buddha," noting, "The Mind in which the irreconcilables – samsara and nirvana – are united is ultimately our mind" (Jung, 1969: 488–489). Jung sets out deconstructing binary oppositions on a diamond path, as it were, toward the collective unconscious. Jung suggests even the binary oppositions which "proclaim the dogmatic ground truths of Buddhism: 'suffering and non-existence, impermanence and non-self,' signifying that all existence is full of suffering, and that everything that clings to the ego is impermanent," are ultimately in error. Further according to Jung, "Not-being and not-being-ego deliver us from these errors" (Jung, 1969: 567).

With psychological interpretations of samsara and nirvana, we have seen a movement from nirvana as an indicator of a trajectory toward biological death to a rereading of the death instinct and the use of "not-being" to signify nirvana. With these different readings we find various valuations of suffering, liberation, life, and death. We might think it appropriate along with Jung, then, to consider two more binary oppositions, true and false, and life and death, in "error." Twisting Hamlet's soliloquy, I express such awareness: It is not to be or not to be, but to be not.

See also: ◎ Archetype ◎ Freud, Sigmund ◎ Hinduism ◎ Jung, Carl Gustav ◎ Koan ◎ Lacan, Jacques ◎ Zen

Bibliography

Anon. (1959). *Buddhist Scriptures* (E. Conze, Trans.). London: Penguin Classics.
Anon. (2004). *Bhagavad Gita* (E. Easwaran, Trans.). New York: Shambhala.
Anon. (2007). *The Upanishads* (E. Easwaran, Trans.). California: Nilgiri Press.
Bhikshu Sangharakshita. (1980). *A survey of Buddhism.* New York: Shambhala.
David-Neel, A. (1978). *Buddhism: Its doctrines and its methods.* New York: St. Martin's Press.
Dogen Z. (1975). Shobogenzo, Vol. 1 (K. Nishiyama & J. Stevens, Trans.) *A complete translation of Dogen Zenji's Shobogenzo,* (pp. 1–165). San Francisco, CA: Japan Publication Trading Company.
Droit, R.-P., Streight, D., & Vohnson, P. (2003). *The cult of nothingness: The philosophers and the Buddha.* Chapel Hill, NC: University of North Carolina Press.
Freud, S. (1955). *The complete psychological works of Sigmund Freud,* Vol. 2 (J. Strachey, Trans.). London: The Hogarth Press.
Freud, S. (1955). *The complete psychological works of Sigmund Freud,* Vol. 18 (J. Strachey, Trans.). London: The Hogarth Press.
Freud, S. (1957).*The complete psychological works of Sigmund Freud,* Vol. 14 (J. Strachey, Trans.). London: The Hogarth Press.
Freud, S. (1961). *The complete psychological works of Sigmund Freud,* Vol. 19 (J. Strachey, Trans.). London: The Hogarth Press.
Guru Rinpoche. (2000). *The Tibetan book of the dead* (F. Fremantle & C. Trungpa, Trans.). Boston, MA: Shambhala.
Jung, C. G. (1969). *The collected works of C.G. Jung,* Vol. 11 (R. F. C. Hull, Trans.). Princeton, NJ: Princeton University Press.
Jung, C. G. (1970). *The collected works of C.G. Jung,* Vol. 4 (R. F. C. Hull, Trans.). Princeton, NJ: Princeton University Press.
Jung, C. G. (1978). *The collected works of C.G. Jung,* Vol. 8 (R. F. C. Hull, Trans.). Princeton, NJ: Princeton University Press.
Lacan, J. (1981). From love to libido. In D. Porter (Trans.) J.-A. Miller (Ed.). *The seminar of Jacques Lacan, Book XI: The four fundamental concepts of psychoanalysis* (pp. 187–200). New York: W. W. Norton.
Lacan, J. (1991). Overture to the seminar. In J. Forrester (Trans.) J.-A. Miller (Ed.). *The seminar of Jacques Lacan, Book I: Freud's papers on technique 1953–1954* (pp. 1–3). New York: W. W. Norton.
Lacan, J. (1992). The demand for happiness and the promise of analysis. In D. Porter (Trans.) J.-A. Miller (Ed.). *The seminar of Jacques Lacan, Book VII: The ethics of psychoanalysis, 1959–1960* (pp. 291–301). New York: W. W. Norton.
Lacan, J. (2006). The direction of the treatment and the principles of its power. In B. Fink (Trans.). *Écrits: A selection* (pp. 489–542). New York: W. W. Norton.
Lacan, J. (2006). The function and field of speech and language in psychoanalysis. In B. Fink (Trans.). *Écrits: A selection* (pp. 197–268). New York: W. W. Norton.
Moncayo, R. (2003). The finger pointing at the moon: Zen practice and the practice of Lacanian psychoanalysis. In J. D. Safran (Ed.), *Psychoanalysis and Buddhism: An unfolding dialogue* (pp. 331–364). Boston, MA: Wisdom Publications.
Plato. (1997). *Phaedo, Plato complete works.* Indianapolis, IN: Hackett Publishing.
Soeng, M. (2000). *The diamond sutra: Transforming the way we perceive the world.* Boston, MA: Wisdom Publications.

Sangha

Paul Larson

In Buddhism the Sanskrit term "sangha" has two meanings. More generally, it refers to the entire community of all practitioners of Buddha dharma, both lay and monastic. It is also used specifically to refer to the monastic community, both monks and nuns. Contemporary Buddhists often refer to themselves not only as Buddhist but as dharma practitioners. This emphasizes the point that they are active in meditation, chanting, or some other spiritual practice or discipline. This is in contrast with the Western monotheisms were the term "believers" emphasizes the cognitive component, what doctrines one holds or affirms.

The sangha is one of the three gems, the other being the dharma and the Buddha. Collectively they are known as the "triple gem." To become a Buddhist one would take refuge in the triple gem. The concept of taking refuge refers to the first of the Four Noble Truths of Buddhism, the pervasiveness of human suffering. As one experiences the reality of suffering one seeks refuge from not only the suffering itself, but with knowledge of the cause of suffering, attachment, one seeks the way out by practicing the methods that lead to enlightenment.

See also: ❂ Buddhism

Bibliography

Behkert, H., & Gombrich, R. (Eds.). (1984). *The world of Buddhism.* London: Thames & Hudson.
Robinson, R. H., & Johnson, W. L. (1997). *The Buddhist religion* (4th ed.). Belmont, CA: Wadsworth Publishing.

Santería

Sana Loue

Origins

Santería originated in Africa and was brought to Cuba by slaves from western Africa, many of whom were from Yoruba-speaking areas that are now part of Nigeria and

Benin. The religion was brought to the United States during the 1940s by immigrants from Cuba. It has been estimated that approximately 10 million individuals in the Americas are adherents to the Afro-Cuban religion Santería; somewhere between half a million and 5 million of them are located in the United States, with approximately 50,000 adherents residing in South Florida. Although many believers may have been raised in the Santería tradition, followers of other faiths are increasingly identifying as believers of Santería.

In many respects, Santería is unlike Western religions. While Western religions such as Christianity, Islam, and Judaism rely on doctrine and liturgy embodied in sacred texts to define their beliefs and boundaries, Santería relies instead on the careful performance of numerous rituals and the fulfillment by its followers of these prescribed rituals and sacrifices. Unlike various denominations within Christianity, Judaism, and Islam, for example, Santería does not have a centralized, hierarchical structure. Each house-temple (*casa de santos*) acts independently of others and may engage in very different practices and have different interpretations of those practices in comparison with other house-temples. Followers of Santería are known as such because they have carried out specific actions during prescribed rituals, not because of an accident of birth.

Significant disagreement exists with respect to the characterization of Santería as a syncretized religion. Santería has been labeled as such because some observers have noted that adherents to Santería appear to be praying to Catholic saints and concluded that Santería followers have merged the Catholic and African belief systems and abandoned their gods (*orishas* or *orichas*) in favor of the Catholic saints. Various scholars, however, have argued that because the Yoruba slaves in Cuba faced religious persecution when they worshiped the orishas, they masked this worship by imbuing a particular Catholic saint with the power and characteristics of a particular orisha. Although it appeared that the slaves were now praying to a saint, they actually continued to worship a particular orisha as manifested in the form of a particular saint. As an example, the orisha Orúnla, who is the god of wisdom, is often manifested as Francis of Assisi, St. Phillip, or St. Joseph. The persecution in Cuba of adherents to Santería continued until relatively recently; the practice of the faith was a punishable crime in Cuba until 1940 and persecution continued until the 1980s. Even in the United States, Santería did not gain formal recognition as a religion until 1993, when the United States Supreme Court ruled that prohibitions against religious rituals involving animal sacrifices were violative of the United States Constitution.

Basic Beliefs

Santería is a highly complex and ritualized faith. The various rituals, proverbs, and relationships that exist between adherents and officiants of the faith and the orishas serve to bind each to the other. As evident from the following discussion, survival of one depends on nourishment of the other.

It is believed that the orishas manifest themselves in other religions in addition to Santería by virtue of ashé, an amoral neutral energy force that serves as the foundation for all that exists and that is possessed by all entities that have life or power. Accordingly, it is believed that every human being who worships the Divine is actually worshiping the orishas. All religions, however, are to be accorded respect since all faiths contain truth.

Every individual is believed to be the spiritual child of an orisha. The identity of the orisha parent will become known once the individual becomes a follower of Santería. The new believer can then begin to foster the relationship with his or her orisha parent and look to the orisha for guidance and assistance with his or her problems. When an individual dies, his or her *ori*, analogous to the Christian concept of a soul, returns to Olodumare, the ultimate god, who causes the ori to be reborn in successive lives until its destiny on earth has been fulfilled. Accordingly, death is viewed not as the end of life, but rather as the beginning of a new existence.

Although the orishas are powerful, they are not immortal. Their survival depends on sacrifices made to them by their believers. The relationship between the orishas and believers is complex; each depends on the other for survival.

Santería's primary purpose is to assist the individual to live in harmony with his or her destiny; they will more easily be able to meet life's challenges and overcome difficulties if they follow the appropriate rituals. These difficulties may include marital strain, financial stress, illness, and problems with children. Although the individual is deemed to be responsible for his or her actions, assistance may be sought from the appropriate spirit. The individual's performance of a prescribed ritual will provide energy to that spirit so that the spirit can provide assistance to the individual.

Santería does not personify the qualities of good and evil as God or Satan, angels or devils. Rather, what is to be considered good or evil depends upon the particular circumstances. Unwelcome events are not deemed to be punishment for having committed a sin or for a human frailty, but are instead seen as the natural consequence of disharmony. Restoration of harmony between the physical and spiritual realms is deemed to be critical. This can be accomplished through the perfect performance of various rituals designed to demonstrate respect to the appropriate orishas and to placate them. If done successfully, the orishas will reward the individual by granting his or her request, even if the fulfillment of that request would be to the detriment of others.

Ritual

Individuals seeking assistance with their difficulties will consult a *santero* or *santera* for a *consulta*. (Santero refers to males and santera to females; the term santero will be utilized in the remainder of this entry to signify both male and females.) Santeros who have developed a reputation of being knowledgeable and powerful may have established a casa de santos, known as an *ilé*. These are often located in a room or basement of a house that has been converted for this purpose and that houses shrines of Santería. Santeros are believed to be extensions of Olodumare, the supreme spiritual source. In their role as mediators between humans and orishas, they are able to officiate at ceremonies and rituals, diagnose illness, effectuate healing, and dispel evil spells. Santeros have been trained by longer-term practitioners of the faith who have "birthed" more junior members (male *padrinos* and female *madrinas*), and are recognized as their mentors' godsons (*ahijados*) and goddaughters (*ahijadas*).

The process of restoring harmony between the physical and spiritual worlds and discovering how to be in balance with one's destiny often begins with divination. Although each individual is believed to have a destiny, actions are not predetermined; rather, each person can pursue actions that are congruent with their destiny and reach their full potential, or they may act in ways that are in opposition to their destiny and create disharmony. Divination will help to clarify the client's situation, reduce anxiety, and identify a solution to the client's difficulties. The santero will ask the client questions about his or her situation; the client is able to clarify for themselves the presenting problem as he or she relates it to the santero.

A detailed description of the varied divination processes is beyond the scope of this entry. In brief, divination may be achieved through reliance on sanctified coconuts which, after being tossed, reveal a yes-no response to a question that has been asked of an orisha; through the use of cowrie shells that constitute the "mouth" of a specified orisha; and through the use of kola nuts or palm nuts.

Only *babalawos*, male high priests whose abilities exceed those of the santeros, are authorized to perform various forms of divination, such as that accomplished through the use of kola nuts or palm nuts. Additionally, only babalawos can perform animal sacrifices. Over time, the power and importance of babalawos has diminished as increasing numbers of santeros learn the rituals involving animal sacrifice and the more advanced forms of divination.

A sacrifice or tribute to a particular orisha may be prescribed at the conclusion of the consulta. Offerings, known as *ebbós*, may be prescribed for a variety of purposes: to give thanks for the favorable resolution of a problem; to obtain an orisha's favor; to appease an angry orisha; to ward off an attack; to mark the beginning of a particular ceremony, such as an ordination; to obtain an orisha's blessing at the start of a new venture or enterprise, among others. Each ritual service necessitates the payment of a monetary offering (*derecho*) to the orisha. The derecho is often needed in advance in order to pay for the various component objects to be used in the ritual, such as food, candles, animals, etc. The blood from animal sacrifices is used to nourish the orisha; the animals are cooked and eaten following most Santería rituals, with the exception of healing and death rites. The ritual of sacrifice or offering serves as a catharsis for the client's emotions that are associated with the difficulties he or she described during the consulta.

A santero, or even an adherent, may become possessed by an orisha during the course of a ritual. A client's belief in spirit possession may in some cases complicate a mental health diagnosis by a Western-trained mental health professional. However, a client's reliance on Santería rituals and consultas may serve to complement therapy by providing additional support, feedback, and opportunity for self-reflection. Accordingly, it is critical that a mental health professional be willing to engage his or her client in a discussion of the client's religious and spiritual beliefs.

Adherence to Santería or membership in the faith is not a prerequisite to a consulta. Individuals who seek entrance to Santería as a full member must proceed through a series of four rituals that includes (1) receipt of the beaded necklaces (*elekes*), containing specific beads that reflect the orishas to whom the individual is responsible; (2) making the image of Elegguá, a warrior orisha responsible for determining human destinies; (3) receiving the warriors (*Guerreros*), that is, receiving from the babalawo objects associated with the warrior orishas Elegguá (his image); Oggún (iron tools), Ochosi (a bow and arrow), and Osún (an iron chalice with a rooster); and

S

(4) *asiento*, an elaborate multi-day ritual through which the individual is reborn into Santería. Various aspects of the asiento serve to distinguish and separate the post-asiento individual from his pre-Santería identity: the initiate's head is shaven, he is given a new name, and he is kept in seclusion. Initiation into the faith through the four rituals typically requires several years and tutelage under a particular santero. The individual is free to halt the process at any stage and may continue as a member of the faith at the level he has attained.

Benefits

Santería has provided and continues to provide its adherents with a sense of family, community, refuge, and belonging, and the possibility of exerting some degree of control within one's current existence. Reincarnation of the ori assures the continued existence of the individual and the regeneration of the community. These physical and emotional benefits are evident throughout the faith's history. During the period of slavery in Cuba, the faith provided a mechanism through which individuals could momentarily escape from their oppression. Cuban immigrants to the United States found fellowship and community in the casas de santos, where fellow clients spoke the same language and held similar worldviews. The santeros and santeras serve as surrogate godparents, while fellow adherents are seen as siblings. The casas de santos also serve as marketplaces, where clients can exchange goods and assist each other economically. In short, the casas de santos and its personages constitute family and community, bound together through an intricate system of ritual and respect and, not infrequently, experiences of oppression.

See also: ❯ Ritual ❯ Sacrifice

Bibliography

Baez, A. B., & Hernandez, D. (2001). Complementary spiritual beliefs in the Latino community: The interface with psychotherapy. *American Journal of Orthopsychiatry, 71*(4), 408–415.

Church of the Lukumi Babalu Aye, Inc v. City of Hialeah. (1993). 508 U.S. 520.

De La Torre, M. A. (2004). *Santería: The beliefs and rituals of a growing religion in America*. Cambridge, England: William B. Eerdmans Publishing Company.

Mason, M. A. (2002). *Living santeria: Rituals and experiences in an Afro-Cuban religion*. Washington, DC: Smithsonian Institution Press.

Powell, E. (n.d.). *The derecho: An anthropological approach to understanding monetary exchange in Santería*. Senior thesis, Department of Anthropology, Haverford College, Haverford, PA.

Satan

❯ Devil

Scapegoat

Tadd Ruetenik

Scapegoating commonly refers to the process by which an individual, or perhaps a group, gets shunned unfairly so that a community can avoid considering a more complex problem. An unremarkable employee, for example, might get fired from a company experiencing major systemic problems, in the hopes that this action will show that the company is serious about reform. Scapegoats can also be found at the more prominent levels of a community. A football coach will often be fired in an attempt to reform a team of weak players, or more seriously, a political leader will be killed in response to problems among the populace.

The common factor here seems to be the defenselessness of the victim or group of victims, and the injustice of the punishment, which is either misapplied or inappropriately harsh. The origin of the scapegoat, however, comes from Leviticus 16, where the process is actually prescribed by law. A priest is instructed to lay his hands on a goat, confess the sins of the people, and send the goat out of the community and into the desert. The consequences of the people's sins, which otherwise would build endlessly, are thus believed to be expulsed expelled from the community along with the animal. The goat is neither guilty nor innocent: it is just a goat. The punishment is thus not misapplied, and the punishment is not too harsh – unless we consider alternative versions of the story in which the goat is pushed off of a cliff. A similar story of scapegoating occurs in the synoptic Gospels in the story of Jesus banishing demons by transferring them into a herd of swine that were sent into the sea. The demons are named "Legion," and require a scapegoat in the plural.

The fact that in both stories the scapegoat is an animal and not a human seems to justify the action morally. When humans are the ones scapegoated, however, the act is regarded as unjust. The problem with scapegoating, however, is that its perpetrators often do not see it for what it is. A myth develops that the sins of the individual are real and justify his exclusion. When Jesus is being crucified, he remarks that the people "know not what they are doing."

Identifying this kind of blindness is important to the work of Rene Girard. According to Girard, a largely unconscious *scapegoat mechanism* is at work in the foundation of human civilization. The mechanism takes the form of unchallenged religious rituals. "Violence and the sacred are inseparable," says Girard in *Violence and the Sacred* "but the covert appropriation by sacrifice of certain properties of violence – particularly the ability of violence to move from one object to another – is hidden from sight by the awesome machinery of ritual."

This machinery results from the pervasiveness of *mimetic desire* within communities. Mimetic desire is a type of rivalry in which its competitors are focused not on objects of desire, but rather for the desire itself. Girard's example involves considering two children who are simultaneously introduced to a new toy. Rivalry develops as soon as one child, perhaps sensing the impending interest of the other, is attracted to that toy. Predictably, the second child will also become interested in that toy, but not because of any intrinsic value in the object. Rather, the child is interested in the other child's interest. The object in question is of secondary importance, and, in the case of pronounced mimetic rivalry, becomes irrelevant.

One does not have to look to the immaturity of children to find examples of mimetic rivalry. The interest of a few customers in a sales bin usually prompts the interest of many others. As clever marketers understand, the contents of the bin are not as important as the fact that someone appears interested in sifting through it, and this interest causes an anxiety in others, who fear they just might be missing out on something. What they are missing out on is the act of looking.

There are of course more intense and important cases of mimetic rivalry involving jealous lovers, business competitors, rival countries, etc. These cases involve more significant and dangerous conflicts, and threaten community stability. According to Girard, mimetic rivalry is both contagious and violence-inducing, and when the threat of mob violence becomes sufficiently acute, a scapegoat is sought by the members of the community. The violence done to the scapegoat by the community serves to dispel the dangerous force by symbolically expelling the agreed-upon object. Yet the symbolic expulsion is not viewed by the community as such. Scapegoat rituals are seen as real solutions, not just symbolic acts. In the case of the witch trials in colonial America, the common interpretation is

that the sacrificed women were victims of some kind of conscious conspiracy by the male elders, who trick the gullible masses. Such an interpretation avoids considering the insidiousness of scapegoat mechanism. According to Girard, both the persecutors and the public are sincere in their beliefs. The primitiveness of a community (and indeed for Girard its lack of Christian revelation) is measured by the extent to which this scapegoat mechanism eludes consciousness.

The importance of Christianity is that it reveals the scapegoating mechanism by showing that the victim, in this case Christ, is innocent. The point however is not that innocence condemns scapegoating while guilt exonerates it; the point is that either way scapegoating is a mistaken response to the problem. The scapegoated individual is not the real threat; it is, rather, an escalation of communal rivalries that threatens peace. The resurrection of Christ is seen as a victory over the dark necessity of violence and scapegoating that constitutes particular communities, and indeed civilization in general. Christianity reveals, according to Jesus, and elaborated by Girard, "things hidden from the foundation of the world."

See also: ❯ Ritual ❯ Sacrifice ❯ Santería

Bibliography

Girard, R. (1972). *Violence and the sacred*. Baltimore, MD: Johns Hopkins University Press.
Girard, R. (1978). *Things hidden since the foundation of the World*. Stanford, CD: Stanford University Press.

Schopenhauer, Nietzsche, and Atheism

David Berman

Schopenhauer's atheism is implied rather than directly stated. For no where in his published works does he either deny the existence of God or describe himself as an atheist. Hence Nietzsche's confident claim, in his *Gay Science* 357, that Schopenhauer was the "first admitted and inexorable atheist among us Germans" (1974) stands in need of qualification. A more accurate statement might be that for a German – rather than a French or British writer of that time – Schopenhauer was an honest and open atheist.

Schopenhauer's Atheism

That having been said, atheism does seem to be a clear implication of Schopenhauer's system: for given that this world is essentially blind eternal will to life, there does not seem to be any need for a intelligent and good God who creates this world.

There is, however, at least one place in Schopenhauer's published work where he comes close to making his atheism explicit, which he does by what is essentially a psychological argument. The argument, in his main work, *The world as will and representation*, vol. 2, xlviii, is based on the fact that we human beings represent the highest possible development of morality and intelligence. Schopenhauer's argument is not just that there is no evidence that there is any being higher than us in these respects, but that there couldn't be. And this is shown, he thinks, by the saints and ascetics of all religions, who, because they are more morally and intellectually sensitive than their fellow human beings, are able to see that this world is the worst of all possible worlds, which moral insight leads them to mortify or deny themselves, with the aim (most clearly expressed in Buddhism) of achieving nirvana or nothingness, which for Schopenhauer is the most perfect state. Hence it is clear to Schopenhauer that if, for the sake of argument, we try to imagine a (supposed) more intelligent and good being, such as God, or a being even marginally superior to the saints, we would realize that such a being would even more instantly annihilate itself when it realized how revolting this world was.

Schopenhauer's psychological-atheistic argument is important not only for the light that it sheds on his mind and metaphysical system, but also as providing the crucial context for Nietzsche's idea of the overman, the central idea of his *Thus Spoke Zarathustra* (Part 1, 1883) and his general attempt to rescue man from nihilism. In his early work, the *Birth of Tragedy* (1872), Nietzsche accepted much of Schopenhauer's pessimism, but still not Schopenhauer's nihilistic belief that the highest good was nirvana. Instead of that bleak prescription, Nietzsche puts forward the more nuanced idea of the tragic life, as exemplified by Aeschylean tragedy, as the highest condition for man. And while he does not repudiate this aesthetic prescription in his later work of the

1880s, Nietzsche does change his focus there, a change that was partly brought on by his break with Richard Wagner and their common mentor, Schopenhauer, who, in 1886 Nietzsche nonetheless describes as "my first and only teacher, the *great* Arthur Schopenhauer". More positively, Nietzsche had by that time come under a new influence, more scientific than aesthetic, namely, the theory of evolution. For now his hope is that a new type of man might be evolved, which will answer the threat of nihilism. Thus Zarathustra's announcement of the death of God, at the beginning of *Thus spoke Zarathustra*, is immediately followed by "I teach you the overman. Man is something that shall be overcome... [and] What is the ape to man? A laughing-stock or a painful embarrassment. And man shall be just that for the overman..." (1962: 124).

Nietzsche's Anti-Atheism

But against such a higher development was Schopenhauer's atheism, as outlined above, which appeared to show that such a development was not possible, since man represented an evolutionary dead end; hence no being more perfect than man can evolve – which, for Nietzsche, was the nightmare of nihilism. So Nietzsche oppposed Schopenhauer's atheism, although not completely, since for one thing he still accepted much of Schopenhauer's pessimistic account of life. So Nietzsche, like his great teacher, rejected the optimistic idea that a scientific or cultural or political improvements might be effected which would improve our happiness quotient – something Nietzsche associated with the shallowness of English Utilitarianism.

In short, for Nietzsche, Schopenhauerian atheism had many roles and implications, sometimes pushing in different directions, which Nietzsche importantly explores in the *Gay Science*, sections 125, 343, 357 and 370 (Berman, 1988). So atheism, thanks to Schopenhauer and others, is going to bring about enormous destruction in our world. A vast amount is going to crumble, "for example, the whole of European morality" (Nietzsche, 1974: section 343). And yet Nietzsche says, in 125, we human beings did it, we are God's "murderers." But then he dramatically asks: "How did we do this? How could we drink up the sea...wipe away the entire horizon?" (1974) And Nietzsche goes on and on about the dire consequences of the deicide, which there is no need to stress here, since it is widely appreciated; but what is not so conspicuous or appreciated is the opposing tendency in Nietzsche, his anti-atheism, according to which the destructive deicide also has a good side, since it is going to clear the way, opening up new possibilities for new creations (1974: section 343), to which Nietzsche alludes even in 125, when he says: "Is not the greatness of this deed too great for us? Must we ourselves not become gods simply to appear worthy of it?" (1974). This is Nietzsche's hope. But it is a hope that is threatened by Schopenhauer's psychological-atheistic argument, a threat that Nietzsche sought to oppose by, among other things, his acute unmasking or transvaluating of what he took to be Schopenhauer's nihilistic concepts of goodness and knowledge, pity and compassion, showing how they worked against life and instinct and hence against the great hope of a new evolutionary development of man (Berman, 1998).

See also: ❯ God ❯ Nirvana

Bibliography

Berman, D. (1998). Schopenhauer and Nietzsche: Honest atheism, dishonest pessimisim. In C. Janaway (Ed.), *Willing and nothingness*. Oxford, England: Oxford University Press.

Nietzsche, F. (1924). *Human, All-too-Human* (Pt. 2. P. V. Cohn, Trans.). London: Allen & Unwin.

Nietzsche, F. (1962). *Thus spoke Zarathustra* (W. Kaufmann, Trans.). In *The portable Nietzsche* (pp. 121–439). New York: Viking Press.

Nietzsche, F. (1967). *Birth of Tragedy* (W. Kaufmann, Trans.). New York: Random House.

Nietzsche, F. (1974). *Gay Science* (W. Kaufmann, Trans.). New York: Vintage.

Schopenhauer, A. (1966). *The world as will and representation*, 2 Vols. (E. F. J. Payne, Trans.). New York: Dover.

Schreber, Daniel Paul

Lorna Lees-Grossmann

Daniel Paul Schreber (1842–1911) was a lawyer and judge by profession, but became infamous as the author of *Denkwürdigkeiten eines Nervenkranken*, or *Memoirs of My Nervous Illness*. In this work he detailed his experiences during his second period of mental illness, lasting from 1893 until 1902. Many well-known psychologists

subsequently adopted Schreber as a case study, although none of them ever met or corresponded with him.

Schreber's illness began with his half-dreaming thought that it must be nice to be a woman submitting to sexual intercourse. He began to experience auditory hallucinations shortly before his hospitalization in October 1893, but in February 1894 his hallucinations became more severe and for the first time visual. From these hallucinations Schreber extrapolated information that he used to create a complex world-view:

God

↑

"Forecourts of Heaven"

↑

"Tested souls"

↑

Hiatus of experience and self-awareness at the moment of death. Ended by God, who examines the soul and judges it

↑

Human beings

Humans have material souls present as "rays" in the nerves of the body. At the moment of death the body is left behind, and God then examines the soul for "blackening," or damage through sinful behavior. Once finished, God assigns the soul a period of time and a method through which it will be purified; it becomes a "tested soul," meaning that it is untested. Schreber's "soul-language" contains several similar antonymic references, e.g., "juice" for "poison." Once the soul is purified it enters the "forecourts of heaven," where it enjoys continued "voluptuousness," defined by Schreber as pleasurable experience caused by the uninterrupted closeness of God. God is split into Upper and Lower Gods, named after Ariman and Ormuzd, the sons of Zurvan, the Persian God of Time. He is unlike the Judaeo-Christian God in that He is neither omnipotent nor benevolent; He is a disinterested observer of the world and only intervenes in exceptional circumstances.

Schreber believed that earthly harmony could only be achieved through his transformation into a woman so that he could bear God's children and thus perpetuate a new and superior race of human beings. To encourage the transformation he took to wearing feminine adornments and asking medical staff to examine his developing breasts. Schreber believed that God was working against the "Order of the World" in this matter: His rays had become dangerously linked with Schreber's, a link that could prove fatal to God were it to be severed while Schreber was still in possession of his wits. For this reason God was involved in an attempt with Schreber's psychiatrist Flechsig to destroy Schreber's reason. This "soul murder," as Schreber termed it, took the form of physical attacks and constant harassment from "tested souls."

The most famous of the multiple analyses of Schreber is Freud's own. Freud, like the others, never met Schreber, and concluded that Schreber's homosexual anxiety was to blame for his breakdown. Freud argued that Schreber turned the love he felt for another man, possibly his father or brother, into hate. He then justified his hatred through delusions of persecution. Schreber's change of sex was therefore an attempt to render his homosexual desires acceptable.

Alternative analyses include Niederland's, who noted the similarity between the miraculous punishments suffered by Schreber with the suggested educational methods of Schreber's father, the pedagogue Moritz Schreber. Schatzman's analysis went further than Niederland's, and blamed Moritz Schreber's "sadistic" teaching methods for Schreber's illness on the grounds of these miraculous punishments. All of these analyses accept the original diagnosis of Schreber as suffering from paranoid schizophrenia, but Koehler suggested that Schreber may originally have been suffering clinical depression and in fact only made the "schizophrenic switch" in February of 1894.

Schreber published his *Memoirs* partly in the hope that they would become the foundational text for a new religion based on the knowledge revealed to him by the "tested souls." His experiences were to be viewed in the context of martyrdom; his suffering led to the acquisition of knowledge of the extraordinary world that is inaccessible to humans under normal circumstances. Comparisons can also be drawn with Biblical Job, Hildegard of Bingen and other religious mystics.

See also: ◎ Freud, Sigmund ◎ God ◎ Job

Bibliography

Baumeyer, F. (1956). The Schreber case. *International Journal of Psycho-Analysis, 37*, 61–67.

Freud, S. (1958). *Psycho-analytic notes on an autobiographical account of a case of paranoia (dementia paranoides), SE* XII (pp. 1–82). London: Hogarth Press. (Translated from the German under the general editorship of J. Strachey, London).

Israels, H. (1989). *Schreber: Father and son*. Madison, CT: International Universities Press.

Koehler, K. G. (1981). The Schreber case and affective illness: A research diagnostic re-assessment. *Psychological Medicine, 11*, 689–696.

Niederland, W. G. (1974). *The Schreber case: Psychoanalytic profile of a paranoid personality*. New York: Quadrangle.

Schatzman, M. (1976). *Soul murder: Persecution in the family*. Harmondsworth: Penguin.

Schreber, D. P. (2000). *Memoirs of my nervous illness* (I. MacAlpine, R. Hunter, Eds.). New York: New York Review of Books.

Search for the Father

◎ Monomyth

Seder

Lynn Somerstein

The Seder, a yearly event celebrated on the 15th and 16th of the month of Nissan, is a part of the Passover celebration that marks the Jew's Exodus from Egypt in the thirteenth Century BCE. The word "Mitzraim," Hebrew for Egypt, comes from the root meaning narrow, so the Jews escaped from a narrow place to a broader world.

Since the Exodus is a prelude to God's revelation on Mount Sinai, the Seder is an opportunity for each participant to relive the Exodus as a personal spiritual event. The Seder meal is supposed to replicate the experience of escaping from bondage to freedom, and can include family references and stories about danger, freedom and redemption. Reciting the family's history is a way to draw individual members closer together; and the Hagadah, the story of the Exodus, says that the more one speaks about liberation, the better. The Hagadah and the family stories together are an oral recitation of history, and a way to remember it.

The word "seder" means order, or order of service, referring to the ritual and the celebratory meal. A thorough house cleaning leads up to the event. Special pots, pans, tableware, and foods, are served, and some foods are prohibited – no leavened foods or grains are eaten.

Matzohs, are allowed because they have been carefully prepared in under 18 min. They commemorate the haste with which the Jews fled the Egyptians, without time to let the bread rise.

The Seder meal teaches about the Exodus. Since it is so different from usual family meals, it inspires people, especially children, to ask questions, like the famous, "Why is this night different from every other night?"

The Seder is quintessentially a *family* meal, usually led by the eldest male in the household. Participation in the Seder at whatever level is a powerful emotional experience of the love and hate occurring in the outside world and within the family as well. Using special cookware and dinnerware, and avoiding prohibited foods for the entire week of Passover can be an exercise in mindfulness or frustration.

The meal concludes with songs, and with the declaration, "Next year in Jerusalem!" This can mean the literal city of Jerusalem, or it can mean Jerusalem as a symbol of personal redemption and freedom. Whichever theme is emphasized, the personal effect of recreating ancestral, family, and individual histories and relationships to bondage and freedom can indelibly mark one's soul with a respect for self-determination and an eternal emotional connection with one's people.

See also: ❂ Exodus ❂ Jerusalem ❂ Judaism and Psychology

Bibliography

http://www.britannica.com/EBchecked/topic/532142/seder#tab = active~ checked%2Citems~checked&title = seder%20–%20Britannica% 20Online%20Encyclopedia

Wigoder, G. (Ed.) (1974). *Encyclopedic Dictionary of Judaica*, NY, Paris: Leon Amiel, p. 539.

Self

Ann Casement

Self lies at the heart of Jung's conceptualizing on the structure and dynamics of the psyche. He first encountered the Self in mid-life during the turbulent years of 1916–1918 while undergoing his "creative illness" following the difficult breakdown of his relationship with Freud. As a result, Jung took mid-life to be universal for experiences of the Self to come into being, a view that has been contested by later analytical psychologists. Jung's definition of the Self is that it is the totality of the psyche as well as being the prime archetype that keeps the psyche from disintegrating at times of stress. Furthermore, it transcends and goes beyond psyche.

If it is conceptualized as the prime archetype, the Self would be the container of opposites, above all perhaps those of good and evil. In this regard, Jung refers to it as a "complexio oppositorum (which) proves to be not only a possibility but an ethical duty" (Jung, 1954:320). This is to be found at the very center of what it is to be human which is also an analogy of God: "Man is God, but not in an absolute sense, since he is man. He is therefore God in a human way. . .every endeavour of our human intelligence should be bent to the achieving of that simplicity where contradictories are reconciled" (Jung, 1954: 320). Here Jung is quoting Nicholas of Cusa of whom he says: "The alchemists are as it were the empiricists of the great problem of opposites, whereas Nicholas of Cusa is its philosopher" (Jung, 1954: 320). Furthermore: "The self is a union of opposites *par excellence,* and this is where it differs essentially from the Christ-symbol. The androgyny of Christ is the utmost concession the Church has made to the problem of opposites" (Jung, 1953: 19).

On the other hand, Jung's writings contain many references to the synonymous nature of the Self with the God-image as follows: "*Christ exemplifies the archetype of the self* " (Jung, 1959: 37) (Original italics). "The Christ-symbol is of the greatest importance for psychology in so far as it is perhaps the most highly developed and differentiated symbol of the self, apart from the figure of the Buddha" (Jung, 1953: 19). However, in so doing Jung was not trying to take on the mantle of a religious thinker but, instead, remained always aware that he was an empirical psychologist. "Strictly speaking, the God-image does not coincide with the unconscious as such, but with a special content of it, namely the archetype of the self. It is this archetype from which we can no longer distinguish the God-image empirically" (Jung, 1958: 469). This image of wholeness rises independently in the conscious mind from the depths of humankind's psychic nature. He goes on to say: ". . .the self is not a philosophical concept like Kant's 'thing-in-itself,' but an empirical concept of psychology, and can therefore be hypostatized" (Jung, 1958: 262).

Self and Individuation

The Self is all important not only in the individuation process of individuals but also in that of collective groups though the symbols of the Self are different at different historical epochs. He elaborated this in his work *Aion,* the name of which is taken from the Mithraic god who rules over time, as follows:

> …"wholeness"…is nevertheless empirical in so far as it is anticipated by the psyche in the form of spontaneous or autonomous symbols. These are the quaternity or mandala symbols, which occur not only in the dreams of modern people…but are widely disseminated in the historical records of many peoples and many epochs. Their significance as *symbols of unity and totality* is amply confirmed by history as well as by empirical psychology (Jung, 1959: 31) (Original italics).

Jung goes so far as to say the Self represents psychic totality and is both conscious and unconscious. From the latter realm it may manifest in dreams, myths and fairy tales in the figure of the "supraordinate personality" (Jung, 1971: 460). In this way, it takes on the form of king, hero, prophet or savior or a symbol of wholeness such as a circle or cross. "I have called this wholeness that transcends consciousness the 'self' The goal of the individuation process is the synthesis of the self.…symbols of wholeness frequently occur at the beginning of the individuation process, indeed they can often be observed in the first dreams of early infancy" (Jung, 1959: 164). This tantalizing glimpse into Jung's interest in infancy was taken up and elaborated by the analytical psychologist, Michael Fordham, whose ideas will be expanded further in this piece.

Encounter with the Self

In exploring the connection between the Self and ego Jung turned to the Biblical story of the *Book of Job.* Similarly, the analytical psychologist, Edward Edinger, depicts the relationship between the story of Job with its relevance for the psyche of modern man, and William Blake's *Illustrations of the Book of Job.* As Edinger states: "…the Job story is an archetypal image which pictures a certain typical encounter between the ego and the Self. This typical encounter may be called the Job archetype" (Edinger, 1986: 11). Edinger further states: "The term 'Self' is used by Jung to designate the transpersonal center and totality of the psyche. It constitutes the greater, objective personality, whereas the ego is the lesser, subjective personality. Empirically the Self cannot be distinguished from the God-image. Encounter with it is a *mysterium tremendum*" (Edinger, 1986: 7).

An encounter between Self and ego always results in a defeat for the latter. However, if it can sustain the ordeal

and at the same time become aware of its meaning, ego may experience an insight into the transpersonal psyche. In the Blake drawings, Job is first depicted as living in a state of unconscious innocent contentment. In the second picture, Satan manifests in a stream of fire between Yahweh and Job and represents the urge to individuation which is a challenge to complacence and living unconsciously. "Dionysian energy of excess has erupted into the Apollonian order" (Edinger, 1986: 19).

The later pictures illustrate the growing dynamism of Dionysian energy and its impact on ego by destroying its containing structures, depicted in the Job story as the loss of his children and their families. Psychologically this corresponds to the onset of bad dreams and neurotic symptoms such as depression and psychosomatic symptoms. Ego may try to deal with these by splitting them off and dissociating them from consciousness, which results in an impoverishment of the conscious personality.

The book goes on to illustrate the complete breakdown of Job (ego) when confronted with the dark side of the Self (Yahweh), which a later picture depicts as Job on high pointing down to the chthonic aspects of the numinosum, Behemoth and Leviathan. "This is the other side of the *numinosum,* which we must always remember is a union of opposites" (Edinger, 1986:55). As Edinger goes on to say: "Job is being shown the abysmal aspect of God and the depths of his own psyche, which contains devouring monsters remote from human values…God reveals his own shadow side, and since man participates in God as the ground of his being he must likewise share his darkness" (Edinger, 1986:55).

Blake's pictures and the *Book of Job* end with Job's fortunes being restored and with an enlargement of his personality through an encounter with the Self. As Jung says: "…the widening of consciousness is at first upheaval and darkness, then a broadening out of man to the whole man" (Jung, 1963:171).

Primal Self

The analytical psychologist, James Astor, views Michael Fordham as the last of the founders of a movement in analysis, who tapped into something essential in the discipline. Fordham's pioneering work led to a developmental model of Jung's ideas of the self. "His most radical departure from Jung was to describe the actions of the self in infancy and childhood such that the infant, far from being uncentered at birth, as Jung originally thought, is a person with an individual identity even in utero" (Astor, 2007).

In this way, Fordham revised Jung's thinking of the self in showing how, through interacting with the environment, it helped to mold and create it. In this way "The self, as Forham conceived it, was the instigator as much as the receptor of infant experience. This conception gave rise to the particularly Jungian theory of ego development in which the interaction between mother and baby ensured the uniqueness of the situation, a uniqueness created as much by the infant as by the mother" (Astor, 2007).

The prospective nature and self-regulating function of the psyche through the self's unifying characteristics "could transcend what seemed to be opposite forces" though in the course of that it could be "'exceedingly disruptive' both destructively and creatively" (Astor, 2007).

Astor sums up Fordham's revised thinking on Jung's theory of the self to include a primary self or original state of integration as follows: "This primal self, he thought, gave rise to structures from interaction with the environment which it in part created. It existed outside of time and space, and was similar to a mystical (or contemporary scientific concept such as emergence), whose manifestations had archetypal form. This primary self was integrated, and in Jung's sense it was an agency of the psyche which transcended opposites" (Astor, 2007). Astor links this to Fordham's innovative thinking about the *dynamic structure* of the self which infant research is arriving at quite separately from analytic thinking. "Fordham took the innateness of Jung's archetypal psychology and demonstrated the way in which the environment affected it" (Astor, 2007). Furthermore, "by having a theory of deintegration we are able to think about the observed behavior of the infant as being continuous with the self. What this means is that the development of the individual baby is in effect an early form of individuation" (Astor, 2007).

Fordham also challenged Jung's thinking about the self as both the totality of the psyche and an archetype. "As for the archetype definition, Fordham notes that it accounts for a range of phenomena related to wholeness (archetypal images) and, in fact, is closer to the data than the totality definition. However this data 'cannot also be the totality' because it excludes the ego, which Jung differentiated from the archetypes" (Urban, 2005: 574).

In conclusion, it is worth noting that the term "Self" is spelt with a capital "S" in some instances and a small 's' in others. The former tends to be used by classical Jungians who view the Self as synonymous with the God-image; in the latter, it is used by analytical psychologists of the developmental school of thought. While Fordham was not an atheist: "Much of Fordham's work has countered this religious aspect of Jungianism"(Astor, 2007). At the same time: "His respect for Jung and his understanding of the value of his studies of the manifestations of the collective unconscious led him to try to take a balanced position with respect to both the psychological and religious perspective" (Astor, 2007).

See also: ❂ Freud, Sigmund ❂ God Image ❂ Individuation ❂ Job ❂ Jung, Carl Gustav ❂ Jungian Self ❂ Mandala ❂ Numinosum

Bibliography

Astor, J. (2007). *Analytical psychology and Michael Fordham*. In A. Casement (Ed.), *Who owns Jung?* (pp. 76, 77, 81–82). London: Karnac Books.

Edinger, E. (1986). *Encounter with the Self: A Jungian commentary on William Blake's illustrations of the Book of Job*. Toronto, Ontario, Canada: Inner City Books.

Jung, C. G. (1953). Introduction to the religious and psychological problems of alchemy. In *Psychology and alchemy* (Vol. 12). London: Routledge & Kegan Paul.

Jung, C. G. (1954). The psychology of the transference. In *The practice of psychotherapy* (Vol. 16). London: Routledge & Kegan Paul.

Jung, C. G. (1958). *Answer to Job*. In *Psychology and religion: West and East* (Vol. 11). London: Routledge & Kegan Paul.

Jung, C. G. (1958). Transformation symbolism in the mass. In *Psychology and religion: West and East* (Vol. 11). London: Routledge & Kegan Paul Ltd.

Jung, C. G. (1959). Christ, a symbol of the self. In *Aion: Researches into the phenomenology of the self*. Princeton, NJ: Princeton University Press.

Jung, C. G. (1959). The psychology of the child archetype. In *The archetypes and the collective unconscious* (Vol. 9). London: Routledge & Kegan Paul.

Jung, C.G. (1959). The Self. In *Aion: Researches into the phenomenology of the self*. Princeton, NJ: Princeton University Press.

Jung, C. G. (1963). The personification of the opposites. In *Mysterium Coniunctionis: An inquiry into the separation and synthesis of psychic opposites in alchemy* (Vol. 14.). London: Routledge & Kegan Paul.

Jung, C. G. (1971). Definitions. In *Psychological types* (Vol. 6). London: Routledge & Kegan Paul.

Urban, E. (2005). Fordham, Jung and the self. *The Journal of Analytical Psychology, 50*(5), 571–594.

Self Object

D. Brian Smothers

Definition

Selfobject: An object which is used in the service of the self, or objects which are experienced as part of the self and provide a function for the self.

Discussion

The selfobject is the central psychic apparatus within Heinz Kohut's theory of self psychology. To understand this ambiguous concept, one must understand Kohut's departure from conventional analytic discourse. Kohut's usage of an object significantly differs from the Freudian usage of an object. Freud's object exists, primarily, as the target of libidinal cathexis; where as Kohut's object is cathected with narcissistic energy in the service of the self. Freud's thinking was bound to the Cartesian dualism of the scientific revolution, in which one is experienced as either a subject (ego) or an object (other). Kohut, on the other hand, recognized the capacity for internalization of the experiences of the subject-in-relation to the object and the object-in-relation to the subject. Accordingly, the selfobject is those dimensions of our experience of another person that relates to this person's functions in establishing our sense of self.

Based on his groundbreaking work with traditionally unanalyzable individuals, narcissistic patients and those with other disorders of the self, Kohut established a bipolar theory of development that contrasted with the traditional drive model proposed by Freud. Extending the works of Margaret Mahler, Heinz Hartmann and Edith Jacobson, Kohut's work sought to develop a theory of self. For Kohut, the infantile or rudimentary self develops along two primary continuums in relation to others, the grandiose self and the idealized parental image.

Kohut viewed narcissism not as pathological, but as a necessary component of healthy development. In his theory, the infant must develop a sense of confirmation through the mirroring of the parent. Thus, the parent must reflect back the grandiosity of the child as a means of her acceptance and participation in the infants developing sense of self and self-agency. Children are biologically and environmentally dependent on an (m) other for food, shelter and nurturance. This other provides critical tasks by fulfilling physiological and psychological needs that the child cannot fulfill herself, though the child will experience the other as an extension of herself. Effective mirroring builds the child's internal confirmation of her self-agency through the development of healthy selfobjects. These internalizations will aid her by mobilizing her to act on the world and to have her needs met. If the need for mirroring is absent or inadequate, the child will grow to feel deficient and will spend her life seeking the selfobject to fulfill this gap within herself. Psychic structures of self are built through the process of transmuting internalizations. Through the process of optimal frustration of the child's narcissistic needs by the parent, the child's emergent self develops. The emergent self will eventually provide mirroring and idealizing through mature relations and the external/internal functions of mature selfobjects.

According to Kohut, one's experience of self is the unconscious experience(s) of self-in-relation to objects, therefore self is selfobjects. Thus, as an individual experiences a sense of 'I', he/she is inextricably bound to the 'I' in relation to the particular 'other' to whom he/she is experientially connected. Therefore the experience of self differs across time, contexts and relationships. The concept of a selfobject refers not to an object in the interpersonal sense of the word, but to the inner experience of an object, therefore, the selfobject is defined by our inner experience of the object and its function in establishing a sense of self. Put more simply, selfobjects are not necessarily selfs or objects, but one's internal subjective experience of the relationship and it's functions for the self.

It is important to note that the rudimentary infantile self is bound to the experience of external others and their selfobject functions. As the individual matures, selfobjects may not necessarily be experiences with a physical manifestation of an other, but may be ones dynamic experience of a piece art, music, literature or religious traditions, beliefs, and associated matters. Mature individuals can turn to selfobject functions of symbolized abstractions to meet their deepest self needs, as we are never fully independent of our deepest self needs.

In his interview with Robert L. Randall, a young theologian, Kohut briefly outlines the theological implications of self-psychology. For Kohut, the role of religion could not be simply reduced to one dimension of the self, though with this said, his focus on the idealizing needs and the role of religion is worth noting. According to Kohut, the core nuclear self is developed through mirroring, idealizing and the optimal frustration of these needs. Through the optimal responsiveness of the caregiver in meeting the mirroring and idealizing needs, and the eventual frustration of those needs, the child slowly internalizes the selfobject functions and the nuclear self emerges. The parent must allow the child to idealize him or her, essentially merging with the perceived strength found within the parent. In the rudimentary child unable to meet her own needs, this process may be internalized in ways such as, "You are perfect, and I am a part of you, so I am perfect." As mentioned above, the mature individual never outgrows the basic self needs, though they are altered through the usage of mature selfobject relations. Accordingly, God is the perfect idealizeable object. The sense of belonging to a religious tradition or having a personal relationship with God, may, through the process of merger and idealization, align one with God's perfection.

A benevolent image of God may provide the mirroring and idealizing functions needed during times of distress. It is not unusual to hear an individual state that "God is my strength;" indeed the psalmist even made this assertion. Thus, faith, or one's faith may function as an organizing selfobject experience, providing psychic structure and experiences of self leading towards equilibrium, cohesiveness, well-being, and esteem. Individual differences are uniquely respected within this conceptualization, as one's experience of a religious experience is not internalized and experienced in the same manner as another's. The religious experience of hearing a moving sermon, participation in the Eucharist, or the symbol of Christ on the cross, become internalized sources of self through the experience and selfobject functions of these abstractions. In the Muslim tradition, the Koran, and recitation of Koranic verses may hold substantial symbolic selfobject functions for individuals of this faith. The Koran soothes, supports and strengthens the Muslim through its subjective and shared selfobject functions.

See also: ❯ Freud, Sigmund ❯ Kohut, Heinz ❯ Narcissism ❯ Object Relations Theory ❯ Psychoanalysis ❯ Relational Psychoanalysis ❯ Self ❯ Self Psychology

Bibliography

Hedayat-Diba, Z. (1997). Selfobject functions of the Koran. *International Journal for the Psychology of Religion, 7*, 211–236.

Kohut, H. (1971). *The analysis of the self: A systematic approach to the psychoanalytic treatment of narcissistic personality disorders*. Madison, CT: International Universities Press.

Kohut, H. (1984). *How does analysis cure?* In A. Goldberg (Ed.), with the collaboration of P. E. Stepansky (pp. 240) Chicago, IL: University of Chicago Press.

Schlauch, C. (1999). Rethinking selfobject and self: Implications for understanding religious matters. *Pastoral Psychology, 48*, 57–78.

Stozier, C. (1997). Heinz Kohut's struggles with religion, ethnicity, and God. In J. L. Jacobs & D. Capps (Eds.). *Religion, Society and Psychoanalysis: Readings in Contemporary Thought*. Boulder, CO: Westview.

Self Psychology

Carol L. Schnabl Schweitzer

The psychology of the self is a psychoanalytic theory of the development of the self which focuses primarily on narcissistic disorders or configurations of the self. With the publication of Heinz Kohut's *The Analysis of the Self* in 1971, the psychology of the self, though widely criticized by psychoanalytic theory purists, began to gain respect as a psychoanalytic treatment for a particular kind of pathology – narcissism. Heinz Kohut understood his work to be an addition to, rather than a replacement of, Freud's groundwork in psychoanalysis. There are several significant points of departure from Freud's metapsychology including Kohut's precise understanding of transference, internalization, and empathy.

Narcissistic patients, according to Kohut, experience the transference not as a projection of their existing internal psychic structures but rather as an expression of a need for internal psychic structures which are missing. Thus, the analytic task focuses on liberating the patient from his or her denial of a need. Likewise, Kohut offers us a somewhat different understanding from Freud of the process of internalization. Building upon Freud's work, Kohut understands internalization as more than the taking in of the qualities of the libidinal object which is lost and mourned; it is a process which includes the taking in (or internalizing) of idealizations of a selfobject when that object has temporarily failed in one of its need-fulfilling functions. One indication that analysis is progressing from Kohut's perspective is the ability of the analysand to tolerate the inevitable empathic failure of the analyst.

Kohut proposed a bi-polar model of the self: one pole is related to ideals (idealized self); the other is related to ambitions (grandiose self); and, the area or space between the two is comprised of inborn skills and talents. The poles of the self are developed in relation to selfobjects (or the original primary caretakers who fulfill the needs of the developing self). The maternal selfobject is associated with the idealized self while the paternal selfobject is associated with the grandiose self (originally the narcissistic self). These selfobjects are not viewed as separate entities but rather in terms of the way they fulfill or fail to meet the needs of the developing infant. Kohut theorized that an infant could tolerate a traumatic failure on the part of one but not both parental selfobjects (or others who may have primary caretaking responsibility). Thus, a paternal selfobject need not be the biological father; it may not even be a male but someone who provides father-like care. The same is true for the maternal selfobject.

The three major constituents of the self (ideals, ambitions, and talents) shape the three major groups of transference experiences in the analytic process. If the area of ambitions (grandiose self) is damaged the patient will likely experience a mirror transference in which the analyst is the person around whom constancy is established. This can be related to the "gleam in a mother's eye as she gazes at her infant." If the area of ideals is damaged then the patient experiences an idealizing transference which means that the analyst provides soothing and tension-regulating functions if the narcissistic injury occurred early in childhood. If the injury occurred later in childhood (or even beyond childhood) then the analyst may become "de-idealized" quickly as the analysand seeks attachment with an omnipotent object. And finally, if the area of skills and talents is damaged then the patient looks for reassurance in an alter ego or twinship transference in which the analyst is experienced as being similar to the analysand's grandiose self. How then, does analysis change from Freud's original understandings according to Kohut's theory of the self? In other words, how does analysis provide a cure?

Freud maintained that a narcissist was not curable because a narcissist was not accessible to the influence of psychoanalysis; thus, the patient lacked the ability to invest in a transference relationship (Freud, vol. 12, 1959 and vol. 14, 1959). The noteworthy difference is Kohut's focus on the treatment and cure of narcissistic personality disorders. The touchstone in Kohut's analytic process is empathy which he understood as a *data-gathering tool* within the analytic relationship, not a cure in itself. (See: *How Does Analysis Cure?* 1984: 300–307.) Why is empathy in and of itself not a cure? Kohut, using an illustration from Nazi Germany, demonstrated that empathy (or the ability to put oneself in another's shoes) can be used for good or ill. The Nazis used empathy to exploit the vulnerabilities of their victims to inflict emotional pain. Nevertheless, Kohut contended that empathy is what ultimately affirms our humanness and makes psychological existence possible (Kohut, *The Search for the Self*, vol. 4, 1990: 531–532). In an attempt to correct the many misunderstandings and misappropriations of empathy in the analytic relationship, Kohut offered the following toward the end of his life (1981); empathy is "the capacity to think and feel oneself into the inner life of another person." (*How Does Analysis Cure?* 1984: 82.) Indeed, the capacity to experience empathy is one of the five qualities identified by Kohut which signal the transformation of narcissism in the therapeutic relationship. The origin of empathy is located in the earliest mother-infant relationship as the developing self of the infant takes in the mother's feelings toward the infant.

Other determinants of a healthy self include creativity, transience, humor and wisdom. The analyst is able to observe these qualities developing in the transference relationship. Creativity, quite simply, is a person's ability to idealize his or her work; it suggests a capacity of playfulness and imagination. One may observe that a patient is now able to celebrate his or her innate skills and talents instead of seeking reassurance.

Transience is the ability to accept one's own mortality. The patient demonstrates an ability to surrender the need to be omnipotent, first in relationship to the analyst, and then subsequently in other relationships. Humor, if it is not a defensive posture (e.g., sarcasm may be a defensive signal), suggests an acceptance of transience. When humor is indicative of a transformation of narcissism, the patient has experienced a strengthening of his or her values and ideals. A genuine sense of humor, according to Kohut, is witnessed by the analyst as the patient's ego is able to experience amusement when reflecting upon old rigid configurations of the ego (e.g., grandiose fantasies and exhibitionistic strivings).

Wisdom, or at the very least a modicum of wisdom, may emerge at the end of a successful analysis. Like Freud, Kohut suggested that analysis never truly ends but he maintained that a successful analysis is eventually terminated. During the concluding phases of analysis, wisdom attained by the analysand helps to maintain self-esteem even upon recognizing personal limitations. The analysand may exhibit a friendly disposition toward the analyst even though there are conflicts remaining and the analyst's limitations have been recognized by the patient as well. In brief, human frailties are now tolerated with composure instead of being defended against with tendencies toward self-aggrandizement or infantile idealization.

Within a religious framework, too much interest in the self may be viewed as pride, self-centeredness, selfishness or sinfulness. Pastoral theologian Donald Capps has written about the narcissist as a tragic self (Capps, 1993) who feels more depleted than ever upon the recognition or observation that others receive the mirroring that one desires for oneself. The unmet desire for mirroring triggers a shame response as the grandiose self receives another disappointment. As Capps observes, many faithful Christians reel from the admonitions against seeking praise and recognition which is in itself a tragedy of faith because "[w]hat was a display of healthy narcissism is redefined as an expression of self-centeredness, and the Christian faith is used to legitimate the renunciation of our desire to be mirrored. This is tragic, for mirroring is at the very heart of the Christian gospel. Quite simply but profoundly, it is the form and means by which the depleted self experiences divine grace, the benediction of God" (Capps, 1993: 64). Thus, in part, Christian faith may be an impediment to the analytic process, especially if the narcissistic vulnerability presented by an analysand is a wounded grandiose self.

Bibliography

Capps, D. (1993). *The depleted self: Sin in a Narcissistic Age* (pp. 60–64). Minneapolis, MN: Fortress Press.

Freud, S. (1959). The Dynamics of Transference. In *The standard edition of the complete psychological works of Sigmund Freud* (J. Strachey, Trans., pp. 89–108) (Vol. 12). London: Hogarth Press.

Freud, S. (1959). On Narcissism. In *The standard edition of the complete psychological works of Sigmund Freud* (J. Strachey, Trans., pp. 67–102) (Vol. 14). London: Hogarth Press.

Kohut, H. (1971). *The Analysis of the Self: A Systematic Approach to the Psychoanalytic Treatment of Narcissistic Personality Disorders*. New York: International Universities Press.

Kohut, H. (1977). *The Restoration of the Self*. New York: International Universities Press.

Kohut, H. (1984). *How does analysis cure?* In Goldberg, A. (Ed.), (pp. 300–307). Chicago, IL: University of Chicago Press.

Kohut, H. (1991). *The search for the self* (P. Ornstein Ed., Vol. 4). NY: International Universities Press.

Siegel, A. M. (1996). *Heinz Kohut and the Psychology of the Self*. New York: Routledge.

Strozier, C. B. (Ed.). (1985). *Self Psychology and the Humanities*. New York: W. W. Norton.

Strozier, C. B. (2001). *Heinz Kohut: The making of a psychoanalyst*. New York: Farrar, Straus, & Giroux.

Sex and Religion

David A. Leeming

▶ Take me to you, imprison me, for I,
Except you enthrall me, never shall be free,
Nor ever chaste, except you ravish me.

(John Donne, *Holy Sonnet 15*)

Sexual and religious experiences have in common characteristics conveyed by such words as *desire, mystery, ritual, passion, ecstasy, and union*. Ideally we go to religious services and "to bed" because our bodies and our psyches *desire* something beyond ourselves. There is a sense of awe and mystery associated with both activities and certain *rituals* that contribute to *passion* and, when things go well, to *ecstasy* in both. The fact that, for some, such an analogy will smack of sacrilege or even heresy only indicates the depth of the split between these two natural human activities. If we have a deeply ingrained horror of mixing sex and religion, this has not always been so.

To begin as far back as we have records of religious experience we would have to look to the Paleolithic (Old Stone Age) period to such sites as the great painted caves and pre-historic settlement ruins in southern France. There we would find, among other objects, abstract and stylized drawings of what appear to be female genitalia and paintings of strange humanoid male figures with animal heads and pronounced genitals dancing before great horned beasts. The themes of the paintings and related figurines, and the dark and moist painted caves themselves, as many scholars have pointed out, suggest, not pre-historic bathroom graffiti, but myths of a goddess-based religion in which human sexuality, centered on the woman, serves as a metaphor for the hoped-for fertility of the humans of the given tribes and of the surrounding earth with its potential plant and animal food sources.

A natural development of the Paleolithic goddess mythology took place in the Mesolithic (Middle Stone Age) and Neolithic (New Stone Age) periods, in which the female, now clearly a mother goddess associated with the emerging practices of agriculture and animal husbandry, was often depicted in the act of giving birth, as, for example, in the famous case of the goddess on sanctuary walls and in figurines at the site called Çatal Hüyük in Anatolia (modern Turkey). Appropriately, the goddess at Çatal Hüyük was accompanied in her many birthing representations by a male fertility principle in the form of a bull.

The sacred marriage of the Great Goddess and the Bull of Heaven – of Earth and Sky – would be celebrated as a central act in the various forms of the Sumero-Babylonian religion in Mesopotamia throughout the Copper and Iron Ages. It was celebrated, for instance, in various "hymns" which today's religious people would probably consider to be pornographic and sacrilegious. In one hymn, the goddess Inanna calls out:

▶ My vulva, the sacred horn,
Heaven's vessel
Is eager, like the new moon, to be full.
My fallow land desires a plow
Who will plow my moist ground?

The goddess being impregnated and giving birth to new life was a logical and almost inevitable early metaphor for hunter gatherers and especially for agriculturalists that depended on the fertility of earth for survival. And it is in this context that the depositing of the male seed in the womb or any plant seed in the ground would have been expressed metaphorically by way of such mythical figures as the god who pours out his life-giving fluid and the dying and buried or "planted" god who returns in the spring.

The process by which sexuality begins to get a bad name in religion seems to coincide with the demise of female power and political importance in the face of a rising male-dominated, warrior-based patriarchy. In ancient Mesopotamia, for example, we find a significant change from early second millennium BCE Sumerian stories of a positive relationship between the hero-king Dumuzi (Tammuz) and the goddess Inanna (Ishtar) to a late Babylonian version of the stories, in which the heroic Gilgamesh scornfully refuses the advances of the same goddess. The situation in which the patriarchal hero refuses the sexual advances of the now suspect, strength-draining female is repeated in other contexts around the world. The Irish hero Cuchulainn's refusal of Queen Maeve – an avatar of the old fertility goddess Morrigan– is a Celtic example. The Bible contains stories of the harm that can come when the otherwise powerful and dominant male is seduced. The stories of Adam and Eve and Samson and Delilah are only two of many such stories in which the *femme fatale* has replaced the old fertility goddess. In Greece it is Pandora, whose name really means "gift giver" and who was in all likelihood once a goddess of agricultural abundance, who is said by Hesiod to have released the evils of the world from her famous box.

Nowhere is the antagonism between sexuality and religion more evident than in the three great monotheistic or Abrahamic religions, Judaism, Christianity, and Islam, as they have evolved. The "People of the Book" envision a world created alone by a distinctly mateless god, Yahweh-God-Allah. Although there are other examples of *ex nihilo* (from nothing) creations by male gods, the more natural metaphor for the conception and birth of the universe has involved the union of male and female. Whether by way of a primal mound (literally a pregnant Earth), the primal maternal waters, the cosmic egg, or intercourse between primal god and goddess, the feminine aspect of nature, with only a few exceptions, plays a significant role in the world's creation stories. This is true, for example, of most animistic religions as well as of Hinduism, Shinto, Taoism, and certain branches of Buddhism, although, it must be said, each of these religious cultures, like the Abrahamic traditions, has tended to place women in an inferior position to men in human society.

The exclusion of the feminine from godhead in the Abrahamic religions developed in part, of course, from the concept of a single deity and the desire of Jews, Christians, and Muslims to separate themselves from so-called Pagan traditions. Furthermore, the depiction of the Abrahamic god–Yahweh, God, or Allah,–as essentially male is a reflection of the realities of cultures that had long been patriarchal. It might well be argued, however, that patriarchy itself, including as it does the insistence on God's maleness and singularity and the relegation of women to secondary status is, as Karen Armstrong, has suggested, "expressive of deep anxiety and repression" (1993:50).

"Repression" is an important word here. We know, for instance, that the Hebrews in Canaan as depicted in the biblical book of *Exodus*, like most peoples of the ancient world, tended to assimilate the deities of conquered or neighboring peoples. It was only the development of priestly law and early rabbinical condemnation of Canaanite religious practices that led to the repression of the popular worship among the Hebrews of the goddess Asherah ("God's wife"), for example, in her many, often erotic, aspects. By being stripped from godhead, sexuality, associated particularly with women, inevitably became tainted by the concept of sin. Women were tempters, women were psychologically and even physically dangerous. Thus, it was Eve who corrupted Adam, initiating, among other things, shameful sex. And it was Delilah who seduced Samson, symbolically castrating him by cutting off his hair.

The repression of the natural relationship between sexuality and religion in the Abrahamic religions has not been limited to story or myth. It is clearly expressed in ritual practices which, whatever their original "religious" or social intent, have resulted in a sense of the essential impurity of certain biological functions associated with human sexuality and an inferior role for women. In effect, religion has been used to reinforce the repressive patriarchal idea of women as the valuable property of men, the necessary but controlled vehicles for pleasure – under certain circumstances – and reproduction.

Christianity and Islam have perpetuated the tradition of the essential impurity of sex and the consequential inferiority of women. The repression of sexuality in Christianity is expressed metaphorically in the depiction of Jesus and his mother in the canonical gospels and dogmas. There the asexuality of Jesus, the virginity of Mary, and Mary's own immaculate conception form a de facto denial of the sacredness of sexuality itself, a denial that is in conflict with the depictions of holy men and avatars of godhead in other religions – Krishna and Moses, for example. Jesus's asexuality undermines the theological position that Jesus is God truly sharing our human nature.

Until very recently, Christians and Jews, did not ordain women to their clergy ranks. And even now such ordination is denied not only by the more orthodox branches of Judaism but by most Muslims and by the largest sect of Christianity, the Roman Catholic Church. It should be pointed out that this is true in spite of the prominent role played by women in the early organization of Christianity and Islam.

Saul of Tarsus (Saint Paul) preached the "head covered, back of the church" doctrine that greatly resembles the early prohibitions against women studying the *Torah* or praying in the synagogues or the present restrictions applied to Muslim women in regard to places of prayer. By the second century CE, the North African theologian Tertullian (160–220) saw women as "the devil's gateway," a point of view developed by one of the most influential of the "church fathers", Saint Augustine (354–430), in the doctrine of Original Sin. The first sin, that of Adam, and especially Eve, was passed on to humans in the sexual act, he announced, an act to which men were enticed by women: "What is the difference, whether it is in a wife or a mother, it is still Eve the temptress that we must beware of in any woman" (see Armstrong, 1993:123–124).

As in the case of Judaism and Christianity, certain Islamic scholars have used often distorted understandings of scripture to justify what can only be called, in spite of various complex and supposedly positive rationales, the oppression of women in such institutions as polygamy, female circumcision, *purdah*, and the denial of basic social and political rights. At the center of this oppression has been the sense of male ownership and a strict double standard in regard to sexual practice. For the Muslim, as for the Christian and Jew, the female and female sexuality are powerful and potentially tempting distractions that can take the believer's mind away from religion and proper order and threaten male control. For many among the Abrahamic faithful – believers in the one god, a wifeless male god, and his prophets – to accept the equality of women would be to accept what are seen as the chaotic ways of the pagan. In short, the secondary status of women is linked to the doctrines of exclusivity associated with Judaism, Christianity, and Islam.

On the other hand, it has been argued by many that the Abrahamic attitude towards sexuality represents an alienation of humans from their humanity. Nietzsche called the Christian God a "crime against life." And there have, of course, always been challenges within religious traditions to the prevailing view of the incompatibility of sex and religion. Like the ancient hymns to Inanna, the biblical *Song of Songs* is a celebration of holy sex. And, implicitly or explicitly, mystics of all three Abrahamic religions (and other religions as well), have turned to sexuality for language that can convey the desire, the mystery, the ritual, the passion, the ecstasy, and the union that together comprise full religious experience.

In a poem of the sixteenth century Christian Spanish mystic Saint John of the Cross, the Soul sings of its intimate union with God:

> O flame of love so living,
> How tenderly you force
> To my soul's inmost core your fiery probe!
> Since now you've no misgiving,
> End it, pursue your course
> And for our sweet encounter tear the robe!

The thirteenth century Sufi (Muslim mystic) Jelaluddin Rumi used similar imagery to convey his sacred love of a friend, a love inseparable from his love of God:

> The Friend comes into my body
> looking for the center, unable
> to find it, draws a blade,
> strikes anywhere.

And later,

> Two hands, two feet, two eyes, good,
> as it should be, but no separation
> of the Friend and your loving.
> Any dividing there
> makes other untrue distinctions like "Jew",
> and "Christian", and "Muslim".

See also: ◉ Christianity ◉ Exodus ◉ God ◉ Great Mother ◉ Islam ◉ John of the Cross ◉ Ritual ◉ Song of Songs ◉ Sufis and Sufism

Bibliography

Armstrong, K. (1993). *A history of God*. New York: Knopf.

Campbell, R. (Trans.) (1967). *Poems of St. John of the Cross*. New York: Universal Library.

Moyne, J. and Barks, C. (Trans.) (1986). *Unseen rain: Quatrains of Rumi*. Putney, VT: Threshold Books.

Wolkstein, D. and Kramer, S. N. (Trans.) (1983). *Inanna: Queen of heaven and earth: Her stories and hymns from Sumer*. New York: Harper & Row.

Shadow

Stephen A. Diamond

For Swiss psychiatrist C. G. Jung (see Jung), the theory of the "shadow" was a metaphorical means of conveying the prominent role of the unconscious in both psychopathology and the perennial problem of evil (see evil). In developing his paradoxical conception of the shadow, Jung sought to provide a more highly differentiated, phenomenologically descriptive version of the unconscious and of the *id* (see id) than previously proffered by Freud. The shadow was originally Jung's poetic term for the totality of the unconscious, a depiction he took from philosopher Friedrich Nietzsche. But foremost for Jung was the task of further illuminating the shadowy problem of human evil and the prodigious dangers of excessive unconsciousness. Especially concerned with those pathological mental states historically known as "demonic possession," Jung's psychological construct of the shadow corresponds to yet differs fundamentally from the idea of the Devil or Satan in theology. As a parson's son, Jung was steeped in the Protestant mythos, digested the rich symbolism of Catholicism, and studied the other great religious and philosophical systems. But, as a physician, he intentionally employed the more mundane, banal, less esoteric or metaphysical and, therefore more rational terminology "the shadow" and "the unconscious" instead of the traditional religious language of god, devil, *daimon* or *mana* (see the daimonic). For Jung, depth psychological (see depth psychology) designations such as *the shadow* or *the unconscious*, were "coined for scientific purposes, and [are] far better suited to dispassionate observation which makes no metaphysical claims than are the transcendental concepts, which are controversial and therefore tend to breed fanaticism" (cited in Diamond, 1996: 97).

The shadow is the unknown "dark side" of our personality – dark both because it tends to consist predominantly of the primitive, benighted, negative, socially or religiously depreciated human emotions and impulses like sexual lust, power strivings, selfishness, greed, envy, aggression, anger or rage, and due to its unenlightened nature, obscured from consciousness. Whatever we deem evil, inferior or unacceptable and deny in ourselves becomes part of the shadow, the counterpoint to what Jung called the *persona* (see persona) or conscious ego personality. According to Jungian analyst Aniela Jaffe, the shadow is the "sum of all personal and collective psychic elements which, because of their incompatibility with the chosen conscious attitude, are denied expression in life...." (cited in Diamond, 1996: 96). Indeed, Jung differentiated between the *personal shadow* and the impersonal or *archetypal shadow*, which acknowledges transpersonal, pure or radical evil (symbolized by the Devil and demons) and collective evil, exemplified by the horror of the Nazi holocaust. Literary and historical figures such as Hitler, Charles Manson, and Darth Vader personify the shadow embodied in its most negative archetypal human form. "The shadow," wrote Jung (1963), is "that hidden, repressed, for the most part inferior and guilt-laden personality whose ultimate ramifications reach back into the realm of our animal ancestors and so comprise the whole historical aspect of the unconscious" (cited in Diamond, 1996: 96). The shadow is a primordial part of our human inheritance, which, try as we might, can never be eluded.

The pervasive Freudian defense mechanism known as "projection" is how most people deny their shadow, unconsciously casting it onto others so as to avoid confronting it in oneself. Such projection of the shadow is engaged in not only by individuals but groups, cults, religions, and entire countries, and commonly occurs during wars and other contentious conflicts in which the outsider, enemy or adversary is made a scapegoat, dehumanized, and demonized. Two World Wars and the current escalation of violence testify to the terrible truth of this collective phenomenon. Since the turn of the twenty-first century we are witnessing a menacing resurgence of epidemic demonization or collective psychosis in the seemingly inevitable violent global collision between radical Islam and Judeo-Christian or secular western culture, each side projecting its collective shadow and perceiving the other as evil incarnate.

For Jung, the shadow is most destructive, insidious and dangerous when habitually repressed and projected, manifesting in myriad psychological disturbances ranging from neurosis to psychosis, irrational interpersonal hostility, and even cataclysmic international clashes. Such deleterious symptoms, attitudes, and behavior stem from being possessed or driven by the dissociated yet undaunted shadow. Robert Louis Stevenson's classic story of *The Strange Case of Dr. Jekyll and Mr. Hyde* can be taken as a cautionary tale par excellence: dissociation of the shadow results in a perilously lopsided development of the conscious personality and renders us susceptible to destructive possession by the disowned shadow. The overly good Dr. Henry Jekyll is at times taken over body and soul by his equally evil shadow: the depraved, nefarious, wicked Edward Hyde, his complete opposite. Indeed, the shadow contains all those qualities we hide from ourselves and others, but which remain active within the unconscious, forming a sort of "splinter personality" or "complex," not unlike the relatively autonomous sub-personalities found in multiple personality (dissociative identity disorder) or in so-called demonic possession or demonism (see devil; exorcism; daimonic). Under stressful circumstances or in states of fatigue or intoxication, this compensatory alter ego or shadow complex can be triggered into temporarily taking total command of the conscious will. The abject negativity and destructiveness of the shadow is largely a function of the degree to which the individual neglects and refuses to take responsibility for it, only inflaming its ferocity and pernicious power. The shadow's sometimes overwhelming strength and disturbing ability to intrude into one's cognitions, affects and behavior has historically been experienced and misinterpreted as demonic possession, for which exorcism is believed to be the only treatment (see exorcism). Yet, it must be emphasized that the shadow is not meant to be taken literally but rather, allegorically: it is not an evil entity existing apart from the person, nor an invading alien force, though it may be felt as such. The shadow is a universal (archetypal) feature of the human psyche for which we bear full responsibility to cope with as creatively as possible.

But despite its well-deserved reputation for wreaking havoc and engendering widespread suffering in human affairs, the shadow – in distinction to the literal idea of the devil or demons–can be redeemed: The shadow must never be dismissed as merely evil or demonic, for it contains natural, life-giving, underdeveloped positive potentialities too. Coming to terms with the shadow and constructively accepting and assimilating it into the conscious personality is central to the process of Jungian analysis. Working with dream material (see dreams) is key to comprehending and dealing constructively with the shadow. The shadow tends to appear in dreams as a figure of the same sex as the dreamer, but Jung draws a distinction between the personal shadow and the *anima* or *animus* (see anima/animus), symbolized in dreams as the opposite sex. Typically, it is the subjective experience of the shadow or evil and its ego-dystonic effects (or, as in the case of the hypercivilized Dr. Jekyll, an inexplicable malaise or vague sense that something vital is missing in us) which motivates the person to seek psychotherapy and spurs one toward new growth, maturation, and individuation (see individuation). Indeed, in many ways we need the shadow, and must therefore learn to develop a more conscious and constructive relationship to it. Becoming conscious of the shadow requires tolerating the inherent tension of opposites within, sometimes "having it out" with the shadow and standing up to its destructive influence; other times permitting it some measured outward expression in the personality; but always treating it with utmost respect.

Notwithstanding its negative influence, Jung understood the *daimonic* nature of the unconscious, and that the compensatory effects of the shadow upon individuals, couples, groups and nations could be beneficial as well: "If it has been believed hitherto that the human shadow was the source of all evil, it can now be ascertained on closer investigation that the unconscious man, that is, his shadow, does not consist only of morally reprehensible tendencies, but also displays a number of good qualities, such as normal instincts, appropriate reactions, realistic insights, creative impulses, etc" (cited in Diamond, 1996: 96). Creativity can spring from the constructive expression or integration of the shadow, as can true spirituality. *Authentic spirituality* requires consciously accepting and relating properly to the shadow as opposed to repressing, projecting, acting out and remaining naively unconscious of its contents, a sort of precarious *pseudospirituality.* "Bringing the shadow to consciousness," writes another of Jung's distinguished followers, Liliane Frey-Rohn (1967),

▶ is a psychological problem of the highest moral significance. It demands that the individual hold himself accountable not only for what happens to him, but also for what he projects... Without the conscious inclusion of the shadow in daily life there cannot be a positive relationship to other people, or to the creative sources in the soul; there cannot be an individual relationship to the Divine (cited in Diamond, 1996: 109).

Acknowledgement

Derived and reprinted by permission from Anger, Madness, and the Daimonic: The Psychological Genesis of Violence, Evil, and Creativity by Stephen A. Diamond, the State University of New York Press ©1996, State University of New York. All rights reserved.

See also: ❯ Anima and Animus ❯ Archetype ❯ Daimonic ❯ Depth Psychology and Spirituality ❯ Devil ❯ Evil ❯ Id ❯ Individuation ❯ Nazism ❯ Persona

Bibliography

Diamond, S. (1996). *Anger, madness, and the daimonic: The psychological Genesis of violence, evil, and creativity* (Foreword by Rollo May. A volume in the SUNY series in the Philosophy of Psychology). Albany, NY: State University of New York Press.

Frey-Rohn, L. (1967). Evil from the psychological point of view. In *Evil*. Evanston, IL: Northwest University Press.

Sanford, J. A. (1987). *The strange trial of Mr. Hyde: A new look at the nature of human evil*. San Francisco, CA: Harper & Row.

Sanford, J. A. (1990). *Evil: The shadow side of reality*. New York: Crossroad Publishing Company.

Stwenson, R. L. (1964). *The Strange case of Dr. Jekyll and Mr. Hyde*. New York: Airmont.

Zweig, C., & Abrams, J. (Eds.). (1991). *Meeting the shadow: The hidden power of the dark side of human nature*. Los Angeles, CA: Tarcher/Putnam.

Shakers

David C. Balderston

The Shakers were the largest, longest lasting, and the most widespread of all the communal or utopian societies that emerged in nineteenth century America, whether secular (Fourierists, Owenites) or religious (at Amana, Bishop Hill, Ephrata, New Harmony, Oneida, and Zoar). Their formal name is the United Society of Believers in Christ's Second Appearing. A Christian millennial sect, they looked to their founder, "Mother" Ann Lee, as a female manifestation of the Christ spirit.

Origin

Described first as "Shaking Quakers" from the free, ecstatic movements that characterized their worship (shaking or trembling is mentioned in several passages in the *Bible* as God's powerful activity and humans' response, e.g., Psalm 99: 1, Ezekiel 38: 19–20, and Philippians 2: 12–13) and because they were mistaken for nonconformist Quakers, the Shakers developed certain religious and psychological practices that helped them to grow, prosper, and endure for many decades, eventually shrinking to currently one small group at Sabbathday Lake, ME – still vibrant and supported by a dedicated organization of Friends of the Shakers.

From humble, working class origins in Manchester, England, at a time of religious ferment and searching outside the Established (Anglican) Church, e.g., the Quaker movement, itinerant preachers such as Methodist George Whitefield, and possibly the immigrant "French Prophets" or Camisards, an illiterate woman named Mrs. Ann Lees Standerin emerged as a charismatic leader in a local revivalist group previously organized by a couple named Wardley. After persecutions, she and a few followers, including her husband who eventually left her, emigrated in 1774 to New York City in the American colonies. Within a few years, they had established themselves near Albany, NY, first at a wilderness site called Niskayuna (now Watervliet), and later at a permanent center not far away in New Lebanon, NY. A nearby revival of "New Light" Baptists was petering out, and Ann Lee's fresh message of salvation found willing converts.

Growth

Missionaries were soon sent from the new center into four New England states. While enduring prejudice, violent opposition, and the death of Ann Lee in 1784 at age 48, the Shakers still managed to establish a total of 11 communities by 1793. Several strong and capable leaders, both female and male, carried on her work, and by 1836, ten additional communities had been founded in Ohio, Kentucky, Indiana, and western New York. Out of a total of 23 Shaker communities, 18 endured for an average of over 125 years. The Shakers reached a peak population of 5000–6000 by ca. 1840.

Religious Practices

Religiously, the Shakers were noted for the following: an emphasis on the female or maternal aspect of God as manifested in Ann Lee; men and women considered equal in their religious contributions and leadership; their "shaking" behavior during worship including strange and spontaneous movements and vocalizations early in their history, and organized marches and patterned gestures later on; celibacy and separation of the sexes by mandating separate sleeping quarters, dining tables, seating in worship, and entrances to major buildings; pacifism; confession of sins; separation from the "world's people" in isolated villages; the inspired creation of many new songs, hymns, and mystical "spirit drawings" – especially in the revival period known as "Mother's Work" (1837–1847). Members turned over all their money and possessions to the community, following the examples of the early first century CE Christians, as recorded in the *Bible's* New Testament at Acts 2:44–45 and 4:32–35 where they "had all things in common." Biblical support for the female aspect of divinity is found in Genesis 1:27 and Rev.12:1 ff., while the breakup of marriage is justified at Luke 20: 34–35, and supported by Jesus' radical challenge to abandon family ties at Matt. 10:35–37 and Luke 14:26. While confession of sins was a universal requirement, and the loss of sexuality, possessions, and family ties was a standard sacrifice, probably the dominant theme of Shaker religion has been an upbeat one: *love*, always available from God and always needed between humans – a succinct principle that exemplifies the Shakers' characteristic simplicity.

Psychosocial Features

Psychologically, the Shakers' egalitarian view of both sexes allowed for the unopposed emergence of several exceptional female leaders. The absolutes of celibacy and separation of the sexes were tempered by the Shakers' enthusiastic worship, e.g., loud singing, synchronized energetic marching and dancing, and physical gestures in which both sexes mirrored each other. During much of the nineteenth century, young men and women would join in "union meetings," small, mid-week gatherings where the sexes would sit in two rows opposite each other and converse, with an elder Shaker monitoring, on various topics of the day – an outlet that helped make the restricted yet close daily proximity of the sexes workable. Individualism was downplayed while the importance of the community was stressed: cemeteries have just one large gravestone marked "Shakers," or small uniform markers recording only names and dates. When whole families joined, they were separated into men's and women's dwellings and their children reared communally. Communities were organized into large, separately sited "Families" for full members, novices, and inquirers, with a leadership hierarchy of elders and eldresses, deacons and deaconesses. Although previous family ties were severed, this community organization provided a larger family, in which all members were known as "brethren" and "sisters," while special leaders were termed "Mother" and "Father." In an age when divorce was nearly impossible and separation usually brought poverty, many women in distressed marriages found refuge among the Shakers, and not just their children but the many orphans left at Shaker villages were given educations considered superior for the times. In general, the austerities of Shaker life seem to have been balanced by spiritual resources and intuitive psychological sensitivity that enabled their remarkably long and fruitful communal existence.

The Shakers' well organized communal life and industrious work ethic produced prosperous farms, innovative crafts, excellent functionally designed chairs and cabinetwork, a widely marketed variety of seeds in standardized packets, and a wholesome, plentiful diet – all of which made possible a unique material culture that also expressed the Shakers' active religious life, summarized in their motto: "Hands to work and hearts to God."

Decline

The all-too-human occasions of youth to rebel against authority, of trustees (who were delegated to conduct business with the outside world) to embezzle funds or invest unwisely, and of illicit lovers and disillusioned apostates to leave the community – all these challenged the Shakers, but after the Civil War external economic and social factors caused an accelerating decline in new members, and the consolidation of communities and then their closing, with some to reopen later as museums. The growth of cities, industrialism, and spreading rail networks reduced the market for Shakers' agricultural and handcrafted products, while also increasing the allure of "the world" with new employment options and personal freedoms available. The proportion of male members shrank, and farming was increasingly done by hired non-Shakers. Women came to dominate in leadership roles, and the average longevity of remaining members increased significantly, due to a healthy lifestyle and the mutual support of communal living. As times changed, so did many aspects of the Shakers' daily life and worship, demonstrating their adaptiveness.

Institutional Strengths

While the Shakers had their origins in spontaneous ecstasies and confrontational testimonies, as their emotional responses to being seized and shaken by the sudden visitation of the Christ spirit, their widespread expansion and long endurance owes as much to the development, after Ann Lee's death, of rational ordering of their social organization, economic structure, and formal worship – all of which were designed to perpetuate, less spontaneously, the original message that was so liberating and spiritually nourishing to so many.

Historiography

Questions remain about the accuracy of some early accounts, and especially about the view that Ann Lee's loss of her four children at very early ages had determined her negative view of sex (although reportedly Mrs. Wardley, an earlier Shaker, had also promoted sexual abstinence). Besides thousands of the Shakers' own publications and manuscripts now in archives, many non-Shakers have written about them; see the bibliography for recommended authors. Aaron Copeland's 1944 music for

Martha Graham's ballet, "Appalachian Spring," incorporated the now-famous tune, "*Simple Gifts*," composed perhaps in 1848. More recent television specials and musical recordings continue to appreciate and publicize aspects of the Shaker legacy.

See also: ❯ Female God Images ❯ Gender Roles

Bibliography

Andrews, E. D. (1962). *The gift to be simple: Songs, dances and rituals of the American shakers*. New York: Dover Publications. (Reprint of 1940 original, published by New York: J. J. Augustin).

The Bible. New Revised Standard Version (1989). New York: Oxford University Press.

Brewer, P. J. (1986). *Shaker communities, Shaker lives*. Hanover, NH: University Press of New England.

Burns, A. S. & Burns, K. (1990). *The Shakers: Hands to work, hearts to God*. New York: Portland House (of Random House). (Reprint of 1987 original by Aperture Foundation, New York, and based on the 1984 film for public television with the same title).

Desroche, H. (1971). *The American Shakers: From Neo-Christianity to Presocialism*. Amherst, MA: University of Massachusetts Press (Translated from the 1955 French original and edited by J. J. Savacool).

Francis, R. (2000). *Ann the Word*. London: Fourth Estate.

Melcher, M. F. (1960). *The Shaker adventure*. Cleveland, OH: The Press of Western Reserve University (Reprint of 1941 original by Princeton, NJ: Princeton University Press).

Morse, F. (1980). *The Shakers and the world's people*. New York: Dodd, Mead.

Sprigg, J. (1987). *Shaker – Life, work and art* (photos by Michael Freeman). New York: Stewart, Tabori & Chang.

Stein, S. J. (1992). *The Shaker experience in America*. New Haven, CT: Yale University Press.

Wertkin, G. C. (1986). *The four seasons of Shaker life* (at Sabbathday Lake, ME) (photos by Ann Chwatsky). New York: Simon & Schuster.

Shakti

David A. Leeming

The Sanskrit for "power" or "energy," Shakti (*sakti*) in Indian religion is the energizing material power of a given Hindu god, a power personified as his wife, especially the wife of Shiva. Often depicted in a state of sexual union, the god and his shakti together represent the Absolute, the god being non-activated Eternity, the goddess being activated Time. The Goddess, Devi, *is* Shakti or "Universal Power." As Prakrti, she is the shakti or female energy by which the original Purusha, the primal male, becomes creation. As Lakshmi, she is the manifestation of the divine energy associated with Vishnu. Shiva's shakti takes many forms – Uma, Durga, the terrifying Kali, the motherly Parvati, for instance. By extension, Sita is the Vishnu avatar Rama's shakti in the *Ramayana*, and Draupadi is the shakti of the Pandavas in the *Mahabharata*. And by further extension, the Hindu wife is a manifestation of her husband's shakti. By still further extension, shakti may be said to be the spiritual equivalent of the Jungian *anima* (Latin for psyche or soul) in which the anima is the subconscious inner self of the male – his feminine principle – and the related animus is the subconscious inner self or masculine principle of the female. The individual might be said to be animated by the anima/animus as the god is animated by his Shakti.

See also: ❯ Anima and Animus ❯ Jung, Carl Gustav

Bibliography

Jung, C. G. (1959). *The archetypes of the collective unconscious* (1934/1954). Princeton, NJ: Princeton University Press.

Jung, C. G. (1973). *Concerning the archetypes, with special reference to the anima concept, CW 9, 1* (pp. 54–72). Princeton, NJ: Princeton University Press.

Leeming, D. A. (2005). *The Oxford companion to World mythology*. New York: Oxford University Press.

Leeming, D. A., & Leeming, M. (1994). *Encyclopedia of creation myths*. Santa Barbara, CA: ABC-CLIO. (Revised as *A Dictionary of Creation Myths*, New York: Oxford University Press, 1994).

Shamanic Healing

Meg Bowles

What is Shamanism?

Shamanism is an ancient method of healing found in many cultures that focuses upon the relief of spiritual pain and suffering through interventions in non-ordinary reality. Non-ordinary reality (see Castaneda, who originally coined the term) can be described as the dimension of the Cosmos that exists outside of and parallel to the linear time-space arena of ordinary awareness. What distinguishes the shaman from other healers is the ecstatic flight or journey into non-ordinary reality in order to contact his or her tutelary spirits for the knowledge and healing needed for a specific patient or community. The shamanic state of consciousness which enables the shaman to see what others do not, is entered into and exited at will, usually with the aid of repetitive drumming or rattling. The drum is often seen as a spirit horse whose sound allows the shaman to ride into the Upper or Lower Worlds of the shamanic Cosmos. It is the helping, compassionate spirits that the shaman interacts with in these realms – the power animals, teachers, and other wise beings – who do the diagnosis as well as the healing work in partnership with the shaman. A master of linking the ordinary with the non-ordinary worlds, the shaman therefore functions as an intermediary or bridge who also interprets and communicates the meaning of what is experienced in these alternate realities.

The resurgence of interest in shamanism and shamanic healing that has been thriving for the past few decades is evidence of a deepening hunger to reconnect with the transcendent dimensions of reality in a direct, revelatory way. Ancient shamanic practices have been resurrected and revitalized throughout the world as indigenous people have become freer to practice their own traditions openly (as in the former Soviet Union for example), and have sought to recover the old ways of their ancestors in order to heal themselves and their communities. Feminine shamanic traditions which possess more of an interpersonal orientation, that encourage and empower patients to become active participants in their own healing are also taking their rightful place of importance alongside the more masculine, heroic shamanic traditions (see Tedlock) where the patient adopts more of a passive role. While some Westerners have been drawn to study with indigenous shamans, many more have been able to explore shamanism through various training programs in what has become known as "core" shamanism that have been offered all over the world through organizations such as the Foundation for Shamanic Studies.

Core Shamanism

The body of work referred to as core shamanism was originally synthesized and brought to Westerners by the pioneering work of anthropologist Michael Harner. During the 1950s, Harner conducted extensive fieldwork with the Jivaro and Conibo people in South America and was eventually initiated as a shaman. After further research into many other shamanic practices throughout the world, Harner began to synthesize and distill the fundamental techniques that he found in common across various traditions into a universal, core practice for integration into Western contemporary life. These techniques, the primary one being the shamanic journey process which enables one to enter into the characteristic ecstatic, shamanic state of consciousness, have proven to be accessible even for those who have no prior training or conscious experience with anything remotely shamanic.

Core shamanism is essentially a modern spiritual practice free of specific religious or cultural requirements. That said, the basic world view embodied in both traditional and core shamanism is an animist one which perceives everything in the Cosmos as being imbued with life essence or spirit, including all members of the varied and wondrous kingdoms that are part of the natural world. Everything is alive and connected within an intricate web or tapestry of energy, both in this physical realm as well as in other parallel realities. In contrast to a psychological perspective of spirits, where the phenomenon might be viewed as an externalization of an unconscious, autonomous complex (Jung), the shamanic experience of spirits is that they have an innate intelligence and a reality of their own that exists outside of the personal and collective psyche.

The Spiritual Origins of Illness

Shamans and practitioners of core shamanism see the phenomenon of illness as a spiritual problem resulting from either a loss of power, a loss of soul, or an intrusion of an energy form which does not belong in the patient, which may be localized somewhere in the energy body or, in the case of spirit possession, systemic. A person suffering from soul loss, for example, does not feel fully alive and engaged with life. Symptoms of soul loss may include experiences of chronic depression, dissociation, addiction, and unresolved grief as well as persistent physical illness. Judging by that list many if not all of us suffer, or have suffered, from some form of soul loss during the course of our lives. There are a number of ways in which the lost soul can spontaneously return to embodiment, such as in a healing dream or even in a luminous moment during analytic work. Sometimes however, a shamanic intervention by another is needed.

Soul Retrieval

One of the most powerful core shamanic healing practices engaged in today is that of soul retrieval, a classic form of shamanic healing (Eliade, 1972) which was spontaneously rediscovered in a journey by shamanic practitioner, author, and therapist Sandra Ingerman during work with a client many years ago. Soul retrieval is a healing ritual where the shamanic practitioner, in partnership with her tutelary spirits, journeys into non-ordinary reality to search for the missing soul parts which are ready to be returned to the patient. The soul parts are located, interacted with, and finally "pulled" or carried out of non-ordinary reality as the journey ends, after which the practitioner restores them to the patient by blowing their essence into the heart and crown chakras of the patient's body. The energy contained in the returned soul essence is often experienced and felt on a subtle yet palpable level by the patient.

According to Ingerman, soul loss is a natural response to unbearable trauma. Trauma triggers a self-protective phenomenon consisting of the splitting off of a part of one's vital essence or "soul," which then literally flees the patient to become stuck in a dimension of non-ordinary reality where it then leads a parallel existence, but one where the gifts and potentials of that soul part (as well as the memories of the trauma) remain inaccessible and no longer incarnated in this world. This view is not so different from that of an analytical psychologist, who might conceive of soul loss as an archetypal defense of the personal spirit (Kalsched, 1996); however, an analytical psychologist might also perceive the phenomenon as taking place in the inner world of the patient (see self care system) whereas according to Harner, the practitioner of core shamanism observes the evidence of soul loss empirically, in the parallel universe known as non-ordinary reality.

Integration with Other Healing Modalities

There is a growing interest with regards to integrating core shamanic healing practices with analytical psychology (and other forms of psychotherapy) as well as with other disciplines such as Western medicine. Having been trained as a psychotherapist, Ingerman sees work of therapy as having tremendous value; however, her pragmatic view is that for the necessary psychological working – through process to progress, the patient's soul must be embodied and therefore in residence or "home"

to engage with the therapist – hence the need for the shamanic approach to bring back the split-off soul parts in order to restore wholeness to the patient. Many analysts who have found themselves working endlessly with a patient's "false self" (Winnicott) as they patiently hold a space for the vulnerable child to appear in their consulting rooms might resonate with Ingerman's position. While the experience of soul retrieval can be a powerful and transformative process standing on its own, or as a complementary practice to deepen the work of psychotherapy, it does not provide a quick fix. As with any other healing modality, there can be pitfalls, such as if the egos of the patient and/or the practitioner get in the way of the process. The work of facilitating and integrating the return of soul into life can be arduous, complex, and humbling, as much as it can be deeply rewarding.

Conclusion

Integrating the two disciplines of analytical psychology and core shamanism in a way that honors the power and essence of each practice without falling into a diluted soup of New Age meaninglessness presents a worthy challenge going forward for all of us who seek wholeness for ourselves and the patients with whom we work.

See also: ◉ Healing ◉ Shamans and Shamanism

Bibliography

Castaneda, C. (1971). *A separate reality*. New York: Simon and Schuster.

Cowan, T. (1996). *Shamanism as a spiritual practice for daily life*. Freedom, CA: Crossing Press.

Eliade, M. (1972). *Shamanism: Archaic techniques of ecstasy*. Princeton, NJ: Princeton University Press.

Harner, M. (1980). *The way of the Shaman*. San Francisco, CA: Harper & Row.

Ingerman, S. (1991). *Soul retrieval: Mending the fragmented self*. San Francisco, CA: Harper San Francisco.

Jung, C. (1920). The psychological foundations of belief in spirits, in *The collected works of C. G. Jung* (Vol. 8, 2nd ed.). Princeton, NJ: Princeton University Press, 1972, pp. 301–318.

Kalsched, D. (1996). *The inner world of trauma*. New York: Routledge.

The Society for Shamanic Practitioners, www.shamansociety.org.

Tedlock, B. (2005). *The woman in the Shaman's body: Reclaiming the feminine in religion and medicine*. New York: Bantam Dell.

The Foundation for Shamanic Studies, www.shamanism.org.

Walsh, R. (2007). *The world of Shamanism: New views of an ancient tradition*. Woodbury, MN: Llewellyn Publications.

Walsh, R. and Grob, C. S. (2005). *Higher wisdom.* Interview with Michael Harner. Albany, NY: State University of New York Press.

Winnicott, D. W. (1960). Ego distortion in terms of true and false self. In *The maturational process and the facilitating environment: Studies in the theory of emotional development* (pp. 140–152). New York: International UP Inc., 1965.

Shamans and Shamanism

Richard W. Voss

Context for the Discussion: Shamans and Non-Ordinary Reality

▶ Shamanism is a great mental and emotional adventure, one in which the patient as well as the shaman-healer are involved. Through his heroic journey and efforts, the shaman helps his patients transcend their normal, ordinary definition of reality, including the definition of themselves as ill. The shaman shows his patients that they are not emotionally and spiritually alone in their struggles against illness and death. The shaman shares his special powers and convinces his patients, on a deep level of consciousness, that another human is willing to offer up his own self to help them. The shaman's self-sacrifice calls forth a commensurate emotional commitment from his patients, a sense of obligation to struggle alongside the shaman to save one's own self. Caring and curing go hand in hand (Harner, 1990: xviii).

The generic term "shaman" describes a wide range of practices among indigenous people wherein "helpers" or "spirits" are called upon to help the patient asking the shaman for help. The term is derived from the language of the Tungus people of Siberia (Eliade, 1964, Harner, 1990), and from the Chinese, *sha men*, as well as the ancient Sanskrit *sramana* which is translated as "ascetic" and from sramati as "he fatigues" (Hopkins, 1918). The term describes the indigenous practitioner who works with spirit helpers, and through whom the spirits "doctor" or treat the individuals that come for help and healing. Often the metaphor of the "hollow bone or tube" is used to describe the power of the shaman – as he or she is one who is simply a tool or conduit for the helping or healing process – the power for the healing comes from something beyond the shaman – often from some other world or realm. Generally the shaman does not seek to become a shaman, but the spirits choose him or her for this purpose or the individual inherits the "helpers" or "medicine" from their family ancestors (Personal communication, 1999, 2001). John A. Grim noted that "Among tribal people the shaman is the person, male or female, who experiences, absorbs, and communicates a special mode of sustaining, healing power. For most tribal peoples the vital rhythms of the natural world are manifestations of a mysterious, all-pervasive power presence" (see van der Leeuw, 1938/1963; Grim, 1983).

In the past other, more pejorative terms were used to describe these healers, such as "witch," "medicine man or woman," "witch doctor," and "sorcerer," etc., so the use of the more generic term "shaman" avoids such prejudicial overlays to this healing tradition, and is preferred (Harner, 1990). The shaman is distinguished from other kinds of healers by his or her use of altered consciousness, which Eliade called "ecstasy" (cited in Harner, 1990). Harner notes that shamanism is the most widespread and ancient methods or systems of mind-body healing known to humanity (1990: 40). Equally remarkable is fact that the assumptions and methods or processes of shamanism are very similar across the various and distant regions of the world (Harner, 1990; Eliade, 1964). Years ago, one of my students showed me a video tape of a spirit-calling ceremony conducted in a remote indigenous community in Brazil – which had many elements I had observed in traditional Lakota spirit-calling ceremonies, such as the use earth in the "altar" as well as the use of six directions' flags (the black, red, yellow, white, blue, and green), tobacco offerings, a darkened room cleared of all furniture.

Harner noted that the shaman

▶ operates in nonordinary reality only a small portion of his [or her] time, and then only as needed to perform shamanic tasks, for shamanism is a part-time activity. Among the Jivaro, the Conibo, the Eskimo, and most other primitive groups, the master shaman is usually an active participant in the economic, social, and even political affairs of the community... The shaman moves back and forth between the two realities deliberately and with serious intention (1990: 46).

The shaman I met in a remote Amazonian community was the president of his community council, a teacher, and also collected Brazil nuts in the forest. When I first met him, his riverboat was on it's way to the market, heading away from his village. When he learned that I had come to interview him, he met me at the small village grocery store where I was told to meet him – I was amazed that he arrived sooner than I did, even though he had been traveling in the opposite direction. He was a highly respected political leader of his community, was modestly dressed, and wore a rosary around his neck. The interview took place on the porch of the small building which served as the local "grocery store." Other traditional "medicine men" or shaman I met often worked tirelessly helping their communities, one actually served as Chairman of the tribe, served on tribal council, and conducted healing ceremonies whenever requested – pretty much at the request of anyone seeking help and assistance (Personal communication, 1999, 2001).

Shamans Do not Operate in the Abstract

I think the best way to discuss C/Shamanism is to describe it in concrete terms. In 2004 I had the opportunity to conduct field research in concert with the Amazon Center for Environmental Education and Research (ACEER) as part of a Faculty Development Grant made possible by West Chester University and the ACEER. As part of this project I visited a traditional indigenous Ese'eja community along the Tambopata River in southeastern Peru. While conducting this field research I had the opportunity to interview numerous individuals about the healing and helping traditions of c/shamans in the area. These interviews included interviews with chaman, patients, community leaders, and other healthcare professionals. As part of this research, I asked a recognized chaman if he would sing a healing song used in his ceremonies. He told me to return later that evening to his casita, not exactly answering my question. Over the years I have learned to follow directions literally, without analysis (which requires a shift from my otherwise usual mode of study). I returned to the little casita at nightfall where he was resting in his hammock. I was invited to sit in one of the adjoining hammocks where we continued our conversation until he invited me into his house.

The Entire Forest Was Dancing!

I was instructed to sit on the edge of his bed. He rolled four tobacco cigarettes, each about 3 in. long, and laid them aside. The C/Shaman stood in front of me. Then he poured rose water over my head from a small bottle which dripped over my face and back. The rose water had a very pleasant fragrance. He then lit one of the cigarettes and blew smoke on me and all around me. He then took a small bunch of long leaves (called a chakra) that were

tied at the stem which formed a handle; the leaf rattle was approximately 10 in. in total length and about 6 in. wide. The C/Shaman then began striking the top of my head with the chakra while he sang a very simple melody in a very soft, subdued birdlike whistle, formed by the air blown against the roof of the mouth through the teeth, not a hollow whistle blown through the lips. All the while the C/Shaman continuously struck the top of my head gently with the chakra. The C/Shaman's song did not have any recognizable words, consisting of a very simple and subdued, yet shrill, whistle. I recall thinking how simple and childlike the tune was – it seemed like a very "happy" tune. I recall feeling very relaxed and that I was "in good hands." There were no explanations given by the C/Shaman; the process was entirely experiential. By this time I had closed my eyes and I focused on the rustling sound of the dry leaves of the chakra. Before I knew it, with each strike of the chakra, I felt as if the entire forest had opened up, and was dancing around me. It was as if the little leaf rattle became the spokesman for the forest, and it was as if I was hearing the entire forest singing and dancing all around me and I was part of it. It was as if the C/Shaman had brought the entire vegetation of the Amazon into that little casita.

Shamanism and Psychology

John A. Grim noted a more universal implication for the interest in shamanism, noting, "Shamanism is not only characteristic of tribal peoples but also is an ongoing and irreducible mode of experiencing the sacred that is not limited to a particular ethnic group. . . 'Elsewhere he noted that ". . . shamanism has a certain attraction for our times, when the more sophisticated, or more rationalized, modes of religious life are often so weak that they no longer communicate the power needed by contemporary man, who must resolve a new and overwhelming set of tensions in a creative manner'" (1983: 29). Shamanism is particularly of interest to those interested in the intersection between religion and psychology, J. A. Grim noted further, that "The meaning of shamanism lies in the depths of the human psyche, which is not yet fully known to itself but is partially manifest in particular human efforts to structure symbols as a way of knowing" (1983: 31).

Conclusion

A discussion of shamans and shamanism provides an important perspective on the intersectionality of

Psychology, Religion, and Ecstatic Experience, and focuses the clinician on the role of "caring and healing" in the therapeutic interaction which is not focused on clinical detachment or objectivity, but rather on ecstatic engagement, connectivity, and the subjectivity of the healer with the patient where both encounter the non-ordinary reality and subsequent psychological and spiritual transformation.

See also: ❯ Eliade, Mircea ❯ Healing ❯ Shamanic Healing

Bibliography

Eliade, M. (1964). *Shamanism: Archaic techniques of ecstasy.* Princeton, NJ: Princeton University Press (Reprint, 2004).

Grim, J. A. (1983). *The Shaman: Patterns of religious healing among the ojibway Indians,* Norman, OK: University of Oklahoma.

Harner, M. (1990). *The way of the Shaman.* San Francisco, CA: HarperSanFranciso, A Division of HarperCollins Publishers.

Harvey, G. (Ed.). (2003). *Shamanism. A reader.* London: Routledge.

Hopkins, E. W. (1918). *The history of religions.* New York: The Macmillan Company, Harvard Despository Brittle Book (AH 5AST D). Retrieved from http://books.google.com/books?id=17sVAAAAYAAJ&dq=history+of+religions+hopkins&printsec=frontcover&source=bl&ots=Se1c0aD5Dj&sig=LbTOq_AXwOvk3UFWg12rRD60d2c&hl=en&ei=WeEvSvnGIpOqtgf2-pCLDA&sa=x&oi=book_result&ct=result&resnum=1#PPP7,M1 on June 10, 2009.

Van der Leeuw, G. (1938/1963). *Religion in essence and manifestation.* London: Allen & Unwin; Harper Paperbacks.

Shame and Depth Psychology

Gerardo James de Jesus

Shame

Shame can be defined simply as the feeling we have when we evaluate our actions, feelings, or behavior, and conclude that what we have done wrong, makes us wrong. It encompasses the whole of us; it generates a wish to hide, to disappear, or even to die. Shame, as the deeper problem of the self, means that one has suffered a loss of being, not merely loss of status. Individuals suffering from a shame-based complex have a characterological style of identification with a given behavior due to internalization. For example, when someone is called "an angry person" an emotion becomes the core of his character or identity. He doesn't *have* anger or depression; he *is* angry or depressed. Similarly, shame-based people identify with this affect – toned complex in a globalized way which becomes characteristic of their behavior. People with shame-based complexes guard against exposing their inner selves to others, but more significantly, will guard against exposing themselves to themselves. The shamed affect is ignited upon hearing a single word, observing a gesture by another that is distorted and catastrophized, or by just about anything that will trigger the complex, creating a negative affect that is felt in a global sense.

One way of understanding a shame-based complex is by noting what shame-based persons are not. Quoting from M. Scott Peck, John Bradshaw notes that to be a non-shame based person "requires the willingness and the capacity to suffer continual self-examination." Such ability requires a good relationship with oneself. This is precisely what no shame-based person has. In fact a toxically shame-based person has an adversarial relationship with himself, often compulsively seeking ways to avoid the affect – toned shame-based feeling. It's this very reason that he projects it away from himself onto others. Other defensive mechanisms which the ego uses to avoid feeling the shame affect are repression, dissociation, distraction, or ownership. This inter-subjective work occurs on an unconscious level; if he understood what he was doing on a conscious level, he would have learned to own it and become conscious of his projections.

The following three points attempt a description of the problem of shame emerging both at an individual and a communal level. First, a normal response of failure to an internalized standard created by an authoritative source such as family, society, or religious affiliation can generate a shame-based complex that has a globalized affect that engulfs one's entire being. Further, shame-based individuals make no distinction between themselves and real and imagined failings. So, often what they imagine to be real is exaggerated.

Secondly, the inability to distinguish between imagined failings and behavior that is not exaggerated is referred to as fusion. Fused feelings blur the self, making it difficult to differentiate clearly. What is cognated, or re-*cognized,* such as inner features, feelings, memories, thoughts, images, standards, God-concepts, are fused with outer features, interpersonal associations such as church, family life, society, culture. Another way to view it is to imagine a co-assembling of inner feelings and thoughts, images, memories, bound to outer shaming events associated with God, church, or family. The church, an outer association where acceptance and purpose is sought can actually be a place where shame is internalized. Feelings of anger, rage, self-contempt, comparison with others and meaninglessness are not relieved with Church activities such as prayer, Bible reading, or hearing homilies. Rather, life becomes a ritualized routine without any connection to a goal or purpose when what is heard is felt to be like shame. For some who have left the church, the hearing of a sermon can become fused with a feeling of shame, and the feeling re-experienced as memories of childhood visits to the house of shame: the church. The sense of "feeling lost," is not unusual in a place where "being found" is preached.

Third, there is no one theory of shame that allows professionals in the field to devise a uniform treatment of the problem. A DSM diagnostic disorder of shame does not exist. Instead, shame is observed as symptomatic of that which stems from mood disorders, or, some would argue, evident in the behavior of personality disorders. It would be helpful to define the state of shame by compiling a list of a unique set of behaviors or a set of stimuli that elicit the particular feeling, informing pastoral psychotherapists on how to treat a patient. What is evident is that those in Christian faith communities who suffer from shame acquire it as a by-product of their theological formation.

As persons of faith process psychological life through theological presuppositions that have helped guide, and at times, misguide them, rather than dismiss the theology or the Christian faith, the pastoral psychotherapist can help the patient discern and re-think metaphors, symbols, and stories that shaped much of the client's identity in a way that is empowering and liberating. Theological concepts such as incarnation, forgiveness, redemption, reconciliation, and unconditional love, can be reframed by re-hearing the sacred narratives in a new way. A healing methodology of pastoral psychotherapy that re-frames the stories, myths, and narratives can be discovered in depth psychology.

The pastoral psychotherapist trained in depth psychology can serve as a primary relational object for the patient's transferences and projections. His or her presence in the therapeutic moment can help to form a healing imago in the memory of the patient of non-shaming episodes. The Christian psychotherapist can discover a theological basis for this encounter in an incarnational theology that is vicarious in its expression, vicarious in the sense that the Christian psychotherapist who utilizes a depth approach to therapy can address shame by speaking in a theological language familiar to the patient. By *re*-presenting the humanity of the Christ that

embraced all people in the light of their psychological formation, the Christian psychotherapists non-shaming presence humanizes the process by moving away from absolute pronouncements of God's will to a declaration that embraces the mystery of the human. By accepting what appears as unrelated phenomena in feeling, thinking and behavior, which, in a more behavioral modification approach would have been avoided, or minimized with absolute biblical principals, the depth approach honors that within the self and outside the self that seeks to bring transformation, including deriving meaning of the shame-based complex and its part in psycho-spiritual renewal.

Depth Psychology

Jung's theory of depth psychology is distinguished by its emphasis on the unconscious as an objective reality. By exerting specific pressures on our subjective consciousness, it produces oppositional, at times compensating viewpoints that guide the process of individuation. The unconscious does not determine consciousness in a fixed way, but operates constantly in the background as a guide to the process of healing and wholeness. To observe this background is to learn how to own the process of individuation. The patient in analysis learns to hear and be conversant with the shame-based complex when it rears its head. By capturing projections, the patient remains conversant with the oppositional voices, embracing the affect rather than avoiding, repressing, denying, or projecting. Differentiation of internalized shame-based affect from outer events is enjoined in the process. By differentiating internalized voices, the patient embraces what once felt oppositional, and in doing so, discovers that what once felt like a feeling to be avoided or projected, can be viewed as a key to understanding the self. From a Jungian depth psychological point of view, transcendence and transformation are possible as the oppositional is now acceptable.

Depth psychology is much broader as a methodology for addressing shame than are Biblical ways of thinking as the source of solving personal complexes and problems. Some approaches to psychotherapy from a Christian perspective assume an anthropology that places the spiritual life as a higher or initial life of the self that is combined with a rational or mental self. By appealing to this spiritual motivation, an appeal that depth psychology also embraces, the cognitive approach seeks to direct the patient towards a Biblical way of thinking as the source of solving problems. The assumption is that if one is spiritually oriented towards God's principles and lives "obediently" in accordance with these principles, all else will follow. For some, this seems to work, but for those unable to accept this principle of spiritual obedience as a solution to all problems, the therapy may not be effective. Consequently, therapy for a non-Christian is not possible, as a prerequisite for successful therapy is to embrace the "truth" of God's principles.

Although depth psychology is similar to a Christian cognitive approach in its emphasis upon the spiritual as a medium for transformation, its universal approach to seeking what is common in all humans and cultures, differs from a Biblical approach to counseling. In depth psychology, prerequisites like embracing Biblical principles are not necessary. It seeks to ask what is it that is longed for in all humans through the symptoms that are expressed by all people. There is no fixed way of being "Christian," rather; to be Christian is an invitation into a way of seeing oneself in its relation to the outer world through a Christ that is transcendent. In the spirit of the Christ of the gospels, the shame-based person learns to reconcile, embrace, and accept all that feels oppositional in him. Rather than seek to impose a conventional form of wisdom that is enculturated as a way of legitimatizing an institution, a depth psychological model can be woven into a theological anthropology that sees the unconscious process as guided by a Spirit that knows of the Christ, an archetypal reality Jung called the Self. The Self is that within all humans that acts as if it knew God or Spirit. It includes both the ego and the unconscious and is encountered when the human need for *transcendence* is understood in the psychotherapeutic moment.

The Transcendent Function is discovered in a process called oppositional dialogue or active imagination. The patient is empowered to hear the "authoritative" voices that once determined approval as a longing to be made whole. By placing oneself in an oppositional relationship with the affect – as if it were alive – one learns to hear and even speak to the affect, seeking meaning for its long and painful manifestation in the life of the shame-based person. Rather than be quick to purge it, or perceive it as a result of a "disobedient life," the process helps to reframe it as a summoning to a more spiritual life. In this approach, "disobedient acts" are less the focus of therapy, and learning to hear what the "acts" and their symptoms mean is a focus of the depth approach. One's overall longing is what is most essential. Ann Belford Ulanov reminds us that "the encounter between Self and transcendence presses for its own resolution, towards what Jung called individuation." The push for transcendence can be manifested in shaming behaviour, and shaming behavior can be conceived as manifesting the need for transcendence. For a Christian psychotherapist practicing within a Jungian theoretical framework, (since as mentioned, Christians tend to address personal issues from within their respective theological presuppositions), the spirit of Christ can be spoken of as the presence that reconciles, embraces, and accepts what felt oppositional and shamed.

By defusing and differentiating the internalized voices discussed above through this active imaginative approach, the patient learns how to capture the unconscious projections. What is projected or transferred is the feeling that is avoided, namely the affective shame-complex. Since passing blame through scapegoating or demonizing is a common transferential phenomenon of the unconscious, it too is an archetypal reality called the shadow. The shadow is that which disrupts and interrupts the ego's need to save face to the outer world. It is the psychological clothing we wear in order to survive an outer world that has shamed us. One cannot act as if the shadow does not exist, for it will manifest itself in projections. Consequently, coming to terms with one's shadow involves clearly defusing and differentiating what is mine, and what belongs to the other. It defuses the internalized images that are fused with the outer world and helps the patient arrest the projections. As the fusion of the inner and outer spheres created the globalized sense of shame, embracing the shadow and differentiating from the ego's need to project contributes to the conscious ownership of the self, as it seeks to become whole.

In the case of a shaming theology, oppositional dialogue seeks to have the patient converse with inner feelings and voices that a shaming theology avoids, since its commitment is the legitimizing of an enculturated religious institution. Depth psychology holds to the legitimization of the objective psyche and its summons towards individuation. A Christian doing psychotherapy from within a Jungian theoretical model might say, "The spirit blows where *it* wills," not where, and how, the institution says it blows! This embracing of the oppositional within as an authentic process of the self is a way of learning about the "truth that sets one free."

See also: ❯ Active Imagination ❯ Complex ❯ Individuation ❯ Shadow ❯ Transcendence ❯ Transcendent Function

Bibliography

Chodorow, J., & Jung, C. G. (Eds.). (1997). *Jung on active imagination*. Princeton, NJ: Princeton University Press.

De Jesus, G. J. (2007). The sabbath and the shadow: An interdisciplinary approach to the healing of shame. An unpublished dissertation, The Claremont School of Theology, Claremont, California.

Dittes, J. E. (1990). Analytical (Jungian) psychology and pastoral care. In R. Hunter (Ed.), *Dictionary of pastoral care and counseling* (pp. 29–33). Nashville, TN: Abingdon Press.

Loftus, R. J. (1990). Depth psychology and religious vocations. In R. L. Moore, & M. Daniel (Ed.), *Jung and Christianity in dialogue* (pp. 208–21). New York: Paulist Press.

McNish, J. L. (2004). *Transforming shame: A pastoral response.* Binghamton, NY: Haworth Pastoral Press.

Ulanov, A. B. (1999). *Religion and the spiritual in Carl Jung.* New York: Paulist Press.

Shame and Guilt

Jill L. McNish

The Shame Affect

According to the influential affect theorist Sylvan Tompkins (1963: 118), shame/humiliation is one of six innate negative affects. By the word "affect," Tompkins means "a physiological mechanism, a firmware script" that is dependent on "chemical mediators that transmit messages, and on the organizing principle stored in the subcortical brain as the affect program" (Nathanson, 1992: 149). "Shame," according to the oft-quoted definition of Tompkins,

▸   ...is the affect of indignity, transgression and alienation. Though terror speaks to life and death and distress makes of the world a vale of tears, yet shame strikes deepest into the heart of man. While terror and distress hurt, they are wounds inflicted from outside which penetrate the smooth surface of the ego; but shame is felt as an inner torment, a sickness of the soul. It does not matter whether the humiliated on has been shamed by derisive laughter or whether he mocks himself. In either event he feels himself naked, defeated, alienated, lacking in dignity or worth (Tompkins, 1963: 118).

The affect of shame manifests in a variety of physiological ways including blushing, sweating, dizziness, lowering or averting of the eyes and increased heart rate.

Shame, as distinguished from guilt (which affect theorists understand to be a subpart of the shame/humiliation affect), is about exposure and the experienced self. Guilt is remorse about acts believed to have been wrongfully committed. Shame is about the experienced wrongness of aspects of one's very being and is often, directly or indirectly, related to the condition, the needs, the desires, limitations and suffering of the human body.

Guilt Distinguished from Shame

It is believed by affect theorists following Sylvan Tompkins (1963) that guilt is subsumed under the affect of shame. Since guilt involves acts believed to have been wrongfully done or left undone, whereas shame involves a sense of the wrongness of the self regardless of acts or omissions, guilt involves less experience of the self than does shame. However, guilt and shame are often fused, with guilt also involving a conscious or unconscious fear of retaliation, or talion dread. Feelings of guilt imply basic trust in one's world, its laws, rules and taboos, and in the persons who are the interpreters of these laws. It is generally understood that guilt feelings develop during the oedipal stage of life when culture's laws are first internalized through fear of the father.

Religions typically are among those societal institutions that create rules, laws and taboos to which persons are expected to adhere. For example in Judeo-Christian religious structures, the Ten Commandments set forth basic laws which must be complied with. Most Christian denominations provide mechanisms and rituals for confessing one's wrongful acts and omissions, thus assuaging feelings of guilt and leading to a sense of forgiveness and reconciliation. It has sometimes been observed that in secular life psychotherapy provides opportunity for "confession."

Implications of Shame

Contemporary psychology understands the affect of shame as being necessary to protect individual boundaries of privacy, and to ensure individuals' social adaptation. Furthermore, psychological theorists following the groundbreaking study of Helen Lynd (1958) see experiences of the affect of shame as providing access to the deepest possible insight into personal identity, since shame is viewed as the affect closest to the experienced self. In her 1971 work *Shame and Guilt in Neurosis* Helen Block Lewis persuasively argued from empirical clinical studies that real psychological healing cannot occur without express analysis of shame issues. However, it is axiomatic that for some individuals shame is the overarching and deeply engrained habitual mode of reacting to others. Large degrees of shame, inappropriately or obsessively fixed, can lead to profound depression and other mental illness. Defenses to the experience of shame include social withdrawal, isolation, addictions, depression, violent acting out, abuse of power, self-righteousness, blaming and projection, shamelessness (a power defense to shame) and perfectionism.

It has been argued that shame is archetypal, as is evidenced in the myth of Adam and Eve's fall and expulsion from the Garden of Eden. It has likewise been asserted that the enduring power of the narratives of the Christian Gospel derive from the shame that is explicit and implicit in Jesus' birth, life, ministry and crucifixion, as well as the shameful circumstances of many of the individuals to whom he ministered (see McNish, 2004).

See also: ❂ Affect ❂ Archetype ❂ Crucifixion ❂ Depression ❂ Fall, The ❂ Jesus ❂ Myth ❂ Oedipus Myth ❂ Power ❂ Projection ❂ Psychotherapy ❂ Taboo

Bibliography

Lewis, H. B. (1971). *Shame and guilt in Neurosis*. New York: International Universities Press.

Lynd, H. (1958). *On shame and the search for identity*. London: Routledge.

McNish, J. (2004). *Transforming shame*. Binghamton, NY: Haworth Press.

Nathanson, D. (Ed.). (1992). *Shame and pride: Affect, sex and the birth of self* (p. 149). New York: W. W. Norton.

Tompkins, S. (1963). *Affect, imagery and consciousness, volume 2, The negative affects* (p. 118). New York: Springer.

Sharia

Amani Fairak

Sharia or Islamic Law, is a set of principles implemented in the Islamic community. Sharia comes from the Arabic word (شرع) Shara'a which means to enforce a code of conduct in order to facilitate a way of life. Islamic Law is integrated into almost all aspects of life, from relationships, education, law to economics and politics. Islam proposes four descending criteria to which Islamic society or individuals can refer as an ideal model for social policies. Sharia has certain sources from which it derives its authority in Islamic society; and characteristics that give it credibility and authenticity among Muslims. Sharia is divided into two major sources and nine sub-sources. The first two sources are *the Quran* and *the Hadith*, which are believed to be directly or indirectly divinely inspired. The sub-sources are mainly based on scholastic interpretation and judgments.

Sources of Sharia

1) Quran: Muslims believe it to be the literal word of God (see Quran).
2) Hadith: the teachings of the Prophet Mohammed (see Hadith).
3) Ijma': the consensus or the collective agreement of Muslim scholars (see Ijma').
4) Qiyas: the standardisation of any issue against Quran and Hadith based on Ijma'a (see Qiyas).
5) Istihsan: it comes from the Arabic word *Istah'sana*, or to prefer something over other possibilities of decisions.
6) Masaleh Morsalah (the Common Good): a jurisprudential agreement can be Islamically approved if it brings about common good for the Islamic community or the public.
7) Sadd al-Dhara'ei (the standardisation of appropriate means and ends): it is to block any means that might cause social disruption even if the ends can be noble. This also means that any means that might bring about a common good should be Islamically facilitated.
8) Al Orf (conventions): it comes from *Arafa* in Arabic, which means an acceptable manner of doing something. It is the social convention or custom in any given Islamic society that may contribute to change in Islamic Law.
9) Math'hab al-Sahabi (the teachings of the Prophet's companions): it is to use the teachings of the Prophet's companions as a raw model in everyday life if there is no direct text from the Quran or Hadith or the previous Islamic laws.
10) Sharia man Qablana (Pre-Islamic Laws): if there is no known source from a companion, Muslims can follow the laws of the previous Messages like Christianity and Judaism as long as they does not conflict with the main sources of the Quran and Hadith.
11) Istis'hab (continuity): the presumption of continuation of a certain status is to remain as is until it can be changed or refuted by evidence.

Characteristics of Sharia

1) Divine law: Muslims believe that the Quran is the third and final literal Message that God has sent to humankind, after al Taurah (*Torah*) and al Injeel (*The later Bible*).

2) Long-term and short-term policy of reinforcements: the Quran speaks of promises and consequences for the short and long-term. The mention of heaven and hell are emphasized throughout Quran. Muslims believe that every action has a reaction that can be either rewarded or disciplined in this life (al-Donia) or the afterlife (al A'khirah).

3) Universality: since the Quran is the last message from God, its message is universal to all humankind in contrast to the previous messages of Jesus and Moses and other prophets whose messages were exclusive to their people.

4) Comprehensiveness: as last Message, the Quran discusses every aspect of human life on every level, personally, socially, politically, spiritually, scientifically, and educationally. Therefore, Muslims believe that the Quran is a divine law that is open to re-interpretation and so applicable at any time anywhere.

Commentary

Several psychologists and sociologists of religion have distinguished between the focus of Islam and western psychology. Islam tends to view religion as the core of the individual's life while psychology tends to view religion as one aspect of the individual's life. Social psychology, therefore, may suggest that abiding by Sharia Law is to confirm the identity of the individual Muslim in society. To follow certain codes of conduct, to adhere to specific policies of discipline or to at least accept such a lifestyle aims at sustaining the religious institution and ensuring its survival.

Islam, as a social system and establishment, introduces the term *umma* or nation to indicate the importance of a "unified Islamic community". This community is governed by particular policies in order to fulfill certain needs and to meet specific goals. Sociology may explain this concept as

▷   ...a cultural and ideological territory in which no Muslim would find himself alien regardless of political or geographical diversities. In one sense, it is comparable to the notion of 'Western World' abundantly used to define a cultural and ideological territory today (Ebrahimi, 1996).

Umma works as "...a common framework in which temporal association of different groups sharing the Islamic values can be maintained" where the goal and the strategy in cultivating the concept of *umma* is already recommended in the Quran.

See also: ◉ Islam ◉ Qur'an

Bibliography

Ebrahimi, M. H. (1996). *Islamic city: Quest for urban cultural identity in the Muslim world*. London: University College London.

Shekhinah

Mark Popovsky

In Rabbinic Literature

In early rabbinic texts such as the Talmud, the term Shekhinah (lit. "dwelling") is used as one of many Hebrew names for God. Deriving from the verb meaning "to dwell," this particular divine appellation suggests imminent divine manifestation in a specific place or at a specific time. For example, the Shekhinah is said to rest at the head of a sick person's bed, to appear when ten men gather for prayer or to rest between a righteous man and his wife. Though this is the only commonly used Hebrew name for God that is grammatically feminine, in Talmudic and contemporaneous sources, overt feminine images are rarely associated with it. In most instances, the term Shekhinah could be replaced with other Hebrew names for God such as "Master of the Universe" or "The Holy One Blesses Be He" without any consequent change in the passage's meaning.

In Medieval Texts

A primary concern of many medieval Jewish philosophers from the post-Talmudic period such as Saadya Gaon, Judah Ha-Levi and Moses Maimonides was to preclude any interpretation of scriptural passages which might suggest divine anthropomorphization. Revelation and prophecy were especially problematic phenomena for these philosophers because they presume that God communicates in human language. Consequently, among these philosophers, the Shekhinah was often understood not as another name for God but rather as a divinely created separate entity. The Shekhinah became the divine intermediary that would appear to prophets in visions; for, God himself does not speak. The Shekhinah is the entity that reflects God's presence in the world and that interacts with human beings because God's ultimate transcendence makes direct human-divine contact impossible.

The concept of the Shekhinah evolved further in the writing of the Kabbalists (Jewish mystics) from the twelfth century on. Kabbalistic thought posits that a profound unity of the divine once existed but was severed because of human sin. With this rupture, the masculine and feminine principles of the divine were separated and remain alienated from each other to this day. The Shekhinah becomes the symbol of the feminine aspect of the godhead, the element of the divine closest to the created world and most directly in contact with human beings. According to the Kabbalists, it is the duty of each individual to work to unite the male and female halves of God by observing the laws of the Torah and living a holy life. Human actions affect the divine, either promoting or hindering progress towards its reunion. Redeeming the Shekhinah from its exile from the remainder of the godhead becomes a primary motivation for behavior in Kabbalistic teachings.

It is in the Kabbalistic literature generally and in the Zohar most prominently that feminine and sometimes even erotic imagery is first associated with the Shekhinah. The Shekhinah is often depicted as a queen or a bride and serves as a foil to the traditional patriarchal images of a transcendent deity. It is not uncommon in Kabalistic texts to find imagery portraying the reunion of the Shekhinah with the remainder of the godhead as sexual intercourse. Some Kabbalists would attempt to visualize such divine coupling when performing religious duties in order to remain aware of the broader theological implications of their righteous acts.

Contemporary Analysis

Reflecting the status of women in the pre-modern period, the Shekhinah is often described in Kabbalistic texts as beautiful and radiant but passive and dependant on the deeds of men for redemption. Some scholars suggest that the popularity of the Shekhinah as a gendered representation of God may have arisen out of the same psychological and theological needs for divine intimacy and accessibility which popularized the Cult of the Virgin Mary among contemporaneous Christians. A number of modern feminists have argued that Jewish women should reclaim the image of the Shekhinah as a counterbalance to the many masculine images of the divine found in scripture and Jewish liturgy. Some Jewish pastoral counselors have reported positive results exploring feminine images of the Shekhinah with women who have suffered trauma and are alienated from more traditional divine imagery.

See also: ❂ Female God Images ❂ God ❂ God Image ❂ Judaism and Psychology ❂ Kabbalah ❂ Talmud

Bibliography

Novick, L. (2008). *On the wings of Shekhinah: Rediscovering Judaism's divine feminine*. Wheaton IL: Quest Books.

Scholem, G. (1995). *Major trends in Jewish mysticism*. New York: Schocken Books.

Shema

Lynn Somerstein

Shema Israel, Adonai Eloheinu, Adonai Ehad – Hear O Israel, the Lord our God, the Lord is One.

This prayer is recited in the morning and afternoon prayers and on the death bed. The word "shema" means listen, or understand, indicating that one is to turn inward and feel God, since God cannot be visualized. "God is one" is a unifying principle.

The word "Lord" is used to replace the name of God, which cannot be said.

Eloheinu means "our God."

Ehad means "one."

This short phrase captures monotheism and identifies the Jew saying it as a dedicated person of God and a member of the Jewish people – it is a statement of belief and of identity. It is an affirmation of Judaism and a declaration of monotheism. It unifies the self as it declares that the individual self belongs with a particular group. This unifying sound of the shema can serve to hold the individual personality and make it feel safe and connected.

See also: ❂ God ❂ Judaism and Psychology ❂ Prayer

Bibliography

Wigoder, G. (Ed.). (1974). *Encyclopedic dictionary of Judaica* (p. 548). New York: Leon Amiel.

Shinto

Robert S. Ellwood

The Nature of Shinto

The word "Shinto" can be translated as "The Way of the Gods," and refers to the traditional religion of Japan. Shinto has roots in the prehistoric past of Japan before the introduction of Buddhism, together with Chinese forms of writing and culture, around the sixth century C.E. "Shinto" then appeared as a term to differentiate the worship of the traditional kami, or gods, from "Butsudo," "The Way of the Buddha." The two faiths became deeply intertwined in the Middle Ages, when Shinto shrines were often closely associated with Buddhist temples, the deities of the former regarded as guardians, students, or even alternative indigenous expressions of the imported Buddhas and bodhisattvas. But during the modernizing and increasingly nationalistic Meiji era (1868–1912) Shinto and Buddhism were separated by the government. Shinto became in effect a state religion. Extreme nationalists favored Shinto, regarding it as the authentic Japanese faith, its deities being ancestors or divine companions of the imperial house. After the end of World War II in 1945, Shinto was separated from the state. Its some 80,000 shrines were placed under local control, and apart from a few controversial relics of the past, such as the Yasukuni Shrine, dedicated to Japanese war dead, the religion went its own way.

Shinto, however, continues in what many consider to be its true nature, a religion centered on the patronal deities of particular places and communities. Most Shinto shrines are *ujigami* shrines, that is, shrines of the patronal deity of a particular community, extended family, place, or occasionally class of persons, such as a certain trade. The kami (or it may be a family or group of kami) is either unique to that shrine, or is a mythological figure of broader background essentially in the same local role. These places of worship are maintained by that community, and their *matsuri*, or festivals, are celebrations reaffirming traditional bonds.

Shinto shrines are easily recognizable by their distinctive *torii* or gate, with two upright pillars and one or two large crossbars, through which one passes to enter the shrine precincts, as though moving from one world to another, from the pollution of everyday life to a realm of sacred purity. The shrine itself will typically have an outer porch, bearing such symbols of kami-presence as a mirror, drums, and hanging *gohei* or zigzag strips of paper. Behind them stands an eight-legged table for offerings. Finally steep steps rise up to massive doors, very seldom opened, concealing the *honden* or inner sanctum where the *shintai*, or token of the divine presence, is reverently kept.

Shinto Worship

Shinto worship typically commences with a stately, highly ritualized offering of food (typically rice, salt, vegetables, fruits, seafood, and rice wine), followed by the chant-like reading of a *norito* or prayer, and the reception by worshippers of a sip of the rice wine as a sort of communion. At major community festivals worship is followed by colorful, celebrative events, ranging from sacred dance and *sumo* wrestling to processions, fairs, and traditional horse or boat races. This last part of the festival, which may go on all day to end with fireworks in the evening, is far from solemn, often having more the atmosphere of Mardi Gras or Carnival in Latin countries.

In any case, the main annual *matsuri* is an important solidifier of community identity; its preparation takes months, and it usually involves special, jealously-maintained customs distinctive to that place. Shinto is fundamentally grounded in archaic agriculture, and most festivals are related to the agricultural year: seedtime, the growing season, harvest. New Year's, the time of renewal in this highly "cosmic" religion, is also very important.

Persons frequently visit shrines at other times as well to pray, customarily approaching the shrine porch, clapping hands twice as it were to attract the deity's attention, then bowing the head for a few moments.

Main Themes of Shinto

Five main themes can be thought of as characterizing Shinto:

1. The importance of the purity versus impurity concept. Shrines, and persons taking part in their rites, must be kept free of contamination by death, disease, or blood. Kami, together with their abodes – which are usually set in green park like spaces as far as possible – bespeak the purity of pristine nature as over against the pollution so often afflicting the city and human life.

2. Tradition. Shinto strives rigorously to maintain traditional practices extending back to the mists of prehistory. For many Japanese, buffeted by the immense and unsettling changes that have affected their country in recent centuries, it is undoubtedly reassuring that one segment of national life changes little and connects them to ancient roots.

3. Matsuri or festival. Shinto fully recognizes the value of "sacred time" that affirms community, permits joyous and even ribald behavior, and is like a release from the tensions of a highly structured, achievement-oriented society.

4. Pluralism. It must always be borne in mind that Shinto is only a part of the Japanese spiritual spectrum; there is also Buddhism, and (while it is not a religion in the strict sense in Japan) Confucian morality, still extremely important in attitudes to family, work, and society. Most Japanese have some connection to all three, having an affiliation with both a traditional family shrine and Buddhist temple, while affirming Confucian ethics. Shinto is typically thought to affirm the joys and relationships of this world, while Buddhism has to do with ultimate metaphysical questions and life after death. Thus marriages are frequently celebrated in Shinto shrines, and funerals (which. having to do with death, would pollute a Shinto shrine) are conducted in Buddhist temples.

   In this regard it should be pointed out that membership figures for Shinto are virtually meaningless; while few Japanese would think of themselves as "a Shintoist" in the western sense of belonging exclusively to one religion, most in fact are likely to visit shrines and participate in Shinto festivals, whatever exactly that may mean in terms of commitment.

5. Polytheism. Shinto, with its many thousands of finite kami, seems to be the only thoroughly polytheistic religion in a major advanced society today.

Shinto and Psychological

All of these points are of great psychological interest. Psychologists know that issues of purity and pollution can be very real to countless people, that the place of tradition as over against other forces is the subject of vehement debate both in society and within individuals, that the need for celebrative release in a world of tension must somehow be dealt with, and that we need to find ways to live with integrity in a highly pluralistic society. In all these matters, undoubtedly there is much to be learned from the Shinto experience.

Polytheism is an especially fascinating case, because it is a challenge to the monotheistic or monistic direction in which most of the world's other religion have gone in the last two thousand years. The theologian Paul Tillich once pointed out that the difference between monotheism and polytheism is not just a matter of quantity, of one God versus more than one, but also of quality. Polytheism involves a different way of seeing the sacred world: not as all centered in one divine power and person, but as diffuse and diverse. The polytheist perceive separate spirits, finite but with distinctive personalities, in this sacred grove and that waterfall, over this town and that, for love and for war. Modern Shinto apologists have argued this is important; that Shinto is the most democratic of religions because it holds the universe runs by processes of divine conflict and consensus, rather than by a single autocratic will. Some psychologists, from William James in *The Pluralistic Universe* to post-Jungians like James Hillman in several works, have perceived modern western society to have become psychologically polytheistic in all but name, and have urged us to come creatively to terms with that vision. Neo-pagans around the world have also lately been paying renewed attention to Shinto.

The psychological significance of Shinto for many Japanese also lies in its symbolic relation to primary social identities, and to nature. Both are very important in Japanese consciousness. In this society, anomie and insecurity can be felt very acutely when the support of a family or peer group is lacking. Families, communities, trades and businesses have their patronal kami and shrines, and collective worship events that reinforce bonding. Shinto has been called a religion of the particular; rather than universal themes, it emphasizes sacredness in particular places and groups, so strengthens attachment to significant locations and people.

Shinto moreover consorts well with the Japanese love of natural beauty. It has been spoken of as a "natural religion" in another, more psychological sense as well: as religion in harmony with the "natural" cycles and social structures of human life, unlike faiths that challenge the merely "natural" on the basis of transcendent revelation. But inspired by Shinto, as well as forms of Buddhism such as Zen, the Japanese appreciate finding the sacred in the world and human life as it is when it is rightly perceived.

Shinto, then, remains an ancient religion with contemporary relevance. It is important for understanding Japan, and also perhaps ourselves.

See also: ◈ Buddhism ◈ James, William ◈ Polytheism ◈ Ritual

Bibliography

Breen, J., & Teeuwen, M. (Eds.). (2000). *Shinto in history*. Honolulu, HI: University of Hawaii Press.

Ellwood, R. (2008). *Introducing Japanese religion*. New York: Routledge.

James, W. (1909). *A pluralistic Universe*. New York: Longmans, Green.

Jillman, J. (1976). *Re-visioning psychology*. New York: Harper & Row.

Kasulis, T. (2004). *Shinto: The way home*. Honolulu, HI: University of Hawaii Press.

Nelson, J. K. (2000). *Enduring identities: The guise of Shinto in contemporary Japan*. Honolulu, HI: University of Hawaii Press.

Philippi, D. L. (Trans.). (1969). *Kojiki*. Tokyo: University of Tokyo Press.

Sin

Morgan Stebbins

The concept of sin can be thought of as a type of error. This can be an error according to either divine or social standards. Furthermore, the concept of sin is active in both religious and secular determinations of group allegiance, human fallibility, suffering, and the cure of suffering. Having said that, the dynamics and repercussions of sin are quite different depending on whether the sin is conceived of as transgressing secular law or divine order. Since there is no sin that is good, it is related to evil. Evil can be seen as relative harm (good for me, bad for you), as distance from the divine (St. Augustine and the *privatio bonum*), or as an absolute and archetypal aspect of the construction of reality.

It may clarify the concept of sin to describe it as a more differentiated and active form of a sense of the taboo that can be seen in relationship with confession, heaven, and hell. Since no significant religious or secular traditions propose a worldview in which humanity is in a state of perfection, sin can be seen as a fairly universal concept although one with incredible variation. Not all religions use a concept of sin in a narrow sense, but it does appear that all religions and indeed all individuals have a way of identifying and dealing with problems, errors, or situations that appear to be beyond the scope of local logic. Local logic (so called because sensible patterns of thought are only comprehensible within a shared emotional, cultural, and metaphysical frame) easily identifies mistakes and can chart the course of their correction. For experiences that supercede this capacity, metaphysics of some kind enters the fray. Metaphysics in this context covers the conceptualization of all non-rational modes, including experiences of love, death, birth, sin, or anything that humans have the capacity to conceptualize but not satisfactorily explain. That is, experiences which are in some way transpersonal are also beyond the normal problem-solving mechanisms of the mind. Not only is the apperception of some types of experiences such as birth, death, and aging beyond the conscious mind's capacity according to psychological theory, evolutionary psychology has shown that there are not any conscious cognition modules for processing them.

Large-scale forms of transpersonal thinking can also be fruitfully described as religions or political ideologies, whereas small-scale forms are called personal projections. Projection is here meant in the broadest and most neutral form: the subject's assumptions about reality are constantly being refined and tested by social interactions and so are in some sense projections. However if personal projections become too detached from social networks of meaning, the subject may be identified by the society as psychotic. This can happen even locally, as many people report having neighbors who are "completely crazy" (see Horwitz, 2004). To further complicate the picture, even individuals who identify as fully secular imagine the transpersonal aspects of sin in a highly uniform and predictable way that is functionally similar to the various religious modes (Boyer, 2002).

Sin is typically defined by dictionaries in two ways: on the one hand it is an offense against God, on the other it is something highly reprehensible, but otherwise secular (Miriam Webster Dictionary). To the religious and secular aspects we will add psychological views in the following discussion. However, from within the structure of religious experience, an offense against God carries definite consequences and demands solutions which are only offered by expert technicians (priests) validated by the religious hierarchy. Thus, as previously stated, we can think of sin as an error or transgression. To whom or what, and what the consequences and solution are, vary by tradition and culture, but in any case the systems are closed and sin is seen as in some way evil.

All of the major religious systems employ a category of sin. Other types of religious or supernatural traditions such as the Greek pantheon or many ancestor or spirit-based traditions have a way to account for actions which anger the supernatural beings and usually need some kind of specialized intervention. It is instructive that the primary Hebrew words for sin are *het*, meaning something that has gone astray or off the path, and *aveira*, or transgression (There are at least 20 Hebrew words that convey variations of the meaning of sin!). What goes astray is *yetzer*, or the human inclinations which must be channeled by the law. The cure for *het* is found in adherence to the law (in Orthodox and Conservative Judaism the law or *Halakha* – meaning the way of walking, or path – is comprised of 248 positive and 365 negative *mitzvoth*) and the expiation of guilt during the celebration of *Yom Kippur*. The *yetzer ha-ra* is the evil inclination which would appear to be a conceptual cognate of original sin except that it is balanced by *yetzer ha-tov*, or the good inclination. This is strongly paralleled (in contradiction to the doctrines of St. Augustine) in the Christian New Testament by Rom. 5:12–19. Psychologically speaking, original sin can be translated as an acknowledgment of feeling estranged or alienated from the law of one's psychic dominant. Spirituality, within this psychological model, depends upon discovering and submitting to a law that comes from a non-conscious aspect of ourselves. In this view, spirituality is not dependent upon social norms or emotional states, but rather upon acting and thinking in ways compatible with the psychological structure that each person comes to discover.

The concept and dynamics of Sin have been gradually differentiated throughout the Hebrew Bible into the New Testament, reaching a crescendo of complexity in the Catholic scheme. The latter includes sins ignorance as well as deliberate action, venal and mortal sins (the mortal seven sins of pride, covetousness, lust, anger, gluttony, envy, and sloth are held to be fatal to spiritual progress), sins of animosity to God, and finally the state of original sin which is not dependent upon an action (The Catholic Encyclopedia; also cf. Genesis 3, as developed originally by St. Augustine but refuted by the monk Pelagius). Sins of commission are expiated through a 5-step process of confession, whereas original sin is only transformed through the mystery of the Eucharist. Original sin, although an unpopular concept in many circles, can be seen psychologically as an intuition that something highly charged needs attention in the very foundation of the human condition and as such has parallels even in the Buddhist tradition.

Buddhism is usually portrayed as having no concept of sin. While it is true that in most forms of Buddhism there is no metaphysical divinity, in practice there are many conceptions of different Buddhas which are beyond space, time, and causality, making them functionally identical with divine beings. Also, the concept of karma, while not implicating a judgmental higher being, is nevertheless a system of punishment and reward for misdeeds (or errors) both of omission and commission. This is further differentiated into a large array of behavioral precepts not unlike the *mitzvoth* or Catholic list of sins (*Nirvana Sutra* and spread around the *Pali Canon*, see Nakamura, 1980). Furthermore, Buddhist texts outline the three poisons, or hindrances to the realization of one's Buddha nature: anger, greed, and ignorance (Watson, 2001). The most potent is ignorance, seen as the root of all suffering. This is the original state of mind of all humans, and is described very specifically as ignorance of the ontological truth of the emptiness of human nature. All suffering, and to put it another way, all sinfulness, is related to this ignorance. Suffering is not the same as pain, and neither Buddhism nor psychology would promise to eliminate the kind of discomfort that comes from making hard choices, or what Jung called conflicts of duty. Rather what can be changed is neurotic suffering, or to put it the other way around, neurotic suffering is often the avoidance of the authentic struggle implied by integrative growth.

The Muslim Qur'an describes also describes sin (like the Jewish and Buddhist traditions) using the error and guidance model (rather than the fall and salvation model). Sura 1:5 describes God sending a succession of prophets to lead the faithful back to the straight path. Sin is thus a kind of distraction correctable by following the examples of the prophets and of course the great prophet, Muhammad.

In all of these descriptions we see a common human experience of something being wrong, and sin locates the problem in the relationship between the personal subject and some transpersonal aspect. Sin moves fully to the psychological realm if conceived of as the description of an experience which leads away from the dominant (and usually unconscious) value in a given personality. Thus sin, radically seen psychologically as a symptom or symbol, also gives shape to a change of attitude which closes the gap between the personal subject and his or her highest value (leaving aside, for the moment, whether that value is conscious, unconscious, ideological, or individual). In other words, sin is the recognition of a projection that is now ready for integration, as well as containing, in itself, as the direction (in symbolic form) of the integrative process.

We can see that this re-contextualizing completely changes the symptom into a complex signifier of psychological progression. An illustration of the flatness of the concept of sin when seen from a pre-determined perspective is contained in the following vignette: President Calvin Coolidge, seeking guidance, attended a sermon on sin. Upon returning, his wife asked what the preacher had said about it. The President shrugged and answered, "He was against it." Instead, the psychological dynamics of sin have a double quality, like the original sin of Adam and Eve being seen as both the cause of expulsion from the Garden as well as the beginning of some correction. The experience of a fall or expulsion can be seen as the first step in moving away from a relationship based on assumption and fusion, and toward a more nuanced and conscious position directed by the very symbol that had been called sin.

An example is found in the treatment of alcoholism. As soon as the subject becomes aware that alcohol has been having a negative effect, the projection on the substance is already beginning to change. However, rather than merely avoiding the concrete usage of alcohol, the cure is found in investigating what exactly was the change in personality that occurred when drinking was engaged (whether this is an increased level of social comfort, an interest in others, relaxation, or even aggression). It is this very change in consciousness that the psyche as a whole is pressing for an awareness of, and experience shows that it will not be satisfied (rather like a jealous god) until this change is accomplished. From the neutral, a-moral side of the psyche, there is no preference for just *how* this is done. However, from the side of personal consciousness, it makes all the difference whether the change takes place through practice and engagement or through drinking.

This double description is not far from a Gnostic view in which the beginning of the path toward gnosis is found in filth, sin, decay, and the experience of alienation (Jonas, 2001). Medieval alchemy, as well, locates the initiation of the *opus* in the experiential feces of the human condition, and for Jung the deep analytic process begins with the cast-off and despised parts of the personal psyche, the shadow (Jung, 1979).

In addition to the religious, secular, and psychological aspects, two others should be mentioned in order to highlight the multiple valences of this concept. Evolutionary anthropology has shown convincingly that religion in general and the embedded concept of sin specifically enable the identification of trusted cohorts, allow room for the problem of de-coupled scenario building (called imagination in other contexts) and provide the economic incentives for a priestly class. From the perspective of a Lacanian critique of the subject (in many ways not different from the Buddhist, see above), the conceptual error is found in the *very idea* of wholeness or healing (Lacan, 1982). Wholeness is thus seen, like the Freudian interpretation of religion in general, as an illusion (Freud, 1989). Instead the subject is constituted at the deepest level by a lack of being which is only painfully exacerbated by collusive and ideological strategies of regaining any concept of wholeness. These strategies actually open the wound through the foreclosing of the natural flow of language.

Both of these latter approaches enable us to ask of sin: what is sin for in the dynamics of the subject? This question allows one to translate from the dogma of a religious tradition to an experiential appreciation of the concept of sin.

See also: ❯ Buddhism ❯ Christianity ❯ Freud, Sigmund ❯ Islam ❯ Judaism and Psychology

Bibliography

Boyer, P. (2002). *Religion Explained*. New York: Basic Books.
Freud, S. (1989). *The Future of an Illusion*. New York: W. W. Norton.
Horwitz, (2004). *Creating Mental Illness*. Chicago, IL: University of Chicago.
Jonas, H. (2001). *The Gnostic Religion*. Boston, MA: Beacon Press.
Jung, C. G. (1979). *Aion, researches into the phenomenology of the self*. Princeton, NJ: Princeton University Press.
Lacan, J. (1982). *Ecrits*. New York: W. W. Norton.
Merriam Webster Dictionary.
Nakamura, H. (1980). *Indian Buddhism*.
The Catholic Encyclopedia. New York: Robert Appleton Company.
Watson, B. (Trans.). (2001). *The essential lotus: Selections from the lotus sutra*. New York: Columbia University Press.

Skinner, Burrhus Frederic

Gilbert Todd Vance

Burrhus Frederic Skinner (1904–1990) is known as the pioneer of radical behaviorism. He was an avowed atheist as an adult and his ideas and methods are not generally associated with religion. However, Skinner's work clearly shows that he was exposed to and influenced by religion and religious ideas. In his autobiography, Skinner describes the influence his Presbyterian Sunday School teacher had on his early love for learning and writing. He also recounts having a "mystical experience" as an adolescent and losing his belief in God after he did not receive additional "signs" to confirm and build on this experience.

A central idea of traditional Presbyterianism is that of predestination, the belief that an omnipotent and omniscient God has determined the fate of the universe from creation until the end of time. This theme is explicitly discussed and contrasted to the idea of free will in Skinner's novel, *Walden Two*. Skinner's radical behaviorism posits that all behavior is determined, not free. In this way, the determinism of radical behaviorism is similar to the religious idea of predestination. While he does not explicitly acknowledge such in his autobiography, it is possible and even likely that the ideas and arguments put forth in *Walden Two* were influenced by Skinner's early exposure to the Presbyterian faith.

See also: ❯ God

Bibliography

Skinner, B. F. (1948/2005). *Walden two*. Indianapolis, IN: Hackett Publishing.
Skinner, B. F. (2008). An Autobiography. Retrieved January 27, 2008 from http://ww2.lafayette.edu/~allanr/autobio.html.

Smith, Joseph

Paul Larson

Joseph Smith (1805–1844) was the founder of Mormonism (cf.). He was only 14 and living with his parents in Palmyra, New York, when he became absorbed with finding out which of the various religions was the true one. The whole region was known as the "burned over" region because of the very active evangelization by preachers; a period known as the second Great Awakening of religion in America. After a period of fervent prayer in a forest grove near his home in 1820 he received a theophany, or divine manifestation where he was told that none of the current religions were true. This is known as the First Vision. Three years later he received another visitation, this time from an angel called Moroni. He was instructed where to look for some plates which he was to recover and then translate the contents with the aid of devices known as the Urim and Thummim. The resulting book was published as the *Book of Mormon*. It claims to be the record of several waves of ancient Hebrew peoples who came to the New World by boat and the civilizations which developed from them over centuries.

From this and several other revelations he was instructed to found a church which was to be a new dispensation of the Gospel with full authority of priesthood to perform sacraments and teach the true religion. In 1830 he and several others including some family members founded the Church of Jesus Christ of Latter Day Saints (LDS), also commonly known as Mormons. The reception to this new proclamation was not generally favorable. Many thought him possessed of the Devil, others just thought he was deluded. Even from an early point in the history of the movement, word surfaced of his association with magical practices such as use of divining rods for finding buried treasure or lost objects (Brodie, 1971; Quinn, 1998). Though later attempts to sanitize his biography have dismissed these claims, there is good evidence for some involvement in folk magic traditions.

Despite critics, the LDS church grew and so did opposition. He moved his flock to Kirtland, Ohio, after a former Campbelite (Disciples of Christ) preacher, Sidney Rigdon converted along with many of his congregation. It was here that the first temple was constructed. Temples are buildings for special rites apart from the regular meeting houses. Persecution of the Church continued as many Christians found the fundamental claim of authenticity of the *Book of Mormon* as a supplementary scripture to the Bible to be unacceptable. Additional practices and beliefs articulated by Smith as Prophet, Seer and Revelator of the new Church were also at odds with orthodox Christian teachings. He rejected all previous creeds, Ecumenical Church Councils and other sources of authoritative teachings held by many Christians. In addition to the *Book of Mormon* he began compiling his revelations in a book now known as the *Doctrine and Covenants*. A third new scriptural book, the *Pearl of Great Price*, contains books whose authorship is claimed to be Abraham and Moses. These are claimed to have been translated from papyri found with a mummy which came into Smith's possession. As a result of continued challenges he moved the church to Independence, Missouri, building a temple there and proclaiming it to be the center of Zion.

From an early period Smith supported aggressive evangelization of others. Missionaries were sent to various parts of the United States and began traveling to Europe, brining in many converts, mostly from northern European countries. Smith moved the church to Missouri, and then after further persecution, to a city he founded on the Mississippi River in Illinois, named Nauvoo. Here, he felt, he and his followers could be secure by building a place where they could be concentrated and thereby hold political control. He founded the Nauvoo Legion, a militia, to guarantee protection for his followers. However, opposition continued and mounted. By this time the Mormon doctrine of polygamy had become widely known and the source of much additional anger from the surrounding community and the American public. Finally, in an outbreak of violence he declared martial law. He and his brother were then taken on criminal charges of treason to the jail in Carthage, Illinois. On June 24, 1844 a mob seized control of the jail and killed both Joseph Smith and his brother Hyrum. Several other followers who were with him were wounded but survived.

His death precipitated a struggle for succession of the church. The largest faction favored election of Brigham Young, who was then a leader of the Quorum of Twelve Apostles, the major body of leadership of the church directly under the President and his counselors. Another faction supported his son, Joseph Smith III. This became known as the Reorganized Church of Jesus Christ of LDS. Young decided to move the flock deep into the far west of the United States to avoid further persecution through isolation and is now known as the Community of Christ. In the winter of 1846, the largest body moved across the river and camped in Iowa, at a place now known as Winter Quarters. From there they migrated across the plains and on July 24, 1847 entered the valley of the Great Salt Lake in what is now Utah. There Young proclaimed that "this is the place" where they could settle and found a new community.

Smith's legacy is established as a founder of a major religious movement, including both the dominant LDS church based in Utah, and several offshoots. The movement was burdened for many years by the doctrine of polygamy, which has been abandoned by all but a few fundamentalist spin-offs. The LDS Church in Utah is one of the most rapidly growing religions and is perhaps the leading example of "restorationist" Christianity, which rejects the bulk of the history of the church as clouded by apostasy and claims that one or more modern prophets have restored the true religion. Brodie's (1971) biography was the first scholarly work which differed from the Church's official hagiography; it stimulated controversy which still reverberates today. Regardless of how one conceives of the status of the *Book of Mormon* or the religion founded by Smith, it is certainly clear that he had a prodigious capacity to formulate a new theological vision and attract followers to that vision.

See also: ◉ Christianity

Bibliography

Brodie, F. M. (1971). *No man knows my history: The life of Joseph Smith.* New York: Alfred A. Knopf.

Brook, J. L. (1994). *The refiner's fire: The making of Mormon Cosmology 1644–1844.* New York: Cambridge University Press.

Quinn, D. M. (1998). *Early Mormonism and the magic world view.* Salt Lake City, UT: Signature Books.

Socrates' Daimonion

David Berman

Probably the fullest description of Socrates's daimonion is in Plato's *Apology* 31c, where Socrates says:

> ▸ I have a divine sign [daimonion] from the god which... began when I was a child. It is a voice, and whenever it speaks it turns me away from something I am about to do, but it never turns me towards anything. This is what has prevented me from taking part in public affairs, and I think it was quite right to prevent me. Be sure, gentlemen of the jury, I should have died long ago otherwise.

One reason that Socrates's daimonion is important is because in *Republic* 496, Socrates suggests that it enabled him to become a true philosopher. This is puzzling, but is made even moreso by the fact that the daimonion does not offer any reasons, but only deters from this or that action. And yet notwithstanding, Socrates, the great rationalist, submits to it. The problem then is squaring Socrates's over-riding commitment to having reasons and his willingness to follow religiously his daimonion.

The Sources

We have two primary sources for the daimonion, the writings of Plato and those of Xenophon, another contemporary follower of Socrates. The data that we need to work from are Plato's *Apology* 31c (as quoted above), also 40 and 41, *Euthyphro* 3b, *Alcibiades* 1, 103, *Euthydemus* 272, *Phaedrus* 242, *Theaetetus* 151b, *Republic* 496; *Theages* 128–30, and probably *Hippias Major* 304 (accepting Reeve's proposal in Smith and Woodruff, 2000: 31–33.) The sources from Xenophon are his *Memorabilia*, I.1.1–9; and 3.5; also IV. 8.1 and 8.5; also *Banquet* viii.5; and Socrates's *Defence* 5 and 13.

On the whole, there is considerable coherence and consistency in these sources. Probably the biggest textual problem is the dialogue called *Theages*, which of all the Platonic dialogues contains the most material on the daimonion. The problem is that in it Socrates says that his daimonion was the dominant element in what he taught his followers. Here Socrates the rational moralist seems to give way to Socrates the man magically possessed by his daimonion, which he says "has absolute power in my dealings with those who associate with me" (129). But since it is agreed by present-day Plato scholars that the *Theages* is not by Plato, we can put its evidence to one side in this article.

Here, then, is what we learn about Socrates's daimonion:

1. It is a divine sign that Socrates had since childhood and which always turns him away from something, never directly towards anything (Ap. 31).
2. Specifically, it stops him: (1) in mid-speech (Ap. 40); (2) from leaving the changing room at the bath house (Euth.); (3) from crossing a river to return to Athens (Phaed.); (4) from initially befriending Alcibiades (Alc.) and from initially associating with Antisthenes (Xen, Banq.); (5) accepting back students that have left him (Theat.); (6) from going into politics (which he believed saved his life) Ap. 40; and also other professions (7) such as becoming a Sophist (Hippias Major) and (8) from twice worrying about or preparing for his defence at his trial (Memorablia 148 and 491).
3. It frequently came to him and sometimes in small things; Ap. 40.
4. It was the source of one of the three accusations made against him at his trial, namely that he introduced new divine things; Euth., Ap. 31; Memo 1.
5. He believes that it was responsible for his becoming a true philosopher; Rep. 496.
6. In Rep. 496 he also says that it was unique or rare.
7. It seems to compel acquiescence; for Socrates always, as far as we know, obeys it.
8. It gives no reason, although this might be qualified by the evidence of the *Phaedrus*, where Socrates says that "just as I was about to cross the river, the familiar divine sign came to me" and adds: "I thought I heard a voice coming from this very spot, forbidding me to leave until I made atonement for some offense to the gods."- which could be taken as the reason for the sign, although hardly a sufficient, justified reason.
9. Unlike the usual divinational signs, such as thunder, birds of omen and sacrificial victims, Socrates's daimonion is not publicly observable. And although he describes it as a voice (in Ap. 31 and Def.), all his other references to it are as a sign. However, here again the evidence of *Phaedrus* might also seem to go against this, since Socrates does talk of a voice speaking to him from "this very spot," although he says that it seemed to be, or he thought it was, a voice speaking to him.
10. In the *Phaedrus* passage the sign is preceded by Socrates feeling uneasy.
11. When Socrates describes his daimonion at his trial (in Ap.31 and Def.), and especially its prescience, it provokes an angry response from his judges.

Interpretations

This, then, is the hard or hardish evidence. The question is: what does it tell us about Socrates's daimonion?

1. Perhaps the most widespread view, recently expressed by Gosling, is that "The voice of the daimonion is pretty clearly what we would call the voice of cautious conscience" (1997: 17). This fits with its subjective character and with Socrates's concern with what is right. But the interpretation seems belied by what Socrates says in Rep. 496, that it is unique or rare, for then Socrates would be saying that that he was unique in having a cautious conscience. Gosling characterization also seems at odds with the outbreak of anger from the judges, which strongly suggests that they thought that Socrates was making an outlandish claim. Seeing the daimonion as a moral manifestation also does not fit the appearance of the sign in the *Euthydemus*, where it stops Socrates from leaving the bath house.
2. Another widely held interpretation is that the daimonion was essentially an indirect manifestion of

Socrates's rationality. Among the proponents of this view is Martha Nussbaum, who speaks of the daimonion as "an ironic way of alluding to the supreme authority of dissuasive reason and elenctic argument" (see Smith and Woodruff, 2000: 32–33). What is attractive about this view and those like it is that if it were right, we would then have a way of dealing with the problem mentioned at the beginning of this article. For then there would be no fundamental conflict between Socrates's rationality and his daimonion. But this suggestion, like Gosling's interpretation, does not fit the evidence of the *Euthydemus*, or (comfortably) most of the other appearances of the daimonion.

3. A variation on (2), which also draws somewhat on (1), is that the daimonion is rational but that its conscious rational operations have become instinctive or intuitive by long use in the service of virtue. This seems to be Montaigne's proposal, that Socrates's daimonion was "a certain impulse of the will that came to him without awaiting the advice of his reason" (p. 35). But, though attractive, it also suffers from the difficulties of (1) and (2).

4. A more searching suggestion, although prima facie less attractive, is made by Nietzsche in his important "The Case of Socrates." This is that the daimonion, which Nietzsche describes as an "auditory hallucination" was an indication that Socrates was suffering from mental illness. I think this is essentially right, but it needs to be honed in important ways. Most important, it needs to be observed that not all mental illnesses are bad. Socrates himself is especially clear about this in the *Phaedrus* 244–5, where he speaks of the valuable things that have come from madness (mania). Also, it is not clear, despite Nietzsche's description, that the daimonion was a psychotic symptom. For unlike the classic psychotics, such as Schreber, Socrates does not believe he was hearing voices that brought him into direct contact with other persons or agents. What all the evidence (with the possible exception of *Phaedrus*) suggests is that he was experiencing (subjective) signs or urgings. Hence, if Socrates was suffering from a mental illness it is probably closer to a neurotic rather than a psychotic illness. And there is evidence that it did resemble an important neurosis, namely obsessional neurosis, now also described as obsessive compulsive disorder or OCD, a condition most famously described by Freud in the seventeenth of the *Introductory Lectures on Psychoanalysis* and the case of the Rat man.

The most important evidence pointing to the daimonion as a form of obsessional neurosis, is that:

1. it compels but without giving a reason; and yet the sufferer feels that it must be obeyed.
2. that those subject to such compulsions often try to rationalize them after the fact, which is what Socrates does.
3. As the obsessional neurotic very frequently believes that he, or his condition, is virtually unique, so did Socrates.
4. Having this condition gives the sufferer a sense of his importance even grandeur. Of course, in one way this does not fit with Plato's picture of the modest Socrates. But this was not how the judges at his trial reacted to his account of his daimonion. It created clamour, since it suggested that he had a special relation with a god.
5. In the *Phaedrus* it goes with or is preceded by uneasiness or anxiety. Obsessional neurosis is also frequently found in people obsessed with morality (as e.g., Zola) which was also Socrates's case.
6. It also very often takes a religious form, most famously shown in Luther and Bunyan.

Of course, in proposing that Socrates's daimonion should be seen as a form of good obsessional madness, I am not claiming that it perfectly fits. Thus we do not know that Socrates found his daimonion oppressive or unwanted. But then it isn't clear what his attitude to it was, or whether it was consistent over the many years that he had it. That he believed it divine and obeyed it does not prove that he liked having it. Another likely objection to this interpretation is that it is crudely reductionistic. In fact, this need not be the case, if we bear in mind Socrates's judgement in the *Phaedrus* that the most valuable things have come from good madness. For then, it is not religion that is being reduced to psychology, but psychology that is being raised to religion. And given Socrates's extraordinary accomplishments- i.e., becoming arguably THE exemplary wise man, even perhaps the noblest human being in history and, through his crucial impact on Plato, the guiding spirit of western philosophy- we have little or no reason to regard anything which was distinctive of him as MERELY psychological or bad psychopathology. Nor, bearing this in mind, should we even exclude the possibility that the daimonion was what Socrates thought it to be, namely a supernatural sign from a god. Seeing the daimonion as some form of good madness does not exclude that. Indeed, if anything the extraordinary character of Socrates's achievements seem to call for some such an extraordinary, paranormal explanation. The daimonion as good or divine psychopathology also offers a way of reconciling the conflict between Socrates daimonion and his rationalism: in short, that it provided the necessary safety net or veto for

Socrates's commitment to reason and rational justification, preventing him from becoming a rational tyrant as well as encouraging his rationalism by the tendency that obsessional's have for finding reasons for their compulsions, or – perhaps we should say in Socrates's case – his repulsions.

Of course, one thing that needs to be mentioned, as lying behind Socrates's unique accomplishments and between the plausibility of the supernatural interpretation and the psychopathological interpretations, was the apparent ability of his daimonaic repulsions to be unerringly, providentially right.

See also: ◉ Daimonic ◉ Plato and Religion

Bibliography

Freud, S. (1986). Introductory lectures on psychoanalysis. In *Standard edition of Freud*, Vol. xv.

Gosling, A. (1997). *Socrates: Philosophy's martyr*. London: Phoenix.

Montaigne, M. (2003). *The complete works* (D. M. Frame, Trans.). London: Everyman.

Nietzsche, F. (1962). Twilight of the idols in *the portable Nietzsche* (W. Kaufmann, Trans.). New York: Viking Press.

Smith, N., & Woodruff, P. (Eds.). (2000). *Reason and religion in socratic philosophy*. Oxford, England: Oxford University Press.

Plato (1997). *Complete works* (J. M. Cooper, Ed.). Indianapolis, IN: Hackett.

Xenophon (1992). *The Memorablia, Banquet and Socrates's Defence* (Vol. 168) (The first translated by E. C. Marchant, the other two by O. J. Todd). Loeb Classical Library, Cambridge: Harvard University Press.

Song of Songs

Ingeborg del Rosario

The Song of Songs, also known as the Canticles of Solomon, is a collection of lyrical love poetry belonging to the Wisdom literature of the Hebrew Scriptures or the Old Testament of Christian Scriptures. The Song's title, the Song of Songs, is in the style of the superlative, similar to other Scriptural references as "the Lord of lords," "the God of gods," "the Holy of holies." While the Song has neither evident moral or ethical teaching nor any mention of God and is highly charged with passion and desire, deeply sensual and earthy in nature, by this designation, the Song is upheld as the Song above and beyond all songs, the godliest and holiest, the greatest of all songs. Within Jewish and Christian traditions, from as early as Rabbi Aqiba (c. 100 CE) and Origen of Alexandria (c. 240 CE) Gregory of Nyssa and Bernard of Clairvaux, to the mystics Teresa of Avila and John of the Cross, the Song is most commonly read and interpreted as an allegorical expression of God's agape, the divine passionate love for Israel, the chosen people, and later, of Christ's intimate love for his Bride, for the individual soul and for his Church. At the same time, while providing an analogue with which to speak of the intensity of divine love, a faithful reading of the Song, which alternates between three voices, a woman, her male lover and a female chorus, needs also to recognize its particular nature as a secular, erotic love poem. From its onset, the Song is eloquent with vivid metaphor and pulsating imagery that playfully express without inhibition or constraint the human experience of sexual yearning, desire and fulfillment:

▶   Let him kiss me with the kisses of his mouth! (Song 1:2).

Oftentimes, the challenge lies in being able to hold together these two ways of reading the Song. Spiritual growth and closeness to the divine do not entail a shunning of the authentic human capacity to be sensual and sexual, to know pleasure, to experience the urgings of desire and the delight of its satisfaction. Development and maturity in the spiritual life does not mean a forsaking of what is innately human, a relinquishment of our embodied nature. Disembodiment deprives and alienates, rather than nourishes and ennobles, the human spirit.

The religious patient in therapy might have profound sexual shame, guilt and inhibition around speaking of and referring to the body, sexual sensations and feelings because of imbibed religious beliefs that have dichotomized and alienated the life of the spirit from felt and sensed human reality. Deep shame can hinder the knowing and trusting of the body's inherent goodness and worth, beauty, loveliness and desirability. Spiritualization as a defense often serves to protect this patient from intense anxiety around being in the body and from experiencing powerful feelings and palpable sensations as well as from having to face and work through internal conflicts around religious beliefs, guilt from the association of the body and pleasure with evil, and sexual shame. Rigid, obsessive attitudes and compulsive behaviors might develop to support and consolidate a defensive spiritualized wish for self-lessness and accompanying disembodiment. Patients might also struggle with repression or dissociation around experiences of relational intimacy and sexuality especially if there is some history of sexual trauma, abuse or trauma to the body. The fear and terror of reawakening or reliving these traumatic experiences can keep patients numb and disconnected from their bodies, unable to feel and, consequently, unable to feel real and in themselves. On the other hand, there are patients who must deal with promiscuity or with sexual addictions and compulsive behaviors that also struggle with a form of this dichotomy between body and spirit. For these patients, there can be an obsessive, insatiable desire for the thrill and pleasure involved in these encounters, a longing that is dissociated from the human reality of the embodied love-object and their potential for a mutually intimate relationship.

A radical experience of the divine as well as an authentic movement towards wholeness and integration involve and presume an immersion in one's body and a growing awareness of the liveliness of its senses, a consciousness of one's sexual nature and robust capacity for mutuality and intimacy. The Song expresses sheer joy in the sensual: fragrant scents and aromas, the taste of sweetness and spice, the roundness of the belly, curve of the cheeks and color of the lips, the radiant ruddiness of the lover and the growing excitement that accompanies the sound of his approach, the heart-piercing desperation and frustration around his leave-taking, the exhilaration of desire and of being desired:

▸ How fair and pleasant you are, O loved one, delectable maiden! You are stately as a palm tree, and your breasts are like its clusters. I say I will climb the palm tree and lay hold of its branches. Oh, may your breasts be like clusters of the vine and the scent of your breath like apples (Song 7:6–8).

The Song touches on deeply human struggles: to take in and receive such profuse admiration of oneself and one's body; to risk physical touch and emotional connection that opens one to vulnerability and the possibility of painful rejection; to experience deep neediness and desperation for love along with the angst that comes with loneliness and abandonment; to deal with familial and cultural stereotypes that affect and distort issues of body image and physical self-care. The Song also provides a vital way of being with and in the body through which the world is known and experienced: allowing the mutuality of sexual desire and delight, palpable affection and playfulness; acknowledging that the human and communal journeys involve comings and goings, searching and finding, finding and losing, want and woo, intimacy that can be left bereft, need and satisfaction, lack and deprivation, assurance and insecurity, the yearning to touch and be touched, to hold and be held, wounding by love and fulfillment in love; recognizing that these same

dimensions are reflected in the spiritual journey and in each one's sacred relationship with the Divine.

The Song calls to a lived consciousness and embrace of the human-divine capacity for passion, yearning and oneness that is both singularly embodied and spirited, allowing each to be deeply moved and affected by the other; that is empowering, vitalizing and transformative, as audacious and bold as the woman of the Song demanding her lover to

▸ Set me as a seal upon your heart, as a seal upon your arm, for love is strong as death, passion fierce as the grave. Its flashes are flashes of fire, a raging flame (Song 8:6).

See also: ❯ Affect ❯ Bible ❯ Body and Spirituality ❯ John of the Cross ❯ Religion and Mental and Physical Health ❯ Sex and Religion ❯ Shame and Guilt ❯ Teresa of Avila ❯ Trauma

Bibliography

Bergant, D. (1998). *Song of songs: The love poetry of scripture.* New York: New City Press.

The Holy Bible: New Revised Standard Version. (1989). New York: Oxford University Press.

Trible, P. (1978). *God and the rhetoric of sexuality.* Philadelphia, PA: Fortress Press.

Sophia

Annabelle Nelson

Origins

Sophia is derived from the Greek word *sophizesthai*, (Cady, Ronanad, and Taussig, 1986) or one who is wise. Her name is also comes from the Greek work *sophos* (Cady, Ronanad, and Taussig, 1986) or to be of the same kind. An interpretation of this definition is that Sophia is contained in all of life; each life form is of the same kind as Sophia. Matthews (1991), describes Sophia as a warrior, dressed in camouflage haunting history. Similarly Schaup (1997) describes Sophia as a red thread who can be traced throughout the history of human experience.

Sophia has been defined as a deity, goddess, creator and archetype. She is referred to a many entities: a Middle

Eastern goddess; the "she" listed in the *Book of Proverbs*; the creator in the Gnostic gospels; a symbol of God in matter in Eastern Orthodox theology; the primordial Jungian archetype of all matter and life in Jungian though; and synonymous with Paramita Prajna, the mother of all Buddhas. Sophia is the spiritual force which formed the material world, and as such her spiritual energy is in each form of creation. Because of this, Sophia can be a conduit from the material world to the spiritual essence in each life form.

Goddess

As a middle eastern goddess, Sophia's name is associated with Barbelo (Ann and Imel, 1993) who is the mother of all the angels, as well as Jehovah's mother. There is an entity called Sophia Prunikos (Ann and Imel, 1993) or the fallen half of Sophia who was thrown out of heaven and became a whore on earth. She experienced the dark side of the human condition, integrated this and then returned to heaven as an aeon. In another form Pistis Sophis (Davidson, 1967) was the serpent who tempted Eve. Pistis is translated as faith. As a deity, Sophia embraces all of life without moralistic judgments.

Creator

Sophia was also named as the creator in the gnostic gospels in the *Nag Hammadi* scrolls (Eliade, 1987). The name for the gnostics comes from the Greek word, *gignoskein* (Eliade, 1987) meaning to know. In the scrolls Sophia is described as a self-generating, emergent force that rippled into existence to begin creation. This story has similar features to the structure of the Jewish kabbalah, where wisdom is *hokhmah* (Seghi, 1995) and is the first manifestation of the unknowable divine energy.

The Gnostic gospels with Sophia as creator are related to Plato's *Timaeus* (Conford, 1959). Speaking through *Timaeus*, Plato described creation as beginning with "one" or the world soul, termed Sophia by the Gnostics, and then subdividing exponentially. In all its varied forms, all matter and life still contained a piece of the world soul, Sophia.

In the *Nag Hammadi*, Sophia is beyond the opposites that define reality, and becomes a paradox that unites.

▶ I am the knowledge of my inquiry
and the finding of those who seek after me,
and the command of those who ask for me
and the power of the powers in my knowledge

of the angels who have been sent at my word
and of the gods in their seasons by my counsel
and of spirits of every man who exists in me (Bonheim, 1997: 216).

Old Testament

Cady, Ronanad, and Taussig (1986) says that the "she" in The Book of Proverbs, Wisdom and Baruch was Sophia. The following quotes exemplify Cady's point (Catholic Family Edition of the Holy Bible, 1953):

▶ For wisdom is more active than all active things; and reacheth everywhere by reason for her purity (Wisdom, Chapter 7, vs. 24).

▶ For she is more beautiful than the sun, and above all the order of the stars being compared with the light, she is found before it (Wisdom, Chapter 7, vs. 29).

▶ Learn where is wisdom, where is strength, where is understanding; that thou mayst know also where is length of days and life, where is the light of eyes and peace (Baruch, Chapter 3, vs. 14).

▶ Receive my instruction, and not money, choose knowledge rather than gold, for my fruit is better than gold and the precious stone and my blossoms than choice silver (Proverbs, Chapter 8, vs. 10 and 11).

Religious Contests

A Russian orthodox mystic, Vadimir Soloviev (1978) created a theology called Sophiology in an attempt to resacralize nature. Bulgakov (1993), one of Soloviev disciple's, makes the point that Sophia is unspeakable and unknowable but she is where the "creaturely world is united with the divine world in divine Sophia" (p. 17). Sophiology teaches that the way to become spiritual is through the material world.

In Tibetan Buddhism, Sophia is Pranaparamita, the Mother of all Buddhas (Macy, 1991). Prana is profound cognition and Paramita is translated as perfect or gone beyond.

▶ Freed from the dichotomies which oppose earth to sky, flesh to spirit, the feminine appears here clothed in light and space, as that pregnant zero point where the illusion of ego is lost, and the world, no longer feared or fled, is re-entered with compassion (Macy, 1991: 107).

Paramita personifies the Buddhist concept of "dependent co-arising." All sentient and insentient life arises from the same energy, consistent with *sophos*, to be of the same kind. Paramita or Sophia symbolize the possibility of transforming the human mind to sense the interconnection of all life.

Sophianic scholars such as Thomas Schiplfinger (1998) and Susan Schaup (1997) conclude that the ecstatic visionary experiences of Hildegard von Bingen and Jacob Boehme were of Sophia. Arne Naess (1992) coined the word Ecosophy to create a philosophy of aligning human life to ecological equilibrium.

Archetype

Maria-Louise von Franz, a Jungian therapist, calls Sophia the self-knowing primordial cause or the energy from "the archetypal world after whose likeness this sensible world was made" (von Franz, 1985: 155f). She also says that Sophia is the fundamental archetype or the blue print of the material, sensible world (von Franz, 1996). Woodman and Dickinson (1996) believe that humans are at the brink of a paradigm shift moving into a state where the spiritual self is the locus of development and interconnectedness will mark consciousness, or the paradigm contained in the archetype, Sophia. The search for wisdom, then, is contained in this quote: "To become like Adam and unite with the inner Sophia and become androgynous" (Eliade, 1987: 13). Sophia transcends religious, racial, tribal, national and even species differences as part of creation, and becomes a method of gaining wisdom of merging human consciousness with the world soul contained in all life.

See also: Archetype Buddhism Eliade, Mircea Female God Images Gnosticism Jung, Carl Gustav Prajna

Bibliography

Ann, M., & Imel, D. M. (1993). *Goddesses in world mythology*. Santa Barbara, CA: ABC-CLIO.

Bonheim, J. (1997). *Goddess, celebration in art and literature*. New York: Street Productions & Welcome Enterprises.

Bulgakov, S. (1993). *Sophia: Wisdom of God*. Hudson, NY: Lindisfurne Press.

Cady, S., Ronanad, M., & Taussig, H. (1986). *Sophia: The future of feminist spirituality*. San Francisco, CA: Harper & Row.

Catholic Family Edition of the Holy Bible. (1953). New York: John. J. Crawley & Co.

Conford, F. M. (1959). *Plato: Timaeus*. New York: MacMillan.

Davidson, G. (1967). *A dictionary of angels including fallen angels*. New York: Free Press.

Eliade, M. (1987). *The Encyclopedia of religion*. New York: MacMillan.

Macy, J. (1991). *World as lover, world as self*. Berkely, CA: Parallax Press.

Matthews, C. (1991). *Sophia, Goddess of wisdom: The divine feminine from the black goddess to the world-soul*. London: HarperCollins.

Naess, A. (1992). Deep ecology and ultimate premises. *Society and Nature, II* (September/December), 108–110.

Schaup, S. (1997). *Aspects of the divine feminine, past and present*. York Beach, ME: Wesier.

Schiplfinger, T. (1998). *Sophia-Maria, a holistic view of creation*. York Beach, ME: Weiser.

Seghi, L. F. (1995). Glimpsing the moon, the feminine principle in Kabbalah. In E. Hoffman (Ed.), *Opening the inner gates: New paths in kabbalah and psychology*. Boston, MA: Shambhala.

Soloviev, V. (1978). *Sophia*. Lausanne, Switzerland: L'Age d'Homme.

Von Franz, M. -L. (1985). *Aurora consurgens*. Princeton, NJ: Princeton University Press.

Von Franz, M. -L. (1996). *The interpretation of fairy tales*. Boston, MA: Shambhala.

Woodman, M., & Dickson, E. (1996). *Dancing in the flames: The dark goddess in the transformation of consciousness*. Boston, MA: Shambhala.

Soteriology

Emily Stetler

Soteriology is the branch of theology dealing with the study of salvation. The term comes from the Greek *soterion*, "salvation," and is also related to *soter*, "savior."

Soteriology relates to several other branches of theology in that it asks who is saved, by whom, from what, and by what means. It asks, as well, what the end goal of this salvation is. In Christianity, soteriology is inextricably linked with christology, for both fields centralize the significance of Christ as savior. Christian soteriology, then, developed vis-à-vis the process of defining doctrinally who Jesus is and what his life, death, and resurrection mean for humankind. While it is outside the scope of this article to give a comprehensive overview of christological developments, we may examine two christological concerns of the early church that are immediately relevant to soteriology: that Christ must be fully God, and that he must be fully human.

The issue of Christ's divinity came to the fore in the early fourth century, when the priest Arius of Alexandria insisted that the Son, Jesus, was not coeternal with the

Father but was created by him. Jesus was the first of all creation, but created, nonetheless. He was, Arius claimed, *homoiousious* with the Father – of *similar* substance. Would Arius' position have been accepted, the soteriological implication would have been that the world's Savior would not have been one with the one wishing the world's salvation.

While the Council of Nicaea condemned Arianism in 325 by declaring the Son to be *homoousious* – of the *same* substance – with the Father, another soteriological challenge soon arose. Apollinaris of Laodicea described Christ as being fully human insofar as his body was concerned; his divinity, however, took the place of a human soul. In this instance, Christ would not be truly human; he would simply be the divine *Logos* enfleshed in a human body. Soteriologically, Jesus the Savior would be, in the Apollonarian view, one with the Father who desires the world's salvation, but unable to be identified with the humans whom he saves. The Council of Chalcedon in 381 condemned Apollonaris and his teaching. Christian soteriology, then, insists that the savior be one with both the God who saves and the people whom he saves.

Certainly, Christianity is unique in being defined by its savior, but there are savior-figures in other religions, too. For instance, some sects of Buddhism see a bodhisattva as helping to bring about salvation. In Pure Land Buddhism, devotees believe that the Dharmākara bodhisattva (also known as the Amitābha Buddha) works to help them enter the perfect land of bliss.

Soteriology, though, deals not only with the *soter*, the savior figure, but also addresses what salvation means. In Christian theology, salvation classically means salvation *from* sin and *for* Heaven. Among and within Christian denominations, however, this statement of salvation still leads to disparate understandings. Western churches traditionally have taught that Christ redeems humankind from personal and original sin; Eastern churches, however, have no doctrine of original sin. Likewise, salvation to Heaven classically means, in the West, that humans can hope to experience the *beatific vision*, seeing God face-to-face in the afterlife. In the East, Heaven has been construed differently; the emphasis has been on Christ bridging the gap between man and God so that, through Christ's saving work, the human experiences *theosis*, a divinization by which he participates in the divine life of the godhead. Heaven, then, is the fulfillment of Athanasius' axiom that God [Christ] became man so that man may become [by adoption, not by nature] God.

Like Eastern Orthodoxy, Islam has no doctrine of original sin, so Muslim soteriology focuses on salvation *for* Heaven. This is accomplished primarily through faith, although some sects of Islam also emphasize adherence to the law and the need for purgation of sin.

In both Buddhism and Hinduism, salvation entails liberation from the illusions of this world. In Hinduism, it is primarily ignorance from which one must be saved; and so the process of salvation is a process of becoming aware of the illusoriness of the world, the transience of all things, and the self as an extension of *brahman*. According to Buddhism, the person escapes suffering through freeing himself from desires and false attachments to the world and the self.

Increasingly across faith traditions in the late twentieth and early twenty-first centuries, soteriology has come to be understood as having ramifications in this world as well as in the afterlife. Liberation theologies emphasize that salvation is not salvation from sin alone, but also from structures of oppression and violence. Faith communities have become more socially engaged to promote human flourishing in this life.

Commentary

In Christianity, soteriology has an undisputable relationship with sin, especially in the Western churches. From a psychological perspective, then, soteriology presupposes a state of guilt, the state in which an individual feels he has committed a violation of moral law. While guilt can be a positive impetus for change, it can also fester and lead to anxiety, depression, and despair.

Freud understands guilt as a state of disjunction between the ego and the superego. More relevant, though, is the notion of existential guilt, associated with Søren Kierkegaard, among others. Kierkegaard denies a concept of original sin that implies that humans cannot resist sinning. Rather, he suggests that humans are free, and in the face of this freedom, they experience anxiety. It is through wrestling with this anxiety that the person becomes authentically human; failure to do so furthers guilt. Ultimately, the person who does not engage his anxiety will fall into despair. Salvation in Kierkegaard's paradigm entails recognizing oneself as a sinner, culpable in ones own right, and acknowledging the need for Christ's saving work.

See also: ❯ Amita Buddha ❯ Anxiety ❯ Atonement ❯ Bodhisattva ❯ Buddhism ❯ Christ ❯ Christianity ❯ Confession ❯ Existentialism ❯ Fall, The ❯ Heaven and Hell ❯ Jesus ❯ Kierkegaard, Søren ❯ Liberation Theology ❯ Original Sin

Bibliography

Athanasius. (1980). *Against the Arians*. In H. Wace (Ed.), *Nicene and Post-Nicene Fathers of the Christian Church* (Vol. IV: St. Athanasius) pp. 306–447. Grand Rapids, MI: William. B Eerdmans Publishing Company.

Aulén, G. (1986). *Christus Victor*. New York: Collier.

Kierkegaard, S. (1980). *The concept of anxiety* (R. Thomte, Ed.). Princeton, NJ: Princeton University Press.

Malkovsky, B. (2001). *The role of divine grace in the soteriology of śamkarācārya*. Boston, MA: Brill.

Mitchell, D. (2008). *Buddhism*. Oxford, England: Oxford University Press.

Norris, R., Jr. (Ed.). (1980). *The Christological controversy*. Philadelphia, PA: Fortress Press.

Rambachan, A. (2006). *The advaita worldview*. Albany, NY: State University of New York Press.

Ricoeur, P. (1967). *The symbolism of evil*. Boston, MA: Beacon Press.

Soul: A Depth Psychological Approach

Lionel Corbett

It has become very fashionable for depth psychologists to speak of the soul, although there is great variation in the way they use this word. Traditionally, the word "soul" refers to a supra-sensory reality, an ultimate principle, a divine essence, or an energy that is essential for organic life, but depth psychologists have appropriated the word as a way of distinguishing themselves from other schools of psychology. Some writers use the word "soul" to deliberately imply an overlap between psychology and spirituality, or to imply depth of experience or a romantic sensibility. For the psychotherapist, the main importance of this word is that it distinguishes between everyday ego concerns and deeper levels of meaning. The word soul is also a useful term for that mysterious, often uncanny sense of presence familiar to all psychotherapists that occasionally pervades the therapy room.

According to Bettelheim (1983), Freud used the term "*die Seele*" not in its religious sense but metaphorically, to indicate our common humanity, or as the seat of human identity and uniqueness. Bettelheim believed that Freud used this word for its psychological impact and to evoke mythological and humanistic resonances in the reader. Bettelheim suggested that Freud was aware of the spiritual nature of his work, but this awareness was ignored by his translators, and the word "soul" was deliberately excised or mistranslated as "mind" to make Freud's work more acceptable to the scientific community. This, even though Freud thought that psychoanalysts could be "secular ministers of souls."

Jung's writing consistently emphasized the soul rather than the mind or the brain. In 1933, in the heyday of behaviorist attempts to rid psychology of words with a religious connotation, he suggested that that the recovery of the soul is an essential task for us. Although he insisted on the reality of the soul as a principle in its own right, he used the term in various ways. Sometimes "soul" was used as if it were synonymous with the whole psyche, which for Jung is an irreducible realm in its own right. Because the psyche creates the reality in which we live, his ontological position is what he calls *esse in anima,* or being in the soul, meaning that our experience of the world is a combination of its material reality and the way the psyche or the soul imagines or fantasizes about it (Jung, 1971). This is an intermediate position between purely materialistic or spiritual perspectives – *esse in re* or *esse in intellectu.*

Jung also uses the term soul as if it were a kind of psychological organ which produces images and symbols which act as a bridge between consciousness and the unconscious. When we dream, or when we have a numinous experience, transpersonal levels of the psyche interact with human levels of consciousness. In this sense, the soul is that which allows us to link with spirit and perceive the sacred – what we know about the spirit comes by means of the soul. The soul casts the experience of spirit into emotions and images that are transmitted into personal awareness and into the body, a process known as the ego-Self axis.

Jung used the term "soul-figures" to refer to a female figure in a man's dream (the anima) or a male figure in a woman's dream (the animus). These parts of the psyche are particularly unconscious to the dreamer, more "other" than same-sex figures in a dream, so they bridge to deeper levels of the psyche. Today, we are reluctant to attribute specific gender qualities to the soul, because these often repeat gender stereotypes. What remains important is the soul's function of linkage to the unconscious.

Hillman (1975) wrote of the soul as "a perspective rather than a substance, a viewpoint rather than a thing itself." He points out that the soul is a way of talking about something that cannot be fully articulated. The soul refers to our capacity for imagination, reflection, fantasy, and "that unknown human factor which makes meaning possible, turns events into experiences, is communicated in love and has a religious concern" (Hillman, 1972). Hillman is fond of Keats's (1958) notion that the world is a "vale of soul-making," although he uses this term in a somewhat different sense than Keats did. Depth psychologists understand "soul-making" to mean the development of interiority, achieved by processing our experience psychologically, by casting our experience into words and images, seeing our situation metaphorically rather than literally, perhaps with a mythic sensibility. Arguably, however, it is the soul itself that allows us to do these things. If the soul is an a priori, supra-ordinate principle, we cannot "make" soul; to do so would imply something beyond the soul that is doing the making. It is more likely that the soul makes us, or makes us human. Our problem is to contact the soul amidst everyday life, whose activities, if understood properly, are a bridge to the soul, which makes the world and the body necessary.

Hillman makes much of the distinction between soul and spirit. He suggests that the soul is deep, moist, and dark while the spirit is fiery, light, impersonal, and ascending. This distinction may be carried too far, since at times the soul can also soar and feel dry, so it is arbitrary to attribute these qualities to spirit alone, not to mention the fact that there are many descent or earth-based spiritualities. But Hillman (1987) makes this distinction so that we do not confuse (soul-centered) psychotherapy with spiritual disciplines such as meditation, which aim at self-transcendence. For him, spirit prefers clarity and order, and is often aloof or image-less, whereas soul is about experiencing the soup of daily life, natural urges, memories, the imagination, fantasies, suffering, and relationships, much of which the spirit considers unimportant. Since only the soul but not the spirit suffers psychopathology, the soul is the proper province and the root metaphor of psychotherapy. For Hillman, it is important to distinguish soul and spirit when we are trying to understand the soul's own logic, its suffering, fantasies, and fears, which is a different project than a metaphysical approach to spirit and its ultimates. While he is correct to point out the danger to the psychotherapist of excessively spiritualizing human concerns, it is also true that the soul has spiritual needs. When we think of soul and spirit as transpersonal processes or qualities, it is overly dualistic to separate them completely. Without actually conflating them, we can think of the soul as an extension of spirit into the body, soul as the way we subjectively experience spirit, or spirit inducing what we call soulful experience.

Other writers in this tradition use the term soul when referring to the deepest subjectivity of the individual, especially to emotionally important experiences. "Soul" is often used synonymously with powerful emotion, especially among psychotherapists with a strong thinking function for whom emotions are numinous. Because emotion is the effect of the archetype in the body, and the archetype is a spiritual principle, soulful emotions such as love, hatred, terror, sadness, and joy are spiritually important to the psychotherapist.

As Jung (1969) puts it, the psyche contains a divine power, or the psyche is a metaphysical principle in its own right. The problem of dualism arises here, of how this essence interacts with the body, or how the body acts as an organ of the soul, which is a preferable attitude to traditional ideas that the soul in trapped in the body. For psychotherapeutic purposes, one can bracket this problem, which does not arise in the consulting room. Here one can think of soul and body as two aspects of the same reality, experienced differently because of the limitations of our perceptual apparatus, emanations of the same source expressing itself on a gradient of different levels of density.

In his seminal work on the soul, which is now rarely acknowledged, Christou (1976) points out that the proper field of psychotherapy is subjective experience, which is not the same as the brain, the body, or the mind. The soul is the experiencing subject, not the mind or the body that is experienced. Just as there is a difference between a physical object and our sense data about it, so there is a distinction between states of mind such as willing, perceiving, thinking, and our *experience* of these states of mind, what we do with them, what they mean to us subjectively. The language of reason and sense perception may vitiate the experience of soul, which is a reality of its own. Just as the body and mind develop in their own ways, so "the soul has its own developmental processes leading to psychic maturity and psychic plenitude" (Christou, 1976: 37).

For Christou, there is a difference between ordinary states of mind and deeply meaningful experiences, which are the province of the soul. Mind is the name we give to ideas and thought, but soul is the name we give to our ability to transform these ideas in our imagination. Mind, body, and emotions are *sources* of psychological experience, but they are not the experience itself – to fail to make this distinction is to confuse different levels. Our imagination elaborates our bodily states and our feelings, and the result is much more than simple conceptual understanding of an original experience. "Soul" therefore implies not just intellectual or aesthetic understanding of an experience, but our gut-level relationship to it, its effects on us, and the ethical demands of the experience on the personality. We participate in soulful experience; we do not just impartially observe it.

The soul cannot be thought of conceptually, because it is that which witnesses thought going on; it is the matrix within which mental life happens. In spite of the claims of cognitive-behavioral approaches, behavior and ideas are of a different order than the order of the soul. There is a distinction between a science of the mind and the reality of the soul, which is not just about behavior. The realm of soul is the realm of meaning that is discovered when we look into ourselves, when we are inspired or deeply affected by music, art, ritual, relationship, nature, love or beauty, whatever really matters to us.

Mainstream psychology rejects the language of the soul because it seems too religious. The soul is impossible to study using empirical criteria; it needs its own methods of study. Dreams and spiritual experiences have no rational explanation, or they have their own rationale – they defy the inductive scientific approach because they produce something new and impossible to replicate, so they are anathema to positivistic approaches.

The word psychotherapy means attending to the soul, and the word psychopathology means the suffering of the soul. If the therapist does not work at the level of the soul, by default we work only with the ego, the sense of personal identity, and with the personal unconscious. But soul is the larger context of experience, so that the ego's attitude may be mistaken from the point of view of the soul. Therefore, psychotherapy that only supports adaptation to the environment may produce a "cure" that ignores the values of the soul. Accordingly, Christou suggests that the "proof of psychotherapeutic cures takes the form of 'testimony,' a 'witness,' rather than that of logical conclusions or empirical observations of an objective event" (Christou, 1976: 3).

See also: ⊗ Anima and Animus ⊗ Depth Psychology and Spirituality ⊗ Dreams ⊗ Freud, Sigmund ⊗ James, William ⊗ Jung, Carl Gustav ⊗ Jung, Carl Gustav, and Religion ⊗ Psychotherapy

Bibliography

Bettelheim, B. (1983). *Freud and man's soul*. New York: Knopf.
Christou, E. (1976). *The logos of the soul*. Zurich, Switzerland: Spring publications.
Gibson, K., Lathrop, D., & Stern, E. M. (1986). *Carl Jung and soul psychology* (pp. 29–35). New York: Haworth Press.
Hillman, J. (1972). *The myth of analysis* (p. 23). Evanston, IL: North-Western University Press.
Hillman, J. (1975). *Re-visioning psychology*. New York: Harper & Row.
Hillman, J. (1989). Soul and spirit. In T. Moore (Ed.), *A blue fire* (p. 122). New York: Harper & Row.
Hillman, J. (1987). Peaks and vales. In J. Hillman (Ed.), *Puer papers*. Dallas, TX: Spring Publications.
Jung, C. G. (1933). *Modern man in search of a soul*. New York: Harcourt, Brace & World.
Jung, C. G. (1969). *Psychology and religion*. In *The collected works of C. G. Jung* (Vol. 11) (R. F. C. Hull, Trans.). Princeton, NJ: Princeton University Press.
Jung, C. G. (1971). *Psychological types. The collected works of C. G. Jung* (Vol. 6) (R. F. C. Hull, Trans.). Princeton, NJ: Princeton University Press.
Keats, J. (1958). Epistles: To my brother George. In D. Bush (Ed.), *Selected poems and letters*. Boston, MA: Harcourt Brace.

Sound

Laurence de Rosen

Sound is scientifically defined as any vibratory disturbance in the pressure and density of a medium (solid, liquid or gas) that stimulates the sense of hearing. It measures the ability to vibrate. Creation myths of a number of ancient religions – African, Australian, Polynesian, Tahitian, Hawaiian, Japanese – reflect the belief that matter is formed and life begins through God's sounds and tones. In Hinduism, the importance of sound, and particularly of chant, is firmly rooted in the belief that sound vibration is the basic nature of the universe, *Nada Brahman*: "Sound is God". The Sanskrit language is essentially a three-thousand-year-old science of sound. For the Greek philosopher Pythagoras, "A stone is frozen music, frozen sound." Hermetic principles tell us the universe is nothing than more an endless number of vibrations and rhythms.

Ancient ideas that sound and vibrations represent the fundamental nature of reality are reflected in the theories of modern particles physics and quantum mechanics.

Most objects, from subatomic particles to planets, have one or more frequencies at which they vibrate. Sound is widely used in modern science (notably in medicine, as in MRI and other technologies) in its re-sonance meaning, literally, re-sound for diagnosis and healing. When a sound wave strikes an object, if there is a match between the frequency of the wave and the frequencies inherent in the object, the object begins to vibrate (creating resonance). The same phenomenon applies at the symbolic level in psychology. The verb "vibrate" means "move, swing to and fro," which is precisely the description Jung gave of the transcendent function, "the psychic function that facilitates a transition from one attitude to another."

The word *persona* is made up of two Latin syllables: *per*, which means "through" and *sonare*, the verb for "sound." Together they mean "sounding through, through sound," an allusion to the hole in the mask worn by actors in ancient times, through which the voice was sounding, moving through.

In psychology, sound is a bridge between Spirit and matter. Through the vibrating energy that is sound, the invisible world can touch this physical plane. In a number of practices (ancient Egypt, Kabala, Sufism, and Buddhism) it is believed that the chanting of particular vowels sounds has the ability to connect the chanter with the energies of the Divine and with the mystery of healing.

See also: ❂ Jung, Carl Gustav ❂ Mantra ❂ Music and Religion ❂ Music Thanatology ❂ Prayer ❂ Transference

Bibliography

Aczel, A. (1999). *God's equation: Einstein, relativity and the expanding universe*. New York: Random House.
Emoto, M. (2004). *The hidden messages in water*. Hillsboro, NY: Beyond Words Publishing.
Goldman, J. (1992). *Healing sounds, the power of Harmonucs*. Rochester, VT: Healing Arts Press.
Lieberman, F. (1999). *Spirit into sound, the magic of music*. San Francisco, CA: Grateful Dead Books.
Sacred Sound and Social Change. (1992). *Liturgical music in Jewish and Christian Experience* Notre Dame, IN: University of Notre Darne Press.

Spirit Writing

Mark Greene

Spirit writing is a popular form of divination used in Taoist temples and folk shrines located principally in Taiwan, Malaysia, Singapore, Hong Kong and Mainland China. The Chinese name for this traditional method is *fuji* (扶乩). The *fuji* diviner uses a stick to convey messages from a god or a spirit by drawing Chinese words in a tray of sand or on a table. Once the character has been identified, a second person transcribes it for later study so that the drawing area can be swept clean to make way for the next word. Although the guiding force behind the stick's movements is thought to be the god or spirit, the diviner participates in the process to the extent that he must be deemed deserving of the post by virtue of his good character. Spirit-writers generally appear to be in a mild trance and do not often show signs of overt spirit-possession.

See also: ❂ Chinese Religions ❂ Taoism ❂ Wong Tai Sin

Bibliography

Lang, G., & Ragvald, L. (1993). *The rise of a refugee God: Hong Kong's Wong Tai Sin*. Oxford, England: Oxford University Press.
Lang, G., & Ragvald, L. (1998). Spirit writing and the development of Chinese cults. *Sociology of Religion, 59*(4), 309–328.

Spiritual Direction

Kenneth L. Nolen

Spiritual direction is the process of one person accompanying another person or persons on their spiritual journey, a journey that emphasizes a growing closer to God, the Holy, or a Higher Power. However, each spiritual director tends to have a modified or different definition of spiritual direction germane to his or her context, background, and experience. Currently Spiritual direction is experiencing a rebirth or resurgence in Christianity, and other faith traditions are discovering or rediscovering spiritual direction as well.

Spiritual direction consists of a director and a directee, or directees in group spiritual direction, that are in a process seeking out the operation and direction of God, the Divine, or the Holy in the directee's life. Although, modern spiritual direction has its root in Catholic and Anglican faith traditions, all Christian faith groups do not universally accept spiritual direction as a valid ministry or expression of faith. Many Evangelical and Pentecostal denominations believe that Christ is the mediator between humankind and God and that the Holy Spirit is the only spiritual guide needed. They fear that using another person as a director is allowing that person to come between the directee and God. In addition, spiritual direction is not a uniquely Christian phenomenon. Witch doctors or shamans perform the role of spiritual guide in primitive cultures and many instances of spiritual guides may be found among eastern traditions. The ascetics of Buddhism, the sages of China and the soul guides of Sufism, with the guru in Hinduism being the closest to the Judeo-Christian concept of a spiritual director, are examples of other spiritual guides or directors.

Although spiritual direction may examine and highlight many issues of life, spiritual direction is not the same as its relative of psychotherapy. While an individual may need and use a combination of psychotherapy and spiritual direction, spiritual direction, although at times overlapping the boundaries of psychotherapy, is a different and distinct helping discipline. Spiritual directors use many of the same techniques such as active listening, compassion, and reflective open-ended questions that psychotherapy practitioners use, but spiritual direction encompasses a differing agenda and stated result.

Commentary

Spiritual direction and psychotherapy have many similarities but they are fundamentally different in content and intent. Psychotherapy focuses on emotional and mental dimensions such as thoughts, feelings, and moods, while spiritual direction focuses more precisely and specifically on spiritual issues such as prayer and the relationship to God and God's direction and work directly in the life of an individual. The intent of psychotherapy is not to facilitate the growth of persons in their relationship with the Divine, the Holy, or God. Modern psychology is valuable in that it gives hope that individuals can really grow and change. It helps to keep individuals moving in life and relationships, but psychology cannot assist in finding the direction that the directee's growth and change should take to facilitate their spirituality. Another major difference between psychotherapy and spiritual direction is that in spiritual direction, the director must be willing to be known in his or her vulnerability and limitations as a child of God, while the psychotherapist remains safely spiritually and many times emotionally unknown to his or her client.

However, it is important to understand that spiritual as used in spiritual direction is not the guidance of a person's spiritual activities alone nor is it particularly directive in nature. The spiritual director is not like a dentist who cares for a patient's teeth or a barber who cares for an individual's hair. A spiritual director is concerned with the whole person including those issues of life that affect an individual's relationship with God and others. Spiritual direction spiritualizes all aspects and activities of the spiritual person's life, but modern spiritual directors do not give answers to their directees nor do they discipline them in the classic image of a master teacher and his or her learner.

Spiritual direction and psychotherapy differ in the degree of training and certification required. Therapists must graduate from an approved and accredited graduate program to meet state requirements for licensure. There are no educational or licensure requirements for one to become a spiritual director. Although spiritual directors may be ordained clergy holding advanced graduate degrees, they may also be laypersons or individuals who are spiritual directors as evidenced by others seeking them out for spiritual direction.

An effective and experienced spiritual director will acquire and use tools from the other helping disciplines as well as attending formation and certification programs for spiritual directors to contribute to acquiring the necessary skills that will contribute to their ministry of spiritual direction. Many of the same active listening and reflective skills used in psychotherapy will aid the spiritual director in hearing God's voice in all of the day-to-day noise experienced by the directee.

See also: ❯ Jung, Carl Gustav, and Religion ❯ Pastoral Counseling ❯ Psychotherapy ❯ Psychotherapy and Religion ❯ Religion and Mental and Physical Health

Bibliography

Bakke, J. A. (2000). *Holy invitations: Exploring spiritual direction*. Grand Rapids, MI: Baker Book House.

Bakke, J. A. (2001, April 23). Making space for God: What spiritual direction is, and why evangelicals are increasingly attracted to it. *Christianity Today*, 88–90.

Demarest, B. (2003). *Soulguide: Following Jesus as spiritual director*. Colorado Springs, CO: Navpress.

Dougherty, R. M. (1995). *Group spiritual direction: Community for discernment*. New York: Paulist Press.

Edwards, T. (1980). *Spiritual friend: Reclaiming the gift of spiritual direction*. New York: Paulist Press.

Ganje-Fling, M. A., & McCarthy, P. R. (1991). A comparative analysis of spiritual direction and psychotherapy. *Journal of Psychology & Theology, 19*, 103–117.

Guenther, M. (1992). *Holy listening, the art of spiritual direction*. Cambridge, MA: Cowley Publications.

Jones, A. (1982). *Exploring spiritual direction*. Boston, MA: Cowley Publications, (Reprint, 1999).

Jones, W. P. (2002). *The art of spiritual direction: Giving and receiving spiritual guidance*. Nashville, TN: Upper Room Books.

Leech, K. (2001). *Soul friend: Spiritual direction in the modern World* (Rev. ed.). Harrisburg, PA: Morehouse.

May, G. G. (1992). *Care of mind/care of spirit: A psychiatrist explores spiritual direction*. New York: HarperCollins.

Merton, T. (1960). *Spiritual direction and meditation*. Collegeville, MN: Liturgical Press.

Moon, G. W., & Benner, D. G. (2004). *Spiritual direction and the care of souls: A guide to Christian approaches and practices*. Downers Grove, IL: InterVarsity Press.

Ochs, C., & Olitzky, K. M. (1997). *Jewish spiritual guidance: Finding our way to God*. San Francisco, CA: Jossey-Bass.

Ruffing, J. K. (2000). *Spiritual direction: Beyond the beginnings*. New York: Paulist Press.

Stone, H. W. (1986). Spiritual direction and pastoral counseling. *Journal of Pastoral Counseling, 21*(1), 60–76.

Vest, N. (Ed.). (2000). *Still listening: New horizons in spiritual direction*. Harrisburg, PA: Morehouse.

Spiritual Emergence

Hillary S. Webb

The term "spiritual emergence" was coined by Dr. Stanislav Grof and his wife Christina Grof, two leaders in the field of transpersonal theory, as a way of referring to breakdowns of meaning that lead to transformative growth and greater psycho-spiritual health on the part of the individual. It is, as the Grofs describe it, "the movement of an individual to a more expanded way of being that involves enhanced emotional and psychosomatic health, greater freedom of personal choices, and a sense of deeper connection with other people, nature, and the cosmos" (Grof and Grof, 1990: 34). The term *spiritual emergence* is often used in conjunction with "spiritual emergency" (also coined by the Grofs), a term used to describe a crisis state in which the process of growth and change stimulated by this "emergence" becomes so overwhelming and unmanageable that the individual is unable to gracefully return to day-to-day functioning.

From Breakdown to Breakthrough

The concept of the "spiritual emergence" is not a new one. The belief in the need to induce states of consciousness in which the individual experiences an oftentimes frightening psycho-spiritual break*down* of meaning in order to achieve an eventual break*through* into higher functioning is the *sine qua non* of many shamanic and mystical traditions around the world. Within these systems of thought, spiritual seekers are encouraged to disengage themselves from their ordinary state of consciousness through practices such as meditation, fasting, the ingestion of psychoactive substances, ecstatic ritual, and so on. Here, the teacher ("guru") and community play a fundamental role in helping the individual move through the process gracefully and in a way that helps assure successful integration and transformation.

In contrast, Western psychological paradigms have historically tended to take a pathologizing approach to any mental state that deviates from what is considered "normalcy." The terms "spiritual emergence" and "spiritual emergency" came about as a response to what the Grofs and others considered to be a failure in the mainstream Western mental health system to distinguish between psycho-spiritual healing crises and actual psychopathologies. They attribute much of Western psychology's inability to see the positive value in transpersonal crises as the result of a superficial and inadequate model of the psyche used by clinicians and academicians, one that is limited to "postnatal biography" and the Freudian individual unconscious. Because conventional psychology is often unable and/or unwilling to distinguish between a spiritual break*through* and a psychological break*down*, individuals going through these experiences are often misdiagnosed.

Says Oscar Miro-Quesada, humanistic psychologist and Peruvian shaman,

▶ As a clinician myself, I have found that about seventy percent of all socio-psychotic states are spiritual emergencies. The other thirty percent are psychopathological illnesses. But in the rest of these cases, if you help the client or the patient interpret his or her experience as a spiritual awakening rather than a sickness, they find purpose and meaning in the experience, rather than condemnation by societal norms (Webb, 2004: 13).

Identification and Diagnosis

Misdiagnosis is understandable, as many of the symptoms of spiritual emergence/emergency manifest in ways that are similar to those of chronic psychosis. Symptoms may include disorientation, disassociation, difficulty in communicating, and visual and/or auditory hallucinations.

An individual may be disturbed by physical feelings and emotions that are seemingly unconnected to anything. Some experience feelings of pressure, claustrophobia, oppression, tightness, restlessness, struggle, and even a sense of losing all reference points towards the self (Grof and Grof, 1990).

▶ Individuals experiencing such episodes may feel that their sense of identity is breaking down, that their old values no longer hold true, and that the very ground beneath their personal realities is radically shifting. In many cases, new realms of mystical and spiritual experience enter their lives suddenly and dramatically, resulting in fear and confusion. They may feel tremendous anxiety, have difficulty coping with their daily lives, jobs, and relationships, and may even fear for their own sanity (Grof and Grof, 1989, back cover).

Within the spectrum of crisis, there are various levels of emergency, which range from mild disorientation and fragmentation to a state in which one undergoes a complete loss of connection to ordinary reality. A spiritual emergence/emergency can occur on its own, or it can co-occur with conventionally diagnosed mental disorders that may, in fact, constitute pathology. In order to help clinicians identify some of the characteristic features of a spiritual emergence/emergency, the Grofs compiled what they had observed to be ten "varieties of spiritual emergency" (Grof and Grof, 1990), many of which are named according to the features that they share with emergences/emergencies found within various spiritual systems. These include: "the shamanic crisis," "the awakening of kundalini," "episodes of unitive (nondual) consciousness" (also referred to as "peak experiences"), "psychological renewal through return to the center (also referred to as "psychological renewal through the central archetype"), "the crisis of psychic opening," "past-life experiences," "communications with spirit guides," "near-death experiences," "experiences of close encounters with UFOs," and "possession states" (Grof and Grof, 1989).

Influence on the Field of Psychology

The Grofs' contribution to the field of psychology has been considerable. In his early studies of LSD and its effects on the psyche, Stanislav Grof constructed a theoretical framework for pre- and perinatal psychology, which mapped early fetal and neonatal experiences, eventually developing into an in-depth cartography of the human psyche. This presented a new perspective on the healing, transformation, and the evolutionary potential of the human psyche, thus challenging psychiatry's perspective on states typically seen as psychoses. In 1991, the Grofs' organization, the Spiritual Emergence Network, petitioned the then-in-development DSM-IV to create a new diagnostic classification that would address issues that involve religio-spiritual content, arguing that such a category would increase the accuracy of diagnostic assessments in cases where religious and/or spiritual issues are involved. The proposal was eventually accepted. Current versions of DSM-IV now include a diagnostic category of "Religious or Spiritual Problems." This change to the DSM-IV is considered to be evidence of an important and necessary shift in the mental health profession's view of religion and spirituality as essential aspects of the human experience. The concepts of "spiritual emergence" and "spiritual emergency" have likewise become key components in Transpersonal Psychology, a field that considers the spiritual dimensions of human experience.

See also: ❱ Spiritual Direction ❱ Transpersonal Psychology

Bibliography

Grof, S., & Grof. C. (1989). *Spiritual emergency: When personal transformation becomes a crisis*. New York: Tarcher/Putnam.

Grof, C., & Grof, S. (1990). *The stormy search for the self: A guide to personal growth through transformational crisis*. New York: Tarcher/Perigee.

Webb, H. S. (2004). *Traveling between the worlds: Conversations with contemporary shamans*. Charlottesville, VA: Hampton Roads Publishing.

Spiritualism

Nicholas Grant Boeving

Broadly defined, Spiritualism is a philosophical orientation that embraces extrasensory epistemologies, an all-knowing infinite God, and the immortality of the soul. With the mid nineteenth century flowering of interest in the occult, however, the word came to signify a largely unchurched religion which espoused not only belief in life after death, but in the ability of mediums to communicate with the departed.

Most authorities agree that the movement first began in the mid-1840s in Hydeville, New York with the Fox Sisters' widely-publicized séances which attracted the attention of thousands. Mental phenomena associated with the movement include clairaudience, clairvoyance, and telepathy, while physical manifestations such as levitation, psychokinesis, table rapping, and any purported supernatural visitations, such as ghosts, are also included.

The writings of Emanuel Swedenborg and Franz Mesmer – although themselves, not Spiritualists – informed much of the movement's thought. Largely a phenomenon of the upper and middle classes, Spiritualism relied on periodicals and trance lectures for dissemination. Lacking both administrative and canonical cohesion and plagued by the constant ousting of frauds, starting in the mid 1920s, membership drastically declined. Although still extent today – both independently and as absorbed by various syncretic movements – it was never to enjoy such widespread devotion again.

Commentary

The modern spiritualist movement arose at a particularly turbulent time, the various scientific and technological revolutions of the age calling into question the very meaning-making matrices of the Occident. A novel resolution to the cognitive dissonance pervasive in Victorian culture, Spiritualism was a way to fuse both faith and faith in science, although efforts to prove its tenets using the latter's methodologies were met resoundingly with failure.

See also: ◉ God ◉ Spiritual Direction ◉ Spiritual Emergence

Bibliography

Brandon, R. (1983). *The spiritualists: The passion for the occult in the nineteenth and twentieth centuries*. New York: Alfred A. Knopf.

Davenport, R. B. (1888). *The death-blow to spiritualism*. New York: G.W. Dillingham.

Deveney, J. P., Rosemont, F., & Randolph, P. B. (1996). *A nineteenth-century black American spiritualist, Rosicrucian, and sex magician*. Albany, NY: State University of New York Press.

Doyle, A. C. (1926). *The history of spiritualism* (Vols. 1 & 2). New York: G.H. Doran.

Stern, Karl

Daniel Burston

Karl Stern (1906–1975) was born in Bavaria to an assimilated Jewish family, and received little formal religions education. After a profoundly alienating experience at his Bar Mitzvah, he repudiated belief in God, and became a Marxist and a Zionist. Stern studied medicine and neuropsychiatry in Munich, Berlin and Frankfurt, and underwent a somewhat unorthodox analytic training with a practitioner who blended Freudian and Jungian perspectives, but leaned strongly toward a belief in "Spirit." During this period, he brief immersed himself in Orthodox Jewish observance, but meanwhile cultivated close friendships with ardent Christians, who seemed to understand his religious longings even better than his own relatives. In 1936, Stern and his family fled Germany to London, where he continued his neuropsychiatric work. Two years later, he arrived in Montreal (via New York), After much study and reflection, in 1943, he finally converted to Roman Catholicism, and was baptized by Father Marie-Alain Couturier (Schwartzwald, 2004).

Stern's first book, *The Pillar of Fire* was published in 1951, and gives a vivid account of his childhood, adolescence and early adulthood, and the various experiences and events that led to his eventual conversion, including his close friendships with Jacques Maritain and Dorothy Day. Like his younger contemporary, Cardinal Jean Marie (Aaron) Lustiger, Stern was unable to understand why most Jews – including many old friends – regarded him as a traitor; a recurrent theme in the literature by "Hebrew Catholics." From a Jewish perspective, of course, his pain and perplexity on this score are odd or disingenuous, since he was quite open about his proselytizing agenda. But regardless of how his actions were experienced and interpreted by his fellow Jews, it is important to note that converts like Edith Stein, Israel Eugenio Zolli, Aaron Lustiger and Karl Stern all worked diligently to overcome anti-Semitism in the Church, paving the way for Vatican II and for the Vatican's gradual recognition of the state of Israel in 1993.

In any case, *The Pillar of Fire* won the Christopher Award, became an international best-seller, and is full of illuminating reflections on the political-religious complexion of different Jewish denominations, the differences between Catholic and Nazi anti-Semitism, and of different currents within Nazism, Marxism and psychoanalysis.

In his next book, *The Third Revolution: A Study of Psychiatry and Religion* (1954), Stern explored the relationship between psychoanalysis and religion, arguing that the two are completely compatible. In his third book, *The Flight From Woman* (1965), Stern explored the pitfalls of (male-centered) Enlightenment rationalism, the denial of the feminine in society, and the roots of militarism and misogyny in the West, anticipating the insights and attitudes of many more recent feminist theorists who are not in the Catholic orbit.

Like Erich Fromm and Erik Erikson, who were also raised in German-Jewish households, Stern was a psychoanalyst who became a public intellectual. Like them, albeit in different ways, he addressed the relationship between science and religion, issues of gender identity, and the nature of religious experience. Stern is well known in Catholic circles as a formative influence on theologian Gregory Baum, another "Hebrew Catholic," and a severe critic of Catholic anti-Semitism, and on psychoanalyst Paul Vitz, whose writings on psychoanalysis and faith are deeply influenced by Stern. Though he wrote from the perspective of a psychoanalytically oriented clinician, Stern's books are informed by a deep knowledge of history, philosophy and sociology, and attest to the yearning for transcendence that persists in the midst of our secular society.

See also: ⊗ Conversion ⊗ Freud, Sigmund ⊗ Jung, Carl Gustav

Bibliography

Fromm, E. (1951, April 15). A modern search for faith: The pillar of fire, by Karl Stern. *New York Herald Tribune Review of Books*.

Graef, H. (1955). *The scholar and the cross*. London: Longmans & Green.

Klein, C. (1983). The new spirit among Jewish converts. *Jewish Christian Relations, 16*, 1.

Neuhaus, D. (1988). Jewish conversion to the Catholic church. *Pastoral Psychology, 37*, 1.

Pigozzi, C., & Rouart, J.-M. (2007, August 15). Le Cardinal Lustiger: Un Destin Exceptionnel D'Ombre Et De Lumiere. *Paris Match*.

Schwartzwald, R. (2004). Father Marie Alain Couturier, O. P., and the Refutation of Anti-Semitism in Vichy France. In L. Ehrlich, et al. (Ed.), *Textures and meaning: Thirty years of Judaic studies at the University of Massachusetts Amherst*. Amherst, MA: Department of Judaic and Near Eastern Studies, University of Massachusetts.

Simon, S. (2001). *Crossing town: Montreal in translation*. Presentation to the MLA annual meeting in New Orleans.

Simon, S. (2004) A. M. Klein et Karl Stern: Le scandale de la conversion. *Etudes Francaises, 3*(37), 53–67.

Stern, K. (1951). *The pillar of fire*. New York: Harcourt Brace.

Stern, K. (1954). *The third revolution: A study of psychiatry and religion*. New York: Harcourt Brace.

Stern, K. (1955). Some spiritual aspects of psychotherapy. In F. J. Braceland (Ed.), *Faith, reason and modern psychiatry; sources for a synthesis* (pp. 125–140). Oxford, England: P. J. Kenedy.

Stern, K. (1965). *The flight from woman*. New York: Farrar Straus & Giroux.

Syrkin, M. (1951, July 7). From Jerusalem to Rome: The pillar of fire by Karl Stern. *The Nation*.

Zolli, I. E. (1954). *Before the dawn*. New York: Sheed & Ward.

Stigmata

Charlene P. E. Burns

Introduction

From the Greek meaning "to prick; to burn in marks; brand" (Perschbacher, 2004). In the ancient Greco-Roman world, stigmata were the brand marks inflicted on slaves by their owners. The term is today most often associated with Christianity and refers to physical wounds, similar to those inflicted on Jesus of Nazareth during his crucifixion, that appear spontaneously on the body of a believer. The first use of the term in connection with Jesus appears in the New Testament, where the apostle Paul refers to his scars from injuries inflicted during imprisonment as "the marks of Jesus branded on my body" (Galatians 6:17); most scholars take his meaning to be that the scars mark him as belonging to Jesus the way a brand marks a slave. This is the sense given to the term in writings of early Christian theologians like Jerome and Augustine. Paul Orosius, a fifth century Spanish theologian, first used it in reference to the actual wounds inflicted on Jesus. In the thirteenth century an Italian monk, Br. Elias of Assisi, first used the word to refer to spontaneously appearing wounds marking the body of Francis of Assisi (Schmucki, 1991).

Historical Background

A few unsubstantiated instances of stigmata have been reported among Muslims in the form of wounds suffered by Muhammad during his efforts to spread Islam, and at least one Jewish case involving a young man who felt an intense identification with Jesus, but the phenomenon has historically been found overwhelmingly among Catholic Christians (Copelan, 1975). The spontaneous appearance of wounds perceived to duplicate those experienced by Jesus is not reported in historical documents before the thirteenth century. There is some disagreement over whether the first witnessed case was that of a British man, Stephen Langton (1222) or the Italian monk, Francis of Assisi (1224). Since that time, the phenomenon has proliferated. Three to five hundred cases have been reported, with peak activity in the nineteenth (20 documented cases) and twentieth centuries (perhaps 100 or more claims). The most famous twentieth century cases were Thérèse Neumann (1898–1962) and Padre Pio (1887–1968). The majority have been Italian Roman Catholic women who experienced significant trauma (physical or mental) prior to first appearance of the stigmata. Sixty two stigmatics have received beatification or canonization by the Catholic Church, although the official position of the Vatican has been that only St. Francis' case is of clearly supernatural origin (Alonso-Fernandez, 1985; Carroll, 1987; Albright, 2002).

Generally, stigmatics experience pain and bleeding intermittently from wounds in the hands or wrists, feet, and one side. Not all experience the same number and type of wounds, not all wounds bleed, and not all are visible; so-called invisible stigmata cause pain in the hands, feet, and side without development of wounds or scaring. Appearance of stigmata tends to be periodic, manifesting at times associated with Christ's Passion (on Fridays or during Lent), on church feast days, or when receiving Holy Communion. Many report a drastic reduction in the need and desire for food, with some claiming to ingest nothing but communion wafers after onset of the phenomenon.

Religious Interpretations

For many devoutly religious people, the stigmata are a sign of sainthood granted to very spiritual men and women as a sign of God's grace. They are miraculous manifestations of divine love and a foreshadowing of the goal of faith-union with God. For the stigmatic, the experience is intensely humbling and painful. In some cases, individuals report having prayed to share Christ's suffering or spending long hours in meditation on the crucifixion before onset. St. Catherine of Siena (1347–1380) was very highly revered during her lifetime, but prayed that the wounds be invisible so that she could continue to function as an influential figure in papal and Italian politics. She was so highly regarded that her head has been preserved in a reliquary which is kept on the altar of her church to this day.

Given the reverence accorded the phenomenon among religious individuals, it is puzzling that there are no records of stigmatization before the thirteenth century. One possible explanation leads us toward psychology and has to do with the fact that Christians did not commonly depict Christ's bodily suffering in art during the first one thousand or so years of the faith. The cross without Christ's body had become a symbol of the faith during Constantine's (272–337 CE) reign. In the early centuries, when Jesus' body was depicted, it was clothed in a shroud and usually without explicit signs of torture. From the ninth century forward, the body appears more and more often either naked or clothed only in a loin cloth, and with the twelfth century we see an upturn in graphic depictions of blood and suffering. By the late Middle Ages, representation of Christ in excruciating pain becomes the norm (Illich, 1987).

Scientific Interpretations

The first attempt to explain stigmata scientifically is found in Alfred Maury's *La Magie et l'astrologie dans l'antiquite et dans le moyen age* (1863). With the advent of scientific investigation during the nineteenth century, a discernable shift in status "from saint to patient" has transpired (Albright, 2002). Growing caution regarding the phenomenon is illustrated in the fact that only one stigmatic living in the last two centuries (Padre Pio canonized in 2002) has been declared a saint by the Catholic Church. The Church hierarchy's prudence regarding stigmata is a function of the difficult questions raised by scientific investigation of religious phenomena. Medically, the wounds are often labeled psychogenic purpura or auto-erythrocyte sensitization syndrome, which involves easy bruising that spreads to adjacent tissues and causes pain. This condition may be due to auto-immune sensitization or to purely psychogenic causes. Because stigmatics are most often devoutly religious and their wounds mimic those of Christ, the tendency among medical professionals is to attribute the condition to psychological factors.

In some cases, the wounds appear to have been self-inflicted. Wovoka (1856–1932), the Pauite leader of the second wave Native American Ghost Dance movement, had a vision of God during a solar eclipse in 1889 after which he preached a message of impending resurrection of the ancestors and end of white rule. He also exhibited the stigmata, which are thought to have been self-inflicted in order to more closely identify his message with Christ. Clearly fraudulent cases have occurred often, with wounds and bleeding caused by everything from self-injury to using makeup or the concealing vials of red food coloring, animal or human blood beneath layers of false skin (Krippner, 2002). Faking of the wounds was substantiated in the case of Magdalena de la Cruz (1487–1560), a Spanish nun. Whereas Wovoka may have inflicted the wounds to achieve ideological goals, stigmatics like Magdalena may suffer from what is now called Factitious Disorder (sometimes called Munchausen Syndrome), the intentional production of medical symptoms. These sufferers have no discernable external incentives, like political or monetary gain, apparently needing to assume the "sick" role for its own sake (DSM-IV, 2000: 471–475).

Psychological Interpretation

Stigmatics have, since the mid-nineteenth century, most often been diagnosed with hysteria or hysterical conversion – somatoform disorder in today's terms (DSM-IV, 2000: 445 or 451–452). In this condition, recurrent clinically significant physical symptoms cannot be explained by a diagnosable medical condition or as resulting from substances or intentional infliction. Pierre Janet (1859–1947) first noted that hysterics tend to be easily hypnotized and Karl Jaspers (1883–1969) discovered that stigmata-like wounds could be induced through hypnotic suggestion (Albright, 2002). The classic Freudian explanation is that stigmata arise due to sexual and aggressive urges originating in childhood (for an interesting Kleinian interpretation, see Carroll, 1987).

Freudian interpretations have been criticized based on the fact that many stigmatics suffered significant physical and/or psychological trauma just prior to first onset. One argument is that Post-traumatic Stress Disorder (DSM-IV, 2000: 309.81) may be more accurately descriptive. Thérèse Neumann, for example, suffered a debilitating back injury when putting out a fire at a neighbor's home when she was 20 years old. Her physical condition deteriorated into temporary blindness, left-sided paralysis, inability to speak normally and lack of appetite. She was bedridden for 6 years, during which time she suffered a seizure and developed infected bed sores. Her condition dramatically and spontaneously improved on the day her namesake, Thérèse of Lisieux, was canonized. Soon afterward she had a vision of Jesus and developed an open wound on her left side, followed by bloody tears and wounds on her hands and feet. She claimed to have ingested nothing but communion wafers for the next 36 years, and experienced the stigmata after entering a trance-like state nearly every Friday through Sunday for the rest of her life. In Albright's analysis, Neumann suffered post-traumatic stress symptoms expressed in disassociative self-mutilation (2002). It must be said, however, that even if science can identify underlying psychological mechanisms at work in the lives of stigmatics, the sufferer's faith that this is a spiritual experience is not thereby disproved. "The fact that an idea satisfies a wish does not mean that the idea is false" (Fromm, 1950).

See also: ❯ Christianity ❯ Freud, Sigmund ❯ Islam ❯ Jesus

Bibliography

Albright, M. (2002). The stigmata: The psychological and ethical message of the posttraumatic sufferer. *Psychoanalysis and Contemporary Thought, 25*(3), 329–358.

Alfred Maury. (1863/1978). *La Magie et l' astrologie dans l' antiquite et dans le moyen age*. Paris, France.

Alonso-Fernandez, F. (1985). Estampas de estigmatizados ccontemporáneosenel campo de la mística. *Psicopatologia, 5*(3), 279–292.

American Psychiatric Association (2000). *Diagnostic and statistical manual of mental disorders* (4th ed.). Washington, DC: Author.

The Bible. New Revised Standard Version.

Carroll, M. P. (1987). Heaven-sent wounds: A kleinian view of the stigmata in the catholic mystical tradition. *The Journal of Psychoanalytic Anthropology, 10*(1), 17–38.

Copelan, R. (1975). Stigmata-passion and punishment: A modern case history. *Journal of the American Society of Psychosomatic Dentistry and Medicine, 22*(3), 85–90.

Early, L. F., & Lifschutz J. E. (1974). A case of stigmata. *Archives of General Psychiatry, 30,* 197–200.

Fromm, E. (1950). *Psychoanalysis and religion.* New Haven, CT: Yale University Press.

Horton, W. (1924). The origin and psychological function of religion according to pierre janet. *The American Journal of Psychiatry, 35*(1), 16–52.

Illich, I. (1987). *Hospitality and pain.* Paper presented at McCormick Theological Seminary. Chicago, IL. Unpublished paper.

Krippner, S. (2002). Stigmatic phenomena: An alleged case in Brazil. *Journal of Scientific Exploration, 16*(2), 207–224.

Littlewood, R., & Bartocci, G. (2005). Religious stigmata, magnetic fluids and conversion hysteria: One survival of 'vital force' theories in scientific medicine? *Transcultural Psychiatry, 42*(4), 596–609.

Perschbacher, W. J. (2004). *The new analytical Greek lexicon.* Peabody, MA: Hendrickson Publishing.

Schmucki, O. (1991). The stigmata of St. Francis of Assisi: A critical investigation in the light of thirteenth century sources (C. F. Connors, Trans.). St. Bonaventure, NY: Franciscan Institute.

Thomas, F. (1946). *The mystery of konnersreuth.* Chicago, IL: Rev. F. Thomas.

Story as Scripture, Therapy, Ritual

Kelly Murphy Mason

Storytelling is known to be a primal human activity, a ritualized interaction between teller and listener that wove the fabric of earliest societies; yet our contemporary conceptualizations of storytelling have, like our societies themselves, grown considerably more complex and sophisticated. The postmodern impulse has had far-reaching implication across such disciplines as literary criticism, psychology, and religious studies, especially in developing greater awareness of the ways in which the collected stories that are constitutive of history could themselves be considered discrete constructions. Increased appreciation for narrative calls for an interdisciplinary approach that makes literature, psychotherapy, and religion more mutually informative in this era. Because humans are by nature storytellers, constructivist investigations into storytelling can reveal something significant about the various meanings ascribed to the human condition.

Constructivist approaches regard endlessly proliferating narratives as proof-positive of the human need for meaning-making (Saleeby, 1994). Many people's understanding of themselves and their larger culture has been shaped by the stories that get told frequently enough to become folklore. Even where meaning appears to be lacking – in needless suffering, for instance, or mass destruction – meaning has been devised through and derived from the stories people told to one another.

The Epic of Gilgamesh, believed to contain the oldest written narratives in history, had Sumerian origins dating to the third millennium BCE, predating the Homeric epics. "It is an old story," the epigraph declares, "but one that can still be told..." In fact, its ancient account of a cataclysmic flood is later retold in the Book of Genesis with the version of the story famously featuring Noah. Across cultures, stories have attempted to describe not only how the world had been created, but also how it had been reconstituted. Like Greek mythology, Sumerian mythology proffered explanations about what exactly separated the human from the godly, the mortal from the immortal, imbuing humans with ever greater self-consciousness.

Even as humans developed a deeper appreciation for the extent to which they were subject to circumstances such as earthly finitude, they also tried to exert individual agency within those confines. The struggle inherent in this dual reality gave rise to tension that created the story dynamic, one that poses questions about whether people are autonomous creations or relationally defined, self-determining, or simply the pawns of fate. By the fourth century BCE, Aristotle had already recognized that stories tended to conform to certain poetic expectations in their imitations of reality. He catalogued three distinct genres emerging: the epic, the comic, and the tragic, with the tragic becoming the most developed dramatically.

Tragedy extends a kind of cautionary tale. The didactic functions of story find their expression not only in tragedies, but also in fables and parables. Stories seem to be educative the sense that they are generally perceived as somehow providing a moral (Coles, 1989). Those stories that give us our most memorable moral instruction come to comprise a kind of sacred scripture. Scripture presumes a moral universe that requires human participation. Scripture also presumes an arc of action that is purposeful. As narrative-based faiths, Jewish and Christian religious traditions maintain a profound historical sensibility that asks believers to consider themselves players in a larger story, namely in God's plan for the salvation of the world.

Although psychotherapy challenged the Judeo-Christian emphasis on the collective experience of a shared reality by privileging instead the role of the individual's inner life, it left unchallenged in the West a fundamentally narrative epistemology. In the early twentieth century, Freud introduced the modality of psychoanalysis through case histories recounting the life stories of his analysands. As the psychological disciplines developed, they framed case histories with a degree of clinical certainty that frequently risked an overdetermined presentation of past events standing in causal relation to present difficulties (Polkinghorne, 1988).

Yet as constructivist approaches such as narrative therapy suggest, persons struggling with significant problems frequently have problematic life scripts (Roberts, 1999). They may have unconsciously concluded that serious troubles have been scripted for them; their troubled re-enactments begin take on a ritualistically repetitive quality that leads them to play caricatured roles in their own lives. Such persons can operate with the assumption of a tragic outcome unchanged in the face of a changing cast of characters in various stages of their life. They live to tell their tales, but again and again. The more regularly these persons tell their tragic tales, the more powerfully they get reinforced as a personal reality.

Storytelling tends not to be an indifferent act. Rather, it evokes certain emotional states for purposive and persuasive effects (Ochberg, 1996). Generally, narratives create an internal logic that must be preserved, often at the cost of curtailing scope and perspective. Stories establish what is and what is not relevant to a given course of action. They determine what knowledge is essential to right understanding.

This essentialism helps to explain why so many of the world's religious communities have established which stories will get told and retold in ritual settings by sealing a canon (Schussler, 1994). Yet there is a two-fold danger in this sealing: first, as stories grow old, they get told so grossly out of context as to be at times almost unintelligible and so are no longer heard in the same spirit as they were originally; and second, newer stories set in familiar contexts that would communicate the proper spirit in intelligible contexts may never be granted a hearing. In the Christian testament, the Pauline commandment to preserve the spirit and not the letter of religious teachings underscores the importance of appreciating the spirit of story, investigating whether it is sufficiently edifying to merit inclusion in scripture. Presumably, scripture offers healing stories that provide people a hopeful glimpse of possible resolutions to their own storied circumstance.

Sometimes sharing life stories provides persons in similar situations the promise of reparative experience by allowing positive identification with others. In recent decades, Alcoholics Anonymous and other Twelve-Step programs have basically provided recovering members the chance to construct a conversion narrative which they then testify to on a regular basis (Kurtz and Ketcham, 1992). Members make important corrections in what would otherwise be tales of woe by confessing all their past errors. With the Twelve Steps providing their narrative framework, they learn a new genre of life story that involves being both psychological and spiritual restored, the ultimate ends of recovery being sanity and serenity.

The potential of storytelling as therapeutic technique lies in its ability not only to provide people with an open hearing and cathartic release, but also to cultivate their awareness of the narrative structures they use to organize their existence. People can be encouraged to become simultaneously author and protagonist in their own stories, carefully crafting intersections of meaning around central themes that can be collected in a coherent self-narrative (Peacock and Holland, 1993). They can become the authorities on their lives as they are lived, recognizing the power of their ability to make choices in the present tense, shaping a storyline as it progresses.

Psychotherapy is usually a narrative undertaking, with persons telling their therapists the stories they want heard. The therapists have greater latitude in the interpretation of those stories if they recognize them as idiosyncratic constructions as opposed to objective factual accounts. Constructivist approaches resemble cognitive approaches in their exploration of the assumed contexts, perceived motives, causal connections, and characterological attributions that are then enlisted as narrative strategies (Mishler, 1995). Recognizing the story as a strategy enables therapists to reframe situations so that alternate narrations become possible. These revisions frequently become far more serviceable than the original versions in the therapeutic process.

Narrative therapists listen for stories that have been that have not yet been told. They challenge the unitary truth posited in a dominant narrative by highlighting the exceptional instance when a problem-saturated story has minimized or excluded a unique outcome which can only be accounted for in a broader narrative framework, one that does not require the narrator to subjugate such realities for the sake of a overall expediency or intended effect (White and Epston, 1990). Instead of overidentifying with the problems memorialized in the story, the narrator is free to externalize the problematic story in order to investigate its narrative logic more thoroughly and modifying it accordingly. In this manner, the narrator achieves a degree of liberation through both narrative competency and self-mastery.

If such liberation is not possible, the narrator becomes stuck in the story and options suddenly seem to narrow. Lacking a sense of authority, the narrator is no longer able to make meaning in and through the story. Should the interests of the story as artifact start to supercede the uses of it as life script, should the story enlist the teller for its ends instead of the opposite thing occurring, the story itself become inviolate in the imagination and a rigid fundamentalism results. It is the letter and not the spirit that triumphs as a mode of instruction and ultimately becomes a method of indoctrination. Because stories deal with animated individuals interacting, they generally represent complicated formulae that generate more questions than they answer (Bruner, 2002). What makes stories useful is their ability to state problems in terms that establish clear analogies.

Story conventions themselves provide people a set of concepts that might otherwise be unavailable. Aristotle recognized that plots turn on both reversals and recognitions, reversals being primarily external occurrences, recognitions being primarily internal ones. The majority of modern literary work does not have an epic sweep; it betrays less fascination with a series of large-scale external events occurring in certain sequence, being more preoccupied with the machinations of inner processing by characters themselves. Point of view now figures prominently and decisively. To an extent it never was before, Western literature has become psychologically minded. It has become an unmistakably humanist endeavor.

This humanist orientation does not mean that literature overlooks the sacred dimension altogether. Rather, modern articulation of the sacred tends to be grounded in a particular perspective rather than in disembodied omniscience. As contemporary sensibilities empower them as storytellers, people become more fully engaged not only as author/protagonists, but also as listeners. They research scriptures and question canons. Testing the spirit of stories, they begin to expect texts to be inspiring as well as inspired. Some old stories may no longer be told with any conviction, while some may need to be told in novel ways. Others in the canon stubbornly resist revision. Other old stories survive because they still invite the kind of participation that elicits personal identification and renewal on the part of their listeners. Such stories have gained credibility by being capacious; they enable connections to continue to be made today.

Commentary

The need for story is evident in young children, just as it was in earliest societies. Children, like the cultures they inhabit, exhibit preference for certain stories by urging that they be retold. Childish efforts to learn a story by heart, to have memorized it in its entirety through ritual repetition, imply a desire for mastery, a developmental drive to parse story grammar and discern the range of narrative elements at play. Some constructivists have posited that narrative is the primary mode humans have for giving the larger world coherence. Without narrative, humans might have difficulty locating themselves in any recognizable context or gaining any sense of direction.

Recognizing stories as fabrications rather than artifacts, people become co-creators capable of restory-ing their lives in meaningful ways. The decisions people make about how they will regard and meet life circumstance enable them to choose with intention the sort of story they will participate in, be it scriptural or secular, conventional or exceptional. They then tell stories that merit their assent and create a significant sense of community. Like psychotherapy itself, storytelling has long been considered as a shamanic practice, a method of channeling numinous energies in the service of human concerns and the greater good. With narrative awareness, constructivists intimate, people can communicate stories that express a conscious desire to heal themselves and their storied world.

See also: ❯ Biblical Narratives Versus Greek Myths ❯ Communal and Personal Identity ❯ Epiphany ❯ Fundamentalism ❯ Meaning of Human Existence ❯ Monomyth ❯ Narrative Therapy ❯ Persona ❯ Purpose in Life ❯ Ritual ❯ Twelve Steps

Bibliography

Anon. (1970). *Gilgamesh: A verse narrative* (H. Mason Trans.). New York: Mariner Books.

Anon. (1976). *Alcoholics Anonymous: The story of how many thousands of men and women have recovered from alcoholism*. New York: Alcoholics Anonymous World Services, Inc.

Aristotle. (1987). *The poetics of Aristotle* (S. Halliwell Trans.). Chapel Hill, NC: University of North Carolina Press.

Bruner, J. (2002). *Making stories: Law, literature, life*. New York: Farrar, Straus and Giroux.

Coles, R. (1989). *The call of stories: Teaching and the moral imagination*. Boston, MA: Houghton Mifflin Company.

Freud, S. (1963). *Three case histories*. New York: Touchstone.

Kurtz, E., & Kethcam, K. (1992). *The spirituality of imperfection: Storytelling and the journey to wholeness*. New York: Bantam Books.

Mishler, E. G. (1995). Models of narrative analysis: A typology. *Journal of narrative and Life history, 5*(2), 87–123.

Ochberg, R. L. (1996). Interpreting life stories. In R. Josselson (Ed.), *Ethics and process in the narrative study of lives* (pp. 97–113). Thousand Oaks, CA: Sage Publications.

Peacock, J. L., & Holland, D. C. (1993). The narrated self: Life stories in process. *Ethos, 21*(4), 367–383.

Polkinghorne, D. E. (1988). *Narrative knowing and the human sciences*. Albany, NY: State University of New York Press.

Roberts, G. (1999). Introduction: A story of stories. In G. Roberts & J. Holmes (Eds.), *Healing stories: Narrative in psychiatry and psychotherapy* (pp. 3–26). New York: Oxford University Press.

Saleeby, D. (1994) Culture, theory, and narrative: The intersection of Meanings in practice. *Social Work, 39*(4), 353–359.

Schussler F. E. (1994). Transgressing canonical boundaries. In E. F. Schussler (Ed.), *Searching the scriptures: A feminist commentary* (Vol. 2, pp. 1–14). New York: Crossroad Publishing company.

White, M., & Epston, D. (1990). *Narrative means to therapeutic ends*. New York: W. W. Norton.

Substance Abuse and Religion

Gilbert Todd Vance

Interest in the relationships between substance use and religion/spirituality has a long history. In *The Varieties of Religious Experience*, first published as a book in 1902,

William James commented on the relationship between alcohol use and mysticism. In 1961, Carl Jung and Bill W. of Alcoholics Anonymous famously corresponded concerning their perceived relationships between alcohol use, recovery from alcohol addiction, and the search for spirituality.

Certain psychoactive substances are associated with use by specific religions for mystical or ceremonial purposes. For example, peyote is associated with use by some indigenous people groups in North America. Kava is associated with use for religious purposes by people groups in the Pacific.

In modern research, an inverse relationship between substance use and religiosity (i.e., higher levels of substance use correlate with lower levels of religiosity and vice versa) has generally been observed across many studies. This relationship has been observed for various aspects of religion/spirituality and well as for the various levels of licit and illicit substance use. However, research has also shown that findings regarding the relationships between substance use and religion/spirituality depend on many factors. These include the specific aspect of religion/spirituality being measured (e.g., frequency of religious service attendance, spiritual practices, scriptural study), the specific aspect of substance use being considered (e.g., lifetime use, substance dependence, abstinence, lifetime risk for substance abuse), and the population being studied (e.g., adolescents, older adults, men, women). It must be noted that inverse relationships observed between substance use and religiosity are not merely a reflection of some religions' prohibitions against substance abuse. As Gorsuch (1995) has said, there is no single set of religious/spiritual norms regarding substance use. Precise research on the relationships between substance use and religion/spirituality requires specification of the various dimensions of religion/spirituality as well as the specific aspect of substance use being examined.

Because of the apparent protective effects of religion/spirituality in relation to substance use, some have proposed that the value of incorporating religion/spirituality should be considering in conceptualizing prevention and treatment programs for substance abuse and dependence. The success of spiritually oriented programs such as Alcoholics Anonymous (AA) suggests that religion/spirituality may play an important role for some persons in recovery from substance dependence. However, it is important to note that the overt spirituality of some AA groups can possibly be seen as a barrier to program participation for those persons who do not identify as religious or spiritual.

See also: ❯ James, William ❯ Jung, Carl Gustav

Bibliography

Gorsuch, R. L. (1995). Religious aspects of substance abuse and recovery. *Journal of Social Issues, 51*(2), 65–83.

James, W. (1902/1997). *The varieties of religious experience: A study in human nature.* New York: Simon & Schuster.

Sufis and Sufism

Fredrica R. Halligan

> ► We are the flute, our music is Yours;
> We are the mountain echoing only You;
> Pieces of chess, You marshall us in line
> And move us to defeat or victory...
>
> (Rumi, cited in Mabley, 2002: 35)

Sufism is the mystical expression of Islamic faith. Numerous orders or brotherhoods (*tariqa*) have been formed over the centuries, many following well-known spiritual leaders (*shaykhs*). Best known in the West is the Whirling Dervishes or Mevlevi, a path of which Rumi was the founder. Jalal al-din Rumi (1207–1273 CE) was born in Persia and settled in Konya in present-day Turkey. His poetry speaks eloquently of love and surrender to the Divine One, and especially of the longing for mystical union (Rumi, 1975). The aim of the Sufi is to perfectly reflect the image of God in one's heart, thus to achieve union with the Divine. For two years, Rumi's closest soul-mate was Shams–i Tabrizi, and after the unexpected departure of this companion, Rumi's grief was expressed passionately as "the dance of the spheres" in which whirling motion served to heighten altered states of spiritual consciousness (Trimingham, 1998). In his longing for Shams, his spiritual companion, Rumi wrote some of his most potent poetry. For example, the longing of the soul for God:

> ► O, make me thirsty, do not give me water! Make me your lover! Banish my sleep! (Mabey, 2002: 21).

Likewise, the willingness to surrender to the Divine One:

> ► My heart has become a pen in the Beloved fingers. . . .The pen says, 'Lo, I obey, for You know best what to do.'

Of Rumi it is written:

▶ Thus the primary goal of the Sufi is to transcend or "naught" the self or ego, which acts as a barrier or "veil" between the human heart and God, distorting our perception of reality and inhibiting our capacity to mature to our full "selfhood" in which we perfectly reflect the attributes of God. The focus is therefore on turning the soul to God; on becoming God-centered rather than self-centered; on the spiritual rather than the material, transitory world; and on inner, spiritual change rather than on the external reality of worldly status and wealth (Mabey, 2002: ix).

Sufi Asceticism

Asceticism and a life of renouncement were highly valued spiritual approaches among the Sufis in the medieval period. Many of the early Sufi ascetics were quite extreme in their behavior. Some Sufi ascetics became hermits and wandered around naked or formed communities that used mind-altering substances such as alcohol, cannabis or hashish. They also followed Islamic law assiduously, fulfilling spiritual duties including prayer, ritual, fasting, cleanliness of body and spirit.

Sufi Mysticism

Ibn 'Arabi (1165–1240 CE) was one of the most articulate of the theologians of Sufism (q.v.). As he pointed out, all Sufis commit themselves to become lovers of God. In Islamic tradition, the ninety-nine beautiful Names of God all refer to the One. So they may describe God, in terms of many attributes, as: The Merciful, the Just, the Wrathful, the Powerful, the Active, the Creator, the Author, the Form-Giver, the Bestower, the Patient, the Separator, the Sustainer, the Wise, the Stability, the Keeper, the Gracious, the Forgiver, the Experiencer, the Self-Sufficient, the Encompassing, the Hearing, the Seeing, the Subtle, the Beloved, and so forth. All Names refer to the One who is God. And that God is infinite Love, infinite Compassion, a feeling-full Person who desires to be known. Following the Tradition of the Prophet Muhammed (the *Hadith*). Ibn 'Arabi wrote that God's Mercy is greater than God's Wrath. "His Mercy encompasses everything existentially and in principle. . . . The Mercy of God flows in [all] created beings and courses through the selves and essences" (Ibn 'Arabi,

1980: 224). In fact, says Ibn 'Arabi, Mercy is inherent in all creation. Not only things and people but also experiences are created by Mercy. Even the experiences we would rather avoid: "Know that Mercy is inherent in all creativity, so that, [even] by the Mercy bestowed on pain, pain was created [brought into existence]" (Ibn 'Arabi, 1980: 224).

In Ibn 'Arabi's psychology, he divides humans into three classes: (1) the disciples of the *science of the heart*. . . . the mystics, and more particularly the perfect among the Sufis; (2) the disciples of the rational intellect. . . .the scholastic theologians; (3) simple believers." The Sufis are disciples of heart; the theologians are disciples of intellect. Never the twain shall meet. For simple believers, he holds out more hope: "Under normal circumstances a simple believer can develop into a mystic through spiritual training; but between mystics and rational theologians there is an unbridgeable gulf" (Corbin, 1969: 230). What Ibn 'Arabi is saying is that essentially we are all blessed. Because of the blessing of our imaginative function, we are at least potentially capable of receiving the theophanies of God. These glimpses of God manifesting to humanity occur definitely, but rarely, for ordinary folk. They occur hardly ever, or are ignored by, intellectualizers who only believe what the rational intellect dictates. But for the prophets, the Sufis, the Shi'ite saints, the mystics, the door is more widely open to receive the frequent glimpses and the revelations of the Divine. Furthermore, one can cooperate with the Divine Intent by making oneself more capable of receiving these Manifestations. This is done through spiritual practices and especially through the loving prayer of the heart (*himma*).

Today, in working therapeutically with spiritually-oriented clients, we can see that Ibn 'Arabi's insights into the difference between heart and intellect can profoundly inform our understanding of passion versus thought in providing access to spiritual growth and development. Creativity itself is "attributed to the heart of the Sufi. . . . here *himma* is defined as the 'cause' which leads God to create certain things, through *himma*, strictly speaking, creates nothing" (Corbin, 1969: 227). This is the power of prayer. As Ibn 'Arabi says, *himma* is "a hidden potency which is the cause of all movement and all change in the world" (cited in Corbin, 1969: 228). When we yearn, as the Sufi does, for God and for His Mercy, and when we surrender to God's Will, then the prayers are heard and the Divine response is according to our best interests.

See also: ❯ Ibn al- 'Arabi ❯ Islam

Bibliography

Corbin, H. (1969). *Alone with the alone: Creative imagination in the sufism of Ibn 'Arabi.* Princeton, NJ: Bollingen Series XCI.

Ibn 'Arabi. (1980). *The bezels of wisdom* (R. W. J. Austin, Trans.) Mahwah, NJ: Paulist Press.

Jalal al-Din Rumi. (1975). *Teachings of Rumi: The Masnavi* (E. H. Winfield, Trans.). New York: E. P. Dutton.

Mabey, J. (2002). *Rumi: A spiritual treasury.* Oxford, England: Oneworld Publications.

Trimingham, J. S. (1998). *The Sufi orders in Islam.* New York: Oxford University Press.

Sullivan, Harry Stack

Melissa K. Smothers

Harry Stack Sullivan (1892–1949) was an American psychiatrist who developed a theory of psychoanalysis which focused on the importance of interpersonal relationships. He grew up in New York State, the son of an Irish-American farmer. His childhood was an impoverished one, in which the Sullivan family often had financially difficulties. Sullivan also may have been isolated at times from other boys during his early years and experienced some degree of loneliness during his childhood. He was brought up in the Catholic faith, but left the church in his adulthood. Sullivan went on to study medicine at the Chicago College of Medicine and Surgery and received an M.D. degree in 1917. It was during medical school that Sullivan first studied psychoanalysis, as well as entered into his own analyses. In the 1920s, Sullivan worked with schizophrenic patients at the Sheppard and Enoch Pratt Hospital in Maryland, which inspired him to reevaluate the current approach in working with this population. He used specially trained ward attendants to work with patients in order to provide them with peer relationships that Sullivan believed the patients had missed during the latency period of development. It was during this time that Sullivan worked closely with William Alanson White, who was interested in the influences of social sciences on psychiatry. White, along with Adolph Meyer, was looking to explain mental illness in more than just physical terms.

Sullivan viewed his patients as being acutely aware of other people, and in order to understand a patient's psychopathology, it was important to view the interpersonal field of the patient as well. He branched out from the typical Freudian approach of the time and began to conceptualize patient's distress as more interactional than intrapsychic. Sullivan asserted that human personality and behaviors are created in interactions between individuals, as opposed to something that resides within the individual. This approach of viewing the patient within the context of others was profound at the time and Sullivan believed one must focus on the past and present relationships of the patient in order to fully understand the individual.

In 1929, Sullivan left Maryland and moved to New York City, where he began work in private practice of psychoanalysis and psychiatry. He did much to advance the study of psychiatry in the 1930s. Following the death of White in 1933, Sullivan and some of his colleagues, established the William Alanson White Psychiatric Foundation. The foundation was originally developed to train psychiatrists in both traditional medical education, as well as the influences of sociocultural factors. He also founded the journal *Psychiatry* in 1938, which he edited until his death. In 1941, Sullivan left clinical practice to work as a consultant to the U.S. Selective Service Commission, which was attempting to improve the psychiatric evaluations of draftees. This experience assisted in the development of a series of lectures, which was published posthumous as *The Psychiatric Interview.* After World War II, Sullivan participated in international mental health seminars and organizations and in 1948, was active in developing the World Federation for Mental Health. He died unexpectedly in Paris, France in 1949 of a cerebral hemorrhage. Sullivan's work in examining interpersonal relationships became the foundation of interpersonal psychoanalysis, a school of psychoanalytic theory that focuses on the detailed exploration of the patients' patterns of interacting and relating with others. Sullivan, along with Clara Thompson, Karen Horney, Erich Fromm, Erik H. Erikson, and Frieda Fromm-Reichmann, laid the groundwork for understanding the individual patient based on the network of the patients' relationships. Sullivan was also the first to introduce the concept of the psychiatrist as a participant observer in therapy. Sullivan acknowledged that the psychiatrist understanding of the current therapeutic interaction stems from his own past experiences. He taught that the psychiatrist must be aware of countertransference feelings within himself. Sullivan credited three well-known therapists with significantly influencing his psychiatric approach: Sigmund Freud, Adolf Meyer, and William A. White. While Sullivan never met Freud, he was an avid follower of his writing and credited him with his fundament orientation. Meyer helped Sullivan to view mental illness as a dynamic pattern of behavior and White assisted him with the practical aspects of therapy. Although Sullivan published little in his lifetime, he influenced generations of mental health professionals and therapists; many of his ideas and writings were collected and published posthumously.

See also: ❯ Erikson, Erik ❯ Freud, Sigmund ❯ Psychoanalysis ❯ Relational Psychoanalysis

Bibliography

Mitchell, S. A., & Black, M. J. (1995). *Freud and beyond*. New York: Basic Books.

Mullahy, P. (Ed.). (1952). *The contributions of Harry Stack Sullivan: A symposium on interpersonal theory in psychiatry and social science*. New York: Science House.

Perry, H. S. (1982). *Psychiatrist of America: The life of Harry Stack Sullivan*. Cambridge, MA: Harvard University Press.

Rychlak, J. F. (1973). *Introduction to personality and psychotherapy: A theory-construction approach*. Boston, MA: Houghton Mifflin Company.

Sunyata

Paul C. Cooper

Sunyata is the Sanskrit term, which has been translated into English as "emptiness or voidness." Along with *pratityasamupadha* (dependent-arising, dependent-origination), sunyata constitutes the foundational cornerstone of Buddhist phenomenology. By emptiness or voidness, Buddhists mean that all phenomena are empty of, lack, or are void of any "own," inherent, permanent or separate existence. All phenomena arise dependently contingent on causes and conditions. Sunyata has been confused with nihilism. This incorrect view has been criticized by both Asian and American Buddhist scholars (Abe, 1985; Hopkins, 1983). On the contrary, Buddhist scholars describe both nihilism and materialism; being and non-being, as dualistic and as a misguided delusion. For example, D. T. Suzuki notes that: "When the mind is trained enough it sees that neither negation (niratta) nor

affirmation (atta) applies to reality, but that the truth lies in knowing things as they are, or rather as they become" (1949: 143).

American psychologists have also addressed this point of misunderstanding and have raised important implications for psychotherapy. For instance, Jack Engler gives an example of the potential misuse of the notion of sunyata among American students of Buddhism. He writes that: "Students may mistake subjective feelings of emptiness for 'sunyata' or voidness; and the experience of not feeling inwardly cohesive or integrated for 'anatta' or selflessness" (Engler, 1984: 39). The complimentary teaching of non-attachment, is then often misunderstood, according to Engler "...as rationalizing their inability to form stable, lasting and satisfying relationships" (Engler, 1984: 37).

Mark Epstein (1989) draws attention to the distinctions between the experience of emptiness associated with depression and that requires treatment and emptiness as a core Buddhist experience and religious principle.

See also: ❯ American Buddhism ❯ Buddhism ❯ Psychotherapy

Bibliography

Abe, M. (1985). *Zen and Western thought*. Honolulu, HI: University of Hawaii Press.

Engler, J. (1984). Therapeutic aims in psychotherapy and meditation: Developmental stages in the representation of self. *The Journal of Transpersonal Psychology, 16*(1), 25–61.

Epstein, M. (1989). Forms of emptiness: Psychodynamic, meditative and clinical perspectives. *The Journal of Transpersonal Psychology, 21*(1), 61–71.

Hopkins, J. (1983). *Meditation on emptiness*. London: Wisdom Publications.

Suzuki, D. T. (1949). *Essays in Zen Buddhism* (1st Series) (p. 68). London: Rider & Co.

Super-Ego

Benjamin Beit-Hallahmi

The basic theory of the development of the super-ego, according to psychoanalytic theory, can be summarized briefly: The child is punished by its parents, either physically or by the withdrawal of love, for indulging in certain behavior, and later experiences anxiety when it does so because of anticipated punishment. The child identifies with the parents and wishes to be like them and conform to their demands. Parental requirements are internalized and the child now feels guilty even if the parents are absent. The psychological structure which represents the parental demands is called the super-ego. In the superego has two parts: The unconscious conscience and the conscious ego-ideal.

The conscience, the bigger part, is harsh and irrational, because aggression towards the parents is redirected to the self; this is particularly likely to happen when the parents are kind, but frustrating in subtle ways. When physical punishment is used, children feel more able to express their frustration in outward aggression.

Psychoanalysts have postulated that the conscience part of the super-ego is projected on to the image of a God. This super-ego projection helps to maintain the adult's typical balance between desire, morality, and action. It may be that the internalization and formation of conscience occur with the image of God serving as a "portable punisher." B. F. Skinner observed that an "all-seeing God" is uniquely effective, because escape from the punisher is impossible. In the search for self-control, external supports are often utilized. This psychological reality is reflected in the familiar philosophical debates about whether morality is at all possible without belief in God, and in many cultures, religion is identified with law and morality.

The super-ego is likely to come into conflict with instinctive desires, particularly sexual and aggressive desires. This conflict is resolved or relieved by projection of the super-ego which now appears as God. For example, the super-ego can be projected on to a doctor, teacher, leader or priest; the repressive demands of the super-ego are then thought to be prohibitions imposed by the person in question, who is felt to be coercing and looking down on the subject. In J. C. Flugel's formulation a more radical type of projection is postulated, in which the super-ego is projected on to the Universe as a God, and the instinctive desires similarly as the Devil. Alternatively, the instinctive desires can be projected on to groups of people such as Jews or Africans who are then thought to be highly sexed and aggressive. The gains for the individual are that the conflict is reduced through being no longer an inner one, while he feels that he can deal with the situation by overt action, instead of by changing himself. The presumed role of religion in impulse control is highly relevant to test this hypothesis. Findings on the effects of religion in controlling aggression, sex, drug use

and in promoting pro-social behavior are relevant to this hypothesis.

Related to the notion of super-ego is the function of religion in relieving guilt feelings. Several psychoanalytic writers have discussed the function of religion in relieving guilt feelings, interpreted as the direction of aggression towards the self, and there is evidence that it is connected with internal conflicts between the self and the ego-ideal or the conscience.

See also: ❱ Ego ❱ Id ❱ Psychoanalysis ❱ Shame and Guilt

Bibliography

Flugel, J. C. (1945). *Man, morals and society.* New York: International Universities Press.

Surrender

Fredrica R. Halligan

Surrender (and/or taming) the ego is an important theme in the mystical traditions of all the major world religions. In the Sanskrit, *saranagathi* connotes personal surrender in terms of acceptance of the Divine Will and devotion to God. It is *not* meant as surrender to another human being, nor as relinquishment of one's own intellectual discrimination. Like asceticism (q.v.) surrender fulfills the spiritual purpose of renouncing the cravings of the ego.

Psychologically, ego is important. According to Jung, ego is built up in the first half of life and performs very necessary functions as center of the conscious psyche. Spiritually, however, there comes a time when ego, with its many desires and propensity to control, must let go of the reins. As the slogan in the 12-step programs articulates it, the essence of the surrender process is to "Let go and let God." Mystics in all of the world's religions have found that higher spiritual states cannot be reached until ego-control is surrendered; the illusion of separation is renounced; and one's actions are dedicated to God, leaving the results in God's hands. This attitude implies acceptance of all aspects of life as they emerge, while continuing to strive to live a virtuous life, according to one's conscience.

See also: ❯ Asceticism ❯ Ego ❯ Jung, Carl Gustav ❯ Twelve Steps

Bibliography

Easwaran, E. (1996). *Original goodness: On the beatitudes*. Tomales, CA: Nilgiri Press.

Hawley, J. (2001). *The Bhagavad Gita: A walkthrough for westerners*. Novato, CA: New World Library.

Halligan, F. R. (2003). *Listening deeply to God: Exploring spirituality in an interreligious age*. Mystic, CT: Twenty-third Publications.

Swamis

Nicholas Grant Boeving

One of the more ubiquitous word acquisitions from Sanskrit, its meaning can roughly be translated as "he who knows and is master of himself" – or her*self*, as the case may be, for swami is an honorific designation for men as well as women. Often indicative of one who has chosen the path of renunciation, it is more often than not attributed to someone who has achieved mastery of a particular Yogic system or demonstrated profound devotion to a god or gods. While there are a multitude of lineages, with a dizzying array of beliefs, perspectives, and loyalties, swami is a pan-traditional designation that tends to mean, simply, "master."

Perhaps the most well known representative of Indian religion in the West to bear this moniker is Swami Vivekananda. The chief disciple of the Bengali saint and mystic Ramakrishna the man born Narendranath Dutt, was one of the early mediators between the religious traditions of the Occident and Orient, appearing before a spellbound audience at Chicago's World's Parliament of Religions in 1893. Vivekananda was instrumental in the founding of the Ramakrishna Order, one of the earliest Vedantic monastic sects to emerge in the West.

Continuing Vivekananda's legacy of spiritual translation to the West was Swami Nikhilananda. Born Dinesh Chandra Das Gupta was instrumental in the founding of the Ramakrishna-Vivekananda Center of New York. He, like Vivekananda, was integral to the process of bringing Eastern spirituality to the West, translating many Hindu holy texts into English, among their number the *Bhagavad-Gita* though perhaps his greatest contribution was the translation of *Ramakrishna Kathamrita* from Bengali into English published under the title *The Gospel of Sri Ramakrishna* in 1942.

The aforementioned religious figures were integral to process of translating Eastern spirituality to West. The Occidental appropriations that naturally unfolded often used psychological concepts and language in making sense of the unfamiliar semantic terrain. The onus of this re-interpretation lay on the first generation of Westerner's to encounter these figures who were part of a larger cultural process of psychologizing religion that continues to this day.

See also: ❯ Bhagavad Gita ❯ Hinduism

Bibliography

Isherwood, C. (1965). *Ramakrishna and his disciples*. New York: Simon & Shuster.

Jackson, C. T. (1994). *Vedanta for the west: The Ramakrishna movement in the United States*. Bloomington, IN: Indiana University Press.

Kripal, J. (1995). *Kali's child: The mystical and erotic in the life and teachings of Ramakrishna*. Chicago, IL: University of Chicago Press.

Vaidyanathan, & Kripal, J. (1999). *Vishnu on Freud's desk: A reader in psychoanalysis and hinduism*. New Delhi: Oxford University Press.

Symbol

Sharn Waldron

According to Carl Jung the development of consciousness has meant that within the psychic processes of civilized humanity there is a capacity for reflection upon the differentiation between psychic and external reality, a capacity which is unknown to the instinctive mind of the primitive. Because of this the psychic system of civilized humanity engenders difficulties that traditional societies never experience. In traditional societies there is no differentiation between psychic and physical reality. The primitive's relationship to the world is one of "participation mystique" that is, the primitive projects his unconscious onto the external environment. Jung writes:

> The fact that all immediate experience is psychic and that immediate reality can only be psychic explains why it is that primitive man puts spirits and magical influences on the same plane as physical events... In his world, spirit and matter still interpenetrate each other... He is like a child, only half born, still enclosed in his own psyche as in a dream (Jung, 1934: par. 682).

For the civilized human being the primitive's way of existence is no longer a valid option. Because of the development of consciousness the unconscious is no longer projected onto the external environment.

Jung writes:

> The psychic life of civilized man, however, is full of problems, we cannot even think of it except in terms of problems. Our psychic processes are made up to a large extent of reflections, doubts, experiments, all of which are completely foreign to the unconscious, instinctive mind of primitive man. It is the growth of consciousness which we must thank for the existence of problems; they are the Danaan gift of civilization. It is just man's turning away from instinct – his opposing himself to instinct – that creates consciousness (Jung, 1954: par. 388).

The primitive psychic life is concrete and symbolic at the same time. As a consequence he can speak of having a totem: a bush brother, or see himself as being a relative of the crocodile who protects him and whom he protects.

By contrast, conscious reason always seeks to find answers, to resolve apparent opposites. It takes a stand, assuming that a logical, understandable and containable answer exists. It can do this because reason is perceived as an unchanging essence. This perspective renders any symbolic view of itself redundant. Objectivity is seen as an inevitable and attainable concomitant of reason. Knowledge is defined by the interest we have in knowing it. For civilized society, knowledge is about controlling the environment, managing its vagaries for the sake of greater prosperity and security. However, reason is always relative and the concept of an unchanging essence of reason is an illusion. Reason, like the totem system, is a means to an end, a symbolic expression, although different in substance to the symbols of the primitive, of a transitional step in the path of development (Jung, 1954: par.47).

For Jung the psyche of both primitive cultures and children are closely connected to the unconscious. It was Jung's view that consciousness began in childhood and developed out of the unconscious. "One can actually see the conscious mind coming into existence through the gradual unification of fragments" (Jung, 1946: par. 103). This process is comparable to the evolutionary process of humanity that Jung regarded as the evolutionary development of consciousness. He writes:

> Consciousness is phylogenetically and ontogenetically a secondary phenomenon... Just as the body has an anatomical pre-history of millions of years, so also does the psychic system. And just as the human body to-day represents in each of its parts the result of this evolution, and everywhere still shows traces of its earlier stages – so the same may be said of the psyche. Consciousness began its evolution from an animal like state which seems to us unconscious, and the same process of differentiation is repeated in every child (Jung, 1977: 381).

The child lives in a world which is understood through the primal relationship with the mother. This relationship is one of "participation mystique." The world for the infant is the mother's body world. The infant has no initial perception of itself as a separate being. With physical touch and stimulation the infant begins to encounter physical realities which stimulate its sense of being and otherness. Therefore, when a child expresses the desire to take, to grasp, to eat, it is attempting to explore and understand the world, and it is in this process that differentiation begins.

Jung argues that if human beings lived by instinct alone, consciousness would be achieved by biological growth and ageing. This is not, however, the experience of all human cultures. It is evident in Jung's analogy of cultural development with early childhood development that Jung, being a creature of his time, perceives culture through the lens of social Darwinism and his language is reminiscent of early Australian explorers who spoke of the Australian Aboriginals as a "child race" (Waldron and Waldron, 2004).

Nevertheless, Jung's contention that intention and determination cannot accomplish psychic development is valid. Psychic development needs symbol to express and grasp realities beyond the scope of consciousness if it is to cognitively apprehend and develop those realities.

The unconscious, out of which symbols emanate, is unknowable and cannot be brought to consciousness because its content would overwhelm the conscious mind. It needs the mediation of symbol.

> A symbol expresses those aspects of the psyche that are differentiated and primal, conscious and unconscious, good and evil; the psychic opposites. Whenever such a symbol spontaneously erupts from the unconscious, it dominates the whole psyche. The symbol is a conduit by which the energy generated from the tension of opposites is channelled so that the psyche can move forward (Jung, 1948: par. 25).

Jung conjectures that the language of all human beings is full of symbols (Jung 1964: 3). For Jung, symbols are language or images that convey, by means of concrete reality, something hidden or unknown. They have a numinous quality only dimly perceived by the conscious mind. These symbols can never be fully understood by the conscious mind. In symbols, the opposites are united in a form that is "never devised consciously, but [are] always produced out of the unconscious by way of revelation or intuition" (Jung, 1964: 48).

The function of a symbol is both compensatory and integrative. It is compensatory in that it illuminates something that belongs to the domain of the unconscious. It compensates for that which is hidden from our conscious. It is integrative in that it is a union of opposites, holding in tension the different aspects of the psyche.

Jung posits individual and collective symbols. Individual symbols are peculiar to individuals. They arise out of the individual's personal unconscious and, as a consequence, have little or no meaning to other individuals. Collective symbols are psychic images that arise out of the collective unconscious of a group, tribe, culture or nation. As such, they possess a functional significance for the community.

For a cultural symbol to be dynamic it must relate to an unconscious factor that the individuals within that culture hold in common. For the symbol to be relevant to a culture it may appear to need to have a functional meaning and this may be seen to contradict the argument that the symbol only needs to relate to unconscious factors. However, the function of meaning will have significance only because its perceived social function is based on a significance that is apprehended and given value by means of the collective unconscious. The more immediate a symbol is to the unconscious reality common to the collective, the greater the effect on that society.

Jung also perceives a "religious function" operative in the psyche, an instinctual drive for a meaningful relationship of the personal self to the transitional source of power, the reality represented by the symbol. This instinctual drive manifests itself in the spontaneous production of religious symbols or "god images." God images are characterized by their central function, to reconcile the opposites within the psyche. In order to creatively engage with a god image it is not required to solve the clash of inner opposites but rather to work with the symbol, to explore its parameters. As we come face to face with the dark side of God, masculine and feminine, we are more able to come to terms with our own dark side and contra-sexual aspects (Jung, 1977: 367).

This transcendent function of the symbol enables a transition from one psychic state to another. Thereby, the drive for religion seems to urge the full development of the individual.

The religious symbols thus generated, become symbols of totality. The god image is an archetype and as such is a source of inexhaustible meaning and intelligibility. It has a numinous quality and cannot be explained or verified through rationale. Because the god image is a symbol it can never be reduced to its subjective origins. Like all symbols, the god image emerges spontaneously from the unconscious and is independent of an individual's religious convictions.

The god image functions as a mediator between the conscious and the unconscious. It is a union within the psyche of male and female, good and evil and all other opposites. It is comprised of unconscious and conscious components and is an essential element in the process of individuation. The goal of the process of individuation is the birth of the Self. The Self is symbolized by the mandala, a mystical circle expressing the totality of the individual. The god image is a reflection of this psychic truth.

It seems evident that there are times when the god image ceases to be an integrative image through which the individual or culture moves towards wholeness. The potential exists for the shadow to be suppressed so that a split occurs in the psyche.

When this happens it is possible for the shadow to erupt in symbolic form. The resultant god image is not integrative but rather expressive of the shadow and suppression of aspects of the psyche. Manifest abuse of power and suppression of minorities and the defenseless elements in society or adjacent societies will demonstrate the non-integrative nature of such a split in the god image.

See also: ◉ Archetype ◉ Consciousness ◉ God Image ◉ Jung, Carl Gustav ◉ Mandala ◉ Participation Mystique ◉ Self ◉ Unconscious

Bibliography

Jung, C. G. (1964). *Man and his symbols*. London: Picador.

Jung, C. G. (1976). *Psychological types*. Princeton, NJ: Princeton University Press.

Jung, C. G. (1977). *Memories, dreams, reflections*. London: Flamingo.

Jung, C. G. (1981). *The development of personality*. Princeton, NJ: Princeton University Press.

Jung, C. G. (1987). *The structures and dynamics of the psyche*. London: Routledge.

Waldron, S., & Waldron, D. (2004). *Jung and the neo-pagan movement*. Quadrant, XXXIV.

Synchronicity

Frances Campbell

As a practicing psychoanalyst, Carl Jung became aware of a process of meaningful coincidence between physical events and the subjective states of his patients. He termed this phenomena *synchronicity* and he came to believe that the acknowledgement and utilization of synchronous phenomena was a valuable tool in the process of understanding and interpreting the expressions and manifestations of the psyche.

The concept of synchronicity is part of a conceptual triad which Jung conceived of as essential to the understanding of the experience of the psyche. The first element is causality, best understood through Freud's ideas of how libidinal energy is managed within the psyche. Repressed energy in one area is likely to express itself in another form in order to be released. In this way the psyche maintains a balance of libidinal energy which becomes converted in response to the principles of cause and affect. Jung broadened this concept into the idea of a more generalized psychic energy. He imagined that the expression of this force is particular to the unfolding of the individual psyche. From this emerged a *teleological* view, in which the psyche contains within itself the potential for self actualization. This forms the second of Jung's developmental triad. This teleological potential for expression is contingent upon opportunities that encompass causality as well as the element of serendipity. Without supporting circumstances, the germ, that is the potential of the self, may never have the opportunity to develop. It is here that synchronicity plays a crucial role. The element of chance may enhance or eliminate opportunities for actualization of the self. Synchronicity, or meaningful chance, can be defined as a seemingly significant coincidence in time and space of two more events that are related, but not causally connected. An image, thought, fantasy or symbol presents itself to consciousness and this is reflected in a meaningful external event that appears to have no causal connection. Synchronicity, then, is the third principle by which the experience of the psyche may be understood or interpreted. Jung considered that a law of synchronicity might contrast with the physical law of causality. Causality propels the objective world, while synchronistic phenomena seems to be primarily connected to conditions of the psyche or processes in the unconscious. Synchronicity takes the coincidence of events in space and time as meaning something more than mere chance, namely a particular interdependence between objective events with the subjective state of the observer.

Jung's exploration of this concept was based on his belief that an emphasis on the rational aspects of consciousness results in a one-sided view of the psyche. This inhibits understanding of the unconscious and it's expression through dreams, fantasy and other non-rational experiences. Synchronicity, as a correspondence theory in which inner events occur simultaneously with exterior events, is a reflection of a deeper perspective found across cultures in which there is the philosophical perception that parts are not only aspects of the whole but reflections of it. That is, the microcosm mirrors the macrocosm. For example, Jung recognized this concept as an aspect of early Taoist Chinese thought. Synchronous events may be generated through the activating of archetypes. These are unconscious preexistent primordial images that yield believed to be a part of the deep structure of the psyche and shared collectively and therefore might be a creation of the collective unconscious, and perhaps even the psychoid strata. The psychoid strata can be equated with a generative yet undifferentiated source that undergirds the collective unconscious. When archetypes are experienced by an individual they are often expressed through dreams and fantasies or through a conscious process Jung applied in his practice called "active imagination." In this process special attention is given to the appearance of archetypal material, and the impact of its presentation on the psyche of the individual. An archetype can act as a mediator between the macrocosm that characterizes the collective unconscious, and the microcosm which is the individual expression. The value of attention to synchronistic phenomena, then, lies in it's ability to illuminate a dimension of the psyche that cannot be reached consciously. For Jung, the fullest potential of the human psyche lies in the integration of unconscious material, both personal and collective, into consciousness. This assimilation expands the individual psyche towards a fuller degree of awareness, or a conscious experience of wholeness.

Because synchronicity may seem to involve the observed as well as the observer, there two possible ways to view synchronous events. In the first there is a relationship between events that can be observed objectively. In the second, synchronicity involves the participation of the observing psyche which in some way becomes reflected in the objective material. In this case synchronicity becomes a type of psycho physical parallelism.

Expressions of Synchronicity

Two forms of synchronous expression most commonly experienced are, 1) the perception that the internal reality of the psyche is being externally manifested in the world through an experience or event. This may take the form of a) a dream, vision or premonition of an experience that has not yet happened, b) two or more external events that appear to be meaningfully, but not causally related.

Synchronous expression appears to serve a significant, if not urgent, purpose, which is to bring attention to a perception or perspective that is needed for the development of the psyche. Synchronous experience may be urgent in presentation, acting as a signpost to bring awareness to the psyche of a situation or state that is in need of attention. In contrast, it may be initially veiled, allowing an idea to be presented to the receiver in a form that will not overwhelm the conscious mind, but allow it to assimilate indirectly. Regardless of presentation, it would seem synchronous phenomena serves to bring to conscious awareness concepts of value for self development.

See also: ◉ Freud, Sigmund ◉ Jung, Carl Gustav

Bibliography

Jung, C. G. (1959). *Psychology and religion: West and East, CW 11*. New York: Pantheon Books.

Jung, C. G. (1959). *The archetypes and the collective unconscious, CW 9*. New York: Pantheon Books.

Jung, C. G. (1960). *The structure and dynamics of the psyche, CW 8*. New York: Pantheon Books.

Jung, C. G. (1960). *Synchronicity: An acausal connecting principle, CW 8*, 424–447. In *Structure and dynamics of the psyche*. New York: Pantheon Books.

Syncretism

Valerie DeMarinis

The term "syncretism" has had different denotations and connotations over time. In current usage in anthropology and religious studies it generally refers to a mixing of elements from different religious systems or traditions. From the perspective of many religious leaders, such a mixing is often viewed as a negative process, as an abandoning of true religion. From the perspective of many anthropologists, psychologists and professionals of other academic disciplines, religious syncretism may assist in a positive acculturation process, whereby elements of different systems emerge in a new format allowing an integration of ideas and behaviors. It is important to bear in mind that whatever example of syncretism is in focus, it always takes place in a psycho-cultural and socio-political context and therefore the psychological effects of such need to include those levels of analysis. Though a central historical concept, globalization as well as the challenges of voluntary and forced migration have given birth to a re-examination of religious syncretism. As Greenfield and Droogers (2001) point to, there is a re-emergence of the concept as a tool for understanding such complex phenomena as ethnicity, postcolonialism and transnationalism. Three examples of religious syncretism are presented here. They are drawn from different cultural contexts and illustrate the complexities for understanding syncretistic systems and behaviors and their varying psychological effects.

Example 1: Syncretism as an Act of Survival

Drawing upon his fieldwork in Afro-Brazilian religions, the French ethnologist Roger Bastide (1978) has emphasized two aspects for historically understanding syncretism in this cultural context. First, attention needs to be given to the systematic way in which elements from different religious sources come together. Second, the role of power mechanisms is emphasized, especially in the contact between two categories of individuals, slaves and slaveholders. Similarity in worldview structures among African, Catholic, and also Amerindian systems has facilitated this syncretism. In this way African gods could be identified with Catholic saints and with Amerindian spirits. Catholic elements were selectively adopted and adapted through the application of African criteria, without the knowledge of the slaveholders. In practice, as strategic devices, identification with and differentiation from the slaveholders' religion were both used for literal and symbolic survival. Thus the apparent adoption of a Catholic ritual attitude in Mass could serve as an alibi for the continuation of African ritual practices. Despite this clever illustration of a survival deception, the reality undergirding this example of syncretism is one of supreme oppression. An examination of the legacy of this syncretism in contemporary Afro-Brazilian expressions of religiosity reveals a variety of mixtures of these religious traditions both in terms of meaning structures and ritual practices.

Example 2: Syncretism as Competitive Sharing

A second example of religious syncretism is found in the article by Robert Hayden (2002) linked to the concept of competitive sharing. This concept explains how sacred sites that have long been shared by members of differing religious communities, perhaps even exhibiting syncretic types of mixtures including the practices of both, may at some point be seized or destroyed by members of one of them in order to manifest dominance over the other. Hayden argues that competitive sharing is compatible with a passive meaning of "tolerance" as noninterference but incompatible with an active meaning of tolerance as an embrace of the Other. This confusion lies at the heart of a critical weakness of most current explanations of nationalist conflict in the Balkans and communal conflict in India. Syncretism, in this example, may be fostered by inequality and is actually endangered by equality between the groups. The term, syncretism, is problematical, however, carrying a negative charge for those concerned with analyzing or maintaining putatively "pure" or "authentic" rituals and a positive one for those who criticize concepts such as cultural purity or authenticity or favor the idea of "multiculturalism" (Shaw and Stewart, 1994). For the former, syncretism is a matter of violating or contaminating categories. For the latter, since supposed boundaries are inherently flexible, syncretism is universal and therefore not an isolable phenomenon (Werbner, 1994). As Hayden notes, the problematical nature of syncretism increases with the growth of the polarizations captured by the word "communalism" in Indian discourse and the comparable "fundamentalisms" elsewhere (Hayden, 2002: 207).

Understanding and approaching syncretism in any given cultural context is dependent upon the framework used for interpretation. Consider the contrast between the following interpretations. Bayly's analysis (1989) has focused on a situation of "paradox" in South India noting a growing tendency for groups and large corporations to be hostile to one another yet at the same time there are persisting or reinvented overlapping religious beliefs and syncretic religious practices. That of van der Veer, on the other hand, has noted that "'syncretism' in India... is a trope in the discourse of 'multiculturalism'" and that

scholarly discussion of "syncretic" phenomena such as Hindu worship of Sufi saints usually omits consideration of conflict or of the processes of expansion and contraction of religious communities (van der Veer, 1994: 200–201). One of the critical differences in these frameworks is that in Bayly's framework syncretism represents tolerance, with a presumed stasis, while for van der Veer, time is brought into the analysis thus creating an approach to syncretism as a dynamic expression that assumes no inherent understanding of tolerance. As Hayden notes, when time is added into the analysis, "syncretism seems to be a measure at a given moment of relations between members of groups that differentiate themselves, and to see it as tolerance instead of competition is misleading" (Hayden, 2002: 207).

Example 3: Syncretism as a Postmodern Choice or Acculturation Survival Tactic

The third example is that of a functional religious/existential syncretism that can be found in what ostensibly has been labeled one of the most secular cultural contexts, Sweden. In this context, organized religious services, based on the Protestant-Lutheran faith and until 2000 expressed through the National Church of Sweden, are not well attended. However, participation in different church-based rituals and ceremonies such as baptism, funerals, and weddings are common. From a functional perspective, ethnic-Swedish participation in ritualized activities remains high though not within the context of a faith or belief tradition. Looking at the results from the multi-country World Values Survey, Sweden appears as an outlier in terms of being the most secular and nontraditional country (Inglehart, 1996). At the same time, there is a growing body of information pointing to an increasing search for existential meaning in this cultural context. The conscious or unconscious expressions of this search not infrequently result in an interesting pattern of existential behaviors and ritual practices that combine elements from different meaning-making traditions and new or alternative religious movements, a mixed existential worldview (DeMarinis, 2003). One illustration of this is an ethnic-Swedish person who may be a member of a Wiccan group and at the same time remain involved in some of the Church of Sweden rituals. Another illustration is of a person with an immigrant or refugee background, involved in both the traditional religious rituals and belief system of the home country and also participating in a religious or other meaning-making system of the new host country.

From the psychological vantage point of postmodernism as defined by Bauman, the individual must create or chose an identity. He also notes that the reverse side of identity choice is that of identity confusion (Bauman, 1998). In this kind of postmodern context syncretic religious/existential patterns are created as part of the internal choice process and expressed in the external sphere where rituals and practices are enacted and experienced. The degree of social support or negative pressure experienced by the individual from the surrounding society in relation to having a mixed existential worldview, can lead to a change in the worldview's structure. In other words, the process is dynamic and open to change.

Psychological Implications of Religious Syncretism

A classic psychological approach to syncretism as a mental function is reflected in the comparison of syncretism with the process of individual cognition (Burger, 1996), in that both create an analogy between the old and the new, and thereby facilitate an innovation acceptance. Syncretism modifies but perpetuates the essence of all impacting sectors, thereby reducing the dangers of cultural shock. Symbolic sectors such as religion can syncretize more easily than artifactual sectors. The psychological mechanics of syncretism need to be understood in relation to the psycho-cultural and socio-political dynamics taking place in the given cultural context. This may seem an obvious need when thinking about the three examples provided, as it is this deeper type of understanding that is essential for mapping the different types of psychological effects of syncretism. The analysis necessary for arriving at this type of understanding is not a standard part of the psychological process of investigation. A valuable resource here is a working approach to cultural analysis that has emerged from the field of cultural psychology (Marsella and Yamada, 2000). Culture is based on shared learned meanings and behaviors that are transmitted from within a social activity context for the purpose of promoting individual/societal adjustment, growth, and development. Cultural representations are both internal (i.e. values, beliefs, patterns of consciousness) as well as external (i.e. artifacts, roles, institutions). Changing internal and external circumstances brings about changes or modifications for shared meanings and behaviors.

Using this approach with respect to understanding a situation involving religious syncretism, the following steps can be taken. First, a cultural mapping needs to be done involving the internal as well as external representations of the syncretistic meanings and behaviors. Such a mapping will provide a means for locating the cultural groups, religious systems, and levels of interaction involved. Second, an historical layer can then be added to this mapping with special focus placed on understanding the power dynamics and socio-political circumstances initially leading to the syncretistic expression and what has happened to that expression over time. The third and most important step is assessing the psychological effects, for both individuals and groups, of engaging in the syncretistic behaviors. Such varied syncretistic behaviors may, as in the very varied examples provided, be associated with psychological consequences ranging from individual and group trauma to a stress-relieving and salutogenic outcome. Each case needs to be assessed on its own, in cultural context, and over time. Clearly, religious syncretism has never been and will never be a simple system with a single design. For this very reason, an understanding of the psychological effects of religious syncretism needs to approached with extreme care and with sufficient, multi-disciplinary methods.

See also: ❷ Cultural Psychology ❷ Migration and Religion ❷ Trauma

Bibliography

Bauman, Z. (1998). Postmodern religion? In P. Heelas (Ed.), *Religion, modernity and postmodernity*. Oxford, England: Blackwell.

Bastide, R. (1978). *The African religions of Brazil, toward a sociology of the interpenetration of civilizations*. Baltimore, MD: Johns Hopkins University Press.

Bayly, S. (1989). *Saints, Goddesses, and kings: Muslims and Christians in South Indian society, 1700–1900*. Cambridge, England: Cambridge University Press.

Burger, H. (1966). Syncretism: An acculturative accelerator. *Human Organization, 25*(2), 103–115.

DeMarinis, V. (2003). *Pastoral care, existential health and existential epidemiology: A Swedish postmodern case study*. Stockholm: Verbum Press.

Droogers, A. (1989). Syncretism: The problem of definition, the definition of the problem. In J. D. Gort, H. M. Vroom, R. Fernhout & A. Wessels (Eds.), *Dialogue and syncretism, an interdisciplinary approach*. Grand Rapids, MI: Eerdmans & Rodopi.

Greenfield, S., & Droogers, A. (Eds.) (2001). *Reinventing religions: Syncretism and transformation in Africa and the Americas*. Lanham, MD: Rowman & Littlefield.

Hayden, R. (2002). Antagonistic tolerance: Competitive sharing of religious sites in South Asia and the Balkins. *Current Anthropology, 43*, 205–231.

Inglehart, R. (1996). Globalization and postmodern values. *The Washington Quarterly, 23*, 215–228.

Marsella, A., & Yamada, A. (2000). Culture and mental health: An introduction and overview of foundations, concepts and issues. In

I. Cúellar, & F. A. Paniagua (Eds.), *Handbook of multicultural health: Assessment and treatment of diverse populations.* San Diego, CA: Academic Press.

Shaw, R., & Stewart, C. (1994). Introduction: Problematizing syncretism. In S. Stewart & R. Shaw (Eds.), *Syncretism/anti-syncretism, the politics of religious synthesis.* London: Routledge.

Van der Veer, P. (1994). Syncretism, multiculturalism and the discourse of tolerance. In S. Stewart & R. Shaw (Eds.), *Syncretism/anti-syncretism, the politics of religious synthesis.* London: Routledge.

Werbner, R. (1994). Afterward. In S. Stewart & R. Shaw (Eds.), *Syncretism/anti-syncretism, the politics of religious synthesis.* London: Routledge.

T

Taboo

Morgan Stebbins

Something that is taboo is so powerful that it must be approached only with the proper attitude and training, or not at all. The concept of taboo derives from the Tongan *tapu* or the Fijian *tabu*. In both cultures it carries a double meaning: it refers to what is both sacred and forbidden. That is, it indicates that which is so powerful that it is dangerous unless treated the right way, or by the right person, under the right circumstances. In original usage, taboo could refer to certain foods, to bodies of the deceased, to the resting places of powerful spirits, to tribal rulers and to warriors who have slain others, and often to women's menstrual periods, as well as even mentioning some of the above in conversation (Frazer, 1990). Thus we see that it can apply to words, objects, actions and concepts (including metaphysical actors such as divinities), and also that there is a temporal aspect, for instance in some warrior cultures we find a taboo on sex, but only before battle. In many religious traditions, the complex mythopoeic indications combined in the term taboo have been differentiated into the categories of sacred, protected, holy, ritual, and sin.

Social usage indicates that a taboo action or conversation is likely to cause shame or embarrassment within a given social group. This is likely only part of the story, since most taboo subjects that are not abhorrent carry an edge of allure or even excitement in the right circumstances, bringing the concept closer to the Tongan sense. Furthermore there are relatively few things that appear to be repugnant in all societies, these being confined to corpses and incest (and even here there is some disagreement). So most things that are taboo in one group or society are not taboo in another, showing that something about the dynamic of the taboo must be more important than the particular item, topic, or action (Durkheim, 1912).

Evolutionary biologists suggest that taboos originated from a hardwired repulsion of disease vectors (in the case of the dead) or social bonding habits (in the case of patricide), however this explanation does little to explain the multiplicity and richness of the concept as it is found in practice or in its religious formulation (Pinker, 1997).

Sigmund Freud noticed a similarity between obsessive states and the descriptions of taboo. This connection shows that taboos can be understood as "a psychological condition that prevails in the unconscious" and states that the only two "universal" taboos are that of incest and patricide which formed the eventual basis of modern society. This conception is not far from the biological, and again does not account for the liminal quality of the concept.

Freud continues with his classic statement about taboo, one which has helped shape a generation of understanding:

> Taboos, we must suppose, are prohibitions of primeval antiquity which were at some time externally imposed upon a generation of primitive men; they must, that is to say, no doubt have been impressed on them violently by the previous generation. These prohibitions must have concerned activities towards which there was a strong inclination. They must then have persisted from generation to generation, perhaps merely as a result of tradition transmitted through parental and social authority (Freud, 1998).

So, for Freud, the incest taboo keeps the subject from doing the abhorrent, and so a more refined outlet must be found through the process of sublimation.

Jung's view of taboo (and especially the incest taboo) is typically prospective, psychological and serves to uncover progressively more subtle layers of process. On one had it does not settle the question, but on the other it allows for the mystery, the social importance, the allure, the horror and the psychological complexity and importance of taboo. Taboo indicates, after all, that which we are inexplicably drawn to and repulsed from at the same time and in certain meaningful ways.

Concepts and impulses that arise from the unknown, regardless of the term used for that other place, are dangerous. Religious symbolic systems, including the forms and laws of the church arise due to the desire of the human subject to avoid revelatory contact with these

D. A. Leeming, K. Madden, S. Marlan (eds.), *Encyclopedia of Psychology and Religion*, DOI 10.1007/978-0-387-71802-6,
© Springer Science+Business Media LLC 2010

unconscious forces. Because of this, from ancient times to the present, societies construct ritual and taboo to protect them from the uncanny voices of dreams and the content of the unconscious in general (Jung, 1960).

For Jung, the pressure to make some personal psychological change is an automatic response to something in the psyche being stuck, like water building up behind an obstruction in a stream. In cases of stuck-ness, or libidinal obstruction (including such symptomatic descriptions such as depression and the various neuroses), the conscious mind feels threatened by an invasion from the unconscious, since the unconscious itself is pressing for a change in conscious attitude. Rather than holding this change at bay, if it is instead possible to be informed by the images that arise (that is, the symbolic form of the symptoms), then the invasion could be completed on its own terms and the conscious mind would break free of the inertia and move forward.

A similar situation is detailed in the poetry of Hölderlin – this theme can be seen as central to the theme of the German aesthetic philosophers in general from Kant to Goethe and Schiller and which is now seeing a resurgence in, of all places, the post-Lacanian work of Slavoj Zizek – particularly in his increasing estrangement from reality. "The god/ Is near and hard to grasp/ But where there is danger/ A rescuing element grows as well" (Hölderlin, 2004). This indicates that regression is an involuntary introversion, of which depression is an unconscious compensation. The psychological task, in this case, is to make the introversion voluntary, both activating the imaginal realm of the mind and lifting the depression (since it has gotten what it was after). Jung uses psychological material as well as Holderlin's poems to illustrate that regression is actually a link with primal material. This primal material contains both the energy that is dammed up and the specific form of a new conscious attitude. However both of these must be assimilated by the conscious mind lest the primal material keep its chaotic form and produce disorientation or even, in severe cases, schizophrenia.

This very regression, being dangerous to the conscious mind as well as social norms, is the subject of taboo. However it is clear that the object of desire is rebirth, not (as in Freud's literalist interpretation) incestuous cohabitation. In this conception, incest refers to the draw towards, and horror of, immersion in the unconscious as the source of the conscious subject. The incest taboo indicates the danger of this regression and religion aids in systematizing the canalization (or routine, even automatic use) of libido into safe and socially acceptable forms. Thus symbolism and symbol formation are civilizing processes at the collective level (such as found in religious traditions), whereas when the symbol is engaged personally it represents an individuating and internal psychological truth (Jung, 1967). Taboo can be seen as a form of collective mediation of overwhelming unconscious forces. However, the advent of neurotic symptoms shows that this collective mediation has broken down, such as when religion no longer seems to mean anything. In these cases, a symbolic interaction with the taboo under carefully controlled circumstances (the container of analysis, for example) allows the instincts to be mediated in a new and personal way, resolving the neurotic suffering.

Finally, since the canalizations or routines surrounding symbol making and the taboo are collective (that is, shared by populations), we can see that the evolutionary instinct has as its goal the *making of meaning.* These instincts manifest also as mythological figures born to the unconscious. That is, it was not the incest taboo that forced mankind forward but rather the evolutionary instinct from which this and other taboos came. Certainly the making of meaning is most safely done in a collective setting, such as a political or religious tradition, since these structures are mediating symbol-systems that let only a small amount of the primal libido through to an individual. When a symbol-system no longer works, the individual must take special precautions not to become overwhelmed by an unconscious and unmediated flood of affect and imagery. To reiterate, the cultural injunction against introversion has led, in modern times, to the rituals of the analytic container (other responses to this injunction occur as well, from the development of the projection of the numinous out onto UFO's to the various new age attempts to encounter the unconscious) and the methodical withdrawal of projections as a safe way to approach the numinous (life-giving but dangerous) core indicated by the term taboo.

See also: ❯ Freud, Sigmund ❯ Jung, Carl Gustav

Bibliography

Durkheim, É. (1912). *The elementary forms of religious life.*

Frazer, J. (1990). *Taboo and the perils of the soul, The golden bough* (3rd ed., Pt. II). New York: St. Martin's Press.

Freud, S. (1998). *Totem and taboo.* New York: Dover Publications.

Hölderlin, F. (2004). *Patmos* (J. Mitchell, Trans.). San Francisco, CA: Ithuriel's Spear.

Jung, C. G. (1960). *Psychology and religion.* New Haven, CT: Yale University Press.

Jung, C. G. (1967). *Symbols of transformation.* Princeton, NJ: Princeton University Press.

Pinker S. (1997). *How the mind works.* New York: W. W. Norton & Company.

Talmud

Mark Popovsky

From the Hebrew verb "to learn," Talmud refers to the central text in the vast corpus of rabbinic literature which serves as a repository of legal discussions, biblical exegesis, theology, philosophy, hagiography, legend, history, science, anecdotes, aphorisms, and humor. The Babylonian Talmud was edited over several generations by the rabbinic authorities of Babylonia, probably attaining a somewhat fixed form in the sixth century. However, individual passages included may be up to several hundred years older having been transmitted orally prior to their inclusion in the text. A second Talmud exists, edited in the land of Israel during the fifth century. Know as the Jerusalem or Palestinian Talmud, it is smaller, more opaque, and less authoritative in later legal debates. The term Talmud unqualified always refers to the Babylonian Talmud which is written primarily in Aramaic though it often cites large passages in biblical or Rabbinic Hebrew.

The Talmud is structured around a second century rabbinic document called the Mishnah or "recitation." Composed in terse Hebrew, the Mishnah compiles unresolved legal debates among rabbis on a wide range of subjects including worship, dietary laws, torts, family law, criminal law, agricultural practices, mourning customs, sexual mores, and holiday observance. These legal discussions are often surrounded by related narratives and relevant biblical interpretations. The Mishnah settles very few of the legal debates it presents and frequently suggests no rationale supporting the various opinions cited. The Talmud begins as a commentary on the Mishnah elucidating its cases and alternatively challenging or defending each of its legal opinions.

While the Talmud retains its structure as a commentary on the Mishnah, it functions much more broadly, citing new legal cases, relating stories about rabbinic figures, and opening moral or theological debates unimagined by the Mishnah. The different material included is woven together in a complicated arrangement that is only sometimes topical. Often, connections between Talmudic passages rely on free associations or any number of other non-linear progressions. The Talmud gives great weight to material from dreams, word play and the exploration of fantasy.

The Talmud's primary method of expression is debate. No legal precedent, biblical passage, or other ostensibly authoritative statement stands immune to challenge. Much like the psychoanalytic process, rather than attempting to avoid or resolve conflict, Talmudic discourse identifies and even elevates disputes among principles, teaching the reader to embrace discord rather than repress it. While the Talmud rarely affirms or rejects one opinion outright, ironically, it often signals its preference for one opinion over another by challenging the favored opinion more extensively. Biblical laws are almost never explicitly repealed, but, with some frequency, problematic biblical passages are interpreted through Talmudic debate to be so narrow in scope as to be practically irrelevant in contemporary society.

The Talmud is traditionally studied in pairs or small groups, reflecting the conversational question-and-answer style of the text itself. Many have argued that the process of studying Talmud parallels the psychoanalytic task as the reader is directed to infer underlying conflicts from surface level ambiguities or inconsistencies in the text. Some scholars claim that Freud fashioned elements of his therapeutic technique from methods of traditional Talmudic analysis. In modern times, the Talmud is almost always printed together with the commentary of Rashi, an eleventh century scholar from Provence, whose glosses guide the reader through the difficult text which often assumes that its readers know the entire contents already.

See also: ❯ Judaism and Psychology

Bibliography

Katz, M., & Schwartz, G. (1998). *Swimming in the sea of Talmud*. Philadelphia, PA: Jewish Publication Society of America.

Rubenstein, J. L., & Cohen, S. J. D. (2002). *Rabbinic stories (Classics of Western spirituality)*. Mahwah, NJ: Paulist Press.

Tantrism

Kathryn Madden

Tantrism is a religious and philosophical movement appearing in India around 400 AD that existed within both Hinduism and Buddhism. In medieval India, Tantrism was a common element of all the major religions. Tantrism focuses upon ritual aspects that involve the use of the physical in sacred and worshipful settings to access the supernatural. Tantrism also can be traced to Jainism and Bön, and elements of Tantric practice are also evident in Burma, China, Japan, Mongolia, and Tibet. The word Tantrism originates from the Sanskrit word *Tantra*: तन्त्र; which is translated variously as "weave, warp, or loom," offering a sense of bringing together, or connecting into a whole. Tantrism is comprised of numerous texts referred to as *Tantras*. The primarily philosophy and goal underlying the practice of Tantrism is that it promotes spiritual growth and leads to personal freedom.

The concept of evolution and involution are central precepts. Tantric practice leads to an outgoing current of energy as well as the return of the current, which is taken back in toward the source of reality rooted in the consciousness of the human being, revealing the pure being of the infinite. In time, with practice, the outgoing current is changed into the return current. This specific interchange is believed to release the chains created by *maya* (the illusion of the phenomenal world) and to free one from illusory existence. Unlike the more orthodox tenets of the Hindu or Buddhist religions, the Tantric aim is to engage with rather than negate reality by undergoing phases of purification, elevation, and finally reaffirming one's identity on the plane of pure consciousness.

Tantric bodily disciplines and techniques in ritual settings are combined with the learning of specific doctrine. The practitioner of Tantrism develops a more expansive internal awareness and ideally achieves union with the divine. In Hindu Tantrism, *Shakti* is active female energy and *Shiva* is passive, male consciousness; whereas in Buddhist Tantrism, *Prajna* is the passive female element and *Upaya* the active, male element. In the Hindu tradition, *Shakti*, the active female energy is promoted as the main deity or god worshiped and is personified as the divine active force. In the Tantric tradition, clearly female energy penetrates male essence.

The doctrine of the *Tantras* claims that an individual practitioner can tap the interplay between these two dynamic universal forces, internalize these energies, and apply them in life. It is believed that the human body itself is a symbol of these universal energies. Sexual union between two persons can become a symbol of liberation when symbolically understood as the union of *Shiva* and *Shakti* or of *Prajna* and *Upaya*. *Shakti* is also understood as a profound force that manifests itself by igniting energy at the base of the spine and winding its way through the chakras (centers of spiritual power in the human body of which there are seven) toward the opening of the third

eye – the highest chakra – enlightenment. In many Tantric forms of meditation, such as *Kundalini* Yoga, the initiate undergoes a ritual in which he or she receives divine *Shaktipat* through the touch of a master who has achieved a level of union with the divine. This touch ignites the movement of *shakti* energy. The central object of the Tantric ritual, then, is to awaken *kundalini* energy and to merge with the Godhead. To sustain the activation of this vibrant energy in meditation, tantric practices focus upon the breath, or *prana*. Concentrating upon the breath relinquishes the practitioner from worldly distractions and removes obstacles from the chakras. Some tantric forms use mantras, incense, chanting, and singing to activate the breath, followed by silent meditation. Meditating upon a specific *yantra* (a geometrical diagram) or *mandala* (a circular figure symbolizing the universe) associated with a deity is a technique employed for the purpose of subjecting the body to the will. As the progressive phases of enlightenment occur and deepen, the experience becomes a mystical one, and the presence of the divinity grows ever more real as the energies of *shakti* weave their way like a double-serpent around the spine, always moving upwards. To learn these meditative practices, an initiate works the guru or a master teacher. Consistency in practice yields a greater response of the universal vibration of *shakti*. If one achieves a state of union with the divine, often depicted in symbol as the opening of a lotus, or as an illumination of the third eye, then one is considered to have become the *Ishta-deva* or meditational deity. Developing the attributes of an *Ishta-deva* is an important phase, for it means one is able to visualize oneself as the deity or to achieve *darshan*, experience a vision of the deity.

Tantric practices are also known for the ritual use of wine, meat, and rituals that involve mystical-erotic sexual practices, emphasizing the primacy of divine union. Participants were prepared in the art of controlled sexual intercourse, *maithuna*, (L., *coitus reservatus*) meaning sex without male orgasm. Through intricate training, the male partner learned to store up his own sexual fluid and to absorb through his penis the fluid engendered by his partner's orgasm. This discipline prolonged the sexual act for an extended period of time. In this way the male partner became similar to *Shiva*, the God in perpetual union with the Goddess. The conserved vital fluids were to be stored in the man's spinal column, working their way through the chakras to unfold into the inspiration of divine wisdom.

For both partners, the goal was to awaken the *kundalini* energy culminated in *samadhi* (contemplative rapture). Each of the persons was to be completely dissolved in the unity of the godhead represented on the earthly plane by the energy field created by the synthesis of *Shiva* and *Shakti* in the couple. The male *linga* and the female *yoni* were symbolic of the generative powers of the two coexisting principles of nature (White, 2000). The production of fluids represented a sacred offering to Tantric deities and was described as an ambrosia-like nectar that permeated the entire spinal cord, genitalia, and brain.

Tantric sexual practices conflicted with Orthodox Buddhism, which promoted chastity and, like Christianity, split the feminine principle into virginal and compassionate, or bodily and sexual opposites. Nonetheless, variations of Tantric practices survived in both Eastern and Western civilizations through forms of goddess worship originating from early Pythagorean and Neoplatonic sources. Certain sects such as the Christian Gnostic *Ophites* performed Tantric sexual rites in devotion to the symbol of the Holy Spirit in the Orthodox Church, Sophia. The Orthodox Church found these practices to be promiscuous and completely unorthodox. Similarly, Islamic religious authorities condemned the Sufi sects who worshiped the feminine principle of love, although Ibn 'Arabi claimed that the most complete union possible was the sexual act between a man and woman, which he associated as a state of bliss beyond pure interior contemplation of God. Thus, Sufism achieved life in sexual mysticism. Sufism was kept alive by troubadours, self-named "Lovers," who worshiped the feminine principle as the source of divine energy. Eventually Sufi influence predisposed European troubadours, following the crusades, to found the renowned movement of Courtly Love. Courtly Love appeared in literature, poetry and song for centuries until the powerful patriarch that was simultaneously branding women as witches and devils, condemned such activity as heterodox Although sexual practices clearly have been an aspect of Tantric rituals, ultimately the *Tantras* stressed sexual ritual more as a conduit to the underlying creative energies of the universe and were practices by a minority of sects. The ritual sexual practices centered upon harnessing the more mundane human impulses of desire toward higher aims in order to replicate the activity of the divine couple. The sexual acts were less for pleasure and intended as an offering toward higher aspirations. The psychological symbolism of the internal male and female energies was the major focus.

Psychology

Carl Jung, along with other academics and intellectuals (Heinrich Zimmer and Mircea Eliade), examined the Hindu and Buddhis Tantric teachings. Sigmund Freud tended to interpret all religiously-endowed and emotionally significant experience as derived from, or a substitute for basic physical sex. Religious and emotional acts were equated as irrational and needed to be sublimated, modified into a cultural higher form. Freud's emphasis was on the biological; thus, sex was primarily a biological function. Unlike Freud, Jung found that there are specific commonalities between the practice of Tantrism and depth psychology. Jung considered sexuality itself to be a symbolic, numinous experience. Analytical psychology compliments the aims of Tantrism by performing a soul-seeking or soul-retrieval function within a ritualized setting that invokes the divine and effects the embodiment of imaginal transformation. This union is analogous to the notion of the *coincidentia oppositorum* in analytical psychology in which the anima and animus – (non-gender specific female soul and non-gender specific male soul) are united with spirit to form a whole, or oneness. Additionally, the internalization of the universal feminine principle is not unlike internalizing the good mother through which a person can relate positively to a feminine principle, fleshing out and healing the wound of previous emptiness of this aspect of the psyche. Tantrism and Jungian depth psychology offer methods for arriving at a more complex and intimate relationship of self (ego in Western psychological terms) with Self. The notion of Self in Jungian psychology would find its analog in the Tantric notion of unity achieved through oneness with the divine feminine. The essence of the psyche as female, following the lineage of *Shakti*, Sophia, and Courtly Love.

Jung affirmed the nature of the opposites as being bi-gendered. The anima and animus are contained within each human psyche. Like the dual-serpents of *Kundalini* energy, these two-fold aspects must be set in motion to realize psychic equilibrium. The combination of these opposites does not depend as much upon two opposite genders but is based more upon the achievement of an embodied non-dualistic consciousness. The ultimate image that guided the practitioner of Tantrism was that of a male and a female conjoined in sexual intercourse. The contemplative aspect of the practice required "meditating upon emptiness and emanating supreme immutable bliss – a state of *passionate desirelessness*,"(Emery, 2005: 6); thus, a unified divine consciousness. Analogously, the *conuinctio* of anima and animus does not pertain to sexual gratification but represents an integrated expression of harmonious wisdom that surpasses mundane sexual longings. The capacity of Tantrism to comprehend the efficacy of the symbolic demonstrates how these early practices offer valuable tools to psychoanalysis in terms of working beyond words, a helpful factor with pre-verbal patients, and dealing directly with the essential being of the person.

Tantric sexual practices more rightly might be compared to the transference between a modern day therapist and patient, although the bodily emphasis is transformed into emphasis upon the imaginal and the symbolic. If desire is ignited in a positive transference, it finds life in the imaginal and sacred realm of the therapeutic space and the third space shared by the two persons. The process of *conuinctio*, or divine marriage is a goal much like that of the early alchemists who projected upon matter symbolically to achieve transformative ends.

Tantrism and Jungian psychology place emphasis upon a *temenos*, a sacred container, and both emphasize the numinous and mystical in the physical and phenomenal realm. Tantrism strives toward internalization of the divine imago. Jungian theory likewise seeks this emphasis. The notion of individuation is analogous to the Tantric understanding of the exchange of currents, once internalized, flowing to and from the source with an ongoing reciprocity (ego and Self, or ego-self axis in analytical terms). Just as the goddess *Shakti* seeks to create an imprint or image in human form, the Self of the psyche seeks us, fueled by the divine source that fuels it. The divine intentionally comes into a human form.

Tantrism, like depth psychology, affirms the tumultuousness of the descent that the individual psyche must undergo into the chthonic realm in order to attain higher consciousness. Similar to Tantric practice, analytical psychology understands the role of the healer as one engaged in a liturgical ritual as a priest. Depth psychology presumes that the therapist, like the master in Tantrism, has sufficiently developed an element of the divine within that enables one to guide the patient in bringing an element of the divine into fruition.

Psychoanalysis in general, mirrors Tantrism, in that it has specific tenets such as the frame (time, place), and an alliance between two persons comparable to the relationship between initiate and guru/master. The authority of the therapist is not derived solely from intellectual theory, any more than the guru's power is a mere derivative of Tantric doctrine. Differences would be that a therapist would not consider himself to be equated with the divine, for this would be an inflation of narcissistic grandeur. Nor does a therapist intend to transform himself into a divinity. The guru, however, is assumed to have achieved a non-dualistic state of being.

In contrast, a therapist will struggle in an ongoing way with various issues of countertransference (individual response to what the patient induces in him or is already a vulnerable aspect of the therapist's psyche). Unlike the psychoanalyst, for whom the transference can induce potentially negative psychic effects, the guru remains untouched by the initiate's damaging energies, having attained high spiritual awareness.

Depth psychology maintains a very structured system of ethics comparable to Tantric doctrine. Yet, unlike some Tantric practices in which the priest enacted sexual practice with virgins representing the divine goddess, a therapist adheres to a completely different code of ethics. If a therapist were to act out with a patient, this would be considered to be not only unethical, but an abuse of the patient's vulnerability in light of the therapist's authority. Further, as the alchemists would say, the bird has flown out of the vessel, meaning that such an action would entirely disrupt the growth of the patient up to this point and that the patient would need to begin all over again in the process of healing.

The downside of removing the bodily aspect from actual proximity to analytic psychology is that the body, along with the desires (*shakti*) aroused within certain psychotherapeutic transferences must find a conduit in life, or these energies will go underground again like a recoiled serpent. The separation of the body from ritual practice has promoted a split between the fields of psychology and "body-work." This split has yet to be resolved successfully in our time.

The Tantric ideals of preparation and initiation are equally evident in psychological practice. Initiation might be compared to the power of the positive or negative transference that the patient transfers onto the therapist, which changes over time as the two persons create an energy field. The individual, like the Tantric initiate, comes to the therapist/master with the projection that the person possesses the capability of changing his or her future. The very existence of the transference maintains a specific kind of authority needed by the therapist to impart "insights" comparable to the hidden truths or mysteries of the *Tantras*.

Tantrism arose historically as a movement that developed in reaction against the authoritative high forms of orthodox Hinduism and Buddhism that neglected the sensation of the body, while also relegating the feminine principle to a secondary or non-existent status. Psychology emphasizes that instinct and imagination are aspects of the bodily senses and thus necessary parts of the ritual healing. Depth psychology, inclusive of both Freudian and Jungian schools of thought arose specifically as a humanistic form of healing practice in response to the inability of medicine, theology, and religion to sufficiently address many of the issues of the ailing person.

Analogous to the notion in analytical psychology that both persons in the therapeutic process undergo transformation, in Tantrism, the initiate transfers his or her inborn self-healing potential to the guru. The guru, like the analyst "holds" this potential until it becomes conscious to the patient/initiate.

Similarly, the guru assists the initiate in realizing images and symbols through the specified preparation and purification processes. Tantrism, with its openness to the instincts and emotions of the body allows considerable access to potent and numinous symbols, accompanied by the psychic energies that are freed along with making the unconscious conscious. The Tantric mind is analogous to the embodied psyche – the experience of the body being penetrated or infused by spirit.

Perhaps the most essential insight is that, in either case – imaginal or actual – desire in relation to the feminine was not despoiled in Tantric practices, but offered multiple levels of conscious spiritual attainment through practices involving mind, body, and psyche. In our contemporary world, how do we embrace the significance of phenomenal experience in relation to spirituality? Is real or imaginal affinity for the feminine figure more significant in the process of spiritual consciousness?

Tantric practice as it informs analytical psychology suggests how feminine consciousness and the inclusion of the body offers a transformational process in spiritual growth that effects the maturation of psychological and spiritual development. We differentiate ourselves through participation with otherness – what is most opposite and other than ourselves – toward a *jouissance* of being that is inclusive of spiritual embodiment.

See also: ❯ Buddhism ❯ Depth Psychology and Spirituality ❯ Freud, Sigmund ❯ Hinduism ❯ Jung, Carl Gustav

Bibliography

Arthur, A. (Sir John Woodroffe). (Ed.). (1960). *Principles of Tantra* (3rd. ed.). Madras, India: Ganesh & Co.

Avalon, A. (1972). *Tantra of the great liberation – Mahanirvana Tantra.* New York: Dover publications.

Emery, L. (2005). *Trans-forming tantra: Tibetan Buddhist Tantra, imaginal Western alchemy and gendered consciousness.* www.adolphus.nl/xcrpts/xckkrsha.html.

Harper, K., & Brown, R. L. (Ed.). (2002). *The roots of Tantra.* Albany, NY: State University of New York Press.

Rosen, S. J. (1994). *Sri Pancha Tattva: The five features of God.* New York: Folk Books.

Tompkins, P. (1984). *The magic of Obelisk.* New York: Harpercollins.

Urban, H. (2003). *Tantra: Sex, secrecy, politics, and power in the study of religions.* Los Angeles, CA: University of California Press.

White, D. G. (Ed.). (2000). *Tantra in practice.* Princeton, NJ: Princeton University Press.

Yeshe, L. T. (1987). *Introduction to Tantra: The transformation of desire.* Boston, MA: Wisdom Publications.

Taoism

Fredrica R. Halligan

Lao Tzu wrote in the sixth to seventh century: "Every being in the universe is an expression of the *Tao*. . . .The *Tao* gives birth to all beings, nourishes them, maintains them, cares for them, comforts them, protects them, takes them back to itself. . . .That is why love of the *Tao* is in the very nature of things" (Lao Tzu in Mitchell, 1989: 13).

The *Tao* (pronounced "Dao") is "The Way" of the ancient Chinese philosophers. The central idea is that harmony with nature is the way to live graciously. To live in harmony with the way the universe works is to keep in tune with natural laws. The concepts of *Yin* (feminine) and *Yang* (masculine) energies flow all through the worldview of the Taoists. The classic text, the *Tao te Ching*, is believed to have been written by the poet and philosopher, Lao Tzu. Much of Chinese culture has been deeply influenced by these Taoist ideas, including statesmanship, religion, medicine (e.g., acupuncture), physical exercise (*Tai Chi* or *Qi Gong*) and even auspicious placement of buildings and interior decorations (*Feng Shui*).

Psychologically, a Toist perspective could be considered to be quite counter-culture in the United States today. The emphasis on yielding, for example, would be contrary to the current psychotherapeutic emphasis on assertiveness. Among Asians, however, this Toist outlook may permeate their worldview, and the influence of Asian culture (including martial arts) has had its impact on the mainstream U.S. culture as well.

See also: ❯ Chinese Religions

Bibliography

Firebrace, P., & Hill, S. (1994). *Acupuncture: How it works, how it cures.* New Canaan, CT: Keats Publishing.

Izutsu, T. (1983). *Sufism and Taoism: A comparative study of key philosophical concepts.* Los Angeles, CA: University of California Press.

Mitchell, S. (Ed.). (1989). *The enlightened heart: An anthology of sacred poetry.* New York: Harper & Row.

Tara

Ann Moir-Bussy

Origins

The goddess Tara, one of many female deities, was first found in early Hinduism and later was adopted by Tibetan Buddhism in the early third century BC. She is worshiped throughout Tibet, Nepal and parts of South-East Asia. Some schools of Buddhism recognize 21 Taras. The Chinese call her Kwan Yin, the Bodhisattva of Compassion, her name meaning "one who hears the cries of the world." Tara is known as the Mother of Mercy, the Goddess of Compassion, the "mother of liberation," the "one who saves." According to one legend she emerged from a lotus that grew in a lake made by the tears of Avalokitesvara as he wept for the world's sufferings. There are different forms of Tara represented by different colors, including blue, green, red, yellow, black and white aspects of White Tara, reflecting her responsiveness to the needs of beings in different circumstances. The colors also represent the many facets of wholeness or balance. The Green Tara is known for her activity of compassion for all beings. Some say the Green Tara represents the night. The White Tara contains all the colors and is also the symbol of compassion, healing and serenity. The Red Tara is recognized as the fierce aspect of Tara, but the fierceness is not about destructiveness, but about magnetizing all good things. Some representations depict her as wrathful, destroying negativity, overcoming disharmonious conditions. In these pictures Tara sits in the center of a raging fire destroying the enemies within: all that is delusion and that gets in the way of liberation and enlightenment. The Black Tara is often associated with power; the Yellow Tara with wealth and prosperity, and the Blue Tara with the transmutation of anger (http://www.crystalinks.com/tara.html).

The Buddhist tradition has 21 different manifestations of Tara and there are mantras or songs of praise to each, describing her attributes (for reference to these see *Praises to the 21 Taras* - http://www.fpmt.org/prayers/21taras94rdr.pdf.).

Other Manifestations

Tara can be likened to the Virgin Mary – known also as Stella Maris – Star of the Sea, or to Aphrodite, also said to be born from water and known as the Morning/Evening Star. In other cultures there are vibrations of her name. In Polynesian myth Tara is a beautiful sea goddess; in Latin, Terra or Mother earth; the Druids' mother goddess was Tara; in Finland the Women of Wisdom were known as Tar; in South America, an indigenous tribe in the jungle called her Tarahumara and, finally, Native American people speak of a Star Woman who came from the heavens and from whom all essential food grew (http://www.crystalinks.com/tara.html). As with many female deities, "Tara governs the Underworld, the Earth and the Heavens, birth, death and regeneration, love and war, the seasons, all that lives and grows, the Moon cycles – Luna – feminine – creation" (http://www.crystalinks.com/tara.html).

Psychological Images

From the standpoint of psychology Tara is symbolic of the Great Mother archetype, the feminine principle. Embodied in men and women, Jung refers to this feminine principle as the *anima* or *soul* (Jung, 1959). It is the principle of relationship and of feeling, eminently expressed in Tara as compassion. The mother is responsible for birth and life, for nurturing and development, for fertility and fruitfulness. "The place of magic transformation and rebirth, together with the underworld and its inhabitants, are presided over by the mother" (Jung, 1982: 16). Hence the task of each individual is the development of all the qualities embodied by Tara, in order to achieve wholeness and completeness and inner wisdom. We can learn from Tara simple and direct means of discovering within oneself the wisdom, joy and compassion of the goddess as we travel along the path to Enlightenment. As a female bodhisattva, Tara, combines the spiritual with the human – heaven and earth. Each human being is a potential bodhisattva, learning to bring into balance, yin and yang, male and female, consciousness and unconsciousness, the self and no-self. The bodhisattva within each of us, challenges us to keep on the journey towards maturation, or individuation and to reach out in compassion to all other sentient beings.

See also: ◉ Bodhisattva ◉ Buddhism ◉ Guan Yin ◉ Individuation

Bibliography

http://www.ackland.org/art/exhibitions/buddhistart/tara.htm. Accessed 6 October 2008.
http://www.crystalinks.com/tara.html. Accessed 6 October 2008.

http://www.fpmt.org/prayers/21taras94rdr.pdf. Accessed 7 October 2008.

Gadon, E. (1989). *The once and future goddess: A symbol for our time.* San Francisco, CA: Harper.

http://www.iloveulove.com/spirituality/buddhist/21tarareference.htm. Accessed 7 October 2008.

Jung, C. G. (1969/1959). Four archetypes – Mother/rebirth/spirit/trickster (R. F. C. Hull, Trans.). In *The collected works of C. G. Jung* (Vol. 9, Pt. I). Princeton, NJ: Princeton University Press, Bollingen Series XX.

Jung, C. G. (1982). Aspects of the feminine (R. F. C. Hull, Trans.). In *The Collected Works of C. G. Jung* (Vols. 6, 7, 9i, 9ii, 10, 17). Princeton, NJ: Princeton University Press, Bollingen Series XX.

Meckel, D. & Moore, R. (Eds.). (1992). *Self and liberation – The Jung/ Buddhism dialogue.* New York: Paulist Press.

Teilhard de Chardin

Fredrica R. Halligan

Many spiritually-oriented individuals have as their personal aim the realization of union with the Divine. Many spiritual paths view the sense of union with all humanity as being preliminary or at least concurrent with Divine union. It is to Pierre Teilhard de Chardin, S.J. that contemporary religion owes its increasing capacity to see humanity as an inter-related whole, and its will to transform religious thinking into global consciousness. Teilhard wrote:

▶ Across the immensity of time and the disconcerting multiplicity of individuals, one single operation is taking place.... one single thing is being made: the Mystical body of Christ (Teilhard, 1960: 143).

Clearly, the earth is on a trajectory toward unification. That we of the twenty-first century can conceptualize this process spiritually is due in large part to the prophetic vision of the Jesuit mystic-scientist. (Cousins, 1985).

Teilhard the Man

Pierre Teilhard de Chardin (1881–1955) was born into an aristocratic family in France, where he acquired both traditional Catholic piety with mystical interests and scholarly, scientific traits. He was educated by the Jesuits and ordained a priest in 1911. As a member of the Society of Jesus he briefly taught physics and chemistry, but devoted most of his life to the pursuit of scientific knowledge. Evolution was his passionate study. Involved in

many archeological digs in China and Outer Mongolia, he was a key member of the paleontology team that discovered *Sinanthropus pekinensis* ("Peiking Man"), an important early link in the evolution of humankind. (Teilhard de Chardin, 1966) Reflecting deeply on the process of evolution, Teilhard brought his contemplative consciousness to bear on what he called the "diaphaneity of matter." In *Hymn of the universe* he wrote:

▶ Blessed be you, mighty matter, irresistible march of evolution, reality ever new-born; you who, by constantly shattering our mental categories, force us to go ever further and further in our pursuit of the truth.

▶ Blessed be you, universal matter, immeasurable time, boundless ether, triple abyss of stars and atoms and generations; you who by overflowing and disordering our narrow standards of measurement reveal to us the dimensions of God (Teilhard de Chardin, 1961: 68f).

Teilhard's Thought

As a mystic, Teilhard viewed evolution in both scientific and spiritual light. He saw repeated patterns, with life emerging from the simple to the complex. From atoms to cells to living creatures, he recognized the processes inevitably requiring first differentiation, then unification. Human life, for example, begins with single cells that differentiate into two, then four, then multiple cells, each cell finding its purpose in the development of neo-natal life. He saw that the process is one of repeated "complexification." Extrapolating from the intelligent, complex beings in the human species, Teilhard foresaw the next phase of development wherein humans will first differentiate and then unite into a higher level of being, i.e., humanity as a whole. This will occur, he predicted, when a shell of intellect, or "noosphere," envelopes the earth. This is an irresistible physical process, the "collectivisation" or "planetisation" of humanity (Teilhard de Chardin, 1964). To Teilhard, the endpoint of this evolutionary unification would be what he called the Omega Point (q.v.), wherein humanity would be united by the force of love. The "fire of love" as he called it, is what Teilhard thought to be the power of Christ.

Teilhard's ideas were so radically new in the 1940s and 1950s that he was prohibited from publishing his *magnum opus*. Although Teilhard's thoughts seemed new, they are really quite in tune with the unitive insights of the mystics both East and West throughout the ages. In 1955 the Jesuit

Order permitted posthumous publication of *The Phenomenon of Man*. Since then, his ideas have had a tremendous impact, not only on Catholic thinking, but also on scientific thought.

Global Consciousness

If Teilhard and all the great mystics are right, then there is de facto unity among us, and what is emerging is global awareness of that underlying unity. Today the internet, which was not yet known in Teilhard's life, is a manifestation of the "noosphere" or shell of intellect enveloping the earth. When Teilhard foresaw the tide of destructive forces that threaten the planet, he called upon all people to unite in building the earth. With today's threats from terrorism as well as climate change, Teilhard's call remains the same.

Our task, from a psychological perspective, is to deepen our personal awareness of the inter-connections among us, and to help others to become aware of those deep spiritual interrelationships. In so doing, we participate as co-creators in the evolution of human consciousness. The inter-religious dialogue is today a vibrant venue for such deepening awareness, helping humanity first to differentiate, to appreciate diversity, and then to integrate, through comprehending our essential spiritual unity.

Teilhard himself always saw the Omega Point in Christian terms. However others who follow him have realized that, in true global unity, no one religion can dominate all the rest. Thus a true sense of dialogue must be established wherein mutual respect is engendered. Psychology has a significant role in fostering and facilitating that dialogue. Seen in breadth and depth of perspective, the world religions have not only different theologies and philosophies but also, in essence, vastly different worldviews. (Panikkar, 1999). Toward furthering cross-cultural understanding and appreciation of religious differences and similarities, psychology has the opportunity to foster understanding with persons from varying cultures and religions. In like manner, in the spirit of Teilhard, psychological understanding can facilitate globalization by dialogue addressing such problems as global warming and combating deleterious climate change.

See also: ❯ Christianity ❯ Creation ❯ Omega Point

Bibliography

Cousins, E. H. (1985). *Global spirituality: Toward the meeting of the mystical paths.* Madras, India: Radhakrishnan Institute.

Panikkar, R. (1999). *The Intrareligious dialogue.* New York: Paulist Press.

Teilhard de Chardin, P. (1959). *The Phenomenon of man* (B. Wall, Trans.). New York: Harper & Row. (Original publication 1955. *Le phenomene humain.* Paris: Editions du Seuil).

Teilhard de Chardin, P. (1960). *The Divine Milieu.* New York: Harper Colophon.

Teilhard de Chardin, P. (1961). *Hymn of the universe.* New York: Harper & Row.

Teilhard de Chardin, P. (1964). *The future of man* (N. Denny, Trans.). New York: Harper & Row.

Teilhard de Chardin, P. (1966). *Teilhard de Chardin album* (J. Mortier & M. -L. Aboux, Eds.). London: Collins.

Temenos

Ronald Madden

Temenos [Greek τέμενος] refers to a piece of land set aside or cut off from everyday use and assigned as a special domain for the veneration of a temporal ruler or a god. It may also be a built structure as in a *temple* that has been consecrated for a sacred purpose, such as a place of sacrifice to a deity or of worship.

A *temenos*, in a narrow sense, is a Greek sanctuary that has been constructed in a specific location that has significance for a ruler or god to be venerated. The temenos dedicated to the chief of the gods at Olympia is called the temenos of Zeus. A temenos may be demarcated by boundary stones possibly erected as a colossal wall or rampart. It is frequently associated with a special tree, such as the Bodhi tree (Sri Maha Bodhi) under which Siddhartha Gautama sat and achieved enlightenment and which was to become the site of the Mahabodhi Temple of Buddhism. The temenos may, itself, take the form of a sacred grove of trees, such as Plato's *grove of Academe* outside of Athens.

The practice of dividing the world into sacred and profane precincts is observed throughout prehistoric, ancient and civilized societies. The temenos universally represents a sacred place set aside from the secular or profane world. It is an integral part of so-called primitive cultures where the sacred place was seen as the center of the cosmos (the Axis Mundi) and was often marked by a sacred tree which represented death and rebirth and the connection between heaven, earth, and hell. Stone and water were usually also a part of the sacred place – stone for its symbolization of permanence and water for purification.

From Celtic spirituality comes the concept of the *thin place*, an idea that is related to that of temenos. A thin place is a sacred place where the veil or membrane between heaven and earth is thin, or where one can pass easily back and forth between the material and spiritual worlds. A thin place may be a specific location where great spiritual energy is experienced by many as being received, such as at Stonehenge, Glastonbury, Luxor, or Mecca. It may be situated on a mountain such as Sinai, Ararat, Machu Picchu, Fuji or Athos. A temenos or temple is often erected at or near the site of a thin place in response to the presence of spiritual energy that is found there. The temenos serves to facilitate passage between the opposing realms of the visible and invisible, conscious and unconscious, inner and outer, spiritual and earthly.

In a certain sense, the work of depth psychology, as experienced in the encounter between analyst and analysand, is soul-work. The work of this interaction is benefited by a space that is experienced by both therapist and patient as quiet, safe, and sacred, where it is possible to access the unconscious without fear of distraction from the profane world outside. The therapist's office is a form of holding place or vessel; its walls and ambiance cut it off from the rest of the world, so that the work of healing can be done. The therapy room may be seen to function as a thin place or temenos for the practice of psychotherapy. It might even be thought of as a sacred enclosure where a symbolic journey through death and rebirth can occur.

See also: ❂ Axis Mundi ❂ Bodhi Tree ❂ Celtic Spirituality ❂ Communitas ❂ Depth Psychology and Spirituality ❂ Gardens, Groves, and Hidden Places ❂ Psychotherapy and Religion ❂ Water ❂ Western Wall

Bibliography

Adams, L. D. (1990). *The world of myth*. New York: Oxford University Press.

Burkert, W. (1985). *Greek religion*. Cambridge, MA: Harvard University Press.

Eliade, M. (1958). *Patterns in comparative religion*. London: Sheed & Ward, Ltd.

Eliade, M. (1974). *The myth of the eternal return*. Princeton, NJ: Princeton University Press.

Eliade, M. (1987). *The sacred and the profane: The nature of religion*. Orlando, FL: Harcourt Brace Jovanovich.

Erich, N. (1989). Mystical man. In J. Campbell (Ed.). *The mystic vision: Papers from the Eranos yearbooks*. Princeton, NJ: Princeton University Press.

Gray, M. *Sacred sites: Places of peace and power*. (http://www.sacredsites.com)

Jung, C. G. (1968). *Psychology and alchemy*. Princeton, NJ: Princeton University Press.

Teresa of Avila

Ann M. Rothschild

St. Teresa was born on March 28th, 1515 in Avila, Spain. She joined the contemplative Carmelite order, taking the habit on November 2, 1535. She founded her first monastery, St. Joseph in Avila, in 1562. She then founded 17 convents, all smaller and simpler and with more discipline than the traditional ones of her times.

Teresa is best known for her three main works. The first was her autobiography, *The Life of Teresa of Jesus*, written when she was in her 40s and completed in 1565. *The Way of Perfection* was written a year later in 1566. Finally near the end of her life, in 1577, when she was 62 years old, she completed *The Interior Castle*, a work she considered a masterpiece, her best work. She died October 4, 1582. She was canonized in 1622. In 1970 Pope Paul VI declared her a Doctor of the Church.

St. Teresa suffered from serious illnesses. She was bed ridden for years. She had emotional issues as well. From the beginning of her religious life, she faced enormous physical and spiritual challenges. She had to find her way, and she began by exploring herself. Her spiritual/psychotherapeutic journey was typically a slow, arduous journey requiring courage. Yet she was always attentive, constantly and consistently moving toward self-integration. She visited those places we might call mad or unreasonable. She noticed and then abstained from her "old passions," her neuroses. She prayed, she meditated, she contemplated, and she looked within, all the time. Her journey to God was a journey to herself. She was a strong individual and example of a woman who strived through discipline, through prayer, through contemplation, and through seeking self-knowledge, to actualize herself. We can easily apply these spiritual struggles to a psychological perspective. She has been called a "psychological mystic." Self-knowledge was very important to her. "This matter of self-knowledge must never be neglected..." (St. Teresa of Avila, 1960: 145).

In *The Interior Castle*, she explores her "interior" self in a journey through seven "mansions." Consistent with modern psychotherapeutic theory, houses often represent the self. This is a spiritual journey but a psychological one as well. As in therapy, it is a voluntary journey. It is also an heroic journey into the unknown. As in therapy there are stages. In St. Teresa's first three stages or "mansions" we are more active. We meet and become aware of our demons. We fight and subdue them. But after the fourth mansion, we can become less active and more receptive. We can go deeper. In the psychological journey, St. Teresa can be a guide to finding and growing an inner self, becoming clearer and deeper room by room. Especially for those with a lack of a sense of self, or those dealing with a narcissist or a schizoid dynamic, reading St. Teresa can be very helpful.

Therapists can find a model in St. Teresa as well. Often a new therapist is very active like the seeker in the beginning mansions. As she notices by exploring her own vices, like the religious person seeing what keeps her away from God, she sees that activity gets in the way. And as she reflects on how her own dynamics contribute to excessive activity, she can become less active, able to use Freud's suspended, free floating attention. Few words are required. There is less effort, more listening.

See also: ❂ Contemplative Prayer ❂ Ecstasy ❂ Individuation ❂ Mysticism and Psychoanalysis ❂ Self

Bibliography

Humphreys, C. (1992). *From ashes to fire.* New York: New City Press.

St. Teresa of Avila. (1960). *The life of Teresa of Jesus* (E. Allison Peers, Ed.). Garden City, NY: Doubleday.

St. Teresa of Avila. (1989). *The interior castle* (E. Allison Peers, Ed.). Garden City, NY: Doubleday.

St. Teresa of Avila. (1991). *The way of perfection.* (E. Allison Peers, Ed.). New York, NY: Doubleday.

St. Teresa of Avila. (2007). *The book of my life.* (M. Starr, Trans.). Boston, MA: Shambhala.

Welch, J. (1982). *Spiritual pilgrims, Carl Jung and Teresa of Avila.* Mawah, NJ: Paulist Press.

Thanatos

Nathan Carlin

The Greek word Thanatos literally means "death." Thanatos also can have metaphorical meanings, such as the personification of death (cf. Romans 5.14 and 1 Corinthians 15.26), as well as spiritual meanings, such as eternal death (cf. 2 Corinthians 7.10). Edward Tripp (1970) notes that in classical mythology, "Thanatos was born of Nyx (Night)," and that Thanatos "and his brother Hypnos (Sleep) lived together in Tartarus" (p. 555). He also notes that "Thanatos appears in Euripides' *Alcestis* to carry off the heroine from her tomb. Heracles wrestles with him, however, and

brings her back to life" (1970: 555). Tripp also directs us to these passages in mythology: *Iliad*, 16.453–455, 16.672–673, 16.682–683; *Theogony*, 211–212 and 758–766.

Freud and Thanatos

In psychological circles, Thanatos always recalls Freud's theory of the death instinct (some prefer the translation "death drive"), despite the fact that, as far as I know, Freud never used the word Thanatos. However, Freud (2001/1930) all but invites the term when he writes in *Civilization and Its Discontents*: "And now it is to be expected that the other two 'Heavenly Powers,' eternal Eros, will make an effort to assert himself in the struggle with his equally immortal adversary. But who can foresee with what success and with what result?" (2001/1930: 145). On the other hand, perhaps the omission of the title Thanatos was intentional, as it could intimate that the powers of Eros are more integrated whereas the powers of the death instincts are more diffuse. In any case, in Freud's thinking, Eros is associated with the sexual and life instincts, instincts that tend to be constructive and have a uniting quality, whereas Thanatos is associated with the death instincts and have a destructive, aggressive, sadist, and even masochistic quality about them.

Freud (2001/1920) first put forth his notion of the death instinct in *Beyond the Pleasure Principle*, and he did so first in speculation to make sense of a problem with his theory of dreams. Since Freud earlier argued that all dreams are wish-fulfillments, anxiety in dreams was problematic for his theory. How, for example, could recurring traumatic dreams possibly be wish-fulfillments? What we normally think of as nightmares, on the other hand, did not pose such a problem, because Freud explained nightmares as repressed wishes coming too close to consciousness. That is, nightmares are revisions of dreams that have come too close to exposing repressed desires. But explaining *recurring* dreams that produce anxiety proved to be much more difficult for Freud, so much so that he eventually postulated the idea of the death instinct. Freud talked of this recurring as a "compulsion to repeat." And he believed that it was an attempt to gain control over past situations retrospectively. He also likened the death instinct to the property of inertia. He observed that there is a tendency in organic life to return to an earlier state of being – in religious language, "from dust to dust." Freud famously proclaimed, "*the aim of all life is death*," and in this sense the death instincts and the life instincts can be thought of as a suicidal impulse. But why, one might object, doesn't all life perish immediately? To this, Freud responded that our life instincts prevent this. And this seems to mean that the death instinct and life instinct, taken together, guide organic life to die on its own terms. The death instinct also provides an explanation for aggression. Aggression, Freud came to believe, is the projection of the death instinct. The upshot of Freud's notion of the death instinct for our purposes is that aggression is instinctual and basic to human nature. This means that attempts to eliminate particular aggressive behaviors will not solve any problems, which is why Freud argued that communism could not contain our aggressive impulses, because these impulses are not rooted in property, they are a part of human nature. Aggression cannot be eliminated; it can only be directed or channeled in better and worse ways.

Freud's views on aggression and the notion of Thanatos have been debated and applied inside and outside of medical and psychological circles (see, e.g., Menninger, 1938 and 1942; Marcuse, 1966; Ricoeur, 1970; Brady, 1974; Stepansky, 1977; Afkhami, 1985; Percy, 1987; Groves, 1999; Hutcheon and Hutcheon, 1999; Bennett, 2005; Arundale, 2006; Cho, 2006).

Norman Brown on Thanatos

One of the more interesting philosophical and theological interpreters of Freud on the death instinct has been Norman Brown. In *Life Against Death: The Psychoanalytical Meaning of History*, Brown (1959) notes that in 1953 he "turned to a deep study of Freud, feeling a need to reappraise the nature and destiny of man" (p. xi). And in this book, Brown argues that "mankind, in all its restless striving and progress, has no idea what it really wants," that "Freud was right: our real desires are unconscious," and that it "also begins to be apparent that mankind, unconscious of its real desires and therefore unable to obtain satisfaction, is hostile to life and ready to destroy itself" (1959: xii). Brown summarizes what he took from his reading of Freud, all the while making his case for a psychoanalytical view of history. He writes, for example, "the theory of neurosis must embrace a theory of history; and conversely a theory of history must embrace a theory of neurosis" (1959: 13). Brown believed that psychoanalysis "can provide a theory of 'progress,' but only by viewing history as a neurosis" (1959: 18). He elaborates:

▶ If therefore we think of man as that species of animal which has the historical project of recovering his own childhood, psychoanalysis suggests the historical proposition that mankind will not put aside its sickness and

its discontent until it is able to abolish every dualism (1959: 52).

"The reunification of Life and Death," Brown writes, "can be envisioned as the end of the historical process" (1959: 91).

David Greenham has written the first systematic work on the work of Norman Brown. Greenham (2006) notes that "Brown is not writing history from a psychoanalytic point of view – a study in the Oedipal motivations of 'great individuals' for example – but he is interpreting the very drives of history using the implications of Freud's late metapsychology" (p. 77). And, in his chapter on Brown's *Life Against Death*, Greenham notes that, "For Brown history has no ontological weight, it is rather only a symptom; it is neurosis pure and simple," for "nature has not history; it just *is*, it does not *become*" (p. 64). He elaborates:

▶ So by the transformation of psychoanalysis into a theory of history... he means a theory of the *end* of history, as we find in the Bible, as well as in Hegel and Marx. Brown's history 'ends' not with revelation or absolute knowledge or the dictatorship of the proletariat – though in part it is all of those things. His history ends by plunging humanity into the immanence of 'nature' (2006: 65).

But, it is still difficult to imagine what it would mean to plunge humankind back into the immanence of nature, and, even if one could imagine it, it is even more difficult to imagine how this might be possible. But, as noted above, Brown is clearly articulating a critique of western civilization in its denial of death, and Greenham clarifies this point made by Brown:

▶ So, according to Brown, humans repress their death and in so doing create history as the history of repression: civilization as neurosis. It is the human failure to recognize, at the most basic level, that life and death are the 'same,' one half of a dialectic; which both fuels history and is its meaning. Freud, perhaps, suggests of this conclusion when he argues that the goal of all life is death, but he shies away from the truth as Brown sees it, and retains a dualism (2006: 79).

Greenham argues that, for Brown, "Eros is the key to unlocking – and ending – history" (2006: 67), and "Religion is important for Brown not because he is putting forward any particular faith, but because he sees religion as 'a half-way house' to curing history" (2006: 66).

It is difficult to understand how religion can cure history in the sense that Brown is suggesting, that is, by reuniting life and death. But another author, Robert Dykstra, a pastoral theologian, has written more clearly about how aggression – what, in the context of this essay, we might call Thanatos – ought to be integrated into the lives of Christian men.

Robert Dykstra on Aggression

In his "Rending the Curtain: Lament as an Act of Vulnerable Aggression," Dykstra (2005) reflects on God's own lament over the death of Jesus to address the lives of contemporary Christen men. His central theme, as his title indicates, is what is called "the rending of the curtain." When Jesus died, Dykstra notes, the biblical text records that the curtain in the temple was torn in two. Dykstra argues that here God not only revealed Himself, but that He *exposed* Himself. Just as the Son was exposed on the cross, literally crucified naked, God the Father likewise exposed His genitals in the rending of the curtain. Dykstra draws on Howard Eilberg-Schwartz (1994) to suggest that "the veiling of God may serve as a theological legitimation of male hegemony. Unable to identify God's sex, Israel's men maintain their status as God's beloved, while at the same time remaining safe from insinuation of homoeroticism" (Dykstra, 2005: 61). He elaborates,

▶ If Eilberg-Schwartz's provocative thesis about ancient Judaism's prohibitions against speculation about God's sexual anatomy is correct, I suggest that Gospel accounts of the rending of the temple curtain change all this, and that the lament is at the very heart of this decisive, even earth-shattering change.... God's own nakedness is at last revealed. In this, God the Father fully identifies with God the Son (p. 62).

Such an interpretation as Eilberg-Schwartz's regarding God's body – i.e., God's body is concealed in the biblical text so as to conceal the implicit homoeroticism of the men of Israel uniting with their male God – accounts, Dykstra believes, for why there seems to be "an enduring underlying anxiety among men that faith somehow threatens masculinity" (2005: 62). However,

▶ God's lament, then, drives God – and this underlying anxiety among men of faith – from the closet; an unbearable grief, shame, and rage in response to Jesus' death compel God to step out from behind the curtain in all God's desperate glory. In Jesus' death, we at last get a full frontal glimpse of God. God's lament removes the dividing line between the holy and the profane. As the curtain is rent in two, so too the old division between sacred and profane is forever torn apart (2005: 62).

For too long, Dykstra rightly notes, "good Christians" have falsely believed that they are not supposed to express or delight in such emotions. Men are to be composed, especially in difficult times, but the result is that men "tend, as a result, to experience a diminished capacity for intimacy, mutuality, and authentic forgiveness with God and one another" (2005: 63). But because of the cross, we find "a God now suddenly revealed in lament, angry and aggressive while naked and vulnerable, a God engaging in a sacred exhibitionism," and Dykstra's hope is, as he so eloquently puts it, "Would that those men who have the most to lose could love a God like this, could love God like this, could finally, in the end, simply love like this" (2005: 68).

Dykstra offers one way – a compelling way, to be sure – to think theologically about Thanatos: God here is destructive and aggressive, ripping the curtain in two, while also naked and vulnerable, breaking the conventions of public decency. There are surely other ways to think theologically about the vicissitudes of Thanatos. In any case, the theme of Thanatos has persisted since ancient days and haunts us even today. Those interested in psychology and religion cannot afford to neglect these forces, whatever their ontological status may be, since they are nevertheless real mythologically and practically (cf. Menninger 1938 and 1942).

See also: ◉ Dreams ◉ Eros ◉ Freud, Sigmund

Bibliography

Afkhami, G. (1985). *The Iranian revolution: Thanatos on a national scale.* Washington, DC: Middle East Institute.

Arundale, A. (2006). Eros and thanatos in context. *British Journal of Psychotherapy, 20*(4), 453–454.

Bennett, E. (2005). *Eros and Thanatos: A psycho-literary investigation of Walter Vogt's life and works.* Oxford, England: P. Lang.

Brady, P. (1974). Manifestations of Eros and Thanatos in *L'Etranger. Twentieth Century Literature, 20*(3), 183–188.

Brown, N. (1959). *Life against death: The psychoanalytical meaning of history.* New York: Vintage Books.

Cho, D. (2006). Thanatos and civilization: Lacan, Marcuse, and the death drive. *Policy futures in education, 4*(1), 18–30.

Dykstra, R. (2005). Rending the curtain: Lament as an act of vulnerable aggression. In S. Brown & P. Miller (Eds.), *Lament: Reclaiming practices in pulpit, pew, and public square* (pp. 59–69). Louisville, KY: Westminster John Knox Press.

Eilberg-Schwartz, H. (1994). *God's phallus and other problems for men and monotheism.* Boston, MA: Beacon Press.

Euripides. (2007). *Alcestis.* Oxford, England: Oxford University Press.

Freud, S. (2001). Beyond the pleasure principle. In J. Strachey (Ed. & Trans.). *The standard edition of the complete psychological works of Sigmund Freud* (Vol. 18, pp. 1–64). London: Vintage. (Original work published 1920).

Freud, S. (2001). Civilization and its discontents. In J. Strachey (Ed. & Trans.), *The standard edition of the complete psychological works of Sigmund Freud* (Vol. 21, pp. 57–145). London: Vintage. (Original work published 1930).

Greenham, D. (2006). *The resurrection of the body: The work of Norman O. Brown.* New York: Lexington Books.

Groves, P. (1999). *Eros and Thanatos.* Chester Springs, PA: Dufour Editions.

Hesiod. (2006). *Theogony; and, works and days.* (C. Schlegel & H. Weinfiled, Trans.). Ann Arbor, MI: University of Michigan Press.

The Holy Bible (King James Version). (1978). New York: American Bible Society. (Original work published 1611).

Homer. (1810). *The Illiad* (A. Pope, Trans.). London: G. Hazard.

Hutcheon, L., & Hutcheon, M. (1999). Death drive: Eros and Thanatos in Wagner's "Tristan und Isolde." *Cambridge Opera Journal, 11*(3), 267–293.

Menninger, K. (1938). *Man against himself.* New York: Harcourt, Brace.

Menninger, K. (1942). *Love against hate.* New York: Harcourt, Brace.

Marcuse, H. (1966). *Eros and civilization: A philosophical inquiry into Freud.* Boston, MA: Beacon Press.

Percy, W. (1987). *The Thanatos syndrome.* New York: Farrar, Straus, Giroux.

Ricoeur, P. (1970). *Freud and philosophy: An essay on interpretation.* New Haven, CT: Yale University Press.

Sears, T. A. (2001). *Clio, eros, thanatos: The "novella sentimental" in context.* New York: P. Lang.

Stepansky, P. (1977). A history of aggression in Freud. *Psychological Issues, 10*(3), Monograph 39.

Tripp, E. (1970). *Crowell's handbook of classical mythology.* New York: Thomas Y. Crowell.

Theodicy

David M. Moss III

The term "theodicy" was adapted from the French *theodicée* which is a compound of the Greek *theós* (God) and *díkē* (justice). Etymologically it means the "justification of God." Generally speaking, theodicy refers to the vindication of divine government given the existence of evil.

Whatever else may be said of evil it is certainly the abuse of a sentient being, a being that can feel pain. It is the pain that matters. Evil is grasped by the mind immediately and felt by the emotions immediately; it is sensed as hurt deliberately inflicted. Evil is never abstract. It is an existential reality and has to be understood in the personal context of suffering.

In fourth century Athens the Epicureans challenged the Stoics with a trilemma: if God could have prevented evil and did not, he is malevolent; if God would have prevented evil but could not, he is impotent; if God could not and would not, why call him God? Here is the primary moral quandary for any monotheism claiming God to be omnipotent, omniscient, and omnipresent. The problem is inescapable, as well as profound. *Si deus bonus, vede malum?* "If God is good, why evil?" The insistence behind this question is the concentration of theodicy, a specific dimension of Natural Theology that attempts to justify or vindicate God's morality *vis-à-vis* the evil that infects mankind.

The word "theodicy" was coined by the German mathematician and philosopher Gottfried Wilhelm Leibniz. In 1710 he used it as a theme and title of a book on metaphysics, *Essais de Théodicée sur la Bonté de Dieu.* Leibniz was a "theodician" who believed: some error is unavoidable in any creature less perfect than its creator; all possible worlds contain some evil; and evil reveals good through contrast. If goodness was constant, we would take it for granted without realizing the blessings of God. In this life evil is a necessary element like the shade in a picture, throwing into relief the beauty and harmony of the whole.

There are numerous dogmatic expressions of theodicy from two basic perspectives. The first emphasizes God's ultimate goodness in spite of the existence of evil. Evil is negative but necessary. It eclipses the good which produces a contrast that ultimately clarifies God's omniscience. Yahweh, for example, allows Job to be tortured and then rewards him. The second perspective is concentrated more on mankind's responsibility than God's because, in creation, the latter endowed the former with free will. The abuse of this freedom originates from within the human psyche. Injustice, cruelty and indifference are not divinely enabled but willfully enacted human behavior.

The subject of theodicy rarely appears in psychology texts or mental health journals. It is periodically addressed by grief literature and thanalology studies. The Pastoral Counseling Movement has made some unique contributions to the literature *via* hospital chaplains who minister to the terminally ill. Pastoral counseling also explores the clinical significance of theodicy and how it can be used to intellectually block the grief process.

Theodicy may be seen as an indirect denial of God's inconceivable nature or *mysterium*. For the justification of God's permission of evil requires a comprehension of the incomprehensible. Nevertheless, the belief in an all-good and all-powerful God naturally leads to a faith in Providence – *bonum ex nocentibus*, "out of evil good emerges." Providence is hope that out of even the most negative experience, no matter how evil, as long as one chooses to look with insight, beneficial results will be revealed. To quote Milton's *Paradise Lost*, ". . .to the height of this great argument I may assert eternal Providence and justify the ways of God to man."

See also: ❂ Evil ❂ God ❂ Pastoral Counseling

Bibliography

Hick, J. (1968). *Evil and the God of love*. London: Macmillan.

Leibniz, G. W. (1985). *Theodicy: Essays on the goodness of God, the freedom of man, and the origin of evil* (A. Farrer, Ed.). La Salle, IL: Open Court.

Lewis, C. S. (1962). *The problem of pain*. New York: Macmillan.

Lowe, W. (1983). *Evil and the unconscious*. Chico, CA: Scholars Press.

Oden, T. C. (1966). *Kerygma and counseling*. Philadelphia, PA: Westminster.

Ward, K. (1983). *Rational theology and the creativity of God*. Oxford, England: Oxford University Press.

Theophany

Emily Stetler

Coming from the Greek *theophaneia*, "appearance of God," a theophany is a revelation of God in which the divine is mediated by sensible matter. A theophany, then, is distinct from other mystical experiences in that it involves material, rather than merely psychic, phenomenon. Indeed, in a theophany, the natural world may exhibit characteristics unable to be explained by laws of nature or unable to be replicated and verified by empirical experimentation. Further, while achievement of a mystical state oftentimes depends upon, or is at least facilitated by, entrance into a receptive emotional or psychological state, a theophanic experience does not; it seems to spring from a source external to the visionary. In scriptural accounts, theophanies seem to be an interruption of the visionary's psychic state rather than an outcropping of it.

Nonetheless, a person *can* induce a hallucination that he describes as theophanic through meditation practices or the use of psychedelic drugs.

It must be noted that a theophany specifically reveals the *deity*. A mystical vision of a saint (such as a Marian apparition in Catholicism) does not qualify as a theophany. "Theophany," thus, is a more restrictive term than is "hierophany," Mircea Eliade's preferred term for a manifestation of the divine.

Theophanies may be found in any theistic religious tradition and, in modern times, have even been reported by individuals not subscribing to any religion. From both a doctrinal and a literary perspective, though, theophanies often function to make immanent a god who is typically characterized as being transcendent.

The Hebrew Bible recounts several theophanies, including Abraham's reception of the divine visitors at Mamre, where God tells him that he will bear a son by Sarah (Genesis 18:1–15); Moses' theophany on Mount Sinai, during which God inscribes his law on the tablets of stone (Exodus 19:16–32:14), and Ezekiel's vision of the four living creatures and the wheels (Ezekiel 1:1–28). Two especially paradigmatic theophanies are Jacob wrestling with God (Genesis 32:22–33) and Moses and the burning bush (Exodus 3:1–4:7). In the former narrative, Jacob's body attests to the contact with God; after the encounter, Jacob's hip is dislocated. In the burning bush account, we see the divine utilizing the material world, yet transcending natural laws: the bush burns, but it is not consumed, as it would be by a merely natural flame.

Although inhabiting the material world, and thus less ephemeral than other mystical experiences, most theophanies are, nonetheless, temporary; after the deity has revealed his purpose to the visionary, the divine presence withdraws, and the natural world assumes its normal workings. The most enduring instances of theophanies are incarnations, in which the god assumes human (or animal) flesh and remains revealed for the duration of its earthly life. For Christianity, the incarnation of the Second Person of the Trinity as the historical Jesus is the ultimate revelation of God. The Eastern Orthodox churches, in fact, observe January 6 as the Feast of the Theophany, commemorating the Baptism of Jesus. (In the Western churches, January 6 is celebrated as the Feast of Epiphany and recalls the visitation of the Magi to the newborn Jesus.) As narrated in the Gospel accounts (Matthew 3:13–17; Mark 1:9–11; Luke 3:21–22), Jesus' baptism portrays a unique theophany in Christianity – one that features the manifestation of all three Persons of the Trinity: the Father speaks, "This is My beloved Son," as the Son emerges from the waters of the Jordan; and the Spirit descends in the visible form of a dove.

Hinduism, too, has incarnational theophanies in its idea of avatars. In Hinduism, a god may become incarnate more than once through the ages, and each incarnation is known as an avatar (from the Sanskrit *avatāra*, "descent"). The most well-known examples are the ten avatars of Vishnu. The versions vary slightly, but the Garuda Purana provides a standard list: a fish; a tortoise; a boar; a lion-man; a dwarf; the man Parashurama; the man Rama (legendary king of Ayodhya and hero of the Ramayana), the god Krishna; and Siddhartha Gautama (the Buddha). The tenth avatar, Kalki, is anticipated to come at the end of the present age (the *Kali Yuga*) to combat evil and corruption and usher in a new golden age (the *Satya Yuga*). In all cases, avatars become incarnate in order to respond to a specific need of the cosmos.

Although generally Islam eschews theophany in order to safeguard the utter transcendence of God, the notion of theophany appears in the thought of some Sufi Muslims. For instance, the Andalusian Sufi Ibn 'Arabī (1165–1240 CE) developed a cosmology in which all of creation, including humankind, is essentially a theophany. According to Ibn 'Arabī, God desired to know himself in others who know him. His being unknown (both to others and, as one who is known, to himself) caused him sorrow, a creative sorrow out of which he reveals himself through creation. Creation is an exhalation of God, or his shadow; God creates *within* the space of his own breath. Ibn 'Arabī's system is panentheistic, a world in which all is in God and is thus not totally other than God. Creation is necessarily theophanic. In particular, according to Ibn 'Arabī, the divine Names of God are theophanic; through each Name, God reveals to his creation (and, therefore, to himself as well) an attribute of himself.

Commentary

In psychoanalytic theory, mystical experience in general can be explained as misdirected sexual feelings, the mystical ecstasy proving for the sexual energy an outlet without directly engaging the sexual. Also, the psychic struggle between a super-ego and a force placing strictures on it can bring about a theophany when the psyche surrenders to exhaustion.

On the other hand, Jung ascribes theophanies to the unconscious. A theophanic experience, then, could be explained as the active imagination probing the unconscious and assigning to the "vision" a particular theological significance.

Additionally, theophanic visions can be induced through the use of psychedelic drugs. The use of peyote in Native American ceremonies and references to *soma* in the Rig Vedas attest the widespread phenomenon of psychedelic theophanies.

Finally, a theophany may also be explained as a symptom of a psychotic or neurotic condition. Schizophrenics, in particular, may experience hallucinations that they describe as theophanic, particularly when the schizophrenia is marked by delusion, as well.

See also: ◉ Active Imagination ◉ Analytical Psychology ◉ Avatar ◉ Baptism ◉ Bible ◉ Buddhism ◉ Christ ◉ Depth Psychology and Spirituality ◉ Eliade, Mircea ◉ Freud, Sigmund, and Religion ◉ God ◉ God Image ◉ Hallucinations ◉ Hierophany ◉ Hinduism ◉ Ibn al-'Arabi ◉ Incarnation ◉ Jesus ◉ Jung, Carl Gustav, and Religion ◉ Mysticism and Psychoanalysis ◉ Sufis and Sufism

Bibliography

Chittick, W. (1982). The five divine presences: From Al-Qūnawīī to Al-Qayṣarīī. *The Muslim world*, 72:2. (pp. 107–128). Maldon: John Wiley & Sons.

Coogan, M. D. (Ed.). (2001). *New Oxford annotated Bible.* Oxford, England: Oxford University Press.

Corbin, H. (1997). *Alone with the alone*, Princeton, NJ: Princeton University Press.

D'Aquili, E., & Newberg, A. (2000). The neuropsychology of aesthetic, spiritual, and mystical states. In *Zygon* 35:1. Maldon, England: Wiley-Blackwell Publishing.

Ibn 'Arabī (1999). *Al-Futūhāt al-Makkīyah* [The meccan revelations], Beirut: Dar al-Kotob al-Ilmiyah.

Ibn 'Arabī (2001). *Fuṣūṣ al-Hikam* [Bezels of Wisdom], Beirut: Dār al-Mahajjah al-Baydā': Dār al-Rasul al-Akram.

Kakar, S. (1991). *The analyst and the mystic.* Chicago, IL: The University of Chicago Press.

Laine, J. (1989). *Visions of God: Narratives of theophany in the Mahābhārata.* Vienna: Gerold & Co.

Merkur, D. (1993). *Gnosis.* Albany, NY: State University of New York Press.

Moloney, J. (1954). Mother, God, and superego. *Journal of the American Psychoanalytic Association, 2*, 120–151.

Parrinder, G. (1970). *Avatar and incarnation.* London: Faber and Faber.

Smith, H. (1970). Psychedelic theophanies and the religious life. *Journal of Psychedelic Drugs 3*(1), 87–91.

Smith, H. (2005). Do drugs have religious import? A forty year follow-up, In R. Walsh & C. S. Grob (Eds.), *Higher wisdom: Eminent elders explore the continuing impact of psychedelics* (pp. 223–239). Albany, NY: State University of New York Press.

Theosophy

Robert S. Ellwood

"Divine Wisdom" A system of thought emphasizing mystical insight into the inner workings of the divine nature. The term is often used more restrictively to refer to the modern movement inaugurated by the creation of the Theosophical Society in New York in 1975. The principal founders were the enigmatic Russian noble-woman Helena P. Blavatsky (1831–1891) and the U.S. lawyer and journalist Henry Steel Olcott (1832–1907).

Blavatsky articulated an ideological basis for modern Theosophy in her writings, especially the monumental *Isis Unveiled* (1877) and *The Secret Doctrine* (1888). Olcott in turn was the first president of the organization. In his inaugural address of 1875 he referred to the conflict between religion and science which so disturbed many Victorian minds. perceiving both pulpit and laboratory as, in his day, representing shallow, dogmatic views of truth. The real solution, he contended, lay in the redis-covery of an "Ancient Wisdom" known in former times but now nearly forgotten, except to various esoteric lodges and teachers, which could show anew the oneness of matter and spirit, and the way to its realization.

Oneness and the Path constituted the essential mes-sage of the Theosophical Society. It was indicated in different words in the Three Objectives stated by the Society, agreement with which is the only criterion for membership. Abbreviated and in current wording, they are: To form a nucleus of the universal brotherhood of humanity; to encourage the comparative study of religion, philosophy, and science; to investigate unexplained laws of nature, and the powers latent in humanity.

Other teachings, developing implications of these principles and found in the writings of H. P. Blavatsky and other classic Theosophical writings, are also asso-ciated with the movement. One is that there are several "planes" or "bodies" in a human being and correspond-ingly in the cosmos. These embody different aspects of nature, but also in their interrelatedness express the ulti-mate oneness of reality. They are named and divided somewhat differently in different sources, but include the physical, etheric or energy field, the "astral" (roughly emotional and mental-image sphere), mental, "buddhic" or intuitive, and "atmic" or divine.

Each individual is seen as a "monad" or "pilgrim" on a long journey, the "cycle of necessity," passing through countless aeons, worlds, and lifetimes out from the One into the realm of manifestation, therein to experience it in innumerable ways, finally returning to the One enriched by all experience.

A corollary of this teaching is that some individuals are well ahead of the common run of humanity on the pilgrimage. They serve as guides and instructors to those willing to accept their tutelage. These persons are often called Masters, Mahatmas, or Elder Brethren. It was said that Blavatsky had a close relationship with certain of them, and that they had a role in the establishment of the Theosophical Society.

Modern Theosophy's history has been sometimes col-orful, producing several divisions. All Theosophical groups have been relatively small, but have had a signifi-cant cultural influence through their promulgation of concepts important particularly to modern art, poetry, and the "new age" movement.

See also: ❯ Pilgrimage

Bibliography

Ashcraft, W. M. (2002). *The dawn of the new cycle; Point Loma Theosphists and American culture.* Knoxville, TN: University of Tennessee Press.
Blavatsky, H. P. (1877). *Isis unveiled.* New York: J. W. Bouton.
Blavatsky, H. P. (1888). *The secret doctrine.* London: Theosophical Publishing Company.
Blavatsky, H. P. (1889). *The key to Theosophy.* London: Theosophical Publishing Company.
Campbell, B. F. (1980). *Ancient wisdom revived: A history of the Theosoph-ical movement.* Berkeley, CA: University of California Press.
Ellwood, R. (1986). *Theosophy: A modern expression of the wisdom of the Ages.* Wheaton, IL: Theosophical Publishing House.
Prothero, S. (1996). *The White Buddhist: The Asian Odyssey of Henry Steel Olcott.* Bloomington, IN: Indiana University Press.

Traditionalism

Marta Dominguez Diaz

Traditionalism is a contemporary esoteric current that develops a philosophy critical of modernity, based on a reinterpretation of the concept of "*Philosophia Perennis.*" The notion is founded upon monotheistic theologies and it understands the world as a created reality that conceals a system of divine signs. Signs, here, are particular man-ifestations of the Truth; an absolute entity of divine nature manifested in all created things and beings. Perennial philosophers sustain that everything is divinely created and that an ontological metaphysical essence exists in every created being. That is to say, it has always been and therefore its existence is not historically or culturally framed. Owing to its immutability and eternity, this spir-itual essence is regarded as divine. According to Peren-nialists, human spirituality in its diverse manifested religious forms is the way that humankind has developed to participate of this Eternal Quintessence. Since it is believed that human participation in godly essence is entirely divine, human reasoning is regarded as not inter-fering in this process of divine apprehension.

From its early formulations in the late antiquity, with thinkers such as the Christian neo-Platonists Ficino and Pico, to its flourishing during the Renaissance and its later modern and post-modern adaptations, Perennial philosophy has been expressed in diverse ways, while remaining faithful to its driving ideas: Firstly, Perennial philosophy is understood to be both divinely received and beyond human action; Secondly, Perennial Philosophy assumes a divine original spirit in each being, who is aware of its originality. This process gradually distances the spirit from its source beginning immediately after Creation. When people wish to regain the absoluteness of the origin, religious experiences are meant to be open accesses to the Divine, a way of returning to the original standpoint; and, lastly, the created world is ectypal of the primordial essence; there exist various explanations – remarkably, the Neo-Platonist and the neo-Pythagorean – on how this reproduction process occurs.

History

Although this tenets have been present in western esoteric thought since the third century AD it was not since the Renaissance that the actual term "*Philosophia perennis*" was literally used. It first appears in Agostino Steuco's (1497–1548) book "*De perenni philosophia libri X*" (1540), and it was used to describe scholasticism as the referential core from which all Christian teachings derive. The notion was later employed by the mathematician Gottfried Leibniz (1646–1716) who uses it to designate a universal mystical core, not only existing in Christianity but common to all the World Religions. The notion "*Philosophia Perennis*" reappears in the twentieth century in the work of the English novelist Aldous Huxley (1894–1963). In his 1945s "*The Perennial Philosophy*," Huxley describes it as a divine metaphysical entity existing in all substantial things and beings, connecting the physical, substantial world to the Transcendent. Furthermore, for Huxley this "*Philosophia Perennis*," is something with basics that have been apprehended and incorporated in the wisdom of peoples of every region in the world since the origins of humankind, but has only been more sophisticatedly articulated by what he called "higher religions" – meaning the main world religions: the three monotheistic creeds, Buddhism and Hinduism. Accordingly, the plurality of religions of the world is, in this view, only a kaleidoscope of diverse manifestations of one unique Divine Truth, generally referred to – among modern authors – with the term "Tradition." Tradition is for Traditionalists what the inner spirit was for former Perennialists, eternal, infinite, unaffected by contextual variables, cross-cultural and a-historical.

Although Huxley's work already made use of the term to build up a criticism towards the "modern world," it was the French thinker René Guénon (1886–1951) who popularized the turned into critique term. Thus, it can be suggested, that Traditionalism uses Perennialism to elaborate a variety of criticisms towards "the Modern."

In Guénonian Traditionalism, European civilization has progressively distanced itself from the "Tradition" that once was part of. This lack of memory, the forgetting of Tradition makes European civilization entering a state of dementia, ultimately responsible for the supposed terminal decline in which Europe is in modern times immersed. Since it is only "Tradition" that can produce the foundation of a genuine civilization, and its wholeness is somewhat quintessentially embodied in "Traditional religions," only the return to this common wisdom can save Europeans or Westerners in general, from the debacle. Christianity is generally discredited of being capable of such transformation. Hence, Traditionalists rely on non-western religious wisdoms with the hope of, individual by individual, return to the West, its original spiritual sense, and with it saving from the moral crisis, if not the whole civilization as such, the souls of those individual spiritually-awakened westerners.

Despite of the fact that Perennialism has a longstanding trajectory, its instrumentalization as a critical discourse is much more recent. Traditionalism as such originates in Europe in the interwar period, taking its inspiration from the writings of René Guénon. The first Traditionalist groups were established before the Second World War, and they were the seed of what was going to become a relevant movement of international dimensions. In 1948–1950, the initial Guénonian school suffered its first division, creating the scission of a group led by one of the most prominent Guénonian disciples, the Swiss Muslim convert Frithjof Schuon (1907–1998). Decades later, Traditionalism has taken three main directions: (1) the one of Schuon, who created the western Sufi order Maryamiyya, that grew in importance in Europe, North-America and uprooted in Iran led by Dr. Seyyed Hossein Nasr (b. 1933), (2) the political orientation of the Italian Julius Evola (1898–1974), who transformed it into a post Second World War fascist-inclined ideology inspiring some Italian terrorist groups of that time, and (3) the scholarly approach of the Romanian Mircea

Eliade (1907–1986), who turned Traditionalism into an hermeneutical perspective to be used for the comparative study of religions.

In Religion

Since its inception, Traditionalism has been closely connected to Western forms of Sufism. The first followers of Sufism appeared in the West at the beginning of the twentieth century – writers such as Doris Lessing and Robert Graves. There have been other famous Traditionalist converts, but it is by far the figure of René Guénon, who has been most influential in inspiring many western Traditionalists' conversion to Islam. Coming from a catholic family, it is sometimes said, although it has not been proved yet, that Guénon was first initiated into Hinduism through the line of Shankarâchârya. However, he is more famous for moving to Cairo in 1911 – where he did live the rest of his live – and where had entered Sufism, adopting the Muslim name of "Abd aw-Wahid Yahya."

Traditionalist thought has also been crucially influential in the academic field of religious studies where instead of Traditionalists are generally called Perennialists. The school initiated by Eliade posed the notion of "mystical experience" at the center of a scholarly debate about the particular/universal nature of religious feelings. Scholars such as Rudolf Otto, Ananda Kentish Coomaraswamy, Walter Terence Stace, Daisetz Teitaro Suzuki and Robert Forman are outspoken voices of this trend, decisive in the emergence of an academic school specialized in comparative religion. Perennialist authors have supported the idea that mystical experiences are ephemeral but ineffable, unmediated contacts with the Divine. They belong to the "One Core" though find expression in multiple forms, becoming what all Traditions worldwide have in common. Furthermore, in the hermeneutics of religious studies, the concept is commonly used to question the authority of empirical methods seeking objectivity to prioritize the value of the individual pulse and subjectivity. Today, authors such as William Chittick, James Cutsinger, Huston Smith, Harry Oldmeadow, and Seyyed Hossein Nasr use markedly Traditionalist perspectives in their scholarly works.

Critics of the Traditionalist approach suggest that Traditionalists apply Perennialist signifying layers to Sacred Texts, meanings that the Text itself does not necessarily contain; critics suggest that such misinterpretation derives from Traditionalists' a priori loyalty to their Traditionalist ideological stance.

In Psychology

Traditionalism has supposed an important influence in the development of new trends of psychological theory, remarkably Transpersonal psychology. Transpersonal psychology is a modality that takes into consideration some aspects hitherto neglected by the previous schools of psychological thought. Transpersonal authors wanted to promote altered states of consciousness and mystical experiences as effective tools to consummate people's potentialities. The term "Transpersonal" is here used to denote that which goes beyond the self. Hence, for Transpersonal psychologists, psychical cure can only occur by abandoning the perceived as constraining self in order to gain access to an Eternal meaningful reality of esoteric nature. This state may eventually help individuals to overcome "negative" feelings such as guilt or unease.

Transpersonal psychology is commonly known as the "fourth force," because it aims to overcome the limitations that Transpersonal psychologists perceive in the so-called "first force" (Freudian thought), "second force" (behaviorist school), and, "third force" (humanist approach). It yearns to develop a radical new perspective by conceptualizing a leveled human psyche. Accordingly, it considers that both psychoanalytical Freudian thought and behavioral theorist have approached the lower levels of this scale, but have failed to address the higher more sophisticated stages, those of the Transpersonal belonging to the transcendental.

The work of the Greek-Armenian Traditionalist George Ivanovich Gurdjieff (1877–1949) has been of particular relevance for the Transpersonal movement, specifically with regard to the insistence on a need for spiritual awakening and his theorization of "The Fourth Way" notion. Among the most prominent predecessor psychologists of the Transpersonal school are William James (1842–1910) and Carl Gustav Jung (1875–1961). In his Gifford lecture (1901) at the University of Edinburgh (published in 1902 under the title of the varieties of religious experience) James became the first in supporting the study of religious experience using psychology's hermeneutics. Well-versed in a wide variety of religiosities, ranging from Sufism, Buddhism and Vedanta, to the New Church, American Transcendentalism, the Theosophical Society, or some forms of Christian mysticism, James perceived the depth of human psyche as primordially spiritual.

Also attracted by several forms of religiosities was the Swiss Carl Gustav Jung. A former disciple of Sigmund Freud, Jung strongly disagreed with the Freudian conceptualization of religion as an outcome of neurosis. In contrast, he considered religion as genuine expressions of the psyche's universal patterns of human behavior. He typified religious feelings (mystical, philosophical, doctrinal and so on) in accordance to the existing behavioral models. Further, in line with Perennialism, he suggested that religiosities were outer expressions of a "universal collective unconscious."

Despite these earlier contributions, it was not until the 1970s that Transpersonal psychology properly became a consistent, though controversial trend of psychological thought. The actual term "Transpersonal psychology" was for the first time employed by the Czech Stanislav Grof (b. 1931) who became famous for using LSD with his patients to help them "recover" pre and peri-natal memories. Since the 1970s, Transpersonal psychology has experienced a significant increase in popularity, when ideas of spiritual growth have extended beyond the psychological arena influencing various forms of New Age ethos and other manifestations of new spiritualities (notably, neo-paganism).

Transpersonal psychology is markedly Perennialist in that it assumes a timeless a-historical dimension common to all human beings, and it proposes a return to the original source – here labeled as "High Consciousness." It also shows a notable Traditionalist influence in that it uses a Perennialist perspective to build up its criticism on modern society in general – its materialist excesses and superficial concerns – and in particular on modern psychological trends. However, Transpersonal psychology differs from Perennialism and Traditionalism alike, in its notorious, sometimes posed as problematic and contradictory, emphasis on the self that contrasts with the claim of abandoning the self to embrace a collective wisdom. Perennial philosophy also attributed a seed of divine nature contained in every individual, but the stress the Transpersonal circles put on self-experience denotes an individualistic shift not present in Perennialist or Traditionalist discourses. Further, even though Transpersonal's Higher Consciousness entails some kind of spirituality, Transpersonal psychology is in most cases detached from the Perennialist and Traditionalist theistic component. Nevertheless, its non theistic approach has not exempted it from criticism. Transpersonal psychology's incorporation of Perennialist/Traditionalist principles into psychology has brought about fierce criticism from more secular-oriented psychologist sectors.

See also: ❯ Eliade, Mircea ❯ James, William ❯ Jung, Carl Gustav ❯ Jung, Carl Gustav, and Eastern Religious Traditions ❯ Jung, Carl Gustav, and Gnosticism ❯ Jung, Carl Gustav, and Religion ❯ Jungian Self ❯ Monotheism ❯ Orthodoxy

Bibliography

Bocking, B. (2006). Mysticism: No experience needed (Vol. 7). *Diskus*. Retrieved 17 August 2008, from www.basr.ac.uk/diskus/diskus7/bocking.htm.

Coomaraswamy, A. K. (1943). Eastern wisdom and western knowledge. *Isis, 4*, 359–363.

Guénon, R. (1975). *The crisis of the modern world*. London: Luzac.

Heelas, P., & Woodhead, L. (2000). Universalization. In *Religion in modern times: an interpretive anthology* (pp. 386–428). Oxford, England: Blackwell Publishers.

Hunter, I. M. L. (1987). James, Williams. In R. L. Gregory (Ed.), *The Oxford companion to the mind*. Oxford, England: Oxford University Press.

Huxley, A. (1945). *The perennial philosophy*. New York: Harper & Brothers.

Huxley, A. (2004). *The perennial philosophy*. New York: Harper Perennial Modern Classics.

King, R. (2005). Mysticism and spirituality. In J. R. Hinnells (Ed.), *The Routledge companion to the study of religion*. London: Routledge.

Lings, M., & Minnaar, C. (2007). *The underlying religion: An introduction to the perennial philosophy*. Bloomington, IN: World Wisdom.

Oldmeadow, H. (2005). *The betrayal of tradition: Essays on the spiritual crisis of modernity*. Bloomington, IN: World Wisdom.

Oldmeadow, H. (2008). *Mediations: Essays on religious pluralism and the perennial philosophy*. San Rafael, CA: Sophia Perennis.

Putnam, R. A. (1997). *The Cambridge companion to William James*. Cambridge, England: Cambridge University Press.

Rooth, G. (2008). *Prophet for a dark age: A companion to the works of René Guénon*. Brighton, England: Sussex Academic Press.

Schmidt-Biggemann, W. (2004). *Philosophia perennis: Historical outlines of Western spirituality in ancient, medieval and early modern thought*. Dordrecht, the Netherlands: Springer.

Schuon, F. (1975). *The transcendent unity of religions*. London: Harper & Row.

Sedgwick, M. (2003). *Western Sufism and traditionalism*. Retrieved August 15, 2008, from www1.aucegypt.edu/faculty/sedgwick/trad/write/WSuf.htm.

Sedgwick, M. J. (2004). *Against the modern world: Traditionalism and the secret intellectual history of the twentieth century*. Oxford, England: Oxford University Press.

Sharf, R. H. (1998). Experience. In M. C. Taylor (Ed.), *Critical terms for religious studies* (pp. 94–115). Chicago, IL: Chicago University Press.

Steuco, A. (1542). *De perenni philosophia libri X*. Basle: Nicolaum Bryling. et Sebastianum Francken.

Tart, C. T. (1992). *Transpersonal psychologies: Perspectives on the mind from seven great spiritual traditions*. New York: Harper San Francisco.

Waterfield, R. E. (1987). *René Guénon and the future of the west: The life and writings of a 20th century metaphysician*. Wellingborough, England: Crucible.

Transcendence

Todd DuBose

Transcendence is an experience central to both spirituality and therapeutic transformation. In fact, it may be considered the most important and distinguishing factor in any form of liberation as transcendence is an experience of moving from one mode of existence to another, for various reasons, and done in a myriad of ways. Understanding the nature of transcendence as a phenomenon is essential to any theory of change.

Transcendence originally meant "going beyond or outside" one's situation. This sense of transcendence is clarified only in relation to what was meant by "immanence." The differentiation of transcendence from immanence was a theological concern as it became central for theologians to distinguish between the nature, relationship and place of God in contradistinction to humankind and the rest of the natural world. While these apologists sought to defend God's existence as immutable and as the uncreated Creator of life, other thinkers took a contrary route than proposed God is immanent within, and as, nature. The latter positions became known as pantheism or pan-en-theism. Either way, the debates, often ending in accusations of heresy, sought to understand and/or explain a metaphysical puzzle of how finite existence comes to know and relate to the infinite.

Part of the difficulty in resolving the puzzle of transcendence and immanence was the presumption that both realities were places in space and time. In other words, transcendence was a state of existence beyond or out of physical existence. Immanence, on the contrary, was finite physical existence. This raised problems for theologians, though, particularly Augustine of Hippo (354–440), who defended the belief that God could not be understood in terms of created existence in time and space because doing so would result in God's eventual decay and mutability along with the rest of immanent reality. A decaying god is not a god at all for Augustine and other likeminded thinkers (Augustine 398/1961; Fitzgerald, 1999).

Moreover, trying to resolve the finite/infinite dilemma by stating that the ability to understand transcendence is simultaneously professing the grandeur of God and stating that the infinite mystery is simply beyond the grasp of the finite mind left a blatant inconsistency unaddressed: How can a finite person "know" an unknowable transcendent reality? Nevertheless, said other apologists, the very fact that one can even *imagine* a transcendent God was evidence enough of the empirical reality of transcendence.

With the impact of logical positivism and naturalistic empiricism, however, transcendence as an immaterial reality is simply rejected as a viable possibility and no amount of faith in the unseen was able to squelch the need among natural scientists for observable proof as a prerequisite for assent. Empirical theologians of "The Chicago School" focused their energies on responding to the apparent scientific/religious rift, gaining particular ground with process theology based on Alfred North Whitehead's thought (Meland, 1969). The tradition of empirical theology opened other possibilities of understanding transcendence as a natural phenomenon that is consistent with natural science convictions while remaining meaningful to human significance.

Transcendence is also understanding in other ways within various religious traditions. In Judaism, for instance, transcendence has been understood as that which is "hidden" or inexhaustible, or, better yet, as the overwhelming power of the numinous. Thus, we hear of the inability to look on the face of God. What is also emphasized in Judaism is the poverty of language to capture and denote what is represented by transcendence. References to the divine are pointed differently in Hebrew or written in transliterated English as G-d. In Buddhism, we experience the possibility of *shunyata*, or emptiness, the void, or no-thing, which transcends attachments and binding images. This is achieved *within* immanence, which is unlike the Hindu goal of escaping rebirth by transcending material desires. Both Buddhism and Hinduism, therefore, see transcendence as the state of relinquishing attachments, a theme which is present in any ascetic tradition. For Islam, and other traditions emphasizing the absolute transcendence of the divine, however, any link of immanence with God drifts lands us in into idolatrous conditions and should be abandoned.

Another very interesting conundrum in the history of transcendence, a nuance of the finite/infinite dilemma, is the paradox of personalistic relationships with God, when God's transcendence is supposedly beyond any personalistic and/or anthropomorphic representation. Nevertheless, transcendent experiences are related to prayerful and mystical experiences of intimate encounters with God as person, despite belief in the Eckhartian flavored understanding of the experience of God as beyond any conceptualization of God. Understanding of God as an enigmatic experience beyond any and all theistic conceptualizations. These challenges to understanding transcendence in theological and religious traditions join other philosophical ones.

Immanuel Kant (1724–1804) stood at the interstices of theology, philosophy, and psychology, and defined the transcendent as that which lies beyond what our faculty of knowledge can legitimately know, thus, placing the transcendent beyond the scope of epistemology. At the same time, Kant saw the "transcendental" as the very conditions of the possibility of knowledge itself (Kant, 1781/2008). The father of transcendental phenomenology, Edmund Husserl (1859–1938), borrowing from his teacher Wilhelm Dilthey (1833–1911), understood transcendence as that which is beyond or separate from the constructs of our consciousness (Husserl, 1962). Martin Heidegger (1889–1976), Husserl's student and assistant, came to a view of transcendence that reversed his teacher's position. For Heidegger, transcendence is always and already occurring within the context of our finitude and throwness (Heidegger, 1962). States of consciousness, therefore, are not separate from the world, but are contextual and co-constructive of experience in the world.

Transcendence, then, becomes a hermeneutical activity for Heidegger in which the interpretive process unveils authentic ways of being in the world. Jean Paul Sartre (1905–1980), the French existential phenomenologist who saw much of his work as a continuation of Heidegger's project, saw transcendence as describing various relations of the self to the object oriented world, including our relations with others. For Sartre, the "for-itself" is sometimes called transcendence, as such a state of existence seeks the freedom to create one's meaningful existence. This is opposed, for Sartre, to an unfree existence in which one forfeits one's subjectivity in collusion with the other's objectifying gaze (Sartre, 1956). Finally, the Swiss psychiatrist Karl Jaspers (1883–1969) saw transcendence as that which is beyond time and space, or what he called the encompassing, which is ultimate non-objectivity (no-thing-ness) (Jaspers, 1971).

Current discussions of transcendence continue to resolved age old dilemmas of describing the experience in ways that are respectful of freedom and transformation while attempting to resist reductionism. This is the case in theology, philosophy, and psychology. A few remaining issue merit address, however, for the future of clarifying transcendence.

Commentary

What is vital in a contemporary understanding of transcendence, particularly as it relates to immanence, is to understand it as a *qualitative* experience and not to equate it with a location in physical space and time, or as something that can be measured. We are still squeamish about immaterial realities. The recent debates on reducing transcendence to genetics and/or neuroscience are cases in point (Hamer, 2005; Zimmer, 2005). Although it can be relieving to align with the "hard" scientists in order to receive their kind of evidence as further legitimization of transcendence. At the same time, it very well may be the inaccurate approach with which to address this matter. Something seems anti-climatic about knowing that God's name is "Gene VMAT2!" Again, the perpetuated mistake in approaching transcendence in this way is in misunderstanding transcendence as a person, place, or thing. Transcendence is an *experience of liberation*, a type of *qualia* that is invisible, immeasurable, and incomparable, because not substantial.

Is the relationship between transcendence and immanence oppositional? Can one hold a respectable postmodern position without fusing transcendence with immanence? If transcendence is immanence then how can we discern one experience from the other? These questions presume a faulty assumption, which is that immanence and transcendence are antagonistic polarities. The morphing of our understanding of transcendence has shown the contrary to this conclusion. The relationship between transcendence and immanence is a dialectical one, and, moreover, one in which each one cannot be understood without presuming the other. Tom Driver (1985) noted how transcendence is radical immanence. As Jean-Luc Nancy (1993) has proposed, we understand freedom only in light of "throwness."

Finally, although discussions of transcendence as ascendance, as escape, as dissociation, or as a Gnostic extrication of our physicality mitigate against an existential conviction of transcendence within immanence, these experiences are nonetheless popular understandings of transcendence. The desire to escape one state of existence for another is at the heart of trance induction and other religious rituals. Opening ourselves to "other worlds" can give perspective to this one. Dissociating during the horrors of physical and sexual abuse can be the only freedom one may have during such a tragic time. Imagination of other worlds, other comportments, and other possibilities is perhaps the most powerful form of transcendence available to any of us, and can be considered an existential. On the other hand, transcendence as escape is the project of the suicidal candidate, though a project carried out through a narrowed attunement to possibilities. Moreover, encouraging otherworldliness as a solution to confronting the complexity, pain, and suffering in this existence can lead to a lack of concern for this life at least, and a hatred for it at best, much like Friedrich

Nietzsche (1844–1900) predicted. Agreeing with the sentiments of Nietzsche, Erich Fromm (1900–1980) noted that the pull away from life and toward a Freudian return to inorganicity is more appropriately driven by an escape from freedom. Contrary to common assumption, we often fear the freedom from which and to which transcendence delivers us (Fromm, 1941).

In fact, what may fuel the pain of this life may be the perpetual desire to transcend-as-escape it. The remedy to our unnecessary suffering, then, may be to give oneself over to another kind of immanent transcendence, which lives out life all its pathos, as Michel Henry (1922–2002) advised, and experience the paradox of transcendence: We transcend existence when we enter it (Henry, 2002). This is not an invitation to ignore oppression or deafen calls for liberation and deliverance. On the contrary, an invitation to live life in its fullness and uniqueness can very well inspire a more vivid respect and sensitivity to creating free, meaningful, and fulfilling lives for each and every person and/or sentient creation.

See also: ❯ Daseinsanalysis ❯ Hermeneutics ❯ Homo Religiosus ❯ Lived Theology ❯ Meaning of Human Existence ❯ Transcendent Function

Bibliography

Augustine, A. (398/1961). *Confessions* (R. S. Pine-Coffin, Trans.). New York: Penguin Books.

Driver, T. (1985). *Patterns of grace: Human experience as word of God.* Landham, MD: University of America Press.

Fitzgerald, A. (Ed.). (1999). *Augustine through the ages: An encyclopedia.* Grand Rapids, MI: W. B. Eerdmans.

Fromm, E. (1941). *Escape from freedom.* New York: Farrar and Rinehart.

Hamer, D. (2005). *The God gene: How faith is hardwired into our genes.* New York: Anchor.

Heidegger, M. (1962). *Being and time.* (J. Macquarrie & E. Robinson, Trans.). Oxford, England: Basil Blackwell.

Henry, M. (2002). *I am the truth: Toward a philosophy of Christianity.* (S. Emanuel Trans.). Stanford, CA: Stanford University Press.

Husserl, E. (1962). *Ideas: General introduction to pure phenomenology.* (W. Gibson Trans.). New York: Collier.

Jaspers, K. (1971). *Philosophy of existence.* (R. Graubau Trans.). Philadelphia, PA: University of Pennsylvania Press.

Kant, I. (2008). *Critique of pure reason.* (M. Weigelt Trans.). New York: Penguin. (Original work published 1781).

Meland, B. (Ed.). (1969). *The future of empirical theology* (Vol. VII). Chicago, IL: The University of Chicago Press.

Nancy, J. L. (1993). *The experience of freedom.* Stanford, CA: Stanford University Press.

Sartre, J. P. (1956). *Being and nothingness: An essay on phenomenological ontology.* (H. Barnes Trans.). New York: Philosophical Library.

Zimmer, C. (2005). *The soul made flesh: The discovery of the brain – and how it changed the world.* Tampa, FL: Free Press.

Transcendent Function

Ann Casement

Transcendent Function is a term that first appears in a paper Jung wrote in 1916 where he states it is neither mysterious nor metaphysical but is, instead, a psychological function "comparable in its way to a mathematical function of the same name, which is a function of real and imaginary numbers. The psychological 'transcendent function' arises from the union of conscious and unconscious contents" (Jung, 1960: 69). As Jung states, the unconscious behaves in a *compensatory* or complementary manner to consciousness and vice-versa. If consciousness is too one-sided, the unconscious may break through via slips of the tongue.

The transcendent function is so called because it enables the transition of contents from the unconscious to consciousness as well as the other way around. In analysis, the analyst can mediate the transcendent function for the analysand through the transference and in this way the patient experiences the analyst as indispensable. Jung defined his approach to transference as "constructive" which is based on evaluating the symbol via dreams and fantasies. It is the symbol that is "the best possible expression for a complex fact not yet clearly apprehended by consciousness" (Jung, 1960: 75).

In his paper on the transcendent function, Jung writes about his constructive approach to dream analysis. In order to exemplify this, he cites the dream of a woman patient in which someone gives her a wonderful, richly ornamented, antique sword dug up out of an ancient burial mound. He interpreted this as her need for the inner father she needs to relate to in order to help her disidentify with remaining in a perpetual passive childlike state. Her actual father was a passionate, energetic man and it is this energy that the patient needs to find in her inner father in order to live life fully.

According to Jung, the self-regulating function of the psyche can be helped through dreams but more importantly through fantasy which enables unconscious material to become activated through activating the transcendent function. In order to do this, he advocates the use of *active imagination* via drawing, painting or sculpting which can give expression to unconscious material which may be expressed in a mood. Critical attention must be eliminated during this process and creative formulation allowed to break through. The second, more important stage of *active imagination* is for ego not to be overwhelmed by unconscious contents. An important way forward is the development of an inner dialog in bringing together the opposites for the production of the third, which is the symbol. Through this transcending of opposites, consciousness is widened by confrontation with unconscious contents and the transcendent function proceeds not without aim and purpose but can enable an individual to move beyond pointless conflict and avoid one-sidedness.

As Jung says, truth, law, guidance is said to be nowhere save in the mind. "Thus the unconscious is credited with all those faculties which the West attributes to God. . .the transcendent function. . .the phenomenon of spontaneous compensation, being beyond the control of man, is quite in accord with the formula 'grace' or the 'will of God'" (Jung, 1958: 506).

The mediatory process of the transcendent function forms the material of construction "in which thesis and antithesis both play their part. . .in the shaping of which the opposites are united (in) the living symbol" (Jung, 1971: 480). This symbol formation through the mediation of the transcendent function in the conflict of opposites is to be found in the struggle between Jesus and Satan, Buddha and Mara, or the regeneration of Faust through the pact with the devil.

Transference, the Transcendent Function, and Transcendence

The analytical psychologist, Ann Ulanov's paper of the above title illustrates how transference, like dreams and symptoms, inevitably introduces the transcendent function in the course of analytic treatment. "The transcendent function is part of the compensatory function of the transference" (Ulanov, 1997: 125). The analyst and analysand consciously take up what the psyche does spontaneously in producing opposite points of view in order to reach its goal of individuating or broadening consciousness. The analysand is dependent on the analyst's involvement and Jung's approach to the analytic process "consisted essentially in a dialogue and a mutuality requiring the emotional involvement of the analyst for change to occur" (Casement, 2001: 79). Ulanov also alerts to the dangers of analyst and analysand "bumping around in the psyche" together which can take the form of inflation, seduction, power plays, and defensive intellectualizing.

"The transcendent function inaugurates transition to arrival of the new" (Ulanov, 1997: 126). This initiates the arrival of a third point of view which surpasses the conflicting opposites and creates a space between consciousness and the unconscious wherein symbols arise. "In the process of the transcendent function we not only struggle with opposites in ourselves, we also inhabit the opposites of our historical time" (Ulanov, 1997: 137).

Ulanov relates the transcendent function and transference to transcendence which is not an abstraction but exists in the here and now. "Spirit and body go together. Transcendence always effects a striking conjunction of the particular and the universal, the awe-inspiring and the humdrum, the vast and the concrete." She quotes Jung as follows: "Analysis should release an experience that grips or falls upon us as from above, an experience that has substance and body . . . . It must be organically true, that is, in and of our own being. If I were to symbolize it I would choose the Annunciation" (Jung, 1925/1989: 80).

Jung and Hegel

The analytical psychologist, Hester Solomon, states that

▸ the schema of psychological functioning that Jung developed in the *Transcendent Function* has a parallel in the philosophical vision of Hegel's dialectic. In the immediacy of the disintegrating psychological experiences that he went through in the years between 1912–1916, Jung swung from one pole of experience to the other... Through this dynamic interplay, he was able to achieve a personal synthesis, a position of relative integration between the conscious and unconscious attitudes. So Jung himself was living the dialectic (Solomon, 2007).

As Solomon goes on to say

▸ Hegel's grand design is an attempt to understand reality as constructed historically in pairs of opposites that are not dichotomous but are rather in intimate, dynamic, albeit oppositional relation to one another. The dialectical model allows for a twofold view of reality, on the one hand in terms of bipolar opposites in dynamic relation to each other, and on the other hand a unity of opposites towards which each strives...The task of dialectical philosophy is to strive for greater and greater comprehension until a kind of totality of understanding is achieved. This is what Hegel called 'absolute reason (Solomon, 2007).

The tripartite structure of the dialectical process, like the transcendent function, expressed as thesis/antithesis/synthesis reflects an archetypal pattern with the third position consisting of a resolution that has the capacity to hold two apparent opposites together. It is through the tension and conflict created by the dynamic relationship that a creative, forward-moving resolution is achieved between, for example, self and another whether it be mother/infant or analyst/analysand. This is also to be met in the "Christian idea of the threefold nature of God as Father, Son and Holy Spirit; Spinoza and Descartes' threefold vision of reality as consisting of three different kinds of substance (thought, nature and God); the Socratic dialectic whereby rigid positions are confronted and thereby changed by adroit questioning...all attest to the ubiquitous, deep structural nature of the tripartite dialectical vision" (Solomon, 2007).

Solomon's conclusion is as follows: "Jung's concept of the transcendent function and Hegel's dialectical vision both seek to address similar understandings of psychic reality and as such demonstrate a remarkable similarity of structure" (Solomon, 2007).

Transcendent Function and Reflective Function

The analytical psychologist, Jean Knox, explores Jung's concept of the transcendent function in relation to research on the reflective function in attachment theory. She states: "The concept of reflective function has emerged to explain the vital role that the parent plays in facilitating the child's capacity to relate to other people as mental and emotional being with their own thoughts, desires, intentions, beliefs and emotions" (Knox, 2003: 10).

Jung was using the term transcendent function to describe an individual's capacity to tolerate difference in others and also in oneself. "In attachment theory it is the development of this capacity which defines reflective function, in that reflective function depends upon the awareness that other people have minds of their own with beliefs and judgments that may differ from one's own...Both transcendent function and reflective function are descriptions of the capacity to relate to other people as psychologically as well as physically separate" (Knox, 2003: 164).

She goes on to say:

▶ There would seem to be sound neurophysiological support for Jung's model of the transcendent function as a dialog between conscious and unconscious processes of appraisal. Allan Schore draws on empirical research to support his view that the right hemisphere is predominant in "performing valence-dependent, automatic, pre-attentive appraisals of emotional facial expressions" and that the orbito-frontal system, in particular, is important in assembling and monitoring relevant past and current experiences, including their affective and social values. Crucially, he extends this appraisal function of the orbito-frontal cortex to underpin reflective function itself (Knox, 2003: 198).

It is this capacity for integrating opposites, emotional appraisal, and psychological separateness that Jung was pointing to in his concept of individuation in which the transcendent function plays such a major role. If "the ego is too unstable and weak to moderate impulsivity enough to allow for the constellation of the transcendent function...Shadow roles and impulses are acted out, without the appearance of a transcendent function to bring about an integration of opposites" (Stein, 1998: 124).

See also: ❧ Active Imagination ❧ Dreams ❧ Jung, Carl Gustav ❧ Psychoanalysis ❧ Transcendence ❧ Transference

Bibliography

Casement, A. (2001). *Carl Gustav Jung.* London: Sage Publications.

Jung, C. G. (1925/1989). *Analytical psychology: Notes of the seminar* (W. McGuire, Ed.). Princeton, NJ: Princeton University Press.

Jung, C. G. (1958). On the Tibetan book of the Great Liberation. In *Psychology and religion: West and East* (Vol. 11, p. 506). London: Routledge & Kegan Paul.

Jung, C. G. (1960). The transcendent function. In *The structure and dynamics of the psyche* (Vol. 8, pp. 69, 75). London: Routledge & Kegan Paul.

Jung, C. G. (1971). Definitions. In *Psychological types* (Vol. 6, p. 480). London: Routledge & Kegan Paul.

Knox, J. (2003). *Archetype, attachment, analysis: Jungian psychology and the emergent mind.* Hove, England: Brunner-Routledge.

Solomon, H. (2007). The transcendent function and Hegel's dialectic vision. In A. Casement (Ed.). *Who owns Jung?* (pp. 270, 271, 273, 288) London: Karnac Books.

Stein, M. (1998). *Jung's map of the soul.* Peru, IL: Open Court Publishing Company.

Ulanov, A. B. (1997). Transference, the transcendent function, and transcendence. *The Journal of Analytical Psychology, 42*(1), 119–138.

Transcendental Meditation

Nicholas Grant Boeving

Transcendental Meditation, popularly known as TM, was introduced by Maharishi Mahesh Yogi (1917–2008) in 1958. Today, its programs and related initiatives are represented on six continents, claim upwards of six million adherents and boast campuses in The United States, Mexico, England, India, and China.

It was not until the Beatles went to India and met with its founder, however, that TM made its appearance on the Western stage. Subsequently, many artists followed suit and brought with them into the Mahrishi's fold innumerable devotees. Such wide-spread – if fleeting - ferver was enough to win The Maharishi the cover of Time Magazine in 1975.

The techniques of meditation are claimed, by its founder to be "a path to God." To follow this path however, TM does not require any change in either faith or belief.

TM has, since its inception, invited and encouraged scientific investigation of its claims. Because of this remarkable openness, a wealth of studies has been conducted on the salutary effects of which practitioners of TM claim to be in receipt. The first wave of these studies was published in the early 1970s and found that the techniques utilized by practitioners of TM led to a state of "restful alertness." Subsequent studies have investigated TM's role in reducing blood pressure, obesity, depression, and a host of other afflictions – somatic and otherwise. These results, however compelling, are far from being undisputed, however.

This scientific turn, while relatively new in the history of religions, is certainly not restricted to TM, though it *is* emblematic of the trend to psychologize religion and in particular spriritual praxes. TM is a particularly salient example of how the religious and psychological horizens can be imperceptibly fused in a single tradition.

Criticism of TM has been harsh – even vituperative. Former members have come forward alleging that it is a cult, entangling the unsuspecting in the insidious web of its rhetoric. Adherents, on the other hand, hail the triumph of TM as the first truly universal spiritual practice scientifically proven to aid in evolution. In any event, TMs reception in the United States has irrevocably altered the landscape of the American religious imagination.

See also: ❂ Contemplative Prayer ❂ Meditation

Bibliography

Gilpin, G. (2006). *The Maharishi effect: A personal journey through the movement that transformed American spirituality.* New York: Tarcher-Penguin.

Mason, P. (2005). *Maharishi Mahesh yogi: The biography of the man who gave transendental meditation to the world.* Merchaxtville, NJ: Evolution Publishing.

Persinger, M. (1980). *TM and cult mania.* Hanover, MA: Christopher Pub House.

Transference

Benjamin Beit-Hallahmi

The idea of transference is at the center of the classical psychoanalytic theory of object relations. Early object-relations patterns, formed by our experiences within the family, become consolidated, and remain relatively fixed throughout adult life. They are revealed as emotional reactions in interpersonal situations which are highly intense and realistically speaking quite improper. Any strong emotional reaction formed quickly in an interpersonal encounter, such as love or hate at first sight represent a transference reaction, i.e., a reaction to a present object which is in reality an acting out of a childhood reaction to one's parents or other close figures.

Sigmund Freud claimed to have discovered transference through the practice of psychotherapy according to his technique of psychoanalysis. He reported that those being analyzed by him were not ready to regard the analyst merely, and realistically, as a helper and adviser. The analysand sees in the analyst "the return, the reincarnation, of some important figure out of his childhood or past, and consequently transfers on to him feelings and reactions" (Freud, 1940: 192). These feelings and reactions are ambivalent, comprising both positive and affectionate as well as negative and hostile attitudes towards the analyst, who is put in the place of the analysand's parents, either father or mother. The transference is made conscious by the analyst, and is handled by showing that the transference, is a re-experiencing of emotional relations which had their origin in the earliest object-relations in childhood.

Positive transference serves to create an attachment to the analyst, as the analysand seeks to please the analyst and win his applause and love. In Freud's phrasing, it becomes the true motive force of the patient's collaboration; his weak ego becomes strong; under its influence he achieves things that would ordinarily be beyond his power; he leaves off his symptoms and seems apparently to have recovered – merely for the sake of the analyst. Another advantage of transference is that the analysand produces and acts out a life-story, with the earliest attachments at its center.

But the transference phenomenon exists outside the analytic situation. As described by Freud, it is a universal phenomenon of the human mind, which dominates the whole of each person's relations to his human environment. In other words, early object relations are acted out in every instance of human contact and in every instance of interpersonal fantasy.

Transference is a particular form of the more general mechanism of projection, and as we know projective hypotheses explain the contents of religious beliefs as reflecting specific human experiences and fantasies. In psychoanalytic writings, projection may be a general perceptual mode, externalizing internal processes or needs. In both cases the result is perceptual distortion. Psychoanalysis suggests an iconic correlation between the internal world and religious ideas, so that these ideas are a reflection of the internal psychic landscape. Psychoanalytic theorists have provided us with various content hypotheses, specifying what is projected. Psychoanalysis also specified the recapitulation mechanism of transference, through which early experiences in the family are recreated as cultural products. The presumably projected humans are the "significant others": father, mother, family relations and dynamics.

Because of the centrality of family dynamics in early childhood, psychoanalysis suggests that all religious traditions would contain projective fantasies which construe the cosmic environment in the shape of the family drama. Parental care varies in different cultures, the child's concept of the parents will similarly vary, and so will the resultant image of the deities. Not only are the images of the gods likely to vary in accordance with early concepts of the parents, but also the means of communicating with them and soliciting their help. A more complex view of the projection process notes that religious images come before us ready-made as part of social learning, but then we as individuals, project our personal, unique experiences on them. What a religious tradition teaches is an ambiguous stimulus, and we develop it in the image of our own private history and our own parents.

See also: ❱ Freud, Sigmund ❱ Object Relations Theory ❱ Projection ❱ Psychoanalysis

Bibliography

Freud, S. (1912/1958). The dynamics of transference. In *The standard edition of the complete psychological works of Sigmund Freud* (Vol. 12, pp. 97–108). London: Hogarth Press.

Freud, S. (1940/1977). An outline of psychoanalysis. In *The standard edition of the complete psychological works of Sigmund Freud* (Vol. 23, pp. 139–207). London: Hogarth Press.

Transfiguration

Kathryn Madden

The word transfiguration derives from the Latin *trānsfigūrāre* and refers to transformation and change in form or appearance. The term is specifically used in reference to the change of appearance in Jesus Christ as narrated in the Christian biblical accounts of Matthew 17:2, Mark 9:2–3, and Luke 9:28–36.

The gospels report the transfiguration event as Jesus taking three of his disciples – John, James, and Peter – to pray with him on a mountain top. Going up on the mountain (óros) is significant in that it is the place set aside for prayer. While he was praying at the top of the mountain, Jesus was transfigured. "The appearance of his countenance was altered, and his raiment became dazzling white" (1952, RSV).

Exegetical Origins

The original Greek term for this phenomenon was *metemorphothe*. Metamorphosis refers to a conspicuous physical and rather sudden change in one's form or structure. In the biblical event, the disciples witnessed Jesus' face shining like the sun and his garments a brilliant white which they described as "light," or "glory." In his altered form, Jesus speaks with Moses and Elijah who also "appear in glory." Glory stresses the concept of visible light (Luke 2:9; 9:31), the divine presence as a luminous manifestation and God's glorious revelation of God's person as borrowed from the Old Testament concept of *kabod*.

In the gospel narrative, the disciples were "heavy with sleep but kept awake." They witness a conversation between Jesus, Moses, and Elijah. Luke tells us that they discussed what Jesus was to accomplish at Jerusalem – his death.

Then "a cloud came and overshadowed them [the disciples], and they were afraid as they entered the cloud; and a voice came out of the cloud" (1952, RSV) proclaiming Jesus to be the Son of God. The voice instructed the disciples to listen to Jesus as the "Chosen one" of God. The disciples are to tell no one of what they have witnessed.

In the image of cloud, (nephélē, néphos), we find a cross-cultural commonality in meaning drawing from the Hellenistic and Greek worlds and in biblical literature. The cloud was an image of religious significance, a theophany, God's visible manifestation.

God indwells the cloud as indicated by the voice arising from it and invites participation. The disciples do not merely observe; they "enter the cloud," even if only as a foretaste of the eschaton (the final event of the divine plan), the resurrected state in the afterlife and the suffering and struggle which is to precede the resurrection with Jesus' death on the cross.

Synchronous Literacy Motifs and Influences

The transfiguration story is influenced both by Hellenistic categories, as well as by the genre of the Old Testament which also bears Egyptian and Persian influences by virtue of the exile of Israel into Babylon. Biblical scholars Helmut Koester and W. G. Kümmel place the transfiguration story in analogy with an epiphany story – Kümmel in association with the Hellenistic motif, (1990: 122) and Koester, with the Old Testament genre and Jewish apocalyptic literature.

Although Hellenistic literature often pursued a more Gnostic strain which rejects the material embodiment of the divine and speaks of the miraculous transformation of a mythical figure, nonetheless, many examples of literature in the Hellenistic religions concerned a metamorphosis. In the story of Apuleius we find persons and deities experiencing transformation and release as a first prediction before a process of suffering.

Thematic similarities also exist in early hermetic literature, in the literature of the mystery cults, in literature informed by Plato, and in parallel themes in other biblical literature. The mystery religions offered an analogous genre to the Christian biblical narrative offering stories of salvation on the basis of divine revelation.

Other literature that may have informed the transfiguration story was *Hermes Trismegistus*. Written between 100 and 200 CE, this series of tractates were astrological or magical. Some tractates contained writing that was religious which demonstrates literary connection with the Greek Old Testament. Hermes, a god, taught secret knowledge about salvation to a disciple. Those who recorded these documents believed that they had received revelation of a gospel, the difference being that the material or physical order is discounted. In *Poimandres*, powers appear before a disciple's eye, and Poimandres receives supreme vision. Receiving the benefaction of Poimandres, the disciple rejoices, for "the sleep of his body had become watchfulness of soul," and he "moves into life and light" (Barrett, 1989: 89).

Literary fragments from the Egyptian magical papyri were also comparable to the definitive style and ethos of Hellenistic magic and, in turn, analogous to themes in the transfiguration: "once purified, the body is fit to receive a ritual vestment...the true new body of immaculate whiteness" (Jacq, 1985: 37).

The Jewish apocalyptic literature and Wisdom literature have narrative similarities: the isolation of a special place, an extraordinary appearance (i.e., a bright, luminous light); and the self-revelation of divinity, followed by a description of the reactions of those who are present, and finally a command (Koester, 1980: 64).

Social Need and Spiritual Longing

Clearly the narrative accounts of the Christian gospel did not arise in a religious-philosophical vacuum. The people of these times sought forms of knowledge and alternative channels of power in a situation that was dominated by Rome. Philosophers emphasized the theme of negotiating in a world that was disoriented.

Epictetus, a lame slave who was a philosopher contemporaneous to the gospel writer Luke, writes of the "universal" phase: an effort to define the free, moral persona as one who has freedom to speak freely regardless of oppressive threat. There was a collective desire for a new disposition of mind and heart. For those who felt marginalized, there was a turning inward, a relativizing of political and social circumstances. By retreating inward, one could discover being part of a principal work, "a fragment of God himself" (Barrett, 1989: 67).

Persons pursued the mystery religions seeking a personal faith that would bring them into immediate contact with deity and would promise them salvation. The inability to negotiate their outer world increased their interest in astrology, fate, mysticism, and esotericism. Many of the mystery religions and cults contemporary to the writing of the gospel literature had existed for centuries. Mostly they were of Eastern origin before Hellenized.

The mystery cult of Cybele, the Great Mother, had come from Asia, the cult of Isis and Osiris from Egypt, and Mithraism from Persia. These cults shared the characteristic of being centered about a god who had died and had been resurrected. An initiate was inducted by specific rituals and secret symbols and participated in mystical union through sacramental means to share in the experience of the god to achieve immortality.

When Mark, the earliest of the gospels was written, the tradition of Jesus had already become saturated with the outlook of Hellenistic magic. The early stages of the interpretation of the miracles of Jesus, particularly his exorcisms and healings, were understood to be magical. Jesus was understood to have entered into the central conflict of the magician's art – the struggle with evil powers.

Informed by the collective psyche of the time, the spiritual world was understood as divided into two realms of power. A battle ensues between Jesus and his foes analogous to a battle between spiritual forces and magic. The folk belief was that Jesus overcame evil by his greater power as indwelt bodily by mana, a charge of divine energy, a vital substance that emanated from the spirit world. This power could be passed from one person to another (Brown, 1978: 560). Those who received this power would undergo an initiation that would come to them as a Pentecostal event, an "inrush of God's kingdom." Christ was the vessel in the event of the transfiguration, the intermediary from whom the disciples received mana directly. A foretaste of the future glory was now *in* them.

Without hesitation, the early church attacked such magical beliefs and stressed that evil power yields to the superior power of God. Jesus was different from the magicians who were concerned with the control of the supernatural by techniques to further their own desires. He desired to do the will of the Father and to teach others to submit to that will.

Spiritual and Psychological Impact

Jesus was fully aware of God's will for him. The intention behind the transfiguration event was to show to the disciples that he would embody the reality of "glory" in the Resurrection. He demonstrates that glory is more than a temporary contact to the divine presence. Glory is a reality that is revealed as a divine mode of being but a reality that is not visible to itself. It is a reality that must be witnessed by an "other." This perception is analogous to the belief in the practice of psychotherapy that healing is most efficacious in that two persons form a relationship in which healing occurs.

Jesus' inclusion of the disciples as witness to the event of the transfiguration indicates the potential of metamorphosis inherent in each person. Analogous to the long years one undergoes psychoanalytic or analytic reflection in the process of therapy, Jesus teaches that the transfiguration is a culmination of a long process and that we have to awaken from our "sleep," our dullness of "seeing and hearing," and recognize the light of the invisible source – the eternal life of the soul in a transfigured reality.

The manifestation of common images in the oral and written traditions point to how these images represent universal motifs that arise within the human psyche. When a people in history find themselves in a disenfranchised stated in which their personal identity is in question or depersonalized, the human psyche reacts by development of a common theme of divine manifestation. From the depths of the human psyche a healing, guiding, presence makes itself known and offers the potential for efficacious change.

The deepest, most far-reaching change possible for human beings is expressed by the word metamorphosis. When we undergo metamorphosis, we are changed at the depths of our being and completely. Psychoanalysis, at its best, works at this level. The deeper psyche becomes the transformative ground for the original unity of soul and spirit. We know that we are in the terrain of deeper psyche when primal archetypal images and symbols grasp us and startle us beyond what we typically know and experience. Aspects of human existence replete with both light and dark sides begin to penetrate our personal consciousness, analogous to the experience of persons in the first century and in all centuries.

From a psychological perspective, in metamorphic change, the ego may feel displaced as it changes experientially into new form in-formed by new knowledge emerging from the psyche as the unconscious becomes conscious. The ego may feel distraught, uncomfortable, as if it is dying unto its new role and existence.

Like the disciples realization in Jesus' transfigured form, the ego in psychological analysis comes to recognize two layers of being. What the ego has known as self is not all that it is. This realization is accompanied by the profound awareness that archetypes and archetypal images do not veil the eternal world. They lead to it. An archetype can arrest us in a mood or a state of biophysical seizure as it announces the new, taking hold of our entire personality, as if, like the disciples, we were entering a cloud. Such in-breakings of the unconscious can transcend the injuries of our childhoods and fuel us with an experiential faith, one that convinces us with impenetrable faith that some precious aspect of our being is impenetrable to death. The psychological movement we make between each image, each point of being, each glimpse of transfigured reality, leads us eventually to a world beyond mere material surfaces.

Transfigured Transfiguration

As the ego surrenders to this process of awareness, we come to realize that an archetype can present itself only in a numinous way if it is clothed in an adequate symbol; a cloud, a mountain top, a cross, for instance. Symbolic expression originates in the body and presents itself as a self-portrait of instinct. As we begin to relate to the unconscious products of dreams, waking imagination, and symbols, our consciousness is ignited into motion. Dreams point to that which is not yet ready to be born but also to the advent of new birth and the eternal.

In modern depth psychological terms, the notion of transfiguration and metamorphosis translates into the goals of the fully individuated individual which emerges in the Self-ego relationship, a psychological reality that finds an analog in religious terms with Christ as exemplar and internal guide. The disciples proclaimed such lived experience and accepted revelation as an ongoing unfolding of divine presence in their lives. They discovered that through the mysteries of the transfigured Christ there is spiritual character that may be embodied in the conscious and visible world that transcends the manifest.

Similarly, the reflective and sacred space of therapy can become the transformative vessel for reaching toward the divine. Human deficiency and lack, as it appears in our most cast off and vulnerable parts may be the source of our greatest offerings. Our depletion may be the stable of incarnation, life that translates into more life in contrast to evil which can translate only into poverty. Therapy is analogous to a parent communing to a child whose healing is greatly aided in feeling "chosen" by a loving, attentive presence.

The transfiguration event attests to the fact that a transformation mystery exists in which the vessel character of the archetypal layer of the psyche houses a creative principle. By means of receptivity, we are enabled to bridge the two worlds of consciousness and unconsciousness. Our receptivity is the only thing that can recover to some form of healing human suffering and despair and give meaning to the inevitability of tragedy, death, dissociation, and developmental traumas. Love has the power to break through our defenses. As the great story teller Ovid once said of metamorphosis, "let me die loving and so never die" (Maidenbaum, 1993: 679–724).

See also: ❯ Archetype ❯ Christ ❯ Christianity ❯ Depth Psychology and Spirituality ❯ Ego ❯ Great Mother ❯ Jesus ❯ Osiris and the Egyptian Religion ❯ Prayer ❯ Psychotherapy ❯ Resurrection ❯ Theophany

Bibliography

Barrett, C. K. (Ed.). (1989). *New Testament background: Selected documents.* San Francisco, CA: Harper & Row.

Brown, C. (1978). Magic. In C. Brown (Ed.), *The new international dictionary of New Testament theology* (3 vols.). Grand Rapids, MI: Zondervan Corporation.

Cloud. (1957). *Nelson's complete concordance of the revised study of the Gospels.* Philadelphia, PA: Fortress Press.

Foerster. W. (1978). Mountain. In C. Brown (Ed.), *The new international dictionary of New Testament theology* (3 vols.). Grand Rapids, MI: Zondervan Corporation.

Jacq, C. (1985). *Egyptian magic* (J. M. Davis, Trans.). Chicago, IL: Bolchazy-Carducci Publishers.

Kittel, G. (1978). Glory. In C. Brown (Ed.), *The new international dictionary of New Testament theology* (3 vols.). Grand Rapids, MI: Zondervan Corporation.

Koester, H. (1980). *Introduction to the New Testament: History and literature of early Christianity* (Vol. 2). New York: Walter De Gruyter & Co.

Koester, H. (1980). *Introduction to the New Testament: History, culture, and religion of the Hellenistic Age* (Vol. 1). Philadelphia, PA: Fortress Press.

Kümmel, W. G. (1990). *Introduction to the New Testament* (H. C. Lee, Trans.). Nashville, TN: Abingdon Press.

Maidenbaum, A. (Trans.) (1993). *The Metamorphosis of Ovid.* Book VIII: 679–724. San Diego, CA: Harcourt, Inc.

Weigle, L. (Trans.) (1952). *The Holy Bible: Revised Standard Version.* New York: Thomas Nelson & Sons.

Transitional Object

Philip Browning Helsel

The term, first coined by analyst D. W. Winnicott, refers to the object that a child might confer with special significance, such as a piece of string, a teddy bear, or a blanket. A popular representation of the transitional object is the "security" blanket that the character Linus always carried in the Peanuts cartoon. In the treatment of this object, the child enacts the love and rage that results from the bond with, and inevitable separation from the mother. Thus, the object can be the treatment of abuse, affection, or idealization and role-play, with the function of allowing the child to create, in a liminal space, a relationship that is reciprocal with and at the same time a working-through of the original mother-child environment. The liminal space in which the object is created by the child is neither the mother-child environment, nor the child separate from the mother, but is the intersection of both settings in the space of play (Winnicott, 2005: 3). The fact that the child chooses the object, uses it and abuses it, but the object continues to exist, represents the child's creativity and the endurance of the earliest bond in spite of inevitable frustration and separation.

Winnicott argued that the space in which the transitional object is chosen, and thereby "created" by the child, is the same space in which culture is developed in adult life. It is not coincidental that Linus, in the Peanuts cartoon, is the character who is the most capable of philosophical reflection. The realms of art, religion, and literature reflect the play of imagination and the "holding" space which is necessary for this play (Winnicott, 2005: 4).

Religion is grasped in a manner similar to that which a child grasps and manipulates the earliest object. Frequent metaphors of "wrestling" or "struggling" with religion are reflective of the child's testing of the object in the liminal space, in which the object's permanence ensures that it will outlast even the rage of the infant. This permanence is reflected in forms of religion which tolerate doubt and even hatred of the deity, reflecting the fact that even after such a powerful struggle with the object, the object will remain.

While the believer may grasp religion as the child holds onto the transitional object, she may simultaneously have the sense of being grasped in relationship to her religion. This reflects the manner in which the psychic object echoes the earliest relations. Forms of Christian Platonism reflected how God seemed familiar to the soul, and seemed to be "recalled" by it even in its encounter with God (Turner, 1995: 70). While religion might be "used" by the adult in a similar manner to which a child uses a transitional object, it also has the quality of an encounter, especially in its mystical forms. In religion, when one may feel enveloped by or chosen by an object which has connotations of fascination, desire, or the uncanny, this sense of resonance with something "beyond" may be reflective of the pre-history of the person, in which mother and child existed in a relationship which predates the historical awareness of the person or personality (Bollas, 1987: 24–25).

See also: ◉ Winnicott, Donald Woods ◉ Winnicott, Donald Woods, and Religion

Bibliography

Bollas, C. (1987). *The shadow of the object: Psychoanalysis of the unthought known.* London: Free Association Books.

Turner, D. (1995). *The darkness of God: Negativity in Christian mysticism.* Cambridge, England: Cambridge University Press.

Winnicott, D. W. (2005) *Playing and reality.* London: Routledge Press.

Transpersonal Psychology

Nicholas Grant Boeving

Often referenced as the Fourth Force of psychology (the previous three being behaviorism, psychodynamism, and

humanism) Transpersonal Theory refers to the intellectual movement and its attendant therapeutic praxes that attempt to redress the perspectival imbalance of its predecessors by integrating the insights of the world's wisdom traditions with the psychological concepts, theories, and methods of the West. Whereas traditional theoretical orientations tend toward the reductive end of the interpretive continuum, transpersonal psychology seeks to include within its purview those regions of the human experience overlooked and unexplored (or utterly reduced/collapsed) by other models. These "higher" states – for curiously, the lower ones are only rarely engaged – are the primary domains with which it is concerned. Transpersonal psychologists are explicit in their mission to unite under one rubric both psychology *and* religion, or, more accurately, psychology and spirituality, however nebulously defined and protean in character the latter may be.

Fueled by the American (read Californian) counterculture of the 1960s, the transpersonal turn was part of a wider cultural process of turning away from the perceived-to-be crumbling Occidental edifices of Church and State. Still, the project was essentially an extension of Enlightenment ideals, its earliest incarnations attempting to wed the methodologies of science to the experiential epistemologies described in various mystical (read Eastern) literatures. The consequence of this spiritually positivistic stance (e.g., there is one unitive ground of all being that can be accessed/realized by practitioners following the various prescriptive technologies described in the various non-dual systems) was the effulgence of all-encompassing meta-theories replete with competing ontological claims. These theories subsumed, into one Ultimate or another, the insights of orthodoxy, Eastern spirituality, indigenous traditions, contemplative prayer, holistic medicine, non-ordinary states of consciousness, ecstatic dance, shamanic trance, yogic breathwork, and spiritual emergencies – to name but a few, as they have arisen in the historical pageant of the world's religious systems.

Transpersonal psychology draws heavily from the hermeneutics of the humanities, such as existentialism, phenomenology, humanism, ethnopsychology, and anthropology and is characterized by its kaleidoscopic inclusion of differing scholastic orientations. Such a promiscuous intermingling of ideas and epistemologies from both psychology and religion, have led many to erroneously conflate it with The New Age, although admittedly, there is much overlap.

Much of Transpersonal Theory is indebted to the pioneering work of William James and Carl Jung, though as a discipline it did not emerge until the late 1960s as a unique efflux within the humanistic school of Carl Rogers and Abraham Maslow, the latter whom, in conjunction with Stanislav Grof, founded, in 1969, the first academic journal devoted exclusively to the exploration of the aforementioned themes, *The Journal of Transpersonal Psychology*.

The two towering pillars of the tradition, however, are undoubtedly Ken Wilber and Stanislav Grof, although Wilber has since distanced himself from the movement in favor of his own epithetical Integral Psychology.

Wilberian Theory views the Kosmos, and by extension the development of consciousness, as a series of unfolding stages, with higher levels superior to lower levels arranged in a progressive paradigm of transcendence and inclusion. His most significant contribution to the field has been his non-dually based spectrum of consciousness.

Grof's model, in counterpoint to Wilber's, is a more laterally oriented approach and arose from his research experiences as one of the first experimenters with LSD. Regression to pre-egoic states is understood in his model to facilitate psychical integration of the individual. At first, these states were encountered with the aid of entheogens, but later with Holotropic Breathwork, a trademarked technique of posturing and breathing designed to activate the same non-ordinary states as its chemical counterparts.

Other theorists of note include: Ralph Metzner, Michael Washburn, Roger Walsh, Frances Vaughan, Robert Assagioli, and Jorge Ferrer. Ralph Metzner's pluralistic model eshews all linearity, while Washburn's calls for a helical process of graduated integration culling insights from both Jungian and psychoanalytic thinking. Jorge Ferrer has reevaluated the entire transpersonal project and is believed by many to have liberated it from the tyranny of any one metasystem, calling for a plurality of intersubjective epistemlogical grounds instead of the various intrapersonal models to which previous theorists had wholeheartedly subscribed.

Criticisms from outside the movement have typically taken several different forms, chiefly among them (1) that transpersonal theorists are guilty of sloppy scholarship, (2) that in selectively privileging certain religious systems over others they unfairly skew the data to support their individual models, and that (3) its continued lack of engagement with the problem of evil impoverishes any attempt to comprehend the Psyche as an integrated whole.

Perhaps most damaging of all, however, is the unfortunate fact of its being mostly ignored by both the academy and the general populace, although evidence is beginning to emerge that this may, indeed, be changing.

Commentary

Although couched as an academic discipline, transpersonal psychology really signifies the dawning of a new species of religiosity – psychology *as* religion.

This alternative expression of the numinous seeks to expand our understanding of the individual outside of the egoic insularity of previous psychological systems. In doing so, it dually uses psychology to read religion and religion to read psychology, neither reductively nor dogmatically collapsing one into the other.

See also: ❷ Jung, Carl Gustav ❷ Rogers, Carl ❷ Wilber, Ken

Bibliography

Cortright, B. (1997). *Psychotherapy and spirit: Theory and practice in transpersonal psychotherapy*. Albany, NY: State University of New York.

Ferrer, J. (2002). *Revisioning transpersonal theory: A participatory vision of human spirituality*. Albany, NY: State University of New York.

Grof, S. (2000). *Psychology of the future: Lessons from modern consciousness research*. Albany, NY: State University of New York.

Scotton, B. W., Chinen, A. B., & Battista, J. R. (Eds.). (1996). *Textbook of transpersonal psychiatry and psychology*. New York: Basic Books.

Walsh, R., & Vaughan, F. (Eds.). (1993). *Paths beyond ego: The transpersonal vision*. New York: Putnam.

Wilber, K. (2000). *Integral psychology: Consciousness, spirit, psychology, and therapy*. Boston, MA: Shambhala.

Trauma

Todd DuBose

Trauma is the description given to an overwhelming, uncanny, or absurd experience, usually involving some kind of violence, abuse, or loss, that threatens death of injury to oneself or another, and that resists one's capacities to process, make meaning of, or schematize the occurrence in typical or familiar ways. Traumatic experiences can be short lived and acute or chronic and seemingly unending. Often accompanied by various experiences and comportments of fear, worry, anger, and crises of meaning, traumatic experiences are encounters with the overwhelming and the overpowering.

Traumatic experiences are often considered experiences that "shatters assumptions" (Janoff-Bulman, 2002; Kauffman, 2002), or belie expectations of how life events should occur. We naturally personalize traumatic events in our lives as we operate from a web of meaning that presumes life is ordered, fair, and benevolent. We live out our existence viewing chaos, chance, random destruction and absurdity as flaws in life rather than as experiences inherent to the very composition of life. The etymology of the word "traumatic," in Greek, means "to incur or inflict a wound or injury." Traumas, or traumata, can be physical, psychological, environmental, and/or spiritual, and can be immediate, acute, chronic, or delayed in their impact. The Diagnostic and Statistical Manual of Mental Disorders-IV-TR describes a traumatic experience as evoking feelings of being overwhelmed and helpless (2000).

It is important to note, though, that a trauma is not only the event itself that occurs, but is shaped as well by how the event is understood by those undergoing it, and how one is cared for before, during, and after such events. Any imposing of generic templates on others of what is considered traumatic should be critically analyzed (Bracken, 2002). What is traumatic for one person may not be so for another. Developmental levels of vulnerability, exposure to life-world situations, meaning-making skills, and cultural sensitivities are all aspects to consider in assessing the nature and intensity of traumatization. Due to its imposing and intimidating nature, traumata evoke our needs to organize, categorize, and make sense of them, even though traumata are by definition experiences that resist these processes. This point testifies to our nature as meaning- making creatures. For instance, habitual ways of defining traumata as horror laden, such as war trauma, rape, physical violence, accidental dismemberment, and so forth, often enframe our definitions of trauma such that we inattend to "positive traumas," such as winning the lottery, being proposed to, finding out your pregnant with triplets, and other experiences.

Psychological perspectives on trauma have included Sigmund Freud's (1856–1939) explications of hysterical neurosis and repetition compulsion (Freud, 1895/2000, 1920/1990) and Otto Rank's (1884–1939) views on birth trauma (Rank, 1929/1994). Much of the field of trauma studies has focused on the neurophysiology of traumatic and post-traumatic reactions as well as on multicultural issues within traumatic experiences and situations, particularly in regards to displacement and torture among refugees. Standard of care for psychological treatment of trauma includes post-traumatic stabilization, integration, and post-integration or reinvestment in relationships and projects in life.

It is the liminal characteristic of traumatic experience, though, that lends itself to comparisons with religious experience. Mircea Eliade (1907–1986) noted how experiences of hierophanies, or the "inbreaking" of the holy, often leave one disoriented, feeling threatened, and "thrown" into an encounter with limitlessness (Eliade, 1959). Rudolf Otto's (1869–1937) descriptions of encounters with the numinous as wholly other include a mixture of awe-filled fascination and terror (Otto, 1917/1958). Gerardus van der Leeuw's (1896–1950) description of the divine as "power," in the sense of profound, impressive and exceptional confrontation with incomparable otherness, concurs with these other phenomenologists of religious experience (van der Leeuw, 1933/1986).

These descriptions of numinous experiences are nearly verbatim of what others have said about traumatic experiences. The traumatic experience is also numinous in its ultimate, encompassing, and boundary oriented in nature, to use Karl Jaspers' language, or "peak experience," to use Abraham Maslow's phrase (Maslow, 1970). For Jaspers (1883–1969), boundary situations, namely, guilt, chance, suffering, conflict, and death, are experiences in which everything is unstable and in flux (Jaspers, 1919/1997; Schlipp, 1981). Traumatic experiences are also apophatic encounters with radical Otherness in that one often finds attempts as description ineffable. When undergoing a traumatic experience, one's very ground of meaning is deconstructed, as evidenced by alienation, guilt, irrevocable loss, and the loss of identity. During the meaning-making crises created by trauma, it is hard to determine the level of existential loss of faith operative. Yet, Stanislov and Christina Grof (1989) have provided extensive scholarship on differentiating spiritual emergencies from spiritual emergence, and how care for each respective phenomenon is different.

Ritual abuse explicitly links traumatic experiences with religious symbolism and ritual in such ways that the religious artifacts and activities are themselves traumatic. In classifying post-traumatic experiences, spiritual abuse is often overlooked, dismissed, or renamed, and can range from sexually and physically violent ritual abuse to proselytizing and theological battery, resulting in devaluation of one's worth and well-being at one's core and banishment from the rejecting community. Although the most overlooked traumatic experience, spiritual abuse may indeed be the most devastating, necessitating a most unique and compassionate response.

Commentary

How one becomes traumatized, *what* is considered traumatizing, and *how* one cares for traumatized individuals remain central to any discussion about trauma. Several issues embedded in these concerns are often overlooked or at least tacked on as supplementary to standard of care protocol regarding traumatic experience. Survivors of traumatic experience often refer to how their spirituality helped them cope. Although researchers such as Kenneth Pargament (2001) have so aptly shown the benefits of religious rituals and beliefs as coping mechanisms, equating spirituality with coping mechanisms can often miss the phenomenology of religious experience on which such coping mechanisms are predicated. Numinosity is inherent in the experiential structure of traumatic phenomenon and not merely a tool of consolation tool that can be chosen or not on an as needed basis.

Another unanalyzed aspect of traumatic experience is a tendency to explain such experiences solely in terms of neurophysiology and cognitive schemas, rather than disclose the phenomenology of the experiences themselves through descriptive analysis of its significance as lived by those undergoing or having undergone such experiences. The field has tended to generically template, categorize, and collate what is counted as a traumatic experience, and how someone should react to it. For instance, a traumatizing experience is not just "caused" by a prior happening in one's immediate or distant past. For an experience to be traumatic, multiple factors have to occur and situations have to provide an arena for traumatic experiences to come into existence, including much that is chance, random, unsolicited, and undeserved. The genericizing of traumatic events and reactions runs the risk of missing the unique and incomparable meaning-making that resists classification. Moreover, addressing trauma requires more than challenging globalizing cognitive distortions. An encounter with the traumatic, much like an encounter with the numinous, is "irrational" in Otto's language (1917), and "absurd" in Camus' (1955) language, and neither experience is a distortion of reality. Life, at times, does not make sense and side-swipes us in undeserved ways. Thinking otherwise is actually the distortion needing correction.

A final point often minimized or not thought about in therapeutically working through traumatic experiences for persons is how prevalent the problem of evil is for traumatized persons, including the often disenfranchised group of traumatized persons: the traumatizers. Whether or not one is theistic, atheistic, or non-theistic, traumas raise the question of the justice, fairness, and benevolence of existence, particularly for the one undergoing the trauma, and therapeutic care must face this often unspoken issue upfront. To do so requires much of the therapist, and given so, one must attend to the perils of vicarious traumatization (Nouwen, 1979; Steed and Downing, 1998). Yet, the model of the wounded healer has guided us though these dark valleys long before the field of trauma was formally conceived. It is often that in caring for those who have survived the undeserved and unexpected visitation of unmitigated destruction that an antidote is offered to soothe the horror. The antidote does not deny that suffering is a part of life, and at the same time, it, too, is undeserved, unexpected, and uncoerced. The antidote may very well be simply the grace of having one's resilient capacities borne witness to and celebrated in order to not only cope, but also to thrive.

See also: ❯ Abyss ❯ Chaos ❯ Dissociation ❯ Evil ❯ Existential Psychotherapy ❯ Existentialism ❯ Frankl, Viktor ❯ Hermeneutics ❯ Holocaust ❯ Homo Religiosus ❯ John of the Cross ❯ Liminality ❯ Lived Theology ❯ Meaning of Human Existence ❯ Phenomenological Psychology ❯ Spiritual Emergence ❯ Theodicy ❯ Vicarious Traumatization

Bibliography

American Psychiatric Publications. (2000). *Diagnostic and statistical manual of mental disorders. Text Review* (4th ed.). Arlington, VA: Author.

Bracken, P. (2002). *Trauma: Culture, meaning, and philosophy.* London: Whurr Publishers.

Camus, A. (1955). *The myth of Sisyphus and other essays.* New York: Random House.

DuBose, T. (1997). The phenomenology of bereavement, grief, and mourning. *Journal of Religion and Health, 36*(4), 367–374.

Eliade, M. (1959). *The sacred and the profane: The nature of religion* (W. Trask, Trans.). New York: Harper & Row.

Freud, S., & Breuer, J. (1990). *Beyond the pleasure principle* (J. Strachey, Trans.). New York: W. W. Norton. (Original work published 1920)

Freud, S., & Breuer, J. (2000). *Studies on hysteria* (J. Strachey, Trans.). New York: Basic. (Original work published 1895)

Girard, R. (1979). *Violence and the sacred.* (P. Gregory, Trans.). Baltimore, MD: John Hopkins University Press.

Grof, S., & Grof, C. (1989). *A spiritual emergency: When personal transformation becomes a crisis.* New York: Tarcher.

Janoff-Bulman, R. (2002). *Shattered assumptions: Toward a new psychology of trauma.* New York: Free Press.

Jaspers, K. (1919/1997). *General psychopathology* (J. Hoenig & M. Hamilton, Trans.). Baltimore, MD: John Hopkins University Press.

Kauffman, J. (Ed.). (2002). *Loss of the assumptive world: A theory of traumatic loss.* New York: Brunner-Routledge.

Kugelmann, R. (1992). The engineering of grief. In *Stress: The nature and history of engineered grief.* London: Praeger.

Maslow, A. (1970). *Religions, values, and peak-experiences* (pp. 19–29). New York: Penguin Books.

Mogenson, G. (1989). *God is a trauma: Vicarious religion and soul-making.* Dallas, TX: Spring.

Nouwen, H. (1979). *The wounded healer: Ministry in contemporary society.* New York: Image.

Otto, R. (1917/1958). *The ideal of the holy: An inquiry into the non-rational factor in the idea of the divine and its relation to the rational* (J. Harvey, Trans.). New York: Oxford University Press.

Pargament, K. (2001). *The psychology of religion and coping.* New York: Guilford.

Rank, O. (1929/1994). *The trauma of birth.* New York: Dover.

Schlipp, P. (1981). *The philosophy of Karl Jaspers.* Chicago, IL: Open Court.

Steed, L., & Downing, R. (1998). A phenomenological study of vicarious traumatization amongst psychologists and professional counselors working in the field of sexual abuse/assault. *The Australasian Journal of Disaster and Trauma Studies, 2*, 1–10.

Van den Berg, J. (1972). *A different existence: Principles of phenomenological psychopathology.* Pittsburgh, PA: Duquesne University Press.

Van den Berg, J. (1983). *The changing nature of man: Introduction to a historical psychology.* New York: W. W. Norton.

Van der Leeuw, G. (1933/1986). *Religion in essence and manifestation.* (J. E. Turner, Trans.). Princeton, NJ: Princeton University Press.

Van der Kolk, B. (1987). *Psychological trauma.* Washington, DC: American Psychiatric Press.

Wilson, J. (1989). *Trauma, transformation and healing: An integrative approach to theory, research, and post-traumatic therapy.* New York: Brunner/Mazel.

Trickster

David A. Leeming

The trickster is a common character in mythology and in certain religious traditions, especially, but not exclusively the animistic – spirit-based – religions of Africa and Native North America. Typically male, the trickster usually has extreme appetites for food and sex. He is immoral, or, at least, amoral, and he is, more often than not, a thief. Yet he often uses his inventiveness to help human beings and is sometimes, in effect, a culture hero. Often his inventiveness interferes with creation, however, and causes such realities as pain and death. The trickster is a shape shifter. He can change shapes at will and, in that sense, is perhaps a mythological relative of the shaman.

In the ancient Greek Religion, Hermes, as a child, has trickster aspects, as, for instance when he steals Apollo's cattle. In India, the great man-god Krishna, the most important of the avatars of the god Vishnu, constantly plays tricks – some of a sexual nature, as when he steals the clothes of his bathing female followers. In these cases, however, the trickster aspect seems to reflect essential inventiveness and creativity and points to later more important achievements. The same is true of stories of tricks played by the boy Jesus in some of the apocryphal gospels.

More typical tricksters are those such as the Native American Coyote and Raven and the African Ananse (the Spider). The fact that these figures take animal forms coincides with their unbridled appetites. Coyote is an expert seducer of women and he constantly steals food from others more needy than himself. The West African Ananse even steals the high god's daughter. Like Hermes and Krishna, these tricksters are highly creative, but their creativity almost always causes trouble for themselves or others.

Tricksters such as Erlik in Central Asia are often close to the creator and manage, while pretending to help, to undermine creation, allowing evil in. In this sense, Satan, in the Abrahamic tradition, is a trickster. A fallen angel, once close to God, he enters the new creation – Eden – as a serpent and uses his natural guile to infect that creation with sin – sin immediately associated with sexuality.

The trickster is a clear representative of an id-dominated ego un-tempered by superego. He is the narcissistic child, whose physical appetites are uppermost in importance. Jung saw the trickster as "an earlier, rudimentary stage of consciousness" (1969: 141) and an expression of shadow, the primitive, irrational "dark side" of the unconscious, but also, in his creativity and inventiveness, as a hint of a later positive figure who takes form, like the Great Hare of the Native American trickster tradition, as a culture hero-savior.

See also: ❂ Animism ❂ Creation ❂ Culture Heroes ❂ Devil ❂ Shamans and Shamanism

Bibliography

Jung, C.G. (1969). *Archetypes of the collective unconscious* (Vol. 9, Pt. 1). Princeton, NJ: Princeton University Press.

Jung, C. G. (1969). *Four archetypes: Mother/rebirth/spirit/trickster.* Princeton, NJ: Princeton University Press.

Leeming, D. A. (1990). *The world of myth* (pp. 163–174). New York: Oxford University Press.

Radin, P. (1969). *The trickster: A study in American Indian mythology.* New York: Greenwood.

Tulku

Paul Larson

In Tibetan Buddhism a tulku is an individual who is deemed to be the current holder of a long chain of lamas who direct the circumstances of their reincarnation through choice, leaving clues to there next incarnation for the students of the lineage to seek out and help train the new embodiment of spiritual power and authority. Reincarnation is a core belief of both Hinduism and Buddhism and is found in many Western esoteric traditions as well. The general view of Buddhism is that all sentient beings are on a wheel of life, endlessly living lives, dying and becoming reborn in another body. There is a broad assumption of an evolutionary process where greater spiritual accomplishments result in moving up the scale of beings. The Mahayana concept of 'bodhisattva' is relevant here, since they postpone their complete enlightment in order to continue to work for the enlightment of all sentient beings. The tulku, as a bodhisattva continues their life stream across particular incarnations in order to facilitate the enlightenment of all. In Tibetan Buddhism, the god realm exists, but enlightenment can only come through a human reincarnation, making it a precious gift. The specific Tibetan twist on this general doctrine of reincarnation involves this special ability of highly developed spiritual leaders; they can direct their own reincarnation and have prescience as to the circumstances so as to be able to guide their followers in finding their next form.

The most widely known of such lineages of lamas is the Dalai Lama, currently held by the 14th lineage holder, formerly known as Tenzin Gyatso. The oldest such lineage line, however, is the Karmapa (head of the Kagyu lineage) which is one of the four major lineages within the monastic community (in order of origination they are Nyingma, Kagyu, Sakya and Gelug). Each of those lineages, as well as many early teachers within each lineage have now recognized lineages of tulkus who are the thread of continuity in spiritual leadership.

Until recently only Tibetan children were recognized as instances of a lineage line, but there are several young Western children who have now been recognized, and whose parents have allowed them to enter monasteries to receive training in Tibetan Buddhism and the specific traditions of their lineage. Individuals who are recognized as reincarnated lamas are generally referred to with the honorific title "rinpoche," or "precious teacher." But this title is also granted to other significant teachers who are not recognized as part of a reincarnated lineage.

These tulkus are themselves manifestations of other transcendental beings. The Dalai Lama, for example is viewed as an embodiment of Chenrezig, the Tibetan equivalent of the Sanskrit Avalokiteshvara, the Boddhisattva of Compassion. All of the great teachers and initiators of lineages are seen as tied to these transcendental Buddhas and Boddhisattvas. The doctrine which provides the theology for understanding this is the "trikaya" (Skt), or three bodies theory. The transcendental Buddha has the capacity to be in three types of bodies, the Dharmakaya body is the truly transcendent realm beyond duality; the Samboghakaya body, or "enjoyment body" is the realm of high bliss as one would experience in the god realm, and the Nirmanakaya body is the "body of transformation," which is how the Buddha manifests in earthly human form. The Buddha's most recent embodiment was the Indian prince Siddhartha Gautama, or Shakyamuni Buddha. Tibetan Buddhism shares the deep involvement in the reality of a pantheon of transcendental Buddhas and Boddhisattvas with the Mahayana tradition found in East Asia.

See also: ❯ Bodhisattva ❯ Buddhism ❯ Dalai Lama ❯ Hinduism ❯ Rinpoche

Bibliography

Ehrhard, F. (1991). Tulku. In I. Fischer-Schreiber, F. Ehrhard, & M. S. Diener (Eds.), *The Shambala dictionary of Buddhism and Zen*. Boston, MA: Shambala.

Thurman, R. (1995). *Inside Tibetan Buddhism: Rituals and symbols revealed*. San Francisco, CA: Collins Publishers.

Twelve Steps

Jennifer Amlen

The 12 step program was founded in Akron, Ohio in 1935 by Dr. Bob Smith (known as Dr. Bob) and Bill Wilson (known as Bill W.). It is based on the 12 steps and 12 traditions of Alcoholics Anonymous. It is an anonymous (using first names only) self-help program based on the goal of attaining sobriety from alcoholism.

The 12 steps are:

1. *We admitted we were powerless over alcohol, that our lives had become unmanageable.*
2. *Came to believe that a Power greater than ourselves could restore us to sanity.*
3. *Made a decision to turn our will and our lives over to the care of God as we understood Him.*
4. *Made a searching and fearless moral inventory of ourselves.*

5. *Admitted to God, to ourselves, and to another human being the exact nature of our wrongs.*

6. *Were entirely ready to have God remove all these defects of character.*

7. *Humbly asked Him to remove our shortcomings.*

8. *Made a list of all persons we had harmed, and became willing to make amends to them all.*

9. *Made direct amends to such people wherever possible, except when to do so would injure them or others.*

10. *Continued to take personal inventory and when we were wrong promptly admitted it.*

11. *Sought through prayer and meditation to improve our conscious contact with God as we understood Him, praying only for knowledge of His will for us and the power to carry that out.*

12. *Having had a spiritual awakening as the result of these steps, we tried to carry this message to alcoholics and to practice these principles in all our affairs.*

The 12 step program aims at helping individuals achieve sobriety by modifying the dysfunctional patterns and defenses of behavior, developing and strengthening their adaptive coping mechanisms, building new supportive social networks through telephone calls and meetings, and utilizing community resources. It teaches individuals to address the feelings that they have avoided through the use of alcohol. It is a non-profit organization based on fellowship of members who share the same goal, a desire to stop drinking.

Total abstinence, in combination with utilizing the tools of the program, is the program's goal for recovery. The tools require one to make a thorough process of working through the 12 steps by obtaining a sponsor (one who has more experience in the program, has long term abstinence and acts as a mentor/primary support). The program stresses the need to help others in order to maintain one's own sobriety. In addition, there is a wide variety of literature that members are encouraged to read daily. Meetings are a strong part of the program, ranging from topic (i.e., serenity, honesty, forgiveness) steps (any one of the 12 steps), and qualification (usually a 20 min description of one's story focused on sharing experience, strength, and hope with fellow members). In the meetings, each member is encouraged to share for 3–4 min, keeping the focus on the solution rather than dwelling on the problem.

According to Carl Jung, alcoholism in Latin is "spiritus" and one uses the same word for the highest religious experience as well as for the most depraving poison. Before Alcoholics Anonymous was established, doctors and psychiatrists didn't have any cure for the alcoholic. It was suggested that many doctors referred to

William James statement that religiomania is the only remedy for dipsomania (Cheever, 2004).

In 1931, it is written that Carl Gustav Jung, the Swiss psychiatrist, told his patient Mr. Rowland H. that the only solution for his recovery from addiction would have to be a religious or spiritual experience. Jung refers to craving for alcohol, on a low level, of the spiritual thirst of our being for wholeness, expressed in medieval language: the union with God. Jung further elaborated that the only cure for alcoholism is a full-fledged religious experience. Rowland H. joined the Oxford Group, led by an old Episcopal clergyman, Dr. Samuel Showemaker, in England. The Oxford Group was a nondenominational evangelical movement, accepting the simple common denominators of all religions that would be potent enough to change the lives of men and women.

The practices of the Oxford Groups were:

1. *Admission of personal defeat (you have been defeated by sin).*

2. *Taking personal inventory (List your sins).*

3. *Confession of one's sins to another person.*

4. *Making restitution of those harmed.*

5. *Helping others selflessly.*

6. *Praying to God for Guidance and the power to put those precepts into practice.*

One of the most important requirements of the Oxford Group was to recruit more members to the group. It was only through helping others selflessly that one was cured. This doctrine was adopted by Alcoholics Anonymous. It was Ebby Thacher that carried the message of the Oxford Group to Bill Wilson in 1934, depicting that a spiritual awakening in combination with the spiritual principals could cure the alcoholic. Bill Wilson teamed up with Dr. Bob Smith and wrote the book for Alcoholics Anonymous, known as the "Big Book." Originally, there were 6 steps of Alcoholics Anonymous, similar to the 6 steps of the Oxford Group's, which were later developed into 12 steps along with the 12 traditions. The 12 step programs stayed true to the tradition of the Oxford Group, remaining nondenominational, using terms as "higher power" and "God," as we understand him.

Although the 12 step programs are rooted in American Protestantism, it is not exclusive to Christian or theistic belief. Eastern spiritual practice such as Transcendental meditation, Native American spirituality, such as sweat lodges, and rituals of singing and medicine circles, are widely practiced, as well. All these spiritual models share a belief that the path to recovery lies in the first 3 steps, which emphasis a belief and a readiness to turn one's will over to a higher power. Other groups have been founded throughout the world based on the same principals: Narcotics Anonymous, Gamblers Anonymous, Debtors Anonymous, Nicotine Anonymous, Al-Anon, Overeaters Anonymous, etc.

Commentary

The most common theoretical approach to curing addiction at the early stages in psychotherapy has been Cognitive Therapy, Behavioral Therapy, and Cognitive Behavioral Therapy (CBT). The theory involves adapting new behavior from old behavior, adjusting one's irrational and faulty thinking to a healthier thought process. It is achieved by setting up a schedule and a contract with a therapist, developing new activities, keeping a journal of feelings and behaviors, cravings and/or triggers. It also involves using positive reinforcement and addressing negative consequences of destructive behavior (Cooper and Lesser, 2002). In the later stages of recovery, ego supportive and ego-modifying work can be undertaken. Many people with substance abuse lack certain ego functioning, such as a state of identity, impulse control, good judgement, frustration tolerance, and object constancy (Goldstein, 1984). Like the ego psychological perspective, the 12 step program promotes growth in ego functioning and ego synthesis, even though the language may be different.

Sigmund Freud's structural theory of the id, the superego and the ego refers to drives by the id's need for immediate gratification, the superego's often punitive and moral perspective of society and the parent, and the ego which acts as the mediator of both the id and the superego. Freud's theories address the treatment of addiction in his discovery of the early defense mechanisms, such as denial, projection, and rationalization. In the 12 step program, steps 1 through 3, address these early defenses of denial and require a willingness and belief in a source (higher power) outside of one's own self. Step 4 through 9, require the review of one's impulses (id drives), address the consequences to oneself and to others, and require taking responsibility for one's actions. This step process requires awareness (observing ego) with a willingness to be able to adapt and modify one's thinking and behavior. Step 10 is a constant review requiring the ego to regulate these drives on a daily basis and to continue to take responsibility for one's actions. Step 11, prayer and meditation, continues to remind the ego to practice further self awareness. Step 12 provides a moral structure for helping others, resisting the potential for grandiosity and narcissism, by focusing on one's strength in order to benefit newcomers to the program who are in need of help.

See also: ⊕ Body and Spirituality ⊕ Compulsion ⊕ Depth Psychology and Spirituality ⊕ Ego ⊕ Faith ⊕ Freud, Sigmund, and Religion ⊕ Freud, Sigmund ⊕ God Image and Therapy ⊕ Healing ⊕ Id ⊕ James, William ⊕ Jung, Carl Gustav ⊕ Jung, Carl Gustav, and Religion ⊕ Religion and Mental and Physical Health ⊕ Jung, Carl Gustav, and Phenomenology ⊕ Meditation ⊕ Personal God ⊕ Prayer ⊕ Psychospirituality ⊕ Psychotherapy and Religion ⊕ Substance Abuse and Religion ⊕ Super-Ego ⊕ Religious Experience

Bibliography

Cheever, S. (2004). *My name is Bill: Bill Wilson-His life and the creation of alcoholics anonymous.* New York: Washington Square Press.

Clark, W. H. (1951). *The Oxford group. Its history and significance.* University of Michigan: Bookmark Associates.

Cooper, M. G., & Lesser, J. G. (2002). Cognitive theory/behavioral theory: A structural approach. In *Clinical social work practice-An integrative approach* (pp. 141–172). Boston, MA: Allyn & Bacon.

Finley, S. W. (2000). *Influence of Carl Jung and William James on the origin of Alcoholic Anonymous.* [Review of General Psychology (Vol. 4(1), pp. 3–12)]. US: Educational Publishing Foundation.

Goldstein, E. G. (1984). *Ego psychology and social work practice* (2nd ed.). New York: Free Press.

Lobdell, J. C. (2004). Dr. Carl Jung's letter to Bill W., Jan 30, 1961. In *This strange illness: Alcoholism and Bill. W.* Hawthorne, NY: Aldine de Gruyter.

Loose, R. (2002). *The subject of addiction.* London: Karnac.

Orange, A. (2006) Bill Wilson writes the twelve steps (Chap. 1). In *The religious roots of alcoholics anonymous and the twelve steps.*

Simmel, E. (1994). Alcoholism and addiction. In *The dynamics of treatment of alcoholism* (Vol. 20, pp. 273–290). Woodstock, VT: Jason Aronson.

Smith, B., & Wilson, B. (1976). *Alcoholics anonymous* (3rd ed.). New York: Alcoholics Anonymous World Services.

Twice Born

John Pahucki

Categorical term in the psychology of religious experience developed and described by William James in his classic work *The Varieties of Religious Experience*. The description is obviously rooted in the exchange between Jesus and Nicodemus in the Gospel of John (3:1–21) where Jesus comments that a man must be "born again" in order to enter the Kingdom of God, although James seems to have directly appropriated the term "twice born" from Francis W. Newman's *The Soul; Its Sorrows and its*

Aspirations (1882). The twice born type is the counterpart of the first born personality, who represents an instance of what James describes as "the religion of healthy-mindedness." These individuals are characterized by a shallow optimism in regard to religious belief and, in extreme cases, an almost pathological aversion to the reality of suffering and evil. In contradistinction to this type, the twice born has passed through the experience of what James describes as "the sick soul," where the individual's greater awareness of manifest evil forestalls the formation of religious conviction. The twice born type has successfully navigated the challenge of religious pessimism, represented by the sick soul, proceeding to an affirmation of life and development of a religious outlook that fully retains its experience of the darker aspects of existence.

The twice born personality, therefore, never represents a relapse into the religion of healthy-mindedness, which is characteristic of the first born type, but indicates a more comprehensive and integrated religious perspective. In this sense, James' description of the twice born bears some resemblance to the successful integration of the shadow in Jungian analytical psychology.

See also: ❯ Jung, Carl Gustav ❯ Shadow ❯ Theodicy

Bibliography

James, W. (1982). *The varieties of religious experience*. New York: Penguin Classics.

U

Unconscious

Nicholas Grant Boeving

Whether structured like a language (Lacan), the submerged base of an iceberg (Freud), or the ocean upon which the iceberg itself is afloat (Jung), the unconscious is that vast "region" of mind that operates below (or para to) the limen of awareness, interacting with, affecting, and determining, to a certain degree, both our actions and our experience of consciousness in a myriad of ways only subtly perceived.

The discovery of this chimerical "entity" and the term which describes it has often been credited to Sigmund Freud, though articulator is perhaps a more a fitting distinction. Innumerable authors have described and foreshadowed what we today call the unconscious, among their number Paracelsus, Schopenhauer, Leibniz, Spinoza, and Shakespeare, but it was Freud who first gave us a language and lattice-work with which to both read and describe it in the form of psychoanalysis.

In the history of psychology, it was this integral insight that shaped the discipline's theoretical orientation(s) and made therapy possible. Much of therapy consists of the seemingly Sisyphean task of unraveling the private mysteries of neurotic conflict, unearthing their roots and exposing these sources to the light of consciousness, and ideally, via the process of therapeutic engagement, successfully working through them.

In the psychology of religion, it is equally important.

Freud's reductive view was rooted in his hydraulically based psychodynamic understanding of the unconscious, believing the entirety of humankind's religious expression to be the glorious, though illusory, processes of projection, psycho-sexual conflict and sublimation. This model has since been applied to virtually every God(dess) and his or her religion that scholars have come in contact with. Freud undoubtedly drew heavily from the work of the German theologian Ludwig Feuerbach, whose cataclysmic pronouncement was that the essence of Christianity (and by natural extension *all* religion) was simply our collective projections of all that is best in us as a species onto the intrinsically non-existent cipher of "God." Although writing long before Freud and the coining of the term "unconscious," the concept is clearly operative in Feuerbach's analysis. Object-Relations Theory further developed these ideas in the context of idealized parental figures, while Jung believed the dazzling infinitude of religious expression could be read as permutations of a pantheon of archetypes.

The reception of these theories has historically been reductive, but recent re-workings of the psychoanalytic method have since seen that this unconscious process known as sublimation is precisely that – sublime. And that the erotic, which so often acts as both medium *and* message in the realm of the unconscious, cannot be collapsed into sex any more than three dimensions can be collapsed into two. And as embodied beings, it is the erotic dimension through which we seem to contact and express our experience of numinosity in its arborescent unfolding throughout the play of time.

See also: ❂ Archetype ❂ Freud, Sigmund ❂ Jung, Carl Gustav ❂ Lacan, Jacques ❂ Psychoanalysis ❂ Psychology of Religion

Bibliography

Feuerbach, L. (1845). *The essence of Christianity.*
Freud, S. (1927/1968). The future of an illusion. In *The standard edition of the complete psychological works of Sigmund Freud* (J. Strachey, Trans.) (Vol. 21). London: Hogarth Press.
Jung, C. *The collected works* (Vols. 1–20). Princeton, NJ: Princeton University Press.
Lacan, J. (1968). *The language of the self: The function of language in psychoanalysis.* Baltimore, MD: The Johns Hopkins University Press.
Rizzuto, A.-M. (1979). *The birth of the living God: A psychoanalytic study.* Chicago, IL: University of Chicago Press.

Underworld

❂ Descent to the Underworld

D. A. Leeming, K. Madden, S. Marlan (eds.), *Encyclopedia of Psychology and Religion*, DOI 10.1007/978-0-387-71802-6,
© Springer Science+Business Media LLC 2010

Urantia Book

Daniel E. Tyler

The Urantia Book was published in 1955 by the Urantia Foundation in Chicago, Illinois. Urantia (you-ranch-ya) is the name assigned by the book to planet Earth, and the book purports to describe the physical and spiritual history of this world and the greater universe. By its own admission, the book claims to be a revelation. The 196 chapters that constitute the 2,093 page text are credited to a variety of angelic and celestial authors. The exact process by which the book was created is a mystery though much is known about the people involved with the publication of the Urantia Book. The central figure in the book's long (by some accounts, almost 50 year) gestation was a prominent Chicago physician and author, William S. Sadler (1875–1969). Sadler; his wife, Lena Kellogg Sadler, also a medical doctor; his son, William, Jr., and his adopted daughter, Emma Christensen, formed the core "contact commission" to whom the contents of the book were first manifested. According to Sadler, a fifth person whose identity has never been revealed was utilized as the agent through whom the information was transmitted by a process never explained. Much of the information imparted by the celestials was in response to questions posed by people associated with the Sadler family, a group known as the "forum." The forum met on a weekly basis for many years to formulate questions and study the material.

The book is organized in four sections: the central and superuniverses; the local universe; the history of Urantia; and the life and teachings of Jesus. The first chapter is titled "The Universal Father" and the book emphasizes the personal and parental nature of God. Consistent with Christian theology, the book is also trinitarian. Jesus is identified as the human incarnation of a divine creator son, Michael of Nebadon. According to the book, Michael incarnated on Urantia as Jesus for many reasons, chief of which was to reveal the nature of God to man. Upon completion of his mission on Urantia, Michael assumed full authority as the supreme ruler of the universe of his creation (Nebadon) which consists of more than three million inhabited planets. From a psychological perspective, the book stresses the unique quality of each person and the evolutionary nature of mortal development. Human beings are ascending creatures on a long journey back to God. Spiritual progress comes as the individual discerns and accepts the will of God. To assist in this process, God has given each human a fragment of Himself called the thought adjuste, which guides a person toward perfection. When an individual has progressed sufficiently to have accepted God's will as his or her own, then the soul and personality fuse with the thought adjuster and the individual attains immortality.

Personality is also a gift from God and every person is a unique and unrepeatable expression of the divine personality, fully endowed with free will. The soul is the product of the personality and thought adjuster working together; human beings create their own souls as they choose to express the divine will, the essence of which is love. The book describes seven psychic circles of advancement a person must attain to achieve immortality, which equates to an eternal existence of learning and service in worlds beyond. Upon mortal death, a person is resurrected on another world consistent with person's spiritual development. The Urantia Book has been translated into a dozen languages and several hundred thousand copies have been printed.

See also: ❯ Christianity ❯ Jesus

Bibliography

Bradley, D. (1998). *An introduction to the Urantia Revelation*. Arcata, CA: White Egret Publications.

Gardner, M. (1995). *Urantia: The great cult mystery*. Amherst, NY: Prometheus Books.

Moyer, E. (2000). *The birth of a divine revelation: The origin of the Urantia papers*. Hanover, PA: Moyer Publishing.

The Urantia Foundation. (1955). *The Urantia book*. Chicago, IL: Author.

Uroboros

John Eric Killinger

Introduction

Uroboros (often *ouroboros*, sometimes *ourovoros*) is a transliteration of the Greek οὐροβόρος (οὐρηβόρος). It has appeared in Latin as *ourvorax*. Uroboros is a composite word meaning "devouring its tail." It is also synonymous with δράκων (*dragon*) and occasionally" ὄφις (*ophis*). Whereas the gnostic Ophites and even contemporary snake handling sects within Pentecostal Christianity (originating in Appalachia) continue to exist sporadically throughout the Southern United States, these are perhaps more derivative of Minoan snake goddess cultic worship than uroboric devotion.

A Powerful Primordial Symbol

Uroboros means "tail devourer." Devouring the tail indicates the eating of one's own flesh (without swallowing – yet). Tertullian (1989) and Chrysostom (1989) remark of the "autocannibalism" within the Eucharistic meal, the Lord's Supper wherein Jesus instituted the bread and cup of wine as his body and blood which his followers are to take, eat, and drink in anamnesis of him. Not only this, but he himself eats his own flesh and drinks his own blood and applies the alpha and omega (the first and the last letters in the apocalypse of John) to himself.

The uroboros is the most dynamic and primitive of all symbols representing the self-sufficient primordial deity. There is a connection between the uroboros and *khut*, the sacred snake that coils around the sun and marks the travel of the solar disk across the heavens in hieroglyphic representations of Ra within Egyptian theology and mythology. Uroboros as a sun depiction in Egyptian papyri is considered a *lemniscate*, or figure eight, the symbol for infinity. In such depictions, the uroboros appears in double and indicates volatility, is associated with the magician card in the Tarot deck, and has affinity with the one-sided Moebius strip that came to symbolize anxiety for Lacan (2004) because of its non-orientability. Representations of the lemniscate uroboros also appear in alchemical texts.

It is a round element, not unlike the Greek α, and because it is a round element, the uroboros is also *omega* (Ω). The eat and be eaten aspects (life and death) are the hallmarks of the uroboros' sustaining of the cosmic process. Not only has it affinity with the Eucharistic meal, but the uroboros is equivalent to the Holy Spirit because it is both actor and the acted-upon and producer and product simultaneously.

There are incidences of triple uroboroi, as well. Charbonneau-Lassay (1991) includes a woodcut depicting such a symbol from a sixteenth-century Italian shield. This insignia is a good ancestor of the Borromean knot matheme in Lacan's psychoanalytic theory of the interconnection between the Real, Imaginary, and Symbolic – this despite the lack of the fourth ring (the *sinthome* or Σ) that would hold the entire knot together should a piece of it be cut. Lacan points out that in the traditional Borromean knot of three interlocking rings, cutting any one of the rings would undo the knot entirely. The presence of the *sinthome* (etymological ancestor of the *symptom*) would keep this from happening. It is worth noting that with this fourth ring we would have not only a quaternity symbol, a squaring of the circle, but also the fourth within the alchemical axiom of Maria Prophetissa (one becomes two, two become three, and out of the third comes the One as the fourth).

Throughout the Septuagint (LXX), the Greek translation of the Old Testament or Hebrew bible, the uroboros appears in various guises as δράκων (*dragon*). There is the serpent in the Garden of Eden; there are epithetical comparisons of the uroboros/dragon to Babylon in the prophets; the uroboros is synonymous with Leviathan whom God tames, makes of it a plaything, and eventually destroys; uroboros/dragon is also epithetically used to describe the pharaoh king of Egypt using the metaphor of the Nile crocodile; and it appears even in apocryphal texts of the prophet Daniel in the stories of Bel and the dragon to be slain as a means to attempt a paradigmatic faith shift in the serpent cults of Babylon.

Interconnections have been made between the triad Leviathan-uroboros-Christ, since the uroboros is viewed as being a *homoousia*. That is, it is of one substance, as Christian creedal statements have attempted to clarify in the relationship between God, Christ, and the Holy Spirit in trinitarian formulae. This is, of course, a throwback to the archetypal incest motif associated with the uroboros. Father, mother, son, and daughter are of the same substance, so that what happens to one happens to all. This ties in with the understanding noted in the Chrysopoeia of Cleopatra in the Egyptian *Codex Marcianus* (Berthelot & Ruelle, 1888) wherein a light and dark uroboros surrounds the Greek phrase "en to pan" (έν τὸ πᾶν), "the One, the All." This is indicative of the uroboros being at one and the same the sacrificer and the sacrificed (i.e., God and Christ), alchemically represented by the spirit Mercurius and his role as both uniter and divider.

In the New Testament, the imagery of the uroboros/dragon appears specifically in the apocalypse (Revelation) of John. In Revelation 12 (Aland, et al., 1998: 654–656), this dragon has been observed to be analogous to the mythologems of Apollo killing the Pythian dragon at Delphi and Zeus' immobilization of Typhon as though to indicate the commonality of the need to overcome/ overthrow/imprison/slay the dragon as offending beast. Indeed, it became common practice in the Middle Ages to dub a knight in the name of God, St. Michael, and St. George as a symbol of Yahweh's overthrowing the great sea serpent Leviathan and making it a plaything – not to mention the obvious affinities with the subduing of Satan by Michael in the Revelation of John. Such imagery also denotes the links the uroboros has with twinship, for example, the story of Castor and Pollux, the pillars of Hermes (Mercurius!) and Hercules (and the Kabbalah's Jachin and Boaz columns), the Mithraic Cautes and Caupartes, as well as the Hero Twins in Pueblo lore: monster slayers and transformers of the old to the new. W. R. Bion (1950/1967) alludes to the poisonous nature in the swallowing of the analytic twin. Ode 22 of the pseudepigraphal *Odes of Solomon* (Charlesworth, 1985: 755) recalls the "poison" of the dragon which is its dark half.

The uroboros motif is also present in the third chapter of the Johannine gospel wherein Jesus and Nicodemus broach the subject of the serpent lifted up by Moses. This is an overt allusion to the lifting up of the Christ on the cross, the sacrifice by the sacrificer for the renewal and redemption of human beings. In this same chapter of John's gospel, the uroboros image first appears in the call to be born from above (water and the spirit). Uroboros is associated with water (as in the Genesis story of creation), and it is affiliated with Okeanos, which has the dual meaning of life (*zoë*) and death (*thanatos*). That the uroboros is capable of fragmenting, separating, and dividing is indicative of life, since *zoë* is an epithet for Dionysos, divine archetypal symbol of fragmentation. But the uroboric dragon is also a symbol of perpetual renewal, which is also indicative of *zoë* as rebirth follows death.

Uroboros in Gnosticism and Mystical Judaism

In gnostic writings, such as the *Pistis Sophia* (Mead, 1921/2005), the body of the mysterious serpent is divided into 12 aeons, corresponding to the 12 months of the solar year. Within the dialogue with the resurrected Christ, Mary Magdalene inquires about the nature of outer darkness. Jesus' response is that the outer darkness is a great dragon with its tail in its mouth outside the whole world and surrounding the whole world. This may well be the same outer darkness into which the improperly attired guest is cast in Jesus' parable of the marriage feast in Matthew 22. Thus the light and dark attributes of the uroboros correspond to the *agathadaimon* (spirit of good) and the *kakadaimon* (spirit of evil), respectively. This is because as serpent, the uroboros gives and sustains life as well as removes and destroys life.

It is important to consider the issue of emanations when speaking of the uroboros. The gnostic texts that comprise the Nag Hammadi codices contain a number of references to the uroboric nature of the creation and dissolution of the cosmos which spring from emanations of the great serpent. These are, psychologically speaking,

projections. Whether we put up barriers (β-screens) to block or repress these projections is something worth taking into consideration. As knowledge of the uroboros is eventually related to the squaring of the circle (which allows us to discern God), contains the union of the opposites (tying it to the hierosgamos [q.v.]), and is, all in all, immune to injury, it is analogous to W. R. Bion's epistemological notion that knowledge leads to absolute reality, which he designates as "O." Put another way, knowledge respectfully leads to the indescribable ultimate reality, godhead (not *imago Dei!*), or "O," remembering that knowledge and ultimate reality are not synonymous.

Referring to Torah, Rabbi Yochanan ben Bag (Ben Bag Bag in the Babylonian Talmud) urges in *Pirke Avot* 5:22, "Turn it and turn it again, for everything can be found therein." It is the uroboric nature of Torah to reach out and draw the world into itself and project it. The same could be said of Kabbalah, since the uroboros is synonymous with Leviathan and this same tamed sea serpent and plaything of God is therein the name for *Yesod* and *Tifereth*.

Uroboros in Psychology

With the uroboros, there is still turbulence, for it encircles the Void or abyss of chaos. This bears on Bion's (1977/2000) concept of emotional turbulence in the analytic encounter – indeed, within any encounter between human beings. This turbulence/chaos holds events that are discernible, and it is up to us to pick our way to them and draw them out. Films (e.g., *Stargate*) have capitalized on the uroboric interconnectedness between other galaxies and times, aeon fluxes, and the like. Joyce (1939/1967) produced an exceptional uroboric text in his *Finnegan's Wake*.

The uroboros is the one that devours, fertilizes, begets, slays, and brings itself, like the phoenix, to life again. It is hermaphroditic and the container of the opposites: poison and panacea, as well as basilisk and savior. As a sexual symbol, the uroboros in fertilizing itself is thus related to hierosgamos. Charbonneau-Lassay (1991) mentions the existence of a gold ring in the form of a uroboros. A wedding band in gold (the highest not-color color both symbolically and alchemically) is already a uroboros, further connecting it with the hierosgamos, or sacred marriage, acted out within the wedding rite.

Despite its lemniscate and Borromean emanations and derivatives, the uroboros is usually depicted as a serpent devouring its tail, ring shaped, a circle without beginning and without end. It's a symbol of infinite time, of death and rebirth, regeneration, dying in order to be born anew. Geometrically, the topology of the uroboros is that of a torus, a donut defined by two circles – one revolving about an axis coplanar with the other. Lacan used the torus to speak of the effect of the irruption of the Real into everyday life. With the torus, there is no inside or outside: only two voids by which to articulate request and desire which never quite find fulfillment and end up creating a spiraling chain of veiled originary remembrance. Because our lives and the world form a continuous order within the toroidal uroboros, when the Real irrupts, it does so everywhere at once, subjecting everything to change. Since the uroboros serpent not only signifies emanation/projection and dissolution but also life-giving and life-taking, such an irruption is threatening because of the potential for the dissolution of everything in its presence. The uroboros is thus a sublation (progress, qualitative change), the sort of *Aufhebung* used in Hegelian terminology. Nevertheless, whatever change occurs is essentially an enantiodromia. There is a return to the originary and the movement is not static but dynamic.

See also: ◉ Apocalypse ◉ Bible ◉ Bion, Wilfred Ruprecht and "O" ◉ Genesis ◉ Gnosticism ◉ Jesus ◉ Kabbalah ◉ Ritual ◉ Symbol

Bibliography

Aland, B., et al. (1998). Ἀποκάλυψις Ἰωάννου [Revelation of John]. In *Greek-English New Testament* (8th Rev. ed., pp. 632–680). Stuttgart, Germany: Deutsche Bibelgesellschaft.

Berthelot, M., & Ruelle, C. -É. (1888). *Collections des anciens alchimistes grecs* (3 Vols.). Paris: G. Steinheil.

Bion, W. R. (1967). The imaginary twin. In *Second thoughts*. pp. 3–22. London: Karnac, (Original work published 1950).

Bion, W. R. (2000). Emotional turbulence. In F. Bion (Ed.), *Clinical seminars and other works* (pp. 295–305). London: Karnac. (Original work published 1977).

Charbonneau-Lassay, L. (1991). *The bestiary of Christ* (Abridged ed.). (D. M. Dooling, Trans.). New York: Parabola.

Charlesworth, J. H. (Ed.). (1985). Odes of Solomon (J. H. Charlesworth, Trans.). In *Old Testament pseudepigrapha: Vol. 2. Expansions of the "Old Testament" and legends, wisdom and philosophical literature prayers, psalms, and odes, fragments of lost Judeo-Hellenistic works* (pp. 725–771). Garden City, NY: Doubleday.

Chrysostom, J. (1989). Concerning the statutes. In P. Schaff (Ed.), *A select library of Nicene and post-Nicene fathers of the Christian church* (pp. 317–489). Grand Rapids, MI: William. B. Eerdmans.

Joyce, J. (1967). *Finnegan's wake*. New York: Penguin. (Original work published 1939).

Lacan, J. (2004). *Le seminaire x: L'angoisse* (J.-A. Miller, Ed.). Paris: Éditions du Seuil.

Mead, G. R. S. (2005). *Pistis sophia: The gnostic tradition of Mary Magdalene, Jesus, and his disciples*. New York: Dover. (Original work published 1921).

Scharfstein, B. (Ed.). (1968). פרקי אבות [*Pirke Avot–Sayings of the fathers*]. New York: Ktav.

Tertullian. (1989). On the resurrection of the flesh. In A. Roberts & J. Donaldson (Eds.), *Latin Christianity: Its founder, Tertullian. Vol. III: The ante-Nicene fathers* pp. 549–596. Grand Rapids, MI: William. B. Eerdmans.

V

Vatican

Anthony J. Elia

The Vatican is a 108-acre territory and independent city-state located in the center of the Italian capital of Rome. It is headed by the Pope, as supreme governor, and administered through the Pontifical Commission. It has its own legal system, based upon the *2000 Fundamental Law of the Vatican City-State*, which was promulgated by Pope John Paul II, as well as a penal system, two jails, a post office, electric plant, bank, and publishing house. Canon law also presides, and in the cases where canon law does not apply, the laws of the city of Rome are employed. Originally, the term "Vatican" referred to the area of Rome called "mons vaticanus," which was a hill sloping away from the center of the ancient city near the Tiber, and a location that was sacred for early Christians, who believed it to be the burial place of St. Peter (Allen, 2004).

In common usage, the terms *Vatican*, *Holy See*, and *Roman Curia* are often interchanged imprecisely. Whereas the Vatican refers specifically to a physical location, the *Holy See* and *Roman Curia* refer to authoritarian and administrative roles. The *Holy See* is the centrality of authority, power, and jurisdiction, coming from the Latin *sedes*, or *seat*. It indicates the "proper term for designating the authority of the papacy to govern the Church. It is a non-territorial institution, an idea rather than a place" (Allen, 2004: 23). The *Roman Curia*, which originally referred to a seat in the ancient Roman Senate, is the "bureaucratic instrument through which the Pope administers the Holy See and carries out his function both as supreme governor of the Catholic Church and as a sovereign diplomatic actor" (Allen, 2004: 28). This said, the use of the term "Vatican" continues to function in media and general discussion as a catch-all for references to the central authority of the Roman Catholic Church.

Freud, Lacan, and the Vatican

Freud visited the Vatican Museum, and was positively enamored by its wealth of art. As Ernest Jones, Freud's biographer writes, "he [Freud] was...in the Vatican Museum and came away from it exhilarated by the beauty of what he had seen" (Jones, 1955: 20). But his feelings about the Vatican as a representative of the New Rome, which he recognized as the empire of Christian Rome, were negative. Unlike Lacan, who is sometimes described as "un cattolico non ortodosso" and a great admirer of Baroque Rome and its Catholic trappings, Freud was greatly conflicted over this new Christian Rome localized in the Vatican, especially as a tension rooted in his vision of Judaism in conflict with the Church (Amati, 1996).

Psychology and the Vatican

In the late nineteenth century, individuals such as Hermann von Helmholtz, Wilhelm Wundt, Pierre Marie Félix Janet, and Sigmund Freud were introducing experimental and clinical methods into the discipline of psychology. It was most significantly Freud, whose writings and psychoanalysis were to become anathema to the Catholic world (Gillespie, 2001). In a 1952 TIME magazine article entitled "Is Freud Sinful?" there is clear consternation from some Vatican officials, but these assertions are notably neither official nor dogmatic. One of the most vocal opponents of Freud was Monsignor Pericle Felici, an official of the Sacred Congregation of the Sacraments, who "loudly attacked 'the absurdity of psychoanalysis.' He stated flatly that anyone who adopts the Freudian method is risking mortal sin" (TIME, 1952). The general concern of most critics, though, had to do with any Freudian issues of sex and sexuality. The Vatican's official status on psychoanalysis in 1952 was expressed in the statement: "should psychoanalytic treatment be judged harmful to the spiritual health of the faithful, the church would not hesitate to take adequate steps to brand it as such. Nothing, so far, indicates that

D. A. Leeming, K. Madden, S. Marlan (eds.), *Encyclopedia of Psychology and Religion*, DOI 10.1007/978-0-387-71802-6,
© Springer Science+Business Media LLC 2010

such steps are about to be taken" (TIME, 1952). Felici continued to criticize the role of psychology and his assertion that "the psychoanalytical school can easily become a school of corruption" resulted in controversy (Gillespie and Kevin, 2001: 19). The official response to the storm over psychoanalysis came when Pope Pius XII spoke at the First International Congress on the Histopathology of the Nervous System, where he vigorously cautioned against "psychotherapeutic treatments that seek to unleash the sexual instinct for seemingly therapeutic reasons" (Gillespie and Kevin, 2001: 19). The following year, on April 13, 1953, Pius XII addressed the Fifth International Congress of Psychotherapy and Clinical Psychology, saying

> be assured that the Church follows your research and your medical practice with her warm interest and her best wishes. You labor in a terrain that is very difficult. But your activity is capable of achieving precious results for medicine, for the knowledge of the soul in general, for the religious dispositions of man and for their development (Pius XII, 1953).

In more recent times, there have been attempts at mollifying the historically tenuous and misunderstood relationship between psychology, psychiatry, and the Vatican. In 1993, Dr. Joseph T. English, then president of the American Psychiatric Association, led a delegation of prominent psychiatrists to meet with Pope John Paul II. The New York Times noted that there was a time when such an event "would have seemed unlikely, if not absurd" (Steinfels, 1993). Some of the issues that were considered in this encounter dealt with the belief by some Catholics that psychological ills are simple moral failings and, thus find psychotherapy something to be shunned (Steinfels, 1993). Five years after this discussion, Pope John Paul II referred to psychoanalysis and psychotherapy in a message on the sacrament of Penance, where he indicated that "the confessional is not and cannot be an alternative to the psychoanalyst's or psychotherapist's office. Nor can one expect the sacrament of Penance to heal truly pathological conditions" (John Paul II, 1998). In the twenty-first century, the Vatican has become more involved in the psychological disciplines, primarily through the work of pastoral care and counseling.

See also: ❂ Confession ❂ Freud, Sigmund ❂ Lacan, Jacques ❂ Pastoral Counseling ❂ Rome

Bibliography

Allen, J. L., Jr. (2004). *All the Pope's Men: The inside story of how the Vatican really thinks*. New York: Doubleday.

Amati, U. (1996). *Freud e Lacan a Roma: Dal Nome del Padre al Padre del Nome*. Roma: Borla.

Gillespie, S. J., & Kevin, C. (2001). *Psychology and American catholicism: From confession to therapy?* New York: The Crossroad Publishing Company.

Jones, E. (1955). *The life and work of Sigmund Freud: years of maturity, 1901–1919* (Vol. 2). New York: Basic Books, Inc.

Pope John Paul II. (1998, March 20). *Child, your sins are forgiven*, Message.

Pope Pius XII. (1953, July). *Psychotherapy and religion: An address to the fifth international congress of psychotherapy and clinical psychology*. Catholic Mind. 435.

Steinfels, P. (1993, January 3). Psychiatrists to Meet With the Pope. *New York Times* (Health).

TIME magazine (1952, Monday April 21).

Vedanta

Fredrica R. Halligan

A philosophy of classical Hinduism, *Vedanta* means "the culmination of the *Vedas*," referring to the *Upanishads* as the final portion of that scripture. In essence *Vedanta* is theology, with its main concern focused on divine power. In the past 100 years, *Vedanta* has been popularized in the West, a movement initiated by Swami Vivekananda who carried the teachings of Sri Ramakrishna from Calcutta to Vedanta Society centers in many major cities of the world.

Principal teachings embody the harmony of all religions: "As many faiths, so many paths." With its aim to experience the oneness of all creation, *Vedanta* preaches kindness to all, non-violence and service to others (*seva.*) God (*Brahman*) can be known as form or formless. In form, for example, God can be found in Divine Incarnations (*Avatars*) and as the Indweller of every human heart (*Atman*). As formless, God is perceived as all-pervading and as pure consciousness.

See also: ❂ Atman ❂ Avatar ❂ Hinduism ❂ Ramakrishna Paramahansa ❂ Vivekananda

Bibliography

Shraddhananda, S. (1996). *Seeing God everywhere: A Practical guide to spiritual living*. Hollywood, CA: Vendanta Press.

Yatiswarananda, S. (1995). *Meditation and Spiritual life*. Bangalore, India: Ramakrishna Math.

Vestments

David A. Leeming

Vestments are the garments worn by priests and other religious leaders in the performance of sacred rites. The term is used especially by Christian denominations which place particular emphasis on the sacrament of Holy Communion, the liturgy of the Eucharist. Thus, priests of the Orthodox, Roman Catholic, Lutheran, and most of the Anglican Communion, wear vestments while celebrating the "Mass" or "Great Liturgy." Vestments of various types and colors, depending on the liturgical season of the church year, are worn. The most common and most visible Eucharistic vestment is the chasuble, a poncho like garment that originated in Roman times.

The psychology behind vestments would seem to have to do with the priest's need during the sacred liturgy (service) to cover his particularity and individuality behind a "uniform" – a recognizable symbolic garment – so that he (or she in some traditions) may become the representative of his church as a whole. It is not Father X saying Mass; it is a representative of Christ and His Church, as the vestments indicate.

See also: ❯ Christianity ❯ Ritual

Bibliography

Norris, H. (2002). *Church vestments, their origin and development.* Mineola, NY: Dover.

Via Negativa

Philip Browning Helsel

The Latin term, which means the "way of negation," refers to the stream of Christian theology which emphasized the unknowability of God and the inability of positive theological attributes to define God. Also known as apophatic (literally "denial") theology, this way of thinking can be seen in the writings of those who would later be known as mystics. The *via negativa* paradoxically uses language to describe what is indescribable, but prefers adjectives of cancellation to those of positive attribution, claiming that positive attributes drawn from human experience can not reflect the divine. This stream of thought, far from being divorced from what preceded it in Christian theology, was present throughout Christian theology, and could be seen as a direct reflection of a strong emphasis on the transcendence of God (Turner, 1995: 1). Rejecting the positive naming of God found in Bonaventure and Aquinas, apophatic theologians emphasized the ineffability of God. Drawing from Pseudo-Dionysus, who in the fifth century described God as "dazzling darkness," thinkers such as Meister Eckhart and the anonymous author of *The Cloud of Unknowing* describe God in terms of negation, reflecting in their language the inexpressibility of God. However, it is important that the via negativa not be objectified by a discussion of it, since it resists fixation and attachment upon it as a particular "correct way." Apophatic theology is also an important stream in Islamic theology, which states the names of Allah, not as direct analogies to Allah, but as "veils put on the mystery of God" (Borrmans, 1993: 63–64).

If, in theistic religions, the via negativa is a reflection of the otherness of God, in a non-theistic religion such as Buddhism, the via negativa could be thought of as a radical immanence. Especially in Zen, the via negativa is strongly exemplified in the use of the prefix "not" in such phrases as "no-mind" and "no-self" and in the tendency to cross out even sacred terms such as sunyata ("emptiness"), emphasizing the limitations of language (Abe, 1995: 51). In Buddhism, the via negativa resists being put into the service of higher goals, or transcendence. In the Zen koan, the paradoxical approach of negation reflects the fact that the practitioner must grapple with the negation and senselessness of the riddle in order to approach meaning which is not positive or negative but transcends dualities (Suzuki, 1927: 250).

The via negativa is not merely semantics, but it points to something central to mysticism, the overcoming of dualities and all notions of the pursuit of sense or purpose. The challenge of apophatic theology is a challenge that is directed against both religion and language, but also inseparable from them.

Commentary

Just as Freud's discoveries unseated the omnipotence of the will and conscious thought, and therefore caused people to look deeper for the complexities of meaning, the via negativa also involves suspicion for the potential of positive language to clearly point to reality. The illuminating character of parapraxes echo negative theology in both

V

the slipperiness of language and the sense of a deep reality being glimpsed. Jung built his theory of opposites upon a valuing of the supposedly paradoxical and contradictory sides of experience. His formulations emphasized mystery and resonated with the via negativa in their suspicion that there maybe something more true than language can explain. The via negativa could be seen as a corollary to depth psychology in its attempts to seek to understand deeper aspects of experience, in its emptying of categories with an openness to what is beyond.

At the same time, the via negativa, in the Christian tradition, seems to rely upon the distance of God, and thus could be seen to imply the distance of the believer from her object of worship. Feuerbach critiqued all expressions of a via negativa as really implying a failure of faith (Feuerbach, 1957: 220). Negative theology could be analyzed as implying doubt or disappointment with a faith object in which one attempts to trust, and thus placing that object beyond all reach. Psychologically, this could be understood as reflecting failure in the earliest environments in which the psychic potential of faith is established for the child. However, apophatic theology should not too quickly be identified with disappointment or loss, or with what John of the Cross called "the dark night of the soul," since it cannot simply be equated with an experience of depression or a purgative stage of faith through which one passes. It is best understood, in theistic settings, as an important stream of thought alongside positive mysticism. In non-theistic traditions, it is the relativity of language in service of non-duality. In either case, it refers to something which certainly has psychological components, but retains its own religious logic and should not be flattened to fit psychological categories.

See also: ❂ Buddhism ❂ Christianity ❂ Depth Psychology and Spirituality ❂ Doubt ❂ Freud, Sigmund ❂ Islam ❂ John of the Cross ❂ Koan ❂ Meister Eckhart ❂ Sunyata ❂ Zen

Bibliography

Abe, M. (1995). Kenotic God and Dynamic Sunyata. In C. Ives (Ed.), *Divine emptiness and historical fullness*. (pp. 25–90) Valley Forge, PA: Trinity Press.

Borrmans, M. (1993). Prayer in Islam. In A. Thottakara (Ed.), *Islamic spirituality*. (pp. 54–72) Mannanam, India: St. Joseph's Press.

Feuerbach, L. (1957). *The essence of Christianity* (G. Eliot, Trans.). Harper: New York.

Johnston, W. (Ed.). (1973). *The cloud of unknowing and the book of privy counsel*. New York: Doubleday.

Suzuki, D. T. (1927). *Essays in Zen Buddhism*. London: Luzac & Co.

Turner, D. (1995). *The darkness of God: Negativity in Christian mysticism*. Cambridge, England: Cambridge University Press.

Theological Seminary Library. http://www.oxfordreference.com/views/ENTRY.html?subview = Main&entry = t174.e5430.s0002.

Uthemann, K.-H., & Kazhdan, A. (1991). Theology. In A. P. Kazhdan (Ed.), *The Oxford dictionary of Byzantium* (pp. 2057–2058). Princeton, NJ: Oxford University Press.

Vicarious Traumatization

Lori B. Wagner-Naughton

Defined as the indirect transmission of distressing symptoms following exposure to an individual who has directly experienced a traumatic event. After empathic and spiritual engagement with a traumatized individual, the listener may experience symptoms consistent with posttraumatic stress disorder (PTSD). These responses can include: distressing imagery or reexperiencing of the event; persistent avoidance and numbing of stimuli, thoughts, or feelings reminiscent of the trauma; increased physiological arousal; somatic ailments; and significant impairment (DSM-IV-TR). In essence, the listener functions as the "container" for the uncomfortable thoughts and feelings that are elicited through exposure to another individual's recollections of traumatic material. The listener may attempt to alleviate these distressing emotions through spirituality or religious affiliation. Shaw, Joseph, and Linley (2005) describe how, "religious beliefs may provide a framework to aid reappraisal of threatening situations as less of a threat and more of a challenge" (p. 3). After reframing the trauma within a different context, the listener can begin to process existential conflicts and seek alternate meanings about life experiences (Frankl, 1984).

See also: ❂ Trauma

Bibliography

American Psychiatric Association. (2000). *Diagnostic and statistical manual of mental disorders* (Rev. 4th ed.). Washington, DC: Author.

Frankl, V. E. (1984). *Man's search for meaning*. New York: Washington Square Press.

Shaw, A., Joseph, S., & Linley, A. (2005). Religion, spirituality, and posttraumatic growth: a systematic review. *Mental health, Religion, & Culture*, 8, 1–11.

Violence and Religion

James W. Jones

All the religions of the world contain storehouses of symbols and metaphors of war and violence. At the beginning of the sacred history of the Bible – the fountainhead of Judaism, Christianity and Islam – God "Himself" hardens Pharaoh's heart to set the Egyptians up for slaughter. The first born child of every Egyptian family is slain until every Egyptian family knew death. Bloody stories of warfare, pillage, rape and conquest fill the opening books of the *Torah*. Such texts lay the basis for the Holy War tradition in Judaism, Christianity, and Islam. The *New Testament* contains bloody portrayals of Jesus' suffering on the cross, Paul's metaphors of continual spiritual warfare, and the horrific images in the *Book of Revelation* so dear to apocalyptic Christians. The crusades, the inquisition, and the European wars of religion following the Reformation are all part of the history of Christianity. Islam tells and retells the stories of the Prophet's battles and conquest and there is the history of Islam's bloody sweep across the Middle East and North Africa. The Pali chronicles contain many tales of the wars and conquests by Buddhist kings, tales that are told and retold among the Buddhists of Sri Lanka in their campaign to subdue the Tamil population there. In 1959 a Sri Lankan Prime Minister was assassinated by a Buddhist monk. Tibetan Buddhism also has many stories of warfare and its divine pantheon contains countless images of bloodthirsty deities and semi-divine beings. And there is a long lineage of warrior Buddhist monks in China and Japan. The Hindu epics like the *Ramayana* and the *Mahabharata* are full of epic battles and warrior heroes. No world religion is without a storehouse of more than enough texts and tales to justify any and all acts of brutality, bloodshed, and terrorism. Historically and textually there are many, many connections between religion and violence. In the sweep of human history there is no evidence that any one world religion is bloodier than any other (Juergensmeyer, 2000; Stern, 2003).

No serious contemporary psychological study has found any evidence for diagnosable psychopathology in those who commit acts horrific violence in the name of religion (see, for example, the review in Horgan, 2006). Most extraordinary acts of inhumanity are committed by very ordinary people. Theologians have said this for centuries; many social psychologists are coming to the same conclusion.

Most contemporary psychological investigations of the connections between religion and violence are done by social psychologists, often in the context of more general investigations into violent behavior. Such studies almost always locate the causes of violent behavior in the dynamics of groups. The two most widely cited social-psychological experiments in the literature of genocide – Milgram's obedience to authority and Zimbardo's prison experiments – illustrate this. In the early 1960s, Stanley Milgram recruited a cohort of forty ordinary men from New Haven, CT and told them to inflict increasing electric shocks on a subject, in response to the subject making mistakes on a word association test. The subject was, in fact, part of the experiment and did not receive any actual shocks. In response to the experimenter's requests, the majority of the participants inflicted increasingly severe shocks on the subject as a punishment for his wrong answers to questions. Even when the subject portrayed signs of severe distress, participants were willing to inflict what they were told was a near-fatal shock to the subject in obedience to the experimenter's commands (Milgram, 1974; Bass, 1999).

In 1971 at Stanford University, Philip Zimbardo recruited a cohort of typical college male undergraduates and randomly assigned one group to play the role of prisoners and the other to play the role of prison guards. He set them up in a mock prison setting. Anyone with noticeable psychological problems was screened out. Within days, a third of those assigned to be guards became increasingly cruel, sadistic, and tyrannical towards the prisoners, whom they knew were really just fellow undergraduates like themselves. This brutality escalated so rapidly that the 2-week long experiment was stopped completely after 6 days (Zimbardo, Maslach and Haney, 1999). These experiments demonstrate the ease with which violent groups can elicit cruel and sadistic behavior even from those not otherwise inclined in that direction.

Waller (2002) suggests four social-psychological factors that permit ordinary people to become perpetrators of extraordinary evil. The first factor claims that all of us have certain genetic predispositions shaped by natural selection that make us susceptible to committing vicious deeds. Religious leaders and institutions are particularly adept at manipulating these inherited inclinations towards ethnocentrism and us-versus-them thinking. Waller's second factor refers to the ways in which these inherited traits are shaped by culture to make us even more potentially available for heinous actions. Among the significant "cultural belief systems" are religious beliefs about the role of authority, about the dichotomy between the ingroup and outgroup, and the demonizing of those considered outside the true fold. Religious beliefs also serve as justifications for killing. By reinforcing ethnocentrism and scapegoating outsiders, religion can facilitate a "moral disengagement," through which we cease to see a horrific deed as immoral, and may redefine, and relabel otherwise abhorrent actions into something justified and even meritorious (Bandura, 2004). The third factor is "a culture of cruelty" in which individuals, already predisposed in this way by genetic inheritance and religious and cultural training, are directly trained as killers. Through escalating commitments (in which an individual is gradually introduced and desensitized to more heinous acts) and a ritual initiation, the individual's conscience is gradually numbed or repressed. Initiation into such violent groups allows for a diffusion of responsibility, creates an ethos of "deindividuation" in which individuals can act with anonymity, and makes them subject to an almost irresistible peer pressure. Religious groups can become cultures of cruelty in this sense. Waller's fourth factor concerns the way in which potential victims are dehumanized, labeled as beyond the pale of human compassion and empathy. Religion has many powerfully effective ways to dehumanize and delegitimize opponents. Religion may be, in fact, one of humanity's most powerful means to the "social death" of the other (Waller, 2002).

Bandura emphasizes that people need a moral justification before they will engage in reprehensible actions. He argues that "the conversion of socialized people into dedicated fighters is achieved not by altering their personality structures, aggressive drives, or moral standards. Rather it is accomplished by cognitively redefining the morality of killing" (Bandura, 2004: 124). Bandura points out that "religion has a long and bloody history" as one of the major vehicles for providing that moral justification of mass bloodshed (Bandura, 2004: 125).

The current psychological discussion of the origins of violence is mainly located here. Most recently published, psychologically oriented articles focus on the group processes and induction procedures by which individuals are recruited to perform violent actions (cf., Miller, 2004). However, not every member of a society from which religious violence arises joins a violent group and not every member of such a group actually commits a violent act. This suggests that the psychology of religious violence cannot completely ignore individual factors.

The clinical question is why certain individuals resonate with the messages of religious violence. In a study of religious violence across three traditions (Muslim jihadis, the Japanese Buddhist group Aum Shinrikyo, American

apocalyptic Christianity) I argue that religions give rise to violent actions when they emphasize shame and humiliation, when they dichotomizes the world into warring camps of the all-good against the totally evil, when they demonize those with whom they disagree and foment crusades against them, when they advocate violence and blood sacrifice as the primary means of purification, when their devotees seek to placate or be unified with a punitive and humiliating idealized figure or institution, when they offer theological justifications for violent acts, and when they promote prejudice and authoritarian behavior (Jones, 2008). Psychological dynamics such as splitting, the rage for purification, the need for absolute certainty, the drive to externalize aggression and demonize an out-group – dynamics historically investigated by clinicians – may predispose individuals to find violent theologies meaningful (Jones, 2002).

From a clinical perspective, religion leads to violence when universal religious themes such as purification or the search for reunion with the source of life or the longing for personal meaning and transformation – the classic instigators of spiritual search and religious conversion – become subsumed into destructive psychological motivations such as a Manichean dichotomizing of the world into all-good, all-evil camps, or the drive to connect with and appease a humiliating or persecuting idealized patriarchal Other. The result is the psychological precondition for religiously sponsored violence. Some factors that might serve as warning signs that a religious group has a high potential for violence are: (1) profound experiences of shame and humiliation either generated by social conditions outside the group and potentiated by it or generated from within the group (Gilligan, 1996), (2) splitting humanity into all-good and all-evil camps and the demonizing of the other, (3) a wrathful, punitive idealized deity or leader, (4) a conviction that purification requires the shedding of blood, and (5) often a fascination with violence (Jones, 2008).

In a book whose title – *Violence and the Sacred* – says it all, Rene Girard offers an account of religion arising out of acts of violence (Girard, 1977, 1996). In tribal societies, violence threatens the entire social order. The solution arrived at by our ancestors, Girard suggests, is the whole society coming together and channeling the urge for violence onto an object, person, animal – the scapegoat – who is then rejected, exiled, and killed. With the scapegoat sacrificed, the community is again reconciled, at least temporarily. The sacrificed victim, bringer of a new order of peace and harmony, is now regarded as a savior, a god. Scapegoating and sacrifice acquire the penumbra of the sacred by their power to contain and mute the devastating possibilities of violence. Because of the scapegoat we are reconciled. Thus the scapegoat comes to be worshiped. So religious ritual develops. For Girard, religious ritual comes after the sacrificial deed, not before it. Religion develops out of the sacrificial action rather than sacrificial rituals being an expression of some religious impulse.

The sacrificers, now bound together by this bloody act, vow not to repeat the violent crime that led to the escalation of violence that only a sacrifice could stop. Thus prohibitions – "thou shall not kill" (unless it is a ritual sacrifice) – arise and become established. Eventually this process must be explicated; it must enter into language and so a narrative grows up to explain the ritual. Thus myth arises and it is established. Here then are the core processes of religion – ritual, prohibition, and myth – all arising out of what Girard calls the "scapegoating mechanism." Religion becomes the major way of containing violence; that is its first and most basic function. So religion and violence are inextricably linked.

A complete psychology of religion must include the psychology of religious violence. Psychological processes such as shame and humiliation, splitting and seeing the world in black-white terms along with the inability to tolerate ambivalence, the dynamic of projection and demonizing the other all contribute to violence apart from religion. But the history and psychology of religion make clear that such dynamics are not only central to the evocation of violence, they also lay close to the heart of much religious experience. By demanding submission to a deity, text, institution, group, or teacher that is experienced as wrathful, punitive, or rejecting, religions inevitably evoke or increase feelings of shame and humiliation that are major psychological causes of violent actions. By continually holding before the devotee an overly idealized institution, book, or leader, religions set up the psychodynamic basis for splitting and bifurcating experience. By teaching devotees that some groups are inferior, evil, satanic, condemned by God, religions encourage the demonizing of others and their "social death," making their slaughter seem inconsequential, justified, or even required. For these reasons any turn to violence is not accidental but is rather close to the heart of much of the religious life (Jones, 2008, 2002).

See also: ❷ Apocalypse ❷ Bible ❷ Christianity ❷ Evil ❷ Jihad ❷ Judaism and Psychology ❷ Psychology of Religion ❷ Sacrifice

Bibliography

Bandura, A. (2004). The role of selective moral disengagement in terrorism and counterterrorism. In F. Moghaddam & A. Marsella (Eds.), *Understanding terrorism*. Washington, DC: American Psychological Association Press.

Bass, T. (Ed.). (2000) *Obedience to authority*. Mahwah, NJ: Erlbaum.

Gilligan, J. (1996) *Violence*. New York: Random House.

Girard, R. (1977). *Violence and the sacred* (P. Gregory, Trans.). Baltimore, MD: Johns Hopkins Press.

Girard, R. (1996). *The Girard reader* (J. Williams, Ed.). New York: Crossroads.

Horgan, J. (2006). *The psychology of terrorism*. London: Routledge Press.

Jones, J. (2002). *Terror and transformation: The ambiguity of religion in psychoanalytic perspective*. London: Routledge.

Jones, J. (2008). *Blood that cries out from the Earth: The psychology of religious terrorism*. New York: Oxford University Press.

Juergensmeyer, M. (2000). *Terror in the mind of God*. Berkeley, CA: University of California Press.

Milgram, S. (1974). *Obedience to authority*. New York: Harper & Row.

Stern, J. (2003). *Terror in the name of God*. New York: Ecco Press.

Waller, J. (2002). *Becoming evil*. New York: Oxford University Press.

Zimbardo, P. (2004). A situationalist perspective on the psychology of evil. In A. Miller (Ed.), *The social psychology of good and evil*. New York: Guilford.

Zimbardo, P., Maslach, C., & Haney, C. (1999). Reflections on the Stanford prison experiment. In T. Bass (Ed.), *Obedience to authority*. Mahwah, NJ: Erlbaum.

Virgin Birth

Jeffrey B. Pettis

In myth and religion virgin birth is central to the life and coming into existence of the divine child. The Buddha, for example, descends from the higher realm into the womb of his mother the Great Queen Maya. He appears in the shape of a milk-white elephant. The conception in her womb occurs without defilement, as he is born coming forth from her side under the shining constellation of Pushya. The birth is miraculous, like those of other Hindu heroes such as Aurva and Prithu, for he does not enter the world in the usual manner. Similarly, Jesus is conceived through the Holy Spirit in the womb of Mary. The conception and birth are acknowledged and celebrated by the cosmos, the Magi from the East, and by Mary herself (Matt. 1.18–2.11; Luke 1.26–58). The virgin as divine bride is set apart from the collective element as a preparation and requirement for divine conception. *The Gospel of Pseudo-Matthew* tells of Mary who as a child was in constant prayer, and that the angels of God spoke with her often. She is called "blessed among women, and blessed is the fruit of her womb" (9). The mother of the Buddha is also marked as having special qualities.

According to Buddha legend, she is the Great Queen Maya, splendid, steadfast, and having the beauty of a goddess after whom she is named. She seeks seclusion in the pure woods where she meditates continuously, and she suffers no discomfort during the birth of the Buddha child. In these examples, both virgin and child are trans-relational and have double-sided natures. The mother, having conceived through *pneuma,* now herself has a sacredness which exists along with her body which gestates, nurtures, and contains the infant child. Likewise, the child conceived as *pneuma* takes on flesh, becoming mortal and collective along with all human beings. This dual nature creates an implicit tension between the divine and human natures which may get played out in the external world. Mary the mother of Jesus is to be divorced by her betrothed Joseph and liable to death by stoning as an adulteress (cf. the Vestil Virgin of Rome who is buried alive for being unchaste). The divine-figure Jesus will be mocked by the mob and executed as "King of the Jews." The Buddha will realize Nirvana only by entering into the suffering and poverty of the collective, mundane world. Virgin birth may be understood ultimately to occur as an act of divine imperative. The virgin's womb becomes the means – the vessel – of divine will and purpose. A spiritualization of matter and the maternal takes place through/by *patēr*-animus. Virgin birth alternately may be seen to be pre-patriarchal in nature, not relying upon sexual intercourse and male human initiative. The virgin mother occurs as the "Great Mother," the "Earth Goddess." She is the true creator, as becomes the Egyptian goddess Isis who re-creates her dismembered husband Osirus, and begets her son Horus to whom she gives the elixir of life.

See also: ❯ Buddhism ❯ Great Mother ❯ Jesus ❯ Mary ❯ Virgin Mary

Virgin Mary

Anthony J. Elia

The Virgin Mary (Heb: *Miryam*; Grk: *Maria*) is the mother of Jesus Christ in the New Testament texts (most notably, the gospels of Luke and Matthew). Throughout history the importance of the mother of Jesus Christ has been interpreted broadly by religious traditions, including Roman Catholicism, Orthodox Christianities, and Protestant denominations, as well as theologians within each of these traditions. Each has contributed to a deep hermeneutical tradition of Marian studies. The Virgin Mary is often referred to as "Maria" (*Ave Maria*), "Mother of God," "The Blessed Virgin," "Mater Dolorosa" (Mother of Jesus providing maternal care at crucifixion), (Pelikan, 1996: 14–15), "The Second Eve," and "Mother of the People." In Eastern Christian traditions, Mary took on the title of "Theotokos," which has often been understood in translations from the Greek as "Mother of God," (Latin: *Mater Dei*; German: *Mutter Gottes*), but is more precisely translated as "the one who gave birth to the one who is God," (Slavic: *Bogorodica*; Latin: *Deipara*), (Pelikan, 1996: 55).

Mary in Islam

In Islam there is favorable discussion about the Virgin Mary (Arabic: *Maryam*) in the Qur'an where she is seen as one of the holiest women to walk the earth. References to the Virgin Mary occur prominently in suras 3 and 19, though the earlier sura 3, which is considered part of the prophet's Medina period, appears to focus on the negation of Jesus's divinity. In contrast, sura 19 strongly draws parallels between the prophet Muhammad and the Virgin Mary as each being bearers of the word of God (Pelikan, 1996).

Cult of Mary

The cult of Mary is relatively absent in the church until about the fourth century C.E. Some scholars (Ashe, Carroll) have noted the rise in the cult at this time to be attributed to changes in the social strata of Roman society. The emergence of the cult of Mary in the fourth century has been partially attributed (in psychological terms) to an increase of proletarian Christians coming from father-ineffective families, which are marked by a "strongly repressed desire for the mother" (Carroll, 1986: 83). The psychoanalytic origins of the cult of Mary have been explained by Freud as a compromise where unconscious desires are redirected through an activity representing disguised fulfillment of the unconscious desire (Carroll, 1986).

Mariology

The scholarly and theological study of Mary, most often through Catholic perspectives, is called *Mariology*.

The history of Mariology dates back to late antiquity, and includes works by Irenaeus of Lyons, Ambrose of Milan, St. Bernard of Clairvaux, and St. Thomas Aquinas. Mariology developed in a more Thomistic vein in the sixteenth and early seventeenth century, specifically beginning with Jesuit scholar Francis Suarez (1548–1617). Francis de Sales (1567–1622), Robert Bellarmine (1542–1621), and St. Lawrence of Brindisi (1559–1619) also contributed to the development of philosophical and highly erudite Mariological texts in the Thomistic tradition.

Of the major theological aspects of Mariological history, there are four dogmas of the Catholic Church which underscore the Mariological narrative and its importance. These are (1) the Perpetual Virginity of Mary; (2) Mary as Mother of God; (3) the Immaculate Conception of Mary by her mother St. Anne; and (4) Mary's Assumption into Heaven. Mary's *Perpetual Virginity* was discussed in Patristic literature (notably Augustine, in his *De Virginitate*, Augustine), and continually reasserted Mary's virginity throughout her entire life. The role of *Mother of God* emphasizes a divine maternity and the unity held between Mary and Christ incarnate. This was first defined ecclesiastically at the Council of Ephesus in 431. The *Mother of God* Feast Day is January 1st. The doctrinal understanding of the *Immaculate Conception* of Mary is not to be confused with the *Virginal Conception* of Jesus. The *Immaculate Conception* is the belief that the Virgin Mother was always without original sin, and specifically, that her mother (traditionally St. Anne) conceived Mary without sin. On December 8th (*Immaculate Conception* Feast Day), 1854, Pope Pius IX solemnly put forth this dogma in a constitution titled *Ineffabilis Deus*. The fourth dogma, the Assumption, was executed in 1950 by Pope Pius XII, and defines that the Virgin Mary was assumed in body and in soul into heaven at the time of her death. August 15th is the Day of Assumption. An additional Feast Day of Marian importance is Annunciation Day, which is March 25th, commemorating the day when the angel Gabriel visited the Virgin Mother.

Jung's Interpretation

The Assumption of Mary is an important aspect of the Marian narrative, which effectively explicates the death of Mary (often referred to as the *dormition* or "falling asleep") and her ascent into heaven. In this context, Mary is often given the title "Queen of Heaven" (Pelikan, 1996). Carl G. Jung's assessment of the Marian Assumption, published in 1952, was in basic agreement with Pius

XII's 1950 apostolic constitution *Munificentissimus Deus*, which defined the dogma of Assumption (Pelikan, 1996). For Jung, Mary is "the pure vessel for the coming birth of God," but also both the daughter, bride, and mother of God, who is free from all original sin. As the bride of God, Jung establishes Mary as the incarnation of her prototype, Sophia, also being a mediatrix, or the one who leads humanity to God and assures immortality (Jung, 1954). Jung also describes the relational aspect of Mary to her son as a closeness where they are not real human beings, but gods. In the twentieth century, the role of Mary as the *coredemptrix*, or one who has an "active collaboration with Christ in the redemption of the world" has been central (Miegge, 1955: 155). These theological roles as *mediatrix* and *coredemptrix* emphasize the *mother as divine* character.

Psychoanalytic Interpretation in Art

Glorification of the Virgin Mary through art has been popular for over a millennium. Marian art has been assessed by the prominent psychological traditions, notably Freudian and Jungian analyses, and includes both analyses of the artists themselves and analyses of symbolism, for example. Psychological interpretations of Renaissance art depicting both Mary and the holy family, including St. Anne, are prominent. Images of the Virgin Mary can be seen in works as varied as Byzantine, Romanesque, Gothic, Renaissance, and Baroque art. Prominent artists, who depicted the Virgin Mary include Jan van Eyck (ca. 1390–1441), Lucas Cranach the Elder (1472–1553), Hans Memling (ca. 1433–1494), Raphael (1483–1520), Michelangelo (1475–1564), Titian (ca. 1485–1576), Leonardo da Vinci (1452–1519), Peter Paul Rubens (1577–1640), Rembrandt (1606–1669), El Greco (1541–1614), as well as more modern artists, such as Paul Gaugin (1848–1903) and Salvador Dali (1904–1989).

Freud himself touched upon Marian studies in his attempt to explicate the painting of the Virgin Mary with Child and St. Anne by Leonardo da Vinci. In this work, (entitled *Leonardo da Vinci and a Memory of His Childhood*, 1910), Freud analyzed the painter through da Vinci's depiction of the Virgin Mary (Freud, 1957: XI). Scholars have studied Freud's own analysis as the first application of psychology to art, and interpreted his study with insight into Freud's inferences that Leonardo depicted two mothers of the Christ child, the biological mother and the stepmother. Other scholars have commented that Freud's mistakes in his analysis of the Da Vinci painting are equally as important as the initial analysis itself, because these errors underscore the role of the analyst in making observations (Thanopulous, 2005).

Marian Apparitions

Apparitions of the Virgin Mary have been numerous and recognized for several centuries. These include apparitions in Guadalupe, Mexico (1531), the French Alps (by Benoite Rencurel) from 1664–1718, Paris (1830), LaSalette (1846), Lourdes (1858), Knock, Ireland (1879), Fatima, Portugal (1917), Beauraing (1932–1933) and Banneux, Belgium (1933), Necedah, Wisconsin (early 1950s), Garabandal, Spain (1961–1965), Zeitoun, Egypt (1968–1971), Bayside, NY (1970), Cuapa, Nicaragua (1980), and Medjugorje (1981).

The study of practitioners of the cult of Mary ranges from Freudian analyses of worship (*latria*), veneration (*dulia*), and hyperveneration (*hyperdulia*) – reserved strictly for the Virgin Mary – to Protestant explanations of visions in psychological terms (Miller, 1992). Psychoanalytic hypotheses have detailed aspects of the relation between the *machismo* complex and the prevalence of the cult of Mary in southern Italy and Spain. Additionally, the concepts of *identification* (defined as "the process of adopting the characteristics of someone else, including only in one's mind") and *sexual attachment* are considered part of the hypothetical schematic for some Marian worship (Carroll, 1986: 52). This continues in the vein of Oedipal frameworks and the sexual explications of both male and female relationships with the Virgin Mary (Carroll, 1986). In the case of excessive Marian devotion by men, some scholars (including Freud) have suggested an association between this excessive devotion and masochism, though evidence is not strong (Carroll, 1986).

Psychological explanations of apparitions range from intentionally fraudulent claims to those manifested by illness. The reasons provided by modern psychiatry include psychological projection, hallucinations, and hysteria (Miller and Samples, 1992). Other explanations of such apparitions, which scholars have deemed illusions, include feelings of anxiety induced by war, such as with the case of the Pontmain, France apparition of 1871, which contextualized, has been understood as a family's deep anxiety produced around its three sons going off to fight in the Franco-Prussian war. The nineteenth century novelist Émile Zola considered the future saint Marie-Bernarde Soubirous (the visionary at Lourdes) to be an exceptional case of hysteria, who suffered a degenerate heredity (Perry and Echeverría, 1988). The example of Zeitoun, Egypt is considered to be an illusion, as an unusual visual stimulus was detected by a large number of observers (Carroll, 1986), while in other cases with fewer observers, the designation has been given as hallucination.

Feminist Perspectives

Freudian analysis of theology and symbolism in contemporary Catholicism through a feminist perspective has yielded an interpretation of Marian femininity as inhibitory to psychological development and a continuation of the dominant patriarchal social structure (Harrington, 1984). The spectrum of feminist approaches to Mariology have been broad, and include such scholars as Elisabeth Gossmann, Daphne Hampson, Elizabeth Johnson, Patricia Noone, Rosemary Radford Reuther, and Catherina Halkes. The underlying and central themes in these perspectives are the issues of passivity, sexuality, gender, and dynamics of hegemony and power (McDonnell, 2005).

See also: ⊙ Christ ⊙ Freud, Sigmund ⊙ Islam ⊙ Jesus ⊙ Jung, Carl Gustav ⊙ Mary ⊙ Qur'an ⊙ Sophia ⊙ Virgin Birth

Bibliography

Ashe, G. (1976). *The virgin.* London: Routledge & Kegan Paul.

Augustine of Hippo. (1887 [1956]). Of Holy virginity. In P. Schaff (Ed.), *First Series Nicene and Post-Nicene Fathers* (Vol. 3, pp. 417–438). Grand Rapids, MI: Wm. B. Eerdmans.

Blum, H. P. (2001). Psychoanalysis and art, Freud and Leonardo. *Journal of the American Psychoanalytic Association, 49,* 1409–1425.

Carroll, M. P. (1986). *The cult of the virgin Mary: Psychological origins.* Princeton, NJ: Princeton University Press.

Ebertshäuser, C. H., et al. (1998). Mary: Art, culture, and religion through the ages. New York: Crossroad.

Freud, S. (1957). *The standard edition of the complete psychological works of Sigmund Freud* (Vol. 11) (J. Strachey, Trans.). London: The Hogarth Press.

Gaventa, B. R., & Rigby, C. L. (Eds.). (2002). *Blessed one: Protestant perspectives on Mary.* Louisville, KY: Westminster John Knox Press.

Harrington, P. A. (1984). Mary and femininity: A psychological critique. *Journal of Religion and Health. 23*(3), 204–217.

Jung, C. G. (1954). *Answer to Job* (R. F. C. Hull, Trans.). London: Routledge & Kegan Paul.

Macquarrie, J. (1990). *Mary for all Christians.* Grand Rapids, MI: William B. Eerdmans Publishing Company.

McDonnell, K. (2005). Feminist mariologies: heteronomy/subordination and the scandal of Christology. *Theological Studies, 66*(3), 527–567.

Miegge, G. (1955). *The Virgin Mary: The Roman Catholic Marian Doctrine.* Philadelphia, PA: Westminster Press.

Miller, E., & Samples, K. R. (1992). *The cult of the Virgin: Catholic Mariology and the apparitions of Mary.* Grand Rapids, MI: Baker Book House.

Pelikan, J. (1996). *Mary through the centuries.* New Haven, CT: Yale University Press.

Perry, N., & Echeverría, L. (1988). *Under the heel of Mary.* London: Routledge.

Thanopulous, S. (2005). Leonardo's phantasy and the importance of Freud's slip: The role of the analyst's phantasies in applied psychoanalysis and in the analytic relation. *International Journal of Psycho-Analysis, 86,* 395–412.

Vision Quest

Richard W. Voss · Robert Prue (Sikangu Lakota)

▶	*Ate wiohpeyata*	Father, to the West
	nawwajin yelo.	I am standing.
	Waayanka yo!	Behold me!
	Ite Otateya nawajin yelo	The wind blowing in my face.
		I am standing.
	Vision Quest Song (Lakota Ceremonial Songs, 1983)	

Introduction

The term "Vision Quest" describes a psychological metaphor based upon or inspired by the spiritual practice among Native American Indians. As a psychological metaphor the "vision quest" has been used by some clinicians to illustrate the journey of understanding one's dreams and experiences in terms of archetypical symbols related to self understanding and individuation (see Temagami Vision Quest Program, http://www.langskib.com/outdoor-programs-for-adults). However, as the indigenous, American Indian practice, "vision quest" is what the traditional Lakota call the *Hanbleceya* or "crying for a vision" ceremony (see B. Elk in J. E. Brown, 1953; Lame Deer, J. (Fire), 1972; Lame Deer, A. (Fire), 1992). Elsewhere, this ceremony is also called a "pipe fast" since the individual faster seeking to complete the vision quest often does so holding a "loaded" pipe, filled with a tobacco mixture that has been prepared by the individual (often a medicine man or holy man, see B. Elk, 1953: 45) who has agreed and committed to assist the individual complete his or her commitment to undergo this ordeal. Native Americans have used ceremonies to encounter the spirit world for thousands of years, and the *Hanbleceya* (pronounced, han-bi-lech-ia) is such a ceremony.

Hanbleceya: Crying for a Vision

"Are you ready to die?" was the question posed to the first author when he spoke to a medicine man about his desire to complete a *Hanbleceya*. That question reflects the traditional indigenous perspective that the "vision quest" or *Hanbleceya* is not something one undertakes lightly or casually. It is something one does under the careful supervision of a recognized medicine man or shaman or spiritual advisor (*Wicasa* waken) who serves as one's spiritual guide and interpreter of the spirits (Little Soldier, 1998, personal communication). Traditionally, only males conduct the *Hanbleceya* ceremony. No "fees" are charged for the ceremony – although a star quilt is generally given to the medicine man in gratitude for the ceremony and there is often a *wopila* or thanksgiving feast which concludes the ceremony where everyone is fed a meal, often comprised of meat (beef or buffalo) soup, fry bread, and chokecherry or berry sauce (*wojape*) by the faster. Traditional beverages offered at the meal include mint tea, coffee, cool aide or gatoraide.

One does not enter into a *Hanbleceya* without proper guidance and preparation. Generally, the preparation requires a year, during which time the individual faster (as he or she is called) gathers all of the materials required for the fast, which includes hosting a feast or closing meal for all those who helped with the ceremony or served as supporters and assistants, as well as prepares spiritually for the ordeal. It is important to note that completing a *Hanbleceya* ceremony does not make one a medicine man.

The *Hanbleceya* may be done by anyone, traditionally it was only done by males, this has changed in recent years where women also fast. Generally, the vision quest or pipe fast ceremony is undertaken by an individual who is drawn by a dream or a spiritual inclination to undergo this ceremony which incorporates a rather strenuous physical ordeal – a total solitary fast from food and water which may last anywhere from a half day or night, up to four days and four nights. The medicine man chooses the location of the ritual site because of the spiritual significance or value rather than "natural beauty" of the place. Typically such sites are often in a remote place without the intrusion of any outside interruptions or distractions. There are some well known sites in North America where Indigenous people seek visions, however, because of extensive exploitation of Indigenous rituals, one should not journey to those locations unless accompanied by a recognized

V

spiritual leader from an Indigenous community. The individual faster's own vision or dream is also taken into consideration in selecting the appropriate site for the fast. For example, one may dream of praying inside the earth, in a pit – close to the Unci (grandmother, Earth) or on a hill close to the Tunka'sila (grandfather) Sky. So, all of this is discussed with the medicine man who then prepares the suitable place for the fast.

Often, people will refer to the entire experience as "going up on the hill" or "going up to pray" which reflect the common location for the *Hanbleceya* as a high elevated point. However, the site or location may also be in a pit or a hole dug into the ground which is then covered with tarps and earth so that the space is completely darkened. One may also complete the fast in an *Inipi* or Sweatlodge, which a small, low lying dome-like structure. So, there is considerable variation here (Little Soldier, 1999, personal communication; Lame Deer, 1992: 190–200). The *Inipikaga* or purification ritual (also called a sweatlodge ceremony) is usually conducted prior to and after the *Hanbleceya*.

After the faster has decided to undergo the *Hanbleceya* or Crying for a Vision Ceremony, he or she seeks out a medicine man-shaman, or spiritual leader (*Wicasa Wakan*) who is willing to take on this responsibility – it is important to note the relational quality to this ceremony. The medicine man who accepts the commitment of a faster also assumes a very serious responsibility for them, and to the spirits, as also, opens himself up to the spiritual consequences of such a commitment. If the faster is not sincere or undergoes the ceremony for the wrong reasons or is not prepared, negative consequences could result. Fr. William Stolzman has prepared an excellent instructional book, *How to take part in Lakota ceremonies* (1995) which has a detailed description of the Vision Quest Ceremony (pp. 23–39). The book is a non-Indian view of the ceremony and provides helpful advise to the non-Indian interested in learning more about the ceremony or if ever asked to assist in such a ceremony. Of course, this does not replace the instruction provided by the medicine man or spiritual advisor, who will give very specific instruction on the way he conducts the ceremony. It is very important if one is taking prescribed medications to inform the medicine man so that this can be taken into consideration in the preparations.

The *Hanbleceya* is often repeated, the second author has participated in numerous vision seeking ceremonies: on the hill, in an inipi (sweatlodge) and in isolated locations for periods from two to five days. Having a vision is important for most Native Americans in the Plains of North America, but having a vision does not make one a shaman or medicine man (Benedict, 1922; Little Soldier,

1999, personal communication). The vision quest is often the precursor to participate in the *Wiwang Wacipi* or Sundance (Standing Cloud, 1987, personal communication; Little Soldier, 1999, personal Communication).

The *Hanbleceya* has the capacity to be a powerful adjunct to psychotherapy (Hawk Wing, 1997), but should not be facilitated by anyone not properly sanctioned to do so. Native American medicine men are the psychologists, psychiatrists, and social workers of their communities. The responsibility of facilitating these rituals often involves as much training as is involved with the training of a sanctioned clinicians, and it would be irresponsible to practice or lead Indian rituals without obtaining the proper training and permission to lead them.

It may be very difficult for non-Indians or individuals not familiar with the traditional ways of native people to comprehend this and other ceremonies. The ceremony is not a "show" or an adventure or some other kind of "personal enrichment experience." It is a real spiritual encounter, which has concrete effects. "Are you prepared to die?" sums up the seriousness of these effects. There have been instances where the spirits "came for the individual" where the faster actually died while undergoing this ceremony (Little Soldier, A. 2001, 2006, personal communication), so the ordeal of the vision quest is very sobering and needs to be understood as such. One does not enter into this without due consideration of the possibility that one may not come back or that one may come back changed by their vision – it may not be the vision that one *wanted*. Archie Fire Lame Deer discusses this, how he went on a vision quest and when he told his visions to the medicine man learned that he was *heyoka* or a contrary, a thunder-dreamer, which meant he would have to do the opposite (1992: 193).

It is important for the non-Indian to be aware of the profound spiritual significance of the Vision Quest ceremony for traditional American Indians, particularly if it is used or appropriated without proper authorization or permissions and preparation as a clinical method or metaphor – srealizing the depth of tradition associated with this ancient ceremony.

See also: ❯ Archetype ❯ Dream ❯ Individuation ❯ Ritual ❯ Shamans and Shamanism ❯ Symbol

Bibliography

Benedict, F. R. (1922). The vision in Plains culture. *American Anthropologist, 24*, 1–23.

Catches, P., & Catches, P. (1997). *Oceti Wakan (Sacred Fireplace)*. Pine Ridge, SD: Oceti Wakan.

Elk, B. (1953). *The sacred pipe: Black Elk's account of the seven rites of the Oglala Sioux.* (recorded & edited by J. E. Brown). Norman, OK: University of Oklahoma Press.

Hawk Wing, P. (1997). Lakota teachings: Inipi, humbleciya, and yuwipi ceremonies. In D. Sandner & S. H. Wong (Eds.), *The sacred heritage the influence of shamanism on analytical psychology* (pp. 193–202). New York: Routledge.

Lakota Ceremonial Songs. (1983). Performed by John Around Him (A. White Hat, Sr., Trans.). Rosebud, SD: Sinte Gleska College, Inc.

Lame Deer, A. F., & Erdoes, R. (1992). *Gift of power: The life and teachings of a Lakota medicine man* (with an introduction by A. M. Josephy, Jr.). Santa Fe, NM: Bear & Company.

Lame Deer, J., (Fire) & Erdoes, R. (1972). *Lame Deer seeker of visions.* New York: Washington Square Press.

Stolzman, W. (1995). *How to take part in Lakota ceremonies.* Chamberlain, SD: Tipi Press.

Temagami Vision Quest Program, Langskib-Canoe Tripping Programs for Young People and Adults. Retrieved 03–13–0, from http://www.langskib.com/outdoor-programs-for-adults/.

Visions

Nicholas Grant Boeving

Metaphorically, visions are often evocations of a scene – whether sordid or sublime. Whether they be of syphilitic agony, paradise or bliss, the word is wedded to an infinitude of metaphor. More prosaic still, visions may refer to nothing more than mere hallucinations or the faculty of sight itself. But in the history of religions, visions are inspirational renderings, often experienced by shamans or prophets, that serve to guide and gild communities of faith.

The Bible is replete with descriptions of visionary encounters. Ezekiel dramatically recalls his experience of witnessing the Lord as a chariot wrought of living creatures with four faces and calf's feet. *The Apocalypse* of Saint John (canonically known as the *Book of Revelation*) describes in phantasmagoric detail the final struggle and apotheosis of the faithful. The previous two examples, along with Paul's vision of Christ while on the road to Damascus, are but three of many visions recorded in the canonical Old and New Testaments.

In later theological developments the concept of The Beatific Vision came to be of central importance. First expounded upon in painstaking detail in the thirteenth century by St. Thomas Aquinas in his *Summae Theologiae*, the Beatific Vision is understood to be the undistilled perception of the unrefracted light of God.

Visions suffuse the literary legacy of Western Esotericism as well. Emanuel Swedenborg's complex theology was both born from and unfolded through a series of visions in which he vividly witnessed the wonders of Heaven and the horrors of Hell. Jakob Bohme (another central figure in the history of Western Esotericism) similarly experienced an ecstatic vision of light reflected in a pewter dish that led him to construct his own mystical philosophy.

Vision Quests are integral to the mechanics of shamanistic societies; in many tribal cultures they herald one's transition from boy or girlhood into the arena of adults. Often this unfolds along the following axes: He or she, upon reaching puberty, sets off into the wilderness to seek a vision, a vision that will direct his or her path for the duration of the life course. Frequently these visions appear in the form of animal teachers, or totems, that become private spiritual guides and shape, in effect, the future of their charges. Once the newly-minted man or woman reintegrates him or herself into the tribe, they are seen as extensions of the vision they experienced and their life's work will unfold accordingly.

Various theoretical apparatuses have been advanced within the field of psychology to account for the occurrence and persistence of visions. Psychoanalysis tends to view them as externalizations of neurotic conflict or simply wish-fulfilling fantasies. Cognitive theories hold them as aberrations of normal mental functioning. Jungian psychology views archetypal images that are regarded as visions crucial to the process of individuation. Newer non-reductive psychoanalytic approaches view visions as transformative and psychically integrative within the interpretive paradigm of psychodynamism.

See also: ❂ Bible ❂ Dreams ❂ Hallucinations ❂ Vision Quest

Bibliography

Alleman, G. M. (1932). *A critique of some philosophical aspects of the mysticism of Jacob Boehme.* Philadelphia, PA: University of Pennsylvania Press.

Berdyaev, N. (1955). *The meaning of the creative act.* (D. Lowrie, Trans.). London: Victor Gollancz.

Eliade, M. (2004). *Shamanism: Archaic techniques of ecstasy.* Princeton, NJ: Princeton University Press (1964; reprint).

Jung, C. (1963). *Memories, dreams, reflections.* New York: Vintage.

Kripal, J. (1995). *Kali's child: The mystical and erotic in the life and teachings of ramakrishna.* Chicago, IL: University of Chicago Press.

LaSor, W. S., et al. (1996). *Old testament survey: The message, form, and background of the old testament.* Grand Rapids, MI: William B. Eerdmans.

Meissner, W. W. (1984). *Psychoanalysis and religious experience.* New Haven, CT: Yale University Press.

Rose, J. S. (Ed.). (2002). *Emanuel swedenborg: Essays for the new century edition on his life, work, and impact.* West Chester, PA: Swedenborg Foundation.

Vivekananda

James H. Stover

Swami Vivekananda (1863–1902), born Narendranath Datta, became the most influential disciple of Sri Ramakrishna Paramahansa. He carried the torch of his guru and established the Ramakrishna Order as well as the Ramakrishna Mission. Arguably the biggest hit of the 1893 World Parliament of Religions in Chicago, he introduced Hinduism to America. As a great reformer and spiritual teacher, he has been called the "patriot saint of modern India."

Living only 39 years, Vivekananda remains one of the most influential people in the history of India and the history of religion. His journey, though brief, was deep and varied. He joined the Brahmo Samaj in college, dedicating himself to its social reforms. Although his interest in social action never waned, he left the Brahmo Samaj, seeking a more spiritual path, ultimately taking Ramakrishna as his guru. Trained in Western history and philosophy and passionate in his search for God, Vivekananda portrayed a keen duet of rationality and spirituality. He often challenged his master who, notwithstanding, appointed him as his spiritual successor. Today, the Ramakrishna Order and Ramakrishna Mission provide charitable, educational, and spiritual services in India and almost 50 other countries. These centers carry out the social and spiritual mission of Vivekananda, with special focus on the teaching of Vedanta.

The basis of Vivekananda's teachings has been characteristically grounded by four themes: the understanding that ultimate reality is non-dual, the soul is divine, existence is unified, and religions are really in harmony with each other. Vivekananda proffered both spiritual freedom and spiritual democracy as ideals to be lived by. He saw the various religions as all sharing the same goal – an experience of God. Replacing secular humanism with spiritual humanism, he taught that serving others was coterminous with serving God, who is visible in all beings. Humanity is one (Adiswarananda).

As a writer he is most recognized by his four classics of Hindu philosophy: *Jnana-Yoga, Raja-Yoga, Karma-Yoga,* and *Bhakti-Yoga.* However, he has an immense collection of lectures and other writings. Throughout both his works and his life, he displayed a rich connection between service to man and contemplation of God. Besides Sri Ramakrishna, he publicly praised Buddha, Christ, Mohammed, and many others. He has been honored by such people as Gandhi, William James, and Max Mueller (Nikhilananda).

Commentary

The challenge of Vivekananda is the challenge of Vedanta – realizing unity and tolerating diversity. He invites us to see the divinity within each individual and therefore relinquish the fear and ignorance caused by differences. From Vivekananda we can learn to give up our attachment to things, realize the need for community, and find a basis for genuine love and service to humanity and God. Jealousy and selfishness become obstacles to be overcome in the realization that injury to others is also injury to oneself. With Vivekananda, the differences are given less attention than the oneness that unites us.

See also: ❂ Hinduism ❂ Ramakrishna Paramahansa ❂ Vedanta ❂ Yoga

Bibliography

Adiswarananda, S. (Ed.) (2006). *Vivekananda world teacher: His teachings on the spiritual unity of mankind.* Woodstock, VT: SkyLight Paths Publishing.

Nikhilananda, S. (1953). *Vivekananda: A biography.* New York: Ramakrishna-Vivekananda Center of New York.

Swami Vivekananda: Life, works and research. CD-ROM. Calcutta: Advaita Ashrama, n.d.

Vocation

Carol L. Schnabl Schweitzer

Career or Calling?

A brief examination of dictionary entries for "vocation" reveals almost immediately the absence of any religious connotation that was once associated with the term. It is associated with a chosen career, trade or profession which *may* include a call or summons to a religious profession or one of public service. Nevertheless, the emphasis is placed upon a paid profession or career track. How one determines precisely what that call to a paid profession is in twenty-first century North American culture is largely determined by a combination of self-interests: strengths, which may be considered gifts, abilities, or personality traits; salary or compensation packages (which include benefits and paid time off); and, the prestige associated with the profession (Schuurman, 2004: xii). There are personality inventories and aptitude tests administered to those with uncertainty, or those experiencing a life transition seeking a new career. The focus is on career as opposed to a call or vocation; and, as Masterson observes "[m]ost people who come to therapy with problems relating to career decisions fall into three categories" (Masterson, 1988: 9–10). In short they are individuals who are: (1) indecisive about what they want to do; (2) successful but don't enjoy their work; and, (3) are able to decide what they want to do, have reason to believe they would be successful but are unable to take the initiative. A shortcoming of vocational testing, meant to identify strengths and abilities, is that it often becomes determinative instead of descriptive; thus, testing becomes restrictive rather than liberating and as Masterson demonstrates, testing will not provide motivation or tell those who engage the process what they *want* to do.

Discernment or Pursuit?

Individuals with a strong sense of self (Kohut), ego (Freud), or identity (Erikson) and a clear sense of purpose frequently *pursue* a vocation with determination. Yet this very act of pursuit is often determined to be an act of violence against the self because one cannot pursue what was given as a birthright from God. One needs to listen to the self or seek guidance from within (Palmer, 2000: 4–10). Here one begins to witness the tension between work and career as a pursuit, and work as a vocation or calling, which is discerned by careful listening to one's inner voice. This inner voice may be understood as the unconscious, a stranger, innate talents, identity, or the mark of one's baptism. If one accepts Palmer's thesis that pursuit of wealth and success, or career is what jeopardizes the soul because the pursuit itself wreaks violence against the soul, then by analogy, one can draw comparisons with Freud's work on "uncanny strangeness" (Freud, 1919: 220) or Kristeva's on the "stranger"

(Kristeva, 1991: 181–188). The act of striving for success may silence the "stranger within" or set us at odds with our true self. We may live with what Palmer calls a dividedness that becomes part of our personal pathology because we don't acknowledge our own identity while attempting to affirm another's (Palmer, 2004: 3–11). This is an indication that we have not learned to make peace with the stranger or foreigner which is our unconscious. There is a strange familiarity when we meet an other who reminds us of the hidden self that lives in conflict with our public role or paid profession. The result of this meeting with the other who is strangely familiar may be that the other is now viewed as enemy. Why? We project our discomfort upon the other so as not to have to acknowledge our own inner conflict.

Faith and Vocation

This is not to argue, however, that wealth and success are necessarily in conflict with vocation but if the pursuit of these things is a denial of true self, the cost may be untenable leading to the undermining of personal "morale, relationships, and the capacity for good work" (Palmer, 2004: 17). The cost of living this way leads to an individual's inescapable feelings of disingenuity, depletion, emptiness, loneliness and despair. These feelings may then become the source of our projections which lead to further isolation. In order to manage living a divided life one may put on a mask which inevitably becomes a sign or symptom of a deeper personality disorder. Even within Protestantism, as Shuurman asserts, there is no univocal agreement upon the meaning of vocation. He cites Christian theologians and ethicists who contend that it is unbiblical and "wrong" to bestow religious meaning or significance upon a secular life (Schuurman, 2004: xii). The point of conflict here is between vocation as a calling solely to a church related occupation and the meaning of vocation as a calling to one's work whatever the occupation or career may be. Those who concur with Shuurman contend that "[v]ocation sets the obligations of one's social locations within larger ethical frames, such as God's revealed law, natural law, and the common good" (2004: xii). Shuurman sees "evoking a sense of God's call" for Christians in all aspects of their lives as a central task in pastoral ministry. Thus Christians discern God's call in their lives "when the heart of faith joins opportunities and gifts with the needs of others" (2004: 4). One may want to raise the question: Are faith and vocation mutually exclusive of paid profession? Or, may life itself be interpreted as vocation? Paul Pruyser, in a discussion of alienation and religious beliefs, sees a convergence particularly when one is speaking of those who are called to a religious profession in that "the actual occupational role one plays in everyday life is one way through which to help realize the kingdom of God on earth" (1974: 35). If one takes the position that all career choices, paid or volunteer, religious or secular, are vocations then all of life may indeed be interpreted as vocation. This would be to conclude with Schuurman that all of life is vocation and infuses the everyday and mundane with religious significance.

See also: ⊗ Consciousness ⊗ Ego ⊗ Projection ⊗ Self ⊗ Soul: A Depth Psychological Approach ⊗ Unconscious

Bibliography

Freud, S. (1919). The Uncanny (J. Strachey, Trans.). *The standard edition of the complete psychological works of Sigmund Freud* (Vol. 17). London: The Hogarth Press.

Kristeva, J. (1991). *Strangers to ourselves* (L. S. Roudiez, Trans.). New York: Columbia University.

Masterson, J. F. (1988). *The search for the real self: Unmasking the personality disorders of our age.* New York: Free Press.

Palmer, P. J. (2000). *Let your life speak: Listening for the voice of vocation.* San Francisco, CA: Jossey Bass.

Palmer, P. J. (2004). *A hidden wholeness: The journey toward an undivided life.* San Francisco, CA: Jossey Bass.

Pruyser, P. N. (1974). *Between belief and unbelief.* New York: Harper & Row.

Schuurman, D. J. (2004). *Vocation: Discerning our callings in life.* Grand Rapids, MI: Eerdmans.

W

Waiting

Ann M. Rothschild

Our current uses of the word "wait" carry derogatory meanings. Words used to define waiting: delayed, stopped or slowed down, postponed, put off, all seem at odds with our Western preoccupation with doing, getting done, action. Holding patterns are a waste, time that doesn't count. Passively receiving or being available rather than achieving diminishes one's dignity. There is discomfort in the ambiguity and disorientation of transitional periods involved in waiting. But in religion and psychology, waiting has not only been necessary and valued, it has been promoted. It is admired and considered a courageous state. Not that it is easy or even wished for, but all major religions and most psychological theories agree that waiting is usually needed and a respected aspect of the search that growth, faith, and change, require.

Often in the spiritual search as well as the psychological one, the changes we are trying to make require that we wait. Making change is never easy. Unless we take time, we repeat patterns, use excessive will, find counterfeits. Religion and psychology suggest we honor the process by waiting. In a new study, psychologist Walter Mischel, found that children who can wait, who can delay gratification, are more likely to be successful adults.

Every religion promotes waiting. Often we hear about the "Slow work of God," the work of the spirit. In the Bible we read "Wait for the Lord; be strong and take heart and wait for the Lord" (Ps. 27:13–14). St. John of the Cross is writing about the difficulty of waiting when he describes the *Dark Night of the Soul*. Jews wait for Elijah at Passover. Every week in silent meeting Quakers "wait in the light." The East has developed techniques for waiting. Buddhists sit in silent meditation. The Tao Te Ching asks "Who can wait quietly while the mud settles?" (Lao Tsu, 1989). Sufis wait for God. References to waiting abound in Islam. In the Qur'an, 2:153 says, "Surely Allah is with the patient." 2:155 admonishes, "Give good news to the patient." And 3:200 says, "Be patient and excel in patience." Great saints and heroes have always waited. Their "arrested" lives have inspired the world. Pauses can be divine gifts not to be avoided.

All therapies promote waiting by both patient and therapist. Self-realization, discovery, exploration of one's path, share the common thread of waiting through all such inquiry. One must stay in the uncomfortable "in between" and wait. Hurrying through the process seems to defeat it and fosters not only mediocrity but a false answer. Haste implies lack of interest and compromise. Waiting honors, and implies caring and hope.

In Spanish the verb to wait, esperar, is the same as to hope. Hope and waiting are intertwined. Waiting is required of both patient and therapist. Is it a coincidence that clients are called Patients and that they often come through "waiting rooms"?

Therapists too must wait. D. W. Winnicott talks about waiting for the patient to make the interpretations. Otherwise it is "stealing something away." As therapists it seems that we regret taking action more than we regret waiting. Waiting for things to emerge, the patient is able to reach for a more profound awareness. Waiting creates the time and space so necessary for this work.

See also: ❂ Christianity ❂ Ego ❂ Erikson, Erik ❂ Freud, Sigmund ❂ Jung, Carl Gustav ❂ Kohut, Heinz ❂ Self

Bibliography

Bonhoeffer, D. (1974). *Letters and papers from prison*. New York: Macmillan.
Guenther, M. (1992). *Holy listening*. Massachusetts: Cowley Publications.
The Holy Bible (New International Version). (2001). Michigan: Zondevan.
Lao Tsu. (1989). *Tao Te Ching*. New York: Vintage Books.
Lehrer, J. (2009, May 18). DON'T, The secret of self control. *The New Yorker Magazine*, 26–32.
Phillips, A. (1993). *On kissing, tickling and being bored*. Cambridge, MA: Harvard University Press.
St. John of the Cross. (2002). *The dark night of the soul* (M. Starr, Trans.). New York: Riverhead Books.
Verhoeven, C. (1972). *The Philosophy of wonder*. New York: Macmillan.
Winnicott. D. W. (1989). *Psycho-Analytic Explorations*. Cambridge, MA: Harvard University Press.

D. A. Leeming, K. Madden, S. Marlan (eds.), *Encyclopedia of Psychology and Religion*, DOI 10.1007/978-0-387-71802-6,
© Springer Science+Business Media LLC 2010

Water

Andrew J. P. Francis

Water is an essential element for life, and of deep spiritual and religious significance. It is an integral part of the ritual practice and symbolic structure of religions throughout the world. Used since antiquity for physical, psychological and spiritual regeneration, water is sustaining, cleansing and rejuvenating. Consistently in creation myths, water is the first principle and *prima materia* from which all else derives or is given birth. As such, it also provides a common and useful metaphor for the origins, evolution and processes of human mind and consciousness, at the level of individual and species. Humans have developed complex relationships with water as natural resource, commercial commodity and religio-spiritual symbol, and there is often conflict between the needs and aims of groups and individuals differentially invested in these various relationships. Most centrally, with respect to its spiritual and psychological significance, water is not only a mirror to our own nature, but also a Levinasian *Other* with which to interact.

Elemental Properties

Along with, variously, earth, fire, air, aether, metal and wood, water is one of the five classical elements present in classical Greek, Hindu and Buddhist philosophies amongst others. Water is unique as an element because it may exist (sometimes simultaneously) in multiple states or "phases": liquid, gaseous (vapor) and solid (ice). As such, it is commonly characterized as the most mutable of the classical elements.

In its liquid state it is flexible, flowing and malleable, taking on the shape of whatever contains it. The surface of liquid water is often translucent or mirrored, reflecting the viewer and concealing much that lies below. In a gaseous state water takes on an ethereal, transitory and insubstantial quality, able to move into confined spaces and range freely over wide expanses. As ice, water becomes fixed and solid, brittle and sharp. Toward theological and psychological points of reference, it is water in its liquid state which most commonly forms the basis for themes of correspondence, metaphor and symbolism, and will be the primary focus for discussion here.

In many theological frameworks, in addition to its physical properties, water is also vital and alive, containing "elemental force" and some varied properties of consciousness and selfness. As an elemental force, water has been the subject of worship and deification from prehistory to current day.

As Part of Ritual Practice and the Symbolic Structure of Religions

Water is the most common physical solvent and cleansing agent. In many religious and spiritual contexts also, water is cleansing and purifying. Water is sprinkled over objects, people and places in order to bless and purify them. Amongst its many ceremonial uses, immersion of individuals in water (or the washing of water over some part of the body) to symbolize a renewal, rejuvenation or rebirth of the self into a new spiritual status is one of the oldest, most familiar and powerful of water rituals.

In Christian faith, the central sacrament of baptism washes away the stain of original sin and opens the gateway to spiritual life; in the New Testament, Jesus begins his ministry following his cleansing by John the Baptist. The ancient Celtic goddess Cerridwen would immerse fallen warriors into her magical cauldron (also known as "the grail of immortality") to restore them to life. For Indian Hindus, ritual bathing in the Ganges River (a goddess deity itself) washes away sin and lessens the karmic burden for the next life. For Jews the mikvah bath is used for a range of purification purposes, some pertaining to ritual practice (e.g., consecration of priests, conversions to Judaism) and others, for example, to cleansing following menstruation, sex or the eating of certain foods. Also in Islam, Shinto, Taoism, Rastafarianism and other major faiths, ritual washing and ablutions are an important part of regular ritual practice.

At a symbolic level, immersion in water is initiation, regeneration, death and rebirth, spiritual and psychological renewal. In immersion (or a token thereof), we return and regress to the waters from which we were born, to the sea, the briny abyss and undifferentiated chaos from which life itself first stepped forth. As such, a ritual immersion and emergence re-enacts creation mythology.

Creation myths and cosmologies, describing how the universe came into being and humanity's relationship to the universe, are cultural artifacts which reflect the most essential theological framework of a collective. Since these myths are ultimately the projected products of human minds, they may be considered to reflect in a very real sense the structure of human nature at its most basic level. Thus in the cosmologies of ancient and contemporary civilizations we see versions of a theory of human nature, a description of how it is that the human psyche has arisen and is structured; we see in creation myths the emergence of human consciousness and self awareness from the undifferentiated unconsciousness of the animal mind.

One of the most ancient creation myths is that of the Babylonians, transcribed in the *Enuma elish* approximately 2000 BCE, and recording a much older oral tradition. In this myth, Tiamat (also known as The Deep) is the originator deity: darkness and primordial chaos, the watery abyss and cosmic sea, the womb from which all else has come. Personified as a sea-dragon, she battles with her progeny, the Gods, in Babylonian myth. Leading the host of younger gods against her is Marduk, principle of light and order. Marduk ultimately slays Tiamat, forming from her body the dome of the heavens, and the other half he lays down to make a floor over the deep. Thus do the younger gods mount of an order of creation, including humanity.

In its essential form, as an archetypal struggle between order and chaos, there is clear parallel in the Babylonian creation myth to the Hebrew account of creation later recounted in Genesis and many others from cultures across the globe. The hidden depths of water – dark, mysterious, chthonic and destructive, are typically associated with the unconscious roots of the human psyche and instinctual energies; in contrast to the en-*light*-ened, celestial and manifesting qualities of a rational and differentiated consciousness.

In Jungian terms, the struggle between these forces, and the eventual victory of Logos over Eros, represents a fundamental ontogenetic process. In each of us, as we progress through cycles of individuation, there is a natural and necessary emergence and further development of individual consciousness and selfness from the undifferentiated abyss of unconscious material. So too does this inner human struggle between light and dark, mythologized in ancient, watery cosmologies of creation, also represent the phylogenetic progression of mind evolution (and which ontogeny recapitulates). Thus does the animal mind, instinct-driven, largely unconscious and undifferentiated, evolve into a human, differentiated, directing and self-aware consciousness.

As a Mirror to Human Nature, and as a Levinasian Other with which to Interact

Mirrors are a common symbol for self-realization and knowledge of self. In everyday living, the reflective surface of water provided a tool for early humans to engage in self-examination, fostering self-awareness and the development of self-consciousness.

In becoming self-aware, our most basic human attribute, we develop a realization of separateness and duality – person from environment, individual consciousness from undifferentiated unconsciousness, self from universe and deity. With this separation can also come estrangement and alienation, and in certain spirito-religious and psychological paths of development and therapy we find the means to "reconnect" these separated parts once more, to experience the divine within and to communicate between the different levels of a multilayered psyche. This conflict between the human drive to individuate on the one hand, and the pull to reconnect with that from which we have separated is reflected in many myths from antiquity, with water again providing the symbolic narrative.

Narcissus of Greek mythology, for example, boasted a watery lineage: born from the dark river nymph Liriope who had been ravished by the river Cephisus. Narcissus is most beautiful, and his mother keeps from him any mirror or reflective surface lest he might see himself and become vain from his own beauty. When Liriope asks of the prophetic seer Tiresias whether her son would live to a ripe age, he answers "yes, if he does not come to know himself" (Ovid, 1955: 83). Narcissus, in his pride, scorns all and sundry amorous advances from boy and girl alike until, one day, separated from his companions in a forest hunt, he finds his way to a pool of water deep in the forest. It is a place, Ovid relates, undisturbed by bird or beast – a place of seclusion and aloneness. There, quenching his thirst in the heat of the day, he catches sight of and is enraptured by his own reflection in the pool. At first he does not realize that it is his own reflection he sees and attempts time and again to embrace and kiss the ravishing beauty he sees before himself, but eventually he recognizes the reflection for his own self and despairs. By the pool he eventually dies of unrequited love and starvation, unable to draw himself away from his own reflection, even for the talkative nymph Echo. In coming to know himself Narcissus thus fulfills the prophecy of Tiresias.

At the surface of this myth is a moral tale warning young boys against the dangers of scornful vanity. But it is also a metaphor for the journey taken toward self-discovery and transformation. Born from the waters of the abyss, and being in a state of "not knowing of his self," Narcissus represents the undifferentiated and unindividuated unconscious. In coming to know himself through seeing his own reflection, he undergoes the transformational process which is the defining moment of all humanity – differentiation, individuation and consciousness. Immediately thereupon he yearns for that which he has lost, and finds oblivion in the further transformational process of death (of the conscious self).

In this way water reflects our own nature, allowing us to see our self. But from a religious perspective water also has its own nature and vitality, and has been deified and worshipped in various forms throughout human history.

Extending Emmanuel Levinas' theory of "the face," water can thus be understood as an Other with whom humans interact. More than projection and reflection, water also has its own selfness and divinity.

See also: ❯ Abyss ❯ Celtic Religions ❯ Chaos ❯ Christianity ❯ Creation ❯ Hinduism ❯ Individuation ❯ Jesus ❯ Myth ❯ Religious ❯ Ritual ❯ Symbol

Bibliography

Campbell, J. (1972). *Myths to live by.* New York: Penguin.

Cooper, J. C. (1978). *An illustrated encyclopedia of traditional symbols.* London: Thames & Hudson.

Cooper, P. C. (2004). The abyss becoming well. *Psychoanalytic Review, 91*(2), 157–177.

Davy, B. J. (2005). Being at home in nature: A Levinasian approach to Pagan environmental ethics. *Pomegranate: The International Journal of Pagan Studies, 7,* 2.

Ezzy, D. (2008). I am the river walking. In S. Shaw & A. Francis (Eds.), *Deep blue: Critical reflections on nature, religion and water* (p. 127). London: Equinox Publishing.

Francis, A. (2008). Creature of water. In S. Shaw & A. Francis (Eds.), *Deep blue: Critical reflections on nature, religion and water* (p. 89). London: Equinox Publishing.

Jung, C. G. (1993). *Memories, dreams and reflections.* London: Fontana Press.

Kirk, G. S. (1970). *Myth: Its meaning and functions in ancient and other cultures.* Cambridge, England: Cambridge University Press.

Muss-Arnolt, W. (1894). The Babylonian account of creation. *The Biblical World, 3*(1), 17–27.

Ovid. (1955). *Metamorphoses.* London: Penguin Books.

Shaw, S., & Francis, A. (Eds.). (2008). *Deep blue: Critical reflections on nature, religion and water.* London: Equinox Publishing.

Slattery, D. P. (1983). Speaking, reflecting, writing: The myth of Narcissus and Echo. *The South Central Bulletin, 43*(4), 127–129.

Strang, V. (2004). *The meaning of water.* Oxford, England: Berg Publishing.

Van Over, R. (1980). *Sun songs: Creation myths from around the world.* New York: Times Mentor.

Weiss, J. (2007, July–August). A river runs through them: How water shaped our beliefs and rituals. *Science and Spirit, 18*(3), 40–43.

Watts, Alan Wilson

Robert S. Ellwood

Alan Wilson Watts (1915–1973) was an Anglo-American writer and lecturer on religion, spirituality, and psychology.

Born in Chislehurst, Kent, England, Watts married an American woman, Eleanor Everett, in 1938, moving to New York the same year. He was ordained a priest in the Episcopal Church in 1944, but left that vocation in 1950 to pursue the study and practice of Eastern mysticism. During his Episcopalian years he had written *Behold the Spirit* (1947), an uneven but sometimes profound synthesis of Eastern and Christian mysticism, and *The Supreme Identity* (1950), articulating a highly monistic mystical philosophy. In 1951–1957 Watts was a member of the faculty of the American Academy of Asian Studies in San Francisco and, under a grant from the Bollingen foundation, in 1956 published *The Way of Zen*, perhaps his best-known book.

With this influential study as a launching-pad, Watts became an independent writer and speaker or, as he liked to call himself, "philosophical entertainer." He produced an unceasing series of lectures, radio addresses, and articles, together with such popular books as *Nature, Man and Woman* (1958), *"This Is It" and Other Essays* (1960), *Psychotherapy East and West* (1961), *The Joyous Cosmology* (1962), *The Two Hands of God* (1963), *Beyond Theology* (1964), *Myth and Ritual in Christianity* (1968), and *In My Own Way* (autobiography; 1972). Serendipitously flourishing in the years the "Beats" of the 1950s and the celebrated "counterculture" of the 1960s were rediscovering the mystic East and going some ways to revolutionize the American spiritual quest, Watts quickly emerged as a major figure in popular culture. Whether speaking or writing, his flow of words was polished and elegant, with never an awkward phrase, and generally informed by just the right metaphor or image to make the piece sing.

Watts knew how to make hearers or readers feel he was letting them in on a great cosmic secret, something sacred hidden behind the scenes that turned the universe and one's life as a part of it into a great and joyous dance. To be sure, in his later books he was sometimes repetitious from one work to another, and his depictions of the God of personal monotheism, whom he clearly disliked, often amounted to caricature. But many found his sparkling evocations of the divine within, realizable in moments of timeless mystical awareness and making all of life holy, to be wonderfully liberating.

Watts' basic ideas were few and simple. Drawing from Hinduism, Zen, and perhaps above all Taoism, he emphasized over and over that we are all parts of the universe, like waves rising and falling on the sea. The universe itself, unceasingly flowing and changing though not "going" anywhere, is expressing itself through us; minds and bodies alike are natural parts of nature. The dualistic

Spirit and Matter of philosophical Idealism and Materialism are mere abstractions. The cosmos in its wholeness cannot be reduced to either, but is what the Buddhists call "Suchness," that indefinable, infinite reality enveloping both consciousness and form. It is known best not by words but, on the human level, in wordlessly joyous activities like meditation, swimming, or dancing, wherein one can feel its flow. All these exercises are rightly done just to be doing them, not for the sake of any extraneous idea of "growth" or of attaining some outside goal. The swimmer does not swim just to get to other side of the pool or lake, or the dancer dance only to reach the end of the number, but for the joy of the activity itself. Meditation too should not be thought of as a task or technique, but as pleasant way of attaining deep and quiet consciousness disconnected from bondage to past or future, and thereby one with the consciousness of the universe.

The good life, then, maintains a sense of joyous wonder toward the unfathomable mysteries of the universe, while enjoying good things as they come. The gift of spontaneity, and of living in the moment, is greatly to be prized. A way of life such as this must steer carefully between true freedom and the deceptive "freedom" of undisciplined self-indulgence. Watts had his inner demons, and was not always responsible in family and other relationships, or in the use of alcohol. But at his best he manifested the exuberant liberty and spiritual excitement of which he could write and speak so eloquently. He died at his home in Marin County, California. His books have remained in print long after his death.

See also: ❷ Buddhism ❷ Hinduism ❷ Taoism ❷ Zen

Bibliography

Furlong, M. (1986). *Zen Effects: The life of Alan Watts*. Boston, MA: Houghton Mifflin.

Watts, A. (1947). *Behold the spirit*. New York: Random House, Pantheon Books.

Watts, A. (1950). *The supreme identity*. New York: Random House, Pantheon Books.

Watts, A. (1957). *The way of Zen*. New York: Random House, Pantheon Books.

Watts, A. (1958). *Nature, man and woman*. New York: Random House, Pantheon Books.

Watts, A. (1960). *"This Is It" and other essays*. New York: Random House, Pantheon Books.

Watts, A. (1961). *Psychotherapy East and West*. New York: Random House, Pantheon Books.

Watts, A. (1962). *The joyous cosmology*. New York: Random House, Pantheon Books.

Watts, A. (1963). *The two hands of God*. New York: Macmillan, Collier Books.

Watts, A. (1964). *Beyond theology*. New York: Random House, Pantheon Books.

Watts, A. (1968). *Myth and ritual in Christianity*. Boston, MA: Beacon Press.

Watts, A. (1972). *In my own way*. New York: Random House, Pantheon Books.

Western Wall

Lynn Somerstein

The Western Wall, in Hebrew, *Ha Kotel haMa'aravi,* is the remaining wall of the Jewish Second temple, the most sacred building in Judaism. It was built on the site of the first temple, also called Solomon's Temple, which was erected in the tenth century BCE. The Gate of Heaven is said to be located directly above *Ha Kotel*. Because it is so near to heaven, people inscribe prayers and wishes on pieces of paper and place them in the cracks in the walls in the hopes that their requests will be granted.

The Dome of The Rock, built in 691 CE, is directly above Ha Kotel. It contains the rock which is considered the foundation from which God created the Universe, and later, where Abraham prepared to slay Isaac. Jacob is said to have slept on this rock and dreamt of a ladder leading to heaven, with angels going up and down on it. In Islamic belief this is the rock from which Muhammad ascended to heaven.

HaKotel is also sometimes referred to as "the Wailing Wall," a derogatory term that refers to Jews wailing about the loss of the temple and other many hardships.

Tisha b'av, the Ninth day of the month of Ab, commemorates the destruction of the temple and is a Jewish religious Day of mourning. The temple is supposed to be remembered in times of joy, too. For example, a traditional Jewish wedding ceremony includes the breaking of a glass, which among other things symbolizes the destruction of the temple. The temple represents irreplaceable joy, an idealized vision of past perfection.

See also: ❷ Jewish Mourning Rituals ❷ Judaism and Psychology

Bibliography

Skolnik, F. (Ed.). (2006). *Encyclopedia Judaica*. New York: MacMillan.

Wicca

David Waldron

Primarily the formation of Wicca, as a sub-category of pagan revivalist movements emerging in the nineteenth and twentieth centuries, is the product of the efforts of Gerald Gardner's attempts to construct an authentically "English" religious system that could revive the traditional religious and cultural practices of England's rich and diverse pagan heritage. It is also a religious tradition replete with archetypal forms, mythological structures and appropriated alchemical models of ritual and religious practice that closely correlates with the analytical psychology of Carl Jung, and in this sense, is extremely significant to the development of psychological theory.

Gerald Gardner and the Origins of Wicca in British Romanticism

Being heavily influenced by nineteenth century Romantic representations of "merry England," Gardner integrated the ideas surrounding Pagan beliefs and practices into a coherent, structured and practical format. Particularly pertinent in his research was the theory of Pagan survivals as propagated in the methodology and historical analytical practices of the Folklore Society in which the rituals, legends and folklore of rural England represented cultural fossils of a primordial pagan past. Similarly, in creating the rituals, symbols and practices of his Wiccan belief system, Gardner drew upon a broad range of established lore and ritual from the occultist and ritual magic traditions of English society. He integrated these strains of English culture within the ideological and cultural matrix of English Romanticism and, so doing, created a body of religious and magical practice that celebrated the Romantic idealization of the countryside, opposition to Enlightenment industrialism and the ideal of an authentic and eternal English national culture. Particularly important in Gardner's Wiccan religion was the centrality of the divine feminine as manifested by a triple aspect lunar goddess of Maiden, Mother and Crone set in symbiotic duality of a nature God, usually associated with the Saxon deity Cernunos (Hutton,1999; Gardner, 1959; Crowley, 2002).

In the formative period of the 1940s wiccans, like their predecessors in the nineteenth century pagan revivalist movements, legitimized their beliefs by appropriating a variety of romanticist histories and interpretations of folklore. Writers such as James Frazer, Jules Michelet and Margaret Murray were perhaps the most principal exponents of this approach. In this context, Gerald Gardner claimed that Wicca was a linear descendant of a pre-Christian Pagan fertility cult, persecuted during the witch hunts of the late middle ages. This model of witchcraft and Wiccan history, as postulated by Gardner, was an almost literal reconstruction (albeit with some significant departures) of the model of witchcraft persecutions presented in Margaret Murray's *Witch Cult in Western Europe* (Murray, 2000) and manifested in a wide array of English folklore (Gardner, 1959; Gardner, 1954; Bishop and Bishop, 2000).

Wicca and Jungian Analytical Psychology

Whilst there is little evidence that psychological theory influenced the construction and evolution of Wicca during its formative phase, the imagery, rituals and religious expressions of Wicca resonated with powerful psychological symbolism. From the eternal duality of the sacred God/Goddess (anima/animas) duality to the use of powerful archetypes developed in romantic literature, folklore and mythology, Gardner's Wiccan movement profoundly illustrated examples of archetypes associated with Jung's collective unconscious. Similarly, the rituals and religious practices of Wicca drew extensively on alchemical traditions relating sacred numbers, geometry and mythology in forms and patterns that closely paralleled that of Carl Jung's use of alchemy as a representation of the search for psychological wholeness (Crowley, 2002; Adler, 1986/1979).

Jungian Archetypes and Wiccan Historicity

Whilst the parallels with Jungian thought are very evident in the powerful and pervasive imagery, ritual and mythology associated with Wicca, the practices and analysis of Wicca only became directly associated with analytical psychology at a much later date. The collapse of the historical and anthropological claims associated with Wicca in the 1970s was closely linked to the perception that empirically verifiable historical antecedents were peripheral to the experience of being a Wiccan. In this context, many Wiccan writers, most notably Starhawk, Vivianne Crowley and Margot Adler, inspired by the increasing popularity of Jung's work in the 1960s and 1970s, took an alternative approach. Using Carl Jung's theories as a tool for understanding the role of the symbolic and the spiritual in human experience, and relying on his concept of the collective unconscious, they described witchcraft history as representative of universal psychic truths, independent of empirical history. From this perspective, the increasingly problematic fixation on empirical history as the primary legitimizing factor in religious belief could be eschewed and the rich network of symbolism, mythology and spiritual belief could be explored in terms of psycho-cultural resonance of religious archetypes and mystical experiences (Adler, 1979; Starhawk, 1989/1979; Crowley, 1989).

Jungian understanding of the nature and function of the symbolic has proved to be an invaluable model for the legitimation of Wiccan rituals, mythology and historical narrative as well as profoundly enriching the understanding of its religious practice and mythology. By giving priority to the psychic significance of symbols that have arisen from the collective unconscious, Wicca had attained a means of legitimating ritual outside of empirical history, whilst at the same time ensconcing itself within the framework of a coherent and relatively respectable psychological and epistemological framework. In this, it has found a contemporary authentication for Pagan beliefs and practice. From this perspective, the rituals and symbols of the neo-Pagan tradition are not so much valued in terms of their indexical relationship to a particular Pagan tradition of the past but rather as indexes of a development into psychological maturity. If radically different cultural traditions are integrated together, such as those of Native Americans and pre-Roman Celts, it is not perceived as a violation of cultural authenticity but rather, recognition of the common source of mythological symbolism in the collective unconscious and the universal search for psychological development.

The Use of Jungian Analytical Psychology in Wiccan Practice

Vivianne Crowley's textbook for Witches, *The Old Religion in the New Age*, is a particularly pertinent example of Jung's impact on the neo-Pagan movement. While the book is certainly based on Gerald Gardner's Wiccan movement and the history of Murray's *Witch cult in Western Europe*, Crowley also incorporates Kundalini meditational practices and Hindu rituals into the practice of Witchcraft. As a practicing Jungian psychoanalyst, she bases the rationale for her work firmly in Jungian theory. She argues that the capacity to integrate the practice of Wicca with the symbols, mythology and rituals of other

traditions is a metaphor of a person's rise to self-fulfillment through the attainment of psychological integration. For Crowley, the growth of neo-Paganism is intrinsically linked with its appropriation of Jungian discourse, even as one's struggle to find religious expression is intrinsically linked to a search for psychological wholeness, Jungian discourse readily translates into the language of magic and mythology and the language of Jungian analytical psychology flows naturally for practicing neo-Pagans because it "reflects back to them their own spiritual experiences." She also argues that from a neo-Pagan perspective, the central issue in Jung's model of religious experience is that of *religare* or rejoining. Through mythology and the embracing of the unconscious, as manifested through deeply resonant archetypal symbols, one can find wholeness and a sense of reconnection in a fundamentally alienated and disconnected world (Crowley, 2002).

From the perspective of the Wiccan appropriation of Jung, the collective unconscious is a common, shared symbolic heritage to all human beings that gives meaning to people's experience. There are certain shared symbols or archetypes that are perceived to represent universals in all human psychic experience. Perhaps the most common example is the concept of *anima* and *animus*, the masculine and feminine components of the human mind, possessed by both men and women. In Jung's analysis there are certain aspects to social and cultural behavior that can be ascribed to universal masculine and feminine qualities that are distinct from gender. These represent unique universal qualities common to both men and women. Crowley illustrates the use of the archetypes of masculine (animus) and feminine (anima) from a neo-Pagan perspective as the underlying psychological truth of the Wiccan postulate that divinity is manifested in a symbiotic God and Goddess, representing universal masculine and feminine qualities intrinsic to both the psyche and the natural world (Crowley, 1989). This is particularly well illustrated in Wiccan author Cassandra Carter's, comment on the significance of Pagan ritual in terms of its capacity to explain Jungian models of psychic development.

> In Jungian terms the descent of the Goddess teaches the need for a woman to go on her own quest in search of her *animus* – not waiting for the knight on a white charger who will rescue her from the need to make her own choices, but going to confront the Dark Lord and solve his mysteries – going of her own choice and will into the Kingdom of the Unconscious mind. For a man, he has been successful, with the help of the Goddess, his anima, in exploring and winning the battles within his

own unconscious, and he and she are happily reunited in the underworld of the unconscious (Carter, 1992: 6).

Wicca and the Search of Psychological Wholeness

For many Wiccans the struggle for psychological wholeness and connectedness is a struggle against the enlightenment definition of progress and universal taxonimization, rationalization and industrialism. It is, at the same time, a re-shaping of the psychic experience of the present as a means to progress. Similarly, Wicca, as a religious tradition tends to be intensely focused on representations of the past and the mythological as a means of coming to a sense of integration of aspects of the self and the *imago dei*. In this context, is not surprising that Wiccans have recognized aspects of Jungian theory with which they could identify and, consequently, incorporate into their own religious framework. This identification and incorporation has also provided the neo-Pagan movement with a teleological orientation, a vehicle that enables their existence to span both the past and the future with intellectual and conceptual integrity.

See also: ❂ Anima and Animus ❂ Female God Images ❂ Femininity ❂ Jung, Carl Gustav ❂ Ritual ❂ Symbol ❂ Witchcraft

Bibliography

Adler, M. (1986/1979). *Drawing down the moon: Witches, druids, goddess worshipers and other pagans in America today*. New York: Penguin Group.

Bishop, C., & Bishop, P. (2000). Embarrassed by our origins. *The Pomegranate: New Journal of Neo-Pagan Thought*, *1*(12), 48–55.

Carter, C. (1992, November 20). *The old religion in the new age*. Lecture given to the C.G. Jung Society. Received transcript at conference.

Crowley, V. (1989). *The old religion in the new age*. New York: Harper Collins.

Crowley, V. (2002, January 12). *Carl Jung and the Development of Contemporary Paganism*. Paper presented at The Development of Paganism: History, Influences and Contexts Conference, Open University, Milton Keynes.

Gardner, G. (1954). *Witchcraft today*. London: Rider & Co.

Gardner, G. (1959). *The Meaning of witchcraft*. Wellingborough, England: Aquarian Press.

Hutton, R. (1999). *Triumph of the moon: A history of modern pagan witchcraft*. Oxford, England: Oxford University Press.

Hutton, R. (2000). Finding a folklore. *The Pomegranate: A Journal of Neo-Pagan Thought*, *1*(12), 4–15.

Jung, C. G. (1980). *The archetypes and the collective unconscious*. Princeton, NJ: Princeton University Press.

Jung, C. G. (1990). *Symbols of transformation*. Princeton, NJ: Princeton University Press.

Murray, M. (1921). *The witch cult in Western Europe*. Oxford, England: Clarendon Press.

Starhawk. (1989/1979). *The Spiral dance*. San Francisco, CA: Harper Collins.

Tacey, D. (2001). *Jung and the new age*. East Sussex, Brunner-Routledge.

Wilber, Ken

Leon Schlamm

Wilber's Integral Psychology

Ken Wilber (1949) is the most influential writer in the field of transpersonal psychology (Wilber, 1977, 1980, 1981a, b, 1983a, b, 1991, 1995, 1996, 1997, 1998, 1999, 2000a, b, 2002, 2006), having for more than two decades been widely acclaimed as its preeminent theoretician. Working self-consciously in the tradition of such systematic philosophers as Hegel, Schelling, and Habermas, he has presented his readers with a cartography of *the spectrum of consciousness* which, in spite of much elaboration on his original speculative model of the development of consciousness, has continued to be one of the defining features of his *integral psychology*. Drawing upon an impressive variety of sources from the world's mystical traditions (particularly Hindu and Buddhist contemplative traditions, as well as twentieth century Indian mystics such as Ramana Maharshi and Sri Aurobindo), developmental psychology (e.g., Alexander, Arieti, Broughton, Graves, Kegan, Kohlberg, Loevinger, Lowen, Piaget, Sullivan, Wade), psychoanalysis (principally Freud and Erikson), analytical psychology (Jung and Neumann), humanistic psychology and psychosynthesis (Maslow and Assagioli), the history of Western philosophy, anthropology (e.g., Beck, Gebser, Lenski), and physics (e.g., Bohm, Capra, Jeans, Pribram), Wilber has consistently argued that human consciousness possesses a hierarchical structure. There are many different psychological and spiritual levels of development, and each level both integrates the properties and achievements of the lower level and transcends its limitations. Identifying an underlying metaphysical pattern assisting integration of the natural and human sciences with the spiritual perspective of the perennial philosophy (e.g., Coomaraswamy, Guenon, Huston Smith),

Wilber introduces the concept of the *holon* which is simultaneously both a whole (in relation to the parts that are at developmentally lower levels) and a part (of a greater whole that is at a higher developmental level). According to Wilber, all human experience (individual and collective) is evolving through a hierarchically organised great chain of holons (or "Great Chain of Being") toward the self-realisation of spirit in non-dual mystical experience, although evolutionary fixation can occur at any developmental level (Wilber, 1977, 1995, 1996, 1997, 2000a, b, 2006; Cortright, 1997; Rothberg, 1998; De Quincey, 2000; Visser, 2003; Reynolds, 2006).

Wilber's Cartography of the Spectrum of Consciousness

It is this vision of *holarchical integration* and the evolution of consciousness (including the correlation of ontogenetic with phylogenetic stages of development) which shapes Wilber's assessment of the relationship between psychological and spiritual development. Wilber identifies many universal, *deep* structures (distinguished from *surface* structures) of consciousness which transcend all cultural conditioning: the prepersonal, prerational, preegoic (fulcrums 0–4: *primary matrix* [pleromatic, uroboric non-differentiation]; *sensoriphysical* [autistic, symbiotic, psychotic]; *phantasmic-emotional* [identification of the ego with the body, typhon, Freudian primary process, sexual energy, libido, *prana*, magical world view, narcissistic-borderline]; *representational mind* [impulsive, self-protective, punishment/obedience, preconventional, mythical world view, psychoneuroses]; *rule/role* [concrete operational, conformist, conventional, approval of others, law and order, mythical world view,]), the personal, rational, egoic (fulcrums 5 and 6: *formal reflexive* [formal operational, individualistic, conscience, postconventional, identity neuroses]; *centaur* [*vision logic*, integration of mind and body and of conflicting points of view, planetary consciousness, gateway to transpersonal]), and the transpersonal (or spiritual), transrational, transegoic (fulcrums 7–9: *psychic* [nature mysticism, body-based spiritual practices as in shamanism and *kundalini-yoga*, paranormal abilities]; *subtle* [deity or theistic mysticism, as in Christian mysticism, Sufism and Indian *bhakti*]; *causal* [formless mysticism celebrated by Hindu and Buddhist canonical literature]), beyond which lies the *non-dual* ground of all experience, of unmanifest formlessness and manifest form (often identified as level 10, and typically associated with the *sunyavadin* tradition of Mahayana Buddhism).

Moreover, he argues that, by integrating the materials of western depth-psychology and developmental psychology with those of the Hindu and Buddhist contemplative traditions, he can delineate the different developmental competences and pathologies of each level of the spectrum of consciousness. Wilber claims that competing schools of psychotherapy and spiritual emancipation (with their different treatment modalities) address different levels of the spectrum and different developmental problems. Since depth-psychology and developmental psychology address the prepersonal and the personal structures of consciousness and mystical traditions are concerned with the transpersonal levels, no school of psychotherapy or spiritual liberation is marginalised. Each is understood to convey partial and complementary truths about human consciousness (Wilber, 1977, 1980, 1981a, 1995, 1996, 1997, 2000a, b, 2006; Cortright, 1997; De Quincey, 2000; Ferrer, 2002; Visser, 2003; Reynolds, 2004, 2006).

The Role of the Ego in Transpersonal Development

It is Wilber's claim, that all types of psychotherapeutic and spiritual practice can be graded by being integrally embraced within the holarchical spectrum of consciousness, which has provoked such intense controversy among transpersonal psychologists. The issue at the heart of this controversy is Wilber's understanding of the role of the ego (the personal self) in transpersonal development. Wilber argues that the ego (fulcrum 5), with its capacity for detached witnessing of the conventional world, is not dissolved but preserved, and typically strengthened, by transpersonal structures. Although exclusive identification of consciousness with the ego is transcended (and thereby dissolved) during spiritual development, the ego, with its rational competences and its scientific worldview, is included within, and utilised by, all transpersonal levels of consciousness. This means, for Wilber, that the acquisition of the ego, as well as modern rationality and science, should not be viewed as an obstacle to spiritual development (the cause of alienation of consciousness from spirit), but rather as a very significant spiritual achievement, a necessary, evolutionary step toward spiritual maturity, a movement of spirit toward spirit. Accordingly, Wilber argues, the spiritual function of science and modern rationality is to strip us of our infantile and adolescent, prerational views of spirit, to dismantle the transitional, *archaic, magical* and *mythic* worldviews associated with the prerational or prepersonal fulcrums, in order to make room for the genuinely transrational insights of authentic mystical traditions. Such a critique by modernity (and postmodernity, as in the *vision logic* of fulcrum 6) of premodernity enables us to realize that mysticism is evolutionary and progressive, not devolutionary and regressive, and thus lies in our collective future, not our collective past (Wilber, 1981b, 1983b, 1991, 1995, 1996, 1997, 1998, 2000a, 2006; Washburn, 1988; Cortright, 1997; Grof, 1998; Kremer, 1998; Rothberg, 1998; Walsh, 1998; De Quincey, 2000; Visser, 2003; Reynolds, 2006).

Wilber's Pre/Trans Fallacy

Moreover, it is this linear model of psychological and spiritual development and the pivotal role of the ego in spiritual transformation which leads Wilber to another defining feature of his integral psychology: his persistent disjunction of spiritual evolution from psychological regression. He criticises many contemporary writers who confuse or equate spiritual development with regression, by obscuring the differences between prepersonal and transpersonal states and stages of development. Because prepersonal and transpersonal states and stages appear to share certain characteristics (e.g., the quality of fusion or union and the lack of a primary focus on rationality), these writers confuse or equate them, and thereby commit what Wilber calls the *pre/trans fallacy*. The pre/trans fallacy can assume two forms. The first (ptf-1) claims that transpersonal, mystical experiences are nothing but a regression to prepersonal, infantile states. It is Freud and his followers who are charged with ptf-1: the fallacy of reductionism. However, Wilber engages more passionately and persistently with ptf 2 than ptf 1: the fallacy of *elevationism*. He argues that Jung and the Romantic movement (and more recently much of New Age and countercultural spirituality) are responsible for the elevation of prepersonal, infantile fusion states (in which a stable personal ego has not yet emerged) to the transegoic and transrational "glory" of mystical union (in which the personal ego has already been transcended). More specifically, Wilber charges Jung with several types of elevationism leading to the misidentification of psychological regression with spiritual evolution: (1) the confusion of primary matrix (fulcrum 0) with causal level, formless mysticism (fulcrum 9), (2) the confusion of magic (fulcrum 2) with psychic level, nature mysticism (fulcrum 7), (3) the confusion of mythic images (fulcrums 3 and 4) with subtle level archetypes (fulcrum 8). Wilber has repeatedly censured Jung for his failure to adopt a linear, evolutionary perspective which differentiates between the "ape side" and the "angel side" of human nature, the prepersonal and the transpersonal levels of the collective unconscious. For

Wilber, this elevationism is particularly evinced by Jung's assumption that archetypes are images of instincts, and by Jung's failure to discriminate between experiences of prepersonal mythic images (which are more self-centric and narcissistic than egoic experiences) and those of transpersonally located archetypes. Wilber concludes that Jung's archetypes are actually a pre/trans fallacy mixture of divine and primitive psychic contents, which "wobble between transrational glory and prerational chaos" (Wilber, 1983b, 1991, 1995, 1996, 1997, 1998, 2000a, 2002, 2006; Washburn, 1988, 1998; Grof, 1989, 1998; Odajnyk, 1993; Cortright, 1997; Visser, 2003; Reynolds, 2004, 2006).

Challenges to Wilber's Integral Psychology

Many transpersonal psychologists have challenged the metaphysical, soteriological, and psychotherapeutic assumptions of Wilber's *integral psychology*. Wilber's Neo-Perennialism, in particular his reification and elevation of deep structures of consciousness to transcendental status, has been questioned because it is not susceptible to empirical verification and falsification, but rather appears to depend on Wilber's experience of meditation for its authority. The essentialism and subtle objectivism of Wilber's metaphysical perspective, which perpetuates false dichotomies between universalism and postmodernism, imposes severe constraints on the variety of forms of spiritual evolution, leading to a misleading homogenization of religious traditions and an unjustifiable privileging of non-dualistic religious traditions. Wilber's claim that progress through the transpersonal levels or fulcrums of consciousness is sequential and unalterable (from psychic to subtle to causal to non-dual) has been challenged, because it is supported neither by clinical materials nor by those of the world's mystical traditions. In the spiritual domain a single invariant sequence of development does not appear to exist. Moreover, some transpersonal psychologists have insisted, contrary to Wilber, that regression can be a powerful tool for spiritual transformation; spiritual evolution typically does not follow a direct linear trajectory, but involves a combined regressive and progressive movement of consciousness. Because the therapeutic process addresses the prepersonal (including the biographical) and the transpersonal bands of the spectrum of consciousness simultaneously (rather than progressively), it is impossible to clearly delineate between psychotherapy and spiritual development (Washburn, 1988, 1998; Cortright, 1997; Grof, 1998; Heron, 1998; Kremer, 1998; McDonald-Smith and Rothberg, 1998; Rothberg, 1998; De Quincey, 2000; Ferrer, 2002).

See also: ❂ Altered States of Consciousness ❂ Analytical Psychology ❂ Archetype ❂ Consciousness ❂ Depth Psychology and Spirituality ❂ Ego ❂ Enlightenment ❂ Freud, Sigmund, and Religion ❂ Individuation ❂ Jung, Carl Gustav ❂ Jungian Self ❂ Mysticism and Psychotherapy ❂ Nonduality ❂ Psyche ❂ Psychology and the Origins of Religion ❂ Psychospiritual ❂ Psychotherapy and Religion ❂ Reductionism ❂ Religious Experience ❂ Transpersonal Psychology

Bibliography

Cortright, B. (1997). *Psychotherapy and spirit: Theory and practice in transpersonal psychotherapy.* Albany, NY: State University of New York Press.

De Quincey, C. (2000). The promise of integralism: A critical appreciation of Ken Wilber's integral psychology. In J. Andresen & R. K. C. Forman (Eds.), *Cognitive models and spiritual maps: Interdisciplinary explorations of religious experience* (pp. 177–208). Bowling Green, OH: Imprint Academic.

Ferrer, J. N. (2002). *Revisioning transpersonal theory: A participatory vision of human spirituality.* Albany, NY: State University of New York Press.

Grof, S. (1998). Ken Wilber's spectrum psychology: Observations from clinical consciousness research. In D. Rothberg & S. Kelly (Eds.), *Ken Wilber in dialogue: Conversations with leading transpersonal thinkers* (pp. 85–116). Wheaton, IL: Quest Books.

Grof, S., & Grof, C. (1989). Spiritual emergency: Understanding evolutionary crisis. In S. Grof & C. Grof (Eds.), *Spiritual emergency: When personal transformation becomes a crisis* (pp. 1–26). Los Angeles, CA: Jeremy P. Tarcher.

Heron, J. (1998). *Sacred science: Person-centred inquiry into the spiritual and the subtle.* Ross-on-Wye, HR: PCCS Books.

Kremer, J. (1998). The shadow of evolutionary thinking. In D. Rothberg & S. Kelly (Eds.), *Ken Wilber in dialogue: Conversations with leading transpersonal thinkers* (pp. 237–258). Wheaton, IL: Quest Books.

McDonald-Smith, M., & Rothberg, D. (1998). Bringing awareness back home: Toward an integrative spirituality. In D. Rothberg & S. Kelly (Eds.), *Ken Wilber in dialogue: Conversations with leading transpersonal thinkers* (pp. 165–178). Wheaton, IL: Quest Books.

Odajnyk, V. W. (1993). *Gathering the light: A psychology of meditation.* Boston, MA: Shambhala.

Reynolds, B. (2004). *Embracing reality: The integral vision of Ken Wilber.* New York: Jeremy P. Tarcher/Penguin.

Reynolds, B. (2006). *Where's Wilber at?: Ken Wilber's integral vision in the new millenium.* St. Paul, MN: Omega Books/Paragon House.

Rothberg, D. (1998). Ken Wilber and the future of transpersonal inquiry: An introduction to the Conversation. In D. Rothberg & S. Kelly (Eds.), *Ken Wilber in dialogue: Conversations with leading transpersonal thinkers* (pp. 1–27). Wheaton, IL: Quest Books.

Visser, F. (2003). *Ken Wilber: Thought as passion.* Albany, NY: State University of New York Press.

Walsh, R. (1998). Developmental and evolutionary synthesis in the recent writings of Ken Wilber. In D. Rothberg & S. Kelly (Eds.), *Ken Wilber in dialogue: Conversations with leading transpersonal thinkers* (pp. 30–52). Wheaton, IL: Quest Books.

Washburn, M. (1988). *The ego and the dynamic ground: A transpersonal theory of human development.* Albany, NY: State University of New York Press.

Washburn, M. (1998). The pre/trans fallacy reconsidered. In D. Rothberg & S. Kelly (Eds.), *Ken Wilber in dialogue: Conversations with leading transpersonal thinkers* (pp. 62–83). Wheaton, IL: Quest Books.

Wilber, K. (1977). *The spectrum of consciousness.* Wheaton, IL: Quest Books.

Wilber, K. (1980). *The Atman project: A transpersonal view of human development.* Wheaton, IL: Quest Books.

Wilber, K. (1981a). *No boundary: Eastern and Western approaches to personal growth.* Boulder, CO: Shambhala.

Wilber, K. (1981b). *Up from Eden: A transpersonal view of human evolution.* Garden City, NY: Anchor Press/Doubleday.

Wilber, K. (1983a). *A sociable God: Toward a new understanding of religion.* Boulder, CO: New Science Library/Shambhala.

Wilber, K. (1983b). *Eye to eye: The quest for the new paradigm.* Garden City, NY: Anchor Press/Doubleday.

Wilber, K. (1991). *Grace and grit: Spirituality and healing in the life and death of Treya Killam Wilber.* Boston, MA: Shambhala.

Wilber, K. (1995). *Sex, ecology, spirituality: The spirit of Evolution.* Boston, MA: Shambhala.

Wilber, K. (1996). *A brief history of everything.* Dublin, Ireland: Gill & Macmillan.

Wilber, K. (1997). *The eye of spirit: An integral vision for a World gone slightly mad.* Boston, MA: Shambhala.

Wilber, K. (1998). *The marriage of sense and soul: Integrating science and religion.* New York: Random House.

Wilber, K. (1999). *One taste: The journals of Ken Wilber.* Boston, MA: Shambhala.

Wilber, K. (2000a). *Integral psychology: Consciousness, spirit, psychology, therapy.* Boston, MA: Shambhala.

Wilber, K. (2000b). *A theory of everything: An integral vision for business, politics, science, and spirituality.* Boston, MA: Shambhala.

Wilber, K. (2002). *Boomeritis: A novel that will set you free.* Boston, MA: Shambhala.

Wilber, K. (2006). *Integral spirituality: A startling new role for religion in the modern and postmodern world.* Boston, MA: Integral Books.

Winnicott, Donald Woods

Jaco J. Hamman

Donald Woods Winnicott (1896–1971) was a prominent British pediatrician and analyst who came to prominence, especially in North America, only after his death. Using understandable terms, he introduced concepts and phrases such as: "the good-enough mother" (Winnicott, Winnicott, Shepherd and Davis, 1987), "the true and false self" (Winnicott, 1994), "holding environment" (Winnicott, 1993; Winnicott et al., 1994), "the transitional object and transitional phenomena" (Winnicott, 1993), and, "there is no such thing as a baby" (Winnicott, 1994). Winnicott never established a school of thought, but his ideas inform especially psychoanalytic thinking about the pre-Oedipal child and the importance of the parent/infant relationship.

Object Relations Theory

As an object relational theorist, he joined others (most notably Margaret Little, W.R.D. Fairbairn, Charles Rycroft, and Masud Kahn) to form the Middle or Independent Group within the British Psychoanalytic Society. This group argued that seeking relationships, and not intrapsychic drives, constitute the fundamental building blocks of mental life.

Described as the master of the in-between (or paradox), Winnicott found a home between the opposing viewpoints of Anna Freud and Melanie Klein. Winnicott's in-between character and especially his interest in transitional objects, transitional phenomena, and the intermediate area of experiencing led him to dialogue extensively with culture.

Area of Faith

Winnicott grew up in a Christian (Methodist) family, but as a self-identified non-traditionalist, showed little interest in religious doctrine. Rather, he stated that tradition and doctrine are things persons should grow out of. Scholars have identified an "area of faith" (Eigen, 1981) in Winnicott's thought. The area of faith is the transitional space between objectivity and subjectivity from which music, art, and religion receive their power to transform. It is an area where transitional experiencing takes place and it speaks to difference and aliveness amidst patterns of destructiveness and survival which lead to new psychic awareness. The area of faith addresses the capacity to project the existence of a god and to experience relationship with that god.

Capacities and Maturity

Winnicott identified six developmental capacities, each enriching our understanding of maturity and the area of faith. Achieving these interrelated capacities requires a nurturing holding environment and is for most persons a life-long maturational process: (1) The *capacity to believe* (Winnicott, Winnicott, Shepherd and Davis, 1986) speaks to being trustful and loving, being able to engage the world confidently with one's complete being: body, mind, and spirit. (2) *The capacity to imagine* (Winnicott, 1993) describes the ability to address realities that are neither purely subjective nor purely objective, but

transitional in nature. Seeing imaginative activity as healthy, Winnicott distinguished himself from the classic psychoanalytic tradition and seeing religious belief as infantile or neurotic. (3) *The capacity for concern* (Winnicott, 1994) addresses the integration of one's constructive and destructive potential. It describes an individual that cares or minds and both feels and accepts responsibility. (4) *The capacity to be alone* (Winnicott, 1994) in turn, speaks to being alone in the presence of others while experiencing significant emotional, spiritual, and relational anxiety. It is overcoming loneliness and experiencing solitude without fleeing into false relationships. (5) *The capacity of object usage* (Winnicott, Winnicott, Shepherd and Davis, 1994) is the ability to discover others for who they are, resisting projection and other projective mechanisms as ways of knowing. In usage, an object becomes valuable when it survives our destructiveness. (6) Lastly, *the capacity to play* (Winnicott, Winnicott, Shepherd and Davis, 1994) indicates entering a sacred space where a person can effortlessly move into the intermediate area of experiencing.

Achieving these capacities implies becoming an emotionally, spiritually, and relationally mature person who can live life with hope and creativity. For Winnicott, a mature person can engage all aspects of culture as forms of play of the imagination. This includes participating in a religious tradition and experiencing religious symbols, and recognizing the relationship between transitional phenomena and religious experience.

See also: ❂ Active Imagination ❂ Mother ❂ Music and Religion ❂ Object Relations Theory ❂ Psychoanalysis ❂ Psychology of Religion ❂ Self ❂ Transitional Object ❂ Winnicott, Donald Woods, and Religion

Bibliography

Clancier, A., & Kalmanovitch, J. (1987). *Winnicott and paradox: From birth to creation.* London: Tavistock Publications.

Davis, M., & Wallbridge, D. (1990). *Boundary and space: An introduction to the work of D.W. Winnicott.* London: H. Karnac Books.

Eigen, M. (1981). The area of faith in Winnicott, Lacan and Bion. *International Journal of Psycho-Analysis, 62,* 413–433.

Finn, M., & Gartner, J. (1992). *Object relations theory and religion: Clinical applications.* Westport, CT: Praeger.

Fromm, G., & Smith, B. L. (1989). *The facilitating environment: Clinical applications of Winnicott's theory.* Madison, CT: International Universities Press.

Grolnick, S. A., Barkin, L., & Muensterberger, W. (1988). *Between reality and fantasy: Winnicott's concepts of transitional objects and phenomena.* Northvale, NJ: Jason Aronson Press.

Hughes, J. M. (1989). *Reshaping the psychoanalytic domain: The work of Melanie Klein, W.R.D. Fairbairn, and D.W. Winnicott.* Berkeley, CA: University of California Press.

Jones, J. W. (1991). *Contemporary psychoanalysis and religion: Transference and transcendence.* New Haven, CT: Yale University Press.

McDargh, J. (1983). *Psychoanalytic object relations theory and the study of religion: On faith and the imaging of God.* Lanham, MD: University Press of America.

Rizzuto, A.-M. (1979). *The birth of the living God: A psychoanalytic study.* Chicago, IL: University of Chicago Press.

Rodman, F. R. (2003). *Winnicott: Life and work.* Cambridge, MA: Perseus Publishing.

Ulanov, A. B. (2001). *Finding space: Winnicott, God, and psychic reality* (1st ed.). Louisville, KY: Westminster John Knox Press.

Winnicott, D. W. (1957). *Mother and child: A primer of first relationships.* New York: Basic Books.

Winnicott, D. W. (1987). *The child, the family, and the outside world.* New York: Addison-Wesley Publishing Company.

Winnicott, D. W. (1988). *Human nature* (1st American ed.). New York: Schocken Books.

Winnicott, D. W. (1993). *Playing and reality.* London: Tavistock.

Winnicott, D. W. (1994). *The maturational processes and the facilitating environment: Studies in the theory of emotional development.* Madison, CT: International Universities Press.

Winnicott, D. W. (1995). *The family and individual development.* London: Tavistock Publications.

Winnicott, D. W., Johns, J., Shepherd, R., & Robinson, H. T. (1996). *Thinking about children.* Reading, MA: Addison-Wesley Publishing Company.

Winnicott, D. W., & Rodman, F. R. (1987). *The spontaneous gesture: Selected letters of D.W. Winnicott.* Cambridge, MA: Harvard University Press.

Winnicott, D. W., Winnicott, C., Shepherd, R., & Davis, M. (1986). *Home is where we start from: Essays by a psychoanalyst* (1st American ed.). New York: Norton.

Winnicott, D. W., Winnicott, C., Shepherd, R., & Davis, M. (1987). *Babies and their mothers* (1st American ed.). Reading, MA: Addison-Wesley Publishing Company.

Winnicott, D. W., Winnicott, C., Shepherd, R., & Davis, M. (1994). *Psycho-analytic explorations.* Cambridge, MA: Harvard University Press.

Winnicott, D. W., Winnicott, C., Shepherd, R., & Davis, M. (1997). *Deprivation and delinquency.* London: Tavistock Publications.

Winnicott, Donald Woods, and Religion

Kathryn Madden

Being and the Feminine Ground

Winnicott grounds his theory on the female element of being as the center of gravity in the relationship between mother, child and environment. "Holding" is important in that it helps the baby to integrate experience and prepares the foundation for what becomes a self experiencing "being." Holding, for Winnicott, refers to the mother's capacity for identification with her infant as well as the literal physical holding of the child–feeding, bathing, dressing–in the phase of "absolute dependence," which includes the mother's empathy, touch, and attentiveness to the infant's sensitivity to falling.

Winnicott also believes that the mother should embrace the infant figuratively in her own being to prevent holding from becoming a mechanical act. Without this experience of being, the infant can feel quite empty. The baby may experience unthinkable anxiety, primitive agonies, or the experience of falling and annihilation. The baby's subjective experience of being merged relies upon the mother's flexibility, which promotes a continuity of being. This merger or un-integration offers a state of rest crucial to creativity and play. As the child integrates the experiences of un-integration and being, these contribute toward doing.

Even before the merger of subject and object, Winnicott speaks of "being" as antedating the merger state because the infant "is" before it feels. Thus, having a good holding environment gives the infant an ability to "be," an experience that contains the child during the period of "absolute dependence." The mother being in a state of "primary maternal preoccupation" provides the ground for this complete dependence. Most important in the early experience of feeding is being and the female element. When a mother offers her breast, and the baby responds to this offering, they share in this element. If the mother does not or cannot provide the baby with a breast that "is" but only with a breast that "does," the child may develop with a crippled capacity to be. The early mother-infant container of un-integration and merger lays the foundation for projective and/or introjective identification and leads to a healthy separation between subject and object, "me" and" not me" in which the object-mother becomes more objective: an "objective-object." As the infant matures, it moves out of the world of subjective-objects, recognizes objects as external to itself and as outside its "omnipotent control". From this sequential development, the child becomes a self who feels real, and who can experience empathy based upon the experience of being at the beginning of his or her own life.

The female element that Winnicott stresses as a crucial container of being for an infant from the beginning moments of life lays the foundations for a strong sense of self. Undergoing human development within a good-enough mother and a sensitive "facilitating environment" gives us access to the creativity that contributes to the formation of culture. In contrast, those who have not known the freedom of healthy omnipotence within the transitional space of early life may experience life as empty compliance to an external reality that is devoid of value and meaning.

Dependence as a Concept of Being

Winnicott's concept of being and the feminine principle has specific developmental shifts or stages through which an infant evolves. In the first to second stage–from absolute dependence to relative dependence–the infant adapts to the failures of the mother in gradual, manageable increments. Provided there is good-enough environmental provision, these first two stages usually are negotiated adequately toward the third stage of independence. This stage lasts roughly into adolescence and adulthood. The external world begins to reflect the person's internal life of external-others. Ideally, the individual develops a sense of confidence in his or her maternal environment and has introjected these memories, which has allowed him to take over part of the mother's function.

The concept of dependence and its stages offers the infant the opportunity to get what he needs because he has *created* it. This function provides the necessary omnipotence to grow and move beyond the subjective-object stage of merger, followed by the psychological ability to use the object ruthlessly (objective-object), and the development of the capacity for creativity, and play.

Being and Doing

The facilitating environment also refers to the id and its instincts and the ego defenses that relate to the instincts but are developmentally important only in the context of the overall relationship with the mother. The infant has to have gone through absolute dependence and the successful negotiation of the subjective-object stage for the instinctual demands to become experienced as part of the self. This successful negotiation gives the infant a strong-enough ego to house the id instincts. Otherwise, the growing child can feel that something is coming "at-it" from outside, which transforms from id-excitement and is experienced as traumatic and without meaning.

In Winnicott's view, being informs doing, the drives as male elements, which come later than being. The male element comes into play as the infant begins to separate from the mother. With the process of separation, there also comes the experience of instinct-backed drives and with this, frustration and anger when the child's id satisfactions are not met. The male element evolves along with the formation of the objective-object and

how the child internally is or is not able to bring together the two aspects of mother.

The Developmental Sequence in the Use of the Object: Two Mothers

Winnicott addresses the development of what happens in infancy in terms of the use of the object. His idea of the facilitating environment includes maternal care as well as the instincts and ego defenses. In this dual context, he originated the theory of "two mothers." The mother of the holding environment is the "environment mother" and the mother of the drives and the objective-object stage is the "object-mother."

The environment mother is experienced by the infant when he is in an un-integrated state, a state associated with rest, being, quiet and an environment that is safe and empathic. The mother receives the infant and is one with him.

The object mother is experienced as the one who the infant knows in his excited states. The mother is fully present to him, as she is in the un-integrated state, but now becomes the target for his crude instinctual-tension, his raw aggression, and his ruthlessness. Both of these aspects of "mother" are needed to modify each other intrapsychically. The mother of eros, resting, and feeding is not sufficient enough to empower the child with all the aggressive energies needed for life.

The object mother introduces the masculine element. The goal, for wholeness and health, is for the infant to achieve fusion internally while separating from the real mother. Fusion represents the primary unity that Winnicott believes precedes the development of infant ego. To acquire fusion – to have both aggression and eros – the baby has to become aware that the two mothers in his fantasy experience are the same mother.

Winnicott conceptualizes how fusion plays out in infantile life by speculating upon what happens internally for the baby during its feeding time at the breast. The infant ego experiences an instinctual id impulse which is spontaneous and impersonal, imaginal and physical: the nipple is in front of the baby and he feels the urge to bite it. The actual breast is not destroyed. Both parties may experience destructive impulses but mostly in fantasized (although sometimes actual) attacks. The mother's survival from these "attacks" helps the infant to separate fantasy from objective reality. The mother is placed outside the arena of projections, outside of the infant's omnipotent control. This separation helps the child to develop an external arena in the sense of relating to objects outside his subjective world.

Further, after the ruthless biting- sucking feed, he not only becomes apprehensive about the hole he has created, he grows anxious about what feels good and what feels bad. An adult example of this anxiety might be going to the grocery store and filling a cart with mounds of incredible food and then, suddenly, feeling really empty, anxious, and awful at the check out stand. Such a feeling relates back to infantile anxiety: "I am feeding, I am fed, I feel good, but there is this hole. I think I feel good, but maybe I feel bad. Now there is stuff coming up from my stomach, and I really feel bad. Or, do I feel good? I am being held. I am being. I am. I think I am?"

An infant has to surrender to his environment. The body is totally hooked into the internal psychic process and vice-versa. To assist with this perceived hole and the struggle which becomes overly personified at the adult level, the mother needs to hold, receive and accept whatever gifts, "good and bad," that the baby gives: his burping, elimination of food, his cries. What is going on in his body is an important part of the development of a psyche-soma unity.

This maternal acceptance is crucial in the joining of the two mothers, aggression and eros. The mother's receiving helps to heal the imagined hole he made in her breast. If she accepts his biting as a gift, no matter how messy, or sloppy it is, this facilitates his gift gesture in being reparative in terms of lessening his anxiety. As with the other instinctive gestures, his anxiety is accepted and tolerated so that he can join the two mothers inside, in fusion, eventually to see the mother as outside, external. This developmental achievement informs the child's capacity to give because he has been helped to sort out the good and bad in the struggle with anxiety that he has experienced within himself. He can tolerate the imagined holes he creates with his instinctual impulses and yet, there is reparation available because these energies have been housed as acceptable. The mother's tolerance enables him to be able to imagine that something can be done about the hole he has created.

In the evolution of this early ruthlessness and aggression, as associated with the fusion of the two mothers, comes a stage of concern. If the mother has been good-enough, the infant comes to experience concern for her even while he becomes aware of his aggression toward her. A healthy guilt begins to form in relationship to his aggression and destruction toward his mother. He learns how to repair when he bursts out with impulses of excitement by giving in social situations.

If the mother is perceived as not surviving, for instance, punishes the baby, the infant can experience her reaction as impingement. The infant fantasizes that his spontaneous impulse-energies have destroyed his source of sustenance and, in its place, he has created a hole. At a baby level, this induces raw anxiety. If the growing ego cannot house this impulse, the infant experiences its own impulses as assaults, which leads to the establishment of a compliant, false self. The false self develops out of what a child is punished for – what is bad or wrong – and this badness is internalized.

Thus, infant development first begins with the subjective-object world and then the objective world which is destroyed, but survives. The infant's aggression serves a developmental purpose. His developing ability to use her as an object fuses instinctual love (aggression) and erotic love (appetite) in him in the act of dependency at the breast. The infant is not aware of his ruthless, destructive intent toward his mother during the first two years or so but at this stage of primitive ruthlessness is simply expressing and releasing instinctual tension.

The importance of aggression is that if there is no space for housing aggression and the destructive, the bad gets split or dissociated. This is extremely difficult to work out in one's body. In adult life, without aggression at the ego's disposal, one has to keep thinking up instances to keep the other person bad. This necessity for projective living is exhausting and uses up energy that could be used more constructively. Without the good-enough mother and environment, primitive ruthlessness and aggression can become anti-social. The child, and later, the adolescent can become destructive in reaction to frustration based upon what he did not receive in terms of mothering.

The ego space of early childhood needs to grow big enough to house these destructive impulses so they do not become permanently un-housed. In such cases, one day one's id impulse might arise in a therapy session. This impulse will need to be receivedas a spontaneous gesture to help repair the dissociation. Only when attention has been given to the destructive impulses in both love (erotic) and aggression (hate, destruction, instinctual love) can the aggressive drives (masculine) become wedded to vulnerable eros (feminine) and become circulated more consciously into a whole-object existence.

Social and Religious Implications of Being and Doing

How do Winnicott's stages of dependence relate to religious concerns and social issues? For us to be able to give continuity of being to another, we have to have experienced it ourselves. If we have not experienced this connection, Winnicott emphasizes that we need to go back to the place of original hurt and suffer through the feelings and images of loss and relive the missed part in the present for the first time.

If we are to engender and pass on an embodied image of a world that "mothers others," we need to internalize the capacity for being. Then, without resentment or envy, we can pass it on and give it to others. Without accepting our needs for dependence, we miss the healing efficacy of gratitude. Gratitude is acknowledged dependence. Our ability to introject unconditional loved enables us to mature into a fourth stage: interdependence, a mutuality of giving.

Winnicott's stages of dependency with the added fourth – interdependency–is a ground for thinking about how to work our way in and out of experiences of resentment within our communities. For clergy persons, faith communities, educators, and caregivers in the psychoanalytic and psychotherapeutic field, the issue of dependence and being informs our means of survival. If we deny our dependence on God and each other and pretend to be able to hold ourselves, our "false self" independence can result in all sorts of disasters, in the body, or in the psyche as a result of our pride. When we cannot get our dependency needs met, we are left frightened. One of the best defenses against fear is pride.

Winnicott's emphasis upon being as an inherited potential has implications for religion if we consider the human individual to be created in the image of God. As we grow and develop toward living in the image of God, we are dependent upon a quality of transcendent Being that makes it possible for us to develop outward from an internal reality. For example, a seed finds incarnation because it has been housed by being in the first place. Otherwise it has no life.

With religious concerns such as mission and outreach, Winnicott's "without being, doing is irrelevant" is a pertinent phrase: who do we include and exclude in social justice concerns? Do our motivations toward fairness arise from being or from doing?

The concept of being pertains to the depth of prayer. Do we pray for things to be done for us, to be on earth as they are in heaven? We cannot do to our neighbor unless we first have been done to. Offering acts of reparation and compassion that are not rooted in being can make our actions superficial and lacking in integrity. If we "are" before we "feel," we can act out of a subjective reality that proceeds to objective reality and then extends to otherness in the world. Thus, "doing unto our neighbors as we would have done unto ourselves" means we do because we have "been," not because we have been "done to."

Winnicott's notion of fusion and the two mothers pertains not only to our relationship to God but our images of the divine. Prayer is not just passive. Relating to God through prayer, which often includes imagery, expands to become both erotic and aggressive. We begin with whatever images we have and, suddenly, the free-flow of instinct-backed impulses can carry us into the most fleshly, tangible places, infusing the wounded body with long-lost energies.

In faith communities, clergy persons might include some healthy aggressive impulses in their sermons and not just tip-toe through the tulips. If a pastor cannot house aggression and eros, such a split can lead to watered-down programs and ineffective sermons: God with no sex appeal. Clergy need to recognize the constructive need for opposition. Conflict plays and important role in objective-object differentiation. We need a certain amount of resistance or disagreement to develop our aggressive potential and for healthy aggression to then lead to a community of concern. Sometimes we have to hate and create a hole in the breast before love can occur.

Too much opposition, however, may prevent fusion, in that it can be received as impingement, a disruption of being. Then we get reactivity instead of responsiveness. Ideally we should be able to use our neighbor for some good and healthy opposition in an interrelated network of dependency.

On an even larger scale, pride, as it is informed by fear can play into big political systems. Instead of working through our inner fantasies of fear of merger, we instead buy into some autocratic or authoritarian mode of political control. For certain groups and individuals, the energies of ruthless aggression needed for healthy development have been forcibly held down by nations, other groups, hierarchies, and/or governments. For those who never had the opportunity to have this stage negotiated, to just forgive may mean a recapitulation of centuries of compliance.

Hostility, anger, and their consequences have roots in maternal/environmental frustration. The mother helps the infant to house aggression, assisting the transformation of this instinct into reparative functions (guilt, giving). In adulthood, if this developmental function is absent, the gap can lead to a defensive splitting of love and hate creating further polarization. The result is that love has less aggression and hate gains more destructiveness. Hostility (racial and relational), can become perpetuated endlessly. We see the unfortunate results of such splitting in Iraq, Afghanistan, North Korea, Palestine, in gangs clustered around urban environments, and in hundreds of other national and global situations. Most unfortunately, if negotiating the ruthless-aggression phase failed, we cannot say, "I'm so sorry that you are deprived. Here, take this hundred dollars and buy yourself a pair of Nikes, or take this welfare check, or accept this affirmative action job and now go get your destructive aggressive energies together." This action does not work and relies upon understanding a much more complex intrapsychic insufficiency.

Winnicott believed that the fear of dependence, specifically absolute dependence, is behind the fear of women and discriminatory acts against them. This fear can pertain to the feminine in either sex and arises in the phallic phase of development according to classical psychoanalytic theory. Dread of the feminine arises particularly in persons who never passed through the stage of absolute dependence successfully with sufficient trust of the primary parent. Or, perhaps the mother was depressed or physically absent for the early months of the child's life because of her own life-traumas. Such a gap can leave a residual apprehension rooted in the primordial fears of our early years.

Winnicott speculates that there exists a male envy of the feminine based upon the fantasy that women possess the female element and can take it for granted. Envy, however, has to do with failure in being and failure in the maternal environment. Both sexes need both elements. Either sex suffers when we lack being and the feminine because being fuels and informs profoundly-grounded doing.

Within the context of depth psychology, much could be done to enable people to better house instinctual impulses and aggression toward fusion within the various maternal/environmental containers we have available in the way of faith communities, social services, therapeutic containers, and social institutions. Both polarities must be housed: eros and aggression. Otherwise, we might buy into a graduate educational institute or a psychoanalytic training institute that needs to dominate the psyche based upon secular modes of doing while interpreting feminine modes of being, passion, and creativity as unresolved pre-Oedipal needs.

If we can tolerate our destructive impulses, we can learn to enjoy ideas, creative projects–religious, social, personal–which include destruction. The body is involved because the bodily excitements that belong to destructive id impulses get activated and add gusto to a person's creative endeavors. This kind of ruthless commitment in the passionate, creative act, receiving and destroying and allowing things to break, carries over to many other creative enterprises in life. Different from Freud's pleasure-seeking principle, the sexual act is considered not so much the erotic desire that needs an object but more the aggressive destructive element of the impulse towards fusion. In mature love, there needs to be enough space for aggressive penetration and we need to know that the object survives our ruthlessness.

This experience of being leads to a continuity of generations. Being is passed on between generations through the female element of both men and women. We hold as we were once held. Our ability to bring these two elements together provides us with the potential for living creatively. If either of these elements is split off, this dissociation interferes with the resources that inform productivity. We do not want to miss the fullness of experience that feminine being has to offer.

See also: ❯ Active Imagination ❯ Defenses ❯ Eros ❯ Mother ❯ Psychotherapy

Bibliography

Winnicott, D. W. (1958). *Collected papers: Through paediatrics to psycho-analysis*. London: Tavistock Publications.

Winnicott, D. W. (1965). *The maturational process and the facilitating environment*. New York: International Universities Press.

Winnicott, D. W. (1986). *Holding and interpretation: Fragment of an analysis*. London: Hogarth Press.

Winnicott, D. W. (1987). *Babies and their mothers*. Beverly, MA: Perseus Publishing.

Winnicott, D. W. (1989). *Psychoanalytic explorations*. Cambridge, MA: Harvard University Press.

Winnicott, D. W., & Winnicott, C. (1971). *Playing and reality*. Kent, England: Tavistock Publications.

Wisdom

Kelly Murphy Mason

Wisdom is a virtue that combines proper understanding with the prudent application of knowledge; it is often believed to be a product of right relation with the Divine. In psychospiritual terms, wisdom melds both acceptance and insight and thereby results in judicious action. Often, wisdom is characterized as having a feminine dimension. It has also been associated with elders at the end of life. Throughout the ages, wise ones have been revered not only by their peers, but also by successive generations who recognized the wisdom of previous generations as timeless wisdom.

Personifications of wisdom have abounded for millennia. In the Greek pantheon, Athena was the embodiment of wisdom; her totem was the round-eyed owl that was able to see through darkness and at wide angles (Warner, 1985). In her nativity myth, Athena springs fully formed from Zeus' head, suggesting the relation of wisdom to flashes of insight. She is a feminine archetype of good counsel, sound strategy, clear thinking, and practical solutions, all of which have frequently assumed to be masculine aspects (Bolen, 2004); rather revealingly, she is the only of the Olympian goddesses to ever be depicted wearing armor.

In the Hebrew scriptures, Wisdom makes several appearances as a goddess-like figure (Cole Ronan and Taussig, 1996), most notably as Hokma in the Book of Proverbs. "Is not Wisdom calling? Is not Understanding raising her voice?" (Ps 8:1). Throughout Proverbs, Wisdom is simultaneously inviting and insistent. "All the words from my mouth are upright, nothing false there, nothing crooked, everything plain, if you can understand, straight, if you have acquired knowledge," she proclaims. "Accept my discipline rather than silver, and knowledge of me in preference to finest gold" (Ps 8:8–10).

Preciousness and primacy alike are repeatedly stressed as characteristics of Wisdom. She declares: "Yahweh created me, first-fruits of his fashioning, before the oldest of his works. From everlasting, I was firmly set, from the beginning, before the earth came into being." Essentially, Wisdom represents the thought that is first creation; a consort of the Creator God, she knows the ways of God and the children of God who constitute humanity (Schroer, 2000).

Proverbs is classified with other "Wisdom books" in the Bible as part of a larger sapiential tradition, including Job, Psalms and Qoholeth/Ecclesiastes (Crenshaw, 1998), as well as Ecclesiasticus/Ben Sira and the Book of Wisdom contained in the Septuagint. In the Book of Wisdom, King Solomon, the greatest sage of ancient Israel and its purported author, exclaims: "Wisdom is brilliant, she never fades. By those who love her, she is readily seen, by those who seek her, she is readily found. She anticipates those who desire her by making herself known first" (Wis 6:12). Her accessibility and nurturing spirit again make Wisdom a maternal figure who is glad to take into her tutelage those who remain educable.

In the Greek New Testament, in the Gospels of Luke and Matthew, Jesus identifies himself as child-student of Wisdom in the Jewish tradition (Fiorenza, 1994). He understands Sophia to be the lost mother of Israelites who have tragically forgotten their parentage. "Yet," Jesus concludes, "Wisdom is justified by all her children" (Lk 7.35). His Sophia bears less resemblance to a Hellenic oracle than to those Hebrew prophets who promulgate teachings

that ultimately prove counter-cultural and occasionally counter-intuitive.

Biblical scholars have noted that Sophia subsequently receded from early Christian writings, becoming a more esoteric figure, almost a theological obscurity. Despite the metaphors depicting Wisdom as mother and sister, bride and wife, Wisdom represented knowledge that refused to be domesticated for convenience or to conform to conventional thought. What has been termed Sophiology quickly became submerged. In the dominant Christian religious discourse, Sophia was replaced with Logos, popularly translated as "the Word" but perhaps more aptly rendered as "the Reason." Effectively, a masculine principle of knowledge supplanted a feminine one.

Medieval mystics such as Hildegard of Bingen exhibited an attraction to the Divine Feminine they saw expressed through Sapientia (Newman, 1987). They understood Wisdom to midwife the manifestation of God's intention, in many senses to actually be the mother of/to God. In Orthodox churches, devotion to Ouisa-Sophia, the Spirit of Wisdom, was once open and institutional (Bulgakov, 1993); icons of her were venerated and Hagia Sophia built in her honor. Only recently have feminist theologians begun to reclaim these stands of thought from the weave of historic Christianity (Camp, 1996; Johnson, 1999).

With the recognition of major world religions as "wisdom traditions" has come greater permission to translate more freely what those traditions might have to say to people in the modern era. Wisdom is still heard speaking through various religions, Eastern as well as Western, and seeking after it is seen as a powerful antidote to the existential anxiety that pervades contemporary society (Watts, 1951). Indeed, one of the ten Buddhist perfections is panna; in allowing its practitioners to witness events with great detachment, panna curbs human affliction.

Perhaps those who most explicitly seek after wisdom in America today are member of a movement that bills itself as spiritual and not religious, members of the programs of 12-Step recovery modeled after Alcoholics Anonymous. In a redaction of a longer prayer authored by theologian Reinhold Neibuhr during the Second World War (Sifton, 2003), those in 12-Step programs pray: "God, grant me the serenity to accept the things I cannot change, courage to change the things I can, and the wisdom to know the difference." The Serenity Prayer has become formative in both popular and psychospiritual formulations on the meaning of wisdom.

What the Serenity Prayer seems to recommend is that people become reconciled with those things they must reconcile themselves to and resist those things they ought to, either for their own good and for the greater good (Alcoholics Anonymous, 1952). Wisdom becomes grounded in a radical acceptance of a sometimes stubborn reality. The challenge is one of discernment: how can divine guidance be channeled to direct (or at times, correct) the course of human events?

Ultimately, Wisdom occupies the intersection of horizontal and vertical concerns, where the highest human ideals meet the most immediate demands of the here-and-now. In her Biblical personifications, Wisdom is hardworking and intimately engaged, calling out to listeners busy with the activities of daily life. Wisdom remains quite distinct from either contemplation or resignation.

In his schedule of virtues, psychoanalyst Erik Erikson positions wisdom as the terminal virtue, maintaining that its antithesis is disdain. In a life review of insights gained, Erikson contends, persons have the choice of adopting an attitude of disgust or a philosophical outlook that leads to deeper understanding of the human condition. The last of the major stages in psychosocial development allows adults to develop into "elders," those defined by being both older and wiser, not merely aged (Erikson, 1982).

According to Erikson, not all elderly persons are able to master this final developmental task and attain wisdom. They are asked to fulfill a demanding grand-generative role, to teach successive generations to live with integrity and die with dignity. This involves a willingness to acknowledge the life cycle itself as somehow purposive, despite the considerable hardships encountered the later years of life, the losses that must be endured. Wisdom is marked by a capacity to vigorously construct some unifying meaning of what may at times appear to be disparate events and experiences; in the end, it serves an integrative function.

Borrowing from Eriksonian schema, psychologist James Fowler posits that wisdom emerges in the penultimate stage of his six theoretical stages of faith development over the lifespan, the stage which he terms "conjunctive." Conjunctive faith is sensitive to the organic interrelatedness of things in a dialogical reality (Fowler, 1981). It blurs boundaries, recognizing how context-dependent and provisional much of human knowledge is, how dimly it apprehends the scope of that which is truly transcendent. Wisdom contains both a comprehension and appreciation for all that is not currently known and may never be known. It may even question what is knowable, humbled by its acquaintance with mystery, simultaneously tolerant and aware of its limits.

Recent psychological research has tried to operationally define and quantify wisdom, but has not yet succeeded in standardizing any metrics or even in delimiting its subject matter satisfactorily. The field of positive psychology has exhibited special interest in wisdom as a "core virtue," exploring material that once seemed to be the purview of transpersonal psychology and acknowledging the possibility of transcendent experience (Cloninger, 2005). Research has suggested that wisdom seems to involve maintaining a sense of perspective, especially in the face of adversity, and maintaining a degree of emotional equanimity; it does not necessarily appear to be an age-related trait, although people can be educated by experiences that accumulate over a lifetime.

Commentary

Personifications and definitions of wisdom appear to share commonalities, mirroring the affective and cognitive aspects alike. Wisdom generally reflects a highly relational way of thinking, one that has stereotypically feminine features. It is often characterized as an experiential mode of knowing.

In sacred scripture, Wisdom is intimately acquainted with the Divine and always desirous of connecting with humanity on a deeper level. The work of Wisdom is to speak some eternal truth in a vernacular that can be easily understood in context, some truth that bears repeating to others. Wisdom simultaneously recognizes and dignifies the human predicament.

In psychological terms, wisdom is demonstrated by a higher comfort level with mixed emotions and ambiguous situations. Those whose sagacity is noted by others are able to put their knowledge base to pragmatic use. They serve a larger cause than narrow self-interest, exhibiting a capacity to take a long-range view of matters, often taking into consideration the welfare of future generations. They have the power to facilitate moral uplift in others.

By exercising empathy, wise persons are able to be tutored by others' experience, as well as their own. For this reason, in many spiritual traditions, the wise are commonly directed to keep the company of the wise. As a religious concept, Wisdom is often represented as somehow accounting for the compendium of all human experience, and in doing so, achieving Ultimate consciousness. Presumably, even the wisest people can only glimpse this.

See also: ❯ Biblical Narratives Versus Greek Myths ❯ Biblical Psychology ❯ Twelve Steps

Bibliography

Alcoholic Anonymous. (1952). *Twelve steps and twelve traditions*. New York: Alcoholics Anonymous World Service.

Bolen, J. S. (2004). *Goddesses in everywoman: Powerful archetypes in women's lives* (20th Anniversary ed.). New York: Quill.

Bulgakov, S. (1993). *Sophia, The wisdom of God: An outline of Sophiology.* Hudson, NY: Lindisfarne Press.

Camp, C. V. (1996). Sophia/Wisdom. In L. M. Russell & J. Shannon Clarkson (Eds.), *Dictionary of feminist theologies.* Louisville, KY: Westminster John Knox Press.

Cloninger, C. R. (2005). Character strengths and virtues: A handbook and classification. *American Journal of Psychiatry, 162*(4), 820–821.

Cole, S., Ronan, M., & Taussig, H. (1996). *Wisdom's feast: Sophia in study and celebration* (New ed.). Kansas City, MO: Sheed & Ward.

Crenshaw, J. L. (1998). *Old Testament wisdom: An introduction* (Revised). Louisville, KY: Westminster John Know Press.

Erikson, E. (1982). *The life cycle completed.* New York: W. W. Norton.

Fiorenza, E. S. (1994). *Jesus: Miriam's child, Sophia's prophet: Critical issues in feminist Christology.* New York: Continuum Publishing.

Fowler, J. W. (1981). *Stages of faith: The psychology of human development and the quest for meaning.* San Franscisco, CA: Harper.

Johnson, E. A. (1999). *She who is: The mystery of God in feminist theological discourse.* New York: Crossroad Publishing.

Newman, B. (1987). *Sister of wisdom: St. Hildegard's theology of the feminine.* Berkley, CA: University of California Press.

Schroer, S. (2000). *Wisdom has built her house: Studies on the figure of Sophia in the Bible.* Collegeville, MN: The Liturgical Press.

Sifton, E. (2003). *The serenity prayer: Faith and politics in times of peace and war.* New York: W. W. Norton.

Wansbrough, H. (Ed.). (1990). *The New Jerusalem Bible.* New York: Doubleday.

Warner, M. (1985). *Monuments and maidens: The allegory of the female form.* New York: Atheneum.

Watts, A. (1951). *The wisdom of insecurity.* New York: Vintage Books.

Witch, The

Ruth Williams

The witch is a character or image of a spell-caster associated with night and death which has manifestations in every world culture and epoch.

Examples include (*inter alia*) Euripides' *Medea* in Greek Mythology; Shakespeare's triumvirate in *Macbeth*; cinema has innumerable versions, notably *The Witches of Eastwick* (Dir. George Miller II, 1987), *The Wizard of Oz* (Dir. Victor Fleming, 1939) and *Batman Returns* (Dir. Tim Burton, 1992) where in modern guise the witch has been merged with her "familiar" and becomes "Catwoman." Pearson (2002) provides an impressive review of (*inter alia*) a raft of artistic and cultural variants.

There are likewise copious fairy tale witches which help children cope, psychologically with feelings of envy and hatred (e.g., Hansel and Gretel, Cinderella).

Witches feature in certain religious traditions such as Voodoo, of which there are several geographical variants.

The images and emotions associated with the witch are generally repellent.

In Mythology and Fairy Tale

The Greek moon goddess Hecate (goddess of witches) is sometimes depicted as having three heads; one of a dog, one of a snake, and one of a horse. Cerberus, the three-headed hound of Hades, is said to have belonged to Hecate. Mythologically witches are often depicted in groups of three. Hecate is said to hold dominion over heaven, earth, and under the earth and this triune quality is often represented in statues showing her as a threefold woman (Harding, 1935/1955: 218) (see, e.g., the frontispiece to Harding (1935/1955) depicting the "Hectarian of Marienbad" from Pausanias, *Mythology and Monuments of Ancient Athens*, 1890). A Classical Jungian amplification of this image (a method whereby an image is filled out by exploring the mythical/fairy tale and archetypal associations to it) might go on to think about this threefold nature as pointing towards the *Moirai*, or Fates, which might suggest there is something *fated* about such a connection, linking also to "past, present, and future" and Karma (Harding, 1955/1971: 218). Hecate is also usually seen with two ghost hounds that are said to serve her. Hecate is sometimes known as "sender of nocturnal visions" (Harding, 1955/1971: 114).

Classical Jungian writers explore the witch in the guise of her many mythical and fairy tale manifestations (e.g., Birkhäuser-Oeri, 1977; von Franz, 1995 and 1999, see also Koltuv, 1986). The most significant Jungian work in this area has been done by Ann and Barry Ulanov in *The Witch and the Clown* (1987).

The witch is seen as appearing in a gap in time. Until the Middle Ages the witch was known as a "hagazussa", meaning the one riding on the fence (Duerr, 1978/1985: 243, n14). According to Duerr (German anthropologist) "the witch is born on the boundary" is a Dinka (African) saying (Duerr, 1978/1985: 243, n14.). (Hecate is known (inter alia) as a goddess of thresholds.)

Psychological Exploration

Dykes' (1980) hypothesis is that the witch occupies the most remote aspect of the psyche making it difficult to access in any psychological exploration (see *psyche*). Dykes describes the mental paralysis associated with the witch's menace as less destructive than aimed at the *prevention* of life (1980: 52). This connects with the witch's mythological solitude (perhaps the source of her loneliness which may fuel her negativity) when she malevolently broods on the objects of her envy and hatred, hatching plans for revenge and retribution. Her bile and envy are represented symbolically in certain examples of witch (e.g., Wizard of Oz) by a green face. She is seen as irritable, power-hungry, malevolent, and greedy.

Jung describes the Shadow, under which rubric the witch would be categorized, as "the thing a person has no wish to be" (1946: par. 470) (see *Shadow*).

Bűhrmann makes a link to depression (1987b: 276). Bűhrmann reports that the victims of witchcraft feel that life is being crushed out of them and they are facing complete annihilation (1987a: 142). This corresponds to the problem when dealing with the witch as an intra-psychic phenomenon in that, during possession, there is similarly a feeling of *metaphorically* being crushed and annihilated.

In Psychoanalysis

Heinemann (2000) provides an excellent psychoanalytic deconstruction of the phenomenon of the witch trials of the sixteenth/seventeenth centuries, arguing against Freud's "hysterical" formulation. She sees the witch as both a "phallic mother" and an early superego imago.

In witchcraft transmission of the witch is seen as being inherited through the maternal line.

In a paper looking at (1) the witch/vampire, (2) the spider and (3) the shark, the images are seen from a psychoanalytic perspective as "three symbols of overwhelming terror" (Lane et al., 1989: 326). Theoretically the images are seen by Lane et al. as symbols deriving from: "the earliest levels of human development [c.f. Dykes, 1980], originating in the preoedipal phases of life. Each symbol expresses a dimension of oral sadism. The witch/vampire bites, the spider stings, and the shark devours its victim totally. All three symbols rely heavily on the use of splitting mechanisms and the polarization of principal identifications (e.g., parasite/host, victim/attacker, idealized/demonic)" (c.f. Dykes, 1980).

The witch is also, more usually, seen as a phallic image: "with a pointed, peaked nose, sharp long finger-nails, and a broom between her legs; she is capable of flying or of going up. She struggles to be like a man and engages in mannish behavior, rivaling and threatening men, argumentative, controlling, casting spells over the potency of men, and the fertility of women. Her evil deeds are carried out by the devil, *the man who resides within her.*

Her dark and dirty side is this masculinity" (c.f. Dykes, 1980) (emphasis added).

Further papers in the psychoanalytic literature which talk of a witch mother are Fenichel (1931), Dahl (1989), Lawson (2000), and the witch as nightmare figure (Jones, 1931 and 1949).

And Sexuality

The image of the witch carries vital characteristics of dark sexuality (her voracious and aggressive appetite, her insatiability and love of control as opposed to vulnerability and intimacy) and for a woman's place in society as an aging crone or shrew with all that implies about her viability as a sexual being.

Brinton Perera views engagement with this "dark" aspect of femininity as being of profound importance in retrieving repressed values (1981: 15). She discusses the feminine by amplifying the Sumerian myth of Inanna whose process into the underworld metaphorically parallels the psychological individuation process. Brinton Perera concludes that it is only by embracing the full, even demonic, range of affects associated with the "dark" feminine, that a woman can truly individuate and make a soul connection in her partnerships on an equal footing (1981: 94).

Mythology

Baring and Cashford (1991) like Neumann (1955) elaborate in exhaustive detail accompanied by copious images, the "eternal feminine" in her many historical manifestations from Palaeolithic times. They amplify the image of the witch in her many guises from Ereshkigal (Inanna's "dark" sister and Queen of the Underworld in Sumerian mythology) to Hecate (Queen of the night in Greek mythology), to Lilith (their counterpart in Hebrew mythology) (1991: 192) as well as Medusa (who quite literally petrified).

Jungian Shadow

De Castillejo places importance on taking responsibility for the Shadow. She believes that, with all women, if you scratch the surface, you would find a witch. She sees the witch in terms of a power complex which perhaps paradoxically often manifests in women in the guise of giving (De Castillejo, 1973: 42).

In her study of *Athene* in tracing the heritage of the feminine, Shearer highlights the importance of the psychological work and regards the need to understand the dual nature of the feminine as being an inescapable task: "in the great cycle of creation we now live in the Kali Yuga, an age as dark as the age of iron" (1996: 52). The Kali Yuga refers to the Hindu goddess Kali (Yuga meaning age or era in Sanskrit), and invokes the dark goddess who is depicted as a destroyer:

> ▶ [s]he stands on a corpse and wears a necklace of skulls . . . She is devourer: her long tongue thrusts out to lick up the blood of sacrifice, her fearsome laughter shows her dreadful teeth, her maw receives all that is created. . . . In one of her hands she wields a sword and in another she carries a severed head. She is always young, bursting with blood, and always ancient, an emaciated hag, whose hunger will never be satiated. She stamps on the body of Lord Shiva (1996: 54).

Shearer tracks the denigration of women and their so-called wickedness which linked them to witchcraft down to the very Fall of Man and her creation from a bent – defective – rib (1996: 165), as did Roberts (1985).

Medusa

Shearer goes on to discuss Medusa (whose severed head Athene wore on her breast) who forms part of yet another triumvirate, the Gorgon sisters:

> ▶ They are a manifestation of the ancient moon goddess (as the Orphics knew when they called the moon 'the Gorgon's head'). The sisters' names honor their power – Stheino means 'strength', Euryale 'the leaping one', and Medusa herself is 'Mistress', 'Queen', 'Ruler' and 'the Cunning One' . . . they have great brazen wings, staring owl-like eyes, serpents for hair and sometimes for girdles as well, tusks like boars and long lolling tongues (1996: 64).

Neumann (in his *magnum opus The Great Mother*) links the negative pole of the feminine with all the dark mythological witch characters so that snake-haired Medusa is seen as belonging to this realm in that "to be rigid is to be dead" (1955: 266), with blood-drinking slayer-of-men, Kali (1955: 72) who is also represented as having three eyes, said to symbolize past, present, and future ("Kala" in Sanskrit meaning time), "'mad'-making Hecate" (see above) and licentious Ishtar. These are placed in direct opposition to "mother" and "virgin"; Mary, Demeter, and Sophia. Although each of the former category are seen as "negative", there is also a transformational quality inherent in the symbol. For instance from Medusa's dead body the giant Chrysaor and the winged horse Pegasus (her son by Poseidon) sprang forth; the blood from Medusa's severed head was given to Asclepius (god of healing) and while blood from the veins on the Gorgon's left side brought harm, that from her right side could raise the dead (March 1999); Kali's usual proximity to cremation grounds where all worldly attachments are dissolved points to the cycle of birth and renewal.

Mother, Depression, Aging

Jung, with his own problematic relationship to his personal mother as described in *Memories, Dreams, Reflections* (1963), was himself only too aware of the dual aspects of woman:

> ▶ Not in vain are little children afraid of their own mothers in the night. Primitive mothers can kill their children. It is absolutely incompatible with the daytime, for then they are most devoted mothers. But in the night they take away the mask and become witches (Jung 1984: 144–5).

On a more ordinary level, a depressive mother may be seen along a continuum which leads to the "Terrible Mother" which links to the witch, particularly in the aging process and menopause.

Bührmann makes the connection between the Terrible Mother and depression when she records:

> ▶ This regressive pull of the elementary feminine is also seen in serious depressions. The ego suffers marked loss of libido, lacking drive or will power, inability to concentrate on work . . . It can be said that the ego is drained of energy, that it is being submerged in the negative world of the elementary feminine in its terrible or devouring aspect (1987a: 151).

Aging women in certain circumstances tend to take on characteristics which are associated with the archetype of the witch. (This has been a cliché in popular culture but perhaps has more serious ramifications.) This can occur when the lacunae associated with this stage of life mean that one is left alone, or children leave the nest, or disappointments build and death comes into one's thoughts. This can be associated with lack of sexual fulfillment, perhaps metaphorically connected to the witch's remoteness from society and engagement with life.

There are also neopagan "white" witches influenced by Wicca.

The nearest equivalent to the witch for men is the vampire, devil, sorcerer, wizard or warlock.

See also: ❂ Archetype ❂ Devil ❂ Feminity ❂ Individuation ❂ Shadow ❂ Wicca ❂ Witchcraft

Bibliography

Baring, A., & Cashford, J. (1991). *The myth of the Goddess: Evolution of an image.* London: Penguin Arkana, 1993.

Birkhäuser-Oeri, S. (1977). *The mother: Archetypal image in fairy tales.* Toronto, ON: Inner City Books, 1988.

Bůhrmann, M. V. (1987a). The feminine in witchcraft: Part I. *Journal of Analytical Psychology, 32,* 139–156.

Bůhrmann, M. V. (1987b). The feminine in witchcraft: Part II. *Journal of Analytical Psychology, 32,* 257–277.

Dahl, E. K. (1989). Daughters and mothers – Oedipal aspects of the witch-mother. *Psychoanalytic Study of the Child, 44,* 267–280.

De Castillejo, I. C. (1973). *Knowing woman: A feminine psychology.* Boston, MA: Shambhala, 1990.

Duerr, H. P. (1978). *Dreamtime: Concerning the boundary between wilderness and civilization.* Oxford, England: Basil Blackwell, 1985.

Dykes, A. (1980). The witch: A severe case and a minor case of witch influence. *Harvest, 26,* 51–61.

Fenichel, O. (1931). The pregenital antecedents of the oedipus complex. *International Journal of Psycho-Analysis, 12,* 141–166.

Harding, M. E. (1955/1971). *Woman's mysteries: Ancient and modern.* London: Rider & Co, 1977.

Heinemann, E. (2000). *Witches: A psychoanalytical exploration of the killing of women.* London: Free Association Books.

Jones, E. (1931). *Nightmare witches & devils.* New York: W. W. Norton.

Jones, E. (1949). *On the nightmare.* London: Hogarth Press.

Jung, C. G. (1946). *The practice of psychotherapy.* London: Routledge & Kegan Paul.

Jung, C. G. (1963). In Jaffé (Ed.), *Memories, dreams reflections.* London: Fontana Press, 1995.

Jung, C. G. (1984). *Dream seminars 1928–30.* London: Routledge & Kegan Paul.

Koltuv, B. B. (1986). *The book of Lilith.* Maine: Nicolas-Hays.

Lane, R. C., & Chazan, S. E. (1989). Symbols of terror: The witch/vampire, the spider, and the shark. *Psychoanalytic Psychology, 6,* 325–341.

Lawson, C. A. (2000). *Understanding the borderline mother.* New York: Jason Aronson.

March, J. (1999). *Dictionary of classical mythology.* London: Cassell.

Neumann, E. (1955). *The great mother.* London: Routledge & Kegan Paul.

Pearson, J. (2002). *Belief beyond boundaries: Wicca, celtic spirituality and the new age.* Milton Keynes, England: Open University.

Perera, S. B. (1981). *Descent to the Goddess: A way of initiation for women.* Toronto, ON: Inner City Books.

Roberts, R. (1985). *From eden to eros: Origins of the put down of women.* San Anselmo, CA: Vernal Equinox Press.

Shearer, A. (1996). *Athene: Image and Energy.* London: Viking Arkana.

Ulanov, A., & B. (1987). *The witch and the clown: Two archetypes of human sexuality.* Wilmette, IL: Chiron Publications.

Von Franz, M.-L. (1995). *Shadow and evil in fairy tales.* Boston, MA: Shambhala.

Von Franz, M.-L. (1999). *The cat: A tale of feminine redemption.* Toronto, Ontario, Canada: Inner City Books.

Witchcraft

David Waldron

The Politicization of Witchcraft History

Witchcraft and its associated imagery is one of the most powerful, pervasive and multi-faceted symbols in western culture. That being said, evaluating the complex webs of representations associated with the image of the Witch and Witchcraft is an enormous task. The issues raised by the historical experience and study of Witchcraft further compound the bewildering array of symbols and themes associated with it. Of particular importance in establishing the links between representations and symbols of Witchcraft with the historical phenomena is the intensely anglo-centric domination of Witchcraft studies and literature, not least of which is the broad association of multiple divergent themes, images, ideas and mythic forms under the category of Witch, despite radically different cultural and historical contexts and localized meanings (Ankarloo and Henningsen, 1990). Similarly, studies of Witchcraft in both its historical context and as a form of archetypal representation, have long served as a battleground between different sectors of society according to a wide array of ideological agendas and religious beliefs (Purkiss, 1996).

Despite this problem of over generalization and politicization, representations of Witchcraft do share certain common themes that link both the term and archetypal image of the Witch together. Essentially, the Witch represents an iconic form of the feminine other and as such lies at the center of a network of social forms, morality, constructions of gender and social order, thus serving as the focal point of a wider array of social projections. Typically, the Witch is associated with the organic, the feminine, the disorder, and there is a close association with the anti-rational and the supernatural (Purkiss, 1996). In this sense, the Witch is both reviled as threat to the social order and associated with anti-human practices and vices yet at the same time can be held up as an iconic antidote to the social ills wrought by sources of authority and social structures symbolically associated with patriarchal control (Briggs, 1996). Similarly, the association of Witchcraft and Witchcraft beliefs with the anti-rational and the supernatural has served as a rallying point for enlightenment models of social structure, warning of the dangers of religious thinking overwhelming the rational/scientific world view with the shadow side of unrestrained superstition and mass hysteria. This contrast is very evident in

W

anthropological interpretations of Witchcraft, especially in the African and Polynesian contexts where the superstition of Witchcraft beliefs is unfavorably contrasted with white rationalism, and Witchcraft is used to label magical practices associated with organic or endemic powers applied emotionally distinct from the learned skills of the sorcerer (Marwick, 1970).

The Witch as a Symbol of Genocide and Oppression

Another important model of Witchcraft is the use of representations of the Witch trials of the early modern period as a vehicle to understand the contemporary experiences of genocide via the work of Norman Cohn (1975) and of the patriarchal oppression of women, primarily through the work of Mary Daly and Robin Morgan (Daly, 1979; Morgan, 1976). In both cases, while the historical parallels are extremely dubious in empirical terms and are subject to much criticism, they have both become pervasive mythologies in contemporary western culture, holding significant emotional appeal and symbolic resonance. Indeed, the images of martyrdom and sexualized tortures implied to both have had a deeply powerful visceral and psychological impact which has afforded this construction of Witchcraft significant popular appeal. Similarly, the model of Witchcraft as a surviving pre-Christian fertility cult, established by Margaret Murray and popularized into modern Wicca and Witchcraft revival movements, also has enormous visceral impact and popular appeal despite the theory being largely discredited in historical terms. In these cases Witches, as the ultimate manifestation of the feminine other, have served as both the projected shadow of mainstream culture and a rallying point for those disaffected by the mainstream social order and patriarchal systems of authority (Purkiss, 1996). Additionally, in much psychological literature and recent anthropological analysis Witchcraft, as a form of demonization and persecution is interpreted as a social feedback phenomenon created out of social anxiety, rumor and gossip akin to phenomena like the Satanic Ritual Abuse panic of the 1980s, McCarthyism of the 1950s and recent panics over suspected terrorists (Stewart and Strathern, 2004; Hicks, 1991).

The Witch in Western Culture

The Witch is a particularly unique figure in western symbolic construction as it is the iconic symbol that stands astride the romantic/enlightenment divide of western culture. For some sectors of society the Witch represents superstition, evil, irrationality and the primitive, i.e., that which limits the potential for human progress and autonomy from nature. To others, the Witch represents beauty, nature, freedom and cultural autonomy from the corrupting and limiting influences of scientific rationalism, commodification and industrialization. In both constructs the Witch serves as the iconic underbelly or shadow side of Western enlightenment associated with femininity, the tribal other, religious superstition, the anti-rational, the magical, sexuality and our organic relationship with nature. As such its psychological impact is enormous and its emotional and archetypal significance is one of the most pervasive and powerful of contemporary symbols emerging from the underbelly of the past.

See also: ❧ Femininity ❧ Wicca ❧ Witch, The

Bibliography

Ankarloo, B., & Henningsen, G. (1990). *Early modern European witchcraft: Centres and peripheries.* Oxford, England: Clarendon Press.

Briggs, R. (1996). *Witches and neighbours the social and cultural context of European witchcraft.* New York: Penguin Group.

Cohn, N. (1975). *Europe's inner demons.* London: Sussex University Press.

Daly, M. (1979). *Gyn/Ecology.* London: Women's Press.

Hicks, R. (1991). *In pursuit of Satan: American police and the occult.* New York: Prometheus.

Marwick, M. (Ed.). (1970). *Witchcraft and sorcery.* Hammondsworth, England: Penguin.

Morgan, R. (1977). *Lady of the Beast.* New York: Random House.

Purkiss, D. (1996). *The witch in history: Early modern and twentieth century interpretations.* London: Routledge.

Stewart, P., & Strathern, A. (2004). *Witchcraft, sorcery, rumors and gossip.* Cambridge, England: Cambridge University Press.

Women and Religion

Benjamin Beit-Hallahmi

The Basic Findings

The greater religiosity of women, demonstrated in numerous and consistent research findings over the past 100 years, is arguably the most important fact about religion. Most research on religion is in reality research about women, who are the backbone of religion globally, and are actively supporting, maintaining, and sometimes keeping alive religious establishments, institutions, and organizations everywhere. If we do some basic ethnographic observations, and visit churches in Rome, Paris, New York City, or Moscow, we will immediately realize that (older) women make up the majority of those in attendance. Anthropological observations in India indicate that women make up the majority of those attending Hindu temples. Only in those traditions where ritual attendance by women is discouraged, such as Islam and Judaism, the majority of those attending will be men.

In the Islamic world, while women are discouraged from attending mosque services, they dominate among those who follow various popular practices, such as pilgrimages to saints' tombs. In these sanctuaries, a popular "women's religion" is practiced, but men are not officially excluded. Television rituals are the perfect opposite to pilgrimage, but we know that among viewers of US televangelists, women are quite over-represented.

When we look at data on levels of religiosity for men and women in all cultures that have been looked at, women are more likely to describe themselves as religious, as compared with men. When it comes to beliefs, the differences between men and women in belief are not always large, but they are the most consistent. Women are more conservative or orthodox; they more often say they hold rather firmly to the central and traditional beliefs in any religion. The differences are especially striking in cultures with an overall low level of religiosity, such as post-Communist Russia. When we look at those with little or no religious beliefs, agnostics and atheists, the probability of finding women among them is extremely low.

The generalization is statistical, which means that not all women are more religious than all men, but any woman chosen randomly anywhere in the world will be more religious than a man similarly chosen. The findings are clearly not tied to Christianity or Western culture, and are just as pronounced in such cultures as India, Japan, China, Israel, Ethiopia, and Turkey.

Research has supported the notion of differential meanings in religion, with women holding different images of deities. For them the gods are seen more as supportive rather than instrumental, and as loving, comforting and forgiving, while males see him as a supreme power, a driving force, a planner and controller.

Activities which are often non-institutionalized, but nevertheless express a belief in a world inhabited by spirits, invisible powers, and miracles, do not differ psychologically from officially recognized religiosity. This view is increasingly found among contemporary theorists.

When it comes to popular and para-religious beliefs, the differences between men and women are even more robust than those relating to institutional religions. Women are the majority of customers for all magical coping practices. The global, and thriving, business of fortune-telling, miracle drugs (alternative medicine), spiritualism or "spiritual channeling," etc. caters mostly to women. They are the customers of practices which offer unofficial contacts with the world of the spirits or claim to operate with the help of invisible powers and energies. Women are much more likely to report beliefs in "telepathy," "psychic healing," and "fortune-telling," as well as being readier to believe in various "miracle drugs."

Explaining the Findings

The greater religiosity of women is often viewed as a puzzle and a paradox. That is because religious organizations, institutions and traditions are developed and controlled by men. Cross-culturally we can say that women are rarely in positions of power and influence in religious institutions and organizations, and in many cases they are formally excluded from positions of liturgical and clerical leadership.

Religious pantheons, which include gods, angels, saints, demons, founders, prophets, priests, and mystics, have little room for women. It is the creation of men, reflecting their wishes and fantasies. When it comes to what religious doctrines everywhere say about women, the content and nature of male fantasies is clear and uniform. Women are the target of taboo and derision in many traditions, described as evil and impure. If the world of religious figures and ideas was created by men, reflecting their wishes, why are women so willing to adopt this masculine universe and commit themselves to it? Attempts to create an alternative female pantheon (Goddess religions) have clearly failed to attract women. If religion is created by the male psyche, does it reflect the male psyche or the human psyche (which should be more female than male)? Our challenge is to explain the significant receptivity of women to messages of the miraculous in various guises, where the common denominator is the illusion of control or understanding.

The most common explanation for female religiosity refers to the reality of deprivation and victimization. Most women in this world are poor, powerless, and have little or no education. We should keep in mind that a 7-year old illiterate Dalit (untouchables) girl in India, already working from dawn to dusk to help her family, is a true representative of womanity and of humanity, rather than a woman with a Ph.D. living in the United States. When we speak of women's religiosity, the Dalit girl is the one we have to understand.

It is clear that while both men and women share the human condition, their location, real and imagined, in human power structures are far apart. Men control all human institutions and organizations, and the status of women in religion, both in the imagined pantheon and in real organizations, reproduces the lot of women in most human collectivities.

Sexuality is the area where women are most deprived and victimized. Women in all cultures suffer from predatory male sexuality. Coercive sexual experiences create lifelong suffering. Early childhood sexual abuse is a relatively common occurrence in the life of too many girls. This is a shattering experience, leading to depression and other problems. This victimization naturally leads to increased fear and insecurity, reinforcing any earlier dispositions.

Religion sometimes offers women a shelter from the male way of defining and controlling sexuality, which views women as sex objects and regards unattached women as easy prey. Religion sacralizes maternity, which is another shelter from male advances. We know that in some religious movements founded or dominated by women (see the Shakers), chastity becomes the rule, and sexuality is avoided. Such groups will have few male members.

Women are more commonly diagnosed as suffering from disorders of internalized conflict, such as anxiety and depression, cyclothymic disorder, panic disorder, attempted suicide, and phobias, with men suffering from acting-out disorders, such as completed suicide, substance abuse or schizotypal, narcissistic, and antisocial personality. Women are more than twice as likely as men to suffer from stress-related disorders, including major depressive disorder, post-traumatic stress disorder, and several anxiety disorders. The lifetime prevalence of PTSD for women, about 10.4%, is more than twice that for men. Females are more prone than males to panic disorder with agoraphobia and to phobias about animals Data from large scale epidemiological surveys indicate that panic disorder is 2.5 times more common in women than in men.

There is much evidence for significant personality differences between men and women; some of which may be relevant to the differences in religious activity. Men and women differ in emotion processing, including perception, experience and expression. Women clearly are readier to express feelings and admit dependence. They are also readier to demonstrate interpersonal caring, sensitivity, and warmth. In all cultures males are less nurturant and less emotionally expressive, while women are more submissive and passive, anxious and dependent. Empathy, defined as the vicarious affective response to another person's feelings, is more prevalent in females.

The greater empathy of women acts to reduce critical thinking, and female neuro-hormones lead to the suppression of negative emotions or judgments. Love is the enemy of critical judgment, and creates acceptance, especially when there is a yearning for consolation, reassurance, and some hope for the relief of suffering.

Some personality differences seem to be innate, such as greater male aggressiveness, verbally and physically, and risk-taking. Males are much more likely to die violently and to commit homicide and suicide at any age. They are responsible for 90% of violent acts in all cultures. Males exceed females on physically risky forms of sensation seeking and these in turn correlate significantly with a variety of physically dangerous activities such as involvement in crime, dangerous sports, injury proneness and volunteering for drug experiments and hazardous army combat. The difference in aggressive tendencies together with the greater conformity of women is reflected in the large differences that have been noted in the occurrence of anti-social behavior, which is so much rarer among women.

Studies of the reported contents of dreams have consistently found females to be significantly more interpersonally oriented than men. Women's dreams involve relationships and loss, while men are likely to dream about fighting, protecting, and competing, almost always with other men. And when ready-made fantasies are consumed, as in watching television, women constitute the audience for soap operas, while men watch aggressive sports (or follow political and economic news, which are often far from fantasies). In popular romance novels, women vicariously live family and relationship conflicts, as well as happy endings.

David Bakan described the dichotomy of orientations in females and males as communion versus agency. Communion is the tendency to be concerned about closeness to others, while agency is the tendency to be self-interested and assertive. Evolutionary psychologists have observed that women feel threatened by isolation and diminished intimacy, while men feel threatened by anything that smacks of diminished prestige and authority.

Looking at the involvement of adult women in the world of spirits, invisible powers, and miracles, we find that many of their activities have little to do with eternal damnation or bliss, but with counter sorcery ideas such as the removal of the evil eye and securing good fortune for one's family. The human condition puts us all in situations of risk and insecurity. Our anxiety and helplessness leads to coping through ritual and fantasy, rather than instrumental action. Men do engage in such acts sometimes, but the challenge is to explain why women do it more often.

The feminine coping strategy may be characterized by anxiety, risk avoidance, and a search for real or imagined security, using comforting others. The male psyche, on average, will be dominated by developmental vulnerability, risk taking, aggression, independence, and relative skepticism, showing the effects of masculine neurohormones. Reacting to distress men will react by externalizing, sometimes harming all involved. In the female psyche, fear, which leads to aggression in males, will lead to attachment, internalization, and help seeking. Low aggression, empathy, suggestibility, guilt, and sympathy will lead to love, but taking care of children and men, and tending to their needs, rather than one's own, is a heavy burden, growing with the victimization of women by violent men.

Turning to the world of supernatural agents and miracles fits with many "feminine" traits and conditions. Women's people-orientation leads to dependence on real and imaginary objects, from fortune-tellers to angels. Those who nurse and nurture humanity seek their compensation in imaginary objects in the absence of real support and the presence of much deprivation. We should think again of Dalit females in India, who may hope for a future incarnation as a male Brahmin (the official version of their own "Pascal's Wager"), but will settle for much less than that, protection from evil spirits for their own children. Any illusion of control will serve to relieve their constant desperation, as the world of spirits and miracles expresses indeed the sigh of the oppressed creature.

See also: ❯ Femininity ❯ Gender Roles ❯ Islam ❯ Shakers

Bibliography

Beit-Hallahmi, B., & Argyle, M. (1997). *The psychology of religious behaviour, belief and experience*. London: Routledge.

Wong Tai Sin

Mark Greene

Known in Hong Kong as Wong Tai Sin (the Great Immortal Sage Wong), where his cult of worship has been flourishing since the 1950s, Wong Cho-ping was born in Zhejiang Province, China in the late third century. Legend has it that under the tutelage of a mountain-dwelling Taoist deity, he mastered the alchemical process of refining cinnabar into a drug which when ingested conferred immortality. Although temples dedicated to Wong Tai Sin exist in Canada, the United States and Mainland China, it is the Wong Tai Sin Temple in Hong Kong – after which the surrounding neighborhood is also named – that annually attracts over five million visitors who seek the god's blessings, proffer donations and thank him for previous kindnesses. The Cantonese pronunciation of his name is Wong Tai Sin (黄大仙) whereas in Mandarin, it is pronounced Huang Daxian.

In the early 1890s, when both Guangzhou and Hong Kong were beset with outbreaks of the bubonic plague, a group of seekers made contact with Wong Tai Sin by means of spirit writing. The god's early messages indicated his original intention was to save humanity. Worshippers believed that the spirit of Wong Tai Sin prescribed combinations of herbs that would invariably cure those who sought his help. Availing themselves of the free prescriptions and traditional Chinese medicine provided by the temple, a large following of commoners who could not afford to see a doctor when ill began to form in his name. From several reported healings, Wong Tai Sin's reputation grew.

The legendary miracle attributed to Wong Tai Sin is his having transformed an outcropping of rocks on the side of a hill into a flock of sheep after his older brother – who had spent years trying to locate him – inquired as to the whereabouts of the flock entrusted to the younger Wong as a teenager. After witnessing his powers, the elder brother became Wong Tai Sin's pupil and eventually also attained immortality.

Within this modern day cult of worship can be found a rich legacy of alchemical imagery that thematically informs worshippers' requests for transformation across spectra including luck, riches and health. The cult of Wong Tai Sin has enjoyed a recent surge in growth on the Mainland since 1990. Due to the mass destruction of most Wong Tai Sin temples and shrines in the 1950s (some dating back 1000 years), it is interesting to note that images of the god in most of the new and reconstructed Mainland temples are emblematic of the Hong Kong version of the cult.

See also: ❯ Astrology and Alchemy ❯ Chinese Religions ❯ Jung, Carl Gustav, and Alchemy ❯ Spirit Writing ❯ Taoism

Bibliography

Chan, S. C. (2005). Temple-Building and Heritage in China. *Ethnology*, 44(1), 65–79.

Ge Hong. (c. 340 CE). *Shenxian Zhuan (Biographies of Immortals)*.

Lang, G., Chan, S. C., & Ragvald, L. (2002). *Return of the refugee God: Wong Tai Sin in China*. Satin, NT, Hong Kong: Chinese University of Hong Kong.

Lang, G., & Ragvald, L. (1993). *The rise of a refugee God: Hong Kong's Wong Tai Sin.* Oxford, England: Oxford University Press.

Unknown. (981 CE). *Taiping Guangji (Extensive Gleanings of the Reign of Great Tranquility).* Chapter 7, p. 1 (Republished in Beijing, 1961).

Wong, S. H. (1985). A study of Wong Tai Sin [in Chinese]. *The Journal of the Institute of Chinese Studies of the Chinese University of Hong Kong, 16,* 223–239.

Worcester, Elwood (Emmanuel Movement)

Curtis W. Hart

Worcester's Life

The Reverend Dr. Elwood Worcester, an Episcopal priest, was the inspirational force and prime mover behind the Emmanuel Movement located at the Emmanuel Church in Boston's Back Bay neighborhood where he was Rector from 1904 to 1929. Worcester was born in Massilon, Ohio into a clerical family. He was educated at Columbia College in New York after which he attended the General Theological Seminary where he completed the 3 year course of study leading to ordination in 1 year as opposed to the normal 3 years. Beyond his theological training he received a Ph.D. in psychology at the University of Leipzig in Germany. There he studied under the great experimentalists Wilhelm Wundt and Gustav Fechner. After returning to the United States he took up a position at St. Stephen's Church in Philadelphia where one of his congregants was the eminent neurologist Weir Mitchell. Worcester records in his autobiography, *Life's Adventure,* (1932) that it was in conversations with Mitchell that he became stimulated to think intentionally about the church's role in the care of the mentally ill or sick of soul. Upon coming to the Emmanuel Church in Boston he became acquainted with Richard Cabot, M.D., then Chief of Medicine at the Massachusetts General Hospital and Isador Coriot, M.D., his psychiatrist colleague who endorsed his idea of a clinic for treatment to be housed at the church. With the support of his clerical colleague at Emmanuel, the Reverend Dr. Samuel McComb, who, like Worcester, was both a priest and a psychologist, the doors opened of Emmanuel for treatment in November of 1906. On the first day there were 198 persons awaiting consultation. The numbers grew as did public interest and use of the clinic. Its success far exceeded any expectation. Worcester wrote and spoke to both professional and lay audiences about the Emmanuel experiment and its program was replicated in several cities across the United States. Its prestige and success were such that it drew heavy criticism from the psychiatric establishment most notably in the person of James Jackson Putnam, M.D. who questioned the use of non-medically trained persons in the provision of treatment. In spite of these objections the Emmanuel Movement continued successfully until Worcester's retirement in 1929.

Worcester's Achievement

Worcester and Emmanuel's accomplishments and contributions were wide and varied. He was ahead of his time by at least a generation in the area of pastoral counseling where he employed a variety of therapeutic techniques that demonstrated his resourcefulness, skill, and familiarity with psychoanalysis. He was able to utilize the processes and perspectives of uncovering, dream analysis, and catharsis as well as more short term approaches to therapy in the case of treatment for grief reactions. The Emmanuel Movement appropriated small group techniques that resemble contemporary modes of psycho education. And the Emmanuel Movement became the scene for use of small groups for addressing issues in alcoholism several years before the founding of Alcoholics Anonymous in 1935. The Emmanuel Movement and Worcester in particular also took a dynamic interest in public health matters related to prevention and treatment of tuberculosis in their urban environment and an open interest in and concern for non-Western religious, most particularly Buddhism, and what they might have to say regarding religion and health.

Emmanuel's Legacy

Worcester and the Emmanuel Movement are largely forgotten in the contemporary world. Their legacy emphasizes the importance of the cooperation between clergy and other health care professionals and the potentially beneficial role of religious institutions and clergy in relation to issues of both mental health care and public education. Palpable signs of their historical influence may be best seen in the way numerous pastoral counseling centers and 12 step groups find a home for their activities within the walls of churches and other religious institutions. Though it is unfortunate that the Emmanuel Movement could not survive without Elwood Worcester's inspired leadership its symbolic importance and actual contributions should never be forgotten or overlooked.

See also: ◉ Pastoral Counseling ◉ Psychotherapy

Bibliography

Gifford, S. (1997). *The Emmanuel movement: The origins of group treatment and the assault on lay psychotherapy.* Boston, MA: Harvard University Press.

Kurtz, E. (1991). *Not-God: A history of alcoholics anonymous.* Center City, MN: Hazelden.

Powell, R. (1974). *Healing and wholeness: Helen Flanders Dunbar (1902–1959): An extra medical origin of the American psychosomatic movement 1906–1936,* Durham, NC: Duke.

Worcester, E. (1932). *Life's adventure.* New York: Charles Scribner's Sons.

World Center

◉ Axis Mundi

World Tree

◉ Axis Mundi

Wounded Healer, The

Bonnie Smith Crusalis

In 1972, a Catholic priest and psychologist, Henri Nouwen, wrote a book that urged ministerial counselors to make their own emotional wounds a source of healing for those they counseled. He called this book *The Wounded Healer.* While the concept of the wounded healer wasn't new, the book's title captured, in a phrase, a perspective of the therapeutic relationship that crosses counseling theories and treatment modalities. Research of the literature suggests that regardless of the counseling theory or technique in play, a therapist who is aware of, and has worked to accept his own wounds, has much to offer a client.

Historical Framework

The concept of the wounded healer is quite old. Seen throughout ancient Greek mythology, healers are portrayed as inseparable from their own persistent wounds. The figures of Chiron and Asklepios are especially prominent as Greek gods and healers who themselves are wounded. Chiron, a centaur, and master of the healing arts, was hit with a poisioned arrow by Heracles. He could not heal himself and thus gave up his immortality. Asklepios is struck by lightning while trying to raise the dead; Asklepios' son is wounded in battle while striving to heal others (Kirmayer, 2003). The concept of the wounded healer appears in medieval Europe in the myth of Parsifal and the Fisher King. The Fisher King, who despite possessing the Holy Grail which can cure all ills, cannot cure his own wound until the Holy Grail is liberated (Miller and Baldwin, 2000). In many primitive societies, the concept is visible in the tradition of the shaman, a healer and often a priest, who represents the wounded healer. In Shamanism, being wounded is linked to knowledge, and the display of wounds represents an authenticity of skills (Miller, Wagner, Britton and Gridley, 1998). According to Miller and Baldwin (2000), the shaman might be referred to as the "ultimate" wounded healer because he is viewed as actually taking on himself the wounds and illnesses of his people. One of the first of the modern healers responsible for advancing the wounded healer paradigm was Carl Jung. "Only the wounded doctor can heal" (Jung, 1951, as cited in Miller & Baldwin, 2000: 246). In 1985, psychologists Remen, May, Young and Berland described wounded healers as those with resolved emotional experiences that sensitized them to working with others (as cited in Gladding, 2004).

Polarities

Fascination with the polarities of life, along with attempts to resolve and connect them, is as old as recorded time. Many cultures created single deities to name opposites, such as *Kali* in India, the goddess of both pox and the healer (Miller and Baldwin, 2000).

The bridging of these polarities in one's personality is of central importance in the wounded healer model. Jung suggests the critical nature of these bridges often, especially in his writings referring to embracing the "shadow," the distinct, "bad/ineffective/wrong" part of one's personality. According to Jung, it is necessary to accept and embrace the shadow as a step toward self actualization (Dunne, 2000). In considering the bridging of polarities as a facet of healing, it is useful to mention the origin of the word "heal," which derives from the Anglo-Saxon word *hal,* meaning whole. To heal is to make whole through a process of unifying all of the elements in a person, good and bad, sick and well (Miller and Baldwin, 2000). Gestalt therapy, with its emphasis on unification, and alcohol and drug counseling, where often the most effective counselors are those who have themselves survived addiction, are examples of this process (Miller and Baldwin, 2000).

Environments in the counseling setting that support wholeness in healers, however, are often difficult to come by. A survey of 229 nurses who experienced depression revealed that 30% did not disclose their condition to their colleagues even though as individual nurses, they expressed the importance of healing from within as having great potential to make an impact on the healing of patients (Jackson, 2004). In a study by Cain (2000), 10 psychotherapists with a history of psychiatric hospitalization reported the stigma associated with their psychiatric histories as the reason for not revealing their illnesses. According to the study's participants, reduced stigma would encourage the disclosure of one's problems and thereby increase the possibility for therapists to explore their own wounds as a means of self-healing and as a technique to use in their professions.

The Inner Healer Archetype

Another concept that emerges in the wounded healer paradigm is that of inner healer. This is the concept that describes a part of the process that promotes healing in either a patient or therapist. It is labeled an archetype because it implies an elemental or universal quality that reflects basic human patterns (Kirmayer, 2003). The archetype of the inner healer is activated whenever a person becomes ill, and healing occurs only if the patient gets help from his inner healer (Guggenbuhl-Craig, 1978, as cited in Miller and Baldwin 2000). This does not always happen, however, according to Grosbeck (1975, as cited in Miller and Baldwin, 2000), because the discomfort of his

wounds blocks the patient from reaching an awareness of his healer within. The patient instead projects the responsibility of healing onto the therapist. The task of the therapist, then, is to help release the inner healer in the patient, a process characterized as "activating dormant or malfunctioning mechanisms of healing and resilience" (Kirmayer, 2003: 250). He says alternately the healer can acknowledge his own wounds as a way of helping the patient to mobilize his inner healer. However activated, functioning inner healers are vital in both the patient and therapist (Miller and Baldwin, 2000).

Wounded Healers

Cain's study (2000) of psychotherapists with personal histories of psychiatric hospitalization reports that Carl Jung was just one of several mental health theorists who sought help in a quest for mental well-being and relief from suffering. Others include Sigmund Freud, Alfred Adler, and Henry Stack Sullivan. Jung might be considered the classic example of the wounded healer, because much of his work was devoted to describing his life struggles or wounds and how he used these struggles to develop his skills as a healer (Dunne, 2000). In her recent biography of Jung, Dunne (2000) describes the wounds and later the healing associated with Jung's troubled childhood, his break with Freud who had designated Jung as his heir apparent, and Jung's efforts to establish his own psychological theories. Albert Ellis (2004) describes himself as "anxious" in an essay entitled "Why I (really) became a therapist." He says that while he wanted to help others and in so doing create a better world, foremost in his choice of psychotherapy as a career was to study and experiment with techniques to help himself. He describes a childhood and adolescence rife with phobias about speaking in public and rejection by girls. He says that having figured out how to solve these phobias in himself, he was able to develop a theory and techniques that could be applied in the healing of others.

On "Wounded" Healing

Carl Jung's view that only wounded doctors can heal is shared by Miller and Baldwin (2000), who say that only healers deeply touched by personal experience of illness can truly heal, and that vulnerability is an integral part of this process (Miller and Baldwin, 2000). They say that an awareness of one's own wounds or conflicts leads to a state of vulnerability which in turn connects the patient and therapist. According to Kirmayer (2003) that connection, and the woundedness and healing in both the patient and therapist, serve as a mechanism for mobilizing the all-important inner healer of each.

It is intuitive that someone who has been afflicted and survives is in the best position to understand illness and cures (Kirmayer, 2003). Kirmayer describes five stages in the development of wounded healers. The first is the healer who will not, can not, or does not confront his own woundedness and instead identifies with the power of healing, seeing himself as different from the patient. The second stage brings the healer into contact with his own problems. The third describes an overwhelming and dark stage where the healer sees himself only as his wounds, loses his identity as healer, sees himself as incurably wounded, identifies with the patient and seeks help. The fourth stage describes the acceptance of the wound which invokes the inner healer. In the fifth stage, the healer realizes that wounding can only be partly healed and that he must descend again and again into his suffering. He realizes that his strengths and weaknesses are one and the same. It is important to note that healing does not occur as a result of the healer describing his own pain or stories about illness and pain to the patient (Nouwen, 1972). Nouwen says healing happens when healer and patient are able to *share the depth* of pain and together experience the action of rising from it. It is this connection, at its deepest level between therapist and patient that is responsible for healing the wounds universally caused by alienation, separation, isolation and loneliness. "I recognize some of the same issues that I grapple with for myself and I discover our shared human condition, even though it is lived somewhat differently by each of us" (van Deurzen, 2001: 49). Thus, a clinician's willingness to remain in contact with the parts of self that are wounded or in pain allow him to meet the patient where the process of true healing may begin (Kirmayer, 2003).

Implications of the Wounded Healer in Counseling

A major concept, which must be emphasized when discussing the wounded healer in the counseling setting, is that of self-knowledge. Miller and Baldwin (2000) describe a medical resident who had grown up with an alcoholic father and who was unsuccessful in counseling an alcoholic patient because of his own anger. Mander (2004) says self-awareness, evidence of the ability to empathize, and life experience are major qualities sought

in candidates applying for professional counseling training programs. Mander (2004) notes that while on the surface there seems to be a recognizable difference between those wanting to study to be therapists and those who want to enter into therapy, both groups are in fact quite similar because both express a desire to understand the psychic process, to explore internal conflict and to repair life wounds.

In the counseling setting, if the wounded side of the healer is devalued, the clinical experience is likely to be distorted (Kirmayer, 2003). Thus it is vital that counseling training and practice environments encourage safety for the expression of a clinician's wounds and vulnerabilities (Mander, 2004) and that practitioners regularly be not only encouraged, but required, to engage in regular self-care behaviors (Jackson, 2004).

Another side of the wounded healer which must be attended to is that of unresolved conflict. A healer's own neglected wounds can result in an inability to activate the inner healer in both the therapist and the patient and in the pathologizing of a patient by the therapist (Kirmayer, 2003). In addition, therapists must always be watchful for their own motivations in the counseling relationship and recognize whether a wish to help is really motivated by immature narcissism (Mander, 2004). The great challenge for healers is to learn to live with their brokenness as a blessing rather than a curse (Nouwen, 1972).

Study findings clearly support the value of "wounded healers" in the field of counseling because consumer/professionals have the potential for modeling collaborative treatment and recovery (Cain, 2000), and because an acceptance by the therapist of his own wounds, through conscious awareness of his own vulnerability, leads to wholeness, which enables a patient to achieve wholeness too (Miller and Baldwin, 2000).

Kirmayer (2003) paraphrases a Pablo Neruda poem when he says that to accept the power of the archetypes of inner healer and wounded healer, we must turn inward to our darkest place and experience confusion until that which hides in us comes out.

> A bough of fruit falls from the sun on your dark garment.
> The great roots of night
> Grow suddenly from your soul
> And the things that hide in you come out again.
> (Neruda, 1969, as cited in Kirmayer, 2003)

See also: ⊙ Archetype ⊙ Daimonic ⊙ Dark Night of the Soul ⊙ Forgiveness ⊙ Holy Grail ⊙ Jung, Carl Gustav ⊙ Psychotherapy ⊙ Shamanic Healing ⊙ Shamans and Shamanism

Bibliography

Cain, N. R. (2000). Psychotherapists with personal histories of psychiatric hospitalization: Countertransference in wounded healers. *Psychiatric Rehabilitation Journal, 24,* 22–28.

Dunne, C. (2000). *Carl Jung: Wounded healer of the soul.* New York: Parabola Books.

Ellis, A. (2004). Why I (really) became a therapist. *Journal of Rational-Emotive & Cognitive Behavior Therapy, 22,* 73–77.

Gladding, S. T. (2004). *Counseling a comprehensive profession.* Upper Saddle River, NJ: Pearson Education, Inc.

Jackson, C. (2004). Healing ourselves, healing others. *Holistic Nursing Practice, 18,* 199–210.

Kirmayer, L. J. (2003). Asklepian dreams: The ethos of the wounded-healer in the clinical encounter. *Transcultural Psychiatry, 40,* 248–277.

Mander, G. (2004). The selection of candidates for training in psychotherapy and counseling. *Psychodynamic Practice, 10*(2), 161–172.

Miller, G. A., Wagner, A., Britton, T. P., & Gridley, B. E. (1998). A Framework for understanding the wounding of healers. *Counseling and Values, 42,* 124–132.

Miller, G. D., Baldwin, D.C., Jr. (2000). Implications of the wounded-healer paradigm for the use of self in therapy. In M. Baldwin (Ed.), *The use of self in therapy* (pp. 243–261). Binghamton, NY: Haworth Press.

Nouwen, H. J. (1972). *The wounded healer.* New York: Doubleday Press.

Van Deurzen, E. (2001). Paradox and passion in psychotherapy. Chichester, England: Wiley.

Y

Yahweh

◈ God ◈ Judaism and Psychology

Yggdrasill

◈ Axis Mundi

Yoga

Magda Schonfeld

As yoga has swept the west, it is now estimated that nearly 20 million people in the United States practice some physical aspect of yoga. But beneath yoga's modern popularity lies an ancient tradition that illuminates knowledge of the Self.

Definition of Yoga

Yoga deals with the most profound of mysteries, the essential nature of the human being in relation to the universe. The term Yoga has its root in the Sanskrit word "yuj" which means to yoke, unite, integrate. What is being united? Yoga is the union between the individual soul and the universal soul. It is the split between the two that is viewed as the root of all suffering.

Many paths evolved in the yoga tradition, originating in India. These include: bhakti yoga, the yoga of devotion, karma the yoga of selfless service, jnana yoga, the yoga of wisdom, and raja yoga, also known as the "royal union." Within the umbrella of raja yoga is the eightfold path (astanga yoga) outlined by the great sage, Patanjali, in the Yoga Sutras of Patanjali, a treatise written about 200 BC. Astanga Yoga, the eight limbed path offers a systematic way of cultivation of the mind so as to ultimately achieve liberation. The first four limbs guide the seeker on a path toward evolution of consciousness, including: yamas, ethics and morals that teach about living in relationship, niyamas, individual practices necessary to build character, asana, physical postures, and pranayama, breath control. The second four limbs teach the path of involution and relate to the true state of Yoga. These include: pratyahara, withdrawal of the senses, dharana, concentration, keeping the mind collected, dhyana, meditation, and Samadhi, profound meditation or complete absorption.

It is interesting to note that Patanjali pays only passing attention to the practice of asana, the third limb of yoga, also known as Hatha yoga. Yet, it is Hatha Yoga, the practice of postures, or asana that has so gripped modern attention. Many individuals are initially drawn to hatha yoga for truly tangible benefits such as stress reduction, increased flexibility, stamina, improved concentration, and overall health and well-being. Hatha Yoga, also refers to the yoga of willpower. It is the way toward realization through rigorous discipline. The power aroused by this discipline clears the energy centers of the body/mind so that union with the supreme is possible.

Patanjali defines yoga more specifically, as *yogas citta vritti nirodahah*: yoga is the cessation of the fluctuations of the mind. What are these mind fluctuations? All the stuff of the mind, memories, thoughts, feelings, beliefs, judgments, the many objects of awareness. It is identification with these objects of awareness that causes suffering. In his yoga sutras, Patanjali shows us a way to free ourselves of this suffering.

Is Yoga a Religion?

Is Yoga a religion? BKS Iyengar (1979), master teacher of Hatha Yoga, whose book Light on Yoga has been a foundation text for the practice of Yoga, says the following:

D. A. Leeming, K. Madden, S. Marlan (eds.), *Encyclopedia of Psychology and Religion*, DOI 10.1007/978-0-387-71802-6,
© Springer Science+Business Media LLC 2010

> Yoga is a subject which cultures the mind and the intelligence of the individual to develop religiousness through practice. It has nothing to do with the man-created religious order; yet it is a religion of human beings, a religion of humanity, as it is filled with the message of goodwill to one and all.

Instead of prayer to a particular god, Patanjali's sutras offer a pathway towards opening to the divine. This divine is referred to as Ishvara, the Universal Soul This divine essence is not bound by place, space or time, not subject to cause and effect, not subject to suffering or the seeds of suffering. This divine nature is, however, not of this religion or that. It is instead a universal truth understood by all religions.

Yoga and Psychology

Patanjali, in a clear, systematic way put forth a treatise to help us understand the nature of mind, its many pitfalls and misidentifications that are the roots of day to day suffering. In modern psychology, we try to comprehend the impact of trauma, archetypal defenses, dissociation as a form of survival, projection, individuation, etc. We have on the other hand, an examination of the mind written centuries ago that sheds light upon the nature of the psyche. But Patanjali takes us beyond psychology to a path of freedom from the entanglements of the mind.

The Five Afflictions

Patanjali enumerates five afflictions (klesas) that disturb the equilibrium of consciousness and perpetuate a state of bondage or suffering.

The first is ignorance, *avidya*, which is the root cause of all affliction. This is the ignorance of our own true nature. We make the mistake of identifying that which is impermanent as permanent. It is taking the day to day self we know, the self that works each day, the self that raises children, the self that succeeds in the world or fails it, the self that takes pride in great accomplishment and the self that feels defeated; it is believing that all these various selves are more real than that which unites them into wholeness.

The second affliction is *asmita*, or pride, ego, which is called an affliction when we misidentify with the ego. A sense of confidence and belief in who you are, is essential to accomplish anything in the world. But ego can trap you into "you're not good enough; you don't deserve to be here," or "you're so great, they don't know anything."

The ego can ensnare you in the "greatness" of your accomplishments, or minimize you into a small suffering being, and lead you into endless comparison between you and the rest of the world. Patanjali warns us not to get ensnared by these voices of ego, for these voices affirm separateness rather than wholeness.

The third and fourth afflictions, *raga and dvesa*, attachment and aversion, likes and dislikes, can easily rule our lives and utterly exhaust us. We run toward what we like and run from what we don't like. Once we attain the possessions we long for, we fear losing them. In order to avoid the pain of what we don't like, or avoid the pain of past suffering, complex defense systems might surface, like acting aggressive when you feel vulnerable, dissociating, disappearing when threatened, turning to addictions like food or alcohol when life doesn't offer what you long for. Chasing after what we long for and running from what we wish never came, keeps us in a state of agitation, restlessness, yearning. Yet if we can practice stillness, witnessing mind with its potent pull in one direction and another, if we can, as referred to in Jungian psychology, hold the tension of the opposites, freedom from misidentification, freedom from suffering is possible.

The fifth and final affliction, abhinivesah, is clinging to life or fear of death. It is the subtlest of all afflictions. Even the wisest of beings are plagued by this affliction and naturally so, it is our instinct to stay alive at all costs. "While practicing Yoga, the aspirant penetrates deep within himself and realizes the life-force, active while one is alive, merges with the universe when it leaves the body at death. Through this understanding, the aspirant can lose his attachment to life and conquer the fear of death" (Iyengar, 1996).

In summary, Patanjali discusses the false identification of thoughts and Self. He teaches that false identification is at the root of all misery. He further teaches that the practices of yoga are about dissolving this false identification.

Asana Practice or Hatha Yoga

Since the western world has embraced yoga as a mainstream activity, it is worthwhile to examine the nature of asana practice. How can the practice of asana teach us about false identification? Often as we move into a pose, the various tight and resistive places in the body reveal themselves. These places of resistance can easily stay hidden from us, if not challenged by touch, movement or some method of conscious awareness. The body, connected to matter, to earth, readily houses our struggles in patterns of tension. These patterns deepen over time and if left unaddressed (unconscious) long enough, will ultimately lead to disease. The body is an extraordinary reflection of the mental/emotional patterns of mind. Yogic practice can help heal the split between the two.

Tightness and resistance can come from many sources and often interweave with one another: (1) physical – structural tightness, injury, repetitive wrong actions, habit patterns, overdoing. (2) chemical – improper diet, drugs, environmental toxins, (3)emotional – distressing thoughts, feelings, memories, anxieties, (4) spiritual – disconnection from the source of one's being.

Whatever the source of resistance is, the body will attempt to express it, often in the manifestation of pain. Whenever we resist the present moment and try to deny what we are experiencing, a split occurs. This split holds energy. It holds tension. It manifests as suffering. By connecting to the body, by witnessing the split, this cut off energy can return to us as wholeness. Asana practice offers us the opportunity to return to ourselves.

Sometimes in practicing an asana, we want to come out of the pose, to jump away from the discomfort that might rise. Or we use too much willfulness and harden the body so that we overdo. Here lies a marvelous analogy to Jung's "holding the tension of the opposites." This has to do with the willingness to be in the pose, the willingness to be with the difficulty or ease and not identify with either. "If we are able to be with what rises, that is remain still long enough to perceive the discomfort, rather than react to it, we can begin the path toward union, Yoga" (Lasater, 2001).

Asana practice can change physiology, brain chemistry and organic function. Backbending poses open the heart, forward bending poses support the digestive organs, twists ring out toxins from the liver and kidneys, inversions support circulation, clear the mind and rejuvenates one from fatigue. "Yoga was invented by our sages in order to overcome bodily impediments, emotional and environmental disturbances of the mind and the wavering qualities of the intelligence, so that the practitioner comes closer and closer to the Self" (Iyengar, 2001).

How can asana bring one closer to the Self? For example, we can look at adho muka virasana, (downward facing hero's pose, sitting with legs folded under you and forehead to the floor); if done with full presence of being, this pose evokes a sense of humbleness. The pose has its own offering.

Another pose, Virabhadrasana II translated as warrior pose, where one stands with legs wide apart, arms fully extended, legs firm, chest and heart open, expansive.

The pose itself invokes a sense of power, extension, and stability, the feet rooted and core of body centered over the pelvis. When fully entering this pose, empowerment manifests, inertia is shed, a sense of energy and will to go forth into the day with vitality rises up.

The notion that poses generate particular patterns in the mind is a more modern interpretation of the powers of yoga. Such ideas are not mentioned by Patanjali. Yet as asana practice has evolved in modern times, we can see that each asana has the capacity to teach us the art of silence. Silence in the brain allows for effortless work. If the effort offered to a pose is done wholeheartedly, effortless practice manifests.

Yoga and Jung

Our past experiences, perceptions impact the nature of our practice. These experiences, instincts and hidden or subliminal impressions make up what is known in Sanskrit as samskaras. If these imprints are good, they act as stimuli to maintain the high degree of sensitivity necessary to pursue the spiritual path. If the imprints are not good, rooted in trauma, abuse or neglect, the seeker has a more complicated journey of learning to see, to perceive habitual reactions to life's events. This might be paralleled to Jung's notion of the "complex," which when activated, triggers an individual to react in a way similar to the initial imprint of wounding. The process of integrating past impressions, so that they no longer trigger unconscious behavior is an important goal in psychotherapy. The yogic tradition understood this long ago. As long as one stays rooted in reactivity to life's phenomena, one is caught in the wheel of "dharma," or an existence bound in cause and effect.

But through practice, these imprints can be transformed. Practice involves the eight limbs of yoga discussed earlier, asana practice being the third limb. Practice, abhyasa involves repeated, committed, devoted effort. Patanjali points out that one must not only practice, but practice with detachment, "vairagya" the discarding of ideas which obstruct progress. Vairagya is a practice where one learns to gain freedom from desires and to cultivate non-attachment to things which hinder pursuit of union with the soul.

It is important here to clarify the difference between the psychological term dissociation and the use of detachment in the sutras. Sometimes withdrawing sense awareness, turning inward, practicing yoga, meditation, silence, can appear as if one was withdrawing from the world at large, retreating from society. This withdrawal, this penetration into silence is necessary to hear the internal voice, the voice of the soul.

But if one gets so captivated by that silence, or so dependent upon it that withdrawal becomes the end of the journey rather than a pathway, the seeker has then cultivated withdrawal as an end rather than the means of realizing the Self.

Practice and detachment are the means to still the movements of consciousness. This sutra brings us back to Pantanjali's earlier definition of yoga. Yoga is the cessation of the fluctuations of the mind. Whenever the mind is fully focused, one pointed, and one is acting in harmony with the nature of all things, one is practicing yoga. Life is filled with moments to enliven this practice.

See also: ◉ Hinduism ◉ Jung, Carl Gustav ◉ Psychotherapy ◉ Self

Bibliography

Arun, H. S. (2007). *Yoga is beyond religion, Iyengar, the yoga master* (B. Kofi, Ed.). Boston, MA: Shambala.

Coulter, H. (2001) *David, anatomy of hatha yoga*. Honesdale, PA: Body & Breath.

Feuerstein, G. (2001). *The Yoga tradition, its history, literature, philosophy and practice*. Prescott, AZ: Hohm Press.

Iyengar, B. K. S. (1966). *Light on Yoga: Yoga Dipika*. New York: Schocken Books.

Iyengar, B. K. S. (1996). *Light on the Yoga sutras of Patanjali*. San Francisco, CA: Thorsons.

Iyengar, B. K. S. (2001). *Astadala Yogamala* (Vol. 2). Mumbai, India: Allied Publishers.

Kraftsow, G., & Yoga, K. (2007). *Transformation through practice, Iyengar, the yoga master* (B. Kofi, Ed.). Boston, MA: Shambala.

Lasater, J. (2001). *Understanding the meaning of Asana*. www.judithlasater.com/writings/no6.html.

Z

Zazen

◈ Koan ◈ Zen

Zen

Paul C. Cooper

"I need to repeat that Zen refuses to be explained, but that it is to be lived" (Suzuki, 1949: 310).

Limitations of Explanation

Keeping the limitations of explanation and the value placed on the primacy of experience in mind, the following will provide an outline sketch of Zen Buddhism. Zen is the Japanese translation of the Sanskrit term, *dhyana*, which means concentration meditation or meditative absorption. Zen is also known as C'han (Chinese), Thien (Vietnamese), and Seon (Korean). However, as Zen is not a monolithic structure, it is important to keep in mind that while there is an historical continuity between C'han and Zen, and that the terms are typically used interchangeably, there are many fundamental socio-cultural and doctrinal differences between these systems as they developed regionally and that integrated various influences of indigenous religions. For example, C'han incorporates elements of Taoism and Confucianism. Recently, a rapidly expanding "interfaith Zen" movement in the United States has integrated many Christian elements (Johnston, 1976; Kennedy, 1996).

History

Historical accounts attribute the Indian monk Bodhidharma with the introduction of C'han into China during the sixth Century. Bodhidharma taught what has been described as a mind-to-mind transmission, outside scriptures, and which does not rely upon words or letters. His teachings were then transmitted through a series of Chinese patriarchs. Given this emphasis on direct transmission, the role of the teacher is essential and supercedes the study of the scriptures. This direct teacher to student "dharma transmission" follows a lineage that can be traced back to preceeding generations to the historical Buddha. Thus, not unlike psychotherapy, Zen is interpersonal, experiential and relies on direct dialog.

Practice and Religious Salvation

The primary experiential activities of Zen are zazen (sitting meditation), dialogues with a teacher, koan study, and moment-to-moment mindfulness during all daily activities and chores. Zen practices engender a liberating awareness of reality through an alteration of perception that includes the derailment of cognitive linear thought. From the Zen perspective, this liberating awareness can be known or intuited experientially, but not known in the cognitive sense. This salvational intention, expressed in the notion of *satori* (enlightenment, literally: "to understand") and engendered through personal experience, qualifies Zen as a religious endeavor. However, it is not a religion in the sense of the word that religion is typically understood in a Western civilizational context. On this point Masao Abe writes, "In one sense, Zen may be said to be one of the most difficult religions to understand, for there is no formulated Zen doctrine or theological system by which one may intellectually approach it" (1985: 3).

This soteriological intention along with supporting practices defines Zen as a religion. The striving for satori (enlightenment) reflects this salvational goal and has resulted in an emphasis on the wisdom or insight aspect of meditation. This emphasis has generated a critique of quietist leanings among certain Buddhist sects. Without an emphasis on the wisdom aspect of zazen, such critics assert that meditation becomes an empty and useless endeavor that can be equated, for example, as "polishing a brick to make a mirror."

D. A. Leeming, K. Madden, S. Marlan (eds.), *Encyclopedia of Psychology and Religion*, DOI 10.1007/978-0-387-71802-6,
© Springer Science+Business Media LLC 2010

Regarding salvation, the Zen scholar D. T. Suzuki notes: "As I have repeatedly illustrated, Buddhism, whether primitive or developed, is a religion of freedom and emancipation, and the ultimate aim of its discipline is to release the spirit from its possible bondage so that it can act freely in accordance with its own principles" (1949: 74).

Zen and Psychoanalysis

The influence of Zen has run through psychoanalysis for over a half of century as a result of D. T. Suzuki's involvement with Eric Fromm (1950, 1956), Fromm, Suzuki & DeMartino (1960), Karen Horney (1945), Harold Kelman (1960), and others. This group of psychoanalysts have approached Buddhist religious experience and associated meditation practices with the true spirit of open-minded inquiry distinctive of the psychoanalytic dialog that Freud fathered and began to look eastward in a search for expanding their psychoanalytic vision. Karen Horney, for example (1945: 163) discusses the "impoverishment of the personality" and refers to the Buddhist notion of "wholeheartedness" or "sincerity of spirit." Susan Quinn (1987), Karen Horney's biographer, chronicles a close association between Horney and D. T. Suzuki.

Harold Kelman, a close colleague of Horney argued in his paper "Psychoanalytic Thought and Eastern Wisdom" (1960), that psychoanalysis is experientially "eastern." While deriving from fundamentally different theoretical assumptions, Kelman observed that Buddhist thought and technique can deeply enhance psychoanalytic technique, particularly regarding the analyst's attentional stance.

Erich Fromm, who was deeply interested in Zen Buddhism, also shared a close association with D. T. Suzuki. He included detailed meditation instructions in his very popular book, *The Art of Loving* (1956). Fromm believed that meditative experience can expand the psychoanalytic process through a positive conceptualization of human potential that goes beyond addressing symptoms. When asked about the benefits of Zen meditation in relation to mental health, Fromm reportedly responded that "It's (Zen) the only way to enduring mental health" (quoted in Kapleau, 1989:14). He viewed both systems as potentially mutually enhancing. A thirst for expanding their vision and looking eastward to do so forms a common thread that ties together the above representative psychoanalysts. They thus paved the way for contemporary contributions, which has expanded to include a wide range of applications from a Zen-influenced short-term crisis intervention (Rosenbaum, 1998) to depth psychoanalysis that

integrates basic Zen principles with contemporary Inter-subjectivity theory and Self Psychology (Magid, 2000).

An examination of the "foundational" (Nagao, 1989) Buddhist principles of emptiness and dependent-arising reveals parallels to the "totalistic" (Kernberg, 1976) understanding of countertransference and can serve as a link between classical and totalistic models. That is, that all experience, including the psychotherapeutic encounter emerges contextually, subject to causes and conditions.

The thirteenth Century Japanese monk Dogen's notion of *gujin* or "total exertion" holds important treatment implications for the psychotherapist who is informed by Zen practice. That is, as the philosopher Joan Stambaugh writes, "Looked at from the standpoint of the situation itself, the situation is totally manifested or exerted without obstruction or contamination" (1999: 6). With regard to the psychoanalytic situation the notion of goal or a stance of removed passivity both contaminate the situation and interfere with presence. Stambaugh asserts that, "The person experiencing the situation totally becomes it. He is not thinking *about* it; he *is* it. When he does this, the situation is completely revealed and manifested." (1999: 6). Thus total exertion refers to an opening that calls for a response that ". . . is never anything passive but can be quite strenuous" (Op. Cit. 1999: 7). From this perspective, the psychotherapist's activity becomes decisive, clean, clear and precise, not encumbered by guilt, anxiety, convention or goals.

In recent years, the conversation between Zen and psychotherapy has been continuously expanding and holds promise for a mutually beneficial cross-fertilization through the open-minded spirit of inquiry that characterizes present studies.

See also: ❯ Buddhism ❯ Chinese Religions ❯ Koan ❯ Psychoanalysis ❯ Self Psychology ❯ Taoism

Bibliography

Abe, M. (1985). *Zen and Western thought*. Honolulu, HI: University of Hawaii Press.

Fromm, E. (1950). *Psychoanalysis and religion*. New Haven, CT: Yale University Press.

Fromm, E. (1956). *The art of loving*. New York: Harper-Collins Publishers.

Fromm, E., Suzuki, D. T., & DeMartino, R. (1960). *Zen Buddhism and psychoanalysis*. New York: Harper & Brothers.

Horney, K. (1945). *Our inner conflicts*. New York: Norton.

Johnston, W. (1976). *Silent music*. New York: Harper & Row.

Kapleau, P. (1989). *The three pillars of Zen*. New York: Random House.

Kelman, H. (1960). Psychoanalytic thought and Eastern Wisdom. In J. Ehrenwald (Ed.), *The history of psychotherapy*. New York: Jason Aronson.

Kennedy, R. (1996). *Zen spirit, Christian spirit: The place of Zen in Christian life*. New York: Continuum Publishing Group.

Kernberg, O. (1976). *Object relations theory and clinical psychoanalysis*. New York: Jason Aronson.

Magid, B. (2000). *Ordinary mind: Exploring the common ground of Zen and psychotherapy*. Boston, MA: Wisdom Publications.

Nagao, G. (1989). *The foundational standpoint of Madhyamika philosophy*. Albany, NY: State University of New York Press.

Quinn, S. (1987). *A mind of her own: The life of Karen Horney*. New York: Summit Books.

Rosenbaum, R. (1998). *Zen and the heart of psychotherapy*. Philadelphia, PA: Brunner/Mazel.

Stambaugh, J. (1999). *The formless self*. Albany, NY: State University of New York Press.

Suzuki, D. T. (1949). *Essays in Zen Buddhism* (First Series). London: Rider & Co.

Zionism

Kate M. Loewenthal

What is Zionism? Does psychology of religion have anything to offer to the understanding of Zionism?

What is Zionism?

The term Zion has traditionally been viewed as synonymous with Jerusalem (Roth and Wigoder, 1971). The most commonly understood use of the term Zionism is the belief that the land of Israel is the homeland of the Jewish people, and every effort is to be made to return Jewish people to the land. There is a detailed biblical definition of the territory in Numbers 34, 1–15, and the territory was then expanded in the time of David and Solomon.

The historical precursors of Zionist ideology are to be found in Jewish history from biblical times, including promises that the descendants of Abraham, Isaac and Jacob (Israel) will inherit the land of Canaan, the process of Jewish settlement of the land, and various persecutions and forced movements of population. Despite the destruction of the second Temple in 70 CE and the creation of diaspora Jewish communities in the former Roman Empire there continued to be Jewish communities in Israel (called Palestine by the Romans) until the present. This included the retention of important Jewish intellectual centres.

Thousands of Jews in Jerusalem were killed by the Crusaders in 1099, who accused them of helping the Arabs. During the later Middle Ages the holy sites in the land and particularly Jerusalem were the focus of pilgrimages and the Jews who lived in Palestine were supported by charitable donations from diaspora communities. References to Israel, Jerusalem and Zion, and the hoped-for return, occur prolifically throughout Jewish liturgy and sacred texts, and the direction of prayer has been towards Jerusalem following a verse in Daniel (6: 11).

In the sixteenth century the northern city of Safed became an important intellectual center, with leading scholars of all traditionalist aspects of Jewish thought among its inhabitants, and this became a significant model for later Cultural Zionism. In the late eighteenth and early nineteenth century, the pace of Jewish return to Israel speeded up with the expansion of the settlements of pious Jews (Hasidim, and also followers of the Vilna Gaon), particularly in Safed, Tiberias and Jerusalem. The Hibbat Zion (Love of Zion) movement was prominent in supporting such settlements philanthropically. Later in the nineteenth century, in the face of persistent pogroms and other persecution in the European diaspora Zionist passion assumed a new, politicised form, sometimes known as "synthetic" Zionism, with active attempts to achieve a political solution, and to develop and support Jewish agricultural settlements. "Cultural" Zionism developed Jewish national awareness and support for the Jewish homeland among diaspora Jews. Landmarks in the history of modern Zionism include the first Zionist congress in 1897 in Switzerland, the Balfour Declaration (1917), asserting the support of the British government for a national home for the Jewish people in Palestine, the founding of the Hebrew University in Jerusalem in 1925, the UN vote to partition the land between Arabs and Jews (1947), followed by war since the Arabs did not accept the partition, and the declaration of the state of Israel (1948). This beleaguered state remains the focus of Jewish immigration from all parts of the diaspora, and also of hostility and repeated attacks from surrounding Arab neighbours. Zionist philosophy has continued to develop pragmatically in response to these developments (Seliktar, 1983).

Secular forms of Zionism, sometimes with a socialist flavor, sometimes purely nationalist, proposed that Jewish religious observance was only needed to preserve Jewish identity (and longing for Zion) while in the diaspora. But once in the Jewish state, Jews were said to no longer need religious observance in order to maintain their identity as Jews. Some observers of the contemporary Israeli scene believe that secular Zionism is no longer the force that it once was, and love of the land is tempered by the complex political difficulties with Arab neighbours, particularly the urgent need to keep peace and survive. Thus modern secular Zionism may entail a willingness to make territorial concessions for the sake of peace. Religious Zionism is based on the philosophy of Rabbi Kook (e.g., 2005), and involves settlements in territories that fall within the biblically-defined boundaries of Israel. Religious Zionism is associated with the view that national security is best served by preserving the biblical boundaries.

Zionist Attitudes

Anti-Zionist attitudes have been noted among Jews. Some strictly orthodox Jews, mainly associated with the Satmar group of Hasidim, believe that the time for the establishment of the Jewish state of Israel is premature, and can only happen after the coming of the Messiah. At another point on the religious spectrum, early Reform Judaism eliminated references to Jerusalem, Israel and Zionism from its liturgy in an attempt to produce truly acculturated citizens of Germany. However, the founding of the State induced a contrary trend. Attitudes which are generally consistent with Zionism have been reported among the majority of Jews. In Seliktar's (1980) study, 75–81% of the 700 young Israelis surveyed were committed to each of the five aspects of Zionist ideology (enumerated below). The majority of American Jews in Cohen and Kelman's (2007) survey considered that "attachment to Israel is an important part of being Jewish," though the percentages agreeing with this statement declined with age: 80% of the over-65s agreed, 60% of the under-35s.

The themes and concepts of Zionism have had a strong impact outside Judaism. In the United States, Zionism is an important feature of fundamentalist Christianity, in which it is held that the settlement of Jews in Israel is foretold by biblical prophecy and is a precursor to the coming of the Messiah. This in turn has impacted on foreign policy attitudes (Cummergen, 2000). In sub-Saharan Africa, particularly in Swaziland, Zionism is widely practiced as a religion. African Zionism was based originally on Christianity but incorporates many indigenous practices and beliefs including animism (Guth, Fraser, Green, Kellstedt, Smidt, 2000).

Zionism and Psychology

What light can the psychology of religion throw on Zionism? There has been negligible study of Zionism as such by psychologists of religion. Nevertheless there are psychological perspectives which may be brought to bear on Zionism among Jews.

Territorial claims are often strongly bound up with national and religious identity: social identity theory offers important discussions on this theme (e.g., Hewstone and Stroebe, 2001).

Band (2005) has discussed the dilemmas faced by religious Zionists in relation to their identities, amid the political complexities of twenty-first century Israel. For example, their pragmatic and religiously-founded wish for peace conflicts with their pragmatic and religiously-founded need to maintain the boundaries of Israel.

The frequent Jewish liturgical and textual references to Israel and Zion reinforce the package of Jewish identity, spirituality and love of the land. In Jewish sacred texts, the land of Israel is given to the Jews and said to be imbued with a special level of holiness (e.g., Genesis 15:18; 2 Chronicles 6, 5–6; Shneur Zalman of Liadi, 1973) and given by G-d to the Jewish people. There are many specific religious commandments associated with the land, for example relating to its agricultural produce, such as observance of the sabbatical year, specific blessings to be pronounced on fruits for which Israel is renowned, and the priestly blessing, recited daily in Israel, and only on festivals in the diaspora. The quantity and spiritual force of biblical and other references to the sacredness of Israel deserve closer study, perhaps using discourse or other linguistic analysis, particularly with the view to the question of the uniqueness of Zionism as a form of nationalist philosophy.

The possible impact of liturgical and religious textual references was supported in a careful study in political psychology examining the socialisation of Zionist ideology among young Israelis: Seliktar (1980) studied the cognitive and affective aspects of five features of Zionist ideology: loyalty to the state of Israel, continuity (of Israel) across time; unity of the Jewish people; Israel as a Jewish national center; the integrative role of the State of Israel (in absorbing new immigrants). Respondents indicated extent of agreement and of emotional commitment to statements relating to these five features (e.g., "We should always think of Israel as a continuation of the ancient kingdom of Judea"). There were significant effects of family religious observance, and of religiosity of the school attended, on strength of commitment to Zionist ideology.

Conclusions

In conclusion, it can be seen that Zionism in all its forms contains powerful ideas about the sacred status of the land of Israel. Although the psychological and spiritual impact of Zionism have not been studied by psychologists of religion, there are conceptual frameworks – for example in social identity theory, attitude theory, and forms of linguistic analysis – which may facilitate closer study.

Acknowledgement

Grateful thanks are due to Dr. Naftali Loewenthal, University College London, for many helpful comments and suggestions on this article.

See also: ◉ Judaism and Psychology ◉ Psychology of Religion

Bibliography

Band, M. (2005). *Religiosity, coping and suicidality within the religious Zionist community of Israel*. London: London University.

Cohen, S. M., & Kelman, A. Y. (2007). *Beyond distancing: Young adult American Jews and their alienation from Israel*. The Jewish Identity Project of Reboot: Andrea and Charles Bronfman Philanthropies. From http://www.acbp.net/pub/BeyondDistancing.pdf. Accessed 16 July 2008.

Cummergen, P. (2000). Zionism and Politics in Swaziland. *Journal of Religion in Africa, 30,* 370–385.

Guth, J. L., Fraser, C. R., Green, J. C., Kellstedt, L. A., & Smidt, C. E. (2000). Religion and foreign policy attitudes: The case of Christian Zionism. In J. Clifford (Ed.), *Religion and the culture wars.* Lanham, MD: Rowman & Littlefield.

Hewstone, M., & Stroebe, W. (2001). *Introduction to Social Psychology.* Oxford, England: Blackwell.

Jewish Publication Society. (1955). *The holy scriptures.* Philadelphia, PA: Jewish Publication Society of America.

Kook, R. A. I. (2005). *When G-d Becomes History: Historical Essays of Rabbi Abraham Isaac Hakoen Kook* (B. Naor, Trans.). Spring Valley, NY: Orot.

Roth, C., & Wigoder, G. (Eds.). (1971). Zionism. In *Encyclopedia Judaica.* Jerusalem: Encyclopedia Judaica.

Seliktar, O. (1980). Socialisation of national ideology: The case of Zionists attitudes among young Israelis. *Political Psychology, 2,* 66–94.

Seliktar, O. (1983). The new Zionism. *Foreign Policy, 51,* 118–138.

Shneur Zalman of Liadi. (1973). Likkutei Amarim – Tanya, (Bilingual edition) (N. Mindel, N. Mandel, Z. Posner, & J. I. Shochet, Trans.). London: Kehot. (Original work published 1796)

Zoroastrianism

Sam Cyrous

Zoroastrianism, also called Zarathustrism, Mazdeism or Parsism, is the religion founded by Zoroaster in Ancient Persia, with approximately 150–250 thousand believers worldwide, mainly concentrated in India and Iran. It is in the *Zend-Avesta*, which literally means *Commentaries on Knowledge*, the holy book of Zoroastrainism, that one can find the principle assertions of this faith. The *Avesta* is divided in the three parts: *Yasna* (sacred *Liturgy* chapters), *Visperad*, *Vendidad* (constituted of purifications laws), and *Khorda*.

Zoroaster's Early Life

Zoroaster (or Zarathustra, as He is known in the West, or Zartosht in Persian), is the founder of Zoroastrianism, considered one of the first non-pantheistic and monotheistic religions. Zoroaster apparently lived in ancient Persia, at an uncertain time in the first millennium before Christ. Joseph Campbell (1962) describes Zoroaster as "the earliest prophet" (7–8). According to Fatheazám (1972), even at the age of 15, He was respected by His fellow countrymen because of His charity work and His kindness to the poor and to animals. At 20 He left His house, spending 7 years in solitude in a cave in the Persian mountains. His family origin, lineage and the context of his birth are unknown, nonetheless it is said that He was born of a virgin mother, like Krishna and Jesus. Campbell pinpoints the mythological birthplace of Zoroaster beside the river Daiti, in the central land of the "seven lands of the earth."

Zoroastrian Cosmology

Arguing that tradition stagnates and knowledge is movement, Zoroaster preached doubt and the need for inquiry to attain knowledge. At the age of 30, he received divine illumination through seven visions that confirmed Him as a demiurge. After 10 years of preaching, miracles, cures and only one confirmed disciple (His own cousin), Zoroaster was incarcerated for disturbing tradition and for the influence and confusion His laws and spiritual and scientific principles caused among the people. Among these laws was the concept of spiritual duality or cosmic dualism, between the spirit of good Ahura Mazda (or Ormuzd) – meaning Supreme Knowledge – and the spirit of evil Ahriman, both preexistent spirits (according to Dual Theology), or twin brothers born of Zurvan (according to Zurvanism). From this dualism comes the "complete freedom of choice exerted by spirits and the consequent responsibility that corresponded entirely to this choice" (Ling, 2005: 87–88). It is this concept that would distinguish Zoroastrianism from Judaism, Christianity and Islam, inasmuch as individuals in Zoroastrianism were not mere receptacles of superior decisions, but the lords of their own destinies, free to act before life's conditionings, what could be seen as "a vision of intentionality" (Frankl, 2002: 214), "without the fundamental supposition that man, simply, 'is', but that he always decides what he is going to be at the next moment" (Frankl, 2001: 73). Decisions are individual responsibilities, hence it is this individual responsibility that permits his spiritual, mental and psychic growth.

Possibly the concept of duality is Zoroastrianism's greatest contribution to modern civilization, manifesting itself in the manifold areas of human knowledge. It is, nevertheless, interesting to note that, perhaps due to Persia's geographical and historical position, we have now what we could speak of as two forms of dualism: oriental dualism, characterized by the intrinsic relationship of good and evil, as in the case of yin and yang, the idea that inside good there is evil and vice versa, according to the principles of mutations; and occidental dualism, in which evil and good are inter-excluding, until, for instance, the final victory of God over the Devil. In the field of psychology, one can find examples of human duality in such concepts as Rotter's internal and external loci of control, Freud's principle of pleasure vs. principle of reality, Piaget's symbolic and logical thoughts, Jung's anima and animus, Nuttin's object-mean and object-end, and Roger's ideal and real self, among others. It is important to underline, however, that these examples are not mere replicas of Zoroastrian dualism. Rather, they are simply useful to illustrate that human thought structure appears to be rooted in the concept of categorization by opposition, a reflection of Zoroastrian cosmology.

Human and Social Progress

Another traditional Zoroastrian element, as quoted here from the *Zend-Avesta*, is the need of three things for human progress: "I celebrate my praises for good thoughts, good words, and good deeds. . . . With chanting praises I present all good thoughts, good words, and good deeds, and with rejection I repudiate all evil thoughts, and words, and deeds" (Yasna 11, 17). In short, the three elements – thoughts, words and actions – should be coherent and congruent. This idea can be found in the lines of Rogerian psychological thought, which postulates the principle of congruence as based on the need of the

therapist to feel and express these feelings to the client, as in the work of Messer and Winokur (1980) whose objective is to be able to help the patient to convert *insight* into action.

In Christianity, in the words of Saint James (2:17) "Even so faith, if it hath not works, is dead, being alone" and, in the Bahá'í religion in a text that Bahá'u'lláh forwards to a Zoroastrian, "Words must be supported by deeds, for deeds are true test of words. Without the former, the latter can never quench the thirst of the yearning soul."

The effect of Zoroaster's vision was stupendous in human history. It allowed the moral, agricultural and economic development of Persian society, inasmuch as its assumptions were based on logic and ethics. Zoroastrianism's best known symbol is fire, an example of the articulation between the material and the immaterial spheres: fire symbolizes true human integrity, in which Zoroastrian psychology is rooted. It is by observing the virtues of fire, the symbol of constancy, purity and sustainability of life created by Ahura Mazda, endowed with movement and creative capacity, that human beings can obtain a true example to follow.

In this sense, hell could not be a place dominated by fire, but by a state of pain:

> On the very first time when that deed has been done, without waiting until it is done again, down there in hell. The pain for that deed shall be as hard as any in this world: even as if one should cut off the limbs from his perishable body with knives of brass, or still worse; down there the pain for that deed shall be as hard as any in this world: even as if one should naildoubtful his perishable body with nails of brass, or still worse; down there the pain for that deed shall be as hard as any in this world: even as if one should by force throw his perishable body headlong down a precipice a hundred times the height of a man, or still worse; down there the pain for that deed shall be as hard as any in this world: even as if one should by force impale his perishable body, or still worse. (Vendidad, Fargard 4, IVb., 49–53)

Hell is a state and not a place, because it is a consequence of incorrect thoughts, words and actions that should be prevented before they happen again.

> The first step that the soul of the wicked man made, laid him in the Evil-Thought Hell; the second step that the soul of the wicked man made, laid him in the Evil-Word Hell; the third step that the soul of the wicked man made, laid him in the Evil-Deed Hell; the fourth step that the soul of the wicked man made, laid him in the Endless Darkness. (Hadhokht Nask [2], 33)

A wise person, therefore, is defined as one who chooses the path of good thoughts, says good words and practices good actions and does not possess useless thoughts, speak lies or practice unjust actions.

At the social level, Zoroastrianism is perhaps the first religion to recognize total equality among all, regardless of creed, race or gender. Zoroaster was also the author of a letter of animal rights and taught that forests should be open, and lands cultivated. At an individual level, He also implemented five daily obligatory prayers, preceded, each one, by ablution.

Zoroastrian Influence in the West

Zoroastrian cosmology, philosophy and faith have had definite historical influence. In Christian culture, besides the previously described confluence, we find in a brief passage in Matthew (2:1–13), the figure of the Wisemen or Three Kings, possibly members of the sacerdotal order of Magi who, according to some historians, were looking for the "Holy Saoshyant" (Visperad, 22:1), an awaited prophet. Historical sources would mention different versions, describing the Magi as being from Persia, Arabia, Chaldea, Yemen, China and other oriental regions, but the term "Magi" itself suggests the astronomically-oriented sacerdotal/philosophical order that articulated, syncretically, Zoroastrianism with its preceding paganism. Ancient paintings and mosaics depicted the Magi in Persian outfits, as in the cases of the Basilica of San Vitale and the Basilica of Sant'Apollinare Nuovo in Ravenna, the Nativity Church in Jerusalem, and Rome's subterranean catacombs.

During the first century of the Christian era, another development of Zoroastrianism resulted from a meeting of Persian and Roman traditions. The result was a form of Mithraism, in which Mithra and Ahura Mazda seemed to be associated with the gods Apollo and Zeus, respectively. This new movement became popular among the Roman soldiers who propagated it, through their legions, in Britain, Germany, and elsewhere (Zeppegno, 1980). The sense of fraternity, hope for a new and better life, and equality among all humans before one single God of love seems to have captivated parts of the Roman population (Spoto, 1995). For Romans, Mithra was a divinity born from immaculate conception, on December 25th, the day of the Winter solstice, the same day that, later on, was defined as the birthday of Jesus. Thus, Zoroastrianism possesses influence, even if indirect, in the context of the yet to be born Christian theology.

In the Hellenic and Greek world it has been suggested that Socrates was in contact with Zoroastrian clergymen, and also with Hebrews in Palestine, assimilating, there, the principles of divine unity and the soul's immortality, concepts foreign until that period to his own cultural background. In his turn, Heraclitus defined *arché* (world's constituent element) as fire and described both divine reality and human existence as possessing dual vision by affirming that we *descend and don't descend in the same rivers* or that God is *day-night, winter-summer, war-peace, satiety-hunger*.

See also: ❯ Analytical Psychology ❯ Campbell, Joseph ❯ Christianity ❯ Frankl, Viktor ❯ Freud, Sigmund ❯ Islam ❯ Jesus ❯ Jung, Carl Gustav ❯ Locus of Control ❯ Monotheism ❯ Pantheism ❯ Psychoanalysis ❯ Religion ❯ Taoism ❯ Virgin Birth ❯ Winnicott, Donald Woods

Bibliography

Bahá'u'lláh (2006). *The Tabernacle of Unity – Bahá'u'lláh's responses to Mánikchí Sáhib and other writings*. Haifa: Bahá'í World Centre.

Campbell, J. (1991). *The Masks of God – Oriental Mythology*. Arkana: Penguin Books (2ª edição: 1991).

Darmesteter, J. (Trans.). (1898a). Avesta: Vendidad in *Sacred Books of the East*. American Edition.

Darmesteter, J. (Trans.). (1898b). Avesta: Fragments (Hadhokht Nask) in *Sacred Books of the East*. American Edition.

Fatheazám, H. (1972). *O Novo Jardim*. Paraná: Editora Bahá'í do Brasil.

Frankl, V. E. (2001). *Psicoterapia y existencialismo – Escritos selectos sobre la logoterapia*. Barcelona, Spain: Editorial Herder.

Frankl, V. E. (2002). *La voluntad del sentido – Conferencias escogidas sobre logoterapia*. Barcelona, Spain: Editorial Herder (4ª edição em espanhol: 2002).

King James Bible.

Ling, T. (1968). *História das religiões*. Lisboa: Editorial Presenta (2ª edição em portugués: 2005).

Messer, S., & Winokur, M. (1980). Some limits to the integration of psychoanalytic and behavior therapy. *American Psychologist, 35*, 818–827.

Mills, L. H. (Trans.). (1898). Avesta: Yasna (Sacred Liturgy and Gathas/Hymns of Zarathushtra) in *Sacred Books of the East*. American Edition.

Spoto, S. (1995). *Misteri e segreti di Ostia antica: Riti magici, giochi proibiti e luoghi di piacere nella Roma «fuori porta» di 2000 anni fa*. Roma: Rendina Editori.

Zeppegno, L. (1980). *Alla scoperta di Roma Sottorranea*. Roma: Edizioni Colosseum.